the Compassionate Congregation

a handbook for

people who care

Pamela,
May this hand-
book be helpful
to you as you
reach out &
care for others.
Keep Caring
Karen

Karen Mulder and

FAITH ALIVE. Christian Resources — Faith Alive Christian Resources
Grand Rapids, Michigan

Reformed Church Press
New York, New York

The Compassionate Congregation: A Handbook for People Who Care was published by Faith Alive Christian Resources and Reformed Church Press. © 2002 by CRC Publications, 2850 Kalamazoo Ave. SE, Grand Rapids, MI 49560. All rights reserved. With the exception of brief excerpts for review purposes, no part of this book may be reproduced in any manner whatsoever without written permission from the publisher. Printed in the United States of America on recycled paper.

We welcome your comments. Call us at 1-800-333-8300 or e-mail us at editors@faithaliveresources.org.

Library of Congress Cataloging-in-Publication Data
Mulder, Karen.
    The compassionate congregation: a handbook for people who care / Karen Mulder and Ginger Jurries.
        p.   cm.
Includes bibliographical references.
    ISBN 1-56212-855-8
    1. Church work—Handbooks, manuals, etc. I. Jurries, Ginger. II. Title.
    BV4400.M83   2002
    253'.7—dc21

                                                                2002010641

10 9 8 7 6 5 4 3 2

Contents

Why

On the street I saw a small girl
cold and shivering in a thin dress,
with little hope of a
decent meal.
I became angry and said to
God,
"Why did you permit this?
Why don't you do something
about it?"
For a while, God said nothing.
That night he replied, quite
suddenly:
"I certainly did something
about it.
I made you."

Author Unknown

Introduction

This handbook is intended to help ordinary pewsitters—as well as pastors and officebearers—be caring and compassionate friends to persons going through a crisis.

Section 1 of *The Compassionate Congregation* consists of first-person accounts of crises faced by individuals whom the authors interviewed. Here you will find stories on nearly two dozen topics, including abortion, abuse, AIDS, aging, cancer, death, depression, illness, substance abuse, unemployment, and much more.

After each story, you'll find a section entitled "Wisdom for the Caregiver"; this section offers down-to-earth advice for caregivers from those who have gone through a particular crisis situation. A section called "Helplines" provides lists of agencies and organizations that might be helpful for caregivers. And for most of the topics, books and other resources are listed as well.

Section 2 takes a more general look at the process of caregiving, dealing with the topics of prayer, listening, and the grief process. Section 3 offers 109+ ways to say, "I Care."

A four-session, self-guided workshop for small groups is found at the back of this handbook (see page 235). The sessions cover—and provide practice in—the basics of caregiving described in section 2. Each session requires at least an hour to complete. While small groups will need a leader to direct the discussion and activities, the sessions are written to the entire small group rather than only to the leader. This tends to give the sessions more of a "seminar" feel, and lessens the need for intensive preparation by group leaders. Some comments intended for use by leaders only are written in the margins.

Karen's Note: The Confession of a Procrastinator

Like Moses resisting God's directive at the burning bush, I avoid, put off, and excuse myself from potentially unpleasant encounters with people in need. So I really don't know why I agreed to become a member of my church's pastoral care team. Sometimes I think God eases us into some situations without our full logical approval. Nevertheless, my first assignment as a member of the care team was to make contact with Joan. Joan had cancer.

Contacting Joan became a personal struggle. My archenemy, procrastination, successfully reigned for days. Finally "The Day" arrived, and I knew that I must do it—I *had* to phone Joan! So I set the timer on the microwave and promised myself that when the buzzer sounded I would make the call. I did, but not before offering what had to be the most urgent prayer of the month, if not the year. "O God," I prayed, "I don't know how to do this. I don't know what to say. What will I say if she starts crying, or if she is angry, or . . . Please, God, *help me!*" (Actually, I hoped that Joan was away at the grocery store, far from her phone.)

So with my heart beating aerobically, I dialed Joan's number and, as her phone started ringing, started counting—one ring, two, three. I had told myself that if Joan didn't answer in six rings I could hang up and try again another day, but she answered! I don't remember what *I* said, but I do remember what *she* said. She told me how much it hurt, not the cancer so much as the way her friends seemed to avoid her and disappear. "My friends don't call much anymore," she said, "and in the grocery store even acquaintances avoid me. That hurts a lot!"

Forty-five minutes later, I hung up the phone and whispered a heartfelt thanks to our faithful God. (The Lord says to each of us, "My grace is sufficient for you, for my power is made perfect in weakness"—2 Corinthians 12:9.) Joan had been very receptive to my call, and with only an occasional question or comment from me, she had shared her thoughts and her feelings. She had actually appreciated the phone call.

During the following twelve months I contacted Joan five times. At the most, I offered five small and quick gestures of caring: maybe two phone calls, one plant, one visit to her home, and one visit to the hospital. That's it.

On September 5, 1988, Joan died. As I was pouring coffee at the reception following the funeral service, Joan's handsome sons gave me a big hug and thanked me for being such a good friend to their mom. I was speechless. I was tempted to say, "Oops, there's been a mistake here. I only offered your mom a few, quick tokens of caring."

Today, years later, the promise running through this book and our caregiving workshops is this: *little* becomes *BIG*. Learning from experiences such as the one with Joan, we realize that our caregiving doesn't have to be polished and perfect and profound. God takes each sincere, small, and clumsy gesture of compassion and turns it into something big, bright, and beautiful.

Ginger's Note: Just Being There

People like Joan constantly confront us in this world. Our parents get old, our children give us headaches, our friends get cancer, and our neighbors lose their jobs. So many people we know are in need of our comfort and thoughtful care. The problem is that too often our hearts say *go* but our heads say *no*. We may have a tendency to avoid these situations because we don't know what to say or do, or we may blunder through a situation, *hoping* that we say and do the right thing.

Karen and I realize the importance of being there for our friends, acquaintances, and relatives in times of crisis, and we understand the importance of sensitivity. We have approached the topic of caregiving by consulting the experts—those who have endured crises and been helped or hurt by caregivers. This handbook is a compilation of some of our interviewees' true stories and their most helpful suggestions.

The Compassionate Congregation can be read straight through, in its entirety. However, *The Compassionate Congregation* is also intended to be used as a handbook, for quick reference when you encounter a particular kind of need. Suppose, for example, you are unsure about caregiving protocol for visiting a hospitalized friend, or what to say to someone who has just learned he or she has cancer, or how to respond to a colleague who has just suffered a miscarriage. By using the table of contents, you can locate an insider's account (in section 1) of what he or she found helpful in a similar situation.

Although the persons we interviewed have much to teach us about caregiving, our model of the perfect caregiver is Jesus Christ. Following Jesus' teaching involves meeting people where they are—feeding the hungry, giving drink to the thirsty, welcoming the stranger, clothing the naked, comforting the sick, and visiting the imprisoned. And whatever we do for one of these, we have done for Christ himself (Matthew 25:35-38).

We all seem to have a desire to rescue our friends from their debilitating situations. However, the experts we interviewed, as well as our supreme model, Jesus Christ, invite us simply to be there, to hold a hand, shed a tear, listen to a story, and give a hug. It seems so little but it means so much to the "Joans" of our world.

A story that Mark Victor Hanson and Jack Canfield tell in their book, *Chicken Soup for the Soul,* illustrates the importance of those acts of kindness that may seem like a proverbial "drop in the bucket":

A friend of ours was walking down a deserted Mexican beach at sunset. As he walked along, he began to see another man in the distance. As he grew nearer, he noticed that the local native kept leaning down, picking something up, and throwing it out into the water. Time and again he kept hurling things into the ocean.

As our friend approached even closer, he noticed that the man was picking up starfish that had been washed up on the beach, and, one at a time, he was throwing them into the water.

Our friend was puzzled. He approached the man and said, "Good evening, friend. I was wondering what you are doing."

"I'm throwing these starfish back into the ocean. You see, it's low tide right now and all of these starfish have been washed up onto the shore. If I don't throw them back into the ocean they'll die."

"I understand," our friend replied, "but there must be thousands of starfish on this beach. You can't possibly get to all of them. There are simply too many, and don't you realize it is probably happening on hundreds of beaches all up and down the coast? Can't you see that you can't possibly make a difference?"

The local native smiled, bent down, and picked up yet another starfish, and as he threw it back into the sea, he replied, "Made a difference to that one!"

—Mark Victor Hanson and Jack Canfield, *Chicken Soup for the Soul,*
pp. 22-23, © 1993, Health Communications, Inc.

Still thinking that caregiving is not "your thing" and should be left to someone else? Then take a few minutes to read some of the first-person accounts in section 1. The crises of life leave us "beached" and in need of a friend to give us "oxygen," that life-giving force that enables us to go on and to find hope in a desperately painful situation. Your simple, caring gestures could be the life-giving "oxygen" your hurting friend needs so urgently.

Karen and I hope and pray that this handbook will help you to be a caring and compassionate friend to those in crisis situations who need you so much.

Additional Resources
Internet Resources
While most of the topics in this handbook include lists of places to get help and information, as well as print resources, you may also want to try the following general "health" websites, a few of the many that are available (please be aware that while these websites were up and running at publication time, they may no longer be available).

⊛ www.about.com
   This site offers information on a number of areas. Click on *health* for topics related to this handbook, including AIDS/HIV, abuse, cancer, death and dying, divorce support, substance abuse, and many more.
⊛ www.ama-assng.org
   This site of the American Medical Society includes news in the health field, reliable health information, and a doctor search (by name of speciality) of more than 690,000 physicians.
⊛ www.drkoop.com
   An advertisement-sponsored website by the former Surgeon General of the United States, C. Everett Koop. Includes health news, family health topics, conditions and concerns, a medical encyclopedia, and more.

Medical Information Line

This handbook offers numerous "helpline" phone numbers on specific topics. In addition, many local hospitals offer free health information on a variety of topics (check your local yellow pages). If you don't mind paying $1.95 per minute (current rate may differ), you can also get reliable health information from the Medical Information Line: 1-900-346-7000. Dial "0" for a directory. Topics include AIDS (#2111), alcoholism (#5113), cancer (by type), substance abuse (by type), Alzheimer's disease (#6111), depression (#5324), suicide (#5326), stress management (#5313), and dozens more. Topics average five minutes each.

SECTION 1

Wisdom of the Wounded: Their Stories and Advice

On a Sabbath, Jesus was teaching in one of the synagogues and a woman was there who had been crippled by a spirit for eighteen years. She was bent over and could not straighten up at all.

—Luke 13:10-11

I remember asking members of my Bible study group to recall a time when they felt like that woman in Luke's gospel, bent over by a problem and quite unable to stand up straight and face the day. After some reflection time, I asked: "Now, what did someone say or do that helped you during that difficult time?"

One by one, individuals told their stories of comfort in the midst of crisis. From this shared folk wisdom, the idea for this book was born. As Karen and I talked with others who had gone through crisis situations and who therefore were "experts" in knowing what helped and what did not, we realized that one does not have to be a trained counselor, psychiatrist, or minister to care effectively for someone who is hurting.

This section of *The Compassionate Congregation* combines true stories of persons in need with "Wisdom for the Caregiver," advice often drawn from their experiences. In addition, you'll find listings of helpful agencies and other resources.

Not every situation of suffering is included in this handbook, of course. If you are interested in a particular crisis that is not included, read about a similar crisis or read *all* the stories and you will glean some ideas for how to help your hurting friend.

—Ginger Jurries

Abortion

God's Forgiveness Brings Healing from Guilt and Shame

But if we walk in the light, as he is in the light, we have fellowship with one another, and the blood of Jesus, his Son, purifies us from all sin.

—1 John 1:7

I was numb. As I talked with my doctor in Michigan's Upper Peninsula, my fears were confirmed: I was pregnant. "Not now!" I wanted to scream.

My marriage was failing, and I wanted out of the relationship. I was twenty-one and had a four-year-old son. "How could this be happening to me?" was all I could think.

Something went off in my head when the doctor queried, "Do you want to terminate?"

One voice (which I now know was God's) said, "This isn't right. Don't do it. You're going to regret it for the rest of your life." Another (mine) said, "You need to do this. You have to get off welfare and get an education."

Not long afterward I found myself in the waiting room at a clinic in Grand Rapids, Michigan, looking at a large poster of beautiful aspens in fall color. I knew the poster was designed to get my mind off the procedure for which I had come. I had already convinced myself not to dwell on my negative feelings. I rationalized that if I could not feel life, this pregnancy had not yet developed into a baby. Although God was simply a "higher power" to me, I prayed to him for strength to do what I had to do.

I can still vividly recall the terrible sound of the vacuum as it sucked the fetus from my womb. I knew at that moment that my womanhood was being traumatized and tortured.

My reaction to the abortion was rebellion. I became a militant feminist. I developed an aversion to submission and to the whole idea of marriage.

In spite of my negative feelings about marriage, while at Ferris State University I met and married a wonderful man named Michael. Of course, the seas of matrimony were not always smooth. But after a few years, I gave birth to a beautiful daughter whom we named Sarah.

While in school we also met a couple who had a wonderfully peaceful attitude about life. Their marriage seemed like the kind that I wanted to have. They invited us to attend Life in the Spirit Seminars. There I learned about a life centered in Jesus, and I asked him to be my personal Savior. As the Spirit took control of my life, an amazing transformation began. I felt at peace; I loved those whom I had not been able to love before; and I was able to forgive others much more easily. My marriage also drastically improved. As if a flame had been lit, I now had a purpose in life, guided and fueled by my love for Jesus: to direct others to new life in Christ and to help prevent women from making the same life-changing mistake that I had made.

Soon I became concerned about the plight of poor women who have abortions and are not presented with options. This brought me in contact with the Right to Life movement. A woman there gave me a Bible study guide, which helped me through the healing process. I was able to come out of denial and release the proverbial ball I was holding under the water. As soon as I confessed my sin of taking the life of my daughter, I felt overwhelmed by God's forgiveness. God was then able to release the blessings he had been holding for me, and I felt an intimacy with my Savior that I never had before. I was also fee to grieve. The child I had been denying became a real person to me. I named her Melissa.

When I gave my testimony to the women at Birthright, they wanted to know how to help other women who were considering abortion. Through a time of prayer and fasting God gave me a vision of a pregnancy center where women could receive Christian counseling and be given options to abortion. It was because of this vision that Lakeshore Pregnancy Center in Holland, Michigan, was born. In just nine years it has grown from a center with a budget of $9,000 to one with a $250,000 budget. Women there receive the kind of counseling I wish I had had at the time I decided to have my abortion.

Another vision took form following a meeting with several other women from Michigan. We had congregated on the steps of the capitol building in Lansing to protest the lack of a law that required giving pregnant women information about alternatives to abortion. Along with a few of these women, I began an organization called Mourning Joy Ministries. Its purpose is to help women toward forgiveness and joy through group Bible study. Through our efforts we were also able to realize another goal: on September 15, 1999, a law was passed in Michigan stating that every woman who comes to an abortion clinic must be given choice options. We were elated!

Well-meaning friends have suggested that God allowed me to have an abortion so that I could help other women avoid the awful experience that termination inevitably brings. Through tears I tell them that I would forego being a savior to the masses if I could only reclaim my precious daughter.

My goal as a pro-life advocate is not to elevate the fetus but to hold up the cross of Christ. It is because of him that I am now free to live the abundant life given to all who believe in him.

Wisdom for the Caregiver

☙ As much as any in this book, this topic—providing care for someone who has had an abortion—requires a prayerful and compassionate heart. You may have strong scriptural and political views about abortion; so might your church. The first-person account above reflects the story of a woman who, years after having an abortion, now devotes much energy to work with a pro-life organization. But your role as caregiver is first and foremost a pro-person endeavor, *not* a platform for your pro-life or pro-choice views. Be more concerned about the person than the issue. (Isn't this what Jesus would do?) Take great care not to be judgmental of the person or in any way tie your presence with them to their acceptance of your personal point of view about abortion. They need to experience the forgiving love of God and complete acceptance from those who are trying to help.

⊛ Most churches in the Reformed/Presbyterian tradition, out of our commitment to covenant—that is, our belonging to God's family—believe that abortion is an option only when the mother's life is in jeopardy. However, all these churches strongly urge their members to fully support those experiencing an unwanted pregnancy, helping them find alternatives to abortion. And all these churches urge showing Christian compassion and support for those who have undergone an abortion.

⊛ Read "Caregiving Basics" (pp. 203-222) and "109+ Ways to Say, 'I Care'" (pp. 223-234). Especially look for ways you can simply be with someone who may be hurting very much. Your presence, in Christ's name, will mean much.

⊛ Recognize that persons who have undergone an abortion often carry a huge burden of loss and guilt. Be ready to show huge amounts of love and acceptance to the person you are trying to help. Spend time with her. Listen uncritically to her story. Give her lots of affirmation and empathy. Laugh and cry with her. And when she is ready, pray with her. If your friend needs the help of a support group or Christian counseling, help her check out some of the local options that are available.

Helplines

1. **American Association of Christian Counselors**, P.O. Box 739, Forest, VA 24551. 1-800-5-COUNSEL; 1-434-525-9470. www.aacc.net. This organization has a directory of counselors who are members of AACC—a great tool for finding a Christian counselor in just about any region in the United States.

2. **CareNet**, 109 Carpenter Dr., Suite 100, Sterling, VA 20164. 1-800-395-HELP; 1-703-478-5661. CareNet is a Christian organization offering abortion education and counseling in crisis centers located throughout

the United States. Check your local phone book or call the number above for the location of a center near you.

3. **London Pregnancy Centre**, London, ON. 1-519-432-7098. Offers post-abortion counseling.

4. **Project Rachel.** 1-800-5-WE-CARE. www.hopeafterabortion.org. An organization of the Catholic church that ministers to women who have had an abortion. Check your phone book for a listing of a local chapter.

5. **Women in Transition**, Houston, TX. 1-713-968-9097; info@wits.org. www.wits.org. Non-denominational post-abortion support.

Books and Other Resources

🕮 Coachman, Judith. *Shaping a Woman's Soul* (Grand Rapids, MI: Zondervan, 1996). Drawing from the wisdom of the Psalms, this book is an inspiring, encouraging, and practical resource for any woman seeking a nourishing relationship with God in the midst of her frazzled life.

🕮 Cloud, Henry, and John Townsend. *Boundaries* (Grand Rapids, MI: Zondervan, 1992). Often Christians focus so much on being loving and unselfish that they forget their own limitations. This book helps the reader answer questions such as "Can I set limits and still be a loving person?" "What are legitimate boundaries?" and "How do I answer someone who wants my time, love, energy, or money?"

🕮 Freed, Luci, and Penny Yvonne Salazar. *A Season to Heal* (Nashville: Cumberland House, 1996). The authors express the hope that their book will provide a road map through the valley of grief, and that women who have experienced abortion will find comfort and help and strength and purpose for their lives.

🕮 Masse, Sydna, and Joan Phillips. *Her Choice to Heal* (Colorado Springs, CO: Victor Publications, 1998). Two women share their post-abortion stories and the hope and healing that come from God's forgiveness and love. This book will help women find spiritual and emotional peace after abortion.

Abuse

No Childhood. No Adulthood.

Turn to me and be gracious to me, for I am lonely and afflicted. The troubles of my heart have multiplied; free me from my anguish.

—Psalm 25:16-17

I buried the memories of being abused until I was thirty-eight years old. When my flashbacks started, I didn't want to believe them. I argued with myself and discounted my memories for a whole year. Finally I had to believe because my mind was so persistent in keeping the memories always in front of me.

Acknowledging the abuse was horrible. Admitting that my grandfather had sexually abused me meant three things: first, he didn't love me; second, no one in my family cared enough about me to know that I was hurting or to protect me; third, I had been a non-person to those who abused me. I felt like a piece of litter that no one even bothered to throw in the trash. Realizing that no one *really* cared about me when I was a child was the most painful part of my healing process.

After hours and hours of tears, I became angry. I wanted to kill my abusers for what they had done to me. Because of them I'd had no childhood. Because of them I didn't trust people. Because of them I felt ashamed and dirty and worthless. They sinned and I got stuck with all the consequences. It isn't fair! When my husband touches me, I freeze up and get scared. My husband suffers because of sins that he did not commit. It's not fair!

After the worst of my anger was over (it will never be completely gone), I began to grieve. I grieved for the little girl who never knew love or joy or how to be carefree. I grieved for the little girl who was always fearful and never peaceful or relaxed. I grieved for the little girl who had no one to turn to with her pain and no one to protect her.

I still grieve for the grown woman who cannot believe that anyone would ever really love her. ("Love" always means people have ulterior motives.) I grieve for the grown woman who struggles to accept God's love.

—Gail

Wisdom for the Caregiver

☘ "The individuals who have been the biggest help to me have been other survivors of abuse, because they can understand the intensity of my feelings and why I don't just 'get over it.' They let me repeat myself. They give me the freedom to be angry over and over again."

—Gail

☘ "A critical moment for getting better is reached when the abused person recalls what happened to him or her and reaches out to share it with someone else. If you are that someone, your attentiveness and caring response helps your loved one—child or adult—continue to talk about his or her abuse and seek the help needed to get well. Such a moment calls for you to set everything else aside, listen, believe, and care."

—M. Gregory Richards, *When Someone You Know Is Hurting* (Zondervan)

☘ Encourage the person to get counseling and to join a support group. Help the person connect with a reputable counselor. (Perhaps you could offer to go with the person the first time. Visits to any type of doctor's office are less scary if someone who cares is there with you.) Help the person connect with a support group by checking with local doctors, ministers, volunteer organizations, and/or newspapers for information on existing support groups.

❧ "The care given to me during the time of a very difficult marriage and divorce was the difference between survival and destruction. My husband was abusive and threatened all manner of things. My deepest gratitude is to friends who walked with me through the agony, gave me literal refuge, and waited until I could see my way clear to leaving. They even let me make the mistake of leaving and returning several times. Through them, God gave me the backbone to call an end to the abuse no matter what might be the cost."

—Robin

❧ "There are times when caregiving requires that you help someone be strong in seeking justice for themselves. For me this has involved confronting. Of course some situations must be accepted, but others require a 'fight,' not another weak accommodation. I've appreciated it when others have stood with me in this way. They are, then, God's strong hands and voice in and for me."

—Robin

❧ A special note and challenge to ministers, church leaders, teachers, staffs of seminaries, and all Christians—from one victim who voices the cry and the need of many victims of abuse:

I long for a place where

I can experience what unconditional love

really can be . . .

a place where I can openly express my

anger at God . . .

a place where I might gradually begin to

believe that God is truly good and

that God loves me and believes that

I am reparable.

❧ Read "Caregiving Basics" (pp. 203-222).

Helplines

1. **American Association of Christian Counselors**, P.O. Box 739, Forest, VA 24551. 1-800-5-COUNSEL; 1-434-525-9470. www.aacc.net. This organization has a directory of counselors who are members of AACC—a great tool for finding a Christian counselor in just about any region in the United States.
2. **Child Help, National Child Abuse Hotline**, 1-800-422-4453.
3. **Cross Canada Search**. www.crosscanadasearch.com. A Christian Internet search engine. Includes information about Christian counseling services (www.crosscanadasearch.com/Ministry_Resources/Counselling).
4. **Domestic Violence Hotline**, 1-800-799-7233. The staff of this 24-hour hotline are trained to offer help to victims of domestic violence who need to find a shelter or other services. Workers also will offer counseling and other information.
5. **Health Canada's National Clearinghouse on Family Violence**, Family Violence Prevention Division, Address Locator 1907D1, Ottawa, ON K1A 1B5. 1-800-267-1291; 1-613-957-2938; TDD 1-800-561-5643. www.hc-sc.gc.ca/hppb/familyviolence.html. www.hc.gc.ca. Resources on where to go for help, suggested books and videos, and a nationwide listing of transition houses and shelters for abused women.
6. **Kids Help Phone**. 1-800-668-6868. www.kidshelp.sympatico.ca. Canada's only national, toll-free, 24-hour, bilingual child and youth telephone counseling service and website.
7. **National Committee for Prevention of Child Abuse**, P.O. Box 94283, Chicago, IL 60690. 1-312-663-3540. This organization offers a variety of publications on abuse. It also can connect you to local chapters.
8. **Salem Christian Mental Health Association**, 1 Young St., Suite 418, Hamilton, ON L8N 1T8. 1-905-528-0353. www.salem.on.ca. Provides counseling and also acts as a clearinghouse for mental health resources.
9. **Survivors Support Ministry**, 1-613-820-0272 (Kathy) or 1-613-792-3275 (Bertina). Run by Classis Eastern Canada of the Christian

Reformed Church, this ministry offers a counseling fund, resources for abuse survivors, education for prevention of abuse, a resources library, and consultation with churches.

Books and Other Resources

⊕ Allender, Dan. B. *The Wounded Heart: Hope for Adult Victims of Childhood Sexual Abuse* (Colorado Springs, CO: NavPress, 1990).

⊕ Frank, Jan. *A Door of Hope* (San Bernardino, CA: Here's Life Publishers, 1987). This book explores the common symptoms of abused individuals and details ten proven steps toward recovery.

⊕ Jansen, Melanie. *From the Darkest Night: Meditations for Abuse Survivors* (Grand Rapids, MI: Faith Alive Christian Resources, 2001). These meditations can help abuse survivors and those who love them walk through the often painful questions they have about God and the church. Useful for individuals, counselors, and support groups. (Call 1-800-333-8300 or visit www.FaithAliveResources.org to order.)

⊕ Jones, Ann, and Susan Schechter. *When Love Goes Wrong: What to Do When You Can't Do Anything Right* (New York: HarperCollins, 1992). A guide to freeing women from abuse, guilt, and blame.

⊕ Swagman, Beth. *Domestic Violence* (Grand Rapids, MI: Faith Alive Christian Resources, 2002). A resource for church leaders and congregation members trying to understand domestic violence and to help those dealing with domestic violence issues. (Call 1-800-333-8300 or visit www.FaithAliveResources.org to order.)

⊕ TRAVARCA. A video library sponsored by the Reformed Church in America and the Christian Reformed Church in North America, TRAVARCA carries thousands of videos on hundreds of topics, including abuse. A yearly membership allows churches and individuals to use an unlimited number of videos; nonmembers may use the videos for established fees. Call 1-800-968-7221 or 1-616-698-7071 for a catalog or to request information and videos.

Aging

A Power Struggle

The length of our days is seventy years—or eighty, if we have the strength; yet their span is but trouble and sorrow, for they quickly pass, and we fly away.
—Psalm 90:10

A Chinese proverb says, "A journey of a thousand miles begins with a single step." One such journey began nearly twenty-five years ago. At that time my husband and I made a decision that the family would relocate to a new home. We invited Grandma (my husband's mother) to move in with the six of us. We thought we would live happily ever after under one roof!

Twenty-four years later, I see Grandma as a very lonely, bitter, old woman who wishes she had the nerve to cease taking her medications. She feels tolerated, and she dislikes being a burden. She finds no joy in living. She has alienated most of those whose paths she has crossed. Even though she needs to be touched, she erects barriers that make her untouchable. Health problems and failing eyesight have taken away her three loves: television, reading, and crossword puzzles.

I question, What is this journey all about? What good has come from it all? All I see is conflict, broken relationships, frustration, and the anger-guilt-anger pattern. Now I realize that perhaps one of the underlying issues is and has been "power." Both she and I continue to struggle to be "queen" of the kingdom, maintaining the power and control.

Evidences of these struggles are many. With little regard for the art of sorting, Grandma decided the laundry would be her daily ritual. Years rolled by. I hid dirty clothes and fumed because I prefer to take care of the laundry. Finally, I stated my preference, and found it necessary to restate and restate it. She was very hurt and angry. "I hope you don't mind me using the machine for my laundry," she said bitterly.

From past experience I know Grandma lacks patience and has little or no expertise when it comes to using a paintbrush, so, when we decided to redecorate, I hid the paint and brushes. She found them and said to one of the kids, "I know that your mother does not want me to paint, but I am going to do it anyway!" I was furious and cried as I viewed the wavy door.

When a doctor suggested to my mother-in-law that she discuss these conflicts with her family, she didn't miss a beat as she informed him, "I make my own decisions. I don't need to talk this over with anyone!"

Recently, I've been anxious about Grandma's ability to see and properly take her medications. So I inquired if perhaps I should take over the sorting and distribution. "No!" she snapped. "I have it all figured out." And she does. She has learned the shapes of the pills, and if there are two with similar shapes she identifies the bottle with a rubber band.

Only now am I beginning to realize how important it is for the aged to have some control over their lives. Only now, twenty-five years late, have I learned about a book that could have helped me along the way: *Your Best Is Good Enough* by Vivian Greenberg. (*Editor's note:* This fine book is now out of print. Your local library may still carry a copy. Also see the book section on p. 32 for a new listing by Greenberg.) In her book Greenberg states, "Old people generally want to do as much as they can for themselves. As old people are able to manage fewer of the tasks of daily living and must depend on others to perform them, whatever they can still do by themselves assumes enormous significance. Polishing the brass candlesticks and peeling and coring apples to make a big pot of applesauce are precious symbols of control and independence. So what if these activities take an hour longer!"

As I view the crooked path this journey has taken, I find myself saying, If I had it to do over again, I would

❧ Increase my knowledge (through reading books and talking with professionals) about the needs of the elderly and how to take care of myself as well as the elderly parent.

- Explore alternative living arrangements.
- Talk more with Grandma.
- Try not to always protect my husband (her son) from knowing what I was feeling.
- Confront as the occasions arise rather than store up resentments.
- Set some ground rules.
- Be more aware of Grandma's need to be productive.
- Realize that I am not her savior and that being a peacemaker does not solve all problems.
- Lovingly question the choices she is making.
- Encourage a greater expansion of her world.
- Touch her more often.
- Realize that I cannot change her, I can only change myself (I can be more faithful and less independent).

Trouble is, all those "if onlys" lie behind me, and I cannot change the route we both chose. However, I still have today and tomorrow. How can I cross the barriers and reenter her life? I ask myself, What does she need? She needs to be needed, wanted and useful. What has she enjoyed in the past? Books, television and crossword puzzles.

- I need to increase my vocabulary and become a better speller. I can ask her to help me work crossword puzzles.
- I like fiction, but do not usually indulge. I have purchased the book *The Gift* by Danielle Steel and plan to read it to Grandma.
- I could listen to a book on tape with her.
- I seldom listen to the news or read a newspaper. I could let her select the headlines and we could keep current together.
- For Christmas the entire family could give Grandma a weekly visit to the hairdresser with various family members providing the transportation.
- I could look for reasons to say "thank you" and affirm her.

I've discovered there are many things I would enjoy doing that would affirm Grandma and at the same time allow her to be productive. Perhaps the twenty-fifth year of this journey is going to be the best ever!

—May

Wisdom for the Caregiver

ஐ Remember the types of activities/hobbies that the aging person enjoyed when younger and more active. Then find a way to make those hobbies a part of his or her present life.

ஐ "All his life, my father enjoyed beautiful classical music. So when it became necessary for Dad to live in a care facility, my brothers and I immediately purchased a small but high-quality stereo system for his room."

—Carl

ஐ "My mother has always enjoyed planting and caring for flowers in her yard and home. Ever since I can remember she has proudly displayed on her windowsill a colorful parade of African violets. So if one day she ends up in a nursing home or other type of smaller living space, one gift I will give her will be a row of African violets, even if I have to replace them often."

—Karen

ஐ Watch for movies and videos that offer motivating insights and encouragement to both the older person and those who care for him or her. Check with TRAVARCA (1-800-968-7221), an audio-visual library serving the Reformed Church in America and the Christian Reformed Church in North America, for listings about aging. (A few significant titles include "A Good Old Age," "My Mother, My Father," "My Mother, My Father: Seven Years Later," and "People with Aging Parents.") Even Hollywood occasionally provides positive films about aging—see, for example, *Dad* and *Roommates*.

ஐ "Be sensitive to changes in their attitudes and likes and dislikes. When my mother was getting very weak toward the end of her life, I continued to recite all my daily activities, thinking she had always been very interested. But one day she said almost angrily, 'You think you are so important—you do this and you do that—you are able to do everything.' I realized that she no longer could relate with joy while she couldn't do anything for herself, not even feed herself. I tried even harder to be aware of her needs."

—Eloise

⊛ Always involve aging parents in the major happenings in your family. To exclude them is to treat them as non-persons! Ask them for their opinions on the big things and little things that make up everyday living. Remember that one of the greatest fears of old people is to be isolated from family activities. You can help keep them connected!

⊛ "If you can't visit your aging parents regularly—or have them visit you—make an extra effort to stay in contact. Call them frequently with all the news of the family. Write as frequently as you can. Many short notes are better than fewer long ones. Include newspaper clippings of interest and discount coupons for things they like. Send them surprise packages: little gifts on occasions other than birthdays and Christmas. That way they'll know you're thinking about them."

—*Household Hints and Handy Tips,* Reader's Digest Assocation, 1988, p. 240

⊛ "When my eighty-two-year-old mother returned home after two weeks of therapy in a rehabilitation hospital for a broken hip, she was apprehensive about filling her time. I decided to send her a box of things to
—Make her smile: foam dart gun, Silly Putty, 'The Honeymooners' videotape (a la Jackie Gleason), 'Lake Wobegon' cassette by Garrison Keillor, checkers
—Give her some intellectual stimulation: 'Quiz Whiz' (an electronic question and answer game), Scrabble
—Help promote her spiritual/emotional well-being: Bernie Siegel audiotapes, booklet: *A Collection of Treasured Bible Verses*
—Make her life more efficient: MagnaDoodle—a 'magic' slate for writing/drawing to record things to remember."

—Ginger

⊛ The following suggestions for caring about and for the elderly are from *Let's Make a Memory* by Gloria Gaither and Shirley Dobson:
—Invite the elderly friend to go along with your family to the ice cream shop, or drop by with an ice cream cone if he or she can't get out.
—Drop by now and then when you or your family are out riding bikes.
—Invite your elderly friend to your birthday party. Make sure he or she has a hat to wear and a horn to blow like everyone else.

—Volunteer to mow the grass, clip around lamp posts, pull some weeds, or paint the mailbox.

—Mail her or him unexpected notes or cards—valentines, Easter cards, school pictures, and so on.

—Share a tape recording (provide a cassette player if needed) of a concert, church service, school program, band recital, and so on.

—Ask your friend's opinion of a paper, a poem, or a song you've written.

—Drop by with one or two of your friends so that your friend can meet them. Make your visits short.

—Offer to pick the cherries, sweep the driveway, wash the car, clean the windows on the outside, shake the rugs, run an errand.

—Have a "read-in" once or twice a week. Suggest to the friend for whom you are reading that he or she invite other friends to share in the "read-in." Choose a "book of the month" that all will enjoy having read aloud.

—Volunteer to write and mail letters or to help with the correspondence involved in paying bills.

⊛ Help the person remember and tell his or her life story. See "Telling Life's Story" (pp. 33-36 of this handbook), or purchase the book *The Story of A Lifetime: A Keepsake of Personal Memoirs* by Pamela and Stephen Pavuk.

⊛ Read "Caregiving Basics" (pp. 203-222).

⊛ Check "109+ Ways to Say, 'I Care'" (pp. 223-234).

Helplines

1. **Abbeyfield Houses Society of Canada**, Box 1, 427 Bloor St. West, Toronto, ON M5S 1X7. 1-416-920-7483; info@abbeyfield.ca. www.abbeyfield.ca. (Chapter offices also in Western Canada and in the U.S. and overseas.) A non-profit organization that aims to provide

accomodation and companionship for lonely older people within their own communities.

2. **Canadian Association of Retired Persons (CARP)**, Suite 1304, 27 Queen St. East, Toronto, ON M3C 2M6. 1-416-363-8748. www.fifty-plus.net.

3. **Medbroadcast Corporation**, Suite 250, Marine Building, 355 Burrard Street, Vancouver, BC V6C 2G8. 1-604-687-7463. www.medbroadcast.com. A comprehensive consumer health and wellness website that has links for medical conditions A-Z, links for support groups both by health topic and by location, and a link with information about prescription drugs.

4. **Ministry of Health National Advisory Council on Aging**, Postal locator 1908A1, Ottawa, ON K1A 1B4. 1-800-277-9914; 1-613-957-1968; TDD 1-800-255-4786. www.hc-sc.gc.ca/seniors.aines.

5. **National Institute on Aging Information Center**, P.O. Box 8057, Gaithersburg, MD 20890-8057. 1-800-222-2225; fax 1-301-589-3014. NIA offers free publications on more than fifty topics of interest to older people and their families (ask for their publications list), such as
   - Arthritis advice
   - Forgetfulness in old age
   - Constipation
   - Stroke: Prevention and treatment
   - Depression
   - Aging and your eyes
   - Urinary incontinence
   - Talking with your doctor

6. **www.wiredseniors.com**. An Internet search directory for the over-50 age group.

Books and Other Resources

ⓒ *Aging Parents: The Family Survival Guide* (San Francisco: Lifetapes Communications by Sybervision Systems, Inc., 1996). This resource provides guidelines for families dealing with a crisis or planning for long-term care. The guide and the accompanying video contain solid, reliable information to help you assist your parents today and in the future. Topics include "Caregiving from a Distance," "Housing Alternatives and Support Services," "Legal Issues," "Government Programs," and "Death and Dying."

⊗ Berman, Claire. *Caring for Yourself While Caring for Your Aging Parents: How to Help, How to Survive* (New York: Henry Holt and Company, Inc., 1996). For those who are involved (or are likely to become involved) in caring for aging parents, this book centers on the emotional needs of caregivers but also addresses all the practical issues they are likely to confront.

⊗ *50 Plus* Magazine, published by the Canadian Association of Retired Persons (CARP). www.50plus.com.

⊗ Greenberg, Vivian E. *Respecting Your Limits When Caring for Aging Parents.* (San Francisco: Jossey-Bass Publishers, 1998). In her practical, down-to-earth style, Greenberg provides compassionate advice on how to lovingly care for aging parents—without letting that care ruin your life! Covers all the issues, including dealing with unrealistic expectations, getting siblings to share responsiblity, loyalty conflicts, dealing with diffiicult parents, and making the decision to place parents in a nursing home.

⊗ Kok, James. *No Such Thing as Over the Hill: Making the Most of Life After 60* (Grand Rapids, MI: Faith Alive Christian Resources, 2000). This is a great read for anyone. Kok says that getting older in many ways means getting "better" and discovering new challenges. (Call 1-800-333-8300 or visit www.FaithAliveResources.org to order.)

⊗ Pipher, Mary. *Another Country: Navigating the Emotional Terrain of Our Elders* (New York: Riverhead Books, 1999). *Another Country* is a field guide for a generation of baby boomers who are finding themselves unprepared to care for those who have always cared for them. Psychologist and bestselling writer Mary Pipher maps out strategies that help bridge the gaps between us and our elders. With respect and realism she offers new ways of supporting each other, of sharing our time, energy, and love.

⊗ Simmons, Henry C., and Mark Peters. *With God's Oldest Friends: Pastoral Visiting in the Nursing Home* (Mahwah, New York: Paulist Press, 1996). This is a valuable resource for all pastoral visitors—both clergy and lay. Topics include old age, terminal illness, Alzheimer's, the use of ritual and sacrament, and empowering nursing home residents to engage in wider ministry through prayer or letter writing. The book contains helpful information on entering a care facility, plus basic information on nursing homes. Resources are suggested for prayer and Bible study, along with many suggestions for further reading.

⊛ Strom, Kay Marshall. *A Caregiver's Survival Guide: How to Stay Healthy When Your Loved One Is Sick* (Downers Grove, IL: InterVarsity Press, 2000). Whether you are caring for an elderly parent or another adult relative, you will be encouraged by the stories the author tells from her own life and from the lives of others. Also offers concrete ideas that will carry you through. (Available from Faith Alive Christian Resources, 1-800-333-8300, www.FaithAliveResources.org.)

⊛ Consider giving a subscription to a large-print edition of a magazine such as *Reader's Digest* (Reader's Digest Fund for the Blind, Large-Type Publication, P.O. Box 241, Mt. Morris, IL 61054) or *Guideposts* (Guideposts, Big Print Edition, Carmel, NY 10512).

Telling Life's Story

Reminiscing is healthy! It's the process by which we make sense out of this mystery we call life. Reminiscing helps those who are older to find meaning and purpose in the years they have lived. It can create new levels of appreciation and intimacy between generations and can transform times spent beside beds or other visits into memorable times together.

The following questions will provide you with hours of worthwhile communication. If possible, tape or write down your discussions. Then the stories can be shared with other family members and friends.

The Family

⊛ How many brothers and sisters do you have?

⊛ Who was/is your favorite sibling? Why? What fun memories do you have of her or him?

⊛ Where did you live?

⊛ Did your father change jobs often? What jobs did he have?

⊛ Did your mother work outside the home?

⊛ Did the family have any pets?

⊛ Did you have your own pet? What was it like?

⊛ Was anyone in the immediate family ever seriously ill?

⊛ Did you think of yourselves as poor, struggling, comfortable, wealthy?

⊛ Did your parents worry about money?

ἒ Did your grandparents live with you?

ἒ Were you close to your grandparents? Describe some fun or special memories that you have of your grandparents.

School

ἒ How did you get to school?

ἒ What was the name of your best friend? What was she or he like?

ἒ Did you like school? Why?

ἒ What was your favorite subject? Why?

ἒ Who was your favorite teacher?

ἒ Did you have any unfulfilled goals, such as becoming a doctor or a farmer?

ἒ What is your earliest happy memory at school?

ἒ Did you want to have more education?

ἒ What games did you play?

ἒ Did you work while you were still in school? Describe job(s).

ἒ How old were you when you left school?

Holidays

ἒ What were the important holidays in your family?

ἒ What were some of your family's traditions?

ἒ Did you go away for holidays? Where did you go?

ἒ What are some of your happiest holiday memories?

Work Experiences

ἒ What was your first job? Describe.

ἒ How did you get to and from work?

ἒ Did you like the job? Why?

ἒ What other jobs have you had?

ἒ What has been your favorite job? Why?

ἒ Did you make any lifelong friends in any of your jobs?

ἒ Who was your favorite boss/employer? Why?

Travel

ἒ What are some special places that you have visited?

ἒ Which destination did you like the most? Why?

ἒ What was your first car?

ἒ What are some places that you would still like to visit? Why?

Married Life

- When did you meet your spouse? What attracted you to him/her?
- How old were you when you got married? How did the proposal go? What was the wedding like?
- How much money did you have then?
- When did you buy your first house? What did you like the most about it?
- What kinds of things do (did) you and your spouse like to do together?
- How many children do you have? Where do they live? What do they do for a job? What do you like the most about each one?

Faith/Church

- Did your family go to church when you were growing up? What did you like and dislike about the church as a child?
- Are you a Christian? When did you become a Christian?
- What's your favorite Bible story? Why?
- What Bible passage or verse has made a great difference in your life? How?
- Can you describe a time when you really felt the presence and power of God?
- What church activities have you participated in and enjoyed?
- What are two of your favorite hymns or songs? What words from those hymns are especially significant to you?

Military Service

- Did you ever serve in the armed forces? Which branch? For how long? What was your rank?
- Did you see any combat duty? If so, what do you remember the most about it?
- Did you make any new friends in the service? Do you ever see them or think about them now?
- What do you think about war?

Friends

- Who is, was, or still is your best friend?
- Why was or is he/she your best friend? What characteristics in that friend do you value the most?
- Whom have you known the longest?
- What is your most treasured memory with your friend?

Politics
⊛ What is your political affiliation? Has it always been the same?
⊛ Who was the "best" president/prime minister? The "worst"?
⊛ Who would you like to be the next president/prime minister?

Challenges/Disappointments/Achievements
⊛ What was your greatest challenge? How did you meet it?
⊛ What did you learn from this challenge? What bit of wisdom would you
   pass on to future generations concerning challenges that they will face?
⊛ What was your greatest disappointment? How did you deal with it?
⊛ What are some of your achievements that you feel proud of?
⊛ What is your greatest achievement?

Changes
⊛ What are the major changes you have seen taking place in your life-
   time? (Technologically, socially, medically, internationally, etc.)
⊛ What change has affected you the most?

Most Admired Person
⊛ Whom have you admired most? Why?

If You Had Your Life to Live Over Again . . .
⊛ Would you make any changes?
⊛ What would they be?

—Adapted from material by the National Caregiving Foundation, 801 N. Pitt Street, #116,
Alexandria, VA 22314-1765. www.caregivingfoundation.org. Used by permission.

AIDS

Healed

This is the message you heard from the beginning. We should love one another.
—1 John 3:11

I am a thirty-seven-year-old male with AIDS. While this disease has caused me a great deal of pain and anguish, it has also been the catalyst for many positive changes and advances in my life.

Although I've suffered confusion, anxiety, surgeries, eye problems, lack of energy, nausea, and ostracism, I have grown so much and learned so many positive things that I can honestly say that AIDS has healed me.

Some of the most important things I have learned:

❧ Life is very precious.
❧ We must give one another unconditional love.
❧ Relationships are of utmost importance.
❧ We need to ask what we can learn from our tragedies.
❧ Spirituality is the backbone of life.
❧ It is important to have a strong sense of self.
❧ We are designed to heal and we can facilitate our own healing.
❧ Even the smallest things that others do for us can be healing (a smile, a warm greeting from a cashier, and so on).

—Thomas

Shortly before Tom died, he sent author Ginger Jurries a note. An excerpt: "I have learned so much through my illness. One thing I have realized is that we are all here together. All here, individual and different, but every one of us must learn the same lessons. I believe that these lessons can all be reduced to "Love one another." We are all on a journey toward the Light. God bless you. Your friend, Tom."

Tending the Wounded

Nothing has ever opened my heart so quickly, so completely, as living through seven years of the AIDS crisis. My heart broke open and stayed open. From early 1985 until the end of 1992, when I finished my fourth book, a novel about AIDS, I served, like hundreds and thousands of others, in this struggle against a plague that seems as yet to have no ending. And I wrote about it. These words are from my novel *Families*.

Into this plague I came, both innocent and ignorant. Into this cauldron of fear, rage, loss, grief, I came.

I was, at the time, a middle-aged, middle-class writer from Texas, not a rebel, never an activist. I was neither nurse nor doctor, neither social worker nor psychiatrist. I was simply an ordinary woman whose son was dying.

I came to take care. I stayed to care. I stayed for seven years. And I will never be the same again.

I was not an observer. I was a participant. And everything that happened to me and the ones I loved is etched indelibly on my mind and in my body.

This plague changed the world. Those of us who served are all changed utterly. We can never go back to being the people we once were. The past is dead. Who we were has disappeared. Innocence has fled forever. Indifference finds no home here.

Those of us who are still alive are survivors in a plague with no ending. We endure. We serve. We attempt to stem the tide of an ocean of pain that keeps on coming. Our sons and daughters, husbands, wives, friends, lovers are scattered bones and ashes in that deep, that ocean with no ending.

We are not swept out to sea. We receive no such mercy. We are the caregivers. We stay on the shore and tend the wounded.

What is the lesson here? Surely there is a life lesson, or two or three or more, to be learned out of every tragedy. Otherwise, nothing makes sense.

Here are some lessons I learned. But at what cost!

I learned that families can come together in love, no matter what their disparate lifestyles, no matter what their unresolved agendas, when a luminous soul draws them together in a circle of unconditional love. I learned that other people's opinions, whether born out of ignorance, indifference, cruelty, or bigotry, have no relevance. I learned that actions of love eclipse rhetoric. I learned that the personal is the political, and the person is the universal, and that even when hearts break, they can serve. Indeed they must. I learned the power of emotions to fuel the words forward, so that the meaning behind the words can touch others and help them to understand. I learned that human beings are both stronger and wiser than I ever dreamed they were. I learned that love lasts beyond bodies. I learned about the essence shining out from within and beyond the body. I learned about the soul.

So, yes, I am changed forever by my son's journey. It has been an integral part of my own journey.

I can no longer stay on the shore and tend the wounded. Caregivers get tired and burnt-out, or "AIDSed-out" as they call it in the jargon of the movement. But I still serve.

Opening the heart is not a pious-sounding platitude. It is a perilous journey indeed. It requires a deepening and a strengthening, as well as a widening. The rewards are nothing less than the practice of unconditional love. But you will be changed at depth. You will be changed forever.

—Excerpted from *Soulwork: Clearing the Mind, Opening the Heart, Replenishing the Spirit* by Bettyclare Moffatt, © 1994. Reprinted with permission of New World Library, Novatao, CA 94949. www.nwlib.com.

Wisdom for the Caregiver

☞ "Most valuable are friends who have allowed me to talk about my fears, friends who were sensitive when referring to my illness (please don't use the term 'full-blown AIDS')."

—Thomas

☞ Encourage the person suffering from AIDS to talk to a counselor who deals specifically with people who have this illness.
☞ Help the person stay connected with friends.
☞ Help the person find and participate in a support group.
☞ Read "Caregiving Basics" (pp. 203-222).
☞ Check "109+ Ways to Say, 'I Care'" (pp. 223-234).
☞ See the suggestions in "Illness (Terminal)" (pp. 135-143).

Helplines

1. **Canadian AIDS Society**, 4th Floor, 309 Rue Cooper St., Ottawa, ON K2P 0G5. 1-613-230-3580. www.cdnaids.ca. National coalition of community-based AIDS organizations.
2. **Health Canada's HIV/AIDS Information**, Health Canada, Address Locator 0900C2, Ottawa, ON K1A 0K9. 1-613-957-2991. www.hc-sc.gc.ca/hpb.lcdc/publicat/stdmts/std_r.html.
3. **Information on Specific AIDS Concerns**. 1-900-346-7000. Offers recordings of information by topic (extension): blood transfusion (2115); men (2121); fact and fiction (2113); sex, stranger (2114); general info (2111); the latest news (2112).

4. **Medbroadcast Corporation**, Suite 250, Marine Building, 355 Burrard Street, Vancouver, BC V6C 2G8. 1-604-687-7463. www.medbroadcast.com. A comprehensive consumer health and wellness website that has links for medical conditions A-Z, links for support groups both by health topic and by location, and a link with information about prescription drugs.
5. **National AIDS Information Clearinghouse**, P.O. Box 6003, Rockville, MD 20849-6003. 1-800-458-5231. This is a national reference, referral, and distribution service for HIV/AIDS-related information. Staff or reference specialists answer questions and provide technical assistance and specific information on AIDS-related organizations, educational materials, etc.
6. **National Association of People with AIDS**. 1-202-429-2856.
7. **National HIV and AIDS Hotline**. 1-800-342-AIDS. In Spanish, 1-800-344-7432. For the hearing impaired, 1-800-AIDS-TTY (243-7889).
8. **RAIN (Regional AIDS Interfaith Network)**. This network offers help for people of faith who have AIDS. Search the Web by typing "Regional AIDS Interfaith Network" to find chapters in various states.

Books and Other Resources

⊗ Moffatt, Bettyclare. *Soulwork: Clearing the Mind, Opening the Heart, Replenishing the Spirit* (Berkeley, CA: Wildcat Canyon Press, 1994). Internationally known lecturer and teacher Bettyclare Moffat explores the soul with warmth, insight, and humor and teaches us how to live abundant lives of compassion, understanding, and joy. Her story will be a comfort and encouragement to clear the mind, open the heart, and replenish the spirit in times of crisis, AIDS or otherwise.

⊗ Stine, Gerald J. *AIDS Update 2002* (New York: Prentice Hall, 2001). This book presents the entire seventeen-year chronology of the AIDS pandemic in a logical manner that interweaves biological, clinical, social, and legal discoveries in a readable presentation. Comprehensive and up-to-date.

⊛ Ungvarski, Peter, Thomas Eoyang, and Jacquelyn Hask Flaskerud. *HIV/AIDS: A Guide to Primary Care* (London: WB Saunders Company, 1999). This book is a Brandon/Hill Nursing List first-purchase selection. It provides a case management approach to the care of people with HIV/AIDS.

⊛ Zylstra, Mignon M., with David Biebel. *When AIDS Comes Home* (Nashville: Thomas Nelson, 1996). A valuable resource for those who have AIDS, those who love them, and those who want to understand and respond to this frightening and deadly disease. Included are a glossary of HIV and AIDS terms, suggestions for a support ministry, and a model for a memorial service.

Alzheimer's Disease

Patience, Please!

Love is patient; love is kind.

—1 Corinthians 13:4

W hen Frank's mom was diagnosed with Alzheimer's disease, I think each one of the family members had the same reaction at first—grief. However, over time we dealt with her illness in different ways. Frank's sister and brother quickly moved into the denial stage and remained there until their mother's death. Frank himself stayed in the grief phase for quite a while, but then moved on to acceptance. "Acceptance" didn't mean, of course, that he gave up all hope—he still longed to see moments of lucidity in his mother.

If I had any advice to others who face taking care of a loved one with Alzheimer's, it would be to first seek the support of others who have gone through or are going through this same devastation. The Alzheimer's Association is a wonderful place to start—or visit your doctor or geriatric hospital. Listen to as many people as you can and form your approach from there.

Frank and I deliberately chose to use humor as much as possible. While it might not work for everyone, for us it helped relieve the overwhelming sense of helplessness we often felt. My goal was to keep his mother happy and not agitated, and I saw no harm in agreeing to some of her most outlandish comments or suggestions, just to keep her calm (as long as she was physically safe, of course). Agreeing with her when she was upset seemed to help ease her agitation. Why try to win an argument that will never have a winner? A case in point—Frank's mom loved to drink wine, but since she was diabetic and her Alzheimer's had progressed to the point that she couldn't control her sugar levels, wine was out of the question. When she asked for wine, I didn't argue. Instead, since she could no longer read, I served her sparkling apple cider or something similar. As long as it came out of a wine-shaped bottle, she was happy.

One more piece of advice: the family must make sure that the primary caregiver has plenty of support and the opportunity to get away from the situation as often as possible. Typically an elderly spouse has the role of primary caregiver; often, he or she—acting as a parent—will protect the rest of the family from knowing what a truly difficult challenge caregiving is. I think Frank's dad sometimes felt as if he were a prisoner in his own home—the doors had to be locked at all times (and preferably with locks out of the patient's reach). Because most Alzheimer's patients don't have a true concept of time, caregivers often find it difficult to rest at night. We think that Frank's dad's taking care of his wife for two years at home contributed to his death as well—he simply wore himself out physically and emotionally.

—Norma Butler

The Cost of Alzheimer's

The devastation of Alzheimer's disease goes far deeper than meets the eye. This horrible disease robbed my husband of his mind and faculties. It also robbed us of our savings, forcing us to sell our home. On the average, nursing care for an Alzheimer's patient costs $36,000 (U.S.) per year. Medicare does not cover this type of medical care.

Often the patient is much better off at home, if circumstances permit. The family member or friend who becomes the primary caregiver then must become the expert.

—Yvonne

Wisdom for the Caregiver (from Yvonne Jonker)

Note: Yvonne is the author of "Alzheimer's: The Bottom Line," a booklet you may order by calling 616-392-3225 or by writing Yvonne Jonker at 30 E. 13th Street, Holland, MI 49423.

- Exercise lots of patience.
- Establish routines. Alzheimer's patients can become very confused and disoriented, and rely heavily on a routine for everything they do. For example, one caregiver takes his patient for an ice cream cone at approximately the same time every day.
- Use distraction tactics when disciplining. Avoid scolding or reprimanding. For example, if the patient is misusing a piece of kitchen equipment or a tool, tell him he could hurt himself by holding it that way, then gently show him the right way to operate it.
- Use compassion as memory begins to fade.
- Humor the patient by diplomatically conceding to his or her wishes. One Alzheimer's patient insisted that she go to Canada. Instead of chiding her by explaining why this was impossible, her wise daughter asked, "What do you remember about Canada? What would you like to see there?" This enabled her mom to "travel" there in her mind.
- Deal with stubbornness diplomatically. *Be creative* when dealing with hygiene issues. For example, if the patient refuses to take a shower, make a game of it by taking one together or by scrubbing him or her down while he or she is seated on the toilet (lid down).
- Reassure frequently. Give the patient as little to worry about as possible. His or her life is fraught with disease. Nothing is the same as it used to be. He or she needs to be assured that all is well.
- Be constantly attentive when walking or doing chores/projects. Loss of balance and concentration are noticeable symptoms.
- Entertain your patient with simple activities, preferably things he or she enjoyed doing prior to the onset of the disease. In the early stages of the disease, perusing photograph albums, cooking, woodworking, walking,

or gardening are all possibilities. In an article for *Guideposts* (June 1995), Cynthia Hall tells how her father, an Alzheimer's sufferer, became productively happy once again after she encouraged him to paint wooden tulips to place on trays for shut-ins receiving Meals-On-Wheels.

⍟ Use humor to lighten the mood. Consult Lila Green's *Making Sense of Humor* (see p. 49) for ideas.

⍟ Treat the patient in a way that respects his or her dignity. Validate feelings and actions. Let the patient know what you are going to do before you do it. For example, "I am going to help you get dressed. Then we can go for a walk."

⍟ Realize that many patients respond only on the spiritual level. Touch, a shared passage of Scripture, and prayer are reassuring and comforting. The Holy Spirit can make inroads in the mind when it seems virtually impossible.

Severe Dementia

Severe dementia necessitates twenty-four-hour monitoring by a caregiver. Patients with severe dementia are noticeably disabled and need a good deal of help. They may be unable to find their way around, to remember moments just passed, to recognize relatives and friends. They may be incontinent, remove clothing in public, and make vulgar or profane remarks. They need to be washed, dressed, and fed. Constant care and attention are necessary.

Unless the patient is entirely alone in the world, there is no doubt that one person will have the burden of his or her everyday care. As the caregiver, it is vital to remember that you are an individual, with needs and interests of your own. You are not doing the patient a favor by becoming frustrated and resentful because your own needs aren't being met.

You must have frequent, regularly scheduled breaks. As one daughter put it, "We'll find help for you somehow. We couldn't cope ourselves if both of you became incapacitated."

Any information presented about Alzheimer's disease would be meaningless without mention of the family. Ironically, the family can be one of the most difficult burdens for the caregiver. Children, grandchildren, brothers, sisters, cousins, nieces and nephews, in-laws—none of these can be fully aware of the stringent demands placed upon a primary caregiver, unless, of course, they have spent a day and night in close contact with the patient as he or she drifts through a twenty-four-hour period.

Usually a family meeting—not just one time but at several intervals as the patient worsens—is beneficial for everyone. At these times, information and updates can be given, feelings explored, suggestions entertained, and the air "cleared." Honesty between family members should be paramount, so that genuine understanding of all the problems involved can be reached, for the betterment of all who are connected to the patient. At the family meeting, everyone should be assured that general coping will be easier if the family is unified. Do not discourage visiting, even by small children, unless the patient becomes overly excited and adversely stimulated by the presence of others. Frequently, children relate especially well to older people with dementia. Give them time to interact.

Be aware that another kind of role reversal exists—that between elderly parents and middle-aged children. When a patient still lives at home, there are times when an elderly parental caregiver fears the interference of middle-aged children; conversely, the middle-aged children often worry about someday having to take on a parental role to their own parents.

As you care for the patient day by day, be his or her ears and eyes. Turn on lights. Establish patterns and routines. Don't change furniture around. Simplify dressing with slip-on shoes, tube socks, zippers, and large buttons. Better yet, use Velcro. If the patient is a messy eater and/or incontinent, let him or her wear washable clothing that doesn't need ironing. Finger foods require less skill to eat. Offer foods that require little chewing, to avoid having the patient choke when he or she forgets how to swallow.

Finally, try not to overreact to negative happenings. While it's difficult—and sometimes impossible—to stay calm, remember that the onus for optimum peace of mind must be on the caregiver, not the patient.

—Yvonne Jonker, "Alzheimer's Disease: The Bottom Line." Used by permission.

Additional Wisdom for the Caregiver

- Check "109+ Ways to Say, 'I Care'" (pp. 223-234).
- Join a support group such as the Alzheimer's Association. (Check your phone directory for one in your neighborhood.)
- Pacing and wandering are very common behavior problems. Upon returning from work in the afternoon, the daughter of an Alzheimer's patient will lie down on the couch and put her head on her mother's lap. Her mother enjoys this closeness and will gently stroke her hair. Both are able to rest, sometimes for as long as thirty minutes.

⊗ If your Alzheimer's-afflicted spouse—or another person of the opposite gender—needs to use a public restroom and there is no help available, you may want to try this tip. One man carries a brass sign which reads "out of order." He places it on the restroom door, after checking that it is not in use. He then is able to assist his wife without embarrassing others.

⊗ Respite time for the caregiver is vital if the patient is to remain in his or her own home. Caregivers must have frequent, regularly scheduled breaks from providing constant care. Contact your Alzheimer's Association chapter and/or support group or ask your doctor.

Helplines

1. **Agevillage.com**. Offers information about Alzheimer's Disease in the French language.
2. **Alzheimer's Association**. 1-800-272-3900. www.alz.org. Literature, referrals, and information on local chapters and support groups.
3. **Alzheimer's Disease Education and Referral Center**, P.O. Box 8250, Silver Spring, MD 20907-8250. 1-800-438-4380; fax 1-301-495-3334. www.alzheimers.org. This organization provides information about Alzheimer's disease diagnosis, treatment, resources, and research. The Center also distributes printed information and makes referrals to other organizations. Services are provided free of charge.

    The following publications are available by calling or writing the ADEAR Center:
    • Alzheimer's Disease Fact Sheet
    • Multi-Infarct Dementia Fact Sheet
    • Progress Report on Alzheimer's Disease
    • Alzheimer's Disease Centers Program Directory

    Also available are a bibliography for caregiver and patient and (for a small fee) a booklet on Home Safety for the Alzheimer's patient.

4. **Alzheimer's Society of Canada**, 20 Eglinton Ave. W. #1200, Toronto, ON M4R 1K8. 1-800-616-8816; 1-416-488-8772; info@alzheimer.ca. www.alzheimer.ca. The website offers a listing of books on the disease

and on caregiving, as well as information about the Wandering Registry and indentification bracelets.

5. **Caregiving.com**. An online support service for caregivers.
6. **Medbroadcast Corporation**, Suite 250, Marine Building, 355 Burrard Street, Vancouver, BC V6C 2G8. 1-604-687-7463. www.medbroadcast.com. A comprehensive consumer health and wellness website that has links for medical conditions A-Z, links for support groups both by health topic and by location, and a link with information about prescription drugs.

Books and Other Resources

☺ Green, Lila. *Making Sense of Humor: How to Add Humor and Joy to Your Life* (Manchester, CT: Knowledge, Ideas, and Trends, Inc., 1994). Humor is entirely too important to be left to chance, says Lila Green. She shows how to inject humor into any situation that needs to be lightened up.

☺ Jonker, Yvonne. "Alzheimer's: The Bottom Line." To order this helpful booklet, call 616-392-3225 or write to 30 E. 13th Street, Holland, MI 49423.

☺ Mace, Nancy, and Peter Rabins. *The 36-Hour Day* (Chicago: John Hopkins University Press, 1981). Available from ADRDA, 360 N. Michigan Ave., Chicago, IL 60601. This guide provides all the practical advice you need to simplify caring for Alzheimer's patients, improve their quality of life, and lift the whole family's spirit. It includes such topics as "How to Cope with an Impaired Person's False Ideas, Suspicion, and Anger" and "How to Get Outside Help from Support Groups, Friends, and Agencies."

☺ Power, Lenore S., and Katie Courtice. *Alzheimer's Disease: A Guide for Families and Caregivers* (Reading, MA: Addison-Wesley Publishing Co., 1983, third edition 2002). Backed by solid medical information about the specifics of the disease—from early signs, testing, and diagnosis to treatments and long-term care—this comprehensive guide will help family and caregivers alike.

⊛ TRAVARCA. A video library sponsored by the Reformed Church in America and the Christian Reformed Church in North America, TRAVARCA carries thousands of videos on hundreds of topics, including Alzheimer's disease. A yearly membership allows churches and individuals to use an unlimited number of videos; nonmembers may use the videos for established fees. Call 1-800-968-7221 or 1-616-698-7071 for a catalog or to request information and videos.

Burnout (Of Pastors, Other Leaders, and Their Spouses)

On Duty Twenty-seven Hours a Day

Like vinegar on a wound is one who sings songs to a heavy heart.
—Proverbs 25:20, NRSV

During my early years as a pastor, I had a hard time balancing the demands of my job with the needs of my wife and family. Putting in long hours, struggling to get organized, and trying to figure out if I was up to this, I considered leaving the ministry. Eventually, the stress contributed to a divorce from my first wife.

During the difficult time when I was going through my divorce there was one person from my church who called daily, took me out for coffee to listen to me, and invited me to dinner. He did not lecture, did not pry, and did not try to get my wife and me back together. He was simply, steadfastly there for me. I will never forget the strength that man gave me.

I have found help in disciplining my time and tending to my needs. I meet with a weekly support group of half a dozen pastors and get together monthly with other fellow clergy. I also take a two-day break each month, retreating to a lake up north for study, planning, fishing, and playing the guitar. That has become as important to me as breathing.

—The pastor cited in this article wishes to remain anonymous.
Based on an interview by the authors of this book and on an
article by Charles Honey, "That Dark Night of the Soul,"
Grand Rapids Press (June 1, 1996), pp. B1-B2.

Wisdom for the Caregiver

Note: The following suggestions were taken from Wes Roberts, "37 Ways to Support Your Pastor," *Discipleship Journal* (no. 92, 1996), pp. 27-31.

- Give time. Tell your pastor you have rearranged your personal schedule and have six free hours per month to give him or her in two three-hour blocks.
- Find out the vision your pastor has for your church, and if something also rings your bells, ask if you can help champion that particular cause.
- Mobilize an army of volunteers. If you can find people who will keep all the volunteer slots filled in your church, your pastor will nominate you for sainthood.
- Give your pastor a call. Limit your call to five minutes or less, focusing on your care and concern. If he or she is busy, leave a message saying he or she was on your mind and you just called to say, "I care about what is happening in your life today. You're in my prayers." What a boost just that much would be!
- Do not stand for gossip. Whenever you hear people criticize your pastor, encourage them to go directly to the pastor with those comments. Do not pass what you hear down the grapevine. That's gossip. If you agree with what the other person is saying, make your own appointment with the pastor and get things settled between the two of you.
- Stand up for your pastor when he or she is not present to defend him- or herself.
- Say it with a note. My office files contain a folder with handwritten notes, and even printed e-mail messages, that I have kept to read on down days when I wonder if I'm fit to serve within the kingdom of God. How about making a practice of sending your pastor a note of appreciation for something you've caught him or her doing very well!
- Recognize your pastor's gifts. Next time you see your pastor, look him or her right in the eye and say with sincerity, "God has really gifted

you in [this area]. It is good to see God using you in that way." Be truthful, and don't gush.

⊛ Pray first. Pray for your pastor first—not as a last resort.

⊛ Pray often. Commit to praying for your pastor or pastors and their families regularly (every day if possible), and let them know you are doing that. Invite them to give you specific prayer requests.

⊛ Allow your pastor to be human. Pastors are regular folk, called and anointed by God for a particular purpose, just as you are. They have struggles, even if they pretend they don't, and they are often tempted in the same ways you are. They get frustrated with the garbage disposal and have lawnmower problems just like everybody else.

⊛ Let the pastor's family be free. Don't require your pastor's spouse or children to fit into a certain mold. Do all that you can to let each of them be uniquely who they are. Don't judge.

⊛ Send each of your pastors and their spouses on a weeklong trip every three to five years. Don't count it as vacation time, study leave time, or a mini-sabbatical, but as a gift of love from the congregation.

⊛ Provide a place for R&R. If both you and your spouse work (outside the home), and you have a home with a quiet backyard or garden, offer it to your pastor as an occasional refuge for rest and reflection while you're at work.

⊛ Allow your pastor to play. Find out your pastor's recreational interests and give him or her a gift certificate to splurge a little.

⊛ Take your pastor to a fun place. Most pastoral couples don't laugh enough. Think hard: Where could you take your pastoral staff just to laugh and be silly? Or what kind of party could you throw to get your church staff laughing?

⊛ Invite your pastor and spouse over for the evening with no agenda other than to be with them—and let them know that.

⊛ Give your pastor professional perks. What is your profession? What skills do you have—tax preparation, medical or dental expertise, home repair, car repair, golf or skiing lessons, gardening? Offer them free to your pastor in a one-time or lifetime deal.

⊛ Help around the house. Offer to help your pastor's family with some job that needs to be done, such as mowing their lawn or painting, to allow their family more time together. On his or her day off, the last thing a pastor probably wants to do is to prune trees, cut grass, trim hedges, and clean up. Offer to bring in a crew to do it all so your pastor can select his or her "rest of choice" for the day of rest and leisure.

ⓦ Respect your pastor's privacy. Give your pastoral families an undisturbed dinner hour between 6:00 and 8:00 p.m. Don't call before 7:00 a.m. or after 10:00 p.m., except in true emergencies. Do not call the pastor on his or her day off.

ⓦ Celebrate your pastor's anniversary. Creatively find some way to mark the anniversary of when your pastor came to your church, either on the very day or on the weekend closest to it.

ⓦ Remember other special dates. How about remembering in some manner the birthdays and wedding anniversaries of your pastors and their families? Release your pastors from any "duty" on their kids' birthdays and on their wedding anniversaries.

ⓦ "Kidnap" your church staff and their spouses, bring them to a central point, and put them in a bus or large van. (Better yet, pick them up in limousines.) Then give them a progressive dinner of appreciation at various members' homes. Provide babysitting and meals for the kids. Take pictures of each couple and of the whole group and have them framed for each couple as a gift of thanks and remembrance.

ⓦ Be an encourager. You have within you all you need to be of tremendous encouragement to your pastor and his or her spouse and family. No one can do exactly what you can to love your pastor well. Be open to the Holy Spirit's leading for just how creative you can be. Stretch yourself a bit and watch what happens with your pastors as they relax and come alive and come forward in their unique calling—ministers of the gospel of Jesus Christ. What an awesome calling. What an awesome task!

—from *Discipleship Journal,* no. 92, 1996, © 1996 by Wes Roberts, Founder/CCO of Leadership Design Group/Life Enrichment Ministries, Parker, CO. Used by permission.

Helplines

1. **American Association of Christian Counselors**, P.O. Box 739, Forest, VA 24551. 1-800-5-COUNSEL; 1-434-525-9470. www.aacc.net. This organization has a directory of counselors who are members of AACC—a great tool for finding a Christian counselor in just about any region in the United States.
2. **Cross Canada Search**. www.crosscanadasearch.com. A Christian Internet search engine. Includes information about Christian counseling services (www.crosscanadasearch.com/Ministry_Resources/Counselling).
3. **Desperate Preachers' Site**. www.desperatepreacher.com/pastor-care/intro_burnout.htm. Several pages of contributions about preventing burnout.
4. **Gray Fox Ranch**, P.O. Box 434, Alto, NM 88312. 1-877-472-9333; 1-505-336-7721; fax 1-505-336-9126. www.grayfox.org. Gray Fox offers clergy restoration, clergy care retreats, marriage counseling and enrichment, and more in the mountain country of New Mexico.
5. **Quiet Waters Ministries**, c/o Bethesda Foundation, Inc., 9185 E. Kenyon Ave., Suite 150, Denver, CO 80237. 1-866-592-8377; info@QWaters.org. www.QWaters.org.

Cancer

A Battle With Cancer

To me healing is letting God write the script of my life. It is choosing to let God's will and my will be one.

—Gerald Jampolsky, M.D.

There are few words that strike terror in the heart like the word *cancer.* It is such a silent, insidious disease. A survivor usually wonders when and where it will strike next. At age 53, I was diagnosed with colon cancer. I was afraid, anxious, and angry. Why had this happened to me?

In the midst of my fear and trembling came God's armor-bearers. They bathed me in prayer and surrounded me with loving words through cards and phone calls.

After abdominal surgery, I returned home and was not allowed to drive for six weeks. Knowing how confining that would be for me, my friends made sure I was "out and about" every day of those six weeks.

Often when a person has a long-term illness, cards and phone calls become less frequent as time passes. However, one friend has continued to remember me with a postcard every day (322 cards so far!). The postcard has an encouraging word, a humorous saying, or words of wisdom that challenge me and give me hope. I have been deeply touched by such long-term care.

During Treatment

I have often asked myself where God is as we suffer through the painful, frightening times in our lives. I have come to the conclusion that for me, God has been with me in many different ways.

God has been present in the encouraging words of a minister friend who said, "I was tempted to quit my treatment, too. But I kept on, knowing that this is the best treatment we have at the moment. I'll always know I used the best that was available." God has been in the words of a book, *Cancer: 50 Essential Things To Do* by Greg Anderson, and in the advice given by Dr. Patrick Quillin in *Beating Cancer with Nutrition*. God has been in the presence of two friends who always played golf with me before I went for chemotherapy so that I wouldn't have to sit home and dread the treatment that was coming. God has been in the continuing presence of a friend who has been my constant companion at therapy appointments. God has been in the cards, phone calls, and voices of friends who have said, "Just remember, Pat, I'm praying for you."

It has been an ongoing battle to stick with the yearlong program that was prescribed, but God's grace-filled presence in people and events has helped me and will enable me to persevere to the end.

The Battle Continues: Years Two and Three

With chemotherapy at an end, life and health returned to normal. The months that followed were good, healthy, fun-filled, and purposeful. Regular checkups during the following year were all normal except for an inexplicable rise in the CEA, a blood test used as a tumor marker for cancer patients. CAT scans revealed nothing, but the CEA continued to climb. Finally, almost a year later, exploratory surgery revealed that the original cancer had spread to the abdominal cavity. It is never good news when cancer returns. It means we are dealing with a more resistant strain of cancer, one that has survived a year of chemotherapy. Since the recurring cancer could not be removed surgically, more chemotherapy was needed. I tried another year of chemo, but even though the CEA dropped significantly, the cancer cells could not be eradicated.

Once again fear and uncertainty returned. Since chemotherapy was not effective, I decided to look for a clinical trial that might prove helpful to me. The September 1996 issue of *Scientific American* was devoted to cancer causes and cures currently being studied by researchers and scientists. My husband and I read through the experimental studies, and, after much prayer and soul-searching, I applied to participate in an experimental study being conducted at Memorial Sloan-Kettering in New York City. I was accepted for a three-month study that involved a trip to New York once a week for treatment. We are uncertain at the moment about the effectiveness of this treatment; however, there are no significant side effects and so I have felt well during this time. We have done things, seen things, and met people we never would have without this experience.

Paul and I have longed for and prayed for a miracle. Whether that request will be granted is still uncertain. But it feels as though God has been involved in the whole process. We have continued to meet with God's prayer warriors as faithfully as we have continued with medical treatments. The elders of our church have met with us weekly, laid hands on me, and anointed me with oil as instructed in James. God has chosen to teach all of us many things about prayer. Waiting patiently, being persistent, accepting God's timetable, learning to not manipulate God or pout like frustrated children, to surrender both the how and when of answered prayer to God—these are some of the things we struggle with as we pray.

Some of the fear and uncertainty remains, and the roller coaster of emotions continues. But Paul and I are learning in new ways to appreciate each day and to offer gratitude for things that happen each day: for the sun at five thousand feet above the clouds on the way to New York; for the birds that are finally finding our Christmas bird feeder; for the commitment of people who take the time to pray with us each week; for a friend who travels with me to New York when Paul is unable to; for friends who are letting us spend two weeks at their condominium in Florida.

Again we ask ourselves where God is in this journey, but again we find God in the grace-filled and compassionate presence of the people of God who are part of the body of Christ. One of the surest signs of God's loving presence through all this struggle is to realize once again that I am married to a man who loves me and who fights with me, and when I am too tired or frightened to fight any more, fights in my place. For this kind of marriage, I am deeply grateful.

—Pat

Wisdom for the Caregiver (from Pat)

- Send cards and notes, frequently. Many people have told us that they save all these cards and reread them often. From each reading they receive much energy and hope.
- Listen. It is the greatest gift we bring to someone. God gave us two ears and one mouth so that we can listen more and talk less.
- Give the following cassettes to the person who has cancer:
  —"Zinger" by Paul Azinger (HarperCollins, 1995). After winning the 1993 PGA Championship, Paul Azinger felt he had overcome an incredible obstacle; but when the doctors found cancer in his shoulder bone, his greatest fight was just beginning. "Zinger" is the inspiring portrait of a great athlete and a great human being who has learned to look at the positive side of such experiences and who wants others to know about the spiritual strength he has found. This tape is available at Amazon.com.
  —"Health Journeys Image Paths." This tape is designed to counteract the negative thinking that patients often have about chemotherapy. Side A features twenty minutes of guided imagery. Side B offers ten minutes of verbal positive affirmations. If not available at your local bookstore, contact: Health Journeys Image Paths, Inc., P.O. Box 5714, Cleveland, OH 44101-0714. 1-800-800-8661.

Additional Wisdom for the Caregiver

- Read "Caregiving Basics" (pp. 203-222).
- Check "109+ Ways to Say, 'I Care'" (pp. 223-234).
- "Please do not avoid or ignore the person because you do not know what to say or do. Don't worry about saying anything. Just be *with* the person, give her a hug, and let her know that you care."

—Dorothy

- Give the person *Today, I Have Cancer: A Daily Journal of Life with Cancer* by Debi Estabrook (Waverly, IA: G&R Publishing, 1995).

Available on Amazon.com. This is a flip-a-page each day journal. Each day a topic is given and a small space is provided to respond.

⊚ When the timing seems right, give your friend a copy of the following poem:

What Cancer Cannot Do
      CANCER is so LIMITED
It CANNOT cripple love
It CANNOT shatter hope
It CANNOT corrode faith
It CANNOT destroy peace
It CANNOT kill friendship

      It CANNOT suppress memories
      It CANNOT silence courage
      It CANNOT invade the soul
      It CANNOT steal eternal life
      It CANNOT conquer the Spirit

—Anonymous

⊚ "Remember, people with cancer still have the same needs and often the same capabilities as they did before. If they are physically able, they need to participate in their normal range of activities and responsibilities—right down to taking out the garbage. Helplessness, or worse, an unnecessary feeling of helplessness, is one of the great woes of the person with cancer. Make every effort not to compound them by ignoring the wishes of the patient, or worse, by trying to make an invalid of a person who is up and around. Pulling one's weight is good exercise."

—*Taking Time—Support for People with Cancer and the People Who Care About Them* (National Institutes of Health, 1992; NIH Publication No. 93-2059). (This booklet is found in the waiting rooms of many doctors.)

Helplines

1. **American Cancer Society,** Park Avenue, New York, NY 10016. 1-212-736-3030. The American Cancer Society is a national voluntary organization whose programs include education, patient services, and rehabilitation. Local ACS units provide information, counseling, and guidance; referral to community health services and other resources; equipment loans for care of the homebound patient; surgical dressings; transportation to and from treatment; and rehabilitation programs.

   For cancer information by recording, call 1-900-346-7000. Extensions:
   ⊛ bladder cancer (1131)
   ⊛ breast cancer (1111)
   ⊛ cervical cancer (1112)
   ⊛ colon cancer (1113)
   ⊛ Hodgkin's disease (1143)
   ⊛ kidney cancer (1135)
   ⊛ leukemia/adults (1123)
   ⊛ liver cancer (1141)
   ⊛ lung cancer (1121)
   ⊛ ovarian cancer (1125)
   ⊛ prostate cancer (1114)
   ⊛ skin cancer (1115)
   ⊛ stomach cancer (1132)
   ⊛ testicular cancer (1144)
   ⊛ throat cancer (1142)
   ⊛ uterine cancer (1124)

2. **Canadian Cancer Society**, Suite 200, 10 Alcorn Avenue, Toronto, ON M4V 3B1. 1-416-961-7223. www.cancer.ca.

3. **Candlelighters Childhood Cancer Foundation Canada**, 55 Eglinton Ave. East, Suite 401, Toronto, ON M4P 1G8. 1-800-363-1062; 1-416-489-6440. This organization is dedicated to improving the quality of life for families experiencing the effects of childhood cancer

through the provision of resources, parent support, and the promotion of research.

4. **Health Canada**, Address Locator 0900C2, Ottawa, ON K1A 0K9. 1-613-957-2991. www.hc-sc.gc.ca. The federal department responsible for helping the people of Canada maintain and improve their health. Options on the website include searching topics A-Z (www.hc-sc.gc.ca/english/diseases/index.html) and finding locations of regional offices (www.hc-sc.gc.ca/english/contact/index.html).

5. **Medbroadcast Corporation**, Suite 250, Marine Building, 355 Burrard Street, Vancouver, BC V6C 2G8. 1-604-687-7463. www.medbroadcast.com. A comprehensive consumer health and wellness website that has links for medical conditions A-Z, links for support groups both by health topic and by location, and a link with information about prescription drugs.

6. **National Cancer Institute**, Building 31, Room 10A24, Bethesda, MD 20892. www.cancer.gov. The National Cancer Institute sponsors a toll-free Cancer Information Service, open seven days a week. By dialing 1-800-422-6237, you will be connected to a trained staff member who can answer your questions and listen to your concerns.

Books and Other Resources

⊛ Anderson, Greg. *Cancer: 50 Essential Things To Do* (New York: Plume Books, 1999). Written by cancer survivor Greg Anderson, this revised version of his earlier book is an invaluable guide to recovery, filled with practical healing "action steps" that have been taken by thousands of cancer survivors.

⊛ Babcock, Elise Needell. *When Life Becomes Precious: A Guide for Loved Ones and Friends of Cancer Patients* (New York: Bantam Books, 1997). Offers hundreds of tips for helping patients, primary caregivers, coworkers, and family members, including: what to say, how to be supportive without being intrusive, how to explain the disease to children, and which gifts and gestures can do the most good.

◉ Canfield, Jack (editor). *Chicken Soup for the Surviving Soul: 101 Healing Stories of Courage and Inspiration* (Deerfield Beach, FL: Health Communications, Inc., 1996). This book is filled with incredible stories from those who have reached beyond the pain of body and soul to survive cancer. Those recovering from a debilitating illness or a serious injury will also find relief from their pain in the warmth of these stories.

◉ Harwell, Amy. *When Your Friend Gets Cancer: How You Can Help* (Wheaton, IL: Harold Shaw Publishers, 1987). Practical advice by a cancer patient on the ways she appreciated her friends' acts of caring in the face of her crisis.

◉ Siegel, Bernie S. *Peace, Love, and Healing: Bodymind Communication and the Path to Self-Healing: An Exploration* (New York: Harper Perennial, 1990). Siegel encourages the ill person (he dislikes the term "patient") to work for peace of mind and to live each moment fully in spite of one's disease.

◉ Sorenson, Sharon, and Suzanne Metzger. *The Complete Idiot's Guide to Living with Breast Cancer* (Indianapolis: Alpha Books, 2000). There is reason for hope, and you'll find this guide will be helpful every step of the way—with information, recommendations, and practical tips. Includes invaluable advice from breast cancer survivors, easy ways to find support groups, and all you need to know about treatments, recovery, and reconstruction.

◉ Vos, Mirth. *Letters to Myself on Dying: A Journal of Hope, Pain, and Courage* (Grand Rapids, MI: Baker Books and Faith Alive Christian Resources, 1999). This account of one woman's battle with cancer gives insight into a love relationship with God that stands up to severe testing and triumphs through faith. Written with both elegance and angst, this book is an unflinching portrait of how Vos learned to grieve her own impending death. (Call 1-800-333-8300 or visit www.FaithAliveResources.org to order.)

Caregivers Taking Care of Caregivers

Stress and the Caregiver

We must accept our vulnerability and limitations in regard to others. This is essential in gaining their confidence. We cannot expect to help others from the "outside."

—Mother Teresa of Calcutta

D on't overlook the major caregiver. He or she needs some uplifting too!

The most difficult time for my wife (Jean) and me was dealing with the two-and-a-half-year losing battle with cancer waged by our nineteen-year-old son, Paul. Within days of the diagnosis, his left leg was amputated two-thirds above the knee, and after metastasis he endured a series of six lung surgeries.

My response was to personally appropriate the stories of Jesus' encounters with heartbroken parents: Mark 5:23 became, "My son is at the point of death. Come and lay your hands on him, so that he may be made well, and live." Matthew 20:30-33 was reduced to, "Lord, have mercy on us, Son of David! Have mercy on us, Lord, Son of David! Lord, let our son be healed."

As mother and homemaker, Jean was Paul's primary caregiver. From the beginning, Paul knew that Jean would willingly have taken his cancer into her body. Through every medical checkup at the Mayo Clinic, through every negative test result, every major surgery in Rochester to remove the cancer from his lungs, Jean waited and worried and walked with him. Devastated within, she exuded strength without for his sake.

When Paul married, he and his wife Ruth settled into an apartment across town, and Jean's emotional stress moved to a new level. Instead of offering some relief and peace, daily physical separation brought the fresh anxiety of wondering hour by hour exactly how he was feeling. Finally, when the spread of the malignancy from the lungs to the rib cage made further surgeries useless, Paul chose to return to his first home to die.

Institutional care was avoided by the installation of oxygen tanks and a hospital bed on our front porch. A hospice nurse taught Ruth and Jean how to administer morphine injections. During those final three months, haunted by morphine and oxygen, Jean never used her bed. Not surprisingly, it was in those months that migratory rheumatoid arthritis permanently invaded Jean's exhausted body.

—Jim Cook

Caring for Caregivers

Caring for children and aging parents can be a profound blessing even while being very difficult. God's Word calls us to honor our parents and to help provide for their needs. At the same time, the needs of our spouse and children also call to us. Most families who care for an ill or aging family member are unable to spend as much time in quality communication or doing things together as they would like.

What can we do about all these competing responsibilities? First, continue to *feed yourself spiritually* so that God can use you in your relationship with others. Living a balanced life provides benefit for this life and the life to come. With our fast-paced lives, it is very easy to neglect our own physical, emotional, and spiritual self-care, but this is a dangerous path to take. Second, *trust the Lord to provide for all your needs* because God cares for you (1 Peter 5:7). Third, *develop a list of family needs and concerns* for yourself, your children, and your parents, deleting those needs that you personally cannot help meet. Of the needs that remain, determine the ones for which you are primarily responsible, then decide which ones are the most important. Fourth, *contact your pastor or your parish nurse* to see if they can help you in some way. You are not alone in your struggles.

Here are few other tips:

- Be confident and hopeful in God's promises to walk with you and not send more than you and he can carry!
- Listen to family members and friends. They often see signs of stress before you do.
- Accept help from family, friends, and professionals.
- Involve others in care. They may be willing and ready, if you let them know what would be helpful.
- Delegation is an art form.
- Find some personal time for yourself *every* day.
- Take care of yourself physically, emotionally, spiritually, and socially.
- Consider being part of a support group, or help form one if none is available.

God has placed us in families for our good and the good of the human family. May you find peace and joy through all the situations life can bring.

—Barb Sychowski, parish nurse

Wisdom for the Caregiver (from Jim and Jean)

- Letters, calls, meals, and prayers continually supported us. One word spoken by a neighbor who had lost a son said so much: "I am so sorry." (Jim)
- We believed that God was present with us, but how God was present was expressed in a letter from a friend who had lost a son in a motorcycle accident: "God incarnates his love in the people who surround us—family, friends, doctors, nurses, and strangers." Some of these people offered prayers that I couldn't even form. When my son said to me, "I need your strength, not your tears," those prayers gave me all the strength, all the love, and all the care I needed to care for Paul. Those prayers gave him the courage to die. (Jean)

⊛ In general, caring people who asked us about our son's condition and how we were doing constantly surrounded us. We thus learned the reality and blessing of the "communion of saints." Specifically, our eldest son took a week of his vacation and joined his brother and us in Rochester, Minnesota, to walk with us all through the biopsy, the amputation of a leg, and the coronary crisis that followed unexpectedly. That was an incredible gift to the sufferer and his parents! (Jim)

⊛ Among all those who offered us pastoral care, the most unacceptable word came from a ministerial student who said, "I know how you feel." The most honest and helpful thing was said by a pastor friend in Rochester who had children: "I *can't* imagine how you must feel!" (Jean)

⊛ Care to those who are in grief over the sufferer means always asking about the crisis, not avoiding it. That crisis is the most important thing in their lives. Normally, they will want to talk about it, perhaps cry about it. Offering care can mean offering them an opportunity to do both in the presence of someone who loves them. (Jim)

⊛ Each person has a special gift, a cup of cold water, which he or she can give to one who suffers. Some have the gift to listen or to speak just the right word. Others have the gift of just being there so that the sufferers do not go through their agony alone. My cup of cold water, my gift, was baking Paul's favorite cookies and learning to give him morphine injections. That is who I am. I think you *do* what you *are*. (Jean)

Additional Wisdom for the Caregiver

⊛ "For three years after her diagnosis for cancer, my wife experienced a continuous degeneration of her condition. As this was occurring she was less and less able to take care of herself and the family. With two adolescent sons, a business to run, and the stress of caring for my wife, my time was strained. So many things needed time and attention. Friends came forward without being asked and organized the supporting acts of other caring people. One assisted in communicating the latest news, another helped by scheduling meals to be brought in several times a week, others stayed with my wife when I was working, and some cared for my wife in any way that was needed. With the help of many, our needs were met."

—Steve

- Help out the tired caregiver by doing little things, like mowing the lawn, driving their kids to school functions, cleaning the house, unloading the dishwasher. Take them out to a movie or out for dinner or for a round of golf. Offer to stay with the patient so that the caregiver can have a break.
- Suggest to your friend that if he or she is too tired from hospital visitation to receive phone calls, he or she might put a message on the answering machine about the loved one's condition.
- Don't tell your own sordid story ("Uncle Jack had the same back injury and he never recovered"). When overloaded with your own concerns, it's difficult to absorb another's problem.
- Don't say, "I'm sure he will be all right." Although well meaning, these rescuing attempts aren't honest or helpful. No one, except God, knows the outcome.
- Share James Cook's booklet with the caregiver: "Shared Pain and Sorrow: Reflections of a Secondary Sufferer" (Pilgrim Press, 1991).
- The person in the hospital receives flowers, cards, visits and other gestures that say, "We care about you!" Meanwhile the non-hospitalized caregiver rushes around trying to care for the patient, the family, the home, and other responsibilities. Remember the major caregiver by inviting him or her for dinner, or inviting him or her to stop by on the way home from the hospital for a sandwich or cup of coffee.
- Call the caregiver and ask how he or she is doing.
- If the hospital is in another area and involves a drive alone, offer to drive the person or ride along with him or her.
- Read "Caregiving Basics" (pp. 203-222).
- Check "109+ Ways to Say, 'I Care'" (pp. 223-234).

Helplines

1. **Canadian Caregivers Coalition**, 110 Argyle Avenue, Ottawa, ON K2P 1B4. 1-888-866-2273; ccc_ccan@von.ca. www.ccc-ccan.ca. A bilin-

gual alliance of individuals, groups, and organizations promoting awareness and action to address the needs of caregivers in Canada.

2. **Caregiver.com**, 6365 Taft St., #3006, Hollywood, FL 33024. 1-954-893-0550; info@caregiver.com. A website with links for Alzheimer's, bipolar disorder, long-term care, caregiver health, elder care, and more.

3. **Veterans Affairs Canada**, www.vac-acc.gc.ca/clients/sub.cfm?source=health/caregiving.burnout. A website about protecting yourself from caregiver burnout.

Books and Other Resources

⛤ Berman, Claire. *Caring for Yourself While Caring for Your Aging Parents: How to Help, How to Survive* (New York: Henry Holt and Company, Inc., 1996). For women and men who are involved (or are likely to become involved) in caring for aging parents, this book centers on the emotional needs of caregivers but also addresses all the practical issues they are likely to confront.

⛤ Kouri, Mark. *Keys to Survival for Caregivers* (Hauppauge, NY: Barrons, 1992). Sickness and infirmity of a loved one can take its toll on caregivers. Here is practical advice on pacing yourself as a caregiver, knowing how and when to seek additional help, and conserving your energy to preserve your own physical and emotional health.

⛤ Strom, Kay Marshall. *A Caregiver's Survival Guide: How to Stay Healthy When Your Loved One Is Sick* (Downers Grove, IL: InterVarsity Press, 2000). Whether you are caring for an elderly parent or other adult relative, you will be encouraged by the stories the author tells from her own life and from the lives of others. Specific ideas will help carry you through. Some of the topics discussed include finding spiritual support, maintaining balanced relationships, and understanding the impact on the whole family.

Criminal Offense

Bars That Separate

Remember those in prison as if you were their fellow prisoners.

—Hebrews 13:3

My son is twenty-eight years old and has spent fifteen of those years in various types of prisons. During his growing-up years our family was actively involved in the life of our church, and yet, since his incarceration, only two church members have ever visited my son in prison. I don't believe that he has ever received a note or card from any of the other members. He often asks me, "Does anyone at church ever ask about me?" I have to say, "That was a long time ago."

—Jan

My daughter pleaded guilty to a felony. If you are a parent, imagine how you would feel. Then you will be able to describe my pain without any additional words from me.

—Anonymous

Wisdom for the Caregiver

ᐁ "When I began to receive notes of comfort and encouragement, I discovered the remarkable healing power of true friendship. Any show of concern will help. The simple sentence 'I'm so sorry about your trouble' says it all.

"I valued friends who shared concern but who did not ask for details. Generally a person experiencing pain wishes to choose his or her ways and with whom they wish to share."

—Anonymous

ᐁ "Real friends showed love, faith, and belief. They were ready to forgive even when things looked the worst. Just being there and expressing unconditional love and friendship is a beautiful grace-filled gift. (Funny thing, for the most part, those who professed to be the most devout Christians didn't call or visit or say anything. This hurt the most.)"

—Sally

ᐁ Read "Caregiving Basics" (pp. 203-222).
ᐁ Check "109+ Ways to Say, 'I Care'" (pp. 223-234).

Helplines

1. **M2/W2 (Man to Man/Woman to Woman)**, 1-604-859-3215; office@m2w2.com. www.m2w2.com. An ecumenical Christian organization in British Columbia that works at building relationships with prisoners who have lost contact with the community.
2. **Prison Fellowship**, P.O. Box 1550, Merrifield, VA 22116-1550. 1-877-478-0100; 1-703-478-0100; correspondence@pfm.org. www.pfm.org.

A non-profit organization whose mission is "to exhort, equip, and assist the Church in its ministry to prisoners, ex-prisoners, victims, and their families, and in its promotion of biblical standards of justice in the criminal justice system."

3. **Prison Fellowship of Canada**, 407 Speers Road, #203, Oakville, ON L6K 3J5. 1-905-339-0213. www.prisonfellowship.ca.

Books and Other Resources

⊛ Stevens, Margaret, and Roger Stevens. *Family of the Jailed* Charlottesville, VA: Walsch Books, 2001). What happens when someone you love is accused of a crime and sent to prison? How do you provide emotional support to him or her during the uncertainties, indignities, and seeming injustices of the legal process and prison life? How do you sustain yourself through such an ordeal? A mother and her imprisoned son—both ordained ministers—have written this memoir to help other families cope with incarceration and with their feelings of shame, bitterness, anger, despair, and hopelessness.

Death of a Parent, Relative, or Friend

Room to Grieve

Rejoice with those who rejoice; mourn with those who mourn.

—Romans 12:15

When my father died three years ago, I was devastated. He had been my best friend and mentor. At the time, I was already being treated for depression (which, I believe, was partially related to my concern for my dad over the last year of his life).

After dad died, many cards came my way. However, what I most appreciated was an agreement among my friends to visit or call me once each day for about two weeks. They held me while I fell apart in torrents of tears and moanings. They listened to me talk about my dad. They let me share as my tears were eventually replaced by moments of laughter. They hugged me, held me, and let me know in every way that they cared and stood with me.

—Robin

I was most helped by those who took note of my mother's death and let me know they shared my sorrow. I did not need sermons, lectures, time-honored sayings. Reminders of the meaning of our faith in this experience were helpful, but I didn't need them. Actually I probably would have been happier without any caregivers around. It was just sufficient to know people cared. What was not helpful was when people said, "I know just what you are going through." They may have lost a mother but their circumstances were not the same as mine. What I remember most of that experience was that one person drove a distance to attend the memorial service—just to be there to experience that service with me.

—Gerald

Wisdom for the Caregiver

⊛ Share a memory. When talking to or writing a note to a friend or relative of a deceased person, try sharing an incident or story that you especially appreciate about the deceased, or simply mention his or her admirable qualities. The following illustrates this suggestion:

> *One wintry day I was having lunch with Mary, an acquaintance whom I hadn't seen since my childhood. She happened to ask how old I was when my father died. When I replied that I was only fourteen, she said, "What a waste. Your father was such a wonderful man!"*
>
> *She then told me about an encounter she had had with my father when she was a teen. Climbing the beach steps to our cottage, she had slipped and slightly injured herself. When an expletive slipped from her lips, my father asked her to sit with him on the landing, and then gently he pointed out the shallowness of such speech. Mary said, "I felt so validated that he took the time to say that to me. It really showed me how much he cared about me."*
>
> *I returned home from our lunch date feeling warm all over despite the subzero temperature. What a gift it was to have someone speak about my father in such glowing terms thirty-seven years after his death!*
>
> —Ginger Jurries

⊛ Read "Caregiving Basics" (pp. 203-222).
⊛ Consider the ideas in "109+ Ways to Say, 'I Care'" (pp. 223-234).

☞ Read other first-person stories about caring for someone who is grieving the death of a loved one. (See pp. 77-98.)

☞ Attend the memorial service. We tend to shy away from funeral homes and memorial services. Is it because such visits make us more aware of our own mortality? Or perhaps we are uncomfortable because we don't know what to say to those who are grieving. Whatever the reason, the important thing is to *be there.* The following article was written following the death of a precious boy whose parents were members of the church I attended. It illustrates the importance of caring within the context of the family of God.

> *Those who attended the memorial service for Matthew Vanderwel, I am sure, felt very deeply the emotions that I experienced—sorrow, anger, regret, compassion, loss. I came to the service because my spirit wanted to touch and comfort the Vanderwels; I felt the need to give. After the service, I felt a warm glow penetrate my sorrow. The glow emanated from an unexpected gift that I had received during that hour.*
>
> *First, I experienced comfort myself. It was as though a bruise had been gently rubbed with a soothing balm. The music, the message, the tears which freely flowed, and the knowledge that God truly is love, that God is still in control—all were healing balm.*
>
> *Second, I felt a unique oneness with others at the service. Matthew not only belonged to the Vanderwels, he belonged to all of us! As the family of God, we experienced the loss collectively. Never have I felt a stronger bond, a more profound closeness with the beloved Body of Christ than that somber Tuesday. Over and over came the thought, "How can one endure a tragedy without a church family such as this?"*
>
> *The treasured gift of such a family is one I have continued to relish with a reverent awe.*
>
> —Ginger Jurries

Helplines

See pages 81-82 for Helplines.

Books and Other Resources

See pages 82-83 and page 98 for books and other resources.

Death of a Spouse

The Process of Grief

Listen, I will tell you a mystery: We will not all die, but we will all be changed—in a flash, in the twinkling of an eye, at the last trumpet. For the trumpet will sound, the dead will be raised imperishable, and we will be changed.

—1 Corinthians 15:51-52

When my husband was killed in a private plane crash, I was completely devastated. Not only was I left a very young widow, but I had also had two teen-aged boys to raise on my own. Raising two children is an awesome task with a mate; now I was alone, almost incapacitated with grief.

It took about fifteen months before I was able to function in a fairly normal capacity without breaking into tears. It's hard to describe all the adjustments I've had to make since Michael suddenly was taken.

Grief is a process. It takes a great deal of time and patience. I will never "get over" my tremendous loss, as some have suggested. When one friend implied that I should be over it by now, I felt like she had thrown cold water in my face. I could not even speak to her, I was so hurt. Another thoughtless remark came after a friend received the news about Michael's death. I'll never forget her comment, "Well, Glenda, you're young; I'm sure you'll marry again." What she didn't understand was that I didn't want to marry again, I wanted Michael back.

—Glenda

Wisdom for the Caregiver (from Glenda)

I appreciated friends who

- came over and answered the phone for me every day for two weeks after Michael's death.
- thought of my needs and acted upon them; for example, my card group gave us six months' worth of restaurant coupons, realizing that I would not feel like cooking.
- said, "Is this a good day?" not, "You're looking good" (implying I should be good).
- talked about Michael.
- mentored my sons.
- included me in dinner parties.
- asked me out to lunch, knowing that then I must get dressed.
- met me at church. (I did not want to sit alone and needed incentive to go since I was angry at God.)
- asked me to Sunday brunch, realizing how lonely Sundays can be.
- gave me a bag of hard candies to suck on when I felt like I was going to cry.
- invited me to go on a trip, and planned a fun event to do that would give me something to look forward to.
- gave me a Walkman and wonderful music tapes. (I especially liked Emile Pandolfi's piano music.)

Some of the things I did for myself:

⊚ Slept on my husband's side of the bed. This made me feel closer to him. As another widow said, "Then I didn't have to look at his empty spot."
⊚ Gave something to Michael's friends that had been meaningful to Michael.
⊚ Journaled what I missed and didn't miss about Michael.
⊚ Wrote notes to friends one year after Michael's death to let them know how much I appreciated their care.

Additional Wisdom for the Caregiver

⊚ "One of the most significant gestures of caring came from my three-and-a-half-year-old grandson, Jacob. One day, after my husband John died, Jacob asked me if I was still sad. Then he said, 'Grandpa John must be really sad not to be able to talk to you.' And during the first Christmas season after John's death, Jacob asked, 'Who makes the Baby Jesus cake in heaven?' Then a few seconds later, he answered his own question: 'I know Grandpa John is baking the Baby Jesus cake.' His comments meant so much to me because (1) he missed Grandpa John too, and (2) his questions invited me to think about and talk about John."

—Ann

⊚ Call and visit often. There is a significant letdown after the funeral when friends return to the living of their own lives. In addition to special days (birthdays, anniversaries, and holidays) widowed persons say that Sunday is the loneliest day of the week.
⊚ "Encourage the person to talk [when the two of you have some private time together]. Help the person express how she or he feels even if you have heard it a few times before. People in pain don't mind talking about it when they have a receptive audience. It helps them to talk about it over and over again."

—Phil

⊚ "'You have been in my thoughts' is a greeting which will elicit a response of the grieving person's choosing. If there is a need to share feelings, the person has permission to share, or he or she can simply say, 'Thank you,' and go on to talk of other things."

—Mickie

❧ "When talking to or writing a note to a friend or relative of a deceased person it is very meaningful to share an incident, story, or an admirable quality that you especially appreciate about the deceased. When my husband died at an early age, I was overwhelmed by the number of people who demonstrated their love and caring. Their remarks like, 'He was the best friend I ever had,' or, 'I remember how he helped me by . . .' or, 'He was a prince among men. I remember one time when he . . .' were a tribute to him and a gift and inspiration to me. I knew that he was a wonderful husband and father and friend, and what a comfort to know others knew too."

—Joyce

❧ "Invite your friend to walk and talk. Both are excellent therapies for grief."

—Mickie

❧ Include your widowed (or divorced) friend just as you would have before his or her partner died. Please start a new trend by inviting one or more persons without partners to your social events and gatherings.

❧ "Take the initiative in inviting your friend out to a specific event. If your friend refuses, call again on another occasion. Be persistent. Suggest things you can do together rather than asking if they want to do something. Your friend may feel lethargic and may say no. Even if you simply go for a walk together, such contacts will help relieve the loneliness and initiate socialization."

—Delores Kuenning, *Helping People Through Grief*
(Minneapolis: Bethany House, 1987), p. 220

❧ "Call frequently to say, 'I'm thinking of you.' If the person is not home, leave a message on the answering machine."

—Mary

❧ "Encourage your friend to cry, knowing that tears bring healing."

—Mary

❧ "After my first wife died, the people who had also suffered the loss of a spouse were the ones who helped me the most. Even though some of them were practically strangers, what they said or did not say meant more to me than the words and comments of some of my friends."

—Phil

⊛ "Since endless repetition of information is draining, suggest that the grieving person leave a message on his or her answering machine announcing pertinent information (time of memorial service, and so on)."

—Amy

⊛ Read "Caregiving Basics" (pp. 203-222).
⊛ Check "109+ Ways to Say, 'I Care'" (pp. 223-234).
⊛ Read other first-person stories about caring for someone who is grieving the death of a loved one. (See pp. 73-76, 84-98.)

Helplines

1. **Accord, Inc. (The American Grief Academy).** 1-800-346-3087. www.accordinc.org. This grief-management agency distributes books, videos, and *Grief Magazine.* Accord also provides grief and bereavement training for clergy, teachers, and social workers. Their programs help grievers identify coping skills for surviving loss.
2. **American Association of Christian Counselors**, P.O. Box 739, Forest, VA 24551. 1-800-5-COUNSEL; 1-434-525-9470. www.aacc.net. This organization has a directory of counselors who are members of AACC—a great tool for finding a Christian counselor in just about any region in the United States.
3. **Bereavement Association of St. John's Region**, Pastoral Care Department, General Hospital, 300 Prince Philip Dr., St. John's, NF A1B 3V6. 1-709-737-6959. www.hccsj.nf.ca.
4. **Bereavement Services**, 18 Suter Cres, Dundas, ON L9H 6R5. 1-905-628-6008. www.bereavement.net/first.htm. Professional grief counseling and support services in the Golden Horseshoe Area of Ontario.
5. **Cross Canada Search**. www.crosscanadasearch.com. A Christian Internet search engine. Includes information about Christian counseling services (www.crosscanadasearch.com/Ministry_Resources/Counselling).

6. **Salem Christian Mental Health Association**, 1 Young St., Suite 418, Hamilton, ON L8N 1T8. 1-905-528-0353. www.salem.on.ca. Provides counseling and also acts as a clearinghouse for mental health resources.

Books and Other Resources

⊛ Colgrove, Melba, Ph.D., Harold Bloomfield, MC, and Peter Williams. *How to Survive the Loss of a Love* (Los Angeles: Prelude Press, 1979). A helpful book on the subject of loss. Clear, simple, comforting, inspiring. Gives the reader what he or she needs at each step in the process of recovering from a loss. A companion workbook is available.

⊛ Deits, Bob. *Life After Loss* (Tucson: Fisher Books, 1999). A personal guide dealing with death, divorce, job change, and relocation.

⊛ Sittser, Gerald L. *A Grace Disguised* (Grand Rapids, MI: Zondervan Publishing, 1998). Sittser plumbs the depth of our sorrows, whether due to illness, divorce, or the loss of someone we love. The author says that coming to the end of ourselves, we can become to the beginning of a new life—one marked by spiritual depth, joy, compassion, and a deeper appreciation of simple blessings.

⊛ TRAVARCA. A video library sponsored by the Reformed Church in America and the Christian Reformed Church in North America, TRAVARCA carries thousands of videos on hundreds of topics, including death. A yearly membership allows churches and individuals to use an unlimited number of videos; nonmembers may use the videos for established fees. Call 1-800-968-7221 or 1-616-698-7071 for a catalog or to request information and videos.

⊛ Westberg, Granger E. *Good Grief* (Philadelphia: Fortress Press, 1971). This timeless book is great for those who want to understand and help others who are grieving over any kind of loss, whether it be the loss of a loved one, a job, a dream, and so on. This small book helps us acknowledge and understand the various stages and emotions in the grief process.

⊛ Zonnebelt-Smeenge, Susan, and Robert C. DeVries. *Getting to the Other Side of Grief: Overcoming the Loss of a Spouse* (Grand Rapids, MI: Baker Book House, 1998). Comfort and guidance from a clinical psychologist and a pastor and professor. The authors' empathy, valuable psychological insights, biblical observations, and male and female perspectives will help readers experience grief in the healthiest, most complete way so that they can move forward to embrace the new life that's waiting for them.

Death of a Child by Miscarriage or Stillbirth

Shattered Dreams

[God] heals the brokenhearted, and binds up their wounds.

—Psalm 147:3

During the first ten years of our marriage, as part of our struggle with infertility, my husband and I experienced the loss of three pregnancies. Each loss was a significant loss for us. Each loss challenged our sense of self, our marriage, and in some significant way, our faith. While surrounded by people able to bring forth the fullness of life, we felt it was ours to know only emptiness and death. When, after extensive invasive procedures, I finally was able to become pregnant, each pregnancy carried all of our hopes and our dreams. To lose each pregnancy, to suffer miscarriage, was to know the pain of our hopes being crushed, our dreams dying. Each pregnancy was the loss of one of our children, someone who in those few and early weeks we had come to love, cherish, and hold closely in our hearts.

I don't believe it was God's will for those three pregnancies to end. The God in whom I believe is a God of life.

I don't believe it was "for the best" because those pregnancies may have produced a child impaired in one way or another. My husband and I have enough love and care within us for children with special needs.

I don't believe a pregnancy loss is an insignificant event. For us each loss was the death of our longed-for child.

Not everyone who suffers pregnancy loss will "get pregnant again right away." It will not be quickly forgotten. It doesn't erase the anguish when one has a child to come home to after such a loss. Death is death, with all its power and pain.

—Diane Maodush-Pitzer

Wisdom for the Caregiver (from Diane)

☙ Worship and liturgy are important for my husband and myself. Friends who were close understood that and helped us put together a service of remembering for the babies we lost. Each child has a name and holds a place in our memories and our hearts.

☙ We appreciated the few people who were willing to listen to our experience: those people who understood it was no small thing we should be over quickly. We appreciated those who simply said, "I'm sorry," or, "I am praying for you"; in times of struggle and loss it can be difficult to pray for oneself. Most of all, we appreciated people who simply let us experience the grief and walked beside us quietly and compassionately.

Additonal Wisdom for the Caregiver

☙ Give the grieving mother (especially a young woman) a teddy bear to hold and hug.

☙ Read "Caregiving Basics" (pp. 203-222).

☙ Check "109+ Ways to Say, 'I Care'" (pp. 223-234).

☙ "Please do not ignore why the parents and family are sad. If you do, it gives them the impression that you think the miscarriage is not a big deal, not even worthy of mentioning."

—Shelly

☙ "Don't avoid the grieving parents. They are still your friends. Call them and let them know you are thinking about them. Ask if they want to talk about their baby. They will usually say yes. Then listen with your heart. They need to talk with friends who care. Grieving is a social process, it requires relationships."

—Delores Kuenning, *Helping People Through Grief*
(Minneapolis: Bethany House, 1987), p. 53.

☞ Keep in mind that a miscarriage is a tragedy. The grieving process is the same when any loved one dies. Individuals need sympathy and time to heal. (See pp. 214-217 for a description of the grieving process.)

☞ "Instead of lecturing the couple to 'get out of the house and do something fun,' send them four coupons (for themselves and some friends) for dinner at their favorite restaurant and a movie."

—Jeff

☞ "Suppress any temptation to say, 'It was for the best,' or, 'It wasn't meant to be,' or, 'At least you can get pregnant again,' or, 'You're young, you can try again,' or, 'Be happy with the two children you have.' And please never say, 'Better this than the baby dying at birth or having a birth defect. This is nature's way.'"

—Shelly

☞ Give the parent(s) the book *Life Line* by Joanie Reid. This book is a journal for parents who are grieving a miscarriage, stillbirth, or early infant death. As the author says, "My sister had the wisdom to bring me a journal while I was in the hospital. I dumped all my emotions and all my confusion on paper. I wrote—without editing, without polish—about how I felt, what had happened, questions I struggled with. I wrote each entry to Dustin, the son we had just lost. Somehow it helped tremendously . . . my sister's gift to me became my life line."

☞ Research the availability of a SHARE support group in the geographical area of the grieving parents. SHARE is a self-help group for parents who have lost a baby through miscarriage, stillbirth, or early infant death. If a group is available, give information about the support group to the parents. For more information write: SHARE, Elizabeth's Hospital, 211 S. Third Street, Belleville, IL 62222.

Helplines

1. **Bereaved Families.** www.cybertap.com/care/bereave/htm. A listing of several Bereaved Family chapters in Ontario, including events and contact information.
2. **Compassionate Friends, Inc.**, P.O. Box 1347, Oak Brook, IL 60521. An organization for parents who have lost a child through death.
3. **Compassionate Friends of Canada**, Box 141 RPO Corydon, Winnipeg, MB R3M 3S7. 1-888-823-0141; 1-204-475-9527. A self-help organization for parents grieving the death of a child of any age. Has 130 chapters and produces national and chapter newsletters.
4. **Empty Cradle**, 6497 Decanture Street, San Diego, CA 92120. A support agency for parents experiencing miscarriage, stillbirth, and infant death.
5. **Perinatal Bereavement Services Ontario**, 6060 Highway 7, Suite 205, Markham, ON L3P 3A9. 1-888-301-7276; 1-905-472-1807; pbso-cares@pbso.ca. http://members.rogers.com/pengel1345/id_bar.html.

Books and Other Resources

⊚ Ilse, Sherokee. *Empty Arms: Coping with Miscarriage, Stillbirth and Infant Death* (Long Lake, MN: Wintergreen Press, revised edition 2000). Ilse offers straightforward information and warm support for getting through the hard times.

⊚ Ilse, Sherokee, and Linda Hammer Burns. *Miscarriage: A Shattered Dream* (Long Lake, MN: Wintergreen Press, 1992). This book includes medical information and helpful coping suggestions that have helped many persons through the agony of a miscarriage.

❧ O'Keefe, Christine, and Phyllis Tickle. *An Empty Cradle, a Full Heart: Reflections for Mothers and Fathers after Miscarriage, Stillbirth, or Infant Death* (Chicago: Loyola Press, 1998). O'Keefe, who has twice lost a child, writes reflections accompanied by Scripture that provide comfort and courage for bereaved parents.

❧ Stetson, Brad. *Tender Fingerprints* (Grand Rapids, MI: Zondervan, 1999). A father writes about his experience of losing a stillborn child.

❧ www.bereavement.net/mtarms/htm. An extensive reading list for those who have lost a child through miscarriage, stillbirth, or neonatal death.

Death of an Infant Child

Each Child's Life Is Precious

Even though I walk through the valley of the shadow of death, I will fear no evil; for you are with me.

—Psalm 23:4

M y valley experience took place when our infant son, Justin, died with no apparent symptoms at the tender age of three and a half months. It happened in the evening just after my husband, a pastor, had left for a meeting. I rushed my baby to the hospital, but the doctors could not revive him. I had one older son, Joshua, who was then 3, and I would later have another son, Christian, but neither of these children would or could replace the precious child whom we lost.

—Donna

Wisdom for the Caregiver (from Donna)

- Many people avoided talking about Justin. It seemed that they were trying to avoid keeping his memory alive. I wanted more than anything to talk about him. It is healing, not hurtful, to hear his name and recall his happy character as well as instances from his life. Some individuals told me that they understood my pain. Even if someone has gone through a similar experience, it is not the same as my experience. Although the words "I understand" may sound comforting, they are not. Please respect the fact that my experience is totally unique.

- Some friends expected that by a certain lapsed time my husband and I should "be over" our grief. The death of a loved one is not something that one day releases its hold and then from that day on the sun shines again. It is like a corner has been torn from one's heart which will never be replaced. Scar tissue will stop the bleeding, but that space will never be filled. The death of a precious child is not the kind of thing one "gets over" like a bump in the road.

- People who helped
    —prayed with us.
    —brought us food. (Although we needed the energy, we did not have the strength or capacity to prepare it.)
    —helped with the funeral arrangements (as did our minister).
    —wrote a letter to express their feelings about our child.
    —talked about Justin.
    —sent a card or note of sympathy. We especially appreciated those who later sent a second note. (This was appreciated more than a phone call.)
    —remembered the anniversary of Justin's death with flowers or a note.
    —did the thoughtful but unexpected thing, as when a friend presented me with a crystal angel for my tree the first Christmas after Justin's death.
    —said, "I'm sorry."

Helplines

See page 87 for a list of organizations.

Books and Other Resources

See pages 87-88 for a list of helpful books.

Death by Suicide

Accepting the Unacceptable

We are hard pressed on every side, but not crushed; perplexed, but not in despair; persecuted, but not abandoned; struck down, but not destroyed. We always carry around in our body the death of Jesus, so that the life of Jesus may also be revealed in our body

—2 Corinthians 4:8-10

A t approximately 2:00 p.m. on November 2, 1993, my husband took his own life. That event brought me and our four children face-to-face with a death we did not understand—indeed, did not want to understand.

My husband's suicide brought us pain that was and is immeasurable. Initially, and for some time after Bill's death, I questioned what I could have done differently. I also experienced some regrets about things said or unsaid during the last few days of his life.

I have not felt a lot of anger this past year, mostly sadness. However, when the anger has spilled out I've tried to channel it in some healthy ways. Some of these ways may sound bizarre, but I'm not the least bit ashamed of them. For example, I have visited the cemetery at all hours of the day and night, and have sworn at him. I have dug through the snow and ice to uncover his grave marker in the dark so that I could stomp on it. I have been known to stand in my garage at night and hurl dishes against the wall. All these actions were very therapeutic.

One of my significant struggles has been moving from "I can't" (*I can't be alone; I can't be a single parent; I can't be a widow*) to "I don't want" (*I don't want to be alone, a single parent, a widow*) to "I am" (*I am alone; I am a single parent; I am a widow*). This whole process of acknowledgment took about nine months. I hesitate to use the word "acceptance," for how do we "accept" what is totally unacceptable?

—Barb Pekich

Note: For the rest of Barb's story, including a touching poem from her daughter, see pages 219-222.

Wisdom for the Caregiver (from Barb)

⊛ People brought dinners every day for two months. This was coordinated by the parish administrator and by my best friend. Two women did my grocery shopping for almost six months. Several others ran errands on Saturday for me. Another woman was at my house after school twice a week from January through June so I could continue to work full time.

⊛ My best friend was here nearly every evening for several months until I could face being alone. She had confidence that the time would come when I wouldn't need someone every night and we'd both know it. She was right. I think I am healthier today because of all the hours she was here grieving with me.

⊛ Men in my church "adopted" each of my children and periodically will call one and invite them to participate in some activity, spend a weekend, and so on. This has been very significant for all of them.

⊛ Remember that it helps to talk and talk and talk about what happened. Let the grieving person talk and you, the caregiver, ask the questions: "Where were you when you heard about . . .?" and so on.

☙ Urge honesty and openness. (Dealing with the fact of suicide openly eliminates speculation and whispered conversations behind your back.)

Additional Wisdom for the Caregiver

☙ Read "Caregiving Basics" (pp. 203-222).

☙ Check "109+ Ways to Say, 'I Care'" (pp. 223-234). Also see first-person accounts and suggestions in "Death of a Spouse" (pp. 77-83).

☙ When talking with the family of the deceased, don't be afraid to talk about his or her death, just as you would normally talk about the death of any friend. Don't be afraid to mention their loved one's name and to recall pleasant memories you shared with the deceased.

☙ If you don't know what to say, just "be there" for the hurting family. Sending a note or making a phone call also shows your love and your acceptance.

Note: The following suggestions come from Lawrence (Bill) Jr. and Elsie Lamb, whose oldest son, Larry, committed suicide at the age of 36.

☙ Hundreds came to the memorial service. They cried. They held us. They said words we've forgotten or didn't hear. We had Communion.

☙ Our church family and friends brought food, smiles, and listening ears. They listened patiently as I poured out my feelings.

☙ Some people still remember the date, January 15, 1987, and on that day they phone us or write a note. Often, I still find a red rose placed on Larry's grave.

☙ Research the availability of support groups such as Compassionate Friends and Survivors of Suicide. Then encourage the grieving person(s) to participate in a support group by providing him or her with information and a phone number.

☙ Write notes/letters. They continue to bring comfort, strength, love, and energy as the grieving persons read and reread them. Elsie shares the following thoughts from conversations and sympathy notes that especially helped her:

—"I hug you to my heart."

—"On Sunday mornings we greet each other with 'the Peace of Christ be with you.' Last Sunday that prayer and promise took on new meaning as we thought of you and your pain. That prayer will continue to be our prayer for you in the days ahead."

—"Sometimes it is not possible to express feelings. This is one of those times." (After the memorial service this former classmate of Larry's and lifelong family friend wept and hugged us.)

—"May you see Larry surrounded by God's love, content and happy at last!"

—"May God hold you in his hand and carry you forward until some understanding of all this comes and healing begins. It will come and it will begin for you and all of your many friends, but for now it is so muddled. We love you dearly."

⊛ The following letter meant a great deal to us:

Dear Elsie and Bill,

Carol and I extend to you our prayerful concern and sympathy in your loss of son Larry.

Struggle and despair do overwhelm, leading people to feel there is nowhere else to go. Larry is now in the hands of our understanding and merciful Heavenly Father and our faithful Savior, our high priest. As the writer of the Epistle to the Hebrews reminds us, "Ours is not a high priest who is incapable of feeling for us in our weakness, but one who has been tempted in every way, exactly as we have been" (Hebrews 4:15). You loved Larry dearly and entered into his struggles as best you could. Our Lord, too, loves him dearly and understands the uncertainties that tormented him.

You miss him and grieve for him and perhaps wish that somehow you could have said or done that one thing that might have dissipated his hurts and struggles. There is a limit to what we can do for one another. Like the waiting father in the parable, too often all we can do is to provide a home to which our children can always return when ready. And this you certainly did. And now he is in God's good hands where hurts are healed.

Henri Nouwen has written a beautiful book, The Wounded Healer, *in which he points out that it is through the wounded Christ that we are healed, and that it is the areas in which we ourselves have been wounded that can, through the grace of God, become the very areas in which we too can become healers for others who are wounded. It is our prayer that in God's good time you may find this to be true. Meanwhile we shall pray for and with you through the difficult days to come.*

Sincerely,

Lars

⊛ Help the person anticipate and prepare for the anniversary of a death or other tragedy. Bob Duvall, a chaplain at Gwinnet Medical who does grief counseling, believes that, for many, the anxiety leading up to the anniversary of a death is worse than what survivors feel when the day arrives. "The anniversary of a death always is very significant," Duvall said in an article in *The Atlanta Journal-Constitution* (April 16, 2000). "The mistake most of us make is that we don't plan for it. We just let it happen. If we make plans for who we want to be with and where we want to be and how we want to mark the anniversary, we are able to handle it better."

⊛ As caregivers we can help others deal with the anticipation of anxious anniversaries by talking to our friends about it. We can ask them how they will be commemorating the special day or we can offer to spend some portion of the day with them: visiting the grave site, going to a show, having dinner, and so on. A gesture such as sending a note or flowers each year to mark the day is also appreciated.

Helplines

1. **American Association of Christian Counselors**, P.O. Box 739, Forest, VA 24551. 1-800-5-COUNSEL; 1-434-525-9470. www.aacc.net. This organization has a directory of counselors who are members of AACC—a great tool for finding a Christian counselor in just about any region in the United States.
2. **American Foundation for Suicide Prevention**. www.afsp.org. Provides news, information, answers to FAQs, research, referrals to

survivor groups, and more. Check the Web for names and phone numbers of area chapters.

3. **Bereavement Association of St. John's Region**, Pastoral Care Department, General Hospital, 300 Prince Philip Dr., St. John's, NF A1B 3V6. 1-709-737-6959. www.hccsj.nf.ca/basj/suicide.html. Has a listing of books and pamphlets for those grieving suicide.

4. **Cross Canada Search**. www.crosscanadasearch.com. A Christian Internet search engine. Includes information about Christian counseling services (www.crosscanadasearch.com/Ministry_Resources/ Counselling).

5. **Salem Christian Mental Health Association**, 1 Young St., Suite 418, Hamilton, ON L8N 1T8. 1-905-528-0353. www.salem.on.ca. Provides counseling and also acts as a clearinghouse for mental health resources.

6. **Suicide Information and Education Centre**, 1615 10th Avenue SW, Suite 201, Calgary, AB T3C 0J7. 1-403-245-3900. www.suicideinfo.ca. The largest English-language suicide center and library in the world. Provides newsletters and referrals to local support services.

7. **The Yellow Ribbon Project**, P.O. Box 644, Westminster, CO 80030. 1-303-429-3530. Suicide is the sixth most common cause of death of children ages 5 to 14 and the third most common among young people ages 15 to 24. Each year suicide takes the lives of over 7,000 children between the ages of 10 and 19. The Yellow Ribbon Project offers a way to help children and young people in need of guidance. This organization distributes a card with a yellow ribbon attached. The card says, "This ribbon is a lifeline." The yellow ribbon is meant to convey the message that there are people available who care and who will help. If you (or anyone else) are in need and don't know how to ask for help, take this ribbon (or any yellow ribbon) to a counselor, teacher, priest, rabbi, minister, parent, or friend and say: "I'd like to use my yellow ribbon." Write or call the Yellow Ribbon Project for free ribbons and suggestions.

Books and Other Resources

ⓦ Chance, Sue, M.D. *Stronger Than Death: When Suicide Touches Your Life: A Mother's Story* (New York: Avon, 1994). Following the death of her son, a psychiatrist shares her professional understanding of suicide and relates her own experiences of anguish, guilt, anger, and healing. A chronicle for survivors, families, and professionals.

ⓦ Dietz, Bob. *Life After Loss: A Personal Guide Dealing with Death, Divorce, Job Changes, and Relocation* (Tucson: Fisher Books, 1999). This book is a roadmap and traveler's guide for those in grief. It includes helpful exercises and charts for working through your grief.

ⓦ Gentzelman, Joan. *God Knows You're Grieving: Things to Help You Through* (Notre Dame, IN: Sorin Books, 2001). Though shared stories, thoughtful insights, and practical suggestions, this book offers encouragement and comfort as we encounter loss.

ⓦ Kübler-Ross, Elisabeth. *Questions and Answers on Death and Dying* (New York: Simon and Schuster, 1997). The author discusses accepting the end of life, suicide, terminal illness, euthanasia, how to tell a patient he or she is critically ill, and how to deal with all the special difficulties surrounding death.

ⓦ Nouwen, Henry. *The Wounded Healer* (Garden City, NY: Doubleday, 1972). In this classic, life-changing book, Nouwen shows us how to transform the shame and guilt into our strengths. By accepting our human frailties we can turn them into helpful resources and extend the gift of emotional healing to others. By becoming a "wounded healer" we are sensitized to the needs of others, offering peace in the midst of human challenges.

ⓦ TRAVARCA. A video library sponsored by the Reformed Church in America and the Christian Reformed Church in North America, TRAVARCA carries thousands of videos on hundreds of topics, including death and suicide. A yearly membership allows churches and individuals to use an unlimited number of videos; nonmembers may use the videos for established fees. Call 1-800-968-7221 or 1-616-698-7071 for a catalog or to request information and videos.

Depression and Mental Illness

Note: Depression is an illness that affects many people, and often goes unnoticed or unrecognized in the church community. Thus, this topic is given prime consideration in this section. However, there are many other forms of mental illness that can be just as devastating for individuals and families, and those should not be neglected. Please see the Helplines on pages 103-105 for a list of organizations that deal with various types of mental illness.

Crazy, Weak, and Worthless?

Why are you downcast, O my soul? Why so disturbed within me? Put your hope in God, for I will yet praise him, my Savior and my God.

—Psalm 42:11

"**D**epression." Even attempting to define the condition is painful for me. Our world does not accept kindly those suffering from depression. We are looked upon as a bit "crazy"; weaklings who feel sorry for ourselves; people who forget to "count their blessings."

To feel depressed is to be "blue" day after day; to experience tiredness that never goes away, not even after ten or twelve hours of sleep; to lack energy for even the smallest of chores; to not be enthusiastic about anything; to be unable to focus or concentrate; to turn molehills into mountains; to be overly sensitive to comments.

My feelings of worthlessness and loneliness were overwhelming. Each day I would pray that God would end my life; at times I even planned how I could do this. I felt like a failure who was all alone in this world.

—Marianne

Wisdom for the Caregiver (from Marianne)

Helpful support during these times came from friends who

- called every morning to wake me.
- extended words of love, care, and affirmation.
- hugged or touched me (very powerful medicine).
- encouraged me to see a professional for help and accompanied me on the first visit.
- invited me to walk or engage in other types of physical activity.
- asked for my help or assistance. These requests added to my feelings of worthiness and also acted as a welcome distraction.
- reached out over and over again.
- prayed for me and with me. (A dear sister-in-law who lives a great distance away would phone and end our visit with prayer. This touched me greatly.)
- gave tangible inspiration. (A friend gave me a daily devotion flip booklet entitled *Never Alone: Comfort in Times of Need.* I still treasure this gift.)

The giving of patience, love, and acceptance are gifts that transmit God's love!

Additional Wisdom for the Caregiver
- "Most appreciated during a period of depression were gestures by a few people who were important to me, which indicated and communicated to me that they cared deeply for me and that I was important, at least to them, and to many others as well—just as I was. It didn't matter to them what I might be like inside. They treated me as if I was

important just because I was who I was. It was true acceptance, unconditional care and love."

—Les

⊛ Listen! Do not offer advice or your own judgments unless asked . . .
and even then avoid it if you can.

⊛ Accept the other person *as he or she is.* You have to start there, and
you need to communicate this acceptance and care.

⊛ Offer anything tangible, if that's wanted, but above all be there *for* and
with the other person.

⊛ Read "Caregiving Basics" (pp. 203-222).

⊛ Check "109+ Ways to Say, 'I Care'" (pp. 223-234).

⊛ Try to talk to the person to discover what he or she is feeling. Ask
questions about his or her feelings.

⊛ A good rule of thumb in determining the degree of the person's depression is to ask questions and actively listen during several meetings with
the person. If the person's mood remains the same over a period of
time, the likelihood of him or her being depressed rather than merely
grieving is high. If the person is not receiving professional help, it's crucial that you recommend this. You may have to make the appointment
yourself if he or she is too depressed to take the initiative. Do not
attempt to diagnose the person. Your role is to be there for him or her.
It's the job of the therapist to help bring him or her back to health.

⊛ Communicate to the depressed person (and remember yourself) that
depression is not a sign of weakness. It is a disorder that responds
very well to various treatment programs. Seeking help is the first step
toward recovery and feeling better.

⊛ "Don't offer simplistic solutions like, 'Things will look better tomorrow.' Avoid quick fixes, for depression cannot be willed or wished
away. The person can't just 'put on a happy face' or 'snap out of it.' "

—Claire

⊛ Free professional help is available for people with undiagnosed clinical
depression. This screening consists of an educational presentation, a
written questionnaire, and the opportunity to discuss the results with a
mental health professional. These screenings are conducted anonymously, so the person can feel comfortable about going. There are
over 2,000 screening sites across the country, so all you need to do is
call 1-800-262-4444 to find the site nearest you.

- ☻ Follow up to make sure the person keeps appointments and takes the prescribed medication.
- ☻ Remember that any kind of healing is a process and takes time. With antidepressants, someone who is severely depressed will normally show improvement in four to six weeks. Psychotherapy takes longer. Many doctors use a combination. Improvement may not occur for six months, and medication may be required for an extended period.
- ☻ Suggest a local support group. Provide the name and telephone number of a support group, and even offer to make the call. Often depressed people can't get themselves to do the very thing that would help. Commit to call a depressed person regularly. Then do it!
- ☻ Don't ignore threats of suicide or discussions of death. Consider these threats serious, not just efforts to gain sympathy.
- ☻ Help the person hold onto hope. Suggest a favorite activity, hobby, or evening out, a trip, and so on. Invite the person to attend church with you, and offer to pick him or her up since this encourages him or her to keep the date.
- ☻ Invite the person to exercise regularly with you. Exercise releases the body's "feel-good" chemicals, which will help the person feel more positive.
- ☻ For a long-term caregiver of a depressed person, it is helpful to remember what depression feels like to the one who is depressed. Perhaps if the caregiver occasionally reads the following description from a sermon by Rev. Timothy Brown, he or she may be able to persevere with more patience and understanding:

> *Depression:*
> —*It feels like being hungry when you know you're well fed.*
> —*It feels like fatigue, tired after a long day, after a long life.*
> —*It feels a little bit like shame and guilt, that feeling you had when you were a little kid and your hand was caught in the cookie jar.*
> —*It feels a little bit like anger. Angry at who, angry at what? "I don't know, I'm just angry."*
> —*It feels something like nothingness. Like a blank screen in an empty theater and you're all alone and it was supposed to be the story of your life.*
> —*It feels something like all of those things.*

⊚ Read, and suggest that your friend read, *Blow Away the Black Clouds* by Florence Littaur (Eugune, OR: Harvest House, 1986). Consider discussing a section together each week.

Helplines

1. **American Association of Christian Counselors**, P.O. Box 739, Forest, VA 24551. 1-800-5-COUNSEL; 1-434-525-9470. www.aacc.net. This organization has a directory of counselors who are members of AACC—a great tool for finding a Christian counselor in just about any region in the United States.
2. **Canadian Mental Health Association**, 2160 Yonge Street, 3rd Floor, Toronto, ON M4S 2Z3. 1-416-484-7750; cmhanat@interlog.com. www.cmha.ca.
3. **Cross Canada Search**. www.crosscanadasearch.com. A Christian Internet search engine. Includes information about Christian counseling services (www.crosscanadasearch.com/Ministry_Resources/ Counselling).
4. **The Depression Screening Website**. www.depression-screening.org. This site is sponsored by the National Mental Health Association. The mission of the website is to educate people about clinical depression, to offer a confidential way for people to be screened for symptoms of the illness, and to guide people toward appropriate help, if necessary.
5. **Free Depression Screening**. 1-800-262-4444. Free screening has helped many people with undiagnosed clinical depression get the treatment they need. The screening consists of an educational presentation, a written questionnaire, and the opportunity to discuss the results with a mental health professional. These screenings are conducted anonymously. There are over 2,000 screening sites across the U.S.; call the phone number above to find the site nearest you. Those who are hearing-impaired can call the AT&T National Long Distance Relay—(voice) 1-800-855-2881; (TDD) 1-800-855-2880—to access the

National Depression Screening Day (NDSD) Toll-Free Site Locator Line. Those who speak only Spanish can access the Locator Line by calling 1-800-789-9800.

6. **Homewood Health Centre**, 150 Delhi St., Guelph, ON N1E 6K9. 1-519-824-1010. www.homewoodhealth.com. A provider of behavioral, addiction, and psychiatric services.

7. **Mennonite Central Committee Mental Health Program**, 134 Plaza Drive, Winnipeg, MN R3T 5K9. 1-888-622-6337; 1-204-261-6381. www.mcc.org.

8. **National Alliance for the Mentally Ill**. 1-800-950-NAMI (6264). This agency is the nation's voice on mental illness. It serves the "whole person" as he or she is affected by mental illness. Contact NAMI for information on specific disorders, medications, and directions to various local support groups.

9. **National Eating Disorder Information Centre**, CW 1-211, 200 Elizabeth Street, Toronto, ON M5G 2C4. 1-866-NEDIC-20; 1-416-340-4156; nedic@uhn.on.ca. www.nedic.ca. Provides information and resources on eating disorders and weight preoccupation.

10. **National Foundation for Depressive Illness, Inc.**, P.O. Box 2257, New York, NY 10116. 1-800-245-4320. This foundation will help you identify the symptoms of depressive illness and manic depression. They state that patients treated with anti-depressive drugs have an 80 percent cure rate. They supply referrals to physicians in your area, as well as information on support groups. A non-profit charitable organization, they request donations for their services.

11. **National Institute of Mental Health**, 5600 Fishers Lane, Rockville, MD 20857. www.nimh.nih/gov. The NIMH can provide material on depression and will send a directory of federally funded mental health centers upon request. The centers have trained workers and round-the-clock emergency services to help those in need.

12. **National Mental Health Association**. 1-800-969-6642. www.nmha.org. The NMHA Resource Center is a nationally recognized resource for information on mental illness and treatments, and referrals for local treatment services. Information provided includes a mental illness fact sheet; information about children and families, serious mental illness, prevention, substance abuse; and much more. Ask about their e-mail newsletter and other resources.

13. **Salem Christian Mental Health Association**, 1 Young St., Suite 418, Hamilton, ON L8N 1T8. 1-905-528-0353. www.salem.on.ca. Provides counseling and also acts as a clearinghouse for mental health resources.
14. **Schizophrenia Society of Ontario**, 885 Don Mills Road, Suite 322, Don Mills, ON M3C 1V9. 1-800-449-6367; 1-416-449-6830; sso@schizophrenia.on.ca. www.schizophrenia.on.ca.

Books and Other Resources

Cronkite, Kathy. *On the Edge of Darkness* (New York: Doubleday, 1994). Kathy Cronkite chronicles her own struggle with depression as well as the struggles of other famous people who have endured and conquered the hopelessness of depression. A helpful book for family and friends of those who suffer from this misunderstood disease. Includes helpful medical information from doctors.

Grissen, Lillian V. *A Path Through the Sea: One Woman's Journey from Depression to Wholeness* (Grand Rapids, MI: William B. Eerdmans, 1993).

Horning, Crystal. *A Christian View of Mental Illness.* Available through the MCC Canada office (1-204-261-6381; ikj@mennonitecc.ca) or through Mennonite Mutual Aid (MMA) in the U.S. (1-800-348-7468). This excellent 52-page book provides a lot of information about mental illness and how congregations can support and include people who live with a mental illness.

Littaur, Florence. *Blow Away the Black Clouds: A Woman's Answer to Depression* (Eugene, OR: Harvest House, 1986). From her own experiences, Littaur speaks to those suffering from depression. She helps us realize that we should not let feelings of inadequacy, insecurity, and inferiority get in the way of living.

Minirth, Frank B., and Les Carter. *Freedom from Depression Workbook* (Nashville: Thomas Nelson, 1996). A twelve-point interactive program to define and identify depression, understand physical and mental factors of depression, and develop keys to lasting change.

ⓦ O'Conner, Richard. *Undoing Depression: What Therapy Doesn't Teach You and Medication Can't Give You* (New York: Berkley Books, 1999). The author, a therapist, shows the reader how to "undo" depression by replacing depressive patterns of thinking, relating, and behaving with a new and more effective set of skills. With a truly holistic approach that synthesizes the best of many schools of thought about this painful disease, O'Conner offers new hope—and new life—for those struggling with depression.

ⓦ Papolos, Demitri, and Janice Papolos. *Overcoming Depression* (New York: HarperCollins, 1997). Clearly and sympathetically, these authors present state-of-the-art medical information and solid practical advice that empowers patients and their families to participate actively in diagnosis and treatment. Their book contains revised information on the latest in anti-depressants and mood-stabilizing drugs, as well as new clinical findings about the risks of anti-depressant treatment in bipolar disorder. An excellent resource for families who live with depression and manic-depression.

Disability (Of an Infant)

Why Did This Happen to My Baby?

So in everything, do to others what you would have them do to you.

—Matthew 7:12

A ndrew Michael Briggs was born six weeks early on January 6, 1995, weighing 4 pounds 15 ounces. As do most "expecting" parents, we had anticipated a healthy baby. We never thought about the possibility of our baby having a birth defect—particularly one as obvious as a facial cleft.

I was more than simply careful while I carried this child. I was obsessed! I had lost a baby boy the year before. So I took every precaution and expected to have a healthy, safe, normal pregnancy. But Andrew Michael was born with a bilateral cleft lip and palate.

My first thoughts and feelings when I saw Andrew Michael were to tell him it wasn't his fault. I took all the blame and guilt upon myself. Somehow, I thought I had caused this defect. My husband and I both wondered if we had done something in the past that warranted this problem. During the first few days in the hospital, I questioned: Why did this happen to my baby? Will he ever be able to kiss his mommy and daddy? Why do people who do not want children have healthy babies? What will people think and say when they see Andrew? Will my family love and accept him?

When we first brought Andrew Michael home, he had to stay inside because his body temperature wouldn't remain constant. So, in a way, we didn't have to face friends or outside people for a couple of months. But, when we did take him out, I would try to cover up his lip with a cloth or blanket. I was embarrassed for us as well as for him.

Andrew's first surgery was at four months of age. It took two hours. The hardest part for me was giving my baby boy to the nurses prior to surgery. The doctor did a wonderful job repairing Andrew Michael's lip.

His second surgery, to repair the soft palate, was at six and a half months of age. He also had tubes placed in both ears. And there will be more surgeries in Andrew's future.

Andrew Michael has been a special blessing to our family. He has brought more tears, laughs, love, and joy to our home than we had previously known. We thank God daily for this little bundle of joy.

—Sara

Wisdom for the Caregiver (from Sara)

☙ Congratulate us on our new arrival.

☙ Send cards and notes saying, "I'm thinking of you."

☙ Tell us that our baby is beautiful. Point out other beautiful features, like his big brown eyes and black hair.

☙ Hold our baby. (Holding the baby says, "This handicap is not a barrier. I accept this special little person.")

☙ Do not say, "I'm sorry about . . ."

Additional Wisdom for the Caregiver

☙ Read "Caregiving Basics" (pp. 203-222).

☙ Check "109+ Ways to Say, 'I Care'" (pp. 223-234).

☙ "Ask the usual questions: 'Does [name] sleep well?' 'Is feeding going okay?' 'How are you feeling?' 'Are you able to get enough rest?'"

—Delores Kuenning, *Helping People Through Grief*
(Minneapolis: Bethany House, 1987), pp. 38-39

☞ "Little things mean a lot. One afternoon, a friend appeared at our door with a game under her arm. 'I've come to play with [name] for a little while,' she said as she greeted me with a big smile. It was one of the nicest things anyone ever did for us."

—Delores Kuenning, *Helping People Through Grief,* pp. 38-39

Helplines

Joni and Friends, P.O. Box 3333, Agoura Hills, CA 91301. 1-818-717-5664. www.joniandfriends.org. This organization can provide you and your church or organization with educational packets that include ways to help a friend with disabilities. Also provides information on starting a disability awareness in Sunday school. Christian school curricula and disability advocacy also provided.

Note: See pages 114-115 for more Helplines.

Books and Other Resources

☞ Beck, Martha. *Expecting Adam* (New York: Berkley Publishing Group, 1999). This is a story about bearing and raising a son with Down Syndrome. Beck tells the story for all parents who have raised children who have disabilities and have ended up feeling privileged.

☞ Kuenning, Dolores. *Helping People Through Grief* (Minneapolis: Bethany House, 1987). This book has a chapter ("When Hello Means Heartache") that includes first-person stories of parents dealing with children who are impaired. Includes advice to parents and caregivers, and lists additional resources.

- Newman, Barbara. *Helping Kids Include Kids with Disabilities* (Grand Rapids, MI: Faith Alive Christian Resources, 2001). This how-to manual for teachers in schools and church programs offers practical suggestions and short session plans for helping groups of elementary-age children understand and welcome into their group a child with a particular disability. (Call 1-800-333-8300 or visit www.FaithAliveResources.org to order.)

- Newman, Gene, and Joni Eareckson Tada. *All God's Children* (Grand Rapids, MI: Zondervan, 1993). *All God's Children* is a handbook for pastors, elders, ministry leaders, and laypeople who want to minister to people with disabilities. This book helps the reader begin to understand some of the issues facing persons with learning disabilities, mental impairments, and hearing and visual impairments.

- Shriver, Maria. *What's Wrong with Timmy?* (Boston: Warner Books, 2001). This little book will help children and adults understand that kids (and adults) with disabilities are not to be feared, pitied, or ridiculed, but are to be embraced, challenged, and included.

Disability (General)

A Person with Disabilities Is First of All a Real Person
Dear children, let us not love with words or tongue but with actions and in truth.

—1 John 3:18

I was born legally blind and became functionally blind at age thirty-two. I have a very supportive husband, two children, and a leader dog. I function very well as director of disabled students at Hope College in Holland, Michigan. Although I have obviously become sensitized to people with disabilities, I still make mistakes in dealing with my students. I have learned that caregiving is an area that takes constant correction. I have found that it is important to give myself permission to make a mistake.

—Louise

Wisdom for the Caregiver

⊚ Remember that the person with disabilities is first of all a real person. If you have questions about a person's disability, ask him or her. If you see a person with a disability who needs assistance, ask if he or she needs help, then wait for an answer.

⊚ It is very important to create a caring church community for persons with disabilities. This can be done by being accepting of such individuals; by learning about disability issues; by realizing that the disabled person often has a family who also needs care; by making the church accessible (wheelchairs and convenient places to place them; ramps or elevators). Think past government regulations to what would be the most humane and thoughtful solution to the disabled person's problem. (For example, the bathroom stall may be large enough to meet regulations but not large enough to enable the person occupying a chair to close the door.)

⊚ Learn the correct language in dealing with a person with disabilities. For example, a person "occupies" a wheelchair; he or she is not "confined" or "bound to" the chair. A person has a disabling condition—he or she is not "inflicted with" or "a victim of" it. A person with a mental illness has an emotional or psychiatric disability—he or she is not "crazy," "insane" or a "mental patient."

⊚ The following are terms never appropriate to use when referring to a person with a disability or a disabling condition: afflicted; crip; crippled; deaf mute; defective; deformed; gimp; invalid; midget or little person or dwarf (use "person who is short" or "person of short stature"); unhealthy; victim.

⊚ Copy the "Rights of Parents with Disabled Children" (see next page) and give it to parents of a child who has a disability.

Rights of Parents With Disabled Children

1. You don't have to devote your entire life to the "cause." You are free to devote as much as you want or to get away from it for a while.
2. You need freedom to take your time in deciding what to do. You have the right to shop around for competent professional help. You have the right not to accept advice or even comfort, especially from people who say such things as, "You think you have troubles?"
3. It is all right to intervene, to arrange parties, and to rendezvous with friends on behalf of your child.
4. It's all right to consider institutionalization, even if it goes against the current trend toward home care.
5. You have the right to feel that it is not God's will, nor is it a punishment.
6. You have the right to feel that it is God's will. (But then you still have to figure out what His will means to you: Does it mean that He would not have given you and your family such a challenge if He didn't think you were strong enough to handle it?)
7. It is your right to consider sending your child to a camp for the summer, even if the child does not want to go. It is amazing how most children end up having a really good experience.
8. You are entitled to good and bad moods. You have the right not to be perfect—even to have hostile thoughts—and the right *not to act* on such thoughts for your own well-being and that of your family. It's all right to feel bad and mourn from time to time.
9. Consider becoming an expert in the disability you are concerned about—even if your motive is initially to help your own child.
10. Don't neglect the comfort your religion can provide.
11. Expect your child to learn to live fully within the family. You can get help to accomplish this.
12. Show by example the need to joke, fool around, and be silly. That's a safety valve for everyone in the family!
13. Consider finding out how to get some use out of all the sorrow, whether it is through writing poetry, painting, or understanding the needs of other people in a more sensitive and compassionate way. Use your tragedy and sorrow constructively, or it will use you. It can be done!
14. Become a health nut. Teach children how to develop healthy life-styles.
15. Use your experiences to be helpful to other parents.
16. Be proud of your accomplishments.
17. There is a powerful need for parents to be on their own, to get away from everything by going on vacations—or just generally doing things—without their children. No healthy, mature family functions well in a posture of constant togetherness.
18. Plan times that are special for the brothers and sisters of the disabled child. Without these breaks, siblings are more likely to resent their responsibilities to their disabled brother or sister.
19. You have the right to expect miracles. Why operate on the assumption that our current scope of knowledge is a verdict of doom?

—Sol Gordon, *Is There Anything I Can Do?* (New York: Delacorte Press, 1994), pp. 104-105

Additional Wisdom for the Caregiver
(from the Easter Seal Foundation)

- ⊛ It's okay to ask a friend about his or her disability, but it's also okay for a friend to not want to talk about it. It should be the person's choice.
- ⊛ It's okay to use words like "see," "hear," "walk," and "run" when talking with a friend who has a disability.
- ⊛ Treat a friend who has a disability the way you like to be treated.
- ⊛ Be considerate of the extra time it might take for a friend with a disability to get things said or done. Let your friend set the pace in walking and talking.
- ⊛ Appreciate what a friend can do. Remember that your friend's difficulties may have more to do with other people's attitudes, or with obstacles your friend may encounter, than with the disability.

Helplines

1. **American Association on Mental Retardation**. 1-800-424-3688. www.aamr.org. The Association is the nation's oldest and largest interdisciplinary organization of mental retardation professionals, advocating the full protection of legal rights of persons with mental impairments.
2. **Autism Society of Canada**, P.O. Box 65, Orangeville, ON. 1-866-874-3334; 1-519-942-8720; info@autismsocietycanada.ca. www.autismsocietycanada.ca.
3. **Canadian Association for Community Living**, Kinsmen Building, York University, 4700 Keele Street, Toronto, ON M3J 1P3. 1-416-661-

9611; TTY 1-416-661-2023; info@cacl.ca. www.cacl.ca. Information and services for those with mental impairments.

4. **Canadian Hearing Society**, 271 Spadina Road, Toronto, ON M5R 2V3. 1-416-964-9595; TTY 1-416-964-0023; info@chs.ca. www.chs.ca.

5. **Canadian Institue for the Blind**, 1929 Bayview Avenue, Toronto, ON M4G 3E8. 1-416-486-2500. www.cnib.ca.

6. **Community Care Access Centres**, Ontario Ministry of Health. 1-800-268-1154; 1-416-314-5518. www.gov.on.ca/MOH/english/news/media/ccac/ccac.html. The point of access to Ontario's long-term care system, including home care, long-term care facilities, community referrals, and more.

7. **Disability Concerns**, 2850 Kalamazoo Ave SE, Grand Rapids, MI. 1-616-224-0838. **Disability Concerns Canada**, 3475 Mainway, P.O. Box 5070 STN LCD 1, Burlington, ON L7R 3Y8. 1-905-336-2920. This agency of the Christian Reformed Church promotes the full participation of people with disabilities in the life of the church. Their work involves helping churches remove the barriers of architecture, communication, and attitude that hinder this participation. It also involves calling churches to discover the needs and employ the gifts of people with disabilities.

8. **Family Network on Disabilities**. 1- 800-825-5736. www.fndfl.org. This network supplies Parent Training Information (PTI) for the state of Florida. However, they will direct callers to the PTI Network for other states as well. They help parents to understand federal laws and to become advocates for their children in special education. They also have various information packages available.

9. **Friendship Ministries**, 2850 Kalamazoo Ave. SE, Grand Rapids, MI 49560. 1-800-333-8300; friendship@friendship.org. www.Friendship.org. **Friendship Groups Canada**, P.O. Box 220, Simcoe, ON N3Y 4L1. 1-519-426-5152. Friendship groups across the United States and Canada, and around the world, help people with mental impairments come to God. They usually meet once a week for sixty to ninety minutes. Participants spend time together as a group and one-on-one with a mentor. A complete curriculum provides the framework for the program. (Friendship also has a Spanish-language equivalent called *Amistad.*) A free information packet is available. Friendship also provides training and workshops on topics relevant to working with people who have mental impairments.

Books and Other Resources

⊛ Bolduc, Kathleen Deyer. *His Name Is Joel: Searching for God in a Son's Disability* (Louisville, KY: Bridge Resources, 1999). This little book would make a wonderful gift to parents struggling to accept a child's disability. The author tells a moving and powerful story of the harsh realities and triumphs of raising a brain-injured child. Inspiring, encouraging, realistic—a "must read" for caregivers.

⊛ Bosch, Henry G. *Rainbows for God's Children in the Storm* (Grand Rapids, MI: Baker Book House, 1990). This devotional gives comfort, counsel, and help to those experiencing life's tragedies and suffering. It provides rays of hope to many who find themselves overwhelmed by the storms of life.

⊛ Eareckson, Joni, and Seven Estes. *When God Weeps* (Grand Rapids, MI: Zondervan, 2000). Joni Eareckson's intimate experiences with suffering give her a special understanding of God's intentions for us in our pain, and how God can use our pain for a greater good than we can imagine.

⊛ Hansel, Tim. *You Gotta Keep Dancin'* (Colorado Springs, CO: Victor Publishing, 1998). The author speaks from his experience of living with continual pain from a climbing accident in the Sierras. In his words, "This book is in no way meant to diminish the awfulness of pain, tragedy, and affliction. I don't want to 'celebrate pain,' but more deeply understand the dignity of what can happen in it."

⊛ Newman, Barbara. *Helping Kids Include Kids with Disabilities* (Grand Rapids, MI: Faith Alive Christian Resources, 2001). This how-to manual for teachers in schools and church programs offers practical suggestions and short session plans for helping groups of elementary-age children understand and welcome into their group a child with a particular disability. (Call 1-800-333-8300 or visit www.FaithAliveResources.org to order.)

⊛ Nouwen, Henri J.M. *Adam, God's Beloved* (Maryknoll, NY: Orbis Books, 1997). Completed a week before Nouwen died, *Adam* tells the moving story of Nouwen's friend, a severely handicapped young man from the L'Arche Daybreak Community, who became Nouwen's "friend, teacher, and guide." Adam led Nouwen to "a new understanding of his Christian faith and what it means to be beloved of God."

⊛ Pierson, Jim. *No Disabled Souls: How to Welcome People with Disabilities into Your Life and Your Church* (Cincinnati: Standard Publishing, 1998). From Jim's stories about his friends with disabilities you'll learn the life-changing eternal impact of being included in community and in church. And you'll understand what friendship with someone with a disability can add to your life. Includes advice on how to deal with needs such as special transportation, medication, and assistive devices.

⊛ Vredevelt, Pam. *Angel Behind the Rocking Chair: Stories of Hope in Unexpected Places* (Sisters, OR: Multnomah Books, 1997). True stories of people who have found God in the dark times of their lives.

⊛ Webb-Mitchell, Bret. *God Plays Piano, Too: The Spiritual Lives of Disabled Children* (New York: Crossroad Publishing Company, 1993). Through powerful stories about children who are disabled, the author shows how much they contribute to society and to the church. "No disabled person's worth should be judged according to our frail, human standards," he says. "We all have dazzling worth in God's presence, in God's eyes."

⊛ Webb-Mitchell, Bret. *Unexpected Guests at God's Banquet: Welcoming People with Disabilities into the Church* (New York: Crossroad Publishing Company, 1994). Using Jesus' parable of the banquet feast, the author shows why and how people who are disabled must be included in congregational life.

Homelessness

I Was Homeless and You Helped

What good is it, my brothers, if a man claims to have faith but has no deeds? Can such faith save him? Suppose a brother or sister is without clothes and daily food. If one of you says to him, "Go, I wish you well; keep warm and well fed," but does nothing about his physical needs, what good is it? In the same way, faith by itself, if it is not accompanied by action, is dead.

—James 2:14-18

The homeless who were fed and covered with blankets at Christmas are still on the streets and in shelters, about to face the coldest and loneliest days of the year. I know; I was homeless once myself. It all began when my husband, Kevin, fell asleep while driving and broke his shoulder.

Our house loan was denied and we owed money to every motel in town. A rainstorm destroyed our tent. We sat staring at our 1981 station wagon. *How did this happen?* We were a normal, Christian family.

I laid aside my pride and asked our church for help. For the next month, our congregation and local agencies supported us. For two months we stayed in a motel that was comfortable, yet inexpensive. One generous church even loaned us a car and offered financial assistance when we found a permanent place to live. I was surprised when people still cared during our leanest months after the holidays. They loved us like Jesus. And they made a difference.

—Martha Jo Walton, "I Was Homeless and You Helped," *Virtue Magazine* (Jan./Feb. 1996). © 1996, Christianity Today International, Carol Stream, IL 60188.

Wisdom for the Caregiver

The following words of wisdom are from Meladee McCarty and Hanoch McCarty, *Acts of Kindness: How To Create a Kindness Revolution* (Deerfield Beach, FL: Health Communications, Inc., 1994), pp. 113-116. Used by permission.

- Get to know one homeless person. You can find them in shelters, soup kitchens, public health clinics, park benches and bus stations. Don't have a set agenda other than just getting to know him. Be honest in your discussion with him. Tell him that you are concerned about the plight of the homeless. . . . Don't apologize for having more than he does, just share yourself as one person to anther.
- Recognize them. The homeless know they are invisible to us. Give them the gift of knowing somebody realizes they exist. Share with them a smile, eye contact, a laugh or an experience. It is so painful to be so totally invisible, many homeless report.
- Simply listen to them. Avoid the urge to blame them for their situation or label them as victims. Such talk is dehumanizing.
- Look for their strengths and their talents. Reinforce them when they speak of options. Stand in line with folks on the street. You don't need to dress up or down or be extremely jovial. As you spend time in the line, it will help you become aware of the forces and choices that put folks on the street. Be authentic with them and absorb and enjoy their stories.
- If you have a talent for problem-solving, help them learn the skills to do so themselves. Not everyone is good at making choices and would do better if they knew how. Practice your own understanding of their condition, then teach skills. Refrain from trying to solve their problems.

❦ Help your friend open a bank account so that his money will be safe. Help him with strategies for money management and be understanding and persistent with him when mistakes challenge his skills.

❦ Educate yourself about the Aid to Families with Dependent Children program (AFDC). Call your local welfare office and ask them about the amount of money a typical family receives, how food stamps are used, and what provisions they offer for rent, medical, and child-care assistance.

❦ Volunteer in a soup kitchen. If the thought frightens you, ask a friend to go with you.

❦ Visit a homeless person in jail. Don't assume you have answers before you get there; just ask about her story. The act of kindness is to listen and learn.

❦ Volunteer in a day shelter for children. Learn and build trust.

❦ Attend a city council meeting when an agenda pertaining to homelessness is being discussed. Speak of your experience with the homeless; be authentic and state the facts.

❦ Build a house for the homeless. There are organizations that do just that. The best known is Habitat for Humanity—in the directory in most cities under Habitat. You can contribute money to them directly, and their group of volunteers will use the money to build houses. Another option is to have your club or organization take on a construction project with their support. This is a good investment of your time and money.

❦ Persuade your church congregation or organization to offer a day shelter for women and children. Work within your community to provide regular, low-cost day care for poor, working mothers with homes. Some families are only one or two house payments away from being on the streets. If you support the opportunities for them to keep working, they can continue to have a roof over their heads.

❦ Make a gift of a public transportation pass to a homeless friend. . . . This can provide the opportunity for the family provider to get to and from work until she gets her feet on steady ground.

❦ If your community or county has a task force for the homeless, join it, learn from it, and see what you can do to help. We have joined the Sacramento County Task Force for Homeless Children, and it has been a real learning experience. We discovered the very special problems of homeless kids. Can you imagine never getting to go to school, or going to a different school every six to eight weeks as your parents wander from county to county seeking benefits? (County welfare benefits in many locations expire cyclically.)

Ⓕ Talk with distributors of children's clothing and ask them if they would be willing to donate seconds to the local clothes closet. Research indicates that homeless students want to attend school, and will, if they are not embarrassed by their clothing.

Ⓕ Some dry cleaners will clean jackets and coats and distribute them to Goodwill or other social service agencies. If you have a coat or jacket you no longer need or care to wear, it might be of great comfort to someone in need of warmth.

Helplines

1. **Habitat for Humanity International**, 121 Habitat St., Americus, GA 31709. 1-229-924-6935, ext. 2551 or 2552. www.habitat.org. Founded in 1976, Habitat is a non-profit, nondenominational Christian housing organization. Homeowners and volunteers contribute the labor to build affordable housing, and homeowners' payments are recycled into building more homes. Habitat's website has a wealth of information about homelessness around the world, as well as information for volunteers and prospective homeowners. The website also contains an affiliate directory that provides contact information for its local chapters, which can be found in all fifty states and in more than eighty countries.

2. **National Law Center of Homelessness and Poverty**. www.nlchp.org. The Center advocates to protect the rights of homeless people and to implement solutions to end homelessless in the United States through impact litigation, policy advocacy, and public education.

3. **Supporting Communities Partnership Initiatives (SCPI)**, National Secretariat on Homelessness, 156 rue Hotel de Ville St., 8th Floor, Hull, PQ K1A 0J2. www21.hrdc-drhc.gc.ca/initiative/i02-1_e.html. This

program of the Canadian government supports collaborative community efforts to address homelessness in ways specific to a local region.

4. **The U.S. Department of Health and Human Services**.
http://aspe.os.dhhs.gov/progsys/homeless/. Check out this site for a wealth of information on the homeless in America, as well as information about HHS assistance programs, publications, research results, and other resources.

Books and Other Resources

- Beukema, George. *Stories from Below the Poverty Line* (Scottdale, PA: Herald Press, 2001). This book is both a message of hope and a challenge to live among the poor as God's people. We can learn much from the faith and courage of people who struggle below the poverty line.
- Hurtig, Mel. *Pay the Rent or Feed the Kids: The Tragedy and Disgrace of Poverty in Canada* (Toronto: McClelland & Stewart, 2000). Combining the latest statistics with the heart-wrenching stories of those living in poverty and the callous comments of politicians and their corporate supporters, Hurtig calls for a reexamination of today's society.
- Layton, Jack. *Homelessness: The Making and Unmaking of a Crisis* (Toronto: Penguin Books, 2000). Layton addresses the crisis from its roots, in order not only to understand the problem, but to find workable solutions. Combines research and personal anecdote, as well as analysis from social scientists, housing economists, mayors, journalists, clergy, and the homeless themselves.
- TRAVARCA. A video library sponsored by the Reformed Church in America and the Christian Reformed Church in North America, TRAVARCA carries thousands of videos on hundreds of topics, including homelessness. A yearly membership allows churches and individuals to use an unlimited number of videos; nonmembers may use the videos for established fees. Call 1-800-968-7221 or 1-616-698-7071 for a catalog or to request information and videos.

Illness (Of an Adult Child)

Ask Me

He who answers before listening, that is his folly and shame.

—Proverbs 18:13

O ne of my sons, blessed with a warm, jovial personality and uncommon brilliance, began part-time college course work as a thirteen-year-old and before high school graduation was a college sophomore with a near straight-A average. Then, to his great dismay, and ours, he was struck by what has since been diagnosed as bipolar disorder (a form of depression).

After six semesters of failed or dropped courses—each begun at his initiative with fresh hopes—he began working, but performed erratically. As we watched his life become a shambles and his faith go dormant, we experienced the gradual death of hope. The son we so loved and celebrated had undergone a living death of the spirit. We grieved, ached, and worried—and gradually adapted our expectations to the new reality, taking joy in small steps toward what—dare we hope?—may be his recovery.

—David

Wisdom for the Caregiver

☞ I appreciated most the few who reached out to *him* with visits or invitations. But I also appreciated the three or four friends who would call or come to me and ask how it was going. Caring is listening, yes, but it's also having the courage to reach out and to broach painful subjects. (It was difficult for me to initiate conversation about such a painful subject, especially given the comparative success my friends were enjoying in their roles as parents.)

—David

Note: For additional Wisdom for the Caregiver, see the following sections on Illness.

Helplines

See pages 132-133, 140, and other sections in this book for Helplines specific to a particular circumstance.

Books and Other Resources

See pages 133-134, 141-142, and other sections in this book for books and other resources specific to a particular circumstance.

Illness (Of a Young Child)

Sharing the Pain, Sharing the Joy

The King will reply, "I tell you the truth, whatever you did for one of the least of these brothers of mine, you did for me."

—Matthew 25:40

W hen my daughter, Crista, was four months old, her pediatrician found a lump on the right side of her abdomen. The first indication of the blood tests, ultrasound, and needle biopsy was that the tumor was malignant. For two and a half weeks we waited anxiously, yet with the peaceful knowledge that God was in control.

The people around us showed their love and care in many wonderful ways. We felt their prayers give us strength every day. People brought dinner. One friend brought us a basket filled with fruit, bagels, juice, crackers, and cheese—all healthy snacks that were appreciated because many times we did not feel like eating big meals, and the last thing on my mind was a trip to the grocery store. One of the most helpful things was a couple of friends volunteering to make phone calls. After exhausting days full of tests and waiting in doctors' offices, we did not feel like making many phone calls, yet we felt it necessary to update all the concerned people. Another friend brought over a gift, an outfit for our daughter. The great thing about the outfit was that it was something that Crista would wear the following summer. That outfit symbolized the hope that Crista would get through this and would grow up. It helped me to focus on that hope.

The above demonstrations of compassion stick out in my memory. But I do not want to underestimate the hundreds of cards we received. Our days were brightened when we could come home and open cards that relayed thoughts, hopes, and prayers.

After those two and a half weeks we found out that Crista's tumor was benign and would disappear on its own. What a miracle! The same people who shared our pain, shared in our celebration. We received "joy" cards, flower arrangements, and many hugs. These gestures were appreciated just as much as the ones we received during the time of crisis. They showed just how sincerely others had felt our anxiety.

—Kim (Crista's mom)

Wisdom for the Caregiver
(from Kim and Michael, Crista's dad)

☙ Please encourage children to "care for" others. One of the most touching notes that we received was the following one from Renee, a ten-year-old girl:

Dear Crista,

I hope you get better fast. I really hope that everything goes fine and Crista is a healthy baby. You are a cute baby. I hope the doctors can cure what she has. When she gets better I will be so happy. I am praying for Crista and I know that a lot of others are praying to.

Love, Renee

☙ I really appreciated it when people who I didn't even know sent us cards. You expect certain people to send cards when you go through a difficult time, but when someone you do not know sends a card, it is very moving.

🕭 Very meaningful was knowing that there were many prayer chains in many geographical areas praying for Crista and us.

🕭 I appreciated people who helped in special ways: One person sent $20 for gas money for the trips to the hospital. Another sent a coupon for long distance phone calls. Another very practical gift (and a symbol of hope) was a year's supply of baby formula.

Additional Wisdom for the Caregiver

🕭 Read aloud the child's favorite books. (If the child is hospitalized, record a reading of the story on video or cassette. The child will feel comforted by hearing the familiar story and your voice.)

🕭 Send cards. Encourage your children to create a card or a picture. If the sick child belongs to a club/group (scouts, Sunday school class, sport teams), suggest that the members of the group make a banner or a giant card with a message from each person.

🕭 Gifts produce lots of smiles! Select a game that can easily be played while the child is in bed. Rather than just giving the game to the child, offer to play the game with her or him "right now!" Other gifts that are almost always a hit: washable markers or crayons, doodle-pad, coloring books, cassettes, and puzzles.

🕭 Send a small gift each day through the mail—a piece of gum, bookmark, balloon, package of plant seeds, miniature puzzle, lollipop, and so on.

🕭 Fill a variety box with the materials for making drawings, collages, posters, and constructing small objects: scissors, crayons, paper, pins, material, buttons, needles, thread, magnifying glass, mirror, pieces of aluminum foil, flashlight, box of paper clips, clay, paper hole-punch, toothpicks, glue, gummed stars, stickers, and so on.

🕭 Give the parents or the child (if he or she can read) the wonderful idea book *Let's Make a Memory* by Gloria Gaither and Shirley Dobson (Dallas: Word Publishing, 1983). This book is filled with activities and special events that can be used to cheer up a family member who is ill. The four ideas above are from this book.

🕭 Give a basket of fun: books, small electronic games (like Quiz Whiz), an "Etch a Sketch," a "Magna Doodle," silly putty, jewelry-making kit, a craft from a craft store, books on tape, and other things that a child can do by him- or herself.

⊛ When caring for a child who is dying, consider the ideas and information in the book *Helping Children Grieve* by Theresa Huntley (Minneapolis: Augsburg, 1991). This book also has helpful information on how to help the other family members and friends of the child.
⊛ Read "Caregiving Basics" (pp. 203-222).
⊛ Check "109+ Ways to Say, 'I Care'" (pp. 223-234).

Helplines

⊛ **Children's Hospice International**. 1-800-242-4453. www.chionline.org. CHI is a non-profit organization started in 1983 to promote hospice support through pediatric care facilities, to encourage the inclusion of children in existing and developing hospice and home care programs, and to provide a hospice perspective for all areas of pediatric care.
⊛ **Make-A-Wish Foundation of America**. 1-800-722-9474. www.wish.org. This foundation allows a child with a life-threatening condition to visit his or her favorite vacation place or be visted by his or her hero, all expenses paid.

Books and Other Resources

See pages 133-134 and 141-142 for a list of helpful books.

Illness (Chronic)

Confronting God

Pleasant words are like a honeycomb, sweet to the soul and healing to the bones.

—Proverbs 16:25

L oss and grief are everywhere in the landscape of our lives. There is nothing in human life to which we are attached that is permanent and unchanging. There is no deep or lasting bond which is not subject to the uncertainties of this world's terrain. Six years ago, at age forty-eight, just when I thought that I had found a sense of permanence, my whole life was thrown into disequilibrium with a diagnosis of Parkinson's disease. I was shaken to the core, left numb and full of fear. . . .

Two things were especially helpful to me in my time of initial shock and outrage with a Parkinson's diagnosis. My pastor invited me to pray with her in our meditation chapel. She took my arm and gently held it in her hands and prayed for my healing. I found it very hard at that time to pray. I had felt God's absence for some weeks, but somehow she connected me with God's presence. I remember her face and touch, a sign of God's comforting presence. I do not remember her words.

A second initiative came as the awareness of loss broke through into my consciousness and the pain sank deeply into the depths of my body and spirit. People in their grief often feel their pain in some part of their stomach or chest. Anger erupts, explodes, or is repressed. Guilt and shame may follow. Self-recrimination comes. We bargain with ourselves and with God. The tears may flow or dry up at unpredictable moments. The circumstances of the loss are repeated again and again as one tries to discover some way of seeing it differently, rehearsing the "if onlys" of life.

Abraham Heschel, the great Jewish biblical scholar, reminds us of the noble vocation of confronting God as we face the losses and injustices that would overpower us. God honors it when we take our call and promise that seriously. God comes close to us in our struggle.

In my case, this confrontation came one morning as I was preparing a sermon on the experience of Jacob at the Jabbok River (Genesis 32) where he wrestled all night with that dark river spirit whom he discovered to be the angel of God. As I sat in my study, wrestling with the text and the reality of Jacob's boldness in confronting God, "I will not let you go, unless you bless me," I held up my shaking hand and shouted in the darkness of the early morning those words. A peace entered my spirit as the light shone in the window. I knew that I had a sign of God's yes in the midst of my many no's. Better to go away from the encounter limping, having risked meeting God in some new way, than to wander in the cold recesses of our own loneliness. Could it be that the heart of God is much more accessible in the midst of our losses, more palpable than we ever dared to believe—in the griefs we bear?. . .

My experience is that even when we do not believe it, or deeply doubt it, that especially then, in the darkest moment of our loss and despair, "nothing will be able to separate us from the love of God" (Romans 8:39). That is the clear witness of God's people in every generation. So to know that each person must die is to begin to learn to live and to care.

—Stanley Rock, "Coming to Terms with Life's Losses," reprinted from the *Church Herald* (Feb. 1992). Copyright © 1992 by the *Church Herald,* Inc. Used with permission.

Wisdom for the Caregiver (from Stan)

- Listen! Help the partner or family member talk about his or her experiences, thoughts, feelings. It's helpful to have careful periodic reviews or "check-in times" of your progress because everything keeps changing with a chronic illness.
- Three major newsletters are committed to Parkinson's research and care, information, and education. Two that I've found especially helpful are the "Parkinson Report" from the National Parkinson's Foundation (www.parkinson.org) and the American Parkinson's Disease Association (www.apdaparkinson.com) newsletter.
- Right now it is particularly difficult for me to deal with the fact that my energy level is significantly reduced. I still work out three or four times a week, but I just can't live at the pace that I use to live at. To slow down is extremely difficult for anyone who has had a busy life.
- A powerful book for personal or small group study is *Journey Through Psalms: A Path To Wholeness* by Denise Hopkins (Cleveland: United Church Press, 1990). This book includes a chapter on praying the psalms of lament and a chapter on confronting God.
- Allow the person with the disease/disability to take charge of his or her own illness. Don't be over-solicitous.
- I like friends to ask how I am doing. My situation changes from day to day and week to week, just like anyone else's. There are things that I get anxious about, there are uncertainties about the future, and I appreciate it when people take an interest.
- What I don't like is when people, in their desire for me to do well and be well, say, "You're looking awfully good." On that day I may not be feeling very well at all, and it's almost like they are trying to make me feel well when I am not.
- The family members certainly care about what's happening to you, but primarily they want you to be their father or husband.
- The church can help by not seeing the disabled as objects, by not denying the reality of the pain, and by fostering a pastoral care ministry.

Additional Wisdom for the Caregiver

⊛ Read "Caregiving Basics" (pp. 203-222).

⊛ Check "109+ Ways to Say, 'I Care'" (pp. 223-234).

⊛ Offer regular, consistent tokens of your care. Suffering people say that fear and loneliness steal in at unexpected moments, and regularity is often more important than the quantity of time a person can give. Regularity becomes increasingly important with illnesses that tend to drag out over long periods of time, such as Parkinson's disease.

⊛ "One man told me the most helpful person during his long illness was an office colleague who called every day, just to check. His visits, usually twice a week, never exceeded fifteen minutes, but the consistency of his calls and visits became a fixed point, something he could count on when everything else in his life seemed unstable."

—Philip Yancey, *Where Is God When It Hurts?* (Grand Rapids, MI: Zondervan, 2001), p. 179

⊛ "Encourage the person to reach out and help others who are suffering. When my physicians noticed how depressed I was in the hospital, they said, 'Be a rabbi—go and counsel other patients.' That made me feel important again. My friends fighting cancer and other diseases tell me the same thing: Helping others cope is the one good thing they can do, the one good thing they feel qualified to do, and the one good thing they find real fulfillment in doing."

—Rabbi Hirshel Jaffe, *Why Me, Why Anyone?* (Northvale, NJ: Jason Aronson, 1994), p. 79

Helplines

1. **Health Canada**, Address Locator 0900C2, Ottawa, ON K1A 0K9. 1-613-957-2991. www.hc-sc.gc.ca. The federal department responsible for helping the people of Canada maintain and improve their health. Options on the website include searching topics A-Z (www.hc-sc.gc.ca/english/diseases/index.html) and finding locations of regional offices (www.hc-sc.gc.ca/english/contact/index.html).

2. **Medbroadcast Corporation**, Suite 250, Marine Building, 355 Burrard Street, Vancouver, BC V6C 2G8. 1-604-687-7463. www.medbroadcast.com. A comprehensive consumer health and wellness website that has links for medical conditions A-Z, links for support groups both by health topic and by location, and a link with information about prescription drugs.

Books and Other Resources

ⓦ Jacobs, Pamela. *500 Tips for Coping With Chronic Illness* (San Franciso: Robert Reed Publishers, 1995). Filled with useful ideas and resources for supporting and nurturing anyone dealing with a chronic illness.

ⓦ Kok, James R. *Waiting for Morning: Seeking God in Our Suffering* (Grand Rapids, MI: Faith Alive Christian Resources, 1997). Kok offers the idea that ongoing suffering can help us grow spiritually and suggests meaningful ways to respond to one's own suffering and that of others. (Call 1-800-333-8300 or visit www.FaithAliveResources.org to order.)

ⓦ Kok, James R. *90% of Helping Is Just Showing Up* (Grand Rapids, MI: Faith Alive Christian Resources, 1996). Want to help people in pain but don't know what to do? Find out why intimacy, not answers, is what people in trouble need most. (Call 1-800-333-8300 or visit www.FaithAliveResources.org to order.)

ⓦ Siegel, Bernie S. *Peace, Love, and Healing: Bodymind Communication and the Path to Self-Healing: An Exploration* (New York: Harper Perennial, 1990). Siegel encourages the ill person (he dislikes the term "patient") to work for peace of mind and to live each moment fully in spite of one's disease.

ⓦ Vanderwell, Howard, and Norma deWaal Malefyt. *Be Still, My Soul* (Grand Rapids, MI: Faith Alive Christian Resources, 2001). A recording of quiet music and reflective thoughts to help bring comfort and encouragement to those who are going through difficult circumstances. Available on CD and cassette. (Call 1-800-333-8300 or visit www.FaithAliveResources.org to order.)

Ⓦ Weiner, William J., Lisa M. Shulman, and Antony Lang. *Parkinson's Disease: A Complete Guide for Patients and Families* (Baltimore: John Hopkins Press, 2001). This comprehensive book helps those who are living with Parkinson's disease adjust to profound life changes, develop expertise in self-monitoring and self-management, and become effective partners in shared decision-making with family members and medical professionals.

Ⓦ Yancey, Philip. *Where Is God When It Hurts?* (Grand Rapids, MI: Zondervan, 1990; revised and expanded edition, 2001). In this popular book, Yancy looks at pain—physical, emotional, and spiritual—and helps us understand why we suffer.

Illness (Terminal)

Caring for a Dying Friend
Some friends play at friendship; but a true friend sticks closer than one's nearest kin.

—Proverbs 18:24, NRSV

My Friend
My friend
Mayo Clinic
Devastating news:
Cancer!
Surgery to remove pancreas, spleen and a portion of the liver.

"O Lord, my friend is very ill.
Grant me the wisdom and the strength
to walk this road with her."
It began with a promise to be there.
She is so brave; so beautiful.
Always there is laughter.
Three more surgeries. Three years.

Teaching is her life, her joy.
Children her love.
She returns to it valiantly, always positive.

I am in awe of her determination,
True grit,
Independence.

How do I fulfill my promise to you, friend?
I listen.
I pray quietly, constantly.
I watch.
I watch for signals.
When to enter, to help.
Then to quietly support her from afar.
Listen.
Love.
Observe.
I push sometimes.
I am rebuffed.
"Lord, help me to listen more carefully."

I pray.
I weep.
I am in awe of her determination.
True grit,
Independence.

Support takes many faces:
making meals
listening
talking
cleaning
doing laundry
laughing

I am angry.
She is composed, resigned, but always determined.
We are so different!
I try to listen,
to read signals and needs.
I try not to push.
We are different.

Listen.
Hold her hand.
Drive her to appointments, wait together.
Choose the "right" wig.
Laugh.
Listen.

I pray,
"Lord, grant me wisdom."

I am blessed to have such a friend.
A new house purchased.
A new focus.
Excitement, celebration.
She is stronger and so happy.
Joy, contentment.
A fireplace.
We share the joy.

And then darkness!
Another surgery, an end to teaching.
Such sadness!
Listen.
Endless trips to doctors, chemotherapy, radiation, MRIs.
She is brave.
No tears from her.
I weep; I pray; I listen.

Medications.
Always laughter
In spite of sadness.
Her skin turns black.
My black, Dutch friend.

She craves artichokes—we lunch.

She prays.
She is leaving me.
Never a complaint.

I weep as she sleeps, so weak.
It won't be long.
I hold her hand.
My friend is gone.

"Lord, thank you for my friend.
I am bettered for being a part of her life."

"And I will raise you up on eagle's wings,
Bear you on the breath of dawn,
Make you to shine like the sun,
And hold you in the palm of my hand."

—Ruth Beckman

Wisdom for the Caregiver (from Billy Graham)

Margaret Vermeer served as a missionary in Nigeria. When she was seven months pregnant, she received the report that a biopsy of a small tumor was malignant. Five weeks after the surgery to remove the tumors, she gave birth to a son, then began chemotherapy and radiation treatments. For two years she had a miraculous remission, but then gradually more tumors appeared. As her condition grew increasingly serious, she became more sensitive about the way people viewed her. Six months before she died, she was speaking for women's church groups, sharing her insights on how to care for others as she wanted to be cared for. Here are some of her thoughts:

Be honest in sharing your feelings. Don't bounce into the room with false cheerfulness, but admit your helplessness and concern. "I would like to help you, but I don't know how," is a straightforward expression of concern. Don't play games and be evasive. Even children can cope better when people talk to them honestly.

Don't preach a well-thought-out sermon. Christians who bring out their Bibles and read lengthy passages are not being sensitive. To share a verse that means something to you may be helpful, but wait for the signals before plunging into a lengthy spiritual discussion.

Be a good listener. People will tell you what they are ready to talk about. Sickness can be a very lonely journey. When Jesus was agonizing in the Garden of Gethsemane, He didn't want to face death alone. He asked the disciples to wait and pray with Him, but they fell asleep. What good were they?

Treat a dying person as a human being. Sometimes we treat a dying person in such a way that we make it harder on that person emotionally. We shut the people up in hospitals, whisper behind their backs, and deprive them of all the things that had made their lives rich. Familiar things *are* important.

Provide spiritual support. When you quote a Bible verse to comfort a person, be sure you know what the verse means. When Margaret Vermeer knew that she only had a short time to live, she said that she was told by her Christian friends to "give thanks in all circumstances, for this is God's will for you in Christ Jesus" (1 Thessalonians 5:18). . . . Look at the verse carefully. It doesn't say give thanks for everything, it says to give thanks in everything. There is a vast difference. When we are told that "God causes everything to work together for good," it doesn't mean that all things are good in themselves, but that God is making them work out for good.

Always have hope. God is greater than the situations we face. Sometimes it's hard to find that which is positive and hopeful, but there is always something to be thankful for. Help the patient look forward to something . . . a visit from someone special . . . a time when you will be returning.

—*Death and the Life After,* Billy Graham, © 1987, W Publishing Group, Nashville, TN. All rights reserved. Used by permission.

Additional Wisdom for the Caregiver

⊛ Be aware of the five stages of dying. Knowing about these stages can be of great help in understanding and comforting a person who is dying. (See page 143 for a description of these stages based on *On Death and Dying* by Elisabeth Kübler-Ross.)

⊛ Read "Caregiving Basics" (pp. 203-222).

⊛ Check "109+ Ways to Say, 'I Care'" (pp. 223-234).

Helplines

1. **AirCare Alliance Mercy Medical Airlift**. 1-800-296-1217. Provides transportation for those who are terminally ill.
2. **Canadian Hospice Palliative Care Association**, Suite 131C, 43 Bruyere St., Ottawa, ON K1N 5C8. 1-800-668-2785; 1-613-241-3663; info@cpca.net. www.cpca.net.
3. **Community Care Access Centre**, Ontario Ministry of Health. 1-800-268-1154; 1-416-314-5518. www.gov.on.ca/MOH/english/news/media/ccac/ccac.html. The point of access to Ontario's long-term care system, including home care, long-term care facilities, services for special needs children, and community referrals.
4. **Medbroadcast Corporation**, Suite 250, Marine Building, 355 Burrard Street, Vancouver, BC V6C 2G8. 1-604-687-7463. www.medbroadcast.com. A comprehensive consumer health and wellness website that has links for medical conditions A-Z, links for support groups both by health topic and by location, and a link with information about prescription drugs.
5. **National Hospice and Palliative Care Organization**, Suite 902, 1901 North Fort Myer Drive, Arlington, VA 22209. 1-800-658-8898. www.nhpco.org. This nonprofit membership organization consists of groups and institutions concerned with or providing care for the terminally ill and their families. The organization furnishes literature, information, and referrals to local hospice programs and to regional and other national resources. Ask for a copy of *A Consumer's Guide to Hospice Care*.

Books and Other Resources

⚘ Byock, Ira, M.D. *Dying Well* (New York: Riverhead Books, 1997).
Dr. Byock encourages those who are dying to find ways to strengthen
bonds with people they love and to create moments of profound meaning in their final passage.

⚘ Callanan, Maggie, and Patricia Kelley. *Final Gifts* (New York: Bantam
Books, 1992). Discover how to listen to a dying person, how to weigh
gesture and meaning so as to avoid responses that alienate and frus-
trate. See how others have approached a death in ways that have
brought comfort and peace, even joy.

⚘ Delbene, Ron. *Into the Light* (Nashville: The Upper Room, 1988). This
book provides a simple way to pray with the sick and the dying. It also
shows the caregiver other ways to be with and care for people who are
sick and dying.

⚘ Huntley, Theresa. *Helping Children Grieve* (Minneapolis: Augsburg,
1991). The second half of this book focuses on providing care for children who are dying.

⚘ Kübler-Ross, Elisabeth. *On Death and Dying* (New York: Macmillan,
1969). Shows how those who are dying can be helped to meet their
death with dignity. Describes the five stages of dying and how to help
meet a person's needs in each of these stages. Includes real-life stories.

⚘ Kübler-Ross, Elisabeth. *Questions and Answers on Death and Dying*
(New York: Simon and Schuster, 1997). The author discusses accepting the end of life, suicide, terminal illness, euthanasia, how to tell a
patient he or she is critically ill, and how to deal with all the special difficulties surrounding death.

⚘ Schwartz, Morrie. *Letting Go: Morrie's Reflections on Living While
Dying* (New York: Dell Publishing Group, Inc., 1996). "With warmth,
wisdom, and humor, Morrie reveals how to . . . live fully in the moment
. . . tap into the power of the mind to transcend physical limitations . . .
use humor to defuse frustration . . . grieve for your losses . . . reach out

to family and friends . . . build support systems and develop an inner space for meditation and spiritual connection."

Ⓥ Vos, Mirth. *Letters to Myself on Dying: A Journal of Hope, Pain, and Courage* (Grand Rapids, MI: Baker Books and Faith Alive Christian Resources, 1999). This account of one woman's battle with cancer gives insight into a love relationship with God that stands up to severe testing and triumphs through faith. Written with both elegance and angst, this book is an unflinching portrait of how Vos learned to grieve her own impending death. (Call 1-800-333-8300 or visit www.FaithAliveResources.org to order.)

How to Handle the Five Stages of Dying

Note: This chart is based on information found in the book *On Death and Dying* by Elisabeth Kübler-Ross (New York: Macmillan Publishing Co., Inc., 1969).

Patient's Behavior	Stage	Caregiver's Response
In effect, the patient says, "No, not me. This cannot be true" (Kübler-Ross, p. 34). Patients often search frantically for a favorable diagnosis. Denial usually occurs during the early stages of an illness, but it may also occasionally be used later, when the patient needs some relief from dealing with the real facts.	Denial	Understand why the patient is grasping at straws. Patience and willingness to talk are important.
The patient says, "Oh, yes, it is me, it was not a mistake . . . but why me?" (p. 44). Deep anger follows, and the patient may bitterly envy those who are well and complain incessantly about almost everything.	Anger	Try to imagine how you would feel if you were in the patient's shoes. Consider that the patient is angry over the impending loss of everything he or she holds dear: family, friends, home, work, play. Treat the person with respect and understanding. If the anger is directed at you, do not take it personally.
The patient says, "Maybe I can bargain with God and get a time extension." Promises of good behavior are made in return for time and some freedom from physical pain.	Bargaining	If the patient's "bargain" is revealed, it should be listened to, not brushed off. This stage typically passes in a short period of time.
The patient grieves and mourns "the impending loss of so many meaningful people and places" (p. 99).	Depression	Attempts to cheer up or reassure the patient mean very little. The patient needs to express sorrow fully and without hindrance.
"If a patient has had enough time . . . and has been given some help in working through the previously described stages, he will reach a stage during which he is neither depressed nor angry about his "fate," a stage of "quiet expectation" of his coming death (p. 99).	Acceptance	News of the outside world means little, and few visitors are required. There will be little talk, and it is time merely for the presence of the close family. During this stage, says Kübler-Ross, the "family needs more help, understanding, and support than the patient" (p. 100).

To gain a deeper understanding of the above process and for a better picture of the variety of reactions and responses demonstrated by patients, read Elisabeth Kübler-Ross' classic, *On Death and Dying* (New York: Macmillan Publishing Co., Inc., 1969). The book features numerous interviews with dying individuals, along with suggested approaches for caregivers.

Illness (General Suggestions and Advice)

Visiting Those Who Are Ill

Following are some common-sense suggestions to guide you in visiting those who are ill. Since circumstances vary, some of the suggestions may not apply in a given situation.

- Be natural. You may not feel "natural" in this unusual circumstance, but try to be yourself. The best thing you can offer is your friendship. Make any necessary adjustments for the person's condition, but treat him or her the way you would if he or she were not sick.
- Permit the person to talk. Respect the person's dignity and give him an opportunity to talk about the things he wants to talk about.
- Be pleasant and cheerful, but do not overdo it. You are not there as an entertainer.
- Avoid talking about illnesses or operations that you or your friends have had.
- Sit where it is easy to be seen (but not on the bed).
- Don't neglect the use of touch. When appropriately used, it is soothing, comforting, and emotionally healing to the ill person. When you touch, use common sense. Watch for any sign that it may be displeasing to the other person. A gentle holding of the hand or arm is usually appropriate and can be very comfortable for both persons.
- Don't shy away from serious conversation. Allow the patient to talk about what he or she wants to talk about.

© Do not come with a little sermon that you intend to deliver. Avoid being "preachy." Talk about encouraging things, give assurances of your love and God's love, rejoice about God's continuing faithfulness as long as these things are natural for you and not contrived.

© Never assume that a person in a coma cannot hear you—she may hear and understand every word, though she is unable to let you know that she is hearing. Speak your words of love and encouragement directly to the person, whether you are sure she understands or not.

Some additional suggestions, mostly quite obvious but sometimes overlooked (from *Amity: Friendship in Action* by Richard P. Walters):

© Don't bump the bed!
© Don't underestimate the value of your silent presence.
© Don't diagnose.
© Don't whisper with others outside the door.
© Don't wear perfume.
© If the patient is sleeping when you arrive, don't awaken him or her.
© Don't have a gab fest with other visitors, unless the patient wants that.
© Don't go if you are sick!

Advice for Medical Patients and Their Families
The following suggestions are from Carol Myers in "Crossing the Line" by David Myers, *Church Herald,* (Nov. 1996), pp. 29-32. Used with permission.

Make Your Wishes Known!
© Give a trusted family member or friend the designation of patient advocate or durable power of attorney with health care decision-making. Such a document, drawn by an attorney, gives this person the legal power to make decisions on your behalf should you become incapacitated. (See "Living Will/Advance Directive" below.)

© If you have a living will/advance directive, recognize that it may not cover all the situations you intend. The applicability of a living will depends on how terms such as *incurable* or *irreversible* are understood. For example, pneumonia —"the old person's friend"—may be treated aggressively against your will. Initial and date the living will regularly to show that it expresses your current intent.

© Inform family members of your wishes. Make sure your patient advocate designee fully understands your intentions.

☯ Discuss with your physicians what you would want in the event of a life-threatening medical crisis.

☯ Request a patient representative or advocate immediately if treatment isn't what you want. This person will represent your interests in working with the hospital and physicians.

☯ Ask to meet with the ethics committee when dialogue with physicians doesn't quickly resolve differences.

Living Will/Advance Directive

If your heart stops, do you want to be resuscitated? If you stop breathing, do you want to be placed on a ventilator? Health care personnel, particularly emergency care teams, operate on the assumption that they must do everything possible to keep a person alive. Generally, this means that medical personnel base their decisions on what can be done, not on whether it should be done on an individual's behalf.

However, there may be occasions or circumstances when a person would prefer to limit the extent of treatment for medical complications: being in an irreversible coma or vegetative state, having a terminal illness, or other circumstances that would impair significantly one's quality of life if further treatment were pursued.

As health care reform comes full circle, individuals need to be prepared to make personal decisions about treatment choices for medical care. Other directives include concerns about antibiotics, any surgical or therapeutic procedure, or life-sustaining treatment of any kind. These instructions or wishes can be made through documents such as a living will or durable power of attorney for health care, allowing you to designate your wishes and who can speak for you to express your wishes. It is necessary to know what is legally approved in your state or province.

Moving

Parting Tears at Heartstrings
There is a time for everything, and a season for every activity under heaven.
—Ecclesiastes 3:1

The following poem powerfully describes the painful feelings and issues that arise when friends (of all ages) are separated by a geographic move. It was written by a ten-year-old boy and given to his friend Jonathan Kleyn, now from Holland, Michigan.

My Best Friend
Jonathan is my very best friend
And he will be until the end.
Laughing, playing, having fun
We loved bright days out in the sun.
Rainy days were fun too,
We never ran out of things to do.
Swimming, gymnastics, spending nights—
We never ever had one fight.
He understood me like no other,
He was more than a friend—he was like a brother.
I liked him
And he liked me.
I thought that was how it would always be.

I thought we'd be together when we were sixty-two,
But it wasn't true,
There was nothing I could do.

He was moving to Michigan—that's far away.
And here I was—I had to stay.
I cried and cried.
Whenever I thought about it—I got sick inside.

I knew I'd miss him forever.
Would I forget him? Never.
When he's gone I'll have the blues,
But he's such a good friend—too good to lose.

Letters are nice, but not enough.
You can't fit in all the little, everyday stuff.
He'll move to Michigan and meet new friends,
And here I'll be alone again.

All the time we spent together
Seems gone on the wind—as light as a feather.
But I'll always have something from times gone past,
Something I know will always last.

—Arthur Hampton

Move to New Town Spells Loneliness

And we know that in all things God works for the good of those who love him, who have been called according to his purpose.

—Romans 8:28

I think it's quite difficult to fathom the emotional stress and loneliness that moving brings unless you have been there.

My most traumatic move was from Chicago, Illinois, where my friends and relatives all lived, to Michigan, where I knew virtually no one. I had been married for six years and was newly pregnant when my husband and I relocated to Holland (Michigan). Precious few people welcomed me. After months of loneliness, I cried out to God to give me just one good friend. In his gracious abundance, God eventually showered me with the best friends a woman could have. The one who became my very best friend is my co-author, Karen Mulder, whom I met at a card party.

Even after I had made numerous friendships, I never forgot the desperately lonely feeling of being a newcomer.

When we moved to one of the first homes in a new neighborhood, I appointed myself official greeter. I gave coffees, invited newcomers to lunch or dinner, and organized a neighborhood Bible study group for women. The Bible study succeeded not only in integrating the women and establishing friendships, but also in introducing many of them to the Lord.

—Ginger Jurries

Wisdom for the Caregiver

❧ "When someone moves into my neighborhood I always offer to help them unpack their kitchen immediately, since this is such a huge job and they can then become functional in the meal department."

—Sue

❧ "When, about a year ago, we moved to Pittsburgh from the South, I was introduced to the most delightful sort of neighborliness I've ever known. Since my husband had to go directly to work, it was my task to meet the moving van at our new apartment. This was my first big moving venture, and I was more than a little overwhelmed when the men departed, leaving me with boxes, cartons, and crated furniture. I had just sat down to map out my first step of unpacking when a knock sounded on the door. Outside stood a youngster holding a tray with sandwiches; a pot of tea, and dainty cakes. A little embarrassed, he handed it to me with a note, then turned and ran down the hall. I opened the envelope and to my astonishment read:

Dear Friend:
I know you're unpacking,
with chores galore.
If you need any help,
I live next door.

If only more people would take the time to be neighborly, how much nicer this old world would be! Knowing the warmth I felt that day, I will never pass up an opportunity to extend a hand to a neighbor."

—Marguerite

- ☙ Give a party; invite your neighbors! Or invite them to your Bible study group, card group, club, and so on.
- ☙ Invite newcomers to your church; pick them up or meet them in the foyer.
- ☙ Offer to watch young children while your new neighbor unpacks.
- ☙ Offer a map of the area with a listing of restaurants, grocery stores, pharmacies, cleaners, and so on marked on the map.
- ☙ Greet newcomers with a pie, loaf of bread, and so on.
- ☙ Check "109+ Ways to Say, 'I Care'" (pp. 223-234).

If you have children and are moving, here's some helpful advice from Gloria Gaither and Shirley Dobson in *Let's Make a Memory* (Nashville: W Publishing Group, 1983, p. 143).

- ☙ Discuss with young children the things in the house that will be moved. Assure them that their beds, trucks, favorite stuffed animals, records, etc., will go along. This is *not* a good time to sort out old toys, games, tennis shoes, etc. Neither should you change from crib to bed, do away with bedtime blanket or pacifier, or drastically change feeding habits.
- ☙ See that the whole family, including young children, is involved in the moving process. Even young children can neatly stack washcloths, towels, or dish towels into a box or fill a container with stuffed toys, paper products, canned goods, utensils or lids, plastic ware, or books.
- ☙ When you arrive at the new place, assemble the children's rooms first and unpack their favorite things. Be sure the children are present for this even if they have to be left with a neighbor or grandparent while the heavy work is done.
- ☙ Encourage children to express their feelings about leaving their home and friends and moving to a new home. If the child likes to write, suggest that he or she keep a journal for a month before the move and for two months after the move.

Helplines

Check your local directory for the number of your "Newcomer's Club" and "Welcome Wagon" if they have not contacted you.

Books and Other Resources

☞ Strannigan, Shawn Alyne. *One Thing Never Changes* (Cincinnati: Standard Publishing, 1995). A heartwarming story about a child's struggle as she moves away from her friends, and how she is helped by knowing that God is with her in the move. The book offers helpful suggestions on easing the trauma of moving for a child.

Parenting Struggles

Communicating with Teens: The Awkward Dance

Do not exasperate your children; instead, bring them up in the training and instruction of the Lord.

—Ephesians 6:4

The awkward dance that parents and their teens do as we move toward greater mutual independence is sometimes difficult and painful. It certainly was for me at times. On one particular day Sara was home from school, due to a scheduled in-service day for the teachers. Sara had slept in later than I thought she should. When she got up, she plopped down in front of the TV. Having the TV on in the middle of the day has always depressed me, so I told her to turn it off. She did, but then she stomped upstairs and slammed the door. Once again we were not communicating. I sat down to reflect on life and meditate, but mostly I felt sad. When would my sweet little girl and I ever get along?

The person who saved the day was Sara herself. As I sat looking out the window, Sara came and handed me a long note. In it she expressed anger at all the ways that I try to take control of her life. She pointed out how inappropriate was my hold on her. Her note was angry and direct. In it she also expressed her fear that I would "blow off" her comments as unimportant, or would laugh or find spelling errors in the note (something I had insensitively done on other occasions). She told me clearly that if that were my response, she did not want to know. In fact, I was deeply moved that she would tell me directly what was bothering her. It was one of several times when Sara's initiative changed our relationship for the better.

—Jane

Wisdom for the Caregiver

🕭 "When you are in a position of power, as a parent or a boss is, listen carefully to criticisms; they are a real gift to you. And if you are the one who is hurt by the person in power, if there is any way to tell that person directly, do it. You may be blessed with a new, more honest relationship."

—Jane

🕭 Encourage the struggling parent to find (or start) a support group of parents with teenagers, or parents with kids who have ADD, and so on.
🕭 Offer the person the book *Caring Enough to Confront* by David Augsburger (Ventura, CA: Regal Books, 1983).
🕭 Suggest the following acronym as a way to CHANGE the way one relates with his or her teenager:

    Communicate openly with your teen.
    Hug (touch) your teen.
    Admit your shortcomings to your teen.
    Negotiate when possible.
    Give your teen specific limits.
    Empathize and affirm.

Helplines

1. **American Association of Christian Counselors**, P.O. Box 739, Forest, VA 24551. 1-800-5-COUNSEL; 1-434-525-9470. www.aacc.net. This organization has a directory of counselors who are members of AACC—a great tool for finding a Christian counselor in just about any region in the United States.
2. **Cross Canada Search**. www.crosscanadasearch.com. A Christian Internet search engine. Includes information about Christian counseling services (www.crosscanadasearch.com/Ministry_Resources/Counselling).
3. **Families Anonymous**, P.O. Box 3475, Culver City, CA 90231-3475. 1-310-815-8010. www.familiesanonymous.org. This organization provides an extensive list of pamphlets on many helpful topics, as well as a list of locations where meetings are held. Many titles are available in Spanish.
4. **Focus on the Family**. 1-800-A-FAMILY. www.Family.org. This popular ministry offers a host of resources for parents and families, including *Family* magazine. A good place to begin is with the "Parent's Place" on their website.
5. **One Parent Family Association**, 1099 Kingston Road, Suite 222, Pickering, ON L1V 1B5. 1-877-773-7714; 1-905-831-7098; opfa222@aol.com. http://hometown.aol.com/opfa222. This parent support organization has local chapters across Canada.
6. **Parents Anonymous**, Fredericton Chapter, P.O. Box 1534, Station A, Fredericton, NB E3B 4Y1. 1-506-472-8255. www.sifn.nb.ca/ community_hall/P/parexxxx.html.
7. **ToughLove International**, P.O. Box 1069, Doylestown, PA 18901. 1-215-348-7090; fax 1-215-348-9874. www.toughlove.org. ToughLove International offers self-help materials to parents, kids in trouble, and the professionals working with them. Helpful audiocassettes are also available (at low cost) on these topics: Things That Stop Us from Changing; Your Kid's Recovery/The Process of Change; Introduction to the ToughLove Program; Drugs and Kids: What You Need to Know;

Especially for Fathers/Family Holidays; ToughLove Program Confrontation/Support.

8. **Worth Unlimited**, 130 Holgate Street, Barrie, ON L4N 2T9. 1-705-734-3817. www.worthunlimited.org. A pre-employment program that helps teenagers discover their God-given gifts and connect these gifts with meaningful work.

Books and Other Resources

⊛ Arp, David, and Claudia Arp. *Suddenly They're 13: Or the Art of Hugging a Cactus* (Grand Rapids, MI: Zondervan, 1999). Through the "four R's" of regrouping, releasing, relating, and relaxing, the Arps help frustrated parents launch their almost-thirteen-year-olds into the teen years.

⊛ Kok, James R. *Family at Work: Building Strong Relationships at Home* (Grand Rapids, MI: Faith Alive Christian Resources, 1999). Find out how to keep peace on the home front. These reflections on family life and marriage will make you laugh, groan, and think. Includes questions for discussion. (Call 1-800-333-8300 or visit www.FaithAliveResources.org to order.)

⊛ Lord, Peter. *Keeping the Doors Open: What to Do When Your Child Wanders from God* (Tarrytown, NY: Chosen Books, 1992). Peter Lord reaches out to parents of "prodigal" children with direction and comfort. Drawing on his experiences with his own once spiritually wayward children, the author offers biblically-based help for parents whose children are far from God. With a sensitive understanding, this pastor of forty-plus years provides principles that you can tailor to your own unique situation. Also offers much needed affirmation for those who feel guilty or insecure about their parental abilities.

⊛ Murdock, Mary Ruth. *Raising a Christian Daughter in an MTV World* (Phillipsburg, NJ: P&R Publishers, 2000). This book provides a wonderful, Scripture-based guide that will encourage and help parents of teen-aged daughters. Practical, full of suggestions and examples.

⊛ Parrott, Les III. *Helping the Struggling Adolescent: A Guide to Thirty Common Problems for Parents, Counselors, and Youth Workers,* rev. ed. (Grand Rapids, MI: Zondervan, 2001).

⊛ Shandler, Nina, and Sara Shandler. *Ophelia's Mom* (New York: Crown, 2001). This book is a collection of essays, poems, stories, and other commentary provided by women across the country. Topics include rejection and bonding, feminism, school, drugs, alcohol, divorce, sibling rivalry, and more.

⊛ Snyderman, Nancy, and Peg Streep. *Girl in the Mirror* (New York: Hyperion, 2002). The authors have crafted a practical, reassuring guide to navigating girls' adolescence. Tackles such issues as sexuality, body image, and family turbulence. Offers advice on how mothers and daughters can thrive during the teen years.

⊛ Tannen, Deborah. *I Only Say This Because I Love You: How the Way We Talk Can Make or Break Family Relationships Throughout Our Lives* (New York: Random House, 2001). Tannen helps the reader understand and redefine family talk. She provides tools for improving relationships with family members of every age.

⊛ TRAVARCA. A video library sponsored by the Reformed Church in America and the Christian Reformed Church in North America, TRAVARCA carries thousands of videos on hundreds of topics, including parenting and family life. A yearly membership allows churches and individuals to use an unlimited number of videos; nonmembers may use the videos for established fees. Call 1-800-968-7221 or 1-616-698-7071 for a catalog or to request information and videos.

⊛ White, Joe, and Jim Weidmann (editors). *Parent's Guide to the Spiritual Mentoring of Teens* (Carol Stream, IL: Tyndale House, 2001). This Focus on the Family publication offers parents advice and techniques to help guide teens into a grace-filled, loving relationship with Jesus Christ.

⊛ Yates, Susan Alexander. *And Then I Had Teenagers* (Grand Rapids, MI: Baker Book House, 2001). Drawing from her experience in raising five teenagers, Yates walks you through everything from preparing for the teen years to letting your teens go. Her insights can help you create open communication, set limits, understand what's normal (and what's not!), take advantage of peer pressure, build your teens' faith, and more.

Relationships: Troubled and Broken (Infidelity)

A Break in Trust

Do not withhold good from those who deserve it, when it is within your power to act.

—Proverbs 3:27

Two weeks before the birth of our son, the most dreadful thing happened: I discovered that my husband was having an affair. I had suspected it, but in every way possible I did not want to believe it. However, what I had been denying inside became a reality; I was face to face with her and my husband. She didn't belong in his arms. *I* did! My arms were empty and so was my heart.

There was anger, screaming anger, that would not stop. I was angry at myself, at God, at the whole world. I screamed until I couldn't scream anymore. I just did.

Being pregnant made the situation more difficult. I felt ugly as it was, and I knew I wasn't going to get any prettier. I kept thinking, "If I wasn't pregnant, he wouldn't be having an affair with another woman." I was filled with guilt: Was this my fault? I felt like a "nothing." There was no energy, joy, or "life." There was a death, a numbness, inside of me and outside of me.

—Mary

Wisdom for the Caregiver (from Mary)

- Every day, for months, a special friend would call and ask me two questions: "I'm here. Do you want me there?" (Sometimes I would ask her to come and be with me because I felt so alone and lonely.) The second question she would ask each day was, "What can I pray about for *you* today?"
- When this friend noticed that my hair needed shaping up, she made appointments for both of us.
- This friend also didn't feel sorry for me. She would say, "You carry the baby, and I will help you carry the hurt, and we will give them both to God."

Additional Wisdom for the Caregiver

- Don't ask for all the juicy details. Ask yourself: What is my motive for asking a particular question?
- Practice strict confidentiality.
- Read "Caregiving Basics" (pp. 203-222).
- Consider "109+ Ways to Say, 'I Care'" (pp. 223-234).
- When the person seems to be immobilized by depression, suggest that she or he write a "to do" list for the day. Then work alongside the person to accomplish the tasks.
- Invite the person to participate in a physical activity/exercise with you. Walking and talking produces healing—so does an intense tennis match or racquetball game.
- Invite the person out for lunch or dinner.
- Encourage the person to become involved in a class or support group on codependency, self-esteem, or assertiveness training. Check with community care persons such as pastors, doctors, nurses, social workers, and so on for information on support groups and for therapist recommendations.
- Read about caring for those who are suffering from depression (pp. 99-106).

Helplines

1. **American Association of Christian Counselors**, P.O. Box 739, Forest, VA 24551. 1-800-5-COUNSEL; 1-434-525-9470. www.aacc.net. This organization has a directory of counselors who are members of AACC—a great tool for finding a Christian counselor in just about any region in the United States.
2. **Covenant Keepers**, P.O. Box 702371, Tulsa, OK 74170-2371. 1-918-743-0365; cki@ifriendly.com (U.S.); covenant@uniserve.com (Canada). www.covenantkeepersinc.org. A ministry to assist Christian couples who are having marital problems.
3. **Cross Canada Search**. www.crosscanadasearch.com. A Christian Internet search engine. Includes information about Christian counseling services (www.crosscanadasearch.com/Ministry_Resources/ Counselling).
4. **Salem Christian Mental Health Association**, 1 Young St., Suite 418, Hamilton, ON L8N 1T8. 1-905-528-0353. www.salem.on.ca. Provides counseling and also acts as a clearinghouse for mental health resources.

Books and Other Resources

Bloomfield, Harold, Melba Colgrove, and Peter McWilliams. *How to Survive the Loss of a Love* (Allen Park, MI: Mary Books/Prelude Press, 2000). This book is about understanding loss, surviving, healing, and growing through the grieving process. If offers many helpful suggestions for persons struggling with grief.

Carder, Dave, and Duncan Jaenicke. *Torn Asunder: Recovering from Extramarital Affairs* (Chicago: Moody Press, 1995). Written to offer couples hope, healing, and encouragement in the face of adultery, this book helps readers understand extramarital affairs and then offers healing for marriages dealing with this betrayal. An excellent resource for pastors, church leaders, pastoral care workers, and those dealing with infidelity in their marriage.

⊛ Gaddy, Welton. *Adultery and Grace: The Ultimate Scandal* (Grand Rapids, MI: Eerdmans Publishing Company, 1996). Welton offers specific suggestions on how God's grace can help adulterers and those affected by their infidelity.

⊛ Gray, John. *Men, Women, and Relationships: Making Peace with the Opposite Sex* (New York: Harper Mass Market Paperbacks, 1996). Dr. Gray argues that the key to creating and maintaining successful relationships between men and women lies in accepting our differences. He suggests simple, practical techniques to help us respect and appreciate each other.

⊛ Smedes, Lewis B. *Forgive and Forget* (New York: Pocket Books, 1984). How can you forgive a friend's betrayal, a parent's limitations, an unfaithful lover? Smedes shows us how to move from hurting and hating to healing and reconciliation. It's not an easy journey but a very necessary one.

⊛ Spring, Janis Abrahams. *After the Affair* (New York: Perennial, 1996). How can partners help themselves through the shattering crisis of an infidelity? The author addresses this and other crucial questions, such as, Why did the affair happen? Once love and trust are gone, can we ever get them back? Can I—should I—recommit when I feel so ambivalent? How do we become sexually intimate again? Is forgiveness possible?

Relationships: Troubled and Broken (Divorce)

Needed: A Nonjudgmental Friend

Rejoice with those who rejoice; mourn with those who mourn.

—Romans 12:15

After we had been in counseling for over a year, my wife and I chose to separate. The decision was very difficult and painful. During the next ten months we continued in counseling, working toward a reconciliation. Most people in our church did not know how to treat us. Ultimately, the reconciliation did not occur.

The most helpful persons showed each of us quiet compassion and support. One family was especially helpful. The husband began by calling me to ask me to meet him for lunch. We were not well acquainted at his first contact. But I welcomed his friendly invitation. On many later occasions, he simply made himself available for conversation at his home or over coffee at a restaurant. However, he did make it clear that he was interested in helping us through this painful time and was hopeful that we could be reunited.

He was alert to the best time to call. For instance, he often called early Sunday night because he knew that was when I would be alone and lonely, having just returned our two children to their mother after a weekend visit. After a few moments of conversation, he might say, "You're really down, aren't you? I can hear it in your voice. Why don't you come over for some popcorn and TV?"

Over a few weeks he gained my heartfelt confidence *because he listened much more than he talked.* And after listening for several weeks, he did not hesitate to point out character traits I needed to work on. He became my most trusted, insightful friend. He always treated me with respect and with unconditional love. He never implied that I had to do any particular thing to gain his love or respect. He took immense amounts of his time, and he took the initiative to contact me several times a week. He knew that when I was most depressed, I did not feel I deserved anyone's attention and was unlikely to initiate contact. He pursued our friendship gently and yet with great professional insight.

Two things are startling about this: first, he did not have any formal education to prepare him for the role. He was a warehouse foreman who had not finished high school. But he had a spiritual gift for caring and showing love. Second, he and his wife were giving almost the same kind of attention to my wife while we were separated. We were each dealt with separately. Their attention included invitations to dinner with them and their family, other casual social evenings, and also some intensive discussions when it seemed the time was right. They never manipulated us so that we would be coming to their house at the same time unawares, or any such stunts.

People who were not helpful were the ones who presented us with propositions from the Bible that proved God did not want us to be divorced. One or two of these folks showed some compassion and concern, but could not get past their own discomfort. Their desire for us to get over this marriage problem was the driving force. Their ability to care was distorted and forced through a narrow conduit. We could only keep their love and respect if we could agree to their solutions, quite the opposite of accepting, unconditional love. They found it hard to believe that we really desired to do the right thing. But we didn't need them telling us we were failing God. We already knew that.

—Jim

Wisdom for the Caregiver

☞ "During the first six months of my marriage I knew that I had made a terrible mistake; however, by then I was pregnant, and the evilness/sinfulness of divorce had been drilled into my head all during my young years. Thirty years later I decided to divorce my husband. When I filed for divorce, friends and acquaintances actually congratulated me on my decision, but then they quickly projected the attitude which said, 'Now that that's over, get on with your life.' What they did not realize was that although I chose to divorce my husband, and although I have never regretted that decision, divorce was ten times more painful than I ever imagined. There were awful fights about the children and settlements. There was dark loneliness and depression. There was a healthy supply of guilt, and my self-esteem was at rock bottom."

—S.J.

☞ "At the time of the divorce I belonged to a small group which met on Sunday evenings. None of those members will ever fully know how important that group was to me. Some weeks I did not know if I could hold myself together until Sunday night. It wasn't so much that I wanted to talk about all of it with the group; I just needed to know that someone cared, that some people still liked me."

—S.J.

☞ "One of the most thoughtful gestures happened on the day that my ex-husband was remarrying. A couple from the small group called, and invited me to go sailing with the declaration, 'You are not going to sit home alone tonight.'"

—S.J.

☞ "Two months after I had filed for divorce a Christian education minister from my church called and asked if I would consider teaching children's church school during the summer. That request meant a great deal to me because it said that I must not be such a bad person if they still want me to teach children. I must be of some usefulness."

—S.J.

Helplines

1. **American Association of Christian Counselors**, P.O. Box 739, Forest, VA 24551. 1-800-5-COUNSEL; 1-434-525-9470. www.aacc.net. This organization has a directory of counselors who are members of AACC—a great tool for finding a Christian counselor in just about any region in the United States.
2. **Covenant Keepers**, P.O. Box 702371, Tulsa, OK 74170-2371. 1-918-743-0365; cki@ifriendly.com (U.S.); covenant@uniserve.com (Canada). www.covenantkeepersinc.org. A ministry to assist Christian couples who are having marital problems.
3. **Cross Canada Search**. www.crosscanadasearch.com. A Christian Internet search engine. Includes information about Christian counseling services (www.crosscanadasearch.com/ Ministry_Resources/Counselling).
4. **The Divorce Site**. www.thedivorcesite.com. Free divorce help and information, plus links to related websites.
5. **Focus on the Family**. 1-800-A-FAMILY. www.Family.org. This popular ministry offers many resources to help families survive a divorce. On the website, search for "divorce." See also "single parents."
6. **Salem Christian Mental Health Association**, 1 Young St., Suite 418, Hamilton, ON L8N 1T8. 1-905-528-0353. www.salem.on.ca. Provides counseling and also acts as a clearinghouse for mental health resources.

Books and Other Resources

Ⓑ Barr-Stewart, Debbie. *Children of Divorce: Helping Kids When Their Parents Are Apart* (Grand Rapids, MI: Zondervan, 1992). This book shows adults how to help the children of divorce. Barr-Stewart speaks frankly about divorce and how it forever changes the lives of kids, but she also explains how Christianity in action can make a big difference in their lives.

Ⓑ Dravecky, Dave, and Jan Dravecky. *Do Not Lose Heart: Meditations of Encouragement and Comfort* (Grand Rapids, MI: Zondervan, 2001). This book offers a collection of meditations for those who must face suffering in their lives, whether due to divorce, the loss of a loved one, the loss of a career, or terminal illness.

Ⓑ Hart, Archibald. *Helping Children Survive Divorce* (Dallas: Word Publishing, 1998). Dr. Hart, professor of psychology at Fuller Theological Seminary and himself a child of divorce, offers invaluable advice on helping parents minimize the psychological and social damage when a family breaks apart. Topics include handling guilt, common mistakes to avoid, steps to help your child cope with anger and depression, step-parenting, blending families, and many more. A highly acclaimed book that has helped many families survive divorce.

Ⓑ Kok, James R. *Waiting for Morning: Seeking God in Our Suffering* (Grand Rapids, MI: Faith Alive Christian Resources, 1997). Kok suggests that suffering can help us grow spiritually. He offers meaningful ways to respond to one's own suffering and that of others. (Call 1-800-333-8300 or visit www.FaithAliveResources.org to order.)

Ⓑ Sittser, Jerry. *A Grace Disguised* (Grand Rapids, MI: Zondervan, 1998). This sensitive book will help you deal with loss, whether due to illness, divorce, or the loss of someone you love. The author shows how we can come through tragedy to a new life—one marked by spiritual growth, joy, compassion, and deeper appreciation of simple blessings.

Ⓑ Smith, Harold Ivan. *A Time for Healing: Coming to Terms with Your Divorce* (Nashville: LifeWay Press, 1994). This course offers insight into principles from God's Word to help you in your personal journey to recovery. The facilitator's guide provides administrative guidance and suggested activities for support-group study. (Available from Faith Alive Christian Resources, 1-800-333-8300 or www.FaithAliveResources.org.)

⊗ Splinter, John P. *The Complete Divorce Recovery Handbook* (Grand Rapids, MI: Zondervan, 1992). Field-tested by hundreds of divorced people, this book details a recovery program suitable for both small group discussion and individual use. Issues covered include coping with feelings, forgiving, dealing with your ex and your children, dating after divorce, a biblical perspective on divorce and remarriage, returning to a sense of wholeness.

⊗ TRAVARCA. A video library sponsored by the Reformed Church in America and the Christian Reformed Church in North America, TRAVARCA carries thousands of videos on hundreds of topics, including divorce. A yearly membership allows churches and individuals to use an unlimited number of videos; nonmembers may use the videos for established fees. Call 1-800-968-7221 or 1-616-698-7071 for a catalog or to request information and videos.

Relationships: Troubled and Broken (Friends and Relatives)

Unwise Counsel

The tongue has the power of death and life.

—Proverbs 18:21

I was devastated. My sister, who had been one of my best friends, and I had had a falling out. Despite my efforts to mend the situation she would not speak to me.

A certain circumstance compelled me to share my heartache with a friend. I briefly spoke of the root of the problem, of my hurt. I expected support and comfort. I certainly did not anticipate the counsel I received. "Well, you know what the Bible says," she snapped. "Forgive 70 times 7." And then she sanctimoniously hurled, "And turn the other cheek."

I was offended; I was furious! I didn't need her sermon. What I did need was her care. A simple "I'm sorry, it must hurt" would have lightened my burdened heart. Instead I actually felt abused. She undoubtedly thought she was God's mouthpiece that gray day. I have filed her remark in my mental folder entitled "What not to say when your friend is hurting."

—Judy

Wisdom for the Caregiver

ⓦ Seek to understand your friend's feelings.

ⓦ Say, "It must hurt."

ⓦ Offer to pray for peace and reconciliation.

ⓦ Give a hug.

ⓦ Refrain from sharing your own stories of broken relationships. Focus all your attention on the hurting friend.

ⓦ Remember that it is best *not* to quote Scripture.

ⓦ Read "Caregiving Basics" (pp. 203-222).

ⓦ Check "109+ Ways to Say, 'I Care'" (pp. 223-234).

Helplines

1. **American Association of Christian Counselors**, P.O. Box 739, Forest, VA 24551. 1-800-5-COUNSEL; 1-434-525-9470. www.aacc.net. This organization has a directory of counselors who are members of AACC—a great tool for finding a Christian counselor in just about any region in the United States.
2. **Cross Canada Search**. www.crosscanadasearch.com. A Christian Internet search engine. Includes information about Christian counseling services (www.crosscanadasearch.com/Ministry_Resources/Counselling).
3. **Focus on the Family**. 1-800-A-FAMILY. www.Family.org. This popular ministry offers a host of resources for parents and families, including *Family* magazine.
4. **Families Anonymous**, P.O. Box 3475, Culver City, CA 90231-3475. 1-310-815-8010. www.familiesanonymous.org. This organization is a

twelve-step self-help and recovery program and fellowship of support groups for relatives and friends of those who have alcohol, drug, or behavioral problems. FA provides an extensive list of pamphlets on many topics, as well as a list of locations where meetings are held. Many titles are available in Spanish.

5. **Salem Christian Mental Health Association**, 1 Young St., Suite 418, Hamilton, ON L8N 1T8. 1-905-528-0353. www.salem.on.ca. Provides counseling and also acts as a clearinghouse for mental health resources.

Books and Other Resources

(ℰ) Lerner, Harriet. *The Dance of Intimacy: A Woman's Guide to Courageous Acts of Change in Key Relationships* (New York: Harper and Row, 1989). Lerner looks into the intimate ways we relate to our loved ones. She poses such questions as, Why are women so concerned about upgrading their relationship skills, especially with men? Why are men relatively unconcerned? Becoming aware of the dynamics of intimacy in personal relationships can help you achieve more satisfying and healthier relationships.

(ℰ) Smedes, Lewis B. *Forgive and Forget* (New York: Pocket Books, 1984). How can you forgive a friend's betrayal, a parent's limitations, an unfaithful lover? Smedes shows us how to move from hurting and hating to healing and reconciliation. It's not an easy journey but a very necessary one.

(ℰ) TRAVARCA. A video library sponsored by the Reformed Church in America and the Christian Reformed Church in North America, TRAVARCA carries thousands of videos on hundreds of topics, including family relationships and reconciliation. A yearly membership allows churches and individuals to use an unlimited number of videos; non-members may use the videos for established fees. Call 1-800-968-7221 or 1-616-698-7071 for a catalog or to request information and videos.

Relationships: Troubled and Broken (Romantic)

A One-Sided Relationship

Carry each other's burdens, and in this way you will fulfill the law of Christ.
—Galatians 6:2

I experienced a difficult time in my life when, as a junior in high school with plans for college and my future scrambling through my head, I fell in love for the first time. It was a one-sided affair—he was a senior in high school who planned to go on to medical school. He didn't want a relationship, only a friend. I knew that, but could not keep myself from wishing and praying otherwise. It was an all-time low for me. He was all I could think about, and I grew extremely depressed; I felt as if the whole universe were against me.

I talked to many people, trying to get advice and guidance. One particular friend helped me the most. Over the months, as I worked myself through my problems, I talked to her often, probably well over forty hours, all told. She always listened, and although she didn't know what to do for me, she was always there. Even after months of hearing me talk about little else other than this guy, she still listened. She listened as I read her poetry I had written. She listened as I told her what went on each day with him. She never told me she was sick of hearing about him, as did some of my other friends, and she never changed the subject when I was talking about him. She always listened and projected the feeling that she cared.

—Rachel

The Power of Empathy

I went through two broken engagements over a five-year period—same girl, both times. After the second and final break, I went to visit my friend. I was numb and tired of hurting. I felt dead inside. We talked for a while, and when I got up to leave he suggested that we pray together. I prayed first, mumbling to God the best theology I could think of under the circumstances. I then waited for him to begin. Nothing came for a long time. I was about to ask what was wrong when I heard something—a sob. I asked him what was wrong. All he could say was, "It hurts so much."

"What hurts?" I asked.

"What's happened to you, stupid!" he said.

Cliff was weeping for me when I could no longer weep for myself! There have been few times in my life when I have felt as comforted. He was a little bit of the Holy Spirit at that moment as he entered into the places in my heart that I could no longer enter. He gave me no lessons to learn nor points to ponder about the human condition. All he gave was himself, and that was enough.

—Ben Patterson, *Waiting: Finding Hope When God Seems Silent*
(Downers Grove, IL: InterVarsity Press, 1989), pp. 43-44

Wisdom for the Caregiver

☺ "Listening is definitely the most important quality to have as a caregiver. Never tell your friend you don't want to hear about his or her problems, even if you are sick of them. Sometimes a person just needs to talk through her or his problems."

—Rachel

☺ Call and visit often. Encourage the person to talk. Help the person express how she or he feels even if you have heard it before.

☺ Invite your friend to walk and talk. Or invite him or her to a specific event. Suggest things you can do together, rather than generally asking if he or she wants to do something.

⊕ Give the person *52 Ways to Mend a Broken Heart* by Lynn Gordon. This is a deck of cards with each card giving a suggestion for healing a wounded heart. Sample suggestions:

—"Be Active: Move your body, even if it's just through little activities like watering your plants, cleaning the house, or walking your neighbor's dog. Find excuses to move and stretch your body. Dust off your bicycle seat or rent roller skates. Don't just sit there, get up and run an errand."

—"Personal Journal: Create a private notebook and allow yourself to write or draw your feelings, thoughts, fantasies, and fears in an uncensored journal. Just putting the words down can help you move through different moods and allow you to see your emotional progress. Since this is your personal journal, take advantage of this privacy to really spill your guts. And hey—have you ever tried writing poetry?"

—"Volunteer: Yup, helping others really can make you feel better about yourself. And even if you don't believe that, do it anyway. Help an elderly neighbor in the garden or run errands for a sick friend. Call your local volunteer center and see what cool nonprofit organizations in your area could really use your time and talents. It's also a great way to meet new people."

—from Lynn Gordon, 52 Ways to Mend a Broken Heart
(San Francisco: Chronicle Books, 1996)

Single Parenting

Carrying the Whole World

A father to the fatherless, a defender of widows, is God in his holy dwelling. God sets the lonely in families.

—Psalm 68:5

I have been a single parent for three and a half years. I decided that there was no hope for my marriage but still a ton of hope for me and for my two sons, Garrett (eight) and Clay (six). However, sometimes it seems like the whole world is on my shoulders. It's not, but it sure feels like it.

I tend to place a lot of expectations on myself and on my performance. I have an overwhelming need to do well in college. I feel an enormous need to have a tight handle on the everyday running of my house. I take care of my children's needs, go to all the conferences, respond to all the problems at school, and drive the boys to soccer and baseball. Sometimes I feel badly because I'm not doing all of these things perfectly. Like all single parents, I need to realize that there are only so many hours in a day, and I can only do so much.

—Amanda

Wisdom for the Caregiver (from Amanda)

ⓘ There are governmental programs to help single parents. They offer assistance with day care, car maintenance, tuition, and so on. (The Department of Social Services can tell you about these services.) At first I was thoroughly embarrassed to ask for this help, but when I convinced myself that this assistance was not a career choice but a means to an end, a way of attaining and maintaining a degree of self-sufficiency, then I appreciated the help.

ⓘ As a college student, I need all the study time I can possibly find in a day. Usually that time gets pushed to 9:00 p.m., after the boys go to bed. However, my parents take my sons for an overnight each week, a tremendous help and gracious gift to me, and a special occasion for my sons. Definitely the most valuable thing that one can do for single parents is give them some time with the kids away from the home.

Additional Wisdom for the Caregiver

ⓘ "Something I did not appreciate was freely given advice. One such 'well-wisher' would consistently remind me, 'Just be strong, the Lord will provide!' I began to wonder just how strong the Lord intended me to be. I'll forever be grateful to my benefactor who opened his wallet instead of his mouth!"

—Martha

ⓘ "One of the things that concerns me as a single mother is providing male role models for my sons. I'm very fortunate here because I have a big family and lots of brothers, who are very interested in the boys. One of my brothers is especially close to them. What a blessing!"

—Dorothy

ⓘ "Single parents, no matter what the conditions, could always use extra sleep, a day off, extra vitamins and a listening ear."

—Meladee McCarty and Hanoch McCarty, *Acts of Kindness*
(Deerfield Beach, FL: Health Communications, Inc., 1994), p. 189

⊚ Read "Caregiving Basics" (pp. 203-222).
⊚ Check "109+ Ways to Say, 'I Care'" (pp. 223-234).

Helplines

1. **Divorce Wizards**, 5001 Birch St., Newport Beach, CA 92660. www.divorcewizards.com. Provides numerous practical articles from a secular perspective, including "How to Be the Best Single Parent You Can Be."
2. **Parents without Partners**, 8807 Colesville Road, Silver Spring, MD 20910. 1-800-637-7974 or 1-301-588-9355. This organization provides printed information and has local support groups. (Ask for the excellent pamphlet "Practical Parenting . . . Tips to Grow By.")

Books and Other Resources

⊚ Benedek, Elessa P. *How to Help Your Child Overcome Your Divorce* (New York: New Market Press, 1998). Benedek provides information that helps divorced parents raise their children (aged twelve and under) to be happy, well-adjusted individuals. Includes numerous examples, commonly asked questions, and abundant resources.
⊚ Hunter, Lynda. *Parenting on Your Own: A Comprehensive Guide* (Grand Rapids, MI: Zondervan, 1997). A good book for caregivers to give to single parents. Based on her own experiences as a single parent, Lynda Hunter offers real-life answers to questions single parents ask. This definitive handbook includes such topics as communication, finances, legal concerns, relationships, discipline, ex-spouses, work, teenagers, and time management.

ᵂ Long, Nicolas. *Making Divorce Easier on Your Child: 50 Effective Ways to Help Children Adjust* (Chicago: Contemporary Books, 2002). This book is filled with practical, sensitive, and highly effective ways to help children cope and adjust during and after a parental divorce. Issues covered include new family combinations, financial issues, looking after your own well-being, and when to seek professional help for your child.

ᵂ Richmond, Gary. *Successful Single Parenting* (Eugene, OR: Harvest House Publishers, 1990). Drawing on the wisdom of God's Word and his experiences as a single-parent pastor, Richmond offers a complete guide to navigating the challenging waters of single parenting. Includes topics such as balancing your your needs with those of your children; dealing with financial changes; talking with your child about love, the absence of the other parent, and more; and how to handle visitation rights, child support, and remarriage issues.

Substance Abuse

Guilt but Never Despair

Sometimes God calms the storm, and sometimes he lets the storm rage and calms his child.

—Anonymous

What did we do wrong? How could we have averted this problem? These and many other questions haunted my husband and me. Our son, Steve, at age 17, had been expelled from military school for using marijuana. This happened in April, just six weeks before he would have completed a very successful year. Prior to this incident we had had some indications of his drinking and drug use, but we did not know the extent of his involvement.

Part of the agreement we made with Steve before he left for military school was that if he were expelled for any reason he would not be welcome in our home. Although it was a difficult decision at which to arrive, we felt it was necessary to prevent Steve from forcing an expulsion should he tire of the regimen. We still feel that it was the right decision (what experts call "tough love"), even though he became more deeply involved with drugs while living with a friend in Chicago. We refused to support him financially as long as he was abusing drugs.

At the same time we demonstrated *tough love* we also exhibited *unconditional love*. We let him know that he could call us anytime, and when we did talk, we always assured him of our love.

The two things that helped us to survive those difficult four months were prayer and support of friends through calls, prayers, and assurances. Once, when especially low, I asked God for a passage from his Word to give me faith. Immediately the story of the Prodigal Son from Luke 15:11-32 came to mind. I knew that God was providing me with hope just when I needed it. I was able to *picture* our son's repentant return to our home.

In August, God sent us an angel dressed in a cook's jacket. Unknown to us, this young caterer was a recovering drug addict. Steve had come home from Chicago for a family party, and the sensitive chef began asking him questions. Before long Steve confessed his addiction to him, and shortly thereafter we enrolled Steve in a recovery program at Hazelden Pioneer House (the juvenile division of Hazelden Recovery Center in Center City, Minnesota).

God worked a miracle in our son, and we are thrilled to report that after six weeks of treatment and countless AA meetings, he is still sober!

Steve has been true to his twelve-step program and helps others with similar problems when the situation arises. His testimonies to the children to whom I teach drug prevention in the public school has made me very proud, as has his agreement to write a letter to a friend's son who is struggling with drug addiction. The frosting was put on the cake when Steve asked for my friend's address, stating, "I wrote a letter to his mom too. I wanted her to know that it was undoubtedly a combination of factors that contributed to her son's addiction, and that she should not feel guilty about anything that she did which might have influenced him to become addicted."

God has not only brought my "prodigal" son back home and given him a new life; God has given me the assurance, through Steve, that he did not blame me or his father for his problem.

—Ginger

Wisdom for the Caregiver

🕊 "My best friend was of tremendous support during our family's crisis with our son. She was able to talk honestly with me as a I tried to search for the 'why?' and the 'How could he be so stupid?' and the 'What did I do wrong as a parent?' She asked those questions and brainstormed with me as I tried to understand his drug and alcohol use. There really weren't answers to all of those questions, but I needed to talk out loud to someone about all of the things that I was thinking. If someone who wasn't a close friend had tried to do the same thing, I would have felt that she was just being nosy or would have turned around and gossiped about it to someone else. I needed to have someone (other than my husband) to take a look at the situation with the eye of an 'outsider.'"

—Leslie

🕊 "I felt that the eyes of the whole town were on our son and our family. It was very difficult to go through the days and months when I felt as though everyone was talking about us. (Not everyone was, of course, but it felt that way!) One day at a younger child's soccer game, another parent asked, 'How's Brian? I haven't seen him in a while.' I briefly but honestly told her. She had had no idea of our family's crisis but she said, 'Isn't it difficult when our children make decisions that we know are wrong for them?' That simple comment helped me so much. To me it said, 'I know you must be hurting and I'm sorry,' and also, 'No child is perfect, all parents struggle.' It was a simple comment on her part, but I needed to hear that I wasn't being judged."

—Alice

🕊 "When my son went to treatment, we had a parent group (I was so grateful to see other 'normal' looking parents with the same problem!). We were told that as parents we had probably punished, talked, begged, screamed, threatened our children over their drug use, but it was all to no avail. We were told that it was *the child's* problem and that he had to deal with it. It was a hard thing to hear, because I wanted to be able to control this problem and solve it, but it was the truth. Our son could only change his life when he took responsibility for himself."

—Catherine

❖ Read "Caregiving Basics" (pp. 203-222).

❖ Call to express your concern.

❖ Pray.

❖ Write a note to family members to tell them you care and are concerned.

❖ Suggest seeking help from a treatment center, AA, and Al-anon. (Al-anon concentrates on the emotional and spiritual health of the friend or relative of the alcoholic).

❖ Realize that the five stages of grief may apply to the person you're trying to help. He or she may be experiencing the loss of the substance abuser as he or she used to be. (See pp. 214-217).

❖ Always offer hope. God never gives up on us, no matter how bleak the situation.

Helplines

1. **Alcoholics Anonymous (AA)**, P.O. Box 459, Grand Central Station, New York, NY 10163. 1-212-870-3400. www.aa.org. AA is a fellowship of alcoholics who help each other stay sober. There are approximately 56,000 AA groups in the United States and Canada. Members meet and share their experiences, providing strength and hope for each other. Check your phone book for local chapters and for information regarding ACOA (Adult Children of Alcoholics).

2. **Al-Anon Family Groups**, 1600 Corporate Landing Parkway, Virginia Beach, VA 23454-5617. 1-800-356-9996. www.al-anon.org. Al-Anon Family Groups, which includes Alateen, is a fellowship for relatives and friends of alcoholics; group members share their experience, their strength, and their help in order to solve their common problems. Materials available include seventeen books and more than fifty

pamphlets, booklets, and videos; an Al-Anon newsletter; and Alateen Talk (teenage newsletter). For further information contact Al-Anon or Alateen through your local telephone directory.

3. **Cocaine Anonymous**. 1-800-347-8998. This organization uses a twelve-step recovery program to help its members stay free of cocaine. The only requirement for joining this group is a sincere desire to stop the use of cocaine or other mind-altering drugs.

4. **Families Anonymous**, P.O. Box 3475, Culver City, CA 90231-3475. 1-310-815-8010. www.familiesanonymous.org. This organization is a twelve-step self-help and recovery program and fellowship of support groups for relatives and friends of those who have alcohol, drug, or behavioral problems. FA provides an extensive list of pamphlets on many topics, as well as a list of locations where meetings are held. Many titles are available in Spanish.

5. **Family Outreach Ontario**, 4002 Hixon St., Beamsville, ON L0R 1B7. 1-905-563-1329. www.vaxxine.com/family. Family Outreach has response teams throughout Ontario that are trained to assist and support ALL family members involved in or affected by alcohol abuse.

6. **Hazelden Admitting Office & Hazelden Substance Abuse Outpatient Treatment**, Center City, MN 55012. 1-612-257-4010, ext. 3307. 1-800-262-5272, ext. 2804. www.hazelden.org. Hazelden is an excellent treatment center that also helps families of substance abusers cope and heal. Helpful books and booklets are available. For a copy of the pamphlet "What Can You Do About Someone Else's Drinking?" send a self-addressed stamped envelope to Hazelden (see address above). To order Hazelden recovery resources call 1-800-328-0098 or check the website.

7. **Homewood Health Centre**, 150 Delhi St., Guelph, ON N1E 6K9. 1-519-824-1010. www.homewoodhealth.com. A provider of behavioral, addiction, and psychiatric services.

8. **Meier New Life Clinics**. 1-800-NEW-LIFE. This nationwide organization provides counseling services to persons struggling with alcohol or drug addiction, as well as help for caregivers. Its "Calvary Center" in Phoenix, Arizona, is a well-known treatment center.

9. **Mission Services of Hamilton**, Men's Residence and Suntrac Recovery, P.O. Box 368, Hamilton, ON L8L 7W2. 1-905-528-4211. www.mission_services.org. A hostel and addiction counseling program for homeless men.

10. **Mission Services of London**, Quintin Warner House, 415 Hamilton Road, London, ON N5Z 1S1. 1-519-433-2807. www.missionservices.ca. A drug and alcohol rehabilitation center, including a residential program for males and a day program for females.

Books and Other Resources

Ackerman, Robert J. *Perfect Daughters: Adult Daughters of Alcoholics* (Deerfield Beach, FL: Health Communications, Inc., 1989).

Bables, Karen. *Beginning with Me* (Grand Rapids, MI: Open Door Books, 1998). A powerful and moving story of a family torn apart by the husband's alcoholism and of his wife's journey to wellness with the help of Al-Anon.

Bartosch, Robert, and Pauline Bartosch. *Overcoming Alcoholism* (Colorado Springs, CO: Focus on the Family, 2000). In this cassette recording, the authors provide clear and helpful advice for beating this destroyer of careers, families, and lives.

Beattie, Melody. *Codependents' Guide to the Twelve Steps* (New York: Prentice Hall, 1993). Discover how recovery programs work and how to find the right one for you. This book explains each of the famous twelve steps and how to apply them to codependent issues. Offers specific exercises and activities to use in group settings and on your own, and provides a directory of twelve-step programs, including Al-Anon, Codependents Anonymous, Codependents of Sex Addicts, Adult Children of Alcoholics, and more.

De Jong, Alexander, and Martin Doot. *Dying for a Drink: A Pastor and a Physician Talk about Alcoholism* (Grand Rapids, MI: Faith Alive Christian Resources and Wm. B. Eerdmans, 1999). The powerful story of how a pastor is successfully recovering from the disease of alcoholism.

Dobson, James C. *Love Must Be Tough* (Nashville: Thomas Nelson, 1983, 1996). This book has become a classic on relationship dynamics. Through questions and answers and patient dialogues, Dobson probes the dynmaics of alcohol's effects on innocent family members.

ⓦ Fletcher, Anne M. *Sober for Good* (New York: Houghton-Mifflin, 2001). Fletcher makes a case that drinking problems can be overcome and that life without alcohol is possible, meaningful, and joyous. A must-read for anyone concerned about their own or another's drinking.

ⓦ Johnson, Vernon E. *Intervention: A Step-by-Step Guide for Families of Chemically Dependent Persons* (Center City, MN: Hazelden, 1989). Johnson describes a process that has successfully motivated thousands of chemically dependent people to accept help. In terms that anyone can understand, this book teaches concerned people how to help and how to do it right. Johnson shows how chemical dependence affects those around the sick person—spouses, children, neighbors, and coworkers. Intervention, he says, is not a clinical process but a personal one that brings families back together.

ⓦ *Living Recovery* (Center City, MN: Hazelden, 1990). Life goes on. These words, familiar to recovering people everywhere, describe the challenging realities we must face when we begin recovering from an addiction. And, as life goes on, there is a tremendous need for meaningful recovery support. Learning to deal with the different stages of growth and the new emotions that surface during the recovery process requires new living skills. This book provides an in-depth look at tools for recovery and offers pragmatic guidance on topics from how to forgive to understanding rejection.

ⓦ Mooney, A. J., M.D. *The Recovery Book* (New York: Workman Publishing, 1992). A guide that answers the questions and concerns of recovering alcoholics and addicts.

ⓦ Quick, Daryl E. *The Healing Journey for Adult Children of Alcoholics* (Downers Grove, IL: InterVarsity Press, 2000). This book pinpoints the specific struggle of grown children of alcoholics. It includes moving stories and helpful exercises that take you step-by-step through new ways of feeling, acting, and thinking. Available through Focus on the Family.

Traumatic Memories

Memories that Haunt

In my anguish I cried to the LORD, and he answered by setting me free.

—Psalm 118:5

It has been twenty-three years since my year of service in Vietnam. For twenty-one years that experience was buried deep inside my consciousness with only an occasional glimpse allowed to others. Then in 1988 I visited the Vietnam Veterans Memorial in Washington, D.C. It was a most profound cathartic event that raised all the emotions that had been suppressed for so long. The memories resurfaced, the anxiety level rose, the pain was great, and the guilt over surviving grew. The catharsis was not complete.

I visited the Memorial again in 1990. This time I was alone and had several hours, and I could allow myself to focus on my emotions and the past. I also was able to visit the booths and displays around the Memorial. I began talking with a man who was selling items to support the memorial. As with all veterans the conversation started with, "When did you serve? What branch, and where in the country were you?" After a few minutes this stranger, yet a comrade, a brother, put forth his hand to me and said with great sincerity, "Welcome home." It was a welcome home that said, "You did what you were expected to do. You are accepted here. This place is yours, you are all right, I understand your pain."

—Steve

Meaningful Touch

*Believe me, every man has his secret sorrows which the world knows not—
and often times we call a man cold, when he is only sad.*

—Henry Wadsworth Longfellow

The young GI stepped into line with the other teenagers to get his barbecued chicken. It's funny how some people can look eighteen—until you
look at their eyes. I think it was his haunted look that caused me to notice
him that evening. From the window of his eyes, he looked like a tired old
man, not like the swarm of happy kids around him.

I was part of a work crew at Trail West, Young Life's beautiful camp
high in the Colorado Rockies. It was my job that night to stand at the
head of the line and hand out the best smelling, best tasting barbecued
chicken I'd ever eaten—before or since.

We had our huge grill fired up in the middle of a large, grassy meadow,
rimmed by massive, solemn pines that stood like a majestic fence around
us. The sun was sliding behind the surrounding mountain peak as the
fragrant smoke from our barbecue drifted across the clearing.

It was 1960, the summer of my junior year in high school. It didn't
occur to me then, but while the laughing, noisy high schoolers waited for
their meal that evening, a number of their dads, friends, schoolmates,
and older brothers were fighting and dying in the rice paddies and jun-
gles of Southeast Asia.

It was easy to spot the young 'Nam vet in our midst. In an era of side-
burns and shaggy haircuts, his government-issue "buzz-cut" drew plenty
of sidelong glances.

He had actually graduated from high school a couple years before, but
his parents had gotten special permission for him to attend the camp.

That's the kind of crazy war it was: Two weeks before, he'd been fighting for his life, watching buddies drop all around him. Then suddenly his
tour was up, he was airlifted out of a fierce firefight to Saigon, got on a
commercial airliner, and headed home. Just like that. Now he was on
leave, standing in line in a Rocky Mountain meadow with a bunch of kids
who didn't seem to have a care in the world.

I first noticed him when he was about the fourth person from the
front of the line. His face was extremely pale, and he was visibly trembling. I remember thinking, *Something's wrong with this guy. He must be
getting sick.*

As he got closer to the grill, he began shaking even harder. I picked up a piece of chicken with my tongs and was just about to serve him when he suddenly dropped his plate, spilling beans and salad on the ground and on the person in front of him. With a choked cry, he took off on a dead run for the forest.

Everyone stopped talking and just stared. We all wondered, *What in the world's wrong with him?*

Our Young Life leader headed off after the young soldier, and after they both disappeared into the trees, the dinner line resumed its onward march.

Doug found him hiding in the trees, shaking like a leaf. The older man, a burly ex-football player, towered nearly a foot above the soldier and probably outweighed him by a hundred pounds. But without saying a word, he gently put his arms around the trembling camper and held him tight.

The young soldier buried his face in our leader's chest and sobbed uncontrollably. They stood together in the twilight for nearly twenty minutes. The young man sobbing, the older man holding him, saying nothing.

When he finally was able to compose himself, they sat on a log together and the vet tried to explain what was going on.

Over in 'Nam, he said, if you were out in open country like that, with so many people milling around, you could expect the mortar rounds to start coming in. He had just seen his sergeant killed, right in front of him, by an incoming shell. And no matter how hard he tried, he couldn't keep the sights and sounds from coming back.

Just before he reached the head of the line, it was as if he could hear the whistle of artillery fire and the screams of "Incoming! Incoming!" He couldn't take it any longer and ran to find cover. That was day two of the camp, of what would become the most important week of this young man's life. Before the week was over, the soldier surrendered his life to a new Commander, Jesus Christ. But not for the reason you might think.

On the final night of camp, as we all sat around a big bonfire, campers were encouraged to stand up and make public their confession of faith if they had come to know Christ that week. Many young men and women responded to the opportunity, citing talks by the speaker, the encouragement of a close friend from home, and other causes as reasons for coming to know Jesus personally. The young soldier was one of the last to stand.

His story was much different from the rest. He began by telling how skeptical he had been about coming to camp. In fact, the only reason he'd agreed to come was that his parents promised to buy him a used car. The thought of his own wheels pushed him over the edge, and he came reluctantly to camp.

While everyone had been "real nice" to him, it wasn't a special friendship that had shaped his decision. And even though he thought the speaker had some good words to say, and made the gospel clear, it wasn't because of him either that he was responding to Christ.

What had really broken through to him was "that big guy," Doug, who had been willing to stand there in the trees with him and hold him until a piece of nightmare loosened its grip. In short, God used a hug—not a lecture, not a long walk through the trees, not a testimony—to win the bigger spiritual battle he was fighting.

—Excerpted from *Leaving the Light On,* © 1994 by Gary Smalley and John Trent. Used by permission of Multnomah Publishers Inc.

Helping the Traumatized

Listening to and comforting those suffering from traumatic memories can be done on an individual level (as Doug did) or in a group setting. Your church might consider starting a support group for such persons.

The director of the church program should be a mental health clinician, such as a psychiatrist, psychologist, licensed family therapist, or licensed social worker with experience and training in working with acute and post-traumatic stress. Consult with professional organizations such as The American Academy of Experts in Traumatic Stress and The International Society of Traumatic Stress Studies.

The optimum size of the support group is between six and twelve. The group leader acts as a facilitator, helping the group understand the problems and suggesting resources that can be used to resolve them. His or her skills should include listening, clarifying, helping to identify needs, acknowledging, summarizing, and acting as manager of the group process.

The task of the group leader or of individuals attempting to help others suffering from traumatic memories includes

- "being with" the person, helping him or her to feel accepted.
- naming the feelings expressed verbally or non-verbally by the individual who has incurred the loss; naming the dilemmas or conflicts implied or expressed (shock, anger, fury, sadness, fear).
- providing information about grief.

⊛ providing some tasks that help the person grieve, move though obstacles, and feel safe within the process.

The following questions can help the traumatized person reduce his or her fears:

⊛ What are you fearing?
⊛ What's the worst that can happen?
⊛ What is the possibility that the worst might actually occur?
⊛ If the worst happened, what would you do?
⊛ What can be done to reduce the possibilities of it occurring?
⊛ What skills can be helpful in getting through the possible situation?

Helping to heal someone from traumatic stress usually occurs in three steps: first, establishing the boundaries of the event; second, filling in the sensory experience related directly to the events; and third, retraining the body to respond to today's stimuli.

The process may take hours or months, but over time persistent counseling should resolve the traumatic flashback episodes. In the meantime, empathetic listening, holding, and other compassionate demonstrations will add much value to the counseling experience.

The authors are indebted to Warren Dale for much of the above information. You are invited to contact him for more information about ministering to persons in trauma. (Warren Dale, 2309 Columbus Parkway, Vallejo, CA 94591. 1-707-643-3108. e-mail: wldbos@aol.com.)

Wisdom for the Caregiver

⊛ "Reach out and touch, hug, or hold the hand of the person who is grieving. The caring touch says all the things that you want to say but don't know how."

—Steve

⊛ Read "Caregiving Basics" (pp. 203-222).
⊛ Check "109+ Ways to Say, 'I Care'" (pp. 223-234).

Helplines

1. **American Association of Christian Counselors**, P.O. Box 739, Forest, VA 24551. 1-800-5-COUNSEL; 1-434-525-9470. www.aacc.net. This organization has a directory of counselors who are members of AACC—a great tool for finding a Christian counselor in just about any region in the United States.
2. **Cross Canada Search**. www.crosscanadasearch.com. A Christian Internet search engine. Includes information about Christian counseling services (www.crosscanadasearch.com/Ministry_Resources/Counselling).
3. **Salem Christian Mental Health Association**, 1 Young St., Suite 418, Hamilton, ON L8N 1T8. 1-905-528-0353. www.salem.on.ca. Provides counseling and also acts as a clearinghouse for mental health resources.

Books and Other Resources

❧ Flynn, Mike, and Doug Gregg. *Inner Healing: A Handbook for Helping Yourself and Others* (Downers Grove, IL: InterVarsity Press, 1993). For those struggling with feelings of abandonment, anger, shame, lust, depression, worry, or fear, inner healing may be God's way of setting a new course in life. The authors offer biblical perspectives and practical know-how from years of experience in this vital ministry.

❧ Fredrickson, Renee. *A Journey to Recovery from Sexual Abuse* (New York: A Fireside Publication, 1992). Most victims of child abuse repress some or all of the memories of the abuse at great expense to their health and emotional well-being. Drawing from her extensive clinical experience, Fredrickson has written a supportive and encouraging book to help abuse victims understand how memory repression happens; what the warning signs are for memory repression; the impact memory repression can have on our lives; why it's vital to recognize all the pieces of the puzzle; and how to recover the memories and begin healing.

ⓦ Sciraldi, Glenn R. *The Post-Traumatic Stress Disorder Sourcebook* (Lincolnwood, IL: Lowell House, 2000). The goal of this book is to help the individual move beyond survival toward the realm of living well. Sciraldi offers a remarkable range of treatment alternatives and self-management techniques that show survivors that the other side of pain is growth and recovery.

ⓦ Seamands, David A. *Healing of Memories* (Wheaton, IL: Victor Books, 1986). Seamands shows how God's healing power can free you from the tyranny of painful memories that affect your behavior and Christian growth. Time alone cannot heal the memories of experiences so painful that we have pushed them from our minds. These subconscious memories can be handled by a special kind of therapy known as "memory healing." This form of Christian counseling, coupled with prayer, focuses the healing power of the Holy Spirit on the root of the problem.

Unemployment

Your Pink Slip Is Showing
You are my fortress, my refuge in times of trouble.

—Psalm 59:16

I n the last fifteen years nearly half of all U.S. companies were restructured, more than 80,000 firms were acquired or merged, at least 700,000 organizations sought bankruptcy protection to continue operation, and more than 450,000 other businesses failed. Beyond this disturbing corporate picture, what happens when people lose jobs?

- 48% change careers
- 10% start their own business
- 33% go back to school
- 16% of married people divorce
- 90% equate the sense of loss to that of a death
- 5% commit suicide

—Sources: U.S. Department of Labor, Bureau of Labor Statistics;
Pritchett & Associates, Inc. of Dallas, Texas; 1995 World Almanac; Challenger,
Gray & Christmas, Inc. of Chicago; Medical College of Virginia

Supporting Your Spouse after a Layoff

"Honey, I've got some good news and some bad news. The good news is that I'd love to meet you for lunch today if you can make it. The bad news is that I don't have to go back to the office again . . . ever. I was just fired."

It's now been many years since I heard those devastating words, but it still seems like yesterday. I couldn't believe my husband had been terminated—after all he'd done for the organization. Our family had sacrificed tremendously to give Clyde the space to perform up to the very high expectations of his boss. We'd even relocated when I was eight months pregnant, leaving behind close friends and family. (Many times, I'd wished we were closer than ten hours away to share all the newness surrounding the birth of our first child.) Still, I'd graciously accepted the move, knowing that it'd be a great career opportunity for Clyde. Now, as the tears welled up, I felt desperately betrayed and remarkably angry. No courses I'd taken, no experiences I'd had prepared me for the profound sense of loss I felt.

What exactly had transpired at the office? I wanted to hear every maddening detail so I could understand how this disaster could've happened. Shell-shocked, my husband couldn't bear to discuss it, except to comment that in those last days, "My boss was such a jerk." His silence made it even harder to respond to insensitive remarks "friends" would make, such as: "He must've done something really wrong because that company just doesn't fire people without cause." Not surprisingly, we found it more comfortable to "retreat" than to face others, yet I resented the lack of social contact. Although the country was in a recession and we'd heard about other friends and relatives in similar situations, I felt very much alone.

I knew in my heart that Clyde was a talented, decent man who'd find another—better—job. I reached out to my loving husband, who'd suffered a greater loss than I had. As we began to put the pieces of our lives back together again, we discovered some friends in our small, northern Wisconsin community who acknowledged the event and supported us, making us feel great.

Thankfully, that difficult time is now behind us. However, some of our hard-earned insights may help you—and your relationship—survive the stresses of unemployment. Spouses occupy a unique place in their partner's job searches. If your mate is unemployed, you won't be making networking calls or going on interviews, but you're directly involved nonetheless.

If you're very lucky, most of your friends and business acquaintances will be supportive. However, it's common to experience some distancing of your relationships. Some friends may not acknowledge that you got "zapped," while others may make you feel completely shunned.

This can be upsetting, but realize that people generally don't know how to handle grief or trauma well. When a significant loss (e.g., of a marriage, a loved one, or a job) occurs either to themselves or someone else, people typically feel awkward and self-conscious. In fact, friends, neighbors, relatives, and acquaintances who seem to be ignoring your plight are probably just trying to keep your mind off the subject.

One wife was so upset when her husband lost his job, she refused to speak to him for two weeks because every time she did, she either yelled at him or cried. She was terrified about the family's finances and about their children's college fund being in jeopardy. Conversely, the husband worried that sharing his deepest concerns would set his wife off. However, she had already experienced the blackest of emotions and thoughts, and his silence only reinforced her greatest fears. Happily, once the couple was able to vent, laugh, and cry a bit, neither of them had to "hide out" anymore and much of the fear went away. After this emotional breakthrough, the husband's campaign accelerated substantially, and he won a fine opportunity in his preferred industry.

—Carolyn Lowstuter

Wisdom for the Caregiver (from Carolyn)

☞ Don't read too much into emotions. They happen for a number of reasons. Recognize that your emotional reactions may be quite different from, or similar to, your spouse's.

☞ Accept each other's behavior as valid considering all the circumstances. Don't call your partner's feelings "wrong" just because they seem uncomfortable or inappropriate to you.

☞ Communicate your own fears or concerns, but balance them with hope.

⊛ Commit to your spouse to do the best you can to support his or her search efforts.

⊛ Express appreciation for the support your partner has given you, acknowledging that it may have been rough for both of you.

⊛ Help your spouse assume complete responsibility for his or her career and life. Don't blame others for your situation. When either of you chooses to act like a "victim," consciously reenter a powerful state in which you both feel confident and in control. It may be uncomfortable, but you must confront each other whenever you resort to blaming others.

⊛ Ask to be involved with your spouse's job-hunting efforts and demonstrate that you're confident he or she will succeed.

⊛ Let as many people as possible know that you're looking for a job. The grapevine is a powerful networking device.

⊛ You don't know where, how, or when the right job will appear, so it's best to keep your options open. Even if you have a terrific job and are both committed to remaining exactly where you are, allowing your partner to interview for out-of-town jobs helps strengthen his or her interviewing skills. And who knows? For the world's best opportunity, you might decide to relocate.

⊛ Finally, help your partner develop his or her resumé and job-search plan. Love and accept your spouse for who he or she is (not who you might like him or her to be) and enthusiastically reinforce positive actions while forgiving the dysfunctional behavior that drives you crazy. Keep your options open. Love and support each other, and never give up. Best of luck!

Authors' note: Carolyn's husband, Clyde, encouraged by a supportive wife, began a business with a partner, David Robertson. Clyde C. Lowstuter is President and CEO and Carolyn E. Lowstuter is Senior Vice-president of *Robertson Lowstuter,* an executive development firm in Chicago. The firm specializes in executive coaching, high performance team building, change leadership, and senior executive outplacement. From her own experience, Carolyn devotes a good portion of her time to coaching spouses through the career transition process. Clyde has written two books that may help you in your job search (see book list, pp. 197-198).

Additional Wisdom for the Caregiver

⊛ Read "Caregiving Basics" (pp. 203-222).

ⓦ Check "109+ Ways to Say, 'I Care'" (pp. 223-234).

ⓦ Between jobs? Transition jobs help, say Christian psychologists Frank Minirth, Paul Meier, and Stephen Arterburn in *The Complete Life Encyclopedia* (Nashville: Thomas Nelson, 1995): "Get a night-job flipping hamburgers or driving a forklift so you can keep looking for your new career during the day. Working and bringing in a paycheck will raise your self-esteem, lower your anxiety level and enable you to feel more confident in job interviews."

Note: The following information comes from a *Focus on the Family* article by Brian J. Waldrop. Out of his own experiences with unemployment, Brian offers some do's and don'ts for "encouraging your unemployed friends and acquaintances."

ⓦ Do inform the individual of employment possibilities, but don't make the person feel that he or she has to jump at the opportunity. Networking is a big part of finding a job, and I've been grateful for friends who've alerted me to openings. But I've felt awkward when I've learned more about the position—and found out it's not a good fit for me. Just because I don't pursue your tip doesn't mean I feel I'm "too good" for the job. I have to do what's best for my family, and if that means not looking into a job that is ill suited for my talents, so be it.

ⓦ Do affirm a person's self-worth and abilities, but don't be condescending. The daily selling of your abilities and worth as an employee to potential employers—through numerous cover letters and interviews—can drain one's self-esteem to dangerously low levels. Unless you've experienced this, it will be hard to understand how frustrating it is to wait for a thumbs-up or thumbs-down from an employer. Reassure your friend of his self-worth in the sight of God, as well as in your sight. Remember: We live in a world that often judges a person based upon what he does for a living, so it's a terrible blow to one's ego to be unemployed.

ⓦ Do ask about an individual's job search but don't let the subject dominate your conversation. I like hearing from friends that they prayed for me during the past week. I like it when my church family asks how my job search is progressing. But sometimes I get tired of talking about it; there is a lot more to me than where I work (or hope to work someday).

ⓦ Don't be judgmental as to why an individual left his or her previous employer. Do be open-minded. Whether you suspect a person left his or her previous employer voluntarily, or was discharged, never assume that it was because of a mistake on his part or because "He couldn't hack it." People find themselves unemployed for numerous and often complicated reasons—many times due to no fault of their own.

⊛ Do be considerate when planning recreational activities. Don't forget that the unemployed friend is probably barely making it. Bowling and burgers may sound like a fun Saturday night outing for the average family, but for the unemployed, such an event is often impossible. When possible, vary activities between the costly and inexpensive. When an outing is going to require money, try to give plenty of notice so that the unemployed person can plan for the added expense. I have found that psychologically it is important for me to still share in recreation and fellowship with other Christians—when I can afford it. Yet most of the time, I am uncomfortable with having someone else pay my way.

⊛ Unemployment can be a rough time, but it is not without its blessings. I have found that my situation has forced me to depend upon God and others. The game of unemployment is a team sport that leaves little room for self-sufficiency.

⊛ Unemployment gives Christians an opportunity to experience the joy of serving others. Don't be afraid to reach out! Your unemployed friends are in need of encouragement that only you can give.

—Brian J. Waldrop, "Encouraging the Unemployed," *Focus on the Family* (October 1995), p. 7. © Brian J. Waldrop, Cincinnati, OH. Used by permission.

Helplines

1. **Human Resources Development Canada**. www.hrdc-drhc.gc.ca/ae-ei/dem-app/2.0_e.shtml. (Or look in the government pages of any local telephone directory.) Provides information about unemployment insurance.

2. **Prodigy**. 1-800-776-3449. www.prodigybusiness.com. A resumé bank and bulletin board with want ads from *USA Today* and the *National Business Employment Weekly*.

If you're seeking work in a Christian organization, consider contacting one of the following:

1. **Larry Burkett's Career Pathways**, P.O. Box 1476, Gainesville, GA 30503. 1-800-722-1976. This arm of the nonprofit Christian Financial Concepts will examine your interests, abilities, skills, work priorities, and temperament in an assessment package, then recommend a representative job.
2. **Intercristo**, 19303 Freemont Ave. N., Seattle, WA 98133. 1-800-426-1343. www.jobsinaflash.org. A Christian placement organization, Intercisto matches skills to openings in Christian organizations.

The following online databases give job listings, but first check with local government employment centers, colleges, and libraries on how to save computer access charges.

1. **Christianity Online**. You can conduct your search by specific job title, skill area, location, job element, or company, as well as advertise products or services you offer.
2. **E-Span**. 1-800-682-2901. www.joboptions.com. A resumé bank for professional, managerial, and technical candidates, available via the Internet, CompuServe, and Genie.

Books and Other Resources

- Bolles, Richard. *What Color Is Your Parachute?* (Berkeley, CA: Ten Speed Press, updated yearly). Offers help in creating a great resumé, advice on how to switch careers, and job listings of specialized industries that are hiring.
- Burkett, Larry, and Lee Ellis. *Your Career in Changing Times* (Chicago: Moody Press, 1993). Career planning from a biblical perspective. The authors describe the workplace and how it is changing, then help you identify your skills and interests and apply them to a

career that's right for now. Includes how to conduct a job search and write a resumé. Best if used in conjunction with the companion workbook (see below).

ⓦ Burkett, Larry and Lee Ellis. *Finding the Career That Fits You: The Companion Workbook to Your Career in Changing Times* (Chicago: Moody Press, 1998). In this book you'll discover the person God made you to be through insightful looks at your personality, skills, values, and vocational interests. The authors walk you through the job search process and give you the confidence you need to start or change a career—and your life.

ⓦ Lowstuter, Clyde. *In Search of the Perfect Job* (New York: McGraw Hill, 1992). Experts refer to this book as the new "Bible" for men and women contemplating a career move in today's uncertain economy. This is a self-help book for the person who does not receive corporate-paid professional career counseling.

ⓦ Lowstuter, Clyde. *Six-Figure Networking and the Self-Directed Job Hunting System.* A six-cassette learning system. To order, call 1-800-398-2665 or fax 1-847-940-7110.

Violation of Privacy and Freedom

A Few Words for a Burglar

"And the second is like it: 'Love your neighbor as yourself.'"

—Matthew 22:39

When you walked in and saw our home did you feel about it the way we do? Did you see the Pocahontas school backpacks laid in the corner all ready for the next day of school? Did you see our faces as we smiled from family photographs? Did you know you'd make us never feel the same way about home again?

Yes, you came in and took advantage of us when we were away. You took our VCR. You took our Camcorder. You took our laptop computer. You took our Seiko watch. You took our jewelry and you took our television.

But when you took those things, did you know you took the VCR that was given as a Christmas present over six years ago?

Did you know that you took our Camcorder with the $10,000.00 video on it? Yes, we were going to copy our two-year-old at the beach and send it to Bob Saget for America's Funniest Home Videos. We don't really care about the $10,000.00 part. We'd just like to have the priceless memories on tape back where they belong.

When you took the laptop computer did you know it had five years of building a business on it? Did you care that inside it were dreams, writings, thoughts and ideas that no one could possibly understand but us?

How about the Seiko watch? How do you feel now that you know this was a gift from a father-in-law to a new son-in-law? It had kept perfect time for more than ten years. It has much more sentimental value than any street price could place on it.

When you traveled up the stairs did you know our two-year-old had just learned to toddle down them? Do you care that our six- and eight-year-old are now scared to sleep at night? Our three-year old knows the police will catch the bad guys. How we pray that he is right.

When you went into our children's rooms did you notice the new school clothes mixed with the old? Did you realize that children in our house are beginning a new school year and that they have enough anxiety? Now we face the knowledge that our children were touched by you and there was nothing we could do about it. You have taken a piece of innocence away that cannot be replaced. Material items are nothing compared to what you really stole.

We wonder what you look like. Are you young? Do we know you, or are you a stranger who feels power making others feel powerless? Are you watching us when we go outside? Do you have anything you'd like to return for, something you didn't get the first time?

We are natives of West Michigan. We grew up in a neighborhood much like this one. Growing up, we never locked our doors. And we took our safe feelings with us as we began our own family. People laugh about how our home looks like Toys-R-Us on a bright sunny day. We leave things in the open. We trust people despite what statistics and headlines say. We leave doors open, garages open, hearts open. Now we feel a closing that hurts us more than the act of violence itself.

When we really think about our anger, we know time will heal us. Will time make your guilt grow? We are sad and confused. And you are the reason for our despair. You have come into our stable lives and made us all feel violated, used and discarded.

—Lynne Jarman-Johnson, "A Few Words for a Burglar," *Grand Rapids Press* (October 22, 1995). © 1995 by Lynne Jarman-Johnson. Used by permission.

Wisdom for the Caregiver

☙ Read "Caregiving Basics" (pp. 203-222).

☙ Check "109+ Ways to Say, 'I Care'" (pp. 223-234).

☙ Don't minimize the crisis by saying unhelpful things like, "Well, it's really fortunate that you were not home!" and, "Aren't you thankful that no one was hurt?" or, "You can always replace material things."

☙ Reread Lynne's story, paying close attention to how she and her family feel. Try to sense her feelings and the issues that plague her thoughts. Then go to the person you're trying to help overcome a violation of his or her privacy, express your feeling of concern, and most importantly, encourage him or her to talk about what happened and how he or she feels about it.

☙ If an object was taken that was extremely important or essential to the person(s), ask a group of friends/relatives to contribute toward replacing the object. Sometimes a concrete expression of caring helps both the receiver and the giver.

☙ The persons who have been victimized will know that you really care if you offer to help them "secure" their home. Maybe it could become a joint project or a neighborhood project where families help each other to "secure" homes. For information on securing a home consult the book *Household Hints and Handy Tips* by Reader's Digest, pages 128-130, or check your local bookstore for other books containing this information.

SECTION 2

Caregiving Basics

A s we have talked with people who have experienced crises, and as we have researched how to care for persons who are hurting, we have identified three basic guidelines that can be applied to any crisis:

1. Pray
2. Listen Well
3. Respect the Grief Process

The following pages describe these guidelines in detail.

Pray

T he most important and helpful guideline for effective caregiving is to pray. To pray is to acknowledge the presence of God.

Trust in the LORD with all your heart and lean not on your own understanding; in all your ways acknowledge him, and he will make your paths straight."

—Proverbs 3:5-6

If any of you lacks wisdom, he should ask God, who gives generously to all without finding fault, and it will be given to him.

—James 1:5

Pray Before
"*Before you are face-to-face with the troubled person, pray about your encounter. Ask God for help. Rely on the strength that Jesus gives each and every one of us. Don't be a know-it-all.*"

—George

Pray your own prayer or use the following caregiver's prayer:

> *Dear God, I want to be your servant, to speak your words of comfort, to demonstrate your unconditional love to [name]. Please show me how to do that. If there is something I should know about this situation, help me discover it. If there is a verse or word of encouragement that I should speak, bring it to my mind. Relieve my fears and doubts. Help me to remember that I do not go alone, that the supreme Comforter, your Holy Spirit, goes with me. Amen.*

Pray During

To pray with someone is to share a treasure of amazing value. Prayer is a powerful way to care for others. By praying with another person, we show them how much we care, and we acknowledge the very presence and power of the Holy Spirit, who is the ultimate comforter, counselor, and healer.

Ask the person if he or she would like you to pray. If the person expresses a desire for prayer, ask, "What issue(s) are you struggling with right now?" (Do not assume that you know what the important issues are in the person's life.) If you have been listening carefully, you may already know the issues that are foremost in the person's mind; however, you might choose to restate or clarify those issues.

Each one of us, whether we feel comfortable doing it or not, can utter a short prayer in the presence of another. It can be as simple as:

> *Dear God, I lift my friend [name] to you. Comfort him/her and give him/her strength in this difficult time. Amen.*

Pray After

After you leave your friend, continue to pray. Let your friend know that you are praying for him or her. At home, consider lighting a prayer candle as a reminder to yourself to keep your promise to pray. Perhaps your next gesture of caring could be a follow-up note that might include a prayer you've written especially for that person.

Never underestimate the power of prayer. Over and over, in books of faith and in conversations, people say, "I knew when someone was praying for me. I could feel it. I became quiet and peaceful," or, "Suddenly I knew what my next step should be," or, "I felt like someone just gave me a hug."

Author Ron Delbene describes this power in his book *Into the Light* (p. 82):

I do not believe we can ever say prayer is wasted; some good always comes of it. Although our prayers may not change a situation and give us the miracle we want, prayer changes us. Through prayer, we are no longer facing our fears and pain alone; God is there beside us, renewing our spirit, restoring our soul, and helping us carry the burden when it becomes too heavy for us to bear.

Listen Well

G ood, empathetic listening is a caregiving guideline that is often taken for granted or overlooked, but it is often the most powerful way you can help a person who is suffering. The following two situations illustrate the importance of this skill.

Fran's Advice

Sally was going through a devastating divorce. Her friend, Fran, encountered her in the foyer at church and asked her how she was doing.

"Everything is so uncertain," Sally said. "I'm not sure what my settlement will be, where I'll live, and with whom the children will be living. I can't sleep nights, I've lost weight, and I can't stop crying. Quite frankly, life is the pits right now."

"Well, life can be pretty cruel, you know," replied Fran. "Sometimes we have to make the most of a bad situation. Maybe God is trying to teach you something through this crisis."

Imagine you are Sally. What are your feelings and thoughts as Fran walks away from you?

Grace's Caregiving

Several days later, another friend, Grace, saw Sally in the grocery store. When Grace asked Sally how she was doing, Sally again described her unfortunate situation. Grace gently offered, "It sounds like you're going through a terrible experience, Sally. You must be devastated! I'm so sorry! Do you have time for a cup of coffee? Sounds like you need to talk."

As Sally poured out her heart to Grace, her friend interjected comments such as, "How upsetting!" "You must be so sad!" and, "I can see you are in a great deal of pain."

Forty-five minutes later, Grace helped Sally put her groceries in her car and asked if she could pray with her friend. Sitting in the car, Grace offered a caring, meaningful prayer for God's comfort and provision. Sally was moved to tears as Grace concluded the prayer. As they said their good-byes Grace offered to babysit for Sally's children the following week when she went to court.

Imagine once more that you are Sally. What are your thoughts and feelings as Grace drives off?

Fran gave advice, but Grace gave care. Most importantly, Grace listened—really listened. An empathetic listener, she "got involved in" Sally's problem. She entered into Sally's feelings; she "suffered with" Sally as if Sally's cares were her own. She listened with love. Grace was an empathetic listener.

An empathetic listener is one who

- gets involved.
- gives full attention to the one who is hurting.
- enters into that person's feelings and suffers with the person.
- listens more than talks.
- speaks primarily to help the sufferer clarify his or her situation and feelings.
- does not interject his or her own problems or situations.

The poem on the following page illustrates this art of listening.

Please Just Listen

When I ask you to listen to me

Come with a desire and commitment to listen.

and you start giving advice,

Avoid judgment statements such as "It's not good to think like that" or "That doesn't make any sense." Initially avoid other forms of advice-giving, including Bible verses and platitudes. Offering advice may make you feel more at ease, but that's not the object here.

you have not done what I asked
nor heard what I need.

When I ask you to listen to me

Just listening has tremendous power to heal. When you don't know what to say or do, just listen.

and you begin to tell me why
I shouldn't feel that way,
you are trampling on my feelings.

Encourage the person to express his or her feelings. Respond to his or her statements by saying things like, "That must have made you angry." "How frightening!" "How did you feel when that happened?"

When I ask you to listen to me
and you feel you have to do something
to solve my problems,

Do not try to "fix" the problem or rescue the one who is suffering. When a person has lost someone or something important, he or she grieves, and grief is a process that takes time—lots of time.

you have failed me—
strange as that may seem.

When you do something for me

In Greek to "comfort" means to come alongside the one who is suffering. That's good advice for caregivers. We ought not to direct the person's steps. Instead, we ought to walk alongside and encourage. Think of it as offering to dry the dishes while the other person washes them.

that I can and need to do for myself
you contribute to my
seeming fearful and weak.

So please listen and just hear me.

Care to those who are in grief means asking about the crisis, not avoiding it. That crisis is the most important thing in their lives. Normally they will want to talk about it, perhaps cry about it. Offering care can mean offering them an opportunity to do both in the presence of someone who loves them.

And if you want to talk,
let's plan for your turn,
and I promise I'll listen to you.

—Anonymous

Respect the Grief Process

Recently Mary, an acquaintance, said to me (Karen), "My neighbor is a mess. I understand her sadness; she misses her husband terribly, but she is a mess. She cries all the time. She looks awful. Her house is chaotic. She doesn't take proper care of her teenage son. I am thinking of being firm with her and simply stating: 'It's time to dry your tears and get on with your life.'"

Then she asked me, "What do you think?" (I was so glad that she asked!)

I inquired, "When was her husband killed in the automobile accident?" Mary responded, "Ten weeks ago."

I told Mary a little about the "grief process" and suggested that she might find help in the classic book *Good Grief* by Granger E. Westberg. (Available online at www.augsburgfortess.org, *Good Grief,* written in 1962, has sold over two million copies.) In contrast to the "quick fix" approach, Westberg explores the predictable and necessary emotional experiences of the good and healthy grief process, a process that takes time (see pp. 214-217, which draw on Westberg's insights).

"Let's face it, grief is just so messy," says Nicholas Wolterstorff, author of *Lament for a Son,* the story of the death of his twenty-five-year-old son, Eric, in a mountain climbing accident. As friends and relatives, says Wolterstorff, we want the grieving person to "get over it," "be done with it," "put it behind them," and "get on with life and living," because we don't know what to say or do, and (truthfully) we don't want to have to deal with the continued pain and messiness of the bereaved. So we are often tempted to rush in with a "quick fix."

Judy Tatelbaum, a therapist, also affirms that the quick fix doesn't work, that wounds do not heal without time and attention. In her book *The Courage to Grieve* (p. 22) she highlights the two major psychological tasks to be accomplished during the grieving process:

⊛ Acknowledging and accepting the truth: that death (or a loss) has occurred and that the relationship is now over.
⊛ Experiencing and dealing with all the emotions and problems this loss creates for the bereaved. These tasks intertwine. Each takes time. Each is necessary for the eventual recovery from grief.

With any of the situations described in section 1 of this book, grief will play a part in the person's road to healing. Some understanding of the grief process, explored in the pages that follow, will help caregivers

⊛ know what to expect.
⊛ be more comfortable with the grieving person.
⊛ respond more effectively by being present, listening, and accepting the person's various emotional responses.

The Emotions and Experiences of the Grief Process

Note: For the information found in this section, we are indebted to a wonderful "classic" on the grief process by Granger E. Westberg. Still in print and still popular, it's called *Good Grief* (Minneapolis: Augsburg Fortress Publishers, 1962).

Grief is the normal and natural process by which a person makes a healthy adjustment to any significant loss in his or her life. Any significant loss (the death of a loved one, the loss of a job, a broken marriage, deterioration of health, a shattered dream) triggers the process. Most people experience some or all of the following emotional responses when they lose anything or anyone important in their lives.

Griever's Behavior	Griever's Response	Caregiver's Response
The person is temporarily anesthetized against the overwhelming experience he or she is facing. May appear zombie-like.	1. Shock, Numbness	Do not assume that the person is "okay." As the hours and days go by, the protective shield will be gradually removed, and the grieving person will increasingly need your loving care.
A person can only accept pain a little at a time. During this stage the mourner says, in actions or words: "It cannot be true!" The person may ignore the loss, and try to live as if it isn't true.	2. Denial	Understand why the person is grasping at straws. Be patient. Stand by.
As one begins to accept the harsh reality, he or she has a sense of utter loneliness and isolation. Despair sets in, and there is no energy to love, live, work, or play. Hopefully, the one who is suffering can vent his or her feelings.	3. Depression	Attempts to cheer up or reassure mean very little to the one grieving. The person needs an empathetic listener (see "Listen Well," pp. 208-211) who helps put his or her feelings and thoughts into words. Some questions that may help that process begin are: "What are you most worried about?" "What's going on in your head today?" The role of a caregiver is to be there, listen, and accept the emotions as they are expressed.

Griever's Behavior	Griever's Response	Caregiver's Response
Many symptoms can appear: nightmares, back pain, inability to concentrate, hallucinations, gagging, sleeplessness, inability to eat, restlessness, hoarseness, feelings that they may die, and others. *The whole of one's being grieves a loss.*	4. Physical Distress	Once again, the caregiver's role is to be there, to listen, to accept the emotions as they are expressed. You might invite the person to share his or her story by saying something like, "I never knew [name of person who died]. Tell me about him/her," or, "Please, if you feel like it now, tell me the whole story of how [name the loss] happened, and if I have questions as you go along, I will ask you." Also encourage the person who becomes physically ill during or after a crisis to see a doctor. Sometimes just knowing that the physical symptoms are "normal" helps.
The person may become panicky because he or she cannot think about anything except the loss. The person cannot concentrate. As anxiety increases, the person may imagine exaggerated physical symptoms.	5. Panic, Fear	Encourage the person to ventilate his or her panic or fear. Never negate any expression of feeling. Instead acknowledge it: "Yes, you have reason to feel frightened." Also assure the person that the inability to concentrate is a normal part of the grieving process. (Instead of just telling the person that panic feelings are normal, it might be more convincing to refer to pp. 45-46 of *Good Grief*.)

Griever's Behavior	Griever's Response	Caregiver's Response
The person says, "What else could I have done?" "Why did I do/say what I did?" "If only." "It's all my fault."	6. Guilt	Allow the person to ask questions, but don't try to answer them. Questions help the person identify and talk about feelings of guilt. Most of this passes in a few months. If not, the individual may require professional help.
Inevitably the grieving person will go through a stage of being very critical. He or she is often angry at God, at the loved one who has died, at doctors and/or medical staff, at a boss, or others. The hostile person is really saying, "They can't do this to me!" "Why did this happen to me?" "I'm scared." "Why me, Lord?"	7. Anger and Resentment	Expect the person to be angry. The expression of this anger may be irrational, and you will not be able to logically resolve it. Again, one of the most helpful things you can do is to allow the person to express anger. You might respond by saying, "When [name the event] happened, it made you very angry because [name the reason]." You might also suggest a way to vent the anger: using a punching bag, writing an angry letter (not to be sent), exercising, yelling at a pillow, or journaling feelings.
Gradually the grieving person may want to get back to his or her normal activities, yet something inside resists returning. Sometimes the person feels he or she must keep the memory of the loved one alive because it appears that most other people have forgotten. Also, getting back into life again can be painful: "Grieving is painful, but not as painful as having to face entirely new [situations] and decisions every hour" (*Good Grief,* p. 54).	8. Resists Returning to Normal Life	The task of caregivers is to help keep the memory of the loved one alive and to show continued care and concern for the grieving person. Gradually encourage the person to get involved again in activities she or he has always enjoyed. "Honor your friend's privacy and need to withdraw, but never withhold sincere offers of help or invitations to get together" (M. Gregory Richards, *When Someone You Know Is Hurting,* p. 91).

Griever's Behavior	Griever's Response	Caregiver's Response
Now and then there is a "glimpse of hope. The cloud which has been so dark begins to break up, and rays of light come through" (*Good Grief*, p. 57). One can never be sure how long the grief process will last. If the loss involves someone important, the most difficult part of the grief process will probably last at the least one year; one needs to go through all the "firsts" without the person: his or her birthday, anniversary, Christmas, and so on. And the grieving person will never entirely "get over" the loss!	9. Gradually Hope Comes Through	Continue to encourage the person to get involved again in activities he or she has always enjoyed. Also invite the person to pursue some new experiences, hobbies, and friends. *Remember that grief is a process and takes time.*
If a person works through the various emotions of grief and allows him- or herself to experience all the pain, such a person will reach a point of affirming that not everything has been taken away. He or she realizes that life will never be the same again but that there is still much in life that can be affirmed (*Good Grief*, p. 63).	10. Struggles to Affirm Reality	If you are a caregiver who has been there for this grieving person for the entire process, you are indeed a precious gift!

Bringing the Chart to Life

The chart on the preceding pages lists the emotional responses that are often experienced when we lose something or someone significant. Perhaps the chart makes the grieving process look too neat, too easy, too programmed. To put breath and life and reality into this grieving process we have two suggestions:

⊛ Read Barb Pekich's story, "One Person's Grieving Process," on the pages that follow.
⊛ Read *Bridge to Terabithia* by Katherine Paterson. This compelling novel, whose main character is a fourth-grader, adds a wonderful human dimension to the emotional responses to grief detailed in the chart.

One Person's Grieving Process
Barb Pekich

Note: The opening of Barb's story is repeated from section 1. The rest of Barb's story comes from an article titled "Why Seek the Dead Among the Living?" *Perspectives* (Oct. 4, 1994). Used by permission.

At approximately 2:00 p.m. on November 2, 1993, my husband took his own life. That event brought me and our four children face-to-face with a death we did not understand—indeed, did not want to understand. The pain is embodied in the words of our oldest daughter, Edie:

> *There's no more laughter in this house*
> *for it has passed away.*
> *You took the joy we once had known*
> *on that awful November day.*
>
> *The pain cuts deep inside my soul*
> *the thoughts that never end*
> *of what has been and what will be*
> *and where you should be now.*
>
> *I want to run away and hide*
> *from all the tears and pain.*
> *But there's nowhere that you didn't touch*
> *that I can find today.*

Depression

My husband's suicide brought us pain that was and is immeasurable. Initially, and for some time after Bill's death, I questioned what I could have done differently. I also experienced some regrets about things said or unsaid during the last few days of his life.

Guilt

I have not felt a lot of anger this past year, mostly sadness. However, when the anger has spilled out I've tried to channel it in some healthy ways. Some of these ways may sound bizarre, but I'm not the least bit ashamed of them. For example, I have visited the cemetery at all hours of the day and night, and have sworn at him. I have dug through the snow and ice to uncover his grave marker in the dark so that I could stomp on it. I have been

Anger

known to stand in my garage at night and hurl dishes against the wall. All these actions were very therapeutic.

One of my significant struggles has been moving from "I can't" (*I can't be alone; I can't be a single parent; I can't be a widow.*) to "I don't want" (*I don't want to be alone, a single parent, a widow.*) to "I am" (*I am alone; I am a single parent; I am a widow.*). This whole process of acknowledgment took about nine months. I hesitate to use the word "acceptance," for how do we "accept" what is totally unacceptable?

I have not been here for five months. Not since May 2 have I stood on this ground and looked at this tree—the site of Bill's suicide nearly one year ago. Then, and in the months after, it was desolate here. Here is where I came alone, with all but one of my children, and with my closest friends. I have been here several times but have not needed to come back since May. Shortly after Bill's death I remarked to a friend of mine on one of these pilgrimages with me that I never wanted things to change here. I never wanted it to look different. It was frightening to think that someday this tree, this huge white oak might not be here.

As I climbed out of the van today with my good friend, Andy, I was struck with how much this site had altered. Everywhere new growth stood firmly and staunchly on the once trampled ground. Grass and wildflowers flourished, unaware of the memories of what was here a year ago. The tire tracks, once so visible, that had plowed a path straight into the tree on that day in November, now made only the smallest indentation in the ground. Eleven months ago the earth was strewn with small pieces of his car: part of a headlight here, a piece of the windshield there. There were reminders everywhere. Now it is hard to walk through the dense growth of weeds, grass, and flowers in front of, beside, and behind the tree. Searching the ground, I find only a small fragment of the side mirror. Oh, there are probably more pieces if I look hard, but what were once precious items that I needed to see and touch are now just the broken things that I don't need anymore.

Sidebar annotations:

Denial

Panic/fear

Remember, there are no quick fixes. Grieving is a complex emotional process. It takes time.

Resists returning to normal

Feels that she must keep the memory alive

Facing the new situation is scary/painful.

Resists returning to normal

"Grieving is painful, but not as painful as having to face entirely new [situations] and decisions every hour" (*Good Grief*, p. 54).

Eleven months ago on a trip here with this same friend, we found part of Bill's glasses, a vivid reminder of the person I loved that cut like a sword into my heart yet brought a strange comfort that part of him had survived. Today in nearly the same spot, amidst the gravel on the shoulder of the road, is a tiny purple flower. Even the tree has begun to heal. After the accident there were deep gouges in the bark and new wood exposed underneath where pieces of the trunk were torn off. Now, the new wood is the same color as the old; some of the old has covered over parts that were exposed. I used to sit on a stump beside the big tree and mourn the act that so quickly left me feeling so desperately alone. Here today, I have to search for the stump. It is surrounded by brush and growth and life, just as my family has been surrounded this past year.

> Gradually, hope comes through.

> We never return to our "old selves" again. Depending upon the way we respond to the loss, we are either stronger than we were before or weaker.

There is little here today to remind me of the violence and the pain that were his a year ago. Thank God. This place has changed. I have changed. My children have changed. But today that thought brings me comfort. As I stand on the spot that once held the dead, I know that there is no longer anything here for me. I have gone so many times before to get in touch with the reality of Bill's death. But today, I wonder, "Why am I seeking the dead among the living?"

> Struggles to affirm reality

At various times these past eleven months I have tried to let go, to hang on, to let go, to hang on—to let go of my identity as a wife and hang on to my new title of "widow." Now I am letting go of "widow" and hanging on to me. It is a process of letting go of the events surrounding Bill's death and remembering the joy we shared in our lives together. It is a process of letting the past be in the past and a part of who I am and who my children are, and yet embracing the promises for the future. It is a process of being able to see life and beauty and feel joy and hope once more. It is a process of moving from trusting the promise that God will be with me to acknowledging the certainty that God has been here and continues to be here. It is the process of resurrec-

> Grieving never wholly ends. "The image, the memory of dreams and things and persons lost, never completely disappears from our minds. What was once a painful wound will become, with successful grieving, a poignant and sometimes pleasant memory, but all the longing will not completely disappear" (Kenneth R. Mitchell, *All Our Losses, All Our Griefs*, p. 95).

"Gradually those individuals who have openly experienced and worked through the various emotions of grief realize that life will never be the same again, but they begin to sense that there is much in life than can be affirmed. And to affirm something is to say that it is good" (*Good Grief*, p. 63).

tion, of moving from death to life, and sorrow to joy, from Good Friday to Easter.

SECTION 3

109+ Ways to Say, "I Care"

Our parents get old.
Our children give us headaches.
Our friends get cancer.
Our neighbors lose their jobs.

Individuals who need our comfort and care surround us. The problem, however, arises when our hearts say, "Go," but our heads say, "No." We may have the tendency to avoid these situations because we don't know what to say or do. This section offers 109 ways to respond to the question "What can I do to help?"

Please read through this menu of ideas. If some of the suggestions do not feel comfortable to you, read on until an idea jumps off the page and a voice within says, "I can do that!"

Meladee McCarty says, "There is a bundle of *kindness energy* in all of us that can come out, given a focus or a strategy for doing so" (*Acts of Kindness: How to Create a Kindness Revolution,* p. 112). Our hope is that the following suggestions will give you concrete ways to express your kindness energy.

Thoughtful Gifts

1. Our family greatly appreciated the gift of **restaurant coupons** when we were going through a crisis. No one felt like cooking, and going to a restaurant got us "up" and "out."

2. I love **chocolate** and so do many other people. So surprise me with a hot fudge sundae or one extra special truffle, or a basket filled with chocolate products: hot fudge sauce, chocolate covered potato chips, and so on.

3. **Cook a dinner** for my family, and offer a choice of two courses. (Bring the food in disposable containers or include your name on returnable containers.)

4. Bake **homemade cookies** or brownies and bring them frozen so I can have the delight of sending fresh goodies in my children's lunch boxes or surprising them with a special after-school snack.

5. Give me a **bag of hard candies** to suck on when I feel like crying in public.

6. One very hot summer day, a neighbor brought me a **frosted glass of freshly squeezed lemonade.** This special gift refreshed my body and soul. (Even better, bring a whole pitcher, and talk to me while we sip the lemonade together.)

7. Kid's version of the above: Bring tall glasses, vanilla ice cream, cold root beer and straws, and make my family and me **root beer floats.** Yum!

8. Who can resist a piece of **homemade apple pie with vanilla ice cream** or other extravagant goodies? Not me.

9. Homemade **chicken soup** has mysterious healing powers. Bring me a pot of this marvelous brew.

10. Bring me a **hostess basket** filled with an array of treats, from chocolate kisses to fresh fruit to home-baked cookies. Then I will have something to offer visitors and/or hospital staff.

11. Perk up my day by bringing me a **special tea cup with a variety of tea bags** or a **pretty mug with flavored coffee.**

12. Receiving a **note or card** is like being hugged. Neither the eloquence of the words nor the elegance of the stationary is as significant as the care expressed.

13. I especially valued those **sympathy cards** which contained some of the **sender's personal thoughts**: words remembering something that they admired or appreciated about my deceased loved one and personal caring prayers. These personal notes continue to bring me quiet joy and courage every time that I read them. (A scrapbook in which to save all the notes and cards is also a long-term meaningful gift.)

14. I enjoy birds, and was delighted when a neighbor built **a bird feeder** for the outside of my window. I spent many pleasant moments watching and identifying the beautiful visitors. (You might want to add a bird book to the gift.)
15. I love receiving **flowers.** They're a wonderful gesture of caring.
16. Share with me some of your favorite **musical tapes or CDs**, or some of my favorite instrumentalists and/or vocalists if you know who they are.
17. Offer to **alleviate my financial crisis** by loaning me funds. (In many cases a loan allows me to maintain my dignity.) Or help me out with an anonymous gift of money.
18. Consider the questions: **What does this person enjoy doing during normal/healthy times? Is he or she able to do that activity now?** Example: I enjoy writing notes and letters, and it would be delightful to receive some attractive writing paper or cards, a new pen, and some stamps, and maybe even one of those wonderful lap desks.
19. When a friend brought me a **comfy new robe** to wear during my stay in the hospital, I was delighted and grateful.
20. Give me **a book of prayers.** Richard J. Foster's *Prayers From the Heart* (Harper San Francisco, 1994) is one of my favorites.
21. Small thoughtful gifts meant so very much to me; for example, a **fragrant votive candle** soothed my senses and a **lavender-filled sachet** to place over my eyes helped me to relax. Little things do mean a lot!
22. Create a basket of **beauty or grooming products** for me. I received one that included lotions to soothe my parched skin, perfume, special shampoo, nail polish in a new color. (Or create a personalized basket filled with items that the person needs or might enjoy.)
23. Hire someone to come to the hospital or to my home and give me a **manicure,** or a professional **back rub** or a **haircut.**
24. At a time when my life was turned upside down, a friend gave me a **daily Bible study guide** titled *This Morning with God.* This programmed study added a necessary structure to each day, and kept me in tune with my faith and my God.
25. "My sister had the wisdom to give me a **journal** while I was in the hospital. I dumped all my emotions and all my confusion on paper.

I wrote—without editing, without polish—about how I felt, what had happened, questions I struggled with. I wrote each entry to Dustin, the son we had just lost" (Joanie Reid, *Life Line,* Pineapple Press, 1994).

26. When my son was tragically killed in an automobile and bike accident, some of our friends started a **memorial scholarship fund** in his name, and have continued to remember our loss each year with a note and a check.

27. When my seven-year-old son died, one of the most thoughtful things that several people did was to give me **pictures** and even a **videotape** of my son, mostly things I hadn't seen before.

28. **Share your special talents and skills** with me. "A story is told about Beethoven, a man not known for social grace. Because of his deafness, he found conversation difficult and humiliating. When he heard of the death of a friend's son, Beethoven hurried to the house, overcome with grief. He had no words of comfort to offer, but he saw a piano in the room. For the next half hour he played the piano, pouring out his emotions in the most eloquent way he could. When he finished playing, he left. The friend later remarked that no one else's visit had meant so much" (Billy Graham, *Hope for the Troubled Heart,* p. 180).

29. **The little book** *Good Grief* by Granger E. Westberg was a very helpful gift. It encourages me to experience the various emotions of the grief process, and it makes me realize that grieving is a *process* that takes time—a lot of time.

30. During a crisis, a friend gave me a **small cross** to remind me of God's constant presence. Every day that cross, which either sets on my desk or is carried in my pocket, continues to remind me of God's love.

Words That Help

31. Say, **"I know you are hurting, and I really care about that. If you want to talk about it, I'll listen."** Then let me talk without interrupting me.

32. Tell me, **"You have been in my thoughts."** That is a greeting which will allow me to choose my response. If I feel a need to share my feelings or thoughts, I can do so, or I can choose to say simply, "Thank you," and go on to talk of other things.

33. Remember: Any show of concern will help. The following simple sentence says it all: **"I'm so sorry about your trouble."**
34. Say, **"I love you!"** Often. We all know that the three little words "I love you" can make a powerful difference in another person's life. There are other three-word powerhouses which can make a big impact. Here are eight to try:
    - "I truly care."
    - "I miss you."
    - "I appreciate you."
    - "It must hurt."
    - "I'm so sorry."
    - "Count on me."
    - "Let me help."
    - "Thinking of you."
35. Say, **"I can't even imagine how much you must hurt or how lonely you must feel or how devastated you must be!"**
36. During a very difficult decision-making time, one friend said to me, "Whatever you decide to do—if you need or choose X, Y, or Z, **I will be here."**
37. **"I'll go with you."** To have a friend go with you when you are facing new and frightening situations (seeing a lawyer, psychologist, or doctor, finding a new apartment, and so on) is a greatly valued gift.
38. Say, **"Call me anytime you need to talk."**
39. Please don't give me advice. Instead **ask me about the options** that are available to me.
40. **Pray with me** in person or over the phone. If this is too difficult for you, **write a prayer** of your own or copy one and give or send it to me. This is helpful because I can read it over and over.
41. A person usually wants to talk about his or her illness (or crisis). They want to tell their story. It's the number one topic on their mind. So gently say, **"Tell me about _____."**
42. As I tell you my crisis story, you don't have to say anything. Just **hum along** by making quiet, compassionate sounds like "hmmm . . . ," "ohhhh . . .," "ahhhh . . .," "oh noooo . . ."
43. "Don't push me to 'get well,' or to 'get on with my life.' After a while, the best advice from a friend was: **'Look, don't even try to get back to normal.** Just make an effort to accomplish one simple thing during the day. It doesn't matter what it is. Make a call, pay a

bill, keep your dental appointment, get a hair cut—and I'll help if you want me to'" (Sol Gordon, *Is There Anything I Can Do?*, p. 181).

44. Sometimes I need a friend who will **ask me questions** that will help me clarify my thinking and unload my heavy heart. Some questions that have been helpful are:
    • What do you feel like talking about today?
    • What are you thinking (or feeling) today?
    • What worries you the most?

45. Even though I'm old or ill or disabled, I still like to think that other people, especially my friends and family, value my opinions, skills, and advice. **So please ask me for help.**

46. **"Be real. Admit your honest feelings to me.** If the news stunned you, say so. If you don't know what to say, say just that. If you suddenly feel tears coming, cry. If you are overwhelmed with pity and compassion, admit it. When you allow your true feelings to show, you give me permission to also 'let go' and express my honest feelings" (Charles Swindol, *Seasons of Life,* p. 172).

47. Phone regularly to say, **"I'm thinking of you."**

48. Don't defend the party with whom I am angry. The fact that he or she may have reasons for doing what he or she did is immaterial. I am angry. **Please help me ventilate my feelings.**

49. Please **do not tell me that you understand how I feel!** Even if you have gone through a similar experience, it is not the same as my experience. Although the words "I understand" may sound comforting, they are not. Please respect the fact that my experience is totally unique.

50. Avoid saying:
    • "You'll get over it."
    • "I'm sure it will be just fine."
    • "You look awful."
    • "You look great." (Implying that the person should also feel great.)
    • "Are you over your loss yet?"
    • "My uncle had the same disease and died (or lived)."
    • "Well, here's what I think you should do . . . "
    • "God doesn't promise us a rose garden." (Or other trite sayings.)
    • "What have you learned from this tragedy?"
    • "Well, you know what the Bible says: 'Forgive 70 times 7.'" (Or some other pulverizing verse.)

Special Services

51. **Make your offer specific.** Say, "I would like to come over Monday at 3:00 to bake cookies," ". . . read you a book," ". . . clean your kitchen," ". . . wash your windows," or whatever. If you say, "Call me anytime for anything," I won't know what you want to do or when you are free, so I probably won't ask.

52. Ask me **who I might like to visit me.** Sometimes I am just too tired or too shy to initiate these contacts.

53. Present me with a **list of videos** (or books or tapes) with **a coupon** attached that says: "I will call on the next four Saturdays for your video order," or, "You may call me to place your order." (Or design your own coupon.)

54. When I was very ill, a group of friends gave me the wonderful gift of a **maid for a month.** They hired a woman to clean my house and to handle other domestic duties once a week. Wow!

55. Offer to **do something for my children:** play with them, tutor them, or take them to the park or to see their grandparents.

56. Offer to **take my children overnight,** or offer to **baby-sit** even if my spouse and I stay home. This gives us some freedom in our home.

57. Offer to **drive me** where I need to go. I may be too tired or too distracted to drive.

58. Offer to **decorate my house** for Christmas or for a birthday party.

59. Ask if there are any **gifts, cards, or wrapping paper** that you could **pick up** for me.

60. Phone me when you go to the **grocery store** to see if I need anything. (I feel so helpless when my family needs or wants something, and I have to ask my friends for another favor.)

61. Help my children attend birthday parties by bringing some **prewrapped children's birthday party gifts** to our home for future use. Indicate the contents with a post-it note.

62. When I must miss a special program or event in which my child is participating, please **take photographs or a video.** This allows me to share the experience with him or her.

63. Offer to do **personal errands and chores** for me:
    - water plants
    - tidy up my house or apartment
    - drop off/pick up dry cleaning

- wash my car and/or fill up gas tank
- bring my mail to the hospital
- ask me for a list of my errand needs

64. Volunteer to **make or return phone calls** during my crisis.
65. Offer to **write thank-you or other types of notes** for me. (I want to show gratitude to those who have helped my family and me, but I am too tired and weak.)
66. Offer to **read my favorite sections of the newspaper** to me. Even though I am ill and do not have the strength to hold a newspaper, I have always been a Detroit Tigers fan, and I would love to hear what the paper said about yesterday's game.
67. **Help the major caregiver in my life.** He or she needs some uplifting too! Help him or her wash the car, mow the lawn, drive the kids to activities, vacuum the house, do the laundry. Invite him or her out to a movie or for dinner or to play tennis, and so on.

Outings

68. Everybody has times during the week when they tend to feel most alone. Evenings—weekend evenings in particular—can be tough. **Make a standing date with me** to go to a movie or out for dinner, or invite me to join you in taking a fun weekly class.
69. I'm lonely. **Invite me to your house for lunch or dinner or coffee regularly.** The companionship, not gourmet food, is what matters the most.
70. Surprise me with a one-month **membership to an athletic club** to help me de-stress and "get out." (This gift becomes even more special if you join me.)
71. **Buy tickets** in advance to a play, symphony, or sporting event that we can enjoy together. This gives me something to anticipate.
72. Instead of lecturing my husband and me to "get out of the house and do something fun" after I had a miscarriage, some friends sent us dated **coupons for a dinner** at our favorite restaurant and **movie coupons.** That gift helped get us out of the house.
73. Invite me to **walk and talk** on a regular basis—great therapy for the mind, body, and soul.
74. When I was too weak to walk but still enjoyed getting out, my friends **took me for walks, to lunch, and shopping via a wheelchair.**

Special Spirit Lifters

75. **Be our dinner guests.** When I was critically ill and confined to my home, it was the highlight of our day when friends not only brought dinner, but also joined us for dinner and conversation. (The dinner-guest schedule was arranged by a caring friend and by my parish nurse.)

76. When I was very ill and in pain, sometimes the only thing that brought me comfort and peace was a **foot massage.** You don't have to know "how." Just start massaging. One caregiver said that she imagined waves of quiet, soothing peace flowing throughout my body. And that's just what I experienced.

77. A friend typed my **favorite Bible verses** in large print on her computer. I posted one verse in each room of my home, so that when I walked into a room I had something positive to read and think about. God's Word gives me hope and courage. Ask the person for a list of their favorite verses or use my favorites: Proverbs 3:5; Psalm 91:4; Psalm 115:1; Isaiah 41:10; Isaiah 49:15,16; Jeremiah 29:11-14.

78. A friend gave me a **daily devotion flip booklet** entitled *Never Alone: Comfort in Times of Need.* It gave me positive encouragement each day. There is a rich variety of these daily flip calendars available. Pick the one that most appeals to you and to the person's situation.

79. **Frequent visits** are treasured, but it is best to call me before you visit to arrange the best time.

80. **Encourage your spouse to come over to visit my husband.** How happy I am when I hear my husband laughing with a friend as they eat popcorn and "coach" a college or pro football game.

81. **Suggest books, support groups, organizations and therapists** who can help me with my problem, but don't try to solve it for me, and don't be hurt if I don't take your advice. I just want you to walk with me during my difficult time.

82. Offer to **link me up with someone who has gone through a similar crisis.** That person may be able to answer some of my questions and concerns.

83. **Watch a television program or a video with me.** This gives me the satisfaction of enjoying your company without the responsibility of entertaining you.

84. If you have been with me during a difficult time, please, before parting, **make a date to get together again.** It offers me another

planned time when I know someone will listen and care. It helps relieve the threat of desperation.

85. Children are so refreshing, honest, and real. **Encourage your children to care for others** by suggesting that they draw a picture, write a poem, learn a song, make up a skit, buy a little gift, and so on. When my eight-year-old son died, one of his friends came to my door with a present. It was a picture of a horse. I don't know why he chose that picture, but it must have been very special to him, and for twelve years it has been special to me. It still is displayed in my guest bedroom.

86. **Hug me often.** I need the physical touch as well as the affirmation!

87. I need to laugh. There is such healing in laughter. So **tell me a joke or tell me about something funny that happened to you,** or bring me a funny cartoon from the newspaper.

88. **"Think of ways to make me smile.** My friend Pat hired a clown to come to the hospital with bright colorful helium balloons. Half of them had 'Amy' on them. The other half said, 'I love you.' Those joyous balloons were a wonderful, blatant denial of the automatic doom and gloom associated with the diagnosis of cancer. They added a welcome contrast to the sterility of the hospital décor. I tied the balloons to the night stand where they could blow in the vent, a bright streamer of color" (Amy Harwell, *When Your Friend Gets Cancer,* p. 38).

89. Make me smile by giving me one of the following **"just for fun" gifts**: foam dart gun, "The Honeymooners" videotape (a la Jackie Gleason), "Lake Wobegon" cassette by Garrison Keillor, checkers, or a handheld electronic game.

90. **Give me a humorous book** to jog my innards. (Someone has said that one hundred good belly laughs are the cardiovascular equivalent of ten minutes of rowing.) Ask a librarian or the manager of your local bookstore for suggestions. Some of our suggestions are:
    - Bill Cosby's books: *Childhood, Love, Marriage,* and *Fatherhood.*
    - Patrick McManus's books: *Never Sniff a Gift Fish* and *The Grasshopper Trap* (especially for hikers/hunters/outdoors people).
    - Any book by Jim Unger or Erma Bombeck.
    - Cartoon books such as *Calvin and Hobbes* or *Dilbert.*

91. Bring me an **inspiring book or gift.** Consider what books have been helpful to you during a crisis or in everyday living. Three gifts that have been very meaningful to me are
    - Lynn Gordon's deck of cards called *52 Ways To Mend a Broken Heart.*
    - *Chicken Soup* books by Canfield and Hansen.
    - A subscription to *Guideposts* magazine (www.guideposts.org or write to Guideposts, Chad Dept., P.O. Box 856, Carmel, NY 10512-0856).
92. **Send me one note a week or call me once a week for a couple of months.** It's the friends who keep visiting, calling, and sending notes who give me hope for the future and courage to work toward it.
93. If you have been with me during a crisis, **follow up your visit with a note of reassurance** that you value me (especially when I have shared very angry, hurtful, painful things).
94. Give me a **tape or CD** that has been especially soothing or inspiring to you.
95. **Allow me to feel sad.** One of the most difficult problems of serious illness is that everyone wants to encourage the patient. However, sometimes having a good cry with a friend allows the tension to escape. You encourage me by letting me talk about my feelings.
96. **Read** my favorite psalm to me.
97. I have one friend who **encourages me to call her** when I feel sad or lonely or ready to give up, and by the time I finish dialing her number and hear her say, "Hello," the fear is gone.
98. Knowing that I needed the emotional support of my family who lived in another state, my friends gave me a generous **gift certificate that helped to pay my phone bill** for six months! What a thoughtful gift. Those phone calls were my life-line during the first six months of my crisis.
99. I don't remember what words people said to me during the first weeks after the death of my young son, but I do remember those who **held my hand, patted my shoulder, and hugged me.** Never underestimate the power of a touch.
100. **Suggest that we do something new** like have a facial or a massage or go to a hockey game or take an aerobic dance class.
101. **Call daily** to check on me, especially during a particularly hard time.

102. **Offer to call my church** to request prayers and/or visitation.
103. **Give me a list of people to pray for.** Praying for others does not take my pain away, but it does change my attitude toward it. By reminding myself that others are also suffering, I can better tolerate my situation.
104. **Suggest that we work on a service project** in the community. My problems seem minimized when I concentrate on another person's need, and I am energized by "reaching out" and helping someone else.
105. **Invite me to participate in projects** that can be done at home (stuffing envelopes, folding programs, cutting/gluing projects) for churches, schools, and charitable organizations.
106. Offer to **start a Bible or book study group** in my home. (An added touch would be if various members took turns coming early to tidy up the house and to make coffee.)
107. Be the kind of caregiver who **visits, calls, or sends a note or flowers** each year on the date when my loved one died. What a loving gift to know that someone else remembers too!
108. **Ask me what food I crave today.** One day I requested pizza, another a turtle sundae. Each made my day! (As an added bonus, my friend stayed and ate with me.)
109. Say, **"I love you. I care."**

Add your own ideas!

110.

111.

112.

113.

114.

115.

SECTION 4

Four Self-guiding Sessions for Small Groups

The following pages contain four session plans for small groups who want to improve their caregiving skills. The sessions are based on caregiving seminars taught by the authors of this handbook, Karen Mulder and Ginger Jurries.

Each session requires at least an hour to complete (leaders should keep an eye on the clock and have some idea of where the session can be trimmed, if necessary).

While small groups will need a leader to direct the discussion and activities, the sessions are addressed to the entire small group rather than only to the leader. This tends to give the sessions more of a "seminar" aspect and lessens the need for intensive preparation by group leaders. Some comments intended for use by leaders only are written in the margins.

Session guides follow each session plan. The guides contain readings and activities that are completed during the time the group meets.

Group members will need a copy of *The Compassionate Congregation* for reference during the sessions. The first three sessions focus on the three skills outlined in section 2 of the handbook: praying, listening, and respecting the grief process. The fourth session invites group members to "follow the model of the Good Samaritan."

Session 1
Go Light Your World

Session Goals
- to state the importance of being an effective caregiver
- to recall two ways of caring that we already know
- to say, "I can do that!" to three new ways of caring for another person
- to name the three basic guidelines for caregiving
- to choose one caring action to do this week

Connecting
1. Connecting with Scripture
Find Session Guide 1, "Why Be a Caregiver?" (p. 243). Take turns reading the biblical principles aloud.

Leader: While you may want to allow some time now for introductions of group members, be aware that throughout the session participants will be sharing information that will help them get to know each other better.

Leader: Please bring the following to this session:
- list of church members who need attention and care
- notecard, pen, and stamped envelope for each participant
- large white pillar candle, small candles for participants, matches
- optional: cassette or CD with song "Go Light Your World" by Kathy Troccoli (or substitute your own choice)

Leader: You may want to reinforce that we all experience losses, times of grief, low times. A spouse gets cancer, a neighbor is unemployed, a child is hospitalized, and a friend is depressed. As author Ginger Jurries states (p. 9), "People are in need of our comfort and thoughtful care. The problem is that too often our hearts say *go* but our heads say *no*. We may have a tendency to avoid these situations because we don't know what to say or do, or we may blunder through a situation, *hoping* that we say and do the right thing."

2. Connecting with Ourselves

Wherever you can find room on Session Guide 1, jot down your reasons for taking this class. What do you hope to get out of it?

Go around the circle and briefly share your response.

3. Connecting with God

If you are willing, name a prayer concern you have about someone who is going through a difficult time. If you'd rather not share, just say, "Remembering someone." For reasons of privacy, you may prefer to use the person's initials rather than reveal his or her name.

Exploring

1. Encouragement

Each of us has just named someone who might benefit from our thoughtful care. Perhaps the task of caring for that wounded person seems too big, and you feel too small and too inadequate. You may want to take a moment to read Karen Mulder's story of procrastination (pp. 8-9). Note her conclusion: "God takes each sincere, small, and clumsy gesture of compassion and turns it into something big, bright, and beautiful." In other words, *little,* caring gestures (our work) become *big, important* gestures (God's work).

Consider how important a little gesture can be:

There are few words that strike terror in the heart like the word cancer. *It is such a silent, insidious disease. A survivor usually wonders when and where it will strike next. At age 53, I was diagnosed with colon cancer. I was afraid, anxious, and angry. Why had this happened to me?*

In the midst of my fear and trembling came God's armor-bearers. They bathed me in prayer and surrounded me with loving words through cards and phone calls.

After abdominal surgery, I returned home and was not allowed to drive for six weeks. Knowing how confining that would be for me, my friends made sure I was "out and about" every day of those six weeks.

Often when a person has a long-term illness, cards and phone calls become less frequent as time passes. However, one friend has continued to remember me with a postcard every day (322 cards so far!). The postcard has an encouraging word, a humorous saying, or words of wisdom that challenge me and give me hope. I have been deeply touched by such long-term care.

—Pat (for the rest of Pat's story, see pp. 56-58)

The authors of this handbook cannot say enough about the value of handwritten notes. One mother keeps a scrapbook of all the notes that were sent to her after her son's suicide. She reads them repeatedly. Other wounded people have shared the value of notes.

2. Activity: Writing a Note

Think of someone in your family, in your church, at your workplace, in your community who is going through a difficult time. Maybe it is the person you mentioned earlier when we shared our prayer concerns. Please take ten minutes right now to write this person a note. (For some help, check out "Words That Help" in "109+ Ways to Say, 'I Care'" (pp. 223-234).

> **Leader:** Supply participants with note-cards and stamped envelopes. You may also want to provide a list of church members who would value a note. If group members need more time to finish their notes, encourage them to do so at home today.

3. Reflection: What Helped You?

In Luke 13:10-13 a woman comes to see Jesus. Luke says she was "crippled by a spirit for eighteen years . . . bent over and could not straighten up at all." Take a moment to think of a time when you may have felt like this woman. (This may be an emotional, mental, physical, or spiritual low time or struggle.)

What did someone say or do which helped you during that difficult time?

Share your recollections and name something someone said or did that encouraged you.

4. Things I Can Do

In your handbooks, turn to "109+ Ways to Say, 'I Care'" on pages 223-234.

Once again think of someone who needs your attention and care. With that person in mind, start reading through "109+ Ways to Say, 'I Care.'"

When you come across an idea that jumps off the page and you think, "I can do that," highlight that suggestion. Take about five minutes to do this.

Share some of your discoveries about actions you feel able to do.

Responding

1. First Guideline: Pray

The authors state three basic guidelines that can be applied to any crisis: pray, listen well, and respect the grief process. In the remainder of this session, we'll look at the first guideline: pray.

Leader: With this section you may begin to feel pinched for time. Be alert to questions or activities you can omit or ask participants to do on their own after your session.

Questions

☞ What are some thoughts/feelings that come to mind when you think about praying with someone?

☞ Why do you think so many people are intimidated by praying with someone?

☞ What can we do to become more comfortable when praying for others?

☞ Why do you think it is so important to pray for each other? How do you feel when someone prays for you? (See James 5:16.)

Pray Before Your Visit

Why do you think it is important to pray before you go to visit a friend? Think about this story:

A man named Bob went to visit a friend in the hospital. Before he entered his friend's room he prayed that God would give him wisdom about Allen's needs.

God revealed to him that Allen needed prayers for comfort and not for healing. When Bob prayed with Allen for comfort and peace, Allen thanked him for not praying for his healing as other friends had done. He acknowledged that he had lived a full life and was truly ready to die and be transported to glory.

How often we think that we know what a person needs! It's important to take time to listen to God and find out what those whom we are caring for really need.

Here is one example of a "before" prayer:

Dear God. I want to be your servant, to speak your words of comfort, to demonstrate your unconditional love to [name]. Please show me how to do that. If there is something I should know about this situation, help me discover it. If there is a verse or word of encouragement that I should speak, bring it to my mind. Relieve my fears and doubts. Help me to remember that I do not go alone, that the supreme Comforter, your Holy Spirit, goes with me. Amen.

> **Leader:** Ask a group member to read this prayer aloud.

Pray During Your Visit

It is vitally important to be sensitive to the other person's situation. Always ask:

- if it is all right to pray with your friend. (Don't assume that they feel comfortable with prayer.)
- how you can *best* pray for your friend.
- if it is all right to hold your friend's hands or place your hand on his or her arm.

Remember to:

- say the person's name in your prayer.
- be concise; don't ramble.

Pray After Your Visit

- Assure the person that you will continue to pray for him or her, and then remember to do so.
- Send a follow-up note or make a call within a few days to see how the person is doing.

Reflect on this:

I do not believe we can ever say prayer is wasted; some good always comes of it. Although our prayers may not change a situation and give us the miracle we want, prayer changes us. Through prayer, we are no longer facing our fears and pain alone; God is there beside us, renewing our spirit, restoring our soul, and helping us carry the burden when it becomes too heavy for us to bear.

—Ron Delbene, *Into the Light* (Nashville: The Upper Room, 1988), p. 82

2. Session Guides 2 and 3

Leader: We are clearly into "optional" territory with Session Guides 2 and 3. It's OK to have participants use these sheets at home.

As time permits, look at Session Guides 2 ("Alternate Ways of Praying," p. 244) and 3 ("Pencil and Paper Prayer," pp. 245-246).

At home or in your session, read the comments about pencil prayer. Then use a sheet of paper to cover the remarks about Psalm 23 in the margin. Write your own thoughts about the prayer.

If time allows, pair up and pray for a specific concern each partner has.

3. Caring Action

Name (silently or aloud) one caring action you will do this week.

4. Go Light Your World

Form a circle. Light a large white candle and place it in the center of the circle. The large white candle represents the light that Jesus, the Light of the World, sheds in our world and our lives.

Listen to the song "Go Light Your World" by Kathy Troccoli. (If the song isn't available, have someone read John 1:1-5 and Matthew 5:14-16 or find a substitute song to play). Each person then lights his or her candle from the Jesus candle, and rejoins the circle.

Conclude by saying in unison two or three times, "Go light your world."

SESSION 1
Session Guide 1
Why Be a Caregiver?

God wants us to:

Be devoted to one another. (Romans 12:10)
Give preference to one another. (Romans 12:10)
Pursue the things that build each other up. (Romans 14:19)
Accept one another. (Romans 15:7)
Care for one another. (1 Corinthians 12:25)
Encourage and comfort others. (1 Corinthians 14:3)
Serve one another. (Galatians 5:13)
Carry each other's burdens. (Galatians 6:2)
Show forbearance (patience) to one another. (Ephesians 4:1-2)
Be kind to one another. (Ephesians 4:32)
Submit to one another. (Ephesians 5:18-21)
Bear with each other and forgive each other. (Colossians 3:12-13)
Increase and abound in love for one another. (1 Thessalonians 3:12)
Comfort one another. (1 Thessalonians 3:12)
Encourage one another. (Hebrews 3:13)
Stimulate one another to love and good works. (Hebrews 10:23-25)
Pray for one another. (James 5:16)
Be hospitable to one another. (1 Peter 4:9)
Clothe ourselves with humility toward one another. (1 Peter 5:5)
Greet one another with a kiss of love. (1 Peter 5:5)
Comfort one another. (2 Corinthians 1:4)
Love one another. (John 15:12; Romans 13:8; 1 Peter 1:22; 1 John 3:11, 23;
    4:7, 11, 12; 2 John 5)

SESSION 1
Session Guide 2
Alternate Ways of Praying

- ⟲ **Phone prayer:** Praying for a person over the phone, as he or she listens.
- ⟲ Short **"arrow"** prayers: "God, please give Susan strength as she goes through this trying time." "Lord, Andy is having a hard time deciding on a new job. Please give him direction."
- ⟲ **Pencil and Paper Prayer:** Together with the person you're caring for, read a prayer of your choosing. Then underline and make notations next to each part that is meaningful (see Session Guide 3 for an example).
- ⟲ **Memorized prayer** of your choice.
- ⟲ **Written prayer**, sent through mail or e-mail.
- ⟲ **Inner healing prayer:** The person receiving care says what he or she needs in order to resolve issues with God or with others. The caregiver then leads in prayer, asking God to meet these needs.
- ⟲ **Listening prayer:** With pencil and paper in hand, listen to God's guidance on a particular issue, write what comes to mind, then thank God for sharing this wisdom.

- ⟲

- ⟲

Session Guide 3
Pencil and Paper Prayer

Pencil and paper prayer is a way to personalize another person's written prayer so that the prayer becomes an expression of your heart and mind. Here's how it works:

- ☙ Each person is given a copy of the chosen prayer.
- ☙ One person slowly and carefully reads the prayer aloud.
- ☙ Each person rereads the prayer silently and writes responses to parts of the prayer that are especially meaningful to them.

The following is an example of this, using Psalm 23.

Psalm 23 For Busy People
by Toki Miyashina

The Lord is my pacesetter, I shall not rush;
he makes me stop and rest for quiet intervals,

> I wish he were!

he provides me with images of stillness,
which restore my serenity.

> Quiet myself—listen to God.

He leads me in ways of efficiency,
through calmness of mind;
and his guidance is peace.

> Lord, teach me to relax and rely on you for guidance.

I can sense you here
with me, Lord.

Even though I have a great many things to accomplish
each day
I will not fret, for his presence is here.

This is exactly what
I need!

His timelessness, his all-importance will keep me
in balance.

He prepares refreshment and renewal
in the midst of activity,
by anointing my mind with his oils of tranquility;
my cup of joyous energy overflows.

How can I get more
of this?

I wonder what
this means?

Surely harmony and effectiveness shall be
the fruits of my hours
and I shall walk in the pace of my Lord,
and dwell in his house forever.

Session 2
Listen Empathetically

Session Goals

⊛ to sense and verbalize the importance of listening in the caregiving process
⊛ to describe four characteristics of empathetic listening
⊛ to commit to practicing one listening technique this week

> **Leader:** Please bring the following to this session:
> ⊛ newsprint; marker
> ⊛ optional: blank sheets of paper

Connecting

1. Connecting with God

As you did last time, please name individuals who are in need of care or attention (they may be from your family, church, community, work, and so on). After listing persons and describing their situations, go around the circle and take turns praying for the persons you've named.

> **Leader:** It may be helpful to list these prayer concerns on a sheet of newsprint, so that the group can refer to them during prayer time and later in the session.

After your prayer time, please choose for yourself one person from among those you prayed for. During the remainder of today's session, listen for one way that might help you care for that particular person.

2. Connecting with Each Other
At the end of our first session, you were invited to name one caring action you would attempt to do during the next week. If you had opportunity to follow through on this, please take a moment to share your caregiving experiences of the previous week.

3. Connecting with Today's Focus: Listening Empathetically

Leader: You may want to read this story to the group. If so, practice reading it a time or two prior to today's session.

Today's session focuses on the second caregiving skill: listening. To introduce this skill, listen to Gregory Richards's description of serving as a chaplain to terminally ill children in a New York City hospital:

One of the first patients I met was a two-year-old attended by his father. The little boy was suffering the advanced stages of his fatal disease. His father, who had given up every other obligation to be with his son constantly, suffered with him.

The father's rage knew no bounds. A Christian convert, he had been victimized by a television preacher who, in reply to his cry for help, sent him a form letter asking for more "seed offerings" to work a divine miracle. The father was angry with God. Since I was God's nearest representative, the anguished parent directed his wrath at me.

Every day I would literally drag myself back to that sad, sad room to face the drawn, pixie-like face of the tiny patient and the bottomless cistern of emotion of his tortured father. For most of each visit, the father would rail at me. One day he pulled back the sheet from his son's distended stomach covered with sores and screamed: "I'd like to have your God here right now! I'd push his nose into the sores on my son's stomach. Where is your God?"

The father didn't want answers to his extended, rhetorical questions. He needed to release pent-up emotions, to lance the infected wound of his spirit, to let the poison of his anger out so healing could begin. The only way I could help him was by soaking up his hurts.

No matter how long I listened, though, no matter how much I soaked up his hurt, nothing seemed to help. The father's rage did not diminish, and I felt helpless and useless. Yet I continued to come. I continued to stand at the bed of this helpless child. I continued to listen *to his father's angry words.*

As the end of my hospital assignment neared, the day came for me to say good-bye to the suffering father and son. I expected to be relieved to go, and I thought the angry father would be glad to see me gone. Instead, the father burst into tears, saying to his weak little one what a nice man I was, how much I'd meant to them, how they would miss me.

Some months later I learned the child died. I was told that the father's grief, while understandably severe, was not volatile. He had apparently gotten out his worst anger in anticipation of his son's death.

In this terrible tragedy, all I could do was be there and listen.

—M. Gregory Richards, *When Someone You Know Is Hurting.* Copyright © 1993 by M. Gregory Richards. Used by permission of Zondervan.

Reflect on this story for a moment, then share your responses.

Exploring

1. Session Guide 4: "Please Just Listen"

Like the story we just read, the poem "Please Just Listen" (Session Guide 4, pp. 243-254) emphasizes the importance of empathetic listening. Please read the poem silently, jotting down key thoughts or suggestions you want to remember.

Now go back and take turns reading each verse aloud. Share your (written) thoughts on that verse with the group.

Leader: You can expand on the comments of the group by using the notes with the poem found on pages 210-211 in the handbook. You may want to refer the entire group to these pages as you talk about the poem.

2. Session Guide 5: "Rescuing vs. Listening Empathetically"

Leader: If time permits, try this more challenging alternative: Have group members cover the right column with a sheet of paper. Read the rescuing statement and then discuss some possible responses that show empathetic listening. Compare your responses with those given in the session guide.

As the poem suggests, we often try to "fix" the situation and "rescue" the person. We do this by giving advice, by offering quick solutions, and by citing clichés and Bible verses.

Session Guide 5 (pp. 255-256) contrasts "rescuing" statements with statements that show empathetic listening. Take turns reading aloud the rescuing statements and the contrasting empathetic listening statements.

3. Session Guide 6: "Caring Response Formula"

Leader: To save time have group members pair off, and assign each pair to one or two of the six items on the session guide. Then review responses.

One helpful way of learning to listen empathetically is to use the "formula" response found in Session Guide 6 (pp. 257-258). The idea is to reflect a person's feelings back to him or her in a way that shows you are listening and you care. Of course, you should feel free to vary the words of the "formula" when you use this approach in real situations.

Try a few of the examples on Session Guide 6 and share your responses with the group.

4. Dramatization

Have two persons from the group dramatize the scene between Sally and Fran from page 208 of the book. Discuss with questions like these:

ⓥ Imagine that you are Sally. What are your thoughts and feelings as Fran walks away from you?

ⓥ How could you improve this care-giving scene?

Leader: If no one in the group wants to show off his or her acting skills, just read the examples aloud and discuss as indicated above.

Now have two other group members dramatize the scene between Sally and Grace on pages 208-209. Discuss this question:

ⓥ Imagine once more that you are Sally. What are your thoughts and feelings as Grace drives off?

5. Summary: An Empathetic Listener

An empathetic listener is one who

⊛ gets involved.

⊛ gives full attention to the one who is hurting.

⊛ enters into that person's feelings and suffers with the person.

⊛ listens more than talks.

⊛ speaks primarily to help the sufferer clarify his or her situation and feelings

⊛ does not interject his or her own problems or situations.

> **Leader:** Be sure to include this important definition in your session. Group members may want to react to it or add their own ideas.

Responding

1. Story

In his book *The Last Thing We Talk About* Joseph Bayly shares his honest feelings about the death of one of his children (the family eventually lost three of their children):

> **Leader:** Ask someone in your group to read this powerful example aloud, slowly and with feeling.

I was sitting, torn by grief. Someone came and talked to me of God's dealings, of why it happened, of hope beyond the grave. He talked constantly. He said things I knew were true. I was unmoved, except to wish he'd go away. He finally did.

Another came and sat beside me. He didn't talk. He didn't ask me leading questions. He just sat beside me for an hour and more, listened when I said something, answered briefly, prayed simply, left. I was moved. I was comforted. I hated to see him go.

2. Sharing

Please share one listening technique you will attempt to practice this week.

3. Closing Prayer

Given today's topic of listening, it's appropriate to close with a time of silence before God. Ask someone in your group to say aloud these words from Psalm 37:7, reading one line at a time and pausing for a moment between lines for reflection (from Don Postema, *Catch Your Breath: God's Invitation to Sabbath Rest,* CRC Publications, 1997):

> *Be still before the LORD and wait patiently for him.*
> *Be still before the LORD and wait patiently.*
> *Be still before the LORD and wait.*
> *Be still before the LORD.*
> *Be still.*
> *Be.*

SESSION 2
Session Guide 4
Please Just Listen

When I ask you to listen to me   **Notes**
and you start giving advice,
you have not done what I asked
nor heard what I need.

When I ask you to listen to me
and you begin to tell me why
I shouldn't feel that way,
you are trampling on my feelings.

When I ask you to listen to me
and you feel you have to do something
to solve my problems,
you have failed me—
strange as that may seem.

When you do something for me
that I can and need to do for myself
you contribute to my
seeming fearful and weak.

So please listen and just hear me.
And if you want to talk
let's plan for your turn,
and I promise I'll listen to you.

—Anonymous

Notes

SESSION 2
Session Guide 5
Rescuing vs. Listening Empathetically

Rescuing
"Everything will be just fine."

"I understand. I have gone through the same thing."

"God must have a good reason for this trial."

"Don't you think you should be finished grieving by now?"

"Be assured that God is in control."

"Be strong/don't cry."

"How wonderful, she's out of her misery and is with the Lord."

Listening Empathetically
"It must be unsettling not to know."

"I can't imagine how much you hurt."

"God's heart must be broken to see you in so much pain."

"Grief is a very long, painful process."

"It must seem like God has turned his back."

"The best thing you can do is cry/talk."

"How lonely you must be with Jane gone."

"Good riddance! You were too good for him anyway!"

"I'm so sorry! You must feel like you've been torn in two!"

"Tomorrow will be a brighter day."

"The world must look very gray."

"You've got to pull yourself together!"

"You must be very upset. Let's go to lunch so you can talk."

Session Guide 6
Caring Response Formula

The "formula" response: "You feel [name the feeling] because [name the reason]."

1. He says to you, "Since I lost that weight, I feel like a million dollars. It's great!"

   He is feeling _____.

   You say to him, using the formula style: "You feel_____
   because_____."

2. She says to you, "I know she was only a dog, but she was like a part of the family. Maybe that's silly, but just the same, I miss her. Somehow, she was a lot more than just a pet."

   She is feeling _____.

   You say to her, using the formula style: "You feel_____
   because_____."

3. He says to you, "Whenever you work as hard as I worked toward a goal and then something like this happens, it's enough to make you want to give up."

   He is feeling _____.

   You say to him, using the formula style: "You feel_____
   because_____"

4. She says to you, "I don't have any idea which would be best—there are so many advantages and disadvantages both ways. The more I think about it, the more things I think of, and they're all important things to consider."

   She is feeling _____.

   You say to her, using the formula style: "You feel_____
   because_____"

5. He says to you, "My job is OK for right now, but things keep changing, so who knows? Maybe I'll get replaced by a machine. And at my age, it's pretty hard to change vocations!"

   He is feeling _____.

   You say to him, using the formula style: "You feel_____
   because_____"

6. She says to you, "How can I ever face them again? They will be laughing about my mistake for years!"

   She is feeling _____.

   You say to her, using the formula style: "You feel_____
   because_____"

Session 3
Respect the Grief Process

Session Goals

☙ to realize that grieving is a process and takes time
☙ to name the emotions that a grieving person often experiences
☙ to describe at least two ways a caregiver can help a person through the grief process

Leader: Prior to today's session study the grief process (see pp. 214-217) so you can talk about it without being tied to reading information from the book. Two books that would add a lot to your understanding of the grief process are *Good Grief* by Granger Westberg (Minneapolis: Augsburg Fortress Publishers, 1962) and *Final Gifts* by Maggie Callanan and Patricia Kelley (New York: Bantam Books, 1992).

Leader: Please bring the following to this session:
☙ a notecard for each person
☙ ten large cards or sheets of paper, each card with the name of one of the ten stages of the grief process (shock, denial, etc.); number the cards and display them around the room
☙ a small starfish (real or cut from construction paper) for each participant
☙ optional: a large starfish to display as you read the story on pages 10-11
☙ optional: invite a grief counselor or hospice nurse to visit the group and talk about the grief process, perhaps in an interview style

Connecting

1. Connecting with Each Other

So far we've talked about two caregiving guidelines: praying and listening empathetically. Talk about how you've used (or attempted to use) these tools in your own caregiving situations during the past week or in previous caregiving situations.

Leader: When you sense that each person has written a name on a notecard, conclude with a short prayer, asking God to give each person in your group (by name) the strength to care for the person whose name he or she has written.

2. Connecting with God

Have someone from the group read the poem "Why?" on page 5 of this handbook. Take a moment to reflect on the poem after it is read.

For your opening prayer, each person should silently ask God to bring to mind the name of a person who needs your care this coming week. Listen for God's response, then write the person's name on a notecard.

Leader: Don't go into a detailed discussion of the grief process at this point. Simply encourage group members to speak out of their own experiences with grief.

3. Connecting with Today's Focus: Respecting the Grief Process

Read the short account on page 212 of the behavior shown by Mary's neighbor, whose husband was killed in an automobile accident. Note her symptoms (crying all the time, looks awful, and so on) and discuss questions like these with the group:

- Are these symptoms true of persons you've encountered who are going through grief of some kind?

- If you have endured a tragedy of some sort, what other feelings/reactions have you experienced?

- Why is it important for caregivers to know about the grief process?

Leader: You may want to refer to the two tasks of the grieving person, as outlined by Judy Tatelbaum on page 213. Stress especially the importance of time in the healing process. Note the purposes of understanding the grief process, as listed on page 213. How do these compare to what the group suggested?

Exploring

1. Defining Grief

Here is a definition of grief from page 213 of the handbook: "Grief is the normal and natural process by which a person makes a healthy adjustment to any significant loss in his or her life. Any significant loss (the death of a loved one, the loss of a job, a broken marriage, deterioration of health, a shattered dream, etc.) triggers the process."

ⓔ How do you react to this definition? Do any parts of it seem to "pop out" at you? Anything you'd like to change or add?

2. The Grief Process

The heart of today's session is the grief process as outlined by Granger E. Westberg in his classic book on this topic, *Good Grief* (Minneapolis: Augsburg Fortress Publishers, 1962). The ten responses to the grief process as he describes them are:

1. shock, numbness
2. denial
3. depression
4. physical distress
5. panic/fear
6. guilt
7. anger and resentment
8. resists returning to normal life
9. gradually hope comes through
10. struggles to affirm reality

See the chart on pages 214-217 for details on each stage. As a group, walk through the ten stages, talking about the various experiences and emotions involved at each level. Please add your own insights and experiences (and critique!) as you go along.

3. One Person's Grieving Process

Have a member of the group read Barb Pekich's story (pp. 219-222) aloud. As the story is read, note the attempts (in the margins) to relate Barb's experience to the various stages of the grief process. After the reading, talk about questions like these:

Leader: We suggest you use the ten cards or signs that you've posted around the room as an organizer for your discussion. Rather than lead the entire discussion yourself, we suggest that you ask group members to work in pairs, with each pair presenting information on one or two of the stages. Have presenters use the chart on pages 214-217 for basic information but also encourage them to use their own experiences and insights. As they give their presentations, have them stand by the card that describes the responses to grief that they're presenting. Invite group participation after each presentation.

⊛ What does Barb's experience illustrate about the grieving process? What insights/comments do you have to share with the group?

⊛ What's your impression of the grieving process (from Barb's story and your own experience): (a) it's a clear and structured process, quite easy to trace? (b) it's a complex and messy process, with definite stages that are not always easy? (c) other? Explain.

⊛ Having applied the grief process to a specific case, to what extent do you think knowing about the process is helpful for caregivers?

Responding

1. Starfish Story

Leader: Distribute a small starfish (real or paper) to each person. If you can find an actual, large starfish, display it as you or someone else reads or tells the starfish story.

Have someone from your group read (or tell) the story about the man on the beach throwing starfish back into the sea on pages 10-11 of this handbook.

2. Gesture of Caring

At the beginning of this session you were invited to write somone's name on a notecard, someone you know who is in need of attention and care. Please look at that notecard now. Ask yourself:

⊛ Do I know this person well enough to know if he or she is going through the "grief process" as we learned about it today? If so, about where in the grief process would I say this person is?

⊛ What can I do this week to show this person that I care and to help him or her through the grief process?

3. Closing Prayer

You may want to use the familiar prayer of St. Francis of Assisi to close the session (have someone read the prayer, or say it in unison):

Lord, make me in instrument of thy peace.
Where there is hatred, let me sow love;
Where there is injury, pardon;

Where there is doubt, faith;
Where there is despair, hope;
Where there is darkness, light;
Where there is sadness, joy.
O Divine Master, grant that I may not so much seek
To be consoled, as to console;
To be understood, as to understand;
To be loved as to love.
For it is in giving that we receive;
It is in pardoning that we are pardoned;
It is in dying that we awaken to eternal life.
Amen.

Leader: Holding the large starfish, dismiss the group by saying something like this: "Go and make a difference to one person. This week care for someone who is hurting."

Session 4
Follow the
Good Samaritan Model

Session Goals

- ☙ to describe at least two caregiving characteristics of the Good Samaritan
- ☙ to evaluate our own caregiving efforts in the light of the parable
- ☙ to know how to find help in this handbook for specific caregiving situations
- ☙ to share something meaningful we've learned about caregiving during the past four weeks
- ☙ to commit to take whatever steps are necessary to provide care when given the opportunity to do so

Connecting

1. Connecting with Each Other

We ended our last session by thinking about where a specific person we know might be in the grief process and how we could show this person that we care or help him or her through the grief process. Share if you were able to

> **Leader:** Please bring the following to this session:
> - ☙ additional names of persons in your church family who might be in need of care
> - ☙ newsprint and marker
> - ☙ notecards
> - ☙ large white pillar candle, small candles for participants, matches
> - ☙ optional: cassette or CD with song "Go Light Your World" by Kathy Troccoli

> **Leader:** Make this a time of mutual encouragement, even if (especially if) people weren't able to follow up on the suggested homework. Recognize that it isn't always possible to tie caregiving down to weekly schedules.

do either of these for the hurting person you listed on the notecard last week.

2. Connecting with God

Leader: Before today's session, you might do a quick check with your pastor or elder/deacon to see if any additional persons in your church family are in need of care.

On a sheet of newsprint, list the names (or initials, if that's necessary for privacy) of the persons group members are helping or who are in need of help. These can be individuals listed on the notecards during session 3 or other individuals in your congregation or community. Please feel free to add new names to your list.

When your list is complete, have someone read a name (or initials) from the list. After each, say in unison:

"Come, Lord Jesus, and touch [name] with your healing touch. Help us to find ways to care for this child of yours."

3. Connecting with Today's Session Focus: The Good Samaritan Model

Leader: The next step will help the group reflect on the insights about caregiving that others have found in this parable, so there's no need to spend much time now going into details. It's important, though, that the group first grapple with the parable on their own, then look at what others have to say. An *optional* approach, should you want to save time, is to omit the session guide in the next step and just focus on insights from your group. If you take this route, be sure to read the session guide as background for yourself.

Today we will be focusing on what the parable of the Good Samaritan teaches us about caregiving. Take a moment now to silently reflect on one individual you are helping or would like to help, someone who is "wounded" alongside a road you travel (this can be the same person you mentioned in previous step). Picture that person in your mind. What might he or she be thinking and feeling right now?

Exploring

1. Reading the Parable

Have someone in the group read aloud the parable of the Good Samaritan (Luke 10:25-37). Others in the group may follow along in their Bibles.

After the reading, take a moment to share some insights about caregiving that you find in this familiar parable.

2. Session Guide 7: "Follow the Good Samaritan Model"

Session Guide 7 (pp. 269-275) lists four insights for caregivers who wish to follow the model set by the Samaritan in Jesus' parable. Your group may have already listed these insights on your own, but take time now to read through the session guide, pausing after each of the four sections to share and reflect.

3. Using the Handbook as a Reference

Use a notecard to:

- name a person you know who is hurting, in need of care of some kind (it can be the same person you listed at the beginning of the session).
- name the crisis he or she is facing (death, divorce, unemployment, and so on).
- jot down the page number in the handbook that describes this specific situation. (Use the table of contents to find the situation/crisis you're looking for; if the specific crisis is not included, select a similar one.)
- jot down one or two insights you learn from the handbook about caring for persons in that situation.

After completing the above, take a moment to share an insight or two with the group.

> **Leader:** Have group members take turns reading the various sections aloud. You will notice that the first "Share and Reflect" question is intended for group discussion or sharing; the second is for private reflection. At the end of the session guide is a prayer that you or someone else can read aloud (or read it with the group, in unison).

> **Leader:** If your group is large, ask participants to share an insight in groups of three or four persons each. Do the same for the first activity of the Responding step.
>
> If you know that your group is familiar with the reference feature of the handbook, you may want to omit this step.

Responding

1. Optional: What's Been Helpful?

If time permits, take a moment to think of one thing that you've learned about caregiving (during these sessions) that's been helpful or meaningful to you.

2. What's Next?

You've had time today to reflect a bit on the Good Samaritan model of caregiving and your own readiness to begin practicing that model. In previous sessions you've had an opportunity to look at some basic caregiving skills. In view of all that, jot down (on the back side of the notecard or

Leader: You may want to encourage group members to pair off with someone who will serve as an "encouragement partner" with them on their caregiving commitments. Partners can agree, if they wish, to get together or phone each other on a regular basis for mutual encouragement in their caregiving endeavors and commitments.

right on these pages) what you are willing to commit to do in the weeks and months ahead for a person in need of care. If there's no one right now for whom you could provide care of some kind, please jot down some things that you will be aware of as you look for persons in need of your care. Share your statements with at least one other person from the group.

3. Go Light Your World

We suggest you end this session as you (may have) ended session 1. Form a circle. Light a large white candle and place it in the center of the circle. The large white candle represents the light that Jesus, the Light of the World, sheds in our world and our lives.

Listen to the song "Go Light Your World" by Kathy Troccoli (if the song isn't available, have someone read John 1:1-5 and Matthew 5:14-16 or find a substitute song to play). Each person then lights his or her candle from the Jesus candle and rejoins the circle.

Conclude by saying in unison two or three times, "Go light your world."

SESSION 4
Session Guide 7
Follow the
Good Samaritan Model

Be Inconvenienced

The Good Samaritan may well have been on a business trip. No doubt he had definite plans for the day—he knew how many miles he wanted to travel and where he wanted to be at the end of the day. Stopping to help a wounded man by the side of the road would mean setting aside his schedule and his plans for the day. Fortunately, the Samaritan had 20/20 peripheral vision and could see the needs of those along his path. He saw the wounded man. He stopped. He got involved. He was willing to be inconvenienced and made caregiving a priority.

If we are going to care for one another, we also must be willing to be inconvenienced, to change our plans, to tear up the day's urgent "to do" list, to choose to do the really important thing.

Here's a contemporary example of being "inconvenienced" for the sake of helping another:

Twenty-two years ago, on Mother's Day, my twelve-year-old son had a bio-logical accident in church school and refused to go into the sanctuary for worship. So we left him in one of the classrooms with some books. After worship we went to pick him up, but he was nowhere to be found. We searched all the church spaces, but he was not there.

When I remember this difficult time, one person comes into my mind: Judy dropped all her plans for the day and came home with me. Once my

son was reported "missing," there wasn't much to do but wait. I don't
remember if we talked or what she did or what I did. All I remember was
the wonderful gift of her caring presence. She stayed all day. She stayed
until my son was found.

—Jan Smith

Share and Reflect

⊛ Share with the group a time when someone was "inconvenienced" to
give you a helping hand or to be with you through a difficult time.

⊛ For personal reflection: How would you rate your personal readiness
to be inconvenienced if someone needs your care? (Let "5" be "I'm willing and ready" and "1" be "This is nearly impossible for me to do!")

Take a Risk

It was risky business for this Good Samaritan to stop and help the wounded man. This particular road was known for its dangers. Obviously, what
happened to the man in the ditch could happen to the rescuer. Maybe the
person in the ditch was only pretending to be seriously wounded and
would attack the good person who stopped to help him. Maybe the man
in the ditch had some terrible disease! Stopping to help one who is hurt
and suffering is often risky business. Caregivers, like the Good
Samaritan, must take risks.

The following is a story about some high school kids who were willing
to take a risk.

It was to be my last day with the students in the alternative high school.
My retirement after many, many years of being a high school counselor
had been announced and became official at the end of the school day. For
some time I had heard the rumors of a "surprise" retirement party to be
given by the students. I was prepared for a perfunctory gathering engi-
neered by the teachers and for the somewhat reluctant participation by
the students. I was prepared for punch and cookies that always mark such
occasions. I was totally unprepared for what really happened.

There is something you must know about these alternative high school
students. They were in this school because they were either ordered to

school by the juvenile court system, had dropped out of traditional high school, or were pregnant or parenting teens. These kids had been hurt and had become committed experts at hiding their vulnerable selves to avoid further hurt. They had years of experience at hiding—behind leather jackets, gang colors, postures of indifference, or weird hairstyles. They entered rooms and fled to the perimeters, leaning against walls always as if to flee if pushed too close to exposure.

The time came. I was called to the large classroom for the "surprise" party. As I entered the room I saw all 57 students standing single file around three sides of the room. After I expressed my "surprise," one student stumbled to the center of the room to announce, "You're supposed to go around the room and hug everyone, because that is what you do at retirement parties." (Where had they gleaned this bit of information?) I looked at the students around the room to see if there was really any agreement to this "unthinkable" activity. There were some hesitant affirmative nods to my questioning looks.

So I began going down the long line of students. There were 57 hugs from these kids who were willing to come out from behind where they had been hiding—57 hugs from kids taking the ultimate risk of showing their extremely vulnerable selves, many for the very first time. One by one they hugged me and we both cried and laughed as they told me goodbye.

What a huge risk those kids took! I learned in those moments that we have to risk showing our vulnerability if we really care for others. I didn't have a single doubt they really cared for me. I will always remember being held in those moments of care, being surrounded by those 57 kids with their leather jackets, gang colors, postures of indifference, and weird hairstyles who cared enough for me to take that risk!

—Bette Williams

Share and Reflect

☙ Share an example of a time when someone took a risk to show they cared for you.

﹇ For personal reflection: How would you rate your readiness to take a risk if necessary to care for someone else? (Let "5" be "I'm ready for risks!" and "1" be "Risks are too risky for me!")

Anticipate Needs

The Good Samaritan anticipated the needs of a suffering man and took care of those needs. He bandaged his wounds, and, knowing that the man needed a safe place in which to recover, he put the wounded man on his own donkey and took him to an inn. The next day, again anticipating his needs, the Good Samaritan gave two silver coins to the innkeeper and said, "Look after him, and when I return I will reimburse you for any extra expense you may have."

When asked, "What can I do to help you?" most people are hesitant. "Oh, nothing, really," they say. "I'm doing just fine." (Perhaps they aren't sure themselves, can't make a decision, don't want to inconvenience you, or are simply shy.) So we need to make an educated guess about what a person's needs might be. It is helpful to imagine oneself in the person's shoes and then ask, "What kind of help and caring would I need and appreciate if I were in her or his situation?" Then, just do it!

Some contemporary examples of anticipating needs:

﹇ Lynn waited all night for news of her boyfriend, Craig, who was the pilot of a missing emergency medical helicopter. When search teams found the wreckage and Lynn's worst fears were confirmed, she headed to the telephone and called her best friend, Susy. "Do you want me to come?" Susy asked.

Lynn said, "I told her, it's not necessary—I'll be okay. Susy lived so far away; I didn't want to inconvenience her. I didn't realize how desperately I would need her when the shock wore off. Thank God she came.

"I also told my friend, Deb, to go on home after the helicopter was reported missing. She had worked a long shift and I hated to make her stay—I knew it could be a long, long time. But she stayed all night. She was with me in the morning when they told me they found the bodies. She cried with me and held me. I'll never forget that."

—Dee Brestin, *The Friendships of Women*
(Colorado Springs, CO: Chariot Victor Publishing, 1997), pp. 88-89

ℬ "After seeing my wife, Dorothy, off to the surgery ward, I returned to the waiting room. As I sat down with a book, in walked Alice and Vic, friends of many years. They said they knew Dorothy was in good hands, but they also knew I needed their support. We talked of the fun times that we had together in the past and also of the things the four of us could do in the future. When I look back, the four hours of surgery seemed like only a few minutes. My friends knew just what I needed."

—Bill Dow

ℬ "My friend was in the hospital recovering from prostate cancer surgery. It was fall and his yard was blanketed with leaves. His son-in-law, knowing that the patient would worry and fuss about this unfinished job, raked all the leaves and carried them away. When the patient returned from the hospital his yard was leafless. What a gift!"

—Karen Mulder

ℬ "For three years after her diagnosis of cancer, my wife experienced a continuous degeneration of her condition. As this was occurring she was less and less able to take care of herself and the family. With two adolescent sons, a business to run, and the stress of the situation along with caring for my wife, my time was strained. The most difficult times were the frequent hospitalizations and the final weeks of my wife's life. So many things needed to be taken care of beyond the normal details of life. I was preoccupied with the swirl of events and activities, but friends came forward without being asked. One assisted in communicating the latest news about my wife, another helped by scheduling meals to be brought in several times a week, others stayed with my wife when I was working, and some cared for my wife in any way that was needed. With the help of many, our needs were met."

—Steve Bassett

Share and Reflect

ℬ Share an example of a time when someone anticipated your needs.

ℬ For personal reflection: How would you rate yourself when it comes to anticipating the needs of others? (Let "5" be "I'm a regular mind-reader" and "1" be "I don't have a clue.")

Practice

Read the following quote from Arthur Gordon's book *A Touch of Wonder* (Grand Rapids, MI: Fleming H. Revell Company, a div. of Baker Books, 1974, p. 28).

What made [the Good Samaritan] sensitive and responsive to the needs of the wounded man when the other travelers who saw that crumpled figure on the road to Jericho simply "passed by on the other side"? One thing I'm sure he had was the habit of helping. Going to the aid of the man on the Jericho road was no isolated incident in the Samaritan's life. He did what he did because he was the kind of man he was—and he didn't get that way overnight. Through the years he had trained himself to respond affirmatively to other people's needs. How? In the same way that any of us can do it, not so much by drastic self-discipline or heroic sacrifice as by the endless repetition of small efforts. By going the extra mile—occasionally. By giving someone in trouble a hand—if you can. By taking a fair share of civic responsibilities when you can manage it. These things may not seem to add up to much. But one day you may look around and discover that to an astonishing degree, self has been pushed off its lonely and arrogant throne and—almost without knowing it—you have become a Samaritan yourself.

Like the Good Samaritan, may God give us the peripheral vision to see, the sensitivity to care, and the love energy to stop and to lend a helping hand to those who have fallen.

Share and Reflect

☺ How do you react to Gordon's idea of becoming a good caregiver by "endless repetition of small efforts"?

☺ For personal reflection: How would you rate your own readiness to commit to practicing the "small efforts" that eventually make one into a "good Samaritan"? (Let "5" be "I'm ready to give it my best shot" and "1" be "I need some strong motivation to get started.")

Prayer

Dear Jesus, why is it you so often place religious leaders in such a bad light? Help me to understand that, Lord. And help me to see that reflected in that light, however dimly, is an image of myself.

As I have traveled down the road to my many responsibilities, how often have I taken a detour around the person in need? How often have I dismissed that need as none of my business?

Forgive me, Lord, for being so concerned about my other commitments that I am unconcerned about my commitment to others. Help me to realize that so much of true ministry is not what I schedule but what comes as an intrusion to my schedule.

Keep my schedule flexible enough, Lord, so that when my path comes across someone in need, I would be quick to change my plans in preference to yours. Give me a heart of compassion that I may love my neighbor the way the Good Samaritan loved him. Give me eyes that do not look away and feet that do not turn to the other side of the road.

Help me to realize that although I cannot do everything to alleviate the suffering in this world, I can do something. And even if that something is a very little thing, it is better than turning my head and walking away. Amen.

—Ken Gire, *Instructive Moments with the Savior*
(Grand Rapids, MI: Zondervan, 1992), pp. 21-22.

CARE AND KINDNESS LITANY

Leader: Oh Lord use us in small ways and in major challenges to bring love and compassion to friends, to neighbors, to strangers.

People: Enable us, oh Lord, to speak, to smile, to encourage.

Leader: Give us simple acts of kindness to spread every day, everywhere.

People: Equip us, oh Lord, with ideas, insights, and fresh words of cheer.

Leader: Give us courage to "show up" in sensitive places and in times of need. Help us to see Jesus in every human being.

People: Encourage us, oh Lord, when we lose confidence.

Leader: Use our listening ears, carefully chosen words, our tears and hugs to the hurt and the discouraged.

People: Use us, oh Lord, everyday, everywhere, with everybody.

Leader: This is our prayer. And all God's people shouted—Yes!! Yes!! Yes!!

People: Yes!! Yes!! Yes!!

Leader: (Benediction)
May the Lord bless you every day with generous attitudes, benevolent spirits, and sensitive hearts as you give birth to Jesus' love everywhere you go. Amen.

People: Amen.

Adaptation of "Care and Kindness Farewell Litany," from "Care and Kindness Conference," Crystal Catheral, 2004.

HEALTH PSYCHOLOGY

SIXTH EDITION

SHELLEY E. TAYLOR
University of California, Los Angeles

Boston   Burr Ridge, IL   Dubuque, IA   Madison, WI   New York   San Francisco   St. Louis
Bangkok   Bogotá   Caracas   Kuala Lumpur   Lisbon   London   Madrid   Mexico City
Milan   Montreal   New Delhi   Santiago   Seoul   Singapore   Sydney   Taipei   Toronto

The McGraw·Hill Companies

HEALTH PSYCHOLOGY
International Edition 2006

Exclusive rights by McGraw-Hill Education (Asia), for manufacture and export. This book cannot be re-exported from the country to which it is sold by McGraw-Hill. The International Edition is not available in North America.

Published by McGraw-Hill, a business unit of The McGraw-Hill Companies, Inc., 1221 Avenue of the Americas, New York, NY, 10020. Copyright © 2006, 2003, 1999, 1995, 1991, 1986 by The McGraw-Hill Companies, Inc. All rights reserved. No part of this publication may be reproduced or distributed in any form or by any means, or stored in a database or retrieval system, without the prior written consent of The McGraw-Hill Companies, Inc., including, but not limited to, in any network or other electronic storage or transmission, or broadcast for distance learning.

Some ancillaries, including electronic and print components, may not be available to customers outside the United States.

Credits: The credits section for this book begins on page 517 and is considered an extension of the copyright page.

10 09 08 07 06 05 04 03 02 01
20 09 08 07 06
CTF   MPM

Library of Congress Control Number : 2005047901

The Internet addresses listed in the text were accurate at the time of publication. The inclusion of a website does not indicate an endorsement by the authors of McGraw-Hill, and McGraw-Hill does not guarantee the accuracy of the information presented at these sites.

When ordering this title, use ISBN 0-07-125193-6

Printed in Singapore

www.mhhe.com

SHELLEY E. TAYLOR is professor of psychology at the University of California, Los Angeles. She received her Ph.D. in social psychology from Yale University. After a visiting professorship at Yale and assistant and associate professorships at Harvard University, she joined the faculty of UCLA in 1979. Her research interests are in health psychology, especially the factors that promote long-term psychological adjustment, and in social cognition. In the former capacity, she is the co-director of the Health Psychology program at UCLA. Professor Taylor is the recipient of a number of awards—most notably, the American Psychological Association's Distinguished Scientific Contribution to Psychology Award, a 10-year Research Scientist Development Award from the National Institute of Mental Health, and an Outstanding Scientific Contribution Award in Health Psychology. She is the author of more than 200 publications in journals and books and is the author of *Social Cognition* and *Positive Illusions*.

CONTENTS

v

PART THREE

STRESS AND COPING

PART FOUR

THE PATIENT IN THE TREATMENT SETTING

When I wrote the first edition of *Health Psychology* nearly 25 years ago, the task was much simpler than it is now. The health psychology field was new and relatively small. In the past 25 years, the field has grown steadily and great research advances have been made. Chief among these developments has been the use and refinement of the biopsychosocial model: the study of health issues from the standpoint of biological, psychological, and social factors acting together. Increasingly, research has attempted to identify the biological pathways by which psychosocial factors such as stress may exert an adverse affect on health and potentially protective factors such as social support may buffer the impact of stress. My goal in the sixth edition of this text is to convey this increasing sophistication of the field in a manner that makes it accessible, comprehensible, and exciting to undergraduates.

Like any science, health psychology is cumulative, building on past research advances to develop new ones. Accordingly, I have tried to present not only the fundamental contributions to the field but also the current form that research takes on these issues. Because health psychology is developing and changing so rapidly, it is essential that a text be up-to-date. Therefore, I have not only reviewed the recent research in health psychology but also obtained information about research projects that will not be available in the general literature for several years. In so doing, I am presenting an edition that is both current and pointed toward the future.

A second goal is to portray health psychology appropriately as being intimately involved with the problems of our times. Because AIDS is now a leading cause of death worldwide, the need for health measures such as condom use is readily apparent if we are going to stop the spread of this disease. The aging of the population and the shift in numbers toward the later years has created unprecedented health needs to which health psychology must respond. Such efforts include the need for a campaign of health promotion for these aging cohorts and an understanding of the psychosocial issues that arise in response to chronic disorders.

Research indicating that health habits lie at the origin of our most prevalent disorders underscores more than ever the importance of modifying problematic health behaviors such as smoking and alcohol consumption. Increasingly, research documents the importance of a healthy diet, regular exercise, and weight control among other positive health habits for maintaining good health. The at-risk role has taken on more importance in prevention, as breakthroughs in genetic research have made it possible to identify when there is a genetic risk for a disease long before disease is evident. How people cope with being at risk and what interventions are appropriate for people at risk represent some of the additions to health prevention coverage in this edition. By expanding the coverage of health promotion issues and integrating them more fully into the later chapters on seeking treatment and managing illness, this edition highlights these developments, forging an integrated presentation of the complex relations among health habits, psychosocial resources, stress and coping, and health and illness outcomes.

Health psychology is both an applied field and a basic research field. Accordingly, in highlighting the research accomplishments of the field, I have not only tried to present a comprehensive picture of the scientific progress but also tried to highlight its very important applications. The chapters on health promotion, for example, put particular emphasis on the most promising methods and venues for changing health behaviors. The chapters on chronic diseases highlight how knowledge about the psychosocial causes and consequences of these disorders may be used to intervene with people at risk—first, to reduce the likelihood that such disorders will develop, and second, to deal effectively with the psychosocial issues that do arise. These applications of the science center around intervention implications for people having difficulty managing their disorders.

Because the field is growing so rapidly and has become so technologically complex, there is a risk that coverage of the field will become needlessly dry and inaccessible for students. In this sixth edition, I have made a conscious effort to make the material more interesting and relevant to the lives of student readers. Each chapter opens with a case history reflecting the experiences of college students. In addition, the presentation of material has been more directly tied to the needs and interest of young adults. For example, the presentation of stress management is tied directly to how students might manage the stresses associated with college life. The presentation of alcoholism and problem drinking includes sections on college students' alcohol consumption and its modification. Health habits relevant to this age group—breast self-examination, testicular self-examination, exercise, and condom use among others—are highlighted for their relevance to the college population. By providing students with anecdotes, case histories, and specific research examples that are relevant to their own lives, I have attempted to show the students how important this body of knowledge is, not only to their growth as developing students but also to their lives as young adults. The success of any text depends ultimately on its ability to communicate clearly to student readers and spark interest in the field.

Health psychology is a science, and consequently it is important to communicate not only the research itself but also some understanding of how studies were designed and why they were designed that way. The explanations of particular research methods and the theories that have guided research have been expanded and clarified throughout the book. Important studies are described in-depth, so that the students may have a sense of the methods researchers use to make decisions about how to gather the best data on a problem or how to intervene most effectively.

Throughout the book, I have made an effort to balance general coverage of psychological concepts with coverage of specific health issues. One method of doing so is by presenting groups of chapters, with the initial chapter offering general concepts and subsequent chapters applying those concepts to specific health issues. Chapter 3 discusses general strategies of health promotion, and Chapters 4 and 5 discuss those issues with specific reference to particular health habits such as alcoholism, smoking, accident prevention, and weight control. Chapters 11 and 12 discuss broad issues that arise in the context of managing chronic and terminal illness. In Chapters 13 and 14, these issues are addressed more concretely, with reference to specific disorders such as heart disease, cancer, and AIDS.

Rather than adopt a particular theoretical emphasis throughout the book, I have attempted to maintain a flexibility in orientation. Because health psychology is taught within all areas of psychology (for example, clinical, social, cognitive, physiological, learning, and developmental), material from each of these areas is included in the text so that it can be accommodated to the orientation of each instructor. Consequently, not all material in the book is relevant for all courses. Successive chapters of the book build on each other but do not depend on each other. Chapter 2, for example, can be used as assigned reading, or it can act as a resource for students wishing to clarify their understanding of biological concepts or learn more about a particular biological system or illness. Thus, each instructor can accommodate the use of the text to his or her needs, giving some chapters more attention than others and omitting some chapters altogether, without undermining the integrity of the presentation.

■ SUPPLEMENTS

For Instructors

Instructor's Resource CD-ROM   The sixth edition is accompanied by a comprehensive CD-ROM for instructors. Resources on the CD include an Instructor's Manual, Test Bank and Computerized Test Bank, and PowerPoint slides. The Instructor's Manual, prepared by Virginia Norris (South Dakota State University) outlines each chapter and provides detailed learning objectives and suggestions for lectures. Also included are ideas for classroom discussion, student projects, paper topics, and other activities. The Instructor's Manual contains an extensive presentation of the methodologies of health psychology, including epidemiology, experiments, surveys, and the like, plus a listing of annotated readings and other materials to enrich the course. The extensive Test Bank of true-false, multiple-choice, and essay questions, also written by Virginia Norris, assess students' recall of material, as well as their ability to comprehend and apply the concepts in the text. The PowerPoint slides were developed for this text by Cathleen Mc-Greal (Michigan State University).

   Classroom Performance System Guide and CD-ROM   Also available to instructors using this text, the Classroom Performance System (CPS) allows instructors to gauge immediately what students are learning during lectures. With CPS from eInstruction, instructors can ask questions, take polls, host classroom demonstrations, and get instant feedback. In addition, CPS makes it easy to take attendance, give and grade pop quizzes, or give formal paper-based class tests with multiple versions of the test using CPS for immediate grading.

   For instructors who want to use CPS in the classroom, we offer a guide containing strategies for implementing the system, specific multiple-choice questions designed for in-class use, and classroom demonstrations for use with this system. For a quick, easy demonstration of CPS, go to www.mhhe.com/wmg/cps/psychology. CPS questions written specifically for use with this text by William Shadel (University of Pittsburgh) are available online at www.mhhe.com/taylor6.

   Online Learning Center   On the book's website, instructors will find the Instructor's Manual, PowerPoints, an Image Gallery with figures from the book, and CPS questions. There materials are available on the password-protected side of the Online Learning Center. (www.mhhe.com/taylor6)

For Students

Online Learning Center   Students will find a number of study tools on the book's website: www.mhhe.com/taylor6. These include learning objectives, chapter outlines, lab exercises, study questions by Jessica Gillooly (Glendale Community College), the book glossary, related publications, and web links.

■ ACKNOWLEDGMENTS

My extensive gratitude goes to Margaret Samotyj and Will Welch for the many hours they put in on the manuscript. I thank my editor at McGraw-Hill, Mike Sugarman, who devoted much time and help to the preparation of the book. I also wish to thank the following reviewers who commented on all or part of the book.

Amy Badura, *Creighton University*

Carlos Escoto, *Eastern Connecticut State University*

Judi Misale, *Truman State University*

Catherine Stoney, *Ohio State University*

Debra VanderVoort, *University of Hawaii*

Evan Zucker, *Loyola University of New Orleans*

Shelley E. Taylor

PART 1

Introduction to Health Psychology

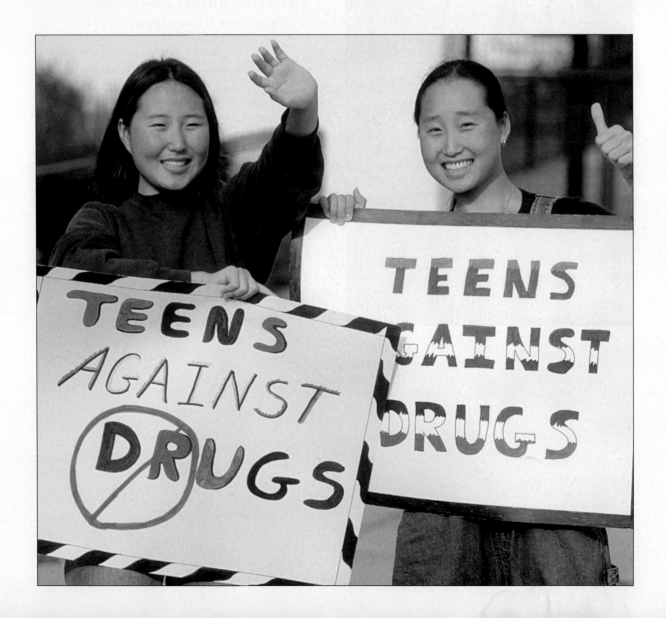

What Is Health Psychology?

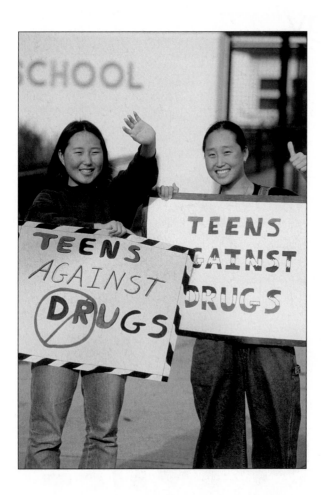

dam arrived at college filled with anticipation. He had had 4 good years of high school, and everyone had told him that college would be the best time of life. He had gotten into his first-choice school, which he had picked both for the first-rate psychology program and for the opportunities to play basketball and run track.

All his life, Adam had been health conscious. From the time he was young, his parents had made sure that he received regular medical checkups, wore his seat belt, and generally stayed out of circumstances in which he was likely to fall into harm. In elementary school, he had learned about the basic food groups, and his family had reinforced this learning by maintaining a healthy diet.

Because Adam had been active in sports from the time he was 7, regular exercise was an integral part of his life. In high school, he had had an occasional beer because everyone did, but he had avoided smoking cigarettes and taking drugs because he knew he couldn't do as well in sports if he abused his body. He got his 8 hours of sleep a night, too, because without them, his concentration in classes lapsed and his coordination on the basketball court fell off.

What would his roommate be like, he wondered, as he carried in the last of his suitcases and finished unpacking.

"Are you Adam?" a voice asked. Adam turned around to meet his new roommate, Greg. He knew im-

mediately that his roommate wasn't an athlete. A skinny, dissipated-looking person, Greg had a cigarette hanging from the corner of his mouth.

"I thought this was a nonsmoking suite," Adam said.

"It's supposed to be," Greg responded. "My mom put down on the application that I didn't smoke, 'cause she thought if I got into a nonsmoking suite, I'd have to stop. I'll try to do it out in the halls."

Over the course of the quarter, Adam learned that there were more surprises in store. Greg liked to sleep until 10:00 or 11:00 in the morning and often stayed up until 4:00 or 5:00 A.M. On weekends, he liked to get drunk, which seemed to be his major recreational activity. Dorm food was not much to his liking, and he often lived on Doritos, and Pepsi for a day or two at a time.

Greg always seemed to be coming down with something, either an upset stomach, a cold, a case of the flu, or just plain fatigue. The medicine cabinet they ostensibly shared was loaded with Greg's over-the-counter medications for every imaginable symptom.

Adam wasn't surprised that Greg was always sick. In high school, Adam had taken a course in psychology and the teacher had taught them about health psychology. Because he was interested in a possible career in sports medicine, he had gotten extra books about the field so he could learn more about it. Now he had his own case history in health psychology: Greg.

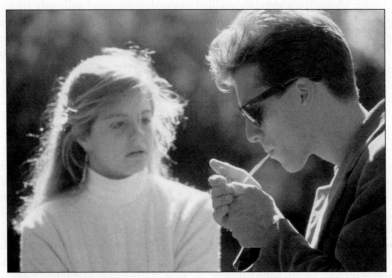

When children leave home for the first time as college students or workers, they often find that the health practices they have taken for granted in their own families are very different than those of their new friends and acquaintances.

■ DEFINITION OF HEALTH PSYCHOLOGY

Health psychology is devoted to understanding psychological influences on how people stay healthy, why they become ill, and how they respond when they do get ill. Health psychologists both study such issues and promote interventions to help people stay well or get over illness. For example, a health psychology researcher might be interested in why people continue to smoke even though they know that smoking increases their risk of cancer and heart disease. Information about why people smoke helps the researcher both understand this poor health habit and design interventions to help people stop smoking.

Fundamental to research and practice in health psychology is the definition of health. In 1948, the World Health Organization defined **health** as "a complete state of physical, mental, and social well-being and not merely the absence of disease or infirmity" (World Health Organization, 1948). This definition, which was very forward looking for its time, is at the core of health psychologists' conception of health. Rather than defining health as the absence of illness, health is recognized to be an achievement involving balance among physical, mental, and social well-being. Many use the term "wellness" to refer to this optimum state of health.

Health psychology is concerned with all aspects of health and illness across the life span (Maddux, Roberts, Sledden, & Wright, 1986). Health psychologists focus on *health promotion and maintenance,* which includes such issues as how to get children to develop good health habits, how to promote regular exercise, and how to design a media campaign to get people to improve their diets.

Health psychologists also study the psychological aspects of the *prevention and treatment of illness.* A health psychologist might teach people in a high-stress occupation how to manage stress effectively so that it will not adversely affect their health. A health psychologist might work with people who are already ill to help them adjust more successfully to their illness or to learn to follow their treatment regimen.

Health psychologists also focus on the *etiology and correlates of health, illness, and dysfunction.* **Etiology** refers to the origins or causes of illness, and health psychologists are especially interested in the behavioral and social factors that contribute to health or illness and dysfunction. Such factors can include health habits such as alcohol consumption, smoking, exercise, the wearing of seat belts, and ways of coping with stress.

Finally, health psychologists analyze and attempt to improve *the health care system and the formulation of health policy.* They study the impact of health institutions and health professionals on people's behavior and develop recommendations for improving health care.

Putting it all together, health psychology represents the educational, scientific, and professional contributions of psychology to the promotion and maintenance of health; the prevention and treatment of illness; the identification of the causes and correlates of health, illness, and related dysfunction; the improvement of the health care system, and health policy formation (Matarazzo, 1980).

In this chapter, we consider why our current state of knowledge about health and health care issues has virtually demanded the field of health psychology. To begin, we consider how philosophers have conceived of the **mind-body relationship** and how we have arrived at our present viewpoint of the mind and body as inextricable influences on health. Next, we discuss the trends in medicine, psychology, and the health care system that have contributed to the emergence of health psychology. We then consider the dominant clinical and research model in health psychology: the biopsychosocial model.

■ THE MIND-BODY RELATIONSHIP: A BRIEF HISTORY

Historically, philosophers have vacillated between the view that the mind and body are part of the same system and the idea that they are two separate ones. When we look at ancient history, it becomes clear that we have come full circle in our beliefs about the mind-body relationship.

In the earliest times, the mind and body were considered a unit. Early cultures believed that disease arises when evil spirits enter the body and that these spirits can be exorcised through the treatment process. Archaeologists have found Stone Age skulls with small holes in them that are believed to have been made intentionally with sharp stone tools. This procedure, called trephination, allowed the evil spirit to leave the body while the "physician," or shaman, performed the treatment ritual (H. I. Kaplan, 1975).

The Greeks were among the earliest civilizations to identify the role of bodily functioning in health and illness. Rather than ascribing illness to evil spirits, they developed a humoral theory of illness, which was first proposed by Hippocrates (ca. 460–ca. 377 B.C.) and later

Sophisticated, though not always successful, techniques for the treatment of illness were developed during the Renaissance. This woodcut from the 1570s depicts a surgeon drilling a hole in a patient's skull, with the patient's family and pets looking on.

expanded by Galen (A.D. 129–ca. 199). According to this view, disease arises when the four circulating fluids of the body—blood, black bile, yellow bile, and phlegm—are out of balance. The function of treatment is to restore balance among the humors. Specific personality types were believed to be associated with bodily temperaments in which one of the four humors predominated. In essence, then, the Greeks ascribed disease states to bodily factors but believed that these factors can also have an impact on the mind.

In the Middle Ages, however, the pendulum swung back toward supernatural explanations of illness. Mysticism and demonology dominated concepts of disease, which was seen as God's punishment for evildoing. Cure often consisted of driving out evil by torturing the body. Later, this "therapy" was replaced by penance through prayer and good works.

Throughout this time, the Church was the guardian of medical knowledge; as a result, medical practice took on religious overtones, including religiously based but unscientific generalizations about the body and the mind-body relationship. Not surprisingly, as the functions of the physician were absorbed by the priest, healing and the practice of religion became indistinguishable (H. I. Kaplan, 1975).

Beginning in the Renaissance and continuing up to the present day, great strides have been made in the tech-

nological basis of medical practice. Most notable among these were Anton van Leeuwenhoek's (1632–1723) work in microscopy and Giovanni Morgagni's (1682–1771) contributions to autopsy, both of which laid the groundwork for the rejection of the humoral theory of illness. The humoral approach was finally put to rest by growing scientific understanding of cellular pathology (H. I. Kaplan, 1975).

As a result of such advances, medicine looked more and more to the medical laboratory and bodily factors, rather than to the mind, as a basis for medical progress. In an effort to break with the superstitions of the past, the dualistic conception of mind and body was strongly reinforced so that physicians became the guardians of the body while philosophers and theologians became the caretakers of the mind. For the next 300 years, as physicians focused primarily on organic and cellular changes and pathology as a basis for their medical inferences, physical evidence became the sole basis for diagnosis and treatment of illness (H. I. Kaplan, 1975).

Psychoanalytic Contributions

This view began to change with the rise of modern psychology, particularly with Sigmund Freud's (1856–1939) early work on **conversion hysteria.** According to Freud, specific unconscious conflicts can produce particular physical disturbances that symbolize the repressed psychological conflicts. In conversion hysteria, the patient converts the conflict into a symptom via the voluntary nervous system; he or she then becomes relatively free of the anxiety the conflict would otherwise produce (N. Cameron, 1963).

The conversion hysteria literature is full of intriguing but biologically impossible disturbances, such as glove anesthesia (in which the hand, but not other parts of the arm, loses sensation) in response to highly stressful events. Other problems—including sudden loss of speech, hearing, or sight; tremors; muscular paralysis; and eating disorders, such as anorexia nervosa and bulimia—have also been interpreted as forms of conversion hysteria. True conversion responses are now less rarely seen.

Psychosomatic Medicine

Nonetheless, the idea that specific illnesses are produced by individuals' internal conflicts was perpetuated in the work of Flanders Dunbar in the 1930s (F. Dunbar, 1943) and Franz Alexander in the 1940s (F. Alexander, 1950). Unlike Freud, these researchers linked patterns of personality rather than a single specific conflict to specific illnesses. For example, Alexander developed a profile of the ulcer-prone personality as someone whose disorder is caused primarily by excessive needs for dependency and love.

A more important departure from Freud concerned the physiological mechanism postulated to account for the link between conflict and disorder. Whereas Freud believed that conversion reactions occur via the voluntary nervous system with no necessary physiological changes, Dunbar and Alexander argued that conflicts produce anxiety, which becomes unconscious and takes a physiological toll on the body via the autonomic nervous system. The continuous physiological changes eventually produce an actual organic disturbance. In the case of the ulcer patient, for example, repressed emotions resulting from frustrated dependency and love-seeking needs were said to increase the secretion of acid in the stomach, eventually eroding the stomach lining and producing ulcers (F. Alexander, 1950).

Dunbar's and Alexander's works helped shape the emerging field of **psychosomatic medicine** by offering profiles of particular disorders believed to be psychosomatic in origin—that is, bodily disorders caused by emotional conflicts: ulcers, hyperthyroidism, rheumatoid arthritis, essential hypertension, neurodermatitis (a skin disorder), colitis, and bronchial asthma. Many of

the early ideas generated by the psychosomatic medicine perspective persist today (B. T. Engel, 1986).

Nonetheless, several important criticisms of this movement have been ventured. First, the work on which many of these formulations was based was methodologically problematic, not conforming to the highest scientific standards of the day. Second and more important, researchers now believe that a particular conflict or personality type is not sufficient to produce illness. Rather, the onset of disease requires the interaction of a variety of factors; these include a possible genetic weakness in the organism, the presence of environmental stressors, early learning experiences and conflicts, current ongoing learning and conflicts, and individual cognitions and coping efforts. A third criticism of the psychosomatic movement was that it cordoned off a particular set of diseases as caused by psychological factors, thereby restricting the range of medical problems to which psychological and social factors were deemed to apply.

Despite the criticisms of the early psychosomatic movement, it laid the groundwork for a profound change in beliefs about the relation of the mind and the body (B. T. Engel, 1986). It is now known that physical health is inextricably interwoven with the psychological and social environment: All conditions of health and illness, not just the diseases identified by the early psychosomatic theorists, are influenced by psychological and social factors. The treatment of illness and prognosis for recovery are substantially affected by such factors as the relationship between patient and practitioner and expectations about pain and discomfort. Staying well is heavily determined by good health habits, all of which are under one's personal control, and by such socially determined factors as stress and social support. The mind and the body cannot be meaningfully separated in matters of health and illness.

An adequate understanding of what keeps people healthy or makes them get well is impossible without knowledge of the psychological and social context within which health and illness are experienced. This current conception of the mind-body interaction is one of the many factors that have spawned the rapidly growing field of health psychology.

■ WHY IS THE FIELD OF HEALTH PSYCHOLOGY NEEDED?

A number of trends within medicine, psychology, and the health care system have combined to make the emergence of health psychology inevitable. It is safe to say that health

FIGURE 1.1 | **Death Rates for the 10 Leading Causes of Death per 100,000 Population, United States, 1900 and 1998**   (*Sources:* M. M. Sexton, 1979; S. L. Murphy, 2000; National Vital Statistics Report, 2003)

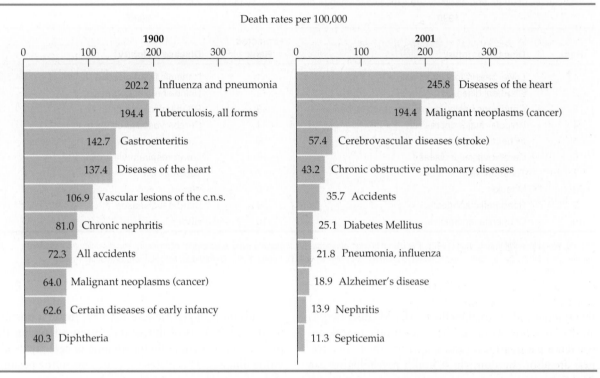

psychology is one of the most important developments within the field of psychology in the past 50 years. What factors have led to the development of health psychology?

Changing Patterns of Illness

The most important factor giving rise to health psychology has been the change in illness patterns that has occurred in the United States and other technologically advanced societies.

As figure 1.1 shows, until the 20th century, the major causes of illness and death in the United States were **acute disorders**—especially tuberculosis, pneumonia, and other infectious diseases. Acute disorders are short-term medical illnesses, often the result of a viral or bacterial invader and usually amenable to cure.

Now, however, **chronic illnesses**—especially heart disease, cancer, and diabetes—are the main contributors to disability and death, especially in industrialized countries. Chronic illnesses are slowly developing diseases with which people live for a long time. Often, chronic illnesses cannot be cured but, rather, only managed by the patient and provider working together. Table 1.1 lists the main diseases worldwide at the present time.

Note how those causes will change over the next decades.

Why have chronic illnesses helped spawn the field of health psychology? First, these are diseases in which psychological and social factors are implicated as causes. For example, personal health habits, such as diet and smoking, are implicated in the development of heart disease and cancer, and sexual activity is critically important in the likelihood of developing AIDS (acquired immune deficiency syndrome). Consequently, health psychology has evolved, in part, to explore these causes and to develop ways to modify them.

Second, because people may live with chronic diseases for many years, psychological issues arise in connection with them. Health psychologists help the chronically ill adjust psychologically and socially to their changing health state. They help those with chronic illness develop treatment regimens, many of which involve self-care. Chronic illnesses affect family functioning, including relationships with a partner or children, and health psychologists both explore these changes and help ease the problems in family functioning that may result. Many people with chronic illnesses use unconventional

TABLE 1.1 | What Are the Worldwide Causes of Death?

The causes of death and disability are expected to change dramatically by the year 2020.

1990		2020	
Rank	Disease or Injury	Projected Rank	Disease or Injury
1	Lower respiratory infections	1	Ischemic heart disease
2	Diarrheal diseases	2	Unipolar major depression
3	Conditions arising during the perinatal period	3	Road traffic accidents
4	Unipolar major depression	4	Cerebrovascular disease
5	Ischemic heart disease	5	Chronic obstructive pulmonary disease
6	Cerebrovascular disease	6	Lower respiratory infections
7	Tuberculosis	7	Tuberculosis
8	Measles	8	War
9	Road traffic accidents	9	Diarrheal diseases
10	Congenital anomalies	10	HIV

Source: World Health Organization (1996). *The global burden of disease: A comprehensive assessment of mortality and disability from diseases, injuries, and risk factors in 1990 and projected to 2020* (C. J. L. Murray & A. D. Lopez, Eds.). Cambridge, MA: Harvard University Press.

therapies outside formal medicine (D. M. Eisenberg et al., 1993). Understanding what leads people to seek unconventional treatments and evaluating their effectiveness are also issues on which health psychologists can shed light.

Advances in Technology and Research

The field of health psychology is changing almost daily because new issues arise that require the input of psychologists. For example, new technologies now make it possible to identify the genes that contribute to many disorders. Just in the past 2 years, genes contributing to many diseases, including breast cancer, have been uncovered. How do we help a college student whose mother has just been diagnosed with breast cancer come to terms with her risk, now that the genetic basis of breast cancer is better understood? Should the daughter get tested? And if she does get tested, and if she tests positive for a breast cancer gene, how will this change her life? How will she cope with her risk, and how should she change her behavior? Health psychologists help answer such questions.

"My father had a heart attack. Should I be making changes in my diet?" asks a student in a health psychology class. Health psychologists conduct research that identifies the risk factors for disease, such as a high-fat diet, and help people learn to change their diet and stick to their resolution. Helping people make informed, appropriate decisions is fundamentally a psychological task.

Advances in genetic research have made it possible to identify carriers of illness and to test a fetus for the presence of particular life-threatening or severely debilitating illnesses. This places some parents in the position of having to decide whether to abort a pregnancy—a wrenching, difficult decision to make.

Certain treatments that may prolong life severely compromise quality of life. Increasingly, patients are asked their preferences regarding life-sustaining measures, and they may require counseling in these matters. These are just a few examples of the increasing role that patients play in fundamental decisions regarding their health and illness and its management and of the help health psychologists can provide in this process.

Impact of Epidemiology   Changing patterns of illness have been charted and followed by the field of epidemiology, a discipline closely related to health psychology in its goals and interests (N. E. Miller, 1992). **Epidemiology** is the study of the frequency, distribution, and causes of infectious and noninfectious disease in a population, based on an investigation of the physical and social environment. For example, epidemiologists not only study who has what kind of cancer but also address questions such as why some cancers are more prevalent than others in particular geographic areas.

In the context of epidemiologic statistics, we will see the frequent use of two important terms, "morbidity" and "mortality." **Morbidity** refers to the number of cases of a disease that exist at some given point in time. Morbidity may be expressed as the number of new cases (incidence) or as the total number of existing cases (prevalence). Morbidity statistics, then, tell us how many people are suffering from what kinds of illnesses at any given time. **Mortality** refers to numbers of deaths due to particular causes.

In establishing the goals and concerns of health psychology and the health care endeavor more broadly, morbidity and mortality statistics are essential. We need to know the major causes of disease in this country, particularly those diseases that lead to early death, so as to reduce their occurrence. For example, knowing that accidents, especially automobile accidents, have historically been the major cause of death among children, adolescents, and young adults has led to the initiation of a variety of safety measures, including child safety restraint systems, mandatory seat belt laws, and airbags. Knowing that cardiac disease is the major cause of premature death (that is, death that occurs prior to the expected age of death for an individual) has led to a nationwide effort to reduce risk factors among those most vulnerable, including smoking reduction efforts, implementation of dietary changes, cholesterol reduction techniques, increased exercise, and weight loss (see M. McGinnis, Richmond, Brandt, Windom, & Mason, 1992).

But morbidity is at least as important. What is the use of affecting causes of death if people remain ill but simply do not die? Increasingly, health psychology is concerned not only with biological outcomes but also with health-related quality of life and symptomatic complaints. Indeed, some have argued that quality of life and expressions of symptoms should be more important targets for our interventions than mortality and other biological indicators (R. M. Kaplan, 1990). Consequently, health psychologists are becoming more involved in the effort to improve quality of life among those diagnosed with chronic illnesses so that individuals may live out their remaining years as free from pain, disability, and lifestyle compromise as possible (J. S. House et al., 1990).

Expanded Health Care Services

Another set of factors that has contributed to the rise of health psychology relates to the expansion of health care services. Health care is the largest service industry in the United States, and it is still growing rapidly. Americans spend more than $1 trillion annually on health (National Center for Health Statistics, 2001). In recent years, the health care industry has come under increasing scrutiny as we have realized that massive increases in health care costs have not brought with them improvement in basic indicators of quality of health.

Moreover, huge disparities exist in the United States such that some individuals enjoy the very best health care available in the world and others receive little health care except in emergencies. As of 2002, 43.6 million Americans had no health insurance at all (U.S. Census Bureau, 2003), placing basic preventive care and treatment for common illnesses out of financial reach. These are among the developments that have fueled recent efforts to reform the health care system to provide all Americans with a basic health care package, similar to what already exists in most European countries.

Health psychology represents an important perspective on these issues for several reasons:

1. Because containing health care costs is so important, health psychology's main emphasis on prevention—namely, modifying people's risky health behaviors before they ever become ill—has the potential to reduce the number of dollars devoted to the management of illness.

2. Health psychologists have done substantial research on what makes people satisfied or dissatisfied with their health care (see chapters 8 and 9). Thus, they can help in the design of user-friendly health care systems.

3. The health care industry employs many millions of individuals in a variety of jobs. Nearly every individual in the country has direct contact with the health care system as a recipient of services. Thus, its impact on people is enormous.

For all these reasons, then, health has a substantial social and psychological impact on people, an impact that is addressed by health psychologists.

Increased Medical Acceptance

Another reason for the development of health psychology is the increasing acceptance of health psychologists within the medical community (Matarazzo, 1994). Although health psychologists have been employed in health settings for many years, their value is increasingly recognized by physicians and other health care professionals.

At one time, the role of health psychologists in health care was largely confined to the task of administering tests and interpreting the test results of individuals who were suspected of being psychologically disturbed.

Like psychiatrists in health settings, psychologists usually saw only the "problem patients" who were difficult for medical staff to manage or whose physical complaints were believed to be entirely psychological in origin. Patients who had complaints that could be readily attributed to medical problems and who were easy to manage were considered not to have psychological problems and were therefore thought to be outside the psychologist's province of expertise.

Now, however, caregivers are increasingly recognizing that psychological and social factors are always important in health and illness. Accordingly, the role of the psychologist in changing patients' health habits and contributing to treatment is increasingly acknowledged.

Demonstrated Contributions to Health

Health psychology has already demonstrated that it can make substantial contributions to health (Melamed, 1995), contributions that form the substance of this book. A few brief examples here can illustrate this point.

Health psychologists have developed a variety of short-term behavioral interventions to address a wide variety of health-related problems, including managing pain; modifying bad health habits, such as smoking; and managing the side effects or treatment effects associated with a range of chronic diseases. Techniques that often take a mere few hours to teach often produce years of benefit. Such interventions, particularly those that target risk factors such as diet or smoking, have contributed to the actual decline in the incidence of some diseases, especially coronary heart disease (M. McGinnis et al., 1992). To take another example, psychologists learned many years ago that informing patients fully about the procedures and sensations involved in unpleasant medical procedures, such as surgery, improves their adjustment to those procedures (Janis, 1958; J. E. Johnson, 1984). As a consequence of these studies, many hospitals and other treatment centers now routinely prepare patients for such procedures. Ultimately, if a discipline is to flourish, it must demonstrate a strong track record, and health psychology has done precisely that.

Methodological Contributions

Health psychologists make important methodological contributions to issues of health and illness. Many of the issues that arise in medical settings demand rigorous research investigation. Although physicians and nurses receive some methodological and statistical education,

their training may be inadequate to conduct research on the issues they wish to address unless they make research their specialty. The health psychologist can be a valuable member of the research team by providing the methodological and statistical expertise that is the hallmark of good training in psychology.

Experiments Much research in health psychology is experimental. In an **experiment,** a researcher creates two or more conditions that differ from each other in exact and predetermined ways. People are then randomly assigned to experience these different conditions, and their reactions are measured. Experiments conducted by health care practitioners to evaluate treatments or interventions and their effectiveness over time are also called **randomized clinical trials.**

What kinds of experiments do health psychologists do? To determine if social support groups improve adjustment to cancer, cancer patients might be randomly assigned to participate in a support group or to participate in a comparison condition, such as an educational intervention, and then evaluated at a subsequent point in time to pinpoint whether one group of patients is better adjusted to the cancer than the other, or in which ways they differ in their adjustment.

Experiments have been the mainstay of science, because they often provide more definitive answers to problems than other research methods. When we manipulate a variable and see its effect, we can establish a cause-effect relationship definitively. For this reason, experiments and randomized clinical trials have been the mainstays of health psychology research. However, sometimes it is impractical to study issues experimentally. People cannot, for example, be randomly assigned to diseases.

Correlational Studies As a result, other research in health psychology is **correlational research,** in which the health psychologist measures whether a change in one variable corresponds with changes in another variable. A correlational study might identify, for example, that people who are higher in hostility have a higher risk for cardiovascular disease. The disadvantage of correlational studies is that it is impossible to determine the direction of causality unambiguously: It is possible, for example, that cardiovascular risk factors lead people to become more hostile. On the other hand, correlational studies often have advantages over experiments because they are more adaptable, enabling us to study issues when the variables cannot be manipulated experimentally.

Prospective Designs   Moreover, some of the problems with correlational studies can be remedied by using a prospective approach to research. **Prospective research** looks forward in time to see how a group of individuals change, or how a relationship between two variables changes, over time. For example, if we were to find that hostility develops relatively early in life, but other risk factors for heart disease develop later, we might feel more confident that hostility is an independent risk factor for heart disease and recognize that the reverse direction of causality—namely, that heart disease causes hostility—is unlikely.

Health psychologists conduct many prospective studies in order to understand the risk factors that relate to certain health conditions. We might, for example, intervene in the diet of one community and not in another and over time look at the difference in rates of heart disease. This would be an experimental prospective study. Alternatively, we might measure the diets that people create for themselves and look at changes in rates of heart disease, as determined by how good or poor the diet is. This would be an example of a correlational prospective study.

A particular type of prospective approach is **longitudinal research,** in which we observe the same people over a long period of time. For example, if we wanted to know what factors are associated with early breast cancer in women at risk for it, we might follow a group of young women whose mothers developed breast cancer in an effort to identify which daughters developed breast cancer and whether there are any reliable factors associated with that development, such as diet, smoking, alcohol consumption, or other co-occurring risk factors.

Retrospective Research   Investigators also use **retrospective research,** which looks backward in time, and attempt to reconstruct the conditions that led to a current situation. Retrospective methods, for example, were critical in identifying the risk factors that led to the development of AIDS.

Initially, researchers saw an abrupt increase in a rare cancer called Kaposi's sarcoma and observed that the men who developed this cancer often eventually died of general failure of the immune system. By taking extensive histories of the men who developed this disease, researchers were able to determine that the practice of anal-receptive sex without a condom is related to the development of the disorder. Because of retrospective studies, researchers knew some of the risk factors for AIDS even before they had identified the retrovirus.

Throughout this text, we will refer to a variety of research methods that have developed to address the manifold problems with which health psychologists have been concerned. The previous general introduction to some of the most important research methods serves as context to clarify the more focused methods that are described in subsequent chapters. Suffice it to say at this point that the research training that health psychologists receive in their undergraduate and graduate school experiences makes them valuable parts of the research teams that attempt to understand how we stay healthy and why we get ill.

■ THE BIOPSYCHOSOCIAL MODEL IN HEALTH PSYCHOLOGY

The idea that the mind and the body together determine health and illness logically implies a model for studying these issues. This model is called the **biopsychosocial model.** As its name implies, its fundamental assumption is that health and illness are consequences of the interplay of biological, psychological, and social factors (G. L. Engel, 1977, 1980; G. E. Schwartz, 1982). Because the biopsychosocial model figures so prominently in the research and clinical issues described in this book, we consider it in some detail here.

The Biopsychosocial Model Versus the Biomedical Model

Perhaps the best way to understand the biopsychosocial model is to contrast it with the **biomedical model.** The biomedical model, which governed the thinking of most health practitioners for the past 300 years, maintains that all illness can be explained on the basis of aberrant somatic processes, such as biochemical imbalances or neurophysiological abnormalities. The biomedical model assumes that psychological and social processes are largely independent of the disease process.

Although the biomedical model has undeniable benefits for studying some diseases, it has several potential liabilities. First, it is a reductionistic model. This means that it reduces illness to low-level processes, such as disordered cells and chemical imbalances, rather than recognizing the role of more general social and psychological processes. The biomedical model is also essentially a single-factor model of illness. That is, it explains illness in terms of a biological malfunction rather than recognizing that a variety of factors, only some of which are biological, may be responsible for the development of illness.

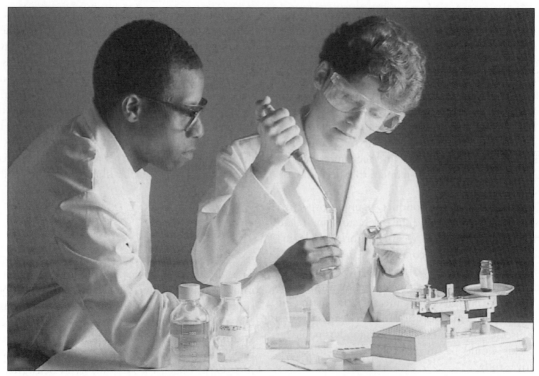

In the 19th and 20th centuries, great strides were made in the technical basis of medicine. As a result, physicians looked more and more to the medical laboratory and less to the mind as a way of understanding the onset and progression of illness.

The biomedical model implicitly assumes a mind-body dualism, maintaining that mind and body are separate entities. Finally, the biomedical model clearly emphasizes illness over health. That is, it focuses on aberrations that lead to illness rather than on the conditions that might promote health (G. L. Engel, 1977).

The shortcomings of the biomedical model are several. First, it has difficulty accounting for why a particular set of somatic conditions need not inevitably lead to illness. Why, for example, if six people are exposed to measles, do only three develop the disease? There are psychological and social factors that influence the development of illness, and these are ignored by the biomedical model. Whether a treatment will cure a disease is also substantially affected by psychological and social factors, and this cannot be explained by the biomedical model. As a consequence, researchers and practitioners have increasingly adopted a biopsychosocial model.

Advantages of the Biopsychosocial Model

How, then, does the biopsychosocial model of health and illness overcome the disadvantages of the biomed-

ical model? The biopsychosocial model, as previously noted, maintains that biological, psychological, and social factors are all-important determinants of health and illness. As such, both macrolevel processes (such as the existence of social support, the presence of depression) and microlevel processes (such as cellular disorders or chemical imbalances) interact to produce a state of health or illness.

The biopsychosocial model maintains that health and illness are caused by multiple factors and produce multiple effects. The model further maintains that the mind and body cannot be distinguished in matters of health and illness because both so clearly influence an individual's state of health. The biopsychosocial model emphasizes both health and illness rather than regarding illness as a deviation from some steady state. From this viewpoint, health becomes something that one achieves through attention to biological, psychological, and social needs rather than something that is taken for granted (World Health Organization, 1948).

But how do biological, social, and psychological variables interact, particularly if biological factors are microlevel processes and psychological and social factors are macrolevel processes? To address this question, researchers have adopted a **systems theory** approach to health and illness. Systems theory maintains that all levels of organization in any entity are linked to each other hierarchically and that change in any one level will effect change in all the other levels. This means that the microlevel processes (such as cellular changes) are nested within the macrolevel processes (such as societal values) and that changes on the microlevel can have macrolevel effects (and vice versa).

Consequently, health, illness, and medical care are all interrelated processes involving interacting changes both within the individual and on these various levels. To address these issues impels researchers toward interdisciplinary thinking and collaboration. It also requires researchers to be sophisticated in multivariate approaches to testing problems and to the often complex statistics needed to analyze them (G. E. Schwartz, 1982).

Clinical Implications of the Biopsychosocial Model

There are several implications of the biopsychosocial model for clinical practice with patients. First, the biopsychosocial model maintains that the process of diagnosis should always consider the interacting role of biological, psychological, and social factors in assessing an individual's health or illness (Oken, 2000). Therefore, an interdisciplinary team approach may be the best way to make a diagnosis (G. E. Schwartz, 1982).

Second, the biopsychosocial model maintains that recommendations for treatment must also examine all three sets of factors. By doing this, it should be possible to target therapy uniquely to a particular individual, consider a person's health status in total, and make treatment recommendations that can deal with more than one problem simultaneously. Again, a team approach may be most appropriate (G. E. Schwartz, 1982).

Third, the biopsychosocial model makes explicit the significance of the relationship between patient and practitioner. An effective patient-practitioner relationship can improve a patient's use of services as well as the efficacy of treatment and the rapidity with which illness is resolved (Belar, 1997).

Summary

In summary, the biopsychosocial model clearly implies that the practitioner must understand the social and psychological factors that contribute to an illness in order to treat it appropriately. In the case of a healthy individual, the biopsychosocial model suggests that one can understand health habits only in their psychological and social contexts. These contexts may maintain a poor health habit or, with appropriate modifications, can facilitate the development of healthy ones. In the case of the ill individual, biological, psychological, and social factors all contribute to recovery.

Consider a high-powered business executive in his early 40s who has a heart attack. A traditional medical approach to this problem would emphasize control of the problem through the regular administration of drugs. The biopsychosocial approach to this man's problem would also identify his health practices that may have contributed to the early heart attack. Treatment efforts might focus on exercise, training in techniques for stress management, and a recommendation to a program to help him stop smoking. In addition, such an assessment might look at his social environment, recognize that he spends relatively little time with his wife and children, and recommend that he make positive social interaction with his family an additional goal for his rehabilitation. Use of the biopsychosocial model informs these kinds of sophisticated assessments, and health psychologists are at the center of these developing trends.

■ WHAT IS HEALTH PSYCHOLOGY TRAINING FOR?

Students who are trained in health psychology on the undergraduate level go on to many different occupations.

Careers in Practice

Some go into medicine, becoming physicians and nurses. Because of their experience in health psychology, they are often able to understand and manage the social and psychological aspects of the health problems they treat better than would be the case if their education had included only training in traditional medicine. Thus, for example, they may realize that no amount of education in a self-care plan for a chronically ill person will be successful unless the family members are also brought in and educated in the regimen. Some of these health care practitioners conduct research as well.

Other health psychology students go into the allied health professional fields, such as social work, occupational therapy, dietetics, physical therapy, and public health. Social workers in medical settings, for example, are often responsible for assessing where patients go after discharge, decisions that are enlightened by knowledge of the psychosocial needs of individual patients. A woman recovering from breast cancer surgery, for example, may need linkages to breast cancer support groups and contacts for obtaining a prosthesis. Occupational therapists are heavily involved in the vocational and avocational retraining of the chronically ill and disabled to improve their occupational abilities and skills for daily living. Dietetics is an increasingly important field as the role of diet in the development and management of certain chronic illnesses, such as cancer, heart disease, and diabetes, becomes clear. Physical therapists help patients regain the use of limbs and functions that may have been compromised by illness and its treatment.

Careers in Research

Many students go on to conduct research in public health, psychology, and medicine. Public health researchers are involved in research and interventions that have the broad goal of improving the health of the general population. Public health researchers typically work in academic settings, in public agencies (such as county health departments), the Centers for Disease Control, family planning clinics, the Occupational Safety and Health Administration and its state agencies, and air quality management district offices, as well as in hospitals, clinics, and other health care agencies.

In these settings, public health researchers can be responsible for a variety of tasks. For example, they may be involved in developing educational interventions for the general public to help people practice better health behaviors. They may formally evaluate programs for improving health-related practices that have already been implemented through the media and through communities. They may be responsible for administrating health agencies, such as clinics or health and safety offices. They may chart the progress of particular diseases, monitor health threats in the workplace and develop interventions to reduce these threats, and conduct research on health issues.

Many undergraduates in health psychology go on to graduate school in psychology, where they learn the research, teaching, and intervention skills necessary to practice health psychology (Sheridan et al., 1989).

Many of these health psychologists then work in university departments of psychology, where they conduct research and train new students; others work in medical schools; many are in independent practice, where they work with patients who have health-related disorders; others work in hospitals and other treatment settings; and others work in industrial or occupational health settings to promote health behavior, prevent accidents and other job-related morbidity, and control health care costs (Quick, 1999; S. Williams & Kohout, 1999).

The remainder of this book focuses on the kind of knowledge, training, research, and interventions that health psychologists undertake, and in the last chapter, chapter 15, information about how to pursue a career in health psychology is provided. At this point, it is useful to turn to the content of this exciting and growing field. ●

SUMMARY

1. Health psychology is the field within psychology devoted to understanding psychological influences on how people stay healthy, why they become ill, and how they respond when they do get ill. It focuses on health promotion and maintenance; prevention and treatment of illness; the etiology and correlates of health, illness, and dysfunction; and improvement of the health care system and the formulation of health policy.

2. The interaction of the mind and the body has concerned philosophers and scientists for centuries. Different models of the relationship have predominated at different times in history, but current emphasis is on the inextricable unity of the two.

3. The rise of health psychology can be tied to several factors, including the increase in chronic or lifestyle-related illnesses, the expanding role of health care in the economy, the realization that psychological and social factors contribute to health and illness, the demonstrated importance of psychological interventions to improving people's health, and the rigorous methodological contributions of expert researchers.

4. The biomedical model, which dominates medicine, is a reductionistic, single-factor model of illness that regards the mind and body as separate entities and emphasizes illness concerns over health.

5. The biomedical model is currently being replaced by the biopsychosocial model, which regards any health or illness outcome as a complex interplay of biological, psychological, and social factors. The biopsychosocial model recognizes the importance of both macrolevel and microlevel processes in producing health and illness and maintains that the mind and body cannot be distinguished in matters of health and illness. Under this model, health is regarded as an active achievement.

6. The biopsychosocial model guides health psychologists in their research efforts to uncover factors that predict states of health and illness and in their clinical interventions with patients.

7. Health psychologists perform a variety of tasks. They research and examine the interaction of biological, psychological, and social factors in producing health and illness. They help treat patients suffering from a variety of disorders and conduct counseling for the psychosocial problems that illness may create. They develop worksite interventions to improve employees' health habits and work in organizations as consultants to improve health and health care delivery.

KEY TERMS

acute disorders
biomedical model
biopsychosocial model
chronic illnesses
conversion hysteria
correlational research
epidemiology

etiology
experiment
health
health psychology
longitudinal research
mind-body relationship
morbidity

mortality
prospective research
psychosomatic medicine
randomized clinical trials
retrospective research
systems theory

The Systems of the Body

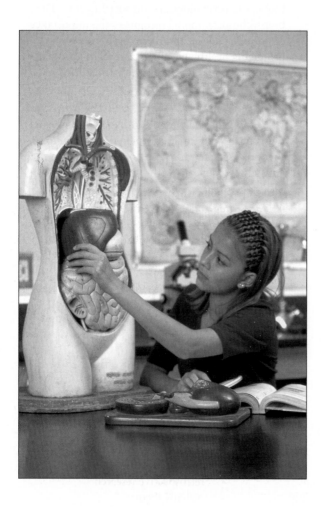

An understanding of health requires a working knowledge of human physiology. This knowledge makes it possible to understand such issues as how good health habits make illness less likely, how stress affects bodily functioning, how repeated stress can lead to hypertension or coronary artery disease, and how cell growth is radically altered by cancer.

Physiology is the study of the body's functioning. The body is made up of many millions of cells which, grouped together form tissues, which form organs whose functions overlap to produce the body's systems. In this chapter, we consider the major systems of the body, examining how each system functions normally and some of the disorders to which the system may be vulnerable.

■ THE NERVOUS SYSTEM

Overview

The **nervous system** is a complex network of interconnected nerve fibers. Sensory nerve fibers provide input to the brain and spinal cord by carrying signals from sensory receptors; motor nerve fibers provide output from the brain or spinal cord to muscles and other organs, resulting in voluntary and involuntary movement.

The nervous system is made up of the central nervous system and the peripheral nervous system. The central nervous system consists of the brain and the spinal cord. The rest of the nerves in the body, including those that connect to the brain and spinal cord, constitute the peripheral nervous system.

The peripheral nervous system is, itself, made up of the somatic nervous system and the autonomic nervous system. The somatic, or voluntary, nervous system connects nerve fibers to voluntary muscles and provides the brain with feedback in the form of sensory information about voluntary movement. The autonomic, or involuntary, nervous system connects the central nervous system with all internal organs over which people do not customarily have control.

Regulation of the autonomic nervous system occurs via the sympathetic nervous system and the parasympathetic nervous system. As will be seen in chapter 6, the **sympathetic nervous system** prepares the body to respond to emergencies; to strong emotions, such as anger or fear; and to strenuous activity. As such, it plays an important role in reactions to stress. Because it is concerned with the mobilization and exertion of energy, it is called a catabolic system.

In contrast, the **parasympathetic nervous system** controls the activities of organs under normal circumstances and acts antagonistically to the sympathetic nervous system. When an emergency has passed, the parasympathetic nervous system restores the body to a normal state. Because it is concerned with the conservation of body energy, it is called an anabolic system. The components of the nervous system are summarized in figure 2.1. We now consider several of these components in greater detail.

FIGURE 2.1 | The Components of the Nervous System

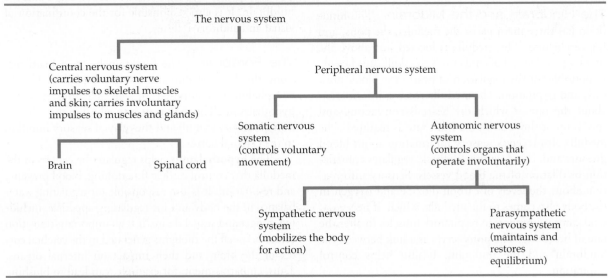

FIGURE 2.2 | The Brain

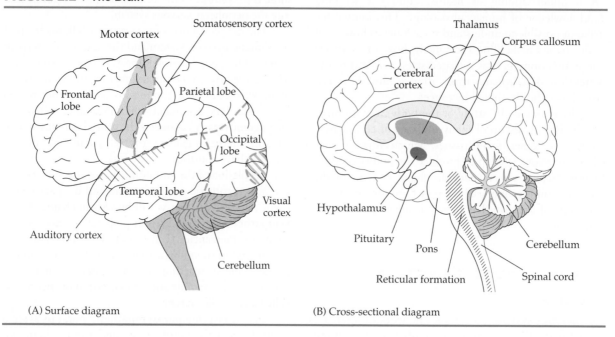

(A) Surface diagram

(B) Cross-sectional diagram

The Brain

The brain might best be thought of as the command center of the body. It receives afferent (sensory) impulses from the peripheral nerve endings and sends efferent (motor) impulses to the extremities and to internal organs to carry out necessary movement. The brain consists of three sections: the hindbrain, the midbrain, and the forebrain. The parts of the brain are shown in figure 2.2.

The Hindbrain and the Midbrain

The hindbrain has three main parts: the medulla, the pons, and the cerebellum. The medulla is located just above the point where the spinal cord enters the skull. It is heavily responsible for the regulation of heart rate, blood pressure, and respiration. The **medulla** receives information about the rate at which the heart is contracting and speeds up or slows down the heart rate as required. The medulla also receives sensory information about blood pressure and, based on this feedback, regulates constriction or dilation of the blood vessels. Sensory information about the levels of carbon dioxide and oxygen in the body also comes to the medulla, which, if necessary, sends motor impulses to respiratory muscles to alter the rate of breathing. The **pons** serves as a link between the hindbrain and the midbrain. It also helps control respiration.

The **cerebellum** coordinates voluntary muscle movement, the maintenance of balance and equilibrium, and the maintenance of muscle tone and posture. Therefore, damage to this area makes it hard for a person to coordinate muscles effectively; such damage produces lack of muscle tone, tremors, and disturbances in posture or gait.

The midbrain is the major pathway for sensory and motor impulses moving between the forebrain and the hindbrain. It is also responsible for the coordination of visual and auditory reflexes.

The Forebrain

The forebrain has two main sections: the diencephalon and the telencephalon. The diencephalon is composed of the thalamus and the hypothalamus. The **thalamus** is involved in the recognition of sensory stimuli and the relay of sensory impulses to the cerebral cortex.

The **hypothalamus** helps regulate the centers in the medulla that control cardiac functioning, blood pressure, and respiration. It is also responsible for regulating water balance in the body and for regulating appetites, including hunger and sexual desire. It is an important transition center between the thoughts generated in the cerebral cortex of the brain and their impact on internal organs. Thus, embarrassment, for example, can lead to blushing via the hypothalamus through the vasomotor center in the medulla to the blood vessels. Likewise, anxiety may result from secretion of hydrochloric acid in the stomach via signals from the hypothalamus. Together with the pituitary gland, the hypothalamus helps regulate the endocrine system, which releases hormones, influencing functioning in target organs throughout the body.

The other portion of the forebrain, the telencephalon, is composed of the two hemispheres (left and right) of the cerebral cortex. The **cerebral cortex** is the largest portion of the brain and is involved in higher order intelligence, memory, and personality. The sensory impulses that come from the peripheral areas of the body, up the spinal cord, and through the hindbrain and midbrain are received and interpreted in the cerebral cortex. Motor impulses, in turn, pass down from the cortex to the lower portions of the brain and from there to other parts of the body.

The cerebral cortex consists of four lobes: frontal, parietal, temporal, and occipital. Each lobe has its own memory storage area or areas of association. Through these complex networks of associations, the brain is able to relate current sensations to past ones, giving the cerebral cortex formidable interpretive capabilities.

In addition to its role in associative memory, each lobe is generally associated with particular functions. The frontal lobe contains the motor cortex, which coordinates voluntary movement. The left part of the motor cortex controls activities of the voluntary muscles on the right side of the body, while the right part of the motor cortex controls voluntary activities on the left side of the body. The parietal lobe contains the somatosensory cortex, in which sensations of touch, pain, temperature, and pressure are registered and interpreted. The temporal lobe contains the cortical areas responsible for auditory and olfactory (smell) impulses, and the occipital lobe contains the visual cortex, which receives visual impulses. Finally, the basal ganglia—four round masses embedded deep in the cerebrum (the main portion of the brain)—help make muscle contractions orderly, smooth, and purposeful.

The Limbic System   The structures of the limbic system, which border the midline of the brain, play an important role in stress and emotional responses. The amygdala and the hippocampus are involved in the detection of threat and in emotionally charged memories, respectively. The cingulate gyrus, the septum, and areas in the hypothalamus are related to emotional functioning as well. The anterior portion of the thalamus and some nuclei within the hypothalamus are important for socially relevant behaviors.

The Role of Neurotransmitters

The nervous system functions by means of chemicals, called **neurotransmitters,** that regulate nervous system functioning. Stimulation of the sympathetic nervous system prompts the secretion of large quantities of two neurotransmitters, epinephrine and norepinephrine, together termed the **catecholamines.** These substances enter the bloodstream and are carried throughout the body promoting the activity of sympathetic stimulation.

The release of catecholamines prompts a variety of important bodily changes. Heart rate increases, the heart's capillaries dilate, and blood vessels constrict, increasing blood pressure. Blood is diverted into muscle tissue. Respiration rate goes up, and the amount of air flowing into the lungs is increased. Digestion and urination are generally decreased. The pupils of the eyes dilate, and sweat glands are stimulated to produce more sweat. These changes are familiar to anyone who has experienced a highly stressful event or a strong emotion, such as fear or embarrassment. As we will see in chapter 6, arousal of the sympathetic nervous system and the production and release of catecholamines are critically important in individual responses to stressful circumstances. Repeated arousal of the sympathetic nervous system may have implications for the development of several chronic disorders, such as coronary artery disease and hypertension, which will be discussed in greater detail in chapter 13.

Parasympathetic functioning is a counterregulatory system that helps restore homeostasis following sympathetic arousal. The heart rate decreases, the heart's capillaries constrict, blood vessels dilate, respiration rate decreases, and the metabolic system resumes its activities.

Disorders of the Nervous System

Approximately 25 million Americans have some disorder of the nervous system, which account for 20% of hospitalizations each year and 12% of deaths. The most common forms of neurological dysfunction are epilepsy and Parkinson's disease. Cerebral palsy, multiple sclerosis, and Huntington's disease also affect a substantial number of people.

Epilepsy   A disease of the central nervous system affecting more than 2.5 million people in the United

States (Epilepsy Foundation, 2003), epilepsy is often idiopathic, which means that no specific cause for the symptoms can be identified. Symptomatic epilepsy may be traced to such factors as injury during birth; severe injury to the head; infectious disease, such as meningitis or encephalitis; and metabolic or nutritional disorders. A tendency toward epilepsy may also be inherited.

Epilepsy is marked by seizures, which range from barely noticeable staring or purposeless motor movements (such as chewing and lip smacking) to violent convulsions accompanied by irregular breathing, drooling, and loss of consciousness. Epilepsy cannot be cured, but it can often be successfully controlled through medication and behavioral interventions designed to manage stress (see chapters 7 and 11).

Cerebral Palsy   Approximately 764,000 children and adults in the United States manifest one or more of the symptoms of cerebral palsy (United Cerebral Palsy Research and Educational Foundation, 2002). Cerebral palsy is a chronic, nonprogressive disorder marked by lack of muscle control. It stems from brain damage caused by an interruption in the brain's oxygen supply, usually during childbirth. In older children, a severe accident or physical abuse can produce the condition. Apart from being unable to control motor functions, sufferers may (but need not) also have seizures, spasms, mental retardation, difficulties of sensation and perception, and problems with sight, hearing, or speech.

Parkinson's Disease   Patients with Parkinson's disease suffer from progressive degeneration of the basal ganglia, the group of nuclei that controls smooth motor coordination. The result of this deterioration is tremors, rigidity, and slowness of movement. As many as one million Americans suffer from Parkinson's disease, which primarily strikes people age 50 and older (Dawson & Dawson, 2003; Parkinson's Disease Foundation, 2002), and men are more likely than women to develop the disease. Although the cause of Parkinson's is not fully known, depletion of the neurotransmitter dopamine may be involved.

Parkinson's patients may be treated with medication, but massive doses, which can cause undesirable side effects, are often required for control of the symptoms. More recently, a technique for making cells within the substantia nigra regenerate has been developed that makes use of a pump implanted in a patient's chest. A brain protein that may restore damaged neurons is pumped through the catheter under the skin and into

the substantia nigra of the basal ganglia. Current trials suggest some success with this method (Arnst & Weintraub, 2002).

Multiple Sclerosis   Approximately 400,000 Americans have multiple sclerosis, and every week about 200 more people are diagnosed (National Multiple Sclerosis Society, 2003). This degenerative disease of certain brain tissues can cause paralysis and, occasionally, blindness, deafness, and mental deterioration. Early symptoms include numbness, double vision, dragging of the feet, loss of bladder or bowel control, speech difficulties, and extreme fatigue. Symptoms may appear and disappear over a period of years; after that, deterioration is continuous.

The effects of multiple sclerosis result from the disintegration of myelin, a fatty membrane that surrounds the nerve fibers and facilitates the conduction of nerve impulses. Multiple sclerosis is an autoimmune disorder, so-called because the immune system fails to recognize its own tissue and attacks the myelin sheath surrounding the nerves.

Huntington's Disease   A hereditary disorder of the central nervous system, Huntington's disease is characterized by chronic physical and mental deterioration. Symptoms include involuntary muscle spasms, loss of motor abilities, personality changes, and other signs of mental disintegration. Because some of the symptoms are similar to those of epilepsy, Huntington's disease is sometimes mistaken for epilepsy.

The disease affects men and women alike, occurring at a rate of about 1 in every 10,000 (Huntington's Outreach Project for Education, 2004). The gene for Huntington's has been isolated, and a test is now available that indicates not only if one is a carrier of the gene but also at what age (roughly) a person will succumb to Huntington's disease (Morell, 1993). As will be seen later in this chapter, genetic counseling with this group of at-risk individuals is important.

Polio   Poliomyelitis is a viral disease that attacks the spinal nerves and destroys the cell bodies of motor neurons so that motor impulses cannot be carried from the spinal cord outward to the peripheral nerves or muscles. Depending on the degree of damage that is done, the individual may be left with difficulties of walking and moving properly, ranging from shrunken and ineffective limbs to full paralysis. Once a scourge of childhood, it is now on the verge of being conquered, although complications late in life from polio contracted years earlier (called post-polio syndrome) are often experienced by those who had the disease.

Paraplegia and Quadriplegia   Paraplegia is paralysis of the lower extremities of the body; it results from an injury to the lower portion of the spinal cord. Quadriplegia is paralysis of all four extremities and the trunk of the body; it occurs when the upper portion of the spinal cord is severed. Once the spinal cord has been severed, no motor impulses can descend to tissues below the cut nor can sensory impulses from the tissues below the cut ascend to the brain. As a consequence, a person usually loses bladder and bowel control. Moreover, the muscles below the cut area may well lose their tone, becoming weak and flaccid.

■ THE ENDOCRINE SYSTEM

Overview

The **endocrine system,** diagrammed in figure 2.3, complements the nervous system in controlling bodily activities. The endocrine system is made up of a number of ductless glands, which secrete hormones into the blood,

FIGURE 2.3 | The Endocrine System

(*Source:* Lankford, 1979, p. 232)

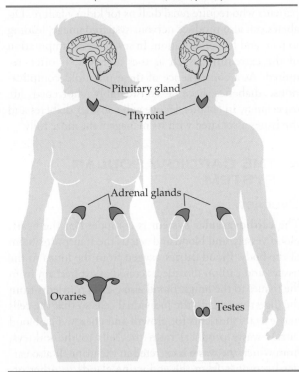

stimulating changes in target organs. The endocrine and nervous systems depend on each other, stimulating and inhibiting each other's activities. The nervous system is chiefly responsible for fast-acting, short-duration responses to changes in the body, whereas the endocrine system mainly governs slow-acting responses of long duration.

The endocrine system is regulated by the hypothalamus and the **pituitary gland.** Located at the base of the brain the pituitary has two lobes. The anterior pituitary lobe of the pituitary gland secretes hormones responsible for growth: somatotropic hormone (STH), which regulates bone, muscle, and other organ development; gonadotropic hormones, which control the growth, development, and secretion of the gonads (testes and ovaries); thyrotropic hormone (TSH), which controls the growth, development, and secretion of the thyroid gland; and adrenocorticotropic hormone (ACTH), which controls the growth and secretions of the cortex region of the adrenal glands (described in the section "The Adrenal Glands"). The posterior pituitary lobe produces oxytocin, which controls contractions during labor and lactation, and vasopressin, or antidiuretic hormone (ADH), which controls the water-absorbing ability of the kidneys.

The Adrenal Glands

The **adrenal glands** are two small glands located one on top of each of the kidneys. Each adrenal gland consists of an adrenal medulla and an adrenal cortex. The hormones of the adrenal medulla are epinephrine and norepinephrine, which were described earlier.

The adrenal cortex is stimulated by adrenocorticotropic hormone (ACTH) from the anterior lobe of the pituitary, and it releases hormones called steroids. These steroids include mineralocorticoids, glucocorticoids, androgens, and estrogens.

As figure 2.4 implies, the adrenal glands are critically involved in physiological and neuroendocrine reactions to stress. Both catecholamines, secreted in conjunction with sympathetic arousal, and corticosteroids are implicated in biological responses to stress. We will consider stress responses more fully in chapter 6.

Diabetes

Diabetes is a chronic endocrine disorder in which the body is not able to manufacture or properly use insulin. It is the third most common chronic illness in this country and one of the leading causes of death. Diabetes consists

FIGURE 2.4 | Adrenal Gland Activity in Response to Stress

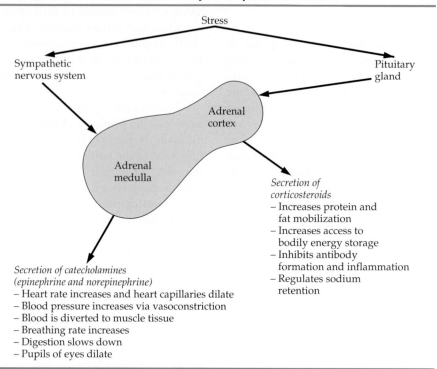

of two primary forms: Type I diabetes (sometimes called insulin-dependent diabetes) is a severe disorder that typically arises in late childhood or early adolescence. At least partly genetic in origin, Type I diabetes is believed to be an autoimmune disorder, possibly precipitated by an earlier viral infection. The immune system falsely identifies cells in the islets of Langerhans in the pancreas as invaders and destroys those cells, compromising or eliminating their ability to produce insulin.

Type II diabetes typically occurs after age 40 and is the more common form. In Type II diabetes, insulin may be produced by the body but there may not be enough of it, or the body may not be sensitive to it. It is heavily a disease of lifestyle, involving a disturbance in glucose metabolism and the delicate balance between insulin production and insulin responsiveness. This balance appears to be dysregulated by such factors as obesity and stress, among other contributing factors.

Diabetes is associated with a thickening of the arteries due to the buildup of wastes in the blood. As a consequence, diabetic patients show high rates of coronary heart disease. Diabetes is also the leading cause of blindness among adults, and it accounts for 50% of all the

patients who require renal dialysis for kidney failure. Diabetes can also produce nervous system damage, leading to pain and loss of sensation. In severe cases, amputation of the extremities, such as toes and feet, is often required. As a consequence of these manifold complications, diabetics have a considerably shortened life expectancy. In chapter 13, we will consider diabetes and the issues associated with its management more fully.

■ THE CARDIOVASCULAR SYSTEM

Overview

The **cardiovascular system** is composed of the heart, blood vessels, and blood and acts as the transport system of the body. Blood carries oxygen from the lungs to the tissues and carbon dioxide, excreted as expired air, from the tissues to the lungs. Blood also carries nutrients from the digestive tract to the individual cells so that the cells may extract nutrients for growth and energy. The blood carries waste products from the cells to the kidneys, from which the waste is excreted in the urine. It also carries hormones from the endocrine glands to other or-

FIGURE 2.5 | The Heart

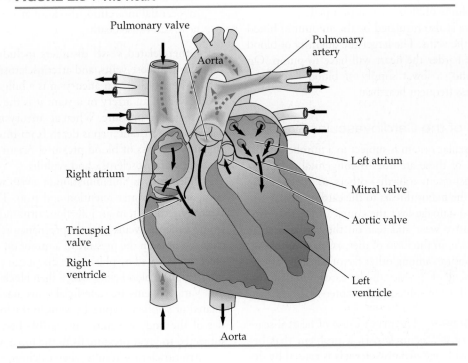

gans of the body and transports heat to the surface of the skin to control body temperature.

The arteries carry blood from the heart to other organs and tissues, where oxygen and nutrients are transported through the arterioles (tiny branches of the arteries) and the capillaries (smaller vessels that branch off from the arteries) to individual cells. Veins return the deoxygenated blood to the heart. Together, these vessels control peripheral circulation, dilating or constricting in response to a variety of bodily events.

The Heart

The heart functions as a pump, and its pumping action causes the blood to circulate throughout the body. The left side of the heart, consisting of the left atrium and left ventricle, takes in heavily oxygenated blood from the lungs and pumps it out into the aorta (the major artery leaving the heart), from which the blood passes into the smaller vessels (the arteries, arterioles, and capillaries) to reach the cell tissues. The blood exchanges its oxygen and nutrients for the waste materials of the cells and is then returned to the right side of the heart (right atrium and right ventricle), which pumps it back to the lungs via the pulmonary artery. Once oxygenated, the blood

returns to the left side of the heart through the pulmonary veins. The anatomy and functioning of the heart are pictured in figure 2.5.

The heart performs these functions through regular rhythmic phases of contraction and relaxation known as the cardiac cycle. There are two phases in the cardiac cycle, systole and diastole. During systole, blood is pumped out of the heart, and blood pressure in the blood vessels increases. As the muscle relaxes during diastole, blood pressure drops and blood is taken into the heart.

The flow of blood in and out of the heart is controlled by valves at the inlet and outlet of each ventricle. These heart valves ensure that blood flows in one direction only. The sounds that one hears when listening to the heart are the sounds of these valves closing. These heart sounds make it possible to time the cardiac cycle to determine how rapidly or slowly blood is being pumped in and out of the heart.

A number of factors influence the rate at which the heart contracts and relaxes. During exercise, emotional excitement, or stress, for example, the heart speeds up and the cardiac cycle is completed in a shorter time. Most of this speedup comes out of the diastolic period so that a chronically rapid heart rate reduces overall time for rest. Consequently, a chronically or excessively rapid heart rate can decrease the heart's strength, which may reduce the volume of blood that is pumped.

Heart rate is also regulated by the amount of blood flowing into the veins. The larger the quantity of blood available, the harder the heart will have to pump. On the other hand, a lower supply of blood leads to a weaker and less frequent heartbeat.

Disorders of the Cardiovascular System

The cardiovascular system is subject to a number of disorders. Some of these are due to congenital defects—that is, defects present at birth—others, to infection. By far, however, the major threats to the cardiovascular system are due to damage over the course of life that produces cumulative wear and tear on the cardiovascular system. Lifestyle, in the form of diet, exercise, smoking, and stress exposure, among other factors, heavily affects the development of diseases of the cardiovascular system, as we will see in subsequent chapters.

Atherosclerosis   The major cause of heart disease in this country is atherosclerosis, a problem that becomes worse with age. **Atherosclerosis** is caused by deposits of cholesterol and other substances on the arterial walls, which form plaques that narrow the arteries. The presence of atherosclerotic plaques reduces the flow of blood through the arteries and interferes with the passage of nutrients from the capillaries into the cells—a process that can lead to tissue damage. Damaged arterial walls are also potential sites for the formation of blood clots, which in themselves can completely obstruct a vessel and cut off the flow of blood.

Atherosclerosis is, in part, a disease of lifestyle, as we will see in chapter 13. It is associated with a number of poor health habits, such as smoking and a high-fat diet. Moreover, it is a very common health problem. These two factors make it of paramount interest to health psychologists and explain the concern over changing these poor health behaviors.

Atherosclerosis is associated with two primary clinical manifestations:

1. **Angina pectoris,** or chest pain, which occurs because the muscle tissue of the heart must continue its activity without a sufficient supply of oxygen or adequate removal of carbon dioxide and other waste products.

2. **Myocardial infarction (MI),** which is most likely to occur when a clot has developed in a coronary

vessel and blocks the flow of blood to the heart. A myocardial infarction, also known as a heart attack, can cause death.

Other related vessel disorders include aneurysms, phlebitis, varicose veins, and arteriosclerosis (or hardening of the arteries). An aneurysm is a bulge in a section of the wall of an artery or a vein; it is the reaction of a weak region to pressure. When an aneurysm ruptures, it can produce instantaneous death from internal hemorrhaging and loss of blood pressure. Aneurysms may be caused by arteriosclerosis and syphilis.

Phlebitis is an inflammation of a vein wall, often accompanied by water retention and pain. The condition typically results from an infection surrounding the vein, from varicose veins, from pregnancy-related bodily changes, or from the pressure of a tumor on the vein. The chief threat posed by phlebitis is that it can encourage the production of blood clots, which then block circulation.

Varicose veins are superficial veins that have become dilated or swollen. Typically, veins in the lower extremities of the body are most susceptible because they are subjected to great pressure from the force of gravity.

Arteriosclerosis results when calcium, salts, and scar tissue react with the elastic tissue of the arteries. The consequence is to decrease the elasticity of the arteries, making them rigid and hard. Blood pressure then increases because the arteries cannot dilate and constrict to help blood move, and hypertension (high blood pressure) may result.

Rheumatic Fever   Rheumatic fever is a bacterial infection that originates in the connective tissue and can spread to the heart, potentially affecting the functioning of the heart valves. The flaps of the valves may be changed into rigid, thickened structures that interfere with the flow of blood between the atrium and the ventricle. People with rheumatic fever, or with congenital heart disease, are particularly vulnerable to endocarditis, the inflammation of the membrane that lines the cavities of the heart, which is caused by staphylococcus or streptococcus organisms.

Blood Pressure

Blood pressure is the force that blood exerts against the blood vessel walls. During systole, the force on the blood vessel walls is greatest; during diastole, it falls to its lowest point. The measurement of blood pressure is a ratio of these two pressures.

Blood pressure is influenced by several factors, the first of which is cardiac output. Pressure against the arterial walls is greater as the volume of blood flow increases. A second factor influencing blood pressure is peripheral resistance, or the resistance to blood flow in the small arteries of the body (arterioles). Peripheral resistance is influenced by the viscosity (thickness) of the blood—specifically, the number of red blood cells and the amount of plasma the blood contains. Highly viscous blood produces higher blood pressure. In addition, blood pressure is influenced by the structure of the arterial walls: If the walls have been damaged, if they are clogged by deposits of waste, or if they have lost their elasticity, blood pressure will be higher. Chronically high blood pressure, called hypertension, is the consequence of too high a cardiac output or too high a peripheral resistance. We will consider the psychosocial issues involved in the management and treatment of hypertension in chapter 13.

The Blood

An adult's body contains approximately 5 liters of blood, which consists of plasma and cells. Plasma, the fluid portion of blood, occupies approximately 55% of the blood volume. The blood cells are suspended in the plasma, which contains plasma proteins and plasma electrolytes (salts) plus the substances that are being transported by the blood (oxygen and nutrients or carbon dioxide and waste materials). The remaining 45% of blood volume is made up of cells.

Blood cells are manufactured in the bone marrow, the substance in the hollow cavities of bones. Bone marrow contains five types of blood-forming cells: myeloblasts and monoblasts, both of which produce particular white blood cells; lymphoblasts, which produce lymphocytes; erythroblasts, which produce red blood cells; and megakaryocytes, which produce platelets. Each of these types of blood cells has an important function.

White blood cells play an important role in healing by absorbing and removing foreign substances from the body. They contain granules that secrete digestive enzymes which engulf and act on bacteria and other foreign particles, turning them into a form conducive to excretion.

Lymphocytes also play an important role in combating foreign substances. They produce antibodies—agents that destroy foreign substances through the antigen-antibody reaction. Together, these groups of cells play an important role in fighting infection and dis-

ease. We will consider them more fully in our discussion of the immune system.

Red blood cells are chiefly important because they contain hemoglobin, which is needed to carry oxygen and carbon dioxide throughout the body.

Platelets serve several important functions. They clump together to block small holes that develop in blood vessels and play an important role in blood clotting. When an injury occurs and tissues are damaged, platelets help form thromboplastin, which, in turn, acts on a substance in the plasma known as fibrinogen, changing it to fibrin. The formation of fibrin produces clotting.

Blood flow is responsible for the regulation of body temperature. When the body temperature is too high, skin blood vessels dilate and blood is sent to the skin, so that heat will be lost. When the body temperature is too low, skin blood vessels constrict and blood is kept away from the skin so that heat will be conserved and body temperature maintained. Alterations in skin blood flow are caused partly by the direct action of heat on skin blood vessels and partly by the temperature-regulating mechanism located in the hypothalamus, which alters the sympathetic impact on the skin blood vessels. Blood flow to the skin is also regulated by the catecholamines, epinephrine and norepinephrine. Norepinephrine generally constricts blood vessels (vasoconstriction), whereas epinephrine constricts skin blood vessels while dilating muscle blood vessels. These changes, in turn, increase the force of the heart's contractions.

Disorders Related to White Cell Production

Some blood disorders affect the production of white blood cells; they include leukemia, leukopenia, and leukocytosis. Leukemia is a disease of the bone marrow, and it is a common form of cancer. It causes the production of an excessive number of white blood cells, thus overloading the blood plasma and reducing the number of red blood cells that can circulate in the plasma. In the short term, anemia (a shortage of red blood cells) will result. In the long term, if left untreated, leukemia will cause death.

Leukopenia is a deficiency of white blood cells; it may accompany such diseases as tuberculosis, measles, and viral pneumonia. Leukopenia leaves an individual susceptible to diseases because it reduces the number of white blood cells available to combat infection.

Leukocytosis is an excessive number of white blood cells. It is a response to many infections, such as leukemia, appendicitis, and infectious mononucleosis. Infection stimulates the body to overproduce these infection-combating cells.

Disorders Related to Red Cell Production

Anemia is a condition in which the number of red blood cells or amount of hemoglobin is below normal. A temporary anemic condition experienced by many women is a consequence of menstruation; through loss of blood, much vital iron (essential for the production of hemoglobin) is lost. Iron supplements must sometimes be taken to offset this problem. Other forms of anemia, including aplastic anemia, may occur because the bone marrow is unable to produce a sufficient number of red blood cells. The result is a decrease in the blood's transport capabilities, causing tissues to receive too little oxygen and to be left with too much carbon dioxide. When it is not checked, anemia can cause permanent damage to the nervous system and produce chronic weakness.

Erythrocytosis is characterized by an excess of red blood cells. It may result from a lack of oxygen in the tissues or as a secondary manifestation of other diseases. Erythrocytosis increases the viscosity of the blood and reduces the rate of blood flow.

Sickle-cell anemia is another disease related to red blood cell production. Most common among Blacks, it is a genetically transmitted inability to produce normal red blood cells. These cells are sickle-shaped instead of flattened spheres, and they contain abnormal hemoglobin protein molecules. They are vulnerable to rupture, leaving the individual susceptible to anemia. The sickle cell appears to be a genetic adaptation promoting resistance to malaria among African Blacks. Unfortunately, although these cells are effective in the short term against malaria, the long-term implications are life threatening.

Clotting Disorders

A third group of blood disorders involves clotting dysfunctions. Hemophilia affects individuals who are unable to produce thromboplastin and fibrin. Therefore, their blood cannot clot naturally in response to injury, and they may bleed to death unless they receive medication.

As noted earlier, clots (or thromboses) may sometimes develop in the blood vessels. This is most likely to occur if arterial or venous walls have been damaged or roughened because of the buildup of cholesterol. Platelets then adhere to the roughened area, leading to the formation of a clot. A clot formed in this manner may have very serious consequences if it occurs in the blood vessels leading to the heart (coronary thrombosis) or brain (cerebral thrombosis) because it will block the vital flow of blood to these organs. When a clot occurs in a vein, it may become detached and form an embolus, which may finally become lodged in the blood vessels to the lungs, causing pulmonary obstruction. Death is a likely consequence of all these conditions.

■ THE RESPIRATORY SYSTEM

The Structure and Functions of the Respiratory System

Respiration, or breathing, has three main functions: to take in oxygen, to excrete carbon dioxide, and to regulate the composition of the blood.

The body needs oxygen to metabolize food. During the process of metabolism, oxygen combines with carbon atoms in food, producing carbon dioxide (CO_2). The respiratory system brings in air, most notably oxygen, through inspiration; it eliminates carbon dioxide through expiration.

The **respiratory system** involves a number of organs, including the nose, mouth, pharynx, trachea, diaphragm, abdominal muscles, and lungs. Air is inhaled through the nose and mouth and then passes through the pharynx and larynx to the trachea. The trachea, a muscular tube extending downward from the larynx, divides at its lower end into two branches called the primary bronchi. Each bronchus enters a lung, where it then subdivides into secondary bronchi, still-smaller bronchioles, and, finally, microscopic alveolar ducts, which contain many tiny, clustered sacs called alveoli. The alveoli and the capillaries are responsible for the exchange of oxygen and carbon dioxide. A diagram of the respiratory system appears in figure 2.6.

The inspiration of air is an active process, brought about by the contraction of muscles. Inspiration causes the lungs to expand inside the thorax (the chest wall). Expiration, in contrast, is a passive function, brought about by the relaxation of the lungs, which reduces the volume of the lungs within the thorax. The lungs fill most of the space within the thorax, called the thoracic cavity, and are very elastic, depending on the thoracic walls for support. Therefore, if air were to get into the space between the thoracic wall and the lungs, one or both lungs would collapse.

Respiratory movements are controlled by a respiratory center in the medulla of the brain. The functions of this center depend partly on the chemical composition of the blood. For example, if the blood's carbon dioxide

FIGURE 2.6 | The Respiratory System   (*Source:* Lankford, 1979, p. 467)

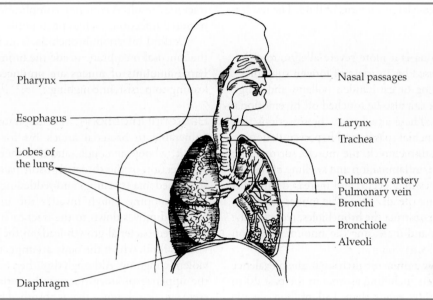

level rises too high, the respiratory center will be stimulated and respiration will be increased. If the carbon dioxide level falls too low, the respiratory center will slow down until the carbon dioxide level is back to normal.

The respiratory system is also responsible for coughing. A large amount of dust and other foreign material is inhaled with every breath. Some of these substances are trapped in the mucus of the nose and the air passages and are then conducted back toward the throat, where they are swallowed. When a large amount of mucus collects in the large airways, it is removed by coughing (a forced expiratory effort).

Disorders of the Respiratory System

Asphyxia, Anoxia, and Hyperventilation
Several disorders of the respiratory system—including asphyxia, anoxia, and hyperventilation—have little significance because they are typically short-lived. When they occur on a long-term basis, however, these disorders can have severe effects.

Asphyxia, a condition of oxygen lack and carbon dioxide excess, may occur when there is a respiratory obstruction, when breathing occurs in a confined space so that expired air is reinhaled, or when respiration is insufficient for the body's needs. Asphyxia increases respiratory activity.

Anoxia, a shortage of oxygen alone, is more serious. People suffering from anoxia may rapidly become disoriented, lose all sense of danger, and pass into a coma without increasing their breathing. This is a danger to which test pilots are exposed when they take their planes to very high altitudes, so pilots are carefully trained to be alert to the signs of anoxia so that they can take immediate corrective steps.

Another disruption of the carbon dioxide–oxygen balance results from hyperventilation. During periods of intense emotional excitement, people often breathe deeply, reducing the carbon dioxide content of the blood. Because carbon dioxide is a vasodilator (that is, it dilates the blood vessels), a consequence of hyperventilation is constriction of blood vessels and reduced blood flow to the brain. As a result, the individual may experience impaired vision, difficulty in thinking clearly, and dizziness.

Severe problems occur when a person stops breathing and becomes unconscious. If artificial respiration is not initiated within 2 minutes, brain damage and even death may result.

Hay Fever
Hay fever is a seasonal allergic reaction to foreign bodies—including pollens, dust, and other airborne allergens—that enter the lungs. These irritants prompt the body to produce substances called histamines,

which cause the capillaries of the lungs to become in-flamed and to release large amounts of fluid. The result is violent sneezing.

Asthma

Asthma is a more severe allergic reaction, which can be caused by a variety of foreign substances, including dust, dog or cat dander, pollens, and fungi. An asthma attack can also be touched off by emotional stress or exercise. These attacks may be so serious that they produce bronchial spasms and hyperventilation.

During an asthma attack, the muscles surrounding air tubes constrict, inflammation and swelling of the lin-ing of the air tubes may occur, and increased mucus is produced, clogging the air tubes. The mucus secretion, in turn, may then obstruct the bronchioles, reducing the supply of oxygen and increasing the amount of carbon dioxide.

Statistics show a dramatic increase in the prevalence of allergic disorders including asthma in the past 20 to 30 years. Currently, more than 130 million people worldwide have asthma, and the numbers are increasing, especially in industrialized countries (eMedicine.com, 2004). Rates are increasing fastest in urban as opposed to rural areas. The reasons for these dramatic changes are not yet fully known. One intriguing fact that may pro-vide a clue to the increase in allergic sensitization is that children who have a lot of childhood infectious diseases are less likely to develop allergies, suggesting that expo-sure to infectious agents may actually have a protective effect against allergies. Thus, paradoxically, the im-proved hygiene of industrialized countries may actually be contributing to high rates of allergic disorders (Yaz-danbakhsh, Kremsner, & van Ree, 2002).

Viral Infections

The respiratory system is vulnera-ble to a number of infections and chronic disorders. Per-haps the most familiar of these is the common cold, a viral infection of the upper and sometimes the lower res-piratory tract. The infection that results causes discom-fort, congestion, and excessive secretion of mucus. The incubation period for a cold—that is, the time between exposure to the virus and onset of symptoms—is 12 to 72 hours, and the typical duration of a cold is a few days. Secondary bacterial infections may complicate the illness. These occur because the primary viral infection causes inflammation of the mucous membranes, reduc-ing their ability to prevent secondary infection.

A more serious viral infection of the respiratory sys-tem is influenza, which can occur in epidemic form. Flu viruses attack the lining of the respiratory tract, killing healthy cells. Fever and inflammation of the respiratory tract may result. A common complication is a secondary bacterial infection, such as pneumonia.

A third infection, bronchitis, is an inflammation of the mucosal membrane inside the bronchi of the lungs. Large amounts of mucus are produced in bronchitis, leading to persistent coughing.

Bacterial Infections

The respiratory system is also vulnerable to bacterial attack by, for example, strep throat, whooping cough, and diphtheria. Strep throat, an infection of the throat and soft palate, is character-ized by edema (swelling) and reddening.

Whooping cough invades the upper respiratory tract and moves down to the trachea and bronchi. The associated bacterial growth leads to the production of a viscous fluid, which the body attempts to expel through violent coughing. Although diphtheria is an infection of the upper respiratory tract, its bacterial organisms se-crete a toxic substance that is absorbed by the blood and is thus circulated throughout the body. Therefore, this disease can damage nerves, cardiac muscle, kidneys, and the adrenal cortex.

For the most part, strep throat, whooping cough, and diphtheria do not cause permanent damage to the upper respiratory tract. Their main danger is the possibility of secondary infection, which results from lowered resis-tance. However, these bacterial infections can cause per-manent damage to other tissues, including heart tissue.

Chronic Obstructive Pulmonary Disease (COPD)

Chronic obstructive pulmonary disease is the fourth leading killer of people in the United States. Some 15 million Americans have COPD, and although lung cancer is deadlier than COPD, COPD is much more common and nearly as deadly. Chronic bronchitis and emphysema are two of the familiar disorders that comprise COPD.

Pulmonary emphysema involves a persistent ob-struction of the flow of air. It occurs when the alveoli be-come dilated, atrophied, and thin, so that they lose their elasticity and cannot constrict during exhalation. As a result, exhalation becomes difficult and forced, so that carbon dioxide is not readily eliminated. Emphysema is caused by a variety of factors, including long-term smoking.

Although COPD is not curable, it is highly pre-ventable. Its chief cause is smoking, which accounts for approximately 85% of all cases of COPD. Specifically, exposure to toxic substances over a long period leads to inflammation and swelling of the cells lining the lungs. In COPD, this swelling is to a point that it restricts the flow of air, thus sapping energy and producing substantial resulting disability, high medical costs, and costs to the economy (Lemonick, 2004).

Pneumonia

There are two main types of pneumonia. Lobar pneumonia is a primary infection of the entire lobe of a lung. The alveoli become inflamed, and the normal oxygen–carbon dioxide exchange between the blood and alveoli can be disrupted. Spread of infection to other organs is also likely.

Bronchial pneumonia, which is confined to the bronchi, is typically a secondary infection that may occur as a complication of other disorders, such as a severe cold or flu. It is not as serious as lobar pneumonia.

Tuberculosis and Pleurisy

Tuberculosis is an infectious disease caused by bacteria that invade lung tissue. When the invading bacilli are surrounded by macrophages (white blood cells of a particular type), they form a clump called a tubercle, which is the typical manifestation of this disease. Eventually, through a process called caseation, the center of the tubercle turns into a cheesy mass, which can produce cavities in the lung. Such cavities, in turn, can give rise to permanent scar tissue, causing chronic difficulties in oxygen and carbon dioxide exchange between the blood and the alveoli.

Pleurisy is an inflammation of the pleura, the membrane that surrounds the organs in the thoracic cavity. The inflammation, which produces a sticky fluid, is usually a consequence of pneumonia or tuberculosis and can be extremely painful.

Lung Cancer

Lung cancer, or carcinoma of the lung, is an increasingly common disease. It is caused by smoking and other factors as yet unknown, including possible environmental carcinogens (air pollution) or cancer-causing substances encountered in the workplace (such as asbestos).

The affected cells in the lungs begin to divide in a rapid and unrestricted manner, producing a tumor. Malignant cells grow faster than healthy cells; they crowd out the healthy cells and rob them of nutrients, causing them to die, and then spread into surrounding tissue.

Conclusion

A number of respiratory disorders are tied directly to health problems that can be addressed by health psy-

chologists. For example, smoking is a major health problem that is implicated in both pulmonary emphysema and lung cancer. The spread of tuberculosis can be reduced by encouraging people at risk to obtain regular chest X rays. Faulty methods of infection control, dangerous substances in the workplace, and air pollution are also factors that contribute to the incidence of respiratory problems.

As we will see in chapters 3, 4, and 5, health psychologists have addressed many of these problems. In addition, some of the respiratory disorders we have considered are chronic conditions with which an individual may live for some time. Consequently, issues of long-term physical, vocational, social, and psychological rehabilitation become crucial, and we will cover these issues in chapters 11, 13, and 14.

■ THE DIGESTIVE SYSTEM AND THE METABOLISM OF FOOD

Overview

Food, essential for survival, is converted through the process of metabolism into heat and energy, and it supplies nutrients for growth and the repair of tissues. But before food can be used by cells, it must be changed into a form suitable for absorption into the blood. This conversion process is called digestion.

The Functioning of the Digestive System

Food is first lubricated by saliva in the mouth, where it forms a soft, rounded lump called a bolus. It passes through the esophagus by means of peristalsis, a unidirectional muscular movement toward the stomach. The stomach produces various gastric secretions, including pepsin and hydrochloric acid, to further the digestive process. The sight or even the thought of food starts the flow of gastric juices.

As food progresses from the stomach to the duodenum (the intersection of the stomach and lower intestine), the pancreas becomes involved in the digestive process. Pancreatic juices, which are secreted into the duodenum, contain several enzymes that break down proteins, carbohydrates, and fats. A critical function of the pancreas is the production of the hormone insulin, which facilitates the entry of glucose into the bodily tissues. The liver also plays an important role in metabolism by producing bile, which enters the duodenum and helps break down fats. Bile is stored in the gallbladder and is secreted into the duodenum as needed.

Most metabolic products are water soluble and can be easily transported in the blood. However, other substances are not soluble in water and therefore must be transported in the blood plasma as complex substances combined with plasma protein. Known as lipids, these substances include fats, cholesterol, and lecithin. An excess of lipids in the blood is called hyperlipidemia, a condition common in diabetes, some kidney diseases, hyperthyroidism, and alcoholism. It is also a causal factor in heart disease (see chapters 4 and 13).

The absorption of food primarily takes place in the small intestine, which produces enzymes that complete the breakdown of proteins to amino acids. The motility of the small intestine is under the control of the sympathetic and parasympathetic nervous systems. Parasympathetic activity speeds up metabolism, whereas sympathetic nervous system activity reduces it.

Food then passes into the large intestine (whose successive segments are known as the cecum and the ascending, transverse, descending, and sigmoid colon), which acts largely as a storage organ for the accumulation of food residue and helps in the reabsorption of water. The entry of feces into the rectum then brings about the urge to defecate, or expel, the solid waste from the body via the anus. The organs involved in the metabolism of food are pictured in figure 2.7.

Disorders of the Digestive System

The digestive system is susceptible to a number of disorders, some of which are only mildly uncomfortable and temporary and others of which are more serious and chronic.

Gastroenteritis, Diarrhea, and Dysentery

Gastroenteritis is an inflammation of the lining of the stomach and small intestine. It may be caused by such factors as excessive amounts of food or drink, contaminated food or water, or food poisoning. Symptoms appear approximately 2 to 4 hours after the ingestion of food; they include vomiting, diarrhea, abdominal cramps, and nausea.

Diarrhea, characterized by watery and frequent bowel movements, occurs when the lining of the small and large intestines cannot properly absorb water or digested food. Chronic diarrhea may result in serious disturbances of fluid and electrolyte (sodium, potassium, magnesium, calcium) balance.

Dysentery is similar to diarrhea except that mucus, pus, and blood are also excreted. It may be caused by a

FIGURE 2.7 | The Digestive System (*Source: Lankford, 1979, p. 523*)

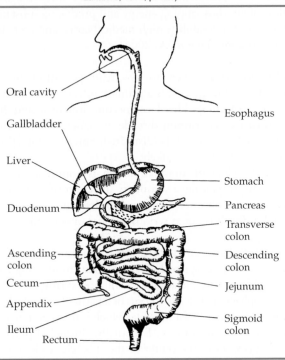

protozoan that attacks the large intestine (amoebic dysentery) or by a bacterial organism. Although these conditions are only rarely life threatening in industrialized countries, in less developed countries, they are common causes of death.

Peptic Ulcer A peptic ulcer is an open sore in the lining of the stomach or the duodenum. It results from the hypersecretion of hydrochloric acid and occurs when pepsin, a protein-digesting enzyme secreted in the stomach, digests a portion of the stomach wall or duodenum. A bacterium called H. pylori is believed to contribute to the development of many ulcers. Once thought to be primarily psychological in origin, ulcers are now believed to be aggravated by stress, but not necessarily caused by it (Goodwin & Stein, 2002).

Gallbladder Gallstones are made up of a combination of cholesterol, calcium, bilirubin, and inorganic salts. When gallstones move into the duct of the gallbladder, they may cause painful spasms; such stones must often be removed surgically. Infection and inflammation of the gallbladder is called cholecystitis and may be a precondition for gallstones.

Appendicitis   A common condition that occurs when wastes and bacteria accumulate in the appendix. If the small opening of the appendix becomes obstructed, bacteria can easily proliferate. Soon this condition gives rise to pain, increased peristalsis, and nausea. If the appendix ruptures and the bacteria are released into the abdominal cavity or peritoneum, they can cause further infection (peritonitis) or even death.

Hepatitis   A common, serious, contagious disease that attacks the liver is hepatitis. "Hepatitis" means inflammation of the liver, and the disease produces swelling, tenderness, and sometimes permanent damage. When the liver is inflamed, bilirubin, a product of the breakdown of hemoglobin, cannot easily pass into the bile ducts. Consequently, it remains in the blood, causing a yellowing of the skin known as jaundice. Other common symptoms are fatigue, fever, muscle or joint aches, nausea, vomiting, loss of appetite, abdominal pain, and sometimes diarrhea.

There are several types of hepatitis, which differ in severity and mode of transmission. Hepatitis A, caused by viruses, is typically transmitted through food and water. It is often spread by poorly cooked seafood or through unsanitary preparation or storage of food. Hepatitis B is a more serious form, with more than 350 million carriers in the world and an estimated 4.8 million in the United States. Also known as serum hepatitis, it is caused by a virus and is transmitted by the transfusion of infected blood, by improperly sterilized needles, through sexual contact, and through mother-to-infant contact. It is a special risk among intravenous drug users. Its symptoms are similar to those of hepatitis A but are far more serious. At present, hepatitis B is a particular risk for people of Asian descent. They are 20 to 30 times more likely to be infected than any other group in the United States, in large part because hepatitis B is so common throughout Asia (Gottlieb & Yi, 2003).

Hepatitis C, also spread via blood and needles, is most commonly caused by blood transfusions; more than 1% of Americans are carriers. Hepatitis D is found mainly in intravenous drug users who are also carriers of hepatitis B, necessary for the hepatitis D virus to spread. Finally, hepatitis E resembles hepatitis A but is caused by a different virus (Margolis & Moses, 1992; National Center for Health Statistics, 1996).

■ THE RENAL SYSTEM

Overview

The **renal system**—consisting of the kidneys, ureters, urinary bladder, and urethra—is also critically important in metabolism. The kidneys are chiefly responsible for the regulation of the bodily fluids; their principal function is to produce urine. The ureters contain smooth muscle tissue, which contracts, causing peristaltic waves to move urine to the bladder, a muscular bag that acts as a reservoir for urine. The urethra then conducts urine from the bladder out of the body. The anatomy of the renal system is pictured in figure 2.8.

Urine contains surplus water, surplus electrolytes, waste products from the metabolism of food, and surplus acids or alkalis. By carrying these products out of the body, urine maintains water balance, electrolyte balance, and blood pH. Of the electrolytes, sodium and potassium are especially important because they are involved in the normal chemical reactions of the body, muscular contractions, and the conduction of nerve impulses. Thus, an important function of the kidneys is to maintain an adequate balance of sodium and potassium ions.

In the case of certain diseases, the urine also contains abnormal amounts of some constituents; therefore, urinalysis offers important diagnostic clues to many disorders. For example, an excess of glucose may indicate diabetes, an excess of red blood cells may indicate a kidney disorder, and so on. This is one of the reasons that a medical checkup usually includes a urinalysis.

FIGURE 2.8 | The Renal System   (*Source:* Lankford, 1979, p. 585)

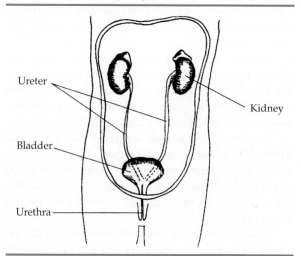

One of the chief functions of the kidneys is to control the water balance in the body. For example, on a hot day when a person has been active and has perspired profusely, relatively little urine will be produced, so that the body may retain more water. This is because much water has already been lost through the skin. On the other hand, on a cold day when a person is relatively inactive or a good deal of liquid has been consumed, urine output will be higher, so as to prevent overhydration.

To summarize, the urinary system regulates bodily fluids by removing surplus water, surplus electrolytes, and the waste products generated by the metabolism of food.

Disorders of the Renal System

The renal system is vulnerable to a number of disorders. Among the most common are urinary tract infections, to which women are especially vulnerable and which can result in considerable pain, especially on urination. If untreated, they can lead to more serious infection.

Acute glomerular nephritis is a disease that results from an antigen-antibody reaction in which the glomeruli of the kidneys become markedly inflamed. These inflammatory reactions can cause total or partial blockage of a large number of glomeruli, which may lead to increased permeability of the glomerular membrane, allowing large amounts of protein to leak in. When there is rupture of the membrane, large numbers of red blood cells may also pass into the glomerular filtrate. In severe cases, total renal shutdown occurs. Acute glomerular nephritis is usually a secondary response to a streptococcus infection. The infection itself does not damage the kidneys, but when antibodies develop, the antibodies and the antigen react with each other to form a precipitate, which becomes entrapped in the middle of the glomerular membrane. This infection usually subsides within 2 weeks.

Another common cause of acute renal shutdown is tubular necrosis, which involves destruction of the epithelial cells in the tubules of the kidneys. Poisons that destroy the tubular epithelial cells and severe circulatory shock are the most common causes of tubular necrosis.

Nephrons are the basic structural and functional units of the kidneys. In many types of kidney disease, such as that associated with hypertension, large numbers of nephrons are destroyed or damaged so severely that the remaining nephrons cannot perform their normal functions.

Kidney failure is a severe disorder because the inability to produce an adequate amount of urine will cause the waste products of metabolism, as well as surplus inorganic salts and water, to be retained in the body. An artificial kidney, a kidney transplant, or **kidney dialysis** may be required in order to rid the body of its wastes. Although these technologies can cleanse the blood to remove the excess salts, water, and metabolites, they are highly stressful medical procedures. Kidney transplants carry many health risks, and kidney dialysis can be extremely uncomfortable for patients. Consequently, health psychologists have been involved in addressing the problems experienced by kidney patients.

■ THE REPRODUCTIVE SYSTEM AND AN INTRODUCTION TO GENETICS

The development of the reproductive system is controlled by the pituitary gland. The anterior pituitary lobe produces the gonadotropic hormones, which control development of the ovaries in females and the testes in males. A diagrammatic representation of the human reproductive system appears in figure 2.9.

The Ovaries and Testes

The female has two ovaries located in the pelvis. Each month, one of the ovaries produces an ovum (egg), which is discharged at ovulation into the fallopian tubes. If the ovum is not fertilized (by sperm), it remains in the uterine cavity for about 14 days and is then flushed out of the system with the uterine endometrium and its blood vessels (during menstruation).

The ovaries also produce the hormones estrogen and progesterone. Estrogen leads to the development of secondary sex characteristics in the female, including breasts and the female distribution of both body fat and body hair. Progesterone, which is produced during the second half of the menstrual cycle to prepare the body for pregnancy, declines if pregnancy fails to occur.

In males, testosterone is produced by the interstitial cells of the testes under the control of the anterior pituitary lobe. It brings about the production of sperm and the development of secondary sex characteristics, including growth of the beard, deepening of the voice, male distribution of body hair, and both skeletal and muscular growth.

Fertilization and Gestation

When sexual intercourse takes place and ejaculation occurs, sperm are released into the vagina. These sperm, which have a high degree of motility, proceed upward

FIGURE 2.9 | The Reproductive System   (*Source:* J. H. Green, 1978, p. 122; Lankford, 1979, p. 688)

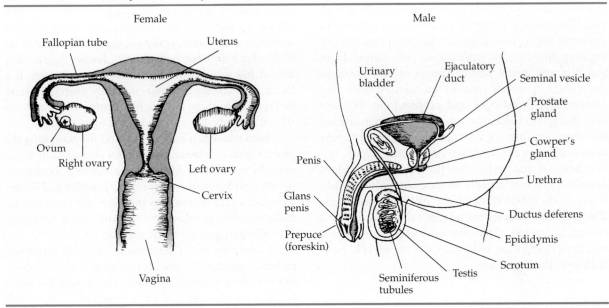

through the uterus into the fallopian tubes, where one sperm may fertilize an ovum. The fertilized ovum then travels down the fallopian tube into the uterine cavity, where it embeds itself in the uterine wall and develops over the next 9 months into a human being.

Disorders of the Reproductive System

The reproductive system is vulnerable to a number of diseases and disorders. Among the most common and problematic are sexually transmitted diseases, which occur through sexual intercourse or other forms of sexually intimate activity. These include herpes, gonorrhea, syphilis, genital warts, chlamydia, and the most serious, AIDS.

For women, a risk of several sexually transmitted diseases is that chronic pelvic inflammatory disease (PID) may result, which may produce a variety of unpleasant symptoms, including severe abdominal pain, and may lead to infections that may compromise fertility. Other gynecologic disorders to which women are vulnerable include vaginitis, endometriosis (in which pieces of the endometrial lining of the uterus move into the fallopian tubes or abdominal cavity, grow, and spread to other sites), cysts, and fibroids (nonmalignant growths in the uterus).

The reproductive system is also vulnerable to cancer, including testicular cancer in men (see chapter 4) and gynecologic cancers in women. Every 6.4 minutes, more than 80,000 times per year, a woman in the United

States is diagnosed with a gynecologic cancer, including cancer of the cervix, uterus, and ovaries (Gynecological Cancer Foundation, 2003). Endometrial cancer is the most common female pelvic malignancy, and ovarian cancer is the most lethal.

Women are vulnerable to disorders of the menstrual cycle, including amenorrhea, which is absence of menses, and oligomenorrhea, which is infrequent menstruation. These problems may originate in the hypothalamus, in the anterior pituitary, or in the ovaries or reproductive tract. Location of the cause is essential for correcting the problem, which may include hormone therapy or surgery.

Approximately 8% of U.S. couples experience fertility problems, defined as the inability to conceive a pregnancy after 1 year of regular sexual intercourse without contraception. Once believed to be emotional in origin, researchers have now concluded that there is little evidence for psychogenesis in infertility (Pasch & Dunkel-Schetter, 1997). Infertility, nonetheless, can create substantial psychological distress. Fortunately, over the past 2 decades, the technology for treating infertility has improved. A variety of drug treatments have been developed, as have more invasive technologies. In vitro fertilization is the most widely used method of assistive reproductive technology, and the success rate for IVF is nearly 30% (American Society for Reproductive Medicine, 2004).

Menopause is not a disorder of the reproductive system but, rather, occurs when a woman's reproductive life ends. Because of a variety of unpleasant symptoms that can occur during the transition into menopause, including sleep disorders, hot flashes, joint pain, forgetfulness, and dizziness, many women choose to take hormone therapy (HT), which typically includes estrogen or a combination of estrogen and progesterone. HT was once thought to reduce the symptoms of menopause but also protect against the development of coronary artery disease, osteoporosis, and even Alzheimer's disease. It is now believed that, rather than protecting against these disorders, HT may actually increase some of these risks (Hays et al., 2003; Hodis et al., 2003; Manson et al., 2003). HT also somewhat increases the risks of breast cancer. As a result of this new evidence, many women and their doctors are rethinking the use of HT, especially over the long term.

Genetics and Health

DNA is coming to a neighborhood near you (Plomin, 1998, p. 53).

The fetus starts life as a single cell, which contains all the inherited information from both parents that will determine its characteristics. The genetic code regulates such factors as eye and hair color, as well as behavioral factors. Genetic material for inheritance lies in the nucleus of the cell in the form of 46 chromosomes, 23 from the mother and 23 from the father. Two of these 46 are sex chromosomes, which are an X from the mother and either an X or a Y from the father. If the father provides an X chromosome, a female child will result; if he provides a Y chromosome, a male child will result.

Genetic Studies   The knowledge produced by genetic studies has provided valuable information about the inheritance of susceptibility to disease (Harmon, 2004). Among several methods, scientists have bred strains of rats, mice, and other laboratory animals that are sensitive or insensitive to the development of particular diseases and then used these strains to study other contributors to illness onset, the course of illness, and so on. For example, a strain of rats that is susceptible to cancer may be used to study the development of this disease and the cofactors that determine its appearance. The initial susceptibility of the rats ensures that many of them will develop malignancies when implanted with carcinogenic (cancer-causing) materials.

In humans, several types of research help demonstrate whether a characteristic is genetically acquired. Studies of families, for example, can reveal whether members of the same family are statistically more likely to develop a disorder, such as heart disease, than are unrelated individuals within a similar environment. If a factor is genetically determined, family members would be expected to show it more frequently than would unrelated individuals.

Twin research is another method for examining the genetic basis of a characteristic. If a characteristic is genetically transmitted, identical twins share it more commonly than fraternal twins or other brothers and sisters. This is because identical twins share the same genetic makeup, whereas other brothers and sisters have only partially overlapping genetic makeup.

Examining the characteristics of twins reared together as opposed to twins reared apart is also informative regarding genetics. Attributes that emerge for twins reared apart are suspected to be genetically determined, especially if the rate of occurrence between twins reared together and those reared apart is the same.

Finally, studies of adopted children also help identify which characteristics are genetic and which are environmentally produced. Adopted children should not manifest genetically transmitted characteristics from their adopted parents, but they would very likely manifest environmentally transmitted characteristics.

Consider, for example, obesity, which is a risk factor for a number of disorders, including coronary artery disease and diabetes. If research indicates that twins reared apart show highly similar body weights, then we would suspect that body weight has a genetic component. If, on the other hand, weight within a family is highly related, and adopted children show the same weight as parents and their natural offspring, then we would look to the family diet as a potential cause of obesity. For many attributes, including obesity, both environmental and genetic factors are involved.

Research like this has increasingly uncovered the genetic contribution to many health disorders and behavioral factors that may pose risks to health. Such diseases as asthma, Alzheimer's, cystic fibrosis, muscular dystrophy, Tay-Sachs, and Huntington's, as well as a number of chromosomal abnormalities, clearly have a genetic basis. There is also a genetic basis for coronary heart disease and for some forms of cancer, including some breast and colon cancers.

Genetic contributions to obesity and alcoholism have emerged in recent years, and even some personality characteristics, such as optimism, which is believed to have protective health effects, appear to have genetic underpinnings (Plomin et al., 1992). Continuing advances in the field of genetics will undoubtedly yield much more information about the genetic role in the behavioral factors that contribute to health and illness.

Genetics and Psychology   Psychologists have important roles to play with respect to the genetic contribution to disorders (Patenaude, Guttmacher, & Collins, 2002). The first role involves genetic counseling. Prenatal diagnostic tests are currently available that permit the detection of a variety of genetically based disorders, including Tay-Sachs disease, cystic fibrosis, muscular dystrophy, Huntington's disease, and breast cancer (Harmon, 2004). Helping people cope with genetic vulnerabilities of this kind will be an important role for psychologists.

In addition, individuals who have a history of genetic disorders in their family, those who have already given birth to a child with a genetic disorder, or those who have repeated reproductive problems, such as multiple miscarriages, often seek such counseling. In some cases, technological advances have made it possible for some of these problems to be treated before birth. For example, drug therapy can treat some genetically transmitted metabolic defects, and surgery in utero has been performed to correct certain neural problems. However, when a prenatal diagnosis reveals that the fetus has an abnormal condition that cannot be corrected, the parents often must make the difficult decision of whether to have an abortion.

In other cases, individuals may learn of a genetic risk to their health as children, adolescents, or young adults. Breast cancer, for example, runs in families, and among young women whose mothers, aunts, or sisters have developed breast cancer, vulnerability is higher. Some of the genes that contribute to the development of breast cancer have recently been identified, and tests are now available to determine whether a genetic susceptibility is present, although, unfortunately, this type of cancer accounts for only 5% of breast cancer. Women who carry these genetic susceptibilities are more likely to develop the disease at an earlier age and thus, these women are at high risk and need careful monitoring and potentially counseling as well (Couzin, 2003; Grady, 2003).

Many scientific investigations attest to the immediate distress and even long-term distress that carriers of genetic disorders may experience (Cella et al., 2002; De-

Wit et al., 1998; Tercyak et al., 2001; Timman, Roos, Maat-Kievit, & Tibben, 2004). In fact, the reactions to this kind of bad news can be so problematic that many people concerned with ethical issues in medicine question the value of telling people about their genetic risks if nothing can be done to treat them. Growing evidence suggests, however, that people at risk for treatable disorders may benefit from genetic testing and not suffer the same degree of psychological distress (e.g., P. B. Jacobsen, Valdimarsdottir, Brown, & Offit, 1997).

Moreover, in some cases, genetic risks are magnified because they interact with environmental factors. For example, some smokers have a genetic susceptibility to lung cancer. Consequently if they are identified early, encouraging them not to begin smoking or to stop smoking if they are already smokers may substantially reduce the likelihood of their going on to develop cancer (Lipkus, McBride, Pollack, Lyna, & Bepler, 2004).

Psychologists have an important role to play in genetic counseling to help people modify their risk status. Knowledge of distress patterns and of who is most likely to be distressed can be helpful for counseling those who learn of their genetic risks (for example, Codori, Slaveny, Young, Miglioretti, & Brandt, 1997). There are not only genetic bases of diseases, there are also genetic bases for fighting diseases. That is, certain genes may act as protective factors against development of a disease. An example is a specific gene that appears to regulate whether the immune system can identify cancer (Carey, 2002). Just as attention to the genetic bases of disease will occupy research attention for decades to come, so the protective genetic factors that keep so many of us so healthy for so long may become better understood as well.

The coming decades will reveal other genetic bases of major diseases, and tests will become available for identifying one's genetic risk. What are the psychosocial ramifications of such technological developments? These issues are addressed in chapter 3, and they take on a special urgency by virtue of the ethical issues they raise. For example, if prospective medical insurers or employers are allowed to conduct genetic screening, could an individual's at-risk status be used to deny that individual health insurance or employment (Faden & Kass, 1993)? How might one avoid such abuses of the technology?

As yet, our ability to deal intelligently with such important psychological, social, and ethical issues has not kept pace with our scientific capacity to elucidate the role of genetics in illness and risk factors. An emerging discussion is essential if we are to make proper use of these valuable and important technologies. Suffice it to say here that the role of health psychologists in this debate is expanding and will evolve further over the coming decades.

■ THE IMMUNE SYSTEM

Disease can be caused by a variety of factors, including genetic defects, hormone imbalances, nutritional deficiencies, and infection. In this section, we are primarily concerned with the transmission of disease by infection—that is, the invasion of microbes and their growth in the body. The microbes that cause infection are transmitted to people in four ways: direct transmission, indirect transmission, biological transmission, and mechanical transmission:

- Direct transmission involves bodily contact, such as handshaking, kissing, and sexual intercourse. For example, genital herpes is generally contracted by direct transmission.

- Indirect transmission (or environmental transmission) occurs when microbes are passed to an individual via airborne particles, dust, water, soil, or food. Influenza is an example of an environmentally transmitted disease.

- Biological transmission occurs when a transmitting agent, such as a mosquito, picks up microbes, changes them into a form conducive to growth in the human body, and passes on the disease to the human. The transmission of yellow fever, for example, occurs by this method.

- Mechanical transmission is the passage of a microbe to an individual by means of a carrier that is not directly involved in the disease process. Transmission of an infection by dirty hands, bad water, rats, mice, or flies are methods of mechanical transmission. For example, hepatitis can be acquired through mechanical transmission. Box 2.1 tells about two people who were carriers of deadly diseases.

Once a microbe has reached the body, it penetrates into bodily tissue via any of several routes, including the skin, the throat and respiratory tract, the digestive tract, or the genitourinary system. Whether the invading microbes gain a foothold in the body and produce infection depends on three factors: the number of organisms, the virulence of the organisms, and the body's defensive powers. The virulence of an organism is determined by its aggressiveness (that is, its ability to resist the body's defenses) and by its toxigenicity (that is, its ability to produce poisons, which invade other parts of the body).

The Course of Infection

Assuming that the invading organism does gain a foothold, the natural history of infection follows a specific course. First, there is an incubation period between the time the infection is contracted and the time the symptoms appear.

Next, there is a period of nonspecific symptoms, such as headaches and general discomfort, which precedes the onset of the disease. During this time, the microbes are actively colonizing and producing toxins.

The next stage is the acute phase, when the disease and its symptoms are at their height. Unless the infection proves fatal, a period of decline follows the acute phase. During this period, the organisms are expelled from the mouth and nose in saliva and respiratory secretions, as well as through the digestive tract and the genitourinary system in feces and urine.

Infections may be localized, focal, or systemic. Localized infections remain at their original site and do not spread throughout the body. Although a focal infection is confined to a particular area, it sends toxins to other parts of the body, causing other disruptions. Systemic infections, by contrast, affect a number of areas or body systems.

The primary infection initiated by the microbe may also lead to secondary infections. These occur because the body's resistance is lowered from fighting the primary infection, leaving it susceptible to other invaders. In many cases, secondary infections, such as pneumonia, pose a greater risk than the primary one.

Immunity

Immunity is the body's resistance to injury from invading organisms. It may develop either naturally or artificially. Some natural immunity is passed from the mother to the child at birth and through breast-feeding, although this type of immunity is only temporary. Natural immunity is also acquired through disease. For example, if you have measles once, it is unlikely that you will develop it a second time; you will have built up an immunity to it.

Artificial immunity is acquired through vaccinations and inoculations. For example, most children and adolescents receive shots for a variety of diseases—among them, diphtheria, whooping cough, smallpox,

BOX 2.1

Portraits of Two Carriers

Carriers are people who transmit a disease to others without actually contracting that disease themselves. They are especially dangerous because they are not ill and are therefore not removed from society. Thus, it is possible for a carrier to infect dozens, hundreds, or even thousands of individuals while going about the business of everyday life.

"TYPHOID MARY"

Perhaps the most famous carrier in history was "Typhoid Mary," a young Swiss immigrant to the United States who apparently infected thousands of people during her lifetime. During her ocean crossing, Mary was taught how to cook, and eventually some 100 individuals aboard the ship died of typhoid, including the cook who trained her. Once Mary arrived in New York, she obtained a series of jobs as a cook, continually passing on the disease to those for whom she worked without contracting it herself.

Typhoid is precipitated by a Salmonella bacterium, which can be transmitted through water, food, and physical contact. Mary carried a virulent form of the infection in her body but was herself immune to the disease. It is believed that Mary was unaware that she was a carrier for many years. Toward the end of her life, however, she began to realize that she was responsible for the many deaths around her.

Mary's status as a carrier also became known to medical authorities, and in the latter part of her life she was in and out of institutions in a vain attempt to isolate her from others. In 1930, Mary died not of typhoid but of a brain hemorrhage (Federspiel, 1983).

"HELEN"

The CBS News program *60 Minutes* profiled an equally terrifying carrier: a prostitute, "Helen," who is a carrier of AIDS (acquired immune deficiency syndrome). Helen has never had AIDS, but her baby was born with the disease. As a prostitute and heroin addict, she is not only at risk for developing the illness herself but also poses a substantial threat to her clients and anyone with whom she shares a needle.

Helen represents a dilemma for medical and criminal authorities. She is a known carrier of AIDS, yet there is no legal basis for preventing her from coming into contact with others. Although she can be arrested for prostitution or drug dealing, such incarcerations are usually short term and would have a negligible impact on her ability to spread the disease to others. For as yet incurable diseases such as AIDS, the carrier poses a frustrating nightmare of complications. Although the carrier can augment the incidence of the disease, medical and legal authorities have been almost powerless to intervene (Moses, 1984).

---

poliomyelitis, and hepatitis—so that they will not contract them should they ever be exposed.

How does immunity work? The body has a number of responses to invading organisms, some nonspecific and others specific. **Nonspecific immune mechanisms** are a general set of responses to any kind of infection or disorder; **specific immune mechanisms,** which are always acquired after birth, fight particular microorganisms and their toxins.

Nonspecific immunity is mediated in four main ways: through anatomical barriers, phagocytosis, antimicrobial substances, and inflammatory response.

Anatomical barriers prevent the passage of microbes from one section of the body to another. For example, the skin functions as an extremely effective anatomical barrier to many infections, and the mucous membranes lining the nose and mouth (as well as other cavities that are open to the environment) also provide protection.

Phagocytosis is the process by which certain white blood cells (called phagocytes) ingest microbes. Phagocytes are usually overproduced when there is a bodily infection, so that sufficient numbers can be sent to the site of infection to ingest the foreign particles.

Antimicrobial substances are chemicals mobilized by the body to kill invading microorganisms. One that has received particular attention in cancer research is interferon, an antiviral protein secreted by cells exposed to a viral antigen to protect neighboring uninfected cells from invasion. Hydrochloric acid and enzymes such as lysozyme are other antimicrobial substances that help destroy invading microorganisms.

The inflammatory response is a local reaction to infection. At the site of infection, the blood capillaries first enlarge, and a chemical called histamine is released into the area. This chemical causes an increase in capillary permeability, allowing white blood cells and fluids to leave the capillaries and enter the tissues; consequently, the area becomes reddened and fluids accumulate. The white blood cells attack the microbes, resulting in the formation of pus. Temperature increases at the site of inflammation because of the increased flow of blood. Usually, a clot then forms around the inflamed area, isolating the microbes and keeping them from spreading to other parts of the body. Familiar examples of the inflammatory response are the reddening, swelling, discharge, and clotting that result when you accidentally lacerate your skin and the sneezing, runny nose, and teary eyes that result from an allergic response to pollen.

Specific immunity is acquired after birth and differs from nonspecific immunity in that it protects against particular microorganisms and their toxins. Specific immunity may be acquired by contracting a disease or through artificial means, such as vaccinations. It operates through the antigen-antibody reaction. Antigens are foreign substances whose presence stimulates the production of antibodies in the cell tissues. Antibodies are proteins produced in response to stimulation by antigens, which then combine chemically with the antigens to overcome their toxic effects.

Humoral Immunity   There are two basic immunologic reactions—humoral and cell mediated. **Humoral immunity** is mediated by B lymphocytes. The functions of B lymphocytes include providing protection against bacteria, neutralizing toxins produced by bacteria, and preventing viral reinfection. B cells confer immunity by the production and secretion of antibodies.

When B cells are activated, they differentiate into two types: (1) mature, antibody-secreting plasma cells and (2) resting, nondividing, memory B cells, which differentiate into antigen-specific plasma cells only when reexposed to the same antigen. Plasma cells produce antibodies or immunoglobulins, which are the basis of the antigen-specific reactions. Humoral immunity is particularly effective in defending the body against bacterial infections and against viral infections that have not yet invaded the cells.

Cell-mediated immunity, involving T lymphocytes from the thymus gland, is a slower-acting response. Rather than releasing antibodies into the blood, as humoral immunity does, cell-mediated immunity operates at the cellular level. When stimulated by the appropriate antigen, T cells secrete chemicals that kill invading organisms and infected cells.

There are two major types of T lymphocytes: cytotoxic T (T_C cells) and helper T (T_H cells). T_C cells respond to specific antigens and kill by producing toxic substances that destroy virally infected cells. T_H cells enhance the functioning of T_C cells, B cells, and macrophages by producing cytokines. T_H cells also serve a counterregulatory immune function, producing cytokines that suppress certain immune activities. Cell-mediated immunity is particularly effective in defending the body against fungi, viral infections that have invaded the cells, parasites, foreign tissue, and cancer.

What, then, does the integrated immune response look like? When a foreign antigen enters the body, the first line of defense involves mechanistic maneuvers, such as coughing or sneezing. Once the invader has penetrated the body's surface, the phagocytes, such as the macrophages, attempt to eliminate it by phagocytosis (engulfing and digesting the foreign invader). Macrophages also release interleukin-1 and display part of the antigen material on their surface as a signal to the T_H cells. These, in turn, secrete interleukin-2, which promotes the growth and differentiation of the T_C cells. Other types of T helper cells secrete substances that promote the development of antigen-specific B cells into antibody-producing plasma cells, which then assist in destroying the antigen. T_H cells also secrete gamma-interferon, which enhances the capacities of the macrophages. Macrophages and natural killer (NK) cells also secrete various types of interferon, which enhance the killing potential of the natural killer (NK) cells and inhibit viral reproduction in uninfected cells. In addition, macrophages, NK cells, and T_C cells directly kill infected cells. During this process, the T_H cells down regulate and eventually turn off the immune response.

The Lymphatic System's Role in Immunity
The **lymphatic system,** which is a drainage system of the body, is involved in important ways in immune functioning. There is lymphatic tissue throughout the body, consisting of lymphatic capillaries, vessels, and nodes. Lymphatic capillaries drain water, proteins, microbes, and other foreign materials from spaces between the cells into lymph vessels. This material is then conducted in the lymph vessels to the lymph nodes, which filter out microbes and foreign materials for ingestion by lymphocytes. The lymphatic vessels then drain any remaining substances into the blood.

The spleen, tonsils, and thymus gland are important organs in the lymphatic system. The spleen aids in the production of B cells and T cells and removes worn-out red blood cells from the body. The spleen also helps filter bacteria and is responsible for the storage and release of blood. Tonsils are patches of lymphoid tissue in the pharynx that filter out microorganisms that enter the respiratory tract. Finally, the thymus gland is responsible for helping T cells mature; it also produces a hormone, thymosin, which appears to stimulate T cells and lymph nodes to produce the plasma cells that, in turn, produce antibodies.

Additional discussion of immunity may be found in chapter 14, where we will consider the rapidly developing field of psychoneuroimmunology and the role of immunity in the development of AIDS (acquired immune deficiency syndrome). As we will see in that context, health psychologists are identifying the importance of social and psychological factors in the functioning of the immune system. Specifically, there is increasing evidence that stressful events can alter immune functioning, in some cases to increase resistance and in other cases to decrease it.

Disorders Related to the Immune System

The immune system and the tissues of the lymphatic system are subject to a number of disorders and diseases. One very important one is AIDS, which is a progressive impairment of immunity. Another is cancer, which is now believed to depend heavily on immunocompromise. We defer extended discussion of AIDS and cancer to chapter 14.

Some diseases of the immune system result when bacteria are so virulent that the lymph node phagocytes are not able to ingest all the foreign matter. These diseases include lymphangitis, an inflammation of the lymphatic vessels that results from interference in the drainage of the lymph into the blood, and lymphadenitis, an inflammation of the lymph nodes associated with the phagocytes' efforts to destroy microbes.

A number of infections attack lymphatic tissue. Elephantiasis is a condition produced by worms; it stems from blockage in the flow of lymph into the blood. Massive retention of fluid results, especially in the extremities. Splenomegaly is an enlargement of the spleen that may result from various infectious diseases. It hinders the spleen's ability to produce phagocytes, antibodies, and lymphocytes. Tonsillitis is an inflammation of the tonsils that interferes with their ability to filter out bacteria. Infectious mononucleosis is a viral disorder marked by an unusually large number of monocytes; it can cause enlargement of the spleen and lymph nodes, as well as fever, sore throat, and general lack of energy.

Lymphoma is a tumor of the lymphatic tissue. Hodgkin's disease, a malignant lymphoma, involves the progressive, chronic enlargement of the lymph nodes, spleen, and other lymphatic tissues. As a consequence, the nodes cannot effectively produce antibodies and the phagocytic properties of the nodes are lost. If untreated, Hodgkin's disease can be fatal.

Infectious disorders were at one time thought to be acute problems that ended when their course had run. A major problem in developing countries, infectious disorders were thought to be largely under control in developed nations. Now, however, some important developments with respect to infectious diseases merit closer looks (Morens, Folkers, & Fauci, 2004). First, as noted in the discussion of asthma, the control of at least some infectious disorders through hygiene may have paradoxically increased the rates of allergic disorders. A second development is that some chronic diseases, once thought to be genetic in origin or unknown in origin, are now being traced back to infections. For example, Alzheimer's disease, multiple sclerosis, and schizophrenia all appear to have infectious triggers, at least in some cases (Zimmer, 2001). The fact that multiple sclerosis shows outbreaks in particular locations is strongly suggestive of an infectious pattern. Ulcers, once thought to be the result of stress, were traced in the 1980s to a microbe known as Helicobacter Pylori; cases of ulcers and even gastric cancers that were once thought to be difficult to treat can now be cured through antibiotics (Zimmer, 2001). Increasingly biologists are suggesting that pathogens cause or actively contribute to, many if not most, chronic diseases. Finally, of considerable concern is the development of bacterial strains that are increasingly resistant to treatment. The overuse of antibiotics is thought to be an active contributor to the development of increasingly lethal strains.

The inflammatory response that is so protective against provocations ranging from mosquito bites and sunburn to gastritis in response to spoiled food is now coming under increasing investigation as a potential contributor to chronic disease as well. The destructive potential of inflammatory responses has long been evident in diseases such as rheumatoid arthritis and multiple sclerosis, but researchers are now coming to believe that inflammation underlies many other chronic diseases including athlersclerosis, diabetes, Alzheimer's disease, and osteoporosis. Inflammation is also implicated in asthma, cirrhosis of the liver, some bowl disorders, cystic fibrosis, and possibly even some cancers (Duenwald, 2002). The inflammatory response, like stress responses more generally, likely evolved in humans' early prehistory and was selected because it was adaptive. For example, among hunter and gatherer societies, natural selection would have favored people with vigorous inflammatory responses because life expectancy was fairly short. Few people would have experienced the long-term costs of vigorous inflammatory responses, which now seem to play such an important role in the development of chronic diseases. Essentially an adaptive pattern of earlier times has become maladaptive, as life expectancy has lengthened (Duenwald, 2002).

Infectious agents have also become an increasing cause for concern in the war on terrorism, as the possibility that smallpox and other infectious agents may be used as weapons becomes increasingly likely (Gruman, 2003).

Autoimmunity is a condition characterized by a specific humoral or cell-mediated immune response that attacks the body's own tissues. Autoimmunity is implicated in certain forms of arthritis, a condition characterized by inflammatory lesions in the joints that produce pain, heat, redness, and swelling. We will discuss arthritis more fully in chapter 14. Multiple sclerosis is also an autoimmune disorder. One of the most severe autoimmune disorders is systemic lupus erythematosis, a gener-

alized disorder of the connective tissue, which primarily affects women and which in its severe forms can lead to eventual heart or kidney failure, causing death.

In autoimmune disease, the body fails to recognize its own tissue, instead interpreting it as a foreign invader and producing antibodies to fight it. Approximately 50 million Americans, or 1 in 5 people, suffer from autoimmune diseases. Women are more likely than men to be affected; some estimates are that 75 percent of those affected are women (American Autoimmune Related Diseases Association, 2003). Although the causes of autoimmune diseases are not fully known, researchers have discovered that a viral or bacterial infection often precedes the onset of an autoimmune disease.

Many of these viral and bacterial pathogens have, over time, developed the ability to fool the body into granting them access by mimicking basic protein sequences in the body. This process of *molecular mimicry* eventually fails but then leads the immune system to attack not only the invader but also the corresponding self-component. A person's genetic makeup may exacerbate this process, or it may confer protection against autoimmune diseases (Steinman, 1993). Stress may aggravate autoimmune disease. ●

SUMMARY

1. The nervous system and the endocrine system act as the control systems of the body, mobilizing it in times of threat and otherwise maintaining equilibrium and normal functioning.

2. The nervous system operates primarily through the exchange of nerve impulses between the peripheral nerve endings and internal organs and the brain, thereby providing the integration necessary for voluntary and involuntary movement.

3. The endocrine system operates chemically via the release of hormones stimulated by centers in the brain. It controls growth and development and augments the functioning of the nervous system.

4. The cardiovascular system is the transport system of the body, carrying oxygen and nutrients to cell tissues and taking carbon dioxide and other wastes away from the tissues for expulsion from the body.

5. The heart acts as a pump to keep the circulation going and is responsive to regulation via the nervous system and the endocrine system.

6. The cardiovascular system is implicated in stress, with cardiac output speeding up during times of stress and slowing down when threat has passed.

7. The heart, blood vessels, and blood are vulnerable to a number of problems—most notably, atherosclerosis—which makes diseases of the cardiovascular system the major cause of death in this country.

8. The respiratory system is responsible for taking in oxygen, expelling carbon dioxide, and controlling the chemical composition of the blood.

9. The digestive system is responsible for producing heat and energy, which—along with essential nutrients—are needed for the growth and repair of cells. Through digestion, food is broken down to be used by the cells for this process.

10. The renal system aids in metabolic processes by regulating water balance, electrolyte balance, and blood acidity-alkalinity. Water-soluble wastes are flushed out of the system in the urine.

11. The reproductive system, under the control of the endocrine system, leads to the development of primary and secondary sex characteristics. Through this system, the species is reproduced, and genetic material is transmitted from parents to their offspring.

12. With advances in genetic technology and the mapping of the genome has come increased understanding of genetic contributions to disease. Health psychologists play important research and counseling roles with respect to these issues.

13. The immune system is responsible for warding off infection from invasion by foreign substances. It does so through the production of infection-fighting cells and chemicals.

KEY TERMS

adrenal glands
angina pectoris
atherosclerosis
autoimmunity
blood pressure
cardiovascular system
catecholamines
cell-mediated immunity
cerebellum
cerebral cortex
endocrine system

humoral immunity
hypothalamus
immunity
kidney dialysis
lymphatic system
medulla
myocardial infarction (MI)
nervous system
neurotransmitters
nonspecific immune mechanisms
parasympathetic nervous system

phagocytosis
pituitary gland
platelets
pons
renal system
respiratory system
specific immune mechanisms
sympathetic nervous system
thalamus

PART 2

Health Behavior and Primary Prevention

CHAPTER 3

Health Behaviors

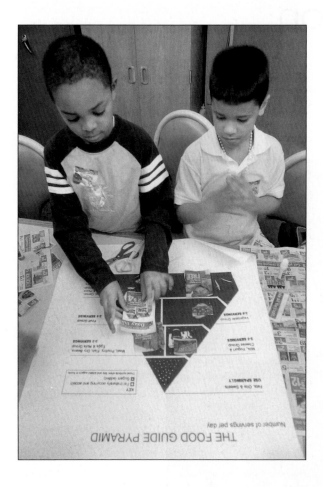

Jill Morgan had just begun her sophomore year in college. Although her freshman year had been filled with lots of required courses, sophomore year was looking more interesting, giving her the chance to really get into her major, biology. The professor whose work she had so admired had an opening in her lab for a research assistant and offered it to Jill. Jill's boyfriend, Jerry, had just transferred to her school, so instead of seeing each other only one or two weekends a month, they now met for lunch almost every day and studied together in the library at night. Life was looking very good.

Tuesday morning, Jill was awakened by the harsh ring of her telephone. Could she come home right away? Her mother had gone in for a routine mammogram and a malignant lump had been discovered. Surgery was necessary, her father explained, and Jill was needed at home to take care of her younger sister and brother. As soon as her mother was better, her father promised, Jill could go back to school, but she would have to postpone the beginning of her sophomore year for at least a semester.

Jill felt as if her world were falling apart. She had always been very close to her mother and could not imagine this cheerful, outgoing woman with an illness. Moreover, it was cancer. What if her mother died? Her mother's situation was too painful to think about, so Jill began to contemplate her own. She would not be able to take the courses that she was currently enrolled in for another year, and she could forget about the research assistantship. And after all that effort so that she and Jerry could be together, now they would be apart again. Jill lay on her dorm room bed, knowing she needed to pack but unable to move.

"Breast cancer's hereditary, you know," Jill's roommate said. Jill looked at her in amazement, unable to speak. "If your mother has it, the chances are you'll get it too," the roommate went on, seemingly oblivious to the impact her words were having on Jill. Jill realized that she needed to get out of there quickly. As she walked, many thoughts came into her head. Would Jerry still want to date her, now that she might get breast cancer? Should she even think about having children anymore? What if she passed on the risk of breast cancer to her children? Without thinking, she headed for the biology building, which now felt like a second home to her. The professor who had offered her the job was standing in the hall as she went in. The professor could sense that something was wrong and invited Jill in for coffee. Jill told her what happened and broke down crying.

"Jill, you should know that breast cancer can now be treated, particularly when it's caught early. If they detected your mother's breast cancer through a mammogram, it probably means it's a pretty small lump. Cure rates are now 90% or better for early breast cancers. On the basis of what your dad has told you so far, your mother's situation looks pretty promising."

"It does?" Jill asked, wiping away tears.

"Not only that, the surgeries they have for breast cancer now are often fairly minimal, just removal of the lump, so you and your father might find that her recovery will be a little quicker than it may look right now. Look, I'm not going to give this research assistantship away. Why don't you go home, find out how things are, and call me in a week or so?"

"My roommate says breast cancer's hereditary," Jill said.

"Heredity is one of the factors that can contribute to breast cancer. The fact that your mother has it does mean you'll have to be aware of your risk and make sure you get screened on a regular basis. But it doesn't mean that you will necessarily get breast cancer. And even if you did, it wouldn't be the end of the world. Early detection and quick treatment mean that most women survive and lead normal lives." The professor paused for a moment. "Jill, my mother had breast cancer, too, about 7 years ago. She's doing fine. I have to go in for regular checkups, and so far, everything has been okay. It's not a risk I'm happy to be living with, but it hasn't changed my life. I have a husband, two great kids, and a wonderful career, and the risk of breast cancer is just something I know about. I'm sure that this feels like a tragedy right now, but I think you'll find that the greatest fears you have probably won't materialize."

"Thanks," said Jill. "I think I'd better go home and pack."

In chapter 3, we take up the important question of health behaviors and risk factors for illness. At the core of this chapter is the idea that good health is achievable by everyone through health habits that are practiced conscientiously. Health promotion means being aware both of health habits that pose risks for future disease and of already existing risks, such as the vulnerability to breast cancer that Jill and the biology professor have. In the following pages, we consider health habits and risk factors with an eye toward their successful modification before they have a chance to lead to the development of illness.

■ HEALTH PROMOTION: AN OVERVIEW

Health promotion is a general philosophy that has at its core the idea that good health, or wellness, is a personal and collective achievement. For the individual, it involves developing a program of good health habits early in life and carrying them through adulthood and old age. For the medical practitioner, health promotion involves teaching people how best to achieve this healthy lifestyle and helping people **at risk** for particular health problems learn behaviors to offset or monitor those risks. For the psychologist, health promotion involves the development of interventions to help people practice healthy behaviors and change poor ones. For community and national policy makers, health promotion involves a general emphasis on good health, the availability of information to help people develop and maintain healthy lifestyles, and the availability of resources and facilities that can help people change poor health habits. The mass media can contribute to health promotion by educating people about health risks posed by certain behaviors, such as smoking or excessive alcohol consumption. Legislation can contribute to health promotion by mandating certain activities that may reduce risks, such as the use of child-restraining seats and seat belts.

The case for health promotion has grown more clear and urgent with each decade. In the past, prevention efforts relied on early diagnosis of disease to achieve a healthy population, with only passing attention paid to promoting healthy lifestyles in the absence of disease. However, on grounds such as cost effectiveness, health promotion appears to be both more successful and less costly than disease prevention (R. M. Kaplan, 2000), making it increasingly evident that we must teach people the basics of a healthy lifestyle across the life span.

■ AN INTRODUCTION TO HEALTH BEHAVIORS

Role of Behavioral Factors in Disease and Disorder

In the past 90 years, patterns of disease in the United States have changed substantially. The prevalence of acute infectious disorders, such as tuberculosis, influenza, measles, and poliomyelitis, has declined because of treatment innovations and changes in public health standards, such as improvements in waste control and sewage. Simultaneously, there has been an increase in

TABLE 3.1 | Risk Factors for the Leading Causes of Death in the United States

Disease	Risk Factors
Heart disease	Tobacco, cholesterol, high blood pressure, physical inactivity, obesity, diabetes, stress
Cancer	Smoking, unhealthy diet, environmental factors
Stroke	High blood pressure, tobacco, diabetes, high cholesterol, physical inactivity, obesity
Accidental injuries	On the road (seat belts), in the home (falls, poisoning, fire)
Chronic lung disease	Tobacco, environmental factors (pollution, radon, asbestos)

Sources: American Cancer Society, 2004; American Heart Association, 2004; Centers for Disease Control and Prevention, 2004.

what have been called the "preventable" disorders, including lung cancer, cardiovascular disease, alcohol and other drug abuse, and vehicular accidents (Matarazzo, 1982).

The role of behavioral factors in the development of these disorders is clear (see table 3.1). It is estimated that nearly half the deaths in the United States are caused by preventable behaviors, with smoking, overeating, and drinking being the top three. This has been true for the last 10 years, the only change being that obesity and lack of exercise are about to overtake tobacco as the most preventable causes of death in the United States (Center for the Advancement of Health, April 2004). Cancer deaths alone could be reduced by 50% simply by getting people to reduce smoking, eat more fruits and vegetables, boost their physical activity, and obtain early screening for breast and cervical cancer (Center for the Advancement of Health, 2003, April 29).

Successful modification of health behaviors, then, will have several beneficial effects. First, it will reduce deaths due to lifestyle-related diseases. Second, it may delay time of death, thereby increasing individual longevity and general life expectancy of the population. Third and most important, the practice of good health behaviors may expand the number of years during which a person may enjoy life free from the complications of chronic disease. Finally, successful modification of health behaviors may begin to make a dent in the more than $1.5 trillion that is spent yearly on health and illness (Center for Medicare and Medicaid Services, 2004). Table 3.2 illustrates the great expense for treat-

TABLE 3.2 | Cost of Treatment for Selected Preventable Conditions

Condition	Avoidable Intervention	Cost per Patient
Heart disease	Coronary bypass surgery	$ 30,000
Cancer	Lung cancer treatment	$ 29,000
Injuries	Quadriplegia treatment and rehabilitation	$570,000 (lifetime)
	Hip fracture treatment and rehabilitation	$ 40,000
Low-birth-weight baby	Respiratory distress syndrome treatment	$ 26,500

Source: M. McGinnis, 1994.

ments of some of the most common chronic problems the country faces. As a result of evidence like this, health care agencies have increasingly devoted their attention to the manifold ways that health can be improved and illness can be prevented (Center for the Advancement of Health, 2000c).

What Are Health Behaviors?

Health behaviors are behaviors undertaken by people to enhance or maintain their health. Poor health behaviors are important not only because they are implicated in illness but also because they may easily become poor health habits.

A **health habit** is a health-related behavior that is firmly established and often performed automatically, without awareness. These habits usually develop in childhood and begin to stabilize around age 11 or 12 (R. Y. Cohen, Brownell, & Felix, 1990). Wearing a seat belt, brushing one's teeth, and eating a healthy diet are examples of these kinds of behaviors. Although a health habit may have developed initially because it was reinforced by specific positive outcomes, such as parental approval, it eventually becomes independent of the reinforcement process and is maintained by the environmental factors with which it is customarily associated. As such, it can be highly resistant to change. Consequently, it is important to establish good health behaviors and to eliminate poor ones early in life.

A dramatic illustration of the importance of good health habits in maintaining good health is provided by a classic study of people living in Alameda County, California, conducted by Belloc and Breslow (1972). These scientists began by defining seven important good health habits:

- Sleeping 7 to 8 hours a night.
- Not smoking.
- Eating breakfast each day.

- Having no more than one or two alcoholic drinks each day.
- Getting regular exercise.
- Not eating between meals.
- Being no more than 10% overweight.

They then asked nearly 7,000 county residents to indicate which of these behaviors they practiced. Residents were also asked how many illnesses they had had, which illnesses they had had, how much energy they had had, and how disabled they had been (for example, how many days of work they had missed) over the previous 6- to 12-month period. The researchers found that the more good health habits people practiced, the fewer illnesses they had had, the better they had felt, and the less disabled they had been.

A follow-up of these individuals 9 to 12 years later found that mortality rates were dramatically lower for people practicing the seven health habits. Specifically, men following these practices had a mortality rate only 28% that of the men following zero to three of the health practices, and women following the seven health habits had a mortality rate 43% that of the women following zero to three of the health practices (Breslow & Enstrom, 1980).

Primary Prevention   Instilling good health habits and changing poor ones is the task of **primary prevention.** This means taking measures to combat risk factors for illness before an illness ever has a chance to develop. There are two general strategies of primary prevention. The first and most common strategy has been to employ behavior-change methods to get people to alter their problematic health behaviors. The many programs that have been developed to help people lose weight are an example of this approach. The second, more recent approach is to keep people from developing poor health habits in the first place. Smoking prevention programs with young adolescents are an example of this approach, which we will consider in chapter 5. Of the two types of primary prevention, it is obviously far preferable to keep people from developing problematic behaviors than to try to help them stop the behaviors once they are already in place.

Practicing and Changing Health Behaviors: An Overview

Who practices good health behaviors? What are the factors that lead one person to live a healthy life and another to compromise his or her health?

Demographic Factors   Health behaviors differ according to demographic factors. Younger, more affluent, better educated people under low levels of stress with high levels of social support typically practice better health habits than people under higher levels of stress with fewer resources, such as individuals low in social class (N. H. Gottlieb & Green, 1984).

Age   Health behaviors vary with age. Typically, health habits are good in childhood, deteriorate in adolescence and young adulthood, but improve again among older people (H. Leventhal, Prohaska, & Hirschman, 1985).

Values   Values heavily influence the practice of health habits. For example, exercise for women may be considered desirable in one culture but undesirable in another (Donovan, Jessor, & Costa, 1991), with the result that exercise patterns among women will differ greatly between the two cultures.

Personal Control   Perceptions that one's health is under personal control also determine health habits. For example, research on the **health locus of control** scale (K. A. Wallston, Wallston, & DeVellis, 1978) measures the degree to which people perceive themselves to be in control of their health, perceive powerful others to be in control of their health, or regard chance as the major determinant of their health. Those people who are predisposed to see health as under personal control may be more likely to practice good health habits than those who regard their health as due to chance factors.

Social Influence   Social influence affects the practice of health habits. Family, friends, and workplace companions can all influence health-related behaviors—sometimes in a beneficial direction, other times in an adverse

direction (Broman, 1993; Lau, Quadrel, & Hartman, 1990). For example, peer pressure often leads to smoking in adolescence but may influence people to stop smoking in adulthood.

Personal Goals   Health habits are heavily tied to personal goals (R. Eiser & Gentle, 1988). If personal fitness or athletic achievement is an important goal, the person will be more likely to exercise on a regular basis than if fitness is not a personal goal.

Perceived Symptoms   Some health habits are controlled by perceived symptoms. For example, smokers may control their smoking on the basis of sensations in their throat. A smoker who wakes up with a smoker's cough and raspy throat may cut back in the belief that he or she is vulnerable to health problems at that time.

Access to the Health Care Delivery System   Access to the health care delivery system can also influence the practice of health behaviors. Using the tuberculosis screening programs, obtaining a regular Pap smear, obtaining mammograms, and receiving immunizations for childhood diseases, such as polio, are examples of behaviors that are directly tied to the health care delivery system. Other behaviors, such as losing weight and stopping smoking, may be indirectly encouraged by the health care system because many people now receive lifestyle advice from their physicians.

Cognitive Factors   Finally, the practice of health behaviors is tied to cognitive factors, such as the belief that certain health behaviors are beneficial or the sense that one may be vulnerable to an underlying illness if one does not practice a particular health behavior.

Barriers to Modifying Poor Health Behaviors

The reason that it is important to know the determinants of health habits is because once bad habits are ingrained they are very difficult to change. Researchers still know little about how and when poor health habits develop and exactly when and how one should intervene to change the health habit. For example, young children usually get enough exercise, but as they get older, a sedentary lifestyle may set in. Exactly how and when should one intervene to offset this tendency? The process is gradual, and the decline in exercise is due more to changes in the environment, such as no longer having to take a compulsory physical education class, than to the motivation to get exercise.

Moreover, people often have little immediate incentive for practicing good health behavior. Health habits develop during childhood and adolescence, when most people are healthy. Smoking, drinking, poor nutrition, and lack of exercise have no apparent effect on health and physical functioning. The cumulative damage that these behaviors cause may not become apparent for years, and few children and adolescents are sufficiently concerned about what their health will be like when they are 40 or 50 years old (R. J. Johnson, McCaul, and Klein, 2002). As a result, bad habits have a chance to make inroads.

Once their bad habits are ingrained, people are not always highly motivated to change them. Unhealthy behaviors can be pleasurable, automatic, addictive, and resistant to change. Consequently, many people find it too difficult to change their health habits because their bad habits are enjoyable. Health habits are only modestly related to each other. Knowing one health habit does not enable one to predict another with great confidence. The person who exercises faithfully does not necessarily wear a seat belt, and the person who controls his or her weight may continue to smoke. It can be difficult to teach people a concerted program of good health behavior, and health behaviors must often be tackled one at a time.

Instability of Health Behaviors   Another characteristic that contributes to the difficulty of modifying health habits is that they are unstable over time. A person may stop smoking for a year but take it up again during a period of high stress. A dieter may lose 50 pounds, only to regain them a few years later. Why are health habits relatively independent of each other and unstable?

First, different health habits are controlled by different factors. For example, smoking may be related to stress, whereas exercise may depend on ease of access to sports facilities. Second, different factors may control the same health behavior for different people. Thus, one person's overeating may be "social," and she may eat primarily in the presence of other people. In contrast, another individual's overeating may depend on levels of tension, and he may overeat only when under stress.

Third, factors controlling a health behavior may change over the history of the behavior (H. Leventhal, 1985). The initial instigating factors may no longer be significant, and new maintaining factors may develop to

replace them. Although peer group pressure (social factors) is important in initiating the smoking habit, over time, smoking may be maintained because it reduces craving and feelings of stress. One's peer group in adulthood may actually oppose smoking.

Fourth, factors controlling the health behavior may change across a person's lifetime. Regular exercise occurs in childhood because it is built into the school curriculum, but in adulthood, this automatic habit must be practiced consciously.

Fifth and finally, health behavior patterns, their developmental course, and the factors that change them across a lifetime will vary substantially between individuals (H. Leventhal et al., 1985). Thus, one individual may have started smoking for social reasons but continue smoking to control stress; the reverse pattern may characterize the smoking of another individual.

Summary   In summary, health behaviors are elicited and maintained by different factors for different people, and these factors change over the lifetime as well as during the course of the health habit. Consequently, health habits are very difficult to change. As a result, health habit interventions have focused heavily on those who may be helped the most—namely, the young.

Intervening with Children and Adolescents

Socialization   Health habits are strongly affected by early **socialization,** especially the influence of parents as role models (Hops, Duncan, Duncan, & Stoolmiller, 1996). Parents instill certain habits in their children (or not) that become automatic, such as wearing a seat belt, brushing teeth regularly, and eating breakfast every day. Nonetheless, in many families, even these basic health habits may not be taught, and even in families that conscientiously attempt to teach good health habits there may be gaps.

Moreover, as children move into adolescence, they sometimes backslide or ignore the early training they received from their parents, because they often see little apparent effect on their health or physical functioning. In addition, adolescents are vulnerable to an array of problematic health behaviors, including excessive alcohol consumption, smoking, drug use, and sexual risk taking, particularly if their parents aren't monitoring them very closely and their peers practice these behaviors (Andrews, Tildesley, Hops, & Li, 2002). Adolescents

The foundations for health promotion develop in early childhood, when children are taught to practice good health behaviors.

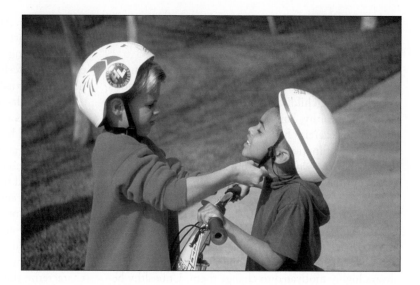

appear to have an incomplete appreciation of the risks they encounter through faulty habits such as smoking and drinking (R. J. Johnson et al., 2002). Consequently, interventions with children and adolescents are high priority.

Using the Teachable Moment   Health promotion efforts capitalize on educational opportunities to prevent poor health habits from developing. The concept of a **teachable moment** refers to the fact that certain times are better than others for teaching particular health practices.

Many teachable moments arise in early childhood. Parents have opportunities to teach their children basic safety behaviors, such as putting on a seat belt in the car or looking both ways before crossing the street, and basic health habits, such as drinking milk instead of soda with dinner (L. Peterson & Soldana, 1996).

Other teachable moments arise because they are built into the health care delivery system. For example, many infants in the United States are covered by well-baby care. Pediatricians often make use of these early visits to teach motivated new parents the basics of accident prevention and safety in the home. Dentists use a child's first visit to teach both the parents and child the importance of correct brushing. Many school systems require a physical at the beginning of the school year or at least an annual visit to a physician. This procedure ensures that parents and children have regular contact with the health care delivery system so that information about

health habits, such as weight control or accident prevention, can be communicated. Such visits also ensure that children receive their basic immunizations.

But what can children themselves really learn about health habits? Certainly very young children have cognitive limitations that keep them from fully comprehending the concept of health promotion, yet intervention programs with children clearly indicate that they can develop personal responsibility for aspects of their health. Such behaviors as choosing nutritionally sound foods, brushing teeth regularly, using car seats and seat belts, participating in exercise, crossing the street safely, and behaving appropriately in real or simulated emergencies (such as earthquake drills) are clearly within the comprehension of children as young as age 3 or 4, as long as the behaviors are explained in concrete terms and the implications for actions are clear (Maddux, Roberts, Sledden, & Wright, 1986).

Teachable moments are not confined to childhood and adolescence. Pregnancy represents a teachable moment for several health habits, especially stopping smoking and improving diet (Center for Advancement of Health, October 2002; Levitsky, 2004). Adults with newly diagnosed coronary artery disease may also be especially motivated to change their health habits, such as smoking and diet, due to the anxiety their recent diagnosis has caused.

Identifying teachable moments—that is, the crucial point at which a person is ready to modify a health behavior—is a high priority for primary prevention.

Adolescence is a window of vulnerability for many poor health habits. Consequently, intervening to prevent health habits from developing is a high priority for children in late elementary and early junior high school.

Closing the Window of Vulnerability   Junior high school appears to be a particularly important time for the development of several health-related habits. For example, food choices, snacking, and dieting all begin to crystallize around this time (R. Y. Cohen et al., 1990). There is also a **window of vulnerability** for smoking and drug use that occurs in junior high school when students are first exposed to these habits among their peers and older siblings (D'Amico & Fromme, 1997). As we will see, interventions through the schools may help students avoid the temptations that lead to these health-compromising behaviors.

Adolescent Health Behaviors Influence Adult Health   A final reason for intervening with children and adolescents in the modification of health habits is that, increasingly, research shows that precautions taken in adolescence may be better predictors of disease after age 45 than are adult health behaviors. This means that the health habits people practice as teenagers or college students may well determine the chronic diseases they have and what they ultimately die of in adulthood.

For adults who decide to make changes in their lifestyle, it may already be too late. Research to date suggests that this is true for sun exposure and skin cancer and for calcium consumption for the prevention of osteoporosis. Diet, especially dietary fat intake and protein consumption in adolescence, may also predict adult cancers. Consequently, despite the sense of invulnerability

that many adolescents have, adolescence may actually be a highly vulnerable time for a variety of poor health behaviors that lay the groundwork for future problems in adulthood.

Interventions with At-Risk People

> I'm a walking time bomb.
> —37-YEAR-OLD WOMAN AT RISK FOR BREAST CANCER

Children and adolescents are two vulnerable populations toward which health promotion efforts have been heavily directed. Another vulnerable group consists of people who are at risk for particular health problems. For example, a pediatrician may work with obese parents to control the diet of their offspring in the hopes that obesity in the children can be avoided. If the dietary changes produce the additional consequence of reducing the parents' weight, so much the better. Daughters of women who have had breast cancer are a vulnerable population who need to monitor themselves for any changes in the breast tissue and obtain regular mammograms. As the genetic basis for other disorders is becoming clearer, health promotion efforts with at-risk populations are likely to assume increasing importance.

Benefits of Focusing on At-Risk People
There are several advantages to working with people who are at risk for health disorders. Early identification of these people may prevent or eliminate the poor health habits that can exacerbate vulnerability. For example,

helping men at risk for heart disease avoid smoking or getting them to stop at a young age may avoid a debilitating chronic illness (Schieken, 1988). Even if no intervention is available to reduce risk, knowledge of risk can provide people with information they need to monitor their situation (Swaveley, Silverman, & Falek, 1987). Women at risk for breast cancer are an example of such a group.

Working with at-risk populations represents an efficient and effective use of health promotion dollars. When a risk factor has implications for only some people, there is little reason to implement a general health intervention for everyone. Instead, it makes sense to target those people for whom the risk factor is relevant.

Finally, focusing on at-risk populations makes it easier to identify other risk factors that may interact with the targeted factor in producing an undesirable outcome. For example, not everyone who has a family history of hypertension will develop hypertension, but by focusing on those people who are at risk, other factors that contribute to its development may be identified.

Problems of Focusing on Risk

Clearly, however, there are difficulties in working with populations at risk. People do not always perceive their risk correctly (Rothman & Salovey, 1997; G. E. Smith, Gerrard, & Gibbons, 1997). Generally speaking, most people are unrealistically optimistic about their vulnerability to health risks (N. D. Weinstein & Klein, 1995). People tend to view their poor health behaviors as widely shared but their healthy behaviors as more distinctive. For example, smokers overestimate the number of other people who smoke. When people perceive that others are engaging in the same unhealthy practice, they may perceive a lower risk to their health (Suls, Wan, & Sanders, 1988).

Sometimes testing positive for a risk factor leads people into needlessly hypervigilant and restrictive behavior. For example, women at genetic risk for breast cancer appear to be more physiologically reactive to stressful events, raising the possibility that the chronic stress associated with this familial cancer risk may actually have consequences of its own through changes in psychobiological reactivity (Valdimarsdottir et al., 2002). People may also become defensive and minimize the significance of their risk factor and avoid using appropriate services or monitoring their condition (for example, Brewer, Weinstein, Cuite, & Herrington, 2004; Croyle, Sun, & Louie, 1993). Providing people with feedback about their potential genetic susceptibility to a

disorder such as lung cancer can have immediate and strong effects on relevant behaviors—in this case, a reduction in smoking (Lerman et al., 1997). As yet, the conditions under which these two problematic responses occur have not been fully identified (Croyle & Jemmott, 1991).

Ethical Issues

There are important ethical issues in working with at-risk populations. At what point is it appropriate to alarm at-risk people if their personal risk may be low? Among people at risk for a particular disorder, only a certain percentage will develop the problem and, in many cases, only many years later. For example, should adolescent daughters of breast cancer patients be alerted to their risk and alarmed at a time when they are attempting to come to terms with their emerging sexuality and needs for self-esteem? Psychological disturbance may be created in exchange for instilling risk-reduction behaviors (Croyle et al., 1997).

Some people, such as those predisposed to depression, may react especially badly to the prospect or results of genetic testing for health disorders (S. W. Vernon et al., 1997). These effects may occur primarily just after testing positive for a risk factor and may not be long term (Lerman et al., 1996; Marteau, Dundas, & Axworthy, 1997; Tibben, Timman, Bannick, & Duivenvoorden, 1997). In many cases, there is no successful intervention for genetically based risk factors, and in other cases, an intervention may not work (A. Baum, Friedman, & Zakowski, 1997; Codori, Slavney, Young, Miglioretti, & Brandt, 1997; M. D. Schwartz, Lerman, Miller, Daly, & Masny, 1995). For example, identifying boys at risk for coronary artery disease and teaching them how to manage stress effectively may be ineffective in changing their risk status.

For other disorders, we may not know what an effective intervention will be. For example, alcoholism is now believed to have a genetic component, particularly among men, and yet exactly how and when we should intervene with the offspring of adult alcoholics is not yet clear.

Finally, emphasizing risks that are inherited can raise complicated issues of family dynamics, potentially pitting parents and children against each other and raising issues of who is to blame for the risk (Hastrup, 1985). Daughters of breast cancer patients may suffer considerable stress and behavior problems, due in part to the enhanced recognition of their risk (S. E. Taylor, Lichtman, & Wood, 1984a; Wellisch, Gritz, Schain, Wang, & Siau, 1991). Intervening with at-risk populations is still a controversial issue.

Health Promotion and the Elderly

> Frank Ford, 91, starts each morning with a brisk walk. After a light breakfast of whole wheat toast and orange juice, he gardens for an hour or two. Later, he joins a couple friends for lunch and if he can persuade them to join him, they fish during the early afternoon. Reading a daily paper and always having a good book to read keeps Frank mentally sharp. Asked how he maintains such a busy schedule, Frank says, "exercise, friends, and mental challenge" are the keys to his long and healthy life.

Ford's lifestyle is right on target. One of the chief focuses of recent health promotion efforts has been the elderly. At one time, prejudiced beliefs that such health promotion efforts would be wasted in old age limited this emphasis. However, policy makers now recognize that a healthy elderly population is essential for controlling health care spending and ensuring that the country's resources can sustain the increasingly elderly population that will develop over the next decades (Maddox & Clark, 1992; Schaie, Blazer, & House, 1992).

Health promotion efforts with the elderly have focused on several behaviors: maintaining a healthy, balanced diet; developing a regular exercise regimen; taking steps to reduce accidents; controlling alcohol consumption; eliminating smoking; reducing the inappropriate use of prescription drugs; and obtaining vaccinations against influenza (Facts of Life, October 2002; Kahana et al., 2002; Nichol et al., 2003).

Exercise is one of the most important health behaviors because exercise helps keep people mobile and able to care for themselves. Even just keeping active also has health benefits. Participating in social activities, running errands, and engaging in other normal activities that probably have little effect on overall fitness nonetheless reduce the risk of mortality, perhaps by providing social support or a general sense of self-efficacy (T. A. Glass, deLeon, Marottoli, & Berkman, 1999). Among the very old, exercise has particularly beneficial long-term benefits, substantially increasing the likelihood that the elderly can maintain the basic activities of daily living (Kahana et al., 2002).

Controlling alcohol consumption is an important target for good health among the elderly as well. Some elderly people develop drinking problems in response to age-related issues, such as retirement or loneliness (Brennan & Moos, 1995). Others may try to maintain the drinking habits they had throughout their lives, which become more risky in old age. For example, metabolic changes related to age may reduce the capacity for alco-

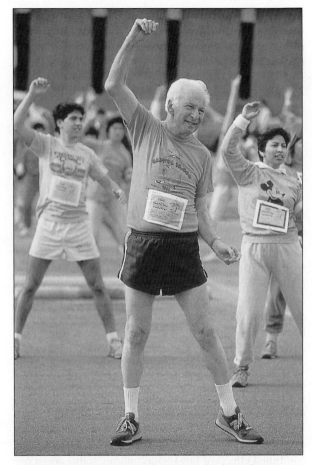

Among the elderly, health habits are a major determinant of whether an individual will have a vigorous or an infirmed old age.

hol. Moreover, many older people are on medications that may interact dangerously with alcohol. Alcohol consumption increases the risk of accidents, which, in conjunction with osteoporosis, can produce broken bones, which limit mobility, creating further health problems (Sheahan et al., 1995). Drunk driving among the elderly represents a problem, inasmuch as diminished driving capacities may be further impaired by alcohol. The elderly are at risk for depression, which also compromises health habits leading to accelerated physical decline. Thus, addressing depression, commonly thought of as a mental health problem, can have effects on physical health as well (Wrosch, Schulz, & Heckhausen, 2002).

Vaccinations against influenza are important for several reasons. First, influenza (flu) is a major cause of death among the elderly. Moreover, it increases the risk of heart disease and stroke because it exacerbates other underlying disorders that an elderly person may have (Nichol et al., 2003). Finding ways to ensure that elderly people get their flu vaccinations each fall, then, is an important health priority.

The emphasis on health habits among the elderly is well placed. By age 80, health habits are the major determinant of whether an individual will have a vigorous or an infirmed old age (McClearn et al., 1997). Moreover, current evidence suggests that health habit changes are working. The health of our elderly population is booming, according to recent statistics (Rosenblatt, 2001).

Ethnic and Gender Differences in Health Risks and Habits

There are ethnic and gender differences in vulnerability to particular health risks, and health promotion programs need to take these differences into account. African-American and Hispanic women get less exercise than do Anglo women and are somewhat more likely to be overweight. In terms of smoking, however, Anglo and African-American women are at greater risk than Hispanic women. Alcohol consumption is a substantially greater problem among men than women, and smoking is a somewhat greater problem for Anglo men than for other groups.

Health promotion programs for ethnic groups also need to take account of co-occurring risk factors. The combined effects of low socioeconomic status and a biologic predisposition to particular illnesses puts certain groups at substantially greater risk. Examples are diabetes among Hispanics and hypertension among African-Americans, which we will consider in more detail in chapter 14.

■ CHANGING HEALTH HABITS

> Habit is habit, and not to be flung out of the window by any man, but coaxed downstairs a step at a time.
> —Mark Twain

In the remainder of this chapter, we address the technology of changing poor health habits. First, we look at attitudinal approaches to health behavior change, which assume that, if we give people correct information about the implications of their poor health habits, they may be motivated to change those habits in a healthy direction. As will be seen, attitude change campaigns may induce the desire to change behavior but may not be successful in teaching people exactly how to do so.

Attitude Change and Health Behavior

Educational Appeals   Educational appeals make the assumption that people will change their health habits if they have correct information. Research has provided us with the following suggestions of the best ways to persuade people through educational appeals:

1. Communications should be colorful and vivid rather than steeped in statistics and jargon. If possible, they should also use case histories (S. E. Taylor & Thompson, 1982). For example, a vivid account of the health benefits of regular exercise, coupled with a case history of someone who took up bicycling after a heart attack, may be persuasive to someone at risk for heart disease.

2. The communicator should be expert, prestigious, trustworthy, likable, and similar to the audience (W. J. McGuire, 1964). For example, a health message will be more persuasive if it comes from a respected, credible physician rather than from the proponent of the latest health fad.

3. Strong arguments should be presented at the beginning and end of a message, not buried in the middle.

4. Messages should be short, clear, and direct.

5. Messages should state conclusions explicitly. For example, a communication extolling the virtues of a low-cholesterol diet should explicitly conclude that the reader should alter his or her diet to lower cholesterol.

6. Extreme messages produce more attitude change, but only up to a point. Very extreme messages are discounted. For example, a message that urges people to exercise for at least half an hour 3 days a week will be more effective than one that recommends several hours of exercise a day.

7. For illness detection behaviors (such as HIV testing or obtaining a mammogram), emphasizing the problems that may occur if it is not undertaken will be most effective (for example, Banks et al., 1995; Kalichman & Coley, 1996). For health promotion behaviors (such as sunscreen use), emphasizing the benefits to be gained may be more effective (Rothman & Salovey, 1997).

8. If the audience is receptive to changing a health habit, then the communication should include only favorable points, but if the audience is not

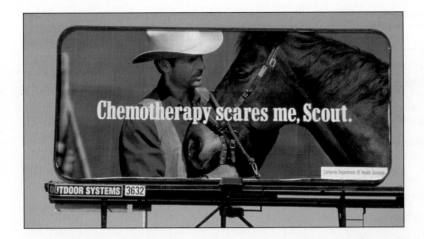

Fear appeals often alert people to a health problem but do not necessarily change behavior.

inclined to accept the message, the communication should discuss both sides of the issue. For example, messages to smokers ready to stop should emphasize the health risks of smoking. Smokers who have not yet decided to stop may be more persuaded by a communication that points out its risk while acknowledging and rebutting its pleasurable effects.

Providing information does not ensure that people will perceive that information accurately. Sometimes when people receive negative information about risks to their health, they process that information defensively (Millar & Millar, 1996). Instead of making appropriate health behavior changes, the person may come to view the problem as less serious or more common than he or she had previously believed (for example, Croyle et al., 1993), particularly if he or she intends to continue the behavior (Gerrard, Gibbons, Benthin, & Hessling, 1996). Smokers, for example, know that they are at a greater risk for lung cancer than are nonsmokers, but they see lung cancer as less likely or problematic and smoking as more common than do nonsmokers.

Fear Appeals   In part because of these issues, attitudinal approaches to changing health habits often make use of **fear appeals.** This approach assumes that if people are fearful that a particular habit is hurting their health, they will change their behavior to reduce their fear. Common sense suggests that the relationship between fear and behavior change should be direct: The more fearful an individual is, the more likely he or she will be to change the relevant behavior. However, research has found that this relationship does not always hold (H. Leventhal, 1970).

Persuasive messages that elicit too much fear may actually undermine health behavior change (Becker & Janz, 1987). Moreover, research suggests that fear alone may not be sufficient to change behavior. Sometimes fear can affect intentions to change health habits (for example, Sutton & Eiser, 1984), but it may not produce long-lasting changes in health habits unless it is coupled with recommendations for action or information about the efficacy of the health behavior (Self & Rogers, 1990).

Message Framing   Any health message can be phrased in positive or negative terms. For example, a reminder letter to get a flu immunization can stress the benefits of being immunized or, alternatively, stress the discomfort of the flu itself (McCaul, Johnson, & Rothman, 2002). Which of these methods is more successful? Messages that emphasize potential problems seem to work better for behaviors that have uncertain outcomes, whereas messages that stress benefits seem to be more persuasive for behaviors with certain outcomes (Apanovitch, McCarthy, & Salovey, 2003). As was the case with fear appeals, recommendations regarding exactly how to take the action increase effectiveness (McCaul et al., 2002).

Health psychologists have now developed approaches to health habit change that integrate educational and motivational factors into more general models for altering health behaviors (see Sturges & Rogers, 1996; N. D. Weinstein, 1993).

The Health Belief Model   The most influential attitude theory of why people practice health behaviors is the **health belief model** (Hochbaum, 1958; Rosenstock, 1966). This model states that whether a person practices a particular health behavior can be understood

FIGURE 3.1 | The Health Belief Model Applied to the Health Behavior of Stopping Smoking

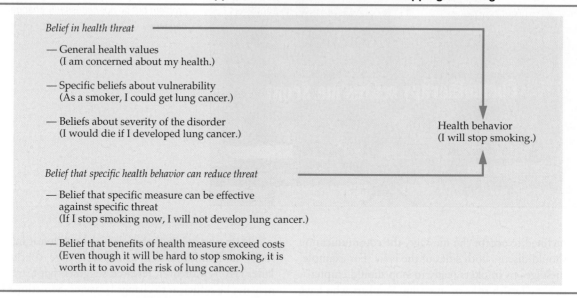

Belief in health threat

— General health values
(I am concerned about my health.)

— Specific beliefs about vulnerability
(As a smoker, I could get lung cancer.)

— Beliefs about severity of the disorder
(I would die if I developed lung cancer.)

Belief that specific health behavior can reduce threat

— Belief that specific measure can be effective
against specific threat
(If I stop smoking now, I will not develop lung cancer.)

— Belief that benefits of health measure exceed costs
(Even though it will be hard to stop smoking, it is
worth it to avoid the risk of lung cancer.)

Health behavior
(I will stop smoking.)

by knowing two factors: whether the person perceives a personal health threat and whether the person believes that a particular health practice will be effective in reducing that threat.

Perception of Health Threat   The perception of a personal health threat is influenced by at least three factors: general health values, which include interest and concern about health; specific beliefs about personal vulnerability to a particular disorder; and beliefs about the consequences of the disorder, such as whether or not they are serious. Thus, for example, people may change their diet to include low-cholesterol foods if they value health, feel threatened by the possibility of heart disease, and perceive that the threat of heart disease is severe.

Perceived Threat Reduction   Whether a person believes a health measure will reduce threat has two subcomponents: whether the individual thinks a health practice will be effective and whether the cost of undertaking that measure exceeds the benefits of the measure (Rosenstock, 1974). For example, the man who feels vulnerable to a heart attack and is considering changing his diet may believe that dietary change alone would not reduce the risk of a heart attack and that changing his diet would interfere with his enjoyment of life too much to justify taking the action. Thus, although his belief in his personal vulnerability to heart disease may be great, if he lacks faith that a change of diet would reduce his

risk, he would probably not make any changes. A diagram of the health belief model applied to smoking is presented in figure 3.1.

Support for the Health Belief Model   The health belief model explains people's practice of health habits quite well. For example, it predicts preventive dental care (Ronis, 1992), breast self-examination (Champion, 1990), dieting for obesity (Uzark, Becker, Dielman, & Rocchini, 1987), AIDS risk-related behaviors (Aspinwall, Kemeny, Taylor, Schneider, & Dudley, 1991), participation in a broad array of health screening programs (Becker, Kaback, Rosenstock, & Ruth, 1975), and drinking and smoking intentions among adolescents (Goldberg, Halpern-Felsher, & Millstein, 2002). Typically, health beliefs are a modest determinant of intentions to take these health measures.

Changing Health Behavior Using the Health Belief Model   The health belief model also predicts some of the circumstances under which people's health behaviors will change. A good illustration of this point comes from the experience of a student in my psychology class a few years ago. This student (call him Bob) was the only person in the class who smoked, and he was the object of some pressure from his fellow students to quit. He was familiar with the health risks of smoking. Although he knew that smoking contributes to lung cancer and heart disease, he believed the relationships were weak. Moreover, because he was in very good health and played a number of sports, his feelings of vulnerability were quite low.

Over Thanksgiving vacation, Bob went home to a large family gathering and discovered to his shock that his favorite uncle, a chain smoker all his adult life, had lung cancer and was not expected to live more than a few months. Suddenly, health became a more salient value for Bob because it had now struck his own family. Bob's perceived susceptibility to the illness changed both because a member of his own family had been struck down and because the link between smoking and cancer had been graphically illustrated. Bob's perceptions of stopping smoking changed as well. He concluded that this step might suffice to ward off the threat of the disease and that the costs of quitting smoking were not as great as he had thought. When Bob returned from Thanksgiving vacation, he had stopped smoking.

Interventions that draw on the health belief model have generally supported its predictions. Highlighting perceived vulnerability and simultaneously increasing the perception that a particular health behavior will reduce the threat are somewhat successful in changing behavior, whether the behavior is smoking (J. R. Eiser, van der Plight, Raw, & Sutton, 1985), preventive dental behavior (Ronis, 1992), or osteoporosis prevention measures (Klohn & Rogers, 1991), for example. However, the health belief model leaves out an important component of health behavior change: the perception that one will be able to engage in the health behavior.

Self-efficacy and Health Behaviors   An important determinant of the practice of health behaviors is a sense of **self-efficacy:** the belief that one is able to control one's practice of a particular behavior (Bandura, 1991; D. A. Murphy et al., 2001). For example, smokers who believe they will not be able to break their habit probably will not try to quit, however much they think that smoking is risky and that stopping smoking is desirable. Self-efficacy affects health behaviors as varied as abstinence from smoking (Prohaska & DiClemente, 1984b), weight control (Strecher, DeVellis, Becker, & Rosenstock, 1986), condom use (Wulfert & Wan, 1993), exercise (B. H. Marcus & Owen, 1992; McAuley & Courneya, 1992), dietary change (Schwarzer & Renner, 2000), and a variety of health behaviors among older adults (Grembowski et al., 1993). Typically, research finds a strong relationship between perceptions of self-efficacy and both initial health behavior change and long-term maintenance of that behavior change.

Summary   To summarize, then, we can say that whether a person practices a particular health behavior depends on several beliefs and attitudes: the magnitude of a health threat, the degree to which that person believes he or she is personally vulnerable to that threat, the degree to which that person believes he or she can perform the response necessary to reduce the threat (self-efficacy), and the degree to which the particular health measure advocated is effective, desirable, and easy to implement.

The Theory of Planned Behavior

Although health beliefs go some distance in helping us understand when people will change their health habits, increasingly health psychologists are turning their attention to the analysis of action. A theory that attempts to link health attitudes directly to behavior is Ajzen's **theory of planned behavior** (Ajzen & Madden, 1986; M. Fishbein & Ajzen, 1975).

According to this theory, a health behavior is the direct result of a behavioral intention. Behavioral intentions are themselves made up of three components: attitudes toward the specific action, subjective norms regarding the action, and perceived behavioral control (see figure 3.2). Attitudes toward the action are based on beliefs about the likely outcomes of the action and evaluations of those outcomes. Subjective norms are what a person believes *others* think that person should do (normative beliefs) and the motivation to comply with those normative references. Perceived behavioral control is when an individual needs to feel that he or she is capable of performing the action contemplated and that the action undertaken will have the intended effect; this component of the model is very similar to self-efficacy. These factors combine to produce a behavioral intention and, ultimately, behavior change.

To take a simple example, smokers who believe that smoking causes serious health outcomes, who believe that other people think they should stop smoking, who are motivated to comply with those normative beliefs, and who believe that they are capable of stopping smoking will be more likely to intend to stop smoking than individuals who do not hold these beliefs.

Benefits of the Theory of Planned Behavior
The theory of planned behavior is a useful addition to understanding health behavior change processes for two reasons. First, it provides a model that links beliefs directly to behavior. Second, it provides a fine-grained

FIGURE 3.2 | The Theory of Planned Behavior Applied to the Health Behavior of Dieting (*Sources:* Ajzen & Fishbein, 1980; Ajzen & Madden, 1986)

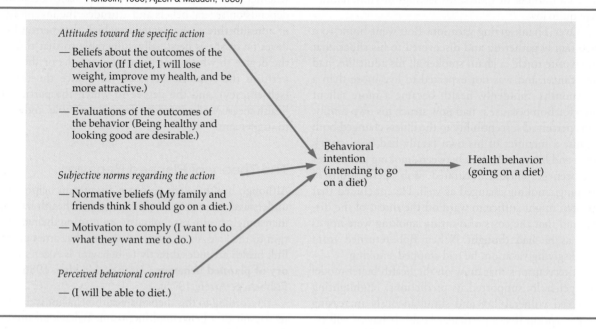

Attitudes toward the specific action

— Beliefs about the outcomes of the behavior (If I diet, I will lose weight, improve my health, and be more attractive.)

— Evaluations of the outcomes of the behavior (Being healthy and looking good are desirable.)

Subjective norms regarding the action

— Normative beliefs (My family and friends think I should go on a diet.)

— Motivation to comply (I want to do what they want me to do.)

Perceived behavioral control

— (I will be able to diet.)

Behavioral intention (intending to go on a diet)

Health behavior (going on a diet)

picture of people's intentions with respect to a particular health habit.

Evidence for the Theory of Planned Behavior

The theory of planned behavior predicts a broad array of health behaviors, including condom use among students (Sutton, McVey, & Glanz, 1999), sunbathing and sunscreen use (Hillhouse, Stair, & Adler, 1996), use of oral contraceptives (J. Doll & Orth, 1993), consumption of soft drinks among adolescents (Kassem & Lee, 2004), mammography participation (Montano & Taplin, 1991), testicular self-examination (Brubaker & Wickersham, 1990), exercise (Baker, Little, & Brownell, 2003), participation in cancer screening programs (B. DeVellis, Blalock, & Sandler, 1990), AIDS risk-related behaviors (W. A. Fisher, Fisher, & Rye, 1995), smoking (Norman, Conner, & Bell, 1999), healthy eating (Baker, Little, & Brownell, 2003), participation in health screening programs (Sheeran, Conner, & Norman, 2001), and several daily health habits, including getting enough sleep and taking vitamins (Madden, Ellen, & Ajzen, 1992).

Attitudes and Changing Health Behaviors: Some Caveats

Despite the success of theories that link beliefs to behavior and modification of health habits, attitudinal approaches are not very successful for explaining spontaneous behavior change, nor do they predict long-term behavior change very well (Kirscht, 1983). An additional complication is that communications designed to change people's attitudes about their health behaviors sometimes evoke defensive or irrational processes: People may perceive a health threat to be less relevant than it really is (A. Liberman & Chaiken, 1992), they may falsely see themselves as less vulnerable than others (Clarke, Lovegrove, Williams, & Machperson, 2000), and they may see themselves as dissimilar to those who have succumbed to a particular health risk (Thornton, Gibbons, & Gerrard, 2002). Continued practice of a risky behavior may itself lead to changes in perception of a person's degree of risk, inducing a false sense of complacency (Halpern-Felsher et al., 2001).

People may also hold irrational beliefs about health, illness, and treatment that lead them to distort health-relevant messages or practice health habits such as the ingestion of dozens of over-the-counter treatments (A. J. Christensen, Moran, & Wiebe, 1999). With these multiple capacities to distort health threats and the relevance of health messages, even carefully designed messages may be unable to get around these biases in the processing of information.

Moreover, thinking about disease can produce a negative mood (Millar & Millar, 1995), which may, in turn, lead people to ignore or defensively interpret their risk. Although some studies have found that inaccurate risk perception can be modified by information and educational interventions (Kreuter & Strecher, 1995), other reports suggest that unrealistic optimism is peculiarly invulnerable to feedback (N. D. Weinstein & Klein, 1995).

Because health habits are often deeply ingrained and difficult to modify, attitude change procedures may not go far enough in simply providing the informational base for altering health habits (Ogden, 2003). The attitude-change procedures may instill the motivation to change a health habit but not provide the preliminary steps or skills necessary to actually alter behavior and maintain behavior change (Bryan, Fisher, & Fisher, 2002). Consequently, health psychologists have also turned to therapeutic techniques.

■ COGNITIVE-BEHAVIORAL APPROACHES TO HEALTH BEHAVIOR CHANGE

Attitudinal approaches to the modification of health behaviors appear to be most useful in predicting when people will be motivated to change a health behavior. **Cognitive-behavior therapy** approaches to health-habit modification change the focus to the target behavior itself—the conditions that elicit and maintain it and the factors that reinforce it (Freeman, Simon, Beutler, & Arkowitz, 1989). Cognitive-behavior therapy also focuses heavily on the beliefs that people hold about their health habits. People often generate internal monologues that interfere with their ability to change their behavior (Meichenbaum & Cameron, 1974). For example, a person who wishes to give up smoking may derail the quitting process by generating self-doubts ("I will never be able to give up smoking"; "I'm one of those people who simply depend on cigarettes"; "I've tried before, and I've never been successful"). Unless these internal monologues are modified, cognitive-behavioral therapists argue, the person will be unlikely to change a health habit and maintain that change over time.

Recognition that people's cognitions about their health habits are important in producing behavior change has led to another insight: the importance of involving the patient as a cotherapist in the behavior-change intervention. Most behavior-change programs begin with the client as the object of behavior-change efforts, but in the therapeutic process, control over behavior change shifts gradually from the therapist to the client. By the end of the formal intervention stage, clients are monitoring their own behaviors, applying the techniques of cognitive-behavioral interventions to their behavior, and rewarding themselves, or not, appropriately.

Self-observation and Self-monitoring

Many programs of cognitive-behavioral modification use **self-observation** and **self-monitoring** as the first steps toward behavior change. The rationale is that a person must understand the dimensions of a target behavior before change can be initiated. Self-observation and self-monitoring assess the frequency of a target behavior and the antecedents and consequences of that behavior (Abel, Rouleau, & Coyne, 1987; Thoresen & Mahoney, 1974). This process also sets the stage for enlisting the patient's joint participation early in the effort to modify health behaviors.

The first step in self-observation is to learn to discriminate the target behavior. For some behaviors, this step is easy. A smoker obviously can tell whether he or she is smoking. However, other target behaviors, such as the urge to smoke, may be less easily discriminated; therefore, an individual may be trained to monitor internal sensations closely so as to identify the target behavior more readily.

A second stage in self-observation is recording and charting the behavior. Techniques range from very simple counters for recording the behavior each time it occurs to complex records documenting the circumstances under which the behavior was enacted as well as the feelings it aroused. For example, a smoker may be trained to keep a detailed behavioral record of all smoking events. She may record each time a cigarette is smoked, the time of day, the situation in which the smoking occurred, and whether or not anyone else was present. She may also record the subjective feelings of craving that were present when lighting the cigarette, the emotional responses that preceded the lighting of the cigarette (such as anxiety or tension), and the feelings that were generated by the actual smoking of the cigarette. In this way, she can begin to get a sense of the circumstances in which she is most likely to smoke and can then initiate a structured behavior-change program that deals with these contingencies.

Although self-observation is usually only a beginning step in behavior change, it may itself produce behavior change. Simply attending to their own smoking may lead people to decrease the number of cigarettes they smoke. Typically, however, behavior change that is produced by self-monitoring is short lived and needs to

FIGURE 3.3 | A Classical Conditioning Approach to the Treatment of Alcoholism

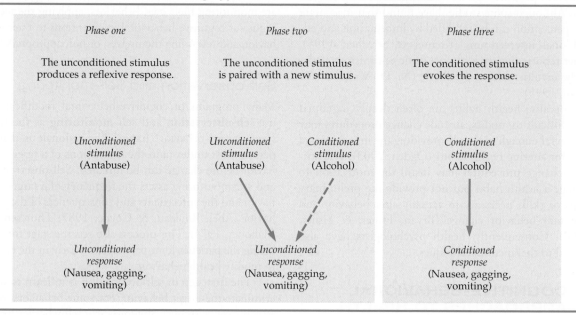

Classical Conditioning

First described by Russian physiologist Ivan Pavlov in the early 20th century, **classical conditioning** was one of the earliest principles of behavior change identified by researchers. The essence of classical conditioning is the pairing of an unconditioned reflex with a new stimulus, producing a conditioned reflex. Classical conditioning is represented diagrammatically in figure 3.3.

Classical conditioning was one of the first methods used for health behavior change. For example, consider its use in the treatment of alcoholism. Antabuse (unconditioned stimulus) is a drug that produces extreme nausea, gagging, and vomiting (unconditioned response) when it is taken in conjunction with alcohol. Over time, the alcohol will become associated with the nausea and vomiting caused by the Antabuse and elicit the same nausea, gagging, and vomiting response (conditioned response).

Classical conditioning approaches to health-habit modification do work, but clients know why they work. Alcoholics, for example, know that, if they do not take the drug, they will not vomit when they consume alco-

hol. Thus, even if classical conditioning has successfully produced a conditioned response, it is heavily dependent on the client's willing participation. Procedures like these produce health risks as well, and as a result, they are no longer as widely used.

Operant Conditioning

In contrast to classical conditioning, which pairs an automatic response with a new stimulus, operant conditioning pairs a voluntary behavior with systematic consequences. The key to **operant conditioning** is reinforcement. When an individual performs a behavior and that behavior is followed by positive reinforcement, the behavior is more likely to occur again. Similarly, if an individual performs a behavior and reinforcement is withdrawn or the behavior is punished, the behavior is less likely to be repeated. Over time, these contingencies build up those behaviors paired with positive reinforcement, and behaviors that are punished or not rewarded decline.

Many health habits can be thought of as operant responses. For example, drinking may be maintained because mood is improved by alcohol, or smoking may occur because peer companionship is associated with it. In both of these cases, reinforcement maintains the poor

be coupled with other techniques (for example, Mc-Caul, Glasgow, & O'Neill, 1992).

health behavior. Thus, using this principle to change behavior requires altering the reinforcement or its schedule.

An important feature of operant conditioning is the reinforcement schedule. A continuous reinforcement schedule means that a behavior is reinforced every time it occurs. However, continuous reinforcement is vulnerable to extinction: If the behavior is occasionally not paired with reinforcement, the individual may cease performing the behavior, having come to anticipate reinforcement each time. Psychologists have learned that behavior is often more resistant to extinction if it is maintained by a variable or an intermittent reinforcement schedule than a continuous reinforcement schedule.

Operant Conditioning to Change Health Behaviors

Operant conditioning is often used to modify health behaviors. At the beginning of an effort to change a faulty health habit, people typically will be positively reinforced for any action that moves them closer to their goal. As progress is made toward reducing or modifying the health habit, greater behavior change may be required for the same reinforcement. For example, suppose Mary smokes 20 cigarettes a day. She might first define a set of reinforcers that can be administered when particular smoking-reduction targets are met—reinforcements such as going out to dinner or seeing a movie. Mary may then set a particular reduction in her smoking behavior as a target (such as 15 cigarettes a day). When that target is reached, she would administer a reinforcement (the movie or dinner out). The next step might be reducing smoking to 10 cigarettes a day, at which time she would receive another reinforcement. The target then might be cut progressively to 5, 4, 3, 1, and none. Through this process, the target behavior of abstinence would eventually be reached.

Modeling

Modeling is learning that occurs by virtue of witnessing another person perform a behavior (Bandura, 1969). Observation and subsequent modeling can be effective approaches to changing health habits. For example, high school students who observed others donating blood were more likely to do so themselves (I. G. Sarason, Sarason, Pierce, Shearin, & Sayers, 1991).

Similarity is an important principle in modeling. To the extent that people perceive themselves as similar to the type of person who engages in a risky behavior, they are likely to do so themselves; to the extent that people see themselves as similar to the type of person who does not engage in a risky behavior, they may change their behavior (Gibbons & Gerrard, 1995). A swimmer may decline a cigarette from a friend because she perceives that most great swimmers do not smoke.

Modeling can be an important long-term behavior-change technique. For example, the principle of modeling is implicit in some self-help programs that treat destructive health habits, such as alcoholism (Alcoholics Anonymous) or drug addiction. In these programs, a person who is newly committed to changing an addictive behavior joins individuals who have had the same problem and who have had at least some success in solving it. In meetings, people often share the methods that helped them overcome their health problem. By listening to these accounts, the new convert can learn how to do likewise and model effective techniques in his or her own rehabilitation.

Modeling can also be used as a technique for reducing the anxiety that can give rise to some bad habits or the fears that arise when going through some preventive health behaviors, such as receiving inoculations. A person's fears can be reduced by observing the model engaging in the feared activity and coping with that fear effectively. For example, Vernon (1974) used modeling in an attempt to reduce children's fears about receiving inoculations. Before they received injections, one group of children saw an unrealistic film of children receiving injections without experiencing any pain or expressing any emotion. A second group saw a realistic film that showed children responding to the injections with short-lived, moderate pain and emotion. A third group of children (the control group) saw no film. The results indicated that children who saw the realistic film experienced the least pain when they subsequently received injections. In contrast, those viewing the unrealistic film experienced the most pain. The results of this study illustrate another important point about modeling. When modeling is used to reduce fear or anxiety, it is better to observe models who are also fearful but are able to control their distress rather than models who are demonstrating no fear in the situation. Because fearful models provide a realistic portrayal of the experience, the observer may be better able to identify with them than with models who are unrealistically calm in the face of the threat. This identification process may enable the person to learn and model the coping techniques more successfully (Kazdin, 1974; Meichenbaum, 1971).

Modeling, or imitative learning, has an important role in the modification of health habits because it exposes an individual to other people who have successfully modified the health habit. Modeling may be most successful when it shows the realistic difficulties that people encounter in making these changes.

Stimulus Control

The successful modification of health behavior involves understanding the antecedents as well as the consequences of a target behavior. Individuals who practice poor health habits, such as smoking, drinking, and overeating, develop ties between those behaviors and stimuli in their environments. Each of these stimuli can come to act as a **discriminative stimulus** that is capable of eliciting the target behavior. For example, the sight and smell of food act as discriminative stimuli for eating. The sight of a pack of cigarettes or the smell of coffee may act as discriminative stimuli for smoking. The discriminative stimulus is important because it signals that a positive reinforcement will subsequently occur.

Stimulus-control interventions with patients who are attempting to alter their health habits take two approaches: ridding the environment of discriminative stimuli that evoke the problem behavior and creating new discriminative stimuli signaling that a new response will be reinforced.

How might stimulus control work in the treatment of a health problem? Eating is typically under the control of discriminative stimuli, including the presence of desirable foods and activities with which eating is frequently paired (such as talking on the phone or watching television). As an early step in the treatment of obesity, individuals might be encouraged to reduce and eliminate these discriminative stimuli for eating. They would be urged to rid their home of rewarding and enjoyable fattening foods, to restrict their eating to a single place in the home, and to not eat while engaged in other activities, such as watching television. Other stimuli might be introduced in the environment to indicate that controlled eating will now be followed by reinforcement. For example, people might place signs in strategic locations around the home, reminding them of reinforcements to be obtained after successful behavior change.

The Self-control of Behavior

Cognitive-behavior therapy, including that used to modify health habits, has increasingly moved toward a therapeutic model that emphasizes **self-control.** In this approach, the individual who is the target of the intervention acts, at least in part, as his or her own therapist

and, together with outside guidance, learns to control the antecedents and consequences of the target behavior to be modified.

Self-reinforcement   **Self-reinforcement** involves systematically rewarding the self to increase or decrease the occurrence of a target behavior (Thoresen & Mahoney, 1974). Positive self-reward involves reinforcing oneself with something desirable after successful modification of a target behavior. An example of positive self-reward is allowing oneself to go to a movie following successful weight loss. Negative self-reward involves removing an aversive factor in the environment after successful modification of the target behavior. An example of negative self-reward is taking the Miss Piggy poster off the refrigerator once regular controlled eating has been achieved.

A study by Mahoney (1974) examined the effects of positive self-reward on weight loss. Mahoney created four experimental conditions: (1) a control condition in which no intervention occurred, (2) a condition in which subjects monitored their weight, (3) a condition in which self-monitoring was accompanied by self-reinforcement with money or gift certificates for successful weight loss, and (4) a condition in which self-monitoring was coupled with gift certificates or money for successful changes in eating. The two self-reward conditions produced greater weight loss than the control or self-observation condition. Interestingly, of the two types of self-reward, the self-reward for habit change (that is, altered eating behavior) produced more weight loss than did the self-reward for weight loss. This result appears to have occurred because self-reward for habit change led these obese individuals to modify their eating habits, whereas self-reward for weight loss was associated only with losing weight and not with the behavior change that produced the weight loss.

An example of negative self-reward was used in a study to control obesity (Penick, Filion, Fox, & Stunkard, 1971). In this study, individuals who were overweight were instructed to keep large bags of suet (animal fat) in their refrigerators to remind themselves of their excess weight. Each time they succeeded in losing a certain amount of weight, they were permitted to remove a portion of the suet from the bag, thereby reducing this unattractive stimulus. Techniques such as these can be very effective in maintaining commitment to a behavior-change program.

Overall, self-reward has proven to be a useful technique in the modification of behavior (Thoresen & Mahoney, 1974). Moreover, self-reward techniques have intrinsic advantages in that no change agent, such as a therapist, is required to monitor and reinforce the behavior; the individual acts as his or her own therapist.

Like self-reward, self-punishment is of two types. Positive self-punishment involves the administration of an unpleasant stimulus to punish an undesirable behavior. For example, an individual might self-administer a mild electric shock each time he or she experiences a desire to smoke. Negative self-punishment consists of withdrawing a positive reinforcer in the environment each time an undesirable behavior is performed. For example, a smoker might rip up a dollar bill each time he or she has a cigarette that exceeded a predetermined quota (Axelrod, Hall, Weis, & Rohrer, 1974).

Studies that have evaluated the success of self-punishment suggest two conclusions: (1) Positive self-punishment works somewhat better than negative self-punishment, and (2) self-punishment works better if it is also coupled with self-rewarding techniques. Thus, a smoker is less likely to stop smoking if he rips up a dollar bill each time he smokes than if he self-administers electric shock; these principles are even more likely to reduce smoking if the smoker also rewards himself for not smoking—for example, by going to a movie.

Contingency Contracting   Self-punishment is effective only if people actually perform the punishing activities. When self-punishment becomes too aversive, people often abandon their efforts. However, one form of self-punishment that works well and has been used widely in behavior modification is **contingency contracting** (Thoresen & Mahoney, 1974; Turk & Meichenbaum, 1991). In contingency contracting, an individual forms a contract with another person, such as a therapist, detailing what rewards or punishments are contingent on the performance or nonperformance of a behavior. For example, a person who wanted to stop drinking might deposit a sum of money with a therapist and arrange to be fined each time he or she had a drink and to be rewarded each day that he or she abstained. A particularly ingenious example of contingency contracting involved an African-American woman who was attempting to control her abuse of amphetamines. She deposited a large sum of money with her therapist and authorized the therapist to give $50 to the Ku Klux Klan each time she abused amphetamines. Not surprisingly, this contract was effective in inducing the patient to reduce her amphetamine intake (Thoresen & Mahoney, 1974).

Covert Self-control   As noted earlier, poor health habits and their modification are often accompanied by internal monologues, such as self-criticism or self-praise. **Covert self-control** trains individuals to recognize and modify these internal monologues to promote health behavior change (Hollon & Beck, 1986). Sometimes the modified cognitions are antecedents to a target behavior. For example, if a smoker's urge to smoke is preceded by an internal monologue that he is weak and unable to control his smoking urges, these beliefs are targeted for change. The smoker would be trained to develop antecedent cognitions that would help him stop smoking (for example, "I can do this" or "I'll be so much healthier").

Cognitions can also be the consequences of a target behavior. For example, an obese individual trying to lose weight might undermine her weight-loss program by reacting with hopelessness to every small dieting setback. She might be trained, instead, to engage in self-reinforcing cognitions following successful resistance to temptation and constructive self-criticism following setbacks ("Next time, I'll keep those tempting foods out of my refrigerator").

Cognitions themselves may be the targets for modification. **Cognitive restructuring,** developed by Meichenbaum (Meichenbaum & Cameron, 1974), is a method for modifying internal monologues that has been widely used in the treatment of stress disorders. In a typical intervention, clients are first trained to monitor their monologues in stress-producing situations. In this way, they come to recognize what they say to themselves during times of stress. They are then taught to modify their self-instructions to include more constructive cognitions. For example, in one study (Homme, 1965), clients who wished to stop smoking were trained to respond to smoking urges by thinking antismoking thoughts ("Smoking causes cancer") and thoughts that favored nonsmoking ("My food will taste better if I stop smoking"). To increase the frequency of these cognitions, the clients were trained to reinforce them with a rewarding activity, such as drinking a soda.

Frequently, modeling is used to train a client in cognitive restructuring. The therapist may first demonstrate adaptive **self-talk.** She may identify a target stress-producing situation and then self-administer positive instructions (such as "Relax, you're doing great"). The client then attempts to deal with his stressful situation while the therapist teaches him positive self-instruction. In the next phase of training, the client attempts to cope with the stress-producing situation, instructing himself out loud. Following this phase, self-instruction may become a whisper, and finally the client performs the anxiety-reducing self-instruction internally.

Behavioral Assignments   Another technique for increasing client involvement is **behavioral assignments,** home practice activities that support the goals of a therapeutic intervention (Shelton & Levy, 1981). Behavioral assignments are designed to provide continuity in the treatment of a behavior problem, and typically, these assignments follow up points in the therapeutic session. For example, if an early therapy session with an obese client involved training in self-monitoring, the client would be encouraged to keep a log of his or her eating behavior, including the circumstances in which it occurred. This log could then be used by the therapist and the patient at the next session to plan future behavioral interventions. Figure 3.4 gives an example of the behavioral assignment technique. Note that it includes homework assignments for both client and therapist. This technique can ensure that both parties remain committed to the behavior-change process and that each is aware of the other's commitment. In addition, writing

FIGURE 3.4 | Example of a Systematic Behavioral Assignment for an Obese Client

(*Source:* Shelton & Levy, 1981, p. 6)

Homework for Tom [client]

Using the counter, count bites taken.

Record number of bites, time, location, and what you ate.

Record everything eaten for 1 week.

Call for an appointment.

Bring your record.

Homework for John [therapist]

Reread articles on obesity.

down homework assignments appears to be more successful than verbal agreements, in that it provides a clear record of what has been agreed to (Cox, Tisdelle, & Culbert, 1988).

The value of systematic homework assignments is widely recognized in the treatment of behaviors. A survey of programs for the treatment of health problems indicated that 75% of obesity programs, 71% of physical illness and rehabilitation programs, and 54% of smoking programs included behavioral assignments (Shelton & Levy, 1981).

In summary, the chief advantages of behavioral assignments are that (1) the client becomes involved in the treatment process, (2) the client produces an analysis of the behavior that is useful in planning further interventions, (3) the client becomes committed to the treatment process through a contractual agreement to discharge certain responsibilities, (4) responsibility for behavior change is gradually shifted to the client, and (5) the use of homework assignments increases the client's sense of self-control.

Skills Training   Increasingly, psychologists have realized that some poor health habits develop in response to or are maintained by the anxiety people experience in social situations (Riley, Matarazzo, & Baum, 1987). For example, adolescents often begin to smoke in order to reduce their social anxiety by communicating a cool, sophisticated image. Drinking and overeating may also be responses to social anxiety. Social anxiety then can act as a cue for the maladaptive habit, necessitating an alternative way of coping with the anxiety. As a result, individuals may need to learn alternative ways of coping with anxiety at the same time that they are altering their faulty health habit.

A number of programs designed to alter health habits include either **social skills training** or **assertiveness training,** or both, as part of the intervention package. Individuals are trained in methods that will help them deal more effectively with social anxiety. The goals of social skills programs as an ancillary technique in a program of health behavior change are (1) to reduce anxiety that occurs in social situations, (2) to introduce new skills for dealing with situations that previously aroused anxiety, and (3) to provide an alternative behavior for the poor health habit that arose in response to social anxiety.

Motivational Interviewing   Motivational interviewing is increasingly used in the battle for health promotion. Originally developed to treat addiction (W. R. Miller & Rollnick, 1991), the techniques have been adapted to target smoking, dietary improvements, exercise, cancer screening, and sexual behavior among other habits (Resnicow et al., 2002).

The idea underlying motivational interviewing is that the interviewer be nonjudgmental, emphatic, and encouraging. The interview is nonconfrontational and supportive, and the goal is for the client to express whatever positive or negative thoughts he or she has regarding the behavior in an atmosphere that is free of negative evaluation. Typically, clients talk at least as much as counselors.

As may be evident, motivational interviewing is an amalgam of principles and techniques drawn from psychotherapy and behavior change theory that draws on many of the principles just discussed. It is a client-centered counseling style designed to get people to work through whatever ambivalence they may be experiencing about changing their health behaviors. It appears to be especially effective for those who are initially wary about whether or not to change their behaviors (Resnicow et al., 2002).

In motivational interviewing, there is no effort to dismantle the denial often associated with the practice of bad health behaviors or to confront irrational beliefs or even to persuade a client to stop drinking, stop smoking, or otherwise improve health. Rather, the goal is to get the client to think through and express some of his or her own reasons for and against change and for the interviewer to listen and provide encouragement in absence of giving advice.

Motivational interviewing has broadened the tools for addressing health promotion efforts, although, like any one-on-one therapeutic technique, it is limited in the number of people it reaches.

Relaxation Training   In 1958, psychologist Joseph Wolpe (1958) developed a procedure known as systematic desensitization for the treatment of anxiety. The procedure involved training clients to substitute relaxation in the presence of circumstances that usually produced anxiety. To induce relaxation, Wolpe taught patients how to engage in deep breathing and progressive muscle relaxation (**relaxation training**).

In deep breathing, a person takes deep, controlled breaths, which produce a number of physiological changes, such as decreased heart rate and blood pressure and increased oxygenation of the blood. People typically engage in this kind of breathing spontaneously when

they are relaxed. In progressive muscle relaxation, an individual learns to relax all the muscles in the body to discharge tension or stress. As just noted, many deleterious health habits, such as smoking and drinking, represent ways of coping with social anxiety. Thus, in addition to social skills training or assertiveness training, people may learn relaxation procedures to cope more effectively with their anxiety.

Broad-Spectrum Cognitive-Behavior Therapy

The most effective approach to health-habit modification often comes from combining multiple behavior-change techniques. This eclectic approach has been termed **broad-spectrum cognitive-behavior therapy,** sometimes known as multimodal cognitive-behavior therapy (A. A. Lazarus, 1971). From an array of available techniques, a therapist selects several complementary methods to intervene in the modification of a target problem and its context.

The advantages of a broad-spectrum approach to health behavior change are several. First, a carefully selected set of techniques can deal with all aspects of a problem: Self-observation and self-monitoring define the dimensions of a problem; stimulus control enables a person to modify antecedents of behavior; self-reinforcement controls the consequences of a behavior; and social skills training may be added to replace the maladaptive behavior once it has been brought under some degree of control. A combination of techniques can be more effective in dealing with all phases of a problem than one technique alone. An example of the application of this kind of therapy to the treatment of alcoholism appears in box 3.1. A second advantage is that the therapeutic plan can be tailored to each individual's problem. Each person's faulty health habit and personality is different, so, for example, the particular package identified for one obese client will not be the same as that developed for another obese client (M. B. Schwartz & Brownell, 1995).

Broad-spectrum approaches to health behavior change have often achieved success when more limited programs have not, but such programs require intelligent application. Overzealous interventionists have sometimes assumed that more is better and have included as many components as possible, in the hopes that at least a few of them would be successful. In fact, this approach can backfire (Brownell, Marlatt, Lichtenstein, & Wilson, 1986). Overly complex behavior-change programs may undermine commitment because

Cognitive-Behavior Therapy in the Treatment of Alcoholism

Mary was a 32-year-old executive who came in for treatment, saying she thought she was an alcoholic. She had a demanding, challenging job, which she handled very conscientiously. Although her husband, Don, was supportive of her career, he felt it was important that evenings be spent in shared activities. They had had several arguments recently because Mary was drinking before coming home and had been hiding liquor around the house. Don was threatening to leave if she did not stop drinking altogether, and Mary was feeling alarmed by her behavior. Mary was seen over a 3-month period, with follow-up contact over the following year.

Mary's first week's assignment was to complete an autobiography of the history and development of her drinking problem—her parents' drinking behavior, her first drinking experience and first "drunk," the role of drinking in her adult life, her self-image, any problems associated with her drinking, and her attempts to control her drinking. She also self-monitored her drinking for 2 weeks, noting the exact amounts of alcohol consumed each day, the time, and the antecedents and consequences.

At the third session, the following patterns were identified. Mary started work at 8:30, typically had a rushed business lunch, and often did not leave work until 6:00, by which time she was tense and wound up. Because she knew Don did not approve of her drinking, she had begun to pick up a pint of vodka after work and to drink half of it during the 20-minute drive home, so that she could get relaxed for the evening. She had also begun stashing liquor away in the house just in case she wanted a drink. She realized that drinking while driving was dangerous, that she was drinking too much too quickly, and that she was feeling very guilty and out of control. Her husband's anger seemed to increase her urges to drink.

Mary agreed to abstain from any drinking during the third and fourth weeks of treatment. During this period, it became apparent that drinking was her only means of reducing the tension that had built up during the day and represented the one indulgence she allowed herself in a daily routine of obligations to external job demands and commitments to her husband and friends. A plan to modify her general lifestyle was worked out that included alternative ways of relaxing and indulging that were not destructive.

Mary joined a local health club and began going for a swim and a sauna every morning on the way to work. She also set aside 2 days a week to have lunch alone or with a friend. She learned a meditation technique, which she began using at the end of the day after getting home from work. She negotiated with Don to spend one evening a week doing separate activities so that she could resume her old hobby of painting.

Mary also decided that she wanted to continue drinking in a moderate way and that Don's support was essential so that she could drink openly. Don attended the sixth session with Mary, the treatment plan was explained to him, his feelings and concerns were explored, and he agreed to support Mary in her efforts to alter her lifestyle as well as to be more accepting of her drinking.

During the next few sessions, Mary learned a number of controlled drinking techniques, including setting limits for herself and pacing her drinking by alternating liquor with soft drinks. She also developed strategies for dealing with high-risk situations, which for her were primarily the buildup of tension at work and feelings of guilt or anger toward Don. She learned to become more aware of these situations as they were developing and began to practice more direct ways of communicating with Don. She also was instructed to use any urges to return to old drinking patterns as cues to pay attention to situational factors and use alternative responses rather than to interpret them as signs that she was an alcoholic.

The final two sessions were spent planning and rehearsing what to do if a relapse occurred. Strategies included the process of slowing herself down, cognitive restructuring, a decision-making exercise to review the consequences and relative merits and liabilities of drinking according to both the old and the new pattern, an analysis of the situation that led to the relapse, problem solving to come up with a better coping response to use next time, and the possibility of scheduling a booster session with her therapist.

At the final follow-up a year later, Mary reported that she was feeling better about herself and more in control, was drinking moderately on social occasions, and was communicating better with Don. She had had a couple of slips but had managed to retrieve the situation, in one case by being more assertive with a superior and in the other by simply deciding that she could accept some mistakes on her part without having to punish herself by continuing the mistake.

Source: J. R. Gordon & Marlatt, 1981, pp. 182–183.
Reprinted by permission.

of the sheer volume of activities they require. A multimodal program must be guided by an intelligent, well-informed, judicious selection of appropriate techniques geared to an individual problem. Moreover, much of the success of such programs comes from the presence of an enthusiastic, committed practitioner, not from the use of lots of techniques (Brownell, Marlatt, et al., 1986).

Relapse

One of the biggest problems faced in health-habit modification is the tendency for people to relapse to their previous behavior following initial successful behavior change (for example, McCaul et al., 1992). This problem occurs both for people who make health-habit changes on their own and for those who join formal programs to alter their behavior. Relapse is a particular problem with the addictive disorders of alcoholism, smoking, drug addiction, and obesity (Brownell, Marlatt, et al., 1986), which have relapse rates between 50 and 90% (Marlatt & Gordon, 1985).

What do we mean by "relapse"? A single cigarette smoked at a cocktail party or the consumption of a pint of ice cream on a lonely Saturday night does not necessarily lead to permanent relapse. However, over time, initial vigilance may fade and relapse may set in. Research suggests that relapse rates tend to stabilize at about 3 months, which initially led researchers to believe that most people who are going to relapse will do so within the first 3 months. However, subsequent research suggests that, although relapse rates may remain constant, the particular people who are abstaining from a bad health habit at one point in time are not necessarily the same people who are abstaining at another point in time. Some people go from abstinence to relapse; others, from relapse back to abstinence.

Why Do People Relapse?   Our knowledge of who relapses is limited. Genetic factors may be implicated in alcoholism, smoking, and obesity (Stunkard et al., 1986). Withdrawal effects occur in response to abstinence from alcohol and cigarettes and may prompt a relapse, especially shortly after efforts to change behavior. Conditioned associations between cues and physiological responses may lead to urges or cravings to engage in the habit (Marlatt, 1990). For example, people may find themselves in a situation in which they used to smoke, such as at a party, and relapse at that vulnerable moment.

Relapse is more likely when people are depressed, anxious, or under stress (Brandon, Copeland, & Saper,

1995). For example, when people are moving, breaking off a relationship, or encountering difficulties at work, they may have greater need for their addictive habits than is true at less stressful times. Relapse occurs when motivation flags or goals for maintaining the health behavior have not been established. Relapse is less likely if a person has social support from family and friends to maintain the behavior change, but it is more likely to occur if the person lacks social support or is involved in a conflictual interpersonal situation.

A particular moment that makes people vulnerable to relapse is when they have one lapse in vigilance. For example, that single cigarette smoked or the single pint of ice cream can produce what is called an **abstinence violation effect**—that is, a feeling of loss of control that results when a person has violated self-imposed rules. The result is that a more serious relapse is then likely to occur as the individual sees his or her resolve falter. This may be especially true for addictive behaviors because the person must cope with the reinforcing impact of the substance itself. Figure 3.5 illustrates the relapse process.

Consequences of Relapse   What are the consequences of relapse? Clearly, relapse produces negative emotions, such as disappointment, frustration, unhappiness, or anger. Even a single lapse can lead a person to experience profound disappointment, a reduced sense of self-efficacy, and a shift in attributions for controlling the health behavior from the self to uncontrollable external forces. A relapse could also lead people to feel that they can never control the habit, that it is simply beyond their efforts. Relapse may be a deterrent to successful behavior change in other ways as well. For example, among the obese, repeated cycles of weight loss and regain make subsequent dieting more difficult (Brownell, Greenwood, Stellar, & Shrager, 1986).

In some cases, however, relapse may have paradoxical effects, leading people to perceive that they can control their habits, at least to a degree. With smoking, for example, multiple efforts to stop often take place before people succeed (Schachter, 1982), suggesting that initial experiences with stopping smoking may prepare people for later success. The person who relapses may nonetheless have acquired useful information about the habit and have learned ways to prevent relapse in the future.

Reducing Relapse   Because of the high risk of relapse, behavioral interventions build in techniques to try to reduce its likelihood. Typically, such interventions have centered on three techniques. Booster sessions

FIGURE 3.5 | A Cognitive-Behavioral Model of the Relapse Process

This figure shows what happens when a person is trying to change a poor health habit and faces a high-risk situation. With adequate coping responses, the individual may be able to resist temptation, leading to a low likelihood of relapse. Without adequate coping responses, however, perceptions of self-efficacy may decline and perceptions of the rewarding effects of the substance may increase, leading to an increased likelihood of relapse.   (*Source:* From Marlatt, G. A., & Gordon, J. R. (1985). *Relapse Prevention: Maintenance Strategies in the Treatment of Addictive Behaviors.* New York: Guilford Press.)

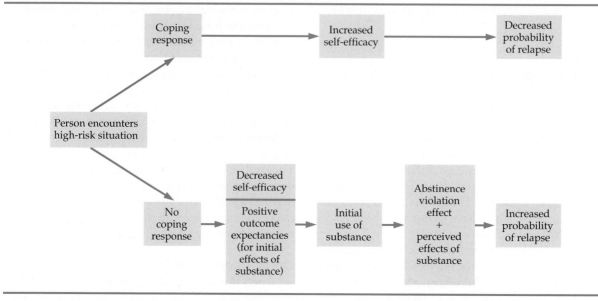

following the termination of the initial treatment phase have been one method. Several weeks or months after the end of a formal intervention, smokers may have an additional smoking-prevention session or dieters may return to their group situation to be weighed in and to brush up on their weight-control techniques. Unfortunately, however, booster sessions have been generally unsuccessful as a method for maintaining behavior change and preventing relapse (Brownell, Marlatt, et al., 1986).

Another approach has been to add more components to the behavioral intervention, such as relaxation therapy or assertiveness training, but, as noted earlier, the addition of components does not appear to increase adherence rates and, under some circumstances, may actually reduce them.

A third approach to relapse prevention is to consider abstinence a lifelong treatment process, as is done in such programs as Alcoholics Anonymous and other well-established lay treatment programs. Although this approach can be successful, it also has certain disadvantages. The philosophy can leave people with the perception that they are constantly vulnerable to relapse, potentially creating the expectation of relapse when vigilance wanes.

Moreover, the approach implies that people are not in control of their habit, and research on health-habit modification suggests that self-efficacy is an important component in initiating and maintaining behavior change (Bandura, 1986; Brownell, Marlatt, et al., 1986).

Relapse Prevention   Researchers have argued that **relapse prevention** must be integrated into treatment programs from the outset. Changing a health habit is not a simple action, but it is a process that may occur in stages (Brownell, Marlatt, et al., 1986; Prohaska & DiClemente, 1984a), and relapse prevention efforts can be built in at all stages.

Some factors are especially relevant when people first join a treatment program. Those people who are initially highly committed to the program and motivated to engage in behavior change are less likely to relapse. These observations imply that one important focus of programs must be to increase motivation and maintain commitment. For example, programs may create a contingency management procedure in which people are required to deposit money, which is returned if they successfully attend meetings or change their behavior.

Another, more controversial approach is the use of screening techniques to weed out people who are not truly committed to behavior change and who are therefore vulnerable to relapse. On the one hand, denying people access to a treatment program that may improve their health may be ethically dubious. On the other hand, including people who will ultimately relapse may demoralize other participants in the behavior-change program, demoralize the practitioner, and ultimately make it more difficult for the person predisposed to relapse to change behavior.

Once motivation and commitment to follow through have been instilled, techniques must be developed in the behavior-change program itself to maintain behavior change and act as relapse prevention skills once the program terminates. One such strategy involves having people identify the situations that are likely to promote a relapse and then develop coping skills that will enable them to manage that stressful event successfully. This strategy draws on the fact that successful adherence promotes feelings of self-control and that having available coping techniques can enhance feelings of control still further (Marlatt & George, 1988). In addition, the mental rehearsal of coping responses in a high-risk situation can promote feelings of self-efficacy, decreasing the likelihood of relapse. For example, some programs train participants to engage in constructive self-talk that will enable them to talk themselves through tempting situations (Brownell, Marlatt, et al., 1986).

Cue elimination, or restructuring the environments to avoid situations that evoke the target behavior, can be used (Bouton, 2000). The alcoholic who drank exclusively in bars can avoid bars. For other habits, however, cue elimination is impossible. For example, smokers are usually unable to completely eliminate the circumstances in their lives that led them to smoke. Consequently, some relapse prevention programs deliberately expose people to the situations likely to evoke the old behavior to give them practice in using their coping skills. The power of the situation may be extinguished over time if the behavior does not follow (Marlatt, 1990). Moreover, such exposure can increase feelings of self-efficacy and decrease the positive expectations associated with the addictive behavior. Making sure that the new habit (such as exercise or alcohol abstinence) is practiced in as broad an array of new contexts is important as well for ensuring that it endures (Bouton, 2000).

Lifestyle Rebalancing   Finally, long-term maintenance of behavior change can be promoted by leading the person to make other health-oriented changes in lifestyle, a technique termed **lifestyle rebalancing** (Marlatt & George, 1988). Making lifestyle changes, such as adding an exercise program or learning stress management techniques, may promote a healthy lifestyle more generally and help reduce the likelihood of relapse. Returning to smoking or excessive alcohol consumption may come to feel inappropriate in the context of a generally healthier lifestyle.

The role of social support in maintaining behavior change is equivocal. At present, some studies suggest that enlisting the aid of family members in maintaining behavior change is helpful, but other studies suggest not (Brownell, Marlatt, et al., 1986). Possibly research has not yet identified the exact ways in which social support may help maintain behavior change.

Overall, at present, relapse prevention seems to be most successful when people perceive their successful behavior change to be a long-term goal, develop coping techniques for managing high-risk situations, and integrate behavior change into a generally healthy lifestyle.

■ TRANSTHEORETICAL MODEL OF BEHAVIOR CHANGE

As the previous analysis implies, changing a bad health habit does not take place all at once. People go through stages while they are trying to change their health behaviors, and the support they need from therapists or formal behavior-change programs may vary depending on the particular stage they are in with respect to their poor health habit (Prohaska, 1994; Rothman, 2000).

Stages of Change

Prohaska and his associates (Prohaska, 1994; Prohaska, DiClemente, & Norcross, 1992) have developed the **transtheoretical model of behavior change,** a model that analyzes the stages and processes people go through in attempting to bring about a change in behavior and suggested treatment goals and interventions for each stage. Originally developed to treat addictive disorders, such as smoking, drug use, and alcohol addiction, the stage model has now been applied to other health habits, such as exercising and obtaining regular mammograms (Rakowski, Fulton, & Feldman, 1993).

Precontemplation   The precontemplation stage occurs when a person has no intention of changing his or her behavior. Many individuals in this stage are not even aware that they have a problem, although families,

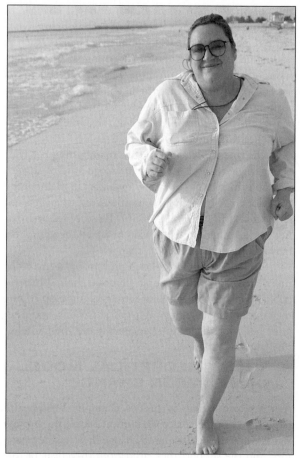

Readiness to change a health habit is an important prerequisite to health habit change.

friends, neighbors, or coworkers may well be. An example is the problem drinker who is largely oblivious to the problems he or she creates for his or her family. Sometimes people in the precontemplative phase seek treatment, but typically they do so only if they have been pressured by others and feel themselves coerced into changing their behavior. Not surprisingly, these individuals often revert to their old behaviors and consequently make poor targets for intervention.

Contemplation   Contemplation is the stage in which people are aware that a problem exists and are thinking about it but have not yet made a commitment to take action. Many individuals remain in the contemplation stage for years, such as the smoker who knows he or she should stop but has not yet made the commitment to do so. Individuals in the contemplation stage are typically still weighing the pros and cons of changing their behavior, continuing to find the positive aspects of the behavior enjoyable. Those who do decide to change their behavior have typically formed favorable expectations about their ability to do so and the rewards that will result (Rothman, 2000).

Preparation   In the preparation stage, individuals intend to change their behavior but may not yet have begun to do so. In some cases, it is because they have been unsuccessful in the past, or they may simply be delaying action until they can get through a certain event or stressful period of time. In some cases, individuals in the preparation stage have already modified the target behavior somewhat, such as smoking fewer cigarettes than usual, but have not yet made the commitment to eliminate the behavior altogether.

Action   The action stage is the one in which individuals modify their behavior to overcome the problem. Action requires the commitment of time and energy to making real behavior change. It includes stopping the behavior and modifying one's lifestyle and environment so as to rid one's life of cues associated with the behavior.

Maintenance   Maintenance is the stage in which people work to prevent relapse and to consolidate the gains they have made. Typically, if a person is able to remain free of the addictive behavior for more than 6 months, he or she is assumed to be in the maintenance stage (Wing, 2000).

Because relapse is the rule rather than the exception with addictive behaviors, this stage model is conceptualized as a spiral. As figure 3.6 indicates, individuals may take action, attempt maintenance, relapse, return to the precontemplation phase, cycle through the subsequent stages to action, repeat the cycle again, and do so several times until they have successfully eliminated the behavior (see Prohaska et al., 1992).

Importance of the Stage Model of Change

The stage model of health behavior change is potentially important for several reasons. It captures the processes that people actually go through while they are attempting to change their behavior, either on their own or with assistance. It illustrates that successful change may not occur on the first try or all at once. It also explicates why many people are unsuccessful in changing their behavior

FIGURE 3.6 | A Spiral Model of the Stages of Change   (*Source:* Prohaska et al., 1992)

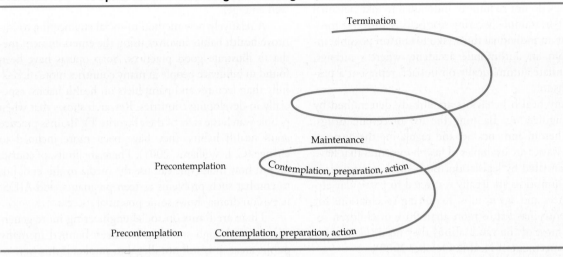

and why relapse rates are so high. Specifically, people who are in the precontemplation stage or the contemplation stage are not ready to be thrust into action. In fact, the research literature suggests that most people with an addictive habit are not in the action phase. For example, a study of smokers revealed that 10 to 15% were prepared for action, 30 to 40% were in the contemplation stage, and 50 to 60% were in the precontemplation stage (Prohaska et al., 1992). These statistics help explain why so many interventions show dismal rates of success. When success rates are recalculated to include only individuals who are ready to change their behavior—namely, those people in the action or preparation stage—most of these programs look more successful.

Using the Stage Model of Change

The stage model of health behavior change is helpful because it suggests that particular interventions may be more valuable during one stage than another. For example, a smoker in the action phase is not going to be helped by information about the importance of not smoking, but information about the importance of controlling alcohol consumption may be valuable to a person who is just beginning to contemplate that he or she has a drinking problem.

At each stage, then, particular types of interventions may be warranted (for example, Blalock et al., 1996; N. D. Weinstein, 1988). Specifically, providing individuals in the precontemplation stage with information about their problem may move them to the contemplation phase. To move people from the contemplation phase into preparation, an appropriate intervention may induce them to assess how they feel and think about the problem and how stopping it will change them. Interventions designed to get people to make explicit commitments as to when and how they will change their behaviors may bridge the gap between preparation and action. Interventions that emphasize providing self-reinforcements, social support, stimulus control, and coping skills should be most successful with individuals already moving through the action phase into long-term maintenance.

The spiral stage model of health behavior change deserves to be true, but so far its applications have shown mixed success. The model has been used with many different health behaviors, including smoking cessation, quitting cocaine, weight control, modification of a high-fat diet, adolescent delinquent behavior, practice of safe sex, condom use, sunscreen use, control of radon gas exposure, exercise acquisition, and regular mammograms (Prohaska et al., 1994). In some cases, interventions matched to the particular stage a person is in have been successful (for example, Park et al., 2003); in other cases, not (Lamb & Joshi, 1996; N. D. Weinstein, Rothman, & Sutton, 1998).

■ CHANGING HEALTH BEHAVIORS THROUGH SOCIAL ENGINEERING

Much behavior change occurs not through behavior-change programs but through social engineering. **Social engineering** involves modifying the environment in ways that affect people's ability to practice a particular health behavior. These measures are called passive because they do not require an individual to take personal action. For example, wearing seat belts is an active measure that an individual must take to control possible injury from an automobile accident, whereas airbags, which inflate automatically on impact, represent a passive measure.

Many health behaviors are already determined by social engineering. Banning the use of certain drugs, such as heroin and cocaine, and regulating the disposal of toxic wastes are examples of health measures that have been mandated by legislation. Both smoking and alcohol consumption are legally restricted to particular circumstances and age groups. Requiring vaccinations for school entry has led to more than 90% of children receiving most of the vaccinations they need (Center for the Advancement of Health, October 2002).

Many times, social engineering solutions to health problems are more successful than individual ones. We could urge parents to have their children vaccinated against the major childhood disorders of measles, influenza, hepatitis, diphtheria, and tetanus, but requiring immunizations for school entry has been very successful. We could intervene with parents to get them to reduce accident risks in the home, but approaches such as using safety containers for medications and making children's clothing with fire-retardant fabrics are more successful (Fielding, 1978). Lowering the speed limit has had far more impact on death and disability from motor vehicle accidents than interventions to get people to change their driving habits (Fielding, 1978). Raising the drinking age from 18 to 21 is more successful in reducing alcohol-related vehicular fatalities than are programs designed to help the drunk driver (Ashley & Rankin, 1988). Fallout from the current negotiations between the tobacco industry and the federal government are likely to lead to further restrictions on smoking, especially those restrictions designed to limit exposure to secondhand smoke.

The prospects for continued use of social engineering to change health habits are great. Controlling what is contained in vending machines at schools, putting a surcharge on foods high in fat and low in nutritional value, and controlling advertising of high-fat and high-cholesterol products, particularly those directed to children, should be considered to combat the enormous rise in obesity that has occurred over the past 2 decades (M. F. Jacobson & Brownell, 2000). Indeed, as the contributions of diet and obesity to poor health and early death become increasingly evident, social engineering

solutions with respect to food sales and advertising may well emerge.

A relatively new method of social engineering to improve health habits involves using the entertainment media to illustrate good practices. Soap operas have been found to influence people in many countries more successfully than lectures and pamphlets on health habits, especially in developing countries. Research shows that when people watch the stars of their favorite TV dramas practice good health habits, they have been more inclined to change (C. J. Williams, 2001). There are limits, of course, on just how much one can use the media to this end, but to combat such problems as teen pregnancy and AIDS, television drama shows some potential success.

There are limits on social engineering more generally. Even though smoking has been banned in many public areas, it is still not illegal to smoke; if this were to occur, most smokers and a substantial number of nonsmokers would find such mandatory measures unacceptable interference with civil liberties. Even when the health advantages of social engineering can be dramatically illustrated, the sacrifice in personal liberty may be considered too great. Thus, many health habits will remain at the discretion of the individual. It is to such behaviors that psychological interventions speak most persuasively.

■ VENUES FOR HEALTH-HABIT MODIFICATION

What is the best venue for changing health habits? There are several possibilities: the private therapist's office, the physician's office, self-help groups, schools, the workplace, the community setting, and the mass media. Each has its particular advantages and disadvantages (Winett, 1995).

The Private Therapist's Office

Some health-habit modification is conducted by psychologists, psychiatrists, and other clinicians privately on a one-to-one basis. These professionals are carefully trained in the techniques of cognitive-behavioral modification that seem to work best in altering health habits.

There are two striking advantages of the one-to-one therapeutic experience for the modification of health habits:

1. Precisely because it is one-to-one, the extensive individual treatment a person receives may make success more likely.

2. Because of the individual nature of the experience, the therapist can tailor the behavior-change package to the needs of the individual.

However, there is a major disadvantage. Only one individual's behavior can be changed at a time. If the modification of health habits is to make any dent in rates of disease, we must find ways of modifying health behaviors that do not require expensive one-to-one attention.

The Health Practitioner's Office

Health-habit modification can be undertaken in the health practitioner's office. Many people have regular contact with a physician or another health care professional who knows their medical history and can help them modify their health habits. Among the advantages of intervening in the physician's office is that physicians are highly credible sources for instituting health-habit change, and their recommendations have the force of their expertise behind them. Nonetheless, as in the case of private therapy, the one-to-one approach is expensive and reduces only one person's risk status at a time.

The Family

Increasingly, health practitioners are recognizing the value of intervening with the family to improve health (Fisher et al., 1998). There are several reasons for this emphasis. First and most obviously, children learn their health habits from their parents, so making sure the entire family is committed to a healthy lifestyle gives children the best chance at a healthy start in life.

Second, families, especially those in which there are children and one or more adults who work, typically have more organized, routinized lifestyles than single people do, so family life often builds in healthy behaviors, such as getting three meals a day, sleeping 8 hours, brushing teeth, and using seat belts. The health-promoting aspects of family life are evident in the fact that married men have far better health habits than single men, in part because wives often run the home life that builds in these healthy habits (for example, Hampson, Andrews, Barckley, Lichtenstein, & Lee, 2000). Single and married women have equally healthy lifestyles, with the exception of single women with children who are disadvantaged with respect to health (Hughes & Waite, 2002).

A third reason for intervening with families is that multiple family members are affected by any one member's health habits. A clear example is secondhand

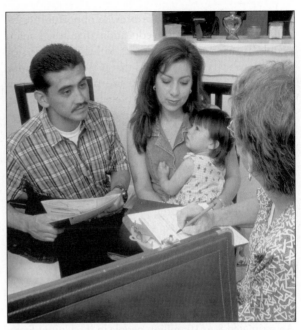

A stable family life is health promoting and, increasingly, interventions are being targeted to families rather than individuals to ensure the greatest likelihood of behavior change.

smoke, which harms not only the smoker but those around him or her.

Finally and most important, if behavior change is introduced at the family level—such as a low-cholesterol diet or stopping smoking—all family members are on board, ensuring greater commitment to the behavior-change program and providing social support for the person whose behavior is the target (D. K. Wilson & Ampey-Thornhill, 2001). Evidence suggests that the involvement of family members can increase the effectiveness of an intervention substantially (Wing & Jeffery, 1999).

As we'll see shortly, the emphasis on individual behavior change is a culturally limited approach that may not be a useful intervention strategy for Latino, Black, Asian, or southern European cultures; people in these latter cultures may be more persuaded to engage in behavior change when the good of the family is at stake (Han & Shavitt, 1994; Klonoff & Landrine, 1999). Consequently, the emphasis on family health behavior change is especially well placed for people from these cultures.

Managed Care Facilities

Increasingly, many of us get our health care from large medical groups, rather than from individual private physicians, and these groups provide opportunities for general preventive health education that reach many people at the same time. Clinics to help smokers stop smoking, dietary interventions that provide information and recipes for changing diet, and programs for new parents that teach home safety are among the many interventions that can be implemented in these larger settings.

Because about half of all early deaths result from preventable behavioral factors, managed care facilities are motivated to provide preventive care; substantial cost savings can result. Many managed care facilities do run alcohol, tobacco, and drug programs, but dietary, exercise, and other preventive interventions are more infrequent (Center for the Advancement of Health, 2000c). Thus, the role of managed care in implementing health behavior change has much room for growth.

Self-help Groups

An estimated 8 to 10 million people in the United States alone attempt to modify their health habits through self-help groups. These self-help groups bring together individuals with the same health-habit problem, and, often with the help of a counselor, they attempt to solve their problem collectively. Some prominent self-help groups include Overeaters Anonymous and TOPS (Take Off Pounds Sensibly) for obesity, Alcoholics Anonymous for alcoholics, and Smokenders for smokers. Many of the leaders of these groups employ cognitive-behavioral principles in their programs. The social support and understanding of mutual sufferers are also important factors in producing successful outcomes. At the present time, self-help groups constitute the major venue for health-habit modification in this country. We will examine the self-help group experience further in chapters 4 and 5.

Schools

Interventions to encourage health behaviors can be implemented through the school system (Center for the Advancement of Health, November 2003). A number of factors make schools a desirable venue for health-habit modification. First, most children go to school; therefore, virtually the entire population can be reached, at least in their early years. Second, the school population is young. Consequently, we can intervene before children have developed poor health habits. Chapter 5 provides examples of smoking prevention programs that are initiated with schoolchildren before they begin smoking.

Moreover, when young people are taught good health behaviors early, these behaviors may become habitual and stay with them their whole lives. Third, schools have a natural intervention vehicle—namely, classes of approximately an hour's duration; many health interventions can fit into this format. Finally, certain sanctions can be used in the school environment to promote health behaviors. For example, some school systems require that children receive a series of inoculations before they attend school and deny admission to those who have not received their shots; this requirement has been extremely successful in increasing compliance with recommended inoculations (W. J. McGuire, 1984).

For these reasons, then, the schools are often used as a venue for influencing health habits. For example, interventions in elementary schools targeted to increasing exercise and knowledge about proper nutrition have documented improvements in diet and exercise patterns that have especially benefited unfit and obese children (Center for the Advancement of Health, November 2003). Moreover, parents are clearly supportive of school efforts to instill better health habits (Center for the Advancement of Health, November 2003). Nonetheless, at present, even in states that require health education, programs may be hit or miss (Center for the Advancement of Health, November 2003).

Work-site Interventions

Very young children and the elderly can be reached through the health care system to promote healthy behavior. Children and adolescents can be contacted through the schools. The bulk of the adult population, however, is often difficult to reach. They do not use medical services regularly, and it is difficult to reach them through other organizational means. However, approximately 70% of the adult population is employed, and consequently, the workplace can be utilized to reach this large percentage of the population (S. G. Haynes, Odenkirchen, & Heimendinger, 1990).

There are at least three ways in which the work site has typically dealt with employees' health habits. The first is the provision of on-the-job health promotion programs that help employees practice better health behaviors. Programs exist to help employees stop smoking, reduce stress, change their diet, exercise regularly, lose weight, control hypertension, or control problem drinking among other problems (for example, Linnan et al., 2002; Theorell, Emdad, Arnetz, & Weingarten, 2001) (see figure 3.7).

FIGURE 3.7 | Percent of Employers Offering Specific Types of Health Promotion Programs in the Workplace   (*Source:* Association for Worksite Promotion et al., *National Worksite Health Promotion Survey,* 2000)

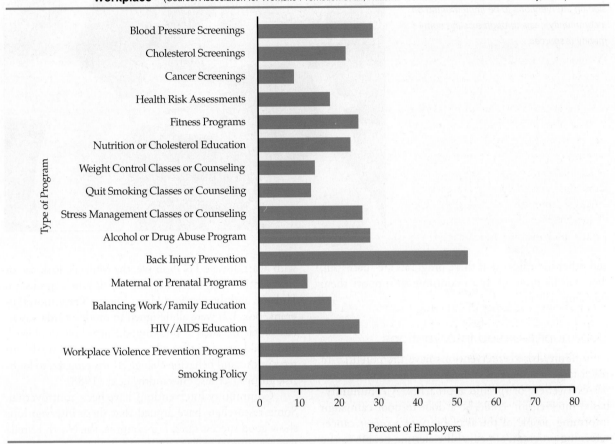

A second way in which industry has promoted good health habits is by structuring the environment to help people engage in healthy activities. For example, many companies ban smoking in the workplace. Others provide health clubs for employee use or restaurant facilities that serve meals that are low in fat, sugar, and cholesterol. Third, some industries provide special incentives, such as reduced insurance premiums for individuals who successfully modify their health habits (for example, individuals who stop smoking). Health psychologists have also been involved in the creation of general wellness programs designed to address multiple health habits.

In addition to being the main venue through which the adult population can be contacted, the work site has other advantages for intervention. First, large numbers of individuals can be educated simultaneously. Second, the work site can provide sanctions for participating in a program. For example, workers may get time off if they agree to take part. Third, the work site has a built-in so-cial support system of fellow employees who can provide encouragement for the modification of health habits. Finally, because people spend so much of their lives at work, changing the reinforcements and discriminative stimuli in the environment can help maintain good health habits instead of poor ones.

How successful are work site interventions? Many such programs have not been formally evaluated. Those that have appear to achieve modest success (Fielding, 1991; R. E. Glasgow, Terborg, Strycker, Boles, & Hollis, 1997), with some caveats. The enrollment is often low, at 20% or less (Winett, 2003). Interventions often reach those with jobs of higher rather than lower occupational prestige (Dobbins, Simpson, Oldenburg, Owen, & Harris, 1998). More efforts need to be made to recruit those in less prestigious occupations and positions. Formal evaluation and high rates of success will be critical in the continuation of such programs. If corporations can see reductions in absenteeism, insurance costs, accidents,

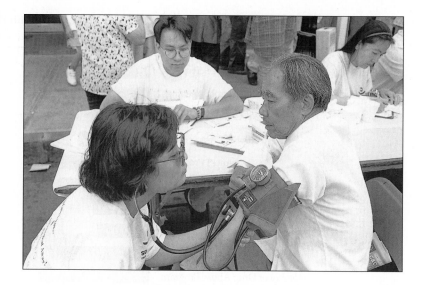

To reach the largest number of people most effectively, researchers are increasingly designing interventions to be implemented on a community basis through existing community resources.

and other indicators that these programs are successful, they will be more likely to continue to support them (Fielding, 1991).

Community-based Interventions

Community-based interventions have the potential to reach large numbers of individuals. The term encompasses a variety of specific approaches. A community-based intervention could be a door-to-door campaign informing people of the availability of a breast cancer screening program, a media blitz alerting people to the risks of smoking, a diet-modification program that recruits through community institutions, or a mixed intervention involving both media and interventions directed to high-risk community members.

There are several potential advantages of community-based interventions. First, such interventions reach more people than individually based interventions or interventions in limited environments, such as a single workplace or classroom. Second, community-based interventions can build on social support for reinforcing compliance with recommended health changes. For example, if all your neighbors have agreed to switch to a low-cholesterol diet, you are more likely to do so as well. Third, community-based interventions can potentially address the problem of behavior-change maintenance. If the community environment is restructured so that the cues and reinforcements for previous risky behaviors are replaced by cues and reinforcements for healthy behaviors, relapse may be less likely (R. Y. Cohen, Stunkard, & Felix, 1986).

Several prominent community-based interventions have been developed to reduce risk factors associated with heart disease. For example, the Multiple Risk Factor Intervention Trial (MRFIT), the North Karelia project in Finland, and the Stanford Heart Disease Prevention Program (box 3.2) were all designed to modify cardiovascular risk factors such as smoking, dietary cholesterol level, and blood pressure through a combination of media interventions and behavior-change efforts targeted to high-risk groups (see also Alexandrov et al., 1988).

Community interventions have been controversial. Some researchers have argued that these interventions show good success rates. For example, the North Karelia project appears to have produced declines in cardiovascular mortality (Tuomilehto et al., 1986), and the MRFIT program brought about reductions in cigarette smoking, reductions in blood pressure, and improvements in dietary knowledge (M. Sexton et al., 1987). Other researchers have argued, however, that these interventions are too expensive for the modest changes they bring about. Moreover, behavior change may not be maintained over time (Klepp, Kelder, & Perry, 1995). Although large-scale, expensive intervention studies that involve individualized behavior therapy for those at high risk are unlikely to be sustainable in the future on the basis of expense, more modest efforts to integrate healthy lifestyle programs into existing community outreach programs are likely to continue.

The Mass Media

One of the goals of health promotion efforts is to reach as many people as possible, and consequently, the mass media has great potential. Evaluations of the effectiveness of health appeals in the mass media suggest some

BOX **3.2**

Portrait of a Media Campaign to Reduce Cardiovascular Risk

An ambitious undertaking to reduce cardiovascular risk was mounted by a team of researchers at Stanford University (A. J. Meyer, Maccoby, & Farquhar, 1980). The Stanford Heart Disease Prevention Program, as it was called, was designed to test a potential model for mass media intervention in communities to get people to change their health habits so as to reduce their risk for cardiovascular disease.

Three communities similar in size and socioeconomic status were identified and compared on risk factors associated with coronary heart disease both before and after the study. One town served as a control town and received no campaign. The second and third towns were both exposed to a massive media campaign on the effects of smoking, diet, and exercise on risk for heart disease over a 2-year period via television, radio, newspapers, posters, billboards, and printed materials sent by mail. In one of these two towns, the media campaign was supplemented by face-to-face instruction, directed at participants at highest risk for coronary heart disease, on how to modify specific risk factors. This intervention was heralded as a potential major breakthrough in the modification of health habits because it employed an experimental design to examine health-habit modification efforts via the mass media and interpersonal interaction.

Only modest attitude and behavior changes were found in the community that was exposed only to the mass media campaign. As a consequence of the campaign, the participants became more knowledgeable about cardiovascular risk factors and reported that they had reduced their consumption of dietary cholesterol and fats relative to the control group. There was some evidence that systolic blood pressure and plasma cholesterol were reduced. More dramatic and lasting effects, however, were found when the mass media campaign was coupled with behavioral instruction of individuals at risk. These individuals did modify their cardiovascular risk status somewhat compared with the other two groups, primarily through reduced smoking (H. Leventhal, Safer, et al., 1980).

The Stanford study was a valuable step in using solid experimental data to evaluate mass media and face-to-face campaigns. The conclusions suggest that the mass media alone are only modestly successful in modifying risk status. Because mass media efforts like the Stanford intervention are very expensive, it seems unlikely that future research efforts will employ a media-only campaign to address health habits. Rather, it is more likely that subsequent community studies will use mass media campaigns as only one component of a more complex, concerted approach to health-habit modification.

Mass media appeals can change the attitudes of the general public toward particular health-related concerns.

qualifications regarding their success (Lau, Kane, Berry, Ware, & Roy, 1980). Generally, mass media campaigns bring about modest attitude change but less long-term behavior change.

The mass media appears to be most effective in alerting people to health risks that they would not otherwise know about (Lau et al., 1980). For example, media attention given to the surgeon general's report (U.S. Public Health Service, 1982) on the health risks of smoking alerted millions of people to the problem faster than any other form of communication.

By presenting a consistent media message over time, the mass media can also have a cumulative effect in changing the values associated with health practices. For example, the cumulative effects of antismoking mass media messages have been substantial, and the climate of public opinion is now clearly on the side of the nonsmoker. In conjunction with other techniques for behavior change, such as community interventions, the mass media can also reinforce and underscore elements in existing behavior-change programs.

The Internet

A promising yet underutilized tool for modifying health habits is the Internet. It provides low-cost access to health messages for millions of people who can potentially benefit from the information, suggestions, and techniques offered on websites. For example, a health screening website on which you enter your date of birth, gender, and basic details about your health history could inform you about the health habits you should be undertaking and whether the degree to which you engage in a health habit (such as the amount of exercise you are obtaining) is sufficient. The Internet also enables researchers to recruit a large number of participants for studies at relatively low cost, thus enabling data collection related to health habits as well (Lenert & Skoczen, 2002).

Conclusions

The choice of venue for health-habit change is an important issue. We need to understand the particular strengths and disadvantages of each venue and continue to seek methods that reach the most people for the least expense possible. By making use of the distinct advantages associated with each venue, we may most successfully modify health habits. Our primary challenge for the future will be to integrate our rapidly accumulating knowledge of how individuals alter their health habits with broader macro-level policies of federal, state, and private health care agencies (such as HMOs) to create a truly integrative approach to building healthy lifestyles (Orleans, 2000). The manifold evidence for the effectiveness of interventions is ultimately successful only if it is translated into practice (Glasgow, Klesges, Dzewaltowski, Bull, & Estabrooks, 2004). ●

SUMMARY

1. Health promotion is the process of enabling people to increase control over and improve their health. It involves the practice of good health behaviors and the avoidance of health-compromising ones. The impetus for health promotion has come from recognizing the impact of lifestyle factors, such as smoking, drinking, and controlling weight, on chronic health disorders.

2. Health habits are determined by demographic factors, social factors (such as early socialization in the family), values and cultural background, perceived symptoms, access to medical care, and cognitive factors (such as health beliefs). Health habits are only modestly related to each other and are highly unstable over time.

3. Health promotion efforts target children and adolescents before bad health habits are in place. They also focus on individuals and groups at risk for particular disorders to prevent those disorders from occurring. An increasing focus on health promotion among the elderly may help contain the soaring costs of health care at the end of life.

4. Attitudinal approaches to health behavior change can instill knowledge and motivation. But approaches such as fear appeals and information appeals have had limited effects on behavior change.

5. Research using the health belief model, the self-efficacy principle, and the theory of planned behavior have identified the attitudes most directly related to health-habit modification. These attitudes are the belief that a threat to health is severe, that one is personally vulnerable to the threat, that one is able to perform the response needed to reduce the threat (self-efficacy), that the response will be effective in overcoming the threat (response efficacy), and that social norms support one's practice of the behavior. Behavioral intentions are also important determinants of behavior.

6. Cognitive-behavioral approaches to health habit change use principles of self-monitoring, classical conditioning, operant conditioning, modeling, and stimulus control to modify the antecedents and consequences of a target behavior. Cognitive-behavior therapy brings patients into the treatment process by teaching them principles of self-control and self-reinforcement.

7. Social skills training and relaxation training methods are often incorporated into broad-spectrum, or multimodal, cognitive-behavioral interventions to deal with the anxiety or social deficits that underlie some health problems.

8. Increasingly, interventions focus on relapse prevention, which is the training of clients in methods to avoid the temptation to relapse. Learning coping techniques for high-risk-for-relapse situations is a major component of such interventions.

9. Successful modification of health habits does not occur all at once. Individuals go through stages, which they may cycle through several times: precontemplation, contemplation, preparation, action, and maintenance. When interventions are targeted to the stage an individual is in, they may be more successful.

10. Some health habits are best changed through social engineering, such as mandated childhood immunizations or banning smoking in the workplace.

11. The venue for intervening in health habits is changing. Expensive methods that reach one individual at a time are giving way to group methods that may be cheaper, including self-help groups and school, work-site, and community interventions. The mass media can reinforce health campaigns implemented via other means and can alert people to health risks.

KEY TERMS

abstinence violation effect
assertiveness training
at risk
behavioral assignments

broad-spectrum cognitive-behavior
     therapy
classical conditioning
cognitive-behavior therapy

cognitive restructuring
contingency contracting
covert self-control
discriminative stimulus

fear appeals
health behaviors
health belief model
health habit
health locus of control
health promotion
lifestyle rebalancing
modeling
operant conditioning

primary prevention
relapse prevention
relaxation training
self-control
self-efficacy
self-monitoring
self-observation
self-reinforcement
self-talk

social engineering
socialization
social skills training
stimulus-control interventions
teachable moment
theory of planned behavior
transtheoretical model of behavior
   change
window of vulnerability

Health-Enhancing Behaviors

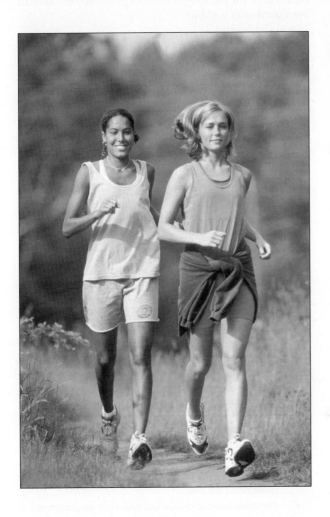

Every New Year's morning, Juanita sat down and took stock of what she wanted to accomplish during the next year. This year's list was like many other New Years' lists. It began with "lose 5 pounds" and included "get exercise every day" and "eat better (cut out junk food and soda)." After making the list, Juanita promptly went out running and returned 45 minutes later with a plan to consume a healthy lunch of steamed vegetables.

The phone rang. It was a friend inviting her to a last-minute New Year's Day brunch. The brunch sounded like a lot more fun than what Juanita had in mind, so off she went. Several hours later, after eggs Benedict and an afternoon of televised football games, soda, and potato chips, Juanita had already broken her New Year's resolve.

Juanita is very much like most of us. We know what we should do to preserve and maintain our health, and we want very much to do it. Given a moment of private reflection, most of us would make decisions similar to Juanita's. In fact, surveys show that the most common New Year's resolutions, in addition to saving money, are losing weight and getting exercise. Although most of us manage to pursue our New Year's resolutions longer than the few hours that Juanita lasted, rarely do we get more than a few weeks into the new year before we lapse back to our more sedentary, less healthy lifestyle. Yet these health habits are important, and changing or maintaining our behavior in the direction of good health habits should be a high priority for all of us.

Chapter 4 employs the attitudinal and behavioral principles identified in chapter 3 and examines how they apply to several self-enhancing behaviors, including exercise, accident prevention, cancer prevention, weight control, and healthy diet. These behaviors are important because each has been systematically related to at least one major cause of illness, disability, and death in industrialized countries. As people in third-world countries adopt the lifestyle of people in industrialized nations, these health habits will assume increasing importance throughout the world.

■ EXERCISE

In recent years, health psychologists have examined the role of aerobic exercise in maintaining mental and physical health. **Aerobic exercise** is sustained exercise that stimulates and strengthens the heart and lungs, improving the body's utilization of oxygen. All aerobic exercise is marked by its high intensity, long duration, and requisite high endurance. Among the forms of exercise that

meet these criteria are jogging, bicycling, rope jumping, running, and swimming. Other forms of exercise—such as isokinetic exercises (weight lifting, for example) or high-intensity, short-duration, low-endurance exercises (such as sprinting)—may be satisfying and build up specific parts of the body but have less effect on overall fitness because they draw on short-term stores of glycogen rather than on the long-term energy conversion system associated with aerobics.

Benefits of Exercise

The health benefits of aerobic exercise are substantial (see table 4.1). A mere 30 minutes of exercise a day can decrease the risk of chronic disease including heart disease and some cancers including breast cancer (Center for the Advancement of Health, March 2004). Exercise, coupled with dietary change, can cut the risk of Type II diabetes in high-risk adults significantly. However, two thirds of American adults do not achieve the recommended levels of physical activity, and about one fourth of American adults do not engage in any leisure-time physical activity (Center for the Advancement of Health, April 2002). Physical inactivity is more common among women than men, among African Americans and Hispanics than Whites, among older than younger adults (R. E. Lee & King, 2003), and among those with lower versus higher incomes (Center for the Advancement of Health, 2002). Sixty-four percent of men and 72% of women do not have any regular leisure time source of physical activity and two thirds

TABLE 4.1 | Health Benefits of Regular Exercise

- Increases maximum oxygen consumption.
- Decreases resting heart rate.
- Decreases blood pressure (in some).
- Increases strength and efficiency of heart (pumps more blood per beat).
- Decreases use of energy sources, such as glutamine.
- Increases slow wave sleep.
- Increases HDL, unchanged total cholesterol.
- Decreases cardiovascular disease.
- Decreases obesity.
- Increases longevity.
- Decreases menstrual cycle length, decreases estrogen and progesterone.
- Decreases risk of some cancers.
- Increases immune system functions.
- Decreases negative mood.

of older adults are not as active as they should be (Facts of Life, March 2004).

Perhaps more surprising is the fact that health practitioners do not uniformly recommend physical exercise, even to their patients who could especially benefit from it, such as their elderly patients (Center for the Advancement of Health, 2000i; Leveille et al., 1998); yet studies show that a physician recommendation is one of the factors that lead people to increase their exercise (Calfas et al., 1997).

Aerobic exercise has been tied to increases in cardiovascular fitness and endurance (B. Alpert, Field, Goldstein, & Perry, 1990) and to reduced risk for heart attack (Paffenbarger, Hyde, Wing, & Steinmetz, 1984). Exercise is considered to be the most important health habit for the elderly, and cardiovascular benefits of exercise have been found even for preschoolers (B. Alpert et al., 1990). Other health benefits of exercise include increased efficiency of the cardiorespiratory system, improved physical work capacity, the optimization of body weight, the improvement or maintenance of muscle tone and strength, an increase in soft tissue and joint flexibility, the reduction or control of hypertension, improved cholesterol level, improved glucose tolerance, improved tolerance of stress, and reduction in poor health habits, including cigarette smoking, alcohol consumption, and poor diet (Center for the Advancement of Health, 2000b; Ebbesen, Prkhachin, Mills, & Green, 1992). People who obtain regular, vigorous exercise may also have lower rates of certain forms of cancer (Brownson, Chang, Davis, & Smith, 1991).

The effects of exercise translate directly into increased longevity. Higher levels of physical fitness in both men and women clearly delay mortality, particularly that due to cardiovascular disease and cancer (Blair et al., 1989). One study estimated that, by age 80, the amount of additional life attributable to aerobic exercise is between 1 and 2 years (Paffenbarger, Hyde, Wing, & Hsieh, 1986). It is also true that, to achieve these extra 2 years of life, a person will have devoted the entire 2 years to exercise over his or her lifetime (Jacoby, 1986). Consequently, the quality of the exercise experience is also an important factor.

How Much Exercise? The typical exercise prescription for a normal adult is to accumulate 30 minutes or more of moderate intensity activity on most, preferably all, days of the week and 20 minutes or more of vigorous activity at least 3 days a week (Center for the Advancement of Health, 2000b; Perri et al., 2002). A person with low cardiopulmonary fitness may derive benefits with even less exercise each week. Even short walks, often recommended for older individuals or those with some infirmities, may have benefits for both physical and psychological health (Schectman & Ory, 2001; Ekkekakis, Hall, VanLanduyt, & Petruzzello, 2000). Lifestyle interventions designed to increase activity levels more generally may eventually lead to a commitment to exercise as well (Heesch, Mâsse, Dunn, Frankowski, & Mullen, 2003). Because it is difficult to get sedentary adults committed to a full-fledged exercise program, a lifestyle intervention aimed at increasing physical activity may represent a good start for aging sedentary adults (Conn, Valentin, & Cooper, 2002).

Exercise Versus Stress One puzzle is why exercise, which produces the release of adrenalin and other hormones, has a beneficial effect on heart functioning, whereas stress, which also produces these changes, has an adverse effect—that is, association with lesions in the heart tissue (Wright, 1988). One theory maintains that infrequent activation and discharge of adrenalin may have beneficial effects, whereas chronically enhanced discharge of adrenalin may not. Another possibility is that adrenalin discharged under conditions for which it was intended (such as running or fighting) is metabolized differently than adrenalin that occurs in response to stress.

A third possibility is that, under conditions of stress, the hypothalamic-pituitary-adrenocortical (HPA) axis is activated (a stress process that we will cover in chapter 6), which may be heavily responsible for the adverse effects of stress on the body, whereas sympathetic nervous system arousal alone or delayed HPA involvement, both of which are common in exercise, may have fewer adverse effects (De Vries, Bernards, De Rooij, & Koppeschaar, 2000). In essence, then, exercise may engage different neurobiological and emotional systems and patterns of activation than stress does.

Effects on Psychological Health Researchers have examined the effect of aerobic exercise on psychological states, such as mood, anxiety, depression, and tension, and have found a beneficial role of exercise on both mental and physical health. Regular exercise improves mood and feelings of well-being immediately after a workout; there may also be some improvement in general mood and well-being as a result of long-term participation in an exercise program (Hansen, Stevens, & Coast, 2001).

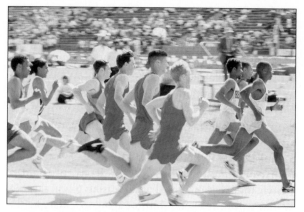

Regular aerobic exercise produces many physical and emotional benefits, including reduced risk for cardiovascular disease.

At least some of the positive effects of exercise on mood may stem from factors associated with exercise, such as social activity and a feeling of involvement with others. For example, bicycling with friends, swimming with a companion, and running with a group may improve mood in part because of the companionship the exercise provides (Estabrooks & Carron, 1999). Social support during exercise increases the likelihood that people will maintain their exercise programs, perhaps because feedback from other people increases feelings of self-efficacy.

An improved sense of self-efficacy can also underlie some of the mood effects of exercise (McAuley, Jerome, Marquez, Elavasky, & Blissmer, 2003). In one study (McAuley, Talbot, & Martinez, 1999), researchers recruited participants for an exercise group and manipulated the experience of self-efficacy during the program by providing contrived feedback to the participants about how well or poorly they were doing. Results indicated that, compared with a control group, people in the efficacy condition had significantly higher levels of perceived self-efficacy, and these perceptions were associated with improvements in mood and psychological well-being (see also Rovniak, Anderson, Winett, & Stephens, 2002).

Because of its beneficial effects on mood and self-esteem (McAuley, Mihalko, & Bane, 1997), exercise has been used as a treatment for depression (Herman et al., 2002) and for symptoms of menopause (Slaven & Lee, 1997). One study assigned depressed women to an exercise condition, a drug treatment session, or a combined treatment. The exercise group improved their mood significantly and as much as those who received only the drug or the combined treatment. More important, once treatment was discontinued, those who continued to exercise were less likely to become depressed again when compared with those who had been on the drug treatment (Babyak et al., 2000).

The impact of exercise on well-being should not be overstated, however. The effects are often small, and the expectation that exercise has positive effects on mood may be one reason that people so widely report the experience. Despite these cautions, the positive effect of exercise on well-being is now quite well established.

Exercise as Stress Management   The fact that exercise improves well-being suggests that it might be an effective way of managing stress. Research suggests that this intuition is well placed. J. D. Brown and Siegel (1988) conducted a longitudinal study to see if adolescents who exercised were better able to cope with stress and avoid illness than those who did not. Results indicated that the negative impact of stressful life events on health declined as exercise levels increased. Thus, exercise may be a useful resource for combating the adverse health effects of stress (for example, C. M Castro, Wilcox, O'Sullivan, Baumann, & King, 2002).

One possible mechanism whereby exercise may buffer certain adverse health effects of stress involves its beneficial impact on immune functioning (Fiatarone et al., 1988). An increase in endogenous opioids (natural pain inhibitors; see chapter 10) stimulated by exercise may also play a role in the modulation of immune activity during periods of psychological stress.

Exercise may also have a beneficial effect on cognitive processes by focusing attention and concentration. However, the evidence on this point is mixed (Blumenthal et al., 1991; Plante & Rodin, 1990). Exercise may initially facilitate attention, but as its intensity increases, these effects may be canceled out by the debilitating effects of muscle fatigue (Tomporoski & Ellis, 1986).

Exercise may offer economic benefits. A review of employee fitness programs, which are now a part of more than 50,000 U.S. businesses, suggests that such programs can reduce absenteeism, increase job satisfaction, and reduce health care costs, especially among women employees (see J. Rodin & Plante, 1989, for a review).

Determinants of Regular Exercise

Although the health and mental health benefits of exercise are well established, most people's participation in exercise programs is erratic. Many children get regular exercise through required physical education classes in school. However, by adolescence, the practice of regular exercise has declined substantially, especially among girls and among boys not involved in formal athletics (Crosnoe, 2002). Smoking, being overweight, and teen pregnancy also account for some of the decline in physical activity (Kimm et al., 2002). Adults cite lack of time and other stressors in their lives as factors that undermine their good intentions (R. S. Myers & Roth, 1997). As humorist Erma Bombeck noted, "The only reason I would take up jogging is so that I could hear heavy breathing again."

Many people seem to share this attitude toward exercise. Evaluations of exercise programs indicate that 6-month participation levels range from 11 to 87%, averaging at about 50% (Dishman, 1982). This statistic means that, on average, only half of those people who initiate a voluntary exercise program are still participating in that program after 6 months. People may begin an exercise program but find it difficult to make exercise a regular activity. Paradoxically, although exercise seems to be a stress buster, stress itself is one of the most common reasons that people fail to adhere to their exercise regimens (Stetson, Rahn, Dubbert, Wilner, & Mercury, 1997). Accordingly, research has attempted to identify the factors that lead people to participate in exercise programs over the long term (B. H. Marcus et al., 2000).

Individual Characteristics   Who is most likely to exercise? People who come from families in which exercise is practiced (Sallis, Patterson, Buono, Atkins, & Nader, 1988), who have positive attitudes toward physical activity, who perceive themselves as athletic or as the type of person who exercises (Salmon, Owen, Crawford, Bauman, & Sallis, 2003), and who believe that people should take responsibility for their health are more likely to get involved in exercise programs initially than people who do not have these attitudes (Dishman, 1982). However, these factors do not predict participation in exercise programs over the long term. Those people who have positive attitudes toward exercise and health are as likely to drop out as those who do not (Dishman, 1982).

Gender predicts who exercises. From an early age, boys get more exercise than girls (for example, Sallis et al., 1993). Middle-aged and older women are especially unlikely to get exercise for several reasons. The lifestyles of older women may not afford opportunities for regular exercise (Cody & Lee, 1999), and exercise has not been a health priority for middle-aged women until relatively recently (C. Lee, 1993; S. Wilcox & Storandt, 1996). Women also report significant barriers to getting exercise, including caregiving responsibilities and concomitant lack of energy (A. C. King et al., 2000).

Some physical factors predict participation in exercise programs. Overweight people are less likely to participate in exercise programs than are those who are not overweight. It may be that exercise is harder for the overweight or that leaner people who had more active lifestyles before getting involved in exercise are better able to incorporate exercise into their activities (Dishman, 1982).

Social support predicts exercise. Among people who participate in group exercise programs such as running groups or walking groups, a sense of support and group cohesion contributes to participation.

The effects of health status on participation in exercise programs are still unclear. Individuals at risk for cardiovascular disease do show greater adherence to exercise programs than do those who are not (Dishman, 1982). However, outside of the cardiovascular area, there is no general relationship between health status and adherence to exercise programs (Dishman, 1982).

People who are high in self-efficacy with respect to exercise (that is, believing that one will be able to perform exercise regularly) are more likely to practice it and more likely to perceive that they are benefiting from it than those people low in self-efficacy. In one study of sedentary, middle-aged adults, those with high self-efficacy beliefs with respect to their exercise plan perceived themselves to expend less effort and reported more positive mood during exercise than did those with low beliefs in self-efficacy. The positive emotions experienced during exercise, in turn, predicted subsequent self-efficacy beliefs, suggesting that positive effect may help maintain the practice of exercise (McAuley, 1993; McAuley & Courneya, 1992). The converse is also true: Those individuals with low self-efficacy beliefs with respect to exercise are less likely to engage in it. Those who do not exercise regularly may have little confidence in their ability to exercise and may regard exercise as entailing nearly as many costs as benefits (B. H. Marcus & Owen, 1992; Motl et al., 2002).

Self-efficacy appears to be especially important for exercise adherence among older men and women. With increasing age, attitudes toward exercise and perceptions of one's self-efficacy with respect to exercise decline, although motivation remains high. Consequently, interventions aimed at modifying attitudes about the importance of exercise and one's ability to perform it might be successful for increasing exercise in older adults (S. Wilcox & Storandt, 1996).

Characteristics of the Setting Which characteristics of exercise programs promote its practice? Convenient and easily accessible exercise settings lead to higher rates of adherence (for example, Humpel, Marshall, Leslie, Bauman, & Owen, 2004). If your exercise program is vigorous walking that can be undertaken near your home, you are more likely to do it than if your source of exercise is an aerobics program in a crowded health club 5 miles from your home. Lack of resources for physical activity may be a particular barrier for regular exercise among those low in socioeconomic status (SES) (Estabrooks, Lee, & Gyurcsik, 2003; Feldman & Steptoe, 2004).

Are people more likely to adhere to exercise if a given amount of exercise has been prescribed for them? To date, research suggests there is no ideal behavioral dosage that improves adherence (Dishman, 1982). An exercise regimen that is consistently near the maximal heart rate (90%), however, tends to produce noncompliance, perhaps because the regimen is too demanding to be sustained on a regular basis (J. E. Martin & Dubbert, 1982).

Perhaps the best predictor of regular exercise is regular exercise. Studies that have assessed attitudinal and motivational predictors of exercise have found that, although exercise intentions are influenced by attitudes, long-term practice of regular exercise is heavily determined by habit (McAuley, 1992). The first 3 to 6 months appear to be critical. People who will drop out usually do so in that time period. Those people who have adhered for 3 to 6 months are significantly more likely to continue to exercise (Dishman, 1982). Developing a regular exercise program, embedding it firmly in regular activities, and practicing it regularly for a period of time means that it begins to become automatic and habitual. However, habit has its limits. Unlike such habitual behaviors as wearing a seat belt or not lighting a cigarette, exercise requires additional thoughtfulness and planning. Exercising takes will power, the recognition that hard work is involved, and a belief in personal responsibility in order to be enacted on a regular basis (P. Valois, Desharnais, & Godin, 1988).

Characteristics of Interventions

Strategies The factors that promote health habits generally are now incorporated into programs designed to increase exercise adherence. Cognitive-behavioral strategies—including contingency contracting, self-reinforcement, self-monitoring, and goal setting—have been employed in exercise interventions and appear to promote adherence (Dishman, 1982). Techniques for maintaining behavior change (see chapter 3) are also successful for enhancing adherence to exercise programs (B. H. Marcus et al., 2000). For example, prompting, in the form of phone calls, was shown in one study to be successful in increasing adherence to a program of walking (Lombard, Lombard, & Winett, 1995).

Relapse prevention techniques have been used to increase adherence to exercise programs. One study (Belisle, Roskies, & Levesque, 1987) compared adherence to exercise among participants in a 10-week exercise group that either did or did not receive training in relapse prevention. Relapse prevention techniques in this intervention centered around increasing awareness of the obstacles people experience in obtaining regular exercise and developing appropriate techniques for coping with them, such as methods of resisting temptation not to exercise. The results indicated superior adherence in the relapse prevention group. With older adults, even simple telephone or mail reminders may help maintain adherence to a physical activity program (C. M. Castro, King, & Brassington, 2001).

Stages of change identified by the transtheoretical model of behavior change suggest that different interventions should be targeted to people at different stages of readiness to exercise. For example, people who are contemplating starting an exercise program may perceive practical barriers to it (R. S. Myers & Roth, 1997), which can be attacked through persuasive communications. Those people already engaged in exercise, however, face the problem of maintenance and relapse to a sedentary lifestyle, so interventions that provide successful techniques for not abandoning an exercise program may be more useful for them (Nigg, 2001). Groups at particular risk for not exercising can be especially well served by stages of change interventions designed to increase exercise. These include sedentary mothers of young children (Fahrenwald, Atwood, Walker, Johnson, & Berg, 2004) and the frail elderly (Leveille et al., 1998).

Many studies confirm the efficacy of the transtheoretical model of behavioral change (that is, the stages of change model) as successful in producing self-efficacy with respect to physical activity and higher levels of physical activity. Generally speaking, interventions designed to increase physical activity that are matched to the stage of readiness of the sample are more successful than interventions that do not have this focus (Blissmer

& McAuley, 2002; Litt, Kleppinger, & Judge, 2002; A. L. Marshall et al., 2003; S. J. Marshall & Biddle, 2001).

Even minimal interventions to promote exercise are showing some success. In an intervention that mailed stage-targeted printed materials encouraging physical exercise to older adults, those who reported receiving and reading the intervention materials were significantly more likely to be exercising 6 months later. The advantage of such an intervention, of course, is its low cost and ease of implementation (A. L. Marshall et al., 2003).

Incorporating exercise into a more general program of healthy lifestyle change can be successful as well. For example, among adults at risk for coronary heart disease, brief behavioral counseling matched to stage of readiness showed success in achieving maintenance to physical activity, as well as smoking reduction and reduction in fat intake (Steptoe, Kerry, Rink, & Hilton, 2001). Although interventions targeted to multiple behaviors are sometimes less easy to undertake because of their complexity, linking health habits to each other in a concerted effort to address risk can be successful, as this intervention study showed.

Individualized Exercise Programs   Because research has identified few individual differences, exercise setting characteristics, or intervention strategies that promote long-term adherence, perhaps the best approach is to individualize exercise programs. Understanding an individual's motivation and attitudes with respect to exercise provides the underpinnings for developing an individualized exercise program that fits the person well. If people participate in activities that they like, that are convenient, for which they can develop goals, and that they are motivated to pursue, exercise adherence will be greater (Dishman, 1982). In addition, as just noted, if interventions are geared to the stage of readiness that individuals are in with respect to exercise, interventions may be more successful (S. J. Marshall & Biddle, 2001). Ensuring that people have realistic expectations for their exercise programs may also improve long-term adherence (Sears & Stanton, 2001).

Exercise interventions may promote more general lifestyle changes. This issue was studied in an intriguing manner with 60 Hispanic and Anglo families, half of whom had participated in a 1-year intervention program of dietary modification and exercise. All the families were taken to the San Diego Zoo as a reward for participating in the program, and while they were there, they were observed, and their food intake and amount of walking were recorded. The results indicated that the families that had participated in the intervention consumed fewer calories, ate less sodium, and walked more than the families in the control condition, suggesting that the intervention had been integrated into their lifestyle (T. L. Patterson et al., 1988).

There may be unintended negative effects of interventions to increase exercise that need to be guarded against in the design of any intervention program. For example, one study (Zabinsky, Calfas, Gehrman, Wilfley, & Sallis, 2001) found that an intervention program directed to college men and women inadvertently promoted an increase in the desire to be thin, despite warnings about dieting. Such pressures can promote eating disorders. Otherwise, exercise interventions do not appear to have negative side effects.

Because of the difficulties that arise in trying to get people to exercise faithfully, some health psychologists have tried simply to increase overall activity level. The more active people become, the more likely they are to maintain a proper body weight. Moreover, recent research has suggested that moderate activity spread throughout the day may be enough to achieve the cardiac gains previously thought to be achievable only through vigorous exercise (Barinaga, 1997), especially for the elderly. However, these findings are controversial, as the relation of activity level to coronary heart disease (CHD) risk factors is still unclear (Barinaga, 1997).

Physical activity websites would seem to hold promise for inducing people to participate in regular exercise (Napolitano et al., 2003). Of course, if one is on the Web, one is by definition not exercising. Indeed, thus far, there is little evidence that physical activity websites provide the kind of individually tailored program that is needed to get people to participate on a regular basis (Doshi, Patrick, Sallis, & Calfas, 2003). To date, then, the Web has demonstrated mixed success modifying physical activity levels. One intervention study via Internet did show modest short-term gains.

Despite the problems psychologists have encountered in getting people to exercise and to do so faithfully, the exercise level in the American population has increased substantially in the past 2 decades. In 1979, the surgeon general articulated a set of goals for the health of the American public, one of which included exercise. This goal has turned out to be the one on which the greatest progress has been made (M. McGinnis, Richmond, Brandt, Windom, & Mason, 1992). The number of people who participate in regular exercise has increased by more than 50% in the past few decades. Increasingly it is not just sedentary healthy adults who are becoming involved in exercise, but also the elderly and patient populations, including patients with heart disease and with cancer (Courneya & Friedenreich, 2001). To be able to sustain and build on these changes in the future suggests that although the population may be aging, it may be doing so in a healthier way than in any previous generation.

■ ACCIDENT PREVENTION

No wonder that so many cars collide;
Their drivers are accident prone,
When one hand is holding a coffee cup,
And the other a cellular phone.

—Art Buck

Despite the jocular nature of this bit of doggerel, it captures an important point. Accidents represent one of the major causes of preventable death in this country. Worldwide, 1.18 million people died as a result of road-traffic injuries in the year 2002, and the estimated economic cost of accidents is $518 billion per year (World Health Organization, 2004). Of particular concern is traffic accidents, which represents one of the largest causes of death among children, adolescents, and young adults.

Several million people are poisoned each year in the United States, 85% of whom are children (S. L. Murphy, 2000). Bicycle accidents cause more than 800 deaths per year, prompt more than 600,000 emergency room visits, and constitute the major cause of head injury, thereby making helmet use an important issue (Center for Disease Control and Prevention, 2000a). Occupational accidents and their resulting impact on disability are a particular health risk for working men. Consequently, strategies to reduce accidents have increasingly been a focus of health psychology research and interventions.

Home and Workplace Accidents

Accidents in the home, such as accidental poisonings and falls, are the most common causes of death and disability among children under age 5. Interventions to reduce home accidents are typically conducted with parents because they have control over the child's environment. Parents are most likely to undertake injury prevention activities if they believe that the recommended steps really will avoid injuries, if they feel knowledgeable and competent to teach safety skills to their children, and if they have a realistic sense of how much time will actually be involved in doing so (L. Peterson, Farmer, & Kashani, 1990).

Increasingly, pediatricians are incorporating such training into their interactions with new parents (M. C. Roberts & Turner, 1984). Parenting classes can be used to teach parents to identify the most common poisons in their household and how to keep these safeguarded or out of reach of young children. A study evaluating training on how to childproof a home suggested that such interventions can be successful (J. R. Matthews, Friman, Barone, Ross, & Christophersen, 1987).

Statistics suggest that, overall, accidents in the home and in the workplace have declined (see figure 4.1). This decline may be due, in part, to better safety precautions by employers in the workplace and by parents in the home. Social engineering solutions, such as safety caps on medications, and strict guidelines for occupational safety have added to the decline. Home and workplace accidents, then, represent a domain in which interventions have been fairly successful in reducing mortality.

Motorcycle and Automobile Accidents

You know what I call a motorcyclist who doesn't wear a helmet? An organ donor.

—Emergency Room Physician

The single greatest cause of accidental death is motorcycle and automobile accidents (Facts of Life, May 2004). To date, little psychological research has gone into helping people avoid vehicular traffic accidents. Instead, efforts

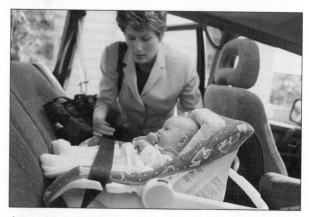

Automobile accidents represent a major cause of death, especially among the young. Legislation requiring child safety restraint devices has reduced fatalities dramatically.

FIGURE 4.1 | Accidental Deaths   (*Source:* National Safety Council, Injury Facts 2002 Edition, 2002)

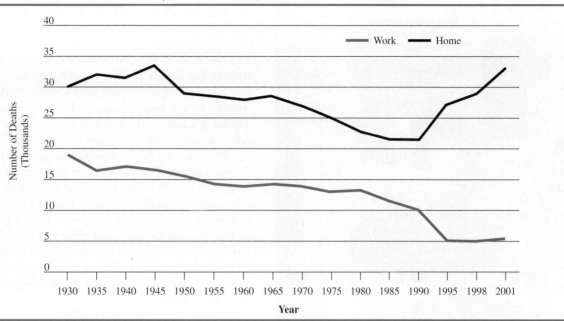

have concentrated on such factors as the maintenance of roadways, the volume of travel, and safety standards in automobiles. However, psychological research can address factors associated with accidents, including the way people drive, the speed at which they drive, and the use of preventive measures to increase safety.

It is clear that safety measures such as reducing highway driving speed to 55 miles per hour, requiring seat belts, and placing young children in safety restraint seats have reduced the number of severe injuries and vehicular fatalities (Facts of Life, May 2004). Making themselves visible through reflective or fluorescent clothing and the use of helmets among bicycle and motorcycle riders has reduced the severity of accidents by a substantial degree, especially preventing serious head injury (Facts of Life, May 2004; Wells et al., 2004).

However, getting people to follow these safety measures is difficult. For example, many Americans still do not use seat belts, a problem that is especially common among adolescents and that heavily accounts for their high rate of fatal accidents (Facts of Life, May 2004). To promote the use of seat belts, a combination of social engineering, health education, and psychological intervention may be most appropriate. For example, most states now require that infants and toddlers up to age 3 or 4 be restrained in safety seats and children up to age 6 wear seat belts. This requirement can lay the ground-

work for proper safety behavior in automobiles, making people more likely to use seat belts in adolescence and adulthood.

Communitywide health education programs aimed at increasing seat belt usage and infant restraint devices can be successful. One such program increased the use from 24 to 41%, leveling off at 36% over a 6-month follow-up period (Gemming, Runyan, Hunter, & Campbell, 1984). In terms of improving seat belt use, one program involving high school students found that frequent but small monetary rewards coupled with an educational campaign stressing the importance of accident prevention substantially increased seat belt use from approximately 25 to nearly 50% (Campbell, Hunter, & Stutts, 1984). On the whole, however, such programs are impractical for instilling the behavior, and legal solutions may be more effective—specifically, penalizing people for not using seat belts. Seat belt use is more prevalent in states with laws that mandate their use.

■ CANCER-RELATED HEALTH BEHAVIORS

Breast Self-examination

Although it is now on the decline, breast cancer remains one of the leading causes of cancer deaths among American women, striking one out of every eight women at

Mammograms are an important way of detecting breast cancer in women over 50. Finding ways to reach older women to ensure that they obtain mammograms is a high priority for health scientists.

some point during her life (S. L. Parker, Tong, Bolden, & Wingo, 1996). Although breast cancer does not usually develop until after age 45, its age of onset is decreasing, and more young women than ever are affected (B. L. Andersen, 1992). Despite medical advances in technology to detect cancerous lumps, 90% of all breast cancer is still detected through self-examination.

Breast self-examination (BSE) is the practice of checking the breasts to detect alterations in the underlying tissue. Ideally, the breasts are palpated once a month, approximately 10 days into the menstrual cycle, in both a standing-up and lying-down position. BSE during a shower or a warm bath sometimes improves the ability to detect lumps. The correct practice of BSE involves checking all the breast tissue, including the nipple and the area under the armpits. But despite its potential for

detecting a common cancer, relatively few women practice BSE, and of those who do, few practice it correctly (V. M. Stevens, Hatcher, & Bruce, 1994).

Barriers to BSE   Several factors may act as deterrents to the regular practice of BSE: not being certain that one is doing it correctly, having difficulty detecting changes in the breast tissue, and fearing what might happen if a lump were detected. Each of these barriers can be addressed by appropriate interventions.

Not knowing exactly how to practice BSE is one of the main factors that keeps women from regular practice (Alagna & Reddy, 1984). Pamphlets and articles in magazines are not usually effective in teaching women how to practice BSE. Personal instruction from a physician or a nurse leads to better and more regular practice of BSE than any other method; yet explicit training of patients by physicians in BSE is still relatively uncommon, so intervening with physicians to encourage their instruction is important.

Many women who practice BSE are discouraged by the fact that it is hard to detect lumps (Kegeles, 1985). Breast tissue tends to be lumpy, and beginners seem to find suspicious lumps all the time. However, research reveals that, when women practice BSE on synthetic models that do and do not contain lumps, their ability to discriminate lumps improves (Atkins, Solomon, Worden, & Foster, 1991). Thus, BSE self-confidence can be augmented by practice on models (for example, S. C. Hall et al., 1980; Stephenson, Adams, Hall, & Pennypacker, 1979). Moreover, such training may improve self-efficacy with respect to the practice of BSE, which is one of the strongest predictors of effective and frequent BSE (Shepperd, Solomon, Atkins, Foster, & Frankowski, 1990).

A family history of breast cancer and worry about breast cancer appear to moderately increase the likelihood of practicing breast cancer–related screening behaviors, including BSE (McCaul, Branstetter, O'Donnell, Jacobson, & Quinlan, 1998). Among some women, however, fear may also act as a deterrent. Publicizing the success rates of breast cancer treatments and the importance of early detection in that success can combat such fears.

Guidelines for the practice of BSE have changed greatly over the past few years. Regular practice of BSE has had little effect on mortality from breast cancer, suggesting that it is not a significant health behavior. Nonetheless, because most abnormalities are self-detected, at least occasional BSE is still recommended for women over 20 (American Cancer Society, 2003).

Mammograms

The recent decrease in breast cancer mortality has been linked in part to better screening. Although the number of women who are screened is increasing, many women still do not get screened (Champion et al., 2002). For women over age 50, national health guidelines recommend a mammogram every year. For at-risk women over age 40, health guidelines also recommend yearly mammograms. (For women not at particular risk but between 40 and 50, the value of a yearly mammogram is less clear.)

Why is screening through mammography so important for older and high-risk women? The reasons are several:

1. The prevalence of breast cancer in this country remains high, with the likelihood rising from 1 in 14 to 1 in 8 and higher in particular geographic locations.

2. The majority of breast cancers continue to be detected in women over age 40, so screening this age group is cost effective.

3. Most important, early detection, as through mammograms, can improve survival rates.

Breast cancer screening programs that include mammograms can reduce deaths from breast cancer by 35 to 40% in older women (S. Shapiro, Venet, Strax, Venet, & Roeser, 1985; Strax, 1984), although mortality rates among younger women do not seem to be as strongly affected.

Getting Women to Obtain Mammograms

Unfortunately, compliance with mammography recommendations is low. Recent reviews suggest that only 59% of women had been screened for breast cancer in the past 2 years, and only 27% had had the age appropriate number of repeat screening mammograms (M. A. Clark, Rakowski, & Bonacore, 2003; K. A. Phillips, Kerlikowske, Baker, Chang, & Brown, 1998). Unfortunately too, the use of mammograms declines with age, even though the risk of breast cancer increases with age (Ruchlin, 1997). Fear of radiation, embarrassment over the procedure, anticipated pain, anxiety, fear of cancer (Gurevich et al., 2004; M. D. Schwartz et al., 1999), and, most important, especially among poorer women, concern over costs act as deterrents to getting regular mammograms (Fullerton, Kritz-Silverstein, Sadler, & Barrett-Connor, 1996; Lantz, Weigers, & House, 1997). Lack of awareness, time, incentive, and availability are also important.

Consequently, research has focused on how to increase women's use of mammographic services. Incentives for obtaining mammograms appear to be effective. One program, which offered women a nutrition information packet as an incentive for making appointments, found significantly higher rates of attendance (J. A. Mayer & Kellogg, 1989). Another study found that mammography use among older women increased substantially when doctors distributed breast cancer brochures with tear-off referral forms and chart stickers for personal calendars (Preston et al., 1998). Counseling and mailed materials promoting mammography are also effective at increasing the use of this important screening procedure (Champion et al., 2002).

Changing attitudes toward mammography may increase the likelihood of obtaining a mammogram. In particular, the health belief model, especially the attitudes of perceiving benefits of mammograms and encountering few barriers to obtaining one, has been associated with a greater likelihood of obtaining a mammogram (Champion & Springston, 1999; McCaul, Branstetter, Schroeder, & Glasgow, 1996).

The theory of planned behavior also predicts the likelihood of obtaining regular mammograms: Women who have positive attitudes regarding mammography and who perceive social norms as favoring their obtaining a mammogram are more likely to participate in a mammography program (Montano & Taplin, 1991). Prohaska's transtheoretical model of behavior change (see chapter 3) also predicts decisions about mammography, with interventions more successful if they are geared to the stage of readiness of prospective participants (Champion & Springston, 1999; Lauver, Henriques, Settersten, & Bumann, 2003).

But interventions with women alone will not substantially alter rates of participation in mammography screening programs if the health care system is not also changed. Mammograms have not been well integrated into standard care for older women. Instead of receiving all necessary diagnostic tests and checkups from one physician, as adult men do, many older women must make at least three appointments—one with a general practitioner, one with a gynecologist, and one with a mammography center. Minority women and older women especially fall through the cracks, because often they do not have a regular source of health care (Champion & Springston, 1999; National Cancer Institute Breast Cancer Screening Consortium, 1990). Interventions need to be directed to health professionals to ensure that physicians routinely refer their older women patients to mammography centers, and health care delivery services need to be established so that mammography is cheaper and more accessible to older and low-income women (Messina, Lane, & Grimson, 2002).

Testicular Self-examination

Testicular cancer is the most common cancer in men between the ages of 15 and 35, and it is one of the leading causes of death for men in this age group. Moreover, its incidence is increasing (National Cancer Institute, 1987). But with early detection, the cure rate is high (Friman & Christophersen, 1986), so interventions to improve early detection are critical.

The symptoms of testicular cancer are typically a small, usually painless lump on the front or sides of one or both testicles, a feeling of heaviness in the testes, a dragging sensation in the groin, accumulation of fluid or blood in the scrotal sac, and pain in advanced cases (Hongladrom & Hongladrom, 1982).

Young men are generally unaware of either their risk or the appropriate health measures to take to reduce it, so instruction in **testicular self-examination (TSE)** can be useful. In many ways, effective testicular self-examination is quite similar to effective breast self-examination. It involves becoming familiar with the surface, texture, and consistency of the testicles, examination during a warm bath or shower, and examination of both testicles rotated between the thumb and forefinger to determine that the entire surface is free of lumps (Hongladrom & Hongladrom, 1982).

A few studies have examined or conducted interventions to assess or improve the frequency and proficiency of TSE. Drawing on the theory of planned behavior, Brubaker and Wickersham (1990) found that men were more likely to perform TSE if they believed it would reduce their risk of testicular cancer and if they believed that others approved of the practice (subjective norms). The researchers then gave these men a persuasive message, derived from the theory of planned behavior, that stressed the value of TSE in early detection and the success of treatments in curing the disorder. The message was successful in increasing the practice of TSE further. Another study (Friman, Finney, Glasscock, Weigel, & Christophersen, 1986) provided young men with a brief checklist of TSE skills and found that the educational intervention produced substantial increases in the efficacy of TSE and more long-term practice.

As is the case with BSE, guidelines for the practice of TSE are ambiguous. There is no documented relation of TSE practice to a reduction in advanced testicular cancer, and so for the present, each young man is urged to decide for himself whether or not to practice TSE (American Cancer Society, 2004b).

Colorectal Cancer Screening

In Western countries, colorectal cancer is the second highest cause of cancerous deaths. In recent years, medical guidelines have increasingly recommended routine colorectal screening for older adults (Wardle, Williamson, McCaffery, et al., 2003). Colorectal screening is distinctive for the fact that people often learn that they have polyps (a benign condition that can increase risk for colorectal cancer) but not detected malignancies. To date, the evidence suggests that colorectal cancer screening does not unduly raise anxiety either among those who have polyps detected or who are vulnerable to cancer (Wardle, Williamson, Sutton, et al., 2003).

Factors that predict the practice of other cancer-related health behaviors also predict participation in colorectal cancer screening, specifically self-efficacy, perceived benefits of the procedure, a physician's recommendation to participate, and low perceived barriers to taking advantage of the screening program (Hays et al., 2003). Community-based interventions that employ such strategies as mass media, community-based education, use of social networks, health care provider recommendations, and reminder notices promote participation in cancer screening programs, including colorectal cancer, and indicate that community-based interventions can attract older populations to engage in appropriate screening behaviors (Curbow, in press). An intervention aimed at a hard to reach group of older adults that provided reassuring information regarding colorectal screening was effective in modifying initially negative attitudes and increasing rates of screening attendance (Wardle, Williamson, McCaffery, et al., 2003).

Sunscreen Use

The past 30 years have seen a nearly fourfold increase in the incidence of skin cancer in the United States. More than 1 million new cases of skin cancer will be diagnosed this year alone. Although common basal cell and squamous cell carcinomas do not typically kill, malignant melanoma takes approximately 7,000 lives each year (Facts of Life, July 2002). In the last two decades, melanoma incidence has risen by 155%. Moreover, these cancers are among the most preventable cancer we

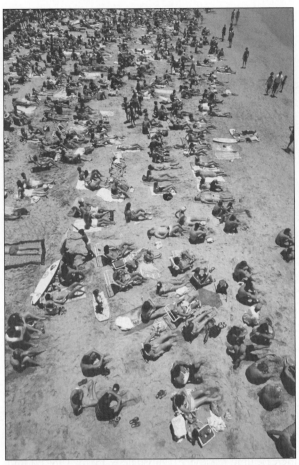

Despite the risks of exposure to the sun, millions of people each year continue to sunbathe.

have. The chief risk factor for skin cancer is well known: excessive exposure to ultraviolet radiation. Living or vacationing in southern latitudes, participating in outdoor activities, and using tanning salons all contribute to dangerous sun exposure (J. L. Jones & Leary, 1994). Sun protective behaviors are practiced consistently by less than one third of American children and more than three quarters of U.S. teens get at least one sunburn each summer (Facts of Life, July 2002). As a result, health psychologists have increased their efforts to promote safe sun practices. Typically, these efforts have included educational interventions designed to alert people to the risks of skin cancer and to the effectiveness of sunscreen use for reducing risk (for example, R. C. Katz & Jernigan, 1991). Based on what we know about attitudinal interventions with other health habits, however, educa-

tion alone is unlikely to be entirely successful (Jones & Leary, 1994).

Problems with getting people to engage in safe sun practices stem from the fact that tans are perceived to be attractive. In fact, young adults perceive people with moderately strong tans as healthier and more attractive than people without tans (Facts of Life, July 2002). Young adults who are especially concerned with their physical appearance and who believe that tanning enhances their attractiveness are most likely to expose themselves to ultraviolet radiation through tanning (Leary & Jones, 1993). Even people who are persuaded of the importance of safe sun habits often practice them incompletely. Many of us use an inadequate sun protection factor (SPF), and few of us apply sunscreen as often as we should during outdoor activities (Wichstrom, 1994). Nonetheless, the type of skin one has—burn only, burn then tan, or tan without burning—is the strongest influence on likelihood of using sun protection (Clarke, Williams, & Arthey, 1997), suggesting that people are beginning to develop some understanding of their risk.

Effective sunscreen use is influenced by a number of factors, including perceived need for sunscreen, perceived efficacy of sunscreen as protection against skin cancer, and social norms regarding sunscreen use, among other factors (Turrisi, Hillhouse, Gebert, & Grimes, 1999). Health communications that enhance these perceptions may be helpful in increasing the practice (Jackson & Aiken, 2000).

Communications to adolescents and young adults that stress the gains that sunscreen use will bring them, such as freedom from concern about skin cancers, appear to be more successful than those that emphasize the risks (Detweiler, Bedell, Salovey, Pronin, & Rothman, 1999). When the risks are emphasized, it is important to stress the immediate adverse effects of poor health habits rather than the long-term risks of chronic illness, since adolescents and young adults are especially influenced by immediate concerns. In one clever investigation, beachgoers were given a photo-aging intervention that showed premature wrinkling and age spots; a second group received a novel ultraviolet photo intervention that made negative consequences of UV exposure very salient; a third group received both interventions; and a fourth group was assigned to a control condition. Those beachgoers who received the UV photo information engaged in more protective behaviors for incidental sun exposure, and the combination of the UV photo with the photo-aging information led to substantially less sunbathing (Mahler,

Kulick, Gibbons, Gerrard, & Harrell, 2003; see also Hillhouse & Turrisi, 2002). Communications drawing on the stages of change model, which aim to move the tanning public from a precontemplative to a contemplative stage and subsequently to implementation of sun protective behaviors, may also be successful (Pagato, McChargue, & Fuqua, 2003).

Social engineering solutions to the sun exposure problem may be needed as well. Few schools have sun protection policies that encourage children and teens to use sunscreen. Most schools provide relatively little shade and some schools do not allow children to wear hats or sunglasses, all of which could be protective (Facts of Life, July 2002). Thus, intervening in the schools represents another point of departure on this important health issue.

■ MAINTAINING A HEALTHY DIET

Developing and maintaining a healthy diet should be a goal for everyone. The dramatic rise in obesity in the United Stated has added urgency to this recommendation. Diet is an important and controllable risk factor for many of the leading causes of death and contributes substantially to risk factors for disease as well. However, only 35% of the population gets the recommended five servings of fruits and vegetables each day. Experts estimate that unhealthful eating contributes to more than 300,000 deaths per year (Centers for Disease Control and Prevention, 2000b; National Center for Health Statistics, 1999). Dietary change is often critical for people at risk for or already diagnosed with chronic diseases, such as coronary artery disease, hypertension, diabetes, and cancer (Center for the Advancement of Health, 2000g). These are diseases for which low-SES people are more at risk, and diet may explain some of the relation between low SES and these disorders. Research consistently shows that supermarkets in high-SES neighborhoods carry more health-oriented food products than do supermarkets in low-income areas. Thus, even if the motivation to change one's diet is there, the food products may not be (Conis, 2003, August 4).

Why Is Diet Important?

Dietary factors have been implicated in a broad array of diseases and risks for disease. Perhaps the best known is the relation of dietary factors to total serum cholesterol level and to low-density lipid proteins in particular

(McCaffery et al., 2001). Although diet is only one determinant of a person's lipid profile, it can be an important one because it is controllable and because elevated total serum cholesterol and low density lipid proteins are risk factors for the development of coronary heart disease and hypertension. Of dietary recommendations, switching from trans fats (as are used for fried and fast foods) and saturated fats (from meat and dairy products) to polyunsaturated fats and monounsaturated fats is one of the most widely recommended courses of action (Marsh, 2002). Diet may be implicated in sudden death, because danger from arterial clogging may increase dramatically after a high-fat meal (G. J. Miller et al., 1989). Salt has been linked to hypertension and to cardiovascular disease in some individuals as well (Jeffery, 1992).

Dietary habits have also been implicated in the development of several cancers, including colon, stomach, pancreas, and breast (Steinmetz, Kushi, Bostick, Folsom, & Potter, 1994). Dietary modification is also important for polyp prevention among individuals at risk for colorectal cancers, specifically a low-fat, high-fiber diet (Corle et al., 2001). Estimates of the degree to which diet contributes to the incidence of cancer exceed 40% (Fitzgibbon, Stolley, Avellone, Sugerman, & Chavez, 1996).

A poor diet may be especially problematic in conjunction with other risk factors. Stress, for example, may increase lipid reactivity (Dimsdale & Herd, 1982). Lipid levels may influence intellectual functioning; in particular, serum cholesterol concentration may be an indicator of levels of brain nutrients important to mental efficiency (Muldoon, Ryan, Matthews, & Manuck, 1997).

The good news is that changing one's diet can improve health. For example, a diet high in fiber may protect against obesity and cardiovascular disease by lowering insulin levels (Ludwig et al., 1999). A diet high in fruits, vegetables, whole grains, peas and beans, poultry, and fish and low in refined grains, potatoes, and red and processed meats has been shown to lower the risk of coronary heart disease in women (Fung, Willett, Stampfer, Manson, & Hu, 2001). Modifications in diet can lower blood cholesterol level (Carmody, Matarazzo, & Istvan, 1987), and these modifications may, in turn, reduce the risk for atherosclerosis. A relatively recent class of drugs, called statins, substantially reduces cholesterol in conjunction with dietary modification. In fact, the effects of statins are so rapid that low-density lipoprotein (LDL) cholesterol is lower within the first month after beginning use. Together, diet modification and a statin regimen appear to be highly successful for lowering cholesterol.

Even people who are usually successful at restraining their food consumption may overeat under certain circumstances. Eating is often disinhibited when a person is under stress, distracted, or otherwise not paying attention to what he or she is eating. This is particularly likely to be true among those who are usually restrained eaters. Thus, the sheer cognitive load of daily life may disinhibit our ability to control our food consumption by preventing us from monitoring the consequences of our eating (Ward & Mann, 2000).

A controversial issue about diet that promises to occupy attention over the next decade concerns reduced calorie diets. In several organisms, caloric restriction or reduced calorie diets have increased life span. It is not yet known if caloric restriction increases life span in humans, but experiments with primates suggests that it may. There is already evidence that caloric restriction is associated with biomarkers that predict longevity in humans (G. S. Roth et al., 2002). Thus, in addition to changing specific patterns of food consumption in the future, we may also all be urged to reduce our caloric intake overall (Lee & Ruvkun, 2002).

Resistance to Modifying Diet

It is difficult to get people to modify their diet, even when they are at high risk for CHD or when they are under the instruction of a physician. Indeed, the typical reason that people switch to a diet low in cholesterol, fats, calories, and additives and high in fiber, fruits, and vegetables is to improve appearance not to improve health. Even so, fewer than half of U.S. adults meet the dietary recommendations for reducing fat and sodium and for increasing fiber, fruit, and vegetable consumption (Kumanyika et al., 2000). Moreover, there is some evidence that in response to a diet lower in fat and cholesterol, people compensate by adjusting their ingestion of other foods (Taubes, 2001). Consequently, the evidence that a low-fat diet actually reduces obesity and prolongs life is equivocal (Taubes, 2001). Any effort to alter diet must be cognizant of these counterveiling forces.

Another difficulty with modifying diet is the problem of maintaining change. Adherence to a new diet may be high at first, but falls off over time. One reason is because of the factors that plague all efforts to change poor health habits: insufficient attention to the needs for long-term monitoring and relapse prevention techniques. In the case of diet, other factors are implicated as well: Self-management is essential because dietary recommendations may be monitored only indirectly by medical authorities, such as physicians, who have only general measures of adherence, such as cholesterol counts, to go on (Carmody et al., 1987). A strong sense of self-efficacy, family support, and the perception that dietary change has important health benefits are critical to successfully making dietary change (E. S. Anderson, Winett, & Wojcik, 2000; Steptoe, Doherty, Carey, Rink, & Hilton, 2000).

Some dietary recommendations are restrictive, monotonous, expensive, and hard to find and prepare. Drastic changes in shopping, meal planning, cooking methods, and eating habits may be required. In addition, tastes are hard to alter. So-called comfort foods, many of which are high in fat and sugars, may help to turn off stress hormones, such as cortisol, thus contributing to eating things that are not good for us (Dallman et al., 2003). Preferences for high-fat foods are so well established that people will consume more of a food they have been told is high in fat than one low in fat, even when that information is false (Bowen, Tomoyasu, Anderson, Carney, & Kristal, 1992). A low sense of self-efficacy, a preference for meat, a low level of health consciousness, a low interest in exploring new foods, and low awareness of the link between eating habits and illness are all associated with poor dietary habits (Hollis, Carmody, Connor, Fey, & Matarazzo, 1986). People who are high in conscientiousness and intelligence also seem to do a better job of adhering to a cholesterol-lowering diet, and people high in depression or anxiety are less likely to do so (Stilley, Sereika, Muldoon, Ryan, & Dunbar-Jacob, 2004).

Stress has a direct effect on eating, especially in adolescence. Greater stress is tied to consuming more fatty foods and less fruit and vegetables and to the lesser likelihood of eating breakfast with more snacking between meals (Cartwright et al., 2003). Thus, stress may contribute to long-term risk for disease by steering the adolescents' and young adults' diet in an unhealthy direction. A lower status job, high workload, and lack of control at work are also associated with less healthful diets, although scientists do not yet know exactly why (Devine, Connors, Sobal, & Bisogni, 2003). It may be that these factors enhance stress and that an unhealthful diet marked by comfort foods reduces it.

Some dietary changes may alter mood and personality. Evidence is mounting that low-cholesterol diets may contribute to poor mood and behavior problems. It may be that people do not like low-cholesterol meals, so they get irritable after consuming them. Diet may also alter levels of neurotransmitters that affect mood as well. The fact that cocaine addicts are more likely to relapse if they have low plasma levels of cholesterol may be consistent with these points (Buydens-Branchey & Branchey, 2003).

Some studies suggest that although low-cholesterol diets lower heart attack rates, they may contribute to deaths from behavioral causes, including suicides, accidents, and murders (K. W. Davidson, Reddy, McGrath, & Zitner, 1996). Research with monkeys suggests that a low-fat diet may increase aggressive behavior (J. R. Kaplan, Manuck, & Shively, 1991); a possible cause of these effects is that the diet produces lower levels of serotonin in the brain (Muldoon, Kaplan, Manuck, & Mann, 1992). Low cholesterol levels have been related to an increased likelihood of depressive symptoms in men as well (Lavigne et al., 1999; Steegmans, Hoes, Bak, van der Does, & Grobbee, 2000).

Conflict over dietary recommendations themselves may undermine adherence. Different diets become fashionable at different times. At this writing, a low-carbohydrate diet is winning over many converts. This diet is unusual because it admits many of the foods that low-cholesterol diets explicitly discourage, such as those that are high in fat. With confusion over what leads to weight loss and what leads to health, would-be dieters do not always know where to turn.

Despite the fact that there may be hardships associated with low-cholesterol diets, evidence suggests that people's quality of life is not seriously compromised and may actually improve under some circumstances (Corle et al., 2001; Coutu, Dupuis, & D'Antono, 2001; Delahanty, Hayden, Ammerman, & Nathan, 2002).

Interventions to Modify Diet

Many efforts to modify diet are done on an individual basis in response to a specific health problem or health risk. Physicians, nurses, dietitians, and other experts work with patients to modify a diet-responsive risk, such as obesity, diabetes, CHD, or hypertension. As with any health habit change, the motivation to pursue dietary change and commitment to long-term health are essential ingredients for success (Kearney, Rosal, Ockene, & Churchill, 2002). Any effort to change diet needs to begin with education and self-monitoring training because many people have a poor idea of the importance of particular nutrients and how much of them their diet actu-

ally includes; estimation of fat intake appears to be poor, for example (O'Brien, Fries, & Bowen, 2000).

Much dietary change has been implemented through cognitive-behavioral interventions. These include self-monitoring, stimulus control, and contingency contracting, coupled with relapse prevention techniques for high-risk-for-relapse situations, such as parties or other occasions where high-fat foods are readily available. One such intervention targeted to African-American adolescents sought to increase fruit and vegetable intake. The intervention produced the desired changes among those who experienced positive shifts in self-efficacy (D. K. Wilson et al., 2002).

Another method of dietary change adopts Prohaska's transtheoretical stages of change model, which assumes that different interventions are required for people at different stages. Research shows that, among people given blood cholesterol tests and a questionnaire assessing diet, those already contemplating dietary change were more likely to enroll in an intervention than those at the stage of precontemplation (B. S. McCann et al., 1996). An intervention that attempted to increase fruit and vegetable consumption also found that those people who were in the stage of contemplation were most receptive to the intervention (Laforge, Greene, & Prohaska, 1994; see also Cullen, Bartholomew, Parcel, & Koehly, 1998).

Family Interventions Recently, efforts to intervene in the dietary habits of high-risk individuals have focused on the family group. There are several good reasons for focusing interventions on the family. When all family members are committed to and participate in dietary change, it is easier for the target family member to do so as well (D. K. Wilson & Ampey-Thornhill, 2001). Moreover, different aspects of diet are influenced by different family members. Whereas wives still usually do the shopping and food preparation, husbands' food preferences are often a more powerful determinant of what the family eats (Weidner, Archer, Healy, & Matarazzo, 1985).

In family interventions, family members typically meet with a dietary counselor to discuss the need to change the family diet and ways for doing so. Family members then talk through the specific changes they might make. Sometimes a family attempting to make these changes will get together with other families who have done the same thing in order to share suggestions and problems that have come up in their efforts to modify the family's diet. Such programs may include social

BOX 4.1

Modifying Diet: Who Are You Fooling?

"The fat around steak is delicious, but you're not supposed to eat it," says one 47-year-old man on a diet. "My daughter tells me, 'Dad, you're going to have a heart attack.' But if I clear the plates from the table, I'll stick it in my mouth when no one is looking." (Baar, 1995, p. B1)

Researchers have found that intervening with the family to change health habits is often successful in improving diet and reducing obesity. Family members can reinforce each other's efforts to lose weight and improve health and give each other social support in the process, yet often members of families cheat on the family diet, trying to outwit those around them, disguising what they eat and how much they eat. One woman noted: "My kids ask, 'Where'd those cookies go?' And I say, 'I don't

know' or 'Daddy ate them'" (Baar, 1995, p. B1). Another man noted:

> It used to be that when people would ask how I eat, I'd tell them I was into grains . . . .I thought that was a socially acceptable answer. What they didn't know was that to me, it meant cookies and cake. (Baar, 1995, p. B1)

A lot of people who mislead their families also lie to themselves. People notoriously underreport how much they eat and what they eat, even when they are deceiving no one but themselves. People tell little lies that don't fool anyone, such as "food that you eat standing up doesn't count" or "eating lots of a food that is low in calories will not lead to weight gain." In fighting the battle to improve diet, then, we need to attack not only what people eat but also the lies they tell themselves and others for continuing to eat it.

---

activities or potlucks, in which people share recipes and bring food, and may use printed media, including newsletters, handouts containing recipes, consumer shopping guides to finding healthier foods, and new meal-planning ideas. Such family interventions appear to have considerable promise in modifying diet (Carmody, Istvan, Matarazzo, Connor, & Connor, 1986).

Community Interventions   Many interventions have been implemented on the community level. One study (Foreyt, Scott, Mitchell, & Gotto, 1979) exposed people in Houston, Texas, to one of four interventions: a diet booklet explaining how individuals can alter their salt and cholesterol intake, formal education in nutrition, a behavioral intervention involving a group discussion, or a combination of all three. Each approach significantly reduced cholesterol levels immediately after the intervention, but none maintained behavior change over time. Although similar community studies have shown similar initial success rates, none has shown impressive long-term change.

Nutrition education campaigns mounted in supermarkets have revealed some success. In one study, a computerized, interactive nutritional information system placed in supermarkets significantly decreased high-fat purchases and somewhat increased high-fiber purchases (Jeffery, Pirie, Rosenthal, Gerber, & Murray, 1982; Winett et al., 1991). Box 4.1 describes a program designed to control hyperlipidemia by modifying diet.

A more recent approach to modifying diet has involved targeting particular groups for which dietary change may be especially important and designing interventions specifically directed to these groups. For example, inner-city, low-income Hispanic Americans are at high risk for cancers because of their diet. An intervention that targeted mothers of young children in a Hispanic community exposed them to a 12-week, culturally sensitive cancer prevention program that encouraged the adoption of a low-fat, high-fiber diet. The intervention was successful in bringing about a reduction in dietary fat consumption (Fitzgibbon et al., 1996).

Change may also come from social engineering solutions to the problem, as well as from individual efforts to alter diet. Factors such as banning snack foods from schools, making school lunch programs more nutritious, and making snack foods more expensive and healthy foods less so will all make some inroads into promoting healthy food choices (Horgen & Brownell, 2002).

■ WEIGHT CONTROL

Maintaining a proper diet and getting enough exercise jointly contribute to weight control, the issue to which we now turn. This issue has become especially urgent in recent years because of the galloping levels of obesity in the population. Consequently, our discussion will begin to cross the line into the area of health-compromising behaviors, as we will look at interventions both for

TABLE 4.2 | Body Mass Index Table

BMI	Normal						Overweight					Obese					
	19	20	21	22	23	24	25	26	27	28	29	30	31	32	33	34	35
Height (inches)	Body Weight (pounds)																
58	91	96	100	105	110	115	119	124	129	134	138	143	148	153	158	162	167
59	94	99	104	109	114	119	124	128	133	138	143	148	153	158	163	168	173
60	97	102	107	112	118	123	128	133	138	143	148	153	158	163	168	174	179
61	100	106	111	116	122	127	132	137	143	148	153	158	164	169	174	180	185
62	104	109	115	120	126	131	136	142	147	153	158	164	169	175	180	186	191
63	107	113	118	124	130	135	141	146	152	158	163	169	175	180	186	191	197
64	110	116	122	128	134	140	145	151	157	163	169	174	180	186	192	197	204
65	114	120	126	132	138	144	150	156	162	168	174	180	186	192	198	204	210
66	118	124	130	136	142	148	155	161	167	173	179	186	192	198	204	210	216
67	121	127	134	140	146	153	159	166	172	178	185	191	198	204	211	217	223
68	125	131	138	144	151	158	164	171	177	184	190	197	203	210	216	223	230
69	128	135	142	149	155	162	169	176	182	189	196	203	209	216	223	230	236
70	132	139	146	153	160	167	174	181	188	195	202	209	216	222	229	236	243
71	136	143	150	157	165	172	179	186	193	200	208	215	222	229	236	243	250
72	140	147	154	162	169	177	184	191	199	206	213	221	228	235	242	250	258
73	144	151	159	166	174	182	189	197	204	212	219	227	235	242	250	257	265
74	148	155	163	171	179	186	194	202	210	218	225	233	241	249	256	264	272
75	152	160	168	176	184	192	200	208	216	224	232	240	248	256	264	272	279
76	156	164	172	180	189	197	205	213	221	230	238	246	254	263	271	279	287

Source: National Heart, Lung & Blood Institute, 2004.

normal, healthy adults to practice weight control and for the obese, who may need to modify their weight to promote their health.

The Regulation of Eating

All animals, including people, have sensitive and complex systems for regulating food. Taste has been called the chemical gatekeeper of eating. It is the most ancient of sensory systems and plays an important role in selecting certain foods and rejecting others.

Although the molecular pathways that govern weight gain and loss are not completely understood, scientists have a fairly good idea what some of these pathways are. A number of hormones control eating. Leptin and insulin, in particular, circulate in the blood in concentrations that are proportionate to body fat mass. They decrease appetite by inhibiting neurons that produce the molecules neuropeptide Y (NPY) and agouti-related peptide (AgRP), peptides that would otherwise stimulate eating. They also stimulate melacortin-producing neurons in the hypothalamus, which inhibit eating.

As may be evident, an important player in weight control is the protein leptin, which is secreted by fat cells. Leptin appears to signal the neurons of the hypothalamus as to whether the body has sufficient energy stores of fat or whether it needs additional energy. The brain's eating control center reacts to the signals sent from the hypothalamus to increase or decrease appetite. As noted, leptin inhibits the neurons that stimulate appetite and activates those that suppress appetite. These effects of leptin have made scientists optimistic that leptin may have promise as a weight-control agent, although thus far the promise of leptin as a pharmacological method of weight control has remained elusive (J. M. Friedman, 2000).

Ghrelin may also play an important role particularly in why dieters who lose weight often gain it back so quickly. Ghrelin stimulates the appetite by activating the NPY-AgRP-expressing neurons. It is secreted by specialized cells in the stomach, spiking just before meals and dropping afterward. When people are given ghrelin injections, they feel extremely hungry. Therefore blocking

Obese				Extreme Obesity														
36	37	38	39	40	41	42	43	44	45	46	47	48	49	50	51	52	53	54
Body Weight (pounds)																		
172	177	181	186	191	196	201	205	210	215	220	224	229	234	239	244	248	253	258
178	183	188	193	198	203	208	212	217	222	227	232	237	242	247	252	257	262	267
184	189	194	199	204	209	215	220	225	230	235	240	245	250	255	261	266	271	276
190	195	201	206	211	217	222	227	232	238	243	248	254	259	264	269	275	280	285
196	202	207	213	218	224	229	235	240	246	251	256	262	267	273	278	284	289	295
203	208	214	220	225	231	237	242	248	254	259	265	270	278	282	287	293	299	304
209	215	221	227	232	238	244	250	256	262	267	273	279	285	291	296	302	308	314
216	222	228	234	240	246	252	258	264	270	276	282	288	294	300	306	312	318	324
223	229	235	241	247	253	260	266	272	278	284	291	297	303	309	315	322	328	334
230	236	242	249	255	261	268	274	280	287	293	299	306	312	319	325	331	338	344
236	243	249	256	262	269	276	282	289	295	302	308	315	322	328	335	341	348	354
243	250	257	263	270	277	284	291	297	304	311	318	324	331	338	345	351	358	365
250	257	264	271	278	285	292	299	306	313	320	327	334	341	348	355	362	369	376
257	265	272	279	286	293	301	308	315	322	329	338	343	351	358	365	372	379	386
265	272	279	287	294	302	309	316	324	331	338	346	353	361	368	375	383	390	397
272	280	288	295	302	310	318	325	333	340	348	355	363	371	378	386	393	401	408
280	287	295	303	311	319	326	334	342	350	358	365	373	381	389	396	404	412	420
287	295	303	311	319	327	335	343	351	359	367	375	383	391	399	407	415	423	431
295	304	312	320	328	336	344	353	361	369	377	385	394	402	410	418	426	435	443

ghrelin levels or the action of ghrelin may help people lose weight and keep it off (Grady, 2002, May 23).

Studies with rats have suggested a possible brain mechanism for the control of at least some eating and its regulation. Rats who have a damaged ventromedial hypothalamus behave like obese humans do: They eat excessive amounts of food, show little sensitivity to internal cues related to hunger (e.g., how long it has been since they last ate), and respond to food-related external cues, such as the presence of food. This evidence implies that at least some obese humans have a malfunctioning ventromedial hypothalamus, which interferes with normal eating habits.

Why Obesity Is a Health Risk

What is obesity? **Obesity** is an excessive accumulation of body fat. Generally speaking, fat should constitute about 20 to 27% of body tissue in women and about 15 to 22% in men. Table 4.2 presents guidelines from the National Institutes of Health for calculating your body mass index and determining whether or not you are overweight or obese.

The World Health Organization estimates that 300 million people worldwide are obese and a further 750 million are overweight, including 25 million children under 5 (Arnst, 2004). Obesity is now so common that it has replaced malnutrition as the most important dietary contributor to poor health worldwide (Kopelman, 2000) and will soon account for more diseases and deaths in the United States than smoking. The global epidemic of obesity stems from a combination of genetic susceptibility, the increasing availability of high-fat and high-energy foods, and low levels of physical activity (Kopelman, 2000).

Although obesity is a worldwide problem, nowhere is it more serious than in the United States. Americans are the fattest people in the world (Critser, 2003). Over the past 15 years, the average body weight of U.S. adults has increased by nearly 8 pounds, and it is continuing to increase rapidly (Mokdad et al., 1999). At present, 60% of the U.S. population is overweight, and about 27% is

FIGURE 4.2 | Percent of Population Overweight and Obese

Overweight is BMI over 25 and obese is BMI over 30.   (*Source:* National Center for Health Statistics, 2002)

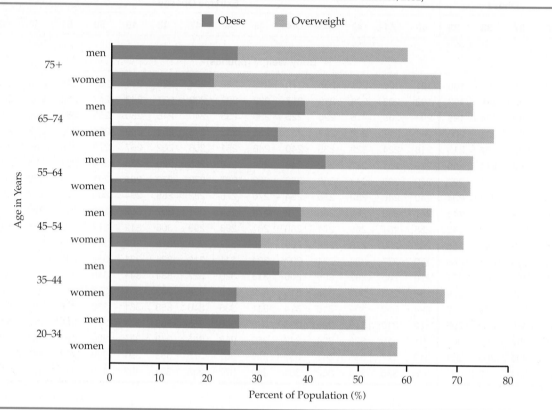

obese (Koretz, 2001), with women somewhat more likely to be overweight or obese than men (see figure 4.2).

There is no mystery as to why people in the United States have become so heavy. The food industry spends approximately $33 billion per year on ads and promotion for food. Portion sizes have increased, and healthful foods are often not available. The average American's food intake rose from 1,826 calories a day in the 1970s to more than 2,000 by the mid 1990s. Soda consumption has skyrocketed from 22.2 gallons to 56 gallons per person per year. Portion sizes at meals have increased substantially over the past 20 years, contributing to the obesity epidemic (Nielsen & Popkin, 2003). So-called supersize portions are very high in calories. For example, whereas the original French fries order at McDonald's was 200 calories, the supersize portion at present is 610. Muffins that weighed 1.5 ounces in 1957 now average half a pound each (Raeburn, 2002). Thus, even those people who are not dieting for obesity should be attentive to their portion sizes, and among dieters, this concern is critical (Nielsen & Popkin, 2003).

The U.S. food industry produces enough food to supply each American with 3,800 calories a day, more than twice what the average American woman needs and at least one third more than the average American man needs. Because supply has exceeded demand, price has fallen, making inexpensive foods more available.

Risks of Obesity   Obesity is a risk factor for many disorders, both in its own right and because it affects other risk factors, such as blood pressure and plasma cholesterol level (Kopelman, 2000). It is estimated to cause in excess of 300,000 deaths annually in the United States (Allison, Fontaine, Manson, Stevens, & VanItallie, 1999). Estimates are that overweight and obesity may account for 14% of all deaths from cancer in men and 20% of all deaths from cancer in women (Calle, Rodriguez, Walker-Thurmond, & Thun, 2003). They have been associated with atherosclerosis, hypertension, diabetes, gallbladder disease, and arthritis; obesity is a risk for heart failure (Kenchaiah et al., 2002). Increased body weight contributes to increased death rates for all

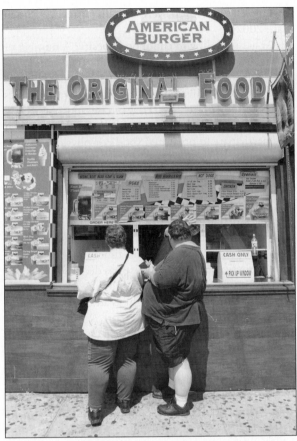

More than one third of the adult population in the United States is overweight, putting them at risk for heart disease, kidney disease, hypertension, diabetes, and other health problems.

TABLE 4.3 | Even Moderate Overweight Can Increase Risk of Death

For women, being even mildly overweight can greatly increase risk of cancer and heart disease. This table, using the example of a woman who is 5 ft 5 in. tall, shows the risk for death among women age 30 to 55 who were followed in this study for 16 years. To put these data into perspective, however, the same woman would have to gain more than 100 pounds to equal the health risks of smoking two packs of cigarettes a day.

Weight in Pounds	Risk
Less than 120 lbs	Lowest risk
120–149 lbs	+20%
150–160 lbs	+30%
161–175 lbs	+60%
176–195 lbs	+110%
Greater than 195 lbs	+120%

Source: Manson et al., 1995.

cancers combined and for the specific cancers of colon, rectal, liver, gallbladder, pancreas, kidney, esophagus, non-Hodgkin's lymphoma, and multiple myeloma. Obesity also increases risks in surgery, anesthesia administration, and childbearing (Brownell & Wadden, 1992). One study found that women who were 30% overweight were more than three times as likely to develop heart disease as women who were of normal or slightly under normal weight (Manson et al., 1990). This risk increased to five times that of normal-weight women among the overweight women who were also smokers (Manson et al., 1990).

Obesity is also one of the chief causes of disability, and rates have soared in the past 15 years. The number of people age 30 to 49 who cannot care for themselves or perform routine household tasks has jumped by 50%. Moreover, this marker bodes poorly for the future. People who are disabled in their thirties and forties are much more likely to have health care expenses and to need nursing home care in older age (L. Richardson, 2004).

As a consequence of its links to chronic disease (especially cardiovascular disease, kidney disease, and diabetes), obesity is associated with early mortality. As a ballpark statistic, people who are overweight at age 40 are likely to die 3 years earlier than those who are thin (Peeters et al., 2003). Even mildly overweight women sustain an increased risk for heart disease and heart attack compared with women who are underweight (Manson et al., 1990). In addition, many of the treatments for overweight that people undertake on their own, such as use of diet pills and other medications, fad diets, fasting, and anorexia or bulimia, create substantial risks of their own. Table 4.3 illustrates these risks.

Often ignored among the risks of obesity is the psychological distress that can result. Although there is a robust stereotype of overweight people as more "jolly," studies suggest that the obese are worse off in terms of psychological functioning, especially depression (Roberts, Strawbridge, Deleger, & Kaplan, 2002; Rydén, Karlsson, Sullivan, Torgerson, & Taft, 2003). Depression may be maintained by increasing recognition that the world is not designed for overweight people. One may have to pay for two seats on an airplane, have little luck finding clothes, endure others' derision and rude comments, and experience other reminders that the obese, quite literally, do not fit.

As just noted, obesity increases the risk for a number of diseases and disorders, yet the obese often avoid

Obesity in childhood is one of the fastest growing health concerns in the United States.

the trips to the physician that might help them. For example, getting in an out of a car and in and out of a doctor's office presents challenges for the morbidly obese. The obese may not fit in standard chairs or in standard wheelchairs. X rays may not penetrate far enough to give accurate readings, blood pressure cuffs are not big enough, and hospital gowns do not cover them (Pérez-Peña & Glickson, 2003, November). If an obese person increasingly withdraws into a reclusive life, by the time he or she seeks treatment, the complications of diabetes, heart disease, and other disorders may be out of control.

Obesity in Childhood

The prevalence of overweight children has doubled over the past 20 years among children 6 to 11 years of age and tripled among those age 12 to 17. African-American and Hispanic children and adolescents are disproportionately affected, and young women are at particular risk for substantial weight gain during their teens and twenties, especially if they have a child during this time (Gore, Brown, & West, 2003).

In the United States, approximately 37% of children are overweight or obese, but other countries are gaining; the figure is 20% in Europe and 10% in China (Nash, 2003). Obesity is becoming a global epidemic. Being overweight in childhood must now be considered a major health problem rather than merely a problem in appearance (Dietz, 2004). Specifically, 60% of overweight children and adolescents are already showing risk factors for cardiovascular disease, such as elevated blood

pressure, elevated lipid levels, or hyperinsulemia (Sinha et al., 2002).

What is leading to childhood obesity? A number of factors are indicated in this epidemic. One important factor is increasingly sedentary lifestyles among children and adolescents, involving television and video games (Dietz & Gortmaker, 2001). Exercise and obesity are clearly related. Children are less likely to be obese when they participate in organized sports or physical activity, if they enjoy physical education, and when their family supports physical activity (L. H. Epstein, Kilanowski, Consalvi, & Paluch, 1999; Sallis, Prochaska, Taylor, Hill, & Geraci, 1999).

The sedentary lifestyle of many children contributes to obesity. As video games and television have increasingly occupied children's leisure time, time devoted to normal physical play and exercise has decreased (Sallis et al., 1993). Overall, 80% of all people who were overweight as children are overweight as adults (S. Abraham, Collins, & Nordsieck, 1971). Figure 4.3 illustrates the high rates of obesity among children.

Early eating habits contribute to obesity. Children who are encouraged to overeat in infancy and childhood are more likely to become obese adults (Berkowitz, Agras, Korner, Kraemer, & Zeanah, 1985). Overweight children also risk rejection, taunting, and mistreatment by their peers (Conis, 2003b). Encouragement by families to avoid sedentary activities like television watching and to engage in sports and other physical activities represents one attack on this problem. School-based interventions directed to making healthy foods available and modifying sedentary behavior may also help combat this problem (Dietz & Gortmaker, 2001). Unfortunately, even with these interventions the majority of overweight children and adolescents will go on to be overweight or obese in adulthood.

Where the Fat Is   Recent epidemiologic evidence suggests that abdominally localized fat, as opposed to excessive fat in the hips, buttocks, or thighs, is an especially potent risk factor for cardiovascular disease, diabetes, hypertension, and cancer. Sometimes called "stress weight," abdominal fat increases especially in response to stress (Rebuffe-Scrive, Walsh, McEwen, & Rodin, 1992). People with excessive central weight (sometimes called "apples," in contrast to "pears," who carry their weight on their hips) are more psychologically reactive to stress and show greater cardiovascular reactivity (M. C. Davis, Twamley, Hamilton, & Swan, 1999) and neuroendocrine reactivity to stress (Epel et

FIGURE 4.3 | **Percent of Young People Who Are Overweight**

Overweight is defined as greater than or equal to the 95th percentile of the age- and sex-specific BMI.   (*Source:* National Center for Health Statistics, 2004)

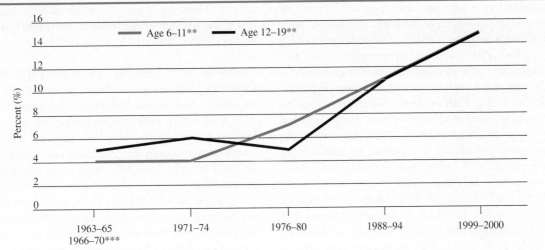

**Excludes pregnant women starting with 1971–74. Pregnancy status not available for 1963–65 and 1966–70.
***Data for 1963–65 are for children 6–11 years of age; data for 1966–70 are for adolescents 12–17 years of age, not 12–19 years.

al., 2000). This reactivity to stress may be the link between centrally deposited fat and increased risk for diseases. Inasmuch as uncontrollable stress may contribute to mortality risk from such diseases as hypertension, cancer, diabetes, and cardiovascular disease, abdominally localized fat may represent a sign that health is eroding in response to stress.

Factors Associated with Obesity

Obesity depends on both the number and the size of an individual's fat cells. Among moderately obese people, fat cells are typically large, but there is not an unusual number of them. Among the severely obese, there is a large number of fat cells, and the fat cells themselves are exceptionally large (Brownell, 1982).

What determines the number and size of fat cells and the propensity to be obese? Childhood constitutes a window of vulnerability for obesity for a number of reasons. One reason is that the number of fat cells an individual has is typically determined in the first few years of life, as by genetic factors or by early eating habits. A high number of fat cells leads to a marked propensity for fat storage, thus promoting obesity in adulthood. In contrast, poor eating habits in adolescence and adulthood are more likely to affect the size of fat cells but not their number.

Our style of eating has changed in ways that promote overweight and obesity. Most obvious is a rise in calorie consumption. However, it appears that people may not be consuming calories at meals, but rather are eating more between meals, with the average number of daily snacks rising nearly 60% over the past three decades (Koretz, 2003b). The time involved in preparing food because of microwave ovens and advances in food processing and packaging had lead to greater convenience for preparing food (Koretz, 2003b). Moreover, it does not take much to produce overweight. The average American weight gain over the past 20 years is the caloric equivalent of just three Oreo cookies or one can of soda a day (Koretz, 2003b).

Family History and Obesity   Family history is clearly implicated in obesity. Overweight parents are more likely to have overweight children than are normal-weight parents. This relationship appears to be due to both genetic and dietary factors (J. M. Meyer & Stunkard, 1994). Evidence for genetic factors comes from twin studies, demonstrating that twins reared apart show a tendency toward obesity when both natural parents were obese, even when the twins' environments are very different (Stunkard, 1988).

The impact of genetics on weight may be exerted, in part, through feeding style. In a study of healthy infants observed from birth to 2 years, Agras and his associates (Agras, Kraemer, Berkowitz, Korner, & Hammer, 1987) found that children who were later to become obese were distinguished by a vigorous feeding style, consisting of sucking more rapidly, more intensely, and longer, with shorter bursts between sucking. This style produced a higher caloric intake and greater overweight. The fact that the feeding style emerged very early suggests that it may be one of the mediators by which a genetic predisposition to obesity leads to obesity. There also appear to be genetically based tendencies to store energy as either fat or lean tissue (Bouchard et al., 1990). Identifying the role of genetics in obesity is important because it helps identify individuals for whom weight management interventions are especially important.

But a family history of obesity does not necessarily implicate genetics. For example, one study found that 44% of the dogs of obese people were obese, compared with only 25% of the dogs of people with normal weight (E. Mason, 1970). Many factors in a home, such as the type of diet consumed, the size of portions, and exercise patterns, contribute to the obesity that runs in families (Klesges, Eck, Hanson, Haddock, & Klesges, 1990). The size of a family may influence the extent to which parents can actively manage their children; with fewer children, parents may be able to bring about concerted weight loss in any one child.

Whether or not one diets is also influenced by family environment. More than two thirds of the population say they are dieting at any given point in time. Efforts to lose weight among daughters are influenced heavily by perceived criticism of parents, whereas sons' weight-loss efforts (or lack of them) seem to be more related to fathers' attitudes toward eating (Baker, Whisman, & Brownell, 2000).

SES, Culture, and Obesity   Additional risk factors for obesity include social class and culture. In the United States, women of low socioeconomic status are heavier than high-SES women, and African-American women, in particular, appear to be vulnerable to obesity (Wardle, Waller, & Jarvis, 2002). Although SES differences in weight have previously been attributed to high-carbohydrate diets early in life, this account does not explain why SES is not associated with obesity in men and children. Interestingly, in developing countries, obesity among men, women, and children is rare, possibly because of insufficient food; in these countries, the prevalence of obesity rises with SES and increasing wealth.

Values are implicated in obesity. Thinness is valued in women from developed countries, which in turn leads to a cultural emphasis on dieting and on physical activity. These social norms prompt most women, not just those who are obese, to be discontented with their bodies (Foster, Wadden, & Vogt, 1997).

Obesity and Dieting as Risk Factors for Obesity   Paradoxically, obesity is also a risk factor for obesity. Many obese individuals have a high basal insulin level, which promotes overeating due to increased hunger. Moreover, the obese have large fat cells, which have a greater capacity for producing and storing fat than do small fat cells. Thus, the obese are at risk to become even more so.

Dieting also contributes to the propensity for obesity. Successive cycles of dieting and weight gain enhance the efficiency of food use and lower the metabolic rate (Bouchard, 2002). (So-called **yo yo dieting.**) When dieters begin to eat normally again, their metabolic rate may stay low, and it can become easier for them to put on weight again even though they eat less food. Unfortunately, too, these decreases in metabolic rate may be more problematic with successive diets.

There may also be a selective preference for foods high in fat following weight loss (Gerardo-Gettens et al., 1991). Thus, people who alternate chronically between dieting and regular eating, yo-yo dieters, may actually increase their chances of becoming obese (Brownell & Rodin, 1996). If these risks weren't enough, yo-yo dieters act as role models, inadvertently increasing their children's likelihood of engaging in the same behaviors and augmenting their risk for obesity (*New York Times,* 2000a).

Set Point Theory of Weight   In the past decade, evidence has accumulated for a **set point theory of weight:** the idea that each individual has an ideal biological weight, which cannot be greatly modified (Garner & Wooley, 1991). According to the theory, the set point acts as a thermometer regulating heat in a home. A person eats if his or her weight gets too low and stops eating as their weight reaches its ideal point. Some individuals may have a higher set point than other people, leading them to be obese (Brownell, 1982). The theory argues that efforts to lose weight may be compensated for by adjustments of energy expenditure, as the body actively attempts to return to its original weight. Psychological changes, such as depression or irritability, can accompany these processes as well (Klem, Wing, McGuire, Seagle, &

Hill, 1998). If this theory is true, this internal regulatory system also contributes to the propensity for the obese to remain so.

Stress and Eating

Stress affects eating, although in different ways for different people. About half of people eat more when they are under stress, and half eat less (Willenbring, Levine, & Morley, 1986). For nondieting and nonobese normal eaters, the experience of stress or anxiety may suppress physiological cues suggesting hunger, leading to lower consumption of food. Stress and anxiety, however, can disinhibit the dieter, removing the self-control that usually guards against eating, thus leading to an increase in food intake both among dieters and the obese (Heatherton, Herman, & Polivy, 1991, 1992). Whereas men appear to eat less in stressful circumstances, many women eat more (Grunberg & Straub, 1992).

Stress also influences what food is consumed. People who eat in response to stress usually consume more low-caloric and salty foods, although when not under stress, stress eaters show a preference for high-caloric foods. Stress eaters appear to choose foods containing more water, which gives the food a chewier texture (Willenbring et al., 1986).

Anxiety and depression appear to figure into **stress eating** as well. One study found that stress eaters experience greater fluctuations of anxiety and depression than do nonstress eaters. Overweight individuals also have greater fluctuations in anxiety, hostility, and depression than do normal individuals (Lingsweiler, Crowther, & Stephens, 1987). Those who eat in response to negative emotions show a preference for sweet and high-fat foods (Oliver, Wardle, & Gibson, 2000).

Whether stress-induced eating can produce obesity in its own right is not yet known, but stress is clearly a complicating factor. Dieters who show increased emotional reactivity to stressors are more likely to eat in response to stress. The perception of stress or the experience of psychological distress may also be psychological markers of the physiologically based need to restore weight to its set point level (C. P. Herman, 1987). As will shortly be seen, stress also figures into eating disorders, such as bulimia and anorexia.

Treatment of Obesity

More people are treated for obesity in the United States than for all other health habits or conditions combined. More than half a million attend weight loss clinics, and Amazon.com currently lists nearly 140,000 book titles that refer to diet or dieting.

Some people attempt to lose weight because they perceive obesity to be a health risk. Others seek treatment because their obesity is coupled with binge eating and other symptoms of psychological distress (Fitzgibbon, Stolley, & Kirschenbaum, 1993). However, most people are motivated by the fact that being overweight is considered to be unattractive and that it carries a social stigma (Hayes & Ross, 1987; see box 4.2). The Duchess of Windsor's oft-quoted statement—"You can never be too thin or too rich"—captures the importance that society places on physical appearance and, in particular, on a thin appearance.

Therefore, the obese are more likely than the nonobese to have a poor self-image. Unlike other groups of people with disabilities, the obese are often blamed for their problem; they are derogated by others because they are seen as lacking sufficient willpower or initiative to lose weight (Teachman, Gapinski, Brounell, Rawlins, & Jeyaram, 2003). Stereotypes of the obese are strongly negative and include the perception that obese people are ugly and sloppy (M. B. Harris, Walters, & Waschull, 1991). These negative stereotypes may extend to outright discrimination; the obese show a decline in their social class and lower levels of socioeconomic attainment overall (Koretz, 2001; Sarlio-Lahteenkorva, Stunkard, & Rissanen, 1995). As a result, obese people are often distressed about their weight problem and are highly motivated to change it (C. E. Ross, 1994). Surprisingly, though, it appears that few health practitioners advise their obese clients to lose weight, despite the clear contribution of obesity to illness (Galuska, Will, Serdula, & Ford, 1999).

Obesity is a very difficult disorder to treat (Brownell & Wadden, 1992). Even initially successful weight-loss programs show a high rate of relapse. In this section, we review the most common approaches to treatment of obesity and consider why weight control is so difficult.

Dieting   Treating obesity through dieting has historically been the most common approach, and most weight-loss programs still begin with dietary treatment. People are trained to restrict their caloric and/or carbohydrate intake through education about the caloric values and dietary characteristics of foods. In some cases, food may be provided to the dieters to ensure that the appropriate foods are being consumed. Providing structured meal plans and grocery lists improves weight loss (Wing et al., 1996; see Surwit et al., 1997).

BOX 4.2

The Stigma of Obesity: Comments on the Obese

Obese people are often the target of insensitive comments about their weight. They are teased by their peers as children, and called names such as whale or fatty. The teasing endures into adulthood, where, while in public, they encounter people staring at them, whispering behind their back about their weight, and calling them names.

Family life for obese people can be even more traumatic than public life. Receiving criticism and comments about their weight from loved ones can irreparably damage family relationships. Lack of family acceptance can remove the home as a buffer against peer cruelty. Some parents push their overweight children to lose weight, using techniques that shame their children into weight loss, such as by withdrawing affection.

The resulting effect of repeated exposure to others' judgments about their weight can be social alienation and low self-esteem. From a young age, overweight children may recognize that they are different from other children. Childhood activities, such as swimming and athletics, when children must wear a swimsuit or change in a locker room, may involve uncomfortable exposure

that leads to more teasing. Unfortunately, obese children learn from a young age to avoid interaction with their peers and may thereby compromise their ability to develop close relationships.

Obese people are one of very few disabled groups to endure public criticism for their disability. Obesity is stigmatized as a disability whose fault lies with obese people. This stigma fuels public sentiments that obese people are responsible for being obese, that they are lazy or gluttonous. Public comments to obese people, such as, "Why don't you lose some weight?," may often be to this effect.

Coping with public views of their weight is difficult for obese people as well. To address teasing directly, especially when the comments are simply a stated fact, such as, "That person is fat," is to admit that being fat is a bad thing. As more people in the U.S. become overweight and obese, these pernicious stereotypes and hostility may ebb. Increasingly, our society will need not only to accommodate the physical needs of obese people but their emotional needs as well.

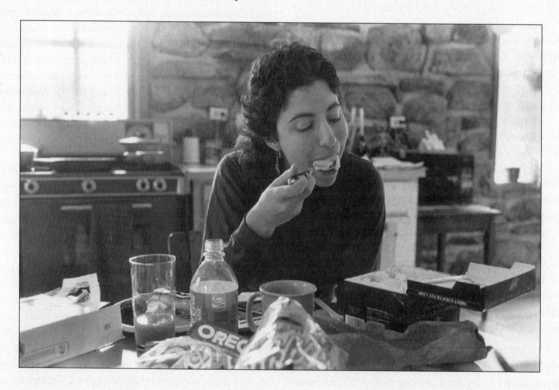

Generally, weight losses produced through dietary methods are small and rarely maintained for long (Agras et al., 1996). Weight losses achieved through dieting rarely match the expectations of clients, whose disappointment may contribute to regaining the lost weight (Foster, Wadden, Vogt, & Brewer, 1997). Very low-carbohydrate or low-fat diets do the best job in helping people lose weight initially, but these diets are the hardest to maintain, and people commonly revert to their old habits. As already noted, repeated dieting, especially yo-yo dieting, may increasingly predispose the dieter to put on weight. Currently popular are low-carbohydrate diets which many people claim are allowing them to lose large amounts of weight. However, formal investigation of low-carbohydrate diets does not suggest that they are necessarily more effective than other kinds of diets (Butler, 2004). Instead, reducing caloric intake, increasing exercise, and sticking with an eating plan over the long term are the only factors reliably related to staying slim.

The risk of yo-yo dieting with respect to CHD may be greater than the risk of obesity alone. The obvious implication of these important findings is that once a dieter has succeeded in taking off weight, every effort should be made to maintain that weight loss. Moreover, because only some people benefit from dieting, it is essential that we identify individuals who will be helped and not harmed by dieting and that we develop safe and effective methods for helping them do so (Brownell & Rodin, 1996). Dieting itself can compromise psychological functioning, leading to impaired concentration, a preoccupation with food, psychological distress, and binge eating (McFarlane, Polivy, & McCabe, 1999). Clinicians who treat obesity now feel that dietary intervention is a necessary but insufficient condition for producing lasting weight loss (Straw, 1983).

Fasting   Fasting is usually employed with other techniques as a treatment for obesity. In fasting, the individual severely restricts food intake over a period of a few days, sometimes consuming little besides low-calorie liquids. For example, in one popular choice, the protein-sparing modified fast, an individual typically consumes between 400 and 800 calories per day of foods consisting primarily of protein and some carbohydrates with carefully balanced vitamins and minerals. Typically, fasting produces dramatic rapid weight losses. However, people cannot fast indefinitely without damaging their health. Moreover, if normal eating habits are resumed, the weight lost through fasting can be rapidly regained (Wadden, Stunkard, & Brownell, 1983). Therefore, fast-

ing is typically supplemented with maintenance strategies designed to help the person keep weight off.

Surgery   Surgical procedures, especially gastric surgeries, represent a radical way of controlling extreme obesity. In the most common surgical procedure, the stomach is literally stapled up to reduce its capacity to hold food so that the overweight individual must restrict his or her intake. As with all surgeries, there is some risk, and side effects, such as gastric and intestinal distress, are common. Consequently, this procedure is usually reserved for people who are at least 100% overweight, who have failed repeatedly to lose weight through other methods, and who have complicating health problems that make weight loss urgent. Despite its drastic nature, use of this surgical treatment for obesity has more than doubled in the past 5 years, attesting again to how common and serious a problem obesity is (Steinbrook, 2004b). Unfortunately, because of its increasing prevalence, many insurance companies are now phasing out coverage for surgery to treat obesity (Costello, 2004).

Appetite-suppressing Drugs   Drugs, both prescription and over-the-counter types, are often used to reduce appetite and restrict food consumption (Bray & Tartaglia, 2000). In some weight-loss programs, drugs may be employed in conjunction with a cognitive-behavioral intervention. Such programs often produce substantial weight loss, but participants can regain the weight quickly, particularly if they attribute the weight loss to the drug rather than to their own efforts (J. Rodin, Elias, Silberstein, & Wagner, 1988). This point underscores the importance of perceived self-efficacy in any weight-loss program. In addition to drugs, certain food additives show potential as adjuncts to weight-control efforts. For example, consumption of fructose prior to a meal reduces caloric and fat intake as compared with consumption of glucose or plain water (J. Rodin, 1990, 1991).

The Multimodal Approach   Many current interventions with the obese use a multimodal approach to maladaptive eating behavior.

Screening   Some programs begin with screening applicants for their readiness to lose weight and their motivation to do so. Unsuccessful prior dieting attempts, weight lost and regained, high body dissatisfaction, and low self-esteem are all associated with less weight loss for behavioral weight reduction programs, and these criteria

Approximately 500,000 Americans participate in organized weight-reduction programs. Many of these programs now include exercise.

can be used to screen individuals before treatment or be used to provide a better match between a particular treatment program and a client (Teixeira et al., 2002).

Self-monitoring   Obese clients are trained in self-monitoring and are taught to keep careful records of what they eat, when they eat it, how much they eat, where they eat it, and other dimensions of eating. This kind of recordkeeping simultaneously defines the behavior and makes clients more aware of their eating patterns (R. C. Baker & Kirschenbaum, 1998). Many patients are surprised to discover what, when, and how much they actually eat. This kind of monitoring is always important for weight loss, but it becomes especially so at high-risk times, such as during the holidays, when weight gain reliably occurs (Boutelle, Kirschenbaum, Baker, & Mitchell, 1999).

Behavioral analysis then focuses on influencing the antecedents of the target behavior—namely, the stimuli that affect eating. Clients are trained to modify the stimuli in their environment that have previously elicited and maintained overeating. Such steps include purchasing low-calorie foods (such as raw vegetables), making access to them easy, and limiting the high-calorie foods kept in the house. Behavioral control techniques are also used to train patients to change the circumstances of eating. Clients are taught to confine eating to one place at particular times of day. They may also be trained to develop new discriminative stimuli that will be associated with eating. For example, they may be encouraged to

use a particular place setting, such as a special placemat or napkin, and to eat only when those stimuli are present. Individualized feedback about one's specific weight problems and their management appears to be especially helpful to success in losing weight (Kreuter, Bull, Clark, & Oswald, 1999).

Control over Eating   The next step in a multimodal behavioral intervention is to train clients to gain control over the eating process itself. For example, clients may be urged to count each mouthful of food, each chew, or each swallow. They may be told to put down eating utensils after every few mouthfuls until the food in their mouths is chewed and swallowed. Longer and longer delays are introduced between mouthfuls so as to encourage slow eating (which tends to reduce intake). Such delays are first introduced at the end of the meal, when the client is already satiated, and progressively moved closer to the beginning of the meal. Finally, clients are urged to enjoy and savor their food and to make a conscious effort to appreciate it while they are eating. The goal is to teach the obese person to eat less and enjoy it more (Stunkard, 1979).

Clients are also trained to gain control over the consequences of the target behavior and are trained to reward themselves for activities they carry out successfully. For example, keeping records, counting chews, pausing during the meal, or eating only in a specific place might be reinforced by a tangible positive reinforcement, such as going to a movie or making a long-distance phone call to a friend. Developing a sense of self-control over eating is an important part of behavioral treatments of obesity. Training in self-control can help people override the impact of urges or temptations.

Adding Exercise   Exercise is a critical component of any weight loss program. In fact, as people age, increasing exercise is essential just to maintain weight and avoid gaining it (Jameson, 2004). High levels of physical activity are associated with initial successful weight loss and with the maintenance of that weight loss among both adults and children (L. H. Epstein et al., 1995; Jeffery & Wing, 1995). Consequently, participants in weight loss programs need to develop a regular program of physical activity that is interesting and convenient for them (see Wadden et al., 1997).

Controlling Self-talk   Cognitive restructuring is an important part of weight-reduction programs. As noted in chapter 3, poor health habits can be maintained through dysfunctional monologues (for example, "I'll never lose weight—I've tried before and failed so many times"). Participants in many weight-loss programs are urged to identify the maladaptive thoughts they have regarding weight loss and its maintenance and to substitute positive self-instruction.

Social Support   Another factor that consistently predicts successfully maintained weight loss is the presence of social support. Because clients with high degrees of social support are more successful than those with little social support, most multimodal programs include training in eliciting effective support from families, friends, and coworkers (Brownell & Kramer, 1989; Brownell & Stunkard, 1981). Even supportive messages from a behavioral therapist over the Internet seem to help people lose weight more successfully (Oleck, 2001).

Relapse Prevention   Relapse prevention techniques are incorporated into many treatment programs. As noted earlier, initial relapse prevention begins with effective screening of applicants to weight-loss programs. In addition, relapse prevention techniques include matching treatments to the eating problems of particular clients, restructuring the environment to remove temptation, rehearsing high-risk situations for relapse (such as holidays), and developing coping strategies to deal with high-risk situations. Taken together, these components of weight-loss treatment programs are designed to address all aspects of weight loss and its maintenance.

We might expect that the stages of change model, by which interventions are tailored to a recipient's stage of readiness, would be successful in managing weight. As yet, however, the success of such efforts is equivocal (Jeffery, French, & Rothman, 1999).

Relapse prevention is important not only for diet control but also for the self-recrimination that occurs when people are unsuccessful. Such negative consequences may fall more heavily on women than men. When their diets fail, women are more likely to blame their own lack of self-discipline, whereas men are more likely to blame external factors, such as work (*New York Times,* 2000b). Often weight loss efforts fail simply because the process of maintaining behaviors needed for weight control is so arduous and there are few long-term rewards for so doing (Jeffrey, Kelly, Rothman, Sherwood, & Boutelle, 2004). Some people may feel that the benefits of weight loss are just simply not worth the effort.

Where Are Weight-Loss Programs Implemented?

Work-Site Weight-Loss Interventions   A number of weight-loss programs have been initiated through the work site, and a technique that has proven especially effective has been competition between work groups to see which group can lose the most weight and keep it off (e.g., Brownell, Cohen, Stunkard, Felix, & Cooley, 1984; Brownell, Stunkard, & McKeon, 1985). Exactly why team competitions are successful is unknown. It may be that team competitions draw effectively on social support or that the arousal produced by a competitive spirit motivates people to work harder to maintain weight loss. However, whether weight loss engaged through such team competitions can be maintained over time remains unknown (Brownell & Felix, 1987; Stunkard, Cohen, & Felix, 1989).

Commercial Weight-Loss Programs   Between $93 and $117 billion are spent annually on health care costs directly related to obesity (Finkelstein, Feibelkorn, & Wang, 2003; U.S. Department of Health and Human Services, 2001). In addition, $33 billion per year goes to commercial weight-loss programs and specialized foods for these programs (Obesity, 2000). More than 500,000 people each week are exposed to behavioral methods of controlling obesity through commercial clinics such as TOPS (Take Off Pounds Sensibly), Weight Watchers, and Jenny Craig. Many of these programs incorporate the behavior change principles just described. Because of the sheer number of people affected by these programs, formal evaluation of their effectiveness is important; yet rarely have such organizations opened their doors to formal program evaluation.

In fact, precisely because of this problem, the Federal Trade Commission has taken action against some commercial weight-loss programs for deceptive advertising, arguing that they provide insufficient and misleading information on success rate, risks of their program, and pricing (*Los Angeles Times,* 1997). Many of the components of commercial weight-loss programs, such as their group nature and the fact that they draw on principles of social support, should enhance success, but whether these programs successfully combat the problem of long-term maintenance of weight loss is unknown.

Evaluation of Cognitive-Behavioral Weight-Loss Techniques

Early evaluations of cognitive-behavioral programs for obesity suggest that modest weight losses, of perhaps a pound a week for up to 20 weeks, could be achieved and maintained for up to a year (Brownell, 1982). More recent programs appear to produce better effects, with weight loss of nearly 2 pounds a week for up to 20 weeks and long-term maintenance over 2 years (Brownell & Kramer, 1989). These improvements may be because the newer programs are longer and because they emphasize self-direction and exercise and include relapse prevention techniques (J. G. Baum, Clark, & Sandler, 1991; Brownell & Kramer, 1989; Jeffery, Hennrikus, Lando, Murray, & Liu, 2000). Nonetheless, responses to these programs are variable. Some people lose weight and are successful in keeping it off, whereas others put the weight back on almost immediately. Moreover, such programs may not be aggressive enough to help the truly obese, who may require the more extreme measures of fasting and surgery. Table 4.4 describes some of the promising leads that current research suggests for enhancing long-term weight loss in cognitive-behavioral programs.

Overall, though, efforts to treat obesity have been only somewhat successful. And because unsuccessful dieting can exacerbate the problem, many health psychologists have come to the conclusion that obesity might also be treated by urging people to develop the healthiest lifestyle they can, involving sensible eating and exercise, rather than specific weight-reduction techniques (Ernsberger & Koletsky, 1999).

Taking a Public Health Approach

The increasing prevalence of obesity makes it evident that shifting from a treatment model to a public health model that emphasizes prevention will be essential for combating this problem (Battle & Brownell, 1996). Although cognitive-behavioral methods are helping at least some people lose weight, clearly weight-loss programs are not a sufficient attack on the problems of overweight and obesity.

Prevention with families at risk for producing obese children is one important strategy. If parents can be trained early to adopt sensible meal planning and eating habits that they can convey to their children, the incidence of obesity may ultimately decline.

Although obesity has proven to be very difficult to modify at the adult level, behavioral treatment of childhood obesity has an impressive record of success. It may be easier to teach children healthy eating and activity habits than to teach adults. Programs that increase activity levels through reinforcements for exercise are an important component of weight-control programs with children (L. H. Epstein, Saelens, Myers, & Vito, 1997). Interventions that reduce TV watching can also reduce weight in children (T. N. Robinson, 1999). Moreover, because parents regulate children's access to food, problems in self-control are less likely to emerge with children. Whether treatment of childhood obesity will have long-term effects on adult weight remains to be seen (G. T. Wilson, 1994).

Another approach to obesity that emphasizes prevention concerns weight-gain prevention programs for normal-weight adults. If exercise can be increased, diet altered in a healthy direction, and good eating habits developed, the weight gains that often accompany the aging process may be prevented (L. H. Epstein, Valoski, Wing, & McCurley, 1994). This approach may be particularly successful for women during menopause, as weight gain is very common during this time (Simkin-Silverman, Wing, Boraz, & Kuller, 2003).

Like many health habits, social engineering strategies may become part of the attack on this growing problem. The World Health Organization has argued for several changes, which include food labels that contain more nutrition and serving size information, a special tax on foods that are high in sugar and fat (the so-called "junk food" tax), and restriction of advertising to children or requiring health warnings (Arnst, 2004).

The Internal Revenue Service has already declared that a person diagnosed by a physician as obese can claim fees paid to weight-loss programs as a tax deduction (Kristof, 2002). In fact, the ruling permits an individual to deduct the cost of the diagnosis, cure, mitigation, treatment, or prevention of the disease. Clearly the ruling covers formal weight-loss programs. It is not yet clear if it would cover gym memberships or exercise equipment, for example. Some individuals have even gone so far as to sue fast food places and food companies. Although these suits may be found to lack merit, the pressure they bring on the industry to engage in responsible food marketing practices and scrutiny of their products, may ultimately be of benefit (Nestle, 2003).

■ EATING DISORDERS

In pursuit of the elusive perfect body (see box 4.3), numerous women and an increasing number of men chron-

TABLE 4.4 | Weight Management Tips

Increasing awareness	Exercise
Keep track of what you eat. Keep track of your weight. Write down when you eat and why.	Track your exercise progress: what do you enjoy doing? Incorporate exercise into your lifestyle—become more active in all areas of life.
While you're eating	**Attitudes**
Pace yourself—eat slowly. Pay attention to your eating process. Pay attention to how full you are. Eat at the same place and at the same time. Eat one portion and serve yourself before beginning the meal.	Think about your weight loss goals—make them realistic. Remember that any progress is beneficial and not reaching your goal does not mean you failed. Think about your desire for foods—manage and work through cravings.
Shopping for food	**Working with others**
Structure your shopping so that you know what you are buying beforehand. Limit the number of already prepared items. Don't shop when you are hungry.	Incorporate friends and family into your goals and your new lifestyle, including meal preparation and exercise routines. Communicate to them what they can do to help you reach your goals.
The eating environment	**Knowing nutrition**
Make healthy foods more available than unhealthy ones. Do your best to stick to your eating routine when dining out. Think about the limitations and possible adjustments to your eating routine before dining out or eating with other people.	Be informed about nutrition. Know your recommended daily intake of calories, vitamins, and minerals. Know which foods are good sources of vitamins, minerals, proteins, carbohydrates, and healthy fats. Eat a balanced diet. Prepare foods that are both healthy and taste good.

ically restrict their diet and engage in other weight-loss efforts, such as laxative use, cigarette smoking, and chronic use of diet pills (Facts of Life, 2002). Females between the ages of 15 and 24 are most likely to be affected, but cases of eating disorders have been documented in people as young as 7 and as old as their mid-eighties (Facts of Life, November 2002), and as many as 20% of people with anorexia nervosa will die prematurely (Center for the Advancement of Health, 2002; Facts of Life, November 2002). These efforts pose serious health risks. Many people are under the impression that thin equals healthy, a misperception that can interfere with the healthy lifestyle all of us should be adopting (Neumark-Sztainer, Wall, Story, & Perry, 2003). The obsession with weight control, coupled with high rates of obesity, have induced many people to diet; 78% of women and 64% of men report that they are trying to lose or at least not gain weight (Centers for Disease Control and Prevention, 2000b). Although some of these concerns are well placed, obsessive concerns with weight can sometimes lead to eating disorders. (See box 4.4.)

The epidemic of eating disorders suggests that the pursuit of thinness is a growing social problem and public health threat of major proportions (Cogan & Ernsberger, 1999). Recent years have seen a dramatic increase in the incidence of eating disorders in the adolescent female population of Western countries. Chief among these are anorexia nervosa and bulimia. Eating disorders result in death for about 6% of those who have them (Facts of Life, November 2002).

Anorexia Nervosa

One of my most jarring memories is of driving down a street on my university campus during Christmas vacation and seeing a young woman clearly suffering from anorexia nervosa about to cross the street. She had obviously just been exercising. The wind blew her sweatpants around the thin sticks that had once been normal legs. The skin on her face was stretched so tight that the bones showed through, and I could make out her skeleton under what passed for flesh. I realized that I was

BOX 4.3

The Barbie Beauty Battle

Many health psychologists have criticized the media and the products they popularize for perpetuating false images of feminine beauty (J. K. Thompson & Heinberg, 1999). The Barbie doll has come under particular criticism because researchers believe that its widespread popularity with young girls may contribute to excessive dieting and the development of eating disorders. Using hip measurement as a constant, researchers have made calculations to determine the changes that would be necessary for a young, healthy woman to attain the same body proportions as the Barbie doll. She would have to increase her bust by 5 inches, her neck length by more than 3 inches, and her height by more than 2 feet while decreasing her waist by 6 inches (Brownell & Napolitano, 1995). This clearly unattainable standard may contribute to the false expectations that girls and women develop for their bodies. Nevertheless, Barbie remains the most popular doll worldwide.

face-to-face with someone who was shortly going to die. I looked for a place to pull over, but by the time I had found a parking space, she had disappeared into one of the dormitories, and I did not know which one. Nor do I know what I would have said if I had successfully caught up with her.

Anorexia nervosa is an obsessive disorder amounting to self-starvation, in which an individual diets and exercises to the point that body weight is grossly below optimum level, threatening health and potentially leading to death. Most sufferers are adolescent females, disproportionately from the upper social classes.

Developing Anorexia Nervosa   Several factors have been identified in the development of the illness. Physiological explanations have been spurred by estimates that amenorrhea (cessation of menstruation, a common symptom of anorexia) often precedes weight loss (Morimoto et al., 1980). Certain neuroactive steroids that are known to regulate eating and mood in animals appear to be present in abnormal levels in girls with anorexia (Monteleone et al., 2001). There appears to be an association between anorexia and Turner's syndrome (a disorder among females who lack a second X chromosome). Hypothalamic abnormalities may also be involved.

Both women who have eating disorders and those who have tendencies toward eating disorders show high blood pressure and heart rate reactivity to stress and high urinary cortisol, suggesting that they may chronically overreact to stress. In addition, women with eating disorders or tendencies toward them are more likely to be depressed, anxious, and low in self-esteem and to have a poor sense of mastery. The fact that this profile is seen in women with eating disorder tendencies, as well as those women with full-blown eating disorders, suggests that they may be precipitating factors rather than consequences of eating disorders (Koo-Loeb, Costello, Light, & Girdler, 2000).

Recent evidence that anorexia nervosa runs in families suggests a genetic contribution to the disorder (Strober et al., 2000). Anorexia and its treatment may be complicated by the psychopathological aspects of obsessive-compulsive disorder, which implicates neuroendocrine mechanisms as well (C. Davis, Kaptein, Kaplan, Olmsted, & Woodside, 1998).

Other researchers have stressed personality characteristics and family interaction patterns as causal in the development of anorexia. Anorexic girls are said to feel a lack of control coupled with a need for approval and to exhibit conscientious, perfectionistic behavior. Body image distortions are also common among anorexic girls,

BOX 4.4

You *Can* Be Too Thin

In the past decade, preoccupation with weight control among adolescents has reached epidemic proportions. In one study conducted in a high school (Rosen & Gross, 1987), 63% of the girls and 16% of the boys reported being on diets. Virtually all these students were already of normal weight. Most of this unnecessary dieting is due to the desire to achieve the thin physique that is currently culturally desirable, a physique that is difficult for most people to achieve without dieting.

Athletes often diet to get ready for events. For example, high school wrestlers may feel the need to "cut weight" for matches. Research, however, suggests that these cycles of weight gain and loss may have adverse health consequences. One result is a lowered metabolic rate, which can lead to a general propensity to gain weight. There may also be changes in fat distribution and risk factors for cardiovascular disease. For example, weight loss is associated with decreased blood pressure and gains with increased blood pressure, and successive gains appear also to produce successive gains in blood pressure. Consequently, these bouts of weight loss and regain may have an adverse long-term effect on blood pressure. Among female athletes who maintain a low body weight overall (such as gymnasts and figure skaters), the low percentage of fat distribution may lead to amenorrhea (cessation of menstrual periods) and problems in the ability to have children (Brownell, Steen, & Wilmore, 1987; Steen, Oppliger, & Brownell, 1988).

Preoccupation with appearance and dieting and a tendency toward eating disorders now appear to be spreading into the gay male community. A study of gay men found that they were more dissatisfied with their bodies and considered their appearance more central to their sense of self than was true for heterosexual men. Gay men were more likely to engage in exercise than were heterosexual men, but this activity was motivated more by a desire to be attractive than to be healthy. Moreover, these men showed attitudes and eating patterns that are usually associated with eating disorders. These findings suggest that a male subculture that emphasizes appearance so heavily may heighten the vulnerability of its members to body dissatisfaction and disordered eating, just as is true for women in our culture (Silberstein, Striegel-Moore, & Rodin, 1987).

---

although it is not clear whether this distortion is a consequence or a cause of the disorder. For example, these girls see themselves as still overweight when they have long since dropped below their ideal weight.

Anorexic girls appear to be more likely to come from families in which psychopathology or alcoholism is found or from families that are extremely close but have poor skills for communicating emotion or dealing with conflict (Garfinkel & Garner, 1983; Rakoff, 1983). The mother-daughter relationship may also be implicated in disordered eating. Mothers of daughters with eating disorders appear to be more dissatisfied with their families, more dissatisfied with their daughters' appearance, and more vulnerable to eating disorders themselves (K. M. Pike & Rodin, 1991).

Treating Anorexia Initially, the chief target of therapy is to bring the patient's weight back up to a safe level, a goal that must often be undertaken in a residential treatment setting, such as a hospital. To achieve weight gain, most therapies use behavioral approaches, such as operant conditioning. Usually, operant conditioning provides positive reinforcements, such as social visits in return for eating or weight gain. However, behavioral treatments in a hospital setting alone may fail to generalize to the home setting (Garfinkel & Garner, 1982) because of family and environmental factors that may induce or maintain the behavior.

Once weight has been restored to a safe level, additional therapies are needed. Family therapy may be initiated to help families learn more positive methods of communicating emotion and conflict. Psychotherapy to improve self-esteem and to teach skills for adjusting to stress and social pressure may also be incorporated into treatments (A. Hall & Crisp, 1983). The outlook for anorexic patients receiving therapy appears to be good, with one behavioral therapy intervention reporting success rates of 85% (Minuchen, Rosman, & Baker, 1978). Other interventions have tried to address social norms regarding thinness directly (for example, Neumark-Sztainer et al., 2003). For example, one study gave women information about other women's weight and body type, on the grounds that women with eating disorders often wrongly believe that other women are smaller and thinner than they actually are (Sanderson, Darley, & Messinger, 2002). The intervention succeeded in increasing women's estimates of their actual and ideal weight (Mutterperl & Sanderson, 2002).

Because of the health risks of anorexia nervosa, research has increasingly moved toward prevention; yet the factors that may prevent new cases from arising may be quite different from those that lead students who already have symptoms to seek out treatment (Mann et al., 1997). An eating disorder prevention program aimed at college freshmen presented the students with classmates who had recovered from an eating disorder, described their experience, and provided information. To the researchers' dismay, following the intervention, the participants had slightly more symptoms of eating disorders than those who had not participated. The program may have been ineffective because, by reducing the stigma of these disorders, it inadvertently normalized the problem. Consequently, as Mann and her colleagues (1997) concluded, ideal strategies for prevention may require stressing the health risks of eating disorders, whereas the strategies for inducing symptomatic women to seek treatment may involve normalizing the behavior and urging women to accept treatment.

Bulimia

Bulimia is an eating syndrome characterized by alternating cycles of binge eating and purging through such techniques as vomiting, laxative abuse, extreme dieting or fasting, and drug or alcohol abuse (M. K. Hamilton, Gelwick, & Meade, 1984). Bingeing appears to be caused at least in part by dieting. A related eating disorder, termed binge eating disorder, describes the many individuals who engage in recurrent binge eating but do not engage in the compensatory purging behavior to avoid weight gain (Spitzer et al., 1993). Binge eating usually occurs when the individual is alone; bingeing may be triggered by negative emotions produced by stressful experiences (Telch & Agras, 1996). The dieter begins to eat and then cannot stop, and although the bingeing is unpleasant, the binger feels out of control, unable to stop it. About half the people diagnosed with anorexia are also bulimic. Bulimia affects between 1 and 3% of women (Wisniewski, Epstein, Marcus, & Kaye, 1997) although up to 10% of people may have episodes.

Who Develops Bulimia?   Whereas many anorexics are thin, bulimics are typically of normal weight or overweight, especially through the hips. In bulimia, as in anorexia, bingeing and purging may be a reaction to issues of control. The binge phase has been interpreted as

an out-of-control reaction of the body to restore weight; the purge phase, an effort to regain control over weight. When a person goes on a diet, the association between physiological cues of hunger and eating break down. Dropping below the set point for her personal weight, the individual reacts as if she may starve: Metabolism slows, and she begins to respond to external food cues instead of internal cues, such as hunger.

Food can become a constant thought. Restrained eating, then, sets the stage for a binge. The control of eating shifts from internal sensations and is replaced by decisions about when and what to eat, which is called a cognitively based regulatory system. This regulatory system is easily disrupted by stress or distraction, and when it is, the dieter is vulnerable to bingeing (Polivy & Herman, 1985). Overvaluing body appearance, a larger body mass than is desired, dieting, and symptoms of depression appear to be especially implicated in triggering binge episodes (Stice, Presnell, & Spangler, 2002).

Families that place a high value on thinness and appearance are more likely to produce bulimic daughters (Boskind-White & White, 1983). Bulimia may have a genetic basis, inasmuch as eating disorders cluster in families and twin studies show a high concordance rate for binge eating (Wade, Bulik, Sullivan, Neale, & Kendler, 2000). Bulimics may suffer from low self-esteem and eat impulsively to control their negative emotions. Girls and women with binge eating disorders appear to be characterized by an excessive concern with body and weight; a preoccupation with dieting; a history of depression, psychopathology, and alcohol or drug abuse; and difficulties with managing work and social settings (Spitzer et al., 1993).

Stress, especially conflict with others, appears to be implicated in the onset of binge-purge cycles, because the cues that normally are used to restrain eating are less salient in times of stress. One study of women in college found that their bulimia worsened in response to stress or to any experience that led to a feeling of being unattractive, overweight, or ineffectual (Striegel-Moore, Silberstein, Frensch, & Rodin, 1989). Their disordered eating symptoms grew worse over the course of the school year, presumably because their level of stress also increased.

Physiological theories of bulimia include hormonal dysfunction (Monteleone et al., 2001), a hypothalamic dysfunction, food allergies or disordered taste responsivity (Wisniewski et al., 1997), a disorder of the endogenous opioid system (Mitchell, Laine, Morley, & Levine, 1986), a neurological disorder, and a combination of these. Bulimia, in turn, disrupts hormonal functioning among those with more chronic and severe diseases, and leptin production is decreased, perhaps because of the malnutrition in bingeing behavior that characterizes bulimia (Monteleone, Martiadis, Colurcio, & Maj, 2002).

Treating Bulimia The first barrier to treating bulimia is the fact that many women do not go in for treatment. Either they do not believe that their problem is a serious one, or they do not believe that any medical intervention will overcome it. Accordingly, one of the first steps for helping bulimics get treatment is to convince them that the disorder threatens their health and that medical and psychological interventions can help them overcome the disorder (Smalec & Klingle, 2000).

A number of therapies have been developed to treat bulimia. Overall, a combination of medication and cognitive-behavioral therapy appears to be the most effective treatment for bulimia (Agras et al., 1992). Typically, this treatment begins by instructing the patient to keep a diary of eating habits, including time, place, type of food consumed, and emotions experienced. Simple self-monitoring can produce decreases in binge-purge behavior (Orleans & Barnett, 1984; G. T. Wilson, 1984).

Most therapies combine monitoring with other behavioral treatments in an individualized effort to bring eating under control (Agras, Schneider, Arnow, Raeburn, & Telch, 1989; Kirkley, Agras, & Weiss, 1985). Specific techniques include increasing the regularity of meals, eating a greater variety of foods, delaying the impulse to purge as long as possible, and eating favorite foods in new settings not previously associated with binges. All these techniques help women to break down patterns that maintained bulimia and to instill better eating habits (Kirkley, Schneider, Agras, & Bachman, 1985). Increased perceptions of self-efficacy with respect to eating facilitate the success of cognitive-behavioral interventions as well (J. A. Schneider, O'Leary, & Agras, 1987).

Relapse prevention techniques are often added to therapeutic programs. For example, the person may be trained to identify situations that trigger binge eating and to develop coping skills to avoid it. Relaxation and stress management skills are often added to these programs as well. When bulimia becomes compulsive, outright prevention of the behavior may be required, with the patient placed in a treatment facility and therapeutic intervention provided to alleviate the emotional problems that may have precipitated the disorder.

The increasing prevalence of eating disorders, coupled with the difficulty of treating them effectively, suggests that health psychologists must begin to think about ways to prevent eating disorders from developing rather than exclusively treating them after they occur (Battle & Brownell, 1996). Exactly how to do this, however, is still being explored (Mann et al., 1997).

■ SLEEP

Michael Foster, a trucker who carried produce, was behind in his truck payments. To catch up, he needed to increase the number of runs he made each week. He could not shave any miles off his trips, so the only way he could make the extra money was to increase the number of trips and reduce his sleep each night. He began cutting back from 6 hours of sleep a night to 3 or 4, stretches that he grabbed in his truck between jobs. On an early-morning run between Fresno and Los Angeles, he fell asleep at the wheel and his truck went out of control, hitting a car and killing a family.

What Is Sleep?

Sleep is a health practice all of us engage in, but many of us abuse our sleep. Sleep consists of four stages. The lightest and earliest stage of sleep is marked by theta waves, when we begin to tune out the sounds around us, although we are easily awakened by any loud sound. In stage 2, breathing and heart rates even out, body temperature drops, and brain waves alternate between short bursts called sleep spindles and large K-complex waves. In stages 3 and 4, known as deep sleep, blood pressure falls, breathing slows, and body temperature drops even lower. These are the phases most important for restoring energy, strengthening the immune system, and prompting the body to release growth hormone. These phases are marked by delta waves. In REM (rapid eye-movement) sleep, eyes dart back and forth, breathing and heart rate flutter, and we often dream vividly. This stage of sleep is marked by beta waves, and it is believed to be important for consolidating memories, solving problems from the previous day, and turning knowledge into long-term memories (Weintraub, 2004). All of these phases of sleep are essential.

Sleep and Health

More than 14 million Americans, most over 40, have major sleep disorders—most commonly, insomnia (Nagourney, 2001). Thirty-nine percent of adults sleep less than 7 hours a night on weeknights, 36% of people over 15 report at least occasional insomnia, and 54% of

Scientists have begun to identify the health risks associated with little or poor-quality sleep.

people over 55 report insomnia at least once a week (Weintraub, 2004). For women, sleep disorders may be tied to hormonal levels related to menopause (Manber, Kuo, Cataldo, & Colrain, 2003).

It has long been known that insufficient sleep (less than 7 hours a night) affects cognitive functioning, mood, performance in work, and quality of life (Pressman & Orr, 1997). Any of us who has spent a sleepless night tossing and turning over some problem knows how unpleasant the following day can be. Poor sleep can be a particular problem in certain high-risk occupations, with nightmares as one of the most common symptoms. This is especially true for occupations such as police work, in which police officers are exposed to traumatic events (Neylen et al., 2002).

Increasingly, we are also recognizing the health risks of inadequate sleep (Leger, Scheuermaier, Phillip, Paillard, & Guilleminault, 2001). Chronic insomnia can compromise the ability to secrete and respond to insulin (suggesting a link between sleep and diabetes), it can increase the risk of developing coronary heart disease (Bonnet & Arand, 1998), and it can reduce the efficacy of flu shots, among its other detrimental effects (Center for the Advancement of Health, January 2004; Weintraub, 2004). More than 70,000 of the nation's annual automobile crashes are accounted for by sleepy drivers, and 1,550 of these are fatal each year. In one study of healthy older adults, sleep disturbances predicted all-cause mortality over the next 4 to 19 years of follow-up (Dew et al., 2003). Even just six nights of poor sleep in a row can impair metabolic and hormonal function, and over time, chronic sleep loss can aggravate the severity of hypertension and Type II diabetes (K. Murphy, 2000).

Sleep deprivation has a number of adverse effects on immune functioning. For example, it reduces natural killer cell activity, which may, in turn, lead to greater receptivity to infection (Irwin et al., 1994), and it leads to reduced counts of other immune cells as well (Savard, Laroche, Simard, Ivers, & Morin, 2003). Poor sleep compromises human antibody response to hepatitis A vaccination (Lange, Perras, Fehm, & Born, 2003). Shift workers, who commonly experience disordered sleep when they change from one shift to another, have a high rate of respiratory tract infections and show depressed cellular immune function. Even modest sleep disturbance seems to have these adverse effects, although after a night of good sleep, immune functioning quickly recovers (Irwin et al., 1994).

Sleep may have particular significance for those low in SES. In particular, the strong relationship between socioeconomic status and health may be partly explained by the poorer sleep quality that people low in SES routinely have (Moore, Adler, Williams, & Jackson, 2002).

People who are going through major stressful life events or who are suffering from major depression especially report sleep disturbances (M. Hall et al., 2000). Particularly when stressful events have been appraised as uncontrollable, insomnia may be the result (Morin, Rodrigue, & Ivers, 2003).

Although the health risks of insufficient sleep are now well known, less well known is the fact that people who habitually sleep more than 7 hours every night, other than children and adolescents, also incur health risks. Long sleepers, like short sleepers, have more symptoms of psychopathology, including chronic worrying (Fichten, Libman, Creti, Balles, & Sabourin, 2004; Grandner & Kripke, 2004).

Apnea

Many of the problems related to sleep disruption have to do with amount of sleep, but in other cases, quality of sleep is the culprit. Recently, researchers have recognized that sleep apnea, an air pipe blockage that disrupts sleep, can compromise health. Each time that apnea occurs, the sleeper stops breathing, sometimes for as long as 3 minutes, until he or she suddenly wakes up, gasping for air. Some people are awakened dozens, even hundreds, of times each night without realizing it. Researchers now believe that sleep apnea triggers thousands of nighttime deaths, including heart attacks. Apnea also contributes to high rates of accidents in the workplace and on the road and to irritability, anxiety, and depression. Sleep apnea is difficult to diagnose because the symptoms, such as grouchiness, are so diffuse, but fitful, harsh snoring is one signal that a person may be experiencing apnea.

Is there any treatment for apnea? Because apnea is caused by excessive tissue in the back of the throat, which blocks the air passages, doctors can in severe cases cut out some of this throat tissue. Other patients sleep with a machine designed to keep airways open or wear sleeping masks that blow air down the throat all night. Such methods improve cognitive functioning, the chief casualty of the exhaustion produced by chronic obstructive sleep apnea (Bardwell, Ancoli-Israel, Berry, & Dimsdale, 2001). Although sleep apnea is a chronic problem for some people, many people also get it occasionally, particularly following a night of heavy drinking or smoking (S. Baker, 1997). The medical community is just beginning to understand how problematic chronic obstructive sleep apnea can be.

The next years promise to enlighten us more fully as to the health benefits of sleep and liabilities of disordered sleeping. For those with persistent sleep problems, a variety of cognitive-behavioral interventions are available that typically make use of relaxation therapies (Perlis et al., 2000; Perlis, Sharpe, Smith, Greenblatt, & Giles, 2001). Such programs also recommend better sleep habits, many of which can be undertaken on one's own (Gorman, 1999; S. L. Murphy, 2000). How can we sleep better? See table 4.5.

■ REST, RENEWAL, SAVORING

An important set of health behaviors that is only beginning to be understood involves processes of relaxation and renewal, the restorative activities that help people reduce stress and restore their personal balance. The ability to savor the positive aspects of life may also have health benefits. We know, for example, that not taking a vacation can be a risk factor for heart attack among people with heart disease (Gump & Matthews, 1998; Step-

**TABLE 4.5	A Good Night's Sleep**
• Get regular exercise, at least three times a week.
• Keep the bedroom cool at night.
• Sleep in a comfortable bed that is big enough.
• Establish a regular schedule for awakening and going to bed.
• Develop nightly rituals that can get one ready for bed, such as taking a shower.
• Use a fan or other noise generator to mask background sound.
• Don't consume too much alcohol or smoke.
• Don't eat too much or too little at night.
• Don't have strong smells in the room, as from incense, candles, or lotions.
• Don't nap after 3 P.M.
• Cut back on caffeine, especially in the afternoon or evening.
• If awakened, get up and read quietly in another place, to associate the bed with sleep, not sleeplessness.

Source: Gorman, 1999; S. L. Murphy, 2000.

toe, Roy, & Evans, 1996). Unfortunately, little other than intuition currently guides our thinking about restorative processes. Nonetheless, health psychologists suspect that rest, renewal, and savoring—involving such activities such as going home for the holidays, relaxing after exams, enjoying a beautiful hiking path or sunset and similar activities—will be shown to have health benefits.

This point underscores the fact that an understanding of health-enhancing behaviors is a work in progress. As new health risks are uncovered or the benefits of particular behaviors become known, the application of what we already know to these new behaviors will take on increasing importance. ●

SUMMARY

1. Health-enhancing behaviors are practiced by asymptomatic individuals to improve or enhance their current or future health and functioning. Such behaviors include exercise, accident prevention measures, cancer detection processes, weight control, and consumption of a healthy diet.

2. Aerobic exercise reduces risk for heart attack and improves other aspects of bodily functioning. Exercise also improves mood and reduces stress.

3. Few people adhere regularly to the standard exercise prescription of aerobic exercise for at least 30 minutes at least three times a week. People are more likely to exercise when the form of exercise is convenient and they like it. If their attitudes favor exercise and they come from families in which exercise is practiced, they are also more likely to exercise.

4. Cognitive-behavioral interventions including relapse prevention components have been at least somewhat successful in helping people adhere to regular exercise programs.

5. Accidents are a major cause of preventable death, especially among children. Recent years have seen increases in the use of accident prevention measures, especially car safety restraint devices for children. These changes have been credited to publicity in the mass media, legislation favoring accident prevention measures, and training of parents by physicians and through interventions to promote safety measures for children.

6. One out of every eight American women will develop breast cancer, yet breast self-examination (BSE) is rarely practiced because women have difficulty detecting lumps, are uncertain if they are doing it correctly, and fear what may happen if a lump is detected.

7. Personalized instruction improves the practice of BSE. Statistics promoting the value of early detection may reduce fear. Regular practice can also be enhanced by monthly prompts or more-than-monthly practice of BSE.

8. Mammograms are recommended for women over age 50, yet few women, especially minority and older women, obtain them because of lack of information, unrealistic fears, and, most important, the cost and lack of availability of mammograms.

9. Testicular self-examination (TSE) can aid in the diagnosis of testicular cancer in men between the ages of 15 and 35, for whom testicular cancer is a leading cause of death.

10. Obesity is a health risk that has been linked to cardiovascular disease, kidney disease, diabetes, and other chronic conditions.

11. Factors associated with obesity include genetic predisposition, early diet, family history of obesity, low SES, little exercise, and cultural values. Ironically, dieting may contribute to the propensity for obesity.

12. Weight may also be regulated by an ideal set point and by prior caloric consumption. Some individuals eat in response to stress, and stress eating may exacerbate existing weight problems.

13. Obesity has been treated through diets, fasting, surgical procedures, drugs, and more recently cognitive-behavioral approaches. Most interventions use a multimodal approach that includes monitoring eating behavior, modifying the environmental stimuli that control eating, gaining control over the eating process, and reinforcing new eating habits. Relapse prevention skills training helps in long-term maintenance.

14. Some success in weight loss has been found in the work site using work-group competition techniques and in commercial weight-loss programs that employ cognitive-behavioral techniques. Such programs can produce weight losses of 2 pounds a week for up to 20 weeks, maintained over a 2-year period.

15. Increasingly, interventions are focusing on weight-gain prevention with children in obese families and with high-risk adults. The role of unrealistic standards of thinness in the causes and perpetuation of eating disorders is receiving increasing attention.

16. Dietary interventions involving reductions in cholesterol, fats, calories, and additives and increases in fiber, fruits, and vegetables are widely recommended, yet long-term adherence to such diets is low for many reasons: Recommended diets are often boring; relation of dietary change to improvement in health is uncertain; tastes are hard to change; attitudes may not favor dietary change;

and despite recommendations for lifetime change, behavior often falls off over time because of sheer inertia. Diets, especially those low in cholesterol, may actually exacerbate some other causes of illness and death.

17. Dietary interventions through the mass media and community resources have promise as intervention techniques. Intervening with the family unit also appears to be useful for promoting and maintaining dietary change.

KEY TERMS

aerobic exercise
anorexia nervosa
breast self-examination (BSE)

bulimia
obesity
set point theory of weight

stress eating
testicular self-examination (TSE)
yo-yo dieting

Health-Compromising Behaviors

Several decades ago, my father went for his annual physical and his doctor told him, as the doctor did each year, that he had to stop smoking. As usual, my father told his doctor that he would stop when he was ready. He had already tried several times and had been unsuccessful. My father had begun smoking at age 14, long before the health risks of smoking were known, and it was now an integrated part of his lifestyle, which included a couple of cocktails before a dinner high in fat and cholesterol and a hectic life that provided few opportunities for regular exercise. Smoking was part of who he was. His doctor then said, "Let me put it this way. If you expect to see your daughter graduate from college, stop smoking *now.*" That warning did the trick. My father threw his cigarettes in the wastebasket and never had another one. Over the years, as he read more about health, he began to change his lifestyle in other ways. He began to swim regularly for exercise, and he pared down his diet to one of mostly fish, chicken, vegetables, fruit, and cereal. Despite the fact that he once had many of the risk factors for early heart disease, he lived to age 83.

In this chapter, we turn our attention to health-compromising behaviors—behaviors practiced by people that undermine or harm their current or future health. My father's problems with stopping smoking illustrate several important points about these behaviors. Many health-compromising behaviors are habitual, and several, including smoking, are addictive, making them very difficult habits to break. On the other hand, with proper incentive and help, even the most intractable health habit can be modified. When a person succeeds in changing a health behavior for the better, often he or she will make other lifestyle changes in the direction of a healthier way of living. The end result is that risk declines, and a disease-free middle and old age becomes a possibility.

■ CHARACTERISTICS OF HEALTH-COMPROMISING BEHAVIORS

Many health-compromising behaviors share several additional important characteristics. First, there is a window of vulnerability in adolescence. Drinking to excess, smoking, illicit drug use, unsafe sex, and risk-taking behavior that can lead to accidents or early death all begin in early adolescence and sometimes cluster together as part of a problem behavior syndrome (S. Donovan & Jessor, 1985; Lam, Stewart, & Ho, 2001).

This is not to suggest that all health-compromising behaviors evolve and are firmly implanted during adolescence. Several health problems, such as obesity, begin early in childhood and others, such as alcoholism, may be special risks for older adults. These exceptions notwithstanding, there is an unnerving similarity in the factors that elicit and maintain many of these health-compromising behaviors.

Many of these behaviors are heavily tied to the peer culture, as children learn from and imitate the peers they like and admire. Wanting to be attractive to others becomes very important in adolescence, and this factor is significant in the development of eating disorders, alcohol consumption, tobacco and drug use, tanning, unsafe sexual encounters, and vulnerability to injury, among other behaviors (for example, Li, Barrera, Hops, & Fisher, 2002).

Several health-compromising behaviors are also intimately bound up in the self-presentation process—that is, in the adolescent's or young adult's efforts to appear sophisticated, cool, tough, or savvy in his or her social environment. The image conveyed by these behaviors, then, is another shared characteristic that must be considered in their modification.

A third similarity is that many of these behaviors are pleasurable, enhancing the adolescent's ability to cope with stressful situations, and some represent thrill seeking, which can be rewarding in its own right; however, each of these behaviors is also highly dangerous. Each has been tied to at least one major cause of death in this country, and several, especially smoking, are risk factors for more than one major chronic disease.

Fourth, development of all these behaviors occurs gradually, as the individual is exposed to and becomes susceptible to the behavior, experiments with it, and later engages in its regular use (Wills, Pierce, & Evans, 1996). As such, these health-compromising behaviors are not acquired all at once, but through a process that may make different interventions important at the different stages of vulnerability, experimentation, and regular use.

Fifth, substance abuse of all kinds, whether cigarettes, alcohol, drugs, or sex, are predicted by some of the same factors. Those adolescents who get involved in such risky behaviors often have high levels of conflict with their parents and poor self-control, suggesting that these behaviors may function in part as coping mechanisms to manage a stressful life (M. L. Cooper, Wood, Orcutt, & Albino, 2003; Wills, Gibbons, Gerrard, & Brody, 2000).

Common to the abuse of many substances, including cigarettes, alcohol, and marijuana, is the profile of those who use these substances. Adolescents with a penchant for deviant behavior, with low self-esteem, and with problematic family relationships often show higher levels of these behaviors (Duncan, Duncan, Strycker, & Chaumeton, 2002; Lam et al., 2001). Those who abuse substances typically do poorly in school. Family problems, deviance, and low self-esteem appear to explain this relationship (Andrews & Duncan, 1997). Likewise, difficult temperament, poor self-control, and deviance-prone attitudes are related to peer and adolescent substance use of tobacco, alcohol, and marijuana (Repetti, Taylor, & Seeman, 2002; Wills & Cleary, 1999).

Finally, problem behaviors are related to the larger social structure in which they occur. Most of these problem behaviors are more common in lower social class individuals. In some cases, these social class differences occur because of greater exposure to the problem behavior and, in other cases, because lower social class raises more stressful circumstances with which the adolescent may need to cope (Wills et al., 1996). Practice of these health-compromising behaviors is thought to be one reason that social class is so strongly related to most causes of disease and death (Adler et al., 1994).

In this chapter, we are especially concerned with two of the most common and commonly treated health-compromising behaviors—alcohol abuse and smoking. Many of the points raised, however, will be relevant to other health-compromising behaviors, such as illicit drug use. In particular, many of these health-compromising behaviors involve addiction.

■ WHAT IS SUBSTANCE DEPENDENCE?

A person is said to be dependent on a substance when he or she has repeatedly self-administered it, resulting in tolerance, withdrawal, and compulsive behavior (American Psychiatric Association, 1994). Substance dependence can include **physical dependence,** the state that occurs when the body has adjusted to the substance and incorporates the use of that substance into the normal functioning of the body's tissues. Physical dependence often involves **tolerance,** the process by which the body increasingly adapts to the use of a substance, requiring larger and larger doses of it to obtain the same effects, eventually reaching a plateau. **Craving** is a strong desire to engage in a behavior or consume a substance. It seems to result from physical dependence and from a condi-

tioning process: As the substance is paired with many environmental cues, the presence of those cues triggers an intense desire for the substance. **Addiction** occurs when a person has become physically or psychologically dependent on a substance following use over time. **Withdrawal** refers to the unpleasant symptoms, both physical and psychological, that people experience when they stop using a substance on which they have become dependent. Although the symptoms vary, they include anxiety, irritability, intense cravings for the substance, nausea, headaches, shaking, and hallucinations. All these characteristics are common to substance abuse involving addiction, which includes smoking, alcohol consumption, and drug abuse (see box 5.1).

■ ALCOHOLISM AND PROBLEM DRINKING

Scope of the Problem

Alcohol is responsible for more than 100,000 deaths each year, making it the third leading cause of preventable death after tobacco and improper diet and exercise. More than 20% of Americans drink at levels that exceed government recommendations (Center for the Advancement of Health, 2001). Originally characterized as a social ill, alcoholism was officially recognized as a disease by the American Medical Association in 1957.

As a health issue, alcohol consumption has been linked to a number of disorders, including high blood pressure, stroke, cirrhosis of the liver, some forms of cancer, and fetal alcohol syndrome, a condition of retardation and physiological abnormalities that arises in the offspring of heavy-drinking mothers (Higgins-Biddle, Babor, Mullahyl, Daniels, & McRee, 1997). Alcoholics can show major sleep disorders; disordered sleep may contribute to immune alterations that elevate risk for infection among alcoholics (Redwine, Dang, Hall, & Irwin, 2003). Excessive drinking also accounts for substantial cognitive impairments, many of them irreversible (M. S. Goldman, 1983; F. L. McGuire, 1982). Approximately 50% of the 50,000 annual highway fatalities are attributed to drinking and driving (F. L. McGuire, 1982), and it is estimated that one in every two Americans will be in an alcohol-related accident during his or her lifetime. Approximately 41% of all traffic-related deaths have been related to alcohol (NHTSA, 2003a).

Economically, alcohol abuse is estimated to cost the nation $184.6 billion, which includes approximately $134 billion in lost productivity; $26 billion in treatment costs for alcohol misuse and related disorders; and

BOX 5.1

Love or Loss: What Sustains Drug Use?

Many of us have an image of a drug user as a nervous, edgy individual who makes a buy, shoots up in an alley, and then experiences the euphoria of the drug state. Recent research on withdrawal and reward, however, questions this account. Although drug use early on can bring euphoria and strong pleasant feelings, later in the drug addict's career, the need to cope with the loss of drugs takes over.

Many drug addicts develop high tolerance, so that taking drugs does not actually make them high anymore. They may have lost their jobs, their homes, their health, and all of the people who once loved them, but they continue to take drugs not because they become euphoric but because of the distress that discontinuing drugs causes.

Two researchers (DuPont & Gold, 1995) who described this problem liken it to the way that people who have been in love talk about the loss of the loved one after the relationship has ended. Just as the adolescent or young adult finds it impossible to imagine life after the lost partner, life loses its value without drugs for the drug addict. The implication is that, as with all health-compromising behaviors, prevention should be the first line of attack.

$24 billion in other costs, including motor vehicle accidents, fire, and crime (NIAAA, 2000a). An estimated 15% of the national health bill goes to the treatment of alcoholism. About 1 of every 10 adult Americans is an alcoholic or a problem drinker (Dorgan & Editue, 1995). The costs of alcohol abuse and alcoholism are estimated to be approximately $184.6 billion and include the following:

1. About $18.9 billion in medical expenditures to treat the medical consequences of alcohol abuse and alcoholism.

2. $5.5 billion for alcohol and drug abuse services.

3. About $134.2 billion due to lost earnings.

4. About $31.5 billion for other effects on society, such as resource expenditures related to drunk driving (Harwood, 2000).

In addition to the direct costs of alcoholism through illness, accidents, and economic costs, alcohol abuse contributes to other health problems. For example, alcohol disinhibits aggression, so a substantial percentage of

homicides, suicides, and assaults occur under the influence of alcohol. Alcohol can also facilitate other risky behaviors. For example, in one study, which analyzed the sexual encounters of sexually active adults, alcohol use led to more impulsive sexuality (Weinhardt, Carey, Carey, Maisto, & Gordon, 2001) and poorer skills for negotiating condom use, relative to those who were more sober (C. M. Gordon, Carey, & Carey, 1997).

Overall, though, it has been difficult to define the scope of alcoholism. Many problem drinkers keep their problem successfully hidden, at least for a time. By drinking at particular times of day or at particular places and by restricting contacts with other people during these times, the alcoholic may be able to drink without noticeable disruption in his or her daily activities.

What Are Alcoholism and Problem Drinking?

Exactly what constitutes alcoholism and problem drinking is fuzzy. **Problem drinking** and **alcoholism** encompass a variety of specific patterns (Jellinek, 1960;

Wanburg & Horn, 1983). The term "alcoholic" is usually reserved for someone who is physically addicted to alcohol. Alcoholics show withdrawal symptoms when they attempt to stop drinking, they have a high tolerance for alcohol, and they have little ability to control their drinking. Problem drinkers may not have these symptoms, but they may have substantial social, psychological, and medical problems resulting from alcohol.

Problem drinking and alcoholism have been defined by a variety of specific behaviors, which range from the milder ones associated with problem drinking to the severe ones associated with alcoholism. These patterns include the need for daily use of alcohol, the inability to cut down on drinking, repeated efforts to control drinking through temporary abstinence or restriction of alcohol to certain times of the day, binge drinking, occasional consumptions of large quantities of alcohol, loss of memory while intoxicated, continued drinking despite known health problems, and drinking of nonbeverage alcohol.

Physiological dependence can be manifested in stereotypic drinking patterns (particular types of alcohol in particular quantities at particular times of day), drinking that maintains blood alcohol at a particular level, the ability to function at a level that would incapacitate less tolerant drinkers, increased frequency and severity of withdrawal, early in the day and middle of the night drinking, a sense of loss of control over drinking, and a subjective craving for alcohol (Straus, 1988).

Symptoms of alcohol abuse include difficulty in performing one's job because of alcohol consumption, inability to function well socially without alcohol, and legal difficulties encountered while drinking, such as drunk driving convictions (American Psychiatric Association, 1980).

Origins of Alcoholism and Problem Drinking

The origins of alcoholism and problem drinking are complex. Based on twin studies and on the frequency of alcoholism in sons of alcoholic fathers, genetic factors appear to be implicated (for example, Hutchison, McGeary, Smolen, Bryan, & Swift, 2002). Men have traditionally been at greater risk for alcoholism than women (C. A. Robbins & Martin, 1993), although with changing norms, younger women and women employed outside the home are beginning to catch up (D. R. Williams, 2002). Sociodemographic factors, such as low income, also predict alcoholism. Overall, however, these

factors account for relatively little alcoholism. Instead, a gradual process involving physiological, behavioral, and sociocultural variables appears to be implicated (Zucker & Gomberg, 1986).

Drinking and Stress   Drinking clearly occurs, in part, as an effort to buffer the impact of stress (M. Seeman, Seeman, & Budros, 1988). People who are experiencing a lot of negative life events, chronic stressors, and little social support are more likely to become problem drinkers than are people without these problems (Brennan & Moos, 1990; Sadava & Pak, 1994). For example, alcohol abuse rises among people who have been laid off from their jobs (Catalano, Dooley, Wilson, & Hough, 1993). Alienation from work, low job autonomy, little use of one's abilities, and lack of participation in decision making at work are associated with heavy drinking (E. S. Greenberg & Grunberg, 1995). Financial strain, especially to the degree that it produces depression, leads to drinking in order to cope (Peirce, Frone, Russell, & Cooper, 1994). A general sense of powerlessness in one's life has also been related to alcohol use and abuse (M. Seeman et al., 1988).

Many people begin drinking to enhance positive emotions and reduce negative ones (M. L. Cooper, Frone, Russell, & Mudar, 1995), and alcohol does reliably lower anxiety and depression and improve self-esteem, at least temporarily (Steele & Josephs, 1990). Thus, there can be psychological rewards to drinking (Steele & Josephs, 1990).

Social Origins of Drinking   Alcoholism is tied to the social and cultural environment of the drinker. Parents and peers influence adolescent drinking by influencing attitudes about alcohol and by acting as role models (Ennett & Bauman, 1991). Many people who eventually become problem drinkers or alcoholics learn early in life to associate drinking with pleasant social occasions. They may develop a social life centered on drinking, such as going to bars or attending parties where alcohol consumption is prominent (Wanburg & Horn, 1983). In contrast, those people who marry and become parents reduce their risk of developing alcohol-related disorders (Chilcoat & Breslau, 1996).

There appear to be two windows of vulnerability for alcohol use and abuse. The first, when chemical dependence generally starts, is between the ages of 12 and 21 (DuPont, 1988). The other window of vulnerability is in late middle age, in which problem drinking may act as a coping method for managing stress (Brennan & Moos,

Adolescence and young adulthood represent a window of vulnerability to problem drinking and alcoholism. Successful intervention with this age group may reduce the scope of the alcoholism problem.

1990). Late-onset problem drinkers are more likely to control their drinking on their own or be successfully treated, compared with individuals with more long-term drinking problems (Moos, Brennan, & Moos, 1991).

Depression and alcoholism may be linked. Alcoholism may represent untreated symptoms of depression, or depression may act as an impetus for drinking in an effort to improve mood. Thus, in some cases, symptoms of both disorders must be treated simultaneously (Oslin et al., 2003). Social isolation and lack of employment can exacerbate these problems. Poor psychological well-being may particularly contribute to increased alcohol use among women (Green, Freeborn, & Polen, 2001) and older problem drinkers. Drinking among older adults may be confounded by the fact that tolerance for alcohol reliably decreases with age, leaving an older person vulnerable to alcohol-related accidents such as falls.

Treatment of Alcohol Abuse

For years, alcohol abuse was regarded as an intractable problem, but substantial evidence now indicates that it can be modified successfully. Between 10 and 20% of all

alcoholics stop drinking on their own, and as many as 32% can stop with minimal help (Moos & Finney, 1983). This "maturing out" of alcoholism is especially likely in the later years of life (Stall & Biernacki, 1986).

In addition, alcoholism can be successfully treated through cognitive-behavioral modification programs. Nonetheless, such programs have high dropout rates. As many as 60% of the people treated through such programs may return to alcohol abuse (Moos & Finney, 1983). This high rate of recidivism may occur, in part, because the people most likely to seek treatment for alcohol abuse are those who had more severe drinking problems (Finney & Moos, 1995).

Earlier, we noted that alcohol consumption is heavily dependent on the social environment in which it occurs, and this fact is prominent in understanding the recovery process as well. Alcoholics who come from high socioeconomic backgrounds and who are in highly socially stable environments (that is, who have a regular job, an intact family, and a circle of friends) do very well in treatment programs, achieving success rates as high as 68%, whereas alcoholics of low socioeconomic status (SES) with low social stability often have success rates of 18% or less. No

BOX 5.2

After the Fall of the Berlin Wall

When the Berlin Wall came down in 1989, there were celebrations worldwide. In the midst of the jubilation, few fully anticipated the problems that might arise in its wake. Hundreds of thousands of East Germans, who had lived for decades under a totalitarian regime with a relatively poor standard of living, were now free to stream across the border into West Germany, which enjoyed prosperity, employment, and a high standard of living. But for many people, the promise of new opportunities failed to materialize. Employment was less plentiful than had been assumed, and the East Germans were less qualified for the jobs that did exist. Discrimination and hostility toward the East Germans was higher than expected, and many migrating East Germans found themselves unemployed.

Unemployment is a severe stressor that has pervasive negative implications for one's entire life. It produces chronic tension, anxiety, and a sense of discouragement. Because alcohol is known to reduce tension and anxiety and can stimulate a good mood, the potential for drinking to alleviate stress among the unemployed is high. Several studies document the fact that alcohol intake often rises among the unemployed (for example, Catalano, Dooley, Wilson, & Houph, 1993). But not everyone responds to the stress of unemployment by drinking.

Two German researchers, Mittag and Schwarzer (1993), examined alcohol consumption among men who had found employment in West Germany and those who had remained unemployed. In addition, they measured self-efficacy with respect to coping with life's problems through such items as "When I am in trouble, I can rely on my ability to deal with the problem effectively." Presumably, individuals who have high feelings of self-efficacy are less vulnerable to stress, and thus they may be less likely to consume alcohol under stressful circumstances than are those with a low sense of self-efficacy.

The researchers found that men with a high sense of self-efficacy were less likely to consume high levels of alcohol. Self-efficacy appeared to be especially important in responding to the stress of unemployment. Those men who were unemployed and had a low sense of self-efficacy were drinking more than any other group. Thus, being male, being unemployed for a long time, and not believing in a sense of personal agency led to heavy drinking.

Although psychologists cannot provide jobs to the unemployed, perhaps they can empower individuals to develop more optimistic self-beliefs. If one believes that one can control one's behavior, cope effectively with life, and solve one's problems, one may be able to deal effectively with setbacks (Mittag & Schwarzer, 1993).

---

treatment program will be highly successful unless it takes account of the alcoholic's environment. Without employment and social support, the prospects for recovery are dim (MedicineNet.com, 2002). Box 5.2 presents an example of these problems.

Treatment Programs

Approximately 700,000 people in the United States receive treatment for alcoholism on any given day (NIAAA, 2000a). A self-help group, especially Alcoholics Anonymous (AA), is the most commonly sought source of help for alcohol-related problems (NIAAA, 2000a) (see box 5.3).

Treatment programs for alcoholism and problem drinking typically use broad-spectrum cognitive-behavioral therapy to treat the biological and environmental factors involved in alcoholism simultaneously (NIAAA, 2000b). The goals of the approach are to decrease the reinforcing properties of alcohol, to teach peo-

ple new behaviors inconsistent with alcohol abuse, and to modify the environment to include reinforcements for activities that do not involve alcohol. These approaches also attempt to instill coping techniques for dealing with stress and relapse prevention methods to enhance long-term maintenance.

For hard-core alcoholics, the first phase of treatment is **detoxification.** Because this can produce severe symptoms and health problems, detoxification is typically conducted in a carefully supervised and medically monitored setting.

Once the alcoholic has at least partly dried out, therapy is initiated. The typical program begins with a short-term, intensive inpatient treatment followed by a period of continuing treatment on an outpatient basis (NIAAA, 2000a). Typically, inpatient programs last between 10 and 60 days, with an average of approximately 28 days (R. K. Fuller & Hiller-Strumhöfel, 1999). After discharge, some patients attend follow-up sessions, whereas others are discharged to supervised living arrangements.

BOX 5.3

A Profile of Alcoholics Anonymous

No one knows exactly when Alcoholics Anonymous (AA) began, but it is believed that the organization was formed around 1935 in Akron, Ohio. The first meetings were attended by a few acquaintances who discovered that they could remain sober by attending services of a local religious group and sharing with other alcoholics their problems and efforts to remain sober. In 1936, weekly AA meetings were taking place around the country.

Who participates in AA? Currently, its membership is estimated to be more than 2 million individuals worldwide (The Columbia Encyclopedia, 2004). The sole requirement for participation in AA is a desire to stop drinking. Originally, the organization attracted hardened drinkers who turned to it as a last resort; more recently, however, it has attracted many people who are experiencing drinking problems but whose lives are otherwise intact. Members come from all walks of life, including all socioeconomic levels, races, cultures, sexual preferences, and ages.

The philosophy of Alcoholics Anonymous is a commitment to the concept of self-help. Members believe that the person who is best able to reach an alcoholic is a recovered alcoholic. In addition, members are encouraged to immerse themselves in the culture of AA—to attend "90 meetings in 90 days." At these meetings, AA members speak about the drinking experiences that prompted them to seek out AA and what sobriety has meant to them. Time is set aside for prospective members to talk informally with longtime members so that they can learn and imitate the coping techniques that recovered alcoholics have used. Some meetings include only regular AA members and cover issues of problem drinking.

AA has a firm policy regarding alcohol consumption. It maintains that alcoholism is a disease that can be managed but never cured. Recovery means that an individual must acknowledge that he or she has a disease, that it is incurable, and that alcohol can play no part in future life. Recovery depends completely on staying sober.

Is Alcoholics Anonymous successful in getting people to stop drinking? AA's dropout rate is unknown, and success over the long term has not been carefully chronicled. Moreover, because the organization keeps no membership lists (it is anonymous), it is difficult to evaluate its success. However, AA itself maintains that two out of three individuals who wish to stop drinking have been able to do so through its program, and one authorized study reported a 75% success rate for the New York AA chapter.

Recent evaluations of alcohol treatment programs have found that people do better if they participate in AA while participating in a medically based formal treatment program, better than they would in the formal treatment program alone (Timko, Finney, Moos, & Moos, 1995). A study that compared AA participation with more formal treatment found comparable effects, a striking finding because the AA attendees had lower incomes and less education initially and thus had somewhat worse prospects for improving. Not incidentally, the treatment costs for the AA group were 45% lower than for the outpatient treatment program, translating into a $1,826 savings per person.

Researchers attempting to understand the effectiveness of AA programs have pointed to several important elements. AA is like a religious conversion experience in which an individual adopts a totally new way of life; such experiences can be powerful in bringing about behavior change. Also, a member who shares his or her experiences develops a commitment to other members. The process of giving up alcohol contributes to a sense of emotional maturity and responsibility, helping the alcoholic accept responsibility for his or her life. AA may also provide a sense of meaning and purpose in the individual's life—most chapters have a strong spiritual or religious bent and urge members to commit themselves to a power greater than themselves. The group can also provide affection and satisfying personal relationships and thus help people overcome the isolation that many alcoholics experience. Too, the members provide social reinforcement for each other's abstinence.

AA is significant as an organization for several reasons. First, it was one of the earliest self-help programs for individuals suffering from a health problem; therefore, it has provided a model for self-help organizations whose members have other addictive problems, such as Overeaters Anonymous and Gamblers Anonymous, among many others. Second, in having successfully treated alcoholics for decades, AA has demonstrated that the problem of alcoholism is not as intractable as had been widely assumed (D. Robinson, 1979).

Cognitive Behavioral Treatments A variety of behavior modification techniques have been incorporated into alcohol treatment programs (NIAAA, 2000a). Many programs include a self-monitoring phase, in which the alcoholic or problem drinker begins to understand the situations that give rise to and maintain drinking. Contingency contracting is frequently employed, in which the person agrees to a psychologically or financially costly outcome in the event of failure. Motivational enhancement procedures have also been included in many cognitive-behavioral interventions with alcoholics and problem drinkers, because the responsibility and the capacity to change rely entirely on the client. Consequently, working to provide individualized feedback about the patient's drinking and the effectiveness of his or her efforts can get the client motivated and on board to continue a program of treatment that may be more resistant to the inevitable temptations to relapse (NIAAA, 2000a).

Some programs have included medications for blocking the alcohol-brain interactions that may contribute to alcoholism. One such medication is naltrexone, which is used as an aid to prevent relapse among alcoholics. It blocks the opioid receptors in the brain, thereby weakening the rewarding effects of alcohol. Another drug, acamprosate (Campral), has also shown effectiveness in treating alcoholism and may help alcoholics maintain abstinence by preventing relapse. It seems to achieve effects by modifying the action of GABA, a neurotransmitter (Elchisak, 2001). Other drugs are being evaluated as well. Although drugs have shown some success in reducing alcohol consumption in conjunction with cognitive-behavioral interventions, successful maintenance requires patients to continue taking the drugs on their own, and if they choose not to do so, they reduce the effectiveness of the chemical treatment.

Many successful treatment programs have attempted to provide alcoholics with stress management techniques that they can substitute for drinking because, as noted earlier, alcohol is sometimes used as a method of coping with stress. Because the occurrence of a major stressful event within the first 90 days after treatment can trigger relapse among apparently recovered alcoholics (Marlatt & Gordon, 1980), stress management techniques can help the alcoholic get through events that raise the temptation to relapse. For example, relaxation training, assertiveness training, and training in social skills help the alcoholic or problem drinker deal with problem situations without resorting to alcohol.

In some cases, family therapy and group counseling are offered as well. The advantage of family counseling is that it eases the alcoholic's or problem drinker's transition back into his or her family (NIAAA, 2000a).

Relapse Prevention Relapse is a major difficulty in treating alcohol abuse. Authoritative studies report relapse rates of 50% or more at 2 to 4 years after treatment. A recent meta-analysis of past alcohol treatment outcome studies estimates that more than 50% of treated patients relapse within the first 3 months after treatment (NIAAA, 2000a). Practicing coping skills or social skills in high-risk-for-relapse situations is a mainstay of relapse prevention interventions. In addition, the recognition that people often stop and restart an addictive behavior several times before they are successful has led to the development of techniques for managing relapses. Understanding that an occasional relapse is normal helps the problem drinker realize that any given lapse does not signify failure or a lack of control. Drink-refusal skills and the substitution of nonalcoholic beverages in high-risk social situations are also important components of relapse prevention skills. Interventions with heavy-drinking college students have made use of these approaches (see box 5.4).

Evaluation of Alcohol Treatment Programs Surveys of alcohol treatment programs suggest several factors that are consistently associated with success: identifying factors in the environment that control drinking and modifying those factors or instilling coping skills to manage them, a moderate length of participation (about 6 to 8 weeks), outpatient aftercare, and active involvement of relatives and employers in the treatment process. Interventions that include these components produce as high as 40% treatment success rate (Center for the Advancement of Health, 2000e; U.S. Department of Health and Human Services, 1981).

Attention has focused on whether alcohol treatment programs must be residential. Such programs are expensive, and if outpatient treatment programs produce the same rates of success, then residential treatment programs may not be needed. It appears that severely deteriorated or socially unstable alcoholics show benefits from inpatient treatment, but the people most likely to be successful—those with jobs, stable relationships, and few other confounding problems—do just as well in outpatient programs (Finney & Moos, 1992; Holden, 1987).

BOX 5.4

The Drinking College Students

Most U.S. college students drink alcohol, and as many as 15 to 25% of them are heavy drinkers (Marlatt, Baer, & Larimer, 1995). If anything, these statistics are increasing, as college women begin to drink as heavily as college men (*New York Times*, 2002a). About 45% of college students overall appear to be involved in occasional binge drinking (Wechsler, Seibring, Liu, & Ahl, 2004). Moreover, if you are a college student who drinks the odds are 7 in 10 that you binge drink (Wechsler et al., 2004). At one time attending a women's college was protective for women against binge drinking, but that is now less common, as binge-drinking has increased in women's institutions as well (Wechsler et al., 2004) (see table 5.1).

Many colleges have tried to deal with the heavy drinking problem by providing educational materials about the harmful effects of alcohol. However, dogmatic alcohol prevention messages may actually enhance intentions to drink (Bensley & Wu, 1991). Moreover, the information conflicts markedly with the personal experiences of many college students who find drinking in a party situation to be satisfying, even exhilarating, behavior. For example, heavy drinking has been associated with active participation in a fraternity or sorority (Bartholow, Sher, & Krull, 2003). Many college students do not see drinking as a problem (Baer, Kivlahan, Fromme, & Marlatt, 1991), and others mistakenly assume that they are alone in their discomfort with campus alcohol practices (Suls & Green, 2003). Those students who would normally be a target for interventions may regard their drinking as a natural outgrowth of their social environment. Consequently, motivating students even to attend alcohol abuse programs, much less to follow their recommendations, is difficult.

Therefore, some of the more successful efforts to modify college students' drinking have encouraged students to gain self-control over drinking rather than explicitly trying to get them to reduce or eliminate alcohol consumption altogether. A program developed by Lang and Marlatt (Baer et al., 1991; Lang & Marlatt, 1982) incorporates techniques derived from attitude-change research and from cognitive-behavioral therapy in a total program to help college students gain such control. The program includes information about the risks of alcohol consumption, the acquisition of skills to moderate alcohol consumption, the use of drinking limits, relaxation training and lifestyle rebalancing, nutritional information, aerobic exercise, relapse prevention skills designed to help students cope with high-risk situations, assertiveness training, and drink-refusal training.

Such programs typically begin by getting students to monitor their drinking and to understand what blood alcohol levels mean and what their effects are. Often, merely monitoring drinking and recording the circumstances in which it occurs actually leads to a reduction in drinking.

The consumption of alcohol among students is heavily under the control of peer influence and the need to relax in social situations (T. J. Murphy, Pagano, & Marlatt, 1986). Thus, many intervention programs include training in cognitive-behavioral alcohol skills designed to get students to find alternative ways to relax and have fun in social situations without abusing alcohol. Such skills training has proven to be an important

TABLE 5.1 | Patterns of College Student Binge Drinking

	1999	2001
All students	44.5%	44.4%
Men	50.2	48.6
Women	39.4	40.9
Live in dormitory	44.5	45.3
Live in fraternity/sorority house	80.3	75.4

Source: Wechsler et al., 2002.

BOX 5.4

The Drinking College Students (continued)

component of successful alcohol abuse programs with college students (Kivlahan, Marlatt, Fromme, Coppel, & Williams, 1990). What are some of these skills?

To gain personal control over drinking, students are taught to identify the circumstances in which they are most likely to drink, and especially to drink to excess. Then students are taught specific coping skills so that they can moderate their alcohol consumption. For example, one technique for controlling alcohol consumption in high-risk situations, such as a party, is **placebo drinking.** This involves either the consumption of nonalcoholic beverages while others are drinking or the alternation of an alcoholic with a nonalcoholic beverage to reduce the total volume of alcohol consumed.

Students are also encouraged to engage in lifestyle rebalancing (Marlatt & George, 1988). This involves developing a healthier diet, engaging in aerobic exercise, and making other positive health changes, such as stopping smoking. As the student comes to think of himself or herself as health oriented, excessive alcohol consumption becomes incompatible with other aspects of the new lifestyle.

Evaluations of 8-week training programs with college students involving these components have shown a fair degree of success. Students reported significant reductions in their drinking, compared with a group that received only educational materials about the dire effects of excessive drinking. Moreover, these gains persisted over a yearlong follow-up period (Marlatt & George, 1988).

Despite the success of such programs, interest has shifted from treatment to prevention, because so many students get into a heavy drinking lifestyle. Alan Marlatt and colleagues (Marlatt et al., 1998) enrolled 348 students in an intervention during their senior year of high school and randomly assigned half to an individualized motivational brief intervention in their freshman year of college or to a no-treatment control condition. The intervention, conducted individually with each student, consisted of guiding the students through their drinking patterns and risks and their knowledge about alcohol's effects. Their rates of drinking were compared with college averages and their risks for current and future problems, such as potential decline in grades, blackouts, and accidents, were identified (see table 5.2). Points on which students lacked information about alcohol were also identified.

The interviewers were careful not to confront the students but did ask them questions such as "What do you make of this?" and "Are you surprised?" Each student was urged, but not forced, to come up with specific goals that might lead them to change their behavior, an intentional low-key effort to place responsibility for this change on the student. Over a 2-year follow-up period, students in the intervention showed significant reductions in both their drinking rates and the harmful consequences that frequently accompany heavy drinking (see table 5.3). Interventions like these emphasize the importance of coming up with effective prevention strategies before problems have a chance to take root (Baer et al., 1991; see also Baer et al., 1992).

TABLE 5.2 | Alcohol-Related Problems of College Students Who Had a Drink in the Past Year

Alcohol-Related Problem	Drinkers Who Reported Problems
Had a hangover	51.7%
Missed class	27.3
Did something you regret	32.7
Forgot where you were or what you did	24.8
Engaged in unplanned sexual activity	19.5
Got hurt or injured	9.3

Source: Wechsler et al., 2002.

TABLE 5.3 | Alcohol Use by U.S. College Students Aged 18 to 24

Alcohol-Related Incidents Per Year
Deaths: 1,400
Injuries: 500,000
Assaults: 600,000 students assaulted by student who had been drinking
Sexual assaults: 70,000 victims of alcohol-related sexual assault or date-rape
Sex: 100,000 said they were too drunk to know if they had consented to having sex
Driving: 2.1 million drove under the influence of alcohol.

Sources: National Institute on Alcohol Abuse and Alcoholism, 2005; Knight Ridder Tribune.

As is true for most behavioral disorders, relapse remains a formidable challenge for those who have drinking problems. People are confronted with urges and cues for drinking constantly. Thus, relapse prevention technology is typically used in the final stages of interventions with people who have problem drinking (Witkiewitz & Marlatt, 2004).

Minimal Interventions   Even minimal interventions can make a dent in drinking-related problems. In one study (Oslin et al., 2003), veterans with depression or who were at risk for problem drinking received either usual care or a telephone alcoholism and depression management program in which a behavioral health specialist provided information and support over a 4-month period. Compared with usual care, the telephone-implemented intervention produced beneficial changes, suggesting that telephone interventions can be a viable, low-cost approach to this problem (Oslin et al., 2003). However, another brief intervention that made use of a self-help manual, personalized feedback from a physician, and telephone counseling calls produced higher dropout rates in the intervention group rather than the control group (Curry, Ludman, Grothaus, Donovan, & Kim, 2003). Thus, the success of brief interventions remains unclear.

The biggest problem facing treatment for alcoholism is that most alcoholics (approximately 85%) do not receive any formal treatment. In response, many health psychologists have suggested that social engineering represents the best attack on the problem. Banning alcohol advertising, raising the legal drinking age, and strictly enforcing the penalties for drunk driving may be the best approaches for reaching this untreated majority.

Can Recovered Alcoholics Ever Drink Again?

A controversial issue in the treatment of alcohol abuse is whether alcoholics and problem drinkers can learn to drink in moderation (Lang & Marlatt, 1982). For decades, research and self-help treatment programs for alcoholism, such as Alcoholics Anonymous, have argued that the alcoholic is an alcoholic for life and must abstain from all drinking.

It does appear that a narrow group of problem drinkers may be able to drink in moderation—namely, those who are young and employed, who have not been drinking long, and who live in a supportive environ-

ment (Marlatt, Larimer, Baer, & Quigley, 1993). Drinking in moderation has some advantages for these problem drinkers. First, moderate drinking represents a realistic social behavior for the environments that a recovered problem drinker may encounter. For example, as box 5.4 indicated, moderating drinking may be a more realistic goal than total abstinence for college students, who are often in heavy-drinking environments. Second, traditional therapeutic programs that emphasize total abstinence often have high dropout rates. Programs for problem drinkers that emphasize moderation may be better able to hold on to these participants.

Preventive Approaches to Alcohol Abuse

Because alcoholism is a serious health problem, many researchers have felt that a prudent approach is to appeal to adolescents to avoid drinking altogether or to control their drinking before the problems of alcohol abuse set in. Social influence programs mounted through junior high schools are typically designed to teach the young adolescents drink-refusal techniques and coping methods for dealing with high-risk situations, so that they will not end up in situations in which drinking is difficult to avoid.

Research suggests some success with these programs, which appears to be due to several factors. First, such programs enhance adolescents' self-efficacy, which, in turn, may enable them to resist the passive social pressure that comes from seeing peers drink (Donaldson, Graham, Piccinin, & Hansen, 1995). In addition, these programs can change social norms that typically foster adolescents' motivations to begin using alcohol, replacing them with norms stressing abstinence or controlled alcohol consumption (Donaldson, Graham, & Hansen, 1994). Third, social influence programs can be low-cost successful treatment programs for low-income areas, which have traditionally been the most difficult to reach.

In addition to interventions with children and adolescents, social engineering solutions hold promise for managing alcohol. These include increasing taxes on alcohol, restricting alcohol advertising and promotion that especially targets young people, cracking down on misleading health claims for alcohol, and strengthening the federal government's focus on alcohol as a major youth problem. As long as alcohol remains the substance of choice for abuse among young people, its prevention will be a high priority (Center for the Advancement of Health, 2001).

Drinking and Driving

Thousands of vehicular fatalities each year result from drunk driving. This aspect of alcohol consumption is probably the one that most mobilizes the general public against alcohol abuse. Programs such as MADD (Mothers Against Drunk Driving) have been founded and staffed by the parents and friends of those killed by drunk drivers. Increasingly, the political impact of these and related groups is being felt, as they pressure state and local governments for tougher alcohol control measures and stiffer penalties for convicted drunk drivers.

Moreover, hosts and hostesses are now pressured to assume responsibility for the alcohol consumption of their guests and for friends to intervene when they recognize that their friends are too drunk to drive. But this can be a difficult task to undertake. How do you know when to tell a friend that he or she is too drunk to drive and to intervene so that the drunk individual will not drive? Knowing the driver well, perceiving that he or she really needs help, feeling able to intervene, and having had conversations in the past that encouraged intervention all enhance the likelihood that an individual will intervene in a situation when a peer is drunk (Newcomb, Rabow, Monto, & Hernandez, 1991). However, the norms to control others' drinking, though growing stronger, still fly in the face of beliefs in individual liberty and personal responsibility. Consequently, many drunk drivers remain on the road.

When drunk drivers are arrested and brought to court, they are typically referred to drinking programs not unlike those we have just discussed. How successful are these referral programs? A review (F. L. McGuire, 1982) examining these programs suggested that light drinkers did well in most of them. Unfortunately, heavy drinkers typically did very poorly. As yet, it seems there is no good rehabilitation program for the heavy-drinking driver, other than getting him or her off the road through stiffer penalties.

With increased media attention on the problem of drunk driving, drinkers seem to be developing self-regulatory techniques to avoid driving while drunk. Such techniques involve limiting drinking to a prescribed number, arranging for a designated driver, getting a taxi, or delaying or avoiding driving after consuming alcohol (S. L. Brown, 1997). Thus, although prevention in the form of eliminating drinking altogether is unlikely to occur, the rising popularity of self-regulation to avoid drunk driving may help reduce this serious problem.

Is Modest Alcohol Consumption a Health Behavior?

Despite the fact that problem drinking and alcoholism remain major health risks and contribute to overall mortality, modest alcohol intake actually adds to a long life. Moderate alcohol intake (approximately one to two drinks a day) may reduce risk of coronary artery disease. The benefits for women may occur at even lower levels of alcohol intake (Center for the Advancement of Health, December 2003).

Moderate drinking is associated with reduced risk of a heart attack, lower blood pressure, lower risk of dying after a heart attack, decreased risk of heart failure, less thickening of the arteries with age, an increase in high-density lipoprotein (HDL) cholesterol (the so-called "good" cholesterol), and fewer strokes among the elderly (Britton & Marmot, 2004; Center for the Advancement of Health, December 2003). These benefits may be especially true for older adults and senior citizens. (Moderate drinking in younger populations may actually enhance risk of death, probably through alcohol-related injuries [Center for the Advancement of Health December, 2003].)

Debate has centered on whether a particular type of alcohol consumption shows more benefits than others. Some researchers have suggested that red wine is healthier because of pigments called polyphenols that may inhibit hardening of the arteries (*New York Times*, 2001), but other studies have suggested that white wine may have more benefits (Center for the Advancement of Health, December 2003). The available evidence suggests that modest consumption of any alcoholic consumption may produce beneficial effects, with the benefits of wine being only slightly greater (Ambler, Royston, & Head, 2003). Although many health care practitioners fall short of recommending that people have a drink or two each day, the evidence is mounting that not only may this level of modest drinking not harm health but it may actually reduce one's risk for some major causes of death.

Postscript

Despite the fact that moderate drinking is now being recognized as a potential health behavior, the benefits appear to occur at fairly low levels. For example, women who drink an average of half a drink a day reduce their risk for high blood pressure but those who have more than one and a half drinks a day can actually raise it as much as 20% (Center for the Advancement of Health, December 2003). The World Health Organization has warned that the message that moderate drinking promotes health may encourage people to continue or increase alcohol consumption to dangerous levels. Overall, the number of deaths attributable to alcohol consumption continues to increase worldwide (Pearson, 2004).

■ SMOKING

Smoking is the single greatest cause of preventable death. By itself and in interaction with other risk factors, it may also be the chief cause of death in developed countries (McGinnis et al., 1992). In the United States, smoking accounts for at least 430,700 deaths each year—approximately 1 in every 5, with the largest portion of these deaths cardiovascular related (American Heart Association, 2001b). Smoking also accounts for at least 30% of all cancer deaths (American Cancer Society, 2001b) (see table 5.4).

In addition to the risks for heart disease and lung cancer, smoking increases the risk for chronic bronchitis, emphysema, respiratory disorders, damage and injuries due to fires and accidents, lower birth weight in offspring, and retarded fetal development (Center for the Advancement of Health, 2000i).

Cigarette smokers also appear to be generally less health conscious and are more likely to engage in other unhealthy behaviors than are nonsmokers (F. G. Castro, Newcomb, McCreary, & Baezconde-Garbanati, 1989). In particular, smoking and drinking often go together, and drinking seems to cue smoking and to make it more difficult to give up smoking (Shiffman, Fischer, et al., 1994). Smokers also have more accidents and injuries at work, take off more sick time, and use more health benefits than nonsmokers, thereby representing substantial costs to employers (Ryan, Zwerling, & Orav, 1992). Smoking appears to serve as an entry-level drug in childhood and adolescence for subsequent substance use and abuse. Trying cigarettes makes one significantly more likely to use other drugs in the future (Fleming, Leventhal, Glynn, & Ershler, 1989; see also Hanson, Henggeler, & Burghen, 1987).

The dangers of smoking are not confined to the smoker. Studies of secondhand smoke reveal that spouses, family members of smokers, and coworkers are at risk for a variety of health disorders (E. Marshall, 1986). Parental cigarette smoking may lower cognitive performance in adolescents by reducing blood oxygen

TABLE 5.4 | U.S. Cigarette Smoking-Related Mortality

Disease	Deaths
Lung cancer	116,920
Heart disease	134,235
Chronic lung disease	84,475
Other cancers	31,402
Strokes	23,281
Other diagnoses	145,297

Source: Centers for Disease Control, 2001.

capacity and increasing carbon monoxide levels (Bauman, Koch, & Fisher, 1989).

Synergistic Effects of Smoking

Smoking has a synergistic effect on other health-related risk factors; that is, it enhances the detrimental effects of other risk factors in compromising health. For example, smoking and cholesterol interact to produce higher rates of morbidity and mortality due to heart disease than would be expected from simply adding together the risk of smoking and high cholesterol (Perkins, 1985). Because nicotine stimulates the release of free fatty acids, it may increase the synthesis of triglycerides, which in turn decreases HDL production. Reducing smoking and modifying diet for people with both risk factors, then, is a high priority for intervention.

Stress and smoking can also interact in dangerous ways. For men, nicotine can increase the magnitude of heart rate reactivity to stress. For women, smoking can reduce heart rate but increase blood pressure responses, also an adverse reactivity pattern (Girdler, Jamner, Jarvik, Soles, & Shapiro, 1997). The stimulating effects of nicotine on the cardiovascular system may put smokers at risk for a sudden cardiac crisis, and the long-term effects on reactivity in response to stress may aggravate coronary heart disease risk factors.

Weight and smoking can interact to increase mortality. Specifically, thin cigarette smokers may be at increased risk of mortality, compared with average-weight smokers (Sidney, Friedman, and Siegelaub, 1987). Thinness is not associated with increased mortality in those people who had never smoked or among former smokers. The reasons for this relationship are unclear.

Smoking also appears to interact with exercise. Smokers engage in less physical activity as long as they

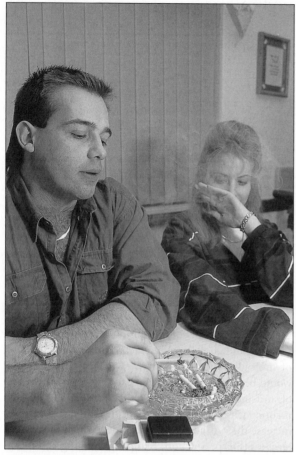

The risks of smoking are not confined to the smoker. Coworkers, spouses, and other family members of smokers are at continued risk for many smoking-related disorders.

continue smoking, but when they quit, their activity level increases (Perkins et al., 1993). Because physical exercise is so important to a variety of health outcomes, the fact that smoking reduces its likelihood represents a further indirect contribution of smoking to ill health.

Smoking is related to a fourfold increase in women's risk of developing breast cancer after menopause. Women who smoke and who carry genes that interfere with their ability to break down certain chemicals in cigarette smoke carry more of those chemicals in their bloodstream, which may set off the growth of tumors (Ambrosone et al., 1996).

Cigarette smoking interacts synergistically with depression such that a depressed person who smokes is at substantially greater risk for cancer. Immune alterations associated with major depression interact with smoking to elevate white blood cell count and to produce a de-

cline in natural killer cell activity. Natural killer cells are thought to serve a surveillance function in detecting and responding to early cancers (Jung & Irwin, 1999). The fact that smoking is now considered to be a potential cause of depression, especially in young people (Goodman & Capitman, 2000), makes the concern about the synergistic impact of smoking and depression on health even more alarming.

Smoking is also related to an increase in anxiety in adolescence; whether smoking and anxiety have a synergistic effect on health disorders is not yet known, but the chances of panic attacks and other anxiety disorders are greatly increased (J. G. Johnson et al., 2000). Whether smoking interacts synergistically with other risk factors, such as obesity, oral contraceptive use, or alcohol consumption, is still under investigation (M. C. Davis, 1999).

The synergistic health risks of smoking are extremely important and may be responsible for a substantial percentage of smoking-related deaths; however, research suggests that the public is largely unaware of the synergistic adverse effects of smoking in conjunction with other risk factors (Hermand, Mullet, & Lavieville, 1997). Nonetheless, the direct effects of smoking on poor health are well established, and its synergistic effects are increasingly being uncovered. Moreover, stopping smoking clearly has beneficial health effects. The risks for CHD and lung cancer are substantially lowered by stopping smoking, which makes smoking the most important health-compromising behavior in existence.

A Brief History of the Smoking Problem

For years, smoking was considered to be a sophisticated and manly habit. Characterizations of 19th- and 20th-century gentry, for example, often depicted men retiring to the drawing room after dinner for cigars and brandy. Cigarette advertisements of the early 20th century built on this image, and by 1955, 53% of the adult male population in the United States was smoking. Women did not begin to smoke in large numbers until the 1940s, but once they did, advertisers began to bill cigarette smoking as a symbol of feminine sophistication as well (Pampel, 2001).

In 1964, the first surgeon general's report on smoking came out (U.S. Department of Health, Education, and Welfare and U.S. Public Health Service, 1964), accompanied by an extensive publicity campaign to highlight the dangers of smoking. Although male smoking subsequently declined (to 39% by 1975), women's

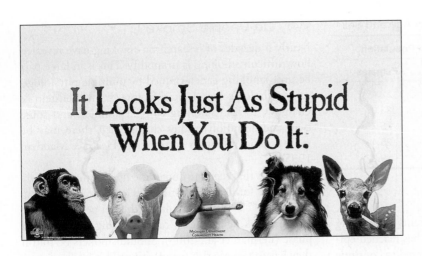

Smoking has been represented by the tobacco industry as a glamorous habit, and one task of interventions has been to change attitudes about smoking.

smoking actually increased during the same period, from 25% in 1955 to 29% by 1979. More frightening still, by 1994 the percentage of female teenage smokers had increased to 22.9% and male teenage smokers to 28.8% (National Center for Health Statistics, 1996). The advantage in life expectancy that women usually enjoy compared with men is shrinking noticeably, and a large part of this decline in women's longevity advantage is due to smoking (Koretz, 2003a). Despite dawning awareness of the threat of smoking, then, smoking continues to be a formidable problem.

The good news is that, in the United States, the number of adults who smoke has fallen substantially, more than 25% since 1979 (see figure 5.1). Nonetheless, smoking continues to be a major health problem (McGinnis et al., 1992). Critics have argued that the to-

bacco industry has disproportionately targeted minority group members and teens for smoking, and indeed, the rates among certain low-SES minority groups, such as Hispanic men, are especially high (for example, Navarro, 1996). These differences may be due in part to differences in cultural attitudes regarding smoking (Johnsen, Spring, Pingitore, Sommerfeld, & MacKirnan, 2002). In 1991, 18.5% of teenagers smoked regularly but by 1997 that figure was 24.6%; happily, as of 2002, it has once again declined to 16.8% (Levin, 2003). Table 5.5 presents current figures on the prevalence of smoking, and figure 5.2 shows the relation of smoking prevalence to smoking-related historical events.

As pressures to reduce smoking among children and adolescents have mounted, tobacco companies have increasingly turned their marketing efforts overseas. In

FIGURE 5.1 | U.S. per Capita Cigarette Consumption   (*Source:* U.S. Department of Economic Research Service, 2002)

TABLE 5.5 | Smoking Prevalence by Age and Sex

	Percentage of Population	
Age	Males	Females
18–24	30.4%	23.4%
25–34	27.2	23.0
35–44	27.4	25.7
45–64	26.4	25.4
65+	11.5	9.2

Source: National Center for Health Statistics, 2001.

developing countries, smoking represents a growing health problem. For example, smoking has reached epidemic proportions in China and is expected to continue to grow. For example, it is estimated that a third of all young Chinese men will die from the effects of tobacco, accounting for 3 million Chinese male deaths each year by the middle of this century (Reaney, 1998).

Why Do People Smoke?

Nearly 3 decades of research on smoking have revealed how difficult smoking is to modify. This is in large part because smoking is determined by multiple physiological, psychological, and social factors (E. Lichtenstein & Glasgow, 1992). Smoking runs in families, and some twin and adoption studies suggest that there may be some genetic influences on smoking (Heath & Madden, 1995).

Genes that regulate dopamine functioning are likely candidates for heritable influences on cigarette smoking (Sabol et al., 1999), particularly whether people are able to stop smoking and resist relapse during the treatment phase (Lerman et al., 2003). Should smokers be told if they have a genetic risk for smoking? This feedback may heighten a sense of vulnerability and promote distress, and it does not appear to enhance quitting in most smokers. Consequently, the value of providing such information is questionable (Lerman et al., 1997).

FIGURE 5.2 | Adult per Capita Cigarette Consumption (Thousands per Year) and Major Smoking and Health Events, United States, 1900 to 2000   (*Source:* U.S. Department of Agriculture, 2000; cited in Novotny, Romano, Davis, & Mills, 1992)

Factors Associated with Smoking in Adolescents   Smoking begins early. The Centers for Disease Control (1989) indicate that more than 15% of the adolescent population between the ages of 12 and 18 already smoke cigarettes regularly and consider themselves to be smokers; if anything, these statistics probably underestimate the adolescent smoking rate. However, smoking does not start all at once. There is a period of initial experimentation, during which an individual tries out cigarettes, experiences peer pressure to smoke, and develops attitudes about what a smoker is like. Following experimentation, only some adolescents go on to become heavy smokers (Pierce, Choi, Gilpin, Farkas, & Merritt, 1996). Moreover, during adolescence, beliefs about the harm of smoking and concern with health may decrease, contributing to receptivity to smoking (Chassin, Presson, Rose, & Sherman, 2001). A further understanding of these dynamics may help address the problem of adolescent smoking (see figure 5.3). Box 5.5

raises the intriguing question of whether beginning smoking represents a true choice in adolescence.

Peer and Family Influences   Peer influence is one of the most important factors in beginning smoking in adolescence. Starting to smoke results from a social contagion process, whereby nonsmokers have contact with others who are trying out smoking or with regular smokers and then try smoking themselves (Presti, Ary, & Lichtenstein, 1992). More than 70% of all cigarettes smoked by adolescents are smoked in the presence of a peer (Biglan, McConnell, Severson, Bavry, & Ary, 1984). As noted, smoking at an early age is generally part of a syndrome of problem behavior in the presence of peers that includes problem drinking, illicit drug use, delinquent behavior, and precocious sexual activity in addition to smoking (Donovan & Jessor, 1985).

Adolescents are also more likely to start smoking if their parents smoke; if they are lower class; if they feel social pressure to smoke; and if there has been a major stressor in the family, such as a family member's job loss (for example, Foshee & Bauman, 1992; Swaim, Oetting, & Casas, 1996; Unger, Hamilton, & Sussman, 2004). Adolescents are also at increased risk to start smoking if their parents separate; these effects are partly due to the increase in stress and depression that may result from separation (Kirby, 2002).

"Chippers" is a term used to describe usually light smokers. Researchers have been interested in what distinguishes them from people who go on to be addicted heavy smokers. Chippers appear to share several risk factors with heavy smokers, including tolerance for deviance, and attitudes and health beliefs that match those of smokers. But they also have more protective factors such as high value placed on academic success, supportive relationships at home, and little smoking among peers and parents. Somewhat surprisingly, the number of chippers has increased, even while smoking problems have declined. The reason why this trend is surprising is because smoking is such an addictive disorder. Low-rate smokers consume only a few (less than five) cigarettes a day and seem to do so without moving on to heavy smoking. In one study, people who gave up smoking fairly easily were those with peers who smoked less frequently, perceived less parental approval of their smoking, did not intend to continue their smoking, were less likely to use marijuana, and had a more stable environment including living in a nuclear family and attending fewer different schools. They also perceived themselves as having more peer support and rated themselves as

FIGURE 5.3 | Teenage Smoking Makes a Comeback

The number of 12th graders who have smoked a cigarette or who are regular smokers had declined until the early 1990s, when it abruptly increased.   (*Source:* Feder, 1997. Copyright © 1997 by The New York Times Company. Reprinted by permission)

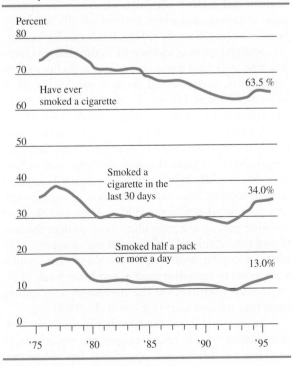

BOX 5.5

Is Smoking an Informed Choice?

Smoking is one of the most controversial health habits. The tobacco industry has argued that the decision to begin to smoke represents an informed choice; that people know what they are doing; and that, by deciding to smoke, they assume responsibility for this habit and its repercussions.

Psychologists have challenged this viewpoint (H. Leventhal, Glynn, & Fleming, 1987). The idea that people choose to smoke assumes that when they begin they have well-informed beliefs about smoking. However, 95% of regular smokers start to smoke during adolescence, and the question arises whether these young people have accurate information. Moreover, the fact that the tobacco industry systematically targets adolescents in their smoking advertising questions the degree of choice that these youngsters experience (Albright, Altman, Slater, & Maccoby, 1988). By playing on their vulnerabilities and needs, the tobacco industry may sway adolescents in the direction of smoking before they are fully able to weigh the evidence concerning this habit.

Moreover, adolescents are badly misinformed about smoking. A study of 895 urban adolescents assessed attitudes and beliefs about smoking and found that most were poorly informed about the prevalence and risks of this habit. They overestimated how many adults smoke and how many of their peers smoke, but they underestimated the extent to which other people hold negative attitudes toward smoking. A large proportion of these adolescents believed that they were less likely than other people to contract a smoking-related illness. They also showed a poor understanding of the unpleasant consequences people experience when they try to quit (H. Leventhal et al., 1987).

Perhaps most significantly, these misperceptions were most common among adolescents who had already begun to smoke, who had friends or family members who smoke, or who intended to begin smoking in the future. These points argue significantly against the tobacco industry's claim that smoking is an informed choice and, rather, suggest that an adolescent's decision to smoke may be based on considerable misinformation and poor assessments of personal risk.

---

healthier (Ellickson, Tucker, & Klein, 2001). Chippers may be informative regarding tobacco control efforts generally and for theories regarding addiction as well (Zhu, Sun, Hawkins, Pierce, & Cummins, 2003).

Self-image and Smoking The image of the smoker is a significant factor in beginning smoking. Early on, preadolescents develop the image of the smoker as a rebellious, tough, mature, iconoclastic individual (Dinh, Sarason, Peterson, & Onstad, 1995). Smoking comes to be regarded as a habit that conveys this image. Thus, youngsters suffering the insecurities of adolescence may find that cigarettes enable them to communicate the image they would like to convey (Aloise-Young, Hennigan, & Graham, 1996).

Consistent with this point, teenagers whose ideal self-image is close to that of a typical smoker are most likely to smoke (Barton, Chassin, Presson, & Sherman, 1982). Low self-esteem, dependency, powerlessness, and social isolation all increase the tendency to imitate others' behavior (Bandura, 1977; Ennett & Bauman, 1993); low-achieving students, female students, students with an external locus of control, and students with a low sense of self-efficacy (J. H. Clark, MacPherson, &

Holmes, 1982) are more likely to smoke than are male students and students with high self-esteem, an internal locus of control, and a high sense of self-efficacy (Stacy, Sussman, Dent, Burton, & Flay, 1992) (see figure 5.4).

Smoking among adolescents is also tied to aggressive tendencies and depressive episodes. Feelings of being hassled, angry, or sad increase the likelihood of smoking (Whalen, Jammer, Henker, & Delfino, 2001). In studies that examine smoking over time for adolescents, feelings of stress and psychological distress were clearly tied to the increase in smoking (Wills, Sandy, & Yaeger, 2002). Schools that look the other way or have poor levels of discipline may inadvertently facilitate a student moving from experimentation to regular cigarette use (Novak & Clayton, 2001). As the prevalence of smoking goes up at a particular school, so does the likelihood that additional students will start smoking. Maladaptive coping styles, especially those that involve withdrawal or repressive coping, and lower levels of exercise may contribute to the depression seen among some teen tobacco users (Vickers et al., 2003).

At one time it was thought that the primary window during which young people are vulnerable to smoking was adolescence, specifically late elementary

FIGURE 5.4 | Percentage of High School Students Who Smoke (*Source:* Centers for Disease Control, May 17, 2002)

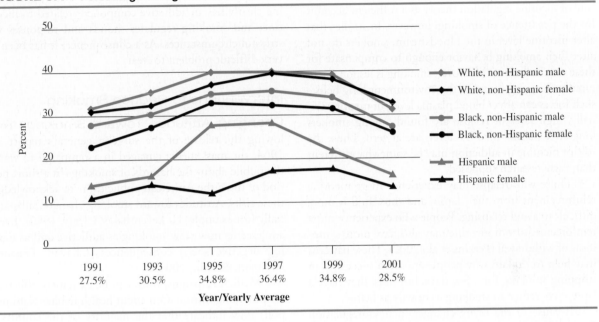

school/junior high school. Now, however, it appears that there is a new window of opportunity when students make the transition to college. Smoking rates among college students have increased substantially over the past few years, and so far little is known about the factors that predict this disturbing trend. As is true in adolescence, peer behavior may be one influential factor. Overall, little is known about the determinants of smoking among college students, although it appears to be more common among those who doubt the health significance of smoking and those who expect smoking will help control their mood (Wetter et al., 2004). Exposure to peers that smoke may have an effect as well (Ellickson, Bird, Orlando, Klein, & McCaffrey, 2003). Clearly increased efforts need to be undertaken to include college students in smoking prevention and cessation programs (Choi, Harris, Okuyemi, & Ahluwalia, 2003).

The Nature of Addiction in Smoking

Smoking is clearly an addiction, reported to be harder to stop than heroin addiction or alcoholism by many who suffer from multiple addictions. Only chippers are able to smoke casually without showing signs of addiction (for example, Shiffman, Kassel, Paty, Gnys, & Zettler-Segal, 1994). Despite the fact that nicotine is known to be a powerfully addictive drug, the exact mechanisms underlying nicotine addiction are unknown (Grunberg & Acri, 1991).

Nicotine Addiction

Theories that stress the role of nicotine addiction and the persistence of smoking argue that people smoke to maintain blood levels of nicotine and to prevent the withdrawal symptoms that occur when a person stops smoking. In essence, smoking regulates the level of nicotine in the body, and when plasma levels of nicotine depart from the ideal levels, smoking occurs.

Nicotine alters levels of active neuroregulators, including acetylcholine, norepinephrine, dopamine, endogenous opioids, and vasopressin. Nicotine may be used by smokers to engage these neuroregulators because they produce temporary improvements in performance or affect. Specifically, acetylcholine, norepinephrine, and vasopressin appear to enhance memory; acetylcholine and beta endorphins can reduce anxiety and tension. Alterations in dopamine, norepinephrine, and opioids improve mood, and people find that their performance of basic tasks is often improved when levels of acetylcholine and norepinephrine are high. Consequently, smoking among habitual smokers increases concentration, recall, alertness, arousal, psychomotor performance, and the ability to screen out irrelevant stimuli.

Consistent with this point, habitual smokers who stop smoking report that their concentration is reduced; their attention becomes unfocused; they show memory impairments; and they experience increases in anxiety, tension, irritability, craving, and moodiness.

A number of factors argue against the addictive nature of nicotine regulation theory as a sufficient account for the persistence of smoking, however. In studies that alter nicotine level in the bloodstream, smokers do not alter their smoking behavior enough to compensate for these manipulations. Moreover, smoking is responsive to rapidly changing forces in the environment long before such forces can affect blood plasma levels of nicotine. Finally, high rates of relapse are found among smokers long after plasma nicotine levels are at zero. Thus, the role of nicotine in addiction may be somewhat different than early research supposed.

Those who relapse may experience more nicotine reinforcement from their lapses and thus, find it more difficult to avoid relapsing. People who experience more reinforcement from nicotine may also have more symptoms of withdrawal (Perkins et al., 2002). These patterns may help to explain why people are often successful in stopping smoking for a few days, but once they have a lapse, may return to smoking as heavily as before.

Because of the many changes in neuroregulation that result from smoking, a large number of both internal bodily cues and external environmental cues that are ostensibly unrelated to the nicotine dependence cycle may come to serve as discriminative stimuli that induce smoking. Many former smokers return to smoking because they have learned that nicotine relieves these problems and can improve coping with the demands of daily living.

Social Learning   Smoking is also maintained by social learning and the pairing of smoking with rewarding experiences (for example, H. Leventhal & Cleary, 1980). How might this conditioning work? Let us adopt a hypothetical example of a novice smoker, an adolescent who is socially anxious. Initially, he may smoke to develop feelings of security and maturity. Smoking, then, reduces his social anxiety. Once he finishes a cigarette, however, the anxiety reappears and plasma nicotine levels begin to drop. Over time, anxiety will become conditioned to declines in nicotine level because of their continual pairing. The sensations produced by a decline in nicotine level will, in turn, become a craving for smoking, since smoking alters both nicotine level and social anxiety. As we will see, these insights need to be incorporated into treatment programs.

In summary, people smoke for a number of reasons (E. Lichtenstein & Glasgow, 1992). Genetic influences may contribute to smoking; smoking typically begins in early adolescence, when youngsters may have little idea

of the problems they face as a result of smoking; smoking clearly has an addictive component related to nicotine; and smoking regulates moods and responses to stressful circumstances. As a consequence, it has been a very difficult problem to treat.

Interventions to Reduce Smoking

Changing Attitudes Toward Smoking   Following the release of the surgeon general's report in 1964, the mass media engaged in a campaign to warn the public about the hazards of smoking. In a short period of time, the American public came to acknowledge these risks. Attitudes toward smoking changed substantially (for example, H. Leventhal & Cleary, 1980). Even adolescents now view smoking as addictive and as having negative social consequences (Chassin, Presson, Sherman, & Kim, 2003).

Media campaigns, thus, can be extremely effective for providing information about health habits. National polls now indicate that the majority of the country's smokers know that smoking is a bad practice and want to stop (Flay, McFall, Burton, Cook, & Warnecke, 1993). Media campaigns against smoking have helped instill antismoking attitudes in the general population. These attitudes have also been very effective in discouraging adults from beginning to smoke as well as persuading them to remain nonsmokers (Warner & Murt, 1982). In essence, then, antismoking messages in the media set the stage for efforts to quit smoking.

The Therapeutic Approach to the Smoking Problem   Attitude-change campaigns alone do not help smokers stop smoking, so psychologists have increasingly adopted a therapeutic approach to the smoking problem.

Nicotine Replacement Therapy   Many therapies begin with some form of nicotine replacement. Nicotine gum was originally used to help motivated smokers with quitting. However, smokers do not like chewing nicotine gum, in part because nicotine is absorbed rather slowly through this method. More recently, therapeutic efforts have made use of transdermal nicotine patches, which are worn by individuals motivated to stop smoking. These patches release nicotine in steady doses into the bloodstream. Transdermal nicotine patches have certain advantages over nicotine gum, including the fact that compliance is significantly better (E. Lichtenstein & Glasgow, 1992). Evaluations show that nicotine replacement therapy produces significant smoking cessation (Cepeda-Benito, 1993; J. R. Hughes, 1993).

Multimodal Intervention   Treatments for smoking generally adopt a multimodal approach. This focus incorporates a variety of specific interventions geared to the stage of readiness that an individual experiences with respect to his or her smoking. In addition, as is true in all multimodal interventions, the goal of these interventions is to engage the smoker's sense of self-control and to enlist active participation in the intervention process (Farkas et al., 1996; K. D. Ward, Klesges, & Halpern, 1997).

Many smoking intervention programs have used the stage model of change as a basis for intervening. Interventions to move people from the precontemplation to the contemplation stage center on attitudes: emphasizing the adverse health consequences of smoking and the negative social attitudes that most people hold about smoking. Motivating a readiness to quit may, in turn, increase a sense of self-efficacy that one will be able to do so, contributing further to readiness to quit (Warnecke et al., 2001). Moving people from contemplation to action requires that the smoker develop a timetable for quitting, a program for how to quit, and an awareness of the difficulties associated with quitting. Moving people to the action phase would employ many of the cognitive-behavioral techniques that have been used in the modification of other health habits.

As this account suggests, smoking would seem to be a good example of how the stage model might be applied. However, interventions matched to the stage of smoking are inconsistent in their effects and do not, at present, provide strong support for a stage approach to helping people stop smoking (Perz, DiClemente, & Carbonari, 1996; Quinlan & McCaul, 2000; Stotts, DiClemente, Carbonari, & Mullen, 2000; Velicer, Prohaska, Fava, Laforge, & Rossi, 1999; Segan, Borland, & Greenwood, 2004).

Social Support and Stress Management   As is true for other health habit interventions, those who wish to quit are urged to enlist social support from their spouse, friends, and coworkers in their resolution to stop. Ex-smokers are more likely to be successful over the short term if they have a supportive partner and if they have nonsmoking supportive friends. Social support from a partner appears to be more helpful to men attempting to stop smoking than for women (Westmaas, Wild, & Ferrence, 2002). The presence of smokers in one's social network is a hindrance to maintenance

and a significant predictor of relapse (Mermelstein, Cohen, Lichtenstein, Baer, & Kamarck, 1986).

Because smoking seems to be relaxing for so many people, relaxation training has also been incorporated into some smoking cessation programs. Teaching former smokers to relax in situations in which they might have been tempted to smoke provides an alternative method for coping with stress or anxiety.

Lifestyle rebalancing, through changes in diet and exercise, may also help people cut down on smoking or maintain abstinence after quitting. Earlier, we noted how important the cool, sophisticated image of the smoker is in getting teenagers to start smoking in the first place. Image is also important in helping people stop. Specifically, research suggests that people who have a strong sense of themselves as nonsmokers may do better in treatment than those who have a strong sense of themselves as smokers (Gibbons & Eggleston, 1996; Shadel & Mermelstein, 1996).

Maintenance   To bridge the transition from action to maintenance, relapse prevention techniques are typically incorporated into smoking cessation programs (Schumaker & Grunberg, 1986). Relapse prevention is important because the ability to remain abstinent shows a steady month-by-month decline, such that, within 2 years after a smoking cessation program, even the best program does not exceed a 50% abstinence rate (H. Leventhal & Baker, 1986).

Like most addictive health habits, smoking shows an abstinence violation effect, whereby a single lapse reduces perceptions of self-efficacy, increases negative mood, and reduces beliefs that one will be successful in stopping smoking. Stress-triggered lapses appear to lead to relapse more quickly than other kinds (Shiffman et al., 1996). Consequently, smokers are urged to remind themselves that a single lapse is not necessarily worrisome, because many people lapse on the road to quitting. Sometimes buddy systems or telephone counseling procedures are made available to help quitters avoid turning a single lapse or temptation into a full-blown relapse (E. Lichtenstein, Glasgow, Lando, Ossip-Klein, & Boles, 1996).

Relapse Prevention   Relapse prevention techniques often begin by preparing people for the management of withdrawal, including cardiovascular changes, increases in appetite, variations in the urge to smoke, increases in coughing and discharge of phlegm, and the like. These problems may occur intermittently during the first 7 to

11 days. In addition, relapse prevention focuses on the long-term, high-risk situations that lead to a craving for cigarettes, such as drinking coffee or alcohol. As just noted, relapse prevention may especially need to focus on teaching people coping techniques for dealing with stressful interpersonal situations. In one study, people who were able to quit smoking had better coping skills for dealing with such situations than those who ended up relapsing (S. Cohen & Lichtenstein, 1990).

Some relapse prevention approaches have included contingency contracting, in which the smoker pays a sum of money that is returned only on condition of cutting down or abstaining. Buddy systems, follow-up booster sessions (for example, see Hunt & Matarazzo, 1973), and follow-up phone calls (McConnell, Biglan, & Severson, 1984) have also been used, but these methods have shown limited success as a maintenance technology (E. Lichtenstein, 1982; G. T. Wilson, 1985).

Factors that predict short-term maintenance and long-term maintenance differ. For example, Kamarck and Lichtenstein (1988) found that people trying to quit smoking were best able to do so in the short term if they had alternative methods of regulating their anxiety and stress. Social support and environmental support for quitting smoking are perhaps the strongest factors for both initial quitting and relapse prevention for both men and women (Nides et al., 1995). Self-efficacy is a strong predictor of success in smoking cessation; research has found that, when a sense of self-efficacy wanes, vulnerability to relapse is high, so interventions that address the dynamics of self-efficacy over time may well improve maintenance rates (Shiffman et al., 2000). Unhappily too, after they relapse, new smokers may increase their positive beliefs about smoking (Chassen, Pressen, Sherman, & Kim, 2002; Dijkstra & Borland, 2003). Over the long term, simply remaining vigilant about not smoking predicts abstinence best.

Evaluation of Multimodal Interventions   How successful have multimodal approaches to smoking been? Virtually every imaginable combination of therapies for getting people to stop has been tested. Typically, these programs show high initial success rates for quitting, followed by high rates of return to smoking, sometimes as high as 90%. Those who relapse are more likely to be young, have a high degree of nicotine dependence, a low sense of self-efficacy, greater concerns about gaining weight after stopping smoking, more previous quit attempts, and more slips (occasions when they used one or more cigarettes) (Ockene et al., 2000).

Although relapse prevention is clearly a vital aspect of successful programs for stopping smoking, no one approach to relapse or maintenance has so far been identified as especially effective in reducing the problem of returning to smoking (Baer & Marlatt, 1991; Center for the Advancement of Health, 2000i). Relapse is least likely when smoking interventions are intensive, when pharmacotherapy is used, and when telephone counseling is available. However, such interventions are expensive to implement and thus reach only some smokers (Ockene et al., 2000).

Brief interventions by physicians and other health care practitioners during regular office visits would help in controlling relapse, but at present advice about stopping smoking is only rarely given by health care practitioners (Ockene et al., 2000). Educating people about the risk of relapse and the fact that lapses do not signify failure or a breakdown in control can reduce the discouragement that many people feel when they resume smoking.

Although the rates of relapse suggest some pessimism with respect to smoking, it is important to consider the cumulative effects of smoking cessation programs, not just each program in isolation (Baer & Marlatt, 1991). Any given effort to stop smoking may yield only a 20% success rate, but with multiple efforts to quit, eventually the smoker may be successful in becoming an ex-smoker (E. Lichtenstein & Cohen, 1990).

In fact, hundreds of thousands of former smokers have successfully stopped, albeit, not necessarily the first time they tried. Factors that predict the ability to maintain abstinence include educational attainment, contemplating quitting smoking, being ready to quit at the beginning of an intervention, and having a sense of self-efficacy (Rosal et al., 1998). Formal smoking cessation programs may look less successful than they actually are because, over time, the individual may amass enough successful techniques and motivation to persist.

Who Is Best Able to Induce People to Stop Smoking?   Is any particular change agent more able to induce people to stop smoking? For example, is a person more likely to stop smoking if a psychotherapist or physician induces that person to do so?

People who seek psychotherapy to quit smoking do no better than those who seek other treatment programs. However, recommendations from physicians fare better (for example, E. Lichtenstein et al., 1996). For example, pregnant smokers who are told to stop by their physicians are more likely to do so than at other points in their lives (L. J. Solomon, Secker-Walker, Skelly, & Flynn, 1996). Patients with symptoms of CHD are more likely to stop when told by a physician that they must do so (Ockene, 1992). Physician recommendations are even more effective if they include an intervention or a referral to a quit-smoking program. Hospitalized patients may be especially able to stop smoking because they are not allowed to smoke while they are hospitalized, and the experience can get them over the first hurdle (R. E. Glasgow, Stevens, Vogt, Mullooly, & Lichtenstein, 1991). All of these circumstances represent teachable moments (see chapter 3). These teachable moments may also be times when family members will be especially motivated to provide support, and thus social support may add to the ability to stop smoking during these important times (Pollak et al., 2001).

Because physician recommendations appear to encourage people to stop smoking, brief interventions for physicians to use with their smoking patients have been attempted. Thus far, however, the results are not as promising as one might hope (G. C. Williams, Gagné, Ryan, & Deci, 2002). Moreover, managed care organizations have not yet developed tobacco use cessation guidelines that can be implemented easily during patient visits to induce people to stop (C. B. Taylor & Curry, 2004). This step alone could improve the quit rate, in that encouragement from a physician contributes to the motivation to stop smoking on one's own (G. C. Williams et al., 2002).

Work Site Initially, work-site interventions were thought to hold promise as successful smoking cessation efforts. In particular, the support provided by the employee peer group should increase the success of such programs. To date, however, interventions at the work site do not seem to be substantially more effective than other intervention programs (Hymowitz, Campbell, & Feuerman, 1991), nor does quitting smoking appear to be successfully sustained in work sites over time (Sorenson et al., 1998).

Commercial Programs and Self-help Commercial stop-smoking clinics, which make use of cognitive-behavioral techniques, enjoy fairly wide attendance. Although cure rates are often advertised to be high, these assessments may be based only on misleading statistics about the short-, but not long-, term effects. Continued evaluation of these popular programs is essential.

A variety of **self-help aids** and programs have been developed for smokers to quit on their own. These in-clude nicotine gum and nicotine patches, as well as more intensive self-help programs that provide specific instruction for quitting. Cable television programs designed to help people stop initially and maintain their resolution have been put in effect in some cities (R. F. Valois, Adams, & Kammermann, 1996). Although it is difficult to evaluate self-help programs formally, studies suggest that self-help programs' initial quit rates are lower, but long-term maintenance is just as high as more intensive behavioral interventions. Because self-help programs are less expensive, they represent an important attack on the smoking problem (Curry, 1993).

Public Health Approach Public health approaches to reducing smoking have included community interventions combining media blitzes with behavioral interventions directed especially at high-risk individuals, such as people who have other risk factors for CHD. As we noted earlier in the discussion of community-focused interventions, such interventions are often expensive, and long-term follow-ups suggest limited long-term effects.

Why Is Smoking So Hard to Change? As we have seen, smoking is a deeply entrenched behavior pattern. Although many people are able to stop initially, relapse rates are very high. Several problems contribute to the difficulty of modifying smoking. Initially, smokers are resistant to interventions because of their lack of knowledge and their health-compromising attitudes. Smokers are less informed and less concerned with the health consequences of smoking than are nonsmokers (for example, McCoy et al., 1992). Because tobacco addiction typically begins in adolescence, adolescents may use tobacco in ways and in social situations that make it particularly difficult to modify, because it comes to be associated with a broad array of pleasurable activities (Gibson, 1997). In addition, because smoking patterns are highly individualized (Chassin, Presson, Pitts, & Sherman, 2000), it is sometimes difficult for group interventions to address all the factors that may influence and maintain any particular smoker's smoking.

Addiction As already noted, dependence on nicotine is another factor that makes it difficult for many people to stop. Immediately after stopping smoking, people experience withdrawal, including decreases in heart rate and blood pressure, a decline in body temperature, and drops in epinephrine and norepinephrine blood levels. These changes are often aversive and lead the former smoker to resume smoking. More long-term difficulties, such as weight gain, distractibility, nausea, headaches, constipation, drowsiness, fatigue, difficulty sleeping, increases in anxiety, irritability, and hostility, are also reported by former smokers and may contribute to the high rate of relapse (Clavel, Benhamou, & Flamant, 1987).

Mood   The fact that smoking appears to be successful in controlling anxiety and reactions to stress is another factor that leads to high rates of relapse (Shadel & Mermelstein, 1993). Smoking is difficult to change because it elevates mood. There has been some effort to mimic the mood-elevation effects of smoking therapeutically, so as to remove this incentive to return to smoking. For example, seratonin-enhancing substances, such as tryptophan and high-carbohydrate diets, enhance mood and may have promise as aids in smoking cessation programs (Bowen, Spring, & Fox, 1991; Spring, Wurtman, Gleason, Wurtman, & Kessler, 1991).

Weight Control   Smoking keeps body weight down, and this factor both contributes to beginning smoking among adolescent girls and to the difficulty many adults have in stopping smoking (Jeffery et al., 2000; Nides et al., 1994).

One reason for the weight gain that so frequently follows smoking is that people change their food habits (S. A. French, Hennrikus, & Jeffery, 1996; Hatsukami, LaBounty, Hughes, & Laine, 1993). People who have quit smoking show a shift in preference for sweet-tasting carbohydrates with a higher caloric value. This shift may occur, in part, because carbohydrates improve mood. Also, nicotine leads to decreases in circulating insulin levels and increases in catecholamines, and a preference for sweets may develop to regulate these processes in the absence of nicotine (Grunberg, 1986).

Another reason that people gain weight after stopping smoking is that nicotine increases energy utilization (J. E. Audrain, Klesges, & Klesges, 1995; Hultquist et al., 1995), and these patterns may be difficult to compensate for once a person stops smoking. Stress-induced eating—namely, eating in response to stressful situations—may also explain part of the weight gain following smoking, inasmuch as a previously successful technique for coping with stress—smoking—has been abandoned (S. M. Hall, Ginsberg, & Jones, 1986).

There is no clear solution to avoiding weight gain after stopping smoking. The best method is to alert people to the potential problem after quitting and get them to develop dietary and exercise habits that will help them avoid putting on extra weight (Klesges, Meyers,

Klesges, & LaVasque, 1989; Perkins, Levine, Marcus, & Shiffman, 1997). However, the prospect of weight gain appears to act as a deterrent to stopping smoking (Jeffery, Boles, Strycker, & Glasgow, 1997).

Many smokers may be unaware of the benefits of remaining abstinent, such as better psychological well-being, higher energy, better sleep, and a higher self-esteem and sense of mastery (A. L. Stewart, King, Killen, & Ritter, 1995). These effects of successful abstinence should be better publicized, in that such knowledge might help the potential relapser maintain his or her resolve.

People Who Stop on Their Own   Despite the difficulties of stopping smoking, more than 45 million Americans have successfully quit smoking (American Cancer Society, 2001b). The impetus for stopping smoking on one's own typically comes from health concerns (for example, McBride et al., 2001).

People who successfully quit on their own have good self-control skills, self-confidence in their ability to stop, and a perception that the health benefits of stopping are substantial (for example, McBride et al., 2001). Stopping on one's own is easier if one has a supportive social network that does not smoke, and if one was a light rather than a heavy smoker (S. Cohen et al., 1989).

People who stop smoking on their own, however, have no magical solution to the smoking problem. They are typically no more successful in maintaining abstinence than are participants in stop-smoking programs, and most smokers who stop on their own eventually relapse (J. R. Hughes et al., 1992). After several efforts to stop, however, many quitters who stop on their own are successful. A list of guidelines for people who wish to stop on their own appears in table 5.6.

Smoking Prevention

Because smoking is so resistant to intervention and because, increasingly, we have come to understand how and why young people begin to smoke, the war on smoking has shifted from getting smokers to stop to keeping potential smokers from starting (Chassin, Presson, Rose, & Sherman, 1996). These **smoking prevention programs** are aimed to catch potential smokers early and attack the underlying motivations that lead people to smoke (Ary et al., 1990).

Advantages of Smoking Prevention Programs
The advantages of smoking prevention programs are several. They represent a potentially effective

TABLE 5.6 | Quitting Smoking

Here are some steps to help you prepare for your Quit Day:

- Pick the date and mark it on your calendar.
- Tell friends and family about your Quit Day.
- Stock up on oral substitutes—sugarless gum, carrot sticks, and/or hard candy.
- Decide on a plan. Will you use nicotine replacement therapy? Will you attend a class? If so, sign up now.
- Set up a support system. This could be a group class, Nicotine Anonymous, or a friend who has successfully quit and is willing to help you.

On your Quit Day, follow these suggestions:

- Do not smoke.
- Get rid of all cigarettes, lighters, ashtrays, an any other items related to smoking.
- Keep active—try walking, exercising, or doing other activities or hobbies.
- Drink lots of water and juices.
- Begin using nicotine replacement if that is your choice.
- Attend stop smoking class or follow a self-help plan.
- Avoid situations where the urge to smoke is strong.
- Reduce or avoid alcohol.
- Use the four "A's" (avoid, alter, alternatives, activities) to deal with tough situations (described in more detail later).

Source: American Cancer Society, 2001b.

and cost-effective assault on the smoking problem that avoids the many factors that make it so difficult for habitual smokers to stop. Smoking prevention programs can be easily implemented through the school system. Little class time is needed and no training of school personnel is required. How do researchers try to prevent smoking before it starts?

Social Influence Interventions   An early program to keep adolescents from smoking was developed by Richard Evans and his colleagues in the Houston School District (Evans, Dratt, Raines, & Rosenberg, 1988). Two theoretical principles were central in the design of Evans's **social influence intervention.** First, the fact that parental smoking and peer pressure promote smoking in adolescents indicates that children acquire smoking at least partly through the modeling of others. By observing models who are apparently enjoying a behavior they know to be risky, the children's fears of negative consequences are reduced and their expectation of positive consequences is enhanced. Thus, Evans reasoned, a successful intervention program with adolescents must include the potential for modeling high-status nonsmokers.

A second theoretical principle on which the social influence intervention is based is the concept of behavioral inoculation developed by W. J. McGuire (1964, 1973). **Behavioral inoculation** is similar in rationale to

inoculation against disease. If one can expose an individual to a weak dose of some germ, one may prevent infection because antibodies against that germ will develop. Likewise, if one can expose individuals to a weak version of a persuasive message, they may develop counterarguments against that message, so that they can successfully resist it if they encounter it in a stronger form.

The following are the three components of the social influence intervention program:

1. Information about the negative effects of smoking is carefully constructed so as to appeal to adolescents.

2. Materials are developed to convey a positive image of the nonsmoker (rather than the smoker) as an independent, self-reliant individual.

3. The peer group is used to facilitate not smoking rather than smoking.

Let us consider each component in turn.

Most adolescents know that smoking is a risky behavior. However, the fact that they continue to smoke suggests that they ignore much of what they know. Therefore, selection of appropriate antismoking materials for this group is critical. Typically, the adolescent's time frame does not include concern about health risks that are 20 to 30 years away. Therefore, antismoking materials must highlight the disadvantages of smoking now, including adverse effects on health, the financial costs of smoking, and negative social consequences of smoking (such as rejection by others), rather than long-term health risks.

The image of the nonsmoker is also addressed in the social influence materials. Specifically, films and posters are developed to appeal to adolescents' need for independence, conveying such messages as "You can decide for yourself" and "Here are the facts so you can make a decision." These messages also show how cigarette advertisers use subtle techniques to try to get people to smoke in the hopes that the students will resist cigarette advertising when they encounter it. Simultaneously, these messages also convey an image of the smoker as someone who is vulnerable to advertising gimmicks.

These interventions address the significance of the peer group in several ways. First, high-status, slightly older peer leaders are typically featured in the films and posters as the primary agents delivering the interventions. They demonstrate through role playing how to resist peer pressure and maintain the decision not to smoke. The films convey techniques that adolescents can use to combat pressure, such as stalling for time or using counterpressure (for example, telling the smoker that she is a fool for ruining her health). In some cases, these messages are reinforced by contact with a peer leader in a small-group interaction after exposure to the filmed material.

Evaluation of Social Influence Programs

Do these programs work? This question has been hard to answer for several reasons. Students may learn how to turn down cigarettes, but this may not lead them to do so (Elder, Sallis, Woodruff, & Wildey, 1993). Smoking prevention programs sometimes delay smoking but may not reduce overall rates when assessed several years later. Validating self-reports of smoking is difficult and often is only successfully accomplished through tests such as saliva thiocyanate and expired air carbon monoxide.

Despite these difficulties, programs such as that developed by Evans have enjoyed wide use and have now been evaluated. Overall, results suggest that social influence programs can reduce smoking rates for as long as 4 years (Murray, Davis-Hearn, Goldman, Pirie, & Luepker, 1988; see also Flay, 1985; Murray, Richards, Luepker, & Johnson, 1987). However, experimental smoking may be affected more than regular smoking; experimental smokers would probably stop on their own (Biglan et al., 1987; Flay et al., 1992). What is needed are programs that will reach the child destined to become a regular smoker, and as yet we know little about the factors that are most helpful in keeping these youngsters from starting to smoke.

The Life-Skills-Training Approach   Another effort to prevent smoking in the adolescent population is called the **life-skills-training approach** (G. J. Botvin et al., 1992). Interestingly enough, this approach to smoking prevention deals with cigarette smoking per se in only a small way. Rather, the rationale for the intervention is that, if adolescents are trained in self-esteem and coping enhancement as well as social skills, they will not feel as much need to smoke to bolster their self-image: The skills will enhance the adolescent's sense of being an efficacious person. The results of these programs to date appear to be as encouraging as the smoking prevention programs based on social influence processes. These programs also show some success in the reduction of smoking onset over time (G. J. Botvin et al., 1992).

Smoking prevention programs are relatively expensive and logistically difficult to implement, so researchers have looked for easier ways to bring about the same positive messages. An interactive CD-ROM program designed to reduce adolescent substance use was developed and made use of several of the same principles on which both the social influence and the life-skills-training programs are based. Directed primarily to marijuana use, students were presented with vignettes that illustrated refusal skills and socially acceptable responses to substance use situations that created temptations—specifically, offers of marijuana. In a randomized experiment with 74 public schools, significant changes were found on adolescents' abilities to refuse an offer of marijuana, their intentions to refuse it, and their perceptions of the social norms that surround it (T. E. Duncan, Duncan, Beauchamp, Wells, & Ary, 2000). These findings present promising prospects for the development of low-cost interventions that may promote substance abuse prevention.

Social Engineering and Smoking

> Since smoking might injure your health, let's be careful not to smoke too much.
> —Warning Label on Cigarette Packages in Japan
> (*Time*, June 25, 2001)

Ultimately, smoking may be more successfully modified by social engineering than by techniques of behavioral change (Heishman, Kozlowski, & Henningfield, 1997;

BOX 5.6

Can Nonsmokers Be Harmed by Secondhand Smoke?

Norma Broyne was a flight attendant with American Airlines for 21 years. She had never smoked a cigarette and yet, in 1989, she was diagnosed with lung cancer, and part of a lung had to be removed. Broyne became the center of a class-action suit brought against the tobacco industry, seeking $5 billion on behalf of 60,000 current and former nonsmoking flight attendants for the adverse health effects of the smoke they inhaled while performing their job responsibilities prior to 1990, when smoking was legal on most flights (G. Collins, 1997).

Until recently, scientists and lawmakers had assumed that smokers hurt only themselves. However, increasing evidence suggests that people exposed to smokers' smoke are also harmed. This so-called **passive smoking,** or **secondhand smoke,** which involves inhaling smoke and smoky air produced by smokers, has been tied to higher levels of carbon monoxide in the blood, reduced pulmonary functioning, and higher rates of lung cancer. Secondhand smoke is the third leading cause of preventable death in the United States, killing up to 65,000 nonsmokers every year (see table 5.7). It is estimated to cause about 3,000 cases of lung cancer annually, as many as 40,000 heart disease deaths, and exacerbation of asthma in 1 million children (American Cancer Society, 2004a). About 60% of deaths from sudden infant death syndrome may be attributed to exposure to parental tobacco smoke before or after birth (Centers for Disease Control, 2004). In addition, babies with prenatal exposure to secondhand smoke have a 7% reduction in birth weight (Environmental Health Perspectives, 2004).

In a dramatic confirmation of the problems associated with workplace smoking, the state of Montana imposed a ban on public and workplace smoking in June 2002 and then overturned it 6 months later. Two physicians charted the number of heart attacks that occurred before the ban, during it, and afterward. They reported that heart attack admissions dropped 40% when the workplace ban on smoking was in place, but immediately bounced back when smoking resumed. Because secondhand smoke causes heart rates to rise, blood vessels to dilate less easily, and blood components to be more sticky, secondhand smoke raises the risk of heart attacks. What is remarkable about the Montana study is its demonstration of its immediate impact on a major

TABLE 5.7 | The Toll of Secondhand Smoke

Disease	Annual U.S. Deaths or Cases
Lung cancer	3,000 deaths
Heart disease	35,000–40,000 deaths
Sudden infant death syndrome	60% of deaths from SIDS may be attributed to parental smoking before or after birth
Low-birth-weight babies	Babies with parental exposure to secondhand smoke had a 7% reduction in birth weight
Asthma in children	Increases in the number and severity of asthma attacks in about 200,000 to 1 million asthmatic children
Bronchitis in children	150,000–300,000 lower respiratory infections

Sources: American Cancer Society, 2004a; Centers for Disease Control, 2004; Environmental Health Perspectives, 2004.

health outcome—heart attacks—in such a short period of time (Glantz, 2004).

Two groups that may be at particular risk are the children and spouses of smokers. A study of 32,000 nonsmoking women conducted by Harvard University researchers (G. Collins, 1997) found that exposure to secondhand cigarette smoke almost doubled their risk of heart disease. A study conducted in Japan (Hirayama, 1981) followed 540 nonsmoking wives of smoking or nonsmoking husbands for 14 years and examined mortality due to lung cancer. The wives of heavy smokers had a higher rate of lung cancer than did the wives of husbands who smoked little or not at all. Moreover, these women's risk of dying from lung cancer was between one third and one half of what they would have faced had they been smokers themselves. Young children of smokers are more vulnerable to ear infections, asthma, bronchitis, and pneumonia than those not exposed to secondhand smoke (K. M. Emmons et al., 2001). Even dogs whose owners smoke are at 50% greater risk of developing lung cancer than are dogs whose owners are nonsmokers (Reif, Dunn, Ogilvie, & Harris, 1992).

The importance of passive smoking has led to interventions designed to reduce its effects. For example, one program attempted to reduce infant passive smoking by intervening with families during the first 6 months of life (R. A. Greenberg et al., 1994). The program, which

BOX 5.6

Can Nonsmokers Be Harmed by Secondhand Smoke? (continued)

targets smoking family members to smoke in places away from the infant, was successful in reducing infant vulnerability to respiratory infection.

Another intervention put nicotine monitors into homes of smokers to show parents exactly the effects smoking has on the air around them. Parents were informed that the monitors in their homes showed nicotine levels comparable to the ones of the bar down the street. In response to this feedback, many of the smokers reported that they would shift their smoking to outside their home or at least away from their children's rooms (Matt et al., 2004). Even with these measures, however, secondhand smoke poses a risk (Emmons et al., 2001).

The fact that passive smoking can be harmful to health adds teeth to the idea that nonsmokers have rights vis-à-vis smokers. Increasingly, we are likely to see the effects of passive smoking used as a basis for legislative action against smoking. Norma Broyne finally saw her day in court. The tobacco companies that she and other flight attendants sued agreed to pay $300 million to set up a research foundation on cancer.

R. M. Kaplan, Orleans, Perkins, & Pierce, 1995). Although it is unlikely that cigarettes will be outlawed altogether, a number of social engineering alternatives may force people to reduce their smoking. Liability litigation is generally considered to be one of the most potentially effective means for the long-term control of the sale and use of tobacco (Kelder & Daynard, 1997). Transferring the costs of smoking to the tobacco industry via lawsuits would raise the price of cigarettes, lowering consumption. Second, access to tobacco may come to be regulated as a drug by the Food and Drug Administration (R. M. Kaplan et al., 1995).

Heavy taxation is a third possibility. Most smokers report that they would reduce their smoking if it became prohibitively expensive (Walsh & Gordon, 1986). Such actions are most likely to influence smoking among teenagers and young adults with little disposable income. A total ban on tobacco advertising is not out of the question, and at the very least, where and how companies may advertise will come under increasing regulation (R. M. Kaplan et al., 1995). Ongoing negotiations with the tobacco industry have centered heavily on the elimination of advertising that appeals to teens, which may reduce the number of young smokers (E. M. Botvin, Botvin, Michela, Baker, & Filazzola, 1991).

Smoking can be controlled by restricting it to particular places (P. B. Jacobson, Wasserman, & Anderson, 1997). The rationale for such interventions is the known harm that can be done to nonsmokers by secondhand smoke (box 5.6). Thus, not permitting smoking in public buildings, requiring nonsmoking sections in restaurants and other public places, and otherwise protecting the rights of nonsmokers have been increasingly utilized legislative options.

Some business organizations have developed smoking cessation programs for their employees, others restrict on-the-job smoking to particular times or places, and still others have banned smoking. No doubt, social engineering interventions to restrict smoking will increase in the coming years.

SUMMARY

1. Health-compromising behaviors are those that threaten or undermine good health, either in the present or in the future. Many of these behaviors cluster and first emerge in adolescence.

2. Alcoholism accounts for thousands of deaths each year through cirrhosis, cancer, fetal alcohol syndrome, and accidents connected with drunk driving.

3. Alcoholism and problem drinking encompass a wide range of specific behavior problems with associated physiological and psychological needs.

4. Alcoholism has a genetic component and is tied to sociodemographic factors, such as low SES. Drinking also arises in an effort to buffer the impact of stress and appears to peak between ages 18 and 25.

5. Most treatment programs for alcoholism use broad-spectrum cognitive-behavioral approaches. Many begin with an inpatient "drying-out" period, followed by the use of cognitive-behavioral change methods, such as aversion therapy and relapse prevention techniques.

6. The best predictor of success is the patient. Alcoholics with mild drinking problems, little abuse of other drugs, and a supportive, financially secure environment do better than those without such supports.

7. Smoking accounts for more than 300,000 deaths annually in the United States due to heart disease, cancer, and lung disorders. Smoking adds to and may even exacerbate other risk factors associated with CHD.

8. Several theories have attempted to explain the addictive nature of smoking, including theories of nicotine regulation and those that emphasize nicotine's role as a neuroregulator.

9. In the past few decades, attitudes toward smoking have changed dramatically for the negative, largely due to the mass media. Attitude change has kept some people from beginning smoking, motivated many to try to stop, and kept some former smokers from relapsing.

10. Many programs for stopping smoking begin with some form of nicotine replacement, such as nicotine gum or transdermal nicotine patches. Operant conditioning techniques disembed smoking from the environmental cues with which it is usually associated. Many multimodal programs include social skills training programs or relaxation therapies. Relapse prevention is an important component of these programs.

11. No particular venue for changing smoking behavior appears to be especially effective. However, physicians working directly with patients at risk may achieve greater success than do other change agents.

12. Smoking is highly resistant to change. Even after successfully stopping for a short period of time, most people relapse. Factors that contribute to relapse include addiction, the loss of an effective coping technique for dealing with social situations, and weight gain, among other factors.

13. Smoking prevention programs have been developed to keep youngsters from beginning to smoke. Many of these programs use a social influence approach and teach youngsters how to resist peer pressure to smoke. Others help adolescents improve their coping skills and self-image.

14. Social engineering approaches to control smoking have also been employed, the rationale being that secondhand smoke harms others in the smoker's environment.

KEY TERMS

addiction
alcoholism
behavioral inoculation
craving
detoxification
life-skills-training approach

passive smoking
physical dependence
placebo drinking
problem drinking
secondhand smoke

self-help aids
smoking prevention programs
social influence intervention
tolerance
withdrawal

Stress and Coping

CHAPTER

6

Stress

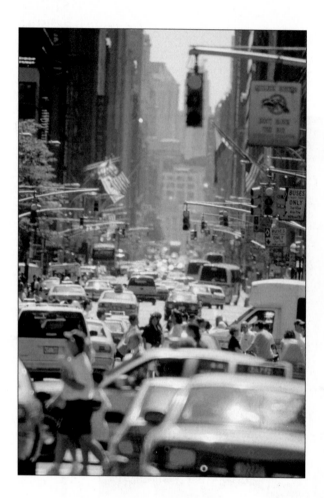

The night before her biology final, Lisa confidently set her alarm and went to sleep. A power outage occurred during the night, and her alarm, along with most of the others in the dorm, failed to go off. At 8:45, Lisa was abruptly awakened by a friend banging on the door to tell her that her final started in 15 minutes. Lisa threw on some clothes, grabbed a muffin and a cup of coffee from the machines in her dorm, and raced to the exam room. Ten minutes late, she spent the first half hour frantically searching through the multiple-choice questions, trying to find ones she knew the answers to, as her heart continued to race.

■ WHAT IS STRESS?

Most of us have more firsthand experience with stress than we care to remember. Stress is being stopped by a police officer after accidentally running a red light. It is waiting to take a test when we are not sure that we have prepared well enough or studied the right material. It is missing a bus on a rainy day full of important appointments.

Psychologists have been studying stress and its impact on psychological and physical health for several decades. **Stress** is a negative emotional experience accompanied by predictable biochemical, physiological, cognitive, and behavioral changes that are directed either toward altering the stressful event or accommodating to its effects (see A. Baum, 1990).

What Is a Stressor?

Initially, researchers focused on stressful events themselves, called **stressors.** Such events include noise, crowding, a bad relationship, a round of job interviews, or the commute to work. The study of stressors has helped define some conditions that are more likely to produce stress than others, but a focus on stressful events cannot fully explain the experience of stress. A stressful experience may be stressful to some people but not to others. If the "noise" is your radio playing the latest rock music, then it will probably not be stressful to you, although it may be to your neighbor. Whereas one person might find the loss of a job highly stressful, another might see it as an opportunity to try a new field, as a challenge rather than a threat. How a potential stressor is perceived determines whether it will be experienced as stressful.

Person-Environment Fit

Stress is the consequence of a person's appraisal processes: the assessment of whether personal resources are sufficient to meet the demands of the environment. Stress, then, is determined by **person-environment fit** (R. S. Lazarus & Folkman, 1984b; R. S. Lazarus & Launier, 1978; Pervin, 1968).

When a person's resources are more than adequate to deal with a difficult situation, he or she may feel little stress and experience a sense of challenge instead. When the individual perceives that his or her resources will probably be sufficient to deal with the event but only at the cost of great effort, he or she may feel a moderate amount of stress. When the individual perceives that his or her resources will probably not suffice to meet an environmental stressor, he or she may experience a great deal of stress.

Stress, then, results from the process of appraising events (as harmful, threatening, or challenging), of assessing potential responses, and of responding to those events. To see how stress researchers have arrived at our current understanding of stress, it is useful to consider some of the early contributions to the field.

■ THEORETICAL CONTRIBUTIONS TO THE STUDY OF STRESS

Fight-or-Flight

One of the earliest contributions to stress research was Walter Cannon's (1932) description of the **fight-or-flight response.** Cannon proposed that, when an organism perceives a threat, the body is rapidly aroused and motivated via the sympathetic nervous system and the endocrine system. This concerted physiological response mobilizes the organism to attack the threat or to flee; hence, it is called the fight-or-flight response (Kemeny, 2003).

At one time, fight-or-flight literally referred to fighting or fleeing in response to stressful events such as attack by a predator. Now more commonly *fight* refers to aggressive responses to stress, whereas *flight* may be seen in social withdrawal or withdrawal through substance use such as alcohol or drugs.

On the one hand, the fight-or-flight response is adaptive because it enables the organism to respond quickly to threat. On the other hand, it can be harmful because stress disrupts emotional and physiological functioning, and when stress continues unabated, it lays the groundwork for health problems.

Selye's General Adaptation Syndrome

Another important early contribution to the field of stress is Hans Selye's (1956, 1976) work on the **general adaptation syndrome.** Although Selye initially intended to explore the effects of sex hormones on physiological functioning, he became interested in the stressful impact his interventions seemed to have. Accordingly, he exposed rats to a variety of stressors—such as extreme cold and fatigue—and observed their physiological responses. To his surprise, all stressors, regardless of type, produced essentially the same pattern of physiological responding. In particular, they all led to an enlarged adrenal cortex, shrinking of the thymus and lymph glands, and ulceration of the stomach and duodenum. Thus, whereas Cannon's work explored adrenomedullary responses to stress—specifically, catecholamine secretion—Selye's work more closely explored adrenocortical responses to stress.

From these observations, Selye (1956) developed his concept of the general adaptation syndrome. He argued that, when an organism confronts a stressor, it mobilizes itself for action. The response itself is nonspecific with respect to the stressor; that is, regardless of the cause of the threat, the individual will respond with the same physiological pattern of reactions. Over time, with repeated or prolonged exposure to stress, there will be wear and tear on the system.

The general adaptation syndrome consists of three phases. In the first phase, *alarm,* the organism becomes mobilized to meet the threat. In the second phase, *resistance,* the organism makes efforts to cope with the threat, as through confrontation. The third phase, *exhaustion,* occurs if the organism fails to overcome the threat and depletes its physiological resources in the process of trying. These phases are pictured in figure 6.1.

The substantial impact of Selye's model on the field of stress continues to be felt today. One reason is that it offers a general theory of reactions to a wide variety of stressors over time. As such, it provides a way of thinking about the interplay of physiological and environmental factors. Second, it posits a physiological mechanism for the stress-illness relationship. Specifically, Selye believed that repeated or prolonged exhaustion of resources, the third phase of the syndrome, is responsible for the physiological damage that lays the groundwork for disease. In fact, prolonged or repeated stress has been implicated in a broad array of disorders, such as cardiovascular disease, arthritis, hypertension, and immune-related deficiencies, as we will see in chapters 13 and 14.

Criticisms of the General Adaptation Syndrome
Selye's model has also been criticized on several grounds. First, it assigns a very limited role to psychological factors, and researchers now believe that the psychological appraisal of events is important in the determination of stress (R. S. Lazarus & Folkman, 1984b). A second criticism concerns the assumption that responses to stress are uniform (Hobfoll, 1989). There is evidence that not all stressors produce the same endocrinological responses (Kemeny, 2003). Moreover, how people respond to stress is substantially influenced by their personalities, perceptions, and biological constitutions. A third criticism concerns the fact that Selye as-

---

FIGURE 6.1 | The Three Phases of Selye's (1974) General Adaptation Syndrome

Plase A is the alarm response, in which the body first reacts to a stressor. At this time, resistance is diminished. Phase B, the stage of resistance, occurs with continued exposure to a stressor. The bodily signs associated with an alarm reaction disappear and resistance rises above normal. Phase C is the stage of exhaustion that results from long-term exposure to the same stressor. At this point, resistance may again fall to below normal.   (*Source: Stress Without Distress* by Hans Selye, M.D. Copyright © 1974 by Hans Selye, M.D. Reprinted by permission of HarperCollins Publishers, Inc.)

sessed stress as an outcome, such that stress is evident only when the general adaptation syndrome has run its course. In fact, people experience many of the debilitating effects of stress while a stressful event is going on and even in anticipation of its occurrence. Despite these limitations and reservations, Selye's model remains a cornerstone of the field of stress.

Tend-and-Befriend

Animals, whether nonhuman or human, do not merely fight, flee, and grow exhausted in response to stress. They also affiliate with each other, whether it is the herding behavior of deer in response to stress, the huddling one sees among female rats, or the coordinated responses to a stressor that a community shows when it is under the threat of flood, tornado, or other natural disaster.

To address this issue, Taylor and colleagues (S. E. Taylor, Klein, et al., 2000) developed a theory of responses to stress termed *tend-and-befriend*. The theory maintains that in addition to fight-or-flight, humans respond to stress with social and nurturant behavior. These responses may be especially characteristic of females. During the time that responses to stress evolved, males and females faced somewhat different adaptive challenges. Whereas males were responsible for hunting and protection, females were responsible for foraging and child care. These activities were largely segregated, with the result that female responses to stress would have evolved so as to protect not only the self but offspring as well. The offspring of most species are immature and would be unable to survive were it not for the attention of adults. In most species, that attention is provided by the mother.

Because tending to offspring, particularly in times of stress, is a complex task, the tend-and-befriend theory maintains that *befriending*—that is, affiliating with others and seeking social contact during stress—may be especially characteristic of females and may help in self-preservation and the protection of offspring.

Like the fight-or-flight mechanism, tend-and-befriend may depend on underlying biological mechanisms. In particular, the hormone oxytocin may have significance for female responses to stress. Oxytocin is a stress hormone, rapidly released in response to at least some stressful events, and its effects are especially influenced by estrogen, suggesting a role in the responses of women to stress.

The potential contribution of oxytocin to stress responses is to act as an impetus for affiliation. Numerous animal and human studies show that oxytocin increases affiliative behaviors of all kinds, especially mothering (S. E. Taylor, 2002). In addition, animals and humans with high levels of oxytocin are calmer and more relaxed, which may contribute to social and nurturant behavior (McCarthy, 1995). Opioids may also contribute to affiliative responses to stress in females (S. E. Taylor, Klein, et al., 2000).

In support of the theory, there is evidence that women are consistently more likely than men to respond to stress by turning to others (Luckow, Reifman, & McIntosh, 1998; Tamres, Janicki, & Helgeson, 2002). Mothers' responses to offspring during stress also appear to be different from those of fathers in ways encompassed by the tend-and-befriend theory. Nonetheless, men, too, show social responses to stress, and at present, less is known about men's social responses to stress than women's.

In addition to offering a biobehavioral approach to differences in male and female responses to stress, the tend-and-befriend theory brings social behavior into stress processes. We are affiliative creatures who respond to stress collectively, as well as individually, and these responses are characteristic of men as well as women.

Psychological Appraisal and the Experience of Stress

In humans, psychological appraisals are an important determinant of whether an event is responded to as stressful.

Primary Appraisal Processes
Lazarus, a chief proponent of the psychological view of stress (R. S. Lazarus, 1968; R. S. Lazarus & Folkman, 1984b), maintains that, when individuals confront a new or changing environment, they engage in a process of **primary appraisal** to determine the meaning of the event (see figure 6.2).

Events may be perceived as positive, neutral, or negative in their consequences. Negative or potentially negative events are further appraised for their possible harm, threat, or challenge. *Harm* is the assessment of the damage that has already been done by an event. Thus, for example, a man who has just been fired from his job may perceive present harm in terms of his own loss of self-esteem and his embarrassment as his coworkers silently watch him pack up his desk.

Threat is the assessment of possible future damage that may be brought about by the event. Thus, the man

FIGURE 6.2 | The Experience of Stress

Primary appraisal
Is the event positive, neutral, or negative in its implications? If negative, to what extent is it presently harmful, threatening for the future, and potentially challenging?

Potential stressor
(external event)

Secondary appraisal
Are coping abilities and resources sufficient to overcome the harm, threat, or challenge posed by the event?

Stress
Physiological, cognitive, emotional, and behavioral responses

who has just lost his job may anticipate the problems that loss of income will create for him and his family in the future. Primary appraisals of events as threats have important effects on physiological responses to stress. For example, blood pressure is higher when threat is higher or when threat is high and challenge is low (Maier, Waldenstein, & Synowski, 2003).

Finally, events may be appraised in terms of their *challenge,* the potential to overcome and even profit from the event. For example, the man who has lost his job may perceive that a certain amount of harm and threat exists, but he may also see his unemployment as an opportunity to try something new. Challenge appraisals are associated with more confident expectations of the ability to cope with the stressful event, more favorable emotional reactions to the event, and lower blood pressure (Maier et al., 2003; N. Skinner & Brewer, 2002).

The importance of primary appraisal in the experience of stress is illustrated in a classic study of stress by Speisman, Lazarus, Mordkoff, and Davidson (1964). College students viewed a gruesome film depicting unpleasant tribal initiation rites that included genital surgery. Before viewing the film, they were exposed to one of four experimental conditions. One group listened to an anthropological account about the meaning of the rites. Another group heard a lecture that deemphasized the pain the initiates were experiencing and emphasized their excitement over the events. A third group heard a description that emphasized the pain and trauma that the initiates were undergoing. A fourth group was given no introductory information, and the film they viewed had no sound track. Measures of autonomic arousal (skin conductance, heart rate) and self-reports suggested that the first two groups experienced considerably less stress than did the group whose attention was focused

on the trauma and pain. Thus, this study illustrated that stress not only was intrinsic to the gruesome film itself but also depended on the viewer's appraisal of it.

Secondary Appraisal Processes   At the same time that primary appraisals of stressful circumstances are occurring, secondary appraisal is initiated. **Secondary appraisal** is the assessment of one's coping abilities and resources and whether they will be sufficient to meet the harm, threat, and challenge of the event. Ultimately, the subjective experience of stress is a balance between primary and secondary appraisal. When harm and threat are high and coping ability is low, substantial stress is felt. When coping ability is high, stress may be minimal. Potential responses to stress are many and include physiological, cognitive, emotional, and behavioral consequences. Some of these responses are involuntary reactions to stress, whereas others are voluntarily initiated in a conscious effort to cope.

Cognitive responses to stress include beliefs about the harm or threat an event poses and beliefs about its causes or controllability. They also include involuntary responses, such as distractability and inability to concentrate; performance disruptions on cognitive tasks (e.g., S. Cohen, 1980; Shaham, Singer, & Schaeffer, 1992); and intrusive, repetitive, or morbid thoughts (Horowitz, 1975). Cognitive responses are also involved in the initiation of coping activities, as we will see in chapter 7.

Potential emotional reactions to stressful events range widely; they include fear, anxiety, excitement, embarrassment, anger, depression, and even stoicism or denial. Emotional responses can be quite insistent, prompting rumination over a stressful event, which in turn, may keep biological stress responses elevated (Glynn, Christenfeld, & Gerin, 2002).

FIGURE 6.3 | The Body's Stress Systems

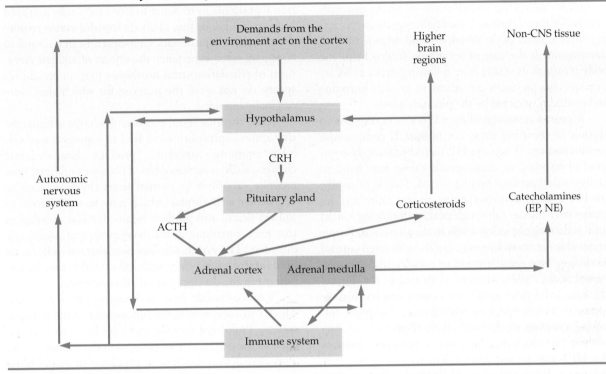

Potential behavioral responses are virtually limitless, depending on the nature of the stressful event. Confrontative action against the stressor ("fight") and withdrawal from the threatening event ("flight") constitute two general categories of behavioral responses. We will examine others in the course of our discussion.

The Physiology of Stress

Stress is important, both because it causes psychological distress and because it leads to changes in the body that may have short- or long-term consequences for health. Two interrelated systems are heavily involved in the stress response. They are the sympathetic-adrenomedullary (SAM) system and the hypothalamic-pituitary-adrenocortical (HPA) axis. These components of the stress response are illustrated in figure 6.3.

Sympathetic Activation   When events are encountered that are perceived as harmful or threatening, they are labeled as such by the cerebral cortex, which, in turn, sets off a chain of reactions mediated by these appraisals. Information from the cortex is transmitted to the hypothalamus, which initiates one of the earliest

responses to stress—namely, sympathetic nervous system arousal, or the fight-or-flight response first described by Walter Cannon.

Sympathetic arousal stimulates the medulla of the adrenal glands, which, in turn, secrete the catecholamines, epinephrine and norepinephrine. These effects result in the cranked-up feeling we usually experience in response to stress. Sympathetic arousal leads to increased blood pressure, increased heart rate, increased sweating, and constriction of peripheral blood vessels, among other changes. As can be seen in figure 6.3, the catecholamines have effects on a variety of tissues and are believed to lead to modulation of the immune system as well.

HPA Activation   In addition to the activation of the sympathetic nervous system, the HPA system is activated. Hans Selye provided the basis for understanding the effects of stress on the HPA in his general adaptation syndrome, the nonspecific physiological reaction that occurs in response to stress and involves the three phases of alarm, resistance, and exhaustion.

The hypothalamus releases corticotrophin-releasing factor (CRF), which stimulates the pituitary gland to secrete adrenocorticotropic hormone (ACTH), which, in turn, stimulates the adrenal cortex to release glucocorticoids. Of these, cortisol is especially significant. It acts to conserve stores of carbohydrates and helps reduce inflammation in the case of an injury. It also helps the body return to its steady state following stress. HPA activation also produces elevations in growth hormone and prolactin, secreted by the pituitary gland.

Repeated activation of the HPA axis in response to chronic or recurring stress can ultimately compromise its functioning. When the HPA axis becomes dysregulated in response to stress, several things may happen. Daily cortisol patterns may be altered. That is, normally, cortisol is high upon wakening in the morning, decreases over the day (although peaking following lunch) until it flattens out at low levels in the afternoon. People under chronic stress, however, can show elevated cortisol levels long into the afternoon or evening (for example, Powell et al., 2002), a general flattening of the diurnal rhythms (McEwen, 1998), an exaggerated cortisol response to a challenge, a protracted cortisol response following a stressor, or alternatively no response at all. Any of these patterns is suggestive of compromised ability of the HPA axis to respond to and recover from stress (McEwen, 1998; Pruessner, Hellhammer, Pruessner, & Lupien, 2003). When researchers study physiological and neuroendocrine stress responses, they look for signs like these (see figure 6.4).

Effects of Long-Term Stress   We have just examined some of the major physiological changes that occur in response to the perception of stress. What do these changes mean? Although the short-term mobilization that occurs in response to stress originally prepared humans to fight or flee, rarely do stressful events require these kinds of adjustments. Consequently, in response to stress, we often experience the effects of sudden elevations of circulating stress hormones that, in certain respects, do not serve the purpose for which they were originally intended.

Over the long term, excessive discharge of epinephrine and norepinephrine can lead to suppression of cellular immune functions; produce hemodynamic changes, such as increased blood pressure and heart rate; provoke variations in normal heart rhythms, such as ventricular arrhythmias, which may be a precursor to sudden death; and produce neurochemical imbalances that may contribute to the development of psychiatric disorders. The catecholamines may also have effects on lipid levels and free fatty acids, all of which may be important in the development of atherosclerosis.

Corticosteroids have immunosuppressive effects, which can compromise the functioning of the immune system. Prolonged cortisol secretion has also been related to the destruction of neurons in the hippocampus. This destruction can lead to problems in verbal functioning, memory, and concentration (Starkman, Giordani, Brenent, Schork, & Schteingart, 2001) and may be one of the mechanisms by which the senility that sometimes occurs in old age sets in. Pronounced HPA activation is common in depression, with episodes of cortisol secretion being more frequent and of longer duration among depressed than nondepressed people, although it is not entirely clear whether HPA activation is

FIGURE 6.4 | Routes by Which Stress May Produce Disease
The text describes how direct physiological effects may result from sympathetic and/or HPA activation. In addition, as this figure shows, stress may affect health via behaviors—first, by influencing health habits directly and second, by interfering with treatment and the use of services.   (*Source:* A. Baum, 1994)

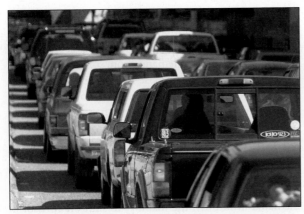

Stressful events, such as being stuck in traffic, produce agitation and physiological arousal.

a cause or an effect of these disorders. Another long-term consequence of the endocrine abnormalities that result from chronic HPA activation is the storage of fat in central visceral areas, rather than to the hips. This accumulation leads to a high waist-to-hip ratio, which is used by some researchers as a marker for chronic stress (Bjorntorp, 1996).

Which of these responses to stress have implications for disease? Several researchers (Dienstbier, 1989; Frankenhaeuser, 1991) have suggested that the health consequences of HPA axis activation are more significant than those of sympathetic activation. Sympathetic adrenal in response to stress may not be a pathway for disease; HPA activation may be required as well. Some researchers have suggested that this reasoning explains why exercise, which produces sympathetic arousal but not HPA activation, is protective for health rather than health compromising.

Stress may also impair the immune system's capacity to respond to hormonal signals that terminate inflammation. A study that demonstrates this point compared 50 healthy adults, half of whom were parents of cancer patients and, the other half, parents of healthy children. Childhood cancer is known to be one of the most stressful events that parents encounter. The parents of the cancer patients reported more stress and had flatter daily slopes of cortisol secretion than was true for the parents of healthy children. Moreover, the ability to suppress production of a proinflammatory cytokine called IL-6 was diminished among parents of the cancer patients. Because proinflammatory cytokines are implicated in a broad array of diseases including coronary artery disease, these findings suggest that the impaired

ability to terminate inflammation may be another pathway by which stress affects illness outcomes (G. E. Miller, Cohen, & Ritchey, 2002).

Researchers are increasingly focusing on poor sleep quality as both an indicator of chronic stress and a consequence of chronic stress. It has long been suspected that chronic insomnia can result from stressful events. Evidence suggests that the combination of emotional arousal and neuroendocrine activation due to chronic stress may indeed underlie chronic insomnia (Shaver, Johnston, Lentz, & Landis, 2002). Because sleep represents a vital restorative activity, this mechanism, too, may represent an important pathway to disease (S. Edwards, Hucklebridge, Clow, & Evans, 2003). The coming years will help clarify the important psychobiological pathways from stress to disease.

Individual Differences in Stress Reactivity

People vary in their reactivity to stress. **Reactivity** is the degree of change that occurs in autonomic, neuroendocrine, and/or immune responses as a result of stress. Reactivity is, in part, a predisposition to respond physiologically to environmental threats or challenges that may be implicated in both short- and long-term health complications due to stress. Some people show very small reactions to stressful circumstances, whereas others show large responses. These differences may be genetic in origin or develop prenatally or in early life.

Reactivity to stress can affect vulnerability to illness. For example, in one study, a group of children ranging in age from 3 to 5 years old were tested for their cardiovascular reactivity (change in heart rate and blood pressure) or their immune response to a vaccine challenge following a stressful task. Parents were then asked to report on the number of family stressors during a 12-week period, and illness rates were charted during this period. The results indicated that stress was associated with increased rates of illness only among the children who had previously shown strong immune or cardiovascular reactions. The less reactive children did not experience any change in illness under stressful circumstances (Boyce, Alkon, Tschann, Chesney, & Alpert, 1995).

Another study found that cardiovascular reactivity predicted stress-induced cortisol changes in a group of young, healthy college students performing a mental arithmetic task; higher reactivity was also related to changes in natural killer cell activity, providing evidence for the pathway between sympathetic activation and immune changes (Uchino, Cacioppo, Malarkey, & Glaser, 1995) and possible risk for infectious disease.

Do changes like this actually lead to illness? S. Cohen and colleagues (2002) found that people who reacted to laboratory stressors with high cortisol responses and who also had a high level of negative life events were especially vulnerable to upper respiratory infections. People who reacted to laboratory stressors with low immune responses were especially vulnerable to upper respiratory infection if they were also under high stress. High immune reactors, in contrast, did not show differences in upper respiratory illness as a function of the stress they experienced, perhaps because their immune systems were quick to respond to the threat that a potential infection posed.

Studies like these suggest that psychobiological reactivity to stress is an important factor that influences the effects that stress has on the body and the likelihood that it will contribute to distress or disease. As will be seen in chapter 13, differences in reactivity are believed to contribute especially to the development of hypertension and coronary artery disease (for example, V. Clark, Moore, & Adams, 1998).

Physiological Recovery Processes   Recovery processes following stress are also important in the physiology of the stress response (Rutledge, Linden, & Paul, 2000). In particular, the inability to recover quickly from a stressful event may be a marker for the cumulative damage that stress has caused. Researchers have paid special attention to the cortisol response—particularly prolonged cortisol responses that occur under conditions of high stress.

In one intriguing study (Perna & McDowell, 1995), elite athletes were divided into groups that were experiencing a high versus a low amount of stress in their lives, and their cortisol response was measured following vigorous training. Those athletes under higher degrees of stress showed a longer cortisol recovery. Because elevated cortisol affects the immune system, the researchers suggested that stress may widen the window of susceptibility for illness and injury among competitive athletes by virtue of its impact on cortisol recovery.

As the research on recovery processes implies, the long-term effects of stress on the body are of great importance when understanding the mechanisms by which physiological changes in response to stress may promote illness.

Allostatic Load   As Selye noted, the initial response of the body to stressful circumstances may be arousal, but over time this response may give way to exhaustion, leading to cumulative damage to the organism. Building on these ideas, researchers have developed the concept of **allostatic load** (McEwen & Stellar, 1993). This concept refers to the fact that physiological systems within the body fluctuate to meet demands from stress, a state called allostasis. Over time, allostatic load builds up, which is defined as the physiological costs of chronic exposure to fluctuating or heightened neural or neuroendocrine response that results from repeated or chronic stress.

This buildup of allostatic load—that is, the long-term costs of chronic or repeated stress—can be assessed by a number of indicators (T. E. Seeman, Singer, Horwitz, & McEwen, 1997). These include decreases in cell-mediated immunity, the inability to shut off cortisol in response to stress, lowered heart rate variability, elevated epinephrine levels, a high waist-to-hip ratio, volume of the hippocampus (which is believed to decrease with repeated stimulation of the HPA), problems with memory (an indirect measure of hippocampal functioning), high plasma fibrinogen, and elevated blood pressure. Many of these changes occur normally with age, so to the extent that they occur early, allostatic load may be thought of as accelerated aging of the organism in response to stress. Over time, this kind of wear and tear can lead to illness. These effects may be exacerbated by the poor health habits practiced by people under chronic stress. The damage due to chronic or repeated stress is only made worse if people also cope with stress via a higher fat diet, less frequent exercise, and smoking, all of which stress can encourage (Ng & Jeffery, 2003).

The physiology of stress and, in particular, the recent research on the cumulative adverse effects of stress are important because they suggest the pathways by which stress exerts adverse effects on the body, ultimately contributing to the likelihood of disease. The relationship of stress, both short and long term, to both acute disorders such as infection, and chronic diseases is now so well established that stress is implicated in most diseases, either in their etiology, their course, or both. We explore these processes more fully when we address different diseases such as heart disease and hypertension in chapter 13 and cancer and arthritis in chapter 14. At this point, suffice it to say, stress is one of the major risk factors for disease that humans encounter.

■ WHAT MAKES EVENTS STRESSFUL?

Assessing Stress

Given that stress can produce a variety of responses, what is the best way to measure it? Researchers have used many indicators of stress. These include self-reports of perceived stress, life change, and emotional distress; behavioral measures, such as task performance under stress; physiological measures of arousal, such as heart rate and blood pressure; and biochemical markers (or indicators), especially elevated catecholamines and alterations in the diurnal rhythm of cortisol or cortisol responses to stress (A. Baum, Grunberg, & Singer, 1982; Dimsdale, Young, Moore, & Strauss, 1987). In each case, these measures have proven to be useful indicators.

However, each type of measurement has its own associated problems. For example, catecholamine secretion is enhanced by a number of factors other than stress. Self-report measures are subject to a variety of biases, because individuals may want to present themselves in as desirable a light as possible. Behavioral measures are subject to multiple interpretations. For example, performance declines can be due to declining motivation, fatigue, cognitive strain, or other factors. Consequently, stress researchers have called for the use of multiple measures (A. Baum et al., 1982). With several measures, the possibility of obtaining a good model of the stress experience is increased.

Dimensions of Stressful Events

As we have just noted, events themselves are not inherently stressful. Rather, whether they are stressful depends on how they are appraised by an individual. What are some characteristics of potential stressors that make them more likely to be appraised as stressful?

Negative Events
Negative events are more likely to produce stress than are positive events. Many events have the potential to be stressful because they present people with extra work or special problems that may tax or exceed their resources. Shopping for the holidays, planning a party, coping with an unexpected job promotion, and getting married are all positive events that draw off substantial time and energy. Nonetheless, these positive experiences are less likely to be reported as stressful than are undesirable events, such as getting a traffic ticket, trying to find a job, coping with a death in the family, or getting divorced.

Negative events show a stronger relationship to both psychological distress and physical symptoms than do positive ones (for example, I. G. Sarason, Johnson, & Siegel, 1978). This may be because negative stressful events have implications for the self-concept producing loss of self-esteem or erosion of a sense of mastery or identity (Thoits, 1986).

There is one exception to this pattern. Among people who hold negative views of themselves, positive life events can have a detrimental effect on health, whereas for people with high self-esteem, positive life events are linked to better health (J. D. Brown & McGill, 1989).

Uncontrollable Events
Uncontrollable or unpredictable events are more stressful than controllable or predictable ones. Uncontrollable events are perceived as more stressful than controllable ones. When people feel that they can predict, modify, or terminate an aversive event or feel they have access to someone who can influence it, they experience it as less stressful, even if they actually do nothing about it (S. C. Thompson, 1981). For example, unpredictable bursts of noise are experienced as more stressful than are predictable ones (D. C. Glass & Singer, 1972).

Feelings of control not only mute the subjective experience of stress but also influence biochemical reactions to it. Believing that one can control a stressor such as noise level (Lundberg & Frankenhaeuser, 1976) or crowding (J. E. Singer, Lundberg, & Frankenhaeuser, 1978) is associated with lower catecholamine levels than is believing that one has no control over the stressor. Uncontrollable stress has been tied to immunosuppressive effects as well (Brosschot et al., 1998; Peters et al., 1999).

Ambiguous Events
Ambiguous events are often perceived as more stressful than are clear-cut events. When a potential stressor is ambiguous, a person has no opportunity to take action. He or she must instead devote energy to trying to understand the stressor, which can be a time-consuming, resource-sapping task.

Clear-cut stressors, on the other hand, let the person get on with the job of finding solutions and do not leave him or her stuck at the problem-definition stage. The ability to take confrontative action is usually associated with less distress and better coping (Billings & Moos, 1984).

Overload
Overloaded people are more stressed than are people with fewer tasks to perform (for example, S. Cohen, 1978; S. Cohen & Williamson, 1988). People who have too many tasks in their lives report higher levels of stress than do those who have fewer tasks. For example, one of the main sources of work-related stress is job overload, the perception that one is responsible for doing too much in too short a period of time.

Which Stressors?
People may be more vulnerable to stress in central life domains than in peripheral ones because important aspects of the self are overly invested in central life domains (Swindle & Moos, 1992). For

Events such as crowding are experienced as stressful only to the extent that they are appraised that way. Some situations of crowding make people feel happy, whereas other crowding situations are experienced as aversive.

example, among working women for whom parental identity was very salient, role strains associated with the parent role, such as feeling that their children did not get the attention they needed, took a toll (R. W. Simon, 1992). Hammen, Marks, Mayol, and DeMayo (1985) found that negative life events affecting personal relationships were stronger predictors of depression among women for whom dependency relationships were important, whereas setbacks in the achievement domain rendered more autonomous women more vulnerable to depression.

To summarize, then, events that are negative, uncontrollable, ambiguous, or overwhelming or that involve central life tasks are perceived as more stressful than are events that are positive, controllable, clear-cut, or manageable or that involve peripheral life tasks.

Must Stress Be Perceived as Such to Be Stressful?

The preceding points suggest that stress is both a subjective and objective experience. In fact, both of these aspects of stress affect the likelihood of resulting health problems. Repetti (1993b) studied air traffic controllers and assessed their subjective perceptions of stress on various days, and she also gathered objective measures of daily stress, including the weather conditions and the amount of air traffic. She found that both subjective and objective measures of stress independently predicted psychological distress and health complaints.

Similarly, S. Cohen, Tyrrell, and Smith (1993) recruited 394 healthy people for a study of the common cold. Participants completed questionnaires designed to obtain objective information about the stressful life events they had encountered, and they completed a

measure of perceived stress. The researchers then exposed participants to a common cold virus and found that both objectively assessed stressful life events and perceived stress predicted whether or not the people developed a cold.

These kinds of studies suggest that, although the perception of stress is important to the physical and psychological symptoms it causes, objectively defined stress also shows a relation to adverse psychological and physiological changes.

Can People Adapt to Stress?

If a stressful event becomes a permanent or chronic part of their environment, will people eventually habituate to it or will they develop **chronic strain?** Will it no longer cause them distress, drain psychological resources, or lead to symptoms of illness? The answer to this question depends on the type of stressor, the subjective experience of stress, and which indicator of stress is considered.

Psychological Adaptation Most people are able to adapt psychologically to moderate or predictable stressors. At first, any novel, threatening situation can produce stress, but such reactions often subside over time (Frankenhaeuser, 1975; Stokols, Novaco, Stokols, & Campbell, 1978). Even monkeys exposed to a shock-avoidance task showed few signs of stress after the first few sessions (J. W. Mason, Brady, & Tolliver, 1968). Research on the effects of environmental noise (Nivison & Endresen, 1993) and crowding (S. Cohen, Glass, & Phillip, 1978) also indicates few or no long-term adverse health or psychological effects, suggesting that most people simply adapt to these chronic stressors. For example, laboratory studies that expose people to noise while they are trying to complete a task find that people may simply change their task strategies or attentional focus to adapt to the noise experience. As a consequence, task performance may suffer little or not at all (D. C. Glass & Singer, 1972).

However, particularly vulnerable populations, especially children, the elderly, and poor people, do seem to be adversely affected by these stressors (S. Cohen et al., 1978); they may show signs of helplessness and difficulty in performing tasks. One possible reason is that these groups already experience little control over their environments and accordingly may already be exposed to high levels of stress; the addition of an environmental stressor, such as noise or crowding, may push their resources to the limits. Consistent with this argument, Karen Matthews and associates (K. A. Matthews, Gump, Block, & Allen, 1997) found that children and adolescents who had recurrent or ongoing stressors in their lives exhibited larger diastolic blood pressure responses to acute laboratory stress tasks, as compared with children and adolescents who had less background stress in their lives.

Thus, the answer to the question of whether people can adapt to chronic stress might best be summarized as follows: People (and animals) show signs of both long-term strain and habituation to chronically stressful events. Most people can adapt moderately well to mildly stressful events; however, it may be difficult or impossible for them to adapt to highly stressful events, and already-stressed people may be unable to adapt to even moderate stressors. Moreover, even when psychological adaptation may have occurred, physiological changes in response to stress may persist. Box 6.1 examines these issues as they affect children.

Physiological Adaptation   In terms of physiological adaptation, animal models of stress suggest evidence for both habituation and chronic strain. For example, rats exposed to relatively low-level stressors tend to show initial physiological responsiveness followed by habituation. When the stimuli employed to induce stress are intense, however, the animal may show no habituation (Pitman, Ottenweller, & Natelson, 1988; R. F. Thompson & Glanzman, 1976). Physiological evidence from studies of humans also suggests evidence for both habituation and chronic strain. Low-level stress may produce habituation in most people, but with more intense stress damage from chronic stress can accumulate across multiple organ systems as the allostatic load model suggests. Habituation is more likely for HPA responses to stress than for sympathetic responses to stress (Schommer,

Hellhammer, & Kirschbaum, 2003). But chronic stress can also impair cardiovascular and neuroendocrine recovery from stressors and through such effects, contribute to an increased risk for diseases, such as cardiovascular disorders, in midlife (K. A. Matthews, Gump, & Owens, 2001).

Recently, researchers have looked at immune responses that are associated with long-term stressful events to address the question of habituation. Herbert and Cohen (1993) found that exposure to a long-term stressful event was significantly related to poorer immune functioning. What this research suggests is that physiological habituation may not occur or may not be complete when stressors are long-term and that the immune system may be compromised by long-term stress.

Must a Stressor Be Ongoing to Be Stressful?

Does the stress response occur only while a stressful event is happening, or can stress result in anticipation of or as an aftereffect of exposure to a stressor? One of the wonders and curses of human beings' symbolic capacities is their ability to conceptualize things before they materialize. We owe our abilities to plan, invent, and reason abstractly to this skill, but we also get from it our ability to worry. Unlike lower animals, human beings do not have to be exposed to a stressor to suffer stress.

Anticipating Stress   The anticipation of a stressor can be at least as stressful as its actual occurrence, and often more so. Consider the strain of anticipating a confrontation with a boyfriend or girlfriend or worrying about a test that will occur the next day. Sleepless nights and days of distracting anxiety testify to the human being's capacity for anticipatory distress.

One study that illustrates the importance of anticipatory stress made use of ambulatory blood pressure monitors to assess natural fluctuations in blood pressure during daily activities. In this study, medical students wore the pressure monitors on an unstressful lecture day, the day before an important examination, and during the examination itself. Although the lecture day was characterized by stable patterns of cardiovascular activity, cardiovascular activity on the preexamination day when the students were worrying about the exam was as high as that seen during the examination (Sausen, Lovallo, Pincomb, & Wilson, 1992). Thus, in this instance, the anticipation of the stressful event taxed the cardiovascular system as much as the stressful event itself.

BOX 6.1

Are Children Vulnerable to Noise?

Although studies of noise generally suggest few long-term negative effects, children do appear to be vulnerable to the stress of noise. S. Cohen, Glass, and Singer (1973) tested children living in apartment buildings built on bridges that spanned a busy expressway. Children who lived in the noisier apartments showed greater difficulty with auditory discrimination tasks and in reading than did children who lived in quieter apartments. These effects were stronger the longer the children had lived there. A study of railroad noise found that children taught in classrooms on the side of an elementary school facing the railroad tracks read less well than children on the quieter side of the building (Bronzaft & McCarthy, 1975). A study of children exposed to aircraft noise (S. Cohen, Evans, Krantz, & Stokols, 1980) found that children who lived and attended school in the air corridor performed less well on both simple and difficult problem-solving tasks than did children not living or attending school in the air corridor. Moreover, children exposed to the aircraft noise were more likely to give up on difficult tasks than were children who lived in the quiet neighborhoods. Clearly, then, children can experience a number of problems as a consequence of sustained exposure to noise, including difficulty in learning, poor task performance, and lack of persistence on tasks. What are some reasons for these effects?

Most people cope with noise by altering their attentional focus—that is, by tuning out extraneous noise and attempting to focus only on relevant information. However, children raised in noisy environments who attempt to use this attentional strategy may have difficulty distinguishing between appropriate and inappropriate cues.

Because they are young, they may not be able to distinguish between speech-relevant and speech-irrelevant sounds as well as adults can. They may consequently lose potentially important verbal experience that would help them develop these skills. One reason that they may end up having more difficulty with verbal skills and reading, then, may be because they tune out sounds in their environment.

The fact that children exposed to long-term stressors give up on tasks more quickly than children not so exposed is particularly chilling. It suggests that these children may have learned to be helpless; they may have experienced repeated unsuccessful efforts to master tasks or to make themselves understood. Over time, they may come to perceive a lack of relationship between their efforts and their outcomes; as a result, they become helpless. Consequently, even when they are placed in new environments where control is possible, they may not recognize this possibility and still give up more quickly (S. Cohen et al., 1980).

A reason that children may be more vulnerable than adults to the learned helplessness effects of noise is that children already experience less control in their lives than adults do. Add to this the fact that children exposed to chronically noisy environments are disproportionately likely to be nonwhite and low socioeconomic, both of which have their own attendant sources of stress (G. W. Evans & Kantrowitz, 2001). It is possible that the additional lack of control that comes from a long-term stressor, such as noise, may be the final straw that impairs their ability to perform well on tasks requiring concentration and the motivation to persist.

Aftereffects of Stress Adverse **aftereffects of stress,** such as decreases in performance and attention span, are also well documented. In fact, one of the reasons that stress presents both a health hazard and a challenge to the health psychology researcher is that the effects of stress often persist long after the stressful event itself is no longer present. Aftereffects of stress have been observed in response to a wide range of stressors, including noise, high task load, electric shock, bureaucratic stress, crowding, and laboratory-induced stress (S. Cohen, 1980). Box 6.2 profiles a particular kind of aftereffect of stress, post-traumatic stress disorder.

In a series of studies, D. C. Glass and Singer (1972) put college student participants to work on a simple task

and exposed them to an uncontrollable, unpredictable stressor in the form of random, intermittent bursts of noise over a 25-minute period. After the noise period was over, these participants were given additional tasks to perform, including solvable and unsolvable puzzles and a proofreading task. The participants who had been exposed to the noise consistently performed more poorly on these tasks. These results have been confirmed by other investigators (S. Cohen et al., 1978).

Stressors can produce deleterious aftereffects on social behavior as well as on cognitive tasks. Several studies have found that, when people are exposed to avoidable stressful events, such as noise or crowding, they are less likely to help someone in distress when the

BOX **6.2**

Post-Traumatic Stress Disorder

Following the Vietnam War, a number of unnerving events were reported in the media regarding veterans who, as civilians, apparently relived some of the experiences they had undergone during battle. In one especially distressing case, a man took charge of a shopping mall, believing that it was under attack by the North Vietnamese, and shot and wounded several police officers before he was shot in an effort to subdue him.

When a person has been the victim of a highly stressful event, symptoms of the stress experience may persist long after the event is over. As we have seen, the aftereffects of stress can include physiological arousal, distractability, and other negative side effects that last for hours after a stressful event has occurred. In the case of major traumas, these stressful aftereffects may go on intermittently for months or years.

Such long-term reactions have been especially documented in the wake of violent wars, such as occurred in Vietnam and the Gulf War (Ford et al., 2001; D. W. King, King, Gudanowski, & Vreven, 1995). But they may also occur in response to assault, rape, domestic abuse, a violent encounter with nature (such as an earthquake or flood) (Ironson et al., 1997), a disaster (such as 9/11) (Fagan, Galea, Ahern, Bonner, & Vlahov, 2003), and being a hostage (Vila, Porche, & Mouren-Simeoni, 1999). Particularly occupations such as employment as an urban police officer (Fagan et al., 2003; D. Mohr et al., 2003) or having responsibility for clearing up remains following war, disaster, or mass death (McCarroll, Ursano, Fullerton, Liu, & Lundy, 2002) increase the risk of traumatic stress exposure and resulting PTSD. Even major diseases and their aggressive treatments can produce effects like these (Widows, Jacobsen, & Fields, 2000).

The term **post-traumatic stress disorder (PTSD)** has been developed to explain these effects. The person suffering from PTSD has typically undergone a stressor of extreme magnitude (Lamprecht & Sack, 2002). One of the reactions to this stressful event is a psychic numbing, such as reduced interest in once enjoyable activities, detachment from friends, or constriction in emotions. In addition, the person often relives aspects of the trauma, as some Vietnam veterans did. Other symptoms include excessive vigilance, sleep disturbances, feelings of guilt, impaired memory or concentration, avoidance of the experience, an exaggerated startle response to loud noise (Carlier, Voerman, & Gersons, 2000; D. Mohr et

al., 2003), and intensification of adverse symptoms associated with other stressful events (National Institute of Mental Health, 2002).

PTSD has been tied to temporary and permanent changes in stress regulatory systems as well. Research suggests that people suffering from PTSD may experience permanent changes in the brain involving the amygdala and the hypothalamic-pituitary-adrenal (HPA) axis. Those suffering from PTSD show substantial variability in cortisol patterns (Mason et al., 2002) as well as higher levels of norepinephrine, epinephrine, testosterone, and thyroxin functioning. These hormonal alterations can last a long time (Buckley & Kaloupek, 2001; Hawk, Dougall, Ursano, & Baum, 2000; J. W. Mason, Kosten, Southwick, & Giller, 1990; Wang & Mason, 1999). Studies have also reported alterations in natural killer cell cytotoxicity following a natural disaster (Hurricane Andrew) (Ironson et al., 1997) and chronically elevated T cell counts among those with combat-related PTSD (Boscarino & Chang, 1999). PTSD is also prognostic of poor health (Deykin et al., 2001), and may interact with pre-existing health risks to increase health-related problems. For example, in the wake of the September 11, 2001, attacks on the World Trade Center, PTSD contributed to severity of symptoms and utilization of urgent health care services among asthmatics in the New York area (Fagan et al., 2003).

BOX 6.2

Post-Traumatic Stress Disorder (continued)

Who is most likely to develop PTSD? In several studies of wartime experiences, researchers have found that men who had more combat experience, who observed atrocities, and who actually participated in atrocities were most likely to experience PTSD (Breslau & Davis, 1987). People who develop the symptoms of PTSD may also have had a preexisting vulnerability to emotional distress as well, inasmuch as many PTSD sufferers have had a prior emotional disorder (Keane & Wolfe, 1990). Avoidant coping, low levels of social support, a history of chronic stress, and general negativity

may also predict who will develop PTSD in the wake of a traumatic stressor (L. D. Butler, Koopman, Classen, & Spiegel, 1999; Widows et al., 2000).

Can PTSD be alleviated? Combining pharmacologic, psychological, and psychosocial treatments into a multimodal intervention program is thought to be the best way of treating PTSD (Shalev, Bonne, & Eth, 1996). With increases in social support and a shift toward problem-focused coping, symptoms of PTSD can decline (Z. Solomon, Mikulincer, & Avitzur, 1988).

---

stressor is over. For example, in one study (S. Cohen & Spacapan, 1978, experiment 2), people shopped in a shopping center that was either crowded or uncrowded and were required to purchase a large or a small number of items in a short period of time. Later, all the shoppers encountered a woman who pretended to have lost a contact lens and who requested help finding it. The people who had had to purchase lots of items in a short period of time or who had been more crowded were less likely to help the woman than were the people who had had few things to buy and more time to shop or who had shopped in less crowded conditions.

The fact that stressful events produce aftereffects should not be surprising. Even simply arriving late to an exam may leave the heart racing for half an hour, interfering with effective performance. Exposure to a stressor over a longer period of time may have cumulative adverse effects so that reserves are drained and resistance breaks down when a person has to cope with a new stressful event. Unpredictable and uncontrollable stressful events appear to be particularly likely to produce deleterious aftereffects (D. C. Glass & Singer, 1972). Stress taxes perceptual and cognitive resources by drawing off attention, overtaxing cognitive capabilities, and depleting cognitive resources for other tasks (D. C. Glass & Singer, 1972). When we devote attention to understanding a stressful event, monitoring it, and attempting to deal with it, these efforts draw the same resources away from other aspects of life, and we have less energy to focus on other tasks. These **cognitive costs** appear to be stronger for unpredictable and uncontrollable events than for stressful events that are more predictable or more amenable to control. Some of these costs are illustrated in box 6.3.

■ HOW STRESS HAS BEEN STUDIED

We now turn to the methods that health psychologists have used for measuring stress and assessing its effects on psychological and physical health. In particular, we look at the measurement of stressful life events, daily hassles, chronic strain, and stress in the workplace and the home.

Studying Stress in the Laboratory

A common current way of studying stress is to bring people into the laboratory, expose them to short-term stressful events, and then observe the impact of that stress on their physiological, neuroendocrine, and psychological responses. This **acute stress paradigm** consistently finds that, when people are induced to perform stressful tasks (such as counting backwards quickly by 7s or delivering an impromptu speech to an unresponsive audience), they show strong indications of sympathetic activity, such as increases in heart rate and blood pressure and strong neuroendocrine responses suggestive of increased HPA activity, such as strong cortisol responses. Such tasks, not surprisingly, also produce short-term psychological distress (for example, Kirschbaum, Klauer, Filipp, & Hellhammer, 1995; S. M. Patterson, Marsland, Manuck, Kameneva, & Muldoon, 1998; Ritz & Steptoe, 2000).

Use of the acute stress paradigm has proven invaluable for understanding what kinds of events produce stress and how reactions to stress are influenced by factors such as personality, social support, and the presence of chronic stress in a person's life. For example, responses to acute stress among those who are also chronically stressed tend to be more exaggerated than among those not going through chronic stress as well (J. Pike et al., 1997).

BOX 6.3

Dormitory Crowding
An Example of Learned Helplessness

Many students have had the experience of arriving at college and finding that the college admitted too many students for the academic year. Rooms designed as singles suddenly become doubles, doubles become triples, and dormitory television rooms are turned into makeshift homes for the overflow. Clearly, these kinds of experiences are stressful, but do they have any impact beyond the trivial annoyances they may produce? Research by A. Baum and his associates suggests that they do.

In a classic study, A. Baum and Valins (1977) studied residents of college dormitories who lived in one of two situations. One group of students lived on long corridors and therefore had prolonged and repeated encounters with the large number of other individuals on their floor. The second group of students lived in short corridors or suites and had relatively few forced encounters with other individuals. Students in these two living situations were taken into the laboratory and exposed to a variety of interpersonal and task situations.

In a series of studies, A. Baum and Valins found that students who lived on the long corridors showed behavior that could be interpreted as helplessness. They initiated fewer conversations with a stranger, spent less time looking at the stranger, and sat farther away from him or her. They were less able to reach a group consensus after a discussion, were more likely to give up in a competitive game situation, and were less likely to assert themselves by asking questions in an ambiguous situation. Responses to questionnaire items confirmed that the students felt helpless.

Baum and Valins argued that because of repeated uncontrollable personal interactions with others, the students had learned to be helpless. The level of stress they experienced in their natural living situation led them to shy away from interpersonal contact with strangers. It also made them less likely to act assertively in ambiguous situations, perhaps because they had learned that they had little control over their environment. Results like these make it clear how stress produced by something as simple as a living situation can affect many other aspects of life.

The acute stress paradigm has also elucidated how individual differences contribute to stress. For example, people who are high in hostility show heightened blood pressure and cardiovascular responsivity to laboratory stress, compared with people who are not as hostile (M. Davis, Matthews, & McGrath, 2000). As we will see in chapter 14, hostile individuals' tendency to respond to interpersonal stressors in a hostile manner and with strong sympathetic responses may contribute to the higher incidence of coronary heart disease in hostile individuals.

The acute stress paradigm has also been proven useful for showing the kinds of factors that ameliorate the experience of stress. For example, when people go through these acute laboratory stressors in the presence of a supportive other person, even a stranger, their stress responses may be reduced (for example, Fontana, Diegnan, Villeneuve, & Lepore, 1999; C. M. Stoney & Finney, 2000). We will explore this phenomenon of social support more fully in chapter 7.

Overall, the acute stress paradigm has proven to be very useful in identifying how biological, psychological, and social factors change and influence each other in situations of short-term stress.

Inducing Disease

A relatively recent way of studying the effects of stress on disease processes has involved intentionally exposing people to viruses and then assessing whether they get ill and how ill they get. For example, S. Cohen, Doyle, and Skoner (1999) measured levels of psychological stress in a group of adults, infected them with an influenza virus by swabbing their nose with a swab soaked in a viral culture, and measured their respiratory symptoms, the amount of mucus they produced, and interleukin-6 (IL-6), a pro-inflammatory cytokine that may link stress through the immune system to illness. They found, as predicted, that psychological stress led to a greater evidence of illness and an increased production of IL-6 in response to the viral challenge than was true of people exposed to the virus whose lives were less stressful.

Stressful Life Events

Another line of stress research has focused more heavily on the psychological experience of stress. One such line of work measures **stressful life events.** These range from cataclysmic events, such as the death of one's spouse or being fired from a job, to more mundane but still problematic events, such as moving to a new home.

Two pioneers in stress research, T. H. Holmes and Rahe (1967) argued that, when an organism must make a substantial adjustment to the environment, the likelihood of stress is high. They developed an inventory of stressful life events in an attempt to measure stress (see table 6.1). Specifically, they identified which events force people to make the most changes in their lives and then assigned point values to those events to reflect the amount of change that must be made. Thus, for example, if one's spouse dies, virtually every aspect of life is disrupted. On the other hand, getting a traffic ticket may be upsetting and annoying but is unlikely to produce much change in one's life. To obtain a stress score, one totals up the point values associated with the events a person has experienced over the past year. Although all people experience at least some stressful events, some will experience a lot, and it is this group, according to Holmes and Rahe, that is most vulnerable to illness.

A number of studies show that stressful life events (SLE) predict illness. Rahe, Mahan, and Arthur (1970), for example, obtained SLE scores on sailors who were about to depart on 6-month cruises. They were able to predict with some success who would get sick and for how long. Life event inventories have been reliably tied both to the onset of acute illness and to the exacerbation of chronic diseases (S. Adams, Dammers, Saia, Brantley, & Gaydos, 1994; Levy, Cain, Jarrett, & Heitkemper, 1997; Yoshiuchi et al., 1998). Overall, however, the relation between the SLE scales and illness is quite modest. The SLE scales do predict illness, but not very well.

Problems Measuring Stressful Life Events

What are some of the problems of using a stressful life event inventory? First, some of the items on the list are vague; for example, "personal injury or illness" could mean anything from the flu to a heart attack. Second, because events have preassigned point values, individual differences in the way events are experienced are not taken into account (Schroeder & Costa, 1984). For example, a divorce may mean welcome freedom to one partner but a collapse in living standard or self-esteem to the other.

Third, inventories usually include both positive and negative events. They include events that individuals choose, such as getting married, as well as events that simply happen, such as the death of a close friend. Some researchers (for example, Billings & Moos, 1982) have argued that these differences matter and that events

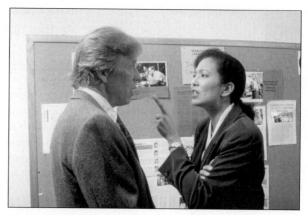

Work strains, like the argument between these co-workers, are common sources of stress that compromise well-being and physical health.

should not be treated the same regardless of valence or choice. As we have seen, sudden, negative, unexpected, and uncontrollable events predict illness better than events that are positive, expected, gradual in onset, or under personal control. In counting up the frequency of life events, researchers typically do not assess whether those events have been successfully resolved or not (Thoits, 1994), and stressful events that have been successfully resolved do not produce adverse effects for an individual. Consequently, this evidence, too, weakens the ability of life event inventories to predict adverse health consequences (R. J. Turner & Avison, 1992).

Another problem is that assessing specific stressful events may also tap ongoing life strain, that is, chronic stress that is part of everyday life. Chronic strain may also produce psychological distress and physical illness, but it needs to be measured separately from specific life events. Additional concerns are that some people may just be prone to report more stress in their lives or to experience it more intensely (S. Epstein & Katz, 1992; Magnus, Diener, Fujita, & Pavot, 1993). Thus, more life events may be checked off by people with a propensity to react strongly to life's stresses and strains. Life event measures may be unreliable because people forget what stressful events they have experienced, especially if the events occurred more than a few weeks earlier (Kessler & Wethington, 1991; Raphael, Cloitre, & Dohrenwend, 1991). Many people have theories about what kinds of events cause illness, so they may distort their reports of stress and reports of illness to correspond with each other.

A final difficulty in trying to estimate the stress-illness relationship concerns the time period between the two. Usually, stress over a 1-year period is related to the

TABLE 6.1 | The Social Readjustment Rating Scale

Rank	Life Event	Mean Value
1.	Death of spouse	100
2.	Divorce	73
3.	Marital separation from mate	65
4.	Detention in jail or other institution	63
5.	Death of a close family member	63
6.	Major personal injury or illness	53
7.	Marriage	50
8.	Being fired at work	47
9.	Marital reconciliation with mate	45
10.	Retirement from work	45
11.	Major change in the health or behavior of a family member	44
12.	Pregnancy	40
13.	Sexual difficulties	39
14.	Gaining a new family member (e.g., through birth, adoption, oldster moving in, etc.)	39
15.	Major business readjustment (e.g., merger, reorganization, bankruptcy, etc.)	39
16.	Major change in financial state (e.g., a lot worse off or a lot better off than usual)	38
17.	Death of a close friend	37
18.	Changing to a different line of work	36
19.	Major change in the number of arguments with spouse (e.g., either a lot more or a lot less than usual regarding child rearing, personal habits, etc.)	35
20.	Taking out a mortgage or loan for a major purchase (e.g., for a home, business, etc.)	31
21.	Foreclosure on a mortgage or loan	30
22.	Major change in responsibilities at work (e.g., promotion, demotion, lateral transfer)	29
23.	Son or daughter leaving home (e.g., marriage, attending college, etc.)	29
24.	Trouble with in-laws	29
25.	Outstanding personal achievement	28
26.	Wife beginning or ceasing work outside the home	26
27.	Beginning or ceasing formal schooling	26
28.	Major change in living conditions (e.g., building a new home, remodeling, deterioration of home or neighborhood)	25
29.	Revision of personal habits (dress, manners, associations, etc.)	24
30.	Trouble with the boss	23
31.	Major change in working hours or conditions	20
32.	Change in residence	20
33.	Changing to a new school	20
34.	Major change in usual type and/or amount of recreation	19
35.	Major change in church activities (e.g., a lot more or a lot less than usual)	19
36.	Major change in social activities (e.g., clubs, dancing, movies, visiting, etc.)	18
37.	Taking out a mortgage or loan for a lesser purchase (e.g., for a car, television, freezer, etc.)	17
38.	Major change in sleeping habits (a lot more or a lot less sleep, or change in part of day when asleep)	16
39.	Major change in number of family get-togethers (e.g., a lot more or a lot less than usual)	15
40.	Major change in eating habits (a lot more or a lot less food intake, or very different meal hours or surroundings)	15
41.	Vacation	13
42.	Christmas	12
43.	Minor violations of the law (e.g., traffic tickets, jaywalking, disturbing the peace, etc.)	11

Source: T. H. Holmes & Rahe, 1967.

BOX 6.4

A Measure of Perceived Stress

Because people vary so much in what they consider to be stressful, many researchers feel that **perceived stress** is a better measure of stress than are instruments that measure whether people have been exposed to particular events. To address this issue, S. Cohen and his colleagues (1983) developed a measure of perceived stress, some items of which follow. Note the differences between this measure of stress and the items on the social readjustment rating scale in table 6.1. Research (for example, Lobel, Dunkel-Schetter, & Scrimshaw, 1992) suggests that perceived stress predicts a broad array of health outcomes.

ITEMS AND INSTRUCTIONS FOR THE PERCEIVED STRESS SCALE

The questions in this scale ask you about your feelings and thoughts during the last month. In each case, you will be asked to indicate how often you felt or thought a certain way. Although some of the questions are similar, there are differences between them, and you should treat each one as a separate question. The best approach is to answer each question fairly quickly. That is, don't try to count up the number of times you felt a particular way, but, rather, indicate the alternative that seems like a reasonable estimate.

For each question, choose from the following alternatives:

0 never
1 almost never
2 sometimes
3 fairly often
4 very often

1. In the last month, how often have you been upset because of something that happened unexpectedly?

2. In the last month, how often have you felt nervous and "stressed"?

3. In the last month, how often have you found that you could not cope with all the things that you had to do?

4. In the last month, how often have you been angered because of things that happened that were outside your control?

5. In the last month, how often have you found yourself thinking about things that you had to accomplish?

6. In the last month, how often have you felt difficulties were piling up so high that you could not overcome them?

---

most recent 6 months of illness bouts, yet is it reasonable to assume that January's crisis caused June's cold or that last month's financial problems produced a malignancy detected this month? After all, malignancies can grow undetected for 10 or 20 years. Obviously, these cases are extreme, but they illustrate some of the problems in studying the stress-illness relationship over time. For all these reasons, stressful life event inventories are no longer used as much. Some researchers, as a result, have turned to perceived stress to assess the degree of stress people experience (see box 6.4).

Daily Stress

In addition to work on major stressful life events and past stressors, researchers have also studied minor stressful events, or **daily hassles,** and their cumulative impact on health and illness. Such hassles include being stuck in a traffic jam, waiting in line, doing household chores, and having difficulty making a small decision. Daily minor problems reduce psychological well-being over the short term and produce physical symptoms (Bolger, DeLongis, Kessler, & Schilling, 1989).

Minor hassles can conceivably produce stress and aggravate physical and psychological health in several ways. First, the cumulative impact of small stressors may wear down an individual, predisposing him or her to become ill. Second, such events may influence the relationship between major life events and illnesses. For example, if a major life event is experienced at a time when minor life events are also high in number, the stress may be greater than it would otherwise be (Monroe, 1983). A traffic ticket that requires a court appearance in the middle of the summer is a nuisance but in the middle of a busy school year can seem like a disaster. Alternatively, major life events may have their effects on distress primarily by increasing the number of daily hassles they create (Pillow, Zautra, & Sandler, 1996).

BOX 6.5

The Measurement of Daily Strain

Psychologists have examined the role of minor stresses and strains in the development of illness. The following are some examples of how psychologists measure these stresses and strains.

INSTRUCTIONS

Each day we can experience minor annoyances as well as major problems or difficulties. Listed are a number of irritations that can produce daily strain. Indicate how much of a strain each of these annoyances has been for you in the past month.

Severity

0	Did not occur
1	Mild strain
2	Somewhat of a strain
3	Moderate strain
4	Extreme strain

Hassles

1.	A quarrel or problems with a neighbor	0	1	2	3	4
2.	Traffic congestion	0	1	2	3	4
3.	Thoughts of poor health	0	1	2	3	4
4.	Argument with romantic partner	0	1	2	3	4
5.	Concerns about money	0	1	2	3	4
6.	Getting a parking ticket	0	1	2	3	4
7.	Preparing meals	0	1	2	3	4

Lazarus and his associates (Kanner, Coyne, Schaefer, & Lazarus, 1981) developed a measure of minor stressful life events termed the hassles scale. In one study (Kanner et al., 1981), 100 middle-aged adults completed the hassles scale for 9 consecutive months and reported psychological symptoms, including depression and anxiety. Hassles proved to be a better predictor of symptoms than were more major life events. Research has also tied daily hassles to declines in physical health (DeLongis, Coyne, Dakof, Folkman, & Lazarus, 1982) and to a worsening of symptoms in those already suffering from illnesses (e.g., R. L. Levy, Cain, Jarrett, & Heitkemper, 1997), although the evidence is inconsistent (Traue & Kosarz, 1999). An example of how daily hassles can be measured is shown in box 6.5.

How does the presence of minor daily hassles interact with major stressful life events or with chronic stress? The answers to these questions are not yet known. In some cases, daily hassles seem to exacerbate psychological distress when they occur in conjunction with chronic stress (Lepore, Evans, & Palsane, 1991; Serido, Almeida, & Wethington, 2004), and in other cases, the presence of chronic stress may actually mute the impact of daily hassles, because the hassles pale in comparison with the more chronic stressful events (McGonagle & Kessler, 1990).

Problems with Measuring Hassles Unfortunately, the measurement of daily hassles is subject to some of the same problems as the measurement of major stressful life events. Individuals who are experiencing a lot of hassles and who are also high in anxiety to begin with also report more psychological distress (Kohn, Lafreniere, & Gurevich, 1991). This suggests that individuals who are predisposed to cope with stress via overreaction and anxiety will respond in this way to daily hassles, thus magnifying their adverse effects. In response, researchers have attempted to disentangle objective daily hassles from psychological and physical symptoms (for example, Kohn, Lafreniere, & Gurevich, 1990; R. S. Lazarus, DeLongis, Folkman, & Gruen, 1985). The results of this work suggest that hassles do, indeed, compromise psychological and physical functioning.

■ SOURCES OF CHRONIC STRESS

Earlier we posed the question, Can people adapt to chronically stressful events? The answer was that people can adapt to a degree but continue to show signs of stress in response to severe chronic strains in their lives. Ongoing stress can exacerbate the impact of life events by straining the person's coping capacities when he or

BOX 6.6

Stress and Human-Made Disasters

Increasingly, stress researchers are examining how people cope with human-made disasters, such as the threats posed by nuclear contamination or toxic wastes. Although in many ways reactions to human-made disasters are similar to reactions to natural disasters, such as fire, tornado, or flood, there are important differences. Natural catastrophes are usually time limited, and they dissipate over time. Also, governments have programs ready to move in almost immediately to ameliorate the effects of natural disasters. In contrast, the threat posed by toxic waste dumps or leaks from nuclear power plants may be ongoing, and solutions for them have yet to be developed.

In a study of the Love Canal, a toxic waste dump adjacent to a neighborhood in the Niagara Falls area, researchers report that the psychological damage from this disaster may ultimately turn out to rival or even exceed the physical damage. Like other human-made disasters, such as the nuclear accident at Three Mile Island, the problems at Love Canal forced residents to cope with several stressors simultaneously. First, they had to face the possibility of serious, life-threatening illness. Residents have highlighted cases of miscarriage, stillbirth, birth defects, respiratory problems, urinary problems, and cancer in an effort to convince scientists and government officials that the threat to their health is real. Second, residents still do not yet know the extent of damage. Unlike flood victims, who can quickly see the nature of their loss, Love Canal residents may spend most of their lives wondering what effects the poisons will have on their systems and worrying about whether these poisons will have effects on their children and grandchildren for generations to come. Third, the residents have had to cope with their feelings of helplessness and betrayal because the government has done so little to help them. The result has been panic, deep distress, and hostility, resulting in mass demonstrations and the taking of government hostages in a vain effort to get action.

Most of the former residents have had a variety of vague psychophysiological problems, including depression, irritability, dizziness, nausea, weakness, fatigue, insomnia, and numbness in the extremities. In addition to these symptoms, family strain was prevalent. More than 40% of the couples evacuated from the area separated or divorced in the 2 years after their departure. Typically, the husband wanted to remain in the neighborhood and salvage what he could of the family's home and possessions, whereas the wife chose to leave for the sake of the children and their health.

Although the Niagara Falls Community Health Center put together a program on coping with stress and publicized available counseling programs, few Love Canal residents used the opportunity. In trying to explain the reasons for this, researchers have suggested two possibilities. First, within this working-class population, counseling may have been viewed as a stigma, an option to be used only by the mentally disturbed and not by normal people coping with a "real" stress. Second, the practice of stress management may have been perceived as indicating that the problem is "all in one's head" rather than objectively "out there" in the dump site itself. Instead of using available mental health services, residents got psychological aid through self-help—that is, talking with one another informally or through organized groups.

The type of stress observed at Love Canal raises an unnerving specter for stress researchers in the future. There are hundreds of chemical dump sites around the country, physical and psychological disasters waiting to be discovered. As researchers increasingly uncover other toxic substances (such as, for example, those posed by herbicides and nuclear accidents), this kind of stress—the stress of not knowing what the damage is and not being able to find ways of overcoming it because of government indecision—will undoubtedly increase.

Source: Holden, 1980.

she is confronted with yet another problem to manage (G. W. Brown & Harris, 1978). Increasingly, stress researchers are coming to the conclusion that the chronic stressors of life may be more important than major life events in the development of illness. There are several kinds of chronic strain, and how they differ in terms of their psychological and physical effects is not yet known.

Post-Traumatic Stress Disorder

One type of chronic strain results from severely traumatic or stressful events whose residual effects may remain with the individual for years. Post-traumatic stress disorder, described in box 6.2, is an example of this kind of chronic stress, as is the response to the Love Canal disaster detailed in box 6.6.

Childhood sexual abuse, rape, and exposure to natural and human-made disasters, such as the World Trade Center attacks, may produce chronic mental health and physical health effects that maintain the virulence of the initial experience (for example, A. Baum, Cohen, & Hall, 1993; Downey, Silver, & Wortman, 1990). In the case of the World Trade Center attacks, the stress of this event has been tied to inflammatory processes potentially enhancing risk for illness (S. Melamed, Shirom, Toker, Berliner, & Shapira, 2004).

Long-Term Effects of Early Stressful Life Experiences

Recent research has focused on the long-term effects of early stressors, including those experienced in early childhood, on disease later in life (Repetti, Taylor, & Seeman, 2002). Some of this work has been prompted by the allostatic load view of stress, which argues that major, chronic, or recurrent stress dysregulates stress systems, which, over time, can produce accumulating risk for disease.

Chronic abuse in childhood or adulthood has long been known to increase a broad array of health risks because it results in intense, chronic stress that taxes physiological systems. It is now clear that even more modest family stress can increase risk for disease as well. Repetti et al. (2002) reported that "risky families"—that is, families that are high in conflict or abuse and low in warmth and nurturance—produce offspring with problems in stress regulatory systems. By virtue of having to cope with a chronically stressful family environment, children from such families may develop heightened sympathetic reactivity to stressors and exaggerated cortisol responses. Moreover, by virtue of exposure to chronic stress early in life, the developing stress systems themselves may become dysregulated, such that physiological and neuroendocrine stress responses across the life span are affected by these early experiences. Because these stress systems and their dysfunctions are implicated in a broad array of diseases, it should not be surprising that an early major stressful event would produce damage later in life. The evidence for this position is quite substantial (for example, Biggs, Aziz, Tomenson, & Creed, 2003; Repetti et al., 2002; Wickrama, Conger, Wallace, & Elder, 2003).

For example, in a retrospective study, Felitti and colleagues (1998) asked adults to complete a questionnaire regarding their early family environment that inquired, among other things, how warm and supportive the environment was versus how cold, critical, hostile, or conflict-ridden it was. The more of these problems these adults reported from their childhood, the more vulnerable they were in adulthood to an array of disorders, including depression, lung disease, cancer, heart disease, and diabetes. At least some of the risk may have occurred not only because of stress-related biological dysregulations but also because of poor health habits, such as smoking, poor diet, and lack of exercise that these early stressful environments prompted.

Of course, there are potential problems with retrospective accounts. People who are depressed or ill, for example, may be especially likely to regard their childhoods as traumatic or stressful. However, substantial evidence from prospective longitudinal investigations supports many of these conclusions (see Repetti et al., 2002, for a review), and consequently distortions in reconstructions of one's childhood family environment may not account for the results.

Other research similarly shows the delayed impact on later illness (Leserman, Li, Hu, & Drossman, 1998) that stress can have. For example, men who had experienced post-traumatic stress disorder from combat experience during the Vietnam War were found in older age to have significantly higher risk for circulatory, digestive, musculoskeletal, metabolic, nervous system, and respiratory disorders (Boscarino, 1997).

Chronic Stressful Conditions

Other chronic strains are of the long-term, grinding kind, such as living in poverty, being in a bad relationship, or remaining in a high-stress job. Compared with research on stressful life events, less research has addressed the role of chronic strain on psychological and physical health outcomes. There is evidence that chronic strain is an important contributor to psychological distress and physical illness (see figure 6.5).

In an early community study of 2,300 people, Pearlin and Schooler (1978) found that people who reported chronic stress in marriage, parenting, household functioning, or their jobs were more likely to be psychologically distressed. Chronic strains lasting for more than 2 years have been implicated in the development of depression (G. W. Brown & Harris, 1978), and uncontrollable stressors may be particularly virulent in this regard (McGonagle & Kessler, 1990). In a survey of Toronto community residents, R. J. Turner and Lloyd (1999) found that the depression that was associated with low social class was completely explained by the

FIGURE 6.5 | Stress Can Compromise Both Mental and Physical Health
This figure shows some of the routes by which these effects may occur.   (*Source:* After S. Cohen, Kessler, & Gordon, 1995)

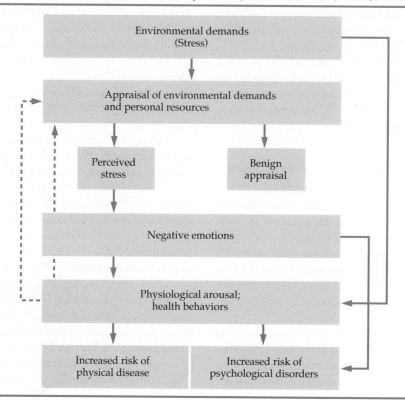

increasing stress exposure of those individuals further down the SES ladder.

Chronic strain may influence the relationship between specific stressors and adverse physical or psychological effects. Jennifer Pike and colleagues (J. Pike et al., 1997) found that people who were undergoing chronic life stress showed exaggerated sympathetic reactivity and corresponding decrements in natural killer cell activity in response to an acute stress in the laboratory, as compared with people who had fewer background stressors (see also Lepore, Miles, & Levy, 1997).

Chronic Stress and Health

Research relating chronic stress to mental and physical health outcomes is difficult to conduct, because it is often hard to demonstrate that a particular chronic stressor is the factor contributing to illness. A second problem is that chronic stress is often assessed subjectively on the basis of self-reports. Unlike life events, which can often be assessed objectively, chronic stress may be more

difficult to measure objectively because it can be more difficult to determine objectively whether particular chronic strains are actually going on.

Third, as in the measurement of life events, inventories that attempt to assess chronic strain may also tap psychological distress and neuroticism rather than the objective existence of stressful conditions. Finally, assessment of stressful life events may also pick up the effects of chronic strain so that the impact of chronic strain on psychological and physical health is obscured. Nonetheless, a wealth of evidence is consistent with the idea that chronic stress is related to illness.

Research showing social class differences in death from all causes and in rates of specific diseases, such as most cancers and cardiovascular disease, is evidence suggestive of a relationship; poverty, exposure to crime, and other chronic stressors vary with social class (N. E. Adler, Boyce, Chesney, Folkman, & Syme, 1993). In addition, many psychological disorders, such as depression, may show the same gradient (R. J. Turner & Lloyd, 1999). For example, people who are low in SES typically have low-prestige occupations, which may expose them to greater interpersonal conflict and arousal at work; the consequences can include psychological distress and changes in cardiovascular indicators, among other stress-related outcomes (K. A. Matthews et al., 2000). Chronic stress has been related to a variety of adverse health-related outcomes, including the likelihood of giving birth prematurely (Rini, Dunkel-Schetter, Wadhwa, & Sandman, 1999) and the likelihood of developing coronary artery disease (see chapter 13). Box 6.7 focuses on a particular type of chronic stress, namely, racism, and its relation to poor health.

As we will next see, the chronic stress of particular jobs, especially those jobs that are high in demands and low in control, has been reliably tied to stress and illness.

Stress in the Workplace

A large body of literature has examined the causes and consequences. Studies of occupational stress are important for several reasons:

1. They help identify some of the most common stressors of everyday life.

2. They provide additional evidence for the stress-illness relationship.

3. Work stress may be one of our preventable stressors and thereby provide possibilities for intervention (Sauter, Murphy, & Hurrell, 1990).

Although not all occupational stress can be avoided, knowledge of job factors that are stressful raises the possibility of redesigning jobs and implementing stress management interventions.

Moreover, as lawmakers are increasingly realizing (Hatfield, 1990; Sauter et al., 1990), stress-related physical and mental health disorders account for an enormous and growing percentage of disability and social security payments to workers. Reining in these substantial costs to the economy has become an important priority.

Physical Hazards   Many workers are exposed as a matter of course to physical, chemical, and biological hazards (G.W. Evans & Kantrowitz, 2001). These risks produce many adverse health outcomes, including injuries, cancers, and respiratory and cardiovascular disease (J. S. House & Smith, 1985). Even noise can produce elevated catecholamines (Center for the Advancement of Health, September, 2003). Recently, workplace stress studies have also focused on such disorders as repetitive stress injuries, such as carpal tunnel

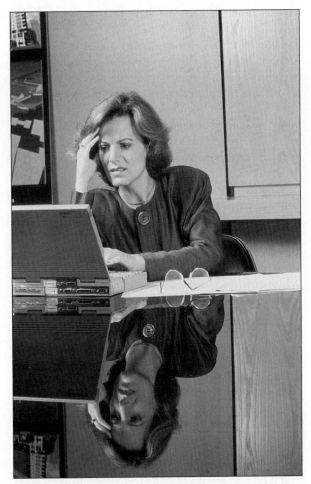

Research shows that workers with high levels of job strain and low levels of control over their work are under great stress and may be at risk for coronary heart disease.

syndrome, which are a product of our sedentary, computerized way of life.

In addition, the changing patterns of work may erode certain health benefits of work that used to occur as a matter of course. For example, the most common work that people undertook before the Industrial Revolution involved agricultural production, in which people engaged in physical exercise as they were going about their work tasks. As people have moved into office jobs or other work contexts that require very little output of physical energy, the amount of exercise that they get in their work life has declined substantially (J. S. House & Smith, 1985). Even those jobs that require high levels of physical exertion, such as construction work and firefighting, may include so much stress that the potential benefits of exercise are negated. Because activity level is

BOX 6.7

Can Racism Kill You?

A young African-American father pulled in front of a house in a largely white neighborhood to pick up his daughter from a birthday party. Because he was early and the party had not ended, he sat in the car to wait until it was over. Within 8 minutes, a security car had pulled up behind him, two officers approached him and asked him to exit his vehicle. Neighbors had reported seeing a suspicious African-American man casing their neighbor.

Stressful events of all kinds can erode health, and recently researchers have explored the effects of prejudice and racism on health. It has long been known that African Americans experience greater health risks than the rest of the population. For example, life expectancy for African-American men is 7.1 years less than for White men, and 12.7 years less than for White women. African-American men die of heart attacks at more than two and half times the rate for White women, and cardiovascular disease is twice as likely to kill African-American men as to kill White women or men. Heart disease has declined dramatically over the past few decades, but that decline has been slower among African-Americans (Zheng, Croft, Labarthe, Williams, & Mensah 2001). The rate of death from cancer for African Americans is also twice than that for White women (National Center for Health Statistics, 1999; Williams, 2001; Williams & Collins, 2001). African Americans are more vulnerable to AIDS and far more likely to die of AIDS than Whites.

Many of these differences can be traced to differences in socioeconomic status. Poverty, lower education attainment, and unemployment are prevalent in many Black communities (Boardman, Finch, Ellison, Williams, & Jackson, 2001; Browning & Cagney, 2003; Steptoe, Kunz-Ebrecht, Owen, Feldman, Willemsen, et al., 2003). The day-in day-out grinding discrimination associated with poor housing, little available employment, poor schools, and poor neighborhoods also contributes to stress through chronic exposure to violence and an enduring sense of danger or trouble to come (C. E. Ross & Mirowsky, 2001). Medical services in minority areas are often inadequate, with the result that African-Americans are less likely to receive preventive services and more likely to suffer the consequences of delayed medical attention (Gornick, 2000; Institute of Medicine, 2002). Racial incidents as well may contribute to the cardiovascular toll that racism plays, such as being treated badly by a store clerk or being stopped by the police for no reason. One study found that although Whites rarely think about race during the course of a day, more than half of Blacks do (Kirchheimer, 2003).

Perceived racism coupled with inhibited angry responses to it is related to higher blood pressure, suggesting that the perception of racism contributes to the high incidence of hypertension seen among African Americans (Brondolo, Rieppi, Kelly, & Gerin, 2003; R. Clark, 2003; Steffen, McNeilly, Anderson, & Sherwood, 2003). Blood pressure usually falls when a person goes to sleep, but in some people it remains elevated, termed *nondipping*. Nondipping may be an indicator of stress exposure. In one study, African-American adolescents who had been exposed to violence in their communities were more likely to show nondipping, especially if they themselves have been victimized (D. K. Wilson, Kliewer, Teasley, Plybon, & Sica, 2002).

Stress exposure may also help to explain the high levels of depression in the African-American population (Forman, 2003; George & Lynch, 2003; Turner & Avison, 2003). Depression is a risk factor for several chronic diseases. Exposure to racism has been tied to problem drinking in African-Americans as well (D. K. Martin, Tuch, & Roman, 2003).

Racism is not the only form of prejudice and discrimination that affects poor health. For example, work discrimination against women has been tied to poor physical and emotional health among women as well (Pavalko, Mossakowski, & Hamilton, 2003; Ryff, Keyes, & Hughes, 2003). Suicide rates among ethnic immigrant groups have been tied to the amount of hate speech directed toward those groups (B. Mullen & Smyth, 2004). Perceived discrimination has been tied to substance abuse among Native American children (Whitbeck, Hoyt, McMorris, Chen, & Stubben, 2001) and to depression among Native American adults (Whitbeck, McMorris, Hoyt, Stubben, & LaFromboise, 2002).

Converging evidence like this indicates clearly that the stressors associated with discrimination and racism can adversely affect health. Although the issue is difficult to study scientifically, mounting evidence leads irresistibly to the conclusion that racism and discrimination contribute to poor health.

related to health, this change in the nature of work creates the possibility of vulnerability to illness (Eichner, 1983; Rigotti, Thomas, & Leaf, 1983).

Overload   Work overload is a chief factor producing high levels of occupational stress. Workers who feel required to work too long and too hard at too many tasks feel more stressed (for example, Caplan & Jones, 1975), practice poorer health habits (Sorensen et al., 1985), and sustain more health risks than do workers not suffering from overload (Repetti, 1993a). Research suggests that the chronic neuroendocrine activation and cardiovascular activation associated with overcommitment can contribute to cardiovascular disease (Steptoe, Siegrist, Kirschbaum, & Marmot, 2004).

An old rock song states, "Monday, Monday, can't trust that day." Increasingly, research suggests that this may be true. Monday appears to be one of the most stressful days of the week. Weekdays are generally associated with more worry and chronic work overload than weekends, resulting in altered cortisol patterns that may be risky for health (Schlotz, Hellhammer, Schulz, & Stone, 2004).

So well established is the relation between work overload and poor health that, in Japan, a country notorious for its long working hours, long work weeks, little sleep, and lack of vacations, there is a term, "karoshi," that refers to death from overwork. One study found that men who worked more than 61 hours a week experienced twice the risk of a heart attack as those working 40 hours or less; sleeping 5 hours or less at least 2 days a week increased this risk by two to three times (Liu & Tanaka, 2002). Under Japanese law, families are entitled to compensation if they can prove that the breadwinner died of karoshi (*Los Angeles Times,* 1993).

Work overload is a subjective as well as an objective experience. The sheer amount of work that a person does—that is, how many hours he or she works each week—is not consistently related to poor health and compromised psychological well-being (A. R. Herzog, House, & Morgan, 1991). The *perception of* work overload shows a stronger relationship to physical health complaints and psychological distress.

Work pressure also leads to stress. In one study, men were interviewed about their job pressures between 1967 and 1970. Those men experiencing more pressures showed more signs of illness and made more visits to health services. More important, when the men were followed through the subsequent decade, those with a moderate or high degree of job pressure or tension were

three times more likely to die than were men who reported lower levels of pressure or tension (J. S. House, Strecher, Meltzner, & Robbins, 1986).

Responsibility at work is a double-edged sword. On the one hand, it gives people a certain amount of latitude, which has been considered an important factor in low job stress, but on the other hand, jobs with high responsibility can also be very stressful (Iwanaga, Yokoyama, & Seiwa, 2000). When one has responsibility for people, rather than responsibility for products, stress may be even greater. One study compared the illness rates of air traffic controllers and second-class airmen. Although both jobs are highly stressful, air traffic controllers have responsibility for many people's lives, whereas airmen do not. The results revealed that hypertension was four times more common among air traffic controllers and that diabetes and peptic ulcers were more than twice as common. All three diseases were more likely to be diagnosed at a younger age among air traffic controllers, and both hypertension and ulcers were more common among controllers at the busier airports (Cobb, 1976).

Ambiguity and Role Conflict   Role conflict and role ambiguity are also associated with stress. As noted earlier, role ambiguity occurs when a person has few clear ideas of what is to be done and no idea of the standards used for evaluating work. **Role conflict** occurs when a person receives conflicting information about work tasks or standards from different individuals. For example, if a college professor is told by one colleague to publish more articles, is advised by another colleague to publish fewer papers but of higher quality, and is told by a third to work on improving teaching ratings, the professor will experience role ambiguity and conflict. Chronically high blood pressure and elevated pulse, as well as other illness precursors, have been tied to role conflict and role ambiguity (for example, J. R. P. French & Caplan, 1973). In contrast, when people receive clear feedback about the nature of their performance, they report lower levels of stress (S. Cohen & Williamson, 1988).

Social Relationships   The inability to develop satisfying social relationships at work has been tied to job stress (J. A. House, 1981), to psychological distress at work (B. P. Buunk, Doosje, Jans, & Hopstaken, 1993), and to poor physical and mental health (Landsbergis, Schnall, Deitz, Friedman, & Pickering, 1992; Repetti, 1993a). Workers who have little opportunity to interact with others are less satisfied with their jobs and may show heightened catecholamine levels (C. J. Cooper & Marshall, 1976).

Having a poor relationship with one's supervisor appears to be especially related to job distress and may also increase a worker's risk for coronary heart disease (M. C. Davis, Matthews, Meilahn, & Kiss, 1995; Repetti, 1993a). Conversely, men and women who are able to develop socially supportive relationships at work have enhanced well-being (Loscocco & Spitze, 1990).

To a degree, having an amiable social environment at work depends on being an amicable coworker. A study of air traffic controllers found that individuals who were not particularly well liked by their coworkers and who consequently did not have much social contact were significantly more likely to become ill and to experience an accidental injury than were individuals who enjoyed and contributed to a more satisfying social climate (Niemcryk, Jenkins, Rose, & Hurst, 1987).

Social relationships may not only be important in combating stress in their own right; they may also buffer other job stressors. For example, one study of New York City traffic enforcement agents found that social support from coworkers and supervisors was associated with lower ambulatory blood pressure, especially during stressful work conditions (Karlin, Brondolo, & Schwartz, 2003).

Control Lack of control over work has been related to a number of stress and illness indicators, including heightened catecholamine secretion, job dissatisfaction, absenteeism, and the development of coronary artery disease in particular (Bosma et al., 1997), as well as the risk of death from all causes (Amick et al., 2002).

The role of several of these job factors in the stress-illness relationship is illustrated in Frankenhaeuser's (1975) classic study of Swedish sawmill workers. In particular, she focused on edgers (those who plane the edges of lumber), sawyers (those who cut the lumber into predetermined sizes), and graders (those who decide on the quality of the lumber). These workers have very dull, repetitive jobs. They have no control over the pace of their work; it is determined by the speed of the machine. The work cycle is about 10 seconds long, requiring that decisions be made quickly. And, quite obviously, these jobs allow little social contact. Frankenhaeuser found that these workers had high levels of catecholamines, as indicated by urinalysis. Compared with other workers in the mill, they also showed high rates of headaches, high blood pressure, and gastrointestinal disorders, including ulcers.

Building on this kind of research, Karasek and his associates (1981) developed a model of job strain that is based on the relation between a worker and the job environment. They hypothesized that high psychological demands on the job with little decision latitude (such as low job control) causes job strain, which, in turn, can lead to the development of coronary artery disease. Research generally supports this idea (Cesana et al., 2003; Marmot, 1998; Pickering et al., 1996; Tsutsumi et al., 1998). The chronic anger that can result from these jobs may further contribute to coronary artery disease risk (Fitzgerald, Haythornthwaite, Suchday, & Ewart, 2003). When high demands and low control are combined with little social support at work, what has been termed as the demand-control-support model, risk for coronary artery disease may be even greater (Muhonen & Torkelson, 2003).

The exact mechanisms whereby work stress contributes to coronary heart disease are unknown, but potentially a broad array of processes are implicated. High levels of work stress can lead to impaired fibrolytic capacity, which may be a result of the impact of chronic stress on insulin resistance (Vrijkotte, van Doornen, & de Geus, 1999; see also Steptoe, Kunz-Ebrecht, Owen, Feldman, Rumley, et al., 2003). Whereas short-term work stress has only temporary effects on lipid activity, lipid activity associated with longer-term stress may well have significance for the development of coronary artery disease (B. McCann et al., 1999; Stoney, Niaura, Bausserman, & Matacin, 1999). Increases in blood pressure prognostic for cardiovascular disease have also been tied to work stress.

Unemployment A final source of stress related to work concerns the impact of unemployment on psychological distress and health. Unemployment can produce a variety of adverse outcomes, including psychological distress (J. R. Reynolds, 1997), physical symptoms, physical illness (V. L. Hamilton, Broman, Hoffman, & Renner, 1990), alcohol abuse (Catalano, Dooley, Wilson, & Houph, 1993), difficulty achieving sexual arousal, low birth weight of offspring (Catalano, Hansen, & Hartig, 1999), and compromised immune functioning (Segerstrom & Miller, 2004).

In a community study of high-unemployment areas in Michigan, R. C. Kessler and associates (1988) found that unemployment was associated with high rates of depression, anxiety, symptom expression, and self-reported physical illness. These effects appear to be accounted for largely by financial strain produced by unemployment and the enhanced vulnerability to other life events that unemployment creates. A follow-up study by J. B. Turner, Kessler, and House (1991) found that those individuals with social support and who coped actively were more buffered against the adverse effects of unemployment. Reemployment largely reversed the adverse effects of unemployment (Kessler, Turner, & House, 1987).

Uncertainty over one's continuing employment and unstable employment have also been tied to physical illness (Heaney, Israel, & House, 1994). For example, a study found that men who had held a series of unrelated jobs were at greater risk of dying over a follow-up period than men who had remained in the same job or in the same type of job over a longer period of time (Pavalko, Elder, & Clipp, 1993). Generally speaking, being stably employed is protective of health (Rushing, Ritter, & Burton, 1992).

Other Occupational Outcomes Stress also shows up in ways other than illness that may be extremely costly to an organization. Many of these factors may represent workers' efforts to control or to offset stress before it ever gets to the point of causing illness. For example, workers who cannot participate actively in decisions about their jobs show higher rates of absenteeism, job turnover, tardiness, job dissatisfaction, sabotage, and poor performance on the job. Moreover, this problem may be getting worse. In essence, workers have taken stress into their own hands and have reduced it by not working as long, as hard, or as well as their employers apparently expect (Kivimaki, Vahtera, Ellovainio, Lillirank, & Kevin, 2002).

Substance abuse, in the form of alcohol abuse and drug abuse, represents another way of coping with occupational stress and alienation from work (E. S. Greenberg & Grunberg, 1995). However, research suggests that such abuse may be more related to general feelings of powerlessness, alienation, and lack of commitment than to specific job characteristics (Mensch & Kandel, 1988; M. Seeman, Seeman, & Budfos, 1988).

Reducing Occupational Stress What are some solutions to these workplace stresses? A blueprint for change has been offered by several organizational stress researchers (for example, Kahn, 1981; McGregor, 1967):

1. Physical work stressors, such as noise, harsh lighting, crowding, or temperature extremes, should be reduced as much as possible.

2. An effort to minimize unpredictability and ambiguity in expected tasks and standards of performance reduces stress. When workers know what they are expected to do and at what level, they are less distressed.

3. Involving workers as much as possible in the decisions that affect their work life reduces stress. Some corporations have given workers control over certain facets of their jobs, including working hours, the rate at which a task is performed, and the order in which tasks are performed, with corresponding increases in productivity and drops in absenteeism and tardiness. Using the primary work group as the decision-making body, rather than more removed authorities in the company, also reduces stress (Kahn, 1981; S. R. Sutton & Kahn, 1986).

4. Making jobs as interesting as possible may contribute to the reduction of stress. In some plants, workers who previously worked on an assembly line and were responsible for assembling a small part of a product were retrained to perform several tasks or even to assemble the entire product. These "job enlargement" or "job enrichment" programs have produced increases in productivity and product quality and increases in job satisfaction.

5. Providing workers with opportunities to develop or promote meaningful social relationships can reduce stress or buffer its impact (B. Buunk, 1989; Moos, 1985). Providing social and recreational facilities for break times, lunch time, and after-hours free time can improve social relations on the job. Extending facilities to workers' families for after-hours and weekend events have all been used to try to bring families into corporations (C. J. Cooper & Marshall, 1976), inasmuch as family support can buffer the impact of work-related stress (Revicki & May, 1985).

6. Rewarding workers for good work, rather than focusing on punishment for poor work, improves morale and provides incentives for better future work (Kahn, 1981).

7. People who are in a supervisory position in work settings can look for signs of stress before stress has an opportunity to do significant damage. For example, supervisors can watch for negative affect, such as boredom, apathy, and hostility, among workers because these affective reactions often precede more severe reactions to stress, such as poor health or absenteeism. In turn, pockets of absenteeism or tardiness may point to particular types of jobs that require redesign or enlargement.

A workplace intervention that addresses some of these issues was conducted by Rahe and colleagues (2002). They randomly assigned 500 participants to one of three groups: an intervention that included assessment for stress-related problems, personalized feedback, and six small group face-to-face counseling sessions; a self-help group that received personalized feedback and assessment by mail; and a wait-list control. Although all three groups experienced less stress and anxiety over the course of the study, the participants in the first intervention showed a more rapid reduction in their stress responses, fewer days of illness, and a large reduction in their health care utilization, suggesting that even a relatively short-term intervention that includes stress management and social support can reduce workplace stress.

Overall, then, the stress-illness relationship has been clearly documented in the workplace and has been tied to a number of specific job-related factors. This knowledge has, in turn, provided the basis for important workplace interventions to reduce stress. In this sense, the occupational stress literature provides a good model for stress prevention. If one can identify stressors early through signs of psychological distress or illness precursors, such as catecholamine excretion, one can intervene in the stress-illness relationship before illness occurs.

Combining Work and Family Roles

So far, our discussion of chronic stress has considered only factors related to employment. But much of the stress that people experience results not from one role in their lives but from the combination of several roles. As adults, most of us will be workers, partners, and parents, and each of these roles entails heavy obligations. Accordingly, recent work has focused on the stress that can result when one is attempting to combine multiple roles simultaneously.

Women and Multiple Roles   These problems have been particularly acute for women. The number of mothers with young children in the American workforce is large, with estimates that more than half of married women with young children are employed (Offerman & Gowing, 1990). Concern has grown over the psychological and health implications of combining demanding family roles and work roles (Eckenrode & Gore, 1990; Repetti, Matthews, & Waldron, 1989).

The task of managing multiple roles is great when both work and family responsibilities are heavy (C. Emmons, Biernat, Teidje, Lang, & Wortman, 1990). Be-

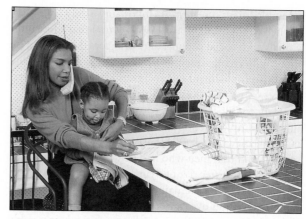

Many women hold multiple roles, such as worker, homemaker, and parent. Although these multiple roles can provide much satisfaction, they also make women vulnerable to role conflict and role overload.

cause concessions to working parents are rarely made at work and because mothers in the workforce usually bear a disproportionate number of household and child-care tasks (C. Emmons et al., 1990; Hochschild, 1989), home and work responsibilities may conflict with each other, enhancing stress. Studies of neuroendocrine responses to stress support this conclusion as well, with working women who have children at home showing higher amounts of cortisol, higher cardiovascular reactivity, and more home strain than those without children at home (Frankenhaeuser et al., 1989; Luecken et al., 1997). Single women raising children on their own are most at risk for health problems (M. E. Hughes & Waite, 2002).

Protective Effects of Multiple Roles   Despite the potential for women to suffer role conflict and role overload by combining work and the homemaker role, there appear to be positive effects of combining home and work responsibilities (Barnett, Davidson, & Marshall, 1991; Waldron, Weiss, & Hughes, 1998).

On the one hand, juggling heavy responsibilities at work with heavy responsibilities at home reduces the enjoyment of both sets of tasks and may leave women vulnerable to depression (K. J. Williams, Suls, Alliger, Learner, & Wan, 1991). However, combining motherhood with employment can be beneficial for women's well-being, improving self-esteem, feelings of self-efficacy, and life satisfaction (Gove & Zeiss, 1987; Kessler & McRae, 1982; Verbrugge, 1983). Combining employment with the family role has also been tied to better health, including lower levels of coronary risk factors (Weidner, Boughal, Connor, Pieper, & Mendell, 1997).

As we will see in chapter 7, whether the effects of combining employment and child rearing are positive or negative can depend heavily on resources that are available. Having control and flexibility over one's work environment (Lennon & Rosenfield, 1992), having a good income (Rosenfield, 1992), having someone to help with the housework (Krause & Markides, 1985), having adequate child care (C. E. Ross & Mirowsky, 1988), having a partner (J. Ali & Avison, 1997), and getting help from one's partner (Rosenfield, 1992) can all reduce the likelihood that juggling multiple role demands will lead to stress and its psychological and physical costs (J. Glass & Fujimoto, 1994).

Men and Multiple Roles   That so much research on combining home and work responsibilities is conducted on women suggests that these issues are not important for men, but this suggestion is not true. To be sure, men and women are distressed by different kinds of events. Evidence suggests that men are more distressed by financial strain and work stress, whereas women are more distressed by adverse changes in the home (Barnett, Raudenbusch, Brennan, Pleck, & Marshall, 1995; Conger, Lorenz, Elder, Simons, & Ge, 1993). But increasingly, studies suggest that satisfaction in the parent role is also important to men (Barnett & Marshall, 1993).

Combining employment and marriage is protective for men with respect to health and mental health (Burton, 1998; Rushing et al., 1992), just as it seems to be for women who have enough help. But multiple roles can take their toll on men as well. Repetti (1989) studied workload and interpersonal strain and how they affected fathers' interactions with the family at the end of the day. She found that, after a demanding day at work (high workload strain), fathers were more behaviorally and emotionally withdrawn in their interactions with their children. After stressful interpersonal events at work (high interpersonal strain), conflict with children increased. In addition, some of the factors that may ameliorate the stress of multiple roles for women may create more stress for men. One study found that, as a woman's employment increased her share of the family's income and increased her husband's share in the domestic labors, her mental health and well-being increased, but her husband's mental health and well-being declined (Rosenfield, 1992). Employed, unmarried fathers may be at risk for psychological distress (R. W. Simon, 1998).

For both men and women, the research on multiple roles is converging on the idea that stress is lower when one finds meaning in one's life. The protective effects of employment, marriage, and parenting on psychological distress and the beneficial effects of social support on health are all testimony to the salutary effects of social roles (Burton, 1998). When these potential sources of meaning and pleasure in life are challenged, as through a demanding and unrewarding work life or stressful close relationships, the effects on health can be devastating (Stansfield, Bosma, Hemingway, & Marmot, 1998).

Children   Children and adolescents have their own sources of stress that can make home life stressful. One study found that social and academic failure experiences at school, such as being rejected by a peer or having difficulty with schoolwork, significantly increased a child's demanding and aversive behavior at home—specifically, acting out and making demands for attention (Repetti & Pollina, 1994). Not surprisingly, children are affected by their parents' work and family stressors as well, and the strains their parents are under have consequences both for the children's academic achievement and the likelihood that they will act out their problems in adolescence (Menaghan, Kowaleski-Jones, & Mott, 1997). Such findings make it clear that, in fully understanding the impact of multiple roles, it is important to study not just working parents but also children. ●

SUMMARY

1. Events are perceived as stressful when people believe that their resources (such as time, money, and energy) may not be sufficient to meet the harm, threat, or challenge in the environment. Stress produces many changes, including adverse emotional reactions, cognitive responses, physiological changes, and performance decrements.

2. Early research on stress examined how the organism mobilizes its resources to fight or flee from threatening stimuli (the fight-or-flight response). Building on this model, Selye proposed the general adaptation syndrome, arguing that reactions to stress go through three phases: alarm, resistance, and exhaustion. More recent efforts have focused on the neuroendocrine bases of social responses to stress—that is, the ways in which people tend-and-befriend others in times of stress.

3. The physiology of stress implicates the sympathetic adrenomedullary (SAM) system and the hypothalamic-pituitary-adrenocortical (HPA) axis. Over the long term, repeated activation of these systems can lead to cumulative damage, termed allostatic load, which represents the premature physiological aging that stress produces.

4. Whether an event is stressful depends on how it is appraised. Events that are negative, uncontrollable or unpredictable, ambiguous, overwhelming, and threatening to central life tasks are likely to be perceived as stressful.

5. Usually, people can adapt to mild stressors, but severe stressors may cause chronic problems for health and mental health. Stress can have disruptive aftereffects, including persistent physiological arousal, psychological distress, reduced task performance, and over time, declines in cognitive capabilities. Vulnerable populations—such as children, the elderly, and the poor—may be particularly adversely affected by stress.

6. Research on stressful life events indicates that any event that forces a person to make a change increases stress and the likelihood of illness. The daily hassles of life can also affect health adversely, as can chronic exposure to stress.

7. Studies of occupational stress suggest that work hazards, work overload, work pressure, role conflict and ambiguity, inability to develop satisfying job relationships, inadequate career development, inability to exert control in one's job, and unemployment can produce increased illness, job dissatisfaction, absenteeism, tardiness, and turnover. Some of these job stresses can be prevented or offset through intervention.

8. Combining multiple roles, such as those related to work and home life, can create role conflict and role overload, producing psychological distress and poor health. On the other hand, such role combinations may also enhance self-esteem and well-being. Which of these effects occurs depends, in large part, on available resources, such as time, money, social support, and help.

KEY TERMS

acute stress paradigm
aftereffects of stress
allostatic load
chronic strain
cognitive costs
daily hassles
fight-or-flight response

general adaptation syndrome
perceived stress
person-environment fit
post-traumatic stress disorder
   (PTSD)
primary appraisal

reactivity
role conflict
secondary appraisal
stress
stressful life events
stressors

Moderators of the Stress Experience

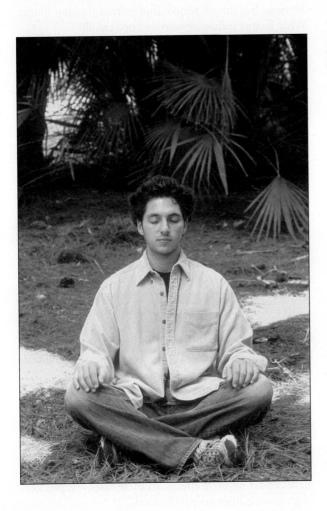

In January 1994, an earthquake measuring 6.7 on the Richter scale struck Los Angeles. Many people were left homeless or suffered damage to their dwellings and property. Some were injured; others had relatives or friends who were hurt or killed. But not everyone was affected in the same way.

Consider four families, all of whom lost the better part of their homes and possessions to the devastation. Despite apparent commonalities in their circumstances, each responded to the stressful experience in a different way. One family, newly arrived from Mexico, who had not yet found friends or employment, lost everything. They were devastated psychologically, peering out from the folds of a relief tent, uncertain what to do next. An older man with a heart condition succumbed to a heart attack, leaving his infirmed wife behind. A third family, who had financial resources and relatives in the area, were quickly cared for and were able to move into an apartment while they looked for another home. Their most immediate concerns were finding a new route to work and a new carpool for their children. A young couple, wiped out by the experience, responded with resilience, determined to make a new start.

The personal accounts that followed on the heels of the Los Angeles earthquake revealed the diversity of individual experiences that people had. What the accounts illustrate, albeit in extreme form, is the degree to which stress is moderated by individual and circumstantial factors. Individuals with many external resources, such as money or social support, may find a potentially stressful experience less so. Others, without resources or coping skills, may cope very poorly.

We term these factors **stress moderators** because they modify how stress is experienced and the effects it has. Moderators of the stress experience may have an impact on stress itself, on the relation between stress and psychological responses, on the relation between stress and illness, or on the degree to which a stressful experience intrudes into other aspects of life.

We begin this chapter with a consideration of the different ways in which stress may affect illness and how moderating variables—such as external resources, social support, and coping styles—might augment or diminish this relationship. We then turn to an analysis of moderators themselves: personality, coping styles, resources, and social support. Finally, we consider stress management techniques that people use to enhance their personal resources for managing stressful events.

■ STRESS AND ILLNESS

As we saw in chapter 6, stress has effects on at least four general physiological systems of the body: the sympathetic-adrenomedullary system, the pituitary-adrenocortical system, the neuropeptide system, and the immune system. To the extent that stress affects these pathways, illness may result, and stress can produce physiological, as well as psychological, changes conducive to the development of illness; precursors (forewarnings) of illness, such as fatigue and achiness, then develop. But not all people under stress develop illness. What factors influence who will become ill?

Initial Vulnerability

Preexisting psychological or physical vulnerabilities are especially important in the stress-illness relationship. Stress may lead to illness among people who have an initial vulnerability. The older man who died in the earthquake illustrates this point. Neither the earthquake nor the heart condition alone were insufficient to cause his heart attack, but their combined effect was fatal.

To illustrate how stress interacts with initial vulnerability to affect health, Tapp and Natelson (1988) examined the impact of stress on hamsters suffering from inherited heart disease. If the animal was stressed early on in the disease process, heart failure did not develop. However, after cardiac changes had developed, stress precipitated heart failure. When the animal was in overt heart failure, stress increased the likelihood that it would die. Moreover, the pattern of results suggests not merely that stress was an additional burden for an animal with a vulnerability but that the effects of stress were multiplied by the existence of the prior vulnerability.

Psychological vulnerability may also interact with stress. Examples of the interactive effects of stress are seen in studies of the effects of crowding and noise. Generally, crowding and noise produce few deleterious health effects. However, among vulnerable populations, such as children, the elderly, and the poor, these stressors have greater negative effects. In these cases, the preexisting vulnerabilities are psychosocial.

Health Behaviors

Stress can indirectly affect illness by altering a person's behavior patterns, especially health behaviors. Consider, for example, the case of a man who is separated from his

FIGURE 7.1 | The Stress-Illness Relationship

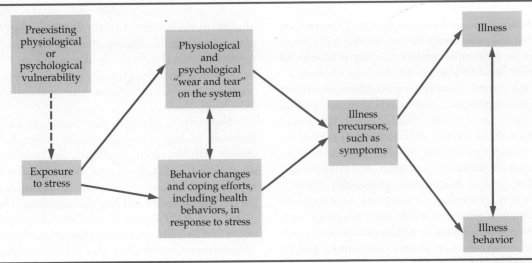

wife. Separation and divorce are known to be major stressful events that produce substantial lifestyle and emotional disruption. If the couple has had a traditional marriage, the husband may be used to having his meals prepared for him; left to his own devices, he may eat poorly or not at all. If he is used to sharing the bed with her, he may have difficulty sleeping without his wife. Because of his distress, he may increase his alcohol consumption or smoking.

S. Cohen and Williamson (1988) found exactly this kind of relationship in a study of stress and health behaviors. People who said they were under more stress reported getting less sleep, were less likely to eat breakfast, and reported using more alcohol and more recreational drugs than people under less stress. To the extent that health habits are altered by stress, then, illness may be a consequence of stress. Figure 7.1 illustrates the interactions among preexisting physiological or psychological vulnerabilities, exposure to stress, and behavior changes that may result, leading to a greater likelihood of illness.

■ COPING WITH STRESS

People respond very differently to stress. We all know people who throw up their hands in despair when the slightest thing goes wrong with their plans, yet we know others who seem able to meet setbacks and challenges with equanimity, bringing their personal and social resources to bear on the problem at hand. The impact of

any potentially stressful event is substantially influenced by how a person appraises it.

As we saw in chapter 6, according to Lazarus's view of stress, any new event or change in the environment prompts the individual to make *primary appraisals* of the significance of the event. An event may be judged to be positive, neutral, or negative in its implications for the self. If an event is judged to be negative, it will be further judged in terms of the *harm or loss* that has already been done, the future *threat* associated with the event, and the potential *challenge* of the event—that is, the perception that gain, growth, or mastery may result from dealing with the event.

At the same time that primary appraisals are undertaken, the individual is also making *secondary appraisals* of his or her ability to cope with the potentially stressful event. Secondary appraisal is the evaluation of one's coping resources and options to determine whether they will be sufficient to overcome the harm and threat that the event represents (R. S. Lazarus & Folkman, 1984b).

What Is Coping?

Coping is the process of managing demands (external or internal) that are appraised as taxing or exceeding the resources of the person (R. S. Lazarus & Folkman, 1984a). "Coping consists of efforts, both action-oriented and intrapsychic, to manage (that is, master, tolerate, reduce, minimize) environmental and internal demands and conflicts among them" (R. S. Lazarus & Launier, 1978, p. 311).

This definition of coping has several important aspects. First, the relationship between coping and a stressful event is a dynamic process. Coping is a series of transactions between a person who has a set of resources, values, and commitments and a particular environment with its own resources, demands, and constraints (R. S. Lazarus & Launier, 1978). Thus, coping is not a one-time action that someone takes; rather, it is a set of responses, occurring over time, by which the environment and the person influence each other. For example, the impending breakup of a romantic relationship can produce a variety of reactions, ranging from emotional responses, such as sadness or indignation, to actions, such as efforts at reconciliation or attempts to find engrossing, distracting activities. These coping efforts will, in turn, be influenced by the way the partner in the relationship responds. With encouragement from the partner, the person may make renewed efforts at reconciliation, whereas anger or rejection may drive the person further away.

A second important aspect of the definition of coping is its breadth. The definition clearly encompasses a great many actions and reactions to stressful circumstances. Viewed within this definition, then, emotional reactions, including anger or depression, can be thought of as part of the coping process, as can actions that are voluntarily undertaken to confront the event. In turn, coping efforts are moderated by the resources that the individual has available. Figure 7.2 presents a diagram of the coping process.

Personality and Coping

The personality that each individual brings to a stressful event influences how he or she will cope with that event. Some personality characteristics make stressful situations worse, whereas others improve them.

Negativity, Stress, and Illness
Certain people are predisposed by their personalities to experience stressful events as especially stressful, which may, in turn, affect their psychological distress, their physical symptoms, and/or their rates of illness. This line of research has focused on a psychological state called **negative affectivity** (Watson & Clark, 1984), a pervasive negative mood marked by anxiety, depression, and hostility.

Individuals high in negative affectivity express distress, discomfort, and dissatisfaction across a wide range of situations (Gunthert, Cohen, & Armeli, 1999). People who are high in negative affectivity are more prone to drink heavily (Frances, Franklin, & Flavin, 1986), to be depressed (Francis, Fyer, & Clarkin, 1986), and to engage in suicidal gestures or even suicide (Cross & Hirschfeld, 1986).

Negativity is related to poor health. In a review of literature relating personality factors to five diseases—asthma, arthritis, ulcers, headaches, and coronary artery disease—H. S. Friedman and Booth-Kewley (1987) found weak but consistent evidence of a relationship between these disorders and negative emotions. They suggested that psychological distress involving depression, anger, hostility, and anxiety may constitute the basis of a "disease-prone" personality that predisposes people to these disorders (see also Scheier & Bridges, 1995). Negative affectivity can be associated with elevated cortisol secretion, and this increased adrenocortical activity may provide a possible biopsychosocial pathway linking negative affectivity to adverse health outcomes (van Eck, Berkhof, Nicolson, & Sulon, 1996). Negative affectivity can also affect adjustment to treatment. One study (Duits, Boeke, Taams, Passchier, & Erdman, 1997) found that people who were very anxious or depressed prior to coronary artery bypass graft surgery were more likely to adjust badly during surgical recovery (see also P. G. Williams et al., 2002).

Although there is now clear evidence that negativity may compromise health, it is also clear that negativity can sometimes create a false impression of poor health when none exists. People who are high in negative affectivity report higher levels of distressing physical symptoms, such as headaches, stomachaches, and other pains, especially under stress (Watson & Pennebaker, 1989), but in many cases, there is no evidence of an underlying physical disorder (Diefenbach, Leventhal, Leventhal, & Patrick-Miller, 1996). For example, Cohen and his associates (S. Cohen, Doyle, Turner, Alper, & Skoner, 2003) obtained both subjective complaints (runny nose and congestion) and objective measures (for example, mucus secretion) of illness from people who had been exposed to a respiratory virus. Negative affectivity was associated with a higher number of complaints but not with more objective measures of disease.

People high in negative affectivity also often appear more vulnerable to illness because they are more likely to use health services during stressful times than are peo-

FIGURE 7.2 | The Coping Process (*Sources:* F. Cohen & Lazarus, 1979; D. A. Hamburg & Adams, 1967; R. S. Lazarus & Folkman, 1984b; Moos, 1988; S. E. Taylor, 1983)

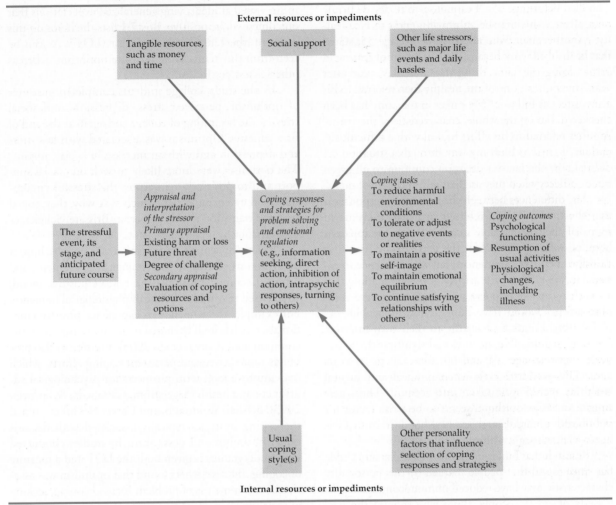

ple low in negative affectivity (S. Cohen & Williamson, 1991). Thus, individuals who are chronically high in negative affect may be more likely to get sick, but they also show distress, physical symptoms, and illness behavior even when they are not getting sick.

Pessimistic Explanatory Style   In related investigations, Seligman and his colleagues (M. O. Burns & Seligman, 1989; C. Peterson, Seligman, & Vaillant, 1988) found evidence for a **pessimistic explanatory style** that may relate to illness. Specifically, some people characteristically explain the negative events of their lives in terms of internal, stable, global qualities of themselves. In so doing, they may lay the groundwork for

poor health. In one study (C. Peterson et al., 1988), interviews completed by graduates of the Harvard University classes of 1942 to 1944 when they were 25 years old were analyzed to see how the men habitually explained the negative events in their lives. Specifically, they were asked about difficult experiences they had encountered during World War II, such as combat situations, relations with superiors, and battles in which they were actively involved, and they were asked whether they felt they had dealt successfully or unsuccessfully with these wartime situations. Some of the men also talked about difficulties they were having getting established in careers and relationships. Their answers were then coded as reflecting an optimistic or a pessimistic style.

An example of explaining a negative event in terms of a pessimistic explanatory style is provided by one man who died before age 55: "I cannot seem to decide firmly on a career…this may be an unwillingness to face reality." Another man, who also died before age 55, stated that he disliked work because he had "a fear of getting in a rut, doing the same thing day after day, year after year." In contrast, one of the healthy men referred to his army career as follows: "My career in the army has been checkered, but on the whole, characteristic of the army." Another referred to his effort to deal with a difficult situation: "I tried to bluff my way through a situation…I didn't know the facts, a situation common to all green junior officers when they are first put in charge of men."

The differences between the two sets of responses is that the first two men referred to negative events in terms of their own stable qualities, with no apparent hope of escape. In contrast, the two healthy men also described negative experiences, but with reference to external factors ("That's the army") or by maintaining that a less than capable response was one that "any green junior officer" would have done. Those men who explained bad events by referring to their own internal, stable, global negative qualities had significantly poorer health between ages 45 and 60, some 20 to 35 years later. This was true even when physical and mental health at age 25 were taken into account. Thus, pessimism in early adulthood seems to be a risk factor for poor health in middle and late adulthood (Maruta, Colligan, Malinchoc, & Offord, 2002).

Research that builds on pessimistic explanatory style has since found that people marked by this personality characteristic may have reduced immunocompetence. In a study of elderly people, those who showed the pessimistic explanatory style were found to have poorer functioning cell-mediated immunity (Kamen-Siegel, Rodin, Seligman, & Dwyer, 1991). This study is important, first, because it shows a direct relationship between pessimistic explanatory style and a biological pathway that can have health implications and, second, because the study was conducted in an elderly population, which is at particular risk for immune-mediated diseases.

Just as negative personality predispositions may exacerbate stress and its relation to illness, other personality factors may enhance the ability to cope with stress effectively. We now turn to some of those personality resources.

Optimism   An optimistic nature can also lead people to cope more effectively with stress and thereby reduce their risk for illness (Scheier & Carver, 1985). Scheier and Carver developed a measure of dispositional optimism aimed at identifying generalized expectations that outcomes will be positive. Box 7.1 lists the items on this measure, the Life Orientation Test (LOT). As can be seen from the items, some measure optimism, whereas others assess pessimism.

In one study, college students completed measures of optimism, perceived stress, depression, and social stress at the beginning of college and again at the end of first semester. Optimism was associated with less stress and depression and with an increase in social support. The optimists were more likely to seek out social support and to positively reinterpret the stressful circumstances they encountered, which was why they coped with the transition to college better (Brissete, Scheier, & Carver, 2002).

Exactly how might optimism exert a positive impact on symptom expression, psychological adjustment, and health outcomes? Optimists have more positive mood, which itself may lead to a state of physiological resilience. For example, the tendency to experience positive emotional states has itself been tied to greater resistance to the common cold (Cohen et al., 2003). Optimism also promotes more active and persistent coping efforts, which may improve long-term prospects for psychological adjustment and health (Segerstrom, Castañeda, & Spencer, 2003). Scheier, Weintraub, and Carver (1986) examined the coping strategies typically associated with dispositional optimism and pessimism. In studies conducted with undergraduates given both the LOT and a measure of coping, the researchers found that optimism was associated with more use of problem-focused coping, seeking of social support, and emphasizing the positive aspects of a stressful situation. Pessimism, in contrast, was associated with denial and distancing from the event, a focus directly on stressful feelings, and disengagement from the goal with which the stressor was interfering. Optimism, then, may help people deal with stressful events by getting them to use their resources more effectively. Optimists also appear to size up stressful situations more positively and seem especially prone to making favorable secondary appraisals, namely that their resources will be sufficient to overcome the threat (Chang, 1998). However, precisely because they are more persistent in pursuing multiple goals, optimists sometimes experience short-term physiological costs in their persistent efforts to pursue goals (Segerstrom, 2001).

Optimism has clear health benefits. To begin with, optimists and pessimists differ in their physiological

BOX 7.1

The Measurement of Optimism

People vary in whether they are fundamentally optimistic or pessimistic about life. Scheier and Carver (1985) developed a scale of dispositional optimism to measure this pervasive individual difference. Items from the life orientation test are as follows. (For each item, answer "true" or "false.")

1. In uncertain times, I usually expect the best.
2. It's easy for me to relax.
3. If something can go wrong for me, it will.
4. I'm always optimistic about my future.
5. I enjoy my friends a lot.
6. It's important for me to keep busy.
7. I hardly ever expect things to go my way.
8. I don't get upset too easily.
9. I rarely count on good things happening to me.
10. Overall, I expect more good things to happen to me than bad.

Scoring:

1. Reverse code items 3, 7, and 9 prior to scoring (0 = 4) (1 = 3) (2 = 2) (3 = 1) (4 = 0)
2. Sum items 1, 3, 4, 7, 9, and 10 to obtain an overall score.

Note: Items 2, 5, 6, and 8 are filler items only. They are not scored as part of the revised scale.

The revised scale was constructed in order to eliminate two items from the original scale, which dealt more with coping style than with positive expectations for future outcomes. The correlation between the revised scale and the original scale is 95.

Source: Scheier, M. F., Carver, C. S. and Bridges, M. W. (1994). Distinguishing optimism from neuroticism (and trait anxiety, self-mastery, and self-esteem): A re-evaluation of the Life Orientation Test. *Journal of Personality and Social Psychology,* 7, 1063–1078.

functioning. Pessimistic and anxious adults not only feel more negative but also have higher blood pressures than more optimistic, less anxious adults during everyday life (Räikkönen, Matthews, Flory, Owens, & Gump, 1999). An optimist style appears to be protective against the risk of coronary heart disease in older men (Kubzansky, Sparrow, Vokonas, & Kawachi, 2001). Pessimism has been tied to the onset of depression in middle age (Bromberger & Matthews, 1996), to cancer mortality among the elderly (Schulz, Bookwala, Knapp, Scheier, & Williamson, 1996), and to illness-related disruption of social and recreational activities among breast cancer patients (Carver, Lehman, & Antoni, 2003). In a study with veterans, optimism was linked to higher levels of pulmonary function and a slower rate of pulmonary function decline in older men (Kubzansky et al., 2002). Optimism also predicts better physical functioning among older patients suffering from knee pain (Brenes, Rapp, Rejeski, & Miller, 2002). In a study with coronary artery bypass patients (Scheier et al., 1989), optimism was also an important predictor of coping efforts in recovery from surgery. Specifically, optimists used more problem-focused coping and made less use of denial. They had a faster rate of recovery during hospitalization and a faster rate of returning to normal life activities after discharge. There was also a strong relationship between optimism and postsurgical quality of life 6 months later, with optimists doing better (see also Carver et al., 1993; T. E. Fitzgerald, Tennen, Affleck, & Pransky, 1993). Optimism also benefits people undergoing serious medical procedures (Curbow, Somerfield, Baker, Wingard, & Legro, 1993; Mroczek, Spiro, Aldwin, Ozer, & Bosse, 1993). In short, optimism is a potent and valuable resource.

Psychological Control Feelings that one can exert control over stressful events have long been known to help people cope effectively with stress (Bandura, 1977; S. E. Taylor, Helgeson, Reed, & Skokan, 1991; S. C. Thompson, 1981). Perceived control is the belief that one can determine one's own behavior, influence one's environment, and bring about desired outcomes. As may be apparent, perceived control is closely related to self-efficacy, which is a more narrow perception that one has the ability to enact the necessary actions to obtain a specific outcome in a specific situation (Bandura, 1977). Both types of cognitions appear to help people cope with a wide variety of stressful events. For example, as we noted in chapter 5, East German migrants to West Germany who found themselves unemployed often turned to alcohol for solace unless they had high feelings of self-efficacy; those migrants with high feelings of self-efficacy, which appeared to buffer them against the stress of unemployment, did not abuse alcohol.

Perceptions of control in one's work life and in the general tasks of living may be especially protective against adopting a risky lifestyle that involves health-compromising behaviors (Wickrama, Conger, & Lorenz, 1995). Across a wide variety of investigations, a feeling that one can control stressful events has been related to emotional well-being, successful coping with a stressful event, good health, behavior change that may promote good health, and improved performance on cognitive tasks (S. C. Thompson & Spacapan, 1991).

Control is important for most people going through stressful events (Compas, Barnez, Malcarne, & Worsham, 1991). For example, among adolescents with asthma, beliefs in personal control are associated with better immune responses related to their disease (E. Chen, Fisher, Bacharier, & Strunk, 2003). A sense of control may be especially important for vulnerable populations, such as medical patients, children, and the elderly, who are at risk for health problems. Because control may be problematic for individuals who already have little opportunity to exercise control (S. C. Thompson & Spacapan, 1991), anything that enhances perceptions of control may benefit such individuals.

So powerful are the effects of psychological control that they have been used extensively in interventions to promote good health habits and to help people cope successfully with stressful events, such as surgery and noxious medical procedures. For example, in chapters 4 and 5, we saw how self-efficacy influences a wide variety of health behaviors, including obtaining exercise and stopping smoking. In chapter 8, we will see how interventions drawing on principles of psychological control help people adjust more successfully to noxious medical treatments. For the moment, it is important to understand that when people are able to perceive events in their environment as controllable, or regard their coping efforts as likely to be successful (Benight et al., 1997), the stress they experience is lessened, their distress is lower, and their physiological responses to stress are reduced.

Additional Coping Resources

High self-esteem may moderate the stress-illness relationship. In one study of students facing exams, those with high self-esteem were less likely to become upset in response to stress (Shimizu & Pelham, 2004). However, self-esteem seems to be more protective at low levels of stress; at higher levels of stress, the stressful events themselves can overwhelm differences in self-esteem (Whisman & Kwon, 1993). In a study of the elderly, high self-esteem was associated with lower levels of cortisol and ACTH in response to a challenge task—namely, an automobile driving simulation task (T. E. Seeman et al., 1995)—suggesting a biopsychosocial route whereby self-esteem may affect illness.

Conscientiousness also moderates the stress-illness relationship. One study (H. S. Friedman et al., 1993) looked at ratings of personality that had been made about youngsters in 1921 and 1922 to see if personality would predict who lived longer. The researchers found that those children who scored high on conscientiousness were more likely to live to an old age (H. S. Friedman, Tucker, Schwartz, Tomlinson-Keasey, et al., 1995). It may be that conscientious people are more successful in avoiding situations that could harm them or they may be more reliable in their practice of good health habits (see also A. J. Christensen et al., 2002).

A cluster of personal qualities called ego strength—dependability, trust, and lack of impulsivity—appears to have health benefits. In a longitudinal investigation (H. S. Friedman, Tucker, Schwartz, Tomlinson-Keasey, et al., 1995), researchers studied children who had first been interviewed in 1947. Some were impulsive and undercontrolled personalities, whereas others showed signs of ego strength. Those who were high in ego strength as children lived longer as adults. One reason was that those high in ego strength were somewhat less likely to smoke and use alcohol to excess.

Being self-confident and having an easygoing disposition also mute the likelihood that stressful events will lead to psychological distress (Holahan & Moos, 1990, 1991), perhaps because self-confident and easygoing individuals cope with stressful events more actively (Holahan & Moos, 1990). However, cheerful people die somewhat sooner than people who are not cheerful (H. S. Friedman et al., 1993). It appears that cheerful people may grow up being more careless about their health and as a result encounter health risks (Martin et al., 2002).

At the other extreme, though, introverts, social isolates, people high in neuroticism or low in mastery or self-efficacy, and people lacking in social skills do appear to be at increased risk for illness behavior and for psychological distress (S. Cohen & Williamson, 1991; Hemenover, 2001; Kempen, Jelicic, & Ormel, 1997).

A sense of coherence about one's life (Jorgensen, Frankowski, & Carey, 1999), a sense of purpose or meaning in one's life (Visotsky, Hamburg, Goss, & Lebovitz, 1961), a sense of humor (Cousins, 1979; R. A.

Religion promotes psychological well-being, and those people with religious faith may be better able to cope with aversive events.

Moody, 1978), trust in others (Barefoot et al., 1998), and religion (see box 7.2) have all been suggested as internal resources that may promote effective coping. Just as some people appear to have an illness-prone personality, then, other people may possess a health-prone personality, characterized by a sense of control, self-esteem, optimism, and resilience.

Coping resources are important because they enable people to manage the demands of job, neighborhood stress, financial strain, and other daily stressful events. People who deal with chronic stress in the absence of protective psychosocial resources have a higher risk of emotional distress, greater health risks, and impaired quality of life, and they show more biological risk factors predictive of coronary heart disease (Steptoe & Marmot, 2003).

Coping Style

In addition to personality traits, which are general ways of responding across situations, coping style represents a more specific individual difference in how people respond to stress. **Coping style** is a general propensity to deal with stressful events in a particular way. As an example, we all know people who deal with stress by talking a lot about it, whereas other people keep their problems to themselves. Coping styles, then, are thought to be like personality traits in that they characterize an individual's way of behaving in a general fashion, but they are more specific than personality traits because they are thought to come into play primarily when events become stressful.

Avoidance Versus Confrontation   Some people cope with a threatening event by using an **avoidant (minimizing) coping style,** whereas others use a **confrontative (vigilant) coping style** by gathering information or taking direct action. Neither style is necessarily more effective in managing stress; each seems to have its advantages and liabilities. Vigilant strategies may be more successful than avoidance for coping with stressful events if one can focus on the information present in the situation rather than on one's emotions (Suls & Fletcher, 1985). Focusing on the negative emotions one is experiencing in responding to stressful events may make the stressful event worse.

Whether avoidant or confrontative strategies are successful also depends on how long term the stressor is. People who cope with stress by minimizing or avoiding threatening events seem to cope effectively with short-term threats (for example, Wong & Kaloupek, 1986). However, if the threat is repeated or persists over time, a strategy of avoidance may not be so successful. People who cope using avoidance may not make enough cognitive and emotional efforts to anticipate and manage long-term problems (Suls & Fletcher, 1985; S. E. Taylor & Clark, 1986).

In contrast, individuals who cope with threatening events through confrontation or vigilance may well engage in the cognitive and emotional efforts needed to deal with long-term threats. In the short term, however, they may pay a price in anxiety and physiological reactivity (S. M. Miller & Mangan, 1983; T. W. Smith, Ruiz, & Uchino, 2000). Thus, the avoider or minimizer may cope well with a trip to the dentist but cope poorly

BOX 7.2

Religion, Coping, and Well-Being

I just prayed and prayed and God stopped that thing just before it would have hit us.

—TORNADO SURVIVOR

Long before researchers were studying coping techniques, individuals going through stressful or traumatic events were encouraged by their family, friends, and religious counselors to turn to their faith and to God for solace, comfort, and insight (W. R. Miller & Thoresen, 2003). Recent surveys (American Religious Identification Survey, 2001; Religious Tolerance Organization, 2003) suggest that the majority of people in the United States believe in God (96%), pray (80%), report attending church services at least once a month (55%), and say that religion is important in their personal lives (71%). Religion, then, appears to be an important part of American life. It may be especially so for women (Gallup, 2003) and some minority groups, such as African-Americans (Holt, Clark, Kreuter, & Rubio, 2003; Steffen, Hinderliter, Blumenthal, & Sherwood, 2001).

Religion can promote a sense of psychological well-being. People with strong religious faith report greater life satisfaction, greater personal happiness, and fewer negative consequences of traumatic life events in comparison with people who are not religious (George, Ellison, & Larson, 2002). Many people report that religion is helpful to them when they must cope with a stressful event (Koenig, George, & Siegler, 1988; Palmer & Noble, 1986). For example, surgery patients with stronger religious beliefs experienced fewer complications and had shorter hospital stays than those with less strong religious beliefs (Contrada et al., 2004).

Religion may be helpful for coping for two main reasons. First, it provides a belief system and a way of thinking about stressful events that lessens distress and enables people to find meaning and purpose in the inevitable stressful events that they encounter (Laubmeier, Zakowski, & Blair, 2004; George et al., 2002; Ironson et al., 2002). Second, it provides a source of social support.

Organized religion often confers a sense of group identity for people because it provides a network of supportive individuals who share their beliefs (George et al., 2002). For example, in a study of parents who had lost an infant to sudden infant death syndrome, both components of religion—its importance as a belief system and active participation in a church—were found to help parents cope with their loss. In particular, the people who were active in their churches perceived that they had more social support and were more able to find meaning in their loss (McIntosh, Silver, & Wortman, 1993).

Some religious beliefs also lead to better health practices (Powell, Shahabi, & Thorsen, 2003), better health (Krause, Ingersoll-Dayton, Liang, & Sugisawa, 1999), and longer life (McCullough et al., 2000). Religion appears to be particularly protective against cardiovascular disease largely because of its promotion of a healthy lifestyle (Powell et al., 2003). However, religious beliefs do not appear to retard the progression of cancer or speed recovery from acute illness (Powell et al., 2003). The links between religion and health appear to be due to underlying physiological processes including cardiovascular, neuroendocrine, and immune function (Seeman, Dubin, & Seeman, 2003).

The socially supportive environment often provided by organized religion may also contribute to the fact that religion improves health and prolongs life (George et al., 2002). For example, orthodox religious groups have lower cancer mortality rates from all cancers (Dwyer, Clarke, & Miller, 1990), presumably because they forbid smoking and drinking and may limit contact with other carcinogens. Individuals who live in the same community but who are not part of a formal religion may benefit inadvertently from diminished exposure to carcinogens and from social disapproval of behaviors related to cancer, such as smoking and alcohol consumption. Religion, then, may not only be an important meaningful part of life, but it also has health and mental health benefits (George et al., 2002; Powell et al., 2003).

with ongoing job stress. In contrast, the vigilant coper may fret over the visit to the dentist but make efforts to reduce stress on the job.

However, studies of short-term threats may have underestimated how unsuccessful avoidant coping strategies are. In a 1-year study of negative life events and emotional and physical distress in 400 adults and their children (Holahan & Moos, 1986), the use of avoidant coping led to higher levels of distress even when initial levels of distress were controlled for. Holahan and Moos concluded that the chronic use of avoidance as a coping style constitutes a psychological risk factor for adverse responses to stressful life circumstances. Moreover, even when avoidant (or repressive) copers report less stress, they may nonetheless show strong physiological responses to stressful events (Nyklicek, Vingerhoets, Van Heck, & Van Limpt, 1998).

Moreover, there is evidence that active coping is associated with other coping resources. Specifically, people who have more personal and environmental resources, such as higher income, more friends, a confident interpersonal style, or a good job, seem to rely more on active coping efforts and less on avoidant coping (Holahan & Moos, 1987).

Problem-Focused Versus Emotion-Focused Coping

Two general types of coping strategies can be distinguished: problem-solving coping and emotion-focused coping (cf. Folkman, Schaefer, & Lazarus, 1979; H. Leventhal & Nerenz, 1982; Pearlin & Schooler, 1978). *Problem-solving coping* involves attempts to do something constructive about the stressful conditions that are harming, threatening, or challenging an individual. *Emotion-focused coping* involves efforts to regulate emotions experienced because of the stressful event.

Sometimes problem-solving efforts and emotional regulation work together. For example, in denying that stressors on the job are causing distress, workers may keep their daily anger low but fail to deal with the cumulative damage that these stressors may cause. Problem-focused coping appears to emerge during childhood; emotion-focused coping skills develop somewhat later in late childhood or early adolescence (Compas et al., 1991).

What determines the kind of coping strategies a person uses? Typically, people use both problem-focused and emotion-focused coping in their stressful episodes, suggesting that both types of coping are useful for most stressful events (Folkman & Lazarus, 1980). However, the nature of the event also contributes to what coping strategies will be used (for example, Vitaliano et al., 1990). For example, work-related problems lead people most commonly to attempt problem-focused coping efforts, such as taking direct action or seeking help from others.

Health problems, in contrast, lead to more emotion-focused coping, perhaps because a threat to one's health is an event that must be tolerated but is not necessarily amenable to direct action. When health problems are amenable to active coping efforts, however,

problem-focused coping is beneficial (Penley, Tomaka, & Wiebe, 2002). Health problems also lead people to seek social support (Vitaliano et al., 1990), whereas individuals with family problems are more likely to use problem-focused coping (Vitaliano et al., 1990). These findings suggest that situations in which something constructive can be done will favor problem-focused coping, whereas those situations that simply must be accepted favor emotion-focused coping (Zakowski, Hall, Klein, & Baum, 2001).

Emotion-focused coping, however, includes coping of two kinds. One involves emotional distress as may be experienced in rumination. Ruminating, that is, negative recurrent thoughts, is detrimental to health. Among other outcomes, rumination has been tied to several indicators of compromised immune functioning in both young and elderly samples (Thomsen et al., 2004).

The other type of emotion-focused coping involves emotional-approach coping, which involves clarifying, focusing on, and working through the emotions experienced in conjunction with a stressor (Stanton, Danoff-Burg, Cameron, & Ellis, 1994). This type of coping has benefits for a broad array of stressful situations. Emotional-approach coping improves adjustment to many chronic conditions, including chronic pain (J. A. Smith, Lumley, & Longo, 2002) and medical conditions such as pregnancy (Huizink, Robles de Medina, Mulder, Visser, & Buitelaar, 2002) and breast cancer (Stanton, Kirk, Cameron, & Danoff-Burg, 2000). Even managing the stressors of daily life can be benefited by emotional-approach coping (Stanton et al., 2000). For example, both emotional-approach coping and problem-focused coping predicted well-being across the first year of medical school in a study of medical students (Park & Adler, 2003). Coping via emotional approach appears to be especially beneficial for women (Stanton et al., 2000).

Individual Differences   Individual differences also influence what coping strategies are used and in a somewhat surprising way. In a study with twins intended to identify what factors contribute to coping (K. S. Kendler, Kessler, Heath, Neale, & Eaves, 1991), three general coping strategies were identified: problem solving, turning to others, and using denial. Based on traditional methodologies of twin studies (see chapter 2), the coping strategies of turning to others and problem solving in response to stress could be explained substantially by genetic factors. In contrast, denial did not appear to have a genetic component but did appear to be explained by early family environment, such as parental child-rearing style, social style, and exposure to childhood stressors. It appears, then, that genetic predispositions may predispose people to cope with stressful events by solving problems directly or turning to others, which in turn, produces better or worse psychological adjustment; early environment contributes to how people learn to cope as well (Busjahn, Faulhaber, Freier, & Luft, 1999).

Disclosure   Considerable research has examined disclosure of emotional experiences and its beneficial effects on health. The rationale for the benefits of disclosure stems, in part, from the research just discussed which shows the benefits of emotional-approach coping. For many years, researchers have suspected that when people undergo traumatic events and cannot or do not communicate about them, those events may fester inside them, producing obsessive thoughts for years and even decades (R. L. Silver, Boon, & Stones, 1983). This inhibition of traumatic events involves physiological work, and the more people are forced to inhibit their thoughts, emotions, and behaviors, the more their physiological activity may increase (Pennebaker, 1997). Consequently, the ability to confide in others or to consciously confront their feelings and perceptions may eliminate the need to obsess about and inhibit the event, and it may reduce the physiological activity associated with the event.

To examine this hypothesis, Pennebaker and Beall (1986) had 46 undergraduates write either about the most traumatic and stressful event ever in their lives or about trivial topics. Although the individuals writing about traumas were more upset immediately after they wrote their essays (see also Pennebaker, Colder, & Sharp, 1990), they were less likely to visit the student health center for illness during the following 6 months.

A subsequent study (Pennebaker, Hughes, & O'Heeron, 1987) found that when people talked about traumatic events, their skin conductance, heart rate, and systolic and diastolic blood pressure all decreased. Emotional disclosure can also have beneficial long-term effects on immune functioning (for example, A. J. Christensen et al., 1996; Petrie, Booth, Pennebaker, Davison, & Thomas, 1995). In another study, people who wrote about traumatic life experiences not only experienced less distress 3 months later but had also changed their self-perceptions in directions reflecting mastery, personal growth, and self-acceptance, suggesting that such interventions may actually lead to a more resilient self-concept (Hemenover, 2003). Together, these changes may influence the long-term positive effects on health that have been found in studies of disclosure.

Other studies have looked at responses to naturally occurring stressors and have found similar results. Pennebaker and O'Heeron (1984), for example, found that individuals whose spouses had died the previous year either by suicide or in an automobile accident were less likely to become ill during the subsequent year if they had talked about the death with others.

Drawing on the value of this method, interventions have employed written exercises designed to encourage emotional expression. Such interventions have led to improved health among AIDS patients (Petrie, Fontanilla, Thomas, Booth, & Pennebaker, 2004), breast cancer patients (Bower, Kemeny, Taylor, & Fahey, 1998), and asthma and rheumatoid arthritis patients, among other conditions (Smyth, Stone, Hurewitz, & Kaell, 1999). Writing may also help people cope with debilitating treatments. For example, a writing exercise also led to a more beneficial, post-operative course in surgery patients (Solano, Donati, Pecci, Persichetti, & Colaci, 2003); those who wrote about their experience, on average, left the hospital several days earlier with lower psychological distress.

There are many reasons why talking or writing about a stressful event or confiding in others may be useful for coping. Talking with others allows one to gain information about the event or about effective coping; it may also elicit positive reinforcement and emotional support from others. In addition, there may be reliable cognitive effects associated with talking about or writing about a traumatic event, such as organizing one's thoughts and being able to find meaning in the experience (Lepore, Ragan, & Jones, 2000). Finally, the benefits of emotional disclosure have increasingly been uncovered. Talking or writing about traumatic or stressful events provides an opportunity for emotional approach coping (Lepore & Smyth, 2002).

Specific Coping Strategies

A seriously ill cancer patient was asked how she managed to cope with her disease so well. She responded, "I try to have cracked crab and raspberries every week." Although her particular choice of coping strategy may be somewhat unusual, her answer illustrates the importance of personal coping strategies for dealing with stressful events.

Research has also focused on more specific coping strategies as well as general coping strategies. This shift has occurred in part because recent research has questioned whether general coping styles measured at the trait level really predict how people behave in specific

BOX 7.3

The Brief Cope

The Brief Cope is a measure of coping that relies on two items to tap each of a broad array of commonly used coping styles for managing stressful events. People rate how they are coping with a stressful event by answering each of these items on a scale from zero ("I haven't been doing this at all") to three ("I've been doing this a lot").

Think of a stressful event that you are currently going through (a problem with your family, a roommate difficulty, problems in a course?) and see which coping methods you use.

1. Active coping

   I've been concentrating my efforts on doing something about the situation I'm in.

   I've been taking action to try to make the situation better.

2. Planning

   I've been trying to come up with a strategy about what to do.

   I've been thinking hard about what steps to take.

3. Positive reframing

   I've been trying to see it in a different light, to make it seem more positive.

   I've been looking for something good in what is happening.

4. Acceptance

   I've been accepting the reality of the fact that it has happened.

   I've been learning to live with it.

5. Humor

   I've been making jokes about it.

   I've been making fun of the situation.

6. Religion

   I've been trying to find comfort in my religion or spiritual beliefs.

   I've been praying or meditating.

7. Using emotional support

   I've been getting emotional support from others.

   I've been getting comfort and understanding from someone.

8. Using instrumental support

   I've been trying to get advice or help from other people about what to do.

   I've been getting help and advice from other people.

9. Self-distraction

   I've been turning to work or other activities to take my mind off things.

   I've been doing something to think about it less, such as going to movies, watching TV, reading, daydreaming, sleeping, or shopping.

10. Denial

    I've been saying to myself "this isn't real."

    I've been refusing to believe that it has happened.

11. Venting

    I've been saying things to let my unpleasant feelings escape.

    I've been expressing my negative feelings.

12. Substance use

    I've been using alcohol or other drugs to make myself feel better.

    I've been using alcohol or other drugs to help me get through it.

13. Behavioral disengagement

    I've been giving up trying to deal with it.

    I've been giving up the attempt to cope.

14. Self-blame

    I've been criticizing myself.

    I've been blaming myself for things that happened.

Source: Carver, 1997.

situations (J. E. Schwartz, Neale, Marco, Shiffman, & Stone, 1999). Such an approach also provides a more fine-grained analysis of exactly how people manage the myriad stressful events they confront each day. Carver, Scheier, and Weintraub (1989) developed a measure called the COPE to assess the specific coping strategies people employ to deal with stressful events. Examples from this widely used instrument appear in box 7.3.

Coping with AIDS

AIDS (acquired immune deficiency syndrome) has killed many thousands of people, and thousands more live, sometimes for years, with the knowledge that they have the disease. Such a threat requires and elicits many forms of coping, some of which are illustrated in the following excerpts from interviews with AIDS patients.

SOCIAL SUPPORT OR SEEKING INFORMATION

A key point in my program is that I have a really good support network of people who are willing to take the time, who will go the extra mile for me. I have spent years cultivating these friendships.

My family has been extremely supportive, and my lover has been extremely supportive, but it really wasn't quite enough. They weren't helping me in the right ways. That's when I went and got a therapist. Basically, she is the one who has helped me cope with [AIDS] and understand it.

DIRECT ACTION

My main concern is making it through another day without getting any disorder. I would really like to completely beat it.

My first concern was that, as promiscuous as I have been, I could not accept giving this to anyone. So I have been changing my lifestyle completely, putting everything else on the back burner.

The main thing I did was to get all my paperwork in order. I was good at it before, but when AIDS hit, I made sure everything was spelled out perfectly, and I figure that makes it easier for my lover left behind. He will go through grief, but he will not have to be sorting through all my junk.

STRATEGIES OF DISTRACTION, ESCAPE, OR AVOIDANCE

I used to depend on drugs a lot to change my mood. Once in a while, I still find that if I can't feel better any other way, I will take a puff of grass or have a glass of wine, or I use music. There are certain recordings that can really change my mood drastically. I play it loud and I dance around and try to clear my head.

There's an old disco song that says, "Keep out of my mind what's out of my hands." I try to do that, to not fret over things I really don't have control over.

It was important to me to focus on something besides AIDS, and my job is the most logical thing. I'm very good at what I do. I have a supervisory position, so I deal with other people's problems, which is good for me, because I take their problems and solve them and I forget about mine. I think that's a real constructive distraction for me.

I drive. I feel so much more at peace when I am driving down the road in a car, listening to music, having my dog next to me. It is wonderful.

Some researchers prefer to look at coping in a more microscopic fashion. A. A. Stone and Neale (1984) developed a measure of daily coping designed for use in studies to see how changes in coping on a day-to-day basis influence psychological and health outcomes (A. A. Stone, Kennedy-Moore, & Neale, 1995). Examples of the coping strategies used to combat the threat of AIDS appear in box 7.4.

People who are able to shift their coping strategies to meet the demands of a situation cope better with stress than those who do not. This point is of course suggested by the fact that the problem-solving and emotional approaches may work better for different stressors. Overall, research suggests that people who are flexible copers may cope especially well with stress (Cheng, 2003).

■ COPING AND EXTERNAL RESOURCES

Coping is influenced not only by the internal resources that an individual has, such as personality traits and coping methods, but also by external resources. These include time, money, education, a decent job, children, friends, family, standard of living, the presence of positive life events, and the absence of other life stressors (Hobfoll, 1989).

Individuals with greater resources typically cope with stressful events better because time, money, friends, and other resources simply provide more ways of dealing with a stressful event. For example, divorce is, generally speaking, an extremely stressful experience. However,

BOX 7.4

Coping with AIDS (continued)

EMOTIONAL REGULATION/ VENTILATION

When you're sad, you cry. That's what I've done a lot lately, over silly, well, not silly things, but over small things, and over reminders of a life that's probably cut short, the expectations of things that you were going to do and planned on doing and don't seem possible now.

I try to be like Spock on *Star Trek*. So this is an emotion. So that's what it makes you feel like. I try to analyze it and look as a third party would, like I am an observer from the fiftieth century.

Sometimes I will allow myself to have darker feelings, and then I grab myself by the bootstraps and say, okay, that is fine, you are allowed to have these feelings but they are not going to run your life.

PERSONAL GROWTH

In the beginning, AIDS made me feel like a poisoned dart, like I was a diseased person and I had no self-esteem and no self-confidence. That's what I have been really working on, is to get the self-confidence and the self-esteem back. I don't know if I will ever be there, but I feel very close to being there, to feeling like my old self.

I've made sure everybody knows how I feel about them. I have given away some of my precious things, some back to the people who gave them to me. I make sure that everyone has something from my past, everyone

who's been important in my life, and for the most part, I've sent them all letters too. Not that it was always received well . . .

When something like this happens to you, you can either melt and disappear or you can come out stronger than you did before. It has made me a much stronger person. I literally feel like I can cope with anything. Nothing scares me, nothing. If I was on a 747 and they said we were going down, I would probably reach for a magazine.

POSITIVE THINKING AND RESTRUCTURING

Everyone dies sooner or later. I have been appreciating how beautiful the Earth is, flowers, and the things I like. I used to go around ignoring all those things. Now I stop to try and smell the roses more often, and just do pleasurable things.

I have been spending a lot of time lately on having a more positive attitude. I force myself to become aware every time I say something negative during a day, and I go, "Oops," and I change it and I rephrase it. So I say, "Wonderful," about 42,000 times a day. Sometimes I don't mean it, but I am convincing myself that I do. The last chapter has not been written. The fat lady has not sung. I'm still here.

Source: G. M. Reed, 1989.

---

men and women with higher income, higher educational achievement, and a greater number of close friends experience less distress (Booth & Amato, 1991). In chapter 6, we saw another example of the moderation of stress by resources. Relative to nonworking women, working women who had adequate child care and whose husbands shared in homemaking tasks benefited psychologically from their work, whereas women without these resources showed higher levels of distress.

One of the most potent external resources with respect to health is socioeconomic status. People who are higher in SES are less likely to have most medical and psychiatric disorders, and they show lower mortality from all causes of death and from a variety of specific causes, including several cancers and cardiovascular dis-

ease. So strong is this relationship that, even in animals, higher-status animals are less vulnerable to infection than lower-status animals are (for example, S. Cohen et al., in press). Figure 7.3 illustrates the relation between social class and mortality (see N. E. Adler, Boyce, Chesney, Folkmann, & Syme, 1993). Studies of both animals and humans show that stable high status is related to reduced neuroendocrine responses to stress (T. E. Seeman & McEwen, 1996).

The presence of other life stressors also moderates coping responses, acting, in essence, as a resource depleter. People who must simultaneously deal with several sources of stress in their lives—such as a failing marriage, financial difficulties, or health problems—will have fewer resources left to use for coping with a new

FIGURE 7.3 | Mortality Rate by Socioeconomic Status

Annual death rate per 1,000 males.   (*Source:* J. Feldman, Makuc, Kleinman, & Corononi-Huntley, 1989)

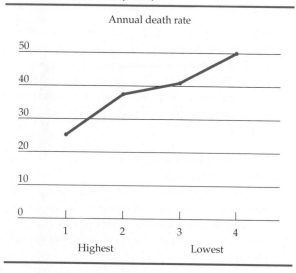

Annual death rate

stressor than will people who do not have to deal with other life stressors (F. Cohen & Lazarus, 1979).

Sources of Resilience

Positive life events (Ryff & Singer, 2000), good mood, and opportunities for rest, relaxation, and renewal may help people cope more effectively with life stressors and/or prevent stressful events from taking a toll on health. Experiencing positive events and having the opportunity to describe them or celebrate them with oth-

Coping researchers have found that direct action often leads to better adjustment to a stressful event than do coping efforts aimed at avoidance of the issue or denial.

ers affects both immediate mood and long-term well-being (Langston, 1994).

Interventions have built on observations like these and are designed to facilitate purposeful living and the development of quality relationships. For example, the Center for Creative Retirement in North Carolina (P. L. Brown, 1990) offers retired people opportunities for continuing education and community volunteer work. Both these efforts are designed to enhance a sense of purpose, foster continued mental growth, and develop meaningful ties to others (Ryff & Singer, 2000).

Whether such activities also have beneficial effects on health has not yet been widely studied. One restful event, however—taking a vacation—is now known to be beneficial for the health of one group—middle-aged men at risk for heart disease (Gump & Matthews, 2000). Whether similar positive experiences are beneficial for other people remains to be seen.

Resilience also comes from individual differences in how people cope with stressful events. Some people seem to recover from stressful events quickly, whereas others do not. Psychological resilience is characterized by the ability to bounce back from negative emotional experiences and by adapting flexibly to the changing demands of stressful experiences (B. L. Fredrickson, Tugade, Waugh, & Larkin, 2003). Being able to experience positive emotions, even in the context of otherwise intensely stressful events, appears to be one of the methods of coping that resilient people draw on (Tugade & Fredrickson, 2004). For example, being able to experience positive emotions, such as gratitude or love, following the 9/11 attacks enabled many people to cope with these distressing events and to experience post-traumatic growth.

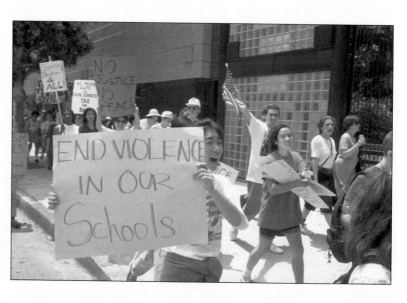

■ SOCIAL SUPPORT

The most vital of all resources against stress is social support. Social ties and relationships with others have long been regarded as emotionally satisfying aspects of life. They can also mute the effects of stress, help an individual cope with stressful events, and reduce the likelihood that stress will lead to poor health.

What Is Social Support?

Social support has been defined as information from others that one is loved and cared for, esteemed and valued, and part of a network of communication and mutual obligations from parents, a spouse or lover, other relatives, friends, social and community contacts (such as churches or clubs) (Rietschlin, 1998), or even a devoted pet (Allen, 2003a). People with high levels of social support may experience less stress when they confront a stressful experience, and they may cope with it more successfully.

Researchers have suggested that social support takes several forms; **tangible assistance** involves the provision of material support, such as services, financial assistance, or goods. For example, the gifts of food that often arrive after a death in a family mean that the bereaved family members will not have to cook for themselves and visiting relatives at a time when their energy and enthusiasm for such tasks is low.

Family and friends can provide **informational support** about stressful events. Information may help an individual understand a stressful event better and determine what resources and coping strategies may be mustered to deal with it. With information, the individual facing a stressful event can determine how threatening the stressful event is likely to be and can profit from suggestions about how to manage the event. For example, if an individual is facing an uncomfortable medical test, a friend who went through the same thing could provide information about the exact procedures, how long the discomfort will last, and the like.

During times of stress, people often suffer emotionally and may experience bouts of depression, sadness, anxiety, and loss of self-esteem. Supportive friends and family can provide **emotional support** by reassuring the person that he or she is a valuable individual who is cared for. The warmth and nurturance provided by other people can enable a person under stress to approach it with greater assurance.

The types of social support just discussed involve the actual provision of help and solace by one person to another. But in fact, many of the benefits of social support may actually come from the *perception* that social support is available. Actually receiving social support from another person can have several potential costs. First, one is using up another's time and attention, which can produce a sense of guilt. Needing to draw on others can also threaten self-esteem because it suggests a need to be dependent on others (Bolger, Zuckerman, &

Humor has long been thought to be an effective defense against stress. Writer Norman Cousins referred to laughter as "inner jogging" (Cousins, 1979). Now research supports that intuition. In one research investigation, a group of college students was shown a silent but highly stressful movie. Half the students were given an opportunity to generate a humorous monologue while watching the stressful film, whereas the other half generated a serious monologue. Compared with the students who produced a serious narrative, the students who produced the humorous narrative had better mood, less tension, and reduced psychophysiological reactivity in response to the stressful movie.

Kessler, 2000). These potential adverse costs of receiving social support can compromise the ability of social support to otherwise ameliorate psychological distress and health. Indeed, research suggests that when one receives help from another, but is unaware of it, that help is most likely to benefit the self. This kind of support is called **invisible support.** Consistent with the idea that implicit or invisible aspects of social support most benefit others, researchers have increasingly uncovered evidence that merely perceiving that one has social support goes considerable distance in providing the health and mental health benefits of social support (Bolger et al., 2000).

Effect of Social Support on Psychological Distress

What, exactly, are the benefits that social support provides? Research demonstrates that social support effectively reduces psychological distress, such as depression or anxiety, during times of stress. For example, a study of residents near the site of the Three Mile Island nuclear accident in 1979 (Fleming, Baum, Gisriel, & Gatchel, 1982) revealed that people with high levels of social support felt less distressed than did people with low levels of social support. Other studies have also found that social support alleviates psychological distress (Haines, Hurlbert, & Beggs, 1996; Lin, Ye, & Ensel, 1999).

Conversely, lack of social support during times of need can itself be very stressful, especially for people with high needs for social support but insufficient opportunities to obtain it. Such people may include the elderly; the recently widowed; and victims of sudden, severe, uncontrollable life events (for example Sorkin, Rook, & Lu, 2002). Loneliness clearly leads to health risks, in large part because lonely people appear to have more trouble sleeping and show more cardiovascular activation (Hawkley, Burleson, Bentson, & Cacioppo, 2003; Cacioppo et al., 2002). People who have difficulty with social relationships such as those who are chronically shy (Naliboff et al., 2004) or who anticipate rejection by others (Cole, Kemeny, Fahey, Zack, & Naliboff, 2003), are at risk for isolating themselves socially, with the result that they experience more psychological distress and are at greater risk for health problems.

Effects of Social Support on Physiological and Neuroendocrine Responses to Stress

Social support can reduce physiological and neuroendocrine responses to stress under a broad array of condi-

tions. Psychologists often study these conditions using the acute stress paradigm—that is, by taking people into the laboratory, putting them through stressful tasks (such as counting backwards quickly by 13s or giving an impromptu speech to an unresponsive audience), and then measuring their sympathetic and HPA axis responses to stress. Quite consistently, these biologic responses to stress are more subdued when a supportive companion is present than when no companion is present (Christenfeld et al., 1997). Even just believing that support is available (Uchino & Garvey, 1997) or contemplating the sources of support one typically has in life (Broadwell & Light, 1999) can yield these beneficial effects. Going through a stressful event in the presence of a pet can keep heart rate and blood pressure lower during that event and lead to faster physiological recovery (K. Allen, Blascovich, & Mendes, 2002). Dogs are somewhat better at providing social support than are other pets.

These calming effects are greater when support comes from a friend than from a stranger (Christenfeld et al., 1997). Both men and women seem to benefit somewhat more when the support provider is female than male (Glynn, Christenfeld, & Gerin, 1999). In fact, when women perform stressful events in the presence of a partner, especially their male partner, they sometimes appear to be more stressed than when they complete stressful tasks alone (Kirschbaum et al., 1995). Even a short encounter with a friendly dog has been found to increase opioid functioning and other hormones associated with companionship and to decrease levels of stress-related hormones such as cortisol; interestingly, the dogs experienced many of these benefits as well (Odendaal & Meintjes, 2002).

Exceptions notwithstanding, on the whole, social support lessens cardiovascular and cortisol responses to short-term stressful events. As box 7.5 shows, even a supportive video companion can have these beneficial effects. Not surprisingly, the advantages of social support during times of stress can be cumulative. Research has found that reoccurring positive social experiences affect a range of biological systems resulting in cumulative differences in risks for a broad array of chronic diseases later in life (Seeman, Singer, Ryff, Love, & Levy-Storms, 2002).

Effect of Social Support on Illness and Health Habits

Social support can lower the likelihood of illness, speed recovery from illness when it does occur, and reduce the risk of mortality due to serious disease (J. S. House, Landis, & Umberson, 1988; Rutledge, Matthews, Lui,

BOX 7.5

Video-Relayed Social Support

Given all the ways that technology has increasingly crept into our lives, it is virtually inevitable that someone would examine whether social support provided via video can actually be supportive. The answer is somewhat surprising: It can (Thorsteinsson, James, & Gregg, 1998).

The researchers brought 40 healthy young men and women into the laboratory and had them perform a demanding computer task. While they were performing the task, their heart rate, blood pressure, and cortisol levels were measured. Half of the participants heard a video-relayed supportive commentary provided by a same-sex person while they were completing the task, whereas the remainder heard no supportive commentary.

Although participants in both conditions performed at the same level, those who had received the social support via video reported feeling supported and rated the task as easier than those in the no-support condition. They also had lower heart rate and lower cortisol levels, compared with those who did not receive the support. Thus, just as a good friend or pleasant stranger can be supportive, so can a videotape of social support.

Stone, & Cavley, 2003). Studies that control for initial health status show that people with a high quantity and sometimes a high quality of social relationships have lower mortality rates (Berkman, 1985; J. S. House et al., 1988). Social isolation is a major risk factor for death for both humans and animals (J. S. House et al., 1988). Thus, the evidence linking social support to a reduced risk of mortality is substantial.

As an example, some impressive evidence for the role of social support in combating the threat of illness came from an early study of adults in Alameda County, California (Berkman & Syme, 1979). Almost 7,000 people were asked about their social and community ties, and their death rate was tracked over a 9-year period. The results showed that people who had few social and community ties were more likely to die during this period than were people with many such ties. Having social contacts enabled women to live an average of 2.8 years longer and men an average of 2.3 years longer. These effects were not caused by differences in socioeconomic status, health status at the beginning of the study, or the practice of health habits.

In a study of the common cold, healthy volunteers reported their social ties, such as whether they had a spouse, living parents, friends, or workmates, and whether they were members of social groups, such as clubs. The volunteers were then given nasal drops containing one of two viruses and were followed for the development of the common cold. Those people with larger social networks were less likely to develop colds, and those who did, had less severe colds (S. Cohen, Doyle, Skoner, Rabin, & Gwaltney, 1997). Social support appears to help people hold off or minimize complications from more serious medical conditions and disorders as well.

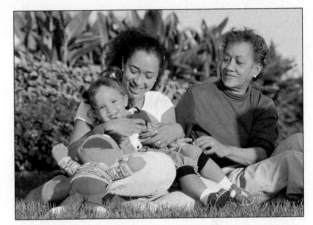

In addition to being an enjoyable aspect of life, social support from family and friends helps keep people healthy and may help them recover faster when they are ill.

People with high levels of social support have fewer complications during pregnancy and childbirth (N. L. Collins, Dunkel-Schetter, Lobel, & Scrimshaw, 1993); report less pain (J. L. Brown, Sheffield, Leary, & Robinson, 2003); are less susceptible to herpes attacks (VanderPlate, Aral, & Magder, 1988); have lower rates of myocardial infarction (Bruhn, 1965); are less susceptible to the development of new brain lesions if they have multiple sclerosis (Mohr, Goodkin, Nelson, Cox, & Weiner, 2002); are less likely to show age-related cognitive decline (Seeman, Lusignolo, Albert, & Berkman, 2001); and are more likely to show better adjustment to coronary artery disease (Holahan, Moos, Holahan, & Brennan, 1997), diabetes, lung disease, cardiac disease, arthritis, and cancer (Penninx et al., 1998; Stone, Mezzacappa, Donatone, & Gonder, 1999).

Social support enhances the prospects for recovery among people who are already ill (B. S. Wallston, Alagna, DeVellis, & DeVellis, 1983). Social support has been associated with better adjustment to and faster recovery from coronary artery surgery (K. B. King, Reis, Porter, & Norsen, 1993; Kulik & Mahler, 1993), kidney disease (Dimond, 1979), childhood leukemia (Magni, Silvestro, Tamiello, Zanesco, & Carl, 1988), and stroke (Robertson & Suinn, 1968), as well as better diabetes control (Marteau, Bloch, & Baum, 1987; L. S. Schwartz, Springer, Flaherty, & Kiani, 1986) and less pain among arthritis patients (R. F. DeVellis, DeVellis, Sauter, & Cohen, 1986).

Although social support has an impact on health independent of any influence on health habits, it also appears to affect health habits directly (Allgöwer, Wardle, & Steptoe, 2001; M. A. Lewis & Rook, 1999). People with high levels of social support are typically more adherent to their medical regimens (DiMatteo, 2004), and they are more likely to use health services, especially when the support network is positively inclined toward those services (Geersten, Klauber, Rindflesh, Kane, & Gray, 1975; B. S. Wallston et al., 1983). Social influences may adversely affect some health habits, however, as when one's peer group smokes, drinks heavily, or takes drugs (Wills & Vaughan, 1989) or when much social contact is coupled with high levels of stress; under these circumstances, risk of minor illnesses such as colds or flus may actually increase (Hamrick, Cohen, & Rodriguez, 2002).

Biopsychosocial Pathways   The frontier of social support research is to identify the biopsychosocial pathways by which social support exerts beneficial or health-compromising effects. Studies suggest that social support has beneficial effects on the cardiovascular, endocrine, and immune systems (T. E. Seeman & McEwen, 1996; Uchino, Cacioppo, & Kiecolt-Glaser, 1996). For example, one study found that the perception of social support was associated with lower systolic blood pressure in working women, suggesting that the presence of or the perception of social support may have enabled these women to go through a stressful workday without experiencing as much sympathetic arousal as was true for women who felt they lacked support (Linden, Chambers, Maurice, & Lenz, 1993). Other studies report similar beneficial effects of social support on blood pressure (for example, Carels, Blumenthal, & Sherwood, 1998). In fact, simply knowing that social support is potentially available leads to reduced cardiovascular reactivity in response to stress, even if that social support is not actually activated (Uchino & Garvey, 1997).

Social support also affects endocrine functioning in response to stress. As an example, a study of older men and women found that the quantity and quality of social relationships that men experienced was strongly related to levels of urinary norepinephrine, epinephrine, and cortisol; less consistent differences were found for women (T. E. Seeman, Berkman, Blazer, & Rowe, 1994). Other studies have found that social support is associated with reduced cortisol responses to stress, which can have beneficial effects on a broad array of diseases, including heart disease and cancer (Turner-Cobb, Sephton, Koopman, Blake-Mortimer, & Spiegel, 2000). Generally speaking, social support is associated with better immune functioning for support recipients (Herbert & Cohen, 1993).

These biopsychosocial pathways, then, provide the links between illness and social support. These links are important because they play critical roles in the leading causes of death—namely, cardiovascular disease, cancer, and respiratory illness.

Genetic Bases of Social Support?   Researchers have questioned exactly why social support is so helpful during times of stress. Certainly, some of these effects are due to benefits that one's close friends, family, and community ties can provide, but there are also advantages to perceiving that social support is available. Research using twin study methodology has discovered genetic underpinnings either in the ability to construe social support as available or in the ability to pick supportive networks (Kessler, Kendler, Heath, Neale, & Eaves, 1992). During periods of high stress, genetic predispositions to draw on social support networks may be activated, leading to the perception that support will be available to mute stress.

Moderation of Stress by Social Support

What is the role of social support in moderating the effects of stress? Two possibilities have been extensively explored. One hypothesis maintains that social support is generally beneficial during nonstressful times as well as during highly stressful times (the **direct effects hypothesis**). The other hypothesis, known as the **buffering hypothesis,** maintains that the health and mental health benefits of social support are chiefly evident during periods of high stress; when there is little stress, social support may have few physical or mental health benefits.

Social support can come not only from family and friends but also from a loved pet. Research suggests that dogs are better at providing social support than cats and other animals.

According to this hypothesis, social support acts as a reserve and resource that blunts the effects of stress or enables the individual to cope with stress more effectively when it is at high levels. Evidence suggesting both direct effects and buffering effects of social support has amassed (S. Cohen & Hoberman, 1983; S. Cohen & McKay, 1984; Penninx et al., 1998; Wills, 1984).

Generally, when researchers have looked at social support in social integration terms, such as the number of people one identifies as friends or the number of organizations one belongs to, direct effects of social support on health have been found. When social support has been assessed more qualitatively, such as the degree to which a person feels that there are other people available who will provide help if it is needed, then buffering effects of social support have been found (J. S. House et al., 1988).

Extracting Support   The effectiveness of social support depends on how an individual uses a social support network. Some people are better than others in extracting the support they need. To examine this hypothesis, S. Cohen, Sherrod, and Clark (1986) assessed incoming college freshmen as to their social competence, social anxiety, and self-disclosure skills. The researchers wanted to see if these skills influenced whether the students were able to develop and use social support effectively and whether the same skills could account for the positive effects of social support in combating stress. Those students with greater social competence, lower social anxiety, and better self-disclosure skills did develop more effective social support and were more likely to form friendships, lending credence to the idea that the use of social support as a coping technique reflects, in part, a difference in personality, social skills, or competence, rather than an external resource (for example, Kessler et al., 1992). The personality of the person seeking social support may predict the emotional support that is perceived but may not predict as strongly the ability to get tangible assistance or information (for example, Dunkel-Schetter, Folkman, & Lazarus, 1987).

What Kinds of Support Are Most Effective?

Not all aspects of social support are equally protective against stress. For example, having a confidant (such as a spouse or partner) may be the most effective social support (Umberson, 1987), especially for men (for example, Broadwell & Light, 1999; Wickrama et al., 1995). The beneficial effects of social support are also not necessarily cumulative. For example, with respect to friends, the critical factor for effective social support is having at least one close friend. Having a dozen close friends may be no more beneficial than having two or three (Langner & Michael, 1960).

In fact, evidence exists that too much or overly intrusive social support may actually exacerbate stress (Shumaker & Hill, 1991). When social support is controlling or directive, it may have some benefits on health behaviors but produce psychological distress (M. A. Lewis & Rook, 1999). People who belong to "dense" social networks (friendship or family groups that are highly interactive and in which everyone knows everyone else) may find themselves besieged by advice and interference in times of stress. As comedian George Burns noted, "Happiness is having a large, loving, caring, close-knit family in another city."

Matching Support to the Stressor   Different kinds of stressful events create different needs, and social support should be most effective when it meets those needs. The hypothesis that a match between one's needs and what one receives from others in one's social network is called the **matching hypothesis** (S. Cohen & McKay, 1984; S. Cohen & Wills, 1985). For example, if a person has someone he or she can talk to about problems but actually needs only to borrow a car, the presence of a confidant is useless. But if a person is upset about how a relationship is going and needs to talk it through with a friend, then the availability of a confidant is a very helpful resource.

Empathetic understanding helps support providers sense what kinds of support will be most helpful to a person going through a particularly stressful event. People who need support, in turn, may be most effectively helped by others when they are able to communicate that they need support and what particular kind of support they need.

Some kinds of support are useful with most kinds of stressors. Having someone to talk to about problems and having a person who makes one feel better about oneself may be especially helpful because these are issues that arise with most stressful events.

Support from Whom?

Providing effective social support is not always easy for the support network. It requires skill. When it is provided by the wrong person, support may be unhelpful or even rejected, as when a stranger tries to comfort a lost child. Social support may also be ineffective if the type of support provided is not the kind that is needed.

Different kinds of support may be valued from different members of one's social support network, in that each member may have unique abilities to be helpful along particular dimensions. Emotional support is most important from intimate others, whereas information and advice may be more valuable from experts. Thus, a person who desires solace from a family member but receives advice instead may find that rather than being supportive, the family member actually makes the stressful situation worse (B. A. Benson, Gross, Messer, Kellum, & Passmore, 1991; Dakof & Taylor, 1990).

Support from a partner, usually a spouse, is very protective of health, especially for men (Kiecolt-Glaser & Newton, 2001). On average, men's health is substantially benefited from marriage. Women's health is only slightly benefited by marriage. The quality of marital relationship influences these outcomes as well. Exiting a marriage, being unmarried, or being in an unsatisfying marriage all entail health risks (Keicolt-Glaser & Newton, 2001; Williams, 2003).

Support from family is important as well. Social support from one's parents in early life and/or living in a stable and supportive environment as a child has long-term effects on coping and on health (Repetti et al., 2002). Experiencing the divorce of one's parents in childhood predicts premature death in midlife (H. S. Friedman, Tucker, Schwartz, Martin, et al., 1995). A study of college students (Valentiner, Holahan, & Moos, 1994) found that students who perceived themselves as having a lot of support from their parents were more likely to make favorable appraisals of potentially stressful events and were more likely to cope actively with those stressful events when they occurred. When faced with uncontrollable events, parental support enabled these students to cope

well emotionally, even when they could not take direct action to reduce the stressor (see also Maunder & Hunter, 2001). Similarly, a long-term study of undergraduate men at Harvard revealed that those men who perceived themselves to have had warm, close relationships with their parents were healthier 35 years later (Russek & Schwartz, 1997). Those men in childhood who did not report a warm relationship with their parents were more likely to be diagnosed in midlife with coronary artery disease, hypertension, ulcers, and alcoholism (see also Russek, Schwartz, Bell, & Baldwin, 1998).

Threats to Social Support

Stressful events can interfere with the ability to use potential social support effectively. People who are under extreme stress may continually express distress to others and drive those others away, thus making a bad situation even worse (for example, G. E. Matt & Dean, 1993; McLeod, Kessler, & Landis, 1992). For example, depressed or ill people can repel their friends and family instead of using them effectively for social support (Alferi, Carver, Antoni, Weiss, & Duran, 2001; Coyne et al., 1987).

Sometimes, would-be support providers fail to provide the support that is needed and, instead, react in an unsupportive manner that actually aggravates the negative event. These negative interactions may have a more adverse effect on well-being than positive social interactions may have on improving it. In a study of 120 widowed women, Rook (1984) found that negative social interactions were consistently and more strongly related to well-being than were positive social outcomes. Dilemmas such as having one's privacy invaded by family and friends, having promises of help broken, and being involved with people who provoked conflict or anger were among the events that worsened psychological adjustment (see also Schuster, Kessler, & Aseltine, 1990).

Hostile and negative behaviors during marital conflict have been associated with immunological downregulation (that is, adverse immunological changes) (Kiecolt-Glaser et al., 1993), increases in epinephrine and norepinephrine, decreases in prolactin (Malarkey, Kiecolt-Glaser, Pearl, & Glaser, 1994), and increases in cortisol (Kiecolt-Glaser, Newton, et al., 1996). As we saw in chapter 6, recurrent or prolonged SAM and HPA axis activation has the potential for compromising health.

Support providers may also be affected by the stressful event. For example, Wortman and Dunkel-Schetter (1979) suggested that the stressful event of cancer in a loved one or friend creates fear and aversion to the cancer but also a simultaneous awareness of the need to provide support. These tensions may produce a variety of negative outcomes, such as physically avoiding the patient, avoiding open communication about the cancer, minimizing its impact, or demonstrating forced cheerfulness that does little to actually raise the patient's spirit (see also Dakof & Taylor, 1990). Any stressful event that alarms or creates conflicts for a would-be support provider can threaten social support.

Effects of Stress on Support Providers

When a close friend, family member, or partner is going through a stressful event, the event also has an impact on close family members who may themselves have resulting needs for social support that go unmet (for example, Aneshensel, Pearlin, & Schuler, 1993). To the extent that family members and friends are adversely affected by the stressful event, they may be less able to provide social support to the person in greatest need (B. G. Melamed & Brenner, 1990).

For example, long-term provision of care for another has been tied to both psychological distress, including anxiety and depression, and compromised health (Schulz, O'Brien, Bookwala, & Fleissner, 1995). For example, as many as one third of primary caregivers of Alzheimer's patients show clinically significant levels of depression (Mintzer et al., 1992), decrements in cellular immunity, and higher rates of disease (Kiecolt-Glaser, Dura, Speicher, Trask, & Glaser, 1991; Kiecolt-Glaser, Marucha, Malarkey, Mercado, & Glaser, 1995; Uchino, Kiecolt-Glaser, & Cacioppo, 1992). Such caregivers, may themselves, be in need of social support, which may, in turn, improve their physiological and psychological functioning.

At the intense levels of social support involved in caregiving, caregivers may experience compromised mental and physical health. On the whole, though, the evidence suggests that giving social support to others has beneficial effects on mental health and health (C. Schwartz, Meisenhelder, Ma, & Reed, 2003; Thoits & Hewitt, 2001). For example, a recent study assessed giving and receiving social support in older married people and related both to mortality rates over a 5-year period (Brown, Nesse, Vinokur, & Smith, 2003). Death was significantly less likely for those people who reported providing instrumental support to friends, relatives, and neighbors and to those who reported providing emotional support to their spouses. Receiving support did not affect mortality. This study, then, provides important evidence that the giving of support can promote health and retard illness progression.

These findings are especially important because social support and helping have long been thought to benefit the beneficiary of the help while taxing the resources of those that provide it. The fact that helping, altruism, and support lead to health and mental health benefits for both the giver and the receiver make social support that much more important. Feeling that one matters to another person improves well-being, especially for women (Taylor & Turner, 2001).

Enhancing Social Support

Health psychologists need to view social support as an important resource in primary prevention. Finding ways to increase the effectiveness of existing or potential support from family and friends should be a high research priority.

Increasingly, researchers are finding ways to increase social support in settings where people may otherwise experience distress, such as in the hospital or just before a noxious medical procedure such as surgery. For example, Mahler and Kulik (2002) gave spouses of coronary bypass graft patients an optimistically slanted information videotape about the surgery, a tape describing the surgery as having more ups and downs, or no tape (a control condition). They found that female spouses of male patients were effective caregivers without the tape, but the tape improved the ability of the male caregivers to provide effective support to their wives; women patients whose spouses had received the optimistically slanted information had fewer post-operative problems (Mahler & Kulik, 2002).

People also need to be encouraged to recognize the potential sources of social support in their environment and be taught how to draw on these resources more effectively. People might also be taught how to develop social support resources, as by joining community groups, interest groups, or informal social groups that meet regularly. Psychologists can contribute to the development of social support mechanisms, explore ways of creating social ties, and develop means of identifying and aiding socially marginal individuals who cannot avail themselves of this valuable resource.

■ COPING OUTCOMES

As we have seen, stressful events can be offset or managed and their adverse health effects muted with the successful recruitment of internal resources, such as coping strategies, and external resources, such as money or social support. But coping must be thought of not only as a set of processes that occurs in reaction to the problems posed by a particular stressor, but also as efforts aimed at the achievement of certain goals. These goals may be thought of as the tasks of coping. Coping efforts center on five main tasks:

1. To reduce harmful environmental conditions and enhance the prospects of recovery.
2. To tolerate or adjust to negative events or realities.
3. To maintain a positive self-image.
4. To maintain emotional equilibrium.
5. To continue satisfying relationships with others (F. Cohen & Lazarus, 1979).

To elaborate, individuals must first deal with the immediate demands of the stressor itself. They must come to terms with any negative and irreversible problems that the stressor has produced. For example, a newly widowed woman must acknowledge the fact that her husband is no longer with her. Next, one must anticipate future threats and take actions that can reduce further risk: The widow must take stock of her financial situation and must pull herself together so that she can continue to perform the tasks of daily living. People under stress must also attempt to reduce emotional distress—both distress caused by already existing harm and distress occasioned by anticipated future stress: The widow must keep her grieving within manageable bounds so that it does not interfere with her ability to go on with her life. Similarly, she must maintain enough emotional control so that subsequent setbacks, such as the discovery that a life insurance policy had expired, do not become devastating experiences. In the face of severe blows and setbacks, the person under stress must try to maintain self-esteem: The widow must remind herself that she is a person of value and worth, even though the person most likely to encourage that self-image is now deceased. Finally, people under stress must revive and maintain social relationships as a source of ongoing sustenance. The widow should turn to her social network of relatives and friends, so that they can ease her loneliness and unhappiness.

Throughout our discussion, we have referred several times to successful coping. What constitutes successful coping? One set of **coping outcomes** has included measures of physiological and biochemical functioning. Coping efforts are generally judged to be more successful if they reduce arousal and its indicators, such as heart rate, pulse, and skin conductivity. If blood or urine levels of catecholamines and corticosteroids are reduced, coping is judged to be more successful.

A second criterion of successful coping is whether and how quickly people can return to their prestress activities. Many stressors—especially severe ones, such as the death of a spouse, or chronic ones, such as excessive noise—interfere with the conduct of daily life activities. To the extent that people's coping efforts enable them to resume usual activities, coping may be judged to be successful. However, there is an implicit bias in this criterion. If a person's prior living situation was not an ideal one, substantial life change may be a sign of successful rather than unsuccessful coping (S. E. Taylor, 1983). For example, a sick person who is overworked and hates his job may not be showing successful adjustment if he returns to the same work situation; revising the work situation would be a more successful form of coping.

Third, and most commonly, researchers judge coping according to its effectiveness in reducing psychological distress. When a person's anxiety or depression is reduced, the coping response is judged to be successful. Finally, coping can be judged in terms of whether it terminates, lessens, or shortens the duration of the stressful event itself (Harnish, Aseltine, & Gore, 2000).

The past few decades have seen great strides in coping research. Researchers have identified many of the common coping strategies that people use, and measures of coping have been developed. The next frontier of coping research is to focus on the biopsychosocial pathways through which coping efforts and those resources that aid in managing stress can influence psychological and health outcomes.

■ THE MANAGEMENT OF STRESS

Individuals' coping responses are often spontaneous; that is, people do whatever comes naturally to them and what has worked in the past. But sometimes these efforts are not enough. The stressor may be so novel, so chronic, or so elusive that people's own efforts may be unsuccessful in reducing stress.

Moreover, as we have seen, individual efforts to control stress are not always adaptive, especially in the long term. Coping with chronic stress through excessive alcohol or drug use, for example, may bring relief in the short run, but often the person is worse off for these efforts; the source of stress itself remains unchanged, and the individual may have an addiction to combat on top of all the other sources of stress.

Who Needs Stress Management?

Because people so obviously have difficulty managing stress themselves, health psychologists have increasingly turned their attention to developing techniques of **stress management** that can be taught. Who participates in stress management programs? Some people obtain help in stress management through private therapists in a one-to-one psychotherapeutic experience.

More commonly, stress management is taught through workshops. For example, increasingly, stress management courses are offered in the workplace. Stress-related disorders account for as much as $17 billion a year in lost productivity, and one estimate places the annual cost of stress-related illness at $69 billion (J. D. Adams, 1978). Consequently, organizations have been motivated to help their workers identify and cope with the variety of stressful events that they experience in their lives and on the job (Ganster, Mayes, Sime, & Tharp, 1982).

People who suffer from or are at risk for illnesses that are aggravated by stress often learn stress management techniques. For example, stress management programs have been used successfully to treat muscle contraction headaches (Holroyd, Andrasik, & Westbrook, 1977), to manage migraine headaches (Turk, Meichenbaum, & Berman, 1979), to manage the symptoms of multiple sclerosis (C. E. Schwartz, 1999), and to control high blood pressure (A. P. Shapiro, Schwartz, Ferguson, Redmond, & Weiss, 1977). Chapters 4 and 5 point out that the treatment of alcohol abuse and obesity also frequently incorporates stress management skills (U.S. Department of Health and Human Services, 1981).

As we will see in chapter 13, individuals with symptoms of cardiovascular disease or a history of angina or myocardial infarction are often trained in techniques for coping with stress (for example, Chesney, Eagleston, & Rosenman, 1981; Roskies, 1980; Roskies, Spevack, Surkis, Cohen, & Gilman, 1978). Effective stress management has clear health benefits in controlling stress-related disorders and in reducing not only the risk factors associated with coronary heart disease but also the development of CHD (Carver & Humphries, 1982; Chesney et al., 1981; Roskies, 1980).

Finally, stress management courses are increasingly being offered to groups experiencing particular kinds of problems.

Basic Techniques of Stress Management

Stress management programs typically involve three phases. In the first phase, participants learn what stress is and how to identify the stressors in their own lives. In the second phase, they acquire and practice skills for coping with stress. In the final phase, participants practice these stress management techniques in the targeted stressful situations and monitor their effectiveness (Meichenbaum & Jaremko, 1983).

As an example, college can be an extremely stressful experience for many students. For some, it is the first time away from home, and they must cope with the problems of living in a dormitory surrounded by strangers. They may have to share a room with another person of a very different background with very different personal habits. High noise levels, communal bathrooms, institutional food, and rigorous academic schedules may all be trying experiences to new students.

In addition, academic life may prove to be more difficult than they had expected. Whereas in high school each student may have been a star, college presents heavier competition because the students are more similar in intellectual caliber. Consequently, course loads are heavier and grades are typically lower. Because the student was able to do well in high school with relatively little effort, he or she may never have developed the concentration, study skills, or motivation required to excel in the college environment. Coping with a first *C, D,* or *F* can be a deflating and anxiety-arousing experience.

If the student sees little prospect for improvement, he or she may become increasingly anxious, find that the college environment is too stressful, and drop out. Recognizing that these pressures exist, college administrators have increasingly made stress management programs available to their students.

A Stress Management Program

One university responded to these problems by developing a stress management program that reaches troubled students before the stresses of academic life lead them to flunk out or drop out. The program, called Combat Stress Now (CSN), makes use of the three phases of education, skill acquisition, and practice.

Identifying Stressors In the first phase of the CSN program, participants learn what stress is and how it creates physical wear and tear. In sharing their personal experiences of stress, many students find reassurance in the fact that so many other students have experiences similar to their own. Students then learn that stress is a process of psychological appraisal rather than a factor inherent in events themselves. Thus, college life is not

There are many stressful aspects of college life, such as speaking in front of large groups. Stress management programs can help students master these experiences.

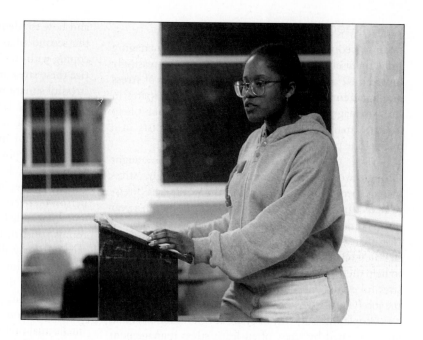

inherently stressful but is a consequence of the individual's perceptions of it. Through these messages, the students begin to see that, if they are armed with appropriate stress management techniques, they will come to experience currently stressful events as less stressful.

Monitoring Stress   In the self-monitoring phase of the CSN program, students are trained to observe their own behavior closely and to record the circumstances that they find most stressful. In addition, they record their physical, emotional, and behavioral reactions to those stresses as they experience them. Students also record their own maladaptive efforts to cope with these stressful events, including excessive sleeping or eating, television watching, alcohol consumption, and other responses.

Identifying Stress Antecedents   Once students learn to chart their stress responses, they are encouraged to examine the antecedents of these experiences. In particular, they learn to focus on what events happen just before they experience subjective feelings of stress. For example, one student may feel overwhelmed with academic life only when contemplating speaking out in class, where as another student may experience stress primarily when thinking about having to use the computer in a particularly demanding course.

Thus, by pinpointing exactly those circumstances that initiate feelings of stress, the students can more precisely identify their own trouble spots.

Avoiding Negative Self-talk   As in many stress management courses, students in the CSN course are trained to recognize the negative self-talk they go through when they face stressful events. Negative self-talk can contribute to irrational feelings that perpetuate stress (Meichenbaum, 1975). For example, the student who fears speaking out in class may recognize how self-statements contribute to this process: "I hate asking questions," "I always get tongue-tied," "I'll probably forget what I want to say."

Take-Home Assignments   In addition to the exercises that students perform in class, they also have take-home assignments. In particular, students keep a stress diary in which they record the events they find stressful and how they responded to them. As they become proficient in identifying stressful incidents, they are encouraged to record the negative self-statements or irrational thoughts that accompany the stressful experience (see Ellis, 1962).

Skill Acquisition   As in most stress management training programs, the second stage of CSN involves skill acquisition and practice. The skills of stress management vary widely and include cognitive-behavioral management techniques, time management skills, and other stress-reducing interventions, such as diet or exercise. Some of these techniques are designed to eliminate the stressful event, whereas others are geared toward reducing the experience of stress without necessarily modifying the event itself.

Setting New Goals

In the CSN program, students begin to attack their stressful events by setting goals, engaging in positive self-talk, and using self-instruction. Specifically, first, each student sets several specific goals that he or she wants to meet to reduce the experience of college stress. For one student, the goal may be learning to speak in class without suffering overwhelming anxiety. For another, the goal may be going to see a particular professor about a problem.

Once the goals have been set, the next challenge is to identify specific behaviors that will meet those goals. In some cases, an appropriate response may be leaving the stressful event altogether. For example, the student who is having difficulty in a rigorous physics course may need to modify his goal of becoming a physicist. Alternatively, students may be encouraged to turn a stressor into a challenge. Thus, the student who fears speaking up in class may come to realize that she must not only master this fearful event but actually come to enjoy it if she is to realize her long-term goal of becoming a trial lawyer.

In other cases, students may have to put up with a stressful event but simply learn to manage it more effectively. If a particular English course is highly stressful but is required for graduation, the student must learn to cope with the course in the best way possible.

Thus, goal setting is important in effective stress management, first, because it forces a person to distinguish among stressful events to be avoided, tolerated, or overcome. Second, it forces the individual to be specific and concrete about exactly which events need to be tackled and what is to be done.

Positive Self-talk

Once students have set some realistic goals and identified some target behaviors for reaching those goals, they learn how to engage in self-instruction and positive self-talk, two skills that can help in achieving those goals. Positive self-talk involves providing the self with specific encouragements. For example, students desiring to overcome a fear of oral presentation might remind themselves of all the occasions in which they have spoken successfully in public.

Once some proficiency in public speaking is achieved, students might encourage themselves by highlighting the positive aspects of the experience (for example, holding the attention of the audience, making some points, winning over a few converts).

As a skill, self-instruction involves reminding oneself of the specific steps that are required to achieve the particular goal. Thus, the would-be trial lawyer should try to create opportunities for public speaking and plan to self-reward when the speaking goes successfully. Each time the student speaks, the steps that go into an effective presentation may need to be carefully rehearsed, composing thoughts before speaking, making notes, rehearsing, and the like. By outlining the speech precisely, the student may make a more effective public presentation.

Other Cognitive-Behavioral Techniques

In some stress management programs, contingency contracting (chapter 3) is encouraged. For example, in the CSN program, students whose problems are motivational are encouraged to make a contract with the self. Thus, the student who fears making oral presentations may define a specific goal, such as asking three questions in class in a week, which is to be followed by a particular reward, such as tickets to a rock concert.

These techniques to control stress present a wide array of cognitive-behavior therapy techniques that an individual can use to combat stress: self-monitoring, the modification of internal dialogues, goal setting, homework assignments, positive self-talk, self-instruction, and contingency contracting. Most stress management programs include this cafeteria-like array of techniques so that people have a broad set of skills from which to choose. People can discover the skills that work best for them. In these ways, individuals can "inoculate" themselves against stress (Meichenbaum & Turk, 1982). This **stress inoculation** training, as Meichenbaum and Turk called it, enables people to confront stressful events with a clear plan in mind and an array of potential measures that they can take before the stressful event becomes overwhelming.

Relaxation Training and Stress Management

Whereas most of the techniques we have discussed so far are designed to give an individual cognitive insights into the nature and control of stress, another set of techniques—relaxation training techniques—is designed to affect the physiological experience of stress by reducing arousal.

Relaxation training therapies include progressive muscle relaxation training, guided imagery, transcendental meditation, and other forms of meditation, including yoga and hypnosis. These techniques can reduce heart rate, skin conductance, muscle tension, blood pressure, inflammatory processes, lipid levels, energy utilization, self-reports of anxiety, and tension (Lucini et al., 1997; Lutgendorf, Anderson, Sorosky, Butler, & Lubaroff, 2000; Scheufele, 2000; R. H. Schneider et al., 1998; Speca, Carlson, Goodey, & Angen, 2000).

Because of the value of relaxation for health and mental health, students in the CSN program are trained in relaxation therapy. First, they learn how to control their breathing, taking no more than six to eight breaths per minute. They are trained to relax the muscles in each part of the body progressively, until they experience no tension (progressive muscle relaxation). They are urged to identify the particular spots that tense up during times of stress, such as a jaw that clamps shut or fists that tighten up. By becoming especially aware of these reactions, they can relax these parts of the body as well. Thus, for example, when students find that the stress of college life is catching up with them, they can take a 5- or 10-minute break in which they breathe deeply and relax completely. They can return to their tasks free of some of their previous tensions.

Supplementary Stress Management Skills

In addition to the basic cognitive and relaxation skills of stress management, many programs also include training in supplementary skills. In many cases, the experience of stress depends heavily on feeling that one has too much to do in too little time. Consequently, many stress management programs include training in **time management** and planning. CSN helps students set specific work goals for each day, establish priorities, avoid time wasters, and learn what to ignore altogether. Thus, a student may learn to set aside 2 hours for a particularly important task, such as studying for a test. In this way, the student has a particular goal and particular time period in which to pursue it and therefore is less subject to interruption. Simple "how to" manuals effectively illustrate the time management approach to stress management.

Many stress management programs emphasize good health habits and social skills as additional techniques for the control of stress (J. D. Adams, 1978). These include good eating habits, exercise, assertiveness in social

situations, and using social support. Stress often affects eating habits adversely: People under stress consume too many stimulants (such as coffee), too much sugar, and too much junk food. By learning to control dietary habits effectively and by eating three balanced meals a day, the student can ameliorate physiological reactions to stress. Likewise, regular exercise reduces stress. At least 20 to 30 minutes of sustained exercise three times a week is widely encouraged for all participants in the CSN program.

Assertiveness training is sometimes incorporated into stress management. Often, people experience stress because they are unable to confront the people who contribute to their stress. For example, in the CSN program, students who have identified other individuals in their environment as causing them special stress (called **stress carriers**) help one another practice dealing with these individuals. One student may practice approaching a professor with whom he is having difficulty communicating; another student may practice dealing tactfully with a roommate who constantly brags about how well she is doing in her classes.

As we have already seen, social support can buffer the adverse effects of stress. Unfortunately, people under stress sometimes alienate rather than effectively engage those people who might provide social support. A harried executive snaps at his wife and children, or a student facing a threatening exam angrily rejects a friend's well-intentioned advice. Students in the CSN program are trained to recognize the important functions that social support can serve in helping them combat stress. They are urged to confide in close friends, to seek advice from people who can help them, and to use their relationships with other people as sources of positive reinforcement after successfully meeting their goals.

In the final stage of the CSN program, stress management techniques are put into effect. Trainees practice the stress management techniques they have learned and monitor their effectiveness in daily situations. If some techniques fail to work, the trainees are urged to figure out why. Students take their experiences of stress management back to the group situation, where successes and failures can be analyzed. If initial efforts to cope with a stressful event are unsuccessful, the student may need to practice the technique more or shift to a different type of stress management technique. Overall, stress management is an important undertaking in a world with many sources of stress. It reliably improves mood (Thayer, Newman, & McClain, 1994) and may have beneficial effects on health as well. ●

SUMMARY

1. Stress can alter health habits, increase the likelihood that one will seek medical attention, increase wear and tear on the physiological system, and interact with preexisting vulnerabilities to produce illness, both psychological and physical. Both stress itself and the stress-illness relationship are importantly influenced by stress moderators—namely, internal and external resources and liabilities that affect people's ability to cope with stress.

2. Coping is the process of managing demands that tax or exceed a person's resources. Coping is influenced by primary appraisals ("Is the event harmful, threatening, or challenging?") and by secondary appraisals ("What are my coping resources and how adequate are they?").

3. Selection of coping efforts is guided by internal and external resources. Internal resources include preferred coping style and other personality factors, such as negativity, hardiness, optimism, and control. External resources include time, money, the presence of other simultaneous life stressors, and social support.

4. Coping styles consist of predispositions to cope with stressful situations in particular ways. Avoidance versus confrontation is one prominently studied coping style. Recent research has explored the value of emotional disclosure.

5. Coping efforts may be directed at solving problems or at regulating emotions. Most stressful events evoke both types of coping, as well as more specific strategies.

6. Social support can be an effective resource in times of stress. It reduces psychological distress and the likelihood of illness. However, some events can undermine or threaten social support resources.

7. The tasks toward which coping efforts are typically directed include reducing harmful environmental conditions and enhancing the adjustment process, tolerating and adjusting to negative events and realities, maintaining a positive self-image, maintaining emotional equilibrium, and continuing satisfying relations with others.

8. Coping efforts are judged to be successful when they reduce physiological indicators of arousal, enable the person to return to prestress activities, and free the individual from psychological distress.

9. Stress management programs exist for those who need aid in developing their coping skills. These programs teach people to identify sources of stress in their lives, to develop coping skills to deal with those stressors, and to practice employing stress management skills and monitoring their effectiveness.

KEY TERMS

avoidant (minimizing) coping style
buffering hypothesis
confrontative (vigilant) coping
   style
coping
coping outcomes
coping style

direct effects hypothesis
emotional support
informational support
invisible support
matching hypothesis
negative affectivity
pessimistic explanatory style

social support
stress carriers
stress inoculation
stress management
stress moderators
tangible assistance
time management

PART 4

The Patient in the Treatment Setting

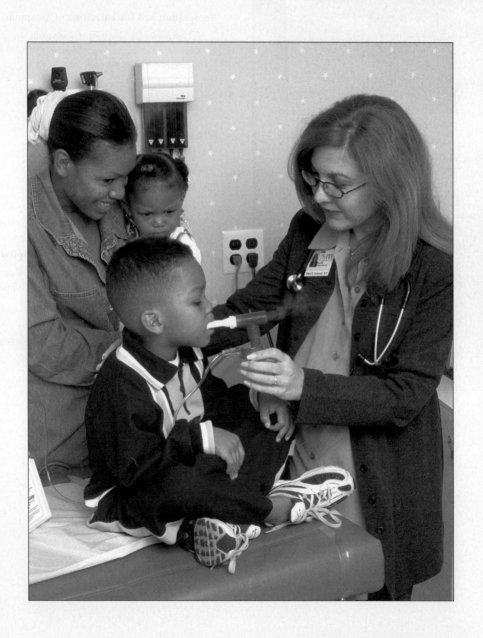

CHAPTER 8

Using Health Services

Some years ago, creative puppeteer Jim Henson died abruptly in his mid-50s from an apparent cold or flu that coursed rapidly through his system. Henson had been working long hours and was run-down from heavy business and travel commitments, and although he knew he should see a doctor—his symptoms were getting worse—he put it off. When he finally did check into a hospital, the infection had spread so far that doctors could not save him. Generations of children and parents who had grown up with *Sesame Street* and who had come to love Kermit the Frog, Oscar, and the other endearing inventions of Henson's mind were stunned, not only by the abrupt ending to his outstanding career but by the form it took.

A few days later, my young son developed a cold and low-grade fever that proved to be surprisingly intractable to his usual medication. I took him to the medical center immediately and was informed by the overworked but patient physician that my son was just fine, the infection was viral in origin, and there was nothing to do but keep him at home, give him lots of rest and fluids, and continue to administer medication on a regular basis. I felt silly and told the doctor that I had probably been a bit overzealous in coming to see him because the Jim Henson account had alarmed me so much. He smiled wearily and said, "Dr. Taylor, you are probably the 30th 'Jim Henson' mother we have seen here this week."

On the surface, the questions of who uses health services and why would seem to be a medical issue. The obvious answer is that people use services when they are sick. But as the preceding anecdote illustrates, this issue can also be psychological. When and how does a person decide that he or she is sick? When are symptoms dismissed as inconsequential? When does a person decide that a symptom requires treatment by a professional, and when do chicken soup, fluids, and bed rest seem to be all that is needed?

■ RECOGNITION AND INTERPRETATION OF SYMPTOMS

Although people have some awareness of what is going on in their bodies, that awareness may be limited (Pennebaker, 1983). This limitation leaves a great deal of room for social and psychological factors to operate in the recognition of symptoms and the interpretation of illness (Petrie & Weinman, 1997).

Recognition of a Symptom

> I have a tumor in my head the size of a basketball. I can feel it when I blink
> —WOODY ALLEN, *HANNAH AND HER SISTERS*

Common observation reveals that some individuals maintain their normal activities in the face of what would seem to be overwhelming symptoms, whereas others take to their beds the moment they detect any minor bodily disturbance.

Individual Differences in Personality   Some of these individual differences are stable. That is, some people are consistently more likely to notice a symptom than other people are. Hypochondriacs, like characters that Woody Allen has played, are people who are preoccupied and worried that normal bodily symptoms are indicators of illness. Although hypochondriacs are only 4 to 5% of the population, because these individuals make such extensive use of medical care services, understanding who experiences symptoms more intensely is an important goal of health psychologists (Lecci & Cohen, 2002).

The most frequent symptoms that show up among patients who convert their distress into physical symptoms are back pain, joint pain, pain in the extremities, headache, abdominal symptoms such as bloating, "allergies" to particular foods, and cardiovascular symptoms such as palpitations (Carmin, Weigartz, Hoff, & Kondos, 2003; Rief, Hessel, & Braehler, 2001). Contrary to stereotypes, women are not more likely than men to report these symptoms. There are pronounced age effects with older people reporting more symptoms than young people.

Neuroticism also affects the perception of symptoms. Neuroticism is a pervasive dimension of personality marked by negative emotions, self-consciousness, and a concern with bodily processes. People who are high in neuroticism recognize their symptoms more quickly, report their symptoms more quickly, or both (P. Feldman, Cohen, Doyle, Skoner, & Gwaltney, 1999). It may be that neurotic, anxious people exaggerate their symptoms, or they may simply be more attentive to real symptoms (Gramling, Clawson, & McDonald, 1996; S. Ward & Leventhal, 1993). Neurotics often erroneously believe they have serious diseases. Some research has found them to account for up to 30% of those who did not have detectable heart disease after being referred for coronary angiography (Pryor, Harrell, Lee, Califf, & Rosatti, 1983).

Cultural Differences   There are reliable cultural differences in how quickly and what kind of symptoms are recognized (Kirmayer & Young, 1998). For example, in a comparative study of Anglos and Mexicans, Burnam, Timbers, and Hough (1984) found that Anglos reported more infrequent symptoms, but Mexicans were more likely to report symptoms that occurred frequently. Cultural differences in symptom experience and reporting have been known about for decades (Zola, 1966), but as yet, the reasons underlying these differences are not fully understood.

Attentional Differences   Attentional differences influence the experience of symptoms. People who are focused on themselves (their bodies, their emotions, and their reactions in general) are quicker to notice symptoms than are people who are focused externally on their environment and activities (Pennebaker, 1983). Thus, people who hold boring jobs, who are socially isolated, who keep house for a living, or who live alone report more physical symptoms than do people who have interesting jobs, who have active social lives, who work outside the home, or who live with others. One possible reason is that these latter people experience more distractions and attend less to themselves than do those people who have little activity in their lives (Pennebaker, 1983).

Situational Factors   Situational factors influence whether a person will recognize a symptom. A boring situation makes people more attentive to symptoms than an interesting situation does. For example, people are more likely to notice itching or tickling in their throats and to cough in response to the sensations during boring parts of movies than during interesting parts (Pennebaker, 1980). A symptom is more likely to be perceived on a day when a person is at home than on a day full of frenzied activity. Intense physical activity takes attention away from symptoms, whereas quiescence increases the likelihood of their recognition.

Any situational factor that makes illness or symptoms especially salient promotes their recognition. For example, a common phenomenon in medical school is **medical students' disease.** As they study each illness, many members of the class imagine that they have it. Studying the symptoms leads students to focus on their own fatigue and other internal states; as a consequence, symptoms consistent with the illness under study seem to emerge (Mechanic, 1972).

Stress   Stress can precipitate or aggravate the experience of symptoms. People who are under stress may believe that they are more vulnerable to illness and so attend more closely to their bodies. Financial strain, disruptions in personal relationships, and other stressors lead people to believe that they are ill (Alonso & Coe, 2001; Angel, Frisco, Angel, & Ciraboga, 2003), perhaps because they experience stress-related physiological changes, such as accelerated heartbeat or breathing, and interpret these changes as symptoms of illness (L. Cameron, Leventhal, & Leventhal, 1995).

Mood   Mood influences self-appraised health. People who are in a positive mood rate themselves as more healthy, report fewer illness-related memories, and report fewer symptoms. People in a bad mood, however, report more symptoms, are more pessimistic that any actions they might take would relieve their symptoms, and perceive themselves as more vulnerable to future illness than do people in good moods (E. A. Leventhal, Hansell, Diefenbach, Leventhal, & Glass, 1996; Salovey, O'Leary, Stretton, Fishkin, & Drake, 1991). Even people who have diagnosed illnesses report fewer or less serious symptoms when they are in a good mood (Gil et al., 2004).

In summary, then, symptom recognition is determined both by individual differences in attention to one's body and by transitory situational factors that influence the direction of one's attention. When attention is directed outward, as by vigorous physical activity or a highly distracting environment, symptoms are less likely to be noticed. When attention is directed toward the body, on the other hand, as by cues that suggest illness, symptoms are more likely to be detected.

Interpretation of Symptoms

The interpretation of symptoms is also a heavily psychological process. Consider the following incident. At a large metropolitan hospital, a man in his late twenties came to the emergency room with the sole symptom of a sore throat. He brought with him six of his relatives: his mother, father, sister, aunt, and two cousins. Because patients usually go to an emergency room with only one other person and because a sore throat is virtually never seen in the emergency room, the staff were understandably curious about the reason for his visit. There was much chuckling about how Italian families stick together and how they panic at any sign of a disturbance

BOX 8.1

Can Expectations Influence Sensations?

THE CASE OF PREMENSTRUAL SYMPTOMS

Many women experience a variety of unpleasant physical and psychological symptoms just before the onset of menstruation, including swollen breasts, cramping, irritability, and depression. These symptoms clearly have a physiological basis, but research indicates that psychological factors may contribute as well. Specifically, it may be that women experience these symptoms more intensely because they expect to experience them (C. McFarland et al., 1989; Ruble, 1972).

To test this idea, Ruble recruited a number of women to participate in a study. She told them she was using a new scientific technique that would predict their date of menstruation. She then randomly told participants that the technique indicated either that their period was due within the next day or two (premenstrual group) or that their period was not due for a week to 10 days (intermenstrual group). In fact, all the women were approximately a week from their periods. All the women

were then asked to complete a questionnaire indicating the extent to which they were experiencing symptoms typically associated with the premenstrual state.

The women who were led to believe that their period was due within the next day or two reported more of the psychological and physiological symptoms of premenstruation than did women who were told their periods were not due for a week to 10 days. Of course, the results of this study do not mean that premenstrual symptoms have no physical basis. Indeed, the prevalence and seriousness of premenstrual syndrome (PMS) bears testimony to the debilitating effect that premenstrual bodily changes can have on physiological functioning and behavior (Kendler et al., 1992; Klebanov & Jemmott, 1992). Rather, the results suggest that women who believe themselves to be premenstrual may be more attentive to and reinterpret naturally fluctuating bodily states as consistent with the premenstrual state. Such research findings also illustrate the significance of psychological factors in the experience of symptoms more generally.

---

in health. But one particularly sensitive medical student reasoned that something more must have caused the man to come to the emergency room with his entire family in tow, so he probed cautiously but persistently during the intake interview with the patient. Gradually, it emerged that the young man's brother had died a year earlier of Hodgkin's disease, a form of cancer that involves the progressive infection and enlargement of the lymph nodes. The brother's first symptom had been a sore throat, which he and the family had allowed to go untreated.

This poignant incident illustrates how important social and psychological factors can be in understanding people's interpretations of their symptoms. To this family, the symptom "sore throat" had special significance. It had a history for them that overrode its usual association with the beginnings of a cold (which is, in fact, what the young man turned out to have). Moreover, it symbolized for them a past failure of the family to respond adequately to an emergency, a failure that they were determined not to repeat. What this incident also illustrates, albeit in a less direct way, is that individual, historical, cultural, and social factors all conspire to produce an interpretation of the symptom experience.

Prior Experience   As the preceding incident attests, the interpretation of symptoms is heavily influenced by prior experience. People who have experience with a medical condition estimate the prevalence of their symptoms to be greater and often regard the condition as less serious than do people with no history of the condition (Jemmott, Croyle, & Ditto, 1988). A symptom's meaning is also influenced by how common it is within a person's range of acquaintances or culture (for example, Croyle & Hunt, 1991). Highly prevalent risk factors and disorders are generally regarded as less serious than are rare or distinctive risk factors and disorders (Croyle & Ditto, 1990). The very fact that the symptom or condition is widespread may be seen as a reason for attaching little significance to it.

Expectations   Expectations influence the interpretation of symptoms. People may ignore symptoms they are not expecting and amplify symptoms they do expect (H. Leventhal, Nerenz, & Strauss, 1982). For example, women who believe they are close to their menstrual periods may interpret otherwise vague sources of discomfort as premenstrual symptoms; women who believe their periods are several days away may ignore the same "symptoms" (see box 8.1).

Seriousness of the Symptoms   Symptoms that affect highly valued parts of the body are usually interpreted as more serious and as more likely to require attention than are symptoms that affect less valued organs. For example, people are especially anxious when their eyes or face are affected, rather than if the symptom involves part of the trunk. A symptom will be regarded as more serious and will be more likely to prompt the seeking of treatment if it limits mobility or if it affects a highly valued organ, such as chest discomfort thought to be indicative of heart disease (Eifert, Hodson, Tracey, Seville, & Gunawardane, 1996). Above all, if a symptom causes pain, it will lead a person to seek treatment more promptly than if it does not cause pain.

Cognitive Representations of Illness

Illness Schemas   People have concepts of health and illness that influence how they react to symptoms (H. Leventhal, Nerenz, & Steele, 1984; Shiloh, Rashuk-Rosenthal, & Benyamini, 2002). Termed **illness representations** (or **schemas**), these organized conceptions of illness are acquired through the media, through personal experience, and from family and friends who have had experience with particular disorders (see Croyle & Barger, 1993, for a review).

Illness schemas range from being quite sketchy and inaccurate to being extensive, technical, and complete. Their importance stems from the fact that they influence people's preventive health behaviors, their reactions when they experience symptoms or are diagnosed with illness, their adherence to treatment recommendations, and their expectations for their health in the future.

Illness schemas include basic information about an illness (H. Leventhal & Benyamini, 1997): The identity, or label, for an illness is its name; its consequences are its symptoms and treatments that result, as well as the extent to which the person believes the illness has ramifications for his or her life; its causes are the factors that the person believes gave rise to the illness, such as environmental or behavioral factors (Shiloh et al., 2002); duration refers to the expected length of time the illness is expected to last; and cure identifies whether the person believes the illness can be cured through appropriate treatment. These illness conceptions appear to develop quite early in life (S. L. Goldman, Whitney-Saltiel, Granger, & Rodin, 1991).

Most people have at least three models of illness (Nerenz & Leventhal, 1983):

- *Acute illness* is believed to be caused by specific viral or bacterial agents and is short in duration with no long-term consequences. An example is the flu.
- *Chronic illness* is caused by several factors, including health habits, and is long in duration, often with severe consequences. An example is heart disease.
- *Cyclic illness* is marked by alternating periods during which there are either no symptoms or many symptoms. An example is herpes.

There is considerable variability in the disease models that people hold for their disorders, and the disease model a person holds can greatly influence their behavior related to that disease. For example, diabetes may be seen by one individual as an acute condition caused by a diet high in sugar, whereas another person with the same disease may see it as a genetic condition lasting for the rest of his or her life with potentially catastrophic consequences. Not surprisingly, these people will treat their disorders differently, maintain different levels of vigilance toward symptoms, and show different patterns of seeking treatment (Weinman, Petrie, Moss-Morris, & Horne, 1996). People's conceptions of disease give them a basis for interpreting new information, influence their treatment-seeking decisions, lead them to alter or fail to adhere to their medication regimens (Coutu, Dupuis, D'Antono, & Rochon-Goyer, 2003), and influence expectations about future health (G. D. Bishop & Converse, 1986). Which conception of disease an individual holds, then, determines health behaviors in important ways.

The Beginning of Treatment

The meaning of a symptom ultimately blends into diagnosis, a process that begins not in the physician's office but in an individual's conversations with friends, neighbors, and relatives. Sociologists have written at length about the **lay referral network,** an informal network of family and friends who offer their own interpretations of symptoms well before any medical treatment is sought (Freidson, 1960). The patient may mention the symptoms to a family member or coworker, who may then respond with personal views of what the symptom is likely to mean ("George had that, and it turned out to be nothing at all") (cf. Croyle & Hunt, 1991). The friend or relative may offer advice about the advisability of seeking medical treatment ("All he got for going to see the doctor was a big bill") and recommendations for various home remedies ("Honey, lemon juice, and a little brandy will clear that right up").

In many communities, the lay referral network is the preferred mode of treatment. A powerful lay figure, such as an older woman who has had many children, may act as a lay practitioner; because of her years of experience, she is assumed to have personal wisdom in medical matters (Freidson, 1960; Hayes-Bautista, 1976). Within ethnic communities, the lay referral network will sometimes incorporate beliefs about the causes and cures of disease that would be regarded as supernatural or superstitious by traditional medicine. In addition, these lay referral networks often recommend home remedies regarded as more appropriate or more effective than traditional medicine.

Nonetheless, folk medicine is on the rise, and as a consequence, the United Nation's World Health Organization has recently taken the unprecedented step of evaluating the efficacy of these treatments (McNeil, 2002). For example, the Chinese herb ma huang helps breathing problems that can cause heart attacks and stroke in some individuals. Ginko biloba stimulates circulation but can also enhance bleeding, which is risky during surgery. The goal of the World Health Organization's effort is to catalog all folk remedies to identify those that are both successful and not risky and to reduce or eliminate use of those that are unsuccessful or risky.

As many as one in three American adults may use an unconventional therapy during the course of a year (D. M. Eisenberg et al., 1993), producing an estimated 425 million visits to providers of unconventional therapy and approximately $13.7 billion in costs (Astin, 1998).

What therapies are people using? Most commonly, unconventional therapies include relaxation techniques, chiropractic, massage, imagery, spiritual healing, diets, herbal medicines, megavitamin therapy, self-help groups, energy healing, biofeedback, hypnosis, homeopathy, and acupuncture. Not all of these therapies are used as alternatives to formal treatment; many are used in conjunction with conventional therapy. But health care providers are typically unaware that their patients are supplementing their care with unconventional therapy.

Some home remedies do work, and simple rest or relaxation can allow an illness to run its course. These actual and apparent cures perpetuate the use of the lay referral network and, consequently, much illness is never formally treated within the medical community. At any given time, between 70 and 90% of the population has a medical condition that can be diagnosed and potentially treated by a health care provider, but between two thirds and three quarters of those people do not consult one.

The Internet

The Internet may well constitute a lay referral network of its own. On a typical day, more than 6 million Americans will look for health care information online (Center for the Advancement of Health, Dec. 23, 2002). Indeed, the amount of health information on the Internet has mushroomed in recent years, with more than 100,000 health-related websites currently in existence (Center for the Advancement of Health, June 2002). Indeed, seeking health information online is a common activity. Sixty-one percent of Internet users report that they have used the Internet to find health information—more than those who shop, get sport scores, or buy stocks. Moreover, more than half the people who have gone online to find health information say it improved the way they took care of themselves (Dias, 2002).

Are these trends worrisome or not? According to a recent study of physicians, 96% said they believe that the Internet will affect health care positively, and many turn to the Internet themselves for the most up-to-date information on illnesses, treatments, and the processing of insurance claims. Nonetheless, some of what is seen on the Internet is not accurate, and some health-related Internet sites want you to pick up a shopping cart and buy their products. One excellent source of health-related issues is the Center for Advancement of Health website (www.cfah.org). Nonetheless, it is evident the Internet is playing an increasingly major role in providing the information that people get about symptoms and illnesses.

■ WHO USES HEALTH SERVICES?

Just as illness is not evenly distributed across the population, neither is the use of health services. Although the presence of atypical symptoms, a serious illness, or disability are the main reasons that people seek help (L. Cameron, Leventhal, & Leventhal, 1993; R. J. Johnson & Wolinsky, 1993), other factors are important as well.

Age

Age influences the use of health care services. The very young and the elderly use health services most frequently

(Aday & Andersen, 1974). Young children develop a number of infectious childhood diseases as they are acquiring their immunities; therefore, they frequently require the care of a pediatrician. Both illness frequency and the use of services decline in adolescence and throughout young adulthood. Use of health services increases again in late adulthood, when people begin to develop chronic conditions and diseases. The elderly use services for a variety of disorders related to the aging process.

Gender

Women use medical services more than men do (Fuller, Edwards, Sermsri, & Vorakitphokatorn, 1993). Pregnancy and childbirth account for much of the gender difference in health services use, but not all. Various explanations have been offered, including, for example, that women have better homeostatic mechanisms than men do: They report pain earlier, experience temperature changes more rapidly, and detect new smells faster. Thus, they may also be more sensitive to bodily disruptions, especially minor ones (for example, H. Leventhal, Diefenbach, & Leventhal, 1992).

Another possible explanation stems from the different social norms for men and women regarding the expression of pain and discomfort. Men are expected to project a tough, macho image, which includes being able to ignore pain and not give in to illness, whereas women are not subject to these same pressures (Klonoff & Landrine, 1992).

Economic factors may also be important. Because more women are part-time workers and nonworkers, they do not have to take time off from work to seek treatment and they do not lose income when they are ill. Consequently, women may use health services more because seeking treatment for illness disrupts their lives less and costs them less (A. C. Marcus & Siegel, 1982). However, the same factors—namely, that women are less likely to be employed, are more likely to work part time, and experience more economic hardship—also contribute to women's poorer health (C. E. Ross & Bird, 1994).

Research suggests that women use health care services more often because their medical care is more fragmented. Medical care for most men occurs through a trip to a general practitioner for a physical examination that includes all preventive care. But women may visit a general practitioner or internist for a general physical, a gynecologist for Pap tests, and a breast cancer specialist

or mammography service for breast examinations and mammograms. Thus, women may use services more than men, in part because medical care is not particularly well structured to meet their basic needs.

Social Class and Culture

The lower social classes use medical services less than do the more affluent social classes (M. Herman, 1972), in part because the poorer classes have less money to spend on health services. However, with Medicare for the elderly, Medicaid for the poor, and other inexpensive health services, the gap between medical service use by the rich and by the poor has narrowed somewhat.

The disadvantaged financial position of the lower classes is not the only reason for their low use of services (L. A. Crandall & Duncan, 1981; Rundall & Wheeler, 1979); there simply are not as many medical services for the poor as for the well-to-do, and what services there are are often inadequate and understaffed. Consequently,

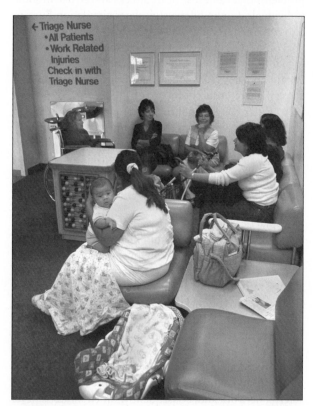

Women use medical services more than men, they may be sick more than men, and their routine care requires more visits than men's. It is often easier for women to use services, and they require services for such gender-related needs as maternity care.

many poor people receive no regular medical care at all and see physicians only on an emergency basis. The social-class differences in use of health services are particularly problematic because the poor are not only sick more often and for longer periods than are the well-to-do, but they die earlier (N. E. Adler et al., 1993). The biggest gap between the rich and the poor is in the use of preventive health services, such as inoculations against disease and screening for treatable disorders, which lays the groundwork for poorer health across the life span.

Cultural factors influence whether a person seeks formal treatment. As already noted, people who live in ethnic neighborhoods may hold beliefs about illness that do not correspond to the beliefs of the medical profession, which lead those people to use a lay referral system of care, instead.

Social Psychological Factors

Social psychological factors—that is, an individual's attitudes and beliefs about symptoms and health services, influence who uses health service. As we saw in chapter 3, the health belief model maintains that whether a person seeks treatment for a symptom can be predicted from two factors: (1) the extent to which the person perceives a threat to health and (2) the degree to which he or she believes that a particular health measure will be effective in reducing that threat.

A large number of studies suggest that the health belief model explains people's use of services quite well. The health belief model does a better job of explaining the treatment-seeking behavior of people who have money and access to health care services than of people who do not.

The use of health care services is influenced by socialization, chiefly by the actions of one's parents. Just as children and adolescents learn other behaviors from their parents, they also learn when and how to use health care services.

Other factors that lead people to seek treatment are interpersonal. For example, an interpersonal crisis may be set off when a symptom threatens a relationship (Zola, 1973). Or, if one member of a couple is always tired, eventually the partner will become annoyed and insist that the other do something about the constant fatigue. Social interference is also a trigger for seeking help. When valued activities or social demands, such as a job or vacation, are threatened by a symptom, a person is more likely to seek prompt treatment than if no such threat is posed. Finally, social sanctioning, as when an employer applies pressure on a symptomatic individual to seek treatment or return to work, can lead to using health services.

Health services, then, are used by people who have the need, time, money, prior experience, beliefs that favor the use of services, and access to services (R. M. Andersen, 1995).

■ MISUSING HEALTH SERVICES

Jerry rolled over when the alarm went off and realized that it was time to get ready to go to work. He'd been up late the night before with some friends, playing cards, and as a result, he'd had only about 4 hours of sleep. As he thought about his assembly-line job, the prospect of getting dressed and getting to work on time seemed less and less attractive. As he swallowed, he noticed some tingling sensations. It could have been too many cigarettes, or maybe he was coming down with a cold. He thought, "If I call in sick today and just spend some time resting, I'll be in better shape for the rest of the week." Having rationalized his situation, Jerry went back to sleep.

Health services may be abused as well as used. In this section, we consider several types of abuse. Some abuse is mild, such as Jerry's decision to sleep off a hangover instead of going to work. But in other cases, abuse is more serious. One type of abuse occurs when people seek out health services for problems that are not medically significant, overloading the medical system. Another significant type of abuse involves delay, when people should seek health care for a problem but do not.

Using Health Services for Emotional Disturbances

Physicians estimate that as much as two thirds of their time is taken up by patients whose complaints are psychological rather than medical. This problem is more common for general practitioners than for specialists, although no branch of medicine is immune. (College health services periodically experience a version of this phenomenon during exam time; see box 8.2.) These nonmedical complaints typically stem from anxiety and depression, both of which, unfortunately, are widespread.

Why do people seek a physician's care when their complaints should be addressed by a mental health specialist? There are several reasons. Stress and the emotional responses to it create a number of physical symptoms and so during stressful times people use

BOX 8.2

College Students' Disease

Visit the health service of any college or university just before exams begin and you will see a unit bracing itself for an onslaught. Admissions to health services can double or even triple as papers become due and examinations begin. Why does this influx occur?

Some of the increase in health service visits is due to an actual increase in illness. Students who are under pressure to do well work long hours and eat and sleep poorly. As they run themselves down, their vulnerability to many common disorders can increase. Moreover, any one individual who develops an infectious disorder can give it to others who live in close proximity.

Some students may not actually be sick, but they think they are. Stressors, such as exams, can produce a variety of symptoms—such as inability to concentrate, sleeplessness, and upset stomach—which may be mistaken for illness. Moreover, exam time may preclude other activities that would provide distraction, so students may be more aware of these symptoms than they would otherwise be. In addition, the "symptoms" may make it hard for students to study, and disruption in important activities often acts as an impetus for seeking treatment.

Finally, there is the chronic procrastinator with four papers due but enough time to complete only two of them. What better excuse than illness for failure to meet one's obligations? Illness legitimizes procrastination, lack of motivation, lack of activity, and a host of other personal failures.

---

health services more. Anxiety, depression, and other psychological disorders are accompanied by a number of physical symptoms. Anxiety can produce diarrhea, upset stomach, sweaty hands, shortness of breath, difficulty in sleeping, poor concentration, and general agitation. Depression can lead to fatigue, difficulty in performing everyday activities, listlessness, loss of appetite, and sleep disturbances. People may mistake the symptoms of their mood disorder for a legitimate medical problem and thus seek a physician's care. Anxiety and depression may not only influence the likelihood of seeking contact initially but lead to recurrent visits and prolong hospital stays as well (De Jonge, Latour, & Huyse, 2003).

Who are these people? One group is the **worried well.** These people are concerned about physical and mental health, inclined to perceive minor symptoms as serious, and believe that they should take care of their own health. Paradoxically, their commitment to self-care actually leads them to use health services more (Wagner & Curran, 1984). The emphasis that our culture places on living a healthy lifestyle and media attention to new health problems and technologies may inadvertently have increased the number of worried well people who use health services inappropriately (Petrie & Wessely, 2002).

Another group of inappropriate users are **somaticizers**—that is, individuals who express distress and conflict through bodily symptoms (Miranda, Perez-Stable, Munoz, Hargreaves, & Heike, 1991). When they have experienced a threat to self-esteem or to their accomplishments, such individuals are especially likely to somaticize, convince themselves they are physically

ill, and seek treatment. This issue is so problematic that a recent study in the *Annals of Internal Medicine* suggested that physicians begin all their patient interviews with the direct questions "Are you currently sad or depressed" and "Are the things that previously brought you pleasure no longer bringing you pleasure?" Positive answers to these questions would suggest that a patient may need treatment for depression as well as, or even instead of, medical treatment (Pignone et al., 2002).

Often patients present with multiple physical symptoms that are chronic, unresponsive to treatment, and unexplained by any medical diagnosis; these patients are *polysymptomatic somaticizers* (Interian et al., 2004). Although a number of psychosocial interventions have been attempted with this group, so far these interventions have not had a lasting impact or reduced the psychiatric problems associated with the physical complaints of these somaticizers (Allen, Escobar, Lehrer, Gara, & Woolfolk, 2002).

There is some evidence that somaticization and related hypochondriasis is more of an interpersonal disorder than a vigilance to or misinterpretation of low-level symptoms. That is, hypochondriacs may be associated with insecure attachment that gives rise to seeking care from others. Thus, people with interpersonal problems may seek reassurance by gaining medical attention (Noyes et al., 2003).

Another reason that people use health services for psychological complaints is that medical disorders are perceived as more legitimate than psychological ones. For example, a man who is depressed by his job and who stays home to avoid it will find that his behavior is more

BOX 8.3

The June Bug Disease

A CASE OF HYSTERICAL CONTAGION

One summer, a mysterious epidemic broke out in the dressmaking department of a Southern textile plant, affecting 62 workers. The symptoms varied but usually included nausea, numbness, dizziness, and occasionally vomiting. Some of the ill required hospitalization, but most were simply excused from work for several days.

Almost all the affected workers reported having been bitten by a gnat or mite immediately before they experienced the symptoms. Several employees who were not afflicted said they had seen their fellow workers bitten before they came down with the disease. However, local, state, and federal health officials who were called in to investigate the incident could obtain no reliable description of the suspected insect. Furthermore, careful inspection of the textile plant by entomologists and exterminators turned up only a small variety of insects—beetles, gnats, flies, an ant, and a mite—none of which could have caused the reported symptoms.

Company physicians and experts from the U.S. Public Health Service Communicable Disease Center began to suspect that the epidemic might be a case of hysterical contagion. They hypothesized that, although some of the afflicted individuals may have been bitten by an insect, anxiety or nervousness was more likely responsible for the onset of the symptoms. On hearing this conclusion, employees insisted that the "disease" was caused by a bite from an insect that was in a shipment of material recently received from England.

In shifting from a medical to a social explanation, health experts highlighted several points. First, the entire incident, from the first to the last reported case, lasted a period of 11 days, and 50 of the 62 cases (80%) occurred on 2 consecutive days after the news media had sensationalized earlier incidents. Second, most of the afflicted individuals worked at the same time and place in the plant. Fifty-nine of the 62 afflicted employees worked on the first shift, and 58 worked in one large work area. Third, the 58 working at the same time and place were all women; one other woman worked on a different shift, two male victims worked on a different shift, and one man worked in a different department. Moreover, most of these women were married and had children; they were accordingly trying to combine a job and motherhood—often an exhausting arrangement.

The epidemic occurred at a busy time in the plant—June being a crucial month in the production of fall fashions—and there were strong incentives for employees to put in overtime and to work at a high pace. The plant was relatively new, and personnel and production management were not well organized. Thus, the climate was ripe for the development of severely anxious feelings among the employees.

Who, then, got "bitten" by the "June bug," and why? Workers with the most stress in their lives (married women with children) who were trying to cope with the further demands of increased productivity and overtime were most vulnerable. Job anxieties, coupled with the physical manifestations of fatigue (such as dizziness), created a set of symptoms that, given appropriate circumstances, could be labeled as illness. The rumor of a suspicious bug and the presence of ill coworkers apparently provided the appropriate circumstances, legitimatizing the illness and leading to the epidemic that resulted.

Source: Kerckhoff & Back, 1968.

---

acceptable to both his boss and his wife if he says he is ill than if he admits he is depressed. Many people are even unwilling to admit to themselves that they have a psychological problem, believing that it is shameful to see a mental health specialist or to have mental problems.

Illness brings benefits, termed **secondary gains,** including the ability to rest, to be freed from unpleasant tasks, to be cared for by others, and to take time off from work. These reinforcements can interfere with the process of returning to good health (some of these factors may have played a role in one famous case of hysterical contagion; see box 8.3).

Finally, the inappropriate use of health services can represent true malingering. A person who does not want to go to work may know all too well that the only acceptable excuse that will prevent dismissal for absenteeism is illness. Moreover, workers may be required to document their absences in order to collect wages or disability payments and may thus have to keep looking until they find a physician who is willing to "treat" the "disorder."

Unfortunately, the worried well and those who seek treatment for psychological symptoms or to meet other needs can be hard to discriminate from patients with legitimate medical complaints (Bombardier, Gorayeb, Jordan, Brooks, & Divine, 1991). Sometimes this differentiation means that patients are put through many tests and evaluations before it is concluded that there may be a psychological basis rather than a physical one for their discomfort.

But because of this difficulty, errors can be made in the opposite direction as well: Individuals with legitimate medical problems may be falsely assumed to be psychologically disturbed. Research suggests that physicians are more likely to reach this conclusion about their female patients than their male patients (Redman, Webb, Hennrikus, Gordon, & Sanson-Fisher, 1991), even when objective measures suggest equivalent rates of psychological disturbance between men and women. Discriminating the truly physically ill from those who use health services to meet other needs can be a very tricky business, complicated by physician bias as well as patient misuse of the system.

Delay Behavior

One morning, while Monica was taking a shower, she discovered a small lump in her left breast. She felt it a couple of times to make sure she wasn't just imagining it, but it was definitely there. A shudder of alarm passed through her, and she thought, "I should go in and get this checked."

After she dried herself off and got dressed, she realized that this week would be a busy one and next week was no better. She had exams the following week, so she couldn't find any time in the next 2 to 3 weeks when she could get to the doctor to have it checked out.

"I'll have to wait until next month," she thought, "when things settle down a bit."

A very different misuse of health services occurs when an individual should seek treatment for a symptom but puts off doing so. A lump, chronic shortness of breath, blackouts, skin discoloration, radiating chest pain, seizures, and severe stomach pains are serious symptoms for which people should seek treatment promptly, yet an individual may live with one or more of these potentially serious symptoms for months without seeking care. This behavior is called **delay behavior.** For example, a major problem contributing to the high rate of death and disability from heart attacks is the fact that patients so often delay seeking treatment for its symptoms, instead normalizing them as gastric distress, muscle pain, and other, less severe disorders.

Delay is defined as the time between when a person recognizes a symptom and when the person obtains treatment. Delay is composed of several time periods, diagrammed in figure 8.1: **appraisal delay,** which is the time it takes an individual to decide that a symptom is serious; **illness delay,** which is the time between the recognition that a symptom implies an illness and the decision to seek treatment; **behavioral delay,** which is the time between actually deciding to seek treatment and actually doing so (Safer, Tharps, Jackson, & Leventhal, 1979); and **medical delay** (scheduling and treatment)**,** which is the time that elapses between the person's making an appointment and receiving appropriate medical care. Obviously, delay in seeking treatment for some symptoms is appropriate. For example, usually a runny nose or a mild sore throat will clear up on its own. However, in other cases, symptoms may be debilitating for weeks or months, and to delay seeking treatment is inappropriate.

Who Delays?   The reasons for delay have been extensively explored. Not surprisingly, the portrait of the delayer generally bears strong similarities to the portrait of the nonuser of services. A major factor in delay is the perceived expense of treatment, especially for poor people. When money is not readily available, people may persuade themselves that the symptoms are not serious enough to justify the expense (Safer et al., 1979). The elderly appear to delay less than middle-aged individuals, particularly if they experience symptoms judged to be potentially serious (E. A. Leventhal, Easterling, Leventhal, & Cameron, 1995). Delay is common among people with no regular contact with a physician, no doubt because in addition to seeking treatment, such individuals have the extra burden of finding someone from whom to seek it. Delay, like nonuse of services in general, is also more common among people who seek treatment primarily in response to pain or social pressure. People who are fearful of doctors, examinations, surgery, and medical facilities generally delay longer than do people who are not fearful. People with generally good medical habits are less likely to delay, and they seek attention quickly for a condition that is unusual or potentially serious.

Because the delayer looks so much like the nonuser of services, one might expect the health belief model to predict delay behavior as well as use of services. In fact, it does explain some delay behavior. For example, people who fail to seek treatment for symptoms that may indi-

FIGURE 8.1 | Stages of Delay in Seeking Treatment for Symptoms

(Reprinted with permission from B. L. Anderson, J. T. Cacioppo, & D. C. Roberts: Delay in seeking a cancer diagnosis: Delay stages and psychophysiological comparison processes. *British Journal of Social Psychology* (1995) 34, 33–52. Fig.1 p. 35. © The British Psychological Society)

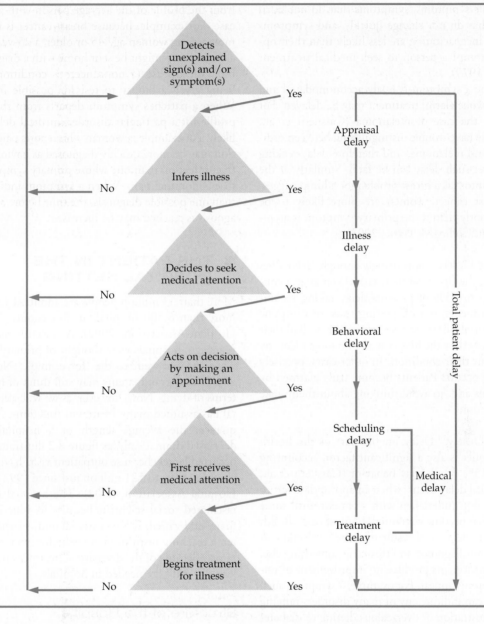

cate cancer are more likely to believe that treatments will be extremely painful (high perceived barriers to, or "costs" of, treatment) and to believe that nothing can be done to cure cancer (low perceived efficacy of treatment) (Safer et al., 1979).

Symptoms and Delaying   Another factor that predicts delay is the nature of the symptoms. When a symptom is similar to one that previously turned out to be minor, the individual will seek treatment less quickly than if the symptom is new (see, for example, Safer et al., 1979). For example, women with a history of benign breast lumps may be less likely to have a new suspicious lump checked out than are women with no such history. Highly visible symptoms, symptoms that do not hurt, symptoms that do not change quickly, and symptoms that are not incapacitating are less likely than their opposites to prompt a person to seek medical treatment (Safer et al., 1979).

Any time a symptom is easily accommodated and does not provoke alarm, treatment may be delayed. For example, in the case of melanoma (Cassileth et al., 1988), people have trouble distinguishing between ordinary moles and melanomas and therefore delay seeking treatment, yet such delay can be fatal. Similarly, if the primary symptom is a breast problem or a lump suggestive of breast cancer, women are more likely to be treated promptly than if the primary symptom is atypical (Meechan, Collins, & Petrie, 2003).

Treatment Delay   Surprisingly enough, delay does not end with the first treatment visit. Even after a consultation, up to 25% of patients delay taking recommended treatments, put off getting tests, or postpone acting on referrals. In some cases, patients have had their curiosity satisfied by the first visit and no longer feel any urgency about their condition. In other cases, precisely the opposite occurs: Patients become truly alarmed by the symptoms and, to avoid thinking about them, take no further action.

Provider Delay   Delay on the part of the health care practitioner is also a significant factor, accounting for at least 15% of all delay behavior (Cassileth et al., 1988). Medical delay occurs when an appropriate test or treatment is not undertaken with a patient until some time after it has become warranted. In most cases, health care providers delay as a result of honest mistakes. A condition is misdiagnosed and treated as something else, either until treatments produce no improvement or until new symptoms appear. For example, a symptom such as blackouts can indicate any of many disorders ranging from heat prostration or overzealous dieting to diabetes or a brain tumor. A provider may choose to rule out the more common causes of the symptom before proceeding to the more invasive or expensive tests needed to rule out a less probable cause. Thus, when the more serious diagnosis is found to apply, the appearance of unwarranted delay exists. Sometimes medical delay is caused by malpractice—for example, failing to do the appropri-

ate tests, misreading test results, or failing to prescribe appropriate medications.

Medical delay is more likely when a patient deviates from the profile of the average person with a given disease. For example, because breast cancer is most common among women age 45 or older, a 25-year-old with a breast lump might be sent home with a diagnosis of fibrocystic disease (a noncancerous condition) without being given a biopsy to test for possible malignancy. When a patient's symptom departs from the standard profile for a particular disorder, medical delay is more likely. For example, a woman who reports pain on urination may be more quickly diagnosed as having a urinary tract infection than one whose primary symptom is diffuse abdominal pain. When a symptom indicates more than one possible diagnosis, the time before a proper diagnosis is reached may be increased.

■ THE PATIENT IN THE HOSPITAL SETTING

More than 33 million people are admitted yearly to the more than 8,500 hospitals in this country (American Hospital Association, 2002). As recently as 60 or 70 years ago, hospitals were thought of primarily as places where people went to die (for example, Noyes et al., 2000). Our grandparents may still think of hospitals in terms of dying. Now, however, as we will see, the hospital has assumed many treatment functions. As a consequence, the average length of a hospital stay has decreased dramatically, as figure 8.2 illustrates. This has occurred largely because outpatient visits have increased, climbing 16% to 521 million just since 1997 (American Hospital Association, 2002). The hospital has always fascinated social scientists because its functions are so many and varied. It is a custodial unit, a treatment center, a teaching institution, a research center, and a laboratory. Because of the diversity of treatment needs, many kinds of skills are needed in hospitals.

Structure of the Hospital

To understand the psychological impact of hospitalization, it is useful to have a working knowledge of its structure and functions. The structure of hospitals depends on the health program under which care is delivered. For example, some health maintenance organizations (HMOs) and other prepaid health care systems have their own hospitals and employ their own physicians. Conse-

FIGURE 8.2 | Hospital Admissions and Length of Stay, 1946–2001

Total of nonfederal, short-term general, and other special hospitals.   (*Source:* American Hospital Association (2003), *Hospital Statistics,* p. 3)

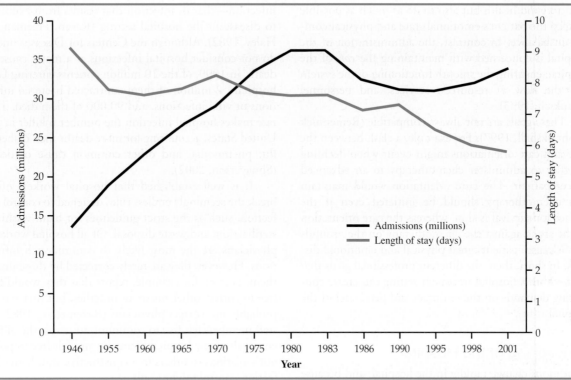

quently, the hospital structure is organized very much as any other hierarchically organized bureaucracy, with administration at the top and physicians, nurses, and technicians as employees.

In the case of the private hospital, a more unusual structure typically dominates. There are two lines of authority—a medical line, which is based on technical skill and expertise, and an administrative line, which runs the business of the hospital. Physicians are at the top of the medical line of authority and are accorded high status because they are chiefly responsible for the treatment of patients. Typically, however, they are not directly employed by the hospital but, rather, act as invited guests, bringing their patients into the hospital in exchange for laboratories, custodial services, equipment, and teaching facilities that the hospital can provide. Because physicians are not directly under the administrative line of authority, the two lines of authority can sometimes be at odds. For example, a teaching physician who brings a class of medical students in to see patients can disrupt

the hospital's custodial procedures. Thus, the relationship between the two lines of authority can be uneasy.

The nurse is part of both lines of authority. Employed by the hospital, he or she is also considered an assistant by the physician and is thus subject to both lines of authority, which can create conflicting requirements and needs. For example, if a doctor asks a nurse to get a piece of equipment that requires him or her to leave the ward, should the nurse follow the directive? Multiple responsibilities to these two lines of authority often produce dissatisfaction and turnover among nurses.

Cure, Care, and Core   The implicit conflict among different groups in the hospital setting relates directly to the goals to which the different professional groups may devote themselves. The goal of *cure* is typically the physician's responsibility: He or she is charged with performing any treatment action that has the potential to restore patients to good health—that is, to cure them. Patient *care,* in contrast, is the orientation of the nursing staff, and it involves the humanistic side of medicine. The goal of care is not only to restore the patient to good health but also to do as much as possible to keep the patient's emotional state and physical comfort in balance. In contrast, the administration of the hospital is concerned with maintaining the *core* of the hospital: ensuring the smooth functioning of the system and the flow of resources, services, and personnel (Mauksch, 1973).

These goals are not always compatible (Remennick & Shtarkshall, 1997). For example, a clash between the cure and care orientations might occur when deciding whether to administer chemotherapy to an advanced cancer patient. The cure orientation would maintain that chemotherapy should be initiated even if the chance for survival is slim, whereas the care orientation might argue against the chemotherapy on the grounds that it causes patients great physical and emotional distress. In short, then, the different professional goals that exist within a hospital treatment setting can create conflicting demands on the resources and personnel of the hospital.

Functioning of the Hospital

Conditions change rapidly in the hospital, and because of these fluctuating demands, the social order in which patient care is delivered is constantly being negotiated (A. Strauss, Schatzman, Bucher, Erlich, & Sarshim, 1963). Although each person involved in patient care, whether nurse, physician, or orderly, has general ideas about his or her functions, it is understood that, under conditions of emergency, each must perform the tasks that he or she knows best while remaining flexible to respond effectively to the changing situation. Television programs such as *ER* capture this aspect of the hospital quite effectively and demonstrate how medical personnel must often grab anyone qualified who is available to help in an emergency situation.

The different goals of different professionals in the hospital setting are reflected in hospital workers' communication patterns. Occupational segregation in the hospital is high: Nurses talk to other nurses, physicians to other physicians, and administrators to other administrators. Physicians have access to some information that nurses may not see, whereas nurses interact with patients daily and know a great deal about their day-to-day progress, yet often their notes on charts go unread by physicians. Other opportunities to communicate may not present themselves.

An example of the problems associated with lack of communication is provided by a study on nosocomial infection—that is, infection that results from exposure to disease in the hospital setting (Raven, Freeman, & Haley, 1982). Although the Centers for Disease control do not consider hospital infections as a major cause of death, in 1999, of the 10 million patients entering U.S. hospitals, 2 million of them contracted bacterial infections or viral infections, and 90,000 of them died. This rate makes hospital infection the number 6 killer in the United States, accounting for more deaths than diabetes, flu, pneumonia, and other common cause of death (Shnayerson, 2002).

It is well established that hospital workers often break the seemingly endless rules designed to control infection, such as the strict guidelines for hand washing, sterilization, and waste disposal. Of all hospital workers, physicians are the most likely to commit such infractions. However, they are rarely corrected by those under them. Nurses, for example, report that they would feel free to correct other nurses or orderlies, but they would probably not correct physicians (Raven et al., 1982). If staff members felt free to communicate across the different levels of the hospital hierarchy and felt free to point out violations to others in a constructive way, better infection control might result.

The preceding discussion has emphasized potential sources of conflict, ambiguity, and confusion in the hospital structure. Burnout, a problem that can result in part from these ambiguities, is described in box 8.4. However, this description presents an incomplete picture. In many respects, hospital functioning is remarkably effective, given the changing realities to which it must accommodate at any given time. Thus, the ambiguities in structure, potential conflicts in goals, and problems of communication occur within a system that generally functions quite well.

Recent Changes in Hospitalization

In recent years, alternatives to traditional hospital treatment have emerged that patients use for many disorders. Walk-in clinics, for example, can deal with less serious complaints and routine surgeries that used to require hospitalization. Clinics handle a large proportion of the smaller emergencies that historically have filled the hospital emergency room. Home help services and hospices provide services for the chronically and terminally ill who require primarily palliative and custodial care rather than active medical intervention. A consequence of removing

BOX 8.4

Burnout Among Health Care Professionals

Burnout is an occupational risk for anyone who works with needy people (Maslach, 2003). It is a particular problem for physicians, nurses, and other medical personnel who work with sick and dying people. As a syndrome, burnout is marked by three components: emotional exhaustion, cynicism, and a low sense of efficacy in one's job. Staff members suffering from burnout show a cynical and seemingly callous attitude toward those whom they serve. Their view of clients is more negative than that of other staff members, and they treat clients in more detached ways (Maslach, 2003).

The effects of burnout are manifold. Burnout has been linked to absenteeism, high job turnover, and lengthy breaks during working hours. When burned-out workers go home, they are often irritable with their families. They are more likely to suffer from insomnia as well as drug and alcohol abuse, and they have a higher rate of psychosomatic disorders. Thus, burnout has substantial costs for both the institution and the individual (P. A. Parker & Kulik, 1995).

Why does burnout develop? It often occurs when a person is required to provide services for a highly needy individual who may not be helped by those services: The problems may be just too severe. For example, imagine the frustration that might develop in trying to provide for a patient who will ultimately die rather than be made better by that assistance. Moreover, such jobs often require the staff member to be consistently empathic; this demand is unrealistic because it is hard for anyone to maintain an empathic orientation indefinitely. Often, caregivers perceive that they give much more than they get back from their patients, and this imbalance aggravates burnout as well (Van YPeren, Buunk, & Schaufelli, 1992). Substantial amounts of time spent with clients, little feedback, little sense of control or autonomy, little sense of success, role conflict, and role ambiguity are job factors that all aggravate burnout (Maslach, 1979).

High rates of burnout have been found among nurses who work in stressful environments, such as intensive care, emergency, or terminal care (Mallett, Price, Jurs, & Slenker, 1991; Moos & Schaefer, 1987). These nurses are expected to be sympathetic to patients and maintain interest, concern, warmth, and caring, yet they are also supposed to be objective. Many nurses find it difficult to protect themselves from the pain they feel from watching their patients suffer or die. To deal with these emotions, they become removed and distant. The

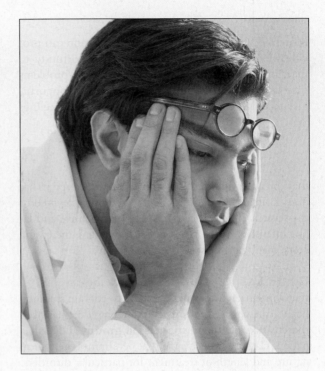

stress of the work environment, including the hectic pace of the hospital and the hurried, anxious behavior of coworkers, also contributes to burnout (P. A. Parker & Kulik, 1995).

Not surprisingly, since burnout results from stress, it is associated with alterations in physiological and neuroendocrine functioning. There is evidence that burnout influences stress hormones, such that people with burnout show elevated cortisol levels after awakening in the morning (Pruessner, Hellhammer, & Kirschbaum, 1999). In addition, burnout has been tied to changes in immune functioning (C. Lerman et al., 1999).

How can burnout be avoided? Interventions that enroll hospital workers in job stress management programs can help them control the feelings of burnout they currently have, as well as head off future episodes (Rowe, 1999). For example, seeing what other people do to avoid burnout can provide a useful model for one's own situation. Research shows that people who have few symptoms of burnout habitually turn to others for help. Institutionalizing this kind of supportive buffer against burnout may also be a way to control the incidence of the syndrome (Moos & Schaefer, 1987; Shinn, Rosario,

BOX 8.4

Burnout Among Health Care Professionals (continued)

Morch, & Chestnut, 1984). A support group can provide workers, such as nurses, with an opportunity to meet informally with others to deal with the problems they face. These groups can give workers the opportunity to obtain emotional support, reduce their feelings of being alone, share feelings of emotional pain about death and dying, and vent emotions in a supportive atmosphere. In so doing, they may ultimately improve client care (Duxbury, Armstrong, Dren, & Henley, 1984).

these bread-and-butter cases from acute care hospitals has been to increase the proportion of resources devoted to the severely ill. Their care tends to be expensive and labor-intensive. With these pressures toward increasing costs, many hospitals are unable to survive.

Cost-Cutting Pressures   Since the early 1970s, there have been increasing pressures to contain spiraling health care costs. One cost-containment effort has been the creation of **diagnostic-related groups (DRGs),** a patient classification scheme that determines the typical nature and length of treatment for particular disorders. Patients in a DRG category (for example, hernia surgery candidates) are assumed to represent a homogeneous group that is clinically similar and that should require approximately the same types and amounts of treatments, length of stay of hospitalization, and cost. DRGs define trim points, which indicate unusually long or short lengths of stay.

If patient care falls within the classification scheme, reimbursement for care will be forthcoming from the third party, whether the federal or state government or an insurance company. In the case of an outlier (for example, a patient who stays in the hospital longer than the DRG specifies), the case is typically subject to review, and the extra costs may not be paid. This procedure puts pressure on hospitals to cut patient stays and treatment costs.

Consequently, with the institution of DRGs, hospitals have gone from being overcrowded to being underused, with vacancy rates as high as 70%. This situation, in turn, creates economic pressures to admit more patients to the hospital (Wholey & Burns, 1991), albeit for shorter stays.

Another cost-containment strategy that has affected the functioning of hospitals is the **preferred provider organization (PPO).** Increasingly, insurance companies and other third-party providers designate the particular hospital or treatment facility that a patient must use in order to be reimbursed for services. Patients are directed to these services because they are judged to provide the least expensive appropriate care and patients who wish to go elsewhere have to pay the additional fees themselves. The consequence has been to keep treatment costs lower than they might otherwise be.

Hospitals are experiencing a variety of other changes as well. Nearly 45% of U.S. hospitals are currently part of a multihospital system (American Hospital Association, 2002). This means that hospitals are no longer as independent as they once were and instead may be subject to rules and regulations established by a higher level of authority.

Changes in the structure and functioning of hospitals involving outside regulation, physician competition, and the corporatization of health services have altered the traditional separation of power between hospital administration and physicians. Administrators are increasingly involved in some of the decisions previously left to physicians, and the reverse is true as well (J. A. Alexander, Morrissey, & Shortell, 1986).

Role of Psychologists   Among the important developments in hospital care has been the increasing involvement of psychologists. The number of psychologists in hospital settings has more than doubled over the past 10 years, and their roles have expanded. Psychologists participate in the diagnosis of patients, particularly through the use of personality, intellectual, and neuropsychological tests. Psychologists also determine patients' general level of functioning, as well as patients' strengths and weaknesses that can help form the basis for therapeutic intervention.

Psychologists are also involved in pre-surgery and post-surgery preparation, pain control, interventions to increase medication and treatment compliance, and behavioral programs to teach appropriate self-care following discharge (Enright, Resnick, DeLeon, Sciara, & Tanney, 1990). They also diagnose and treat psychological problems that can complicate patient care. As our country's medical care system evolves over the next decades, the role of psychologists in the hospital will continue to change.

Impact of Hospitalization on the Patient

> The patient comes unbidden to a large organization which awes and irritates him, even as it also nurtures and cares. As he strips off his clothing so he strips off, too, his favored costume of social roles, his favored style, his customary identity in the world. He becomes subject to a time schedule and a pattern of activity not of his own making. (R. Wilson, 1963, p. 70)

Patients arrive at the hospital with anxiety over their illness or disorder, confusion and anxiety over the prospect of hospitalization, and concern over all the role obligations they must leave behind unfulfilled. The hospital does little, if anything, to calm anxiety and in many cases exacerbates it. The admission is often conducted by a clerk, who asks about scheduling, insurance, and money. The patient is then ushered into a strange room, given strange clothes, provided with an unfamiliar roommate, and subjected to peculiar tests. The patient must entrust him- or herself completely to strangers in an uncertain environment in which all procedures are new. The patient is expected to be cooperative, dependent, and helpful without demanding excessive attention. The patient quickly learns that the hospital is organized for the convenience of staff rather than patients. He or she is also physically confined, making adjustment to the new situation that much more difficult.

Hospital patients may show a variety of problematic psychological symptoms, especially anxiety and depression. Nervousness over tests or surgery and their results can produce insomnia, terrifying nightmares, and a general inability to concentrate. Procedures that isolate or immobilize patients are particularly likely to produce psychological distress. Hospital care can be highly fragmented, with many as 30 different staff people passing through a patient's room each day, conducting tests, taking blood, bringing food, or cleaning up. Often, the staff members have little time to spend with the patient beyond exchanging greetings, which can be very alienating for the patient.

At one time, patients complained bitterly about the lack of communication they had about their disorders and their treatments. In part, precisely because of these concerns, hospitals have now made substantial efforts to

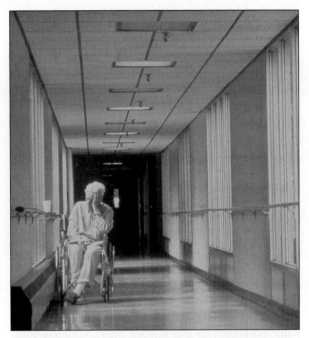

The hospital can be a lonely and frightening place for many patients, leading to feelings of helplessness, anxiety, or depression.

ameliorate this problem. Patients are now typically given a road map of the procedures they can expect to go through and what they may experience as a result.

In truth, many hospitalized patients are too ill to care about whether they are getting sufficient information about their disorder and treatment or not. Moreover, whereas once patients' hospital stays were long, now people are typically hospitalized primarily on a short-term basis for specific treatments. Often prepared for those treatments in advance, the patient may be discharged shortly after they are over.

■ INTERVENTIONS TO INCREASE CONTROL IN HOSPITAL SETTINGS

In part because of the issues just noted, many hospitals now provide interventions that help prepare patients generally for hospitalization and, more specifically, for the procedures that they will undergo.

Coping with Surgery Through Control-Enhancing Interventions

In 1958, psychologist Irving Janis conducted a landmark study that would forever change the preparation of patients for surgery. Janis was asked by a hospital to study its surgery patients to see if something could be done to reduce the stress that many of them experienced both before and after operations. One of Janis's earliest observations was that, without some anticipatory worry, patients were not able to cope well with surgery. He termed this the "work of worrying," reasoning that patients must work through the fear and loss of control that are raised by surgery before they are able to adjust to it.

To get a clearer idea of the relationship between worry and adjustment, Janis first grouped the patients according to the level of fear they experienced before the operation (high, medium, and low). Then he studied how well they understood and used the information that the hospital staff gave them to help them cope with the aftereffects of surgery. Highly fearful patients generally remained fearful and anxious after surgery and showed many negative side effects, such as vomiting, pain, urinary retention, and inability to eat. Patients who initially had little fear also showed unfavorable reactions after surgery, becoming angry or upset or complaining. Of the three groups, the moderately fearful patients coped with post-operative stress most effectively as determined by both interviews and staff reports.

In interpreting these results, Janis reasoned that very fearful patients had been too absorbed with their own fears pre-operatively to process the preparatory information adequately and that patients with little fear were insufficiently vigilant to understand and process the information effectively. Patients with moderate levels of fear, in contrast, were vigilant enough but not overwhelmed by their fears, so they were able to develop realistic expectations of what their post-surgery reactions would be; when they later encountered these sensations and reactions, they expected them and were ready to deal with them.

Subsequent studies have borne out some but not all of Janis's observations. Whereas Janis believed that fear and the work of worrying are essential ingredients in processing information about surgery. Most researchers now believe that the effect is primarily determined by the informational value of the preparatory communication itself (J. E. Johnson, Lauver, & Nail, 1989). That is, patients who are carefully prepared for surgery and its aftereffects will show good post-operative adjustment; patients who are not well prepared for the aftereffects of surgery will show poor post-operative adjustment.

Janis's initial work sparked a large number of intervention studies. An example of this kind of research is the work of Egbert and his colleagues with patients facing intra-abdominal surgery (Egbert, Battit, Welch, & Bartlett, 1964). In this study, half the patients were alerted to the likelihood of post-operative pain and were given information about its normality, duration, and severity. They were also taught breathing exercises that would help them control the pain. The other half of the patients received no such information or instructions. When examined post-operatively, patients in the instruction group showed better post-operative adjustment: They required fewer narcotics and were able to leave the hospital sooner than were the patients who had not received the preparatory instructions.

Research on the role of preparatory information in adjustment to surgery overwhelmingly shows that such preparation has beneficial effects on patients. Most surgical preparation interventions provide information about the procedures and sensations that can be expected. Patients who have been prepared in these ways are typically less emotionally distressed, regain their functioning more quickly, and are often able to leave the hospital sooner. One study (Kulik & Mahler, 1989) even found that the person who becomes your post-operative roommate can influence how you cope with the aftermath of surgery, because of the information a roommate conveys (see box 8.5).

Preparation for patients is so beneficial that many hospitals show videotapes to patients to prepare them for upcoming procedures. In another study by Mahler and Kulik (1998), patients awaiting coronary artery bypass graft (CABG) were exposed to one of three preparatory videotapes or to no preparation. One videotape conveyed information via a health care expert; the second featured the health care expert but also included clips of interviews with patients who reported on their progress; and the third presented information from a health care expert plus interviews with patients who reported their recovery consisting of "ups and downs." Compared with patients who did not receive videotaped preparation, patients who saw a videotape—any videotape—felt significantly better prepared for the recovery period, reported higher self-efficacy during the recovery period, were more adherent to recommended dietary and exercise changes during their recovery, and were released sooner from the hospital. Similar interventions have been employed successfully for patients awaiting other medical procedures (for example, Doering et al., 2000).

To summarize, **control-enhancing interventions** with patients awaiting surgery can have a marked effect

Social Support and Distress from Surgery

Patients who are hospitalized for serious illnesses or surgery often experience anxiety. From our discussion of social support, we know that emotional support from others can reduce distress when people are undergoing stressful events. Researchers have made use of these observations in developing interventions for hospitalized patients. Kulik and Mahler (1987) developed a social support intervention for patients about to undergo cardiac surgery. Some of the patients were assigned a roommate who was also waiting for surgery (pre-operative condition), whereas others were assigned a roommate who had already had surgery (post-operative condition). In addition, patients were placed with a roommate undergoing surgery that was either similar or dissimilar to their own.

The results suggested that patients who had a post-operative roommate profited from this contact (see also Kulik, Moore, & Mahler, 1993). Patients with a post-operative roommate were less anxious before surgery, were more ambulatory after surgery, and were released more quickly from the hospital than were patients who had been paired with a roommate who was also awaiting surgery. Similarity versus dissimilarity of the type of

surgery made no difference, only whether the roommate's surgery had already taken place.

Why exactly did rooming with a post-operative surgical patient improve the adjustment of those awaiting surgery? It may be that post-operative patients were able to provide relevant information to patients about the post-operative period by telling them how they felt and what the patient might expect (Thoits, Harvey, Hohmann, & Fletcher, 2000). Post-operative roommates may also have acted as role models for how one might feel and react post-operatively. Alternatively, those awaiting surgery may simply have been relieved to see that somebody who had undergone surgery had come out all right.

Whatever the specific explanation, the social contact produced by the presence of the post-operative roommate clearly had a positive impact on the pre-operative and post-operative adjustment of these surgery patients. These results have intriguing implications and may well be used to design future interventions to improve the adjustment of those awaiting unpleasant medical procedures, such as surgery (Kulik & Mahler, 1993; Kulik et al., 1993).

on postoperative adjustment, as evidenced both by patients' emotional reactions and by objective indicators, such as amount of medication required and length of hospital stay.

Coping with Stressful Medical Procedures Through Control-Enhancing Interventions

Although control-enhancing interventions were first used in hospitals to help patients cope with surgery, they are also used increasingly to help patients cope with other stressful medical procedures. Anticipating an invasive medical procedure can be a crisis situation for patients who have extreme anxiety about such procedures (Auerbach & Kilmann, 1977). Accordingly, any intervention that can reduce anxiety both before the procedure and during it will achieve welcome benefits for both patients and the medical staff.

Control-enhancing interventions, similar to those used for surgery, have now been used with a variety of these procedures, including gastroendoscopic examina-

tions (J. E. Johnson & Leventhal, 1974), childbirth (E. A. Leventhal, Leventhal, Schacham, & Easterling, 1989), the management of peptic ulcers (Putt, 1970), chemotherapy (T. G. Burish & Lyles, 1979), hysterectomy (J. E. Johnson, Christman, & Stitt, 1985), radiation therapy (J. E. Johnson et al., 1989), cardiac catheterization (Kendall et al., 1979), and sigmoidoscopy (examination of the sigmoid colon via a small scope inserted through the anus) (R. M. Kaplan, Atkins, & Lenhard, 1982).

Reviewing a large number of studies, Ludwick-Rosenthal and Neufeld (1988) concluded that information, relaxation, and cognitive-behavioral interventions, such as learning to think differently about the unpleasant sensations of a procedure, are all successful in reducing anxiety, improving coping, and enabling people to overcome the adverse effects of medical procedures more quickly.

The evidence on the beneficial effects of psychological control should not be taken to suggest that control is a panacea for all aversive situations. People who have a high desire for control may especially benefit from control-based interventions (S. C. Thompson, Cheek, & Graham, 1988). But control may actually be aversive if it gives people more responsibility than they want or feel able to assume. And too much control, such as being instructed to focus on too much information or to make too many choices, may be stressful, exacerbating distress over the medical procedure (see, for example, R. T. Mills & Krantz, 1979; S. C. Thompson et al., 1988).

■ THE HOSPITALIZED CHILD

Were you ever hospitalized as a child? If so, think back over the experience. Was it frightening and disorienting? Did you feel alone and uncared for? Or was it a more positive experience? Perhaps your parents were able to room in with you, or other children were around to talk to. You may have had either of these experiences because procedures for managing children in the hospital have changed dramatically over the past few decades.

Although it is generally acknowledged that people should be hospitalized only when it is absolutely necessary, this caution is particularly important in the care of the ill child. Some hospitalized children show adverse reactions, ranging from regressive, dependent behavior, such as social withdrawal, bed-wetting, and extreme fear, to rebelliousness and temper tantrums. And some problematic responses to hospitalization often do not become evident until the child returns home.

Anxiety

Anxiety is the most common adverse response to hospitalization. At young ages (2 to 4), children's anxiety may arise from their wish to be with the family as much as possible and more than may be practical. Children between ages 3 and 6 may become upset because they feel they are being rejected, deserted, or punished by their families. Between 4 and 6, children may act out their anxiety by developing new fears, such as a fear of darkness or of hospital staff. Sometimes, too, anxiety will be converted into bodily symptoms, such as headaches or stomachaches. In somewhat older children (ages 6 to 10), anxiety may be more free floating: It may make the child irritable and distractible without being tied to any particular issue.

Until recent years, psychologists usually attributed adverse reactions to hospitalization entirely to **separation anxiety.** Bowlby (1969, 1973) suggested that long-term separation of a child from the mother can produce ex-

Recent changes in hospitalization procedures for children have made hospitals less frightening places to be. Increasingly, medical personnel have recognized children's needs for play and have provided opportunities for play in hospital settings.

treme upset, even grief and mourning reactions under some circumstances. To address this issue, one study (Branstetter, 1969) divided hospitalized children into three groups: One third of the children saw their mothers only during visiting hours, the hospital's standard custom; one third had their mothers with them for extended periods during their hospitalization; and one third were assigned a "substitute mother," a student nurse or graduate student who talked with and played with them for extended periods. The results indicated that the children with mothers present for extended periods or with the companion showed less emotional disturbance than the group that saw their mothers only during visiting hours. These results suggest that a warm, nurturant relationship with a caregiver can offset some of the adverse effects of hospitalization and that the mother need not be the person who provides that relationship.

The fact remains, however, that it is hard for a child to be separated from family and home. Some children may not understand why they have been taken away from their families and mistakenly infer that they are being punished for some misdeed. The hospital environment can be lonely and isolating. Physical confinement in bed or confinement due to casts or traction keeps children from discharging energy through physical activity. The dependency that is fostered by bed rest and reliance on staff can lead to regression. Children, especially children just entering puberty, can be embarrassed or ashamed by having to expose themselves to strangers. The child may also be subject to confusing or painful tests and procedures.

Preparing Children for Medical Interventions

Major breakthroughs have been made in treating children for the often painful medical procedures they must endure, especially in response to childhood cancer. For example, conscious sedation has been a major breakthrough in distress management for children going through bone marrow aspirations and lumbar punctures in their cancer treatments (Pringle, Dahlquist, & Eslenazi, 2003). These techniques are especially useful with infants who do not have the cognitive capacities to process other kinds of coping interventions (L. L. Cohen, 2002).

Nonetheless, children still face many noxious procedures for which psychological preparation is valuable. Under some circumstances distraction may be effective for managing pain or discomfort (Dahlquist, Pendley, Landthrip, Jones, & Steuber, 2002). In an earlier section, we considered how principles of **psychological control** have been used to create interventions for adult patients undergoing stressful medical procedures, such as surgery. The principles of psychological control have also been used with children, and the results suggest that control-based interventions can reduce distress (for example, Jay, Elliott, Woody, & Siegel, 1991; Manne et al., 1990).

In one study (B. G. Melamed & Siegel, 1975), children about to undergo surgery were shown either a film of another child being hospitalized and receiving surgery or an unrelated film. Results suggested that those children exposed to the relevant film showed less pre-operative and post-operative distress than did children exposed to the irrelevant film. Moreover, parents of the children exposed to the modeling film reported fewer problem behaviors after hospitalization than did parents of children who saw the control film. Older children seem to be well served by seeing a film several days before hospitalization, whereas younger children may need exposure to information immediately before the relevant events.

Coping skills preparation has been found to be helpful with children (L. Cohen, Cohen, Blount, Schaen, & Zaff, 1999). For example, Zastowny, Kirschenbaum, and Meng (1986) gave children and their parents information describing typical hospitalization and surgery experiences, relaxation training to reduce anxiety, or a coping skills intervention to teach children constructive self-talk. Both the anxiety reduction and the coping skills interventions reduced fearfulness and parents' distress. Overall, the children exposed to the coping skills intervention exhibited the fewest maladaptive behaviors during hospitalization, less problem behavior in the week before admission, and fewer problems after discharge.

Preparation of children often focuses not only on the hospitalization experience but also on the illness itself and its treatment (for example, O'Byrne, Peterson, & Saldana, 1997). When a child understands what the illness is, what it feels like, and how soon he or she will get better, anxiety may be reduced. Researchers now believe that even very young children should be told something about their illness and treatment and encouraged to express their emotions and to ask questions.

Just as is true for adults, children's responses to preparation for hospitalization or treatment are influenced by how they prefer to cope with stress. Children who are vigilant copers may profit more from such interventions than children who characteristically use avoidant coping (L. Peterson & Toler, 1986; Reid, Chambers, McGrath, & Finley, 1997).

Different forms of preparation may be needed for children who face many medical procedures. For example, children with cancer undergo numerous invasive medical procedures, many of which are repeated. Whereas preparation may be important initially, sometimes distraction from the painful procedures are better on subsequent occasions (Manne, Bakeman, Jacobsen, Gorfinkle, & Redd, 1994).

Some preparation can be undertaken by parents. If a parent prepares a child for admission several days before hospitalization—explaining the reason for it, what it will be like, who will be there, how often the parent will visit—this preparation may ease the transition. During admission procedures, a parent or another familiar adult can remain with the child until the child is settled into the new room and engaged in some activity. Parents who remain with the child in the hospital can be partially responsible for explaining procedures and tests, knowing what the child will best understand. The presence of parents during stressful medical procedures is not an unmitigated benefit however. Parents do not always help reduce children's fears, pain, and discomfort (P. B. Jacobsen et al., 1990; Lumley, Abeles, Melamed, Pistone, & Johnson, 1990; Manne et al., 1992). When present during invasive medical procedures, some parents can become distressed and exacerbate the child's own anxiety (J. P. Bush, Melamed, Sheras, & Greenbaum, 1986). Nonetheless, parental support is important, and most hospitals now provide opportunities for extended parental visits, including 24-hour parental visitation rights.

Despite some qualifications, the benefits of preparation of children for hospitalization are now so widely acknowledged that it is more the rule than the exception. The area of working with hospitalized children has been

a story with something like a happy ending. Truly substantial changes have been made in a short time, and children's adverse reactions to hospitalization have declined as a result (Koetting, O'Byrne, Peterson, & Saldana, 1997). Hospitals now have more busy, active children with things to do and people to play with them than they had 25 years ago. ●

SUMMARY

1. The detection of symptoms, their interpretation, and use of health services are all heavily influenced by psychological processes.

2. Personality and culture, focus of attention, the presence of distracting or involving activities, mood, the salience of illness or symptoms, and individual differences in the tendency to monitor threat influence whether a symptom is noticed. The interpretation of symptoms is influenced by prior experience and expectations about their likelihood and meaning.

3. Illness schemas (which identify the type of disease, its consequences, causes, duration, and cure) and disease prototypes (conceptions of specific diseases) influence how people interpret their symptoms and whether they act on them by seeking medical attention.

4. Social factors, such as the lay referral network, can act as a go-between for the patient and the medical care system.

5. Health services are used disproportionately by the very young and very old, by women, and by middle- to upper-class people.

6. The health belief model, which ascertains whether a person perceives a threat to health and whether a person believes that a particular health measure can overcome the disorder, influences use of health services. Other social psychological factors include an individual's social location in a community and social pressures to seek treatment.

7. Health services may also be abused. A large percentage of patients who seek medical attention are depressed or anxious and not physically ill. People commonly ignore symptoms that are serious, resulting in dangerous delay behavior.

8. The hospital is a complex organizational system buffeted by changing medical, organizational, and financial climates. Different groups in the hospital develop different goals, such as cure, care, or core, which may occasionally conflict. Such problems are exacerbated by communication barriers.

9. Hospitalization can be a frightening and depersonalizing experience for patients. The adverse reactions of children in hospitals have received particular attention.

10. Control-restoring and control-enhancing interventions improve adjustment to hospitalization and to stressful medical procedures in both adults and children. The benefits of information, relaxation training, and coping skills training are well documented.

KEY TERMS

appraisal delay
behavioral delay
control-enhancing interventions
delay behavior
diagnostic-related groups (DRGs)
illness delay

illness representations (schemas)
lay referral network
medical delay
medical students' disease
preferred provider organization (PPO)

psychological control
secondary gains
separation anxiety
somaticizers
worried well

Patient-Provider Relations

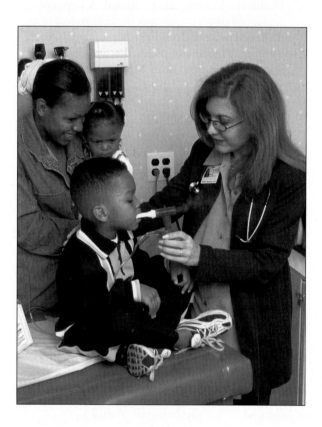

"I've had this cold for 2 weeks, so finally I went to the Student Health Services to get something for it. I waited more than an hour—can you believe it? And when I finally saw a doctor, he spent a whole 5 minutes with me, told me what I had was viral, not bacterial, and that he couldn't do anything for it. He sent me home and told me to get a lot of rest, drink fluids, and take over-the-counter medications for the stuffiness and the pain. Why did I even bother?!" (Student account of a trip to the health services)

Nearly everyone has a horror story about a visit to a physician. Long waits, insensitivity, apparently faulty diagnoses, and treatments that have no effect are the stuff of these indignant stories (Pescosolido, Tuch, & Martin, 2001), yet in the same breath, the storyteller may expound on the virtues of his or her latest physician with an enthusiasm bordering on worship. To what do we attribute this seemingly contradictory attitude toward health care practitioners?

Health ranks among the values we hold most dear. Good health is a prerequisite to nearly every other activity, and poor health can interfere with nearly all one's goals. Moreover, illness is usually uncomfortable, so people want to be treated quickly and successfully. Perhaps, then, it is no wonder that physicians and other health care professionals are alternately praised and vilified: Their craft is fundamental to the enjoyment of life.

In this chapter, we take up the complex issue of patient-provider interaction. First, we consider why patient-provider communication is important. Next, we look at the nature of patient-provider communication and the factors that erode it. Then, we consider some of the consequences of poor communication, including noncompliance with treatment regimens and malpractice litigation. Finally, we consider efforts to improve patient-provider communication.

■ WHAT IS A HEALTH CARE PROVIDER?

In the following pages, we refer to the "provider" rather than to the "physician." Although physicians continue to be the main providers of health care, Americans are increasingly receiving much of their primary care from individuals other than physicians (Hartley, 1999).

Nurses as Providers

Advanced-practice nursing is an umbrella term given to registered nurses who have gone beyond the typical 2 to 4 years of basic nursing education and who have many responsibilities for patients. For example, many **nurse-practitioners** are affiliated with physicians in private practice; they see their own patients, provide all routine medical care, prescribe for treatment, monitor the progress of chronically ill patients, and see walk-in patients with a variety of disorders. As a consequence, they must often explain disorders and their origins, diagnoses, prognoses, and treatments. Even in medical practices that do not employ nurse-practitioners, much patient education falls to nurses. Nurses frequently give treatment instructions or screen patients before they are seen by a physician.

Other advanced-practice nurses include certified nurse midwives, who are responsible for some obstetrical care and births; clinical nurse specialists, who are experts in a specialty, such as cardiac or cancer care; and certified registered nurse anesthetists, who administer anesthesia (*Los Angeles Times,* 1993a). Given the directions of current U.S. health policy, an expanded role for nurses in primary health care is likely.

Physicians' Assistants as Providers

Physicians' assistants perform many routine health care tasks, such as taking down medical information or explaining treatment regimens to patients. Physicians' assistants are educated in one of more than 50 special programs in medical schools and teaching hospitals, as well as throughout the armed forces. Such programs typically require at least 2 years of college and previous experience in health care. The physicians' assistant program itself lasts 2 years. In many instances, physicians' assistants take the same classes as medical students during the first year, and the second year is spent in clinical rotation with direct patient contact.

As medical practice has become increasingly complex, other professionals, such as biofeedback technicians and psychologists, have also become involved in specialized care. Consequently, issues of communication—especially poor communication—that arise in medical settings are not the exclusive concern of the physician.

■ NATURE OF PATIENT-PROVIDER COMMUNICATION

Criticisms of providers usually center on volumes of jargon, little feedback, and depersonalized care. Clearly, the quality of communication with a provider is important to patients, but does good communication do anything more than produce a vague sense of satisfaction or dissatisfaction in the patient's mind? The answer is yes. Poor patient-provider communication has been tied to outcomes as problematic as nonadherence to treatment recommendations and the initiation of malpractice litigation.

Judging Quality of Care

People often judge the adequacy of their care by criteria that are irrelevant to its technical quality (Yarnold, Michelson, Thompson, & Adams, 1998). Although we might be able to discern a case of blatant incompetence, most of us are insufficiently knowledgeable about medicine and standards of practice to know if we have been treated well or not. Consequently, we often judge technical quality on the basis of the manner in which care is delivered (Ben-Sira, 1980). A warm, confident, friendly provider is often judged to be both nice and competent, whereas a cool, aloof provider may be judged less favorably, as both unfriendly and incompetent (for example, Bogart, 2001). Moreover, if a physician expresses uncertainty about the nature of the patient's condition, patient satisfaction declines (C. G. Johnson, Levenkron, Suchman, & Manchester, 1988). In reality, technical quality of care and the manner in which care is delivered are unrelated.

Patient Consumerism

Another factor that may heavily influence patient-provider interaction is patients' increasing desire and need to be involved in the decisions that affect their health. Whereas at one time the physician's authority was accepted without question or complaint (Parsons, 1954), increasingly patients have adopted consumerist attitudes toward their health care (Haug, 1994). This change has come from several factors.

First, to induce a patient to follow a treatment regimen, one must have the patient's full cooperation and participation in the treatment plan. Giving the patient a role in the development of the plan and how it will be enacted can help ensure such commitment. Moreover, as we have seen, lifestyle is a major cause of disability and illness. Modifying lifestyle factors such as diet, smoking, and alcohol consumption must be done with the patient's full initiative and cooperation if change is to be achieved. In fact, patients who regard their behavior as under the control of providers instead of themselves are less likely to adhere to lifestyle change (Lynch et al., 1992).

Patients often have considerable expertise about their illness, especially if it is a recurring or chronic problem. A patient will do better if this expertise is tapped and integrated into the treatment program. For example, a diabetic may have a better sense of how to control his or her own blood glucose level than does a physician unfamiliar with the particular case. A study of pediatric asthma patients (Deaton, 1985) found that parents' modifications of a child's asthma regimen on the basis of severity of the disease, seasonal changes, symptoms, and side effects produced better asthma control than strict adherence to the prescribed medical regimen.

Clearly, then, the relationship between patient and provider is changing in ways that make better communication essential. The factors that erode communication include aspects of the office setting itself, the changing nature of the health care delivery system, provider behaviors, patient behaviors, and qualities of the interaction. We will consider each in turn.

Setting

On the surface of it, the medical office is an unlikely setting for effective communication. The average visit only lasts 12 to 15 minutes, and when you are trying to explain your symptoms to the physician, he or she will, on average, interrupt you before you get 23 seconds into your comments (N. Simon, 2003). Moreover, if you are ill, you must communicate that fact to another person, often a stranger; you must respond to specific and direct questions and then be content to be poked and prodded while the diagnostic process goes on. At the very least, it is difficult to present one's complaints effectively when one is in pain or has a fever, and a patient's ability to be articulate may be reduced further by any anxiety or embarrassment about the symptoms or the examination.

The provider, on the other hand, has the task of extracting significant information as quickly as possible from the patient. The provider is often on a tight schedule, with other patients backing up in the waiting room. The difficulties presented by the patient may have been made more complex by the use of various over-the-counter remedies so that symptoms are masked and distorted. Moreover, the patient's ideas of which symptoms are important may not correspond to the provider's knowledge, so important signs may be overlooked. With the patient seeking solace and the provider trying to maximize the effective use of time, it is clear that there are many potential sources of strain.

When physicians treat patients in a warm, friendly, confident manner, they are judged to be competent as well as nice.

Structure of Health Care Delivery System

Until a few decades ago, the majority of Americans received their health care from private physicians, whom they paid directly on a visit-by-visit basis (termed **private, fee-for-service care**). Each visit was followed by a bill, which the patient typically paid out of his or her own pocket.

That picture has changed. More than 103 million Americans now receive their health care through a prepaid financing and delivery system termed a **health maintenance organization (HMO)** (Spragins, 1996). By this arrangement, an employer or employee pays an agreed-on monthly rate, and the employee is then entitled to use services at no additional (or a greatly reduced) cost. This arrangement is called **managed care.** In some cases, HMOs have their own staff, from which enrollees must seek treatment. In preferred-provider organizations (PPOs), a network of affiliated practitioners have agreed to charge preestablished rates for particular services. Enrollees in the PPO must choose from these practitioners when seeking treatment. Table 9.1 describes the differences among types of health care plans.

Patient Dissatisfaction in Managed Care

The changing structure of the health care delivery system has contributed to dissatisfaction with health services by altering the nature of patient-provider interactions (C. E. Ross, Mirowsky, & Duff, 1982). Prepaid plans often operate on a referral basis so that the provider who first sees the patient determines what is wrong and then recommends any number of specialists to follow up with treatment. Because providers are often paid according to the

TABLE 9.1 | Types of Health Care Plans

Name	How It Works
Health maintenance organization (HMO)	Members select a primary-care physician from the HMO's pool of doctors and pay a small fixed amount for each visit. Typically, any trips to specialists and nonemergency visits to HMO network hospitals must be preapproved.
Preferred-provider organization (PPO)	A network of doctors offers plan members a discounted rate. They usually don't need prior authorization to visit an in-network specialist.
Point-of-service plan (POS)	These are plans, administered by insurance companies or HMOs, that let members go to doctors and hospitals out of the network—for a price. Members usually need a referral to see a network specialist.
Traditional indemnity plan	Patients select their own doctors and hospitals and pay on a fee-for-service basis. They don't need a referral to see a specialist.

Source: American Association of Health Plans, 2001; National Committee for Quality Assurance (NCQA), 2001.

FIGURE 9.1 | Percentage of Physicians in Various Forms of Practice   (*Sources:* Bureau of Labor Statistics, 2004; Bianco & Schine, 1997)

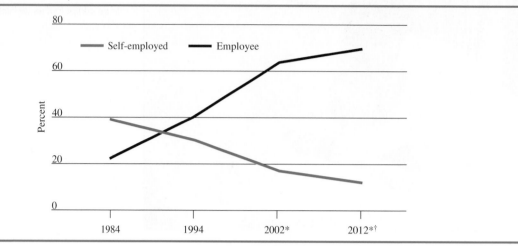

*Physicians & surgeons; †Projected

number of cases they see, referrals are desirable. There-fore, a colleague orientation, rather than a client or pa-tient orientation, can develop (Mechanic, 1975). Because the patient no longer pays directly for service and because the provider's income is not directly affected by whether the patient is pleased by the service, the provider may not be overly concerned with patient satis-faction. The provider is, however, concerned with what his or her colleagues think, because it is on their recom-mendations that he or she receives additional cases. In theory, such a system can produce high technical quality of care because providers who make errors receive fewer referrals; however, there is less incentive to offer emo-tionally satisfying care (I. K. Barr, 1983).

In recent years, the question of whether HMOs of-fer a higher technical quality of care has come into ques-tion. As efficiency and cost-cutting pressures have assumed increasing importance and as physicians have been urged to avoid expensive tests and shorten hospital stays, there is some evidence that quality of care has eroded (see box 9.1). One study found that the ill elderly and poor fared especially poorly in HMOs, compared with people in fee-for-service practices. Because fee-for-service insurance allowed patients a much broader choice of doctors and placed fewer restrictions on services, their care was better, the study reported (Ware, Bayliss, Rogers, & Kosinski, 1996). An extensive evaluation of HMOs by an independent organization showed that quality of care ranged from barely satisfactory to excel-lent, depending on the facility (Spragins, 1996). Overall,

changes in the practice of medicine have led to a rise in negative attitudes about physicians and medical practice (Pescosolido et al., 2001). Clearly, then, managed care does not guarantee a higher standard of care.

HMOs may undermine care in other ways. When providers are pressured to see as many patients as possi-ble, the consequences can be long waits and short visits. These problems are compounded if a patient is referred to several specialists because each referral may lead to an-other long wait and short visit. Patients may feel that they are being shunted from provider to provider with no continuity in their care and no opportunity to build up a personal relationship with any one individual. Indeed, a nationwide study of more than 170,000 HMO patients revealed widespread dissatisfaction (Freudenheim, 1993). Increasingly, as figure 9.1 suggests, third-party payment systems adopt cost-saving strategies that may inadver-tently restrict clients' choices over when and how they can receive medical services. Because patients value choice, these restrictions contribute to dissatisfaction.

Precisely because problems have developed, some HMOs have taken steps to reduce long waits, to allow for personal choice, and to make sure a patient sees the same provider at each visit. But it is clear that the chang-ing structure of medical practice generally may under-mine emotional satisfaction and does not guarantee a high standard of care.

DRGs and Patient Care   In chapter 8, we dis-cussed DRGs (diagnostic-related groups), which are

BOX 9.1

The Frustrations of Managed "Care"

Although many patients find their managed care plans to be highly satisfactory, others face frustrating, time-consuming, and seemingly arbitrary rules about the type of care they can and cannot receive. One patient describes her experiences as follows:

I didn't want to join a managed care plan. I loved my [old plan], but it didn't love my employer and dropped us like a hot potato one year when "not enough" employees had chosen it.

I'm not sick, fortunately. I have routine and relatively trivial ailments, and one not-serious chronic problem for which I take a daily pill. I've gradually discovered what all those managed care advocates mean when they say managed care plans are more efficient and cut out unnecessary expenditures. They mean they shift a lot more of their costs onto me and my doctors.

For my chronic problem, I get checked out twice a year by a specialist to make sure that nothing's changed. My HMO said a referral form was good only for three months. So I started having to procure one of those forms for each visit to the specialist. At first, I could only get a form with a phone call to Dr. Gatekeeper's office, but his staff got swamped with all this paperwork and asked me to send a written request with a stamped envelope addressed to the specialist. The little costs to me of my HMO's cost-saving strategies were starting to add up. I can't begin to calculate the costs to Dr. Gatekeeper as more of his and his staff's time went to referral paperwork.

Then there was the matter of my once-a-day pill. Last year I went abroad for two months and wanted a sixty-day supply of pills to take along. But when my pharmacist tried to fill the prescription and bill it to my HMO, my HMO denied the request, saying they allow only a one-month supply, and will not pay for another refill until twenty-eight days have elapsed. I contacted my HMO, explaining my situation. I got an unhelpful response: sorry, we can't bend our rules, but you can pay for your second-month stock now and file for reimbursement later. More time and money costs to me.

Recently I hurt my knee and needed physical therapy. In order for my insurance to cover the treatment, I had to have a referral from Dr. Gatekeeper. Eventually a referral came, but it authorized only three visits. I've already had seven visits and I clearly need lots more. So I called Dr. Gatekeeper's office once more to try to secure more referrals for more visits. This time, I was told that they now have a special telephone number for referral requests. I called the number, only to get a lengthy recording, reeling off at least ten items of information I was supposed to leave if I wanted a prescription refill and then another ten or so items of information if I wanted a referral. I furiously scribbled notes, fished for my insurance card in my wallet and left the information. No referral has shown up at the physical therapist's office. I'm still liable for the payment. The bureaucratic snafus are getting deeper and deeper, and I can't talk to a real person in my internist's office anymore.

I may be out money, if Dr. Gatekeeper's staff doesn't understand my recorded message or forgets to back-date the referral forms to cover the visits I've already had. The physical therapist is out money because she can't get reimbursed until my referral forms show up. One day, while she was pushing and poking at my knee, the therapist explained to me how insurance has kept her payments so low that she has had to cut back each treatment session from one hour to forty-five minutes.

In effect, while managed care plans are bragging about how they are providing more care for less money, their members are getting less care for more money and more lost time. (C. Thomas, 1995, pp. 11–12)

guidelines for patient care in particular disease or disorder categories. The argument is that DRGs can produce efficient patient care, thereby producing reductions in costs. The impact of DRGs on medical care are several. First, because the DRG system implicitly rewards institutions for the detection and treatment of complications or co-occurring medically problematic conditions, the system provides an impetus for diagnostic vigilance. It is to the practitioner's advantage to find everything that is wrong with the patient before treatment. However, DRGs implicitly adopt biomedical criteria for how and how long a disease should be treated, often ignoring psychosocial issues. As a result, DRGs are quite poor predictors of patients' need for services and length of stay. One patient may be fine with a 2-day hospital stay, for example, whereas another patient with the same problem may require 4 days because of complications or no help with aftercare at home. Finally, DRGs can potentially undermine effective treatment, in that they may create a tendency to discharge patients before the DRGs' boundaries for length of stay are exceeded. Thus, although the presence of DRGs can have some positive effects on quality of care (such as attentiveness to the diagnostic process), they may also compromise care.

Summary The changing structure of the health care delivery service from private, fee-for-service practice to third-party arrangements can inadvertently exert adverse effects on patient-provider communication and on patient choice. The colleague orientation of the third-party system makes it less necessary for physicians to please patients; although it may increase technical quality of care, a colleague orientation may undermine the quality of interactions with patients. In addition, cost-saving strategies may restrict patient choices of treatment options and overly constrain the length of care and kind of treatments they receive.

Changes in the Philosophy of Health Care Delivery

A number of changes underlying the philosophy of health care delivery are altering the face of health care delivery. The physician's role is changing. The development of new organizational systems for delivering services, such as HMOs, and the rising number of women in the medical profession have changed what was once a very clear physician role characterized by dominance and authority (Goldstein, Jaffe, Sutherland, & Wilson, 1987). Although these changes promote more egalitarian attitudes among physicians (Lavin, Haug, Belgrave, & Breslau, 1987), they also challenge the physician's dominance, autonomy, and authority (Hartley, 1999; Warren, Weitz, & Kulis, 1998). Responsibilities that once fell exclusively to physicians are now shared with many other authorities, including administrators and patients.

Holistic Health Movement and Health Care
Western medicine is increasingly incorporating Eastern approaches to medicine and nontraditional therapies, such as meditation and biofeedback. The philosophy of **holistic health,** the idea that health is a positive state to be actively achieved, not merely the absence of disease, has gained a strong foothold in Western medicine. This viewpoint acknowledges psychological and spiritual influences on achieving health, and it gives patients responsibility for both achieving health and curing illness

through their behaviors, attitudes, and spiritual beliefs. Holistic health emphasizes health education, self-help, and self-healing. Natural, low-technology interventions and non-Western techniques of medical practice may be substituted for traditional care and include herbal medicine, acupuncture, acupressure, massage, psychic diagnosis, spiritual healing, the laying on of hands, and dance therapy.

These changes alter the relationship between provider and patient, making it more open, equal, and reciprocal and potentially bringing emotional contact into the relationship between patient and provider (Astin, 1998). Even some physicians who do not subscribe to holistic health beliefs are trying to structure more egalitarian relationships with their patients and recognize that there may be less intrusive alternatives to traditional medical management that can achieve the same outcomes (Goldstein, Jaffe, Garell, & Berk, 1986).

Provider Behaviors That Contribute to Faulty Communication

Not Listening Communication between the patient and physician can be eroded by certain provider behaviors. One problematic provider behavior is not listening. In a study of physicians' initial responses to patient-initiated visits, Beckman and Frankel (1984) studied 74 office visits. In only 23% of the cases did patients have the opportunity to finish their explanation of concerns before the provider began the process of diagnosis. In 69% of the visits, the physician interrupted, directing the patient toward a particular disorder. On an average, physicians interrupted after their patients had spoken for only 18 to 22 seconds.

The consequence of this controlling effort to manage the interaction not only prevents patients from discussing their concerns but may also lead to loss of important information. Because physicians knew their behavior was being recorded during the office visits, the study may actually underestimate the extent of this problem.

Use of Jargon The use of jargon and technical language is another important factor in poor communication. Studies reveal that patients understand relatively few of the complex terms that providers often use. Why do providers use complex, hard-to-understand language? In some cases, jargon-filled explanations may be used to keep the patient from asking too many questions or from discovering that the provider is not certain what the patient's problem is.

Physicians have long used medical jargon to impress gullible laymen. As far back as the 13th century, the medieval physician, Arnold of Villanova, urged colleagues to seek refuge behind impressive-sounding language when they could not explain a patient's ailment. "Say that he has an obstruction of the liver," Arnold wrote, "and particularly use the word obstruction because patients do not understand what it means" (*Time,* 1970, p. 35). One physician explained, with great amusement, that if the term "itis" (meaning "inflammation of") was connected to whatever organ was troubled (for example, "stomachitis"), this would usually forestall any additional questions from the patient.

More commonly, however, providers' use of jargon may be a carryover from their technical training. Providers learn a complex vocabulary for understanding illnesses and communicating about them to other professionals; they often find it hard to remember that the patient does not share this expertise. The use of jargon may also stem from an inability to gauge what the patient will understand and an inability to figure out the appropriate nontechnical explanation. How much should one tell a patient? Does the patient need to know how the disorder developed? If so, how should that explanation be provided?

Baby Talk   Because practitioners may underestimate what their patients will understand about an illness and its treatment, they may resort to baby talk and simplistic explanations.

> "Nurse, would you just pop off her things for me? I want to examine her." In the hospital, everything is "popped" on or off, slipped in or out. I don't think I met a single doctor who, in dealing with patients, didn't resort to this sort of nursery talk. I once heard one saying to a patient, an elderly man, "We're just going to pop you into the operating theater to have a little peep into your tummy." Nurses, too, had people "popping" all over the place—in and out of lavatories, dressing gowns, beds, scales, wheelchairs, bandages. (Toynbee, 1977)

As these remarks indicate, overly simple explanations coupled with infantilizing baby talk can make the patient feel like a helpless child. Moreover, such behavior can forestall questions. Having received a useless explanation, the patient may not know how to begin to ask for solid information. The tendency to lapse into simple explanations with a patient may become almost automatic. One woman, who is both a cancer researcher and a cancer patient, reports that when she goes to see her cancer specialist, he talks to her in a very complex and technical manner until the examination starts. Once she is on the examining table, he shifts to very simple sentences and explanations. She is now a patient and no longer a colleague.

The truth about what patients can understand lies somewhere between the extremes of technical jargon and infantilizing baby talk. Typically, providers underestimate the ability of patients to understand information about the origins, diagnosis, prognosis, and treatment of their disorders (McKinlay, 1975; Waitzkin, 1985).

Nonperson Treatment   Depersonalization of the patient is another problem that impairs the quality of the patient-provider relationship (Kaufman, 1970). This nonperson treatment may be employed intentionally to try to keep the patient quiet while an examination, a procedure, or a test is being conducted, or it may be used unintentionally because the patient (as object) has become the focus of the provider's attention.

> When I was being given emergency treatment for an eye laceration, the resident surgeon abruptly terminated his conversation with me as soon as I lay down on the operating table. Although I had had no sedative, or anesthesia, he acted as if I were no longer conscious, directing all his questions to a friend of mine—questions such as, "What's his name? What occupation is he in? Is he a real doctor?" etc. As I lay there, these two men were speaking about me as if I were not there at all. The moment I got off the table and was no longer a cut to be stitched, the surgeon resumed his conversation with me, and existence was conferred upon me again. (Zimbardo, 1969, p. 298)

To understand the phenomenon of nonperson treatment, consider what a nuisance it can be for a provider to have the patient actually there during a treatment—fussing, giving unhelpful suggestions, and asking questions. If the patients could drop their bodies off, as they do their cars, and pick them up later, it would save both the provider and the patient a lot of trouble and anxiety. As it is, the provider is like an auto mechanic who has the misfortune of having the car's owner following him or her around, creating trouble, while he or she is trying to fix the car (E. Goffman, 1961). Goffman suggests that providers cope with their bad luck by pretending that the patient is not there: "The patient is greeted with what passes for civility, and said farewell to in the same fashion, with everything in between going on as if the patient weren't there as a social person at all, but only as a possession someone has left behind" (pp. 341–342).

Nonperson treatment may be employed at particularly stressful moments to keep the patient quiet and enable the practitioner to concentrate. In that way, it may serve a valuable medical function. But patient depersonalization can also have adverse medical effects. Medical staff making hospital rounds often use either highly technical or euphemistic terms when discussing cases with their colleagues. Unfortunately, these terms may confuse or alarm the nonparticipating but physically present patient, an effect to which the provider may be oblivious. In fact, one study found that the number of heart disease complications increased among patients after physicians' rounds (Jarvinen, 1955).

Patient depersonalization also provides emotional protection for the provider. It is difficult for a provider to work in a continual state of awareness that his or her every action influences someone's state of health and happiness. The responsibility can be crushing. Moreover, every provider has tragedies—as when a patient dies or is left incapacitated by a treatment—but the provider must find a way to continue to practice. Depersonalization helps provide such a way.

The emotion communicated by a provider in interaction with a patient can have a substantial impact on the patient's attitude toward the provider, the visit, and his or her condition (J. A. Hall, Epstein, DeCiantis, & McNeil, 1993). One study, for example, found that women getting their mammogram results from a seemingly worried physician recalled less information, perceived their situation to be more severe, showed higher levels of anxiety, and had significantly higher pulse rates than women receiving mammogram results from a nonworried physician (D. E. Shapiro, Boggs, Melamed, & Graham-Pole, 1992).

Stereotypes of Patients   Communication may be especially eroded when physicians encounter patients or diseases that they would prefer not to treat (Morgan, 1985; Schmelkin, Wachtel, Schneiderman, & Hecht, 1988). Negative stereotypes of patients may contribute to problems in communication and subsequent treatment. Research shows that physicians give less information, are less supportive, and demonstrate less proficient clinical performance with Black and Hispanic patients and patients of lower socioeconomic class than is true for more advantaged patients, even in the same health care settings (van Ryn & Fu, 2003). When a person is seen by a physician of the same race or ethnicity, satisfaction with treatment tends to be higher, underscoring the importance of increasing the number of minority physicians (Laveist & Nuru-Jeter, 2002).

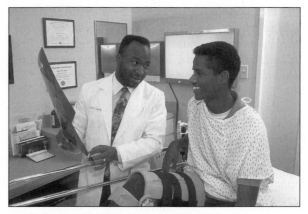

Patients are often most comfortable interacting with a physician who is similar to themselves.

Many physicians also have negative perceptions of the elderly (Haug & Ory, 1987). Older patients may also be less likely to be resuscitated in emergency rooms or given active treatment protocols for life-threatening diseases (J. Roth, 1977). These problems may be exacerbated by any communication difficulties the elderly person has (Haug & Ory, 1987; Morgan, 1985). The negative attitudes of physicians seem to be reciprocated in the elderly, in that among those 65 and over, only 54% express high confidence in physicians.

Sexism is a problem in medical practice as well. For example, in three experimental studies that attributed reported chest pain and stress to either a male or female patient, medical intervention was perceived to be less important for the female patient (R. Martin & Lemos, 2002). Male physicians and female patients do not always communicate well with each other. Research suggests that in comparison with male physicians, female physicians generally conduct longer visits, ask more questions, make more positive comments during a visit, and show more nonverbal support, such as smiling and nodding (J. A. Hall, Irish, Roter, Ehrlich, & Miller, 1994). The matching of gender between patient and practitioner appears to foster more rapport and disclosure (Levinson, McCollum, & Kutner, 1984; C. S. Weisman & Teitelbaum, 1985). However, physicians of both genders still prefer male patients (J. A. Hall et al., 1993).

Patients who are regarded as seeking treatment largely for depression, anxiety, or other forms of psychological disorder also evoke negative reactions from physicians. With these patients, physician attention may be especially cursory. Physicians also prefer healthier patients to sicker ones (J. A. Hall et al., 1993), and they prefer acutely ill to chronically ill patients; chronic illness poses uncertainties and questions about prognosis, which acute disease does not (R. N. Butler, 1978). Chronic illness can also increase stress and distress over having to give bad news (L. Cohen et al., 2003).

Patients' Contributions to Faulty Communication

Within a few minutes of having discussed their illness with a provider, as many as one third of patients cannot repeat their diagnosis; up to one half do not understand important details about the illness or treatment (Golden & Johnston, 1970). Some of these problems stem from faulty communication, but some of it also stems from patients themselves. Whereas dissatisfied patients complain about the incomplete or overly technical explanations they receive from providers, dissatisfied providers complain that even when they give clear, careful explanations to patients, the explanation goes in one ear and out the other.

Patient Characteristics   Several factors on the patient's part contribute to poor patient-provider communications. Neurotic patients often present an exaggerated picture of their symptoms (for example, Ellington & Wiebe, 1999). This style can, unfortunately, compromise a physician's ability to effectively gauge the seriousness of a patient's condition. When patients are anxious, their learning can be impaired (Graugaard & Finset, 2000). Anxiety makes it difficult to focus attention and process incoming information and even harder to retain it. Because anxiety is often high during a visit to a provider, it is not surprising that patients retain so little information. Focusing directly on the patient's concerns can alleviate this barrier to effective communication (Graugaard & Finset, 2000).

Patient Knowledge   Some patients are unable to understand even simple information about their case. Physicians are usually upper middle class and often White and male, whereas their patients may be of a lower social class, a different race, and a different sex. Consequently, there may also be class-based, sociolinguistic factors that contribute to poor communication (Waitzkin, 1985).

As people age, their number of medical problems usually increases, but their abilities to present their complaints effectively and follow treatment guidelines can decrease. About 40% of patients over 50 have difficulty understanding their prescription instructions. Extra time and care may be needed to communicate this vital information to older patients.

In contrast, patients who have had an illness before, who have received a clear explanation of their disorder and treatment, or who know that their illness is not serious show relatively little distortion of information. Patients for whom the illness is new and who have little prior information about the disorder show the greatest distortion in their explanations (DiMatteo & DiNicola, 1982).

Patient Attitudes Toward Symptoms   Patients respond to different cues about their illness than do practitioners (R. Martin & Lemos, 2002). Patients place considerable emphasis on pain and on symptoms that interfere with their activities. But providers are more concerned with the underlying illness—its severity and treatment. Patients may misunderstand the provider's emphasis on factors that they consider to be incidental, they may pay little attention when vital information is being communicated, or they may believe that the provider has made an incorrect diagnosis.

Patients sometimes give providers misleading information about their medical history or their current concerns. Patients may be embarrassed about their health history (such as having had an abortion) or their health practices (such as being a smoker) and often do not report these important pieces of information to the physician (L. Smith, Adler, & Tschann, 1999).

Patients may fear asking questions because they do not think they will receive straight answers, and providers may erroneously assume that because no questions have been asked, the patient does not want any information. The following episode illustrates the lengths to which such misconceptions can be carried:

> At the age of 59, [Mr. Tischler] suffered progressive discomfort from a growing lump in his groin. He did not discuss it with his wife or anyone else until six weeks prior to his admission to the hospital, when he began to fear that it was cancer. When Mrs. Tischler heard about it, she, too, was fearful of cancer, but she did not mention this to her husband. She did, however, discuss his condition with a close friend who was the secretary of a local surgeon. Through this friend, Mr. Tischler was introduced to the surgeon who examined him, made a diagnosis of a hernia, and recommended hospitalization for repair of the hernia. Both Mr. and Mrs. Tischler thought the surgeon was trying to be kind to them since Mr. Tischler, in their fearful fantasies, was afflicted with cancer.

The surgeon scheduled admission to the hospital for elective repair of the hernia. After the surgery, the hernia disappeared, the incision healed normally, and there were no complications. Mr. Tischler then realized that the surgeon had been accurate in his diagnosis and prognosis. He returned to work in three weeks, free from pain and all disability. (Duff & Hollingshead, 1968, p. 300)

Interactive Aspects of the Communication Problem

Qualities of the interaction between practitioner and patient can perpetuate faulty communication (J. A. Hall, Rotter, & Katz, 1988). A major problem is that the patient-provider interaction does not provide the opportunity for feedback to the provider. Providers rarely know whether information was communicated effectively because they rarely learn about the results of the communications (Sicotte, Pineault, Tilquin, & Contandriopoulos, 1996).

Specifically, the provider sees the patient, the patient is diagnosed, treatment is recommended, and the patient leaves. When the patient does not return, any number of things may have happened: The treatment may have cured the disorder; the patient may have gotten worse and decided to seek treatment elsewhere; the treatment may have failed, but the disorder may have cleared up anyway; or the patient may have died. Not knowing which of these alternatives has actually occurred, the provider does not know the impact and success rate of the advice given. Obviously, it is to the provider's psychological advantage to believe that the diagnosis was correct, that the patient followed the advice, and that the patient's disorder was cured by the recommended treatment, but the provider may never find out for certain.

The provider may also find it hard to know when a satisfactory personal relationship has been established with a patient. Many patients are relatively cautious with providers. If they are dissatisfied, rather than complain about it directly, they may simply change providers. The provider who finds that a patient has stopped coming does not know if the patient has moved out of the area or switched to another practice. When providers do get feedback, it is more likely to be negative than positive: Patients whose treatments have failed are more likely to go back than are patients whose treatments are successful (Rachman & Phillips, 1978).

Two points are important here. First, learning is fostered more by positive than by negative feedback; positive feedback tells one what one is doing right, whereas negative feedback may tell one what to stop doing but not necessarily what to do instead. Because providers get more negative than positive feedback, this situation is not conducive to learning. Second, learning occurs only with feedback, but in the provider's case, lack of feedback is the rule. Clearly, it is extremely difficult for the provider to know if communication is adequate and, if not, how to change it. It is no wonder, then, that when social scientists display their statistics on poor patient-provider communication, each provider can say with confidence, "Not me," because he or she indeed has no basis for self-recrimination.

■ RESULTS OF POOR PATIENT-PROVIDER COMMUNICATION

The patient-provider communication problems would be little more than an unfortunate casualty of medical treatment were it not for the toll they take on health. Dissatisfied patients are less likely to use medical services in the future (C. E. Ross & Duff, 1982; Ware, Davies-Avery, & Stewart, 1978). They are more likely to turn to nontraditional services that satisfy emotional needs rather than medical needs (D. M. Eisenberg et al., 1993). Dissatisfied patients are less likely to obtain medical checkups and are more likely to change doctors and to file formal complaints (Hayes-Bautista, 1976; Ware et al., 1978).

Thus, it appears that patient dissatisfaction with patient-provider interaction not only fosters health risks by leading patients to avoid using services in the future but also poses costly and time-consuming dilemmas for the health care agencies themselves.

Nonadherence to Treatment Regimens

Chapters 3, 4, and 5 examined **adherence** to treatment regimens in the context of health behaviors and noted how difficult it can be to modify or eliminate poor health habits, such as smoking, or to achieve a healthy lifestyle. In this section we examine the role of health institutions, and particularly the role of the provider, in promoting adherence.

A 17th-century French playwright, Moliere, aptly described the relationship that physicians and patients often have with respect to treatment recommendations:

THE KING: You have a physician. What does he do?

MOLIERE: Sire, we converse. He gives me advice which I do not follow and I get better. (Treue, 1958, as cited in Koltun & Stone, 1986)

When patients do not adopt the behaviors and treatments their providers recommend, the result is termed **nonadherence** (DiMatteo, 2004). Estimates of nonadherence vary from a low of 15% to a staggering high of 93%. On average, nonadherence is about 26% (DiMatteo, Giordani, Lepper, & Croghan, 2002). For short-term antibiotic regimens, one of the most common prescriptions, it is estimated that at least one third of all patients fail to comply adequately (see Rapoff & Christophersen, 1982). Between 50 and 60% of patients do not keep appointments for modifying preventive health behaviors (DiMatteo & DiNicola, 1982). As many as 80% of patients drop out of lifestyle change programs designed to treat smoking or obesity (J. M. Dunbar & Agras, 1980; Turk & Meichenbaum, 1991). Of 750 million new prescriptions written each year, approximately 520 million are responded to with partial or total nonadherence (Buckalew & Sallis, 1986). In a study of children treated for ear infection, it was estimated that only 5% of the parents fully adhered to the medication regimen (Mattar, Markello, & Yaffe, 1975). Adherence is typically so poor that researchers believe that the benefits of many medications cannot be realized at the current levels of adherence that patients achieve (R. B. Haynes, McKibbon, & Kanani, 1996). Adherence is highest in HIV disease, arthritis, gastrointestinal disorders, and cancer and lowest among patients with pulmonary disease, diabetes, and sleep disorders (DiMatteo et al., 2002).

More than 80% of patients who receive behavioral change recommendations from their doctors such as stopping smoking or following a restrictive diet fail to follow through on these recommendations. Even heart patients, who should be motivated to adhere, such as patients in cardiac rehabilitation, show an adherence rate of only 66 to 75% (Center for the Advancement of Health, March 2003).

Measuring Adherence   Obtaining reliable indications of nonadherence is not an easy matter (Turk & Meichenbaum, 1991). One study that attempted to assess use of the drug theophylline for patients suffering from chronic obstructive pulmonary disease (COPD) found that physicians reported that 78% of their COPD patients were on the medication, chart audit revealed 62% of the patients were on the medication, videotaped observation of patient visits produced an estimate of 69%, and only 59% of the patients reported they were on theophylline (Gerbert, Stone, Stulbarg, Gullion, & Greenfield, 1988). And the study did not even assess whether theophylline was administered correctly, only if it was prescribed at all.

Asking patients about their adherence yields unreliable and artificially high estimates (for example, R. M. Kaplan & Simon, 1990; Turk & Meichenbaum, 1991). Because most patients know they are supposed to adhere, they may bias their answers to appear more compliant than they really are (H. P. Roth, 1987; Turk & Meichenbaum, 1991). As a consequence, researchers draw on indirect measures of adherence, such as the number of follow-up or referral appointments kept, but even these measures can be biased. Treatment outcome might be a way to assess nonadherence, but there is little evidence of a clear relationship between the extent of adherence and health outcomes. In short, many factors obscure the relationship between adherence and recovery (Turk & Meichenbaum, 1991). The unnerving conclusion is that, if anything, the research statistics underestimate the amount of nonadherence that is actually going on.

Causes of Adherence

When asked to explain nonadherence, physicians usually attribute it to patients' uncooperative personalities, to their ignorance, to lack of motivation, or to their forgetfulness (M. S. Davis, 1968a; W. C. House, Pendelton, & Parker, 1986). In fact, efforts to identify the types of patients that are most likely to be nonadherent have been unsuccessful (R. M. Kaplan & Simon, 1990; Meichenbaum & Turk, 1987). Nonetheless, the greatest cause of nonadherence is poor communication.

Good Communication   Good communication fosters adherence. The patient must understand the treatment regimen, be satisfied with the relationship and treatment regimen, and decide to adhere.

The first step in adherence is understanding the treatment regimen. Much nonadherence occurs because the patient does not understand what the treatment regimen is (Hauenstein, Schiller, & Hurley, 1987; Stanton, 1987). Accordingly, adherence is highest when a patient receives a clear, jargon-free explanation of the etiology, diagnosis, and treatment recommendations. Adherence is also enhanced by factors that promote good learning: Adherence is higher if the patient has been asked to repeat the instructions, if the instructions are written down, if unclear recommendations are pointed out and clarified, and if the instructions are repeated more than once (DiMatteo & DiNicola, 1982). Box 9.2 addresses some ways in which adherence errors may be reduced.

Reducing Error in Adherence

The Center for the Advancement of Health is a non-profit organization whose goal is to promote greater recognition of the many ways that psychological, social, behavioral, economic, and environmental factors influence health and illness (Center for the Advancement of Health, 2000c; Center for the Advancement of Health, 2005).

Among its concerns has been low levels of patient adherence to treatment generally, as well as the many errors that can occur if physicians are unaware of patients' other medications or if patients misuse or combine treatments on their own. Included in the recommendations the center has proposed for treating this formidable problem are the following:

1. Make adult literacy a national priority.

2. Require all prescriptions be typed on a keyboard.

3. Make commonplace a secure electronic medical record for each individual that records his or her complete medication history and that is accessible by both patients and their physicians.

4. Enforce requirements that pharmacists provide clear instructions and counseling along with prescription medication.

5. Develop checklists for both patients and doctors, so they can ask and answer the right questions before a prescription is written.

Satisfaction with the patient-provider relationship also predicts adherence. When patients perceive the provider as warm and caring, they are more compliant; providers who show anger or impatience toward their patients, or who just seem busier, have more nonadherent patients (Sherbourne, Hays, Ordway, DiMatteo, & Kravitz, 1992). On the other hand, providers who answer patients' questions have more adherent patients (DiMatteo et al., 1993).

The final step in adherence, one that is frequently overlooked, involves the patient's decision to adhere to a prescribed medical regimen. Many providers simply assume that patients will follow their advice, without realizing that the patients must first decide to do so.

Treatment Regimen   Qualities of the treatment regimen also influence the degree of adherence a patient will exhibit (R. B. Haynes, 1979a). Treatment regimens that must be followed over a long period of time, that are highly complex, and that interfere with other desirable behaviors in a person's life all show low levels of adherence (Turk & Meichenbaum, 1991). As box 9.3 illustrates, sometimes these can be the very treatment regimens on which survival depends. In contrast, keeping first appointments and obtaining medical tests (J. J. Alpert, 1964; for a review, see DiMatteo & DiNicola, 1982) show high adherence rates.

Adherence is high (about 90%) when the advice is perceived as "medical" (for example, taking medication) but lower (76%) if the advice is vocational (for example, taking time off from work) and lower still (66%) if the advice is social or psychological (for example, avoiding

stressful social situations) (Turk & Meichenbaum, 1991). Adherence is higher for treatment recommendations that seem like medicine (taking pills) but much lower when the treatment seems nonmedical (such as instructions to rest). Adherence is very poor (20 to 50%) when people are asked to change personal habits, such as smoking or drinking (DiMatteo & DiNicola, 1982).

Complex self-care regimens show the lowest level of overall adherence (Blumenthal & Emery, 1988). People with diabetes, for example, must often take injections of insulin, monitor their blood glucose fluctuations, strictly control their dietary intake, and in some programs, engage in prescribed exercise programs and efforts at stress management. Even with the best of intentions, it is difficult to engage in all the required behaviors, which take up several hours a day (Turk & Meichenbaum, 1991).

Avoidant coping strategies on the part of patients are associated with poor adherence to treatment recommendations. In a longitudinal study of patients with a variety of chronic disorders, patients who relied on avoidant coping strategies were less likely to follow their doctors' specific recommendations and to adhere to treatment goals in general (Sherbourne et al., 1992). Consistent with our analysis of avoidant coping in chapter 7, it may be that patients who cope with stressful events via avoidance are less attentive or responsive to information about threatening events, such as health problems.

Another patient factor that influences adherence is the presence of life stressors. Nonadherent patients cite lack of time, no money, or distracting problems at home, such as instability and conflict, as impediments

BOX 9.3

Protease Inhibitors: An Adherence Nightmare?

People living with AIDS who once believed they were at death's doorstep now have a life-prolonging treatment available to them in the form of protease inhibitors. Protease is an HIV enzyme that is required for HIV replication. Protease inhibitors prevent the protease enzyme from cleaving the virus-complex into pathogenic virions (the infective form of a virus). Taken regularly, protease inhibitors not only stop the spread of HIV but in some cases, following treatment, people once diagnosed with AIDS show no trace of the virus in their bloodstreams.

But taking protease inhibitors regularly is the trick. Protease inhibitors have several qualities that make adherence problematic. First, many protease inhibitors must be taken four times a day. Most people can barely remember to take one tablet a day, and estimates of levels of compliance with antibiotic regimens requiring two tablets a day put adherence at less than one third. Moreover, on these other regimens, a skipped date does not mean failure, whereas with protease inhibitors, missing even one dose may make the medication permanently unsuccessful. Many protease inhibitors require refrigeration, and consequently, the patient must remain close to the refrigerated drug throughout the day so as to take the medication on time. This factor is impractical for some people with AIDS.

For middle-class people with stable lives, regular employment, and socially supportive networks, adherence may be likely. However, for the poor, the homeless, and the unemployed, who may lack even a refrigerator for keeping protease inhibitors cold, much less the stable

life that promotes their regular use, adherence is a difficult task. Moreover, drug use, chronic anxiety, and other affective or psychotic disorders interfere with the ability to use the drugs properly, and these states characterize some of the people who are eligible for protease inhibitors. Protease inhibitors have unpleasant side effects, including diarrhea and nausea. Unpleasant side effects often produce high levels of nonadherence.

In short, although protease inhibitors represent a life-saving discovery, they have many features that make their faithful use problematic. Integrating medication into busy, often chaotic and changing lives is difficult, yet adherence holds the key to survival, so psychologists will be heavily involved in the effort to help people with AIDS adhere faithfully to the medication regimen.

to adherence. In contrast, people who enjoy the activities in their lives are more motivated to adhere to treatment (Irvine et al., 1999). Adherence is substantially higher in patients who live in cohesive families but lower with patients whose families are in conflict (DiMatteo, 2004). Likewise, people who are depressed show poor adherence to treatment medication (DiMatteo, Lepper, & Croghan, 2000).

Creative Nonadherence   One especially interesting form of nonadherence is termed **creative nonadherence,** or intelligent nonadherence, because it involves modifying and supplementing a prescribed

treatment regimen. For example, a poor patient may change the dosage level of required medication to make the medicine last as long as possible or may keep some medication in reserve in case another family member comes down with the same disorder. Creative nonadherence may also be a response to concerns or confusion over the treatment regimen. Not understanding the dosage level may lead some people not to take any at all in the fear that they will overmedicate. Others may stop a medication because of unpleasant side effects. One study of nonadherence among the elderly estimated that 73% of nonadherence was intentional rather than accidental (J. K. Cooper, Love, & Raffoul, 1982).

TABLE 9.2 | Some Determinants of Adherence to Treatment Regimens and Care

	Following Prescribed Regimen	Staying in Treatment
Social Characteristics		
Age	0	+
Sex	0	0
Education	0	0
Income	0	0
Psychological Dispositions		
Beliefs about threat to health	+	+
Beliefs about efficacy of action	+	+
Knowledge of recommendation and purpose	+	+
General attitudes toward medical care	0	0
General knowledge about health and illness	0	0
Intelligence	0	0
Anxiety	−?	−
Internal control	0?	0
Psychic disturbance	−	2
Social Context		
Social support	+	+
Social isolation	−	−
Primary group stability	+	+
Situational Demands		
Symptoms	+	+
Complexity of action	−	−
Duration of action	−	−
Interference with other actions	−	−
Interactions with Health Care System		
Convenience factors	+	+
Continuity of care	+	+
Personal source of care	+	+
General satisfaction	0	0
Supportive interaction	+	+

Table entries indicate whether a factor encourages compliance (+), works against it (−), has no impact (0), or has uncertain impact (?).

Source: Adapted from Kirscht & Rosenstock, 1979, p. 215.

Creative nonadherence can also result from private theories about a disorder and its treatment (Wroe, 2001). For example, patients may decide that particular symptoms that merit treatment were ignored by the provider; they may then supplement the treatment regimen with over-the-counter preparations or home remedies that interact with prescribed drugs in unpredictable, even dangerous ways. Alternatively, the patient may alter the dosage requirement, reasoning, for example, that if four pills a day for 10 days will clear up the problem, eight pills a day for 5 days will do it twice as quickly. One motive for this potentially risky behavior may be to

overcome the sense of loss of control that illness and its treatment brings (Turk & Meichenbaum, 1991). Non-adherence, then, is a widespread and complex behavior. Some of the contributing factors are listed in table 9.2.

Patient-Provider Communication and Malpractice Litigation

Dissatisfaction and nonadherence are not the only problematic outcomes of poor patient-provider communication. Malpractice suits are another. Once rare, the number of malpractice suits has exploded over the past decades. Some of this malpractice litigation can be tied to increases in the technical complexity of medicine. The overuse of new and complex machinery can lead to patient harm, either because the treatment is not necessary or because the side effects of the technology are not known. A 1999 report by the Institute of Medicine estimated that between 48,000 and 98,000 errors occurred every year and that most of these are medication errors, such as giving the wrong drug or wrong dosage (Institute of Medicine, 1999). Malpractice litigation has also been tied to the administrative complexity of the health care system. Patients may be unwilling to sue an individual physician, but if they can sue an institution and convince themselves that the settlement money will never be missed, they are more likely to sue (Halberstam, 1971).

Although the most common grounds for a malpractice suit continue to be incompetence and negligence, patients are increasingly citing factors related to poor communication as a basis for their suits, such as not being fully informed about a treatment. Studies designed to unearth the causes of discretionary malpractice litigation confirmed the importance of communication factors. The research found that more suits were initiated against physicians who were fearful of patients, insecure with them, or derogatory in their manner toward them. When patients felt their medical complaints had been ignored or rudely dismissed, they were more likely to file suit, perhaps as retaliation against the rude treatment. According to a health care negotiator, patients are seeking three things when a medical mistake has occurred:

1. They want to find out what happened.
2. They want an apology from the doctor or hospital.
3. They want to know that the mistake will not happen again (Reitman, 2003a).

An explanation, apology, and reassurance can go some way in muting the effects of malpractice. In a study designed to test this point, 958 members of a health maintenance organization were given a fictitious situation involving a doctor who made a mistake with varying consequences and then disclosed it with varying degrees of candor. For example, in one situation the doctor prescribed a drug without asking the patient whether he or she had allergies, and the patient suffered a reaction as a result. In another case the doctor prescribed a drug to an elderly patient that affected balance, and the patient subsequently fell. In some cases the doctor apologized unreservedly ("this was my mistake and I feel terrible"), whereas in other cases the doctor was

more evasive ("it is an unfortunate thing that happens every now and then"). Patients were then asked what they thought they would do in response to such a circumstance, namely, staying with the doctor, changing doctors, or talking with an attorney. On the whole, the physician was viewed more favorably when he admitted to making the mistake (Mazor et al., 2004).

The long-term fallout from the escalating frequency and costs of malpractice suits are that many physicians have to change the way they conduct their practices, and others have had to leave medicine altogether. For example, malpractice premiums are so high for obstetricians that some have decided to move to other specialties where malpractice insurance is lower (Eisenberg & Sieger, 2003).

■ IMPROVING PATIENT-PROVIDER COMMUNICATION AND REDUCING NONADHERENCE

The fact that poor patient-provider communication appears to be so widespread and tied to problematic outcomes suggests that improving the communication process should be a high priority. One attack on the problem is to teach providers how to communicate more effectively.

Teaching Providers How to Communicate

Providers have known for some time that the course of medical treatment can be affected by communication (see, for example, Shattuck, 1907), yet many may see communication as a knack that some people have and others do not. However, efforts to identify the personalities of physicians who communicate effectively have revealed only one reliable predictor of physician sensitivity: the physician's reported interest in people. This fact suggests that physician sensitivity is more a matter of motivation than skill; hence, anyone, given the desire, has the potential to be an effective communicator.

Training Providers   Talking to patients takes time. With pressures toward cost-effective treatment in mind, what constitutes realistic training in communication skills? "Patient-centered communication" is an important way to improve the patient-provider dialogue. This type of communication enlists the patient directly in decisions about medical care: Physicians try to see the disorder and the treatment as the patient does, and in so doing enlist the patient's cooperation in the diagnostic and treatment process. Not only is this approach successful in improving doctor-patient communication, it seems to be especially effective with "difficult" patients, such as those who are high in anxiety (M. Sharpe et al., 1994; Langewitz, Eich, Kiss, & Wossmer, 1998).

Any communication program should teach skills that can be learned easily; that can be incorporated in medical routines easily; and that, over time, come to be automatic. For example, many communication failures in medical settings stem from violation of simple rules of courtesy. These rules can be incorporated into the provider's behavior with a minimum of effort and are as follows: greeting patients, addressing them by name, telling them where they can hang up their clothes if an examination is necessary, explaining the purpose of a procedure while it is going on, saying goodbye, and, again, using the patient's name. Such simple behaviors add a few seconds at most to a visit, yet they are seen as warm and supportive (DiMatteo & DiNicola, 1982).

Communication courses should also be taught in settings that mirror the situations in which the skills will later be used. Training that uses direct, supervised contact with patients and gives students immediate feedback after a patient interview works well for training both medical and nursing students (for example, H. Leigh & Reiser, 1986). Many courses include videotaping the student's interactions with patients so that good and bad points in the interview can be pointed out (for example, Levenkron, Greenland, & Bowlby, 1987). Specially made tapes that illustrate common problems can be used so that students can see both the right and the wrong ways to handle them (see, for example, Jason, Kagan, Werner, Elstein, & Thomas, 1971; Kagan, 1974).

Nonverbal communication can create an atmosphere of warmth or coldness. A forward lean and direct eye contact, for example, can reinforce an atmosphere of supportiveness, whereas a backward lean, little eye contact, and a postural orientation away from the patient can undercut verbal efforts at warmth by suggesting distance or discomfort (DiMatteo, Friedman, & Taranta, 1979). The ability to understand what patients' nonverbal behaviors may mean can also be associated with better communication and adherence (DiMatteo, Hays, & Prince, 1986).

Once these basic skills are learned, they should be practiced so that they come automatically to the provider. At this point, too, more complex material may be introduced, such as how to draw out a reticent patient, how to deal with a patient's guilt or shame over particular symptoms, and how to learn what a symptom means to the patient so as to better understand the patient's reaction to it.

Training Patients   Interventions to improve patient-provider interaction include teaching patients skills for eliciting information from physicians (Greenfield, Kaplan, Ware, Yano, & Frank, 1988). For example, a study by S. C. Thompson, Nanni, and Schwankovsky (1990) instructed women to list three questions they wanted to ask their physician during their visit. Compared with a control group, women who listed questions in advance asked more questions during the visit and were less anxious. In a second study, Thompson and her colleagues added a third condition: Some women received a message from their physician encouraging question asking. These women, too, asked more of the questions they wanted to, had greater feelings of personal control, and were more satisfied with the office visit. This pair of studies suggests that either thinking up one's own questions ahead of time or perceiving that the physician is open to questions improves communication during medical office visits, leading to greater patient satisfaction.

Reducing Nonadherence

Reducing nonadherence is important, made all the more so as research increasingly reveals the importance of lifestyle change to promote health and avoid illness. Counseling patients on issues related to health promotion and health habit modification are activities physicians have traditionally not had to undertake, but increasingly they are urged to do so (Wechsler, Levine, Idelson, Rothman, & Taylor, 1983). Because lifestyle changes are the very behaviors that show low levels of adherence, teaching physicians to communicate effectively to increase treatment adherence has become a critical goal. Strategies for reducing nonadherence are many and varied (Roter et al., 1998).

Health Care Institution Interventions   Several interventions at the institutional level can foster adherence. Postcard reminders or telephone calls to patients reminding them to return can reduce high rates of no-shows (Friman, Finney, Glasscock, Weigel, & Christopherson, 1986). Reducing the amount of time a patient must wait before receiving service also improves the rate of following through on appointments (P. D. Mullen & Green, 1985). Although some research has used incen-

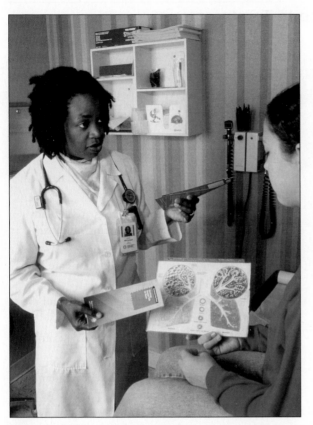

When physicians present concrete advice about lifestyle change, patients are more likely to adhere.

TABLE 9.3 | Why the Health Practitioner Can Be an Effective Agent of Behavior Change

- The health practitioner is a highly credible source with knowledge of medical issues.
- The health practitioner can make health messages simple and tailor them to the individual needs and vulnerabilities of each patient.
- The practitioner can help the patient decide to adhere by highlighting the advantages of treatment and the disadvantages of nonadherence.
- The private face-to-face nature of the interaction provides an effective setting for holding attention, repeating and clarifying instructions, extracting commitments from a patient, and assessing sources of resistance to adherence.
- The personal nature of the interaction enables a practitioner to establish referent power by communicating warmth and caring.
- The health practitioner can enlist the cooperation of other family members in promoting adherence.
- The health practitioner has the patient under at least partial surveillance and can monitor progress during subsequent visits.

tives, such as money, to get patients to show up, these techniques may backfire; once incentives are removed, patients may be even less likely to keep their appointments (Finney, Lemanek, Brophy, & Cataldo, 1990).

Treatment Presentation Interventions   The presentation of the treatment regimen can also influence adherence. Treatment recommendations should be written down and the patient should be tested for understanding and recall. Giving the patient a medication information sheet that describes the treatment, the dosage level of medication, and possible side effects can also improve compliance (Peck & King, 1982). Take-home pill calendars, special pill packaging designed to aid recall, and pill containers with time-alarm buzzers are also helpful devices (R. B. Haynes, 1979b).

Skills Training   As has been noted, nonadherence is also tied to provider communication skills. Box 9.4 summarizes the specific steps that should be incorporated into communication efforts to help patients com-

ply with medical advice. The provider's personal authority can also be used to instill compliance once the foundations for effective communication have been laid. Providers, especially physicians, are high-status figures for most patients, and what they say is generally accepted as valid. Accordingly, the information about the disorder and recommendations for treatment have high credibility. The provider is in a position to underscore the patient's personal vulnerability to the disorder: He or she has intimate personal knowledge of the patient. The provider can help the patient decide to adhere to a medical treatment regimen by highlighting its advantages, downplaying attendant disadvantages, and stressing the disadvantages of nonadherence (J. H. Brown & Raven, 1994). Reasons the health provider can change patients' health behaviors are listed in table 9.3.

Probing for Barriers   The provider can also probe for potential barriers to adherence. Patients are remarkably good at predicting how compliant they will be with treatment regimens (R. M. Kaplan & Simon, 1990). By making use of this personal knowledge, the physician may discover what some of the barriers to adherence will be. For example, if the patient has been told to avoid stressful situations but anticipates several high-pressure meetings the following week at work, the patient and provider together might consider how to resolve this

BOX 9.4

Improving Adherence to Treatment

Nonadherence to treatment is a formidable medical problem, and many of the reasons can be traced directly to poor communication between the provider and the patient. The following are some guidelines generated by research findings that can help improve adherence.

1. Listen to the patient.
2. Ask the patient to repeat what has to be done.
3. Keep the prescription as simple as possible.
4. Give clear instructions on the exact treatment regimen, preferably in writing.
5. Make use of special reminder pill containers and calendars.
6. Call the patient if an appointment is missed.
7. Prescribe a self-care regimen in concert with the patient's daily schedule.
8. Emphasize at each visit the importance of adherence.
9. Gear the frequency of visits to adherence needs.
10. Acknowledge at each visit the patient's efforts to adhere.
11. Involve the patient's spouse or other partner.
12. Whenever possible, provide patients with instructions and advice at the start of the information to be presented.
13. When providing patients with instructions and advice, stress how important they are.
14. Use short words and short sentences.
15. Use explicit categorization where possible. (For example, divide information clearly into categories of etiology, treatment, or prognosis.)
16. Repeat things, where feasible.
17. When giving advice, make it as specific, detailed, and concrete as possible.
18. Find out what the patient's worries are. Do not confine yourself merely to gathering objective medical information.
19. Find out what the patient's expectations are. If they cannot be met, explain why.
20. Provide information about the diagnosis and the cause of the illness.
21. Adopt a friendly rather than a businesslike attitude.
22. Avoid medical jargon.
23. Spend some time in conversation about nonmedical topics.

Source: Based on R. B. Haynes, Wang, & da-Mota-Gomes, 1987; Ley, 1977; DiMatteo, 2004.

---

dilemma—one option may be to have a coworker take the patient's place at some of the meetings.

For the vocational and social advice on which nonadherence rates are known to be high, special measures are needed. The health care provider can begin by explaining why these seemingly nonmedical aspects of the treatment regimen are, in fact, important to health. For example, the benefits of regular exercise can be concretely explained. Finally, because of the face-to-face nature of patient-provider interaction, the provider may be in a good position to extract a commitment from the patient—that is, a promise that the recommendations will be undertaken and followed through. Such verbal commitments are associated with increased adherence (Kulik & Carlino, 1987).

Breaking advice down into manageable subgoals that can be monitored by the provider is another way to increase adherence. For example, if patients have been told to alter their diet and lose weight, intermediate weight-loss goals that can be checked at successive appointments might be established (for example, "Try to lose 3 pounds this week").

The importance of the physician's recommendation should not be underestimated. When lifestyle change programs are "prescribed" for patients by physicians, patients show higher rates of adherence than if they are simply urged to make use of them (Kabat-Zinn & Chapman-Waldrop, 1988).

In short, then, adherence is a formidable issue that can be attacked on several fronts simultaneously. Modifying institutional procedures for following patients, presenting the treatment regimen clearly, and increasing the skill of the practitioner in communicating with the patient all have potential for increasing adherence.

This 16th-century woodcut shows the preparation of theriac, a supposed antidote to poison. If theriac was a successful treatment, it was entirely due to the placebo effect.

■ PLACEBO AS A HEALER

- Inhaling a useless drug improved lung function in children with asthma by 33%.

- People exposed to fake poison ivy develop rashes.

- Forty-two percent of balding men taking a placebo maintained or increased their hair growth.

- Sham knee surgery reduces pain as much as real surgery. (Blakeslee, 1998)

All of these astonishing facts are due to one effect—the placebo.

Historical Perspective

In the early days of medicine, few drugs or treatments gave any real physical benefit. As a consequence, patients were treated with a variety of bizarre, largely ineffective therapies. Egyptian patients were medicated with "lizard's blood, crocodile dung, the teeth of a swine, the hoof of an ass, putrid meat, and fly specks" (T. Findley, 1953), concoctions that were not only ineffective but dangerous. If the patient did not succumb to the disease, he or she had a good chance of dying from the treatment. Medical treatments of the Middle Ages were somewhat less lethal, but not much more effective. These European patients were treated with ground-up

"unicorn's horn" (actually, ground ivory); bezoar stones (supposedly a "crystallized tear from the eye of a deer bitten by a snake" but actually an animal gallstone or other intestinal piece); theriac (made from ground-up snake and between 37 and 63 equally exotic ingredients); and, for healing wounds, powdered Egyptian mummy (A. K. Shapiro, 1960).

In some cases, a clear, if somewhat naïve, logic was present in these treatments. For example, consumption (tuberculosis of the lung, which is marked by short-windedness) was treated with ground-up fox lung because the fox is a long-winded animal. As late as the 17th and 18th centuries, patients were subjected to bloodletting, freezing, and repeatedly induced vomiting to bring about a cure (A. K. Shapiro, 1960).

Such accounts make it seem miraculous that anyone survived these early medical treatments. But people did; moreover, they often seemed to get relief from these peculiar and largely ineffective remedies. Physicians have, for centuries, been objects of great veneration and respect, and this was no less true when few remedies were actually effective. To what can one attribute the success that these treatments provided? The most likely answer is that these treatments are examples of the **placebo effect.** Placebo effects continue to be powerful today, even though medicine now boasts a large number of truly effective treatments.

What Is a Placebo?

A **placebo** is "any medical procedure that produces an effect in a patient because of its therapeutic intent and not its specific nature, whether chemical or physical" (R. Liberman, 1962, p. 761). The word comes originally from Latin, meaning "I will please." Any medical procedure, ranging from drugs to surgery to psychotherapy, can have a placebo effect. The role of placebos in reducing pain and discomfort is substantial. Many patients who ingest useless substances or who undergo useless procedures find that, as a result, their symptoms disappear and their health improves.

Moreover, placebo effects extend well beyond the beneficial results of ineffective substances. Much of the effectiveness of active treatments that produce real cures on their own include a placebo component. For example, in one study (Beecher, 1959), patients complaining of pain were injected with either morphine or a placebo. Although morphine was substantially more effective in reducing pain than was the placebo, the placebo was a successful painkiller in 35% of the cases. Another study

Cancer and the Placebo Effect

A dramatic example of the efficacy of the placebo effect is provided by the case history of a cancer patient, Mr. Wright. The patient thought he was being given injections of a controversial drug, Krebiozen, about which his physician was highly enthusiastic. In fact, knowing that Krebiozen was not an effective treatment, the physician gave Mr. Wright daily injections of nothing but fresh water. The effects were astonishing:

> Tumor masses melted. Chest fluid vanished. He became ambulatory and even went back to flying again. At this time he was certainly the picture of health. The water

injections were continued since they worked such wonders. He then remained symptom-free for over two months. At this time the final AMA announcement appeared in the press—"Nationwide Tests Show Krebiozen to Be a Worthless Drug in Treatment of Cancer."

Within a few days of this report, Mr. Wright was readmitted to the hospital in extremis; his faith was now gone, his last hope vanished, and he succumbed in less than 2 days.

Source: Klopfer, 1959, p. 339.

---

demonstrated that morphine loses as much as 25% of its effectiveness in reducing pain when patients do not know they have been injected with a painkiller and are therefore not preset to experience the drug's effects. In summarizing placebo effects, A. K. Shapiro (1964) stated:

> Placebos can be more powerful than, and reverse the action of, potent active drugs . . . The incidence of placebo reactions approaches 100% in some studies. Placebos can have profound effects on organic illnesses, including incurable malignancies . . . Placebos can mimic the effects usually thought to be the exclusive property of active drugs. (p. 74)

How does a placebo work? The placebo effect is not purely psychological, as stereotypes would have us believe. That is, people do not get better only because they *think* they are going to get better, although expectations of success play an important role (Stewart-Williams, 2004). The placebo response is a complex, psychologically mediated chain of events that often has physiological effects. For example, if the placebo reduces anxiety, then activation of stress systems may be reduced, thus increasing the body's ability to recover from illness. Placebos may also work in part by stimulating the release of opioids, the body's natural pain killers (J. D. Levine, Gordon, & Fields, 1978). Exciting new research that examines brain activity using fMRI technology reveals that when patients report reduced pain after taking a placebo, they also show decreased activity in pain-sensitive regions of the brain (Wager et al., 2004). Evidence like this suggests that placebos may work via some of the same biological pathways that account for the effects of "real"

treatments (Lieberman et al., 2004; Petrovic, Kalso, Peterson, & Ingvar, 2002). Box 9.5 describes a case of a successful placebo effect with a cancer patient.

In some cases, a placebo produces an apparently successful recovery, whereas in other cases it has no effect. What factors determine when placebos are most effective?

Provider Behavior and Placebo Effects

The effectiveness of a placebo varies, depending on how a provider interacts with the patient and how much the provider seems to believe in the curative powers of the treatment being offered. Providers who exude warmth, confidence, and empathy get stronger placebo effects than do more remote and formal providers. Placebo effects are also strengthened when the provider radiates competence and provides reassurance to the patient that the condition will improve. Taking time with patients and not rushing them strengthens placebo effects (R. Liberman, 1962; A. K. Shapiro, 1964).

The provider's faith in the treatment increases the effectiveness of placebos (A. H. Roberts, Kewman, Mercier, & Hovell, 1993). Signs of doubt or skepticism may be communicated subtly, even nonverbally, to a patient, and these signs will reduce the effect. Even clearly effective drugs will lose much of their effectiveness when providers express doubt over their effectiveness. In one study, for example, patients were given chlorpromazine (a tranquilizer commonly used with psychiatric patients) by a provider who either expressed great confidence in its effectiveness or who voiced some doubt as to its ability to reduce symptoms. This usually effective drug's actual effectiveness dropped from 77 to 10% when the provider was doubtful regarding its effectiveness (P. E. Feldman, 1956; see also Volgyesi, 1954).

Patient Characteristics and Placebo Effects

Although there is no placebo-prone personality, some types of patients show stronger placebo effects than others. People who have a high need for approval (R. Liberman, 1962), who have low self-esteem, who are externally oriented toward their environment, and who are persuasible in other contexts show somewhat stronger placebo effects. Anxious people show stronger placebo effects. This effect seems to result less from personality, however, than from the fact that anxiety produces physical symptoms, including distractibility, racing heart, sweaty palms, nervousness, and difficulty sleeping. When a placebo is administered, anxiety may be reduced, and this overlay of anxiety-related symptoms may disappear (A. K. Shapiro, 1964; see also T. R. Sharpe, Smith, & Barbre, 1985).

Despite the fact that some personality differences do predict placebo effects, these findings must be set in the context of many dozens of studies that have failed to show effects. Sex, age, hypochondriasis (the tendency to report physical symptoms), dependency, and general neuroticism do not discriminate those who show placebo effects from those who do not. Likewise, results on personality tests, such as the MMPI or the Rorschach (inkblot) test, do not predict who will show a placebo response (for reviews, see R. Liberman, 1962; A. K. Shapiro, 1964).

Patient-Provider Communication and Placebo Effects

As noted in this chapter, good communication between provider and patient is essential if patients are to follow through successfully on their prescribed treatment regimens. This point is no less true for placebo responses. For patients to show a placebo response, they must understand what the treatment is supposed to do and what they need to do. When the provider-patient relationship is based on effective communication, placebo effects will be stronger.

Another aspect of the patient-provider relationship that enhances the placebo effect is the symbolic value the placebo may have for the patient. When patients seek medical treatment, they want an expert to tell them what is wrong and what to do about it. When a disorder is diagnosed and a treatment regimen is prescribed, however ineffective, the patient has tangible evidence that the provider knows what is wrong and that the provider has done something about it (A. K. Shapiro, 1964).

Situational Determinants of Placebo Effects

The characteristics of the placebo itself and the setting in which it is administered influence the strength of the placebo response. A setting that has the trappings of medical formality (medications, machines, uniformed personnel) will induce stronger placebo effects than will a less formal setting. If all the staff radiate as much faith in the treatment as the physician, placebo effects will be heightened.

The shape, size, color, taste, and quantity of the placebo also influences its effectiveness: The more a drug seems like medicine, the more effective it will be (A. K. Shapiro, 1964). Thus, for example, foul-tasting, peculiar-looking little pills that are taken in precise dosage ("take two" as opposed to "take two or three") and that are taken at prescribed intervals will show stronger placebo effects than will good-tasting, candy-like pills with dosage levels and intervals that are only roughly indicated ("take one anytime you feel discomfort"). Similarly, treatment regimens that seem medical and include precise instructions, medications, and the like will produce stronger placebo effects than will regimens that do not seem very medical; for example, exercise prescriptions and dietary restrictions show weaker placebo effects than do pills and other medications.

Social Norms and Placebo Effects

The placebo effect is facilitated by norms that surround treatment regimens—that is, the expected way in which treatment will be enacted. Drug taking is clearly a normative behavior (see T. R. Sharpe et al., 1985). In the United States, people spend more than $100 billion each year on prescription drugs (NIHCM, 2000). One study of a random sample of nonhospitalized adults found that 55% of them had taken some medication within the previous 24 hours, and 40% of them took some form of medication on a regular basis (Dunnell & Cartwright, 1972). A study of hospitalized patients found that the average patient was receiving 14 drugs simultaneously; one patient had received 32 drugs, and no patient had less than 6 (Dunlop, 1970, cited in Rachman & Phillips, 1978).

A large number of people are killed or seriously injured by overzealous drug taking. Drugs cause adverse side effects or disabilities in more than 770,000 Americans each year and cost hospitals at least $1.5 billion in longer hospital stays and other complications. The more general cost to society of adverse drug reactions is estimated to be $47 billion a year (Bales et al., 1997; Classen, Pestotnik, Evans, Lloyd, & Burke, 1997; Lesar, Briceland, & Stein, 1997). However, the drug-taking epidemic continues unabated. Clearly, there is enormous faith in medications, and the psychological if not the physical benefits can be quite substantial. Thus, placebos are effective in part because people believe that drugs work and because people have a great deal of experience in drug taking (A. H. Roberts et al., 1993).

Equally important is the fact that most people have no experience that disconfirms their drug taking. If one is ill, takes a drug, and subsequently gets better, as most of us do most of the time, one does not in reality know exactly what caused this result: A drug may be responsible; the disease may have run its course; or one's mood may have picked up, altering the body's physiological balance and making it no longer receptive to an invader. Probably a combination of factors is at work. Regardless of the actual cause of success, the patient acting as his or her own naïve physician will probably attribute success to whatever drug he or she took, however erroneous that conclusion may be.

Generalizability of Placebo Effects

As noted earlier, virtually any medical procedure can have placebo effects (N. E. Miller, 1989). For example, many surgical patients show improvement simply as a function of having had surgery and not as a result of the actual procedure employed (Stolberg, 1999a). Psychiatry and clinical psychology also show placebo effects; some patients feel better simply knowing that a psychiatrist or

psychologist has found a cause for their problems, even if this cause is not the real one. Adherence to a placebo can even be associated with lower death rates due to illness (Irvine et al., 1999).

The efficacy of the placebo should not be thought of as either a medical trick or a purely psychological response on the part of the patient. Placebo effects merit respect. The placebo achieves success in the absence of truly effective therapy (A. H. Roberts et al., 1993). It increases the efficacy of a therapy that has only modest effects of its own. It reduces substantial pain and discomfort. It is the foundation of most of early medicine's effectiveness, and it continues to account for many of medicine's effects today. Its continued success should be encouraged (N. E. Miller, 1989).

Placebo as a Methodological Tool

The placebo response is so powerful that no drug can be marketed in the United States unless it has been evaluated against a placebo. The standard method for so doing is termed a **double-blind experiment.** In such a test, a researcher gives half a group of patients a drug that is supposed to cure a disease or alleviate symptoms; the other half receives a placebo. The procedure is called double-blind because neither the researcher nor the patient knows whether the patient received the drug or the placebo; both are "blind" to the procedure. Once the effectiveness of the treatment has been measured, the researcher looks in the coded records to see which treatment the patient got. The difference between the effectiveness of the drug and the effectiveness of the placebo is considered to be a measure of the drug's effectiveness. Comparison of a drug against a placebo is essential for accurate measurement of a drug's success. Drugs may look four or five times more successful than they really are if there is no effort to evaluate them against a placebo (N. E. Miller, 1989; A. K. Shapiro, 1964). ●

SUMMARY

1. Patients evaluate their health care based more on the quality of the interaction they have with the provider than on the technical quality of care.

2. Many factors impede effective patient-provider communication. The office setting and the structure of the health care delivery system are often designed for efficient rather than warm and supportive health care. Pressures toward more humane health care treatment are fueled by movements toward holism and wellness.

3. Providers contribute to poor communication by not listening, using jargon-filled explanations, alternating between overly technical explanations and infantilizing baby talk, communicating negative mood or expectations, and depersonalizing the patient.

4. Patients contribute to poor communications by failing to learn details of their disorder and treatment, failing to give providers correct information, and failing to follow through on treatment recommendations. Patient anxiety, lack of education, lack of experience with the disorder, and incomplete information about symptoms interfere with effective communication as well.

5. Because the provider usually receives little feedback about whether the patient followed instructions or if the treatments were successful, it is difficult to identify and correct these problems in communication.

6. Communication is one of the main factors leading to high rates of nonadherence to treatment. Poor communication has also been related to the initiation of malpractice litigation.

7. Adherence is lower when recommendations do not seem medical, when lifestyle modification is needed, when complex self-care regimens are required, and when patients have private and conflicting theories about the nature of their illness or treatment.

8. Adherence is increased when patients have decided to adhere; when they feel the provider cares about them; when they understand what to do; and when they have received clear, written instructions.

9. Efforts to improve communication have included training in communication skills and taking full advantage of the provider's potent professional role, a movement termed patient-centered communication. Face-to-face communication with a physician can enhance adherence to treatment because of the personalized relationship that exists.

10. A placebo is any medical procedure that produces an effect in a patient because of its therapeutic intent and not its actual nature. Virtually every medical treatment shows some degree of placebo effect.

11. Placebo effects are enhanced when the physician shows faith in a treatment, the patient is preset to believe it will work, these expectations are successfully communicated, and the trappings of medical treatment are in place.

12. Placebos are also a useful methodological tool in evaluating drugs and other treatments.

KEY TERMS

adherence
creative nonadherence
double-blind experiment
health maintenance organization
  (HMO)

holistic health
managed care
nonadherence
nurse-practitioners

physicians' assistants
placebo
placebo effect
private, fee-for-service care

Pain and Its Management

Jesse woke up to the sun streaming in through the windows of his new home. It was his first apartment and, with a sigh of contentment, he reveled in the experience of finally being on his own. Yesterday had been a busy day. He and several of his friends had moved all the stuff he had accumulated from college up two flights of narrow stairs to his small but cozy new place. It had been a lot of work, but it had been fun. They'd had a few beers and some pizza afterward, and everyone went home tired and sore but contented.

As Jesse rolled over to admire his apartment, he experienced a sharp pain. Muttering an unprintable epithet to himself, he realized that his back had gone out on him. It must have been from carrying all those boxes. Slowly and carefully, he eased himself into a sitting, and then a standing, position. He was definitely stiff, probably aggravated by the injuries he had acquired during years of football. It was not the first time he had had this experience, and he knew that over-the-counter painkillers and moving around would help him feel better as long as he did not exert himself too much that day.

Jesse is fortunate because he is young and his pain is only short term in response to the exertion of carrying boxes and using muscles not accustomed to regular use.

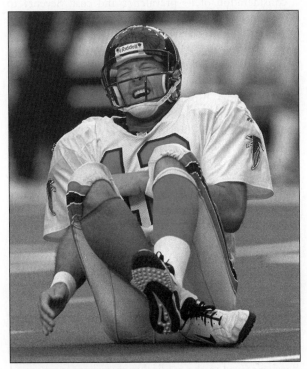

Pain is a valuable cue that tissue damage has occurred and activities must be curtailed.

For many people, though, the kind of experience that Jesse has is a chronic one—that is, long term, painful, and difficult to treat. In fact, chronic back pain is one of the most common causes of disability in this country, and large numbers of middle-aged and older Americans deal with back pain on a daily or intermittent basis. Even his short-term experience leads Jesse to realize that he has to moderate his physical activity the following day.

Chronic pain lasting at least 6 months or longer affects between 30 and 50 million people in the United States. Costs in disability and lost productivity add up to more than $100 billion annually (Thernstrom, 2001). Indeed, pain typically leads people to change their activity level and other aspects of their behavior. As this chapter explains, such pain behaviors are an important component of the pain experience. Jesse is annoyed with himself for not taking basic precautions in lifting and carrying that might have spared him this agony. For people who experience chronic pain, the emotional reactions are more likely to be anxiety and depression. As we will see, emotional reactions to pain are also integral to the pain experience (Severijns, Vlaeyen, Van den Hout, & Picavet, 2004).

■ SIGNIFICANCE OF PAIN

On the surface, the significance of pain would seem to be obvious. Pain hurts, and it can be so insistent that it overwhelms other, basic needs. But the significance of pain goes far beyond the disruption it produces. Pain is significant for managing daily activities. Although we normally think of pain as an unusual occurrence, we live with minor pains all the time. These pains are critical for survival because they provide low-level feedback about the functioning of our bodily systems, feedback that we then use, often unconsciously, as a basis for making minor adjustments, such as shifting our posture, rolling over while asleep, or crossing and uncrossing our legs.

Pain also has important medical consequences. It is the symptom most likely to lead an individual to seek treatment (see chapter 8). Unfortunately, though, the relationship between pain and severity of an underlying problem can be weak. For example, a cancerous lump rarely produces pain, at least in its early stages, yet it is of great medical importance.

Pain is also medically significant because it can be a source of misunderstanding between a patient and the medical provider. From the patient's standpoint, pain may be the problem. To the provider, in contrast, pain is a by-product of a disorder. In fact, pain is often considered by practitioners to be so unimportant that many

At least $532 million is spent annually in the United States on over-the-counter remedies to reduce the temporary pain of minor disorders.

medical schools have virtually no systematic coverage of pain management in their curriculum. One student, reporting on his medical school experience, stated that pain had been mentioned exactly four times in the entire 4-year curriculum, and only one lecture had even a portion of its content devoted to pain management.

Although the practitioner focuses attention on symptoms, which, from a medical standpoint, may be more meaningful, the patient may feel that an important problem is not getting sufficient attention. As we saw in chapter 9, patients may choose not to comply with their physician's recommendations if they feel they have been misdiagnosed or if their chief symptoms have been ignored.

Pain has psychological as well as medical significance (Keefe et al., 2002). For example, both depression and anxiety worsen the experience of pain (for example, Vowels, Zvolensky, Gross, & Sperry, 2004). When patients are asked what they fear most about illness and its treatment, the common response is pain. The dread of not being able to reduce one's own suffering arouses more anxiety than the prospect of surgery, the loss of a limb, or even death. In fact, inadequate relief from pain is the most common reason for patients' requests for euthanasia or assisted suicide (Cherny, 1996).

No introduction to pain would be complete without a consideration of its prevalence and cost. Seventy to 85% of people in the United States suffer from back pain at some time in their life, 40 million people suffer from daily arthritis pain, 45 million have chronic headaches, and the majority of patients in intermediate or advanced stages of cancer suffer moderate to severe pain (University of Alabama, Birmingham Health System, 2004). At least $532 million is spent every year on over-the-counter drugs (ABC News, 2004). The worldwide pain management prescription drug market totaled approximately $24 billion in 2002 and is projected to surpass $30 billion by 2006 (Global Information Inc., 2003). The pain business is big business, reflecting the chronic and temporary suffering that millions of people experience.

■ ELUSIVE NATURE OF PAIN

Pain has been one of the more mysterious and elusive aspects of illness and its treatment. It is fundamentally a psychological experience, and the degree to which it is felt and how incapacitating it is depend in large part on how it is interpreted. Howard Beecher, a physician, was one of the first to recognize this (1959). During World War II, Beecher served in the medical corps, where he observed

BOX 10.1

A Cross-Cultural Perspective on Pain

THE CHILDBIRTH EXPERIENCE

Although babies are born in every society, the childbirth experience varies dramatically from culture to culture, and so does the experience of pain associated with it. Among Mexican women, for example, the word for labor ("dolor") means sorrow or pain, and the expectation of giving birth can produce a great deal of fear. This fear and the anticipation of pain can lead to a more painful experience with more complications than is true for women who do not bring these fears and expectations to the birthing experience (Scrimshaw, Engle, & Zambrana, 1983).

In stark contrast is the culture of Yap in the South Pacific, where childbirth is treated as an everyday occurrence. Women in Yap perform their normal activities until they begin labor, at which time they retire to a childbirth hut to give birth with the aid of perhaps one or two other women. Following the birth, there is a brief period of rest, after which the woman again resumes her activities. Problematic labors and complications during pregnancy are reported to be low (Kroeber, 1948).

There is no simple and direct relationship between expectations about pain and the childbirth experience, but expectations do play an important role in how labor

The meaning attached to an experience substantially determines whether it is perceived as painful. For many women, the joy of childbirth can mute the pain associated with the experience.

is experienced. Cultural lore and customs are a significant source of these expectations.

The meaning attached to an experience substantially determines whether it is perceived as painful. For many women, the joy of childbirth can mute the pain associated with the experience.

many wartime injuries. In treating the soldiers, he noticed a curious fact: Only one quarter of them requested morphine (a widely used painkiller) for what were often severe and very likely to be painful wounds. When Beecher returned to his Boston civilian practice, he often treated patients who sustained comparable injuries from surgery. However, in contrast to the soldiers, 80% of the civilians appeared to be in substantial pain and demanded painkillers. To make sense of this apparent discrepancy, Beecher concluded that the meaning attached to pain substantially determines how it is experienced. For the soldier, an injury meant that he was alive and was likely to be sent home. For the civilian, the injury represented an unwelcome interruption of valued activities.

Pain is also heavily influenced by the context in which it is experienced. Sports lore is full of accounts of athletes who have injured themselves on the playing field but stayed in the game, apparently oblivious to their pain. Such action may occur because sympathetic arousal, as it occurs in response to vigorous sports, seems to diminish pain sensitivity (Fillingham & Maixner,

1996; Zillman, de Wied, King-Jablonski, & Jenzowsky, 1996). In contrast, stress and psychological distress may aggravate the experience of pain (for example, L. Porter et al., 1998). In addition, shut-ins who have little to occupy their time other than minding their aches and pains may feel each one acutely (Pennebaker, 1983).

Pain has a substantial cultural component. Although there are no ethnic or racial differences in the ability to discriminate painful stimuli, members of some cultures report pain sooner and react more intensely to it than individuals of other cultures (Edwards & Fillingham, 1999; Zatzick & Dimsdale, 1990). These ethnic and cultural differences may derive both from differences in cultural norms regarding the expression of pain and in some cases from different pain mechanisms (Sheffield, Biles, Orom, Maixner, & Sheps, 2000). An example of these kinds of cultural differences appears in box 10.1. There are also gender differences in the experience of pain as well, with women typically showing greater sensitivity to pain (C. D. Myers, Robinson, Riley, & Sheffield, 2001; Lowery, Fillingim, & Wright, 2003).

Measuring Pain

One barrier to the treatment of pain is the difficulty people have describing it objectively. If you have a lump, you can point to it, or if a bone is broken, it can be seen in an X ray. Pain does not have these objective referents.

Verbal Reports   One solution to measuring pain is to draw on the large, informal vocabulary that people use for describing pain. Medical practitioners usually use this source of information in trying to understand patients' complaints. A throbbing pain, for example, has different implications than does a shooting pain or a constant, dull ache.

Other researchers have developed pain questionnaires (for example, Osman, Breitenstein, Barroos, Gutierrez, & Kopper, 2002) (see figure 10.1). Such measures typically provide indications of the nature of pain, such as whether it is throbbing or shooting, as well as its intensity (Dar, Leventhal, & Leventhal, 1993; Fernandez & Turk, 1992). Measures have also been developed to address the psychosocial components of pain, such as the fear it causes or the degree to which it has been catastrophized (Osman et al., 2000). Combinations of measures like these can help those who treat pain patients get a full picture of all the dimensions of a patient's pain.

Pain Behavior   Other measures of pain have focused on **pain behaviors.** Pain behaviors are behaviors that arise as manifestations of chronic pain, such as distortions in posture or gait, facial and audible expressions of distress, and avoidance of activity (Turk, Wack, & Kerns, 1995). Analyses of pain behaviors provide a basis for assessing how pain has disrupted the life of particular patients or groups of patients, distinguishing, for example, between how people manage lower back pain versus chronic headaches.

Because pain behavior is observable and measurable, the focus on pain behaviors has helped define the characteristics of different kinds of pain syndromes. Pain is now viewed as a complex biopsychosocial event involving psychological, behavioral, and physiological components (Kroner-Herwig et al., 1996).

Physiology of Pain

The view of pain as having psychological, behavioral, and sensory components is useful for making sense of the manifold pathways and receptors involved in the pain experience.

Overview   The experience of pain is a protective mechanism to bring into consciousness the awareness of tissue damage. At the time of the pain experience, however, it is unlikely to feel very protective. Unlike other bodily sensations, the experience of pain is accompanied by motivational and behavioral responses, such as withdrawal and intense emotional reactions, such as crying or fear. These experiences are an integral part of the pain experience and thus become important in its diagnosis and treatment.

Scientists have distinguished among three kinds of pain perception. The first is mechanical **nociception** (pain perception) that results from mechanical damage to the tissue of the body. The second is thermal damage, or the experience of pain due to temperature exposure. The third is referred to as polymodal nociception, a general category referring to pain that triggers chemical reactions from tissue damage.

Nociceptors in the peripheral nerves first sense injury and, in response, release chemical messengers, which are conducted to the spinal cord, where they are passed directly to the reticular formation and thalamus and into the cerebral cortex. These regions of the brain, in turn, identify the site of the injury and send messages back down the spinal column, which lead to muscle contractions, which can help block the pain and changes in other bodily functions, such as breathing.

Two major types of peripheral nerve fibers are involved in nociception. A-delta fibers are small, myelinated fibers that transmit sharp pain. They respond especially to mechanical or thermal pain, transmitting sharp brief pains rapidly. C-fibers are unmyelinated nerve fibers, involved in polymodal pain, that transmit dull or aching pain. (Myelination increases the speed of transmission, so sudden and intense pain is more rapidly conducted to the cerebral cortex than is the slower, dull, aching pain of the C-fibers.)

Peripheral nerve fibers enter the spinal column at the dorsal horn. Sensory aspects of pain are heavily determined by activity in the A-delta fibers, which project onto areas in the thalamus and the sensory areas of the cerebral cortex.

The motivational and affective elements of pain appear to be influenced more strongly by the C-fibers, which project onto different thalamic, hypothalamic, and cortical areas. The experience of pain, then, is determined by the balance of activity in these nerve fibers, which reflects the pattern and intensity of stimulation.

Neurotransmitters also affect the transmission of pain. In particular, Substance P and glutamate appear to

FIGURE 10.1 | The McGill Pain Questionnaire

Patient's name _____   Date _____   Time _____   A.M./P.M.

| 1 Flickering —
  Quivering —
  Pulsing —
  Throbbing —
  Beating —
  Pounding — | 11 Tiring —
   Exhausting —
12 Sickening —
   Suffocating — | Brief —
Momentary —
Transient — | Rhythmic —
Periodic —
Intermittent — | Continuous —
Steady —
Constant — |

1 Flickering —
  Quivering —
  Pulsing —
  Throbbing —
  Beating —
  Pounding —
2 Jumping —
  Flashing —
  Shooting —
3 Pricking —
  Boring —
  Drilling —
  Stabbing —
  Lancinating —
4 Sharp —
  Cutting —
  Lacerating —
5 Pinching —
  Pressing —
  Gnawing —
  Cramping —
  Crushing —
6 Tugging —
  Pulling —
  Wrenching —
7 Hot —
  Burning —
  Scalding —
  Searing —
8 Tingling —
  Itchy —
  Smarting —
  Stinging —
9 Dull —
  Sore —
  Hurting —
  Aching —
  Heavy —
10 Tender —
   Taut —
   Rasping —
   Splitting —

11 Tiring —
   Exhausting —
12 Sickening —
   Suffocating —
13 Fearful —
   Frightful —
   Terrifying —
14 Punishing —
   Grueling —
   Cruel —
   Vicious —
   Killing —
15 Wretched —
   Blinding —
16 Annoying —
   Troublesome —
   Miserable —
   Intense —
   Unbearable —
17 Spreading —
   Radiating —
   Penetrating —
   Piercing —
18 Tight —
   Numb —
   Drawing —
   Squeezing —
   Tearing —
19 Cool —
   Cold —
   Freezing —
20 Nagging —
   Nauseating —
   Agonizing —
   Dreadful —
   Torturing —
   PPI
0 No pain —
1 Mild —
2 Discomforting —
3 Distressing —
4 Horrible —
5 Excruciating —

E = External
I = Internal

Comments:

be implicated in pain transmission. Several other regions of the brain are also involved in the modulation of pain. The periductal gray, a structure in the midbrain, has been tied to pain relief when it is stimulated. Neurons in the periductal gray connect to the reticular formation in the medulla, which make connections with the neurons in the substantia gelatinosa of the dorsal horn of the spinal cord. Sensations are modulated by the dorsal horn in the spinal column and by downward pathways from the brain that interpret the pain experience.

FIGURE 10.2 | The Experience of Pain

The signal goes to the spinal cord, where it passes immediately to a motor nerve ① connected to a muscle, in this case, in the arm. This causes a reflex action that does not involve the brain. But the signal also goes up the spinal cord to the thalamus ② , where the pain is perceived.

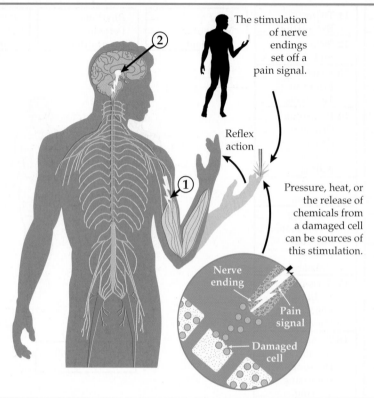

Processes in the cerebral cortex are involved in cognitive judgments about pain, including the evaluation of its meaning. The psychological and neural mechanisms of the affective dimension of pain are a critical aspect of the pain experience. The affective dimension of pain is made up of feelings of unpleasantness and negative emotions associated with future concerns. Researchers call these concerns secondary affect (Price, 2000).

Pain sensation, intensity, and duration interact to influence pain, its perceived unpleasantness, and related emotions through a central network of pathways in the limbic structures and the thalamus which direct their inputs to the cortex. In the cortical regions of the brain, nociceptive input is integrated with contextual information about the painful experience, which contributes to the strong emotions often experienced during pain and which can themselves exacerbate pain (Meagher, Arnau, & Rhudy, 2001). The overall experience of pain, then, is a complex outcome of the interaction of these elements of the pain experience (see figure 10.2). An example of just how complex pain and its management can be is provided in box 10.2.

Neurochemical Bases of Pain and Its Inhibition

The brain can control the amount of pain an individual experiences by transmitting messages back down the spinal cord to block the transmission of pain signals. One landmark study that confirmed this hypothesis was conducted by D. V. Reynolds (1969). He demonstrated that, by electrically stimulating a portion of the rat brain, one

BOX 10.2

Phantom Limb Pain

A CASE HISTORY

Nerve injury of the shoulder is becoming increasingly common because motorcycles are widely accessible and, all too often, their power is greater than the skill of their riders. On hitting an obstruction, the rider is catapulted forward and hits the road at about the speed the bike was traveling. In the most severe of these injuries, the spinal roots are avulsed—that is, ripped out of the spinal cord—and no repair is possible.

C. A., age 25, an Air Force pilot, suffered such an accident. After 8 months, he had completely recovered from the cuts, bruises, and fractures of his accident. There had been no head injury, and he was alert, intelligent, and busy as a student shaping a new career for himself. His right arm was completely paralyzed from

the shoulder down, and the muscles of his arm were thin. In addition, the limp arm was totally anesthetic so that he had no sensation of any stimuli applied to it. On being questioned, he stated that he could sense very clearly an entire arm, but it had no relationship to his real arm. This "phantom" arm seemed to him to be placed across his chest, while the real, paralyzed arm hung at his side. The phantom never moved and the fingers were tightly clenched in a cramped fist, with the nails digging into the palm. The entire arm felt "as though it was on fire." Nothing has helped his condition, and he finds that he can control the pain only by absorbing himself in his work.

Source: Melzack & Wall, 1982, pp. 21–22.

---

could produce such a high level of analgesia that the animal would not feel the pain of abdominal surgery, a phenomenon termed stimulation-produced analgesia (SPA). Reynolds's findings prompted researchers to look for the neurochemical basis of this effect, and in 1972, Akil, Mayer, and Liebeskind (1972, 1976) uncovered the existence of endogenous opioid peptides.

What are **endogenous opioid peptides?** Opiates, including heroin and morphine, are drugs manufactured from plants that help control pain. Opioids are opiate-like substances produced within the body that constitute a neurochemically based, internal pain regulation system. Opioids are produced in many parts of the brain and glands of the body, and they project onto specific selective receptor sites in various parts of the body.

The endogenous opioid peptides fall into three general families:

1. Beta-endorphins, which produce peptides that project to the limbic system and brain stem, among other places.
2. Proenkephalin, which are peptides that have widespread neuronal, endocrine, and central nervous system distributions.
3. Prodynorphins, found in the gut, the posterior pituitary, and the brain (Akil et al., 1984).

Each of these families of opioids has several forms with differing potencies, pharmacological profiles, and recep-

tor selectivities (Akil et al., 1984). For example, one opioid receptor may be receptive to beta-endorphins but not to proenkephalin or prodynorphins. Thus, the system of endogenous opioid peptides in the body is highly complex.

Endogenous opioid peptides, then, are important in the natural pain suppression system of the body. Clearly, however, this pain suppression system is not always in operation. Particular factors must trigger its arousal. Research on animals suggests that stress is one such factor. Acute stress reduces sensitivity to pain. This phenomenon is called stress-induced analgesia (SIA), and research demonstrates that SIA can be accompanied by an increase in brain endogenous opioid peptides (J. W. Lewis, Terman, Shavit, Nelson, & Liebeskind, 1984). As we saw in chapter 6, endogenous opioid peptides are secreted in response to stress in humans as well as animals.

Researchers do not yet know all the functions of endogenous opioid peptides. They are one method of inhibiting pain, particularly under stressful circumstances. Because the endogenous opioid peptides can be found in the adrenal glands, the pituitary gland, and the hypothalamus, they are clearly involved in responses to stress. Opioid peptides have been implicated in immune functioning and cardiovascular control as well (Akil et al., 1984; Holaday, 1983), and thus, release of opioid peptides may represent one route by which stress depresses immune functioning (see chapter 14).

The release of endogenous opioid peptides may be one of the mechanisms underlying various techniques of pain control (Bolles & Fanselow, 1982). Because opioids are powerful analgesics they are now used to treat chronic pain, including that due to malignancies (Brody, 2002).

■ CLINICAL ISSUES IN PAIN MANAGEMENT

Historically, pain has been managed by physicians and other health care workers. Traditional pain management techniques include pharmacological, surgical, and sensory techniques. Increasingly, psychologists have become involved in pain management and, as a result, techniques that include a heavily psychological component have been used to combat pain. These techniques include biofeedback, relaxation, hypnosis, acupuncture, distraction, guided imagery, and other cognitive techniques. As these methods have gained centrality in the treatment of pain, the importance of patients' self-management, involving responsibility for and commitment to the course of pain treatment, has assumed centrality in the management of chronic pain (Glenn & Burns, 2003).

Acute and Chronic Pain

There are two main kinds of clinical pain: acute and chronic. **Acute pain** typically results from a specific injury that produces tissue damage, such as a wound or broken limb. As such, it is self-limiting and typically disappears when the tissue damage is repaired. Jesse's pain, from moving into his new apartment, is an example of acute pain. Acute pain is usually short in duration and is defined as pain that goes on for 6 months or less. While it is going on, it can produce substantial anxiety and prompts its sufferer to engage in an urgent search for relief. The pain decreases and anxiety dissipates once painkillers are administered or the injury begins to heal.

Types of Chronic Pain   **Chronic pain** typically begins with an acute episode, but unlike acute pain, it does not decrease with treatment and the passage of time. There are several different kinds of chronic pain. **Chronic benign pain** typically persists for 6 months or longer and is relatively intractable to treatment. The pain varies in severity and may involve any of a number of muscle groups. Chronic low back pain and myofascial pain syndrome are examples.

Recurrent acute pain involves a series of intermittent episodes of pain that are acute in character but chronic inasmuch as the condition persists for more than 6 months. Migraine headaches, temporomandibular disorder (involving the jaw), and trigeminal neuralgia (involving spasms of the facial muscles) are examples.

Chronic progressive pain persists longer than 6 months and increases in severity over time. Typically, it is associated with malignancies or degenerative disorders, such as cancer or rheumatoid arthritis.

It is estimated that more than 100 million Americans suffer from chronic pain at any given time (C. Hall, 1999). Such pain is not necessarily present every moment, but the fact that it is chronic virtually forces sufferers to organize their lives around it.

Acute Versus Chronic Pain   The distinction between acute and chronic pain is important in clinical management for several reasons. First, acute and chronic pain present different psychological profiles because chronic pain often carries an overlay of psychological distress, which complicates diagnosis and treatment. The realization that pain is interfering with desired activities and the perception that one has little control over that fact often produce depression in pain patients (Maxwell, Gatchel, & Mayer, 1998). Depression, anxiety, and anger are common among chronic pain patients and may exacerbate pain and pain-related behaviors (Lautenbacher, Spernal, Schreiber, & Krieg, 1999; Plehn, Peterson, & Williams, 1998). One study found that pain is present in two thirds of patients who seek care from physicians with primary symptoms of depression (Bair et al., 2004). Thus, pain and depression appear to be heavily intertwined.

Some chronic pain patients develop maladaptive coping strategies, such as catastrophizing their illness, engaging in wishful thinking, or social withdrawal, which can further complicate treatment and enhance care-seeking (Severeijns et al., 2004). When patients have endured their pain for long periods of time without any apparent relief, it is easy to imagine that the pain will go on forever, only get worse, and be a constant part of the rest of their life—beliefs that magnify the distress of chronic pain and feed back into the pain itself (for example, R. Bishop & Warr, 2003). When these psychological issues are effectively treated, this fact may in itself reduce chronic pain (Fishbain, Cutler, Rosomoff, & Rosomoff, 1998). The sheer duration of chronic pain can account for the fact that many chronic pain patients become nearly completely disabled over the course of their pain treatment (Groth-Marnat & Fletcher, 2000).

A second reason to distinguish between acute and chronic pain is that most of the pain control techniques presented in this chapter work well to control acute pain but are less successful with chronic pain, which requires individualized multiple techniques for its management.

Third, chronic pain involves the complex interaction of physiological, psychological, social, and behavioral components, more than is the case with acute pain. For example, chronic pain patients often experience social rewards from the attention they receive from family members, friends, or even employers; these social rewards, or secondary gains, of pain can help maintain pain behaviors (Osterhaus, Lange, Linssen, & Passchier, 1997).

The psychological and social components of pain are important in part because they are an integral aspect of the experience of pain and they influence the likelihood of successful pain programs (for example, J. Burns, 2000). As such, chronic pain management is complicated and must be thought of not as a particular pain that simply goes on for a long period of time but as an unfolding physiological, psychological, and behavioral experience that evolves over time into a syndrome (Flor, Birbaumer, & Turk, 1990).

Who Becomes a Chronic Pain Patient?

Of course, all chronic pain patients were once acute pain patients. What determines who makes the transition to chronic pain? One might assume that pain intensity determines making the transition into chronic pain, but, in fact, functional disability appears to play a more important role. Patients for whom pain interferes with life activities make the transition into the chronic pain experience (Epping-Jordan et al., 1998). Chronic pain patients may experience pain especially acutely because of high sensitivity to noxious stimulation, impairment in pain regulatory systems, and an overlay of psychological distress (Hassinger, Semenchuk, & O'Brien, 1999; Maixner et al., 1997).

Unlike acute pain, chronic pain usually has been treated through a variety of methods, used both by patients themselves and by physicians. Chronic pain may be exacerbated by these inappropriate prior treatments, by misdiagnosis, and/or by inappropriate prescriptions of medications (Kouyanou, Pither, & Wessely, 1997).

Chronic pain may result from a predisposition to respond to a bodily insult with a specific bodily response, such as tensing one's jaw or altering one's pos-

ture. This response may then be exacerbated by stress. The chronic jaw pain or back pain that may result can be aggravated by inadequate coping, further exacerbating the pain syndrome and leading to pain behaviors that occur in the process of attempting to cope with pain (for example, taking time off from work or cutting back on activities in the home).

Lifestyle of Chronic Pain

By the time a pain patient is adequately treated, this complex, dynamic interaction of physiological, psychological, social, and behavioral components is often tightly integrated, making it difficult to modify (Flor et al., 1990). The following case history suggests the disruption and agony that can be experienced by the chronic pain sufferer:

> A little over a year ago, George Zessi, 54, a New York furrier, suddenly began to have excruciating migraine headaches. The attacks occurred every day and quickly turned Zessi into a pain cripple. "I felt like I was suffering a hangover each morning without even having touched a drop. I was seasick without going near a boat," he says. Because of the nausea that often accompanies migraines, Zessi lost fifty pounds.
>
> At his workshop, Zessi found himself so sensitive that he could not bear the ringing of a telephone. "I was incapacitated. It was difficult to talk to anyone. On weekends, I couldn't get out of bed," he says. A neurologist conducted a thorough examination and told Zessi he was suffering from tension. He took several kinds of drugs, but they did not dull his daily headaches. (M. Clark, 1977, p. 58)

As this case history suggests, chronic pain can entirely disrupt a person's life. Many such sufferers have left their jobs, abandoned their leisure activities, withdrawn from their families and friends, and evolved an entire lifestyle around pain. Typically, chronic pain sufferers have little social or recreational life and may even have difficulty performing simple tasks of self-care. Because their income is often reduced, their standard of living may decline, and they may need public assistance. Their lifestyle becomes oriented around the experience of pain and its treatment. A good night's sleep is often elusive for months or years at a time (Currie, Wilson, & Curran, 2002). Work-related aspirations and personal goals may be set aside because life has become dominated by chronic pain (Karoly & Ruehlman, 1996). Therefore, the loss of self-esteem that is experienced by these patients can be substantial.

More than 90 million Americans, many of them elderly, suffer from chronic pain.

Some patients receive compensation for their pain because it has resulted from an injury, such as an automobile accident. Compensation can actually increase the perceived severity of pain, the amount of disability experienced, the degree to which pain interferes with life activities, and the amount of distress that is reported (Ciccone, Just, & Bandilla, 1999; Groth-Marnat & Fletcher, 2000) because it provides an incentive for being in pain.

The Toll of Pain on Relationships   Chronic pain can take a special toll on marriage and other family relationships. Chronic pain patients often do not communicate well with their families, and sexual relationships almost always deteriorate. Ironically, among those chronic pain patients whose spouses remain supportive, such positive attention may inadvertently maintain or increase expression of pain and the experience of disability (Ciccone et al., 1999; Turk, Kerns, & Rosenberg, 1992).

Social relationships, in addition to the marital relationship, can be threatened by chronic pain as well. The resulting reduction in social contact that pain patients experience may contribute to their tendency to turn inward and become self-absorbed. Neurotic behavior, including preoccupation with physical and emotional symptoms, can result. Pain patients often have to deal with negative stereotypes that physicians and other providers hold about chronic pain patients, and this experience, too, may exacerbate adverse psychological responses to pain (Marbach, Lennon, Link, & Dohrenwend, 1990). Many chronic pain patients are clinically depressed; a large number have also contemplated or attempted suicide.

Chronic Pain Behaviors   Chronic pain leads to a variety of pain-related behaviors that can also maintain the pain experience. For example, they may avoid loud noises and bright lights, reduce physical activity, and avoid social contacts. These alterations in lifestyle then become part of the pain problem and may persist and interfere with successful treatment (Philips, 1983). Understanding what pain behaviors an individual engages in, knowing whether they persist after the treatment of pain, and determining how they can be eliminated are important factors in treating the total pain experience.

Pain and Personality

Because psychological factors are so clearly implicated in the experience of pain and because at least some pain serves clear functions for the chronic pain sufferer, researchers have examined whether there is a **pain-prone personality:** a constellation of personality traits that predispose a person to experience chronic pain.

Research suggests that this hypothesis is too simplistic. First, pain itself can produce alterations in personality that are consequences, not causes, of the pain experience. Second, individual experiences of pain are far too varied and complex to be explained by a single personality profile. Nonetheless, certain personality correlates are reliably associated with chronic pain, including neuroticism, introversion, and the use of passive coping strategies. Because findings like these provide clues to the treatment of pain, researchers have continued to refine their understanding of profiles of pain patients.

Pain Profiles   Developing psychological profiles of different groups of pain patients has proven to be helpful for treatment, and so, although these profiles are not thought of as pain-prone personalities, they are useful in specifying problems that patients with particular types of pain have or may develop.

To examine these issues, researchers have drawn on a variety of personality instruments, especially the Minnesota Multiphasic Personality Inventory (MMPI) (Johansson & Lindberg, 2000). Chronic pain patients typically show elevated scores on three MMPI subscales: hypochondriasis, hysteria, and depression. This constellation of three factors is commonly referred to as the "neurotic triad" because it frequently shows up in the personality profiles of patients with neurotic disorders as well.

Depression reflects the feelings of despair or hopelessness that can often accompany long-term experience with unsuccessfully treated pain. Pain does not appear to be a sufficient condition for the development of depression but, rather, leads to a reduction in activity level and in perceptions of personal control or mastery, which, in turn, can lead to depression (Nicassio, Radojevic, Schoenfeld-Smith, & Dwyer, 1995). Depression itself increases perceptions of pain (Dickens, McGowan, & Dale, 2003). Depression can, then, feed back into the total pain experience, both aggravating the pain itself and increasing the likelihood of debilitating pain behaviors, such as leaving work (for example, Linton & Buer, 1995). This profile has implications for the treatment of pain because interventions with depressed pain patients must address chronic depression and the thought disorders that result, in addition to the pain itself (Ingram, Atkinson, Slater, Saccuzzo, & Garfin, 1990).

Chronic pain is also associated with psychopathology including depression and anxiety disorders, substance use disorders, and other psychiatric problems. The reason chronic pain and psychopathology are so frequently associated is not fully known. One possibility is that chronic pain activates and exacerbates a latent psychological vulnerability that was not previously recognized, leading to diagnosable psychopathology (Dersh, Polatin, & Gatchel, 2002).

Pain and Stereotyped Responses to Stress

Some chronic pain patients have physiologically stereotypic responses to stress that aggravate particular groups of muscles, exacerbating their pain. For example, patients suffering from myofascial pain dysfunction syndrome (a set of disorders in which the chronic pain originates within the head or neck muscles) show increased activity in particular facial muscles in response to stress (Kapel, Glaros, & McGlynn, 1989). Other research suggests distinctive patterns of cephalic blood flow for people predisposed to muscle contraction or migraine headaches in response to stress (S. N. Haynes, Gannon, Bank, Shelton, & Goodwin, 1990).

Knowing that these distinctive patterns are aggravated by stress provides the potential for pain management that teaches patients to recognize the sources of stress in their lives and to cope in ways that counteract their stereotypic bodily responses to stress.

■ PAIN CONTROL TECHNIQUES

We now turn to pain control techniques, examining individual techniques that have been used to reduce or control pain. What exactly is pain control? **Pain control** can mean that a patient no longer feels anything in an area that once hurt. It can mean that the person feels sensation but not pain. It can mean that he or she feels pain but is no longer concerned about it. Or it can mean that he or she is still hurting but is now able to stand it.

Some pain control techniques work because they eliminate feeling altogether (for example, spinal blocking agents), whereas others may succeed because they reduce pain to sensation (such as sensory control techniques), and still others succeed because they enable patients to tolerate pain more successfully (such as the more psychological approaches). It will be useful to bear these distinctions in mind as we evaluate the success of individual techniques in the control of pain.

Pharmacological Control of Pain

The traditional and most common method of controlling pain is through the administration of drugs. In particular, morphine (named after Morpheus, the Greek god of sleep) has been the most popular painkiller for decades (Melzack & Wall, 1982). A highly effective painkiller, morphine does have the disadvantage of addiction, and patients may become tolerant to it. Nonetheless, it is a mainstay of pain control, especially in the case of severe pain.

Any drug that can influence neural transmission is a candidate for pain relief. Some drugs, such as local anesthetics, can influence transmission of pain impulses from the peripheral receptors to the spinal cord. The application of an analgesic to a wounded area is an example of this approach. The injection of drugs, such as spinal blocking agents that block the transmission of pain impulses up the spinal cord, is another method.

Pharmacological relief from pain may also be provided by drugs that act directly on higher brain regions involved in pain. Antidepressants, for example, combat pain not only by reducing anxiety and improving mood but also by affecting the downward pathways from the brain that modulate pain. As such, antidepressant administration is often a successful pain reduction technique for depressed pain patients, as well as for pain patients not showing clinical signs of depression.

Pharmacological control is the mainstay of pain control techniques. It is typically the first line of defense against pain, and it is often sufficient and successful in the management of acute pain. In addition, for chronic patients it may be employed in conjunction with other techniques. Over the long term, however, analgesic medications have limitations.

Sometimes these treatments make the pain worse rather than better. Patients may consume large quantities of painkillers, which are only partially effective, and they have a variety of undesirable side effects, including inability to concentrate and addiction. Nerve-blocking agents may be administered to reduce pain, but these can also produce side effects, including anesthesia, limb paralysis, and loss of bladder control; moreover, even when they are successful, the pain will usually return within a short time.

The main concern practitioners have about the pharmacological control of pain is addiction. However, it now appears that this threat is less than was once thought to be the case. One estimate is that about 15% of patients with cancer-related pain and as much as 80% with noncancer chronic pain do not receive sufficient pain medication, leading to a cycle of stress, distress, and disability (Chapman & Gavrin, 1999). In three studies involving 25,000 patients treated with opioids who had no history of drug abuse, only seven cases of addiction were reported (Brody, January 2002), suggesting that the concern over addiction is indeed exaggerated. (Box 10.3 pursues this issue further.) Even long-term use of prescription pain drugs for such conditions as arthritis appears to produce very low rates of addiction.

However, concerns of potential addiction are so great that patients with legitimate complaints requiring pain medication are often undermedicated. At present, this issue is one of the most controversial and significant ones faced by researchers and practitioners concerned with pain management.

Surgical Control of Pain

The surgical control of pain also has an extensive history. Surgical treatment involves cutting or creating lesions in the so-called pain fibers at various points in the body so that pain sensations can no longer be conducted. Some surgical techniques attempt to disrupt the conduct of pain from the periphery to the spinal cord, whereas others are designed to interrupt the flow of pain sensations from the spinal cord upward to the brain.

Although these surgical techniques are sometimes successful in reducing pain temporarily, the effects are often short-lived. Therefore, many sufferers who have submitted to one or more operations to reduce pain may find that only short-term benefits were gained at substantial cost: the risks, possible side effects, and tremendous expense of surgery. It is now believed that the nervous system has substantial regenerative powers and that blocked pain impulses find their way to the brain via different neural pathways.

Moreover, there is some indication that surgery can ultimately worsen the problem because it damages the nervous system, and this damage can itself be a chief cause of chronic pain. Hence, whereas surgical treatment for pain was once relatively common, researchers and practitioners are increasingly doubtful of its value, even as a treatment of last resort.

Sensory Control of Pain

One of the oldest known techniques of pain control is **counterirritation,** a sensory method. Counterirritation involves inhibiting pain in one part of the body by stimulating or mildly irritating another area. The next time you hurt yourself, you can demonstrate this technique on your own (and may have done so already) by pinching or scratching an area of your body near the part that hurts. Typically, the counterirritation produced when you do this will suppress the pain to some extent.

This common observation has been increasingly incorporated into the pain treatment process. An example of a pain control technique that uses this principle is dorsal column stimulation (Nashold & Friedman, 1972). A set of small electrodes is placed or implanted near the point at which the nerve fibers from the painful area enter the spinal cord. When the patient experiences pain, he or she activates a radio signal, which delivers a mild electrical stimulus to that area of the spine, thus inhibiting pain.

Sensory control techniques have had some success in reducing the experience of pain. However, their effects are often only short-lived, and they may therefore be appropriate primarily for temporary relief from acute pain or as part of a general regimen for chronic pain.

In recent years, pain management experts have turned increasingly to exercise and other ways of increas-

BOX 10.3

Managing Pain . . . or Not

The management of pain in the hospital setting is controversial. Many physicians and other medical providers fear that if patients receive too much medication during their hospitalizations, they will become addicted to painkillers (L. A. Rose, DeVellis, Howard, & Mutran, 1996). As a result, in hospital settings, patients are often undermedicated, and pain is a significant problem.

In recent years, many prominent pain researchers have called for the reevaluation of these policies. The rate of addiction among people hospitalized for surgeries or other procedures who have received painkillers on a short-term basis is very small. Addiction, quite simply, is not a risk for most people. Moreover, consider the following letters to the editor of *Time* magazine following an article on precisely this problem:

> My father died in 1994 after a long illness. In the end, his heart simply wore out, and morphine was the wonderful drug that allowed him to relax and breathe easily. My father wasn't "snowed under" but, rather, was kept comfortable with small doses as needed. He no longer worried about dying (as he had for years), because he felt good mentally, emotionally, and physically. And when his time came, he died in peace.

> When I had an operation several years ago, I asked my surgeon to start giving me pain killers while I was still in surgery, since I had read that this procedure would help curb post-operative pain. Not only did he do so, but he also gave me a morphine pump so I could administer my own pain medication. But most important, I was controlling a part of my recuperation. I didn't end up a drug addict and was out of the hospital sooner than expected.

These reports are not unusual, and increasingly medical providers are finding that proper medication for pain is not the risky venture it was once thought to be and that patients can participate actively and responsibly in controlling the amount of medication they receive.

---

ing mobility to help the chronic pain patient. At one time, it was felt that the less activity, the better, and patients with problems ranging from back trouble to nerve problems (such as sciatica) and other disorders were urged to take it easy and not to put too much strain on those parts of the body. In recent years, exactly the opposite philosophy has become increasingly popular, and patients are urged to stay active in the hopes of keeping as much of their functioning as possible. This approach has been especially successful with older people in helping manage the discomfort of musculoskeletal disorders (Avlund, Osler, Damsgaard, Christensen, & Schroll, 2000).

We now turn to psychological techniques for the management of pain. Unlike the pharmacological, surgical, and sensory pain management techniques considered so far, these more psychological techniques require active participation and learning on the part of the patient. Therefore, they are more effective for managing slow-rising pains, which can be anticipated and prepared for, than sudden, intense, or unexpected pains.

Biofeedback

Biofeedback, a method of achieving control over a bodily process, has been used to treat a variety of health problems, including stress (see chapter 6) and hypertension (see chapter 13). It has also been used as a pain control technique.

Biofeedback comprises a wide variety of techniques that provide biophysiological feedback to a patient about some bodily process of which the patient is usually unaware. Biofeedback training can be thought of as an operant learning process. First, a target body function to be brought under control, such as blood pressure or heart rate, is identified. This function is then tracked by a machine, and information about the function is passed on to the patient. For example, heart rate might be converted into a tone, so the patient can hear how fast or slowly his or her heart is beating. The patient then makes efforts to change the bodily process. Through trial and error and continuous feedback from the machine, the patient learns what thoughts or behaviors will modify the bodily function.

Thus, for example, a patient might learn that blocking out all sounds, concentrating, and breathing slowly help reduce heart rate. Although it is not always clear to the patient exactly what he or she is doing that achieves success, often the patient can nonetheless become proficient at controlling a bodily function that was once automatic. Once patients are able to bring a process under bodily control with feedback from the machine, they can usually come to make the same changes on their own without the need for the machine.

Biofeedback has been used to treat several chronic disorders, including Reynaud's disease (a disorder of the cardiovascular system in which the small arteries in the extremities constrict, limiting blood flow and producing a cold, numb aching), temporomandibular joint pain (Glaros & Burton, 2004), and hypertension (see chapter 13). Biofeedback has been used to treat a broad array of pains. For example, a study of patients with temporomandibular disorders had more significant pain reduction when they were trained in biofeedback techniques to reduce tension in the jaw, as compared with those who did not receive a biofeedback intervention (Mishra, Gatchel, & Gardea, 2000).

Success of Biofeedback How successful is biofeedback in treating pain patients? Despite widely touted claims for the efficacy of biofeedback, there is only modest evidence that it is effective in reducing pain (White & Tursky, 1982). Even when biofeedback is effective, it may be no more so than less expensive, more easily used techniques, such as relaxation (for example, Blanchard, Andrasik, & Silver, 1980; C. Bush, Ditto, & Feuerstein, 1985).

In addition, when biofeedback training is successful, it is not clear exactly why. There is little evidence that success at controlling a target process and corresponding reduction of pain are related, which raises the possibility that the beneficial effects of biofeedback are resulting from something other than modification of the target process, such as relaxation, suggestion, an enhanced sense of control, or even a placebo effect.

Biofeedback has been used successfully to treat muscle-tension headaches, migraine headaches, and Reynaud's disease. However, evidence to date suggests that other, less expensive relaxation techniques may be equally successful.

Although biofeedback training may prove to be effective in combination with other treatments for particular patients, as a general method of pain intervention, it is expensive and complicated, and simpler interventions may be just as effective.

Relaxation Techniques

Relaxation training has been employed with pain patients extensively, either alone or in concert with other pain control techniques. Originally developed to treat anxiety-related disorders (E. Jacobson, 1938), relaxation is known to promote coping with stress (see chapter 6). One rationale for teaching pain patients relaxation techniques, then, is that it enables them to cope more successfully with stress and anxiety, which may also ameliorate pain.

Relaxation may also affect pain directly. For example, the reduction of muscle tension or the diversion of blood flow induced by relaxation may reduce pains that are tied to these physiological processes.

What Is Relaxation? In relaxation, an individual shifts his or her body into a state of low arousal by progressively relaxing different parts of the body. Controlled breathing is another component of relaxation, in which breathing shifts from relatively short, shallow breaths to deeper, longer breaths. Anyone who has been trained in prepared childbirth techniques will recognize that these procedures are used for pain management during early labor.

An alternative method of inducing relaxation is through meditation. In this process, a person attempts to focus attention fully on some very simple and usually unchanging stimulus. For example, one may repeat a very simple syllable (such as "Om") slowly over and over again; this process is used in transcendental meditation, and the syllable is called a mantra. Box 10.4 gives two examples of the use of relaxation in pain control.

Success of Relaxation How successful have relaxation strategies been in the management of pain? Meditation per se does not appear to be successful, primarily because it does not reliably achieve the target state of relaxation (D. S. Holmes, 1981). Relaxation is modestly successful with some acute pains and may be of value in treating chronic pain when used in conjunction with other methods of pain control. Some of the beneficial physiological effects of relaxation training may be due to the release of endogenous opioid mechanisms,

BOX 10.4

Using Relaxation to Combat Pain

The following are case histories of patients treated with relaxation to reduce pain that, in some instances, proved resistant to other pain control methods.

CASE 1

A 65-year-old ex-steeplejack was hospitalized for evaluation of increasingly severe intermittent chest pain which had been present for over 10 years. An extensive workup revealed esophagitis (inflammation of the esophagus). The patient used relaxation exercises frequently both for general relaxation and for relief of moderate pain. "I get into it and just sort of forget all about the pain." Over a period of six months, he found the method very useful. "If I catch the pain early enough, I can stop it before it gets too bad." He typically used the method for 10 to 15 minutes, following which he went directly to sleep.

CASE 2

A dramatic response was seen in a 22-year-old man who was hospitalized following extensive bullet wounds in the abdomen and hip. During the three months of hospitalization, he suffered severe pain, which responded partially to surgery. He was anxious, depressed, irritable, and occasionally panicky due to the continual pain. He ate poorly and steadily lost weight. Using relaxation, he was able to sleep if the pain was not severe. He stated, "I stay there as long as I can—maybe 30 minutes. The trouble is, I go to sleep." There was a marked improvement in his general mood and he began eating well.

Source: A. P. French & Tupin, 1974, pp. 283, 285.

---

and there seem to be some beneficial effects of relaxation on immune system functioning as well (McGrady et al., 1992; Van Rood, Bogaards, Goulmy, & von Houwelingen, 1993).

Hypnosis

Hypnosis is one of the oldest techniques for managing pain, and it is one of the most misunderstood. Its mere mention conjures up visions of Svengalilike power seekers forcing others to do their bidding by inducing a hypnotic trance. In one of his most troublesome cases, Sherlock Holmes was nearly assassinated by a young man ordered to kill him while under the hypnotic control of a bewitching woman.

In fact, there are strict limitations on what a hypnotized subject will do while in a trance. Although such subjects may perform some minor feats that they do not customarily perform, they typically cannot be induced to do injury to themselves or others (Hilgard, 1965, 1971). So much for mythology.

That hypnosis can help control pain has been noted for centuries. Old medical textbooks and anthropological accounts of cultural healing rituals provide anecdotes of such extreme interventions as surgery conducted with no apparent pain while the patient was under a hypnotic trance:

> In 1829, prior to the discovery of anesthetic drugs, a French surgeon, Dr. Cloquet, performed a remarkable operation on a sixty-four-year-old woman who suffered from cancer of the right breast. After making an incision from the armpit to the inner side of the breast, he removed both the malignant tumor and also several enlarged glands in the armpit. What makes this operation remarkable is that, during the surgical procedure, the patient, who had not received any drugs, conversed quietly with the physician and showed no signs of experiencing pain. During the surgery, her respiration and pulse rate appeared stable and there were no noticeable changes in her facial expression. The ability of this patient to tolerate the painful procedures was attributed to the fact that she had been mesmerized immediately prior to the operation (cited in Chaves & Barber, 1976, p. 443).

Cloquet's case is one of the first reports of painless surgery with mesmerism, or, as it was later called, hypnosis.

How Does Hypnosis Work?   As an intervention, hypnosis relies on several pain reduction techniques (Barber, 1965; Hilgard, 1978). First, a state of relaxation is brought about so that the trance can be induced; relaxation alone can, of course, help reduce pain. Next, patients are explicitly told that the hypnosis will reduce pain; the suggestion that pain will decline is also sufficient to reduce pain. Hypnosis is itself a distraction from the pain experience, and distraction can reduce the experience of pain.

In the hypnotic trance, the patient is usually instructed to think about the pain differently; as noted earlier in this chapter, the meaning attached to pain influences its occurrence. And finally, patients undergoing painful procedures with hypnosis are often given painkillers. The beneficial effects of hypnosis in reducing pain are due at least in part to the composite effects of relaxation, reinterpretation, distraction, and drugs. Debate has centered on whether hypnosis is merely the sum of these other methods or whether it adds an altered state of consciousness to the experience. This issue has not yet been resolved.

In a recent study that made use of hypnotherapy, 28 patients with irritable bowel syndrome were randomly assigned either to receive hypnotherapy directed to modifying gastric experiences or a supportive verbal therapy as a control group. The hypnotherapy was found to reduce discomfort associated with the gastric, colonic response to their syndrome, suggesting that hypnotherapy may have clinical benefits for this patient group (Simrén, Ringström, Björnsson, & Abrahamsson, 2004).

Regardless of the exact mechanism by which it works, the efficacy of hypnosis for the management of some acute pains is now established (Linden, 1994). It has been used successfully to control acute pain due to surgery, childbirth, dental procedures, burns, and headaches, as well as pain due to a variety of laboratory procedures (Hilgard, 1978). It has also been used with success in the treatment of chronic pain, such as that due to cancer (Kogan et al., 1997), and may be especially successful in conjunction with other pain control techniques (Allison & Faith, 1996).

Acupuncture

Acupuncture has been in existence in China for more than 2,000 years. In acupuncture treatment, long, thin needles are inserted into specially designated areas of the body that theoretically influence the areas in which a patient is experiencing a disorder. Although the main goal of acupuncture is to cure illness, it is also used in pain management because it appears to have an analgesic effect. In fact, in China, a substantial percentage of patients are able to undergo surgery with only the analgesia of acupuncture. During surgery, these patients are typically conscious, fully alert, and able to converse while the procedures are going on.

How Does Acupuncture Work?

How acupuncture controls pain is not fully known. It is possible that acupuncture functions partly as a sensory method of controlling pain. Researchers also believe that

acupuncture may work because it is associated with other psychologically based techniques for pain control. In particular, patients believe that acupuncture will work, and their expectations may help reduce pain. The belief that acupuncture will reduce pain can reduce anxiety, inducing a state of relaxation.

Before acupuncture begins, patients are usually fully prepared for it and are told what the sensations of the needles will be and how to tolerate them. Such informed preparation often reduces fear and increases tolerance of pain (see chapter 9). Acupuncture needles and the process of inserting them are distracting; accordingly, attention may be directed away from pain. Patients undergoing acupuncture often receive analgesic drugs of various kinds, which also reduce the pain experience.

Finally, it is possible that acupuncture triggers the release of endorphins, thus reducing the experience of pain. When naloxone (an opiate antagonist that suppresses the effects of endorphins) is administered to acupuncture patients, the success of acupuncture in reducing pain is reduced (D. J. Mayer, Price, Barber, & Rafii, 1976).

Overall, is acupuncture an effective method of pain control? It can help reduce some kinds of short-term pain, but it may not be as effective for chronic pain. An evaluation of the effectiveness of acupuncture is also limited by its relatively uncommon use in the United States and by a lack of formal studies of the technique. As a result, acupuncture and other less traditional treatments for pain are sometimes regarded with suspicion by managed care organizations, who may not pay for these techniques even though they may lessen pain that has proven intractable to other methods (J. Lee, 2000).

Distraction

Individuals who are involved in intense activities, such as sports or military maneuvers, can be oblivious to painful injuries. These are extreme examples of a commonly employed pain technique: **distraction.** By focusing attention on an irrelevant and attention-getting stimulus or by distracting oneself with a high level of activity, one can turn attention away from pain.

There are two quite different mental strategies for controlling discomfort. One is to distract oneself by focusing on another activity. Some examples of control techniques that rely on distraction are provided by children describing how they deal with stressful or painful events (Bandura, 1991). For instance, an 11-year-old boy described how he reduced pain by distracting himself while in the dentist's chair:

When the dentist says, "Open," I have to say the Pledge of Allegiance to the flag backwards three times before I am even allowed to think about the drill. Once he got all finished before I did.

The other kind of mental strategy for controlling stressful events is to focus directly on the events but to reinterpret the experience. The following is a description from an 8-year-old boy who confronted a painful event directly:

As soon as I get in the dentist's chair, I pretend he's the enemy and I'm a secret agent, and he's torturing me to get secrets, and if I make one sound, I'm telling him secret information, so I never do. I'm going to be a secret agent when I grow up, so this is good practice.

According to Albert Bandura, who reported these stories, occasionally the boy "got carried away with his fantasy role-playing. One time the dentist asked him to rinse his mouth. Much to the child's own surprise, he snarled, 'I won't tell you a damned thing,' which momentarily stunned the dentist."

Does Distraction Work?

Distraction appears to be a successful technique of pain control, especially with acute pain (for example, L. Cohen, Cohen, Blount, Schaen, & Zaff, 1999). In one study, 38 dental patients were exposed to one of three conditions. One third of the group heard music during the dental procedure; one third heard the music coupled with a suggestion that the music might help them reduce stress; and the third group heard no music. Patients in both music groups reported experiencing less distress than did patients in the no-treatment group (R. A. Anderson, Baron, & Logan, 1991).

Distraction appears to be most effective for coping with low-level pain. Its practical significance for chronic pain is limited by the fact that such patients cannot distract themselves indefinitely. Moreover, distraction by itself lacks analgesic properties (McCaul, Monson, & Maki, 1992). Thus, while effective, distraction may be most useful when used in conjunction with other pain control techniques.

Coping Techniques

Coping skills training has been increasingly used for helping chronic pain patients manage pain. For example, one study with burn patients found that brief training in cognitive coping skills, including distraction and focusing on the sensory aspects of pain instead of their painful qualities, led to reduced reported pain, increased satisfac-

tion with pain control, and better pain coping skills (Haythornthwaite, Lawrence, & Fauerbach, 2001). Active coping skills have been found to reduce pain in patients with a variety of chronic pains (Mercado, Carroll, Cassidy, & Cote, 2000; S. R. Bishop & Warr, 2003).

Is any particular coping technique effective for managing pain? The answer appears to depend on how long patients have had their pain. In a study of 30 chronic pain patients and 30 recent-onset pain patients, researchers found that those with recent-onset pain experienced less anxiety and depression and less pain when employing avoidant coping strategies rather than attentional strategies. Because the pain was short term, putting it out of mind worked (B. Mullen & Suls, 1982).

In contrast, for chronic pain patients, attending directly to the pain, rather than avoiding it, was more adaptive, enabling these chronic pain patients to mobilize their resources for reducing or controlling the pain (J. A. Holmes & Stevenson, 1990). Such studies suggest that pain patients might be trained in different coping strategies, avoidant versus attentive, depending on the actual or expected duration of their pain (J. A. Holmes & Stevenson, 1990).

Patients' assessments of their own coping techniques may be useful information for planning interventions with chronic pain patients. A recent study found that patients who appraised their problem-solving abilities as poor suffered increased pain, depression, and disability whereas those with a more favorable assessment of their problem-solving competence did better (Kerns, Rosenberg, & Otis, 2002).

About 30–50 million people in the United States experience chronic pain that requires treatment.

Guided Imagery

Guided imagery has been used to control some acute pain and discomfort. In **guided imagery,** a patient is instructed to conjure up a picture that he or she holds in mind during the painful experience.

Some practitioners of guided imagery use it primarily to induce relaxation. The patient is encouraged to visualize a peaceful, relatively unchanging scene, to hold it in mind, and to focus on it fully. This process brings on a relaxed state, concentrates attention, and distracts the patient from the pain or discomfort—all techniques that have been shown to reduce pain.

The use of guided imagery to induce relaxation can control slow-rising pains, which can be anticipated and prepared for, or it can be used to control the discomfort of a painful medical procedure. As an example of the former use, advocates of prepared childbirth encourage a woman in labor to develop a focal point—a real or an imagined picture that she can focus on fully when labor pains begin. An example of using guided imagery to control the discomfort of a medical procedure is provided by a patient undergoing radiation therapy:

> When I was taking the radiation treatment, I imagined I was looking out my window and watching the trees and seeing the leaves go back and forth in the wind. Or, I would think of the ocean and watch the waves come in over and over again, and I would hope, "Maybe this will take it all away."

A very different kind of visualization technique may be used by patients trying to take a more personally aggressive stance toward pain. Instead of using imagery to calm and soothe themselves, these patients use it to rouse themselves into a confrontive stance by imagining a combative, action-filled scene. The following examples are from patients who used aggressive imagery in conjunction with their chemotherapy treatment.

> I happened to see something my husband was watching on TV. It was on World War II and the Nazis were in it. They were ruthless. They killed everything. I visualized my white blood cells were the German Army, and that helped me get through chemotherapy.
>
> I imagined that the cancer was this large dragon and the chemotherapy was a cannon, and when I was taking the chemotherapy, I would imagine it blasting the dragon, piece by piece.

What Does Guided Imagery Do?   Aggressive imagery may improve coping with the uncomfortable effects of illness or treatment. When the body is in a state of excitement or arousal, pain can be inhibited. Moreover, aggressive imagery can serve as a distraction to pain, and it gives the patient something to focus on.

Although relaxation imagery is more often used to combat pain than is aggressive imagery, aggressive imagery may work, too. In fact, one chemotherapy patient apparently profited from the use of both:

> It was kind of a game with me, depending on my mood. If I was peaceful and wanted to be peaceful, I would image a beautiful scene, or if I wanted to do battle with the enemy, I would mock up a battle and have my defenses ready.

It is interesting to note that these two virtually opposite forms of imagery may actually achieve some beneficial effects in controlling pain through the same means. Both may induce a positive mood state (relaxation or excitement), which contributes to the reduction of pain, and both focus attention and provide a distraction from pain—one by concentrating attention on a single, unchanging or repetitive stimulus, the other by diverting attention to the drama of an active scene.

How effective is guided imagery in controlling pain? Guided imagery is typically used in conjunction with other pain control techniques, so its unique contribution to pain reduction, if any, is, as yet, unknown. If it does add to the control of pain, it will likely be in the treatment of acute, slow-rising pain.

Additional Cognitive Techniques to Control Pain

In recent years, psychologists have attempted to expand the arsenal of cognitive and behavioral techniques for controlling pain. These have several objective approaches. First, they encourage patients to reconceptualize the problem from overwhelming to manageable. The rationale is that the pain problem must be seen as modifiable for cognitive and behavioral methods to have any impact.

Second, clients must be convinced that the skills necessary to control the pain can and will be taught to them, thereby enhancing their expectations that the outcome of this training will be successful (Gil et al., 1996).

Third, clients are encouraged to reconceptualize their own role in the pain management process, from being passive recipients of pain to being active, resourceful, and competent individuals who can aid in the control of pain. These cognitions are important in the pain experience and may promote feelings of self-efficacy.

Fourth, clients learn how to monitor their thoughts, feelings, and behaviors to break up maladaptive cognitions that may have resulted in response to pain. As we noted in chapter 3, patients often inadvertently undermine behavior change by engaging in discouraging self-talk. Leading pain patients to develop more upbeat monologues increases the likelihood that cognitive-behavioral techniques will be successful.

Fifth, patients are taught how and when to employ overt and covert behaviors in order to make adaptive responses to the pain problem. This skills training component of the intervention may include biofeedback training or relaxation.

Sixth, clients are encouraged to attribute their success to their own efforts. By making internal attributions for success, patients come to see themselves as efficacious agents of change and may be in a better position to monitor subsequent changes in the pain and bring about successful pain modification.

Seventh, just as relapse prevention is an important part of health habit change, it is important in pain control as well. Patients may be taught to identify situations likely to give rise to their pains and to develop alternative ways of coping with the pain rather than engaging in the usual pain behaviors they have used in the past, such as withdrawing from social contact.

Do Cognitive-Behavioral Interventions Work?

Evaluation of cognitive-behavioral interventions suggests that these techniques have considerable promise (Keefe, Dunsmore, & Burnett, 1992). Those techniques that enhance perceptions of self-efficacy may be especially successful. Self-efficacy is important, both because it leads patients to undertake steps to control their pain and because perceptions of efficacy may offset the potential for depression that is so often seen in chronic pain patients.

■ MANAGEMENT OF CHRONIC PAIN: PAIN MANAGEMENT PROGRAMS

As we noted in our previous discussion, no single pain control technique has been clearly effective in modifying chronic pain. Thus, often the chronic pain patient runs the gamut of techniques and finds them all to be unsuccessful.

Until 45 years ago, the patient who suffered from chronic pain had few treatment avenues available, save the tragedy of addiction to morphine or other pain-killers and rounds of only temporarily successful operations. Now, however, a coordinated form of treatment has developed to treat chronic pain.

These interventions are termed **pain management programs,** and they make available to patients all that is known about pain control. Pain management programs have evolved greatly over the past 2 decades. Initially, many pain treatment programs were in-patient, multiweek endeavors designed to decrease use of pain medication and restore daily living skills. Presently, however, most chronic pain management efforts are outpatient programs, both because they appear to be successful and because they are less costly.

The first pain management program was founded in Seattle at the University of Washington by John Bonica, MD, in 1960. At present, there are numerous such clinics around the country. Typically, these programs are interdisciplinary efforts, bringing together neurological, cognitive, behavioral, and psychological expertise concerning pain (Rains, Penzien, & Jamison, 1992). As such, they involve the expertise of physicians, clinical psychologists or psychiatrists, and physical therapists, with consultation from neurology, rheumatology, orthopedic surgery, internal medicine, and physical medicine. The goals of programs in pain management are to enable patients to reduce their pain as much as possible, to increase their levels of activity, to reduce perceptions of disability, to return to work, and to lead meaningful and rewarding lives, even if the pain cannot be entirely eliminated (Vendrig, 1999).

Initial Evaluation

Initially, all patients are evaluated with respect to their pain and pain behaviors. Typically, such evaluation begins with a qualitative and quantitative assessment of the pain, including its location, sensory qualities, severity, and duration, as well as its onset and history. Functional status is then assessed, with patients providing information about the degree to which their work and family lives have been impaired.

Exploring how the patient has coped with the pain in the past helps establish treatment goals for the future. For example, patients who withdraw from social activities in response to their pain may need to increase their participation in social activities or their family life.

Most patients are evaluated for their emotional and mental functioning as well. Many patients are very distressed and may suffer significant emotional and cognitive disruption in their lives (Iezzi, Archibald, Barnett,

Klinck, & Duckworth, 1999). Formal testing for psychological symptomatology, illness behavior, and degree of psychosocial impairment is often a part of this phase in pain management, and a wide variety of tests are available to help pain management experts derive a complete and complex profile of each patient (Rains et al., 1992).

Individualized Treatment

Individualized programs of management are developed following completion of the profile of the patient's pain and how it has affected their lives. Such programs are typically structured and time limited. They provide concrete aims, rules, and endpoints so that each patient has specific goals to achieve.

Typically, these goals include decreasing the intensity of the pain, increasing physical activity, decreasing reliance on medications, improving psychosocial functioning, reducing perception of disability, returning to full work status, and reducing the need to use health care services. An overarching goal has been to get patients to adopt a self-management approach for dealing with their pain. As we saw earlier in a discussion of self-efficacy, accepting the role of self-management for controlling pain may be helpful in reducing pain severity and interference with lifestyle (Glenn & Burns, 2003).

Components of Chronic Pain Management Programs

Pain management programs include several common features. The first is patient education. All patients are provided with complete information about the nature of their condition. Often conducted in a group setting, the educational component of the intervention may include discussions of medications; assertiveness or social skills training; ways of dealing with sleep disturbance; depression as a consequence of pain; nonpharmacological measures for pain control, such as relaxation skills and distraction; posture, weight management, and nutrition; and other topics related to the day-to-day management of pain.

Most patients are then trained in a variety of measures to reduce pain. Typically, such programs include relaxation training and exercise and may include other components, such as temperature biofeedback for muscle-contraction headaches or stretching exercise for back pain patients.

Because many pain patients are emotionally distressed and suffer from some degree of depression, anxiety, or irritability, group therapy is often conducted to help patients gain control of their emotional responses.

Pain management programs also target the maladaptive cognitions that may arise in response to chronic pain. Given what has often been a history of unsuccessful treatment of their pain, patients often catastrophize, and so interventions are aimed at the distorted negative perceptions patients hold about their pain and their ability to overcome and live with it (Ukestad & Wittrock, 1996).

Increasingly, pain management programs are taking into account patients' typical coping strategies and the need to match pain treatments to preferred coping styles. By matching treatments to patients' methods of coping, treatment benefits may be maximized (Rokke & Al Absi, 1992).

Involvement of Family

Many pain management programs intervene at the family level, combining family therapy with other interventions. On the one hand, chronic pain patients often withdraw from their families, but on the other hand, efforts by the family to be supportive can sometimes inadvertently reinforce pain behaviors. Working with the family to reduce such counterproductive behaviors may be necessary. For example, negative responses of caregivers to a family member's chronic pain such as depression, may actually exacerbate the patient's pain. Intervening with caregivers to help them develop a less negative model of their loved one's pain can ameliorate this problem (Williamson, Walters, & Shaffer, 2002).

Relapse Prevention

Finally, relapse prevention and follow-up activities are typically initiated in pain management programs so that patients will not backslide once they are discharged from the outpatient program. As is true for other treatments, nonadherence to pain regimens is a common problem among pain patients. The incidence of relapse following initially successful treatment of persistent pain appears to range from about 30 to 60% (Turk & Rudy, 1991a), and it appears that, for at least some pains, relapse is directly related to nonadherence to treatment. Consequently, the use of relapse prevention techniques and adherence-enhancement tactics may provide valuable assistance in the maintenance of post-treatment pain reduction (Turk & Rudy, 1991a).

Evaluation of Pain Management Programs

Pain management programs appear to be successful in helping control chronic pain. Studies that have evaluated behavioral interventions in comparison with nontreatment have found that the behavioral interventions reduce reports of pain disability and psychological distress (Center for the Advancement of Health, 2000e; Haythornthwaite et al., 2001; Keefe et al., 1992). These interventions improve psychological and social functioning as well (V. Stevens, Peterson, & Maruta, 1988).

As the importance, complexity, and costs of pain have become increasingly clear, pain is now taken more seriously in the medical management of patients and is recognized as an important medical issue in its own right rather than the inconvenient symptom it was once regarded to be (Turk, 1994). Originally directed largely to the alleviation of pain itself, programs designed to manage chronic pain now acknowledge the complex interplay of physiological, psychological, behavioral, and social factors, representing a truly biopsychosocial approach to pain management.

Pain management programs extend a promise of relief to thousands of sufferers who previously had little to aid them. These programs offer not only the possibility of a pain-free existence but also the dignity that comes from self-control of pain management and freedom from a life of pain, addiction, and depression. ●

SUMMARY

1. Pain is a significant aspect of illness because it is the symptom of chief concern to patients and leads them to seek medical attention. However, pain is often considered of secondary importance to practitioners.

2. Pain is intensely subjective and, consequently, has been difficult to study. It is heavily influenced by the context in which it is experienced. To objectify the experience of pain, pain researchers have developed questionnaires that assess its dimensions and methods to assess pain behaviors.

3. A-delta fibers conduct fast, sharp, localized pain; C-fibers conduct slow, aching, burning, and long-lasting pain; higher-order brain processes influence the experience of pain through the central control mechanism.

4. Neurochemical advances in the understanding of pain center around endogenous opioid peptides, which regulate the pain experience.

5. Acute pain is short term and specific to a particular injury or disease, whereas chronic pain does not decrease with treatment and time. More than 100 million Americans suffer from chronic pain, which may lead them to disrupt their entire lives in an effort to cure it. Chronic pain is complicated to treat because it has a functional and psychological overlay.

6. Efforts to find a pain-prone personality have been largely unsuccessful. Nonetheless, personality profiles based on the MMPI do suggest that chronic pain patients have elevated scores on the neurotic triad.

7. Pharmacologic (for example, morphine), surgical, and sensory stimulation techniques (for example, dorsal column stimulator) have been the mainstays of pain control. Increasingly, treatments with psychological components, including biofeedback, relaxation, hypnosis, acupuncture, distraction, and guided imagery, have been added to the pain control arsenal. Although all these techniques show at least some success, the exact mechanisms by which they do so are still elusive.

8. Most recently, cognitive-behavioral techniques that help instill a sense of self-efficacy have been used successfully in the treatment of pain.

9. Chronic pain is often treated through coordinated pain management programs oriented toward managing the pain, extinguishing pain behavior, and reestablishing a viable lifestyle. These programs employ a mix of technologies in an effort to develop an individualized treatment program for each patient—a truly biopsychosocial approach to pain.

KEY TERMS

acupuncture
acute pain
biofeedback
chronic benign pain
chronic pain
chronic progressive pain

counterirritation
distraction
endogenous opioid peptides
guided imagery
hypnosis
nociception

pain behaviors
pain control
pain management programs
pain-prone personality
recurrent acute pain

Management of Chronic and Terminal Illness

Management of Chronic Illness

During a race at a high school track meet, a young runner stumbled and fell to the ground, caught in the grips of an asthma attack. As her mother frantically clawed through her backpack, looking for the inhaler, three other girls on the track team offered theirs. As this account implies, asthma rates have skyrocketed in recent years, particularly among children and adolescents. More than 5 million children have asthma, an increase of 92% over the past 10 years, and more than a third of those children require treatment in a hospital emergency room for an asthmatic attack each year (National Heart, Lung, & Blood Institute, 1999). Scientists are not entirely sure why asthma is on the increase, but the complications that it creates for young adults are evident (Gregerson, 2000). Caution in activities, medication, and inhalers become a part of daily life. Psychosocial factors are clearly an important part of this adjustment, helping us answer such questions as "What factors precipitate an asthma attack?" and "What does it mean to have a chronic disease so early in life?"

At any given time, 50% of the population has a chronic condition. Taken together, the medical management of these chronic disorders accounts for three quarters of the nation's health spending (Hoffman, Rice, & Sung, 1996), not including nursing home care. The chronically ill account for 90% of home care visits, 83% of prescription drug use, 80% of the days spent in hospitals, 66% of doctor visits, and 55% of visits to hospital emergency rooms. As the opening example implies, these conditions are not confined to the elderly. More than one third of young adults ages 18 to 44 have at least one chronic condition.

Chronic conditions range from relatively mild ones, such as partial hearing losses, to severe and life-threatening disorders, such as cancer, coronary artery disease, and diabetes. For example, in the United States, arthritis in its various forms afflicts 49 million people (Centers for Disease Control and Prevention, 2004a); 9.6 million people have had cancer (American Cancer Society, 2004); diabetes afflicts 18.2 million people (American Diabetes Association, 2004); more than 4.8 million people have sustained a stroke (American Heart Association, 2004); and 14.6 million people have a history of heart attack and/or chest pain (American Heart Association, 2004). Fifty million people have diagnosed hypertension (American Heart Association, 2004).

A more startling statistic is that most of us will eventually develop at least one chronic disability or disease, which may ultimately be the cause of our death. Thus, there is every likelihood that, at some time, each of us will hear a physician say that our condition is chronic and cannot be cured; it can only be managed.

In this chapter, we consider some of the problems posed by chronic illness. We begin with a consideration of quality of life and how it may be assessed. Next, we consider patients' psychological reactions to chronic illness. We consider patients' spontaneous efforts to deal with the problems and emotional reactions posed by illness, their individual coping efforts, and their illness-related cognitions. We then turn to the specific issues of rehabilitation posed by chronic illness, including physical management, vocational problems, and problems in social functioning, and examine some general strategies for comprehensive rehabilitation programs. The vital importance of **self-management** of illness by the chronically ill is a central concept that guides this discussion (Lorig & Holman, 2003; Glasgow, et al., 2002). Self-management refers to involvement of the patient in all aspects of a chronic illness and its implications, including medical management, changes in social and vocational roles, and coping.

■ QUALITY OF LIFE

Until recently, quality of life was not considered an issue of psychological importance. For many years, it was measured solely in terms of length of survival and signs of presence of disease, with virtually no consideration of the psychosocial consequences of illness and treatments (S. E. Taylor & Aspinwall, 1990).

However, medical measures are only weakly related to patients' or relatives' assessments of quality of life. In fact, one classic study of hypertension (Jachuck, Brierley, Jachuck, & Willcox, 1982) found that although 100% of the physicians reported that their patients' quality of life had improved with the regular use of hypertensive medication, only half the patients agreed and virtually none of the relatives did (see also Brissette, Leventhal, & Leventhal, 2003; Gorbatenko-Roth, Levin, Altmaier, & Doebbeling, 2001). Moreover, some illnesses and treatments are perceived by patients to be "fates worse than death" because they threaten valued life activities so completely (Ditto, Druley, Moore, Danks, & Smucker, 1996).

Perhaps the most important impetus for evaluating quality of life stems from the psychological distress chronically ill patients often experience. The chronically ill are more likely to suffer from depression, anxiety, and distress (for example, De Graaf & Bijl, 2002; Mittermaier et al., 2004). Depression, psychological distress, and neuroticism contribute to substantially increased

In the past decade, researchers have begun to consider psychosocial functioning as an important aspect of quality of life among the chronically ill and disabled.

risks for mortality from chronic conditions (Christensen, Moran, Wiebe, Ehlers, & Lawton, 2002). Stress exacerbates the symptoms and course of many chronic illnesses, and since depression and anxiety are common consequences of stress, reducing stress levels and managing those stressors that cannot be eliminated are paramount for the management of chronic illness.

What Is Quality of Life?

Because of findings like these, quality of life is now given attention in the management of chronic illness. **Quality of life** has several components, specifically physical functioning, psychological status, social functioning, and disease- or treatment-related symptomatology (Kahn & Juster, 2002; S. T. Katz, Ford, Moskowitz, Jackson, & Jaffee, 1983; Power, Bullinger, Harper, & The World Health Organization Quality of Life Group, 1999). Quality of life among the chronically ill is now assessed with emphasis especially placed on how much the disease and its treatment interferes with the activities of daily living, such as sleeping, eating, going to work, and engaging in recreational activities. For patients with more advanced diseases, such assessments include whether the patient is able to bathe, dress, use the toilet, be mobile, be continent, and eat without assistance. Essentially then, quality of life assessments gauge the extent to which a patient's normal life activities have been compromised by disease and treatment. A broad array of measures is now available for evaluating quality of life (for example, Hazuda, Gerety, Lee, Mulrow, & Lichtenstein, 2002; Logsdon, Gibbons, McCurry, & Teri, 2002).

Why Study Quality of Life?

Why should we study quality of life among the chronically ill? There are several reasons:

1. Documentation of exactly how illness affects vocational, social, and personal activities, as well as the general activities of daily living, provides an important basis for interventions designed to improve quality of life (Devins et al., 1990; Maes, Leventhal, & DeRidder, 1996).

2. Quality of life measures can help pinpoint which problems are likely to emerge for patients with diseases. Such a measure, for example, might indicate that sexual functioning is a problem for patients with certain kinds of cancer but that depression is a more common problem for patients with other kinds of cancer. Such information would be helpful in anticipating the interventions that are required (Schag & Heinrich, 1986).

3. Such measures assess the impact of treatments on quality of life. For example, if a cancer treatment has disappointing survival rates and produces adverse side effects, the treatment may be more harmful than the disease itself (Aaronson et al., 1986). Quality of life measures have made it possible to assess the impact of unpleasant therapies and to identify some of the determinants of poor adherence to those therapies.

4. Quality of life information can be used to compare therapies. For example, if two therapies produce approximately equivalent survival rates but one

TABLE 11.1 | **Quality of Life Scores for U.S. Population and Several Groups of Chronically Ill Individuals**

A look at the typical score for the U.S. population indicates how each of several chronic conditions affects functioning in each area. For example, pain and vitality are most problematic for migraine sufferers, osteoarthritis compromises physical activities related to roles, diabetes undermines general health, and so on. An important point is that compared with the debilitating effects of clinical depression, which is an emotional disorder, the chronically ill generally fare quite well on quality of life, with the exception of areas directly affected by their diseases.

	Physical Functioning	Role— Physical	Bodily Pain	General Health	Vitality	Social Functioning	Role— Emotional	Mental Health
U.S. Population	92.1	92.2	84.7	81.4	66.5	90.5	92.1	81.0
Clinical depression	81.8	62.8	73.6	63.6	49.0	68.5	47.8	53.8
Migraine	83.2	54.0	51.3	70.1	50.9	71.1	66.5	66.4
Hypertension	89.5	79.0	83.8	72.6	67.2	92.1	79.6	77.3
Osteoarthritis	81.9	66.5	69.7	70.4	57.0	90.1	85.5	76.5
Type II diabetes	86.6	76.8	82.8	66.9	61.4	89.4	80.7	76.6

Source: Based on Ware, 1994; U.S. population estimates are for those reporting no chronic conditions. Scores take into account other chronic conditions, age, gender.

lowers quality of life substantially, one would be inclined to go with the treatments that keep quality of life at a higher level (S. E. Taylor & Aspinwall, 1990, for a review).

5. Quality of life information can inform decision makers about care that will maximize long-term survival with the highest quality of life possible. Such information enables policy makers to compare the impact of different chronic diseases on health care costs and to assess the cost effectiveness of different interventions, given quality of life information (R. M. Kaplan, 1985; R. M. Kaplan & Bush, 1982; Lubeck & Yelin, 1988).

Attention to quality of life issues has been useful in pinpointing some of the areas that require particular attention and interventions following the diagnosis of a chronic disease (see table 11.1), to which we now turn.

■ EMOTIONAL RESPONSES TO CHRONIC ILLNESS

Many chronic diseases affect all aspects of a patient's life (T. G. Burish & Bradley, 1983; Maes et al., 1996; S. E. Taylor & Aspinwall, 1990). As in acute diseases, there is a temporary first phase, when all life activities are disrupted. Chronic disease, however, may also carry the need to make intermittent or permanent changes in physical, vocational, and social activities. In addition, people with chronic illnesses must integrate the patient

role into their lives psychologically if they are to adapt to their disorders.

Immediately after a chronic disease is diagnosed, patients can be in a state of crisis marked by physical, social, and psychological disequilibrium. They find that their habitual ways of coping with problems do not work. If the problems associated with a chronic disease fail to respond to coping efforts, the result can be an exaggeration of symptoms and their meaning, indiscriminate efforts to cope, increasingly neurotic attitudes, and worsening health (Cheng, Hui, & Lam, 1999; Drossman et al., 2000; Epker & Gatchel, 2000). Anxiety, fear, and depression may temporarily take over.

Eventually, the crisis phase of chronic illness passes, and patients begin to develop a sense of how the chronic illness will alter their lives. At this point, more long-term difficulties that require ongoing rehabilitative attention may set in. These problems and issues fall into the general categories of physical rehabilitation, vocational rehabilitation, social rehabilitation, and psychological issues. In the next sections, we first consider emotional issues and coping with chronic illness and then turn to more general issues of rehabilitation.

Denial

Denial is a defense mechanism by which people avoid the implications of an illness. It is a common reaction to chronic illness that has been observed among heart patients (Krantz & Deckel, 1983), stroke patients (Diller,

1976), and cancer patients (Meyerowitz, 1983). Patients may act as if the illness were not severe, as if it will shortly go away, or as if it will have few long-term implications. However, immediately after the diagnosis of illness, during the acute phase of illness, denial can serve a protective function. It can keep the patient from having to come to terms with the full range of problems posed by the illness at a time when he or she may be least able to do so (T. P. Hackett & Cassem, 1973; R. S. Lazarus, 1983). One study of patients with myocardial infarction (MI) found that high initial denial was associated with fewer days in intensive care and fewer signs of cardiac dysfunction (M. N. Levine et al., 1988). Denial can also reduce the experience of unpleasant symptoms and side effects of treatment (S. E. Ward, Levanthal, & Love, 1988). Denial can mask the fear associated with a chronic disease until the patient is more accustomed to the diagnosis and better able to sort out realistically the restrictions that it will pose.

During the rehabilitative phase of illness, denial may have adverse effects if it interferes with the ability to take in necessary information that will be part of the patient's treatment or self-management program. For example, in the study that found initial benefits of denial among MI patients (M. N. Levine et al., 1988), high deniers showed poorer adaptation to disease in the year following discharge. The high deniers were less adherent to their treatment regimen and required more days of rehospitalization, suggesting that denial was interfering with successfully adopting a comanagement role in the illness. When patients must be actively involved with a treatment regimen—that is, when they must be able to assess their activities realistically and comply with medications and other changes in their lifestyle—denial can be an impediment.

Overall, then, denial may be useful in helping patients control their emotional reactions to illness, but it may interfere with their ability to monitor their conditions, to take the initiative in seeking treatment, or to follow through when they must act as responsible comanagers of their illness.

Anxiety

Following the diagnosis of a chronic illness, anxiety is common. Many patients become overwhelmed by the potential changes in their lives and, in some cases, by the prospect of death. Every twinge of chest pain may raise concern over another heart attack for the patient recuperating from MI. Many cancer patients are constantly vigilant to changes in their physical condition, and each minor ache or pain may prompt fear of a possible recurrence. Anxiety is especially high when people are waiting for test results, receiving diagnoses, awaiting invasive medical procedures, and anticipating or experiencing adverse side effects of treatment (for example, Rabin, Ward, Leventhal, & Schmitz, 2001; P. B. Jacobsen et al., 1995). It is also high when people expect substantial lifestyle changes to result from an illness or its treatment, when they feel dependent on health professionals, when they experience concern over recurrence (S. E. Taylor & Aspinwall, 1990), and when they lack information about the nature of the illness and its treatment (Marks, Sliwinski, & Gordon, 1993).

Anxiety is a problem not only because it is intrinsically distressing but also because it can interfere with good functioning. Anxious patients may be debilitated by their emotional distress even before therapy begins (Stauder & Kovacs, 2003; P. B. Jacobsen et al., 1995), anxious patients cope more poorly with treatments such as radiation therapy or chemotherapy (M. P. Carey & Burish, 1985), anxious diabetic patients report poor glucose control and increased symptoms (Lustman, 1988), anxiety can increase the frequency of attacks of Raynaud's disease (K. M. Brown, Middaugh, Haythornthwaite & Bielory, 2001) and lead to hyperreactivity in the gut for patients suffering from irritable bowel syndrome (Blomhoff, Spetalen, Jacobsen, & Malt, 2001), and anxious MI patients are less likely to return to work on schedule (Maeland & Havik, 1987). Anxiety is especially prevalent among people with asthma and pulmonary disorders and, not surprisingly, compromises quality of life (Katon, Richardson, Lozano, & McCauley, 2004).

Although anxiety directly attributable to the disease may decrease over time, anxiety about possible complications, the disease's implications for the future, and its impact on work and leisure-time activities may actually increase with time (Christman et al., 1988). Thus, both assessment and treatment of anxiety may be needed, an issue we turn to later in this chapter.

Depression

Depression is a common and often debilitating reaction to chronic illness. Up to one third of all medical inpatients with chronic disease report at least moderate symptoms of depression, and up to one quarter suffer from severe depression (L. Moody, McCormick, & Williams, 1990; G. Rodin & Voshart, 1986). Although there is evidence that depression may occur somewhat later in the adjustment process than does denial or severe anxiety, it can also occur intermittently. Depression is common among stroke patients, cancer patients, and heart disease patients, as well as for those suffering from many other chronic diseases (see S. E. Taylor & Aspinwall, 1990, for a review).

At one time, depression was treated as an unfortunate psychological result of chronic illness, but its medical significance is increasingly being recognized. Depression can be a sign of impending physical decline, especially among elderly men (Anstey & Luszcz, 2002). Depression exacerbates the risk and course of several chronic disorders, most notably coronary heart disease. Depression complicates treatment adherence and medical decision making. It interferes with patients adopting a comanagerial role, and it confers enhanced risk of mortality from a broad array of chronic diseases (Anstey & Luszcz, 2002). For all these reasons, the assessment and management of depression in chronic illness has become of paramount importance to health care providers and health psychologists.

Depression is sometimes a delayed reaction to chronic illness because it often takes time for patients to understand the full implications of their condition. During the acute phase and immediately after diagnosis, the patient may be hospitalized, be awaiting treatments, and have other immediate decisions to make. There may be little time to reflect fully on the implications of the illness. Once the acute phase of chronic illness has ended, the full implications of the disorder may begin to sink in. For example, a stroke patient comments on his discharge from the hospital:

> That was a glorious day. I started planning all the things I could do with the incredible amount of free time I was going to have, chores I had put off, museums and galleries to visit, friends I had wanted to meet for lunch. It was not until several days later that I realized I simply couldn't do them. I didn't have the mental or physical strength, and I sank into a depression. (Dahlberg, 1977, p. 121)

Significance of Depression   Depression is important not only for the distress it produces but also because it has an impact on the symptoms experienced and on the overall prospects for rehabilitation or recovery (J. J. W. Schaeffer et al., 1999). Depressed stroke patients have longer hospital stays and are more often discharged from the hospital to nursing homes than are other patients (Cushman, 1986). They show less motivation to undergo rehabilitation (S. C. Thompson, Sobolew-Shubin, Graham, & Janigian, 1989), they are less likely to maintain gains during rehabilitation (Sinyor et al., 1986), and they are less likely to restore their quality of life to prestroke levels (Niemi, Laaksonen, Kotila, & Waltimo, 1988). Depression is very common among patients with irritable bowel syndrome, an emotional overlay that can complicate treatment (Trikas et al., 1999). Rheumatoid arthritis patients with high levels of depression are more likely to catastrophize, overgeneralize, and negatively interpret their situation (T. W. Smith, Peck, Milano, & Ward, 1988). MI patients who were depressed while in the hospital are less likely to be back at work 1 year later and are more likely to be rehospitalized compared with those patients who were not depressed (Stern, Pascale, & Ackerman, 1977). Depression can exacerbate the symptoms and complicate the treatment of major chronic diseases, including diabetes (De Groot, Anderson, Freedland, Clouse, & Lustman, 2001), cancer, coronary heart disease, and hypertension.

Depression over illness and treatment has also been linked to suicide among the chronically ill (Goodwin, Kroenke, Hoven, & Spitzer, 2003; Rollman & Shear, 2003). For example, one out of every six long-term dialysis patients over the age of 60 stops treatment, resulting in death (Neu & Kjellstrand, 1986). The rate of suicide among cancer patients is approximately one-and-a-half times greater than that among adults who are not ill (J. Marshall, Burnett, & Brasure, 1983), and the rate of suicide among men with AIDS is higher than the national rate for their age group. Perhaps most important, depression is a potent risk factor for death among the chronically ill (Herrmann et al., 1998; Wulsin, Vaillant, & Wells, 1999).

Unlike anxiety, which ebbs and flows during the course of a chronic illness, depression can be a long-term reaction. For many illnesses, it may last a year or more following onset of the disorder (Lustman, Griffith, & Clouse, 1988; Meyerowitz, 1980; R. G. Robinson & Price, 1982).

Assessing Depression   Assessing depression in the chronically ill can be problematic. Many of the physical signs of depression, such as fatigue, sleeplessness, or weight loss, may also be symptoms of disease or side effects of a treatment. If depressive symptoms are attributed to aspects of illness or treatment, their significance may be less apparent, and, consequently, depression may go untreated (Massie & Holland, 1987). For example, one study of depressed stroke patients found that only one third had been referred for treatment of the depression (Lustman & Harper, 1987). These issues are especially problematic for illnesses that can affect brain functioning, such as cancer, stroke, diabetes, AIDS, and epilepsy (J. S. House, 1987; Massie & Holland, 1987; Primeau, 1988). Depression, as well as anxiety, is so prevalent among chronically ill patients that many experts recommend routine screening for these symptoms during medical visits (for example, Löwe et al., 2003).

Who Gets Depressed?   Depression increases with the severity of the illness (for example, Cassileth et al., 1985; L. Moody et al., 1990). The experiences of pain and disability, in particular, lead to depression (for example, R. J. Turner & Noh, 1988; Wulsin et al., 1999), which, in turn, increases pain and disability. These problems are aggravated in those who are experiencing other negative life events, social stress, and lack of social support (Bukberg, Penman, & Holland, 1984; S. C. Thompson et al., 1989).

Physical limitations may predict depression somewhat better earlier in chronic illness, whereas psychological factors may better explain depression later on. For example, one study of stroke patients found that the location of stroke damage predicted depression in the first 6 months, whereas later on, cognitive impairment, physical disability, social support, changes in body image and self-esteem, and the adverse mood effects of therapeutic drugs were stronger determinants of depression (Morris & Raphael, 1987).

In recent years, a variety of effective cognitive and behavioral interventions have been developed to deal with the depression that so frequently accompanies chronic illness (Center for the Advancement of Health, 2000f). Treatment for depression may not only alleviate psychological distress but also improve functioning by reducing symptoms associated with the illness (Mohr, Hart, & Goldberg, 2003).

■ PERSONAL ISSUES IN CHRONIC DISEASE

To fully understand changes in response to chronic illness requires a consideration of the self, its sources of resilience, and its vulnerabilities. The self is one of the central concepts in psychology. Psychologists refer to the **self-concept** as a stable set of beliefs about one's qualities and attributes. **Self-esteem** refers to the general eval-

uation of the self-concept—namely, whether one feels good or bad about personal qualities and attributes.

A chronic illness can produce drastic changes in self-concept and self-esteem. Many of these changes will be temporary, but some may be permanent, such as the mental deterioration that is associated with certain diseases (see box 11.1). The self-concept is a composite of self-evaluations regarding many aspects of one's life, which include body image, achievement, social functioning, and the private self.

The Physical Self

Body image is the perception and evaluation of one's physical functioning and appearance. Studies of hospitalized patients indicate that body image plummets during illness. Not only is the affected part of the body evaluated negatively, the whole body image may take on a negative aura (Schwab & Hameling, 1968). For acutely ill patients, changes in body image are short lived; however, for the chronically ill, negative evaluations may last. For several reasons, body image is importantly implicated in chronic illness. First, a poor body image is related to low self-esteem and an increased likelihood of depression and anxiety. Second, body image may influence how adherent a person is to the course of treatment and how willing he or she is to adopt a co-management role. Finally, body image is important because it can be improved through psychological and educational interventions (Wenninger, Weiss, Wahn, & Staab, 2003). Many chronic disorders including cancers, cystic fibrosis, multiple sclerosis, and other disabling conditions have adverse effects on body image. In most cases, body image can be restored to a degree, although it may take time (Wenninger et al, 2003).

Two exceptions are patients with facial disfigurements or with extensive burns (for example, Fauerback et al., 2002). Patients whose faces have been scarred or disfigured may never truly accept their altered appearance. There appear to be two reasons that facial disfigurements produce chronic alterations in body image. First, the face is often associated with personality, and, when the face is deformed, both patients themselves and others reacting to them may see the individual's whole nature as tainted (S. A. Richardson, Goodman, Hastorf, & Dornbusch, 1961). Second, facial disfigurements cannot be masked: They are apparent to all passersby, who may act with involuntary disgust or withdrawal. An example of the potent impact of facial disfigurement is the case of Mrs. Dover:

BOX 11.1

Future of Fear

Mollie Kaplan can remember half a century ago when she was 12 and met her husband, Samuel, at a Halloween party in the Bronx. What she can't remember is whether she had breakfast, so sometimes she eats it twice. She doesn't cook much anymore because if the recipe calls for salt, she can't remember whether she added it. "It's so frustrating," she said. "I can't read a book anymore, because if I stop and put a bookmark where I leave off, when I pick the book up again, I don't know what I have read."

If nothing else, Mollie retains a disarming sense of humor. When asked about anything in the recent past, she often replies, "Who remembers? You are talking with an Alzheimer's." It isn't much of a humorous matter to Sam, now 64, who still loves the woman he met half a century ago but wearily confesses: "You don't know what this is like until you get there. I never thought this would happen to me. People say to me, 'Join a support group.' I say, 'Fine, but what is Mollie supposed to do while I'm at the group?'" (D. Larsen, 1990, pp. E1, E8).

Mollie Kaplan is a victim of Alzheimer's disease. Alzheimer's is the fourth leading cause of death among adults, behind heart disease, cancer, and strokes. Given the aging of the population, by the year 2050, more than 14 million people in the United States could be suffering from Alzheimer's disease (Cowley, 2002). Alzheimer's disease accounted for at least 53,852 deaths in 2001 (Centers for Disease Control and Prevention, 2004), and 4.5 million American's currently have the disease (Hebert, Scherr, Bienias, Bennett, & Evans, 2003). Typical symptoms of Alzheimer's disease (named after Dr. Alois Alzheimer, who described it in 1906) include gradual progression of memory loss or other cognitive losses (language problems, motor skills), personality change, and eventually loss of function. Personality changes include hostility, withdrawal, inappropriate laughing, agitation, and paranoia.

The strain of Alzheimer's on both the patient and the caregiver can be great. For the patient, the distress of being increasingly unable to do simple routine tasks or to remember an activity just completed is disruptive, frustrating, and depressing. For caregivers, the emotional toll is substantial, and the effect on family finances can be huge. Often, the family is left with little alternative but to place the loved one in a nursing home. Despite this grim picture, many treatments for Alzheimer's disease are in development, and many are currently being tested or are generally available. Getting those treatments to the people who need them and doing so at an early stage of the disease is a top priority (Cowley, 2002).

Before her disfigurement (amputation of half of her nose), Mrs. Dover, who lived with one of her two married daughters, had been an independent, warm, and friendly woman who enjoyed traveling, shopping, and visiting her many relatives. The disfigurement of her face, however, resulted in a definite alteration in her way of living. The first two or three years she seldom left her daughter's home, preferring to remain in her room or to sit in the backyard. "I was heartsick," she said; "the door had been shut on my life." (E. Goffman, 1963, p. 12)

When illness threatens sexual functioning—as it does for stroke, paralysis, and some cancers and heart conditions—body image may be affected. Disease severity and the presence of debilitating symptoms also clearly affect body image and overall quality of life (L. Moody et al., 1990).

Body image can be improved by stressing other aspects of appearance and health. Researchers have sometimes noted spontaneous increases in physical exercise and improvement of other aspects of physical appearance or health as a reaction to illness (S. E. Taylor, Wood, & Lichtman, 1983).

The Achieving Self

Achievement through vocational and avocational activities is also an important aspect of self-esteem and self-concept. Many people derive their primary satisfaction from their job or career; others take great pleasure in their hobbies and leisure activities (Kahn, 1981). If chronic illness threatens these valued aspects of the self, the self-concept may be damaged. The converse is also true. When work and hobbies are not threatened or curtailed by illness, the patient has these sources of satisfaction from which to derive self-esteem, and they can come to take on new meaning.

Chronic disease or disability can interfere with some life activities, but a sense of self that is based on broader interests and abilities will sustain self-esteem.

The Social Self

As we have already seen, rebuilding the social self is an important aspect of readjustment after chronic illness. Interactions with family and friends can be a critical source of self-esteem. Social resources provide chronically ill patients with badly needed information, help, and emotional support. On the other hand, a breakdown in the support system has implications for all aspects of life. Perhaps for these reasons, fears about withdrawal of support are among the most common worries of chronically ill patients. Consequently, family participation in the rehabilitation process is widely encouraged. Providing all family members, even young children, with at least some information about the disorder, its course, and its treatment can offset the potential for confusion and miscommunication (P. D. Williams et al., 2002).

The Private Self

The private self may be severely strained by chronic illness. Many illnesses create the need to be dependent on others; the resulting loss of independence and the strain of imposing on others represent major threats to the self (van Lankveld, Naring, van der Staak, van't Pad Bosch, & van de Putte, 1993).

The residual core of a patient's identity—ambitions, goals, and desires for the future—are also affected by chronic illness. Occasionally, adjustment to chronic illness may be impeded because the patient has an unrealized secret dream, which is now out of reach, or at least appears to be. Encouraging the patient to discuss this difficulty may reveal alternative paths to fulfillment and awaken the ability to establish new ambitions, goals, and plans for the future.

■ COPING WITH CHRONIC ILLNESS

Despite the fact that most patients with chronic illness suffer at least some adverse psychological reactions as a result of the disease, most do not seek formal or informal psychological treatment for their symptoms. Instead, they draw on their internal and social resources for solving problems and alleviating psychological distress. How do they cope so well?

Coping Strategies and Chronic Illness

The appraisal of a chronic disease as threatening or challenging leads to the initiation of coping efforts (see chapter 7; R. S. Lazarus & Folkman, 1984a, 1984b). Relatively few investigations have looked systematically at coping strategies among chronically ill patient groups.

In one of the few such studies (Dunkel-Schetter, Feinstein, Taylor, & Falke, 1992), cancer patients were asked to identify the aspect of their cancer they found to be the most stressful. The results indicated that fear and uncertainty about the future were most common (41%); followed by limitations in physical abilities, appearance, and lifestyle (24%); followed by pain management (12%).

Patients were then asked to indicate the coping strategies they had used to deal with these problems. The five identified strategies were social support/direct problem solving (for example, "I talked to someone to find out more about the situation"), distancing (for example, "I didn't let it get to me"), positive focus (for example, "I came out of the experience better than I went in"), cognitive escape/avoidance (for example, "I wished that the situation would go away"), and behavioral escape/avoidance (for example, efforts to avoid the situation by eating, drinking, or sleeping) (cf. Felton & Revenson, 1984).

The strategies identified in this investigation are not substantially different from those employed to deal with other stressful events (see chapter 7). One notable difference, though, is that the chronically ill report fewer active coping methods, such as planning, problem solving, or confrontative coping, and more passive coping strategies, such as positive focus and escape/avoidant strategies. This discrepancy may reflect the fact that some chronic diseases, such as cancer, raise many uncontrollable concerns that active coping strategies cannot directly address. One might find that in coping with the aftermath of MI, for example, confrontative coping and problem solving would emerge as people attempt to modify their health habits and lifestyle, with the hope of reducing subsequent risk.

Which Coping Strategies Work?   Do any particular coping strategies facilitate psychological adjustment among the chronically ill? As is true for coping with other stressful events, the use of avoidant coping is associated with increased psychological distress and thereby may be a risk factor for adverse responses to illness (for example, Heim, Valach, & Schaffner, 1997). It may also exacerbate the disease process itself. For example, avoidant coping has also been related to poor glycemic control among insulin-dependent diabetics (Frenzel, McCaul, Glasgow, & Schafer, 1988).

Active coping, in contrast, has been found to predict good adjustment to multiple sclerosis (Pakenham, 1999). Also, those patients who actively solicit health-related information about their condition may cope better with it (for example, A. J. Christensen, Ehlers, Raichle, Bertolatus, & Lawton, 2000). Research has also found lower psychological distress when patients cope using positive, confrontative responses to stress; with a high internal locus of control (Burgess, Morris, & Pettingale, 1988); and with beliefs that one can personally direct control over an illness (Affleck, Tennen, Pfeiffer, & Fifield, 1987; S. E. Taylor, Helgeson, Reed, & Skokan, 1991).

Because of the diversity of problems that chronic diseases pose, people who are flexible copers may cope better with the stress of chronic disease than do those who engage in a predominant coping style. Coping strategies may be most effective when they are matched to the particular problem for which they are most useful. If people have available to them multiple coping strategies, they may be more able to engage in this matching process than those who have a predominant coping style (for example, Cheng, Hui, & Lam, 2004).

Patients' Beliefs About Chronic Illness

If patients are to adjust to chronic illness satisfactorily, they must somehow integrate their illness into their lives. Virtually all chronic illnesses require some alteration in activities and some degree of management. For example, diabetic patients must control their diet and perhaps take daily injections of insulin. Cancer patients, even those whose cancer is not currently active, must re-

main vigilant to possible signs of recurrence. Both stroke and heart patients must make substantial alterations in their daily activities as a consequence of their physical and psychological impairments.

Patients who are unable to incorporate chronic illness into their lives may fail to follow their treatment regimen and be nonadherent. They may be improperly attuned to possible signs of recurrent or worsening disease. They may engage in foolhardy behaviors that pose a risk to their health, or they may fail to practice important health behaviors that could reduce the possibility of recurrence or other complicating illnesses. Thus, developing a realistic sense of one's illness, the restrictions it imposes, and the regimen that is required is an important process of coping with chronic illness.

Beliefs About the Nature of the Illness   One of the problems that often arises in adjustment to chronic illness is that patients adopt an inappropriate model for their disorder—most notably, the acute model (see chapter 8). For example, hypertensive patients may believe incorrectly that, if they feel all right, they no longer need to take medication because their hypertension must be under control; accordingly, they may fail to monitor their condition closely (Nerenz, 1979; Ringler, 1981). Thus, it is often important for health care providers to probe patients' beliefs about their illness to check for significant gaps and misunderstandings in their knowledge that may interfere with self-management (Guzman & Nicassio, 2003).

Beliefs About the Cause of the Illness   People suffering from both acute and chronic illness often develop theories about where their illness came from (Affleck, Tennen, Croog, & Levine, 1987; A. Ali et al., 2000). These theories include stress, physical injury, disease-causing bacteria, and God's will. Of perhaps greater significance is where patients ultimately place the blame for their illness. Do they blame themselves, another person, the environment, or a quirk of fate?

Self-blame for chronic illness is widespread. Patients frequently perceive themselves as having brought on their illness through their own actions. In some cases, these perceptions are to some extent correct. Poor health habits, such as smoking, improper diet, or lack of exercise, can produce heart disease, stroke, or cancer. But in many cases, the patient's self-blame is ill placed, as when a disease is caused by a genetically based defect.

What are the consequences of self-blame? Unfortunately, a definitive answer to this question is not available.

Some researchers have found that self-blame can lead to guilt, self-recrimination, or depression (Glinder & Compas, 1999), but perceiving the cause of one's illness as self-generated may represent an effort to assume control over the disorder; such feelings can be adaptive in coping with and coming to terms with the disorder. It may be that self-blame is adaptive under certain conditions but not others (Schulz & Decker, 1985; S. E. Taylor et al., 1984a).

Research uniformly suggests that blaming another person for one's disorder is maladaptive (Affleck et al., 1987; S. E. Taylor et al., 1984a). For example, some patients believe that their disorder was brought about by stress caused by family members, ex-spouses, or colleagues at work. Blame of this other person or persons may be tied to unresolved hostility, which can interfere with adjustment to the disease.

Beliefs About the Controllability of the Illness

Researchers have also examined whether patients who believe they can control their illness are better off than those who do not see their illness as under their control. Patients develop a number of control-related beliefs with respect to chronic illness. They may believe, as do many cancer patients, that they can prevent a recurrence of the disease through good health habits or even sheer force of will. They may believe that by complying with treatments and physicians' recommendations, they achieve vicarious control over their illness (Helgeson, 1992). They may believe that they personally have direct control over the illness through self-administration of a treatment regimen. These control-related beliefs may or may not be accurate. For example, if patients do maintain a treatment regimen, they may very well be exercising real control over the possibility of recurrence or exacerbation of their illness. On the other hand, the belief that one's illness can be controlled through a positive attitude may or may not be correct.

Recall from earlier chapters that feelings of psychological control are generally beneficial for good mental functioning. As noted in chapter 8, interventions that attempt to instill feelings of control are often highly successful in promoting good adjustment and in reducing physiological arousal and emotional distress caused by illness and its treatment. Do feelings of control have the same beneficial effects when they are self-generated by patients attempting to deal with chronic illness?

Belief in control and a sense of self-efficacy with respect to the disease and its treatment are generally adaptive. For example, cancer patients who believed that they

had control over their illness were better adjusted to their cancer than were patients without such beliefs (S. E. Taylor et al., 1984a; S. C. Thompson, Nanni, & Levine, 1994). A sense of control or self-efficacy has been found to lead to improved adjustment among people with rheumatoid arthritis (Tennen, Affleck, Urrows, Higgins, & Mendola, 1992), sickle-cell diseases (R. Edwards, Telfair, Cecil, & Lenoci, 2001), chronic obstructive pulmonary disease (Kohler, Fish, & Greene, 2002), AIDS (S. E. Taylor et al., 1991), spinal cord injuries (Schulz & Decker, 1985), and patients recovering from angioplasty (Helgeson & Fritz, 1999), among many others. Even for patients who are physically or psychosocially badly off, adjustment is facilitated by high perceptions of control (McQuillen, Licht, & Licht, 2003). Thus, control appears to be helpful not only in coping with acute disorders and treatments but also with the long-term debilitation that may result from chronic illness (Schiaffino & Revenson, 1992).

The experience of control or self-efficacy may prolong life. A study of patients with chronic obstructive pulmonary disease found that those with high self-efficacy expectations lived longer than those without such expectations (R. M. Kaplan, Ries, Prewitt, & Eakin, 1994). Several studies that have attempted to enhance feelings of control in cardiac patients also suggest beneficial effects (for example, Cromwell, Butterfield, Brayfield, & Curry, 1977). Box 11.2 describes a study that further addresses these issues. Not all studies find that feelings of control are adaptive in adjusting to chronic conditions. When real control is low, efforts to induce it or exert it may be unsuccessful and backfire (T. G. Burish et al., 1984; Tennen et al., 1992; Toshima, Kaplan, & Ries, 1992).

■ REHABILITATION AND CHRONIC ILLNESS

Chronic illness raises specific problem-solving tasks that patients encounter on the road to recovery. These tasks include physical problems associated with the illness, vocational problems, problems with social relationships, and personal issues concerned with chronic illness. Some of these problems become so severe that they can be handled only through institutionalization (figure 11.1), but more commonly, these problems are managed through short-term residential or outpatient treatment programs. Even more than acute illness, chronic illness depends critically on patient comanagement of the disorder (for example, Goldring, Taylor, Kemeny, & Anton, 2002).

BOX 11.2

Causal Attributions, Feelings of Control, and Recovery from Myocardial Infarction

Studies of patients recovering from myocardial infarction (MI) illustrate the importance of both causal attributions for illness and feelings of control (Bar-On, 1986, 1987). In one study, patients were asked (1) why they thought they had had a heart attack and (2) what health measures they planned to take as a result of the attack. Several months later, their work and social functioning were measured.

Patients who attributed the cause of their MI to modifiable factors under their personal control (such as stress or smoking) were more likely to have initiated active plans for their recovery (for example, changing jobs or starting exercise) and to have returned to work and resumed other activities. In contrast, patients who attributed the MI to external factors beyond their personal control (bad luck or fate, for instance) were less likely to have generated active plans for recovery or to have returned to work; they were also less likely to have resumed other activities (cf. Affleck et al., 1987).

Bar-On also looked at the attributions that spouses made for the heart attack. Under most circumstances,

when spouses made the same attributions for the heart attack as their mates, short-term rehabilitation progressed well. However, if the patient's attributions were to external, uncontrollable factors or if the patient denied the infarct, long-term rehabilitation progressed better when the spouse's attribution was incongruent with the patient's attributions. In this case, the spouse's attribution to internal and controllable factors may have counteracted the patient's tendency toward denial, nudging him or her in the direction of becoming more aware of the things he or she could do to reduce the risk for a second heart attack (Bar-On & Dreman, 1987).

These results strongly suggest that, when an illness is perceived as being modifiable and under one's personal control, the process of recovery from chronic disease is enhanced (cf. Affleck et al., 1987). Moreover, these kinds of perceptions may be even more important predictors of successful rehabilitation than more traditional physical indicators used by physicians in predicting rehabilitation (Bar-On, 1986, 1987).

FIGURE 11.1 | Who Uses Long-Term Care?

Long-term nursing care is among the most expensive treatments available for chronic conditions. Who uses this care? The following statistics are from John Hancock and are considered representative of other insurers. In 1996, the average cost for a year in a nursing home was approximately $40,000. (*Source:* John Hancock Financial Services, cited in *BusinessWeek*, 1996a)

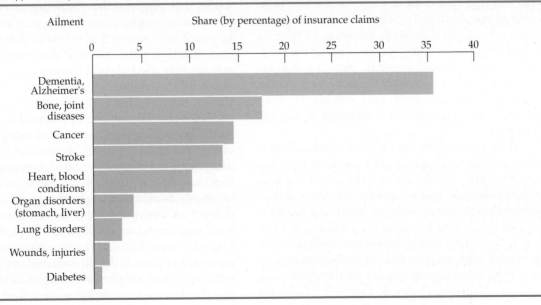

Patients are effective collaborators in managing their chronic conditions because they have personal knowledge of its development, symptoms, and course over a period of time. They are vital to effective treatment because the often complex and long-term treatment regimens that are recommended may require the active, committed participation of the patient (Center for the Advancement of Health, 1999). We next turn to these issues.

Physical Problems Associated with Chronic Illness

Physical rehabilitation is an important aspect of chronic illness. Chronic disability leads to anxiety, depression, and even thoughts of suicide. Consequently, any measures that can be taken to improve activity level, physical independence, and the ability to mange the tasks of daily living will have positive effects, not only on daily functioning but also on psychosocial adjustment (Zautra, Maxwell, & Reich, 1989).

Goals of Physical Rehabilitation   **Physical rehabilitation** of chronically ill or disabled patients typically involves several goals: to learn how to use one's body as much as possible, to learn how to sense changes in the environment in order to make the appropriate physical accommodations, to learn new physical management skills, to learn a necessary treatment regimen, and to learn how to control the expenditure of energy.

Patients must develop the capacity to read bodily signs that signal the onset of a crisis, know how to respond to that crisis, and maintain whatever treatment regimen is required (Gartner & Reissman, 1976). Even general exercise goes a long way in reducing the symptoms of many chronic disorders, including diabetes, chronic obstructive pulmonary disease (Emery, Schein, Hauck, & MacIntyre, 1998), and arthritis. For heart patients exercise is a critical component of recovery programs.

Many patients who require physical rehabilitation have problems resulting from prior injuries or participation in athletic activities earlier in life, including knee problems, shoulder injuries, and the like. Many of these problems simply worsen with age. Functional decline in the frail elderly who live alone is a particular problem (Gill et al., 2002). Physical therapy can ameliorate these age-related aches and pains and can also help patients recover from treatments designed to alleviate them, such as surgery (Stephens, Druley, & Zautra, 2002). Recent

Physical rehabilitation concentrates on enabling people to use their bodies as much as possible, to learn new physical management skills if necessary, and to pursue an integrated treatment regimen.

studies have suggested that group cognitive-behavioral interventions may be successful in getting people to adhere to physical activity than individual therapy (Rejeski et al., 2003). Regular exercise is also critical because it may not only affect physical functioning but also beneficially affect cognitive and psychological functioning (Emery, Shermer, Hauck, Hsaio, & MacIntyre, 2003).

Some physical problems are produced by the disease itself. They include physical pain, such as the chest pain experienced by heart patients; the discomfort associated with cancer; and the chronic pain of rheumatoid arthritis (van Lankveld et al., 1993). Breathlessness associated with respiratory disorders, metabolic changes associated with diabetes and cancer, and motor difficulties produced by spinal cord injuries are also important physical problems. Cognitive impairments may occur, such as the language, memory, and learning deficits associated with stroke. In many cases, then, the physical consequences of a chronic disorder place severe restrictions on an individual's life.

Treatment of primary symptoms and the underlying disease can also produce difficulties in physical functioning. Cancer patients receiving chemotherapy sometimes face nausea, vomiting, hair loss, skin discoloration, and other unattractive and uncomfortable bodily changes. Those cancer patients who receive radiation therapy must cope with burning of the skin, gastrointestinal problems, and other temporary disturbances (Nail, King, & Johnson, 1986). Chemotherapy can produce changes in taste acuity and taste aversions, sometimes leading to anorexia (Grunberg, 1985). Medications for hypertension can produce a variety of unpleasant side effects, including drowsiness, weight gain, and impotence. Sexual dysfunction as a result of illness and/or treatment may occur in patients with hypertension, myocardial infarction, and cancer (for example, B. L. Andersen, Anderson, & deProsse, 1989a, 1989b). Restrictions on the activities of patients who have had a heart attack—including dietary changes, elimination of smoking, and exercise requirements—may pervade their entire way of life. (A disease for which this is the case is profiled in box 11.3). In many cases, patients may feel that in terms of the discomfort and restrictions they impose, the treatments are as bad as the disease.

Developing a Comprehensive Program
Comprehensive physical rehabilitation must take into account all the illness- and treatment-related factors. Patients may need a pain management program for the alleviation of discomfort. They may require prosthetic devices, such as an artificial limb after amputation related to diabetes. They may need training in the use of adaptive devices; for example, a patient with multiple sclerosis or a spinal cord injury may need to learn how to use crutches or a wheelchair. Certain cancer patients may elect cosmetic surgery, such as breast reconstruction after a mastectomy or the insertion of a synthetic jaw after head and neck surgery. Parkinson's disease patients may require behavioral interventions to improve their motor skills and reduce their tremors. Disorders such as stroke, diabetes, and high blood pressure may compromise cognitive functioning, requiring active intervention (Zelinski, Crimmins, Reynolds, & Seeman, 1998).

As these examples indicate, chronic illness often creates a need for assistive technologies—namely, those aids and types of training that enable people with disabilities to perform the daily tasks of independent living. Unfortunately, access to such technologies remains uneven. Patients with good medical care, good insurance, and access to technology receive such assistance; those with fewer resources, no insurance, and little access to high-quality care are less likely to receive them (Seelman, 1993). Thus, one of the tasks facing those who work in physical rehabilitation is making assistive technologies more generally available to those patients who need them.

In addition to physical rehabilitation, a program for identifying and controlling factors that contribute to recurrence or that exacerbate the disease may be required. For example, stress has been implicated in the course of diabetes (Surwit, Schneider, & Feinglos, 1992), heart disease (see Krantz, 1980), hypertension (Harrell, 1980), multiple sclerosis (Mei-Tal, Meyerowitz, & Engel, 1970), cancer (Visintainer, Volpicelli, & Seligman, 1982), and Crohn's disease (Garrett, Brantley, Jones, & McKnight, 1991). As a consequence, stress management programs are increasingly incorporated into the physical treatment regimens of many chronically ill patients.

Adherence Physical rehabilitation must also tackle the very complex and serious problem of adherence to a long-term medical regimen. Cognitive and behavioral interventions may be needed to help a patient adhere to a medication regimen. For example, diabetic patients may be trained in how to recognize and treat symptoms as they change.

Unfortunately, the features that characterize the treatment regimens of chronically ill patients are those typically associated with high levels of nonadherence. As will be recalled from chapter 9, treatment regimens that must be followed over a long time period, that are complex, that interfere with other desirable life activities, and that involve lifestyle change show very low levels of adherence (Turk & Meichenbaum, 1991).

Moreover, some of these treatment regimens bear an uncertain relationship to outcome. For example, patients diagnosed with coronary artery disease must often stop smoking, lose weight, exercise, lower their cholesterol, and modify their volume of food intake simultaneously. However, once a diagnosis of coronary heart disease has already been made, the relation of these changes to subsequent risk may be weak (for example, Blumenthal & Emery, 1988). Moreover, adherence to one aspect of a complex regimen does not guarantee adherence to other aspects of that regimen.

Side effects of treatment also contribute to high rates of nonadherence. This problem is seen particularly with hypertensive medication (Love, Leventhal, Easterling, & Nerenz, 1989) but is also apparent with chemotherapy (J. L. Richardson et al., 1987; S. E. Taylor, Lichtman, &

BOX 11.3

Chronic Fatigue Syndrome and Other Functional Disorders

In recent years, health psychologists have become increasingly interested in **functional somatic syndromes** characterized by an intriguing pattern: These syndromes are marked by the symptoms, suffering, and disability they cause rather than by any demonstrable tissue abnormality. In short, we don't know why people have these disorders.

Functional somatic syndromes include chronic fatigue syndrome, irritable bowel syndrome, and fibromyalgia, as well as chemical sensitivity, sick building syndrome, repetitive stress injury, complications from silicone breast implants, Gulf War syndrome, and chronic whiplash.

Chronic fatigue syndrome (CFS), one of the most common, is a disorder of uncertain etiology marked by debilitating fatigue present for at least 6 months. The onset of CFS may be related to a prior viral condition, muscle abnormalities, and/or immunological or neurological changes. To date, though, no clear distinguishing biological cause has been found (Moss-Morris & Petrie, 2001). Some have nicknamed the disorder "yuppie flu," implying that the disorder may be a reaction to the stress of modern society.

Fibromyalgia is a syndrome involving widespread pain with particular tenderness in multiple sites. About 6 million individuals suffer from this disorder. As with chronic fatigue syndrome, the pathogenesis remains unclear, but the disorder is associated with sleep distur-

bance, disability, and psychological distress (Affleck et al., 1998). Sympathetic and HPA axis system stress responses may also show alterations (Peckerman et al., 2003; Buske-Kirschbaum et al., 2003; Gaab et al., 2002; LaManca et al., 2001).

Functional disorders have proven to be extremely difficult to treat inasmuch as their etiology is not well understood. Because of their insidious way of eroding quality of life, the functional syndromes are typically accompanied by a great deal of psychological distress, including depression, and the symptoms of the illness have sometimes been misdiagnosed as depression.

Who develops functional somatic disorders? Functional somatic syndromes are more common in women than men, and those who suffer from these disorders often have a prior history of emotional disorders, especially anxiety and depression (Skapinakis, Lewis, & Mavreas, 2004). Low SES, unemployment, and minority status have been tied to a somewhat higher likelihood of chronic fatigue (R. R. Taylor, Jason, & Jahn, 2003). Twin studies of chronic fatigue syndrome suggest that there may be genetic underpinnings of these disorders (Buchwald et al., 2001). A history of childhood maltreatment and abuse may also be implicated.

Substantial overlap exists among the individual syndromes in terms of symptoms and consequences (Ciccone & Natelson, 2003; Schmaling, Fiedelak, Katon, Bader, & Buchwald, 2003). Many of the disorders are

Wood, 1984b). On the other hand, the inclination to not follow an unpleasant treatment regimen can be offset by the recognition that it represents a potentially lifesaving measure.

An important first step in ensuring adherence to a treatment regimen is appropriate education. Some patients fail to realize that aspects of their treatment regimen are important to their successful functioning. For example, some patients may believe that exercise is a discretionary lifestyle decision rather than an essential ingredient in the restoration of physical functioning.

Self-efficacy beliefs are an important determinant of adherence to treatment regimens among the chronically ill (Strecher, DeVillis, Becker, & Rosenstock, 1986). In particular, high expectations for controlling one's health, coupled with knowledge of the treatment regimen, predict adherence among hypertensives (Stanton, 1987),

diabetics (Grossman, Brink, & Hauser, 1987), and end-stage renal disease patients (M. S. Schneider, Friend, Whitaker, & Wadhwa, 1991), among others.

Sometimes chronically ill patients employ creative nonadherence. Such actions may occur because the chronically ill know their disease extremely well, perhaps even better than some medical personnel, and so they make adjustments in their treatment in response to internal feedback. Nonetheless, creative nonadherence can lead to mistakes. For example, the use of unproven remedies or unconventional therapies may produce problematic interactions with prescribed medications. Consequently, an ongoing dialogue about supplementary treatments or treatment modification between provider and patient is essential (R. M. Kaplan, 1990). For a full consideration of adherence, refer to chapter 9. On the whole, though, cognitive behavioral interventions that marked by abdominal distention, headache, fatigue, and disturbances in the HPA axis, for example (Gaab et al., 2002). Among the common factors implicated in their development are a preexisting viral or bacterial infection and a high number of stressful life events (for example, Theorell, Blomkvist, Lindh, & Evengard, 1999). For example, the chronic aftermath of Lyme disease (caused by ticks) shows strong similarities to these disorders as well.

The similarity among the functional symptoms should not be interpreted to mean that these disorders are psychiatric in origin or that the care of patients suffering from them should be shifted to psychology and psychiatry; rather, it suggests that breakthroughs in understanding the etiology and treatment of these disorders may be made by pooling knowledge from the study of all these functional syndromes rather than by treating them as completely separate disorders. The core symptoms of fatigue, pain, sick-role behavior, and negative affect are all symptoms of chronic, low-level inflammatory processes, and it is possible that this sustained or recurrent immune response is what ties these disorders together.

What helps people cope with these debilitating disorders? Although social support is helpful to those with functional somatic syndromes, particularly solicitous behavior from significant others may actually aggravate the disorder by increasing sick-role behavior (Schmaling,

Smith, & Buchwald, 2000). As is true for most chronic disorders, positive reinterpretation and a sense of self-efficacy predict good psychological adjustment to the disorder, whereas avoidant coping strategies and emotional venting are associated with greater disability and poorer psychological well-being (J. C. Findley, Kerns, Weinberg, & Rosenberg, 1998; Moss-Morris, Petrie, & Weinman, 1996).

How are these disorders treated? Generally speaking, medical practitioners have combined pharmacological interventions for such symptoms as sleep deprivation and pain with behavioral interventions, including exercise and cognitive-behavioral therapy, efforts that appear to achieve some success (for example, Rossy et al., 1999). The specific treatment recommended for functional disorders varies, of course, with the particular nature of the problem. Those whose chronic fatigue developed in the wake of an infectious disorder may require different treatments than those whose chronic fatigue is unrelated to a prior infection; the latter group may require more psychological counseling (Masuda, Munemoto, Yamanaka, Takei, & Tei, 2002).

Overall, functional somatic syndromes are common, persistent, disabling, and costly. Simultaneous attention to the medical symptoms and the psychosocial distress generated by these disorders is essential for successful treatment.

explain therapies to the chronically ill or disabled and enlist their cooperation as comanagers achieve considerable success in adherence (Christensen et al., 2002).

Summary Effective physical rehabilitation requires consideration of all the illness- and treatment-related factors that may influence a patient's level of functioning. It requires pooling the skills of many specialists, including physical therapists and health psychologists, to make sure that the most effective methods of meeting treatment goals are employed. An eclectic collection of physical, behavioral, and cognitive interventions may be needed to develop the ideal physical management program that is individually tailored to each patient to control disabilities and treatment-related side effects, as well as to promote adherence. Such a program should be initiated early in the patient's recovery, with provision for

alterations in training as illness and treatment goals change. This kind of programmatic assistance, when effective, can be of enormous benefit to chronically ill patients. Not only can it help them resume the activities of daily living, but it may also contribute to a reduction in illness-related emotional disturbances as well (Emery et al., 1998). A crucial element in all such programs is the patient's active role as a comanager in rehabilitation. That is, rehabilitation is not something that is done to a patient. It is done with his or her full cooperation and participation.

Unfortunately, this programmatic approach to physical rehabilitation is still the exception rather than the rule. Although patients' physical rehabilitative needs do receive attention in the recovery process, an organized, concerted effort is rare. Perhaps more important is the fact that the crucial educational, behavioral, and

BOX 11.4

Epilepsy and the Need for a Job Redesign

In infancy, Colin S. developed spinal meningitis, and although he survived, the physician expressed some concern that permanent brain damage might have occurred. Colin was a normal student in school until approximately age 11, when he began to have spells of blacking out. At first, his parents interpreted these as a form of acting out, the beginnings of adolescence. However, as it became clear that Colin had no recollection of these periods and became angry when questioned about them, they took him to a physician for evaluation. After a lengthy workup, the doctor concluded that Colin was suffering from epilepsy.

Shortly thereafter, Colin's blackouts (known as petit mal seizures) became more severe and frequent; soon after that, he began to have grand mal seizures, involving severe and frightening convulsions. The doctors tried several medications and eventually were able to control the seizures successfully. Indeed, so successful was the medication that Colin eventually was able to obtain a driver's license, having gone 5 years without a seizure. After he completed high school and college, Colin chose social work as his career and became a caseworker. His livelihood depended on his ability to drive because his schedule involved visiting many clients for in-home evaluations. Moreover, Colin had married, and he and his wife together were supporting two young children.

In his early thirties, Colin began to experience seizures again. At first, he and his wife tried to pretend that nothing was wrong, but quite quickly they knew that the epilepsy was no longer under successful control. Colin's epilepsy represented a major threat to the family's income because Colin would no longer be able to keep his job as a caseworker. Moreover, his ability to find reemployment could also become compromised by the revocation of his driver's license. With considerable anxiety, Colin went to see his employer, the director of the social service unit.

After consultation, Colin's supervisor determined that he had been a valuable worker and they did not want to lose him. They therefore redesigned his position so that he could have a desk job that did not require the use of a car. By having his responsibilities shifted away from monitoring cases to the evaluation of cases and by being given an office instead of a set of addresses to visit, Colin was able to use in very similar ways the skills he had worked so hard to develop. In this case, then, Colin's employer responded sympathetically and effectively to the compromises that needed to be made in Colin's job responsibilities. Unfortunately, not all victims of epilepsy or other chronic diseases are as fortunate as Colin (Mostofsky, 1998).

---

cognitive training efforts that enlist the patient's cooperative comanagement are even more rare. Comprehensive physical rehabilitation is a goal toward which we are currently striving. The health psychologist is a key figure in this emerging effort.

Vocational Issues in Chronic Illness

Many chronic illnesses create problems for patients' vocational activities and work status. Some patients may need to restrict or change their work activities. For example, a salesman who previously conducted his work from his car but is now newly diagnosed as an epileptic may need to switch to a job in which he can use the telephone instead. Patients with spinal cord injuries who previously held positions that required physical activity will need to acquire skills that will let them work from a seated position. This kind of creative job change is illustrated in box 11.4.

Discrimination Against the Chronically Ill

Many chronically ill patients, such as heart patients, cancer patients, and AIDS patients, face job discrimination (for example, Heckman, 2003). One survey, reported in *Time,* indicated that employees with cancer are fired or laid off five times as often as other workers. When these patients return to their jobs, they may be moved into less demanding positions, and they may be promoted less quickly because the organization believes that they have a poor prognosis and are not worth the investment of the time and resources required to train them for more advanced work (*Time,* 1996).

Because of these potential problems, any job difficulties that the patient may encounter should be assessed early in the recovery process. Job counseling, retraining programs, and advice on how to avoid or combat discrimination can then be initiated promptly. Box 11.5 focuses on some health care professionals who deal with such problems.

BOX 11.5

Who Works with the Chronically Ill?

A variety of professionals are involved in the rehabilitation of the chronically ill. Many of these professionals are physicians, nurses, and psychologists. However, a number of other individuals with technical training in particular aspects of rehabilitation also work with the chronically ill.

PHYSICAL THERAPISTS

Physical therapists typically receive their training at the college undergraduate level or in a graduate master's program, both of which lead to required licensure. About 135,000 people work as licensed physical therapists in hospitals, nursing homes, rehabilitation centers, and schools for disabled children (U.S. Department of Labor, 2003). Physical therapists help people with muscle, nerve, joint, or bone diseases or injuries to overcome their disabilities. They work primarily with accident victims, disabled children, and older people.

Physical therapists are responsible for the administration and interpretation of tests of muscle strength, motor development, functional capacity, and respiratory and circulatory efficiency. On the basis of these tests, they then develop individualized treatment programs, the goals of which are to increase strength, endurance, coordination, and range of motion.

Physical therapists are also responsible for the ongoing evaluation and modification of these programs in light of treatment goals. In addition, they help patients learn to use adaptive devices and become accustomed to new ways of performing old tasks. They may use heat, cold, light, water, electricity, or massage to relieve pain and improve muscle function.

OCCUPATIONAL THERAPISTS

Occupational therapists work with individuals who are emotionally and physically disabled to determine skills, abilities, and limitations. They evaluate the existing capacities of patients, help them set goals, and plan a therapy program with other members of a rehabilitation team to try to build on and expand these skills. They help patients regain physical, mental, or emotional stability; relearn daily routines, such as eating, dressing, writing, or using a telephone; and prepare for employment. They plan and direct educational, vocational, and recreational activities to help patients become more self-sufficient.

Patients who are seen by occupational therapists range from children involved in craft programs to adults who must learn new skills, such as typing or using power tools. In addition, occupational therapists teach creative tasks, such as painting, weaving, leatherworking, and other craft activities that help relax patients, provide a creative outlet, and offer some variety to those who are institutionalized. Occupational therapists usually obtain their training through one of the occupational therapy training programs located in universities and colleges around the country, and, like physical therapists, they must be formally licensed.

DIETITIANS

Many of the country's 46,000 dietitians are involved in management of the chronically ill (U.S. Department of Labor, 2003). Although many **dietitians** are employed as administrators and apply the principles of nutrition and food management to meal planning for hospitals, universities, schools, and other institutions; others work directly with the chronically ill to help plan and manage special diets. In particular, these clinical dietitians assess the dietetic needs of patients, supervise the service of meals, instruct patients in the requirements and importance of their diets, and suggest ways of maintaining adherence to diets after discharge. Many dietitians work with diabetics and with patients who have disorders related to obesity, because both groups need to control their caloric intake and types of foods. Dietitians are formally licensed and must complete a 4-year degree program and clinically supervised training to be registered with the American Dietetic Association.

SOCIAL WORKERS

Social workers help individuals and families with the many social problems that can develop during illness and recovery by providing therapy, making referrals to other services, and engaging in more general social planning. These social workers work in hospitals, clinics, community mental health centers, rehabilitation centers, and nursing homes.

A medical social worker might help a patient understand his or her illness more fully and deal with emotional responses to illness, such as depression or anxiety, through therapy. A social worker can also help a desperate patient and family find the resources they need to

BOX 11.5

Who Works with the Chronically Ill? (continued)

solve their problems. For example, if the patient has been a homemaker—responsible for cooking, cleaning, and coordinating family activities—the social worker can help the family find temporary help to fulfill these tasks. If the patient will need vocational retraining after a chronic illness, the social worker can help find or even develop the facilities to make this possible. If the patient needs to transfer from the hospital into a special facility, such as a nursing home or rehabilitation center, the social worker is often the one who will make these arrangements.

In 2003, approximately 460,000 individuals were employed as social workers; two thirds worked for the local, state, or federal government. The minimum qualification for social work is a bachelor's degree, but for many positions a master's degree (MSW) is required. About 440 colleges nationwide offer accredited undergraduate programs in social work, and about 150 colleges and universities offer graduate programs (U.S. Department of Labor, 1998).

Financial Impact of Chronic Illness A difficulty related to the vocational problems of chronic illness concerns the enormous financial impact that chronic illness can have on the patient and the family. Many people are not covered by insurance sufficient to meet their needs. In other cases, patients who must cut back on their work or stop working altogether will lose their insurance coverage, adding enormous financial costs to the burden of their care. In this sense, then, the threat to vocation that chronic illness sometimes raises can be a double whammy: The chronically ill patient's capacity to earn income may be reduced, and simultaneously, the benefits that would have helped shoulder the costs of care may be cut back.

Social Interaction Problems in Chronic Illness

The development of a chronic illness can create problems of social interaction for the patient. After diagnosis, patients may have trouble reestablishing normal social relations. They may complain of others' pity or rejection but behave in ways that inadvertently elicit these behaviors. They may withdraw from other people altogether or may thrust themselves into social activities before they are ready.

Negative Responses from Others Patients are not solely responsible for whatever difficulties and awkwardness arise in interaction with others. Acquaintances, friends, and relatives may have problems of their own adjusting to the patient's altered condition. Many people hold pejorative stereotypes about certain groups of chronically ill patients, including those with cancer or AIDS (Fife & Wright, 2000).

Studies of reactions to people with disabilities reveal that they tend to elicit ambivalence. Acquaintances may give verbal signs of warmth and affection while nonverbally conveying revulsion or rejection through their gestures, contacts, and body postures (Wortman & Dunkel-Schetter, 1979). Distant relationships with friends and acquaintances appear to be more adversely affected in these ways than intimate relations (Dakof & Taylor, 1990). The newly disabled patient has difficulty interpreting and reacting to these behaviors.

Intimate others may themselves be distressed by the loved one's condition (for example, P. N. Stein, Gordon, Hibbard, & Sliwinski, 1992) or may be worn down by the constant pain, disability, and dependency of the partner (S. L. Manne & Zautra, 1990). Moreover, they may be ineffective in providing support because their own support needs are unmet (for example, Horwitz, Reinhard, & Howell-White, 1996).

Chronically ill patients may need to think through whether they want to disclose the fact of their illness to those outside their immediate family. If they decide to do so, they may need to consider the best approach because certain illnesses—particularly cancer, AIDS, and epilepsy—may elicit negative responses from others.

Working through problems with family members often helps patients lay the groundwork for reestablishing other social contacts. As the first social group with whom the patient interacts, the family can be a social microcosm on whom the patient tries out his or her coping efforts and who react to him or her in turn. By developing effective ways of dealing with family members and friends in various contexts, the patient simultaneously builds skills for dealing with other people in a variety of social situations.

Impact on Family   It has been said that individuals do not develop chronic diseases; families do. The reason for this belief is that the family is a social system and disruption in the life of one family member invariably affects the lives of others (for example, P. D. Williams et al., 2002). One of the chief changes brought about by chronic illness is an increased dependency of the chronically ill individual on other family members. If the patient is married, the illness inevitably places increased responsibilities on the spouse.

Simultaneously, other responsibilities may fall to children and other family members living at home. Consequently, the patient's family may feel that their lives have gone out of control and may have difficulty coping with the changes (Compas, Worsham, Ey, & Howell, 1996). Role strains of all kinds can emerge as family members find themselves assuming new roles and simultaneously realize that their time to pursue recreational and other leisure-time activities has declined (Pavalko & Woodbury, 2000; Quittner et al., 1998; Williamson, Shaffer, & Schulz, 1998).

Increased responsibilities may be difficult to handle. If family members' resources are already stretched to the limit, accommodating new tasks is very difficult. The wife of one stroke patient suggested some of the burdens such patients can create for their families:

> In the first few weeks, Clay not only needed meals brought to him, but countless items he wanted to use, to look at, and so forth. He was not aware of how much Jim [the patient's son] and I developed our leg muscles in fetching and carrying. When he was on the third floor I would say "I am going downstairs. Is there anything you want?" No, he couldn't think of a thing. When I returned he remembered something, but only one thing at a time. There are advantages to a home with stairs, but not with a stroke victim in the family. (Dahlberg, 1977, p. 124)

Young children who are suddenly forced into taking on more responsibilities than would normally be expected for their age group may react by rebelling or acting out. Disturbances may include regression (such as bedwetting), problems at school, truancy, sexual acting out, drug use, and antagonism toward other family members.

Despite the clear sources of strain that develop when a member of a family has a chronic illness, there is no evidence that such strains are catastrophic. There is no higher divorce rate among families with a chronic illness, nor do such families show less cohesion. Moreover, some families are actually drawn closer as a consequence

of chronic illness (Masters, Cerreto, & Mendlowitz, 1983).

Caregiving Role   Nonetheless, substantial strains may fall on family members, as just seen. In no case is this strain more evident than in the case of the primary caregiver.

Care for the chronically ill is notoriously irregular (Stolberg, 1999b). Few facilities are available to give the kind of custodial care that is often required for chronically ill patients. Consequently, the burden often falls on a family member to provide this often intense, unrelenting care for another. Both men and women may be involved in caregiving, although on the whole, the role more commonly falls to women. The typical caregiver is a woman in her sixties caring for an elderly spouse, but caregivers also provide help for their own parents and for disabled children.

Caregiving may be intermittent or supplementary in the case of patients who can contribute actively to their own disease management; many cancer patients and heart patients fall into this category. In other cases, it may be intense for a period until recovery progresses; some stroke patients fall into this category. In other cases, caregiving needs increase, as the disease progresses to the point where the caregiver has responsibility for virtually every activity the patient must undertake, including brushing their teeth, feeding them, cleaning them, and the like; progressive cancers, Alzheimer's disease, Parkinson's disease, and advanced multiple sclerosis are among the illnesses that may create this need for intense caregiving.

Not surprisingly, family members who provide caregiving are at risk for distress, depression, and declining health (Bigatti & Cronan, 2002). To begin with, caregivers are often elderly, and, consequently, their own health may be threatened when caregiving begins. The process of caregiving may further erode health (von Kaenel, Dimsdale, Patterson, & Grant, 2003). Many studies attest to the risks that caregiving poses to immune functioning (Glaser, Sheridan, Malarkey, MacCallum, & Kiecolt-Glaser, 2000; Mills, Yu, Ziegler, Patterson, & Grant, 1999), long-term changes in stress responses (Grant, Adler, Patterson, & Irwin, 2002), an increased risk of infectious disease, and even death (Schulz & Beach, 1999).

Caregiving can also strain the relationship between patient and caregiver (Martire, Stephens, Druley, & Wojno, 2002). Patients are not always appreciative of the help they receive and may resent the fact that they need help. Their expression of resentment can contribute to the depression and distress so often seen in caregivers (Newsom & Schulz, 1998). The anxiety and depression that can result from caregiving may, in turn, feed back into the health of the caregiver (for example, Shewchuk, Richards, & Elliott, 1998). Caregivers fare better when they have a high sense of personal mastery and active coping strategies (for example, K. A. Christensen, Stephens, & Townsend, 1998; Goode, Haley, Roth, & Ford, 1998).

Caregivers themselves may be in need of interventions, especially those involving social support, because the demands of caregiving may tie them to the home and give them little free time. Recently, the possibility that the Internet can be used to provide support to caregivers has been explored. One study (Czaja & Rubert, 2002) found that caregivers who were able to communicate online with other family members, a therapist, and an online discussion group found the services to be extremely valuable, suggesting that this intervention has substantial promise for caregivers who might otherwise be isolated from others.

Impact on Sexuality Many chronic illnesses—including heart disease, stroke, and cancer—lead to a decrease in sexual activity. In some cases, the condition itself prompts temporary restrictions on sexual activity; more commonly, however, the decline can be traced to psychological origins (such as loss of desire, fears about aggravating the chronic condition, or impotence). The ability to continue physically intimate relations can be protective of mental health and relationship satisfaction among the chronically ill, but attention to issues of physical intimacy can improve emotional adjustment to chronic illness and quality of life (Perez, Skinner, & Meyerowitz, 2002).

Gender and the Impact of Chronic Illness Chronically ill women may experience more deficits in social support than do chronically ill men. One study found that disabled women receive less social support because they are less likely to be married or get married than disabled men (Kutner, 1987; see also Bramwell, 1986). Stern et al. (1977) found that women who had sustained heart attacks were less likely to get married, and, if they were married, their prognosis was worse after the myocardial infarction than was true for men. Because ill and/or elderly women may experience reduced quality of life for other reasons as well, such as poor income and high levels of disability (Haug & Folmar, 1986), problems in social support may exacerbate these already existing differences.

Even when chronically ill women are married, they are more frequently institutionalized for their illnesses than are husbands. Being married appears to protect men, but not women, from being institutionalized after a stroke (Kelly-Hayes et al., 1988), and married men spend fewer days in nursing homes than married women (Freedman, 1993). It may be that husbands feel less capable providing care than wives, or, because husbands are older than wives, they may be more disabled than are wives of chronically ill husbands.

Following the diagnosis of a chronic illness, women may nevertheless continue to carry a disproportionate burden of household responsibilities and activities, a burden that may pose a threat for progressive illness (J. S. Rose et al., 1996). Gender differences in the availability and effects of social support among the chronically ill clearly merit concern.

Positive Changes in Response to Chronic Illness

At the beginning of this chapter, we considered quality of life, and throughout the chapter, we have focused on many of the adverse changes that chronic illness creates and what can be done to ameliorate them. This focus tends to obscure an important point, however—namely, that chronic illness can confer positive outcomes as well as negative ones (S. E. Taylor, 1983, 1989).

Research has focused disproportionately on the negative emotions that are produced by chronic illness. However, many people experience positive reactions (Ryff & Singer, 1996), such as joy (S. M. Levy, Lee, Bagley, & Lippman, 1988) and optimism (Scheier, Weintraub, & Carver, 1986; Cordova, Cunningham, Carlson & Andrykowski, 2001). These reactions may occur because chronically ill people perceive that they have narrowly escaped death or because they have reordered their priorities in a more satisfying way. They may also find meaning in the daily activities of life in response to the illness (McFarland & Alvaro, 2000).

In one study (R. L. Collins, Taylor, & Skokan, 1990), more than 90% of cancer patients reported at least some beneficial changes in their lives as a result of the cancer, including an increased ability to appreciate each day and the inspiration to do things now in life rather than postponing them. These patients reported that they were putting more effort into their relationships and believed they had acquired more awareness of others' feelings and more empathy and compassion for others. They reported feeling stronger and more self-assured as well.

A study of patients who had had a heart attack found that 46% reported that their lives were unchanged by the disease, 21% reported that it had worsened, but 33% felt that their lives had improved overall (Mohr et al., 1999). Half of the patients reported increased joy in life and increased value in families, hobbies, and health. A study of people with multiple sclerosis found that many had experienced a deepening of their relationships, an enhanced appreciation of life, and an increase in spiritual interests (Mohr et al., 1999). Two studies compared the quality of life experienced by cancer patients with a normal sample free of chronic disease, and both found the quality of life experienced by the cancer sample to be higher than that of the non-ill sample (Danoff, Kramer, Irwin, & Gottlieb, 1983; Tempelaar et al., 1989; see also Cassileth et al., 1984).

The ability to reappraise one's situation positively has been tied to a more positive mood and to posttraumatic growth in women with breast cancer (Sears, Stanton, & Danoff-Burg, 2003), especially among people with more advanced disease. Finding meaning in a chronic illness and coping through religion can also improve adjustment to chronic illness (Calhoun, Cann, Tedeschi, & McMillan, 2000).

How do people with chronic disease so often manage to achieve such a high quality of life? Many people perceive control over what happens to them, they have positive expectations about the future, and they have a positive view of themselves. These kinds of beliefs are adaptive for mental and physical health much of the time (S. E. Taylor, 1983; S. E. Taylor & Brown, 1988) but become especially important when a person faces a chronic illness. In a recent investigation, Helgeson (2003) examined these beliefs in men and women treated for coronary artery disease with an angioplasty and then followed them over 4 years. These beliefs not only predicted positive adjustment to disease, but also associated with a reduced likelihood of sustaining a repeat cardiac event.

Finding benefits in illness is often, but not invariably, associated with good adjustment (Tomich & Helgeson, 2004). Regardless of why they occur, these positive reactions usually serve a beneficial function in recovery from illness and imply that health psychologists should be attentive to this fact (for example, O'Carroll, Ayling, O'Reilly, & North, 2003). In short, people rearrange their priorities and their beliefs in such a way that they are able to extract benefit and meaning from the event (J. A. Schaefer & Moos, 1992), as figure 11.2 reveals.

When the Chronically Ill Patient Is a Child

Chronic illness can be especially problematic when the chronically ill patient is a child. First, children may not fully understand the nature of their diagnosis and treatment and thus experience confusion as they are trying to cope with illness and treatment (Strube, Smith, Rothbaum, & Sotelo, 1991). Second, because chronically ill children often cannot follow their treatment regimen by themselves, the family must participate in the illness and treatment process even more than is the case with a chronically ill adult (for example, Gross, Eudy, & Drabman, 1982). Such interdependence can lead to tension between parent and child (for example, S. L. Manne, Jacobsen, Gorfinkle, Gerstein, & Redd, 1993). Sometimes, children must be exposed to isolating and terrifying procedures to treat their condition (Kellerman, Rigler, & Siegel, 1979). All these factors can create problems of adjustment for both children and parents (E. J. Silver, Bauman, & Ireys, 1995).

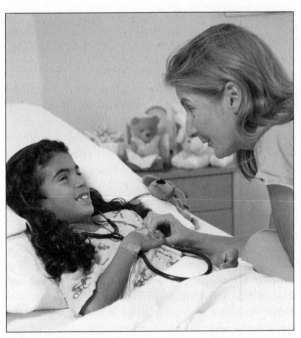

Children's needs to be informed about their illness and to exert control over illness-related activities and over their lives have prompted interventions to involve children in their own care.

FIGURE 11.2 | This figure shows the positive life changes experienced by MI patients and cancer patients in response to their illness. An interesting point is that most of the benefits reported by MI patients involve lifestyle changes, perhaps reflecting the fact that the course of heart disease is amenable to changes in personal health habits. Cancer patients, in contrast, report more changes in their social relationships and meaning attached to life, perhaps because cancer may not be as directly influenced by health habits as heart disease but may be amenable to finding greater purpose or meaning in other life activities.   (*Source:* Petrie, Buick, Weinman, & Booth, 1997)

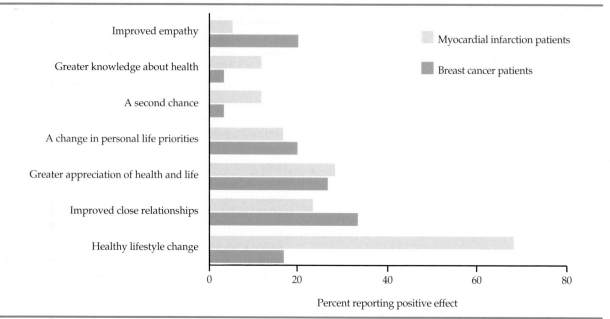

Although many children adjust to these radical changes in their lives successfully, others do not. Children suffering from chronic illness exhibit a variety of behavioral problems, including rebellion and withdrawal from others. They may suffer low self-esteem, either because they believe that the chronic illness is a punishment for bad behavior or because they feel cheated because their peers are healthy. Nonadherence to treatment, underachievement in school, and regressive behavior, such as bedwetting or throwing temper tantrums, are not uncommon. These problems can be aggravated if families do not have adequate styles of communicating with each other and of resolving conflict (for example, S. L. Manne et al., 1993). In addition, chronically ill children may develop maladaptive coping styles involving repression, which may interfere with their understanding of and ability to comanage their disorders (Phipps & Steele, 2002). Like other chronic diseases, childhood chronic diseases can be exacerbated by stress. For example,

among children with asthma, number of hospitalizations was associated with family conflict and strain and with the strain experienced by caregivers as well (E. Chen, Bloomberg, Fisher, & Strunk, 2003).

Improving Coping   Several factors can improve a chronically ill child's ability to cope. Parents with realistic attitudes toward the disorder and its treatment can soothe the child emotionally and provide an informed basis for care. If the parents are free of depression, have a sense of mastery over the child's illness, and can avoid expressing distress, especially during treatments (DuHamel et al., 2004), this may also aid adjustment (Timko, Stovel, Moos, & Miller, 1992). If children are encouraged to engage in self-care as much as possible and only realistic restrictions are placed on their lives, adjustment will be better. Encouraging regular school attendance and reasonable physical activities is particularly beneficial. If the parent can learn to remain calm in crisis situations, maintain emotional control, and become familiar with the child's illness, these factors can contribute positively to the child's functioning.

When families are unable to provide help for their chronically ill child and develop ineffective communication patterns, interventions may be needed. Family therapy and training the family in the treatment regimen can improve family functioning. Alternatively, interventions may need to be directed separately to parents and to children. Children's and parents' views of illness are not necessarily the same (Strube et al., 1991), so interventions directed at either parents or children to the exclusion of the other may be limited in their effectiveness. Thus, different but complementary interventions may be required for parents and children.

■ PSYCHOLOGICAL INTERVENTIONS AND CHRONIC ILLNESS

As we have seen, the majority of chronically ill patients appear to achieve a relatively high quality of life after diagnosis and treatment for their illness. In fact, many who are free from pain or advancing disease achieve at least as high, if not higher, a quality of life than before the illness, by their self-reports. However, as we have also seen, there are reliable adverse effects of chronic disease, such as anxiety, depression, and disturbances in interpersonal relations. Increasingly depression, psychological distress, and neuroticism are being targeted for intervention to reduce risk for mortality from chronic conditions (Christensen et al., 2002). In addition, because stress aggravates so many chronic diseases and conditions (for example, Ackerman et al., 2002), assistance in managing the demands of daily life may be required. Consequently, health psychologists have increasingly focused on ways to ameliorate these problems.

The fact that anxiety and depression are intermittently high among chronically ill patients suggests that evaluation for these problems should be a standard part of chronic care. Researchers and clinicians need to develop ways to identify people who are at high risk for emotional disorders. For example, patients who have a history of depression or other mental illness prior to the onset of their chronic illness are at particular risk and therefore should be evaluated early for potential interventions (Goldberg, 1981; Morris & Raphael, 1987). A variety of interventions have been developed to deal with these and other problems associated with chronic illness.

Pharmacological Interventions

A chief target of pharmacological interventions is depression. Pharmacological treatment may be appropriate for patients suffering from major depression associated with chronic illness. Antidepressants are fairly commonly prescribed under such circumstances, especially if the prognosis is poor.

Individual Therapy

Individual therapy is one of the most common interventions for patients who have psychosocial complications due to chronic illness. But there are important differences between psychotherapy with medical patients and psychotherapy that is conducted with patients who have primarily psychological complaints (Wellisch, 1979).

First, therapy with medical patients is more likely to be episodic than continuous. Chronic illness raises crises and issues intermittently that may require help. For example, problems with an adolescent daughter after her mother has been treated for breast cancer may not occur immediately but may develop over the subsequent months (Lichtman et al., 1984). Recurrence or worsening of a condition may present a crisis that needs to be addressed with a therapist, as for a heart patient who has had a second heart attack or a cancer patient who has developed a new malignancy.

Second, collaboration with the patient's physician and family members is critical in therapy with medical patients. The physician can inform the psychologist or other counselor of a patient's current physical status. Problems experienced by the patient will have implications for other family members' activities; accordingly, family members are almost inevitably involved in the problems created by illness.

Third, therapy with medical patients more frequently requires respect for patients' defenses than does traditional psychotherapy. In traditional psychotherapy, one of the therapist's goals may be to challenge a patient's defenses that may interfere with an adequate understanding of his or her problems. However, in the case of chronically ill patients, the same defenses may serve a benign function in protecting them from the full realization of the ramifications of their disease.

Fourth and finally, the therapist working with a medical patient must have a comprehensive understanding of the patient's illness and its modes of treatment. Because many of the issues are centered around particular aspects of illness and treatment, the therapist who is uninformed about the illness will not be able to provide adequate help. Moreover, illness and treatments themselves produce psychological problems (for example, depression due to chemotherapy), and a therapist who is ignorant of this fact may make incorrect interpretations.

Brief Psychotherapeutic Interventions

Several short-term interventions ranging from informal communication with a health care professional to brief psychotherapy are available to alleviate emotional distress in chronically ill patients. Some brief informational interventions can be accomplished on a preventive basis within the medical setting (for example, Dobkin et al, 2002). For example, telling patients and their families what they can expect during the course of diagnosis and treatment can substantially alleviate or even forestall anxiety (for example, Egbert, Battit, Welch, & Bartlett, 1964; Maguire, 1975). Simply telling patients that anxiety is a normal response to the stress of chronic illness (Welch-McCaffrey, 1985) or that depression is a common consequence of certain disorders, such as stroke (Goodstein, 1983; R. G. Robinson, 1986), may alleviate patients' and family members' concerns over whether the patient is reacting normally to illness. This kind of patient-staff communication can improve the detection of mood disorders and improve the flow of information.

Increasingly, psychologists have made use of short-term, structured therapeutic interventions to help the most people in the shortest period of time (for example, van Dulmen, Fennis, & Bleijenberg, 1996). For example, Telch and Telch (1986) compared group coping skills training to supportive group therapy for highly distressed cancer patients. After 6 weeks, the coping skills patients showed less emotional stress and more vigor than did the group therapy or no-treatment patients. Patients in the coping skills training group also reported heightened feelings of self-efficacy and fewer problems. The success of the coping skills instruction appears to be due to its highly specific nature directed toward enhancing perceptions of control. Even briefer therapies, such as those conducted over the telephone, have been shown to benefit patients, enhancing a sense of personal control (Sandgren & McCaul, 2003).

Although many interventions focus on coping skills, others have made use of more novel techniques for attempting to improve a patient's emotional and behavioral responses to chronic illness. These include music, art, and dance therapies (see, for example, Pacchetti et al., 2000).

Patient Education

Patient education programs that include coping skills training relative to particular disorders have been found to improve functioning for a broad variety of chronic diseases, including endstage renal disease, stroke, cardiovascular disease, and cancer. Such programs can increase knowledge about the disease, reduce anxiety, increase patients' feelings of purpose and meaning in life (Brantley, Mosley, Bruce, McKnight, & Jones, 1990; J. Johnson, 1982), reduce pain and depression (Lorig, Chastain, Ung, Shoor, & Holman, 1989), improve coping (Lacroix, Martin, Avendano, & Goldstein, 1991), increase adherence to treatment (Greenfield, Kaplan, Ware, Yaw, & Frank, 1988), and increase confidence in the ability to manage pain and other side effects (J. C. Parker et al., 1988), relative to waitlist patients who have not yet participated in the program or to patients who did not participate at all (Helgeson, Cohen, Shulz, & Yasko, 2001).

Internet The Internet poses exciting possibilities for providing interventions in a cost-effective manner. Information about illnesses can be presented in a clear and simple way, and even information about skills for coping with common illness-related problems or side effects of treatment can be posted at appropriate websites for use by patients and their families (Budman, 2000). Many websites now offer information to a broad array of chronically ill patients. In one study, breast cancer patients who used the Internet for medical information were surveyed, and the results showed that they experienced greater social support and less loneliness than those who did not use the Internet for information. Moreover, the time involved was less than an hour a week, suggesting that these psychological benefits may result from only a minimal time commitment (Fogel, Albert, Schnabel, Ditkoff, & Neugut, 2002).

Expressive Writing In chapter 7, we discussed the benefits of expressive writing for coping with stress. These interventions have been especially beneficial to chronically ill patients. A study of metastatic renal cell carcinoma patients, for example, found that those who wrote about their cancer (versus those who wrote about a neutral topic) had less sleep disturbance and better sleep quality and duration and fewer problems with activities of daily life, suggesting that expressive writing has benefits for terminally ill patients (de Moor et al., 2002).

Relaxation, Stress Management, and Exercise

Relaxation training is a widely used intervention with the chronically ill. Along with other stress management techniques, it can reduce the likelihood that asthmatics will have an asthma attack for example (Lehrer, Feldman, Giardino, Song, & Schmaling, 2002). It can decrease anxiety and nausea from chemotherapy and decrease pain for cancer patients (M. P. Carey & Burish, 1988). Combinations of relaxation training with stress management and blood pressure monitoring have proven useful in the treatment of essential hypertension (Agras, Taylor, Kraemer, Southam, & Schneider, 1987) and asthma (Smyth, Soefer, Hurewitz, & Stone, 1999).

In recent years, mindfulness-based stress reduction has been used to improve adjustment to medical illness. Mindfulness-based stress reduction (MBSR) refers to systematic training in meditation to enable people to self-regulate their reactions to stress and the negative emotions that may result (K. W. Brown & Ryan, 2003). Mindfulness meditation teaches people to strive for a state of mind in which one is highly aware and focused on the reality of the present moment, accepting and acknowledging it without becoming distracted or distressed by stress. Thus, the goal is to induce people to approach stressful situations mindfully rather than reacting to them automatically (S. R. Bishop, 2002). At present, the long-term efficacy of this approach is not known, but at least some studies suggest that MBSR may be effective in reducing stress, anxiety, and distress (S. R. Bishop, 2002; Roth & Robbins, 2004).

Exercise interventions have been most commonly undertaken with MI patients. It is unclear whether exercise has a direct impact on mood in patients. However, physical fitness is reliably improved, and exercise can improve quality of life (Blumenthal & Emery, 1988).

Social Support Interventions

As we noted in chapter 7, social support is an important resource for people suffering from chronic disease. Chronically ill patients who report good social relationships are more likely to be positively adjusted to their illness. The importance of social support to adjustment has been found for cancer patients (Neuling & Winefield, 1988), arthritis patients (Goodenow, Reisine, & Grady, 1990), patients suffering from endstage renal disease (K. Siegel, Mesagno, Chen, & Christ, 1987), and patients with spinal cord injuries (Schulz & Decker, 1985),

among others. Social support can also influence health outcomes favorably, promoting recovery or longevity (A. J. Christensen, Wiebe, Smith, & Turner, 1994; Grodner et al., 1996; R. M. Kaplan & Toshima, 1990; V. L. Wilcox, Kasl, & Berkman, 1994; see chapter 7).

However, social support resources can be threatened by a chronic illness. Consequently, interventions around chronic illness may need to deal with issues of social support. Patients need to recognize the potential sources of support in their environment and be taught how to draw on these resources effectively (Messeri, Silverstein, & Litwak, 1993). For example, patients might be urged to join community groups, interest groups, informal social groups, and self-help groups.

Family Support

Family support of the chronically ill patient is especially important, not only because it enhances the patient's physical and emotional functioning but also because it can promote adherence to treatment (for example, M. S. Davis & Eichhorn, 1963; B. S. Wallston, Alagna, DeVillis, & DeVillis, 1983). Family members may not only remind the patient about activities that need to be undertaken but also tie treatment to already existing activities in the family so that adherence is more likely. For example, the family may undertake a daily jog through the neighborhood just before breakfast or dinner.

Sometimes family members also need guidance in the well-intentioned actions they should nonetheless avoid because such actions actually make things worse (for example, Dakof & Taylor, 1990; R. Martin, Davis, Baron, Suls, & Blanchard, 1994). For example, many family members think they should encourage a chronically ill patient to be relentlessly cheerful, which can have the unintended adverse effect of making the patient feel unable to share distress or concern with others.

At different times during the course of an illness, patients may be best served by different kinds of support. Tangible aid, such as being driven to and from medical appointments, may be important at some points in time. At other times, however, emotional support may be more important (for example, Dakof & Taylor, 1990; R. Martin et al., 1994).

In helping separate supportive from potentially unsupportive behaviors, friends and relatives may themselves require interventions. Even the simple provision of information may be helpful to family members who must provide social support to a chronically ill individual

BOX 11.6

Help on the Web

Janet and Peter Birnheimer were thrilled at the arrival of their newborn but learned almost immediately that he had cystic fibrosis. Shocked at this discovery—they had no idea that both were carrying the recessive gene for CF—they tried to learn as much as they could about the disease. Their hometown physician was able to provide them with some information, but they realized from newspaper articles that there was breaking news as well. Moreover, they wanted help dealing with the coughing, wheezing, and other symptoms, so they could provide their youngster with the best possible care.

The couple turned to the Internet, where they found a website for parents of children with cystic fibrosis. From conversations, they learned much more about the disease, found out where they could get articles providing additional information, chatted with other parents about the best ways to manage the symptoms, and had the opportunity to share the complex and painful feelings they had to manage every day (Baig, 1997).

As this account implies, the Internet is increasingly a source of information and social support to the chronically ill. Although support groups may be available for patients with relatively common disorders, such as breast cancer, many people have less common diseases or live in an area that contains few other individuals like themselves with whom they can share information and emotional support. Websites provide instant access to other people going through the same events. The Birnheimers, for example, found that the website was one of their best sources for new breakthroughs in understanding the causes and treatments of the disease as well as the best source for advice from other parents on the psychosocial issues that arose.

Websites are only as good as the information they contain, of course, and there is always the risk that patients and families will receive misinformation as well as help. However, some of the better known websites that are available to patients to provide health information are scrupulously careful about the information they post. Among such services currently available is WebMD, devoted to providing consumer and health information on the Internet. Websites have created opportunities for chronically ill patients and their families to obtain information and gain social support that never existed before, bringing together people who were once isolated, so that they can solve their problems collectively.

over the long term. In one study of wives of men who had heart attacks, the majority reported feeling poorly informed about myocardial infarction, they reported few opportunities to ask experts questions, and they consequently experienced considerable stress (D. R. Thompson & Cordle, 1988). A short intervention designed to acquaint family or friends with a disease could ameliorate such situations.

Support Groups

Social **support groups** represent a resource for the chronically ill. Such groups are available for many patients with chronic illnesses, including stroke patients, patients recovering from myocardial infarction, and cancer patients. Some of these groups are initiated by a therapist, and in some cases they are patient-led.

These support groups discuss issues of mutual concern that arise as a consequence of illness. They often provide specific information about how others have successfully dealt with the problems raised by the illness and provide people with an opportunity to share their emotional responses with others facing the same problems (B. H. Gottlieb, 1983, 1988). Social support groups can satisfy unmet needs for social support from family and caregivers or they may act as an additional source of support provided by those going through the same event. Although traditionally social support groups have met on a face-to-face basis to exchange personal accounts and information, the Internet now provides manifold opportunities for giving and receiving social support and information, see box 11.6.

Studies that have evaluated the efficacy of social support groups vis-à-vis people waiting to participate or nonparticipants have found beneficial results. Social support groups have been shown to be beneficial for rheumatoid arthritis patients (for example, Bradley et al., 1987), men with prostate cancer (Lepore, Helgeson, Eton, & Schulz, 2003), and MI patients (for example, Dracup, 1985), among others. Self-help groups may help victims especially cope with the stigma associated with certain disorders, such as cancer or epilepsy (Droge, Arntson, & Norton, 1986), and such groups may help patients develop the motivation and techniques to adhere to complicated treatment regimens (Storer, Frate, Johnson, & Greenberg, 1987).

Support groups may encourage adherence for several reasons:

1. People must commit themselves to change their behavior in front of other individuals. Commitment to a decisional course can frequently improve adherence (Cummings, Becker, Kirscht, & Levin, 1981; Janis, 1983).

2. In the course of interacting with others, people may also learn techniques that others have used successfully to maintain adherence and adopt them to combat their own problems.

3. The emotional support and encouragement that others with similar problems provide can also encourage adherence.

Participation in social support groups may even promote better health and long-term survival. One study of patients in a weekly cancer support group found that participants survived longer than nonparticipants (Spiegel & Bloom, 1983).

Although widely heralded as a low-cost, convenient treatment option for people to deal with a wide variety of problems, self-help groups currently reach only a small proportion of chronically ill patients (S. E. Taylor, Falke, Shoptaw, & Lichtman, 1986). Moreover, they appear to appeal disproportionately to well-educated, middle-class White women. Not only is this the segment of the population that is already served by traditional treatment services, but these participants in self-help groups may actually be the same individuals who use helping services of all kinds (S. E. Taylor et al., 1986). The potential for self-help groups to be a general resource for the chronically ill, then, has yet to be fully realized.

To summarize, several psychotherapeutic interventions are available to chronically ill patients who are trying to cope with complex problems. These interventions include crisis intervention, family therapy, individual therapy, group therapy, and support groups. Each has distinctive features and benefits, and different options may be better suited to some problems than others. Evaluations of these kinds of interventions suggest consistent beneficial effects.

Despite these advances in care for the chronically ill and our expanded understanding of the psychosocial issues that the chronically ill face, medical and psychoso-

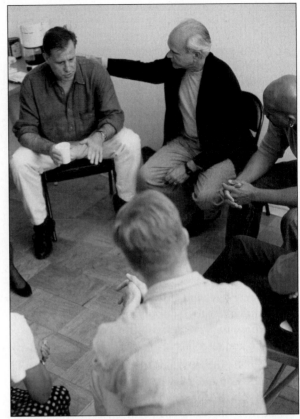

Social support groups can satisfy unmet needs for social support from family and friends and can enable people to share their personal experiences with others like themselves.

cial care for the chronically ill is still irregular, as the burden on caregivers clearly attests. Consequently, managed care may need to assume responsibility for broader-based behavioral and psychological approaches to improving health among the chronically ill. Physicians and other health practitioners need better training in behavioral and psychosocial approaches to chronic disorders. Techniques for teaching self-management of chronic illness need to be refined, and educational interventions for communicating them to patients need to be undertaken; monitoring the success of programs like these will be important as well (Center for the Advancement of Health, 1999).

SUMMARY

1. At any given time, 50% of the population has a chronic condition that requires medical management, yet only recently has attention turned to the psychosocial aspects of quality of life. Quality-of-life measures pinpoint problems associated with diseases and treatments and help in policy decision making about the effectiveness and cost effectiveness of interventions.

2. Chronically ill patients often experience denial, intermittent anxiety, and long-term depression. But too often, these reactions, especially anxiety and depression, are underdiagnosed, confused with symptoms of disease or treatment, or presumed to be normal and therefore not appropriate for intervention.

3. Anxiety is reliably tied to illness events, such as awaiting test results or obtaining regular checkups. Depression increases with the severity of disease, pain, and disability.

4. Despite problems, most patients cope with chronic illness as they cope with other stressful events in life. Active coping and multiple coping efforts may be more successful than avoidance, passive coping, or use of one predominant coping strategy.

5. Patients also develop concepts of their illness, its cause, and its controllability that relate to their coping. Perceived personal control over illness and/or treatment is associated with good adjustment.

6. Rehabilitation centers around physical problems, especially recovering functioning and adherence to treatment; vocational retraining, job discrimination, financial loss, and loss of insurance; gaps and problems in social support; and personal losses, such as the threat that disease poses for long-term goals.

7. The majority of patients appear to achieve some positive outcomes of chronic illness as well as negative ones. These positive outcomes may occur because patients compensate for losses in some areas of their lives, with value placed on other aspects of life.

8. Interventions with the chronically ill include pharmacological interventions, individual therapy, brief psychotherapeutic interventions oriented toward solving crises or providing information, relaxation and exercise, social support interventions, and support groups. Support groups appear to be an underused but potentially helpful resource for the chronically ill.

KEY TERMS

body image
denial
depression
dietitians
functional somatic syndromes

occupational therapists
patient education
physical rehabilitation
physical therapists
quality of life

self-concept
self-esteem
self-management
social workers
support groups

CHAPTER 12

Psychological Issues in Advancing and Terminal Illness

At the first assembly of freshman year in a suburban high school, the principal opened his remarks by telling the assembled students, "Look around you. Look to your left, look to your right, look in front of you, and look in back of you. Four years from now, one of you will be dead." Most of the students were stunned by this remark, but one boy in the back feigned a death rattle and slumped to the floor in a mock display of the principal's prophecy. He was the one. Two weeks after he got his driver's license, he crashed his car into a stone wall, when the car spun out of control at high speed.

The principal, of course, had not peered into the future but had simply drawn on the statistics showing that even adolescents die, especially from accidents. By the time most of us are 18, we will have known at least one person who has died, whether it be a classmate from high school, a grandparent, or a family friend. Many of these causes of death are preventable as we will see. Many children die from accidents in the home. Adolescents, as well as children, die in car crashes often related to risky driving, drugs, alcohol, or a combination of factors. Even death in middle and old age are most commonly due to the cumulative effects of bad health habits, such as smoking, poor eating, lack of exercise and accompanying obesity (Mokdad, Marks, Stroup, & Gerberding, 2004).

■ DEATH ACROSS THE LIFE SPAN

Comedian Woody Allen is said to have remarked on his 40th birthday, "I shall gain immortality not through my work but by not dying." Many of us would echo this desire to live forever, but life inevitably ends in death. A mere 100 years ago, people died primarily from infectious diseases, such as tuberculosis, influenza, or pneumonia. Now those illnesses are much less widespread because of substantial advances in public health and preventive medical technologies that developed in the 20th century. On average, people in the United States can now expect to live 77.4 years (National Center for Health Statistics, 2004). When death does come, it will probably stem from a chronic illness, such as heart disease or cancer, rather than from an acute disorder as tables 12.1 and 12.2 indicate. This fact means that, instead of facing a rapid, unanticipated death, the average American may know what he or she will probably die of for 5, 10, or even more years.

Understanding the psychological issues associated with death and dying first requires a tour, a rather grim tour, of death itself. What is the most likely cause of

TABLE 12.1 | Deaths: Leading Causes in the United States

Rank and Cause	Number of Deaths
1. Heart disease	700,142
2. Cancer	553.768
3. Stroke	163,538
4. Chronic respiratory diseases	123,013
5. Accidents (unintentional injuries)	101,537
6. Diabetes	71,372
7. Influenza/pneumonia	62,034
8. Alzheimer's disease	53,852
9. Nephritis*	39,480
10. Septicemia	32,238

*Includes nephrotic syndrome and nephrosis.

Source: Centers for Disease Control and Prevention, 2004. Statistics are for 2001.

death for a person of any given age, and what kind of death will it be?

Death in Infancy or Childhood

Although the United States is one of the most technologically developed countries in the world, our **infant mortality rate** is high (6.9 per 1,000) (Centers for Disease Control and Prevention, 2004), higher than is true for most Western European nations. Although these figures represent a substantial decline in infant mortality since 1980 (from 12.6 per 1,000) (National Center for Health Statistics, 2002), African-American infants are still more than twice as likely to die during the first year as White infants are (Centers for Disease Control and Prevention, 2004).

To what do we attribute such upsetting statistics? The countries that have a lower infant mortality rate than the United States all have national medical programs that provide free or low-cost maternal care during pregnancy. We are one of the few developed nations without such a program. When infants are born prematurely or die at birth, the problems can frequently be traced to poor prenatal care for the mother.

Remarkably, as reproductive technology has improved, racial disparities in infant mortality rates have actually increased, reflecting continued inequities in access to and allocation of health care resources. The availability of health care to all Americans would ameliorate these inequities and have the beneficial effect of bringing down the overall infant mortality rate.

TABLE 12.2 | Leading Causes of Mortality Among Adults, Worldwide, 2002

Mortality—Adults Ages 15–59			Mortality—Adults Ages 60 and Over		
Rank	Cause	Deaths	Rank	Cause	Deaths
1	HIV/AIDS	2,279,000	1	Ischaemic heart disease	5,825,000
2	Ischaemic heart disease	1,332,000	2	Cerebrovascular disease	4,689,000
3	Tuberculosis	1,036,000	3	Chronic obstructive pulmonary disease	2,399,000
4	Road traffic injuries	814,000	4	Lower respiratory infections	1,396,000
5	Cerebrovascular disease	783,000	5	Trachea, bronchus, lung cancers	928,000
6	Self-inflicted injuries	672,000	6	Diabetes mellitus	754,000
7	Violence	473,000	7	Hypertensive heart disease	735,000
8	Cirrhosis of the liver	382,000	8	Stomach cancer	605,000
9	Lower respiratory infections	352,000	9	Tuberculosis	495,000
10	Chronic obstructive pulmonary disease	343,000	10	Colon and rectum cancers	477,000

Source: World Health Organization, 2003.

During the first year of life, the main causes of death are congenital abnormalities and **sudden infant death syndrome (SIDS).** The causes of SIDS are not entirely known—the infant simply stops breathing—but epidemiologic studies reveal that it is more likely to occur in lower-class urban environments, when the mother smoked during her pregnancy (R. R. Robinson, 1974) and when the baby is put to sleep on its stomach or side (Lipsitt, 2003). Mercifully, SIDS appears to be a gentle death for the child, although not for parents: The confusion, self-blame, and suspicion of others who do not understand this phenomenon can take an enormous psychological toll on the parents (Downey, Silver, & Wortman, 1990). News stories detailing how some infant deaths blamed on SIDS were, in fact, murders has not helped parents of SIDS babies cope well, either. SIDS may be confused with homicide and vice versa, leading to substantial legal and emotional complications (Nowack, 1992). For mothers of SIDS infants, adjustment seems to be better if they already have children, if they do not blame themselves for the death, and if they have had some contact with the infant before death (Graham, Thompson, Estrada, & Yonekura, 1987).

The fact that sleeping position has now been reliably related to SIDS is a great breakthrough in its reduction. About 30% fewer babies in the United States are dying of SIDS now that parents are being taught to put infants to sleep on their backs instead of their stomachs, representing a saving of more than 1,500 infant lives a year (*New York Times,* 1995).

After the first year, the main cause of death among children under age 15 is accidents, which account for 40% of all deaths in this group. In early childhood, accidents are most frequently due to accidental poisoning, injuries, or falls in the home. In later years, automobile accidents take over as the chief cause of accidental death (National Center for Injury Prevention and Control, 2001). The good news is that both accidental deaths in the home and automobile deaths have declined in recent years (M. McGinnis et al., 1992), in part because of the increasing attention to these causes of childhood death and the preventive technologies, such as infant car seats, that have resulted.

Cancer, especially leukemia, is the second leading cause of death in youngsters between ages 1 and 15, and its incidence is rising. Leukemia is a form of cancer that strikes the bone marrow, producing an excessive number of white blood cells and leading to severe anemia and other complications. As recently as 30 years ago, a diagnosis of leukemia was a virtual death sentence for a child. Now, because of advances in treatment, including chemotherapy and bone marrow transplants, more than 70% of its victims survive the disease (M. McGinnis et al., 1992). Unfortunately, these procedures, especially bone marrow transplants, can be very painful and produce a variety of unpleasant side effects. But they have given leukemia sufferers and their families hope when there used to be none. Box 12.1 outlines some of the issues faced by victims of childhood leukemia. Overall, the mortality rates for most causes of death in infants and children have declined.

BOX 12.1

Mainstreaming the Leukemic Child

At one time, a diagnosis of leukemia inevitably meant death for a child. Now, however, many children who have had leukemia are living long, full lives, some with intermittent periods of disease and treatment, others with no sign of disease at all. Because so many leukemic children have periods of remission (the symptom-free state), many are being mainstreamed back into their communities instead of being cared for in separate treatment facilities, as was once the case (see Michael & Copeland, 1987).

Although there are many advantages to mainstreaming, there are some difficulties as well. Leukemic children may look different from other children. They may be thin, pale, and bald from treatments such as chemotherapy. They may have little energy for physical activities and may need to go back to the hospital from time to time for treatments. Because leukemia is a form of cancer, it has the stigma of cancer associated with it, and its earlier association with death makes it upsetting to many people who do not understand it. Therefore, mainstreaming the leukemic child can require careful, sensitive preparation.

One large metropolitan children's hospital has developed several programs for such mainstreaming. The primary goal of the program is to work with the entire family (the ill child, parents, and siblings) and the child's total environment (home and school) to make the transition as smooth as possible. Several steps are undertaken while the child is in the acute phase of illness. The hospital provides a residential hotel for families of children undergoing radiation therapy so that the parents can be near the child throughout treatment. A community kitchen, dining room, and living room enable parents to meet and share information and concerns with each other.

Special recreational programs developed by trained patient activity specialists enable sick children to play and, at the same time, to work out conflicts about illness and treatment. Doctor-patient games and body-image games, for example, can reveal adjustment problems and can help the child make the transition back to normal life. Siblings who are having trouble adjusting to their brother's or sister's illness also participate in the playrooms and work on their own confusion.

Other interventions help the family understand the leukemic child's situation. Parents can participate in educational programs that are designed to allay fears, to teach the parents to provide daily home care, and to help the parents help the child adjust to the disease.

Patient activity specialists also work with the schools to ease the child's transition back into the school environment. Following interviews with the child and family to identify potential problems and strains, the specialist will meet with the child's principal, teachers, school nurse, and other staff both to educate them about the child's disease and needs and to help them make the child feel comfortable in the school setting. The specialist may also meet with the other children in the child's class to inform them about the disease and allay any fears. Alternatively, the specialist may help the child prepare a talk for the class about leukemia and its treatments. These steps help the peers of leukemic children relate to them normally.

Other interventions help children develop a positive self-image by exposing them to other children who have leukemia, as through a summer camp for leukemic and other children with cancer or blood disorders. If the counselors have themselves been leukemia patients, they act as living, positive role models for the younger children.

Programs for mainstreaming leukemic children are impressive examples of what can be done when a conscientious effort is made to address all of the chronically ill patient's social and psychological needs.

Children's Understanding of Death   A discussion of death in childhood is incomplete without some understanding of how children develop a concept of death. The child's idea of death appears to develop quite slowly. Up to age 5, most children think of death as a great sleep. Children at this age are often curious about death rather than frightened or saddened by it, partly because they may not understand that death is final and irreversible. Rather, the dead person is thought to be still around, breathing and eating, but in an altered state, like Snow White or Sleeping Beauty waiting for the prince (Bluebond-Langner, 1977).

Between ages 5 and 9, the idea that death is final may develop, although most children of this age do not have a biological understanding of death. For some of these children, death is personified into a shadowy figure, such as a ghost or the devil. They may, for example, believe that death occurs because a supernatural being comes to take the person away. The idea that death is universal and inevitable may not develop until age 9 or 10. At this point, the child typically has some understanding of the processes involved in death (such as burial and cremation), knows that the body decomposes, and realizes that the person who has died will not return (Bluebond-Langner, 1977; Kastenbaum, 1977).

Death in Young Adulthood

When asked their view of death, most young adults envision a trauma or fiery accident. This perception is somewhat realistic. Although the death rate in adolescence is low (about 0.82 per 1,000 for youths ages 15 to 24), the major cause of death in this age group is unintentional injury, mainly involving automobiles (National Center for Health Statistics, 2004c). Homicide is the second leading cause of death and is the leading cause of death for young Black males. In fact, the homicide rate among young Black males ages 15 to 24 is nearly five times that for young White males (National Center for Health Statistics, 2004c). Suicide, largely through firearms, is the third leading cause of death in this age group, with heart disease the fourth. Cancer and AIDS account for most of the remaining mortality in this age group.

Reactions to Young Adult Death   Next to the death of a child, the death of a young adult is considered the most tragic. Young adults are products of years of socialization and education and are on the verge of starting their own families and careers. Their deaths are tragic both because of the seeming waste of life and because they are robbed of the chance to develop and mature (Kalish, 1977).

Not surprisingly, when young adults do receive a diagnosis of a terminal illness, such as cancer, they may feel shock, outrage, and an acute sense of injustice. Partly for these reasons, medical staff often find it difficult to work with these patients. They are likely to be angry much of the time and, precisely because they are otherwise in good health, may face a long and drawn-out period of dying. For them, unlike older people, there are simply fewer biological competitors for death, so they do not quickly succumb to complications, such as pneumonia or kidney failure. Of particular concern is the terminally ill parent of young children. These parents feel cheated of the chance to see their children grow up and develop and concerned over what will happen to their children without them.

One of the chief causes of death among adolescents and young adults is vehicle accidents.

BOX 12.2

A Confrontation with Mortality

Personal contact with death can prompt a person to reevaluate the course of his or her life and, sometimes, to make radical life changes. In the following excerpt from *Passages,* writer Gail Sheehy (1974, pp. 2–3, 5) describes the circumstances that led to her own personal crisis:

> Without warning, in the middle of my thirties, I had a breakdown of nerve. It never occurred to me that while winging along in my happiest and most productive stage, all of a sudden simply staying afloat would require a massive exertion of will. Or of some power greater than will.
>
> I was talking to a young boy in Northern Ireland where I was on assignment for a magazine when a bullet blew his face off. That was how fast it all changed. We were standing side by side in the sun, relaxed and triumphant after a civil rights march by the Catholics of Derry. We had been met by soldiers at the barricade; we had vomited tear gas and dragged those dented by rubber bullets back to safety. Now we were surveying the crowd from a balcony. "How do the paratroopers fire those gas canisters so far?" I asked.
>
> "See them jammin' their rifle butts against the ground?" the boy was saying when the steel slug tore

into his mouth and ripped up the bridge of his nose and left of his face nothing but ground bone meal.

> "My God," I said dumbly, "they're real bullets." I tried to think how to put his face back together again. Up to that moment in my life I thought everything could be mended . . . When I flew home from Ireland, I couldn't write the story, could not confront the fact of my own mortality . . .
>
> Some intruder shook me by the psyche and shouted: Take stock! Half your life has been spent. What about the part of you that wants a home and talks about a second child? Before I could answer, the intruder pointed to something else I had postponed: What about the side of you that wants to contribute to the world? Words, books, demonstrations, donations—is this enough? You have been a performer, not a full participant. And now you are 35.
>
> To be confronted for the first time with the arithmetic of life was, quite simply, terrifying.

Source: From *Passages* by Gail Sheehy. Copyright 1974, 1976 by Gail Sheehy. Used by permission of Dutton Signet, a division of Penguin Books USA, Inc.

Death in Middle Age

In middle age, death begins to assume more realistic and, in some cases, fearful proportions, both because it is more common and because people develop the chronic health problems that may ultimately kill them. The much popularized midlife crisis that may occur in the forties or early fifties is believed to stem partly from the gradual realization of impending death. It may be touched off by the death of a parent, an acquaintance, or a friend or by clear bodily signs that one is aging (Kastenbaum, 1977). The fear of death may be symbolically acted out as a fear of loss of physical appearance, sexual prowess, or athletic ability. Or it may be focused on one's work: the realization that one's work may be meaningless and that many youthful ambitions will never be realized. The abrupt life changes that are sometimes made in response to this crisis—such as a divorce, remarriage to a much younger person, or radical job change—may be viewed partly as an effort to postpone death (Gould, 1972). Box 12.2 offers a poignant example of such an experience.

Premature Death The main cause of **premature death** in adulthood—that is, death that occurs before the projected age of 77—is sudden death due to heart attack or stroke. Members of a cancer conference some years ago were startled to hear the keynote speaker say that he wished everyone would die of a heart attack. What he meant is that, compared with a slow and painful death, such as that caused by cancer, sudden death is quick and relatively painless. When asked, most people reply that they would prefer a sudden, painless, and nonmutilating death. Although sudden death has the disadvantage of not allowing people to prepare their exit, in some ways it facilitates a more graceful departure, because the dying person does not have to cope with physical deterioration, pain, and loss of mental faculties. Sudden death is, in some ways, kinder to family members as well. The family does not have to go through the emotional torment of watching the patient's worsening condition, and finances and other resources are not as severely taxed. A risk is that families may be poorly prepared financially to cope with the loss, or family members may be estranged, with reconciliation now impossible.

Overall, death rates in the middle-aged group have declined, due in large part to a 60% drop in cancers. This drop has been chiefly in lung cancers because of reduced smoking. Heart disease and stroke have also declined over the past decade (American Heart Association, 2001a).

Death in Old Age

> In olden times, as was the custom, an elderly woman went out of sight of others to become young again. She swam off a little way and discarded her aged skin, but on her return she was not recognized by her grand-daughter, who became frightened and drove her away. The aged woman recovered her old skin from the water and resumed it. From then on, this power was lost to man; aging and death was inevitable. (Melanesian folk tale, Hinton, 1967, p. 36)

Dying is not easy at any time during the life cycle, but it may be easier in old age. The elderly are generally more prepared to face death than are the young. They may have thought about their death and have made some initial preparations. The elderly have seen friends and relatives die and often express readiness to die themselves. They may have come to terms with issues associated with death, such as loss of appearance and failure to meet all the goals they once had for themselves, and may have withdrawn from activities because of their now limited energy.

Typically, the elderly die of degenerative diseases, such as cancer, stroke, heart failure, or just general physical decline that predisposes them to infectious disease or organ failure. The terminal phase of illness is generally shorter for them because there is often more than one biological competitor for death. As an age group, the elderly may have a greater chance to achieve death with dignity.

Health psychologists have begun to investigate the factors that predict mortality in the elderly age group. Why do some individuals live into their seventies, whereas others live into their nineties or longer? Obviously, new illnesses and the worsening of preexisting conditions account for many of these differences. But changes in psychosocial factors also appear to be important. Reduced satisfaction with life and depression predict declines in health among the elderly (J. Rodin & McAvay, 1992). Close family relationships appear to be protective, especially when a widowed parent has close

relationships with adult children (Silverstein & Bengtson, 1991). Clearly, psychosocial factors play an important role in health and illness throughout the life course.

In part because of such findings, health goals for the elderly now focus less on the reduction of mortality than on improving quality of life. In the United States, older people age 65 and up now experience less morbidity and fewer restricted activity days than was true 15 years ago. However, the worldwide picture is quite different. People are living longer, averaging 64 years in third-world countries, but the prevalence of chronic diseases in those countries, especially those caused by smoking, bad diet, sedentary lifestyle, and alcohol abuse, means that many older people are living poor-quality lives.

As our emphasis on morbidity and the importance of enhancing quality of life takes precedence in health policy concerns, we may see improvement in these figures. With the baby boom generation moving into old age in the next 10 years, the need to reduce morbidity and improve quality of life still further will assume a special urgency so that the baby boomers do not completely consume health care resources.

One curious fact about the elderly is that typically women live longer than men, women to age 80, men only to age 75 (Centers for Disease Control and Prevention 2004). Box 12.3 explores some of the reasons for this difference in mortality rates between men and women. Table 12.3 provides a formula for roughly calculating personal longevity.

■ PSYCHOLOGICAL ISSUES IN ADVANCING ILLNESS

Although many people die suddenly, most of the terminally ill know that they are going to die for some time before their death. As a consequence, a variety of medical and psychological issues arise for the patient.

Continued Treatment and Advancing Illness

Advancing and terminal illness frequently brings the need for continued treatments with debilitating and unpleasant side effects. For example, radiation therapy and chemotherapy for cancer may produce discomfort, nausea and vomiting, chronic diarrhea, hair loss, skin discoloration, fatigue, and loss of energy. The patient with advancing diabetes may require amputation of extremities, such as fingers or toes. The patient with advancing cancer may require removal of an organ to which the

BOX 12.3

Why Do Women Live Longer Than Men?

Women live an average of nearly 6 years longer than men in the United States, a difference that also exists in most other industrialized countries. Only in underdeveloped countries, in which childbirth technology is poorly developed or in countries where women are denied access to health care, do men live longer. What are the reasons that women typically live longer than men?

One theory maintains that women are biologically more fit than men. Although more male than female fetuses are conceived, more males are stillborn or miscarried than are females. This trend persists in infancy with more male than female babies dying. In fact, the male death rate is higher at all ages of life. Thus, although more males than females are born, there will be more females than males left alive by the time young people reach their 20s. Exactly what biological mechanisms might make females more fit are still unknown. Some factors may be genetic; others may be hormonal. For example, women's buffered X chromosome may protect them against certain disorders to which men are more vulnerable (Holden, 1987). Males are more prone to infectious disease and parasites (I. P. F. Owens, 2002).

Another reason that men die in greater numbers at all ages than do women is that men engage in more risky behaviors (D. R. Williams, 2003). Chief among these is smoking, which accounts for as much as 40% of the mortality difference between men and women. Men are typically exposed to more occupational hazards and more hold hazardous jobs, such as construction work, police work, or firefighting. Men's alcohol consumption is greater than women's, exposing them to liver damage, and they consume more drugs than do women. Men are more likely to participate in hazardous sports and to use firearms recreationally. Men's greater access to firearms, in turn, makes them more likely to use guns to commit suicide—a method that is more effective than the methods typically favored by women (such as poison). Men also use automobiles and motorcycles more than women, contributing to their high death rate from accidents. Men's tendencies to cope with stress through fight (aggression)-or-flight (social withdrawal or withdrawal through drugs and alcohol) may thus, also account for their shorter life span.

A third theory maintains that social support may be more protective for women than for men. On the one hand, being married benefits men more than women in terms of increased life span. In fact, marriage for women seems to serve little or no protective function. However, women report having more close friends and participating in more group activities, such as church, that may offer support. Social support keeps stress systems at a low ebb and thus may prevent some of the wear and tear that men, especially unattached men, sustain (S. E. Taylor, Kemeny, Reed, Bower, & Gruenewald, 2000). Thus, women's tendencies to tend-and-befriend in response to stress may account for part of their longevity as well (S. E. Taylor, 2002).

Which of these theories is correct? The evidence suggests that all of them account for some of the sex difference in mortality. Whether the factors that have protected women from early mortality in the past will continue to do so is unknown. Changes in women's roles may erode their current advantage in life span (J. Rodin & Ickovics, 1990). Smoking, for example, which did not reach high levels in women for some decades after men had begun to smoke, is now taking its toll on women's health. The next decades will elucidate further whether the changes in men's and women's roles that expose them to similar activities and risks will eventually produce similar mortality rates.

---

illness has now spread, such as a lung or part of the liver. The patient with degenerative kidney disease may be given a transplant, in the hope that it will forestall further deterioration.

Many patients find themselves repeated objects of surgical or chemical therapy in a desperate effort to save their lives; after several such efforts, the patient may resist any further intervention. Patients who have undergone repeated surgery may feel that they are being disassembled bit by bit. Or the person who has had several rounds of chemotherapy may feel despair over the apparent uselessness of any new treatment. Each procedure raises anew the threat of death and underscores the fact that the disease has not been arrested, and in many cases, the sheer number of treatments can lead to exhaustion, discomfort, and depression. Thus, there comes a time when the question of whether to continue treatments becomes an issue. In some cases, refusal of treatment may indicate depression and hopelessness, but in many cases, the patient's decision may be supported by

TABLE 12.3 | How Long Will You Live?

This is a rough guide for calculating your personal longevity. The basic life expectancy for males in the United States is 74 and for females is 80 (National Vital Statistics System, 2001). Write down your basic life expectancy. If you are in your fifties or sixties, you should add 10 years to the basic figure because you have already proven yourself to be quite durable. If you are over age 60 and active, add another 2 years.

Basic Life Expectancy

Describe how each item below applies to you and add or subtract the appropriate number of years from your basic life expectancy.

1. Family history
   Add 5 years if 2 or more of your grandparents lived to 80 or beyond. _____
   Subtract 4 years if any parent, grandparent, sister, or brother died of a heart attack or stroke before 50;
   subtract 2 years if anyone died from these diseases before 60. _____
   Subtract 3 years for each case of diabetes, thyroid disorders, breast cancer, cancer of the digestive system,
   asthma, or chronic bronchitis among parents or grandparents. _____

2. Marital status
   If you are married and male, add 10 years; if married and female, add 4 years. _____
   If you are over 25 and not married, subtract 1 year for every unwedded decade. _____

3. Economic status
   Subtract 2 years if your family income is over $400,000 per year. _____
   Subtract 3 years if you have been poor for the greater part of your life. _____

4. Physique
   Subtract 1 year for every 10 pounds you are overweight. _____
   For each inch your girth measurement exceeds your chest measurement deduct 2 years. _____
   Add 3 years if you are over 40 and not overweight. _____

5. Exercise
   Regular and moderate (jogging 3 times a week), add 3 years. _____
   Regular and vigorous (long-distance running 3 times a week), add 5 years. _____
   Subtract 3 years if your job is sedentary. Add 3 years if it is active. _____

6. Alcohol*
   Add 2 years if you are a light drinker (1–3 drinks a day). _____
   Subtract 5 to 10 years if you are a heavy drinker (more than 4 drinks a day). _____
   Subtract 1 year if you are a teetotaler. _____

7. Smoking
   Two or more packs of cigarettes per day, subtract 8 years. _____
   One to two packs per day, subtract 4 years. _____
   Less than one pack, subtract 2 years. _____
   Subtract 2 years if you regularly smoke a pipe or cigars. _____

8. Disposition
   Add 2 years if you are a reasoned, practical person. _____
   Subtract 2 years if you are aggressive, intense and competitive. _____
   Add 1–5 years if you are basically happy and content with your life. _____

9. Education
   Less than high school, subtract 2 years. _____
   Four years of school beyond high school, add 1 years. _____
   Five or more years beyond high school, add 3 years. _____

10. Environment
    If you have lived most of your life in a rural environment, add 4 years. _____
    Subtract 2 years if you have lived most of your life in an urban environment. _____

11. Sleep
    More than 9 hours a day, subtract 5 years. _____

12. Temperature
    Add 2 years if your home's thermostat is set at no more than 68°F. _____

13. Health care
    Regular medical checkups and regular dental care, add 3 years. _____
    Frequently ill, subtract 2 years. _____

*It should be noted that these calculations for alcohol consumption are controversial and require additional evidence. It is not clear that moderate drinking is healthful relative to teetotaling, and indeed the reverse may be true.

Source: R. Schulz, *Psychology of Death, Dying, and Bereavement,* © 1978 by the McGraw-Hill Companies. Reproduced with permission of the McGraw-Hill Companies.

thoughtful choice. For example, a recent study of patients with end-stage renal disease who decided to discontinue kidney dialysis found that the decision was not influenced by a major depressive disorder or by ordinary suicidal thought, but rather represented a decision to forego aggressive painful therapy (L. M. Cohen, Dobscha, Hails, Pekow, & Chochinov, 2002).

Is There a Right to Die?   In recent years, the right to die has assumed importance due to several legislative and social trends. In 1990, Congress passed the Patient Self-determination Act, requiring that Medicare and Medicaid health care facilities have written policies and procedures concerning patients' wishes for life-prolonging therapy. These policies include the provision of a Do Not Resuscitate (DNR) order, which patients may choose to sign or not, in order to provide explicit guidance regarding their preference for medical response to cardiopulmonary arrest.

An important social trend affecting terminal care is the right-to-die movement, which maintains that dying should become more a matter of personal choice and personal control. Derek Humphry's book *Final Exit* virtually leaped off bookstore shelves when it appeared in 1991. A manual of how to commit suicide or assist in suicide for the dying, it was perceived to give back to

In recent years, grass roots movements expressing the rights to die and to physician-assisted suicide have gained strength in the U.S.

dying people the means for achieving a dignified death at a time of one's choice.

Receptivity to such ideas as suicide and assisted suicide for the terminally ill has increased in the American population. In a 1975 Gallup Poll, only 41% of respondents believed that someone in great pain with no hope of improvement had the moral right to commit suicide, but by 1999 that figure had reached 61% (Gillespie, 1999). A similar poll found that 84% of U.S. residents said that they would want treatment withheld if they were maintained completely by a life-support system (Ames, Wilson, Sawhill, Glick, & King, 1991). Although some have expressed concerns that these preferences may change when people realize that they are facing death, in fact, declines in functioning appear to lead to even less interest in life-sustaining treatments (Ditto et al., 2003).

However, there is by no means agreement on the criteria under which requests for assisted suicide might be honored (Pfeifer & Brigham, 1996), and many people have regarded the assisted suicide movement with concern (for example, Byock, 1991). Until genuine access to comprehensive hospice and good-quality care becomes a reality for dying patients and their families, assisted suicide may result from unmet needs rather than a genuine choice (see box 12.4).

Moral and Legal Issues   Increasingly, our culture must struggle with the issue of **euthanasia,** that is, ending the life of a person who is suffering from a painful terminal illness. "Euthanasia" comes from the Greek word meaning "good death" (Pfeifer & Brigham, 1996). Terminally ill patients most commonly request euthanasia or assisted suicide when they are experiencing extreme distress and suffering, often due to inadequate relief from pain (Cherny, 1996).

In 1994, Oregon became the first state to pass a law permitting physician-assisted dying. Generally, at the patient's request, the physician provides a lethal dose of medication or sleeping pills that the patient can then ingest to end his or her life. Although a 1997 Supreme Court ruling did not find physician-assisted dying to be a constitutional right, they nonetheless left legislation to individual states and so the 1997 Oregon Death with Dignity Act became official, with the first physician-assisted death occurring in 1998 (Sears & Stanton, 2001).

At one time, surveys suggested that 45% of oncologists (cancer specialists) supported the idea of physician-assisted suicide; but that figure has now dropped to 22.5%. Support for euthanasia has fallen even more,

BOX 12.4

A Letter to My Physician Concerning My Decision About Physician Aid-in-Dying

Dear Dr. _____ ,

It is important to me to have excellent and compassionate medical care—to keep me healthy and alive and, at the end of my life, to alleviate suffering and ensure that I have a peaceful and dignified death. When there are measures available to extend my life, I would like to know their chances of success and how they will impact my quality of life.

I would like the reassurance:

- That if I am able to speak for myself, my requests will be honored; if I am not, the requests from my health care proxy and advance directives will be honored.

- That you will make an appropriate referral to hospice should I request it.

- That you will support my desire to die with dignity and in peace if the burdens of an incurable condition became too great.

I believe in physician aid-in-dying as one option at the end of life. If the end is inevitable, the quality of my life is more important than the quantity. My dignity, comfort and the burden I may be to those I love are critical considerations for me.

Thank you.

_____   _____
Signature   Date

Source: From Compassion & Choices (formerly the Hemlock Society). For more information, visit www.compassionandchoices.org.

---

from 27.7% to 6.5% (Emanuel et al., 2000). These changes may reflect general social trends that have been increasingly critical of assisted suicide, or they may stem from the fact that physicians now feel better able to handle the psychological issues that arise at the end of life.

More passive measures to terminate life have also received attention. A number of states have now enacted laws enabling people with terminal diseases to write a **living will,** requesting that extraordinary life-sustaining procedures not be used if they are unable to make this decision on their own. The will, which is signed in front of witnesses, is usually developed when the person is diagnosed as having a terminal illness. It provides instructions and legal protection for the physician, so that life-prolonging interventions, such as respirators, will not be indefinitely undertaken in a vain effort to keep the patient alive. This kind of document also helps to ensure that the patient's preferences, rather than a surrogate's (such as a relative) preferences are respected (Fagerlin, Ditto, Danks, Houts, & Smucker, 2001) (see box 12.5).

Unfortunately, research suggests that many physicians ignore the wishes of their dying patients and needlessly prolong pain and suffering. One study (Seneff, Wagner, Wagner, Zimmerman, & Knaus, 1995) found that although one third of the patients had asked not to be revived with cardiopulmonary resuscitation, half the time this request was never indicated on their charts.

Thus, at present, the living will and related tools available to patients are not completely successful in allowing patients to express their wishes and ensure that they are met. Box 12.6 presents a daughter's perspective on some of these issues with regard to her dying father.

The complex moral, legal, and ethical issues surrounding death are relatively new to our society, prompted in large part by substantial advances in health care technologies. Life-sustaining drugs, cardiopulmonary resuscitation, advanced cardiac life support, renal dialysis, nutritional support and hydration, mechanical ventilation, organ transplantation, antibiotics, and other interventions that prolong life were unheard of as recently as 30 years ago. Our understanding of how to make appropriate use of these technologies has not kept up with their increasing sophistication. First, there is substantial inequity in access to life-sustaining technologies (Henifin, 1993). Those patients better-off financially and with better health insurance have greater access to and are more likely to receive life-sustaining technology. Second, we do not yet have guidelines regarding cost-effectiveness and appropriateness of use. That is, life-sustaining technologies are often extremely expensive, and guidelines must be developed as to when and with whom such interventions are appropriate (Kapp, 1993). Third, our society has yet to achieve consensus on the appropriate role that the individual may play in choosing the time and means of his

BOX 12.5

Ready to Die: The Question of Assisted Suicide

Frans Swarttouw, former chairman of the Fokker aircraft company and one of the Netherlands' most colorful businessmen, bid an unusual farewell to his countrymen. Stricken with throat cancer, the executive, 64, who once characterized an entrepreneur as "a guy who works hard, drinks himself into the ground, and chases women," said he had stopped his painful therapy and opted out of a life-saving operation that would have left him an invalid. "I want to be able to draw the line myself," he said on TV. Three days later, he was put to death by a doctor. "His last evening at home was so cozy," his wife said. "Frans gave himself another quarter of an hour: 'One last gin and tonic and a cigarette, then we'll get down to work.'"

The touch of bravura was uniquely Swarttouw, but the candor about voluntary death was typically Dutch. While euthanasia and physician-assisted suicide remain taboo subjects in much of Europe and are contentious topics in the United States, they have been openly debated and researched for more than 20 years in Holland, which has a record of pragmatism in dealing with thorny social issues like drugs and abortion. Euthanasia is still, under Dutch law, a crime punishable by up to 12 years in prison. But in fact, the Netherlands has tolerated the practice for more than a decade, and the number of cases has risen dramatically over the past five years. Have the Dutch found a sensible and humane way of dealing with the unbearable pain and suffering that often comes at the end of life? Or is this a policy run amuck? (Branegan, 1997, p. 30)

The United States is only beginning to address these questions.

Source: Branegan, 1997 Time, Inc. Reprinted by permission.

or her own death and the roles that health care practitioners may or may not play in assisting this process. These issues will assume increasing importance in the coming decades with the aging of the population.

Psychological and Social Issues Related to Dying

Changes in the Patient's Self-concept   Just as chronically ill patients must engage in new health-related activities and continued monitoring of their physical condition, so must patients with advancing illness adjust their expectations and activities according to the stage of their disorder. The difference is that, for patients with progressive diseases such as cancer or severe diabetes, life is a constant act of readjusting expectations and activities to accommodate an ever-expanding patient role.

Advancing illness can threaten the self-concept. As the disease progresses, patients are increasingly less able to present themselves effectively (Liegner, 1986–1987). It may become difficult for them to maintain control of biological and social functioning. They may be incontinent (unable to control urination or bowel movements); they may drool, have distorted facial expressions, or shake uncontrollably. None of this is attractive either to the patient or to others.

These patients may also be in intermittent pain; may suffer from uncontrollable retching or vomiting; and may experience a shocking deterioration in appearance due to weight loss, the stress of treatments, or the sheer drain of illness. Even more threatening to some patients is mental regression and inability to concentrate. Such losses may be due either to the progressive nature of the disease itself or to the tranquilizing and disorienting effects of painkillers.

Issues of Social Interaction   The threats to the self-concept that stem from loss of mental and physical functioning spill over into threats to social interaction. Although terminally ill patients often want and need social contact, they may be afraid that their obvious mental and physical deterioration will upset visitors. Patients may begin a process of social withdrawal, whereby they gradually restrict visits to only a few family members (Hinton, 1967). Family and friends can help make this withdrawal less extreme: They can prepare visitors in advance for the patient's state so that the visitor's reaction can be controlled; they can also screen out some visitors who cannot keep their emotions in check.

Some disengagement from the social world is normal and may represent the grieving process through which the final loss of family and friends is anticipated (R. D. Abrams, 1966). This period of anticipatory

BOX 12.6

A DAUGHTER'S PERSPECTIVE

My father sleeps, I sit writing. . . trying to get something on paper I know is there, but which is as elusive and slippery as the life that's ending before me.

My father has cancer. Cancer of the sinuses, and as the autopsy will show later, of the left occipital lobe, mastoid, cerebellum. . . .

I have not seen my father for nine months, when the lump was still a secret below his ear. A few months later I heard about it and headaches, and then from time to time all the diagnoses of arthritis, a cyst, sinusitis . . . even senility. Then finally—the lump now a painful burden to be carried—he was subjected to nine days of tests of bowels, bladder, blood. And on the last day a hollow needle was inserted into the growth; the cells gathered, magnified, interpreted, and pronounced cancer. Immediate surgery and/or cobalt treatment indicated. . . .

And after the trauma of no dentures, no hearing aid, and one unexpected cobalt treatment, triumphant that his mind functioned and his voice was firm, he stated unfalteringly: "Let me alone. No more treat-

ments. I am 75. I have had an excellent life. It is time for me to die in my own way." His decision was not to be met with approval. . . .

Death is not easy under any circumstances, but at least he did not suffer tubes and IVs and false hope, and we did not suffer the play-acting, the helpless agonies of watching a loved one suffer to no purpose, finally growing inured to it all or even becoming irritated with a dying vegetable that one cannot relate to any longer. In the end, I have learned, death is a very personal matter between parents and offspring, husbands and wives, loving neighbors and friends, and between God or symbols of belief and the dying ones and all who care about them.

There comes a point where it is no longer the business of the courts, the American Medical Association, the government. It is private business. And I write now publicly only because it needs to be said again, and my father would have agreed. . . .

Source: "Death Is a Personal Matter." Carol K. Littlebrant, originally published January 12, 1976, in *Newsweek* under the name of Carol K. Gross. Selected excerpts—by permission of author.

grieving may exacerbate communication difficulties because it is hard for the patient to express affection for others while simultaneously preparing to leave them.

In other cases, withdrawal may be caused by fear of depressing others and becoming an emotional burden. The patient may feel guilty for taking up so much of the family's time, energy, and money and may, therefore, withdraw so as not to be even more of a burden (R. G. Carey, 1975). In such cases, it is easy for misunderstandings to arise. The family may mistakenly believe that the patient wishes to be left alone and may therefore respect these wishes. Instead, family and friends may need to make a strong and concerted effort to draw out the patient to forestall a potential severe depression (Hinton, 1967), in part because depression appears to precipitate death (Hermann et al., 1998; Wulsin, Vaillant, & Wells, 1999). Yet another cause of withdrawal may be the patient's bitterness over impending death and resentment of the living. In such cases, the family may need to understand that such bitterness is normal and that it usually passes.

Social interactions during the terminal phase of illness, then, are complex and often marked by the patient's

gradual or intermittent withdrawal. In determining how to respond to this withdrawal, one must try to understand which of several reasons may be producing the behavior.

Communication Issues As long as a patient's prognosis is favorable, communication is usually open; however, as the prognosis worsens and therapy becomes more drastic, communication may start to break down. Medical staff may become evasive when questioned about the patient's status. Family members may be cheerfully optimistic with the patient but confused and frightened when they try to elicit information from medical staff. The potential for a breakdown in communication as illness advances can be traced to several factors.

First, death itself is still a taboo topic in our society. The issue is generally avoided in polite conversation; little research is conducted on death; and even when death strikes within a family, the survivors often try to bear their grief alone. The proper thing to do, many people feel, is not to bring it up.

A second reason that communication may break down in terminal illness is because each of the participants—medical staff, patient, and family—may believe

Many terminally ill patients who find themselves repeated objects of intervention become worn out and eventually refuse additional treatment.

that others do not want to talk about the death. Moreover, each of the participants may have personal reasons for not wanting to discuss death as well. Some patients do not want to hear the answers to their unasked questions because they know the answers and fear having to cope with the finality of having them confirmed. Family members may wish to avoid confronting any lingering guilt they have over whether they urged the patient to see a doctor soon enough or whether they did everything possible. Medical staff may fear having to cope with the upset or angry reproaches of family members or the patient over whether enough was done.

The Issue of Nontraditional Treatment

As both health and communication deteriorate, some terminally ill patients turn away from traditional medical care. Many such patients fall victim to dubious remedies offered outside the formal health care system. Frantic

family members, friends who are trying to be helpful, and patients themselves may scour fringe publications for seemingly effective remedies or cures; they may invest thousands of dollars in their generally unsuccessful search.

What prompts people to take these often uncomfortable, inconvenient, and useless measures? Some are so frantic and unable to face the prospect of death that they will use up both their own savings and those of the family in the hope of a miracle cure. In other cases, the turn to nontraditional medicine may be a symptom of a deteriorating relationship with the health care system and the desire for more humanistic and optimistic care. This is not to suggest that a solid patient-practitioner relationship can prevent every patient from turning to quackery. However, when the patient is well informed and feels cared for by others, he or she is less likely to look for alternative remedies.

Strong criticism of nontraditional medicine frequently prompts strenuous objections coupled with loudly touted case histories of dramatic improvement due to some unlikely treatment. The criticism offered here should not be taken to mean that no patient ever survives nontraditional treatments or that some will not be found eventually to be effective treatments. Indeed, as chapter 9 clearly indicates, placebos alone effect miracle cures in some cases. However, these instances are relatively rare, and the small chance of being among them may not justify the great expense and hardship involved in undergoing these dubious therapies.

■ ARE THERE STAGES IN ADJUSTMENT TO DYING?

Do people pass through a predictable series of **stages of dying?**

Kübler-Ross's Five-Stage Theory

Kübler-Ross suggested that people pass through five predictable stages as they adjust to the prospect of death: denial, anger, bargaining, depression, and acceptance.

Denial   The first stage, *denial,* is thought to be a person's initial reaction on learning of the diagnosis of terminal illness. Denial is a defense mechanism by which people avoid the implications of an illness. They may act as if the illness were not severe, as if it will shortly go away, or as if it will have few long-term implications. In extreme cases, the patient may even deny that he or she has the illness, despite having been given clear information about the diagnosis (Ditto et al., 2003). Denial, then, is the subconscious blocking out of the full realization of the reality and implications of the disorder.

The diagnosis of a terminal illness can come as a shock to a person. The immediate response may be that a mistake has been made, that the test results or X rays have been mixed up with those of someone else, or that the diagnosis will shortly be reversed. Shortly thereafter, everything suddenly seems to change. Plans—ranging from what to do tomorrow to what to do for the rest of one's life—may have to change. The initial diagnosis may be so disorienting that the person has difficulty gauging the degree of change that will be required. He or she may be as likely to wonder who will stop at the dry cleaner's tomorrow as to wonder about returning to school, moving into a new home, having another child, or going on a long-planned trip.

It may be days or even weeks before these questions fall into place, arranging themselves in a proper hierarchy. The sheer quantity of issues to be considered may make the patient appear unresponsive, preoccupied by the wrong problems, and unable to understand the scope and limits of the treatments that will be required. The emotions most likely to accompany these initial feelings of disorientation are denial and anxiety.

For most people, this shock and the denial that anything is wrong lasts only a few days. Denial early on in adjustment to life-threatening illness is both normal and useful because it can protect a patient from the full realization of impending death (R. S. Lazarus, 1983). Sometimes, denial lasts longer than a few days. When it does, it may require psychological intervention. Extreme denial ("This is not happening to me; it is happening to someone else") may be manifested by terrified patients who are unable to confront the fact of their illness or the likelihood of their eventual death. But is it not helpful to a patient to be able to deny death? Denial may give the appearance of being a successful psychological shelter from reality, but it is a primitive and ultimately unsuccessful defense (A. D. Weisman, 1972). It may mask anxiety without making it go away. The patient who is denying the implications of illness often appears rigidly overcontrolled, as if a crack in the defense would cause the entire facade to crumble. In fact, reality can break through for a few minutes or hours at a time, leaving the patient vulnerable and frightened. Long-term denial of one's illness, then, is a defensive pattern from which a patient should be coaxed through therapeutic intervention.

Anger   Denial usually abates because the illness itself creates circumstances that must be met. Decisions must

be made regarding future treatments, if any, where the patient will be cared for, and by whom. At this point, according to Kübler-Ross, the second stage, *anger*, may set in. The angry patient is asking the question "Why me?" Considering all the other people who could have gotten the illness, all the people who had the same symptoms but got a favorable diagnosis, and all the people who are older, dumber, more bad-tempered, less productive, or just plain evil, why should the patient be the one who is dying? Kübler-Ross quotes one of her dying patients:

> I suppose most anybody in my position would look at somebody else and say, "Well, why couldn't it have been him?" and this has crossed my mind several times. An old man whom I have known ever since I was a little kid came down the street. He was eighty-two years old, and he is of no earthly use as far as we mortals can tell. He's rheumatic, he's a cripple, he's dirty, just not the type of person you would like to be. And the thought hit me strongly, now why couldn't it have been old George instead of me? (Quoted in Kübler-Ross, 1969, p. 50)

The angry patient may show resentment toward anyone who is healthy, such as hospital staff, family members, or friends. Angry patients who cannot express their anger directly by being irritable may do so indirectly by becoming embittered. Bitter patients show resentment through death jokes, cracks about their deteriorating appearance and capacities, or pointed remarks about all the exciting things that they will not be able to do because those events will happen after their death.

Anger is one of the harder responses for family and friends to manage. They may feel they are being blamed by the patient for being well. The family may need to work together with a therapist to understand that the patient is not really angry with them but at fate; they need to see that this anger will be directed at anyone who is nearby, especially toward people with whom the patient feels no obligation to be polite and well-behaved. Unfortunately, family members often fall into this category.

Bargaining   *Bargaining* is the third stage of Kübler-Ross's formulation. At this point, the patient abandons anger in favor of a different strategy: trading good behavior for good health. Bargaining frequently takes the form of a pact with God, in which the patient agrees to engage in good works or at least to abandon selfish ways in exchange for health or more time. A sudden rush of charitable activity or uncharacteristically pleasant behavior may be a sign that the patient is trying to strike such a bargain.

Depression   *Depression,* the fourth stage in Kübler-Ross's model, may be viewed as coming to terms with lack of control. The patient acknowledges that little can now be done to stay the course of illness. This realization may be coincident with a worsening of symptoms, tangible evidence that the illness is not going to be cured. At this stage, patients may feel nauseated, breathless, and tired. They may find it hard to eat, to control elimination, to focus attention, and to escape pain or discomfort.

Kübler-Ross refers to the stage of depression as a time for "anticipatory grief," when patients mourn the prospect of their own deaths. This grieving process may occur in two stages, as the patient comes to terms with the loss of past valued activities and friends and later begins to anticipate the future loss of activities and relationships. The stage of depression, though far from pleasant, can be functional in that patients begin to prepare for what will come in the future. As a consequence, it may sometimes be wise not to intervene immediately with depression but, rather, to let it run its course, at least for a brief time (Kübler-Ross, 1969).

The advice to let depression run its course obviously does not extend to clear cases of pathological depression, in which the patient is continually morose, unresponsive to friends and family, unable to eat, and basically uninterested in activity. In these cases, a therapist may have to intervene. In so doing, however, it is important that depression be distinguished from further physical deterioration. In advanced illness, patients often have so little energy that they cannot discharge activities on their own. What such patients may need—rather than a therapist—is a quiet companion, someone to spoonfeed them, and someone to sponge them off from time to time.

Acceptance   The fifth stage in Kübler-Ross's theory is *acceptance.* At this point, the patient may be too weak to be angry and too accustomed to the idea of dying to be depressed. Instead, a tired, peaceful, though not necessarily pleasant calm may descend. Some patients use this time to make preparations, deciding how to divide up their last personal possessions and saying goodbye to old friends and family members.

Evaluation of Kübler-Ross's Theory

How good an account of the process of dying is Kübler-Ross's stage theory? As a description of the reactions of dying patients, her work has been invaluable. She has chronicled nearly the full array of reactions to death, as those who work with the dying will be quick to ac-

knowledge. Her work is also of inestimable value in pointing out the counseling needs of the dying. Finally, along with other researchers, she has broken through the silence and taboos surrounding death, making them objects of both scientific study and sensitive concern.

What her work has not done is to identify stages of dying. Patients do not go through five stages in a predetermined order. Some patients never go through a particular stage. Others will go through a stage more than once. All the feelings associated with the five stages may be experienced by some patients on an alternating basis. The resigned patient has moments of anger or depression. The angry patient may also experience denial. The depressed patient may still be hoping for a last-minute reprieve.

In fairness to Kübler-Ross, it should be noted that she readily acknowledged that her "stages" can occur in varying, intermittent order. Unfortunately, this point is sometimes missed by her audience. Nurses, physicians, social workers, and others who work with the dying may expect a dying person to go through these stages in order, and they may become upset when a patient does not "die right" (Liss-Levinson, 1982; R. L. Silver & Wortman, 1980).

Kübler-Ross's stage theory also does not fully acknowledge the importance of anxiety, which can be present throughout the dying process. Next to depression, anxiety is one of the most common responses (Hinton, 1967). What patients fear most is not being able to control pain; they may welcome or even seek death to avoid it (Hinton, 1967). Other symptoms, such as difficulty breathing or uncontrollable vomiting, likewise produce anxiety, which may exacerbate the patient's already deteriorating physical and mental condition.

Is Kübler-Ross's stage theory wrong and some other stage theory correct, or is it simply inappropriate to talk about stages of dying? The answer is that no stage model can be infallibly applied to the process of dying. Dying is a complex and individual process, subject to no rules and few regularities.

■ PSYCHOLOGICAL MANAGEMENT OF THE TERMINALLY ILL

Medical Staff and the Terminally Ill Patient

Approximately 60% of Americans die in hospitals each year (Mayo Clinic, 2001). Unfortunately, death in the institutional environment can be depersonalized and fragmented. Wards may be understaffed, so the staff may be unable to provide the kind of emotional support the patient needs. Hospital regulations may restrict the number of visitors or the length of time that they can stay, thereby reducing the availability of support from family and friends. Pain is one of the chief symptoms in terminal illness, and in the busy hospital setting, the ability of patients to get the kind and amount of pain medication that they need may be compromised. Moreover, as we saw in chapter 10, prejudices against drug treatments for pain still exist, so terminal patients run the risk of being undermedicated for their pain (Turk & Feldman, 1992a, 1992b). Death in an institution can be a long, lonely, mechanized, painful, and dehumanizing experience.

The Significance of Hospital Staff to the Patient

Hospital staff can come to be very significant to a patient. Physical dependence on hospital staff is great because the patient may need help for even the smallest thing, such as brushing teeth or turning over in bed. Patients are entirely dependent on medical staff for amelioration of their pain. Frequently, staff are the only people to see a dying patient on a regular basis if he or she has no friends or family who can visit regularly.

Moreover, staff can also be the only people who know the patient's actual physical state; hence, they are the patient's only source of realistic information. They may also know the patient's true feelings when others do not; often, patients put up a cheerful front for family and friends so as not to upset them. The patient, then, may welcome communication with staff because he or she can be fully candid with them. Finally, staff are important because they are privy to one of the patient's most personal and private acts, the act of dying.

Risk of Terminal Care for Staff

Terminal care is hard on hospital staff. It is the least interesting physical care because it is often **palliative care**—that is, care designed to make the patient feel comfortable—rather than **curative care**—that is, care designed to cure the patient's disease. Terminal care involves a lot of unpleasant custodial work, such as feeding, changing, and bathing the patient. Even more important is the emotional strain that terminal care places on staff. The staff may burn out from watching patient after patient die, despite their efforts.

Staff may be tempted to withdraw into a crisply efficient manner rather than a warm and supportive one so as to minimize their personal pain. Physicians, in par-

Medical staff can be very significant to a dying patient because they see the patient on a regular basis, provide realistic information, and are privy to the patient's last personal thoughts and wishes.

ticular, want to reserve their time for patients who can most profit from it and, consequently, may spend little time with a terminally ill patient, yet terminally ill patients may interpret such behavior as abandonment and take it very hard. Accordingly, a continued role for the physician in the patient's terminal care in the form of brief but frequent visits is desirable. The physician can interpret new and confusing physical changes and allay anxiety by providing information and a realistic timetable of events. The patient and the physician may also make decisions about subsequent medical interventions, such as the use of life support systems and the living will, as noted earlier.

One of the most controversial issues regarding patient-staff interaction during the terminal phase of illness concerns what information patients should be told about their illness. At one time, it was widely believed that patients did not want to know if they were terminally ill, although research subsequently proved that belief groundless. Nonetheless, great disparities remain regarding preferences for information and beliefs about the amount of information that patients should have. Although 69% of European Americans believe a patient should be told if the prognosis is terminal, only 63% of African Americans, 48% of Mexican Americans, and a mere 35% of Korean Americans agree (Blackhall, Murphy, Frank, Michel, & Azen, 1995). Similarly, whereas 65% of Americans of European origin believe that patients should make the decision about the use of life support, only 41% of Mexican Americans and 28% of Korean Americans agree. Consequently, it may be best to take cues from the patient and family regarding how much to disclose.

Achieving an Appropriate Death   Psychiatrist Avery Weisman (1972, 1977), who worked with dying patients for many years, outlined a useful set of goals for medical staff in their work with the dying:

1. *Informed consent*—Patients should be told the nature of their condition and treatment and, to some extent, be involved in their own treatment.

2. *Safe conduct*—The physician and other staff should act as helpful guides for the patient through this new and frightening stage of life.

3. *Significant survival*—The physician and other medical staff should help the patient use his or her remaining time as well as possible.

4. *Anticipatory grief*—Both the patient and his or her family members should be aided in working through their anticipatory sense of loss and depression.

5. *Timely and appropriate death*—The patient should be allowed to die when and how he or she wants to, as much as possible. The patient should be allowed to achieve death with dignity.

These guidelines, established many years ago, still provide the goals and means for terminal care. Unfortunately, a "good death" is still not available to all. A recent survey of the survivors of 1,500 people who had died found that dying patients most often did not get enough medication to ease their pain or enough emotional support. Open communication and lack of respect from medical staff were also two of the most common complaints (Teno, Fisher, Hamel, Coppola, & Dawson, 2002).

Individual Counseling with the Terminally Ill

Many patients need the chance to talk with someone about how they feel about themselves, their lives, their families, and death, and they need the opportunity to

regain a sense of control over their lives. Typically, medical staff cannot devote the kind of time required for this support. Accordingly, therapy for dying patients is becoming an increasingly available and utilized option (Sobel, 1981).

Therapy with the dying is different from typical psychotherapy in several respects. First, for obvious reasons, it is likely to be short term. The format of therapy with the dying also varies from that of traditional psychotherapy. The nature and timing of visits must depend on the inclination and energy level of the patient, rather than on a fixed schedule of appointments. The agenda should be set at least partly by the patient. If an issue arises that the patient clearly does not wish to discuss, this wish should be respected.

Terminally ill patients may need help in resolving unfinished business. Uncompleted activities may prey on the mind, and preparations may need to be made for survivors, especially dependent children. Through careful counseling, a therapist may help the patient come to terms with the need for these arrangements, as well as with the need to recognize that some things will remain undone (R. D. Abrams, 1966).

Some **thanatologists**—that is, those who study death and dying—have suggested that behavioral and cognitive-behavioral therapies can be constructively employed with dying patients (Sobel, 1981). For example, progressive muscle relaxation can ameliorate discomfort and instill a renewed sense of control. Positive self-talk, such as focusing on one's life achievements, can undermine the depression that often accompanies dying.

Therapy with the dying is challenging. It can be emotionally exhausting to become intimately involved with people who have only a short time to live. Few guidelines are available for **clinical thanatology**—that is, therapy with the dying. Nonetheless, such efforts can be important in that they can help the dying place their lives into perspective prior to death. Many people find meaning in **symbolic immortality,** a sense that one is leaving behind a legacy through one's children or one's work or that one is joining the afterlife and becoming one with God (Lifton, 1977). Thus, the last weeks of life can crystallize the meaning of a lifetime.

Family Therapy with the Terminally Ill

Sometimes, the preferable therapeutic route with dying patients is through the family. Dying does not happen in a vacuum but is often a family experience. As a consequence, family therapy can be an appropriate way to deal with the most common issues raised by terminal illness: communication, death-related plans and decisions, and the need to find meaning in life while making a loving and appropriate separation. Sometimes, the therapist will need to meet separately with family members as well as with the patient.

Family and patient may be mismatched in their adjustment to the illness. For example, family members may hold out hope, but the patient may be resigned to the prospect of death. Moreover, the needs of the living and the dying can be in conflict, with the living needing to maintain their resources and perform their daily activities at the same time that the patient needs a great deal of support. A therapist can help family members find a balance between their own needs and those of the patient.

Other conflicts may arise that require intervention. If a patient withdraws from some family members but not others, a therapist can anticipate the issues that may arise so that the patient's withdrawal is not misunderstood, becoming a basis for conflict. Both patients and family members may have difficulty saying what they mean to each other. Therapists can interpret what patients and family members are trying to express. For many families, terminal illness can be a time of great closeness and sharing. It may be the only time when the family sets aside time to say what their lives within the family have meant.

The Management of Terminal Illness in Children

Working with terminally ill children is perhaps the most stressful of all terminal care. First, it is often the hardest kind of death to accept. Hospital staff typically serve only limited rotations in units with terminally ill children because they find the work so psychologically painful. Death in childhood can also be physically painful, which adds to the distress it causes. A common cause of childhood death is leukemia, which is not only painful in itself but is treated through a variety of stressful medical procedures, such as bone marrow transplants. Moreover, one must work not only with a confused and often frightened child but usually also with unhappy, frightened, and confused parents (Whittam, 1993).

For these reasons, terminally ill children often receive even less straightforward information about their condition than do terminally ill adults (Spinetta, 1974). Their questions may go unanswered, or they and their parents may be led to falsely optimistic conclusions so that medical staff can avoid painful confrontations. To what extent is this a defensible policy? Precisely because they are children, it is easy to rationalize not giving children true information about their treatments and condition on the grounds that they will not understand it or that it will make them fearful, yet it is clear that, just as is true for terminally ill adults, terminally ill children know more about their situation than they are given credit for (Spinetta, 1974, 1982). As Bluebond-Langner's (1977) work with leukemic children demonstrates, children use cues from their treatments and from the people around them to infer what their condition must be. As their own physical condition deteriorates, they develop a conception of their own death and the realization that it may not be far off:

> TOM: Jennifer died last night. I have the same thing. Don't I?
>
> NURSE: But they are going to give you different medicines.
>
> TOM: What happens when they run out? (Bluebond-Langner, 1977, p. 55)

It may often be difficult to know what to tell a child. Unlike adults, children may not express their knowledge, concerns, or questions directly. They may communicate the knowledge that they will die only indirectly, as by wanting to have Christmas early so that they will be around for it. Or they may suddenly stop talking about their future plans:

> One child, who when first diagnosed said he wanted to be a doctor, became quite angry with his doctor when she tried to get him to submit to a procedure by explaining the procedure and telling him, "I thought you would understand, Sandy. You told me once you wanted to be a doctor." He screamed back at her, "I'm not going to be anything," and then threw an empty syringe at her. She said, "OK, Sandy." The nurse standing nearby said, "What are you going to be?" "A ghost," said Sandy, and turned over. (Bluebond-Langner, 1977, p. 59)

In some cases, death fantasies may be acted out by burying a doll or holding a funeral for a toy (Bluebond-Langner, 1977; Spinetta, 1974; Spinetta, Spinetta, Kung, & Schwartz, 1976). Some of these problems will require counseling. Counseling with a terminally ill child can, in certain respects, proceed very much like counseling with a terminally ill adult. The therapist can take cues of what to say directly from the child, talking only when the child feels like talking and only about what the child wants to talk about.

In many cases, it is not just the terminally ill child who requires some kind of counseling but the family as well. Parents may blame themselves for the child's disease, and, even in the best of cases, family dynamics are often severely disrupted by the terminal illness of a child. The needs of other children may go relatively ignored, and they may come to feel confused and resentful about their own position in the family. Parents may have needs for assistance in coping that are going ignored because of their child's needs. It may be difficult for parents to get good information about the nature of their child's treatment and prognosis (Barbarin & Chesler, 1986). A therapist working with the family can ameliorate these difficulties.

■ ALTERNATIVES TO HOSPITAL CARE FOR THE TERMINALLY ILL

Hospital care for the terminally ill is palliative, emotionally wrenching, and demanding of personalized attention in ways that often go beyond the resources of the hospital. This has led to the development of treatment alternatives. As a result, two types of care have become increasingly popular: hospice care and home care.

Hospice Care

In the past 2 decades, **hospice care** has emerged as a type of care for the dying. The idea behind hospice care is the acceptance of death in a positive manner, emphasizing the relief of suffering rather than the cure of illness. Hospice care is designed to provide palliative care and emotional support to dying patients and their family members (Plumb & Ogle, 1992).

In medieval Europe, a **hospice** was a place that provided care and comfort for travelers. In keeping with this original goal, hospice care is both a philosophy concerning a way of dying and a system of care for the terminally ill. Hospice care may be provided in the home, but it is also commonly provided in free-standing or hospital-affiliated units called hospices. Typically, painful or invasive therapies are discontinued. Instead, care is aimed toward managing symptoms, such as reducing pain and controlling nausea.

Most important, the patient's psychological comfort is stressed. Patients are encouraged to personalize their living areas as much as possible by bringing in their

Hospice care, an alternative to hospital and home care for the terminally ill, is designed to provide personalized palliative treatment without the strains that home care can produce. This photograph shows a 73-year-old woman in a hospice, surrounded by photos of her family.

own, familiar things. Thus, in institutional hospice care, each room may look very different, reflecting the personality and interests of its occupant. Patients also wear their own clothes and determine their own activities in an effort to establish the kind of routine they might develop on their own at home. Hospice care is particularly oriented toward improving a patient's social support system. Restrictions on visits from family or friends are removed as much as possible. Family may be encouraged to spend full days with the patient, to stay over in the hospice if possible, to eat together with the patient. Staff are especially trained to interact with patients in a warm, emotionally caring way. Usually, therapists are made available—either on an individual basis or through family therapy—to deal with such problems as communication difficulties and depression. Some programs also make discussion groups available to patients who wish to discuss their thoughts with others who are also facing death (Aiken & Marx, 1982; Young-Brockopp, 1982).

When hospice care was first initiated, there was some concern that moving a patient to a facility that specialized in death—as hospices, in essence, do—would depress and upset both patients and family members. Such fears have largely proved groundless.

Evaluations of hospice care suggest that it can provide palliative care on a par with that in hospitals—and more emotionally satisfying care for both patients and their families. However, there are sometimes problems attracting trained nursing and medical staff to such units, because palliative care is less technically challenging than other forms of medical care (Sorrentino, 1992).

Although hospices were originally developed to be facilities separate from hospitals, their success as a treatment model has led to their increasingly being incorporated into traditional hospitals. In addition, many hospice programs now involve home care, with residential hospice care as a backup option. In many ways, this flexible program can meet all needs: Patients can remain home as long as the family members are able to manage it and receive professional care, once the patients' needs exceed the families' abilities (Buckingham, 1983).

Home Care

In recent years, we have witnessed renewed interest in **home care** for dying patients. Home care appears to be the care of choice for a substantial percentage of terminally ill patients, 50% in one study (Mor & Hiris, 1983). Because hospital costs have escalated so markedly, many people cannot afford hospitalization for terminal illness, particularly if the death is long and drawn out. Also, some managed care programs do not fully cover hospital or residential hospice costs for some terminal illnesses.

Although home care would solve many logistical difficulties, the important question of quality of care arises. Can patients receive as competent care at home as in the hospital? Researchers who have examined this issue believe that usually they can, provided that there is regular contact between medical personnel and family members and that the family is adequately trained (Rutman & Parke, 1992; but see A. Cartwright, 1991).

Psychological factors are increasingly raised as legitimate reasons for home care. In contrast to the mechanized and depersonalized environment of the hospital, the home environment is familiar and comfortable. The patient is surrounded by personal items and by loving family rather than by medical staff. The ability to make small decisions, such as what to wear or what to eat, can be maintained. The strongest psychological advantages of home care, then, are the opportunity to maintain personal control and the availability of social support.

Although home care is often easier on the patient psychologically, it can be very stressful for the family (Aneshensel, Pearlin, & Schuler, 1993). Even if the family is able to afford around-the-clock nursing, often at least one family member's energies must be devoted to the patient on an almost full-time basis. Given work schedules and other daily tasks, it may be difficult for any family member to do this. Such constant contact with the dying person is also stressful. Family members may be torn between wanting to keep the patient alive and wanting the patient's suffering to be over. Home care does give the family an opportunity to share their feelings and to be together at this important time. These benefits may well offset the stresses, and studies often find that families prefer home to hospital care.

■ PROBLEMS OF SURVIVORS

The death of a family member may be the most upsetting and dreaded event in a person's life. For many people, the death of someone close is a more terrifying prospect than their own death or illness. Even when a death is anticipated and, on some level, actually wished for, it may be very hard for survivors to cope successfully.

We have already discussed several methods of helping families prepare for death. Family therapy, participation in a hospice program, and contact with sensitive medical staff members all help prepare the family. But

BOX 12.7

Cultural Attitudes Toward Death

Each culture has its own way of coming to terms with death (Pickett, 1993; M. Stroebe, Gergen, Gergen, & Stroebe, 1992). Whereas in some cultures death is feared, in others it is seen as a normal part of life. Each culture, accordingly, has developed death-related ceremonies that reflect these cultural beliefs.

Within traditional Japanese culture, death is regarded as a process of traveling from one world to another. When someone dies, that person goes to a purer country, a place often described as beautifully decorated with silver, gold, and other precious metals. The function of death rituals is to help the spirit make the journey. Thus, a series of rites and ceremonies takes place, aided by a minister, to achieve this end. The funeral events begin with a bedside service, in which the minister consoles the family. The next service is the *Yukan,* the bathing of the dead. An appreciation service follows the funeral, with food for all who have traveled long distances to attend. When the mourning period is over, a final party is given for friends and relatives as a way of bringing the mourners back into the community (Kübler-Ross, 1975).

The Andaman Islanders, in the Bay of Bengal, are one of many societies that respond to death with ritual weeping. Friends and relatives gather together with the mourners during the funeral to weep and show other signs of grief. This ritual of weeping is an expression of the bonds among individuals within the society and reaffirms these bonds when they are broken arbitrarily by death. Mourners are separated from the rest of society for a short time after the death; during this time, they become associated with the world of the dead. At the end of the mourning period, they are reunited with the rest of the community (Radcliffe-Brown, 1964).

In Hinduism, which is the main religion of India, death is not viewed as separate from life or as an ending. Rather, it is considered a continuous, integral part of life. Because Hindus believe in reincarnation, they believe that birth is followed by death and death by rebirth; every moment one is born and dies again. Thus, death is like any transition in life. The Hindus teach that one should meet death with tranquillity and meditation. Death is regarded as the chief fact of life and a sign that all earthly desires are in vain. Only when an individual neither longs for nor fears death is that person capable of transcending both life and death and achieving nirvana—merging into unity with the Absolute. In so doing, the individual is freed from the fear of death, and death comes to be seen as a companion to life (Kübler-Ross, 1975).

What would people from another culture think about attitudes toward death in the United States if they were to witness our death practices? First, they would see that the majority of deaths take place in the hospital without the presence of close relatives. Once death has occurred, the corpse is promptly removed without the help of the bereaved, who see it again only after morticians have made it acceptable for viewing. In some cases, the corpse is cremated shortly after death and is never again seen by the family. A paid organizer, often a director of a funeral home, takes over much of the direction of the viewing and burial rituals, deciding matters of protocol and the timing of services. In most subcultures within the United States, a time is set aside when the bereaved family accepts condolences from visiting sympathizers. A brief memorial service is then held, after which the bereaved and their friends may travel to the cemetery, where the corpse or ashes are buried. Typically, there are strong social pressures on the friends and relatives of the deceased to show little sign of emotion. The family is expected to establish this pattern, and other visitors are expected to follow suit. A friend or relative who is out of control emotionally will usually withdraw from the death ceremony or will be urged to do so by others. Following the ceremony, there may be a brief get-together at the home of the bereaved, after which the mourners return home (Huntington & Metcalf, 1979).

---

few such programs can really help the family prepare for life after the death. Nonetheless, it is often at this point that family members need the most help, and it can be when they are least likely to get it (Feifel, 1977).

The weeks just before the patient's death are often a period of frenzied activity. Visits to the hospital increase, preliminary legal or funeral preparations may be made, last-minute therapies may be initiated, or the patient may be moved to another facility. Family members are kept busy by the sheer amount of work that must be done. Even after the patient dies, there is typically a great deal of work (Raether & Slater, 1977). Although there are large cultural differences in reactions to death and the formalities that follow (see box 12.7), typically funeral arrangements must be made, burial and tombstone details must be worked out, family members who have ar-

Grief involves a feeling of hollowness, a preoccupation with the deceased person, and guilt over the death. Often, outsiders fail to appreciate the depth of a survivor's grief or the length of time it takes to get over the bereavement.

rived for the services must be housed and fed, and well-intentioned friends who drop by to express their condolences must be talked to. Then, very abruptly, the activities cease. Visitors return home, the patient has been cremated or buried, and the survivor is left alone.

The Adult Survivor

During the period of terminal illness, the survivor's regular routine was probably replaced by illness-related activities. It may be hard to remember what one used to do before the illness began; even if one can remember, one may not feel much like doing it.

The survivor, then, is often left with lots of time and little to do but grieve. Moreover, the typical survivor is a widow in her sixties or older, who may have physical problems of her own. If she has lived in a traditional marriage, she may find herself with tasks to do, such as preparing her income tax return and making household repairs, that she has never had to do before. Survivors may be left with few resources to turn to (Kastenbaum, 1977). Increasingly, psychological researchers are turning their attention to the problems experienced by the bereaved (for example, N. Stein, Folkman, Trabasso, & Richards, 1997; R. S. Weiss & Richards, 1997).

Grief, which is the psychological response to bereavement, is a feeling of hollowness, often marked by preoccupation with the image of the deceased person, expressions of hostility toward others, and guilt over the death. Bereaved people often show a restlessness and an inability to concentrate on activities, and they may experience adverse physical symptoms as well (W. Stroebe & Stroebe, 1987).

It may be difficult for outsiders to appreciate the degree of a survivor's grief. They may feel that, especially if the death was a long time in coming, the survivor should be ready for it and thus show signs of recovery shortly after the death. Widows report that often, within a few weeks of their spouse's death, friends are urging them to pull out of their melancholy and get on with life. In some cases, the topic of remarriage is brought up within weeks after the death (Glick et al., 1974). However, normal grieving may go on for months, and a large percentage of widows and widowers are still deeply troubled by their spouse's death several years later (R. L. Silver & Wortman, 1980; W. Stroebe & Stroebe, 1987).

The question of whether it is adaptive to grieve or to avoid prolonged grief in response to a death has received research attention recently. In contrast to psychologists' usual caution that the avoidance of unpleasant emotion can be problematic, some emerging evidence suggests that emotional avoidance (Bonanno, Keltner, Holen, & Horowitz, 1995) and positive appraisals (N. Stein et al., 1997) actually lead to better adjustment in the wake of a death. Bereaved adults who ruminate on their losses are less likely to have good social support, more likely to have higher levels of stress, and more likely to be depressed (Nolen-Hoeksema, McBride, & Larson, 1997).

The grief response appears to be more aggravated in men and in those whose loss was sudden and unexpected (W. Stroebe & Stroebe, 1987). Nonetheless, the majority of widows and widowers are resilient in response to their loss, especially if the partner's death had been long and they had had the opportunity to accept its inevitability (Bonnano et al., 2002). Although many women have short-term difficulties adjusting to widowhood, over the long term the majority do well, with social support being a chief resource from which they draw (Wilcox et al., 2003). Among women who are depressed in widowhood, financial strain appears to be the biggest burden. For men, the strains associated with household management can lead to distress (Umberson, Wortman, & Kessler, 1992). As we will see in chapter 14, the experience of bereavement can lead to adverse changes in immunologic functioning, increasing the risk of disease and even death (Janson, 1986; Osterweis, 1985; W. Stroebe & Stroebe, 1987). In addition, increases in alcohol and drug abuse and inability to work are common among survivors (Aiken & Marx, 1982). Programs designed to provide counseling to the bereaved have the potential to offset these adverse reactions (Aiken & Marx, 1982).

The Child Survivor

Explaining the death of a parent or sibling to a surviving child can be particularly difficult (J. W. Ross, 1985). As noted earlier, the child's understanding of death may be incomplete and as a consequence, the child may keep expecting the dead person to return. This is troubling both to the child and to other family members. Even if the child does understand that the dead person is not going to return, he or she may not understand why. The child may believe either that the parent intended to leave or that the parent left because the child was "bad." It may take counseling to make a child see that this conclusion is not true.

The death of a sibling raises particular complications, because many children have fervently wished, at one time or another, that a sibling were dead. When the sibling actually does die, the child may feel that he or she somehow caused it. The likelihood that this problem will arise may be enhanced if the sibling was ill for some time before death.

Very possibly, the surviving child did not get much attention during that time and may thus feel some temporary elation when the sibling is no longer around as a source of competition (Lindsay & McCarthy, 1974). As one child remarked on learning of his sibling's death, "Good. Now I can have all his toys" (Bluebond-Langner, 1977, p. 63). Such reactions are typically only temporary and may exacerbate the sorrow or guilt the child feels later on:

> Lars was seven when his sister died of leukemia. He was never told that she was sick and when she did die, he was sent away to a relative. After the funeral he returned home to find his sister gone and his parents in a state of grief. No explanation was offered and Lars was convinced he had done something that caused his sister's death. He carried this burden of guilt with him until he was fifteen. Academically, he had many problems. His math and reading remained at about the second-grade level. His parents were concerned and cooperative, but it was impossible for them to identify the problem. After leukemia was discussed in a health science class, Lars hesitantly told the teacher his story. Lars wanted to believe that he was not responsible for his sister's death, but he needed to hear it directly from his parents. A conference was set up, and with the support of his teacher, Lars told his parents his feelings of guilt. The parents were astonished. They had no idea their son felt any responsibility. Through many tears, they told him the entire story and tried to reassure him that in no way was he responsible. In fact, he had been a source of comfort and support to both his sister and his parents. (Spinetta et al., 1976, p. 21)

In leading a child to cope with the death of a parent or a sibling, it is best not to wait until the death has actually occurred. Rather, the child should be prepared for the death, perhaps by drawing on the death of a pet or a flower to aid understanding (Bluebond-Langner, 1977). The child's questions about death should be answered as honestly as possible, but without unwanted detail. Providing only what is asked for when the timing is right is the best course.

Death Education

Some educators and researchers have maintained that one way to make surviving easier is to educate people about death earlier in their lives, before they have had much personal experience with it.

Because death has been a taboo topic, many people have misconceptions about it, including the idea that the dying wish to be left alone, without talking about their situation. Because of these concerns, some courses on dying, which may include volunteer work with dying patients, have been developed for college students. This approach is believed to eliminate myths and to promote realistic perceptions about what can be done to help the dying (Schulz, 1978). A potential problem with such courses is that they may attract the occasional suicidal student and provide unintended encouragement for self-destructive leanings. Accordingly, some instructors have recommended confronting such problems head-on, in the hopes that they can be forestalled.

Whether college students are the best and the only population that should receive death education is another concern. Unfortunately, organized means of educating people outside the university system are few, so college courses remain one of the more viable vehicles for death education. Yet a book about death and dying, *Tuesdays with Morrie* (Albom, 1997), was a bestseller in recent years, a fact that underscores how much people want to understand death. Moreover, causes of death, especially diseases with high mortality, dominate the news (Adelman & Verbrugge, 2000). At present, though, the news and a few books are nearly all there is to meet such needs. Through **death education,** it may be possible to develop realistic expectations, both about what modern medicine can achieve and about the kind of care the dying want and need.

SUMMARY

1. Causes of death vary over the life cycle. In infancy, congenital abnormalities and sudden infant death syndrome (SIDS) account for most deaths. From ages 1 to 15, the causes shift to accidents and childhood leukemia. In young adulthood, death is often due to auto accidents, homicide, suicide, cancer, and AIDS. In adulthood, cancer or sudden death due to heart attack is the most common cause of death. Death in old age is usually due to heart attacks, stroke, cancer, and physical degeneration.

2. Concepts of death change over the life cycle. In childhood, death is conceived of first as a great sleep and later as a ghostlike figure that takes a person away. Finally, death is seen as an irreversible biological stage. Many believe that middle age is the time when people first begin to come to terms with their own death.

3. Advancing disease raises many psychological issues, including treatment-related discomfort and decisions of whether to continue treatment. Increasingly, issues concerning living wills (the patient's directive to withhold extreme life-prolonging measures), assisted suicide, and euthanasia have been topics of concern in both medicine and law.

4. Patients' self-concepts must continually change in response to the progression of illness, change in appearance, energy level, control over physical processes, and degree of mental alertness. The patient may withdraw from family and friends as a result. Thus, issues of communication are a focal point for intervention.

5. Kübler-Ross's theory of dying suggests that people go through a series of predictable stages, progressing through denial, anger, bargaining, depression, and finally acceptance. Research shows, however, that patients do not go through these stages in sequence but that all these phenomena describe reactions of dying people, to a degree.

6. Much of the responsibility for psychological management of terminal illness falls on medical staff. Medical staff can provide information, reassurance, and emotional support when others may not.

7. Psychological counseling needs to be made available to terminally ill patients, because many need a chance to develop a perspective on their lives. Developing methods for training therapists in clinical thanatology, then, is an educational priority. Family therapy may be needed to soothe the problems of the family and to help the patient and family say goodbye to each other.

8. Counseling terminally ill children is especially important because both parents and children may be confused and frightened. Families of dying children may need help in developing effective coping, which can be influenced by the medical environment.

9. Hospice care and home care are alternatives to hospital care for the dying. Palliative care in the home or in a homelike environment can have beneficial psychological effects on dying patients and their survivors.

10. Grief is marked by a feeling of hollowness, preoccupation with an image of the deceased person, guilt over the death, expressions of hostility toward others, and restlessness and inability to concentrate. Many people do not realize how long normal grieving takes.

KEY TERMS

clinical thanatology
curative care
death education
euthanasia
grief
home care

hospice
hospice care
infant mortality rate
living will
palliative care
premature death

stages of dying
sudden infant death syndrome (SIDS)
symbolic immortality
terminal care
thanatologists

13

Heart Disease, Hypertension, Stroke, and Diabetes

Andrea's father had a heart attack during her junior year in college. It was not entirely a surprise. He was overweight, suffered from hypertension, and had diabetes—all of which are risk factors for heart disease. Fortunately, the heart attack was a mild one, so, after a brief hospitalization, he returned home and began a program of cardiac rehabilitation.

Many aspects of his life required change. Although he had always had to watch his diet, dietary intervention now became especially important to his recovery. Previously, he had enjoyed watching sports from his armchair, but he now found that he had to take up physical exercise. And the cigarettes he had always enjoyed were out of the question. On weekends, Andrea called to make sure everything was okay.

First, her mother would get on the phone. "Your father is impossible, Andrea. He doesn't eat the things I fix for him, and he's not doing the exercise he's supposed to be doing. He stops after about 5 minutes. I think he's even sneaking a cigarette when he goes out to run errands."

Then Andrea's father would get on the phone. "Your mother is driving me crazy. It's like having a spy following me around all the time. I can't do anything without her getting on my case, constantly nagging me about my heart. My blood pressure's going up just having to deal with her."

Unfortunately, Andrea's parents' situation is not unusual. Adjustment to chronic disease, as we have seen, is a difficult process, and one that often requires major changes in lifestyle that are very difficult to make.

In this chapter, we take up four major chronic disorders: heart disease, hypertension, stroke, and diabetes. All four involve the circulatory and/or metabolic system and often represent co-occurring disorders, especially in older adults. Moreover, due to their frequency, they affect large numbers of people.

■ CORONARY HEART DISEASE

Coronary heart disease (CHD) is the number one killer in the United States, accounting for more than one out of every five deaths (American Heart Association, 2004). It was not a major cause of illness and death until the 20th century because, in earlier decades, most people died of infectious diseases, so many people did not live long enough to develop heart disease.

But CHD is also a disease of modernization, due at least in part to the alterations in diet and reduction in activity level that have accompanied modern life. Be-

cause of these factors, around the turn of the 20th century, coronary heart disease began to increase, although it has recently begun to level off. Nonetheless, it is estimated that, in the United States, 865,000 new cases are identified annually. One of the most significant aspects of CHD is that 32% of the deaths that occur each year are premature deaths; that is, they occur well before age 75 (American Heart Association, 2004).

In addition to its high death rate, CHD is also a major chronic disease. Millions of Americans live with the diagnosis and symptoms. Because of its great frequency and the toll it takes on relatively young people, finding the causes and cures of heart disease has been a high priority of health research.

What Is CHD?

Coronary heart disease (CHD) is a general term that refers to illnesses caused by atherosclerosis, the narrowing of the coronary arteries, the vessels that supply the heart with blood. As we saw in chapter 2, when these vessels become narrowed or closed, the flow of oxygen and nourishment to the heart is partially or completely obstructed. Temporary shortages of oxygen and nourishment frequently cause pain, called angina pectoris, that radiates across the chest and arm. When severe deprivation occurs, a heart attack (myocardial infarction) can result.

A number of factors are involved in the development of coronary artery disease (see chapter 2). Recent research has especially implicated inflammatory processes in the development of the disease. A particular proinflammatory cytokine (IL-6) is thought to play a role in heart disease by stimulating processes that contribute to the buildup of atherosclerotic plaque (Suarez, 2003). Low-grade inflammation appears to underlie many, if not most, cases of cardiovascular disease. A particularly strong predictor of heart disease is the level of c-reactive protein in the blood stream, which assesses inflammatory activity (Ridker, Rifai, Rose, Buring, & Cook, 2002). C-reactive protein is produced in the liver and released in the bloodstream in the presence of acute or chronic inflammation. Because inflammation can promote damage to the walls of the blood vessels, c-reactive protein is a prognostic sign that this damage may be occurring. Because c-reactive protein levels are not particularly strongly related to other risk factors for heart disease, this risk factor may help predict heart disease in many thousands of individuals who unexpectedly experience an acute coronary event in the absence of prior symptoms. As a result of research like this, coronary heart disease is now considered to be a systemic disease rather than a disease of the coronary arteries because it is responsive to inflammatory processes.

Risk factors for CHD include high blood pressure, diabetes, cigarette smoking, obesity, high serum cholesterol level, and low levels of physical activity (American Heart Association, 2004). Identifying patients with metabolic syndrome also helps predict heart attacks. Metabolic syndrome is diagnosed when a person has three or more of the following problems: obesity centered around the waist; high blood pressure; low levels of HDL, the so-called good cholesterol; difficulty metabolizing blood sugar, an indicator of risk for diabetes; and high levels of triglycerides, which are related to bad cholesterol. High cardiovascular reactivity may also be a component of this cluster (Waldstein & Burns, 2003). Routine screening for metabolic syndrome and inflammation (by assessing c-reactive protein) is increasingly recommended for most middle-aged adults in order to initiate drug treatments and health behavior change early to prevent escalating development of coronary heart disease. Heart disease has a family history component, being more common among the offspring of people who have had heart disease. This component may include a genetically based predisposition to cardiovascular reactivity, which may emerge early in life (Boyce, Alkon, et al., 1995; Yamada et al., 2002) and which is exacerbated by lifestyle-related risk factors, including exposure to stress. However, taking all known risk factors together accounts for less than half of all newly diagnosed cases of CHD; accordingly, a number of risk factors remain to be identified, which could target people who are at risk for CHD early in the disease process.

Role of Stress

Extensive research links chronic stress to coronary heart disease (Vitaliano et al., 2002). Hostility, depression, and cardiovascular reactivity to stress are heavily implicated in the development of CHD (Krantz & McCeney, 2002; T. W. Smith & Ruiz, 2002; Wulsin & Singal, 2003). Cardiovascular reactivity contributes to the development of coronary heart disease in part by damaging endothelial cells, which facilitates the deposit of lipids, increases inflammation, and ultimately contributes to the development of atherosclerotic lesions (Black & Garbutt, 2002; T. W. Smith & Ruiz, 2002; Treiber et al., 2003). Acute stress, negative emotions, and sudden bursts of activity (Brody, 1993) can precipitate sudden clinical events, such as a heart attack, that lead to diagnosed disease. Reactivity to stress or coping with it via hostility may interact with other risk factors, such as elevated cholesterol level, in enhancing overall risk (for example, Lombardo & Carreno, 1987; Pradhan, Rifai, & Ridker, 2002).

Heart disease is more common in individuals low in socioeconomic status (SES), especially males, and the symptoms and signs of cardiovascular disease develop earlier (Krantz & McCeney, 2002) (see figure 13.1). These patterns are believed to reflect the greater chronic stress that people experience, the lower they are on the

FIGURE 13.1 | Annual Rate of First Heart Attacks by Age, Sex, and Race, 1987–2000 (*Source:* Heart Disease and Stroke Statistics–2005 Update. © 2004 American Heart Association. Reproduced with permission.)

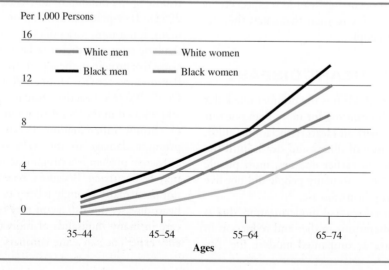

BOX **13.1**

Can a New York Minute Be Fatal?

Residents of New York City have an unusually high rate of death due to heart disease. Is it stress? The joke about the "New York Minute" that actually lasts about 20 seconds maintains that New Yorkers are exposed to a chronically pressured, highly stressed environment. Does it actually compromise their health?

To test this question, Christenfeld and his associates (1999) examined all U.S. death certificates for a 10-year period and looked especially at three groups: New York City residents who died in the city, non–New York City residents who were visiting the city, and New York City residents who were traveling outside of the city.

Among New York City residents, the death rate was 155% higher than the expected number of deaths, and among visitors to the city, the death rate was 134% of the expected deaths. But for New York City residents dying outside of the city, the death rate was only 80%.

Thus, can life in New York City kill you? It looks as if it can.

socioeconomic ladder (for example, Adler et al., 1994). Consequently, as one might expect, low SES is also associated with poor prospects for recovery (Ickovics, Viscoli, & Horwitz, 1997). African Americans are disproportionately exposed to chronic stress and, as a result, for coronary heart disease (Troxel, Matthews, Bromberger, & Sutton-Tyrrell, 2003). Although both African-American and White deaths from heart disease have decreased in recent years, the racial gap has actually increased (Zheng, Croft, & Williams, 2002).

As already noted, CHD is a disease of modernization and industrialization (see box 13.1). As we saw in chapter 6, occupational stress has been related to its incidence (Repetti, 1993a). Research on CHD and the workplace reveals that several job factors are reliably related to increased risk: job strain, especially the combination of high work demands and low control; a discrepancy between one's educational level and one's occupation; low job security; little social support at work; high work pressure; and a vigilant coping strategy. Although men with low medical risk may not develop CHD in response to these factors, among men with higher initial risk, these job factors enhance risk of CHD (Siegrist, Peter, Runge, Cremer, & Seidel, 1990; see also Falk, Hanson, Isaacsson, & Ostergren, 1992).

More recently, research has suggested that the balance of control and demand in daily life more generally (not only at work) is a risk for atherosclerosis. That is, people whose lives are characterized by high levels of demands coupled with low levels of control outside the workplace experience a higher risk for atherosclerosis (Kamarck et al., 2004).

Stress due to social instability may also be tied to higher rates of CHD. Urban and industrialized countries have a higher incidence of CHD than do underdeveloped countries. Migrants have a higher incidence of CHD than do geographically stable individuals. People who are occupationally, residentially, or socially mobile in a given culture have a higher frequency of coronary heart disease than do those who are less mobile (Kasl & Berkman, 1983). Men married to highly educated women or to women in white-collar jobs may be at greater risk (Frankish & Linden, 1996).

Women and CHD

Coronary heart disease is the leading killer of women in the United States and most other developed countries (Center for the Advancement of Health, February 2002). Although the onset of CHD is typically about 15 years later in women than men, more women die of heart disease than men do. One in 10 women between the ages of 45 and 64 has some form of heart disease, a rate that increases to 1 in 4 over the age of 65. In 2001, it accounted for 54% of all female deaths. Studies of risk factors, diagnosis, prognosis, and rehabilitation have all focused primarily on men. Less is known about patterns of women's heart disease (Burell & Granlund, 2002).

FIGURE 13.2 | Percentage of U.S. Heart Disease Deaths in 2001, by Age Group

Heart disease killed more than 700,000 Americans in 2001—roughly half women and half men. Following menopause, women face greater risks than men of the same age.   (*Source:* National Vital Statistics Report, 2003)

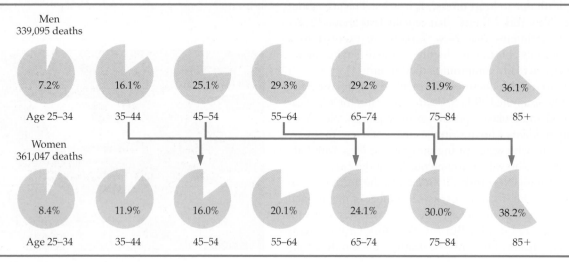

This discrepancy may occur, in part, because premature death from cardiovascular disease does not occur as often for women as for men (see figure 13.2). Nonetheless, women have a 50% chance of dying from a first heart attack, compared with 30% for a man. Of those who survive their heart attack, 38% will die within a year compared with 25% of men. Forty-six percent of women are disabled by heart failure after a heart attacked, compared with only 22% of men. Although heart disease typically occurs later for women, it is more dangerous when it does occur (Gorman, 2003). And young women (under the age of 50) who experience a heart attack may never have been diagnosed at all (Reitman, 2003b).

Women seem to be protected at young ages against coronary disease relative to men. One reason may be their higher levels of high-density lipoprotein (HDL), which appears to be linked to premenopausal women's higher levels of estrogen. Estrogen also diminishes sympathetic nervous system arousal, which may add to the protective effect against heart disease seen in women (K. A. Matthews & Rodin, 1992); in response to stress, premenopausal women show smaller increases in blood pressure, neuroendocrine, and some metabolic responses than do men and older women.

Women experience a higher risk of cardiovascular disease after menopause. They typically gain weight during menopause, and this weight gain may partly explain the enhanced risk; increases in blood pressure, choles-

terol, and triglycerides, also risk factors for CHD (Wing, Matthews, Kuller, Meilahn, & Plantinga, 1991), may also occur. However, the belief that estrogen replacement therapy following menopause would keep rates of CHD among women low has proven to be groundless; HRT may actually increase the risk for heart disease. Consequently, the relation of estrogen to heart disease remains unclear.

As noted, relatively little research on CHD has been conducted on women. Some researchers believe that this gap is due to sexism in the allocation of funds; more concern is placed on "male" problems than "female" ones (Altman, 1991). The bias favoring men occurs both for risk factors as well as for treatment. That is, although the risk factors for CHD in men have been well established, considerably less research has explored risk factors for women or has checked to see if the same risk factors for men are implicated in the development of disease in women. Heart disease in men is diagnosed earlier and treated more aggressively than is the case for women (for example, Gan et al., 2000). Because of recent national attention to this bias, research is now beginning to clarify the determinants, behavioral risk factors, and success of treatments in women (Roan, 1993).

Nonetheless, the fact that women have been so underexamined in research on CHD has meant not only that we know less about women's heart disease and its treatment but also that less information about women's

BOX 13.2

Can Male and Female Qualities Affect Your Health?

As scientists have explored the risk factors for the development of coronary heart disease, for the most part they have examined factors that may characterize both men and women. However, recently researchers have begun to realize that there may be personality qualities associated with masculine or feminine construals of the world that may be differentially associated with health risks.

In particular, research has focused on *agency,* which is a focus on the self, versus *communion,* which is a focus on others, and on *unmitigated communion,* which is an extreme focus on others to the exclusion of the self. Men typically score higher than women do on measures of agency. Agency has been associated with good physical and mental health outcomes in several studies (Helge-

son, 1993; Helgeson & Fritz, 1999; Helgeson & Lepore, 1997), and it is associated with reduced psychological distress.

Communion, a focus on other people in relationships, reflects a positive caring orientation to others, and it is typically higher in women than in men. However, it has few relations to mental and physical health outcomes. Unmitigated communion, however, exemplified in a self-sacrificing individual who fails to focus on his or her own needs, has been tied to adverse health outcomes. Like communion, it is higher in women than it is in men, but it is reliably associated with poorer mental and physical health outcomes (Fritz, 2000; Helgeson & Fritz, 1998).

---

heart disease has been present in the media, leaving women misinformed about their health risks (S. Wilcox & Stefanick, 1999). Women are less likely to receive counseling about heart disease than men or learn about the benefits of exercise, nutrition, and weight reduction in preventing heart disease. They are also significantly less likely to get risk factor interventions for heart disease (Center for the Advancement of Health, February 2002). And they are significantly less likely than men to receive and use drugs for the treatment of heart disease including aspirin, beta blockers, and lipid lowering agents (Vittinghoff et al., 2003).

What research there is suggests that CHD risk factors in women are relatively similar to those in men. As is true for men, women who are more physically active, who get regular exercise, and who have lower cholesterol and triglycerides (Owens, Matthews, Wing, & Kuller, 1990) are less likely to develop heart disease. As is true of men, social support, especially in the marriage, is associated with less advanced disease in women (Gallo, Troxel, Kuller, et al., 2003). Among women, depression is a risk factor for metabolic syndrome, a precursor of heart disease (Kinder, Carnethon, Palaniappan, King, & Fortmann, 2004). Low SES is associated with greater early stage atherosclerosis in women as it is in men (Gallo, Matthews, Kuller, Sutton-Tyrrell, & Edmunowicz, 2001). Employment as a clerical worker as opposed to a white-collar worker enhances risk for coronary artery disease (Gallo, Troxel, Matthes, et al., 2003). However, the effects of job characteristics on CHD risk in women is not yet known, although some evidence suggests that the same job factors that predict coronary

heart disease in men may not do so for women (Riese, Houtman, Van Doornen, & De Geus, 2000). (See box 13.2 for a discussion of other factors that may affect men's and women's heart disease rates).

Relatively little is known about the differences in men's and women's responses to treatment. Women do not experience the same quality of life following coronary bypass surgery as men do (Bute et al., 2003). Women experience more anxiety after a heart attack than men do, which may go unrecognized or untreated (Moser et al., 2003). Female cardiac patients experience poorer quality of life than men do (Emery et al., 2004).

Much of what we have learned about women's heart disease has come from long-term clinical studies, such as the Nurses' Health Study, and this study presents some basis for cautious optimism regarding women and CHD. The Nurses' Health Study began in 1976, when more than 120,000 female nurses, then between ages 30 and 55, participated in a long-term study of medical history and lifestyle (Nurses' Health Study, 2004). Over the past 25 years, the expected incidence of heart disease in this sample has not appeared—in large part because more older women have stopped smoking and have changed their diets in healthy directions (C. M. Stoney, Owens, Guzick, & Matthews, 1997). Indeed, among women who have adhered to recommended guidelines involving diet, exercise, and abstinence from smoking, there is a very low risk of coronary heart disease (Stampfer, Hu, Manson, Rimm, & Willett, 2000). As levels of obesity increase in this population, the incidence of heart disease may rise again (Hu et al., 2000), but at present, the study is testimony to the payoffs of good health habits.

Cardiovascular Reactivity, Hostility, and CHD

Type A Behavior In their efforts to identify psychological risk factors for cardiovascular disease, behavioral scientists initially identified a behavioral style termed the **Type A behavior pattern.** The Type A behavior pattern was formulated by two physicians (M. Friedman & Rosenman, 1974) as a behavioral and emotional style marked by an aggressive, unceasing struggle to achieve more and more in less time, often in competition with other individuals or forces. The Type A behavior pattern was thought to be characterized by three components: easily aroused hostility, a sense of time urgency, and competitive achievement strivings. So-called Type Bs, with whom Type As are frequently compared, are less driven individuals who do not show these behavior patterns.

The Type A behavior pattern made considerable sense as a potential risk factor for cardiovascular disease because these individuals fit the stereotype of the coronary-prone individual. For example, Type A individuals lead fast-paced lives, working longer and more discretionary hours than do Type Bs. They are impatient with other people's "slow" behavior; they are likely to challenge and compete with others, especially in circumstances that are only moderately competitive; and they may suffer from free-floating (unfocused) hostility (Rosenman, 1978; Yoshimasu et al., 2001). Their relations with others may be more strained and difficult, and they may have trouble coping in situations that require slow, careful work that calls for a broad focus of attention (K. A. Matthews, 1982). In recent years researchers have come to doubt that Type A behavior is itself a cause of coronary heart disease. However, Type A may be a strong predicator of when a coronary incident occurs because Type A behavior increases exposure to potential triggers such as acute stress (Gallacher, Sweetnam, Yarnell, Elwood, & Stansfeld, 2003).

Importance of Hostility Researchers now suspect that some aspects of Type A behavior are more lethal than others. Specifically, anger and hostility are more strongly implicated as risk factors for CHD than are the other dimensions of Type A behavior (Gallacher, Yarnell, Sweetnam, Elwood, & Stansfeld, 1999; R. B. Williams, Barefoot, & Shekelle, 1985). A proneness to the expression of anger has been implicated not only as a potential risk factor for the development of heart disease (Gallacher et al., 1999) but also as a potential trigger for

heart attack (Moller et al., 1999). As we will see, anger has also been implicated in hypertension and also to a lesser degree in stroke and diabetes as well, suggesting that it may be a general risk factor for coronary heart disease, cardiovascular disease, and their complications. Hostility has been tied to higher levels of proinflammatory cytokines and to the metabolic syndrome which may explain its relation to coronary heart disease (Niaura et al., 2002).

A particular type of hostility may be especially implicated—namely, cynical hostility, characterized by suspiciousness, resentment, frequent anger, antagonism, and distrust of others. Individuals who have negative beliefs about others, including the perception that other people are being antagonistic or threatening, are often highly verbally aggressive and exhibit subtly antagonistic behavior. Individuals who are high in cynical hostility may have difficulty extracting the social support that they need from their environment (Benotsch, Christensen, & McKelvey, 1997), or they may fail to make effective use of available social support (Lepore, 1995) (see box 13.3). People high in cynical hostility also appeared to have more conflict with others, more negative affect, and more resulting sleep disturbance, which may further contribute to their risk (Brissette & Cohen, 2002).

Hostility combined with defensiveness may be particularly problematic for adverse cardiovascular changes (Helmers & Krantz, 1996). Specifically, people who are both hostile and defensive (that is, who do not report socially undesirable aspects of themselves) show the greatest association between cardiovascular response and coronary heart disease (Helmers & Krantz, 1996).

Who's Hostile? Overall, men show higher hostility generally, which may partially explain their heightened risk for CHD, relative to women (K. A. Matthews, Owens, Allen, & Stoney, 1992). Higher hostility is found among non-Whites and those of lower socioeconomic status (Barefoot, 1992; Siegman, Townsend, Civelek, & Blumenthal, 2000). Hostility can be reliably measured at a young age and shows considerable stability among boys but not girls (Woodall & Matthews, 1993).

Developmental Antecedents Hostility reflects an oppositional orientation toward people that is developed in childhood, stemming from feelings of insecurity about oneself and negative feelings toward others (Houston & Vavak, 1991). Consistent with this point, research has suggested that particular child-rearing practices may foster hostility—specifically, parental in-

BOX 13.3

Hostility and Cardiovascular Disease

Research has implicated cynical hostility as a psychological culprit in the development of cardiovascular disease. Many studies have employed measures of hostility to look at this association. Some sample items are below:

1. I don't matter much to other people.
2. People in charge often don't really know what they are doing.
3. Most people lie to get ahead in life.
4. People look at me like I'm incompetent.
5. Many of my friends irritate me with the things they do.
6. People who tell me what to do frequently know less than I do.
7. I trust no one; life is easier that way.
8. People who are happy most of the time rub me the wrong way.
9. I am often dissatisfied with others.
10. People often misinterpret my actions.

terference, punitiveness, lack of acceptance, conflict, or abuse. Family environments that are nonsupportive, unaccepting, and high in conflict tend to promote the development of hostility in sons (K. A. Matthews, Woodall, Kenyon, & Jacob, 1996), and early hostility is related to certain risk factors for later cardiovascular disease (K. A. Matthews, Woodall, & Allen, 1993). Hostility runs in families and both genetic and environmental factors appear to be implicated (Weidner et al., 2000). Evidence that hostility in childhood predicts the development of coronary artery disease risk factors later in life is mounting. For example, hostility in children and adolescents predicts the development of metabolic syndrome (Räikkönen, Matthews, & Salomon, 2003).

Expressing Versus Harboring Hostility Is hostility lethal as a psychological state or only in its expression? Research suggests that the expression of hostile emotions, such as anger and cynicism, may be more reliably associated with enhanced cardiovascular reactivity than is the state of anger or hostility (Siegman & Snow, 1997). For example, among men low in socioeconomic status, the overt behavior expression of anger is related to CHD incidence, but trait anger, or the experience of anger without expressing it, bears no relationship (Mendes de Leon, 1992). Although anger suppression and hostile attitudes have been related to atherosclerosis in women (K. A. Matthews, Owen, Kuller, Sutton-Tyrrell, & Jansen-McWilliams, 1998), the relation between hostile style and enhanced cardiovascular reactivity to stress may not be as reliable for women as for

men (K. W. Davidson, Hall, & MacGregor, 1996; Engebretson & Matthews, 1992).

Hostility and Social Relationships Hostile individuals have more interpersonal conflict in their lives and less social support, and this fallout may also contribute to their risk for disease. Their reactivity to stress seems especially to be engaged during these episodes of interpersonal conflict. For example, in one study, 60 couples participated in a discussion under conditions of high or low threat of evaluation by others while they were either agreeing or disagreeing with each other. Husbands who were high in hostility showed a greater blood pressure reactivity in response to stressful marital interaction in response to threat; the same relationship was not found for wives, however (T. W. Smith & Gallo, 1999; see also Newton & Sanford, 2003).

Hostile people may produce or seek out more stressful interpersonal encounters in their daily lives and, at the same time, undermine the effectiveness of their social support network (J. Allen, Markovitz, Jacobs, & Knox, 2001). Researchers are uncertain whether the enhanced CHD risk of hostile people is caused by the deficits in social support that hostility produces, by the hostile anger itself, or by the underlying cardiovascular reactivity that hostility may reflect.

Hostility and Reactivity Some health psychologists now suspect that hostility is, at least in part, a social manifestation of cardiovascular reactivity and the likelihood of overresponding sympathetically to stressful circumstances. Among the evidence suggesting this relation are findings that cardiovascular reactivity in social situations explains the relation between hostility and the development of coronary heart disease (Guyll & Contrada, 1998). That is, when a hostile person is provoked in interpersonal situations, the hostility-hyperreactivity relation is seen (Suls & Wan, 1993). Chronically hostile people show more pronounced physiological reactions in response to interpersonal stressors (Guyll & Contrada, 1998). In response to provocation, hostile individuals have larger and longer-lasting blood pressure responses to anger-arousing situations (Fredrickson et al., 2000).

Hostile Type A individuals appear to exhibit a weak antagonistic response to sympathetic activity in response to stress, suggesting that their reactivity to stress is not only greater initially but also may last longer (Fukudo et al., 1992). Hostile individuals also show different patterns of immune activation in response to sympathetic activation, which may further contribute to accelerated development of heart disease (R. B. Williams et al., 1997). Highly hostile individuals appear to take longer to recover physiologically from stress (Suarez et al., 1997).

The fact that hostility may reflect underlying tendencies toward cardiovascular reactivity in stressful circumstances does not undermine or deny the importance of childhood environment in the development of hostility or the significance of the social environment in eliciting it. For example, to the extent that hostility reflects a genetically based underlying physiological reactivity, parents and children predisposed to reactivity may create and respond to the family environment differently. For reactivity to assume the form of hostility, particular environmental circumstances—such as the parental child-rearing practices noted earlier or the interpersonal conflictual stressful circumstances that evoke hostile behavior—may need to be in place. Consequently, the reactivity-hostility relationship may be thought of as a biopsychosocial process.

Mechanisms Linking Reactivity and Psychological Factors   How might greater physiological and psychological reactivity in conflictive situations promote heart disease? (Lovallo & Gerin, 2003). In some individuals, stress causes vasorestriction in peripheral areas of the heart and at the same time accelerates heart rate. Thus, these individuals attempt to transfer more and more blood through ever-shrinking vessels. Presumably, this process produces wear and tear on the coronary arteries, which, in turn, produces atherosclerotic lesions. Blood pressure variability may have adverse effects on the endothelial tissue of the coronary arteries and may promote plaque formation (Sloan, Shapiro, Bagiella, Myers, & Gorman, 1999).

Catecholamines exert a direct chemical effect on blood vessels. The rise and fall of catecholamine levels, as may occur in chronic or recurrent exposure to stress, may prompt continual changes in blood pressure that undermine the resilience of the vessels. Whether the effect of the catecholamines on the endothelial cells that maintain the integrity of the vessels is a mechanism that links psychosocial factors to coronary heart disease is not yet known (K. F. Harris & Matthews, 2004). Sympathetic activation also causes lipids to be shunted into the bloodstream, another possible contributor to atherosclerosis. Low levels of tonic vagal cardiac control may impede recovery from stress and act as another mechanism increasing the risk of cardiovascular disease (Mezzacapa, Kelsey, Katkin, & Sloan, 2001). Hostility is also related to increased lipid profiles (Richards, Hof, & Alvarenga, 2000) and increased platelet activation in coronary heart disease patients, which can precipitate secondary heart disease events (Markovitz, 1998). Cynical hostility does not appear to be linked to inflammatory processes, however (G. E. Miller, Freedland, Carney, Stetler, & Banks, 2003).

Stress and anxiety may be linked to heart disease via changes in blood coagulation and fibrinolytic activity (von Kaenel, Mills, Fainman, & Dimsdale, 2001). Stress can contribute to increased migration and recruitment of immune cells to sites of infection and inflammation. This increase in leukocyte trafficking and consequent increase in inflammatory activity may contribute to endothelial damage and the buildup of plaque (Redwine, Snow, Mills, & Irwin, 2003).

Hostile individuals may engage in high-risk health behaviors that enhance CHD risk. Higher hostility is associated with more caffeine consumption, higher weight, higher lipid levels, smoking, greater alcohol consumption, and hypertension (Greene, Houston, & Holleran, 1995; Lipkus, Barefoot, Williams, & Siegler, 1994; Siegler, Peterson, Barefoot, & Williams, 1992). Expressed hostility has also been related to higher total cholesterol and higher low-density lipoprotein (LDL) in both men and women (Dujovne & Houston, 1991). It has also been tied to a lower likelihood of complying with interventions, such as those involving diet (A. J. Christensen, Wiebe, & Lawton, 1997).

Depression and CHD

Considerable research now suggests a central role for depression in the development and exacerbation of coronary heart disease. As one newspaper headline put it, a life of quiet desperation is as dangerous as smoking. Reviews of the literature reveal a strong association between CHD and depression (Musselman & Nemeroff, 2000). Depression is not a psychological by-product of other risk factors for CHD but an independent risk factor in its own right, environmentally rather than genetically based (Lett et al., 2004). The risk that depression poses with respect to coronary artery disease is greater than that posed by secondhand smoke but sufficiently strong to consider depression a major independent factor in the onset of coronary disease (Wulsin & Singal, 2003).

Research also supports a strong link between depression and the likelihood of a heart attack (Pratt et al., 1996), between depression and heart failure among the elderly (Williams et al., 2002), and between hopelessness and heart attack (Everson et al., 1996; see also N. Adler & Matthews, 1994; Markovitz, Matthews, Wing, Kuller, & Meilahn, 1991). This additional risk is not explained by health behaviors, social isolation, or work characteristics; this relation is more consistent in men than it is in women (Stansfeld, Fuhrer, Shipley, & Marmot, 2002). The exhaustion and depression characteristic of the phase just before an acute coronary event is thought by some to represent a reactivation of latent viruses and a concomitant inflammation of coronary vessels. Some evidence suggests that the mental state of patients awaiting angioplasty for heart disease is positively associated with blood markers of inflammation (Appels, Bar, Bar, Bruggeman, & DeBaets, 2000). Symptoms of depression before coronary artery bypass graft surgery is an important predictor of long-term mortality (Burg, Benedetto, Rosenberg, & Soufer, 2003).

How does depression predict heart disease? As is true for hostility, depression has been tied to inflammatory processes. Depression is strongly related to elevated c-reactive protein, a marker of low-grade systemic inflammation. As already noted, atherosclerosis is an inflammatory process, and, because depression promotes inflammation, this may account for the relation between depression and atherosclerosis (Danner, Kasl, Abramson, & Vaccarino, 2003; G. E. Miller et al. 2003; Suarez, Krishnan, & Lewis, 2003). Inflammatory processes appear to explain the relation of depression to heart failure as well (Pasic, Levy, & Sullivan, 2003). Depressive symptoms are also associated with indicators of the metabolic syndrome, which may represent a related pathway to disease (McCaffrey, Niaura, Todaro, Swann, & Carmelli, 2003).

Treatment of depression may improve the prospects of long-term recovery from heart attack. Depression is typically treated by serotonin reuptake inhibitors, which prevent serotonin from attaching to receptors. When the receptors in the blood stream are blocked, it may reduce the formation of clots by preventing the aggregation of platelets in the arteries (Schins, Honig, Crijns, Baur, & Hamukyak, 2003). Essentially, antidepressants may act as blood thinners (Gupta, 2002). As yet, whether treatment for depression improves coronary heart disease prevalence and survival remains to be seen (Lett et al., 2004).

Other Psychosocial Risk Factors and CHD

Vigilant coping—that is, chronically searching the environment for potential threats—has also been associated with risk factors for heart disease (Gump & Matthews, 1998). Anxiety has been implicated in sudden cardiac death, perhaps because anxiety appears to reduce vagal control of heart rate (L. L. Watkins, Grossman, Krishnan, & Sherwood, 1998).

Recently, researchers have explored whether social dominance contributes to risk for coronary heart disease. Social dominance reflects a pattern of attempting to dominate social interactions through verbal competition, a fast speaking rate, and the tendency to jump on other people's responses before they have had a chance to finish. Evidence suggests that social dominance may be related to all-cause mortality (Houston, Babyak, Chesney, Black, & Ragland, 1997), and it may be especially related to mortality due to coronary heart disease.

Investigators have related vital exhaustion, a mental state characterized by extreme fatigue, a feeling of being dejected or defeated, and enhanced irritability to cardiovascular disease (Wirtz et al., 2003); vital exhaustion, in combination with other risk factors, predicts the likelihood of a heart attack (Bages, Appels, & Falger, 1999) and of a second heart attack after initial recovery (Kop, Appels, Mendes de Leon, de Swart, & Bar, 1994).

As we saw earlier, hostility can interfere with the ability to get social support. Social isolation in its own right confers increased risk for coronary heart disease as well as does chronic interpersonal conflict (T. W. Smith & Ruiz, 2002). Unchecked inflammatory processes may

BOX 13.4

Coronary Heart Disease and the Web

The computer age has made it increasingly possible to improve the process of diagnosis and treatment in heart disease. Over many years, databases have been painstakingly constructed as physicians have provided details of thousands of cases of people with coronary heart disease. Duke University, for example, has a databank that contains detailed information on thousands of heart attack patients, including age, family history, and enzyme levels, that, among other things, can be used to project the kind of treatment a patient should receive and generate a prediction of how that patient will respond (Ramos, 1996). From this database, practitioners and researchers get a much clearer picture of the factors that predict heart attacks and how risk factors can be identified early and treated most effectively.

In addition, as in many fields of health psychology, advances in the diagnosis and treatment of coronary heart disease are coming rapidly, so textbooks are out of date before they come out. Even journals provide

information that may be old news. Computer databanks and the Web provide access to the most current information, greatly increasing the chances that every patient can receive the best possible treatment, whatever that treatment may be.

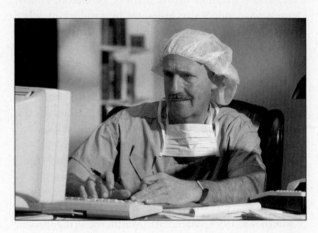

account for these findings (Wirtz et al., 2003). On the protective side, optimism appears to guard against the development of depressive symptoms in heart disease (Shnek, Irvine, Stewart, & Abbey, 2001) and the development of coronary heart disease in older adults (Kubzansky, Sparrow, Vokonas, & Kawachi, 2001).

Overall, there is still much to be learned about environmental and social factors that contribute to coronary heart disease, and especially how they differ between the genders and races. We have considerable knowledge about White men, somewhat less about Black men, relatively little about women in general, and very little about Black women. These differences are a high priority for future research (Saab et al., 1997; Vogele, Jarvis, & Cheeseman, 1997). (See box 13.4 for a discussion of the role that the Internet is increasingly playing concerning information about cardiovascular diseases.)

Modification of CHD Risk-Related Behavior

In keeping with the general shift toward prevention, interventions have increasingly focused on those at risk for heart disease. People with high cholesterol or poor lipid profiles may be targeted for preventive dietary interventions. Programs to help people stop smoking have been heavily targeted toward those at risk for heart disease. Ex-

ercise has been recommended for the modification of coronary-prone behavior, and it can achieve positive effects in both physiological and psychological functioning.

In one study (Blumenthal et al., 1988), healthy Type A men were assigned to either an aerobic exercise training group or a strength and flexibility training group. After 12 weeks, both groups showed declines in behavioral reactivity to stress. In addition, the aerobic exercise group showed attenuation of heart rate, systolic and diastolic blood pressure, and estimated myocardial oxygen consumption during a behavioral challenge, as well as lower blood pressure, heart rate, and myocardial oxygen consumption during recovery. Subsequent studies with both men and women have confirmed these early results (Blumenthal, Matthews, et al., 1991). Thus, exercise interventions have the potential for reducing cardiovascular risk.

Interventions may be targeted to particular windows of vulnerability, during which time educational interventions to help people control their risk factors may be especially helpful. As we saw earlier, women's risk for heart disease increases after menopause, so targeting diet and exercise interventions to this high-risk group is a promising intervention strategy (Simkin-Silverman et al., 1995).

Modifying Hostility
Researchers have now established that the relationship between hostility and CHD

is clear enough to have policy implications. That is, interventions designed to reduce anger and hostility may well reduce rates of coronary heart disease and related diseases, such as hypertension.

Some such interventions have used principles of relaxation therapy, helping those with enhanced reactivity to stress learn to substitute relaxation and deep breathing instead. In one study, 36 men were trained in progressive relaxation techniques, transcendental meditation, or a control condition. Relaxation training did not reduce cardiovascular responses during stress, but it did result in more rapid blood pressure reduction during the recovery period (English & Baker, 1983).

Modification of the speech style of hostile individuals has also been used as an intervention to manage responses to stress. As noted earlier, one of the characteristics of individuals who show heightened cardiovascular reactivity to stress is speaking quickly and loudly, especially when they are angry or upset. Researchers have found that people who are trained to reduce their speech rate and their loudness experience a significant reduction in cardiovascular reactivity (Siegman, Dembroski, & Crump, 1992).

Management of Heart Disease

Approximately 700,000 individuals suffer a heart attack each year in the United States. Of these, it is estimated that 400,000 die before reaching the hospital or in the emergency room (American Heart Association, 2004).

Role of Delay   One of the reasons for high rates of mortality and disability following heart attacks is that patients often delay several hours or even days before seeking treatment. Some patients are simply unable to face the fact that they have had a heart attack. Others interpret the symptoms as more mild disorders and treat themselves.

Older patients and African-American heart attack victims appear to delay longer, as do patients who have consulted with a physician or engaged in self-treatment for their symptoms. Experiencing the attack during the daytime, as well as having a family member present, enhances delay, perhaps because the environment is more distracting under these circumstances. Surprisingly, too, a history of angina or diabetes actually increases, rather than decreases, delay (Dracup & Moser, 1991).

One of the psychosocial issues raised by heart attack, then, is how to improve treatment-seeking behavior and reduce the long delays that patients often demonstrate. At minimum, patients at high risk for an acute coronary event and their family members need to be trained in recognizing the signs of an impending or actual acute event, so as to avoid the delay that can compromise long-term recovery.

Initial Treatment   During the acute phase of illness, the myocardial infarction (MI) patient is typically hospitalized in a coronary care unit in which cardiac functioning is continually monitored. Many MI patients experience anxiety as they cope with the possibility of a recurrence and see their cardiac responses vividly illustrated on the machines before them. Commonly, however, MI patients in the acute phase of the disease cope by using denial and thus may be relatively anxiety-free during this period.

Most heart attack victims return home after hospitalization. Therefore, a number of long- and short-term issues of rehabilitation arise. The process of adjusting emotionally to the experience of a heart attack begins almost immediately. A number of heart attack patients experience cardiac arrest during their myocardial infarction and have to be resuscitated through artificial means. Being a victim of cardiac arrest can produce a number of psychological difficulties, including nightmares, chronic anxiety, depression, and low expectations of regaining health and vigor.

Cardiac Rehabilitation   Once the acute phase of illness has passed, patients are encouraged to become more active. At this point, a program of education and intervention begins, covering such topics as medical regimen, health risks, exercise, diet, work, and emotional stress. Heart patients, especially women, report receiving far less information about their disease and treatment than they want from health professionals. Most patients want and expect a shared or autonomous treatment decision-making role with their physician, but very few patients experience this (Stewart, Abbey, Shnek, Irvine, & Grace, 2004). Because adherence to treatment regimens is so much better when patients are actively involved, providing more information to patients and involving them actively in the process is essential.

Cardiac rehabilitation is defined as the active and progressive process by which individuals with heart disease attain their optimal physical, medical, psychological, social, emotional, vocational, and economic status (Dracup, 1985). The goals of rehabilitation are to produce relief from symptoms, to reduce the severity of the disease, to limit further progression of disease, and to promote psychological and social adjustment. Underlying the philosophy of cardiac rehabilitation is the belief that such efforts can stem advancing disease, reduce the likelihood of a repeat myocardial infarction, and reduce the risk of sudden death.

As will be evident throughout this discussion, successful cardiac rehabilitation depends critically on the patient's active participation and full commitment to the behavior-change efforts that must be undertaken. An underlying goal of such programs is to restore a sense of mastery or self-efficacy. Because a sense of self-efficacy has been related to beneficial outcomes of treatments, in the absence of self-efficacy, adherence to the goals of rehabilitation may be low (for example, Helgeson & Fritz, 1999; Sullivan, LaCroix, Russo, & Katon, 1998). As such, a sense of self-efficacy is especially critical in recovery in treating the disease and forming a commitment to the rehabilitation phase (Bastone & Kerns, 1995; Bock et al., 1997).

Indeed, it is becoming increasingly clear that the beliefs that patients develop about their disorders are reliably related to successful recovery. A surprising finding is that a repressive coping style is adaptive for immediate and long-term adjustment to MI. Because repressive coping style has generally not been found to be an adaptive coping style otherwise (see chapter 7), its importance in recovery from MI is somewhat startling. It appears that repressive coping style acts as a stress buffer, protecting against signs of post-traumatic stress disorder that may result from MI and its treatment. Heart patients who respond to their disease and treatment with optimism, efforts to maintain high self-esteem, and sense of mastery over the disorder are at less risk for a new cardiac event and better adjusted (Helgeson, 1999; Helgeson & Fritz, 1999). Cardiac rehabilitation is, thus, most likely to be successful when the patient is fully engaged psychologically.

The components of the typical cardiac rehabilitation program are very similar to the interventions used for people at risk for CHD and include exercise therapy with some psychological counseling, as through support groups, nutritional counseling, and education about coronary heart disease (Dracup et al., 1984).

Treatment by Medication   Treatment for coronary heart disease begins immediately after diagnosis. Much of the drop in deaths for CHD can be attributed to the administration of clot-dissolving drugs and medical procedures such as angioplasty and coronary artery bypass surgery.

Once the acute phase of treatment is over, preparation for the rehabilitation regimen begins. Such a regimen often includes self-administration of beta-adrenergic blocking agents on a regular basis. Beta-blocking agents are drugs that resist the effects of sympathetic nervous system stimulation. Because heightened sympathetic nervous system activity aggravates cardiac arrhythmia, angina, and other conditions associated with heart disease, beta-blocking agents are useful in preventing this kind of stimulation. Beta-blockers, however, may have a variety of unpleasant side effects, including fatigue and impotence, which may lead people to take them only intermittently. Interventions have been developed to teach recovering heart patients behavioral stress management procedures that can be used if beta-blockers are not desired, are not practical, or are medically unwise for some reason (Gatchel, Gaffney, & Smith, 1986).

Aspirin is commonly prescribed for people recovering from or at risk for heart attacks. Aspirin helps prevent blood clots by blocking one of the enzymes that cause platelets to aggregate. Research on aspirin now shows that men who take half an aspirin a day are at significantly reduced risk for fatal heart attacks (O'Neil, 2003). Women, too, appear to be benefited by aspirin therapy. As with many drugs, adherence is problematic (Vittinghoff et al., 2003).

A relatively new class of drugs called statins are now frequently prescribed for patients following an acute coronary event, particularly if they have elevated lipids. Statins target LDL cholesterol, reducing risk for a repeat event (Cannon et al., 2004). So impressive have statins been that they are now recommended for patients and at-risk individuals as well to lower lipids before any diagnosis of heart disease is made. In fact, statin drugs have surpassed all other drug treatments for reducing the incidence of death, heart attack, and stroke. Not incidentally, statins appear to be protective against a wide range of diseases including multiple sclerosis, neurodegerative disorders such as Alzheimer's disease, and some types of cancer (Topol, 2004).

Diet and Activity Level   Dietary restrictions may be imposed on the recovering MI patient in an attempt to lower his or her cholesterol level. Instructions to reduce smoking, lose weight, and control alcohol consumption are also frequently given. Most patients are put on an exercise program involving medically supervised walking, jogging, bicycling, or calisthenics at least three times a week for 30 to 45 minutes (DeBusk, Haskell, Miller, Berra, & Taylor, 1985). Exercise appears to improve not only cardiovascular functioning but also psychological recovery. Adherence to exercise regimens is a problem, and

The treadmill test provides a useful indicator of the functional capacity of recovering myocardial infarction patients.

therefore, building in relapse prevention is essential (Kugler, Dimsdale, Hartley, & Sherwood, 1990).

Patients also receive instructions about resumption of their previous activities. Most are urged to return to their prior employment as soon as possible, in part because low economic resources and a decline in income are associated with lower survival (R. B. Williams et al., 1992). Because employment is sometimes affected by heart disease, economic problems may result that require counseling. Because 20% of MI patients do not return to their previous jobs, they often suffer a loss of income. These families may require financial counseling or retraining to help them offset their losses. The problems experienced by one man in returning to work after a myocardial infarction are described in box 13.5. However, patients in high-stress jobs may be advised to cut back, to work part-time, or to take a position with fewer responsibilities. Unfortunately, adherence is not high in this area of life, typically ranging from 50 to 80%. One reason for this low rate of adherence is that advice to cut back on work activities is often phrased in very vague

terms, and patients may not understand exactly how they should implement this goal.

Stress Management   Stress management is an important ingredient in cardiac rehabilitation as well, because stress can trigger fatal cardiac events (Jiang et al., 1996). Younger patients, female patients, and those with social support gaps, high social conflict, and negative coping styles appear to be most at risk for high stress levels following a diagnosis of coronary artery heart disease, and therefore might be especially targeted for stress management interventions (Brummett et al., 2004).

Yet at present, stress management with coronary artery disease patients is hit-or-miss and often haphazard. Patients are urged to avoid stressful situations at work and at home, but these comments are often presented as vague treatment goals. Moreover, as many as 50% of patients say that they are unable to modify the stress in their lives. These problems are solved by employing methods such as those outlined in chapter 6—namely, stress management programs.

The patient is taught how to recognize stressful events, how to avoid those stressful activities when possible, and what to do about stress if it is unavoidable. Training in specific techniques, such as relaxation therapy, improves the ability to manage stress (P. A. Cole, Pomerleau, & Harris, 1992). Coping strategies may need to be targeted as well. Avoidant coping is associated with poor quality of life, whereas approach coping and optimism predict a higher quality of life (Echteld, van Elderen, & van der Kamp, 2003). Because a reliable predictor of survival and repeat events following interventions with cardiac patients is depression, all such patients should be screened for depression routinely (Zipfel et al., 1999).

Recently, stress management interventions have targeted risk factors thought to be especially implicated in cardiovascular disease and MI, including hostility. Hostility ebbs and flows across the life span, and risk factors for coronary heart disease ebb and flow with it. Declines in hostility in midlife, for example, are associated with lower risk (Siegler et al., 2003). Accordingly, one program developed an intervention for modifying hostility and found that eight weekly sessions designed to alter antagonism, cynicism, and anger were somewhat successful in reducing hostility levels (Gidron & Davidson, 1996; Gidron, Davidson, & Bata, 1999). Because anger is a risk factor not only initially for heart disease but also for a second heart attack following a first one (Mendes de Leon, Kop, de Swart, Bar, & Appels, 1996), modifying

BOX 13.5

The Heart Patient Returns to Work

People who have gone through a heart attack often experience difficulties when they try to return to work. They may be warned against certain activities, particularly those that are stress related or that may tax sympathetic nervous system activity. The following shows how one man attempted to cope with this advice, and the repercussions that followed.

> The physician instructed the patient that he could carry out all usual activities, except, "Avoid lifting." "Don't pick up heavy boxes at the office." In the first weeks of work return, he finds a sympathetic attitude among coworkers and pleasant relationships. As the occasion arises, he calls upon one or another to lift heavy boxes for him. Coworkers assist him, most willingly, in the first days after his return to work. Eventually, the tone in the office changes, and resentment stirs among those who are called upon to interrupt their own work and lift the occasional heavy boxes. The character of his informal associations alters, and he begins to have the feeling of becoming an outsider. Yet he has received doctor's orders on lifting, and he is unwilling to risk his health or his life by picking up boxes.

Occasional mild chest pain and shortness of breath remind him that he is not the man he used to be. One day he asks a fellow worker to lift a box for him. The response comes, "Why don't you go ahead and drop dead, you lazy son-of-a-bitch!"

The solutions are limited for this 55-year-old man. Transferring to another department is not possible, as the company is a small one. Leaving for another job is not possible for many reasons: limited employment opportunities in the marketplace during a recession; a record of years of personal attachment to the company; the strains of job hunting, relocating, and adjusting to a new work situation. Trying to win understanding and cooperation from fellow workers is a fruitless task, since the intermesh of personalities, resentments, and personal rivalries common to many offices continues to interfere.

So picking up the heavy boxes seems the easiest solution—but for how long can he continue? What will be the eventual effects on his heart? Anxiety about health, death, and his family colors his life.

Source: Croog, 1983, pp. 300–301.

---

how people experience and manage anger is a high priority for interventions.

Do these programs work? A review of 37 interventions involving health education and stress management found strong beneficial effects. The programs yielded a 34% reduction in cardiac mortality; a 29% reduction in recurrences of heart attacks; and significant beneficial effects on blood pressure, cholesterol, body weight, smoking, exercise, and eating habits (Dusseldorp, van Elderen, Maes, Meulman, & Kraaij, 1999).

Targeting Depression   Depression is a significant problem during cardiac rehabilitation, as it is throughout the management of CHD (T. W. Smith & Ruiz, 2002). The prevalence is sufficiently great and the relation of depression to reoccurring events is sufficiently strong that depression represents an important target for rehabilitative efforts (Davidson, Rieckmann, & Lesperance, 2004; Freedland et al., 2003). CHD patients with high depression or high anxiety have decreased heart rate variability as compared with the norms, suggesting that they may have sustained alterations in their auto-

nomic nervous system modulation over time (Krittayaphong et al., 1997). Depression and anxiety not only compromise quality of life, but they also predict poor recovery from treatment and mortality among people already diagnosed with coronary heart disease (T. W. Smith & Ruiz, 2002). Psychological factors, such as depression, may also moderate responses to drug treatments (Rutledge, Linden, & Davies, 1999).

Years after initial treatment, depression is associated with increased health care costs and increased need for treatment for coronary artery disease (Sullivan, LaCroix, Spertus, Hecht, & Russo, 2003). When depressed coronary heart disease patients are treated with cognitive-behavioral therapy to reduce depression, it can have beneficial effects on risk factors for advancing disease, including the reduction of heart rate and increases in heart rate variability (Carney et al., 2000). As might be expected, optimism and the presence of social support contribute to good long-term health outcomes among patients in cardiac rehabilitation, in part, by increasing effective coping and lowering symptoms of depression (Shen, McCreary, & Myers, 2004).

Evaluation of Cardiac Rehabilitation

Cardiac rehabilitation is now a standard part of the aftercare of patients who have had heart attacks or who have been hospitalized for heart disease. More than 130 published studies have evaluated cardiovascular disease management programs. Most of these studies find that interventions targeted to weight, blood pressure reduction, smoking, and, in increasing number, quality of life are successful in reducing patients' standing on risk factors for heart disease and, in some cases, reducing the risk of death from cardiovascular disease (Center for the Advancement of Health, 2000d). Evaluations show that the addition of psychosocial treatments to standard cardiac rehabilitation programs reduces psychological distress and can reduce the likelihood that cardiac patients will experience symptoms, suffer a recurrence, or die following an acute cardiac event (for example, Ketterer et al., 2000; Linden, Stossel, & Maurice, 1996).

As must be evident, a complicating issue in recovery from MI is that many patients need to modify several health habits simultaneously. As we have repeatedly seen, adherence to lifestyle change is often low and may be lower still if several health habits must be modified at the same time. Moreover, the active involvement of the patient is required for successful rehabilitation following MI or another CHD-related event.

For both men and women already diagnosed with CHD, modifying risk factors may help prevent further damage and subsequent heart attacks. Stopping smoking reduces the incidence of CHD, although switching to low-tar-and-nicotine cigarettes does not. The benefits of treating substantially elevated blood pressure are indisputable, although the benefits of treating milder hypertension are inconclusive. Reducing cholesterol has beneficial effects, with approximately a 2% reduction in disease for every 1% reduction in total cholesterol (Criqui, 1986). Modifying behavioral methods of coping with stress also appears to reduce the risk of a repeat infarct, at least in men (M. Friedman et al., 1986). Given the likelihood of being able to reduce further damage with interventions, the role of the health psychologist in research about and interventions for heart disease is indisputably important.

Problems of Social Support

As is true for other diseases, social support can help heart patients recover, reducing distress and improving cardiac symptoms, especially in the months just following hospitalization (Elizur & Hirsh, 1999; Kulik & Mahler, 1993). Indeed, in one study, heart patients without a spouse or a confi-

dant were twice as likely to die within 6 months of their first heart attack, compared with those patients who were married or had friends (Case, Moss, Case, McDermott, & Eberly, 1992; see also Collijn, Appels, & Nijhuis, 1995). Social support during hospitalization predicts depressive symptoms during recovery, and depression itself is a risk factor for mortality related to CHD (Brummett et al., 1998). So important is social support for long-term prognosis that it is now targeted for intervention during recovery (ENRICHD, 2001).

However, many factors may erode the potential for social support. In the home setting, one of the MI patient's chief complaints is loss of independence. MI sharply reduces an individual's physical stamina, and many patients are surprised by the extent of their disability. Feelings of shame, helplessness, and low self-esteem may result. Conflict over changes in lifestyle can result in marital strife (Croog & Fitzgerald, 1978; Michela, 1987). The patient may find it difficult to adhere to dietary restrictions and exercise, whereas the spouse may be highly motivated to help the patient comply. Stressful interactions over the need to modify daily activities can aggravate the patient's perceptions of dependence and exacerbate already existing depression, as was evident in the example that opened this chapter.

Spouses of recovering heart attack patients tend to see the patient as dependent and irritable, whereas the recovering patient may regard the spouse as meddling and overprotective. Unfortunately, to the extent that the spouse is successful in helping the patient cope and develop feelings of self-efficacy, the spouse's own distress may increase (Coyne & Smith, 1991). An overly solicitous partner can aggregate severity of symptoms, disability, and symptoms of depression as well (Itkowitz, Kerns, & Otis, 2003). In addition, spouses of heart attack victims often show severe psychological responses to the MI, including nightmares and chronic anxiety over the patient's survival (Skelton & Dominian, 1973). Although there is no evidence that heart attacks drive married couples apart, neither does it necessarily bring them closer together. It is a difficult situation for everyone involved. Marital counseling or family therapy may be needed to deal with marital strain.

Cardiac invalidism can be one consequence of MI; that is, patients and their spouses both see the patient's abilities as lower than they actually are. In a study designed to reduce this problem (C. B. Taylor, Bandura, Ewart, Miller, & DeBusk, 1985), wives of recovering MI patients were provided with information about their husbands' cardiovascular capabilities, observed their husbands' performance on a treadmill task, or took part in the treadmill activity personally. Wives who personally experienced the treadmill task increased their perceptions of their husbands' physical and cardiac efficiency after observing their husbands' treadmill attainments. Wives who were simply informed about their husbands' performance or who observed treadmill activity continued to regard their husbands as impaired.

Despite these problems, the family has the potential to play an important role in follow-up care. Both patients and family members should be taught how to recognize the symptoms of an impending heart attack; how to differentiate them from more minor physical complaints, such as heartburn; and how to activate the emergency system. In this way, delay behavior can be reduced and treatment can be improved in the event of a repeat event.

Family members of the MI patient should also be trained in **cardiopulmonary resuscitation (CPR).** Approximately 70% of potential sudden deaths from heart attacks occur in the home rather than the workplace, but relatively few programs have been initiated to train family members in CPR. More such training programs should be available for MI families (Dracup, Guzy, Taylor, & Barry, 1986; Nolan et al., 1999).

As we have repeatedly seen, the beliefs one holds about illness, treatment, and recovery are important determinants of adjustment, and this importance is certainly true for recovering heart patients as well. To the extent that interventions enhance feelings of self-efficacy and personal control, the beneficial contribution that they make to psychological and physical health may go well beyond specific training in diet, exercise, and other components of standard cardiac rehabilitation.

■ HYPERTENSION

Hypertension, or high blood pressure, occurs when the supply of blood through the vessels is excessive. It can occur when cardiac output is too high, which puts pressure on the arterial walls as blood flow increases. It also occurs in response to peripheral resistance—that is, the resistance to blood flow in the small arteries of the body.

Hypertension is a serious medical problem for several reasons. According to recent estimates, one in four U.S. adults has high blood pressure, but because there are no symptoms, nearly one third of these people don't know they have it (American Heart Association, 2004). Moreover, hypertension is a risk factor for other disorders, such as kidney failure (American Heart Association, 2001b).

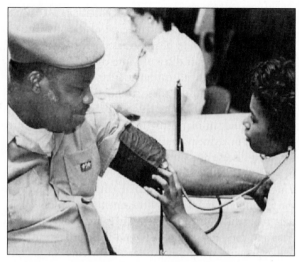

Hypertension is a symptomless disease. As a result, unless they obtain regular physical checkups or participate in hypertension screening programs, many adults are unaware that they have this disorder.

Untreated hypertension can also adversely affect cognitive functioning, producing problems in learning, memory, attention, abstract reasoning, mental flexibility, and other cognitive skills. Even in healthy adults, elevated blood pressure appears to compromise cognitive functioning (Suhr, Stewart, & France, 2004). These problems appear to be particularly significant among young hypertensives (Waldstein et al., 1996). Given the risks and scope of hypertension, early diagnosis and treatment are essential.

How Is Hypertension Measured?

Hypertension is assessed by the levels of systolic and diastolic blood pressure as measured by a sphygmomanometer. As noted in chapter 2, systolic blood pressure is the greatest force developed during contraction of the heart's ventricles. It is sensitive both to the volume of blood leaving the heart and to the arteries' ability to stretch to accommodate blood (their elasticity). Diastolic pressure is the pressure in the arteries when the heart is relaxed; it is related to resistance of the blood vessels to blood flow.

Of the two, systolic pressure has somewhat greater value in diagnosing hypertension. Mild hypertension is defined by a systolic pressure consistently between 140 and 159; moderate hypertension involves a pressure consistently between 160 and 179; and severe hypertension means a systolic pressure consistently above 180. Keeping systolic blood pressure under 120 is best.

People at risk for hypertension show a less rapid recovery following sympathetic arousal. That is, after blood pressure has been elevated, as in response to a stressful event, it remains so for a significantly longer period of time than is true for people who do not have hypertension or who have no family history of hypertension (Gerin & Pickering, 1995). Hypertension, then, may be characterized both by greater reactivity to stress and by slower recovery.

What Causes Hypertension?

Approximately 5% of hypertension is caused by failure of the kidneys to regulate blood pressure. However, almost 90% of all hypertension is *essential*—that is, of unknown origin.

Some risk factors have been identified. Prior to age 50, males are at greater risk for hypertension than are females; above the age 55 however, both men and women living in the United States face a 90% chance of developing hypertension. Cardiovascular disease risk factors are higher among minorities than among Whites in the United States. This increased risk appears to be due in part largely to low socioeconomic status. For example, compared with White women, Hispanic women and African-American women have higher blood pressure, greater body mass index, lower levels of physical activity, and higher rates of diabetes, all of which contribute to cardiovascular disease (Winkleby, Kraemer, Ahn, & Varady, 1998).

Genetic factors clearly also play a role (see T. W. Smith et al., 1987): If one parent has high blood pressure, the offspring have a 45% chance of developing it; if two parents have high blood pressure, the probability increases to 95%. Blood pressure reactivity in childhood and adolescence predicts later development of hypertension, consistent with the possibility of a genetic mechanism (Ingelfinger, 2004; K. A. Matthews, Salomon, Brady, & Allen, 2003). As is true for coronary heart disease more generally, the genetic factor in hypertension may be reactivity, a hereditary predisposition toward elevated sympathetic nervous system activity, especially in response to stressful events (DeQuattro & Lee, 1991; Everson, Lovallo, Sausen, & Wilson, 1992; Jeffery, 1991). Further evidence for the importance of a genetically based predisposition to sympathetic nervous system reactivity comes from studies of people with a family history of hypertension but who do not themselves have hypertension. These individuals show reliably greater cardiovascular reactivity in response to stress

and in anticipation of stress, despite the fact that they have not yet developed hypertension (Jorgensen & Houston, 1981).

Emotional factors are also implicated in this constellation of risk. In particular, negative affect and frequent experiences of intense arousal predict increases in blood pressure over time (Jonas & Lando, 2000; Pollard & Schwartz, 2003). A tendency toward anger (Harburg, Julius, Kacirotti, Gleiberman, & Schork, 2003; E. H. Johnson, Schork, & Spielberger, 1987), cynical distrust (R. B. Williams, 1984), and excessive striving in the face of significant odds (S. A. James, Hartnett, & Kalsbeek, 1983) have all been implicated in the development of hypertension. A family environment that fosters chronic anger may contribute to development of hypertension (Ewart, 1991). In contrast, children and adolescents who develop social competence skills may have a reduced risk for cardiovascular disease (E. Chen, Matthews, Salomon, & Ewart, 2002; Ewart & Jorgensen, 2004). Such observations suggest the importance of intervening early in the family environment to prevent or modify deficits in communication. Although much of the research concerning negative affect and hypertension has focused on men, longitudinal research suggests that anger and other negative emotional states may be related to blood pressure changes over time in women as well (Markovitz et al., 1991).

Relationship Between Stress and Hypertension

Stress has been suspected as a contributor to hypertension for many years (Henry & Cassel, 1969). Repeated exposure to stressful events during which heightened blood pressure reactions occur may contribute over the long term to development of chronically high blood pressure (D. Carroll et al., 2001). High blood pressure can result from exposure to chronic social conflict and from job strain—namely, the combination of high demands with little control (Pickering et al., 1996). Crowded, high-stress, and noisy locales produce higher rates of hypertension. Groups that have migrated from rural to urban areas have higher rates of hypertension. As we noted in chapter 6, job stress and unemployment have also been tied to higher blood pressure (Pickering et al., 1996). In women, elevated blood pressure has been related to having extensive family responsibilities, and among white-collar women, the combined impact of large family responsibilities and job strain has been tied to higher blood pressure (Brisson et al., 1999). At present, the suspicion is that hypertension results from high-stress reactivity, possibly genetically based, in conjunction with high-stress exposure (al'Absi & Wittmers, 2003; Schwartz, Meisenhelder, Ma, & Reed, 2003).

How Do We Study Stress and Hypertension?

To study the effects of stress on hypertension, researchers have adopted several research methods. One method brings people into the laboratory, often people at risk for or already diagnosed with hypertension, to see how they respond to physical or mental challenges that are stressful, such as a difficult arithmetic task. Laboratory studies that expose people to stressors, such as bright lights, or to stressful tasks such as holding one's breath for a long time, reliably show increased blood pressure responses (Girdler et al., 1996).

Another line of work identifies stressful circumstances, such as high-pressure jobs, and examines the rates of hypertension and how blood pressure ebbs and flows in response to environmental demands (Steptoe, Roy, & Evans, 1996).

Building on this method, a third type of research makes use of ambulatory monitoring to examine the relationship between lifestyle factors and blood pressure in natural settings, as people go through their daily lives. That is, a person wears a blood pressure cuff, which assesses blood pressure at intervals throughout the day. This method has the advantage of charting the ebb and flow of blood pressure for each individual in response to different events. It has revealed, among other observations, that variation in blood pressure over the course of a day is considerable (Pickering, Schwartz, & James, 1995). These variations are especially high among people who smoke, who drink heavily, who experience job strain, and who experience other stressful life conditions, lending support to the idea that blood pressure fluctuations may contribute to the development of essential hypertension (Pickering et al., 1995).

All three types of studies provide evidence that links increases in or increased variability in blood pressure to stressful events.

The role of stress in the development and exacerbation of hypertension may be different for people at risk for hypertension than for those who are not, and it may change as hypertension progresses. People without preexisting signs of hypertension show large and reliable blood pressure responses to stressors, primarily when they must make an active behavioral response to that stress (Sherwood, Hinderliter, & Light, 1995). People

with borderline hypertension show a similar pattern, although they also show exaggerated stress-induced cardiovascular responses to stress at a relatively young age (K. A. Matthews et al., 1993) and a stronger blood pressure response to laboratory stressors than do people with normal blood pressure (Tuomisto, 1997).

People already diagnosed with hypertension show large blood pressure responses to a wide range of stressors, both passive stressors not requiring a behavioral response and active stressors that do require a behavioral response (Fredrickson & Matthews, 1990). The fact that diagnosed hypertensives show blood pressure responses to a wide array of stressors is consistent with the idea that excessive sympathetic nervous system activity—that is, reactivity in response to stress—may be significant in the development of hypertension.

The findings also suggest that factors that usually help people cope successfully with stressful events may not do so with hypertensives. For example, people who feel they have personal control over stressful events usually show less sympathetic nervous system activity. This decrease does not appear to be true for people diagnosed with hypertension, however. Chronically hypertensive individuals appear to be stress sensitive (see Frederikson, Robson, & Ljungdell, 1991).

Psychosocial Factors and Hypertension

Originally, hypertension was thought to be marked by a constellation of personality factors, dominated by suppressed anger (F. Alexander, 1950; F. Dunbar, 1943). What is the evidence for the role of psychological factors in the development of hypertension? Although personality factors are now known to be insufficient for the development of hypertension, research continues to show that hostility may play a role (for example, Dimsdale et al., 1986; Sommers-Flanagan & Greenberg, 1989).

Research has focused heavily on the experience of anger and its expression. Originally, suppressed hostility was thought to be associated with higher blood pressure levels and hypertension, although evidence for this hypothesis has been mixed. More recently, researchers have suggested that expressed anger and the potential for hostility are associated with exaggerated blood pressure responses, especially under conditions of stress or harassment. Evidence relating anger to hypertension is now quite substantial. Ruminating on the source of one's anger, whether one suppresses or expresses it, is associated with elevated blood pressure (Everson, Goldberg, Kaplan, Julkunen, & Salonen, 1998; Hogan & Linden, 2004; Schum, Jorgensen, Verhaeghen, Sauro, & Thibodeau, 2003).

Social support is a resource for combating most health problems. In the case of people with hypertension, however, those who are also high in hostility can compromise the social support that they receive. Thus, the quality of personal relationships may influence whether social support has a beneficial effect on CVD (Uno, Uchino, & Smith, 2002). Hypertensives who are high in hostility can often drive those who might otherwise be supportive away. Recent research suggests that hostility may be associated with hypertension via its effects on interpersonal interaction, namely by increasing the number of conflict-ridden or unpleasant interactions in daily life (Brondolo, Rieppi, & Erickson, 2003). Other evidence suggests that negative emotions, including depression and anxiety, may be prospective risk factors for hypertension as well (Jonas & Lando, 2000; Rutledge & Hogan, 2002; Scherrer et al., 2003). Depression and hostility and (lack of) social support are quite closely tied (Benotsch et al., 1997; Räikkönen, Matthews, Flory, & Owens, 1999; Raynor, Pogue-Geile, Kamarck, McCaffery, & Manuck, 2002; Suarez, Kuhn, Schanberg, Williams, & Zimmermann, 1998).

Stress and Hypertension Among African Americans   Hypertension is a particular medical problem in African-American communities. Its high prevalence in this population is tied to stress, including the stress associated with racial discrimination (Blascovich, Spencer, Quinn, & Steele, 2001; Fang & Myers, 2001; Guyll, Matthews, & Bromberger, 2001).

An early study of hypertension among African Americans was conducted by Earnest Harburg and his associates among Black men in Detroit (Harburg et al., 1973). Their analysis focused on several factors: high stress, suppressed hostility, minority status, and skin color. First, the researchers identified high- and low-stress locales in the city of Detroit. High-stress locales were defined as areas characterized by low socioeconomic status, high population density, high geographical mobility, high rates of marital breakup, and high crime; low-stress areas had more favorable ratings on all these variables. Suppressed rage was measured as guilt and inwardly directed anger; these variables were coded from each individual's responses to a series of vignettes about injustices (such as an arbitrary rent hike) frequently faced by residents of the inner city.

The results indicated that several factors were related to hypertension. First, higher rates of hypertension were found in high-stress than in low-stress locales. Second, Black men had higher blood pressure than White men, especially dark-skinned Black men who lived in the high-stress areas. Overall, the highest blood pressure ratings were found among dark-skinned Black men in high-stress locales who dealt with their anger by suppressing it. This important, now classic study shows the interplay of environmental and individual risk factors in the development of hypertension.

As this study suggests, hypertension is especially prevalent among lower-income Blacks. Part of this risk appears to be associated with such factors as parental history of hypertension. Racial differences in neuropeptide and cardiovascular responses to stressors also appear to influence the development of hypertension (for example, Saab et al., 1997); however, psychosocial factors are implicated as well (R. Clark, 2003). Low-income Blacks are likely to live in stressful neighborhoods, which are associated with the development of hypertension (Fleming, Baum, Davidson, Rectanus, & McArdle, 1987; Harburg et al., 1973). Low-income Blacks report more psychological distress than do higher income Whites and Blacks, and chronic life stress may interfere with sympathetic nervous system recovery in response to specific stressors (Pardine & Napoli, 1983). Exposure to racism may also aggravate high blood pressure among Blacks (Armstead, Lawler, Gordon, Cross, & Gibbons, 1989; Blascovich et al., 2001). Recent evidence suggests that dark-skinned African Americans experience more frequent racial discrimination than their lighter-skinned counterparts, estimated in one study to be 11 times more common (Klonoff & Landrine, 2000).

African Americans are more likely to be obese, a risk factor tied to hypertension. Dietary factors, such as patterns of eating that develop in infancy (M. M. Myers, 1996), or salt intake may play a causal role. Compared with Whites, African Americans also show a lower nocturnal decrease in blood pressure (Ituarte, Kamarck, Thompson, & Bacanu, 1999); nondipping of blood pressure at night is a risk factor for hypertension (Räikkönen et al., 2004). Hostility and anger may account for this ethnic difference (K. S. Thomas, Nelesen, & Dimsdale, 2004).

Cardiovascular reactivity among African Americans, especially older African Americans, may be part of a more general syndrome that implicates multiple risk factors for cardiovascular disease. A study by Waldstein and colleagues (Waldstein, Burns, Toth, & Poehlman, 1999) found that elevated blood pressure was associated with greater heart rate reactivity, greater fasting insulin levels, lower high-density lipoprotein cholesterol levels, a higher waist-to-hip ratio, and greater body mass overall. This clustering of metabolic factors, termed **metabolic syndrome,** may predispose older African Americans to a higher risk for cardiovascular disease and metabolic disorders, such as diabetes.

John Henryism   Because hypertension is a particular risk for Blacks, some research has examined a phenomenon known as **John Henryism.** John Henry, the "steel-driving" man, was an uneducated Black laborer who allegedly defeated a mechanical steam drill in a contest to see which could complete the most work in the shortest period of time. However, after winning the battle, John Henry reportedly dropped dead from exhaustion. S. A. James et al. (1983) coined the term "John Henryism," which refers to a personality predisposition to cope actively with psychosocial stressors. It becomes a lethal predisposition when active coping efforts are likely to be unsuccessful. The person scoring high on John Henryism would try harder and harder against ultimately insurmountable odds. Consequently, one would expect to find John Henryism to be especially lethal among the disadvantaged, especially low-income and poorly educated Blacks. Research tends to confirm these relations (S. A. James, Keenan, Strogatz, Browning, & Garrett, 1992). The specific factors tying John Henryism to an increased risk for hypertension appear to be increased cardiovascular reactivity to stress and prolonged difficulty recovering from stress (Merritt, Bennett, Williams, Sollers, & Thayer, 2004).

Treatment of Hypertension

Overview   Hypertension has been controlled in a variety of ways. Commonly, patients are put on low-sodium diets, and reduction of alcohol intake is also recommended. Weight reduction in overweight patients is strongly urged, and exercise is recommended for all hypertensive patients.

Caffeine restriction is often included as part of the dietary treatment of hypertension, because caffeine, in conjunction with stress, elevates blood pressure responses among those at risk for or already diagnosed with hypertension (Lovallo et al., 2000). Indeed, caffeine intake may more generally contribute to rising levels of hypertension and thus be considered a strategy for the primary prevention of hypertension as well as its treatment (J. E. James, 2004).

Drug Treatments   Most commonly, hypertension is treated pharmacologically. Diuretics reduce blood volume by promoting the excretion of sodium. Another common treatment is beta-adrenergic blockers, which exert their antihypertensive effects by decreasing cardiac output and decreasing plasma renin activity. Central adrenergic inhibitors are also used to reduce blood pressure by decreasing the sympathetic outflow from the central nervous system. Peripheral adrenergic inhibitors are also used to deplete catecholamines from the brain and the adrenal medulla. Alpha-adrenergic blockers, vasodilators, angiotensin-converting enzyme inhibitors, and calcium channel blockers have also been used in the treatment of hypertension.

Recently, drug treatments for hypertension have become controversial. Hypertension is only one of a cluster of factors that lead to the development of coronary heart disease. Certain of the drug treatments may have positive effects in reducing blood pressure but augment sympathetic nervous system activity overall, thereby aggravating rather than reducing the likelihood of coronary heart disease. Research, in fact, suggests that some drug treatments are more likely to enhance sympathetic nervous system activity than reduce it. Recent evidence suggests that the most effective treatment for lowering blood pressure with the fewest complications is the oldest, traditional form of drug intervention, namely, diuretics (Altman, December 2002).

Cognitive-Behavioral Treatments   The fact that antihypertensive medications can actually aggravate sympathetic nervous system activity, coupled with the success of cognitive-behavioral therapy in other areas of health psychology, has led to an increasing use of cognitive-behavioral modification techniques in the treatment of hypertension.

A variety of behavioral and cognitive-behavioral methods have been evaluated for their potential success in lowering blood pressure (for a review, see M. S. Glasgow & Engel, 1987). Methods that draw on relaxation include biofeedback, progressive muscle relaxation, hypnosis, and meditation, all of which reduce blood pressure via the induction of a state of low arousal. Deep breathing and imagery are often added to accomplish this task. Evaluations of these treatments suggest modestly positive effects (Davison, Williams, Nezami, Bice, & DeQuattro, 1991; Jacob, Chesney, Williams, Ding,

& Shapiro, 1991; Nakao et al., 1997), although hypertensive patients may not practice them as much as they should (Hoelscher, Lichstein, & Rosenthal, 1986). Giving patients feedback about exactly how poor their compliance efforts are can improve blood pressure control (Zuger, 1999).

Other stress management techniques have also been employed in the treatment of hypertension. Such techniques train people to identify their particular stressors and to develop plans for dealing with them. The programs include training in self-reinforcement, self-calming talk, goal setting, and time management.

Exercise may also help in blood pressure control (Brownley, West, Hinderliter, & Light, 1996). One study (Perkins, Dubbert, Martin, Faulstich, & Harris, 1986) found that aerobically trained mild hypertensives reacted to mildly stressful situations with smaller blood pressure increases than did untrained mild hypertensives. Thus, aerobic training, which itself may reduce blood pressure in mild hypertensives, may also help people manage stress more effectively, perhaps by reducing cardiovascular reactivity in response to stress (Blumenthal, Siegel, & Appelbaum, 1991).

Because obesity is implicated in the development of hypertension, interventions to promote weight loss may also be successful in reducing hypertension. However, the treatment of obesity itself remains difficult (see chapter 4), and so a combination of diet, exercise, and behavioral strategies may be most desirable for maintaining weight loss (Jeffery, 1991).

The fact that anger has been tied to hypertension implies that teaching people how to manage their anger might be useful. In fact, studies suggest that training hypertensive patients how to manage confrontational scenes through such behavioral techniques as role playing can produce better skills for managing such situations and can lower blood pressure reactivity (Davidson, MacGregor, Stuhr, & Gidron, 1999; Larkin & Zayfert, 1996).

Evaluation of Cognitive-Behavioral Interventions How do behavioral techniques fare comparatively in the treatment of hypertension? Of the nondrug approaches, weight reduction, physical exercise, and cognitive-behavioral therapy appear to be quite successful (Linden & Chambers, 1994). Although not all hypertensive patients benefit from such training, many do. Moreover, cognitive-behavioral methods have the advantage of being inexpensive as well as easy to implement: They can be used without supervision, and they have no side effects.

Cognitive-behavioral interventions may reduce the drug requirements for the treatment of hypertension (D. Shapiro, Hui, Oakley, Pasic, & Jamner, 1997). For some hypertensives, drug treatments have risks, and may, for example, impair their ability to manage work responsibilities well. Under these circumstances, cognitive-behavioral therapies may enable hypertensives to reduce or replace their drugs (Kristal-Boneh, Melamed, Bernheim, Peled, & Green, 1995). Behavioral treatments appear to be especially successful with mild or borderline hypertensives and, with these groups, may actually substitute for drug control.

Other patients, however, may profit less from behavioral treatments, and adherence to cognitive-behavioral interventions is not particularly high. At present, then, the combination of drugs and cognitive-behavioral treatments appears to be the best approach to the management of hypertension, better than any other (Hoelscher et al., 1986).

Problems in Treating Hypertension

The Hidden Disease One of the biggest problems in the treatment of hypertension is that so many people who are hypertensive do not know that they are. Hypertension is largely a symptomless disease, so, rather than seeking treatment for hypertension, people are often diagnosed when they go in for a standard medical examination. Thus, many thousands of people who do not get regular physicals suffer from hypertension without realizing it.

National campaigns to educate the public about hypertension have been somewhat successful in getting people diagnosed (Horan & Roccella, 1988). Early detection is important because, as we have seen, more treatments may be available for borderline or mild hypertensives than for people with more serious forms of the disorder.

Untreated hypertension is related to a lower quality of life, compromised cognitive functioning, and fewer social activities, so, despite the fact that it is symptomless, it nonetheless has adverse effects on daily life (Horan & Roccella, 1988; M. A. Robbins, Elias, Croog, & Colton, 1994; Saxby, Harrington, McKeith, Wesnes, & Ford, 2003).

In addition to physician diagnosis, work site-based screening programs have been successful in identifying people with hypertension (Alderman & Lamport, 1988). Increasingly, community interventions enable people to have their blood pressure checked by going to mobile units, their churches or community centers, or even the local drugstore. The widespread availability of these screening programs has helped with early identification of people with hypertension.

Adherence   A second major problem facing the management of hypertension is the high rate of nonadherence to therapy. This, too, is affected by the symptomless nature of the disease. Because hypertensive patients "feel fine," it can be difficult to get them to take medications on a regular basis. Many of us believe that, when we are "cranked up," under stress, or annoyed, our blood pressure is high. In fact, the correlation between beliefs about level of blood pressure and actual blood pressure is low. Unfortunately, hypertensives tend to have such theories and may choose to medicate themselves on the basis of them, thus showing nonadherence with their prescribed regimen and sustaining substantial health risks (D. Meyer, Leventhal, & Gutmann, 1985).

What can be done to increase adherence? Clearly, one solution is to educate patients fully about the largely symptomless nature of the disease and the critical importance of treatment for controlling it (Zimmerman, Safer, Leventhal, & Baumann, 1986). It may be necessary, too, to demonstrate to patients that their theories about their blood pressure are wrong. Unfortunately, research data suggest that hypertensives and borderline hypertensives are only moderately responsive to information, indicating that they are unable to control their blood pressure (Baumann, Zimmerman, & Leventhal, 1989; Brondolo, Rosen, Kostis, & Schwartz, 1999).

Compliance with a hypertension regimen is also influenced by factors that predict adherence more generally. Patients who expect greater control over health and hypertension have greater knowledge of the treatment regimen, have stronger social support, and are more likely to adhere to their hypertension regimen (Dunbar-Jacob, Dwyer, & Dunning, 1991; Stanton, 1987). Interventions may be able to draw on these findings as well.

■ STROKE

Lee Phillips, 62, was shopping at a San Diego mall with her husband, Eric, when she felt an odd tugging on the right side of her face. Her mouth twisted into a lurid grimace. Suddenly she felt weak. "What kind of game are you playing?" asked Eric. "I'm not," Lee tried to respond—but her words came out in a jumble. "Let's go to the hospital," Eric urged her. All Lee wanted to do

People who have had strokes often must relearn some aspects of cognitive functioning.

was go home and lie down. Fortunately, it turned out, her husband summoned an ambulance instead. Like 730,000 other Americans each year, Lee was suffering a stroke. (Gorman, 1996 Time Inc. Reprinted with permission.)

Stroke, the third major cause of death in the United States, results from a disturbance in blood flow to the brain. Some strokes occur when blood flow to localized areas of the brain is interrupted, a condition that can be due to arteriosclerosis or hypertension. For example, when arteriosclerotic plaques damage the cerebral blood vessels, the damaged area may trap blood clots (thrombi) or produce circulating blood clots (emboli) that block the flow of blood.

Stroke can also be caused by cerebral hemorrhage (bleeding caused by the rupture of a blood vessel in the brain). When blood leaks into the brain, large areas of nervous tissue may be compressed against the skull, producing widespread or fatal damage. Strokes cause approximately 10% of all deaths. The mortality rate is around 30% during the first month after a stroke, and those who survive may suffer some degree of permanent physical impairment. In the United States, approximately 600,000 individuals experience a stroke every year, and currently, more than 5 million stroke survivors live with significant cognitive and emotional problems (American Heart Association, 2001b). The warning signs of stroke are listed in table 13.1.

A chief risk of stroke is that more will follow in its wake, ultimately leading to severe disability or death. Researchers have recently discovered that a simple intervention—aspirin—can greatly reduce this risk. Aspirin has immediate benefit for stroke patients by preventing

TABLE 13.1 | Stroke Warning Signs

The American Stroke Association says these are the warning signs of stroke:
- Sudden numbness or weakness of the face, arm or leg, especially on one side of the body
- Sudden confusion, trouble speaking or understanding
- Sudden trouble seeing in one or both eyes
- Sudden trouble walking, dizziness, loss of balance or coordination
- Sudden, severe headache with no known cause

Source: American Heart Association, 2004.

coagulation. Following a stroke, even a few weeks of aspirin's use can reduce the risk of recurrent strokes by as much as a third (Z. Chen et al., 2000). As we saw in the section "Coronary Heart Disease," aspirin is believed to be helpful in reducing risk of coronary events as well, so this little drug, that has been with us for so long, may prove to be the wonder drug of the century.

Risk Factors for Stroke

Risk factors for stroke overlap heavily with those for heart disease. Some factors are hereditary, others result from lifestyle, and still others come from unknown causes. Risk factors include high blood pressure, heart disease, cigarette smoking, a high red blood cell count, and transient ischemic attacks. Transient ischemic attacks are little strokes that produce temporary weakness, clumsiness, or loss of feeling in one side or limb; a temporary dimness or loss of vision, particularly in one eye; or a temporary loss of speech or difficulty in speaking or un-

derstanding speech (American Heart Association, 2000a). In addition, psychological distress is related to the likelihood of having a fatal stroke (May et al., 2002). Anger expression also appears to be related to stroke as it is for coronary heart disease and hypertension; low levels of anger expression appear to be mildly protective (Eng, Fitzmaurice, Kubzansky, Rimm, & Kawachi, 2003).

In addition, the likelihood of a stroke increases with age, occurs more often in men than in women, and occurs more often in African Americans and among those who have diabetes. A prior stroke or a family history of stroke also increases the likelihood. Increasingly, health practitioners are recognizing the significance of psychosocial factors in stroke. Depression and anxiety are predictive of stroke (May et al., 2002) and appear to be especially strong predictors for White women and for African Americans (Jonas & Mussolino, 2000).

The incidence of first stroke by gender and race is shown in figure 13.3. As can be seen, one of the groups at high risk for stroke is Black men ages 45 to 64. During this period, strokes kill Black men at about three times the rate for White men (Villarosa, 2002). As is true for heart disease, depression is a risk factor for stroke. In the case of stroke, cerebrovascular reactivity appears to be reduced in patients with depression, which may account for this relation (P. Neu, Schlattmann, Schilling, & Hartmann, 2004).

Consequences of Stroke

Stroke affects all aspects of one's life: personal, social, vocational, and physical (S. C. Thompson et al., 1989). Although many victims have already reached retirement

FIGURE 13.3 | Stroke Incidence Rates for First-Ever Stroke, 2001 (*Source:* American Heart Association, 2004a)

Note: Incidence rates are age-adjusted.

age, stroke can also attack younger people. Patients who are minimally impaired following a stroke may return to work after a few months, but many patients are unable to return to work even part-time (for reviews, see W. A. Gordon & Diller, 1983; Krantz & Deckel, 1983). Stroke almost inevitably leads to increased dependence on others, at least for a while; as a consequence, family or other social relationships may be profoundly affected.

Motor Problems Immediately after a stroke, motor difficulties are common. Because the right side of the brain controls movement in the left half of the body and the left side of the brain controls movement in the right half of the body, motoric impairments occur on the side opposite to the side of the brain that was damaged in the stroke. It is usually difficult or impossible for the patient to move the arm and leg on the affected side; therefore, he or she usually requires help walking, dressing, and performing other physical activities. With physical therapy, some of these problems are greatly diminished (W. A. Gordon & Diller, 1983).

Cognitive Problems The cognitive difficulties that the stroke victim faces depend on which side of the brain was damaged. Patients with left-brain damage may have communication disorders, such as aphasia, which involves difficulty in understanding others and expressing oneself. A stroke patient described a relevant incident:

> One of my first shopping expeditions was to a hardware store, but when I got there I couldn't think of the words, "electric plug," and it took me a while to get the message across. Naturally, I was humiliated and frustrated. I was close to tears at the store, and let them out to Jane [the patient's wife] at home. I was learning day by day the frustrations of a body and mind I could not command. (Dahlberg, 1977, p. 124)

Other problems of left-brain dysfunction include cognitive disturbances, an apparent reduction in intellect, and difficulty in learning new tasks. In particular, cognitive tasks that require the use of short-term memory seem to be particularly affected after a stroke that causes left-brain damage:

> Everyone repeats some stories, but within 15 minutes I told three stories that Jane had just heard—from me. Such experiences have not brought me humility, but I have lost some confidence, and I have developed patience with people. In the past, I have sometimes been arrogant. But since the stroke I have learned to say, "excuse me" and "I don't know." (Dahlberg, 1977, p. 126)

Patients with right-brain damage may be unable to process or make use of certain kinds of visual feedback. As a result, such a patient may shave only one side of his face or put makeup on only half her face. The patient may eat only the food on the right side of the plate and ignore the food on the left. Patients may have trouble reading a clock, dialing a phone, or making change. These patients sometimes have difficulty perceiving distances accurately and may bump into objects or walls.

Patients with right-brain damage may also feel that they are going crazy because they cannot understand the words they read or seem to be able to perceive only the last part of each word. They may also think they are hearing voices if a speaker is physically positioned on the impaired side and can thus be heard but not seen (W. A. Gordon & Diller, 1983). Although some stroke patients seem to have a good idea of how much damage has been done, a fact that is depressing in its own right, others are quite inaccurate in their assessment of how the stroke has changed their cognitive abilities, their memory, and their moods (Hibbard, Gordon, Stein, Grober, & Sliwinski, 1992). These misperceptions lead them to misjudge what they are capable of doing and to inaccurately assess how well they have done.

Emotional Problems Emotional problems after a stroke are common. Patients with left-brain damage often react to their disorder with anxiety and depression; patients with right-brain damage more commonly seem indifferent to their situation. These differences in emotional response appear to be due to neurological damage. Right-brain-damaged patients have alexithymia, which involves difficulty in identifying and describing feelings (Spaletta et al., 2001).

As we have seen, depression is a serious problem for stroke patients, and its degree depends on the site of the stroke and its severity. However, psychosocial factors also predict the degree of depression. Depression depends, in part, on the relationship the stroke patient has to the caregiver. Overprotection by a caregiver, a poor relation with a caregiver, and a caregiver who views the caregiving situation negatively all lead to depression on both sides. In addition, depression is aggravated if the person must live in worsened circumstances after the stroke, has a poor perception of the future, and perceives little meaning in life (S. C. Thompson et al., 1989).

Relationship Problems The stroke patient may have problems with social relationships. Strokes produce symptoms that interfere with effective communication. For example, facial muscles may fail to work properly, producing the appearance of disfigurement. Cognitive impairment leads to memory loss, difficulties in concentrating, and other socially disruptive impairments, such as inappropriate emotional expression. A condition known as *multiinfarct dementia,* which results from the accumulating effects of small strokes, may produce Alzheimer's-like symptoms. Thus, the consequences of stroke can be socially stigmatizing, and patients may find they are avoided or rejected by their colleagues and friends (S. Newman, 1984).

Types of Rehabilitative Interventions

Interventions with stroke patients have typically taken four approaches: psychotherapy, including treatment for depression; cognitive remedial training to restore intellectual functioning; training in specific skills development; and the use of structured, stimulating environments to challenge the stroke patient's capabilities (Krantz & Deckel, 1983). Although individual counseling is employed with some stroke patients, group therapy is more common (Krantz & Deckel, 1983). Home visits from volunteers or counselors can provide help for the confused and frightened stroke patient who is too ill to go to a facility.

Treatment for depression usually takes the form of antidepressants, although in some cases, patients cannot take these medications because they aggravate other medical conditions. Consequently, psychotherapy is employed to help stroke patients learn ways of coping with their altered circumstances. The progress is often slow (Hibbard, Grober, Stein, & Gordon, 1992).

Interventions designed to deal with cognitive problems after stroke address several goals (W. A. Gordon & Diller, 1983). First, patients must be made aware that they have problems. Often, the stroke patient thinks he or she is performing adequately when this is simply not so. A risk of making patients aware of these problems is the sense of discouragement or failure that may arise. Thus, it is important for patients to see that these deficits are correctable.

Hopefulness regarding the optimism of patients to recover their faculties is based on a new approach, called *neurorehabilitation,* that relies on the brain's ability to rebuild itself and learn new tasks. Essentially the idea is to rewire the brain so that other areas of the brain than the area affected by the stroke can come to take on those functions, thus improving patients' ability to move, speak, and articulate clearly. Whereas it was once believed that stroke patients would achieve their maximum recovery within the first 6 months after stroke, it now

appears that these gains can occur over subsequent years (J. E. Allen, 2003a). Certain drugs such as antidepressants and cholesterol-lowering drugs appear to promote the growth of new neurons and may consequently be employed in the future to treat stroke (Abbott, 2004).

There are a variety of techniques to help right-brain-damaged stroke patients regain a full visual field (for example, W. A. Gordon & Diller, 1983; Weinberg et al., 1977). One method is to spread out an array of money before a patient and ask him or her to pick all of it up. The right-brain-damaged patient will pick up only the money on the right side, ignoring that on the left. When the patient is induced to turn his or her head toward the impaired side, he or she will see the remaining money and can then pick it up as well.

A scanning machine can improve this process further. Patients are first instructed to follow a moving stimulus with their eyes. When the stimulus moves to the left side of the stimulus array, it is out of sight of right-brain-damaged patients unless they turn their heads. Thus, patients quickly learn to turn their heads so they can pick up all information when the scanner moves into the left side of the visual field. Various tasks that require scanning, such as number canceling, are then introduced, so the patient can get practice using the entire visual field. Gradually, the patient is led to do tasks without benefit of the artificial scanner. Through these kinds of retraining efforts, many stroke patients are able to regain many of their lost capabilities. Eventually, they can negotiate the world much as they did before the stroke (W. A. Gordon & Diller, 1983).

Cognitive remediation is a slow process, and skills retraining needs to proceed in an orderly fashion, beginning with easy problems and moving to more difficult ones. As each skill is acquired, practice is essential (W. A. Gordon & Hibbard, 1992).

■ DIABETES

Diabetes is the third most common chronic illness in this country and one of the leading causes of death (Centers for Disease Control and Prevention, 2001). Nearly 6.3% of the U.S. population has diabetes, and of the roughly 18 million individuals who have it, 5.2 million cases remain undiagnosed (American Diabetes Association, 2002a). People with diabetes are at high risk for hypertension and stroke as well (Roan, 2003). Diabetes costs the United States more than $132 billion a year in medical costs, not including the indirect costs that result from disability and work loss (American Diabetes Association, 2003; Diamond, 2003).

In the past 40 years, the incidence of diabetes has increased sixfold, and each year physicians diagnose nearly 1.3 million new cases (American Diabetes Association, 2002a). Approximately 1 in every 400 to 500 children is diagnosed with diabetes. Altogether, diabetes contributes to 213,062 deaths yearly (American Diabetes Association, 2002a). Diabetes is estimated to cause approximately 41,000 cases of kidney failure, 24,000 cases of blindness, and 82,000 amputations yearly. In addition, about 65% of deaths among people with diabetes are due to heart disease and stroke (American Diabetes Association, 2002a). At present, about 1 million Americans have Type I diabetes, and 17 million have Type II diabetes. The incidence of cases of Type II diabetes is increasing so rapidly that it is considered a pandemic (R. Taylor, 2004). The complications of diabetes are pictured in figure 13.4.

Diabetes is a chronic condition of impaired carbohydrate, protein, and fat metabolism that results from insufficient secretion of insulin or from insulin resistance. The cells of the body need energy to function, and the primary source of energy is glucose, a simple

FIGURE 13.4 | The Potential Health Complications of Diabetes Are Extensive, Life-Threatening, and Costly

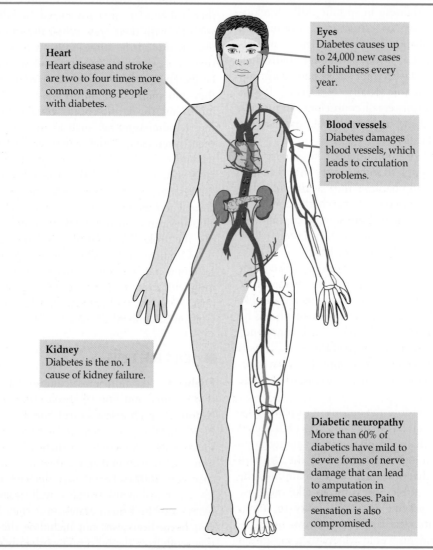

Heart
Heart disease and stroke are two to four times more common among people with diabetes.

Eyes
Diabetes causes up to 24,000 new cases of blindness every year.

Blood vessels
Diabetes damages blood vessels, which leads to circulation problems.

Kidney
Diabetes is the no. 1 cause of kidney failure.

Diabetic neuropathy
More than 60% of diabetics have mild to severe forms of nerve damage that can lead to amputation in extreme cases. Pain sensation is also compromised.

sugar that results from the digestion of foods containing carbohydrates. Glucose circulates in the blood as a potential source of energy for cells that need it.

Insulin is a hormone, produced by the beta cells of the pancreas, that bonds to the receptor sites on the outside of a cell and acts essentially as a key to permit glucose to enter the cells. When there is not enough insulin produced or when insulin resistance develops (that is, the glucose can no longer be used by the cells), glucose stays in the blood instead of entering the cells, resulting in a condition called hyperglycemia. The body attempts to rid itself of this excess glucose, yet the cells are not receiving the glucose they need and send signals to the hypothalamus that more food is needed.

Types of Diabetes

There are two major types of diabetes, insulin-dependent (or Type I) diabetes and non-insulin-dependent (or Type II) diabetes. They differ in origin, pathology, role of genetics in their development, age of onset, and treatment.

Type I Diabetes

Type I diabetes is characterized by the abrupt onset of symptoms, which result from lack of insulin production by the beta cells of the pancreas. The disorder may result from viral infection or autoimmune reactions, and probably has a genetic contribution as well. In Type I diabetes, the immune system falsely identifies cells in the pancreas as invaders and accordingly destroys these cells, compromising or eliminating their ability to produce insulin. Type I diabetes usually develops relatively early in life, earlier for girls than for boys, between the ages of 5 and 6 or later between 10 and 13.

The most common early symptoms are frequent urination, unusual thirst, excessive drinking of fluids, weight loss, fatigue, weakness, irritability, nausea, uncontrollable craving for food (especially sweets), and fainting. These symptoms are due to the body's attempt to find sources of energy, which prompts it to feed off its own fats and proteins. By-products of these fats then build up in the body, producing symptoms; if the condition is untreated, a coma can result.

Type I diabetes is a serious, life-threatening illness accounting for about 10% of all diabetes. It is managed primarily through direct injections of insulin—hence the name insulin-dependent diabetes (American Diabetes Association, 1999). The Type I diabetic is especially vulnerable to hyperglycemia. When this occurs, the skin is flushed and dry, and the individual feels drowsy and has deep, labored breathing. Vomiting may

occur, and the tongue is dry; feelings of hunger are rare, but thirst is common. Abdominal pain may occur, and a large amount of sugar is detectable in the urine. Hyperglycemia may require medical intervention because coma may result, requiring hospitalization.

Type II Diabetes

Type II (or non-insulin-dependent) diabetes is milder than the insulin-dependent type. Type II diabetes is typically a disorder of middle and old age, striking those primarily over the age of 40. As obesity has become rampant, Type II diabetes, to which obesity is a major contributor, has become more prevalent, especially at earlier ages. Many children and adolescents are now Type II diabetics. This type of diabetes is increasing at astronomical rates.

A good deal is known about the mechanisms that trigger Type II diabetes. Glucose metabolism involves a delicate balance between insulin production and insulin responsiveness. As food is digested, carbohydrates are broken down into glucose. Glucose is absorbed from the intestines into the blood, where it travels to the liver and other organs. Rising levels of glucose in the blood trigger the pancreas to secret insulin into the blood stream. When this balance goes awry, it sets the stage for Type II diabetes. First, cells in muscle, fat, and liver lose some of their ability to respond fully to insulin, a condition known as insulin resistance. In response to insulin resistance, the pancreas temporarily increases its production of insulin. At this point, insulin-producing cells may give out, with the result that insulin production falls, and the balance between insulin action and insulin secretion becomes disregulated, resulting in Type II diabetes (Alper, 2000). The symptoms include frequent urination; fatigue; dryness of the mouth; impotence; irregular menstruation; loss of sensation; frequent infection of the skin, gums, or urinary system; pain or cramps in legs, feet, or fingers; slow healing of cuts and bruises; and intense itching and drowsiness.

The majority of Type II diabetics are overweight (90%), and Type II diabetes is more common in women and individuals of low socioeconomic status (American Diabetes Association, 2002a). Type II diabetes is heavily a disorder of aging. More than 17% of people 65 or older have diabetes, compared with 1.2% among those 20 to 64 (Centers for Disease Control and Prevention, 2002b). Diabetes strikes the minority communities in the United States especially heavily. African Americans are 1.7 times as likely to develop diabetes as Whites, and Hispanic Americans are nearly twice as likely. In some Native American tribes, 50% of the population has diabetes

TABLE 13.2 | Risk Factors for Type II Diabetes

You are at risk if:
- You are overweight
- You get little exercise
- You have high blood pressure
- You have a sibling or parent with diabetes
- You had a baby weighing over 9 pounds at birth
- You are a member of a high-risk ethnic group, which includes African Americans, Latinos, Native Americans, Asian Americans, and Pacific Islanders

Source: American Diabetes Association, 1999.

(American Diabetes Association, 1999). Type II diabetes is on the increase because of an increase in the prevalence of a sedentary lifestyle and obesity, both of which are risk factors for the development of the disorder. Risk factors for Type II diabetes are listed in table 13.2.

Health Implications of Diabetes

The reason that diabetes is such a major public health problem stems less from the consequences of insufficient insulin production per se than from the complications that may develop. Diabetes is associated with a thickening of the arteries due to the buildup of wastes in the blood. As a consequence, diabetic patients show high rates of coronary heart disease.

Diabetes is the leading cause of blindness among adults, and it accounts for 50% of all the patients who require renal dialysis for kidney failure. Diabetes may also be associated with nervous system damage, including pain and loss of sensation. In severe cases, amputations of the extremities, such as toes and feet, are required. As a consequence of these complications, diabetics have a shorter life expectancy than do nondiabetic individuals. Diabetes may also exacerbate other difficulties in psychosocial functioning, contributing to eating disorders (P. Carroll, Tiggemann, & Wade, 1999) and sexual dysfunction in both men and women (Spector, Leiblum, Carey, & Rosen, 1993; Weinhardt & Carey, 1996), as well as depression (Talbot, Nouwen, Gingras, Belanger, & Audet, 1999), among other problems. Diabetes may produce central nervous system impairment that interferes with memory (L. A. Taylor & Rachman, 1988), especially among the elderly (Mooradian, Perryman, Fitten, Kavonian, & Morley, 1988).

Diabetes is one component of the so-called deadly quartet, the other three of which are interabdominal body fat, hypertension, and elevated lipids. This cluster of symptoms, also known as the metabolic syndrome, is potentially fatal because it is strongly linked to an increased risk of myocardial infarction and stroke (Weber-Hamann et al., 2002). Hostility may also foster the metabolic syndrome as well (Niaura et al., 2000).

Stress and Diabetes   Both Type I and Type II diabetics are sensitive to the effects of stress (Gonder-Frederick, Carter, Cox, & Clarke, 1990; Halford, Cuddihy, & Mortimer, 1990). Stress may precipitate Type I diabetes in individuals with the affected gene (Lehman, Rodin, McEwen, & Brinton, 1991). People at high risk for diabetes show abnormal glycemic responsiveness to stress, which, when coupled with the experience of intermittent or long-term stress, may be implicated in the development of the disease (Esposito-Del Puente et al., 1994). Stress also aggravates both Type I and Type II diabetes after the disease is diagnosed (Surwit & Schneider, 1993; Surwit & Williams, 1996).

At least 14 studies have reported direct links between stress and poor diabetic control (see Brand, Johnson, & Johnson, 1986; Hanson & Pichert, 1986). This relationship is not caused by differences in adherence to medications (Hanson, Henggeler, & Burghen, 1987), coping efforts (Frenzel, McCaul, Glasgow, & Schafer, 1988), insulin regimen, diet, or exercise (Hanson & Pichert, 1986), although stress can also adversely affect adherence and diet (Balfour, White, Schiffrin, Dougherty, & Dufresne, 1993; Halford et al., 1990).

Just as they appear to be implicated in the development of coronary heart disease and hypertension, anger and hostility may be implicated in higher glucose levels (Vitaliano, Scanlan, Krenz, & Fujimoto, 1996), and an examination of their role in the potential aggravation of diabetes is warranted. Diabetic patients with depression appear to be at enhanced risk for coronary heart disease (Kinder, Kamarck, Baum, & Orchard, 2002).

Although the actual mechanisms involved in the aggravation of diabetes by stress are still being explored, it is clear that glucose metabolism is influenced by stress. As noted, glucose supplies cells with energy, and insulin is responsible for glucose storage. In the presence of stress hormones, such as cortisol, however, insulin is less effective in facilitating glucose storage. This process may result in increased insulin secretion. When insulin is high, systolic blood pressure and heart rate also tend to be elevated. When these processes are combined with overeating and inactivity, the results can lead to obesity, causing further insulin resistance and higher insulin secretion.

Just as sympathetic nervous system reactivity is implicated in the development of coronary heart disease and hypertension, it likewise appears to be involved in the pathophysiology of Type II diabetes. In particular, a hyperresponsivity to epinephrine, higher levels of circulating catecholamines, and elevated levels of endogenous opioid-peptides are found in many diabetes patients. Thus, theoretically, as is the case with heart disease and hypertension patients, interventions to reduce sympathetic nervous system activity can be useful for modulating hyperglycemia.

Problems in Self-Management of Diabetes

The key to the successful control of diabetes is active self-management (Auerbach et al., 2001). Indeed, Type II diabetes can be completely prevented by changes in the lifestyle of high-risk individuals (Tuomilehto et al., 2001), and the trajectory of the disease in already diagnosed patients can be greatly improved by changes in lifestyle. The lifestyle factors most strongly implicated are the need for exercise, weight loss among those that are overweight, stress management, and dietary control. However, adherence to lifestyle change is problematic, so a therapeutic approach is often undertaken. The ideal treatment is patient centered and patient directed, rather than physician directed.

Management of Type I Diabetes   Because very tight control of glucose levels can make a huge difference in the progression of this disease, patients with Type I diabetes need to monitor their glucose levels throughout each day and take immediate action when it is needed.

The treatment goal for diabetes is to keep blood sugar at normal levels. This regulation is typically accomplished through regular insulin injections, dietary control, weight control, and exercise. The number of calories taken in each day must be relatively constant. Food intake must be controlled by a meal plan and not by temptation or appetite. Insulin injections are most often recommended on a regular basis for Type I diabetes, whereas diet, weight control, and exercise figure prominently in the management of both types of diabetes. When blood glucose levels can be actively controlled through such methods, onset and progression of diabetes-related disorders, including eye disease, kidney disease, and nerve disorders, may be reduced by more than 50% (National Institute on Diabetes and Digestive and Kidney Disorders, 1999).

Adherence   Unfortunately, adherence to self-management programs appears to be low. For example, one set of investigations found that 80% of diabetic patients administered insulin incorrectly, 58% administered the wrong dosage, 77% tested their urine for sugar

The management of Type I diabetes critically depends on proper monitoring of blood glucose level and regular injections of insulin, yet many adolescents and adults fail to adhere properly to the treatment regimen.

content inaccurately, 75% were not eating at sufficiently regular intervals, and 75% were not eating prescribed foods (Watkins, Roberts, Williams, Martin, & Coyle, 1967; Wing, Nowalk, Marcus, Koeske, & Finegold, 1986). Overall, only about 15% of patients appear to adhere to all their treatment recommendations.

Moreover, many of the severe complications that arise from diabetes are not evident for 15 or 20 years after its onset. Therefore, complications do not frighten people into being adherent. They may feel no symptoms and, because the disease does not seem insistent on a day-to-day basis, fail to adhere to their treatment regimen. Many of the errors made by diabetics in adhering to their treatment regimen, then, are errors of omission rather than errors of commission. That is, it is relatively unusual for diabetics to intentionally relapse but common for them to forget to undertake particular behaviors they are supposed to do regularly (Kirkley & Fisher, 1988).

One of the dilemmas involved in adequate adherence is that diabetic patients often fail to self-monitor their blood glucose level (Wysocki, Green, & Huxtable, 1989). Instead, like hypertensive patients, they rely on what their blood glucose level "feels like" (Hampson, Glasgow, & Toobert, 1990), and they rely strongly on their mood for making this judgment (Gonder-Frederick, Cox, Bobbitt, & Pennebaker, 1986). And, as is also the case in hypertension, even training in glucose level awareness fails to produce very accurate estimates of blood sugar levels (Diamond, Massey, & Covey, 1989). Depression, too, complicates glycemic control in Type I diabetic patients (Van Tilberg et al., 2001).

Adherence is improved when patients and physicians share treatment goals. One study that uncovered a high level of nonadherence to treatment among parents regulating their children's Type I diabetes found that parents and physicians had quite different goals. The parents' efforts to control diet were designed to avoid hypoglycemia, which is a short-term threat. In contrast, the physicians' goals were centered on the long-term threat of diabetes complications and the need to keep blood glucose levels steady. These differences in goals accounted for many of the departures from the prescribed regimen (Marteau, Johnston, Baum, & Bloch, 1987).

Effective diabetes management involves multiple aspects of behavior change, and as we have seen, complex regimens directed to multiple health habits are often difficult to implement. As a result, interventions with diabetics often pull together into a single treatment program all the self-regulation techniques that are required.

Diabetics are trained in monitoring blood sugar accurately, using the information as a basis for making changes in behavior as through self-injection, reinforcing themselves for efforts to improve blood sugar control, managing stress, controlling diet, exercising, and developing social and problem-solving skills to deal with situational pressures to break with their treatment regimen (Goodall & Halford, 1991; Jenkins, 1990a; Wing, Epstein, Nowalk, & Lamparski, 1986). By seeing the relations among all the components in an organized program of self-regulation, adherence to the separate aspects of the regimen may be improved (R. E. Glasgow et al., 1989). Evidence suggests that intensive treatment interventions are more successful than less intensive programs in promoting long-term weight loss and maintaining adherence to treatment.

Management of Type II Diabetes   Type II diabetics are often unaware of the health risks they face. A recent survey found that only one third of diagnosed diabetic patients realized that heart disease was among the most serious complications for which they were at risk (*New York Times,* 2001). Clearly, education is an important component of intervention.

Dietary intervention involves reducing the sugar and carbohydrate intake of diabetic patients. Obesity especially seems to tax the insulin system, so patients are encouraged to achieve a normal weight. Exercise is encouraged because it helps use up glucose in the blood (Feinglos & Surwit, 1988) and helps reduce weight.

Adherence is problematic for Type II diabetics as well. Poor adherence seems to be due more to transient situational factors, such as psychological stress and social pressure to eat (Goodall & Halford, 1991). However, people with good self-control skills do a better job achieving glycemic control by virtue of their greater adherence to a treatment regimen (Peyrot, McMurry, & Kruger, 1999). The nature of the diabetes treatment regimen also contributes to poor rates of adherence. Specifically, the chief factors that require self-control, diet and exercise, are lifestyle factors, and, as we noted in chapter 3, adherence to recommendations to alter lifestyle is very low.

One reason for this fact is that such advice is often not seen as medical but as advisory and discretionary, and patients often fail to follow their regimen or modify it according to their own theories and desires. Another reason is that dietary control and exercise are very difficult health habits to follow regularly. The person attempting to exert rigorous dietary control is constantly besieged by temptations to depart from a preset course, and the person trying to fit exercise into an already busy day may find it easy to forget this activity when other demands seem more pressing or necessary. Voluntarily restricting calories, avoiding desired foods, and engaging in an exercise program may seem like self-punishment, something that many patients are unwilling to do.

Improving Adherence Nonadherence to treatment programs is also influenced by knowledge and health beliefs. Many diabetic patients simply do not have enough information about glucose utilization and metabolic control of insulin. A patient may simply be told what to do without understanding the rationale for it. Patients who are threatened by their disease show poor metabolic control, and those who have strong feelings of self-efficacy seem to achieve better control (S. B. Johnson, Tomer, Cunningham, & Henretta, 1990; Kavanaugh, Gooley, & Wilson, 1993). Consequently, education is vital.

Does social support improve adherence to a diabetes regimen? Generally, support improves adherence, but this generalization may not be so true for diabetes. Although social support can have beneficial effects on adjustment to the disease, active participation in a social network often leads diabetics to be exposed to norms about diet and temptations to eat that compromise diabetic functioning (R. M. Kaplan & Hartwell, 1987; Littlefield, Rodin, Murray, & Craven, 1990). Thus, the effects of social support are mixed.

As is true of all chronic diseases, patients with diabetes must play an active role in their own care. Consequently, any intervention that focuses on improving a sense of self-efficacy and the ability to independently regulate one's behavior has the potential to improve adherence and glycemic control (Macrodimitris & Endler, 2001; Senecal, Nouwen, & White, 2000; G. C. Williams, McGregor, Zeldman, Freedman, & Deci, 2004).

Diabetes Prevention Increasingly, health psychologists and policy makers are recognizing that diabetes is a major public health problem. Proactive responses to its increasing incidence are on the rise and include more active efforts to control obesity as the first defense against this common, costly, and rapidly growing disorder (R. E. Glasgow et al., 2002).

A recent investigation (Diabetes Prevention Program Research Group, 2002) identified 3,000 adults whose blood sugar levels were high but not yet high enough to be diagnosed with diabetes. These high-risk individuals were then assigned to one of three groups. One group received a placebo medication and lifestyle recommendations; a second received lifestyle recommendations and a medication that lowers blood sugar; and a third group received an intensive lifestyle intervention focused on weight loss, physical activity, and diet change. After only 4 years, the incidence of diabetes was decreased by 58% in the lifestyle intervention group, and by 31% in the medication group when compared to the placebo group. The fact that only modest weight loss and small increases in physical activity were needed to achieve these results suggests that intervening with high-risk individuals to modify a lifestyle can be successful in reducing the incidence of diabetes.

Interventions with Diabetics

As noted, treatment of Type I diabetes involves an exacting insulin regimen; although some Type II diabetics must also take insulin, most do not. Current recommendations are that most people diagnosed with Type II diabetes should begin to take statins, the cholesterol-lowering drugs, in order to guard against the heart disease that often accompanies diabetes (O'Neil, 2004).

A variety of cognitive-behavioral interventions have been undertaken with diabetics to improve adherence to aspects of their regimen. Some programs have focused on helping diabetics engage in appropriate self-injection (see Wing, Nowalk, et al., 1986). Others have focused more on training patients to monitor blood sugar levels effectively (Wing, Epstein, Nowalk, Scott, et al., 1986). As a result of ties between stress and diabetes (for example, Herschbach et al., 1997), behavioral investigators have examined the effect of stress management programs on diabetic control. An example of combating stress to control diabetes appears in Box 13.6.

Weight control improves glycemic control and reduces the need for medication, and so behavioral interventions that help diabetic patients lose weight have been undertaken and appear to show at least some success (Wing, Epstein, Nowalk, Scott, et al., 1986). However, as with most weight-loss programs, following initial success, people often relapse to their poor habits and may gain back much of the weight (Wing, Blair, Marcus, Epstein, & Harvey, 1994). Self-management is an important focus for all interventions with people with chronic disease but is especially true with diabetes. Because the diabetes regimen is complex, involves lifestyle change, and implicates multiple risk factors,

BOX 13.6

Stress Management and the Control of Diabetes

Mrs. Goldberg had had Type II diabetes for some time. Her doctor had made the diagnosis 10 years earlier, just after her 40th birthday. She watched her diet, got sufficient exercise, and was able to control her blood glucose with oral medication. During the past several months, however, Mrs. Goldberg's diabetes control had begun to deteriorate. Despite the fact that she continued to follow her diet and exercise regimen, her blood glucose levels became elevated more frequently.

Mrs. Goldberg consulted her physician, who asked her if her lifestyle had changed in any way over the past several months. She told him that her boss had added several new responsibilities to her job and that they made her workday much more stressful. Things were so bad that she was having trouble sleeping at night and dreaded going to work in the morning. Mrs. Goldberg's physician told her that this additional stress might be responsible for her poor diabetes control. Rather than

initially changing her medications, he suggested that she first speak with her boss to see if some of the stress of her job might be relieved. Fortunately, her boss was understanding and allowed Mrs. Goldberg to share her responsibilities with another employee. Within several weeks, she no longer dreaded going to work, and her diabetes control improved significantly.

This case illustrates how a relatively simple change in a patient's environment may have a clinically significant impact on blood glucose control. It underscores the need for the physician to be aware of what is happening in the patient's life in order to determine requirements for treatment. Under the circumstances described, it would have been inappropriate to have altered this patient's medication.

Source: Feinglos & Surwit, 1988, p. 29.

---

technical skills to manage the regimen as well as problem-solving skills and active coping methods are needed. Thus, training in self-management skills is a vital part of many interventions with diabetes (Hill-Briggs, 2003). Because of problems involving adherence, a focus on maintenance and relapse prevention is essential.

The fact that stress and social pressure to eat have such major effects on adherence to treatment regimens has led researchers to focus increasingly on social skills and problem-solving skills training in diabetes management (for example, R. E. Glasgow, Toobert, Hampson, & Wilson, 1995). That is, in addition to information about the treatment regimen, diabetic patients often need training in how to maintain the treatment regimen in the face of circumstances that undermine it (M. S. Glasgow, Engel, & D'Lugoff, 1989; Goodall & Halford, 1991). Thus, for example, just as the smoker is trained to resist social pressure to smoke, the diabetic is trained in resisting influences to consume foods that would have adverse effects on blood sugar (Toobert & Glasgow, 1991).

A complication of diabetes is the depression that often accompanies it. Especially as symptoms increase and the disease intrudes increasingly on life activities, patients may become depressed (Talbot et al., 1999). Depression is tied to poor glucose control and poor compliance with the diabetes treatment regimen (Lust-

man et al., 1997). Depression is linked to an enhanced risk of coronary heart disease risk among women diagnosed with diabetes; thus, it represents a particularly problematic complication (Clouse et al., 2003). As a result, depression is often an object of treatment, as well as a symptom of the disease.

Because diabetes is so clearly linked to other disorders, including cardiovascular disease, stroke, and heart attack, interventions that aim toward multiple risk factors may be especially successful. One study that employed behavior modification and pharmacological therapy that targeted hyperglycemia, hypertension, elevated lipids, and cardiovascular disease (treated by an aspirin) found substantial reduction not only in diabetes but in cardiovascular events as well (Goede et al., 2003).

Special Problems of Adolescent Diabetics

The management of diabetes is a particular problem with adolescents (for example, S. B. Johnson, Freund, Silverstein, Hansen, & Malone, 1990). To begin with, adolescents often have Type I diabetes, so their disease is severe. They are entangled in issues of independence and developing self-concept; diabetes and the restrictions that it imposes are inconsistent with these developmental tasks. Adolescents may see their parents' limitations on food as efforts to control them and may regard the need to monitor diet or to be conscientious about injections as rules and regulations imposed from the outside. Moreover, within the adolescent peer culture, those who are different are often stigmatized. Thus, the adolescent diabetic may neglect proper care to avoid rejection. Emotionally stable and conscientious adolescents are more likely to follow the complex regimen that diabetes requires than those who do not have these qualities (Skinner, Hampson, & Fife-Schaw, 2002).

Relations with Family   Problems of managing Type I diabetes among adolescents are not confined to the diabetic's own difficulties of accepting the limitations imposed by the disease. Other family members may also react in ways that defeat management efforts. Parents, for example, may treat their newly diagnosed adolescent diabetic as a child and restrict activities beyond what is necessary, infantilizing the adolescent and increasing dependence. Alternatively, the parents may try to convince the child that he or she is normal, like everyone else, yet the adolescent quickly learns otherwise.

The family environment can be important to diabetic control and adherence (for a review, see Hanson, Henggeler, Harris, Burghen, & Moore, 1989). One study (Minuchin et al., 1978) found that diabetic children with poor control improved substantially after fam-

ily therapy that attempted to break down faulty methods of communication and conflict resolution. Individual therapy failed to achieve the same outcomes.

Studies suggest that when parents are actively involved in diabetes management tasks, such as helping their adolescents monitor blood glucose levels, better metabolic control over the disease can be obtained (B. L. Andersen, Ho, Brackett, Finkelstein, & Laffel, 1997).

Adherence   Increasingly, health psychologists have been involved in the development of interventions to improve adherence and adjustment and control over Type I diabetes. The health psychologist can help with the delineation of problems in achieving control over diabetes (R. E. Glasgow & Anderson, 1995) and with the identification of complicating psychological and social factors not yet identified that may compromise the treatment of diabetes (Talbot, Nouwen, Gingras, Gosselin, & Audet, 1997).

The health psychologist, then, has an important role to play in the management of diabetes, by developing the best format for teaching the complex treatment regimen, ensuring adherence, developing effective means for coping with stress, and helping the diagnosed diabetic develop the self-regulatory skills needed to manage the multiple factor treatment program that is required.

SUMMARY

1. Coronary heart disease is the number one killer in the United States. It is a disease of lifestyle, and risk factors include cigarette smoking, obesity, elevated serum cholesterol, low levels of physical activity, chronic stress, and hostility.

2. Coronary proneness is associated with hostility and with hyperreactivity to stressful situations, including a slow return to baseline. These exaggerated cardiovascular responses to stress may be genetically based, related to heightened neuroendocrine reactivity to environmental stressors.

3. Efforts to modify excessive reactivity to stress and hostility through training in relaxation and stress management show promise in reducing morbidity and mortality due to CHD.

4. Cardiac rehabilitation is designed to help diagnosed CHD patients obtain their optimal physical, medical, psychological, social, emotional, vocational, and economic status. Components of these programs typically include education in CHD, drug treatments, nutritional counseling, supervised exercise, stress management, and, under some circumstances, psychological counseling and/or social support group participation.

5. MI patients often have difficulty managing the stress-reduction aspects of their regimens, and sometimes marital relations can be strained as a result of the changes forced on the patient and the spouse by the post-MI rehabilitative regimen.

6. Hypertension, or high blood pressure, affects one in four Americans. Most hypertension is of unknown origin, although risk factors include family history of hypertension. Low-SES Blacks are particularly vulnerable to the disorder.

7. Hypertensives show heightened reactivity to stressful events. Hostility is also implicated.

8. Hypertension is typically treated by diuretics or beta-blocking drugs, which may have adverse side effects. Cognitive-behavioral treatments, including stress management, have been used to control the disorder and to reduce drug dosages.

9. The biggest problems related to the control of hypertension concern high rates of nondiagnosis and nonadherence to therapy. The fact that the disease is symptomless helps explain both problems. Low rates of adherence are also explained by the adverse side effects of drugs.

10. Stroke results from a disturbance in blood flow to the brain. It may disrupt all aspects of life. Motor difficulties, cognitive impairments, and depression are particular problems associated with stroke.

11. Interventions for stroke patients have typically involved psychotherapy, including treatment for depression; cognitive remedial training to restore intellectual functioning; skill building; and structured, stimulating environments to challenge the stroke patient's capabilities.

12. Diabetes is the third most common chronic disease in the United States. Insulin-dependent, or Type I, diabetes typically develops in childhood and is more severe than non-insulin-dependent, or Type II, diabetes, which develops typically after age 40. Stress is known to exacerbate glycemic control in both types of diabetes.

13. The diabetes self-care regimen is complex, involving testing urine for sugar content, administering insulin, (Type I), eating prescribed foods, eating at regular intervals, and exercising regularly. Adherence to this regimen is poor.

14. Interventions can improve adherence, especially if the different components of the regimen are logically linked to each other in a programmatic effort toward effective self-care. Training in diabetes-specific social management skills and problem-solving skills are especially important components.

KEY WORDS

cardiac invalidism
cardiac rehabilitation
cardiopulmonary resuscitation
   (CPR)

coronary heart disease (CHD)
diabetes
hypertension
John Henryism

metabolic syndrome
stroke
Type A behavior pattern

CHAPTER 14

Psychoneuroimmunology, AIDS, Cancer, and Arthritis

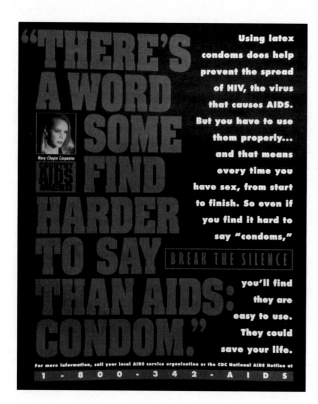

Using latex condoms does help prevent the spread of HIV, the virus that causes AIDS. But you have to use them properly... and that means every time you have sex, from start to finish. So even if you find it hard to say "condoms," you'll find they are easy to use. They could save your life.

Mei-ling was facing the toughest semester she had ever had. Her father had lost his job, so in addition to trying to provide social support to her parents, she had been forced to take on a part-time job to help pay for her college expenses.

She had scheduled all her courses for the first few hours of the morning so that by 1:30, she was able to get over to the accountant's office, where she answered phones and billed clients until 6:00 at night. Then she headed back to the dorm to study long into the night.

Her boyfriend, Mark, was complaining that he never saw her anymore. When he was free and wanted to go out to a movie or to a fraternity party, she was always studying, trying to make up for the time she lost while she was working. He hadn't actually said that he was going to start dating other women, but she suspected he might soon reach that point.

And now she faced exams. All of them promised to be challenging, and she would have to rearrange her work hours to accommodate the exam schedule. Her boss was annoyed enough at the fact that she sometimes had to reduce her hours to complete course requirements, and he was not going to appreciate the further complications in her schedule that the exams would create.

Mei-ling made it through her exams, but just barely. Following her last exam, in Spanish, she headed back to her room and collapsed into bed with a temperature of 102, where she stayed, nursing a respiratory flu, for the next 10 days.

In this chapter, we take up the question of immunity, the factors that influence it, and the situations that compromise it. Mei-ling's case is not unusual. Stress and problems in social support are among the most clearly documented conditions that compromise the ability of the body to mount resistance to potential infection.

For many years, the immune system was one of the most poorly understood systems of the human body. However, in the past 2 decades, research advances in this area have been substantial, leading to the burgeoning field of psychoneuroimmunology.

Psychoneuroimmunology refers to the interactions among behavioral, neuroendocrine, and immunological processes of adaptation (Ader, 1995). In this chapter, we consider developments in this rapidly growing field and then turn in more detail to three disorders believed to be related to immunologic functioning: AIDS, cancer, and arthritis.

■ PSYCHONEUROIMMUNOLOGY

The Immune System

As noted in chapter 2, the immune system is the surveillance system of the body. It is implicated in infection, allergies, cancer, and autoimmune diseases among other disorders. The primary function of the immune system is to distinguish between what is "self" and what is foreign and then to attack and rid the body of foreign invaders.

Profile of the Immune System   To understand the relationship of psychosocial factors to the immune system, the distinction between natural and specific immunity is important. Natural immunity is involved in defense against a variety of pathogens. That is, the cells involved in natural immunity do not provide defense against a particular pathogen, but rather against many pathogens. As noted in chapter 2, the largest group of cells involved in natural immunity is granulocytes, which include neutrophils and macrophages; both are phagocytic cells that engulf target pathogens. Neutrophils and macrophages congregate at the site of an injury or infection and release toxic substances. Macrophages release cytokines that lead to inflammation and fever, among other side effects, and promote wound healing. Natural killer cells are also involved in natural immunity; they recognize nonself material (such as viral infections or cancer cells) and lyse (break up and disintegrate) those cells by releasing toxic substances. Natural killer cells are believed to be important in signaling potential malignancies and in limiting early phases of viral infections.

Specific immunity is slower and, as its name implies, more specific than natural immunity. The lymphocytes involved in specific immunity have receptor sites on their cell surfaces that fit with one, and only one, antigen, and thus they respond to only one kind of invader. When they are activated, these antigen-specific cells divide and create a population of cells called the proliferative response.

Essentially, natural and specific immunity work together, such that natural immunity contains an infection or wound rapidly and early on following the invasion of a pathogen, whereas specific immunity involves a delay of up to several days before a full defense can be mounted. Figure 14.1 illustrates the interaction between lymphocytes and phagocytes.

FIGURE 14.1 | Interaction Between Lymphocytes and Phagocytes

B lymphocytes release antibodies, which bind to pathogens and their products, aiding recognition by phagocytes. Cytokines released by T cells activate the phagocytes to destroy the material they have taken up. In turn, mononuclear phagocytes can present antigen to T cells, thereby activating them.   (*Source:* Roitt, Brostoff, & Male, 1998)

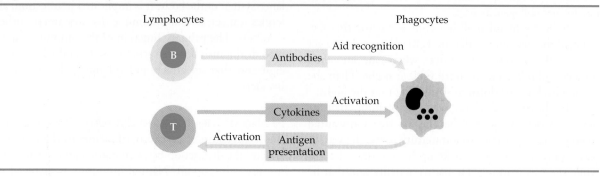

Humoral and Cell-Mediated Immunity   As explained in chapter 2, specific immunity is of two types—humoral and cell mediated. Humoral immunity is mediated by B lymphocytes, which provide protection against bacteria, neutralize toxins produced by bacteria, and prevent viral reinfection. Cell-mediated immunity, involving T lymphocytes from the thymus gland, operates at the cellular level. Cytotoxic (T_C) cells respond to specific antigens and kill by producing toxic substances that destroy virally infected cells. Helper T (T_H) cells enhance the functioning of T_C cells, B cells, and macrophages by producing lymphokines. Lymphokines also appear to serve a counterregulatory immune function that suppresses immune activity. Components of the immune system are pictured in figure 14.2.

Assessing Immunocompetence

There are many potential indicators of immune functioning. Two general approaches have been used:

1. Measuring the numbers of different kinds of cells in the immune system by looking at blood samples.
2. Assessing the functioning of immune cells.

Examples of the first approach involve counting the numbers of T, B, and NK cells and assessing the amount of circulating lymphokines or antibody levels in the blood.

Assessing the functioning of cells involves examining the activation, proliferation, transformation, and cytotoxicity of cells. Common assessments include the ability of lymphocytes to kill invading cells (lymphocyte cytotoxicity), the ability of lymphocytes to reproduce when artificially stimulated by a chemical (mitogen), and the ability of certain white blood cells to ingest foreign particles (phagocytotic activity). For example, in the mitogenic stimulation technique, it is assumed that the more proliferation that occurs in response to the mitogen, the better the cells are functioning.

Another measure of how well the immune system is functioning has to do with the degree to which an individual produces antibodies to a latent virus. All of us carry around viruses that are latent, that is, not active. If our bodies begin to produce antibodies to these inactive viruses (such as Epstein-Barr virus or herpes simplex virus), this is a sign that the immune system is not working well enough to control these latent viruses. Consequently, levels of antibodies to these latent viruses constitute a third type of measure of how well the immune system is functioning.

Producing antibodies to a vaccine is also a measure of immune functioning. When people have received vaccination for particular disorders, the degree to which the body is able to produce antibodies to the vaccine is a sign of good functioning. For example, in studies in which participants received a course of hepatitis B vaccinations, lower antibody response was predicted by a poorer initial T cell proliferation response to mitogenic stimulation and by negative affect (A. L. Marsland, Cohen, Rabin, & Manuck, 2001; see also V. E. Burns, Drayson, Ring, & Carroll, 2002). Subsequent to vaccination, those with higher stress exposure were more

FIGURE 14.2 | Components of the Immune System   (*Source:* Roitt, Brostoff, & Male, 1998)

Stress and Immune Functioning
-->

Stress and Immune Functioning

likely to show an inadequate antibody titre. Level of antibody titre was also compromised by substance use. Those who coped with stressful life events through emotion-focused coping—that is, by accepting the reality of the situation—were more likely to have an adequate antibody titre 1 year later.

When indicators such as these suggest that the immune system is working effectively, a state of **immunocompetence** is said to exist. When these indicators suggest that immune functioning may have been disrupted or reduced below a normal level, a state of **immunocompromise** is said to exist.

Another way of studying the effects of stress and psychosocial resources on immune functioning is to examine wound healing. Wounds heal faster when the immune system is functioning more vigorously. Using this method, researchers make a small puncture wound usually in the forearm then examine how quickly the wound heals over and shrinks in people who are under stress or not. Psychological distress impairs the inflammatory response that initiates wound repair (Broadbent, Petrie, Alley, & Booth, 2003; Glaser et al., 1999). Although this method may only indirectly assess the relation of stress to the immune system, it is of critical importance because it demonstrates a relation to health outcomes. For example, stress impairs wound repair due to surgery and thus may prolong the recovery period (Broadbent et al., 2003).

Stress and Immune Functioning

Despite the methodological difficulties of psychoneuroimmunology research, a number of studies suggest that many commonplace stressors can adversely affect the immune system. This research began with animal studies showing that experimentally manipulated stressors altered immunologic functioning and increased susceptibility to disorders under immunologic regulation. Exposures of rats to loud noise, electric shock, and separation from the mother, for example, are all stressful events that produce adverse immunologic effects (Moynihan & Ader, 1996).

Research on humans shows similar effects (Segerstrom & Miller, 2004). In an early classic study, Ishigami (1919) observed decreases in phagocytic activity of tuberculosis patients' white blood cells when the patients were emotionally excited; this result suggested to him that immunologic functioning is suppressed during times of excitement.

Stress and Immunity in Humans
There are more than 300 studies examining the relation of stress to immune functioning in humans (Segerstrom & Miller, 2004). Different kinds of stressors create different demands on the body, so they may be expected to show different effects on the immune system. Human beings likely evolved so that in response to sudden stress, changes in the immune system could take place quickly,

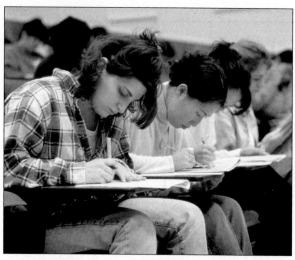

Studies show that exams and other stressful aspects of academic life can adversely compromise immune functioning.

leading to wound repair and infection prevention. For example, short-term stressors (of a few minutes' duration) produce a fight-or-flight response and would be expected to elicit immune responses that anticipate risk of injury and possible entry of infectious agents into the blood stream. Although short-term stressors now rarely involve wounds and the subsequent threat of infection, the system that evolved to deal with these threats is, nonetheless, mobilized in response to short-term stressors. Thus, for example, a short-term stressor, such as being called on in class or having to rapidly compute mental arithmetic in one's head, leads to marked increases in both natural killer cells and large granular lymphocytes. These increases in cell numbers are consistent with the idea that an acutely stressful event causes immune cells to redistribute themselves to fight off infection. In contrast, some measures of specific immunity decrease in response to acute short-term stressors. Recall that specific immunity is quite slow to develop, so specific immunity would be of little, if any, help for combatting short-term stressors. Thus, immediate short-term stressors produce a pattern of immune responses involving upregulation of natural immunity accompanied by downregulation of specific immunity (Segerstrom & Miller, 2004).

Brief naturalistic stressors of several days' duration, such as preparing for an examination, show a different pattern. Rather than altering the number or percentage of cells in the blood, short-term stressors mobilize immune functioning, particularly changes in cytokine pro-

duction, indicating a shift away from cellular immunity toward humoral immunity. Essentially then, real-life, short-term challenges seem to mobilize the immune system to fight off invaders (Segerstrom & Miller, 2004).

Chronically stressful events—including living with a disability; being unemployed; or engaging in long-term, difficult caregiving—are reliably tied to adverse effects on almost all functional measures of the immune system, involving both cellular and humoral downregulation. These effects are stronger among people with pre-existing vulnerabilities, such as old age or disease.

Thus, different types of stressful events (short term versus a few days versus long term) make different demands on the body that are reflected in different patterns of immune activity, in ways consistent with evolutionary arguments. Intense, short-term stressors recruit cells that may help defend against wounds and infection. Acute stressors of several days' duration upregulate immune functioning in ways likely to ward off threats posed by pathogens. However, chronic stressors seem to affect most measures of immune functioning adversely, ultimately leaving a person vulnerable to diseases (Segerstrom & Miller, 2004).

The body's stress systems appear to partially regulate these effects. As we saw in chapter 6, stress engages the sympathetic nervous system and the HPA axis, both of which also influence immune functioning (E. M. Friedman & Irwin, 1995). Sympathetic activation in response to stress has immediate effects of increasing immune activity, especially natural killer cell activity. Stress-related changes in hypothalamic adrenocortical functioning has immunosuppressive effects. That is, activation of the HPA axis leads to the release of glucocorticoids such as cortisol; cortisol reduces the number of white blood cells, affects the functioning of lymphocytes, and reduces the release of cytokines, which can reduce the ability of these substances to signal and communicate with other aspects of the immune system. Cortisol can also trigger apoptosis (cell death) of white blood cells. There may also be downward modulation of the immune system by the cerebral cortex, possibly via the release of neuropeptides, such as beta-endorphins (S. M. Levy, Fernstrom, et al., 1991; Morley, Kay, & Solomon, 1988).

Examples of Stress Studies   An example of the kind of study that relates stress to immunologic changes is an investigation of the impact of space flight on astronauts' immune functioning. Eleven astronauts who flew five different space shuttle flights ranging in length from

4 to 16 days were studied before launch and after landing. As expected, space flight was associated with a significant increase in number of circulating white blood cells, and natural killer cells decreased. At landing, catecholamines (epinephrine and norepinephrine) increased substantially as did white blood cells. These effects were stronger for astronauts who had been in space approximately a week, but in those who had experienced long-term flight (about 2 weeks), the effects were attenuated. This evidence suggests that the stress of space flight and landing produces a sympathetic nervous system response that mediates redistribution of circulating leukocytes, but this response may be attenuated after longer missions. Perhaps the stress of landing is muted by the relief of being at home (Mills, Meck, Waters, D'Aunno, & Ziegler, 2001). Another study of astronauts found that space flight resulted in decreased T-cell immunity and reactivation of the Epstein-Barr virus (a latent virus), consistent with the idea that the immune system was showing the effects of stress (Stowe, Pierson, & Barrett, 2001).

Most studies of stress, however, are literally quite closer to home and involve the effects of natural disasters and other traumas on immune functioning. A study of community responses to Hurricane Andrew damage, for example, revealed substantial changes in the immune systems of those most directly affected, changes that appeared to be due primarily to sleep problems that occurred in the wake of the hurricane (Ironson et al., 1997).

Stress involving threats to the self may be especially likely to produce changes in immune functioning. A study by Dickerson and colleagues (2004) had healthy participants write about traumatic experiences in which they had blamed themselves or more neutral experiences. Those who wrote about traumas in which they blamed themselves showed an increase in shame and guilt, coupled with elevations in proinflammatory cytokine activity. These findings suggest that self-related emotions can cause changes in inflammatory processes.

Several studies have examined whether daily hassles are associated with reduced immunocompetence. One study focused especially on a group of people who are chronically low in NK cell activity. They found that the two factors that best predicted this group were age and severity of daily hassles. The authors concluded that people who perceived the events that occurred to them as especially serious were likely to exhibit chronically low NK cytotoxic activity (S. M. Levy et al., 1989).

Anticipatory stress can also compromise immune functioning. In a longitudinal study of patients vulnerable to genital herpes recurrences, Kemeny and her colleagues (1989) found that over a 6-month period, the number of stressful events experienced was associated with a decreased percentage of T_H cells. More interesting is the fact that anticipated stressors, those that had not yet occurred but that were expected, also related to decreased percent of T_H cells. See box 14.1 which illustrates how academic stress affects immune functioning.

Interestingly, the effects of stress on immune functioning can be somewhat delayed. A study of antibody responses to influenza vaccine suggested that psychological stress just before the vaccine was not related to the response, but in the 10 days following vaccination, stress had shaped long-term antibody responses. These effects may have been mediated by the effect of stress on sleep loss (G. E. Miller et al., 2004).

Long-Term Stress As noted, other research has focused on adjustment to long-term stressors. Two investigations, for example, studied people living near the Three Mile Island nuclear power station after the nuclear accident. M. A. Schaeffer et al. (1985) found significantly lower levels of saliva IgA and lower percentages of B cells, total T cells, and T_H cells among the residents, suggesting that the stress of living near the site had adversely compromised their immune functioning. McKinnon and colleagues (1989) found fewer B cells, alterations in types of T cell frequencies, a lower level of NK cells, and high antibody titres to several viruses among the residents. Both studies are notable for having compared residents with a matched control sample from a demographically similar area and controlling for diet, smoking history, and health—factors that can alter immune profiles.

Health Risks Is the immune modulation that is produced by psychological stressors sufficient to lead to actual effects on health? The answer seems to be yes.

Research suggests that both children and adults under stress show increased vulnerability to infectious disease, including colds, flus, and herpes virus infections, such as cold sores or genital lesions, chicken pox, mononucleosis, and Epstein-Barr virus (for example, S. Cohen & Herbert, 1996; S. Cohen, Tyrrell, & Smith, 1993; Kiecolt-Glaser & Glaser, 1987). Among people who are already ill, such as people with a respiratory infection, stress predicts more severe illness and higher production of cytokines (S. Cohen, Doyle, & Skoner, 1999). Diseases whose onset and course may be influenced by proinflammatory cytokines are also potential

BOX 14.1

Academic Stress and Immune Functioning

Students are a captive population who are often willing and able to participate in research; consequently, much of the groundbreaking work on stress and the immune system has involved coping with the stress of school. Students may take grim satisfaction from studies indicating that, indeed, examinations, public speaking, and other stressful events of academic life can lead to enhanced cardiovascular activity, changes in immunologic parameters, and even illness (for example, Gerritson, Heijnen, Wiegant, Bermond, & Frijda, 1996; R. Glaser et al., 1992; Vedhara & Nott, 1996).

One study (R. Glaser, Kiecolt-Glaser, Stout, et al., 1985), for example, assessed immune parameters in a sample of 40 second-year medical students at 6 weeks before finals and then again during final exams. The students showed an increase in distress from the first to the second time period, and the percentages of total T and T_H lymphocytes were significantly lower during exams. There was also a decrease in NK cells and a significant depression in NK cell cytotoxic activity. Lymphocyte responsivity was lower during the exam period than at baseline, as was the quantity of interferon produced by stimulated leukocytes.

Several subsequent studies have confirmed these earlier observations (L. Cohen, Marshall, Cheng, Agarwal & Wei, 2000; R. Glaser et al., 1999; R. Glaser et al.,

1992; Tomei, Kiecolt-Glaser, Kennedy, & Glaser, 1990). Even 5-year-old kindergarten children attending school for the first time showed elevations in cortisol and changes in certain immune measures in response to this stressor (Boyce, Adams, et al., 1995). Moreover, these immune changes may have implications for health.

In another study, children who had recently begun kindergarten experienced a mild earthquake about 6 weeks into the school year. Those who had shown significant alterations in immune functioning in response to beginning kindergarten were more likely to experience a respiratory infection, such as a cold, following the earthquake (Boyce et al., 1993), suggesting that the earlier compromise of their stress systems had left them vulnerable to an illness following the second stressor.

School-related stress, then, does appear to compromise immune functioning. Are these changes inevitable? If people take care of themselves, can they avoid adverse changes in immunity in response to stress? As noted earlier, Segerstrom (1998) and her colleagues found that students who were optimistic about their ability to manage school-related stress and who made active efforts to cope with it fared better both psychologically and immunologically than those who did not. Good coping, then, may help offset the adverse effects of stress on the immune system.

---

health risks associated with stress-related immune changes. These include cardiovascular disease, arthritis, and other major chronic disorders (Kiecolt-Glaser, McGuire, Robles, & Glaser, 2002). Autoimmune disorders, which are described in box 14.2, are also affected by stress.

Negative Affect and Immune Functioning

Stress may compromise immune functioning, in part, because it increases negative emotions such as depression or anxiety. Depression has been heavily studied as a culprit in the stress-immune relationship (S. Cohen & Herbert, 1996; Irwin, 1999). A review relating clinical depression to immunity (Herbert & Cohen, 1993) found depression to be associated with several alterations in cellular immunity—specifically, lowered proliferative response of lymphocytes to mitogens, lowered NK cell activity, and alterations in numbers of white blood cells (see G. E. Miller, Cohen, & Herbert, 1999).

These immune effects were stronger among older people and people who were hospitalized, suggesting that already vulnerable people are at special risk.

Moreover, the research suggests a fairly straightforward relationship between depression and immunity such that the more depressed a person is, the more compromise of cellular immunity is likely to be found. Evidence is accumulating that some of the adverse effects of depression on immunity may be mediated by sleep disturbance that results from depression (for example, Cover & Irwin, 1994).

Stress, Immune Functioning, and Interpersonal Relationships

Both human and animal research suggests the importance of personal relationships to health (S. Cohen & Herbert, 1996). One of the earliest investigations examined bereavement. In a prospective study, Bartrop and associates (1977) studied 26 bereaved individuals and

BOX 14.2

Autoimmune Disorders

In autoimmune diseases, the immune system attacks the body's own tissues, falsely identifying them as invaders (Medzhitov & Janeway, 2002). Autoimmune diseases include more than 80 conditions, and virtually every organ is potentially vulnerable. Some of the most common disorders include Graves' disease, involving excessive production of thyroid hormone; chronic active hepatitis, involving the chronic inflammation of the liver; lupus, which is chronic inflammation of the connective tissue and which can affect multiple organ systems; multiple sclerosis, which involves the destruction of the myelin sheath that surrounds nerves and which produces a range of neurological symptoms; rheumatoid arthritis, in which the immune system attacks and inflames the tissue lining the joints; and Type I diabetes. The conditions range from mildly annoying to severe, progressive, and fatal. Nearly 80% of people who have these and other autoimmune disorders are women.

Exactly why women are so vulnerable is not yet completely understood. One possibility is that hormonal changes relating to estrogen modulate the occurrence and severity of symptoms. Consistent with this point, many women first develop symptoms of an autoimmune disorder in their twenties, when estrogen levels are high. Another theory is that testosterone may help protect against autoimmune disorders, a hormone that women have in short supply (Angier, 2001). A third theory is that during pregnancy, mother and fetus exchange bodily cells, which can remain in the mother's body for years. Although these cells are very similar to the mother's own, they are not identical and, the theory suggests, the immune system may get confused and attack both the leftover fetal cells and the maternal cells that look similar.

Because autoimmune disorders are a related group of conditions, the likelihood of suffering from one and then contracting another is relatively high. Genetic factors are implicated in autoimmunity (Ueda et al., 2003); one family member may develop lupus, another develop rheumatoid arthritis, and a third develop Graves' disease. Efforts to understand autoimmune diseases have recently been given extra urgency by the fact that immune-related disorders now appear to be implicated in such disorders such as atherosclerosis or even diabetes. For example, people with lupus are at risk for premature coronary artery atherosclerosis (Asanuma et al., 2003) and for accelerated atherosclerosis (Ham, 2003; Roman et al., 2003). As noted, Type I diabetes may be best understood as an autoimmune disorder as well. Thus, increasing attention to autoimmune disorders, their relation to other disorders, and gender differences in them merits additional intention.

Autoimmune conditions appear to be on the rise, and consequently understanding their causes and effective management will become a high priority for both scientists and health care practitioners.

---

26 comparison subjects matched for age, sex, and race. A number of immunologic parameters were examined 3 weeks after bereavement and again 6 weeks later. At the second time point, the bereaved group showed less responsiveness to mitogenic challenge than did the comparison group. More recent research, however, suggests that impaired immunity in response to bereavement is found largely among those people who become depressed in response to the bereavement (Zisook et al., 1994).

Loneliness also appears to adversely affect immune functioning. Lonely people have poorer health and show more immunocompromise on certain indicators than do people who are not lonely (R. Glaser, Kiecolt-Glaser, Speicher, & Holliday, 1985).

Marital Disruption and Conflict   Marital disruption and conflict have also been tied to adverse changes in immunity. In a study by Kiecolt-Glaser et al. (1987), women who had been separated 1 year or less showed poorer functioning on some immune parameters than did their matched married counterparts. Among separated and divorced women, recent separation and continued attachment or preoccupation with the ex-husband were associated with poorer immune functioning and with more depression and loneliness. Similar results have been found for men facing separation or divorce (Kiecolt-Glaser & Newton, 2001).

Even short-term marital conflict can have a discernible effect on the immune system. Kiecolt-Glaser and colleagues (1993) assessed the relationship between problem solving and immune functioning in 90 newly-wed couples. The couples were asked to spend 30 minutes discussing their marital problems. Those who showed negative or hostile behaviors during the discussion showed impairment on several functional immunologic tests. These results are especially noteworthy because adjustment among newlyweds is generally very high, and the couples had been initially selected because they had good physical and mental health. A subsequent study showed similar effects in couples who had been married, on average, 42 years, suggesting that even in long-term marriages, people are not protected against the adverse immunologic effects of marital conflict (Kiecolt-Glaser et al., 1997). Adverse effects of marital problems and conflict appear to fall more heavily on women than on men (see Kiecolt-Glaser & Newton, 2001, for a review).

Caregiving   In chapter 11, we saw how stressful caregiving can be for people who provide care for a friend or family member with a long-term illness, such as AIDS or Alzheimer's disease. Caregiving has been investigated for its impact on the immune system (for example, Esterling, Kiecolt-Glaser, & Glaser, 1996; Kiecolt-Glaser, Glaser, Gravenstein, Malarkey, & Sheridan, 1996). In one study, the caregivers for Alzheimer's patients were more depressed and showed lower life satisfaction than did a comparison sample. The caregivers had higher EBV antibody titres (an indication of poor immune control of latent virus reactivation) and lower percentages of T cells and T_H cells. These differences did not appear to be related to nutrition, alcohol use, caffeine consumption, or sleep loss.

Other studies have found that the stress of caregiving has adverse effects on wound repair (Kiecolt-Glaser, Marucha, Malarkey, Mercado, & Glaser, 1995), on defects in NK cell function (Esterling et al., 1996), and on reactions to flu vaccine (Kiecolt-Glaser, Glaser, et al., 1996). Caregivers who experience emotional distress such as anger or depression may be at particular risk for adverse effects on the immune system (Scanlan, Vitaliano, Zhang, Savage, & Ochs, 2001).

This research suggests that severe and long-term stressors, such as those that result from caregiving, particularly in the elderly, may leave caregivers vulnerable to a range of health-related problems. Moreover, these immune alterations can persist well beyond the end of the stressful situation—that is, after caregiving activities have ceased (Esterling, Kiecolt-Glaser, Bodnar, & Glaser, 1994).

Protective Effects of Social Support   Emerging evidence suggests a potentially important role for social support in buffering people against adverse immune change in response to stress. Studies with monkeys, for example, suggest that affiliating with fellow monkeys protects against decreases in lymphocyte response to mitogens that would normally be elicited by a chronic stressor (S. Cohen, Kaplan, Cunnick, Manuck, & Rabin, 1992). In a study of breast cancer patients, S. M. Levy et al. (1990) found that perceived social support buffered NK cell activity in response to stress. Specifically, the tendency to seek social support and the perception that one had good emotional support from one's spouse, from an intimate other, or from the physician were associated with high NK cell activity.

Coping and Coping Resources as Moderators of the Stress–Immune Functioning Relationship

In chapter 7, we saw that the impact of stressful events on distress and adverse health outcomes can sometimes be muted by coping methods, such as problem solving, stress management, and relaxation. Research suggests that these resources may also moderate the relation between stress and immune functioning.

Optimism   Segerstrom and colleagues (1998) found that optimism and active coping strategies were protective against stress. In this study, 90 first-year law students, tested at the beginning of law school and again halfway through the first semester, completed questionnaire measures regarding how they coped with the stress of law school, and they had blood drawn for an assessment of immune measures. The optimistic law students and students who used fewer avoidant coping methods showed less increase in distress across the quarter; pessimism, avoidance coping, and mood disturbance, in turn, predicted less NK cell cytotoxicity and fewer numbers of T cells, suggesting that optimism and coping can be important influences on stress-related distress and immune changes.

Self-Efficacy/Personal Control   Feelings of self-efficacy and the ability to exercise control over stressful events are associated with less immunocompromise under stress. Such changes could conceivably come about in three ways (Bandura, 1989):

1. Perceived self-efficacy may reduce the experience of stress itself.

2. It may reduce the tendency to develop depression in response to stressful events.

3. It may create some expectancy-based central nervous system modulation of immunologic reactivity.

Evidence shows that, when people are exposed to controllable or uncontrollable stressors, such as noise, those who perceive that they can control the noise show little change in immune parameters. In contrast, those people exposed to uncontrollable stressors are more likely to show adverse effects (Sieber et al., 1992).

Similar findings have emerged with clinical populations suffering from immune-related disorders. For example, a study of female rheumatoid arthritis patients (Zautra, Okun, Roth, & Emmanual, 1989) found that those who perceived themselves as able to cope with stressful events and who felt satisfied with their ability to cope had higher levels of circulating B cells.

Finding benefits in stressful events may improve immune functioning or at least undercut the potential damage that stress may otherwise do. A study by Bower and colleagues (2003) found that women who wrote about positive changes in important personal goals over a month-long period showed increases in natural killer cells cytotoxicity. Potentially then, prioritizing goals and emphasizing relationships, personal growth, and meaning in life may have beneficial biological effects on immune functioning.

Other coping styles may also be related to the stress–immune functioning relationship (S. Cohen & Herbert, 1996). For example, exercise activates beta-endorphins, which may stimulate NK cell activity (Fiatarone et al., 1988); therefore, exercise may be an important buffer against stress-related immune changes. Active methods of coping may be particularly helpful at high stress levels for maintaining immune function while at lower stress levels avoidance coping may be more helpful (Stowell, Kiecolt-Glaser, & Glaser, 2001).

Interventions to Enhance Immunocompetence

A number of investigators have examined whether stress management interventions can mute the impact of stressful events on the immune system. In chapter 7, we saw that emotional disclosure appears to enhance health and mood in individuals who have suffered a traumatic event. These results may be immunologically mediated. In one study (Pennebaker, Kiecolt-Glaser, & Glaser, 1988), 50 undergraduates wrote about either traumatic experiences or superficial topics for 20 minutes on each of 4 consecutive days. Those students who wrote about traumatic or upsetting events demonstrated a stronger mitogenic response, compared with baseline, than did the control subjects.

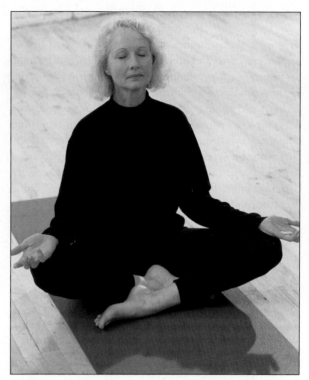

Training in relaxation may help people learn how to mute the adverse effects of stress on the immune system.

Relaxation Relaxation may mute the effects of stress on the immune system. In a study with elderly adults (a group at risk for illness because of age-related declines in immune functioning generally), participants were assigned to relaxation training, social contact, or no intervention (Kiecolt-Glaser et al., 1985). Participants in the relaxation condition had significantly higher levels of NK cell activity after the intervention than at baseline and significantly lower antibody titres to herpes simplex virus I, suggesting some enhancement of cellular immunity associated with the relaxation intervention.

In a study of malignant melanoma patients, Fawzy, Kemeny, et al. (1990) found that those patients assigned to a group intervention program that involved relaxation, problem-solving skills, and effective coping strategies showed higher NK activity, higher percentages of NK cells, lower percentages of T_H cells, and higher interferon-augmented NK cell cytotoxic activity than did a comparison group 6 months after the intervention was completed. They also found that those patients who received the intervention were less likely to have a melanoma recurrence (Fawzy et al., 1993). Similar interventions have shown success with people suffering from herpes simplex virus type 2 (S. Cruess, Antoni, Cruess,

BOX 14.3

A Profile of Patient Zero

In the 1970s, a number of seemingly isolated cases of Kaposi's sarcoma and other rare opportunistic infections broke out in the gay community. By the early 1980s, the Centers for Disease Control (CDC) was able to put together these anomalous and seemingly unrelated disorders into a pattern defined as acquired immune deficiency syndrome. As the cluster of disorders associated with this syndrome became more clear, agents from the CDC began to track the cases in an effort to identify common links. They soon became aware that one name was turning up repeatedly as a sexual partner of those now suffering from AIDS, the name of Gaetan Dugas:

> Gaetan Dugas was an attractive, sexually active French-Canadian airline flight attendant. His job and sexual proclivities made him an effective and deadly carrier for spreading the AIDS virus as far and wide as possible.
>
> Gaetan was the man everybody wanted, the ideal for this community, at this time and in this place. His sandy hair fell boyishly over his forehead, his mouth easily curled into an inviting smile, and his laugh could flood color into a room of black and white. He bought his clothes in the trendiest shops of Paris and London. He vacationed in Mexico and on the Caribbean beaches. Americans tumbled for his soft, Quebecois accent and sexual magnetism.

There was no place that the 28-year-old airline steward would rather have the boys fall for him than in San Francisco. Here, Gaetan could satisfy his voracious sexual appetite with the beautiful California men he liked so much. He returned from every stroll down Castro Street with a pocketful of match covers and napkins that were crowded with addresses and phone numbers. He recorded names of his most passionate admirers in his fabric-covered address book. But lovers were like suntans to him: they would be so wonderful, so sexy for a few days, and then fade. At times, Gaetan would study his address book with genuine curiosity, trying to recall who this or that person was.

He didn't feel like he had cancer at all. That was what the doctor had said after cutting that bump from his face. Gaetan had wanted the small purplish spot removed to satisfy his vanity. The doctor had wanted it for a biopsy. Weeks later, the report came back that he had Kaposi's sarcoma, a bizarre skin cancer that hardly anyone got . . . He was terrified at first, but he consoled himself with the knowledge that you can beat cancer. He had created a life in which he could have everything and everyone he wanted. He'd figure a way around this cancer, too. (Shilts, 1987, pp. 21–22)

---

et al., 2000). Training in mindfulness meditation has produced demonstrable effects on immune functioning, specifically increasing antibody titres to influenza vaccine (R. J. Davidson et al., 2003). A study using tai chi chih (TCC) as an intervention for older adults reduced the intensity and severity of herpes oster (shingles), suggesting that this may be a useful intervention as well (Irwin, Pike, Cole, & Oxman, 2003).

Overall, the evidence suggests that these kinds of interventions can have significant effects on the immune system and even on health outcomes (Kiecolt-Glaser et al., 2002; G. E. Miller & Cohen, 2001). Stress management interventions including relaxation show more consistent benefits (G. E. Miller & Cohen, 2001).

Stress and the Developing Immune System

In addition to understanding the neuroendocrine regulation of immune functioning, the impact of stress on the developing immune system merits extensive investigation. The developing immune system may be especially vulnerable to effects of adverse psychological states such as stress, depression, or grief; moreover, these experiences may permanently affect the immune system in ways that persist into adulthood (Schleifer, Scott, Stein, & Keller, 1986).

■ AIDS

A Brief History of AIDS

Exactly when **acquired immune deficiency syndrome (AIDS)** first appeared is unknown. It seems to have begun in Central Africa, perhaps in the early 1970s. It spread rapidly throughout Zaire, Uganda, and other central African nations, largely because its origins were not understood. A high rate of extramarital sex, little condom use, and a high rate of gonorrhea also facilitated the spread of the AIDS virus in the heterosexual population.

BOX 14.3

A Profile of Patient Zero (continued)

When he was finally tracked down by the CDC in 1982, Dugas readily and happily acknowledged his sexual activities, apparently unaware that he had infected dozens of homosexual men. "Including his nights at the baths, he figured he had 250 sexual contacts a year. He'd been involved in gay life for about 10 years, and easily had had 2,500 sexual partners" (p. 83). By the time he learned he was contagious, he had had the disease for almost 2 years and it had progressed only minimally. Although Dugas was urged to stop having sex by the CDC, he responded: "Of course I'm going to have sex. Nobody's proven to me that you can spread cancer. Somebody gave this to me; I'm not going to give up sex" (p. 138).

Nonetheless, he cooperated by providing as many names and phone numbers of his previous lovers as he could locate. Time after time, these connections led back to small enclaves of AIDS in San Francisco, New York, and other gay communities. "By April, 1982, epidemiologists found that 40 of the first 248 gay men diagnosed could be tied directly to Gaetan Dugas. All had either had sex with him or sex with someone who had. In fact, from just one tryst with Gaetan, 11 early cases could be connected. He was connected to nine of the first 19 cases in L.A., 22 in New York City, and nine in eight other American cities" (p. 147). The odds that these connections could be a coincidence were calculated to be zero.

CDC officials started talking to the San Francisco city attorneys to see if any laws existed to enable them to take formal action against Dugas. There weren't. "It was around this time that rumors began on Castro Street about a strange guy at the 8th and Howard bathhouse, a blonde with a French accent. He would have sex with you, turn up the lights in the cubicle, and point out his Kaposi's sarcoma lesions. 'I've got gay cancer,' he'd say. 'I'm going to die and so are you'" (p. 165). Eventually, he became well enough known in the San Francisco gay community that other gay men tried to stop him from having anonymous sex at the bathhouses. Finally, after having AIDS for 4 years, Gaetan Dugas died in March 1984.

Originally, the CDC speculated that Dugas was *the* person who brought AIDS to North America. It now appears that he may have been one of several, but it is evident that he "played a key role in spreading the virus from one end of the United States to the other" (p. 439). Author Randy Shilts summarized the legacy of Gaetan Dugas: "At one time, Gaetan had been what every man wanted from gay life; by the time he died, he had become what every man feared" (p. 439).

Source: Shilts, 2000.

Medical clinics may have inadvertently promoted the spread of AIDS because, in attempting to vaccinate as many people as possible against the common diseases in the area, needles were used over and over again, promoting the exchange of fluids. From Africa, the disease appears to have made its way slowly to Europe and to Haiti, and from Haiti into the United States, as Americans vacationing in Haiti may have brought the virus back. A profile of one of the earliest and most notorious carriers of HIV appears in box 14.3. The current location and prevalence of HIV infection is listed in figure 14.3.

As of the end of 2003, an estimated 40 million people worldwide—37 million adults and 2.5 million children younger than 15—were living with HIV/AIDS. Approximately two thirds of these people (26.6 million) live in Sub-Saharan Africa; another 18% (7.4 million) live in Asia and the Pacific. Worldwide, approximately 11 of every 1,000 adults ages 15 to 49 are infected with HIV. The Centers for Disease Control and Prevention (CDC) estimates that 850,000 to 950,000 U.S. resi-

dents are living with HIV, many of whom are unaware of their infection (Centers for Disease Control and Prevention, 2002; UNAIDS, 2003). Table 14.1 shows how AIDS is transmitted.

AIDS researchers are projecting an estimated 65 million deaths from AIDS by the year 2020—more than triple the number who died in the first 20 years of the epidemic—unless major efforts toward primary prevention or major developments in treatment take place (Altman, July 2002). That is, despite the large numbers of people who have already died of AIDS, the epidemic is actually still in its early stages and is now being transmitted to every part of the world. Currently AIDS is the fourth leading cause of death worldwide (Altman, July 2002).

AIDS in the United States

What Are AIDS and HIV Infection? The first case of AIDS in the United States was diagnosed in 1981. It now appears, however, that there may have

FIGURE 14.3 | Regional HIV/AIDS Statistics, 2003   (*Source:* UNAIDS Report on the Global AIDS Epidemic, 2004)

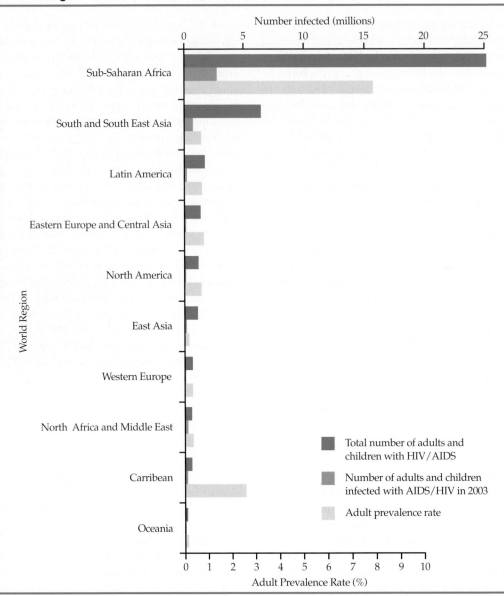

been isolated cases of AIDS before that date. The viral agent is a retrovirus, the **human immunodeficiency virus (HIV),** and it attacks the helper T cells and macrophages of the immune system. The virus appears to be transmitted exclusively by the exchange of cell-containing bodily fluids, especially semen and blood.

The period between contracting the virus and developing symptoms of AIDS is highly variable, with some individuals developing symptoms quite quickly and others free of symptoms for years. Thus, a person

may test HIV-seropositive (HIV+) but be free of AIDS and, during the asymptomatic period, pass on the virus to many other people.

How is HIV transmitted? Among drug users, needle sharing leads to the exchange of bodily fluids, thereby spreading the virus. Among homosexual men, exchange of the virus has been tied to sexual practices, especially anal-receptive sex involving the exchange of semen without a condom. In the heterosexual population, vaginal intercourse is associated with the transmission of AIDS,

TABLE 14.1 | How We Get AIDS: Cases by Mode of Transmission (World, 1996; U.S., 2003)

	World	United States
Heterosexual	70–75%	31%
Homosexual	5–10	42
Homosexual and intravenous drug use		4
Intravenous drug use	5–10	22
Other	3–22	1

Source: National Center for HIV, STD & TB Prevention, 2004.

The possibility that the AIDS virus may move into the adolescent population is substantial, but as yet there are few signs that adolescents have changed their sexual practices in response to the threat of AIDS.

with women more at risk than men. The likelihood of developing AIDS increases with the number of sexual partners a person has had and with the number of anonymous sexual partners; thus, these behaviors are also considered to be risk related (see table 14.2 for a breakdown of AIDS exposure categories).

How HIV Infection Progresses Following transmission, the virus grows very rapidly within the first few weeks of infection and spreads throughout the body. Early symptoms are mild, with swollen glands and mild, flulike symptoms predominating. After 3 to 6 weeks, the infection may abate, leading to a long asymptomatic period, during which viral growth is slow and controlled. The amount of virus typically rises gradually, eventually severely compromising the immune system by killing the helper T cells and producing a vulnerability to opportunistic infections that leads to the diagnosis of AIDS.

Some of the more common opportunistic infections that result from the impaired immune system include Pneumocystis carinii pneumonia and unusual neoplasms, such as Kaposi's sarcoma or non-Hodgkin's lymphoma. Early in the disease process, people infected with HIV also begin to show abnormalities in their neuroendocrine and cardiovascular responses to stress (for example, Starr et al., 1996). Chronic diarrhea, wasting,

TABLE 14.2 | Cases by Exposure Category

Following is the distribution of the estimated number of diagnoses of AIDS among U.S. adults and adolescents by exposure category. A breakdown by sex is provided where appropriate.

Exposure Category	Male	Female	Total
Male-to-male sexual contact	420,790	—	420,790
Injection drug use	172,351	67,917	240,268
Male-to-male sexual contact and injection drug use	59,719	—	59,719
Heterosexual contact	50,793	84,835	135,628
Other*	14,350	6,519	20,869

*Includes hemophilia, blood transfusion, perinatal, and risk not reported or not identified.

Source: Centers for Disease Control, 2004g.

skeletal pain, and blindness are also complications. One of the most common symptoms for women with AIDS is gynecologic infection, but because gynecologic infection was not considered an AIDS-related condition, often women were diagnosed very late. This late diagnosis means that experimental treatments may not be available to women at the time they could be helpful.

AIDS also eventually leads to neurological involvement. Early symptoms of central nervous system (CNS) impairment are similar to those of depression and include forgetfulness, inability to concentrate, psychomotor retardation, decreased alertness, apathy, withdrawal, diminished interest in work, and loss of sexual desire. In more advanced stages, patients may experience confusion, disorientation, seizures, profound dementia, and coma. CNS disturbance is variable, not appearing until the late stages in some patients but developing early among others (U.S. Department of Health and Human Services, 1986). This variability has led to controversy about whether individuals diagnosed with AIDS should continue to hold sensitive jobs, such as airline pilot, when cognitive impairment may have resulted from their infected state (Mapou, Kay, Rundell, & Temoshok, 1993).

The rate at which these changes take place can differ widely. Low-income Blacks and Hispanics who test positive for HIV go on to develop AIDS much faster than Whites. Not all the reasons for the heightened vulnerability of minorities to HIV and AIDS are clear. One possible reason is the greater prevalence of intravenous (IV) drug use in these populations. Drug users who live on the streets often succumb to the complications from the disease in less than a year due to lifestyle factors and generally poor health. But another reason is that low-income Blacks and Hispanics do not get new medications as quickly as Whites do, so at any given time, they are less likely to have state-of-the-art treatment (Stolberg, 2002).

Consequently, individuals from higher socioeconomic status (SES) groups have a much greater chance of long-term survivorship. Such individuals have greater access to drug treatment programs through private physicians who are participating in studies. Thus, socioeconomic factors have a major impact on both the time between progression from HIV+ status to a diagnosis of AIDS and how quickly an individual dies after a diagnosis of AIDS.

Antiretroviral Therapy   Highly active antiretroviral therapy (HAAVT) is a combination of antiretroviral medications that has dramatically improved the health of HIV individuals. So successful have these drug combinations been proven to be that, in some patients, HIV can no longer be discerned in the bloodstream. However, people on protease inhibitors must take these drugs faithfully, often several times a day, or the drugs will fail to work. Yet because the treatments are complex and can disrupt activities, adherence to the drugs is variable, posing a major problem for stemming the progress of the virus (Catz, Kelly, Bogart, Benotsch, & McAuliffe, 2000). Nonetheless, the drugs have made it possible for people with AIDS to live increasingly normal lives. Unhappily, the number of new HIV infections that involve drug-resistant strains of the virus is increasing, meaning that some antiretroviral therapies will fail, as this problem increases (Little et al., 2002).

Who Gets AIDS?   Early on in the U.S. AIDS epidemic, the two major at-risk groups were homosexual men and intravenous drug users. While these groups continue to have the largest number of AIDS cases, low-income Blacks, Hispanics, and other minority populations are increasingly at risk.

In all populations, adolescents and young adults are the most at risk because they are the most sexually active group, having more sex with different partners than any other age group. Child and adolescent runaways represent a particularly at-risk group, largely because they sometimes exchange sex for money in order to live. Of particular concern is the fact that AIDS infections are climbing again. Whereas the estimated number of new cases of HIV infections among gay and bisexual men decreased steadily, it has increased steadily from 1999 to the present (R. Stein, 2003).

The CDC currently reports that the number of AIDS cases is growing faster among women, especially minority women, than for any other group. In 1992, women accounted for 14% of adults/adolescents living with AIDS—by 1999, the proportion had grown to 20%. Since 1985, the proportion of all AIDS cases reported among adult and adolescent women has more than tripled, from 7% in 1985 to 25% in 1999. The epidemic has increased most dramatically among women of color. African-American and Hispanic women together represent less than one fourth of all U.S. women, yet they account for more than 80% of cases reported in women (Centers for Disease Control & Prevention, 2004b).

Providing knowledge about treatments for AIDS is assuming increasing importance, as research advances have brought treatments that prolong the lives of those infected with HIV. Surveys show that the availability of antiretroviral therapeutic agents has relieved psychological distress in the gay community (Rabkin, Ferrando, Lin, Sewell, & McElhiney, 2000). However, optimism regarding AIDS may have indirectly fueled an increase in risk-related behavior because the new treatments relieve worries about unsafe sex (Huebner & Gerend, 2001; Vanable, Ostrow, McKirnan, Taywaditep, & Hope, 2000). Unprotected anal intercourse appears to be on the increase again among the high-risk, gay population (Kalichman, Kelly, & Rompa, 1997).

Ignorance about the risks of contracting HIV from a partner with a low viral load may fuel risky practices. An anonymous survey of gay men found that younger, less-well-educated men who were more likely to believe that it is safe to have intercourse with a person with an undetectable viral load were more likely to practice unprotected anal intercourse (Kalichman, Nachimson, Cherry, & Williams, 1998). Consequently, education remains a high priority for intervention with high-risk groups.

Psychosocial Impact of HIV Infection

Thousands of people currently test positive for HIV but have not yet developed AIDS. Most health experts believe that the majority will eventually go on to develop AIDS. Thus, this group of people lives with a major threatening event (HIV+ status) coupled with substantial uncertainty and fear. How do these people cope?

The initial response to testing seropositive appears to be a short-term increase in psychological distress. Also, people who test seropositive and learn their serostatus appear to sharply curtail their HIV risk-related behavior. But over time, the psychosocial response to testing positive is modest (L. S. Doll et al., 1990). People seem to cope with the threat of AIDS surprisingly well (for example, Blaney, Millon, Morgan, Eisdorfer, & Szapocznik, 1990), although a subset of people diagnosed with AIDS reacts with extreme depression and thoughts of suicide (Kelly et al., 1993).

The majority of people diagnosed with AIDS appear to make positive changes in their health behaviors almost immediately after diagnosis. Changing diet in a healthier direction, getting more exercise, quitting or reducing smoking, and reducing or eliminating drug use are among the most common changes people report having made to improve their quality of life and helpfully the course of illness as well (R. L. Collins et al.,

2001). Many of these improve psychological well-being, and they may affect course of health as well. Interventions that reduce depression are potentially valuable in the fight against AIDS because depression exacerbates many immune-related disorders (Motivala et al., 2003).

Disclosure   Not disclosing HIV status or simply lying about risk factors, such as the number of partners one has had, is a major barrier to controlling the spread of HIV infection (Kalichman, DiMarco, Austin, Luke, & DiFonzo, 2003). Moreover, those less likely to disclose their HIV serostatus to sex partners also appear to be less likely to use condoms during intercourse (DeRosa & Marks, 1998). Not having disclosed to a partner is associated with low self-efficacy for disclosing, suggesting that self-efficacy interventions might well address the disclosure process as well (Kalichman & Nachimson, 1999). Disclosure may have some surprising benefits. Several studies have shown the positive health consequences of disclosure on health, and in one study, those who had disclosed their HIV+ status to their friends had significantly higher levels of CD4 cells than those who had not (Sherman, Bonanno, Wiener, & Battles, 2000).

Whether or not to disclose HIV-seropositive status is influenced by cultural factors. For example, historically, family values have been an especially important part of Hispanic culture, values that have often had healthy effects on risk-related behaviors. In the case of HIV, however, there may be a desire to protect family members, which acts as a barrier to disclosing HIV status (H. R. C. Mason, Marks, Simoni, Ruiz, & Richardson, 1995; Szapocznik, 1995). The fact of nondisclosure may also mean that these young men are unable to get the social support they need from their families (H. R. C. Mason et al., 1995).

Women and HIV   The lives of HIV-infected women, particularly those with symptoms, are often chaotic and unstable. Many of these women have no partners, they may not hold jobs, and many depend on social services and Medicaid to survive. Some of these women have problems with drugs. Many have experienced trauma from sexual or physical abuse (Simoni & Ng, 2002). To an outsider, being HIV+ would seem to be their biggest problem, but in fact, getting food and shelter for the family is often far more salient. Low-income women who are HIV seropositive experience considerable stress, especially related to family issues (Schrimshaw, 2003), and depressive symptoms that

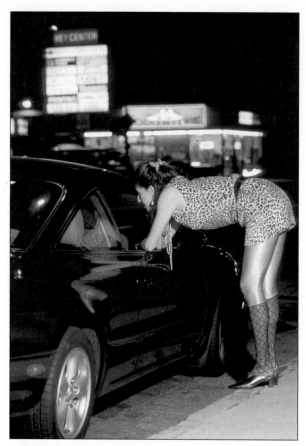

Prostitution is one source of the increasing numbers of women who are infected with HIV.

result from stress may exacerbate the course of disease (D. J. Jones, Beach, Forehand, & Foster, 2003). To date, agencies and interventions to help women deal with these problems have been slow to develop.

Despite problems that women encounter once they have been diagnosed as HIV-seropositive, many women are able to find meaning in their lives, often prompted by the shock of testing positive. A study of low-income, seropositive women (Updegraff, Taylor, Kemeny, & Wyatt, 2002) found that the majority reported positive changes in their lives, including the fact that the HIV diagnosis had gotten them off drugs, gotten them off the street, and enabled them to feel better about themselves. Some people who test seropositive encounter barriers to health care and badly needed social services, which can further erode quality of life (Heckman, 2003).

Depression commonly accompanies an HIV diagnosis. Depression is most likely to occur among those

with little social support, who engage in avoidant coping, and/or who have more severe HIV symptoms (Heckman et al., 2004). Thoughts of suicide may be common especially among geographically isolated infected people (Heckman et al., 2002). Some people who test HIV-seropositive live in communities where many other people are seropositive or have AIDS as well. Consequently, repeated bereavement is often a risk for people trying to cope with HIV (Sikkema, Kochman, DiFranceisco, Kelly, & Hoffman, 2003). Bereavement and its corresponding grief are important because the bereavement experience itself can increase the likelihood that the disease will progress (Bower, Kemeny, Taylor, & Fahey, 1997).

The stigma associated with AIDS and the negative ways in which people respond to those who have HIV infection or AIDS is a problem for those already diagnosed and may act as a deterrent to those not yet tested (Herek, Capitanio, & Widaman, 2003).

Interventions to Reduce the Spread of AIDS

Interventions to reduce risk-related behavior loom large as the best way to control the spread of HIV infection. These interventions center around practices that involve the exchange of bodily fluids. Refraining from high-risk sex, using a condom, and not sharing needles if one is an IV drug user are the major behaviors on which interventions have focused. Given the diversity of groups at special risk for AIDS—adolescents, homosexuals, low-income women, minorities—intensive, community-based interventions aimed at particular at-risk populations seem most likely to be effective.

Education Most interventions begin by educating the target population about risky activity, providing knowledge about AIDS and modes of transmission. Studies suggest a high degree of "magical thinking" about AIDS, with people overreacting to casual contact with HIV+ individuals but underreacting to their own sexual risk resulting from casual sex and failure to use a condom.

In addition, people seem to see HIV as socially discriminating, such that the harmfulness of germs depends on the relationship to the person with those germs. Lovers' germs are seen as less threatening than are the germs of people who are disliked or unfamiliar (Nemeroff, 1995). On the whole, gay men are well informed about AIDS, heterosexual adolescents considerably less,

The overwhelming majority of early AIDS cases occurred among gay men. The gay community responded with dramatic and impressive efforts to reduce risk-related behaviors.

and some at-risk groups are very poorly informed (LeBlanc, 1993). A study of urban female adolescents revealed that about half the participants underestimated the risks entailed in their sexual behavior (Kershaw, Ethier, Niccolai, Lewis, & Ickovics, 2003). Studies of single, pregnant, inner-city women, likewise, reveal poor knowledge about AIDS, little practice of safe sex, and little knowledge of their partner's current or past behavior and the ways in which it places them at risk (for example, Hobfoll, Jackson, Lavin, Britton, & Shepherd, 1993).

There may be particular teachable moments when AIDS education is vital. Mayne and colleagues (1998) found that men who had been bereaved of a partner were more likely to engage in unprotected anal intercourse in the following months. Men with a new primary partner are also more likely to practice risky behavior. Consequently, education with respect to these time points may be especially valuable.

As more women have become infected with HIV, issues surrounding pregnancy have assumed concern. Many women lack knowledge regarding the transmission of HIV to infants, so their decision making with respect to pregnancy may be poorly informed. Only about 15 to 30% of infants born to HIV-seropositive mothers will be seropositive, and treatment with AZT can reduce that incidence to 4 to 8%. Providing education with respect to HIV and pregnancy, then, is an important educational priority as well (D. A. Murphy, Mann, O'Keefe, & Rotheram-Borus, 1998).

How successful are educational interventions? A review of 27 published studies that provided HIV counseling and testing information found that this type of

education was an effective means of secondary prevention for HIV+ individuals, reducing behaviors that might infect others, but was not as effective as a primary prevention strategy for uninfected participants (Weinhardt, Carey, Johnson, & Bickman, 1999; see also Albarracín et al., 2003).

Culturally sensitive interventions pitched to a specific target group may fare somewhat better. A study of African-American, male, inner-city adolescents showed that providing knowledge could be an effective agent of behavior change in populations in which the level of information may initially be somewhat low (Jemmott, Jemmott, & Fong, 1992). The young men in this study were randomly assigned to an AIDS risk-reduction intervention aimed at increasing their knowledge about AIDS and risky sexual behavior or to a control group. The intervention was conducted by African-American adults, and the materials were developed so as to be especially interesting to inner-city, African-American adolescents. The results indicated that this culturally sensitive intervention was successful over a 3-month period. The adolescents exposed to the intervention reported fewer instances of intercourse, fewer partners, greater use of condoms, and less anal intercourse, compared with adolescents not exposed to the intervention.

Health Beliefs and AIDS Risk-Related Behavior   Knowledge, of course, provides only a basis for effective interventions. In addition to knowledge, one must perceive oneself to be capable of controlling risk-related activity (Forsyth & Carey, 1998). As is true for so many risk-related behaviors, perceptions of self-efficacy with respect to AIDS risk-related behavior is critical. Gay men who are higher in a sense of self-efficacy are more likely to use condoms for example, as are African-American adolescents (Jemmott, Jemmott, Spears, Hewitt, & Cruz-Collins, 1992), African-American and Latina women (Nyamathi, Stein, & Brecht, 1995), and college students (O'Leary, Goodhardt, Jemmott, & Boccher-Lattimore, 1992; Wulfert & Wan, 1993; see Forsyth & Carey, 1998). Gay men who are high in self-efficacy beliefs have fewer sexual partners and fewer anonymous sexual partners as well (Aspinwall, Kemeny, Taylor, Schneider, & Dudley, 1991; Wulfert, Wan, & Backus, 1996).

The health belief model (see chapter 3) has shown modest ability to predict the number of sexual partners and number of anonymous partners of gay men (Aspinwall et al., 1991). It also predicts condom use among adolescents (C. Abraham, Sheeran, Spears, & Abrams,

BOX 14.4

| Safe Sex

THE MAGIC CONDOM

In a recent television program, a man and a woman are fondling each other, removing each other's clothes, and making steady progress toward the man's bed. As they approach it, she whispers, "Have you had a blood test?" He responds, "Last month. Negative. You?" She responds, "Negative, too. Do you have protection?" His response: "I'm covered." They fall to the bed and . . . (fade out).

This scene is Hollywood's idea of a safe-sex encounter. But where did the magic condom come from? Did he put it on in the taxi on the way back to his apartment? Did he put it on in the kitchen while he was pouring them each a glass of wine?

Hollywood's safe-sex encounters may be seamless, but in real life safe sex is not. A first important step is getting people to recognize that safe sex is important— that is, that they are at risk for AIDS and other sexually transmitted diseases. AIDS is beginning to spread into the sexually active young adult population and is spreading fastest among Blacks and Hispanics, yet levels of knowledge about sexuality in general and AIDS in particular are problematic, especially among less acculturated Hispanics (Marin & Marin, 1990).

Inducing young people to take steps to practice safe sex is also problematic. Sexual counselors advocate asking prospective partners about their sexual histories, yet many young adults indicate that they would lie to a partner to minimize their HIV risk history (Cochran & Mays, 1990). Moreover, young adults who ask questions in the hopes of reducing their HIV risk are less likely to use condoms (Cochran & Mays, 1990).

Many adolescents who report risky behavior, such as promiscuity, are unlikely to use condoms consistently (Biglan et al., 1990). Adolescents and young adults typically regard condom use as "not cool" (B. E. Collins & Aspinwall, 1989). The very factors that the Hollywood encounter overlooked—namely, the interpersonal awkwardness and logistics of actually using condoms—act as barriers to their use.

Clearly, then, safe sex takes more than a couple of hurried questions and a claim of protection. Interventions to increase the practice of safe sex need to address knowledge about sex and sexually transmitted diseases, such as AIDS; attitudes toward sexual protection; cultural differences that may bear on these attitudes; and the ways condoms are perceived by young adults.

1992). The theory of reasoned action (see chapter 3) has been somewhat more informative, in part because social norms are so important to several of the populations at risk for AIDS, especially adolescents (Winslow, Franzini, & Hwang, 1992). Jemmott, Jemmott, and Hacker (1992), for example, studied inner-city, African-American adolescents and found that those with more favorable attitudes toward condoms and those who perceived subjective norms to be supportive of condom use reported greater intentions to use condoms over the next few months. Fear of AIDS, perceived susceptibility, and believed behavioral control with respect to condom use also predict condom use.

Targeting Sexual Activity   Interventions to address AIDS risk-related sexual behavior also need to account for the dynamics of sexuality. Sexual activity is a very personal aspect of life, endowed with private meaning by every individual. Consequently, knowledge of how to practice safe sex and the belief that one is capable of doing so may not translate into behavior change if spontaneous sexuality is seen as an inherent part of one's

personal identity. For example, for many gay men, being gay is associated with the belief that they should be free to do what they want sexually; consequently, modifying sexual activity can represent a threat to identity and lifestyle (L. McKusick, Horstman, & Coates, 1985). In addition, even among men who show high rates of condom use, sexual risk-taking behavior can vary over time, as personal circumstances change (Mayne et al., 1998).

Past sexual practice is, nonetheless, an important predictor of AIDS risk-related behavior. As people become more sexually experienced, they develop a sexual style that may become integrated into their life more generally. Consistent with this point, people who have had a large number of partners, especially anonymous partners, and who have not used condoms in the past tend to continue these behaviors, perhaps because those behaviors are well integrated into their sexual style (Aspinwall et al., 1991; van der Velde & van der Pligt, 1991) (see box 14.4).

Some interventions have focused on improving skills relating to sexual activity. Sexual encounters, particularly with a new partner, are often rushed, nonverbal, and passionate, conditions not very conducive to a rational discussion of safe-sex practices. To address these issues, health psychologists have developed interventions that involve practice in sexual negotiation skills (for example, L. C. Miller, Bettencourt, DeBro, & Hoffman, 1993). For example, in a cognitive-behavioral intervention (Kelly, Lawrence, Hood, & Brasfield, 1989), gay men were taught how to exercise self-control in sexual relationships and how to resist pressure to engage in high-risk sexual activity through modeling, role playing, and feedback. With this training, the men became somewhat more skillful in handling sexual relationships and were able to reduce their risky sexual behaviors and use condoms (see also NIMH Multisite HIV Prevention Trial Group, 2001).

Sexual negotiation skills may be especially important for intervening with adolescents. One of the reasons that young women engage in unsafe sex is the coercive sexual behavior of their young male partners. Teaching sexual negotiation skills to both young men and women, and especially teaching young women how to resist coercive sexual activity, is therefore important (M. P. Carey, 1999).

Interventions may also be successful if they directly address some of the barriers to safe-sex practices. Sanderson (1999) showed college students videos that portrayed communication skills (such as persuading a sexual partner to use a condom) and technical skills (using a condom correctly without ruining the mood) and found that the technical skills video was especially associated with increased self-efficacy for condom use. Overall, messages that focused on both technical and communication skills were most successful in leading to behavior change (Sanderson, 1999).

Risky sexual activity may be part of a more generally risky experimental lifestyle, involving cigarette smoking, illicit drug and alcohol use, and antisocial activity (Kalichman, Weinhardt, DiFonzo, Austin, & Luke, 2002). Unfortunately, these activities can put temptations or deterrents to condom use in place. For example, one study found that the thought of envisioning a new lover reduced perceptions of risk (Blanton & Gerrard, 1997; Corbin & Fromme, 2002). Moreover, attitudes toward condoms are not positive. Among adolescents, both gay and straight, the effort to modify AIDS risk-related behavior, then, needs to challenge peer norms about what constitutes erotic sex, eroticizing safer sexual activity, and enhancing a sense of personal efficacy about practicing safe sex (L. McKusick, Coates, Morin, Pollack, & Hoff, 1990). Interventions that di-

rectly address condom negotiation skills in a manner that is sensitive to these dynamics can be effective among both Black and White adolescents (Jemmott & Jones, 1993; M. Z. Solomon & De Jong, 1989). Debunking the myth that alcohol enhances sexual performance and pleasure may also contribute to reducing the behaviors that facilitate risky sex (Kalichman et al., 2002). Even brief but intensive interventions addressing risk factors and skills may have these beneficial effects (Patterson, Shaw, & Semple, 2003).

Cognitive-Behavioral Interventions Cognitive-behavioral stress management interventions have been employed with some HIV+ groups, including homosexual men and poor African-American women (N. Schneiderman, 1999). These interventions can decrease distress, buffer the psychological and immunologic consequences of learning about positive serostatus, and improve surveillance of opportunistic infections, such as herpes; in turn, the improved psychological adjustment may retard the progress of the HIV virus, thus contributing to better health.

In a major review of behavioral interventions conducted with adolescents, gay and bisexual men, inner-city women, college students, and mentally ill adults—all groups at significant risk for AIDS—interventions oriented toward reducing their sexual activity and enhancing their abilities to negotiate condom use with partners were beneficial for reducing risk-related behavior (Kalichman, Carey, & Johnson, 1996).

More recently, many programs have built in not only educational interventions and skills training but also motivational components to try to increase the motivation for at-risk groups to change their risk-related behavior. Recall that "motivation training" refers to inducing a state of readiness to change, as by helping individuals develop behavior-change goals, recognize the discrepancy between their goals and their current behavior, and develop a sense of self-efficacy that they can change. An empathetic, nonjudgmental style on the part of the therapist is thought to promote this motivational component. Research suggests that adding a motivational component to education and skills training can enhance the effectiveness of interventions designed to reduce HIV risk-related behavior (Carey et al., 1997; Carey et al., 2000).

Targeting IV Drug Use Interventions with IV drug users need to be targeted toward reducing contact with infected needles as well as toward changing sexual activity. Information about AIDS transmission, needle exchange programs, and instruction on how to sterilize needles can reduce risky injection practices among IV drug users (Des Jarlais, 1988). Methadone maintenance treatments, coupled with HIV-related education, may help reduce the spread of AIDS by reducing the frequency of injections and shared needle contacts, by reducing health risk behaviors, by increasing use of condoms, and by reducing the number of sexual partners (Margolin, Avants, Warburton, Hawkins, & Shi, 2003). Working with the drug-abusing peer group may result in more success than trying to reach individual drug users (Latkin, Sherman, & Knowlton, 2003). However, the cognitive-behavioral intervention programs that work with other populations may not work as well with IV drug users because they may lack good impulse control.

HIV Prevention Programs   Prevention programs are now being introduced in U.S. public schools to warn adolescents about the risks of unprotected sexual intercourse and to help instill safe-sex practices. Teenagers who are HIV+ sometimes pitch these programs, making the risk graphically clear to the audience. There is some evidence that adolescents try to distance themselves from peers who have HIV in an effort to control the threat that such an encounter produces, so interventions that stress information, motivation, and sexual negotiation skills, as opposed to peer-based interventions, may be more successful in changing adolescent behavior (Fisher, Fisher, Bryan, & Misovich, 2002). Research is still exploring which elements of school-based prevention programs are most successful.

When prominent public figures, such as Magic Johnson, make their HIV infection public, the desire for more information about AIDS and concern about AIDS increase (Zimet et al., 1993). This finding suggests that the effective timing and use of such announcements might be helpful in getting people tested and getting them to reduce their AIDS-related risk behaviors.

Recent interventions in schools have made use of HIV prevention videos that provide training in communication skills and condom use skills. Results suggest that this cost-effective intervention can be an effective way of decreasing risky sexual behavior (Sanderson, 1999). Increasing self-efficacy regarding condom use also improves the likelihood of using them (Longmore, Manning, Giordano, & Rudolph, 2003).

The stage model of behavior change may be helpful in guiding interventions to increase condom use. Some people have gaps in their knowledge about AIDS or

about their own behaviors or their partners' behavior that may put them at risk (Hobfoll et al., 1993). Therefore, they may profit from knowledge-based interventions that move them from a precontemplation to a contemplation phase with respect to safe-sex practices. In contrast, moving from contemplation to preparation, or from preparation to action, may require specific training in condom negotiation skills so that the individual follows through on the commitment to refrain from risky sex during specific sexual encounters (cf. Catania, Kegeles, & Coates, 1990).

Efforts to prevent risk-related behavior may need to target not only high-risk sexual practices themselves but also other behaviors that facilitate high-risk sex. Chief among these are drug and alcohol use. That is, people who may be otherwise aware that they should not engage in risky sexual activities may be less inhibited about doing so when under the influence of drugs or alcohol (Corbin & Fromme, 2002).

Interventions that address the norms surrounding sexual activity are needed as well. Any intervention that supports norms favoring more long-term relationships or decreasing the number of short-term sexual relationships an individual has is a reasonable approach to prevention (Pinkerton & Abramson, 1993).

Coping with HIV+ Status and AIDS

Now that AIDS is a chronic rather than an acute disease, a number of psychosocial issues raised by chronic illness come to the fore. One such issue is employment. Research suggests that men with HIV who were working at the time of diagnosis continue to work but that those who are unemployed may not return to work. Interventions may be needed to help those who can return to work do so (Rabkin, McElhiney, Ferrando, Van Gorp, & Lin, 2004).

People with AIDS must continually cope with the fear and prejudice that they encounter from the general community. Many people have an intense fear of AIDS, especially those with an intense antigay reaction (homophobia) (Kunkel & Temple, 1992). Consequently, many individuals blame victims of AIDS for their disease, especially if they are gay (B. L. Andersen, 1992) or IV drug users (Hunter & Ross, 1991).

Despite advances in the treatment of AIDS and the discovery of resources that help people with AIDS cope more successfully, many people with HIV infection and AIDS do experience deteriorating health and worsening symptoms. Depression is one of the most common psychological concomitants of these changes. Changes in physical symptoms, an increased number of bed days, fatigue, and the perception that one's social support is insufficient are the factors most consistently associated with depression (Siegel, Karus, & Raveis, 1997; Ferrando et al., 1998). What factors foster successful coping with AIDS? We next address some of these factors.

Coping Skills   The chronic burdens associated with HIV infection necessitate coping resources, and those who lack such coping skills are at risk for psychological distress (Penedo et al., 2003). Coping effectiveness training appears to be successful for managing the psychological distress that can be associated with HIV-seropositive status (Chesney, Chambers, Taylor, Johnson, & Folkman, 2003). In one study, a cognitive-behavioral stress management program designed to increase positive coping skills and the ability to enlist social support was associated with improvement of psychological well-being and quality of life among HIV-seropositive individuals (S. K. Lutgendorf et al., 1998).

Perceiving that one has control over a stressor is usually associated with better adjustment to that stressor. As has been found with other chronic or advancing diseases, a sense of personal control, or self-efficacy, is important in successful adjustment to AIDS (Benight et al., 1997; Rotheram-Borus, Murphy, Reid, & Coleman, 1996; S. E. Taylor et al., 1991; S. C. Thompson, Sobolew-Shubin, Galbraith, Schwankovsky, & Cruzen, 1993).

Social Support   Social support is very important to people with AIDS. Men with AIDS who have emotional, practical, and informational support are less depressed (Turner-Cobb et al. 2002). Informational support appeared to be especially important in buffering the stress associated with AIDS-related symptoms (R. B. Hays, Turner, & Coates, 1992; K. Siegel et al., 1997).

The ability to talk to family members about AIDS is important, too. Unfortunately, although families appear to have the potential to be especially helpful to men infected with AIDS, when men are depressed or have a large number of AIDS-related symptoms, they are less likely to receive the support that they need (H. A. Turner, Hays, & Coates, 1993). Such findings suggest that augmenting natural social support and providing social support to people with AIDS should be an important mental health services priority.

The Internet represents an important resource for people with AIDS. Research suggests that those who use the Internet in conjunction with managing their seropositive status had more HIV disease knowledge, had more active coping skills, engaged in more information-seeking coping, and had more social support than those not using the Internet (Kalichman et al., 2003). The Internet appears to be a promising, potentially important resource in HIV/AIDS care in the future.

Psychosocial Factors That Affect the Course of AIDS

In recent years, studies have provided evidence that psychosocial factors can influence the rate of immune decline from AIDS. In one study of HIV-infected gay men, those who were under considerable stress had a more rapid course of HIV disease, whereas those with more social support had a slower course (Leserman et al., 1999).

Several studies have found that negative beliefs about the self and the future are associated with helper T cell (CD4) decline and onset of AIDS in individuals with HIV (Segerstrom, Taylor, Kemeny, Reed, & Visscher, 1996), and other studies have found that negative expectations about the course of illness can lead to an accelerated course of disease (Byrnes et al., 1998; Reed, Kemeny, Taylor, & Visscher, 1999; Reed, Kemeny, Taylor, Wang, & Visscher, 1994).

On the positive side, the ability to find meaning in one's experiences appears to slow declines in CD4 levels and has been related to less likelihood of AIDS-related mortality (Bower et al., 1997). Optimists have been shown to perform more health-promoting behaviors than pessimists, so one recent intervention (Mann, 2001) assigned HIV-infected women to write about positive events that would happen in the future, or they were in a no-writing control group. Among participants who were initially low in optimism, the writing intervention led to increased optimism, a self-reported increase in adherence to medication, and less distress from medication side effects. The results suggest that future-oriented, positive writing intervention may be a useful technique for decreasing distress and increasing medication adherence, especially in pessimistic individuals. Optimism may also help people already infected with HIV withstand additional stressors better (S. Cruess, Antoni, McGregor, et al., 2000).

Research has also linked psychological inhibition to physical illness or a more rapid course of illness, and this relationship also appears to be true for people with HIV. In one investigation, HIV infection advanced more rapidly in men who concealed their homosexual identity relative to men who were openly gay (S. W. Cole, Kemeny, Taylor, Visscher, & Fahey, 1996). Psychological inhibition is known to lead to alterations in sympathetic nervous system activation and immune function, which may have accounted for these differences in physical health. This may also help explain the beneficial effects of disclosure of HIV status on CD4 levels. However, in an apparent reversal of the usually maladaptive effects of avoidant coping, Mulder and colleagues (1999) found that avoidant copers had a slower decline in CD4 cells, perhaps because their avoidant coping protected them against psychological distress. Stress itself may foster a more rapid course of illness in people with AIDS and/or foster more opportunistic symptoms or more aggressive opportunistic symptoms (Pereira et al., 2003).

Bereavement of a partner can have adverse effects on the immune systems of HIV+ men (Kemeny et al., 1994) and women (Ickovics et al., 2001). For example, Kemeny et al. (1995) found that HIV+ men who had been bereaved by the death of their partner showed a significant increase in immune activation and a significant decrease in proliferative response to mitogenic stimulation. Depression may also play a role in T cell declines. Kemeny et al. (1994) found that HIV+ men who were depressed (but not due to bereavement) had significantly fewer helper/inducer T lymphocytes and more activated suppressor/cytotoxic T cells, as well as lower proliferative responses to mitogenic stimulation. Positive affect lowers the risk of AIDS mortality (Moskowitz, 2003). By contrast, the research that ties psychosocial factors to the course of illness—such as beliefs about one's illness, coping strategies, and social support resources—is especially exciting, because it not only clarifies the factors that may promote long-term survival in people with HIV infection but may also provide more general hypotheses for understanding how psychological and social factors affect the course of illness (S. E. Taylor et al., 2000).

■ CANCER

Cancer is a set of more than 100 diseases that have several factors in common. All cancers result from a dysfunction in DNA—that part of the cellular programming that controls cell growth and reproduction. Instead of ensuring the regular, slow production of new cells, this malfunctioning DNA causes excessively rapid cell growth and proliferation (Kiberstis & Marx, 2002). Unlike other cells, cancerous cells provide no benefit to the body. They merely sap it of resources.

Cancer is second only to heart disease in causes of death in the United States and most developed countries (see figure 14.4). From 1900 until 1990, death rates from cancer progressively climbed. From 1993 to 1999, however (the latest year for which figures were available), the U.S. cancer death rate dropped an average of about 1% annually. Most of the decline in death rates occurred in lung, colorectal, breast, and prostate cancer, which account for more than half of all U.S. cancer deaths (CNN, 2002). The decline in smoking accounts for much of this change. The rest of the decline in cancer deaths can be attributed to improvements in treatment (Brody, 1996a). Nonetheless, more than 500,555 people in the United States will die of cancer this year.

Because psychosocial factors are so clearly implicated in the causes and course of cancer, the health psychologist has an important role in addressing issues involving etiology and progression of cancer. Moreover, because cancer is a disease with which people often live for many years, interventions to reduce it and to improve coping with it are essential (Holland, 2002).

Why Is Cancer Hard to Study?

A number of factors make cancer very difficult to study, in terms of identifying causes and factors that may exacerbate or ameliorate the disease. Many cancers are species specific, and some species are more vulnerable to cancer than others. For example, mice typically contract a lot of cancers, whereas monkeys get very few. Moreover, even a cancer that develops in more than one species may develop in different ways. For example, breast cancer in dogs is very different from breast cancer in humans. As a consequence, it is difficult to use animal models to understand factors that influence the development and course of some human cancers.

Many cancers have long or irregular growth cycles, which contribute to difficulties in studying them. Tumors are measured in terms of their doubling time—that is, the time it takes a tumor to double in size. Doubling time ranges from 23 to 209 days; thus, a tumor may take anywhere from 2 to 17 years to reach a size that can be detected (Fox, 1978).

There is also high within-species variability such that some subgroups within a species are susceptible to certain cancers, whereas other subgroups are susceptible to different ones. Thus, for example, three individuals all exposed to the same carcinogen may develop different tumors at different times, or one individual may develop a tumor, whereas the others remain tumor free.

FIGURE 14.4 | **Leading Sites of New Cancer Cases and Deaths, 2003 Estimates (Excluding Basal and Squamous Cell Skin Cancer and Carcinomas in Situ Except Urinary Bladder)**   (*Source:* The American Cancer Society, Inc.)

Cancer cases by site and sex		Cancer deaths by site and sex	
Male	**Female**	**Male**	**Female**
Prostate 220,900	Breast 211,300	Lung and bronchus 88,900	Lung and bronchus 68,800
Lung and bronchus 91,800	Lung and bronchus 80,100	Prostate 28,900	Breast 39,800
Colon and rectum 72,800	Colon and rectum 74,700	Colon and rectum 28,300	Colon and rectum 28,800
Urinary bladder 42,200	Uterine corpus 46,100	Pancreas 19,700	Pancreas 15,300
Non-Hodgkin's lymphoma 28,300	Ovary 25,100	Non-Hodgkin's lymphoma 12,200	Ovary 14,300
Melanoma of the skin 29,900	Non-Hodgkin's lymphoma 25,100	Leukemia 12,100	Non-Hodgkin's lymphoma 11,200
Oral cavity 18,200	Melanoma of the skin 24,300	Esophagus 9,900	Leukemia 9,800
Kidney 19,500	Urinary bladder 15,200	Liver 9,200	Uterine corpus 6,800
Leukemia 17,900	Pancreas 15,800	Urinary bladder 8,600	Brain 5,800
Pancreas 14,900	Thyroid 16,300	Stomach 7,000	Stomach 5,100
All sites 675,300	**All sites 658,800**	**All sites 291,300**	**All sites 205,700**

Who Gets Cancer? A Complex Profile

Many cancers run in families. To a degree, this tendency occurs because many cancers have a genetic basis. Recent research implicates genetic factors in a subset of colon cancers and breast cancer, discoveries that will help in assessing the risk status of many people. However, family history does not always imply a genetically inherited predisposition to cancer. Many things run in families besides genes, including diet and other lifestyle factors that influence the development of cancer, and on the whole cancer is more closely tied to lifestyle than to genetics (P. Lichtenstein et al., 2000).

Some cancers are ethnically linked. For example, in the United States, Anglo men have a bladder cancer rate twice that of other groups and a relatively high rate of malignant melanoma. Hispanic men and women have the lowest lung cancer rates, but Hispanic women show one of the highest rates of invasive cancers of the cervix. The prostate cancer rate among African Americans is higher than the rate for any other cancer in any other group. Japanese Americans have an especially high rate of stomach cancer, whereas Chinese Americans have a high rate of liver cancer. Breast cancer is extremely common among northern European women and is relatively rare among Asians (World Health Organization, 1995–1996).

Some cancers are culturally linked through lifestyle. For example, Japanese-American women are more susceptible to breast cancer the longer they have lived in the United States and the more they have adopted the American culture (Wynder et al., 1963). This change in vulnerability is believed to be heavily linked to changes in diet. Infectious agents are implicated in some cancers. For example, the human papillomavirus (HPV) is the main cause of cervical cancer (Waller, McCaffery, Forrest, & Wardle, 2004). Heleopactor pylori is implicated in some types of gastric cancer. Most cancers are related to socioeconomic status with low SES individuals more at risk. Moreover, even as incidence rates for major cancers have slowed or decreased, declines in mortality have been slower in minority populations than among Whites (Glanz, Croyle, Chollette, & Pinn, 2003).

The probability of developing some cancers changes with socioeconomic status. For example, White women are more likely than African-American women to develop breast cancer, but among African-American women who have moved up the socioeconomic ladder, the breast cancer rate is the same as for White women at that economic level (Leffall, White, & Ewing, 1963). Figure 14.5 shows cancers of all types broken down by different ethnic groups in the United States, both by incidence and by mortality.

Married people, especially married men, develop fewer cancers than single people. The sole exception to

FIGURE 14.5 | Average Annual Incidence and Mortality Rates of All Types of Cancer in the United States by Ethnicity (Adjusted to Eliminate Age as a Determining Factor)   (*Source:* American Cancer Society, 2001a)

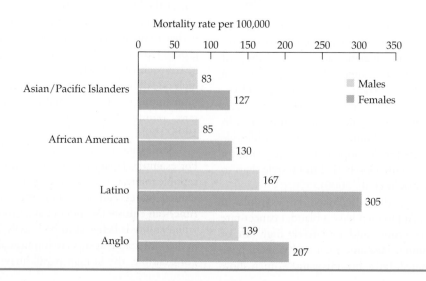

this pattern is gender-linked cancers, such as prostate or cervical cancer, to which married people are somewhat more vulnerable than single people. These health benefits may derive from having a regular source of social support, regularity in health habits, and as yet unidentified factors.

Dietary factors are also implicated in cancer development. Cancers are more common among people who are chronically malnourished and among those who consume high levels of fats, certain food additives (such as nitrates), and alcohol (American Cancer Society, 1997).

Research is beginning to identify interactions among risk factors that may contribute to particular cancers. For example, women who are sedentary and significantly overweight have a higher risk of pancreatic cancer if their diets are also high in starch and starchy foods such as potatoes and rice (Michaud et al., 2002). As researchers increasingly identify risk factors and focus on their co-occurrence, other such relationships may be found.

Psychosocial Factors and Cancer

Psychosocial factors can affect cancer in a number of ways. In terms of initiation of the disease, behavioral factors are involved in exposures to carcinogens, such as tobacco and occupational carcinogens. Psychosocial variables may also indirectly affect the initiation of cancer through consumption of a fatty diet or exposure to stress (S. M. Levy, 1983).

Psychosocial factors are also involved in the progression of a cancer after it is initiated. For example, stress exposure and certain ways of coping may affect progression of cancer. Behavioral factors are also involved indirectly in the progression of a cancer, for example, through failing to adhere to a low-cancer diet, not adhering to treatment, or not using screening or early detection methods (S. M. Levy, 1983).

We have already considered many of the factors that initiate and lead to a progression of cancer, including such risk factors as smoking, alcohol consumption, or fatty diet (chapters 4 and 5), and variables that promote delay behavior and nonadherence (chapters 8 and 9). In this chapter, we focus more heavily on the evidence regarding stress and personality in the initiation and progression of cancer.

Who Gets Cancer? A Psychological Profile

The role of personality factors in the development of cancer has been suspected for centuries (see LeShan &

Worthington, 1956). Early research attempted to tie specific cancers to particular personality structures. For example, breast cancer was attributed to conflicts surrounding motherhood and femininity and to masochistic tendencies involving an inability to discharge negative emotions and unresolved hostility toward the mother (Renneker & Cutler, 1952). As in the case of other personality-specific models of illness, there is no evidence for such speculation.

Another line of investigation explored the idea of a cancer-prone personality. For decades, there has been a stereotype of a cancer-prone personality as an individual who is easygoing and acquiescent, repressing emotions that might interfere with smooth social and emotional functioning. As Woody Allen remarked in the film *Manhattan,* "I can't express anger. That's one of the problems I have. I grow a tumor instead." Some studies of cancer-prone personality traits have suffered from methodological problems that make it impossible to determine whether cancer patients develop cancer because they have these particular personality factors or whether these personality factors develop as a consequence of cancer.

Research has found a positive association between depression and cancer (for example, Carney, Jones, Woolson, Noyes, & Doebbeling, 2003; Dattore, Shontz, & Coyne, 1980; Persky, Kempthorne-Rawson, & Shekelle, 1987). Depression can be associated with elevated neural endocrine responses such as cortisol and norepinephrine, which may, in turn, have implications for cancer via their impact on the immune system.

Modest relationships between cancer development and use of denial or repressive coping strategies have been found as well (McKenna, Zevon, Corn, & Rounds, 1999), but other studies have failed to identify any psychosocial predictors of cancer (for example, Joffres, Reed, & Nomura, 1985; Keene, 1980). At present, evidence suggests only a modest association between psychosocial factors and the development of at least some cancers and questions any general relationship between personality and the development of cancer (McKenna et al., 1999).

Stress and Cancer   Does stress cause cancer? One approach to this question has focused on major life events and their relationship to cancer development. Generally, studies on both animals and humans suggest such a link. Animals exposed to stressors, such as crowding, show higher malignant tumor rates (for example, Amkraut & Solomon, 1977). A few prospective studies in humans have found evidence of a link between uncontrollable stress and cancer (McKenna et al., 1999; Sklar & Anisman, 1981).

A particular type of stress, lack or loss of social support, may affect the onset and course of cancer. The absence of close family ties in childhood may predict cancer (Felitti et al., 1998; Grassi & Molinari, 1986; Shaffer, Duszynski, & Thomas, 1982). The absence of a current social support network has been tied to both a higher incidence of cancer (C. B. Thomas & Duszynski, 1974) and a more rapid course of illness (P. Reynolds & Kaplan, 1986; Worden & Weisman, 1975).

A long-term study of factors related to cancer incidence, mortality, and prognosis in Alameda County, California, found that women who were socially isolated were at a significantly elevated risk of dying from cancer of all sites (G. A. Kaplan & Reynolds, 1988). However, other studies have found no relationship between social support problems and cancer (see Joffres et al., 1985). Consequently, evidence relating cancer to gaps in social support remains inconclusive.

Psychosocial Factors and the Course of Cancer

Researchers have also examined the role of psychosocial factors in the course of cancer, specifically whether the cancer progresses rapidly or slowly. Avoidance, or the inability to confront the disease and its implications, has been associated with a more rapid course of the disease (J. A. Epping-Jordan, Compas, & Howell, 1994). Depression is implicated in the progression of cancer, both by itself (K. W. Brown, Levy, Rosberger, & Edgar, 2003) or in conjunction with other risk factors. For example, R. W. Linkins and Comstock (1990) found a 18.5-fold increase in risk for smoking-related cancers among smokers who were depressed, as well as a 2.9-fold increase for non-smoking-associated cancers. Avoidant or passive coping is also a risk factor for psychological distress and depression, which may represent another way in which these forms of coping may adversely influence course of disease (Kim, Valdimarsdottir, & Bovbjerg, 2003). Repressive coping appears to be especially common in children with cancer, so this coping style warrants particular consideration in their care (Phipps, Steele, Hall, & Leigh, 2001).

In addition to depression, negative expectations regarding one's situation have been related to a more rapid course of illness in young cancer patients (Schulz, Bookwala, Knapp, Scheier, & Williamson, 1996). Inasmuch as negative expectations also affect time to death among

diagnosed AIDS patients (Reed et al., 1994) as well as among people who have HIV infection (Reed et al., 1997), pessimism about the future merits continued examination.

Stress itself has been tied to a higher likelihood of cancer in both animal and human studies. For example, confronting major stressors such as divorce, infidelity, marital quarreling, financial stress, and the like increases risk for diagnosed cervical cancer (Coker, Bond, Madeleine, Luchok, & Pirisi, 2003). Animal studies in which tumor material is transplanted into mice suggests that although stress may not play a critical role in whether the transplant develops into a tumor, it may play an important role in the progression of malignancy once a tumor has taken root (Kerr, Hundal, Silva, Emerman, & Wienberg, 2001). On the whole, the evidence relating psychological distress and pessimism to cancer survival is increasingly persuasive and underscores the importance of identifying and intervening in distress early, so as to mute its impact on survival course.

Mechanisms Linking Stress, Coping, and Cancer

How, exactly, might stressful events and cancer be linked? A number of researchers have implicated the immune system. As noted earlier, NK cells are involved in the surveillance and destruction of tumor cells and virally infected cells, and therefore, they are believed to have a role in tumor surveillance in the body. NK cell activity is also believed to be involved in whether or not a carcinogen takes hold after exposure.

Psychological stress appears to adversely affect the ability of NK cells to destroy tumors (for example, R. Glaser, Rice, Speicher, Stout, & Kiecolt-Glaser, 1986; Locke, Kraus, & Leserman, 1984), an important finding because NK cell activity appears to be important in survival rates for certain cancers, especially early breast cancer (S. M. Levy, Herberman, Lippman, D'Angelo, & Lee, 1991). Consistent with this analysis is the fact that cancer patients show reduced immunologic competence and are sometimes successfully treated with therapies designed to enhance immune functioning (G. F. Solomon, Amkraut, & Kasper, 1974).

Researchers have also begun to explore the pathways by which coping may affect the course of cancer. Inflammatory cytokines, specifically interleukin-6 (IL-6) may be involved in disease progression in gynecologic cancers. In one study (S. K. Lutgendorf, Anderson, Sorosky, Buller, & Lubaroff, 2000), patients who sought instrumental support from others at the time they were diagnosed had lower IL-6 (a proinflammatory cytokine) and better clinical status and less disability a year later. These findings were independent of psychological distress and suggest that the ways patients cope with the stress of cancer may be associated with inflammatory processes implicated in tumor progression. The pathways by which stress may have an impact on the initiation and course of cancer will continue to be a fruitful avenue for research over the next decades.

Adjusting to Cancer

One out of every four people will eventually develop cancer, and each year cancer causes approximately 542,000 deaths in the United States (Centers for Disease Control and Prevention, 2000a). The psychosocial toll of cancer is enormous. Two out of every three families will have a family member who develops cancer, and virtually every member of these families will be affected by the disease. This burden will fall disproportionately on minority and low-SES populations in the United States (Bach et al., 2002). However, more than one third of cancer victims live at least 5 years after their diagnosis, thus creating many issues of long-term adjustment. Many of the issues that we explored in chapters 11 and 12 in the context of chronic, advancing, and terminal illness are especially relevant to the cancer experience. We highlight a few additional issues in this section.

Coping with Physical Limitations   Cancer takes a substantial toll, both physically and psychologically. The physical difficulties usually stem from the pain and discomfort cancer can produce, particularly in the advancing and terminal phases of illness.

Cancer can lead to downregulation of the immune system, which may enhance vulnerability to a variety of other disorders, including respiratory tract infections. These persistent health problems can compromise quality of life (B. L. Andersen, Kiecolt-Glaser, & Glaser, 1994). Fatigue due to illness and treatment is also one of the main complaints of cancer patients (Andrykowski, Curran, & Lightner, 1998).

Treatment-Related Problems   Difficulties also arise as a consequence of treatment. Some cancers are treated surgically. Removal of organs can create cosmetic problems, as for patients with breast cancer who may have a breast removed (mastectomy) or for patients with head-and-neck cancer who may have a portion of this area removed. Body image concerns stem not only from concern about appearance following surgery but also from concerns about a sense of wholeness, bodily integrity, and the ability to function normally. Either concern can complicate reactions to treatment (Carver et al., 1998).

In some cases, organs that are vital to bodily functions must be taken over by a prosthesis. For example, a urinary ostomy patient must be fitted with an apparatus that makes it possible to excrete urine. A patient whose larynx has been removed must learn to speak with the help of a prosthetic speech device. Side effects due to surgery are also common. A colostomy (prosthetic replacement of the lower colon) produces a loss of bowel control.

Some cancer patients receive debilitating follow-up treatments. Patients undergoing chemotherapy may expect and experience debilitating nausea and vomiting and may develop anticipatory nausea and vomiting that occurs even before the chemotherapy session begins (for example, Montgomery & Bovbjerg, 2003). As a result, symptoms of nausea, distress, and vomiting can continue to adversely affect quality of life among cancer patients long after the treatment has ended (C. L. Cameron et al., 2001). Because chemotherapy is often administered in the same place by the same person under the same circumstances, patients may develop conditioned nausea to a wide variety of stimuli, including the hospital staff (P. B. Jacobsen et al., 1993a). One chemotherapy nurse remarked that once she saw one of her chemotherapy patients in a supermarket. She said hello, and the patient threw up in the aisle. One risk of these extreme side effects of treatments is that they sometimes compromise long-term compliance (Love, Cameron, Connell, & Leventhal, 1991). Fortunately, in recent years, chemotherapies with less virulent side effects have been developed. Patients may also develop conditioned immune suppression in response to repeated pairings of the hospital, staff, and other stimuli with the immunosuppressive effects of chemotherapy (Cameron et al., 2001; Lekander, Furst, Rotstein, Blomgren, & Fredrikson, 1995), which can have adverse effects on the course of cancer.

These physical problems are not only important in their own right, but they can often feed into psychological adjustment problems, increasing the likelihood of depression (Given et al., 1993). Research suggests that stress management skills may contribute to a more positive state of mind following radical treatments (Penedo et al., 2003).

Psychosocial Issues and Cancer

Because of early identification techniques and promising treatments, many people who are diagnosed with cancer live long and fulfilling lives free of disease. Others may have recurrences but nonetheless maintain a high quality of life for 15 or 20 years. Others live with active cancers over the long term, knowing that the disease will ultimately be fatal. All of these trajectories, however, indicate that cancer is now a chronic disease, which poses long-term issues related to psychosocial adjustment.

Intermittent and long-term depression are among the most common difficulties experienced as a result of cancer. Depression not only compromises quality of life in its own right, but it can have adverse effects on physical health outcomes as well, including the progression of cancer (B. L. Andersen et al., 1994). Adjustment problems appear to be greatest among women who have a history of life stressors or a lack of social support (L. D. Butler, Koopman, Classen, & Spiegel, 1999). Although cancer patients do not have more psychological distress than people without cancer for the most part, they are more susceptible to depression (van't Spijker, Trijsburg, & Duivenvoorden, 1997). Restriction of usual activities is a common outcome of the disease and its treatment, which can foster depression and other adverse psychosocial responses (Williamson, 2000).

Issues Involving Social Support   Despite the fact that many cancer patients receive considerable emotional support from their families and friends, social support can be problematic. Problems in social support are especially significant, because negative aspects of close relationships appear to affect psychological distress and well-being among cancer patients in an adverse direction more than emotional support enhances it (S. L. Manne & Glassman, 2000; S. L. Manne, Taylor, Dougherty, & Kemeny, 1997).

Effective support is important for several reasons. It improves psychological adjustment to cancer, and it can help patients deal with intrusive thoughts and rumination about the cancer (Lewis et al., 2001). Support may improve immunologic responses to cancer as well. If there was any doubt of the importance of social support to cancer survival, a recent investigation (Lai et al., 1999) found that married patients with cancers have significantly better survival than single, separated, divorced, or widowed patients. How spouses provide support matters. Hagedoorn et al. (2000) found that actively engaging in conversations with the patient about

the cancer and finding constructive methods for solving problems were beneficial, whereas hiding one's concerns and overprotecting the patient were less beneficial. Interventions directed to these issues can significantly improve quality of life (Graves, 2003).

Problems concerning a cancer patient's children are relatively common. Young children may show fear or distress over the parent's prognosis (Compas et al., 1994). Older children may find new responsibilities thrust on them and may respond by rebelling. Problems with children may be especially severe if the cancer is one with a hereditary component because children may blame the parent for putting them at increased risk (Lichtman et al., 1984).

Marital and Sexual Relationships   A strong marital relationship is important in cancer because marital adjustment predicts psychological distress following cancer diagnosis (Banthia et al., 2003). Unfortunately, disturbances in marital relationships after a diagnosis of cancer are not uncommon (Ybema, Kuijer, Buunk, DeJong, & Sanderman, 2001). Sexual functioning is particularly vulnerable. Body image concerns and concerns about a partner's reactions represent psychosocial vulnerabilities, especially when there has been disfiguring surgery, as in the case of breast cancer (Spencer et al., 1999). Breast-conserving techniques, such as lumpectomy, lead to moderately better psychological, marital, sexual, and social adjustment than the more extensive mastectomy surgery (Moyer, 1997).

Sexual functioning can be directly affected by treatments, such as surgery or chemotherapy, and indirectly affected by anxiety or depression, which often reduce sexual desire (B. L. Andersen, Woods, & Copeland, 1997). Sexual functioning problems have been particularly evident in patients with gynecologic cancers and prostate cancer and underscore the fact that different types of cancers create different kinds of problems (for example, Moyer & Salovey, 1996).

Psychological Adjustment and Treatment
Adverse psychological reactions to cancer can also be severe when the treatments are severe or if the patient has a poor understanding of the disease and treatment or both. Survivors of childhood leukemia, for example, sometimes show signs of post-traumatic stress disorder (PTSD), which may persist for years following treatment (Somerfield, Curbow, Wingard, Baker, & Fogarty, 1996; Stuber, Christakis, Houskamp, & Kazak, 1996).

Among adult patients, however, signs of PTSD appears to be relatively rare, suggesting that trying to understand the experience of cancer patients through our understanding of trauma may be misleading (Palmer, Kagee, Coyne, & DeMichele, 2004).

Identifying and attending to psychological distress in response to cancer is an important issue, not only for maintaining quality of life but also because psychological distress may itself be related to prospects for long-term survival. For example, research shows that cancer survivors may show elevated cortisol and alterations in their HPA axis responses to stress subsequent to cancer treatment; this may be due to fear of recurrence, stress associated with cancer treatment and the disease, or a combination (Porter et al., 2003). These hormones may, in turn, exert a regulatory effect on the immune system that may influence the likelihood of a recurrence (see also Luecken & Compas, 2002).

Self-Presentation of Cancer Patients Vocational disruption may occur for patients who have chronic discomfort from cancer or its treatments (Somerfield et al., 1996), and job discrimination against cancer patients has been documented. Difficulties in managing social interactions can result from alterations in physical appearance, disrupting social and recreational activity. An ostomy patient, for example, described his fear of revolting others:

> When I smelled an odor on the bus or subway before the colostomy, I used to feel very annoyed. I'd think that the people were awful, that they didn't take a bath, or that they should have gone to the bathroom before traveling. I used to think that they might have odors from what they ate. I used to be terribly annoyed; to me it seemed that they were filthy, dirty. Of course, at the least opportunity I used to change my seat and if I couldn't, it used to go against my grain. So naturally, I believe that the young people feel the same way about me if I smell. (Goffman, 1963, p. 34)

There is now cause for considerable optimism. Many people with active malignant disease live long, active, satisfying, unrestricted lives. The sense of doom that a cancer diagnosis once conveyed no longer casts a shadow over cancer patients. The stigma attached to cancer has largely lifted. Nonetheless, cancer does pose a variety of issues including physical disabilities, family and marital disruptions, sexual difficulty, self-esteem problems, social and recreational disruptions, and psychological distress for which coping and interventions may be needed.

Coping with Cancer

Certain coping strategies appear to be helpful in dealing with the problems related to cancer. In a study of 603 cancer patients, Dunkel-Schetter et al. (1992) identified five patterns of coping:

1. Seeking or using social support.
2. Focus on the positive.
3. Distancing.
4. Cognitive escape-avoidance.
5. Behavioral escape-avoidance.

look for on papers on coping

Coping through social support, focusing on the positive, and distancing were all associated with less emotional distress from cancer. Patients high in optimism also experience less psychological distress (J. E. Epping-Jordan et al., 1999).

Patients who cope with their cancer-related problems through cognitive and behavioral escape-avoidant strategies show more emotional distress (for example, Manne, Glassman, & DuHamel, 2000). When spouses cope with their partner's illness using these same avoidance strategies, a patient's distress may also be high (Ben-Zur, Gilbar, & Lev, 2001).

Despite documented psychosocial problems associated with cancer, many people clearly have cancer experiences that they weather quite well from a psychological standpoint, adjusting successfully to major changes in their lives (Reaby & Hort, 1995). With the exception of depression, the psychological distress experienced by cancer patients does not differ from people without cancer and is significantly less than people suffering from psychiatric disorders (van't Spijker et al., 1997).

Finding Meaning in Cancer Indeed, some cancer patients report that their lives have been made better in important ways by the cancer experience, permitting them to experience growth and satisfaction in personal relationships that they might not otherwise have achieved (Fromm, Andrykowski, & Hunt, 1996; Katz, Flasher, Cacciapaglia, & Nelson, 2001; S. E. Taylor, 1983). Such growth experiences may mute neuroendocrine stress responses, which may, in turn, have a beneficial effect on the immune system (D. G. Cruess, Antoni, McGregor, et al., 2000).

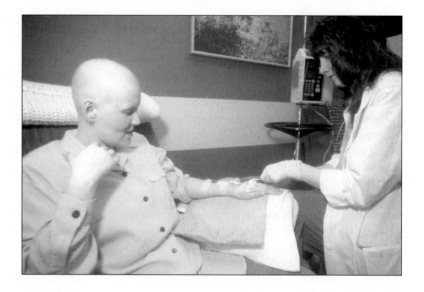

Many cancer patients who receive intra- venously administered chemotherapy experience intense nausea and vomiting. Interventions using relaxation and guided imagery can substantially improve these problems.

These positive adaptations to the cancer experience can be enhanced by feelings of control or self-efficacy in response to the cancer experience. People who are able to experience a sense of personal control over their cancer, its treatments, or their daily activities cope more successfully with cancer (Newsom, Knapp, & Schulz, 1996; S. E. Taylor et al., 1991). Control over emotional reactions and physical symptoms appear to be especially important for psychosocial adjustment (S. C. Thompson et al., 1993).

Interventions

Rehabilitative interventions for cancer patients generally fall into three categories: pharmacologic interventions, behavioral interventions, and psychotherapeutic interventions.

Pharmacologic Interventions   Pharmacologic management of the cancer patient typically centers on four issues:

1. Nausea and vomiting induced by chemotherapy.
2. Anorexia and other eating difficulties.
3. Emotional disorders, such as depression and anxiety (P. B. Jacobsen, Bovbjerg, & Redd, 1993b).
4. Pain.

Nausea and vomiting are usually treated by the use of drugs. Marijuana has proven to be particularly successful in combating the nausea and vomiting associated with chemotherapy, and drugs such as thorazine, val-

ium, and compazine help. Anorexia is treated most successfully through dietary supplements because appetite stimulants do not seem to work very well. Depression and anxiety may be managed pharmacologically with the help of such drugs as valium, and pain may be managed by using morphine, methadone, or antianxiety drugs and antidepressants. In the end stage of cancer, pain may significantly increase requiring immediate intervention (Butler et al., 2003).

Cognitive-Behavioral Interventions   Cognitive-behavioral approaches to the management of cancer-related problems have focused on depression, stress, pain, appetite control, and side effects associated with chemotherapy, radiation therapy, and other cancer treatments (Holland & Rowland, 1981; Antoni et al., 2001). Interventions directed to these issues can significantly improve quality of life (Graves, 2003). In one study of a cognitive-behavioral, stress management intervention with women newly diagnosed with breast cancer, the intervention successfully reduced the prevalence of depression and increased the women's ability to find benefits in their experience (Antoni et al., 2001). This intervention also reduced cortisol levels in these women, which may have positive implications for the course of their cancer (D. G. Cruess, Antoni, McGregor, et al., 2000).

Mindfulness-based, stress reduction interventions have also been undertaken with cancer patients. For example, a study with breast and prostate cancer patients employed a mindfulness intervention involving the active cultivation of conscious awareness through relaxation, meditation, and yoga, with daily practice. The intervention not only enhanced quality of life and decreased stress symptoms but also produced a shift in immune profile from one associated with depressive symptoms to a more normal profile (Carlson, Speca, Patel, & Goodey, 2003).

Recently, practitioners have recommended exercise as a general intervention to improve quality of life following cancer. A review of 24 research studies found that physical exercise had a positive effect on quality of life following cancer diagnosis, including both physical functioning and emotional well-being (Courneya & Friedenreich, 1999; 2001). Exercise is beneficial generally for health in the later years of life and for psychosocial adjustment, and it is recommended for people at risk for cancer as well as those already diagnosed (Audrain, Schwartz, Herrera, Goldman, & Bush, 2001).

Pain is a relatively common problem among cancer patients and often provokes anxiety or depression, which, as we saw in chapter 10, may exacerbate its severity. Although painkillers remain the primary method of treating cancer-related pains, increasingly behavioral interventions are being adopted (M. Davis, Vasterling, Bransfield, & Burish, 1987). Relaxation therapy, hypnosis, cognitive-reappraisal techniques, visual imaging, and self-hypnosis have all proven to be at least somewhat useful in the management of pain due to cancer (Turk & Fernandez, 1990).

A recent concern has been the fact that cancer patients' complaints of pain, fatigue, nausea, and breathlessness receive insufficient attention and that, in advancing and terminal cancers, these patients' lives are compromised severely by inattention to these important problems (Grady, 2000b).

Chemotherapy   Because it is the most debilitating of the side effects of cancer treatment, chemotherapy has also been a particular focus of behavioral interventions. Distraction is one intervention that has been used successfully with chemotherapy, especially among children. For example, the severity of nausea in response to chemotherapy was lower among children who were permitted to play video games during chemotherapy administration, and playing the video games also somewhat reduced the anxiety associated with chemotherapy (Redd et al., 1987).

Cognitive distraction may work for adult chemotherapy patients as well (Vasterling, Jenkins, Tope, & Burish, 1993). Biofeedback appears to have minimal effects on coping with chemotherapy (Burish & Jenkins, 1992).

Relaxation and guided imagery are two additional techniques that can help control chemotherapy side effects (Carey & Burish, 1988). In this approach, patients are taught the techniques and urged to practice them at home before the chemotherapy sessions, in the hopes that this counterconditioning will enable them to cope more successfully. In an evaluation of this procedure, patients who received relaxation training and guided imagery reported feeling less anxious and less nauseated during chemotherapy. They were less physiologically aroused, and they felt less anxious and depressed immediately afterward. They also reported less severe and protracted nausea at home.

Although research continues to suggest that relaxation and guided imagery are successful treatments for chemotherapy, even shorter and more easily administered coping preparation packages may be equally successful (Burish, Snyder, & Jenkins, 1991). In one study, researchers instituted a simple, one-session coping preparation intervention involving relaxation and guided imagery and found that it reduced many sources of distress associated with chemotherapy (Burish & Trope, 1992). Fortunately, chemotherapy regimens are becoming less toxic, which has reduced the distressing side effects.

Psychotherapeutic Interventions   In contrast to pharmacologic and behavioral interventions, which are directed primarily toward reducing the physical discomfort associated with cancer and its treatment, psychotherapeutic interventions—including individual psychotherapy, group therapy, family therapy, and cancer support groups—attempt to meet the psychosocial and informational needs of cancer patients.

Individual Therapy   Patients seeking individual therapy after a diagnosis of cancer are most likely to experience:

1. Significant anxiety, depression, or suicidal thoughts.

2. Central nervous system dysfunctions produced by the illness and treatment, such as the inability to concentrate.

3. Specific problems that have arisen as a consequence of the illness, its management, or family dynamics.

4. Previously existing psychological problems that have been exacerbated by cancer.

Individual therapy with cancer patients typically follows a crisis-intervention format rather than an intensive psychotherapy model. That is, therapists working with cancer patients try to focus on the specific issues faced by the patient rather than undertaking a more general, probing, long-term analysis of the patient's psyche. The most common issues arising in individual therapy are fear of recurrence (Vickberg, 2003), pain, or death; fear of loss of organs as a consequence of additional surgeries; interference with valued activities; practical difficulties, such as job discrimination and problems with dating and social relationships; and communication problems with families.

As cancer patients approach death, there is often a spike in psychological distress; thus, end-stage clinical interventions are especially needed at this time point (Butler et al., 2003). Psychotherapeutic interventions best focus on helping a cancer patient make use of and build personal resources such as optimism and control as well as social recourses such as social support. These psychological resources are most important for mental and physical functioning over the long term (Helgeson, Snyder, & Seltman, 2004).

Psychotherapeutic interventions with children who have cancer follow many of the same guidelines and issues as is true for therapy with adult cancer patients. Generally, therapy is focused on the psychosocial issues that inevitably arise in childhood cancer, including relations with peers and family. Pediatric cancer patients are also likely to develop learning problems in concentration or attention. Child cancer patients are vulnerable to neurocognitive "late" effects, which result from both the disease and its treatment. These are changes in the brain structure and development that do not appear until after treatment is over but often impair intellectual functioning. These deficits may not be evident for simple tasks but may become more evident with difficult tasks or may be manifested as difficulty learning new cognitive tasks such as long division. In essence the brain's ability to process new information may be compromised. Early assessments and interventions to address these cognitive problems and to help children avoid lifelong problems in attention and concentration are essential (DeAngelis, 2003).

Family Therapy   As previously noted, cancers almost always have an impact on other family members. Including family members in therapy is important because families can either help or hinder an individual cancer patient's adjustment to illness. By providing social support, the family can smooth the patient's adjustment, whereas a reaction of fear or withdrawal can make the

patient's problems more difficult. Issues that commonly arise in family therapy are problems with children, especially adolescents; role changes and increased dependency; and problems of sexual functioning (Wellisch, 1981).

Especially when a patient's quality of life is impaired, and he or she experiences psychological distress, these effects can spill over into the marital relationship, leading to distress in the spouse as well (Fang, Manne, & Pape, 2001). Emotional support from family is highly desired by cancer patients, and it promotes good psychological adjustment (Helgeson & Cohen, 1996; Northouse, Templin, & Mood, 2001). Not all families are able to communicate freely with each other. Moreover, cancer patients' distress may be hard for families to bear and accordingly may actually contribute to a loss of social support from the family (Alferi, Carver, Antoni, Weiss, & Duran, 2001). Therefore, family therapy provides an opportunity for family members to share their problems and difficulties in communicating.

Support Groups   A number of cancer service programs have been developed to help the patient adjust to problems posed by a particular cancer. Several of these programs are sponsored by the American Cancer Society; they include Reach to Recovery for breast cancer patients and groups for patients who have had ostomies. These programs provide either a one-on-one or a group experience in which individuals can discuss some of their common problems. Reach to Recovery is one of several such groups that has adopted a peer counseling approach, in which a well-adjusted breast cancer patient acts as an adviser to a newly diagnosed patient. This kind of educational and informational support has been found to be valuable in promoting psychological adjustment to cancer (Helgeson & Cohen, 1996).

Self-help groups in which patients share emotional concerns are also available to many cancer patients (Helgeson & Cohen, 1996). Although the self-help experience currently appeals to a fairly limited portion of the cancer population, it appears to be beneficial for many who try it. On the whole, social support groups appear to be most helpful to women who have more problems, who lack support, or who have fewer personal resources, but they may provide few if any benefits for those who already have high levels of support (Helgeson, Cohen, Schulz, & Yasko, 2000; K. L. Taylor et al., 2003). When such groups do provide benefits, a possible reason is that the self-help format presents patients with an array of potential coping techniques from which they can draw skills that fit in with their particular styles and problems (S. E. Taylor et al., 1986). Spending time with well-adjusted people who have had the same disorder can satisfy patients' needs for information and emotional support (Stanton, Danoff-Burg, Cameron, Snider, & Kirk, 1999).

Such interventions may also have unanticipated health benefits. Specifically, social support interventions may actually prolong life among some patient groups (S. M. Levy, Herberman, Lee, Lippman, & d'Angelo, 1989). Spiegel and colleagues (1989), for example, found that metastatic breast cancer patients who had been randomly assigned to a weekly support group intervention lived significantly longer than did nonparticipants by an average of nearly 18 months. These findings held up when various indicators of disease had been controlled for (see also Fawzy, Cousins, et al., 1990; Fawzy, Kemeny, et al., 1990). The intervention may have succeeded because it helped patients control their pain more successfully and alleviated their depression; both of these effects may allow for a better immune response to cancer.

In closing our discussion of cancer, we return to the issue of SES disparities and the fact that low-income people are both at greater risk for cancer initially and for a faster course of illness once detected. It is clear that more investigations into how SES exerts these effects and to why SES is related to higher incidence and mortality is vital. In addition, the development of culturally appropriate interventions and research is also needed to identify the needs of these obviously underserved groups (Glanz, Croyle, Chollette, & Pinn, 2003).

■ ARTHRITIS

We learned in chapter 2 about a set of diseases known as autoimmune diseases, in which the body falsely identifies its own tissue as foreign matter and attacks it. The most prevalent of these autoimmune diseases is arthritis, and we examine it both because of its relationship to immune functioning and because it is one of the most common chronic disorders and causes of disability.

Arthritis has been with humankind since the beginning of recorded history. Ancient drawings of people with arthritic joints have been found in caves, and early Greek and Roman writers described the pain of arthritis (S. Johnson, 2003). *Arthritis* means inflammation of a joint; it refers to more than 80 diseases that attack the joints or other connective tissues. More than 43 million people in the United States are afflicted with arthritis

severe enough to require medical care, a figure that is projected to rise to 60 million by 2025, due to the aging of the population (National Institute of Arthritis and Musculoskeletal and Skin Diseases, 2002). Although it is rarely fatal, arthritis ranks second only to heart disease as the most widespread chronic disease in the United States today. Arthritis costs the U.S. economy nearly $86.2 billion per year in medical care and indirect expenses such as lost wages and production (Arthritis Foundation, 2004).

The severity of and prognosis for arthritis depend on the type; the disease ranges from a barely noticeable and occasional problem to a crippling, chronic condition. The three major forms of arthritis are rheumatoid arthritis, osteoarthritis, and gout.

Rheumatoid Arthritis

Rheumatoid arthritis (RA) affects 2.1 million Americans, mostly women (Arthritis Foundation, 2004), and is the most crippling form of arthritis. The disease first strikes primarily the 40 to 60 age group, although it can attack people of any age group, including children. It usually affects the small joints of the hands and feet, as well as the wrists, knees, ankles, and neck. In mild cases, only one or two joints are involved, but sometimes the disease becomes widespread. In severe cases, there may be inflammation of the heart muscle, blood vessels, and tissues just beneath the skin.

Rheumatoid arthritis may be brought on by an autoimmune process (Firestein, 2003): Agents of the immune system that are supposed to protect the body instead attack the thin membranes surrounding the joints. This attack leads to inflammation, stiffness, and pain. If not controlled, the bone and surrounding muscle tissue of the joint may be destroyed. Almost half of RA patients recover completely, nearly half remain somewhat arthritic, and about 10% are severely disabled.

The main complications of rheumatoid arthritis are pain, limitations in activities, and the need to be dependent on others (van Lankveld et al., 1993). In addition, because rheumatoid arthritis primarily affects older people, its sufferers often have other chronic conditions present as well, such as poor cognitive functioning and poor vision, which may interact with arthritis to produce high levels of disability (Shifren, Park, Bennett, & Morrell, 1999; Verbrugge, 1995). Not surprisingly, one of the most common complications of rheumatoid arthritis is depression (Dickens, McGowan, Clark-Carter, & Creed, 2002). Depression may feed back into

Approximately 1 to 2% of the population of the United States has rheumatoid arthritis, and it is especially common among older women. The frustration of being unable to do things that one used to do and the need to be dependent on others are problems for this group.

the pain process enhancing pain from RA (Zautra & Smith, 2001). Negative affect may increase arthritis disease activity (B. W. Smith & Zautra, 2002). A vicious spiral may be sent into effect: As the disease progresses, greater disability results. Patients may come to doubt their abilities to manage vital life activities, which can contribute to a high level of depression, which, in turn, exacerbates physical impairment (Neugebauer, Katz, & Pasch, 2003).

At one time, psychologists speculated that there might be a "rheumatoid arthritis personality." This personality type was said to be perfectionistic, depressed, and restricted in emotional expression, especially the expression of anger. Recent research now casts doubt on the accuracy and value of such a profile, at least as a cause of arthritis (for example, C. A. Smith, Wallston, & Dwyer, 1995). However, cognitive distortions and feelings of helplessness can aggravate depression and other emotional responses to arthritis (for example, Clemmey & Nicassio, 1997; Fifield et al., 2001; T. W. Smith, Christensen, Peck, & Ward, 1994). Gaps in social support may also be a consequence (Fyrand, Moum, Finset, & Glennas, 2002).

Stress and RA   Stress may play a role both in the development of rheumatoid arthritis and in its aggravation. In particular, disturbances in interpersonal relationships may contribute to the development of the disease (K. O. Anderson, Bradley, Young, McDaniel, & Wise, 1985) and/or its course (Affleck, Tennen, Urrows, & Higgins, 1994; Zautra, Burleson, Matt, Roth, & Burrows, 1994). Increased reactivity to stress and pain may

be increased by the depression felt by RA patients (Zautra & Smith, 2001).

The aggravation of rheumatoid arthritis by stress appears to be mediated by the immune system, inasmuch as those with rheumatoid arthritis show stronger immune responses to stress than do comparison groups (for example, Harrington et al., 1993; Timko, Baumgartner, Moos, & Miller, 1993; Zautra & Smith, 2001). Unfavorable social reactions to people with rheumatoid arthritis may also contribute to disability (McQuade, 2002).

Treatment of RA   Treatments to arrest or control the problems of rheumatoid arthritis include aspirin (which relieves both pain and inflammation), rest, and supervised exercise. Surgery is rarely needed, and hospitalization is necessary only in extreme cases or for extreme pain or flareups. Exercise is strongly recommended for rheumatoid arthritis patients so that they can gain more control over the affected joints (Waggoner & LeLieuvre, 1981). Unfortunately, adherence is often low.

Increasingly, psychologists have used cognitive-behavioral interventions in the treatment of rheumatoid arthritis (McCracken, 1991). In one study (O'Leary, Shoor, Lorig, & Holman, 1988), rheumatoid arthritis patients were randomized into a cognitive-behavioral treatment that taught skills in managing stress, pain, and symptoms of the disease, or they received an arthritis self-help book containing useful information about arthritis self-management. The cognitive-behavioral treatment was designed to increase perceptions of self-efficacy with respect to the disease. Results indicated that patients in the cognitive-behavioral treatment experienced reduced pain and joint inflammation and improved psychosocial functioning. The degree to which people improved was correlated with the degree of self-efficacy enhancement, suggesting that the enhancement of perceived self-efficacy to manage the disease was responsible for the positive effects.

Indeed, because a chief side effect of rheumatoid arthritis is the sense of helplessness over the inability to control the disease and the pain it causes, any intervention that enhances feelings of self-efficacy should have beneficial effects on psychological adjustment (Schiaffino & Revenson, 1992; C. A. Smith & Wallston, 1992). As one patient in such an intervention put it, "I went from thinking about arthritis as a terrible burden that had been thrust upon me to something I could control and manage. I redefined it for myself. It's no longer a tragedy, it's an inconvenience." As this comment also suggests, optimism can lead people to cope more actively with rheumatoid arthritis, improving adjustment over time (Brenner, Melamed, & Panush, 1994). Nonetheless, as is true for all cognitive-behavioral interventions, relapse to old habits is likely; therefore, relapse prevention strategies to preserve both behavioral changes and a sense of self-efficacy and optimism must be an important part of these interventions with rheumatoid arthritis patients (Keefe & Van Horn, 1993).

Overall, cognitive-behavioral interventions, including biofeedback, relaxation training, problem-solving skills, and cognitive pain-coping skills training, have been modestly successful in aiding pain management for rheumatoid arthritis patients. Interventions such as these appear to be modestly successful in improving both joint pain and psychological functioning, although the interventions appear to be more effective for the patients who have had the illness for a shorter period of time (Astin, Beckner, Soeken, Hochberg, & Berman, 2002). Coordinating these cognitive-behavioral interventions with the use of drug therapies to control pain appears to provide the most comprehensive approach at present (Zautra & Manne, 1992).

Juvenile RA   Another form of rheumatoid arthritis is juvenile rheumatoid arthritis. Its causes and symptoms are similar to those of the adult form, but the victims are children between the ages of 2 and 5. Among them, the disease flares up periodically until puberty. The disease is rare and affects girls four times as often as boys. With treatment, most children are managed well and experience few adverse effects. However, there is a juvenile form

of rheumatoid disease that can be severely crippling and can lead to extensive psychological and physical problems for its sufferers, including missed school and participation in few social activities (Billings, Moos, Miller, & Gottlieb, 1987). Social support from family members is also important in helping the juvenile rheumatoid arthritis patient adjust successfully to the disorder.

Osteoarthritis

Osteoarthritis affects an estimated 20.7 million Americans, mostly after age 45. Women are more commonly affected than men (Arthritis Foundation, 2004).

The disorder develops when the smooth lining of a joint, known as the articular cartilage, begins to crack or wear away because of overuse, injury, or other causes. Thus, the disease tends to affect the weight-bearing joints: the hips, knees, and spine. As the cartilage deteriorates, the joint may become inflamed, stiff, and painful. The disease afflicts many elderly people and some athletes. As is true for other forms of arthritis, more serious and extensive symptoms require more aggressive treatment and lead to a poorer quality of life (Hampson, Glasgow, & Zeiss, 1994). Depression may result, and depressive symptoms may in turn elevate pain and distress (Zautra & Smith, 2001).

With proper treatment, osteoarthritis can be managed through self-care. Treatment includes keeping one's weight down and taking aspirin. Exercise is also recommended, although adherence to exercise recommendations is mixed; exercise can initially aggravate the discomfort associated with osteoarthritis, but over time, ameliorate pain and improve physical functioning (Focht, Ewing, Gauvin, & Rejeski, 2002). Occasionally, use of more potent pain relievers, anti-inflammatory drugs, or steroids is needed. Those who manage the pain of osteoarthritis through active coping efforts and spontaneous pain control efforts appear to cope better with the disease (Keefe et al., 1987).

Gout

The third form of arthritis is **gout.** About 1 million Americans suffer from gout, and it is nine times more prevalent in males than in females (National Institute of Arthritis and Musculoskeletal and Skin Diseases, 2002). This condition is caused by a buildup of uric acid in the body due to the kidneys' inability to excrete the acid in the urine. Consequently, the uric acid forms crystals, which may become lodged in the joints.

The area most likely to be affected is the big toe (because the blood supply there is too small to carry away the uric acid crystals). The joint then becomes inflamed, causing severe pain. Occasionally, the uric acid crystals can become lodged in the kidney itself, causing kidney failure.

The exact cause of the buildup of uric acid is unknown. A genetic component is believed to play a role, and the condition can be triggered by stress as well as by certain foods. Other causal factors include infections and some antibiotics and diuretics.

Gout can be managed by limiting the intake of alcohol and certain foods and by maintaining proper weight, exercise, and fluid intake. Aspirin is not used because it slows the removal of uric acid. For severe cases, anti-inflammatory drugs or drugs that control uric acid metabolism may be used. Gout can usually be controlled; when left untreated, however, it can lead to death from kidney disease, high blood pressure, coronary heart disease, or stroke (Kunz, 1982; National Health Education Committee, 1976; Rubenstein & Federman, 1983).

To summarize, arthritis is the second most prevalent chronic disease in the United States. Although it rarely kills its victims, it causes substantial pain and discomfort, creating problems of management. The self-care regimen of arthritis patients centers largely around pain control, dietary control, stress management, and exercise; therefore, the health habits and issues of adherence that we have discussed throughout this book are clearly important in the effective management of arthritis.

SUMMARY

1. The immune system is the surveillance system of the body; it guards against foreign invaders. It involves a number of complex processes, comprising humoral immunity and cell-mediated immunity.

2. Studies suggest that stressors, such as academic exams and stressful interpersonal relationships, can compromise immune functioning.

3. Negative emotions, such as depression or anxiety, may also compromise immune functioning. Coping methods may buffer the immune system against adverse changes due to stress.

4. Studies have evaluated the potential of conditioned immune responses and interventions such as relaxation and stress management as clinical efforts to augment immune functioning in the face of stress.

5. Acquired immune deficiency syndrome (AIDS) was first identified in the United States in 1981. It results from the human immunodeficiency virus (HIV) and is marked by the presence of unusual opportunistic infectious diseases that result when the immune system, especially the helper T cells, has been compromised in its functioning.

6. Gay men and intravenous, needle-sharing drug users have been the primary risk groups for AIDS in the United States. More recently, AIDS has spread rapidly in minority populations, especially among minority women. Heterosexually active adolescents and young adults are also at risk.

7. Primary prevention, in the form of condom use and control of number of partners, is a major avenue for controlling the spread of AIDS. Such interventions focus on providing knowledge, increasing perceived self-efficacy to engage in protective behavior, changing peer norms about sexual practices, and communicating sexual negotiation strategies.

8. Many people live with asymptomatic HIV-seropositivity for years. Exercise and active coping may help prolong this state. Drugs such as protease inhibitors now hold promise for enabling people with HIV and AIDS to live longer, healthier lives.

9. AIDS itself creates a variety of debilitating physical and psychosocial problems. The main psychosocial tasks faced by people diagnosed with AIDS are dealing psychologically with the likelihood of a shortened life, dealing with negative reactions from others, and developing strategies for maintaining physical and emotional health. A variety of interventions have been developed to aid in these tasks.

10. Cancer is a set of more than 100 diseases marked by malfunctioning DNA and rapid cell growth and proliferation. Research investigations have attempted to relate psychosocial factors to the onset and progression of cancer. Helplessness, depression, and repression of emotions may be implicated, especially in the progression of cancer, but as yet the evidence is not definitive.

11. Cancer can produce a range of physical and psychosocial problems, including surgical scarring, the need for prostheses, debilitating responses to chemotherapy, avoidance or rejection by the social network, vocational disruption, and adverse psychological responses such as depression. Behavioral and psychotherapeutic interventions are being used successfully to manage these problems.

12. Arthritis, involving inflammation of the joints, affects about 37 million people in the United States. Rheumatoid arthritis is the most crippling form. Stress appears to exacerbate the disease.

13. Interventions involving cognitive-behavioral techniques to help people manage pain effectively and increase perceptions of self-efficacy have proven helpful in alleviating some of the discomfort and psychosocial difficulties associated with arthritis.

KEY TERMS

acquired immune deficiency
  syndrome (AIDS)
gout

human immunodeficiency virus
  (HIV)
immunocompetence
immunocompromise

osteoarthritis
psychoneuroimmunology
rheumatoid arthritis (RA)

PART 6

Toward the Future

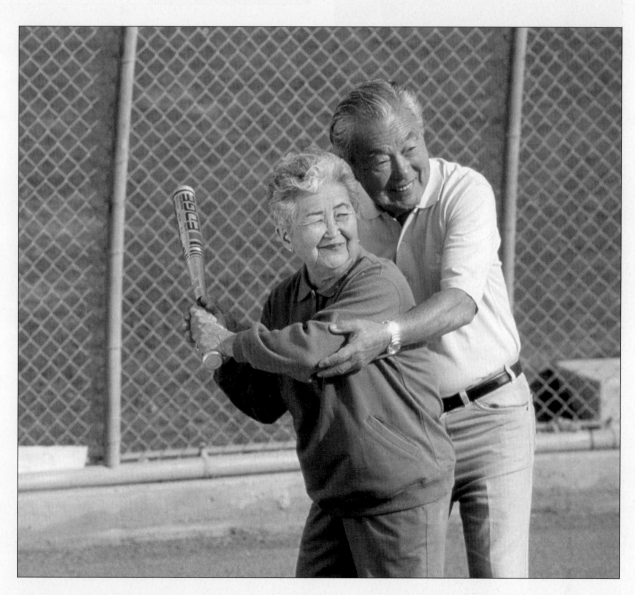

15

Health Psychology: Challenges for the Future

In the past 25 years, health psychology has made dramatic and impressive advances. This last chapter highlights some of the research accomplishments and likely future directions of the field. We then turn to general issues facing health psychology. Some challenges are internal to the discipline and represent coming trends in the research and practice of health psychology. Others are dictated by changes in medicine. As patterns of disease and disorders shift, new causes are identified, and new methods of treatment develop, so inevitably must health psychology change.

■ HEALTH PROMOTION

In recent years, Americans have made substantial gains in altering their poor health habits. Many people have successfully stopped smoking, and many have reduced their consumption of high-cholesterol and high-fat foods. Coronary heart disease and other chronic diseases have shown dramatic decreases as a result. Although alcohol consumption patterns remain largely unchanged, exercise has increased. Despite these advances, overweight and obesity are currently endemic and will shortly take over from smoking as the major avoidable contributor to mortality.

Clearly, most people know that they need to practice good health behaviors and many have tried to develop or change them on their own. Not everyone is successful, however. Thus, the potential for health psychology to make a contribution to health promotion remains.

Increasingly, we will see efforts to identify the most potent and effective elements of behavior-change programs in order to incorporate them into cost-effective, efficient interventions that reach the largest number of people.

In particular, we can expect to see the design of interventions for mass consumption at the community level, the workplace level, and the schools. By reaching people through the institutions in which they live and work and by integrating health behavior–change materials into existing work and community resources, we may reach the goal of modifying the most people's behavior in the most efficient and cost-effective manner.

Focus on Those at Risk

As medical research increasingly identifies genetic and behavioral risk factors for chronic illness, the at-risk role will be increasingly important. Individuals who are identified early as at risk for particular disorders need to learn how to cope with their risk status and how to change their modifiable risk-relevant behaviors. Psychologists can aid substantially in both these tasks.

Studies of people who are at risk for particular disorders are very useful in identifying additional risk factors for various chronic disorders. Not everyone who is at risk for an illness will develop it, and by studying which people do and do not, researchers can identify the further precipitating or promoting factors of these illnesses.

Prevention

Preventing poor health habits from developing will continue to be a priority for health psychology. As noted earlier, adolescence is a window of vulnerability for most bad health habits, and closing this window is of paramount importance. **Behavioral immunization** programs are already in existence for smoking, drug abuse, and, in some cases, diet or eating disorders. Programs that expose fifth and sixth graders to antismoking or antidrug campaigns before they begin these habits appear to be somewhat successful in keeping some adolescents from undertaking such habits. Behavioral immunization for other health habits—including safe sex, condom use, and diet—also holds promise.

For some health habits, we may need to start even earlier and initiate behavioral pediatric programs to teach parents how to reduce the risks of accidents in the home; how to practice good safety habits in automobiles; and how to instill in their children good health habits such as exercise, proper diet, regular immunizations and medical checkups, and regular dental care.

Focus on the Elderly

The rapid aging of the population means that within the next 20 years, we will have the largest elderly cohort ever seen in this and other Western countries. This cohort can be an ill one, placing a drain on medical and psychological services, or it can be a healthy, active one (Koretz, 2000). Interventions should focus on helping the elderly achieve the highest level of functioning possible through programs that emphasize diet, exercise, and other health habits.

Refocusing Health Promotion Efforts

Some refocusing of health promotion efforts is in order. In the past, we have stressed mortality more than morbidity (R. M. Kaplan, 1989). Although the reduction of

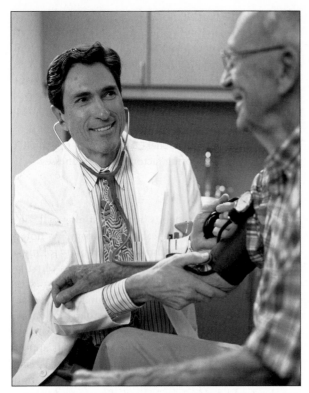

The health needs of the elderly will take on increasing importance with the aging of the population. Helping the elderly achieve a high level of functioning through interventions that emphasize diet, exercise, and other health habits is a high priority for the future.

factor at a time, addressing the difficult issue of continued maintenance, and integrating individual-level interventions with the broader environmental and health policy levels that support and sustain individual efforts (Orleans, 2000).

Promoting Resilience

Future health promotion efforts should place greater weight on positive factors that may reduce morbidity or delay mortality. For example, although eliminating heart disease and cancer would lengthen lives by several years, marriage would add several years to a man's life. As W. J. McGuire (1984) suggested facetiously, health psychologists could make a giant leap forward by going after this health-related factor and opening a marriage bureau. The point is well taken.

Health psychologists have focused most of their research on risk factors for chronic illnesses and have largely ignored the positive experiences that may keep some people from developing these disorders (Ryff & Singer, 1998). Studying how people spontaneously reduce their levels of stress, for example, and how they seek out opportunities for rest, renewal, and relaxation may provide knowledge for effective interventions. Personal resources, such as optimism or a sense of control, may prove to be protective against chronic illness. Can these resources be taught? Recent research suggests that they can (for example, Mann, 2001). The coming decades may explore these and related possibilities.

Promotion as a Part of Medical Practice

A true philosophy of health promotion cannot be adequately implemented until a focus on health promotion becomes an integral part of medical practice (Orleans, 2000). Although some progress in this direction has been made, we are still far away from having a health care system that is oriented toward health promotion.

As noted in chapter 3, there is as yet no formal diagnostic process for identifying and targeting preventive health behaviors on an individual basis. If the annual physical that many people obtain were to include a simple review of the particular health issues and habits that the individual should focus on, this step would, at the very least, alert each of us to the health goals we should consider and would perhaps prod us in the direction of taking necessary action.

Physicians are high in status and tend to be persuasive when other change agents are not. A 28-year-old man in a high-stress occupation might be urged by his

mortality, especially early mortality, is an important priority, there will always be 10 major causes of death (Becker, 1993). Refocusing our effort toward morbidity is important for a number of reasons.

One obvious reason is cost. Chronic diseases are expensive to treat, particularly when those diseases persist for years, even decades. For example, conditions such as rheumatoid arthritis and osteoarthritis have little impact on mortality rates but have a major impact on the functioning and well-being of the population, particularly the elderly population. Keeping people as healthy as possible for as long as possible will help reduce the burden of chronic illness costs. Moreover, maximizing the number of good years during which an individual is free from the burdens of chronic illness produces a higher quality of life.

Priorities for the future include developing interventions that can address more than one behavioral risk health care practitioner to practice stress management, be given a self-help program for stopping smoking, and be reminded to practice testicular self-examination on a regular basis. A young woman who wolfs down a burrito between classes might be given information about the need for a healthy diet and simple steps she can undertake to improve her current diet, such as having a yogurt, fruit, and cereal instead. In the future, we may begin to see practicing physicians integrate prevention into their daily practice with their healthy patients as well as their ill ones.

SES and Health Disparities

But efforts to postpone morbidity and disability into the last years of life will be unsuccessful without attention to our country's large socioeconomic differences in health and health care (Powell, Hoffman, & Shahabi, 2001). One of the most potent risk factors for early disease, disability, and death is low socioeconomic status (SES). From birth throughout life, those of us who are born into the lower social classes experience more and more intense stressors of all kinds, which have a cumulative toll on health risks (Steinbrook, 2004a). Lower income and educational and occupational attainment leads to exposure to a broad array of stressors including inadequate housing, violence, danger, lack of vital goods and services, inadequate medical facilities, poor sanitation, exposure to environmental pollutants, and numerous other hazards (for example, Center for the Advancement of Health, April 2003; Ewart & Suchday, 2002; Grzywacz, Almeida, Neupert, & Ettner, 2004). In contrast, people with higher income and educational attainment have a broad array of psychosocial resources and a lower risk of illnesses and disabilities across the life span (Kubzansky, Berkman, Glass, & Seeman, 1998).

The effect of low SES on poor health is true for both men and women (McDonough, Williams, House, & Duncan, 1999) and at all age levels, although the effect of SES tends to narrow toward the end of life (Beckett, 2000). Among the many risk factors tied to low socioeconomic status are alcohol consumption, high levels of lipids, obesity, tobacco use, and fewer psychosocial resources such as a sense of mastery, self-esteem, and social support. Each of these has an effect on health (J. S. House, 2001; Kubzansky et al., 1998). Low SES is tied to a higher incidence of chronic illness, a heightened risk of low-birth-weight babies and infant mortality, and a heightened risk of accidents among numerous other causes of death and disability (Center for the Advancement of Health, December 2002). In fact, the over-

whelming majority of diseases and disorders show an SES gradient, with poor people experiencing greater risk. Even in the case of diseases that lower- and upper-class individuals are equally likely to develop, such as some cancers, mortality is earlier among the more disadvantaged (Leclere, Rogers, & Peters, 1998). Designing interventions targeted specifically to low SES individuals to modify risk factors associated with social class such as smoking, drug use, alcohol consumption, and consumption of an unhealthy diet need to assume very high priority (for example, Droomers, Schrijivers, & Mackenbach, 2002).

Increasingly, health psychologists are exploring racial differences in health, and the picture is bleak. African Americans have poorer health at all ages and higher levels of depression, hostility, anxiety, and other emotional risk factors for chronic disease (for example, Eaton, Mutaner, Bovasso, & Smith, 2001; Matthews & Grasseau, 1999). The life expectancy gap between African Americans and Whites remains high, at a more than 6-year difference (R. N. Anderson, 2001). African Americans have a higher infant mortality rate than Whites and higher rates of most chronic diseases and disorders, with racial differences especially dramatic for hypertension, HIV, diabetes, and trauma (Wong, Shapiro, Boscardin, & Ettner, 2002). Some of the racial differences in health stems from the fact that African Americans are, on average, lower in socioeconomic status, so they are disproportionately subject to the stressors that accompany low SES. But some of the differences, as was noted in chapter 6, are due to the stresses of racism.

Social Change to Improve Health

Individual health behavior changes alone may not substantially improve the health of the general population. What is needed is individual change coupled with social change. Although the United States spends more on health care than any other country in the world (see figure 15.1), we have neither the longest life expectancy nor the lowest infant mortality rate. As just noted, our political and economic system has produced great disparities in the conditions under which people in the United States live, and many people live in intrinsically unhealthy environments (S. E. Taylor, Repetti, & Seeman, 1997)—that is, environments that threaten safety, undermine the creation of social ties, or are conflictual, abusive, or violent. Many people live in unsafe, high-conflict neighborhoods and thus are exposed to these stressors continually and often unrelentingly (Adler,

FIGURE 15.1 | Comparative Health Spending   (*Source:* Organisation for Economic Cooperation and Development, 2004)

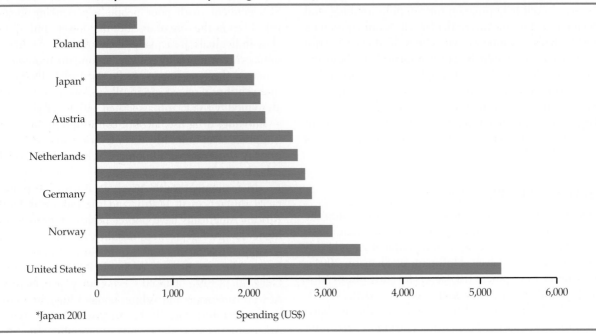

*Japan 2001

Marmot, McEwen, & Stewart, 1999). Social conditions that breed social conflict and lack of control have been tied to the development of coronary heart disease and to indicators of allostatic load, as described in chapter 6. The hostility and depression that may evolve in people living in these chronically stressful environments appear to have health risks as well.

By contrast, healthy environments provide safety, opportunities for social integration, and the chance to experience a sense of personal control over important life tasks. A successful policy of health promotion needs to address not just individual risk but also the social conditions in which they are embedded (Center for the Advancement of Health, June 2003).

Stressful living situations with noise, crowding, and crime take a particular toll on vulnerable populations, such as children, the elderly, and the poor. Increasingly, research must focus on interventions to alleviate the impact of these conditions.

Nor are disparities in health attributable solely to the social conditions in which people live. There are enormous SES and ethnic differences in the delivery of medical treatment as well (Dimsdale, 2000). More than 39 million people under the age of 65 are without health insurance, statistics which include nearly 4.5 million children. These statistics represent more than 16% of the population, and this gap disproportionately affects the poor (National Center for Health Statistics, 2004c). Although Medicaid, instituted in 1965, was designed to help the poor achieve high-quality health care, in many states it has eroded to the point that families with poverty-level incomes are not eligible for benefits. We currently have what is essentially a two-tiered medical system: High-quality and high-technology care go to the well-to-do and not to the poor. Unless the health care available to the poorer segments of society begins to match that available to the wealthier parts of society, morbidity may not be significantly reduced by intervention efforts (J. S. House et al., 1990).

Gender and Health

Another significant gap in health care and research concerns gender (K. A. Matthews, Gump, Block, & Allen, 1997). As one critical article put it, "Women are studied for what distinguishes them from men—their breasts and genitals" (Meyerowitz & Hart, 1993). Thus, for example, breast, ovarian, and other sexual cancers have received substantial attention, but many other disorders have not.

Weak justification for such discrimination has sometimes been based on the fact that women live, on average, 7 years longer than men. But women are sick more than men, and their advantage in mortality has been decreasing in recent years (Rodin & Ickovics, 1990), a trend that appears to be due heavily to women's use of cigarettes. Women are less likely than men to have health insurance, and even if they do, their policies may fail to cover basic medical care, such as Pap smears for the detection of cervical cancer, a standard part of any gynecologic examination. More women are insured through their husbands' jobs than through their own jobs, but because of instability in marriage, coverage for women is irregular. These issues are especially problematic for African-American women (M. H. Meyer & Pavalko, 1996).

Women are not included as research subjects in studies of many major diseases because cyclical variations in hormones are thought to obscure results or because pharmaceutical companies fear lawsuits if experimental drugs have adverse effects on women of child-bearing age, harming fetuses or putting future children at risk (S. E. Taylor et al., 2000). Heart disease research has been based largely on men, and women are often ignored in studies of cancers, except for reproductive cancers. Fewer than half of all new drugs receiving FDA approval between January 1988 and June 1991 were examined for different effects in men and women. Some drugs that are used primarily to treat health problems in women have been tested only on men and male laboratory animals. For example, women with lung cancer respond differently to certain cancer drugs, a fact that goes unnoticed if only men are included in clinical trials (Grady, 2004). Legislation now exists that has helped to reverse this trend (Ezzel, 1993).

It is essential to include women in medical studies for many reasons (K. A. Matthews, Shumaker, et al., 1997). First, women may have different risk factors for major diseases, or existing risk factors may be more or less virulent (Grady, 2004). For example, some research suggests that smoking may be two to three times more hazardous for women than for men (Taubes, 1993). Men and women differ in their biochemistry, and they differ in their physiological reactions to stress (A. Baum & Grunberg, 1991). Consequently, their symptoms may be different, their age of onset for the same diseases may differ, and their reactions to treatment and needed dosage levels of medications may be different. For example, women's risk for coronary heart disease increases greatly following menopause.

Until recently, however, research unearthing these important relationships was not even conducted. Without a systematic investigation of women's health and their particular risk factors, as well as changes in both over the life span, women will simply be treated more poorly than men for the same diseases.

■ STRESS AND ITS MANAGEMENT

Substantial advances in stress research have been made in the past 2 decades. Physiological, cognitive, motivational, and behavioral consequences of stress have been identified. Moreover, the biopsychosocial routes by which stress adversely affects bodily functions and increases the likelihood of illness are increasingly well understood.

Recent attention to stress and inflammatory processes represents a significant knowledge breakthrough of the past few years. Advances have been made in research on environmental and occupational stress. Stressors such as noise or crowding do not show consistently adverse effects but do appear to adversely affect vulnerable populations. Thus, the health needs of children, the elderly, and the poor have taken special priority in the study of stress and its reduction.

Occupational stress researchers have identified many of the job characteristics that are tied to stress such as low control, high demands, and little opportunity for social support. As a consequence, promising workplace interventions have been developed to redesign jobs or reduce on-the-job stressors.

Nonetheless, the demographics of stress may be offsetting whatever concessions can or might be made in the workplace. The majority of American families find that both parents must work in order to make ends meet, yet, like all families, the two-career family must absorb an extra month a year of housework, home activities, and child care. Typically, this extra month a year is taken on by women (Hochschild, 1989). Moreover, increasing numbers of adult children have responsibility for their aging parents, and these responsibilities, too, more frequently fall to women than to men.

These trends put the adult American female population under unprecedented degrees of stress, patterns that may be increasing in other countries as well. One consequence is that women are sick more than men (Verbrugge, 1985, 1990). Additional health and mental health consequences, as well as effective solutions to these dilemmas, have yet to fully emerge.

Where Is Stress Research Headed?

Research should focus on those populations at particular risk for stress-related disorders in an attempt to reduce or offset their stressful circumstances. In theory, knowledge of how people adjust successfully to stressful events can be translated into interventions to help those coping unsuccessfully to cope more successfully.

Many important advances in stress research will come from research on the neurophysiology of stress, particularly the links between stress and corticosteroid functioning, temperamental differences in sympathetic nervous system activity, and factors influencing the release of endogenous opioid peptides and their links to the immune system including inflammatory processes. Through these studies, we may increasingly understand the pathways by which stress exerts adverse effects on health.

One of the most significant advances in stress research is the discovery that social support can buffer stress. For example, intervention studies with disabled, chronically ill, and recovering populations show that social support can have positive effects on both physical and psychological outcomes. These findings suggest that we need to do more to help people draw effectively on this important resource. Helping people build social ties is critical at this time in our social history. The two-job family, coupled with high rates of living alone because of divorce or never marrying, may provide fewer opportunities for building socially supportive networks. Families have fewer children and are less likely to live in extended families, and they may belong to fewer clubs or have fewer long-term opportunities for social contact. Even children, who historically spent many hours with at least one parent, may now see parents less than children once did, instead developing ties with child care workers (cf. Scarr, Phillips, & McCartney, 1989). Fostering social support systems to offset the trends that isolate individuals should be a high priority for prevention.

In addition, we should teach people how to provide support for others. We know that difficult and stressful relationships can adversely affect health and mental health and that positive social relations can protect against those outcomes.

Self-help groups, both real and virtual via the Internet, are possible ways of providing social support for those who otherwise might lack it. Through these formats, people can discuss a common problem with each other and try to help each other work it out. Once oriented primarily around particular illnesses, such as cancer, or particular health problems, such as obesity, these groups are becoming increasingly available for those going through divorce, the loss of a child, and other specific stressful events.

■ HEALTH SERVICES

Health care reform is one of the most urgent issues facing the United States (Clinton, 2004). Our health care system is marked by at least three basic problems: Health care costs too much; the system is grossly inequitable, favoring the wealthy over the poor; and health care consumers use health care services inappropriately (R. M. Kaplan, 1991a).

Building Better Consumers

Decades of research have indicated that people who are ill and those who are treated for illness are frequently not the same individuals. For financial or cultural reasons, many ill people do not find their way into the health care delivery system, and at least two-thirds of people who seek and receive treatment have complaints that are related to distress. Building responsible and informed health care consumers is an especially high priority.

Increasingly, patients need to be involved in their own care, monitoring their symptoms and treatments in partnership with physicians and other health care practitioners. It does little good to diagnose a disorder correctly and prescribe appropriate treatment if the patient cannot or will not follow through on treatment recommendations. Moreover, as preventive health behaviors become increasingly important in the achievement of good health and in secondary prevention with the chronically ill, the fact that 97% of patients fail to adhere properly to lifestyle recommendations takes on added significance.

Trends within medical care suggest that the problem of patient-provider communication is likely to get worse, not better. Increasingly, patients are receiving their medical care through prepaid, colleague-centered services rather than through private, fee-for-service, client-centered practices. As noted in chapters 8 and 9, these structural changes can improve the quality of medical care, but they may sacrifice the quality of communication.

The probability that communication suffers in these settings is strengthened by the fact that the clientele served by prepaid plans is disproportionately poor, poorly educated, and non-English-speaking. Although the well-to-do can pay for emotionally satisfying care, the poor increasingly cannot. Health settings that rob patients of feelings of control can breed anger or depression, motivate people not to return for care, and possibly even contribute to a physiological state conducive to illness or its exacerbation. Thus, there is an expanding role for psychologists in the development and design of health services.

Containing Costs of Health Care

The appropriate use of health services assumes increasing urgency in the context of current changes in its structure, technology, and costs. Medicine is high technology, and high technology is expensive (Callahan, 2003). Although policy makers often assume that patients are driving the development of this technology, in fact, this may not be the case. Most surveys suggest that patients want less, not more, expensive, high-technology treatment, especially in the terminal phase of illness

(Schneiderman, Kronick, Kaplan, Anderson, & Langer, 1992). The increasing use of technology may have more to do with physicians' desire to provide state-of-the-art care.

Deficit financing of federal health care costs has added billions of dollars to the national debt, and the inability of the government to cover the uninsured and the increasing costs of Medicare and Medicaid have contributed to the rapid rise in costs (Kerry & Hofschire, 1993). These factors have prompted the scrutiny of health care by the government in recent years, and the widespread movement in the direction of managed care represents an institutional-level response to try to manage these issues.

Indeed, by far the biggest change in health care that has implications for health psychology is the rapid growth of managed care. Millions of Americans have found that their health insurance has changed as they have been moved into health maintenance organizations (HMOs) and away from more traditional health insurance programs. Many of these HMOs are for-profit organizations, creating an uneasy relationship between business and medicine. Physicians employed by HMOs may not necessarily put their patients' interests first if administrative pressures nudge them in the direction of cost containment. The full ramifications of this unprecedented and rapid switch toward managed care have yet to emerge (Koop, 1996).

■ MANAGEMENT OF SERIOUS ILLNESS

Because chronic illness has become our major health problem, its physical, vocational, social, and psychological consequences have been increasingly recognized. Although a number of specific programs have been initiated to deal with particular problems posed by chronic illness, these efforts are as yet not systematically coordinated or widely available to the majority of chronically ill patients.

Quality-of-Life Assessment

A chief goal for health psychologists in the coming years, then, should be to develop programs to assess quality of life in the chronically ill and to develop cost-effective interventions to improve quality of life. Initial assessment during the acute period is an important first step. In addition, supplementing initial assessment with regular needs assessment over the long term can help identify potential problems, such as anxiety or depression, before they fully disrupt the patient's life and bring about additional costs to the health care system. Because psychosocial states such as depression and hostility affect both the development and exacerbation of chronic disorders, psychological interventions directed to these important cofactors in illness will be a high priority. No intervention that fails to improve psychological functioning is likely to profoundly affect health or survival (B. H. Singer, 2000).

Pain Management

Among the advancements in the treatment of chronic disease is progress in pain management. Recent years have witnessed a shift away from dependence on expensive pharmacologic and invasive surgical pain control techniques to ones that favor cognitive-behavioral methods, such as biofeedback or relaxation. This change has brought about a shift in responsibility for pain control from practitioner to comanagement between patient and practitioner. The enhanced sense of control provided to the chronic pain patient is a treatment advance in its own right, as research on self-efficacy also underscores. The development of pain management programs has been valuable for consolidating what is known about pain control technology.

Psychologists may need to become involved in the ongoing controversies that surround alternative medicine. Increasingly, both the worried well and those with chronic illnesses are treating themselves in nontraditional ways, through herbal medicine, homeopathy, and other untested regimens. What these sources of care do for those who make use of them may be heavily, perhaps primarily, psychological. Psychologists may need to become involved not only in evaluating these alternative medical practices but also in helping develop interventions that will address the psychological needs currently met by these treatments.

Adherence

The management of specific chronic disorders contains both accomplishments and gaps in knowledge. One of the chief remaining tasks is to identify the best ways to gain adherence to multiple treatment goals simultaneously. That is, how does one induce a patient to control diet, alter smoking, manage stress, and get exercise all at the same time? How does one maximize compliance with the often aversive or complex regimens used to treat such diseases as hypertension or diabetes? Finding answers to these questions is one of the challenges of the future.

Terminal Care

The past 20 years have witnessed substantial changes in attitudes toward terminal illness as well. Health psychology research has been both a cause and an effect of these changing attitudes, as clinical health psychologists have turned their attention to the needs of the terminally ill and the gaps in psychological care that still exist.

The appearance of AIDS has added weight to these issues. Following more than a decade of watching thousands of America's talented gay men die in their youth, medical research has now uncovered the promise of longer-term survival in the form of protease inhibitors.

However, the face of AIDS is changing, and it has spread heavily into the poor urban populations of the country, involving many Black and Hispanic men and women. Women are at special risk, and as a result, a growing population of infants is infected with HIV as well. Moreover, these people are less likely to have expensive protease inhibitors available, so their prospects for long-term survival may be low. AIDS is becoming a disease of families, and adequate attention needs to be paid to helping mothers, especially single mothers with HIV, manage their families while coping with their own deteriorating health and to helping the HIV-infected children who will survive their mothers.

With the prevalence of chronic disease increasing and the aging of the population occurring rapidly, ethical issues surrounding death and dying—including assisted suicide, living wills, the patient's right to die, family decision making in death and dying, and euthanasia—will increasingly assume importance. If a beginning resolution to these complex issues cannot be found by medical agencies and allied fields, including health psychology, then the solutions will undoubtedly be imposed externally by the courts.

The Aging of the Population

The substantial shift in the population toward the older years poses a challenge for health psychologists to anticipate what the health problems of the coming decades will be. What kinds of living situations will these increasing numbers of elderly people have, and what kinds of economic resources will they have available to them? How will these resources influence their health habits,

FIGURE 15.2 | Population by Age Group   (*Source: Population Division of the Department of Economic and Social Affairs of the United Nations Secretariat, World Population Prospects: The 2002 Revision and World Urbanization Prospects: The 2001 Revision,* http://esa.un.org/unpp, 20 October 2004)

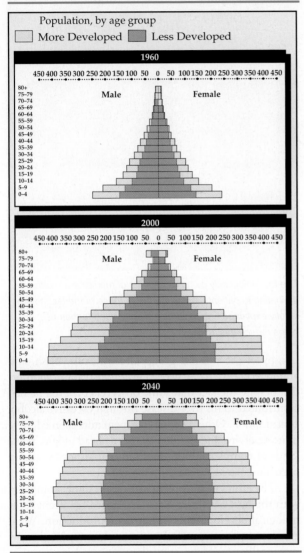

conditions, such as arthritis, osteoporosis, hearing losses, incontinence, and blindness. Some effort to control these disorders must necessarily focus on prevention. For example, the incidence of deafness is rising, attributable in part to the blasting rock music that teenagers in the 1950s and 1960s (who are now in their fifties, sixties, and seventies) listened to. Because rock music is not getting any quieter and because adolescents now go to rock concerts and use headphones as well, prevention of deafness will take on increasing significance in the coming years. This is just one example of the kinds of problems that are created for health psychologists as a result of the shift in age of the population and a shift in leisure-time activities (figure 15.2).

■ TRENDS FOR THE FUTURE

The Changing Nature of Medical Practice

Health psychology is continually responsive to changes in health trends and medical practice. For example, as the population has aged, the significance of prostate cancer as a cause of mortality, especially among older men, has become evident. Understanding the impact of prostate disease on a patient's psychosexual self-concept and on social and emotional functioning is important, especially given that most of the available treatments substantially compromise sexual functioning.

One of the factors that has made health psychology such a vital discipline is that important psychological and social issues are raised by the changing patterns of illness that favor chronic over acute disease; paradoxically, the face of health psychology may change yet again as patterns of infectious disease have altered. Although the past century has brought substantial control over infectious diseases, they remain a public health problem globally and are still responsible for 13 million deaths each year. Moreover, changes in society, technology, and microorganisms themselves are leading to the emergence of new diseases, the reemergence of diseases that were once successfully controlled, and problems with drug-resistant strains of once successfully controlled disorders. Just one example of such an issue is getting people to use antibiotics correctly and not to overuse them (M. L. Cohen, 2000). A bigger role in health psychology may emerge from this important and frightening trend.

As technology has improved, organ donation has become an important issue for health psychologists (Radecki & Jaccard, 1997; Shih et al., 2001). More than

their level of health, and their ability to seek treatment? How can we evaluate and monitor care in residential treatment settings, such as nursing homes, to guard against the risks of maltreatment?

As our population ages, we can expect to see a higher incidence of chronic, but not life-threatening

88,166 people are currently waiting for donor organs, a statistic that does not include all of those who could profit from such intervention (United Network for Organs Sharing Bulletin, 1996). The shortage of donor organs suggests that this may be an area in which health psychologists could be increasingly helpful. Psychologists can help people discuss their wishes for organ donation with family and help people make the decision of whether to sign donor cards (Burroughs, Hong, Kappel, & Freedman, 1998). There appears to be a gap in that many people who are willing in theory to donate their organs have not yet made a commitment to do so. Psychologists may be able to facilitate this process (Amir & Haskell, 1997).

Another example of a medical trend that has fueled research and debate within health psychology is the increasing availability of risk factor testing for a variety of relatively common disorders. Tests are now available, or will shortly be available, on a widespread basis for identifying genes implicated in such diseases as Huntington's disease, breast cancer, and colon cancer (for example, V. A. McKusick, 1993), yet our understanding of how people deal psychologically with the knowledge that they possess a gene or another risk factor that may ultimately lead to fatal disease is scanty.

A handful of prescient health psychologists (for example, Croyle & Lerman, 1993) have begun to explore why some people fail to minimize their risk on learning that they may be vulnerable, as opposed to becoming more vigilant by taking effective preventive action or monitoring themselves more closely. But much of this work continues to be conducted in the laboratory on hypothetical risk factors, and more understanding of how people manage their risk is essential.

Impact of Technology Technological advances in medicine have contributed greatly to the enormous costs of contemporary medicine (Reinhardt, 2004). These complex aspects of medicine itself also are often daunting for many patients. Explaining the purposes of these technologies and using control-enhancing interventions to enable people to feel like active participants in their treatment can help reduce fear. The growth of medical technology also raises complex questions about how it should be used. Consider transplantation. At present, insufficient numbers of transplantable organs are available; consequently, how to increase the supply of transplantable organs and how to develop priorities as to who should receive transplants have been highly controversial issues (Singh, Katz, Beauchamp, & Hannon, 2002). David

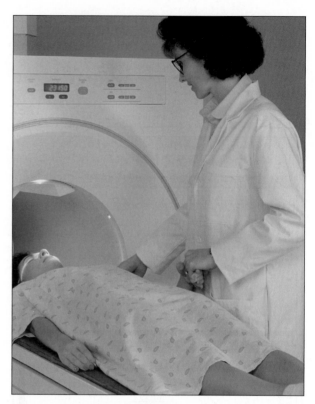

The technologically complex aspects of medicine are often intimidating to patients, but when the purpose of the technology is fully explained and patients are committed to their use, it helps reduce this anxiety.

Crosby of the musical group Crosby, Stills, Nash, and Young received a badly needed liver transplant in short order, despite the fact that some observers believed he had contributed to his liver disease through excessive alcohol consumption. Other people, commentators claimed, were more deserving and should have been ahead in line. These kinds of complex ethical questions could not even have been anticipated a mere 20 years ago.

The ethics of transplantation seem tame, compared with the host of ethical questions raised by recent technological developments in human reproduction. What are the implications of cloning for humans? It is now technically possible to transplant eggs and even ovaries from aborted female fetuses into women who have been unable to conceive a child on their own (Kolata, 1994). What are the ethics of using one life to create another? What psychosocial issues are raised by these dilemmas? As a science, health psychology must begin to anticipate many of these controversial issues to help provide a blueprint for considering the psychosocial and ethical issues that will arise.

FIGURE 15.3 | Continuum of Care and Types and Levels of Intervention   (*Source:* D. B. Abrams et al., 1996)

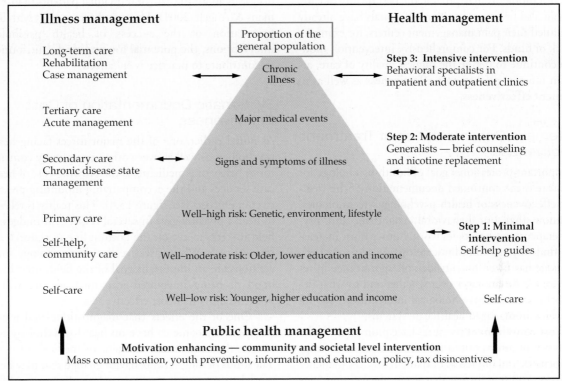

As medical care has grown more technologically complex, it has also, paradoxically, begun to incorporate psychological and spiritual sides of healing, especially those approaches that draw on Eastern healing traditions. Relaxation and other nontraditional treatment methods are a boon to HMOs because those methods are typically low cost and yet can be remarkably effective for treating stress-related disorders, including such severely problematic conditions as hypertension.

Comprehensive Intervention   Another trend within medicine that affects health psychology is the movement toward **comprehensive intervention models**. There are several models that concentrate and coordinate medical and psychological expertise in well-defined areas of medical practice. One is the pain management program, in which all available treatments for pain have been brought together so that individual regimens can be developed for each patient. A second model is the hospice, in which palliative management technologies and psychotherapeutic technologies are available to

the dying patient. Coordinated residential and outpatient rehabilitation programs for coronary heart disease patients, in which multiple health habits are dealt with simultaneously, constitute a third example. Similar interventions for other chronic diseases, such as cancer and AIDS, may be developed in the coming years.

Most comprehensive intervention models thus far have been geared to specific diseases or disorders, but, increasingly, researchers are urging that this model be employed for concerted attacks on risk factors as well (for example, D. B. Abrams et al., 1996). Making use of the mass media, youth prevention projects, educational interventions, social engineering solutions, and tax solutions to such problems as smoking, excessive alcohol consumption, and drug abuse, for example, may represent badly needed supplements to programs that currently focus primarily on health risks that are already in place. The coordination of public health management at the institutional and community levels, with individual health management and illness management for those already ill, is represented in figure 15.3.

Although comprehensive interventions for particular health problems may provide the best quality of care, they can also be expensive. Some hospitals have already dismantled their pain management centers, for example, for lack of funds. For comprehensive intervention models to continue to define the highest quality of care, attention must be paid to **cost effectiveness** as well as to **treatment effectiveness**.

Systematic Documentation of Treatment Effectiveness

An important professional goal of health psychology for the future is the continued documentation of the treatment effectiveness of health psychology's technologies. We know that our behavioral, cognitive, and psychotherapeutic technologies work, but we must increasingly find ways to communicate this success to others. This issue has taken on considerable significance in recent years as debate rages over whether and to what degree behavioral and psychological interventions should be covered in managed health care systems.

Cost containment pressures have prompted the development of interventions that are time limited, symptom focused, and offered as outpatient services (Sanchez & Turner, 2003), a format that is not always conducive to change through behavioral intervention. Moreover, this has been accompanied by a shift in treatment decision-making power from behavioral health care providers to policy makers. These changes affect health psychology in several ways. A lack of empirical data regarding treatment outcomes and efficacy represents a striking gap in how behavioral scientists and practitioners present their interventions to policy makers (Sanchez & Turner, 2003). This gap occurs, in part, because behavioral scientists may fail to recognize or document the treatment implications of their work and because practitioners may lack the interest or expertise to conduct the formal scientific investigations that would make the scientific case for their interventions. Continued training of health psychologists in both the science and practice aspects of health psychology is clearly needed (Center for the Advancement of Health, 2001). Developing convincing methods of measuring successful psychosocial interventions is of paramount importance.

The potential for health psychology to make major contributions to medicine and medical practice has never been greater. **Evidence-based medicine** is now the criterion for adopting medical standards. Evidence-based medicine refers to the conscientious, explicit, judicious use of the best scientific evidence for making decisions about the care of individual patients (Timmermans & Angell, 2001). This trend means that, with documentation of the success of health psychology interventions, the potential for empirical contributions to contribute to practice is enhanced.

Systematic Documentation of Cost Effectiveness

As noted earlier, one of the major forces facing health psychology, as well as every other disciplinary contributor to behavioral medicine, is the growing cost of health care services and the accompanying mounting pressure to contain costs (see figure 15.4). This reality is relevant to health psychologists in several respects. It nudges the field to keep an eye on the bottom line in research and intervention. While effective health psychology interventions are an important goal of the field, their likelihood of being integrated into medical care will be influenced by their cost effectiveness.

One of the effects that diagnostic-related groups (DRGs) may come to have on health psychology is to restrict the behavioral treatment of medical disorders. The kinds of long-term behavior change that may be essential to treatment success, such as dietary modification, smoking cessation, and exercise prescriptions for cardiac patients, may fall outside the time period specified in the DRG treatment guidelines (see chapter 9). Moreover, because DRGs require nonphysician expenses to be bundled together, psychologists are often not able to bill separately for services. Consequently, any long-term behavior-change programs must be initiated and followed through only within the time period of the DRG. The incentive to include psychologists in care, then, exists only to the extent that such services can reduce length of stay and increase profitability.

Subtly, the pressures of cost containment push the health psychology field in the direction of research that is designed to keep people out of the health care system altogether. On the clinical practice side, interventions include self-help groups, peer counseling, self-management programs (for example, Kirschenbaum, Sherman, & Penrod, 1987), and other inexpensive ways to provide services to those who might otherwise not receive care. Writing about intensely traumatic or stressful events is also a low-cost, easily implemented intervention that has demonstrated beneficial effects (for example, Ullrich & Lutgendorf, 2002). Another example is the stress reduction and pain amelioration benefits that can be achieved

FIGURE 15.4 | National Health Care Expenditures: Selected Calendar Years, 1990–2013* (*Source:* Centers for Medicare and Medicaid Services, Office of the Actuary, 2004)

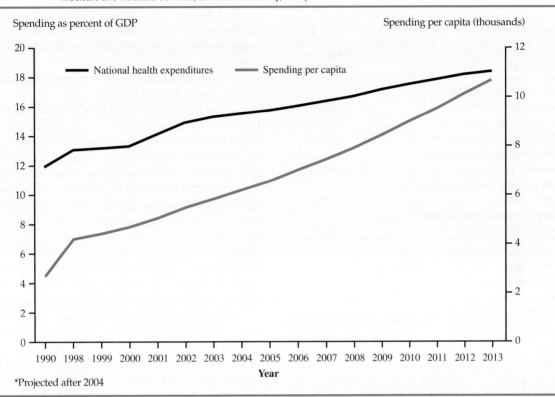

by simple, inexpensive techniques of relaxation and other cognitive-behavioral interventions (Blanchard et al., 1988).

There are benefits and risks to the formidable role that economic factors play in the field of health psychology. On the one hand, the field cannot afford to pursue its scientific and clinical mission without regard to cost. On the other hand, cost-containment issues can compromise scientific and intervention missions of the field by prematurely choking off areas of inquiry that do not immediately appear to be cost-effective. The relative lack of attention to issues of rehabilitation in contrast to the heavy preponderance of research in primary prevention activities can be regarded as one casualty of these pressures.

Documenting Savings   Many interventions have the potential to save substantial funds and other resources, and documenting this fact should increasingly be a high priority. Interventions designed to enhance

feelings of control among patients awaiting unpleasant medical procedures have clear cost-saving benefits. As noted in chapter 8, these interventions can lead patients to require less medication, make fewer complaints, demand less staff time, and leave the hospital early. The monetary gains of these cost-saving measures versus the minimal costs incurred (the time and personnel necessary to provide patients with information) are substantial.

Similarly, training practitioners in effective communication improves patient satisfaction with medical care, can enhance adherence, and may reduce malpractice litigation. The savings to health institutions that could be gained by this training have yet to be systematically documented. Similar documentation of the cost effectiveness of other health psychology interventions can and should be developed in other areas so that these interventions may be judged as successful not only on their own merits but also on cost-saving grounds.

In addition, health psychology could help develop interventions to save costs. For example, finding ways of

TABLE 15.1 | The Bottom Line

This chart shows the reduction in frequency of treatments as a result of various clinical behavioral medicine interventions.

Treatment	Frequency Reduction
Total ambulatory care visits	−17%
Visits for minor illnesses	−35%
Pediatric acute illness visits	−25%
Office visits for acute asthma	−49%
Office visits by arthritis patients	−40%
Cesarean sections	−56%
Epidural anesthesia during labor and delivery	−85%
Average hospital length of stay for surgical patients (in days)	−1.5

Source: American Psychological Society, 1996.

identifying and drawing off the two thirds of patients whose medical complaints are believed to be primarily of psychological origin would save the health care delivery system billions of dollars yearly and would direct these people more appropriately into psychological services (R. M. Kaplan, 1991b). Table 15.1 shows the reduction in health care visits that can occur as a result of health psychology interventions.

It is unlikely that health psychology will be able to achieve these gains on its own. Moreover, to the extent that the health psychology endeavor is focused only in departments of psychology, it runs the risk of becoming an ivory tower endeavor that is divorced from medical care. The integration of health psychology into the medical curriculum; the development of departments of behavioral medicine within traditional medical schools (Agras, 1992; S. Williams & Kohout, 1999); and the integration of behavioral medicine into health care institutions, such as hospitals and clinics, are important ways of ensuring that advances in health psychology can have an impact on patient care and health care policy (Carmody & Matarazzo, 1991).

International Health

There is also an important role for health psychologists in international health. Disease prevalence varies greatly by country. Poverty, lack of education, and lack of health care resources contribute to a high incidence of acute infectious disease, for example. As smoking has begun to decline in the United States, its incidence is rising in many developing countries. Whereas Americans are beginning to exercise more, countries that are becoming modernized are losing the exercise benefits that accompanied a less sedentary lifestyle.

There is a role for health psychology in carrying the hard-won lessons of the past few decades in the United States to countries in which exactly the same problems are now beginning to emerge. Moreover, psychologists and other behavioral scientists are more likely than people in traditional medical disciplines to understand the significance of varying cultural norms and expectations, how social institutions function, and the roles that culturally specific attitudes and behaviors may play in health care practices and decisions (Jenkins, 1990b). In the battle for a high level of international health care, then, the health psychologist appears to be well positioned to make a substantial and lasting contribution.

Foretelling the future is never an easy task. Some trends, such as the aging of the population, are obvious and have clear implications for the field. Others are not so easily anticipated; thus their implications for health psychology are still elusive.

■ BECOMING A HEALTH PSYCHOLOGIST

If, after reading this textbook and taking a course in health psychology, you think you want to pursue a career in this field, what would you need to do?

Undergraduate Experience

As an undergraduate interested in continuing in health psychology, you would be wise to do several things. First, try to take all the health psychology courses that you can at your undergraduate institution. These courses might include topics such as health habits, wellness, and stress and coping. Second, develop a broad background in psychology by sampling heavily from the many courses available to you. Take courses in physiological psychology, neuroscience, or human physiology, if they are offered at your school. Understanding the biological underpinnings of health psychology is critical to going into the field.

Use your summers effectively. Find a psychologist who does research in health psychology, and see if you can get a research assistantship. Volunteer if you have to. Acquiring research experience is the best preparation you can get. Of course, such positions are hard to obtain and may not be available where you are.

You can look for summer employment opportunities in a medical school or hospital, which might give you patient contact or contact with medical care providers. If you are a candy striper or an aide, ask lots of questions. Find out why the nurses are doing what they're doing and why the doctors are recommending particular treatments. Find out why one patient is going to physical therapy while another is obtaining relaxation treatments.

Or you might try to find a health maintenance organization or another managed care program that has learning opportunities. Even if you are involved only in paperwork, find out how the organization works. What kinds of patients does it see? In what areas are its costs higher than it would like, and how is the organization trying to reduce costs? Whatever position you undertake, ask a lot of questions.

As a college student, you may not be able to get the position of status or responsibility that you would like to have, but you can make the most of the position if you use it as the learning opportunity it can be.

Graduate Experience

If, after additional coursework and summer experiences, you decide you want to go on in health psychology, you will need to acquire a Ph.D. At this point, you should decide whether your interests lie chiefly in research investigations, chiefly in clinical practice (that is, direct contact with individual patients), or both.

If your interest is in research, what kind of research excites you the most? Is it the study of the biology of infection or transmission? Is it the understanding of how social support affects health? Is it research on increasing exercise or changing diet? Try to define your interests as clearly as possible because you may need to select a subfield of psychology to go into. Your choices are likely to be physiological psychology, where you will focus heavily on the biology and neurological aspects of health psychology; social psychology, which examines social and psychological processes in adopting preventive health behaviors, managing stress, and coping with chronic dis-

ease, among other issues; clinical health psychology, in which patient contact will be one of your primary tasks; or developmental psychology, in which you will look especially at the health of children and the factors that affect it. A few health psychology programs around the country do not require you to declare a subspecialty when you apply, but many do.

During your 4 years in graduate school, if your interests are even partly in research, you will need to take courses in research methodology and statistics. You may take a course in epidemiology, as many health psychologists do, a course that would probably be taught in a school of public health. Most important, get practical experience. Work with a health psychologist on several research or clinical projects. Try to get into the field so that you gain experience not just in a university laboratory but also in a hospital, a clinic, or another health care delivery situation.

Look for opportunities to get practical hands-on field experience. If you're interested in exercise, for example, go to a fitness center. If you want to understand how people cope with AIDS, help out at your local volunteer organization that delivers food or other essentials to people with AIDS. If you're interested in aging, go to senior citizen centers or other facilities for the elderly. Research training under the guidance of a skilled health psychologist is essential, but there is no substitute for the practical experience and insight that you acquire when you are doing work in the field.

If you are interested in patient contact and apply to a clinical psychology program, you will be expected to take the standard clinical curriculum, which includes courses and practica addressing major mental disorders and community intervention and therapy, including cognitive-behavior therapy. Your patient contact not only will involve people with medical problems but also will be heavily geared toward people with depression, obsessive-compulsive disorder, anxiety problems, or behavioral problems. You will be expected to complete a year's internship in a field setting, so if your interests are in health, you should try for a field setting in a medical hospital, medical clinic, or health maintenance organization that gives you direct patient contact.

During the course of your graduate training, you will be involved in a number of projects, and at the time of your dissertation, you will be expected to mount a major research project on your own. By this time, you will have a clear idea of what your interests are and can pursue a health-related project in depth. This project will take you a year or more to complete.

On completion of the dissertation and the receipt of the Ph.D., you have several options: If your plan is to go into clinical psychology, you may want to find a clinical setting in which you can get practical expertise in addition to that acquired during your internship. This training, coupled with your internship and coursework, should put you in a good position for getting licensed in the state in which you choose to practice. You will be expected to take several hours of licensure exams, the exact form of which varies from state to state; on receipt of your license, you will be able to practice clinical psychology.

Postgraduate Work

Following graduate school, you can go on the job market, or you can get additional training in the form of a postdoctoral research opportunity. Many health psychologists choose to acquire postdoctoral training, because, at the present, health psychology training is not uniform across universities. You may, for example, receive excellent instruction in stress and coping processes, for example, but be poorly informed about health habits. Or your program may provide you with lots of patient contact but very little in the way of training in neuroscience.

You may decide that you want to concentrate on a particular disease, such as cancer or heart disease, but have insufficient knowledge about the risk factors and physiology of the illness for your research to be well informed. Identifying the gaps in your training reveals the type of postdoctoral training you should seek out.

Typically, postdoctoral training is undertaken at a laboratory different from the place at which you completed your Ph.D. and takes place under the guidance of a senior scientist whose work you admire. You spend a year or 2 in this individual's lab, after which you are ready to go on the job market.

Employment

What kinds of jobs do health psychologists obtain? Table 15.2 shows where health psychologists most typically work. About 45% of health psychologists go into academic settings or teach in medical schools (American Psychological Association, 1996; Williams & Kohout, 1999). In academic positions, health psychologists are responsible

TABLE 15.2 | Where Do Health Psychologists Work?

Colleges and universities	24.9%
Medical schools	15.9
Other academic settings	3.0
Schools and other educational settings	1.0
Independent practice	27.4
Hospitals and clinics	17.4
Other	11.0

Source: American Psychological Association, 1996.

for educating undergraduate as well as graduate students, physicians, nurses, and other health care workers.

Most health psychologists in academic settings also conduct research programs to try to uncover the factors associated with the maintenance of health and the onset of illness. The preceding chapters attest to the breadth of research topics that health psychologists address.

About 35% of health psychologists work with medical patients in a hospital or another treatment setting. Many health psychologists, about 28%, are involved in private practice, in which they provide therapy and other mental health services to people with medically related problems. These health psychologists often deal individually with patients who need help managing their health problems. The short-term cognitive-behavioral interventions that work well in modifying health habits, controlling pain, managing side effects of treatments, and the like represent the kind of activities that health psychologists in these settings undertake. For example, a clinician might initiate individual psychotherapy to help a cancer patient recover from bouts of depression. Another clinician may work with family members to set up a self-care treatment regimen for an adolescent recently diagnosed with diabetes (see Belar, 1997).

Increasingly, health psychologists are employed in the workplace (Keita & Jones, 1990) or as consultants to the workplace. They advise employers attempting to set up new health care systems about what kind of system will provide the best care for the least money. They establish work-site interventions to teach employees how to manage stress, they set up exercise programs, or they establish work-site competitions to help overweight employees lose weight. Health psychologists consult with governmental agencies on how to reduce health care costs. They advise health care services about how to improve patient satisfaction or reduce inappropriate use of health services. In short, health psychologists deliver a wide range of services to an ever-growing and diverse group of employers, as table 15.2 indicates.

The number of health psychologists in the United States and other countries is growing rapidly. Since the beginning of the field approximately 20 years ago, the number of health psychology training programs in the country has also grown exponentially. Health psychologists have proven vital to medical research and health services delivery in this country. The opportunities for the fledgling health psychologist are boundless, as table 15.3 indicates.

TABLE 15.3 | What Do Health Psychologists Do?

Research	57.1%
Education	58.6
Health/mental health services	71.5
Educational services	20.9
Management/administration	20.4
Other	36.6

Source: American Psychological Association, 1996.

SUMMARY

1. Health psychology research and practice have identified the complexity of faulty health habits and how best to modify them. Health promotion priorities for the future include the modification of the most consequential risk factors, incorporation of the most potent and effective elements of behavior-change programs into cost-effective interventions, and the continuing search for the best venue for intervention.

2. Health psychology interventions will continue to focus on people at risk for particular disorders, on preventing poor health habits from developing, and on developing effective health promotion interventions with the elderly. Health promotion efforts must consider not only mortality but also the reduction of morbidity and the importance of enhancing overall quality of life.

3. As medicine develops a health promotion orientation, the potential for collaborative interventions between psychologists and medical practitioners through the media, the community, and the physician's office may come to be more fully realized.

4. An effective health promotion program must involve not only health behavior change but also social change that makes high-quality health care available to all elements of the population, especially those low in SES.

5. Research on stress will continue to focus on vulnerable populations and on trends in the economy and culture that increase the stress on particular subpopulations, such as children, the elderly, and the poor.

6. In the future, many important advances in stress research will likely come from research examining the pathways by which stress exerts adverse effects on health.

7. The appropriate use of health services is an important target for the future. Communication issues are important for reducing health costs that relate to improper use of services, initiation of malpractice litigation, and failure to adhere appropriately to medication and lifestyle recommendations.

8. The management of chronic illness will increasingly focus on quality of life and appropriate ways to measure it. The management of terminal illness will increasingly focus on ways of enabling people to die physically and psychologically comfortable deaths. In addition, ethical issues involving assisted suicide, living wills, the patient's right to die, family decision making in death and dying, and euthanasia will continue to be prominent.

9. A target for future work is identification of the health and lifestyle issues that will be created by the aging of the population. Anticipating medical disorders and developing interventions to offset their potential adverse effects should be targets for research now.

10. Health psychology needs to be responsive to changes in medical practice, including changes in disease demographics (such as age). The changing face of medicine creates challenges for health psychologists in anticipating the impact of technologically complex interventions and helping prepare patients for them.

11. Important goals for health psychology's future are systematic documentation of treatment effectiveness using the criteria of evidence-based medicine, systematic documentation of the cost effectiveness of interventions, and continued efforts to find ways to reduce health costs. In addition, there is an emerging and important role for health psychologists in the international health care arena.

12. Health psychology can be a rewarding career for anyone willing to gain the necessary education and research and field experience.

KEY TERMS

behavioral immunization	cost containment	evidence-based medicine
comprehensive intervention models	cost effectiveness	treatment effectiveness

abstinence violation effect A feeling of loss of control that results when one has violated self-imposed rules, such as not to smoke or drink.

acquired immune deficiency syndrome (AIDS) Progressive impairment of the immune system by the human immunodeficiency virus (HIV); a diagnosis of AIDS is made on the basis of the presence of one or more specific opportunistic infections.

acupuncture A technique of healing and pain control, developed in China, in which long, thin needles are inserted into designated areas of the body to reduce discomfort in a target area of the body.

acute disorders Illnesses or other medical problems that occur over a short period of time, that are usually the result of an infectious process, and that are reversible.

acute pain Short-term pain that usually results from a specific injury.

acute stress paradigm A laboratory procedure whereby an individual goes through moderately stressful procedures (such as counting backwards rapidly by 7s), so that stress-related changes in emotions and physiological and/or neuroendocrine processes may be assessed.

addiction The state of physical or psychological dependence on a substance that develops when that substance is used over a period of time.

adherence The degree to which an individual follows a recommended health-related or illness-related recommendation.

adrenal glands Two small glands, located on top of the kidneys, that are part of the endocrine system and secrete several hormones, including cortisol, epinephrine, and norepinephrine, that are involved in responses to stress.

aerobic exercise High-intensity, long-duration, and high-endurance exercise, believed to contribute to cardiovascular fitness and other positive health outcomes. Examples are jogging, bicycling, running, and swimming.

aftereffects of stress Performance and attentional decrements that occur after a stressful event has subsided; believed to be produced by the residual physiological, emotional, and cognitive draining in response to stressful events.

alcoholism The state of physical addiction to alcohol that manifests through such symptoms as stereotyped drinking, drinking to maintain blood alcohol at a particular level, increasing frequency and severity of withdrawal, drinking early in the day and in the middle of the night, a sense of loss of control over drinking, or a subjective craving for alcohol.

allostatic load The accumulating adverse effects of stress, in conjunction with preexisting risks, on biological stress regulatory systems.

angina pectoris Chest pain that occurs because the muscle tissue of the heart is deprived of adequate oxygen or because removal of carbon dioxide and other wastes interferes with the flow of blood and oxygen to the heart.

anorexia nervosa A condition produced by excessive dieting and exercise that yields body weight grossly below optimal level, most common among adolescent girls.

appraisal delay The time between recognizing that a symptom exists and deciding that it is serious.

assertiveness training Techniques that train people how to be appropriately assertive in social situations; often included as part of health behavior modification programs, on the assumption that some poor health habits, such as excessive alcohol consumption or smoking, develop in part to control difficulties in being appropriately assertive.

atherosclerosis A major cause of heart disease; caused by the narrowing of the arterial walls due to the formation of plaques that reduce the flow of blood through the arteries and interfere with the passage of nutrients from the capillaries into the cells.

at risk A state of vulnerability to a particular health problem by virtue of heredity, health practices, or family environment.

autoimmunity A condition in which the body produces an immune response against its own tissue constituents.

avoidant (minimizing) coping style The tendency to cope with threatening events by withdrawing, minimizing, or avoiding them; believed to be an effective short-term, though not an effective long-term, response to stress.

behavioral assignments Home practice activities that clients perform on their own as part of an integrated therapeutic intervention for behavior modification.

behavioral delay The time between deciding to seek treatment and actually doing so.

behavioral immunization Programs designed to inoculate people against adverse health habits by exposing them to mild versions of persuasive communications that try to engage them in a poor health practice and giving them techniques that they can use to respond effectively to these efforts.

behavioral inoculation See **behavioral immunization.**

biofeedback A method whereby an individual is provided with ongoing, specific information or feedback about how a

437

particular physiological process operates, so that he or she can learn how to modify that process.

biomedical model   The viewpoint that illness can be explained on the basis of aberrant somatic processes and that psychological and social processes are largely independent of the disease process; the dominant model in medical practice until recently.

biopsychosocial model   The view that biological, psychological, and social factors are all involved in any given state of health or illness.

blood pressure   The force that blood exerts against vessel walls.

body image   The perception and evaluation of one's body, one's physical functioning, and one's appearance.

breast self-examination (BSE)   The monthly practice of checking the breasts to detect alterations in the underlying tissue; a chief method of detecting breast cancer.

broad-spectrum cognitive-behavior therapy   The use of a broad array of cognitive-behavioral intervention techniques to modify an individual's health behavior.

buffering hypothesis   The hypothesis that coping resources are useful primarily under conditions of high stress and not necessarily under conditions of low stress.

bulimia   An eating syndrome characterized by alternating cycles of binge eating and purging through such techniques as vomiting or extreme dieting.

cardiac invalidism   A psychological state that can result after a myocardial infarction or diagnosis of coronary heart disease, consisting of the perception that a patient's abilities and capacities are lower than they actually are; both patients and their spouses are vulnerable to these misperceptions.

cardiac rehabilitation   An intervention program designed to help heart patients achieve their optimal physical, medical, psychological, social, emotional, vocational, and economic status after the diagnosis of heart disease or a heart attack.

cardiopulmonary resuscitation (CPR)   A method of reviving the functioning of heart and lungs after a loss of consciousness in which the patient's pulse has ceased or lungs have failed to function appropriately.

cardiovascular system   The transport system of the body responsible for carrying oxygen and nutrients to the body and carrying away carbon dioxide and other wastes to the kidneys for excretion; composed of the heart, blood vessels, and blood.

catecholamines   The neurotransmitters, epinephrine and norepinephrine, that promote sympathetic nervous system activity; released in substantial quantities during stressful times.

cell-mediated immunity   Slow acting immune response, involving T lymphocytes, that operates at the cellular level.

cerebellum   The part of the hindbrain responsible for the coordination of voluntary muscle movement, the maintenance of balance and equilibrium, and the maintenance of muscle tone and posture.

cerebral cortex   The main portion of the brain, responsible for intelligence, memory, and the detection and interpretation of sensation.

chronic benign pain   Pain that typically persists for 6 months or longer and is relatively intractable to treatment. The pain varies in severity and may involve any of a number of muscle groups. Chronic low back pain and myofascial pain syndrome are examples.

chronic illnesses   Illnesses that are long lasting and usually irreversible.

chronic pain   Pain that may begin after an injury but which does not respond to treatment and persists over time.

chronic progressive pain   Pain that persists longer than 6 months and increases in severity over time. Typically, it is associated with malignancies or degenerative disorders, such as skeletal metastatic disease or rheumatoid arthritis.

chronic strain   A stressful experience that is a usual but continually stressful aspect of life.

classical conditioning   The pairing of a stimulus with an unconditioned reflex, such that over time the new stimulus acquires a conditioned response, evoking the same behavior; the process by which an automatic response is conditioned to a new stimulus.

clinical thanatology   The clinical practice of counseling people who are dying on the basis of knowledge of reactions to dying.

cognitive-behavior therapy   The use of principles from learning theory to modify the cognitions and behaviors associated with a behavior to be modified; cognitive-behavioral approaches are used to modify poor health habits, such as smoking, poor diet, and alcoholism.

cognitive costs   An approach to the study of stress that emphasizes how stressful events tax perceptual and cognitive resources, draw off attention, or deplete cognitive resources for other tasks.

cognitive restructuring   A method of modifying internal monologues in stress-producing situations; clients are trained to monitor what they say to themselves in stress-provoking situations and then to modify their cognitions in adaptive ways.

comprehensive intervention model   A model that pools and coordinates the medical and psychological expertise in a well-defined area of medical practice so as to make all available technology and expertise available to a patient; the pain management program is one example of a comprehensive intervention model.

confrontative (vigilant) coping style   The tendency to cope with stressful events by tackling them directly and attempting to develop solutions; may ultimately be an especially effective method of coping, although it may produce accompanying distress.

contingency contracting   A procedure in which an individual forms a contract with another person, such as a therapist, detailing what rewards or punishments are contingent on the performance or nonperformance of a target behavior.

control-enhancing interventions   Interventions with patients who are awaiting treatment for the purpose of enhancing their perceptions of control over those treatments.

conversion hysteria   The viewpoint, originally advanced by Freud, that specific unconscious conflicts can produce physical disturbances symbolic of the repressed conflict; no longer a dominant viewpoint in health psychology.

coping   The process of trying to manage demands that are appraised as taxing or exceeding one's resources.

coping outcomes   The beneficial effects that are thought to result from successful coping; these include reducing stress, adjusting more successfully to it, maintaining emotional equilibrium, having satisfying relationships with others, and maintaining a positive self-image.

coping style   An individual's preferred method of dealing with stressful situations.

coronary heart disease (CHD)   A general term referring to illnesses caused by atherosclerosis, which is the narrowing of the coronary arteries, the vessels that supply the heart with blood.

correlational research   Measuring two variables and determining whether they are associated with each other. Studies relating smoking to lung cancer are correlational, for example.

cost containment   The effort to reduce or hold down health care costs.

cost effectiveness   The formal evaluation of the effectiveness of an intervention relative to its cost and the cost of alternative interventions.

counterirritation   A pain control technique that involves inhibiting pain in one part of the body by stimulating or mildly irritating another area, sometimes adjacent to the area in which the pain is experienced.

covert self-control   The manipulation and alteration of private events, such as thoughts, through principles of reinforcement and self-instruction.

craving   A strong desire to engage in a behavior or consume a substance, such as alcohol or tobacco, which appears, in part, to occur through the conditioning of physical dependence on environmental cues associated with the behavior.

creative nonadherence   The modification or supplementation of a prescribed treatment regimen on the basis of privately held theories about the disorder or its treatment.

curative care   Care designed to cure the patient's disease.

daily hassles   Minor daily stressful events; believed to have a cumulative effect in increasing the likelihood of illness.

death education   Programs designed to inform people realistically about death and dying, the purpose of which is to reduce the terror connected with and avoidance of the topic.

delay behavior   The act of delaying seeking treatment for recognized symptoms.

denial   A defense mechanism involving the inability to recognize or deal with external threatening events; believed to be an early reaction to the diagnosis of a chronic or terminal illness.

depression   A neurotic or psychotic mood disorder marked especially by sadness, inactivity, difficulty with thinking and concentration, a significant increase or decrease in appetite and time spent sleeping, feelings of dejection and hopelessness, and sometimes suicidal thoughts or an attempt to commit suicide.

detoxification   The process of withdrawing from alcohol, usually conducted in a supervised, medically monitored setting.

diabetes   A chronic disorder in which the body is not able to manufacture or use insulin properly.

diagnostic-related groups (DRGs)   A patient classification scheme that specifies the nature and length of treatment for particular disorders; used by some third-party reimbursement systems to determine the amount of reimbursement.

dieticians   Trained and licensed individuals who apply principles of nutrition and food management to meal planning for institutions, such as hospitals, or for individuals who need help planning and managing special diets.

direct effects hypothesis   The theory that coping resources, such as social support, have beneficial psychological and health effects under conditions of both high stress and low stress.

discriminative stimulus   An environmental stimulus that is capable of eliciting a particular behavior; for example, the sight of food may act as a discriminative stimulus for eating.

distraction   A pain control method that may involve either focusing on a stimulus irrelevant to the pain experience or reinterpreting the pain experience; redirecting attention to reduce pain.

double-blind experiment   An experimental procedure in which neither the researcher nor the patient knows whether the patient received the real treatment or the placebo until precoded records indicating which patient received which are consulted; designed to reduce the possibility that expectations for success will increase evidence for success.

emotional support   Indications from other people that one is loved, valued, and cared for; believed to be an important aspect of social support during times of stress.

endocrine system   A bodily system of ductless glands that secrete hormones into the blood to stimulate target organs; interacts with nervous system functioning.

endogenous opioid peptides   Opiatelike substances produced by the body.

epidemiology   The study of the frequency, distribution, and causes of infectious and noninfectious disease in a population, based on an investigation of the physical and social environment. Thus, for example, epidemiologists not only study who has what kind of cancer but also address questions such as why certain cancers are more prevalent in particular geographic areas than other cancers are.

etiology   The origins and causes of illness.

euthanasia   Ending the life of a person who has a painful terminal illness for the purpose of terminating the individual's suffering.

evidence-based medicine   The conscientious, explicit, judicious use of the best scientific evidence for making decisions about the care of individual patients.

experiment   A type of research in which a researcher randomly assigns people to two or more conditions, varies the treatments that people in each condition are given, and then measures the effect on some response.

fear appeals   Efforts to change attitudes by arousing fear to induce the motivation to change behavior; fear appeals are used to try to get people to change poor health habits.

fight-or-flight response   A response to threat in which the body is rapidly aroused and motivated via the sympathetic nervous system and the endocrine system to attack or flee a threatening stimulus; the response was first described by Walter Cannon in 1932.

functional somatic syndrome   Marked by the symptoms, suffering, and disability it causes rather than by any demonstrable tissue abnormality.

general adaptation syndrome   Developed by Hans Selye, a profile of how organisms respond to stress; the general adaptation syndrome is characterized by three phases: a nonspecific mobilization phase, which promotes sympathetic nervous system activity; a resistance phase, during which the organism makes efforts to cope with the threat; and an exhaustion phase, which occurs if the organism fails to overcome the threat and depletes its physiological resources.

gout   A form of arthritis produced by a buildup of uric acid in the body, producing crystals that become lodged in the joints; the most commonly affected area is the big toe.

grief   A response to bereavement involving a feeling of hollowness and sometimes marked by preoccupation with the dead person, expressions of hostility toward others, and guilt over death; may also involve restlessness, inability to concentrate, and other adverse psychological and physical symptoms.

guided imagery   A technique of relaxation and pain control in which a person conjures up a picture that is held in mind during a painful or stressful experience.

health   The absence of disease or infirmity, coupled with a complete state of physical, mental, and social well-being; health psychologists recognize health to be a state that is actively achieved rather than the mere absence of illness.

health behaviors   Behaviors undertaken by people to enhance or maintain their health, such as exercise or the consumption of a healthy diet.

health belief model   A theory of health behaviors; the model predicts that whether a person practices a particular health habit can be understood by knowing the degree to which the person perceives a personal health threat and the perception that a particular health practice will be effective in reducing that threat.

health habit   A health-related behavior that is firmly established and often performed automatically, such as buckling a seat belt or brushing one's teeth.

health locus of control   The perception that one's health is under personal control; is controlled by powerful others, such as physicians; or is determined by external factors, including chance.

health maintenance organization (HMO)   An organizational arrangement for receiving health care services, by which an individual pays a standard monthly rate and then uses services as needed at no additional or at greatly reduced cost.

health promotion   A general philosophy that maintains that health is a personal and collective achievement; the process of enabling people to increase control over and improve their health. Health promotion may occur through individual efforts, through interaction with the medical system, and through a concerted health policy effort.

health psychology   The subarea within psychology devoted to understanding psychological influences on health, illness, and responses to those states, as well as the psychological origins and impacts of health policy and health interventions.

holistic health   A philosophy characterized by the belief that health is a positive state that is actively achieved; usually associated with certain nontraditional health practices.

home care   Care for dying patients in the home; the choice of care for the majority of terminally ill patients, though sometimes problematic for family members.

hospice   An institution for dying patients that encourages personalized, warm palliative care.

hospice care   An alternative to hospital and home care, designed to provide warm, personal comfort for terminally ill patients; may be residential or home-based.

human immunodeficiency virus (HIV)   The virus that is implicated in the development of AIDS.

humoral immunity   Fast-acting immune response that defends the body against bacterial and viral infections that have not yet invaded the cells; mediated by B lmphocytes.

hypertension   Excessively high blood pressure that occurs when the supply of blood through the blood vessels is excessive, putting pressure on the vessel walls; a risk factor for a variety of medical problems, including coronary heart disease.

hypnosis   A pain management technique involving relaxation, suggestion, distraction, and the focusing of attention.

hypothalamus   The part of the forebrain responsible for regulating water balance and controlling hunger and sexual desire; assists in cardiac functioning, blood pressure regulation, and respiration regulation; has a major role in regulation of the endocrine system, which controls the release of hormones, including those related to stress.

illness delay   The time between recognizing that a symptom implies an illness and the decision to seek treatment.

illness representations (schemas)   An organized set of beliefs about an illness or a type of illness, including its nature, cause, duration, and consequences.

immunity   The body's resistance to injury from invading organisms, acquired from the mother at birth, through disease, or through vaccinations and inoculations.

immunocompetence   The degree to which the immune system functions effectively.

immunocompromise   The degree to which the immune system responds suboptimally, because of either reduced numbers of cells or reduced functioning.

infant mortality rate   The number of infant deaths per thousand infants.

informational support   The provision of information to a person going through stress by friends, family, and other people in the individual's social network; believed to help reduce the distressing and health-compromising effects of stress.

invisible support   When one receives help from another, but is unaware of it; support that is most likely to benefit a person.

John Henryism   A personality predisposition to cope actively with psychosocial stressors; may become lethal when those active coping efforts are unsuccessful; the syndrome has been especially documented among lower-income Blacks at risk for or suffering from hypertension.

kidney dialysis   A procedure in which blood is filtered to remove toxic substances and excess fluid from the blood of patients whose kidneys do not function properly.

lay referral network   An informal network of family and friends who help an individual interpret and treat a disorder before the individual seeks formal medical treatment.

life-skills-training approach   A smoking prevention program characterized by the belief that training in self-esteem and coping skills will boost self-image to the point that smoking becomes unnecessary or inconsistent with lifestyle.

lifestyle rebalancing   Concerted lifestyle change in a healthy direction, usually including exercise, stress management, and a healthy diet; believed to contribute to relapse prevention after successful modification of a poor health habit, such as smoking or alcohol consumption.

living will   A will prepared by a person with a terminal illness, requesting that extraordinary life-sustaining procedures not be used in the event that the person's ability to make this decision is lost.

longitudinal research   The repeated observation and measurement of the same individuals over a period of time.

lymphatic system   The drainage system of the body; believed to be involved in immune functioning.

managed care   A health care arrangement in which an employer or employee pays a predetermined monthly fee to a health care or insurance agency that entitles the employee to use medical services at no additional (or a greatly reduced) cost.

matching hypothesis   The hypothesis that social support is helpful to an individual to the extent that the kind of support offered satisfies the individual's specific needs.

medical delay   A delay in treating symptoms, which results from problems within the medical system, such as faulty diagnoses, lost test results, and the like.

medical students' disease   The relabeling of symptoms of fatigue and exhaustion as a particular illness resulting from learning about that illness; called medical students' disease because overworked medical students are vulnerable to this labeling effect.

medulla   Part of the brain that regulates heart rate, constriction of blood vessels, and rate of breathing.

metabolic syndrome   A pattern of risk factors for the chronic health problems of diabetes, heart disease, and hypertension, characterized by obesity, a high waist-to-hip ratio, and insulin resistance. Metabolic syndrome is exacerbated by inactivity, overeating, age, and hostility.

mind-body relationship   The philosophical position regarding whether the mind and body operate indistinguishably as a single system or whether they act as two separate systems; the view guiding health psychology is that the mind and body are indistinguishable.

modeling   Learning gained from observing another person performing a target behavior.

morbidity   The number of cases of a disease that exist at a given point in time; it may be expressed as the number of new cases (incidence) or as the total number of existing cases (prevalence).

mortality   The number of deaths due to particular causes.

myocardial infarction (MI)   A heart attack produced when a clot has developed in a coronary vessel, blocking the flow of blood to the heart.

negative affectivity   A personality variable marked by a pervasive negative mood, including anxiety, depression, and hostility; believed to be implicated in the experience of symptoms, the seeking of medical treatment, and possibly illness.

nervous system   The system of the body responsible for the transmission of information from the brain to the rest of the body and from the rest of the body to the brain; it is composed of the central nervous system (the brain and the spinal cord) and the peripheral nervous system (which consists of the remainder of the nerves in the body).

neurotransmitters   Chemicals that regulate nervous system functioning.

nociception   The perception of pain.

nonadherence   The failure to comply fully with treatment recommendations for modification of a health habit or an illness state.

nonspecific immune mechanisms   A set of responses to infection or a disorder that is engaged by the presence of a biological invader.

nurse-practitioners   Nurses who, in addition to their training in traditional nursing, receive special training in primary care so they may provide routine medical care for patients.

obesity   An excessive accumulation of body fat, believed to contribute to a variety of health disorders, including cardiovascular disease.

occupational therapists   Trained and licensed individuals who work with emotionally and/or physically disabled people to determine skill levels and to develop a rehabilitation program to build on and expand these skills.

operant conditioning   The pairing of a voluntary, nonautomatic behavior to a new stimulus through reinforcement or punishment.

osteoarthritis   A form of arthritis that results when the articular cartilage begins to crack or wear away because of overuse of a particular joint; may also result from injury or other causes; usually affects the weight-bearing joints and is common among athletes and the elderly.

pain behaviors   Behaviors that result in response to pain, such as cutting back on work or taking drugs.

pain control   The ability to reduce the experience of pain, report of pain, emotional concern over pain, inability to tolerate pain, or presence of pain-related behaviors.

pain management programs   Coordinated, interdisciplinary efforts to modify chronic pain by bringing together neurological, cognitive, behavioral, and psychodynamic expertise concerning pain; such programs aim not only to make pain more manageable but also to modify the lifestyle that has evolved because of the pain.

pain-prone personality   A constellation of personality traits that predisposes a person to experience chronic pain.

palliative care   Care designed to make the patient comfortable, but not to cure or improve the patient's underlying disease; often part of terminal care.

parasympathetic nervous system   The part of the nervous system responsible for vegetative functions, the conservation of energy, and the damping down of the effects of the sympathetic nervous system.

passive smoking   Nonsmokers' inhaling of smoke as a result of exposure to smokers; believed to cause health problems such as bronchitis, emphysema, and lung cancer.

patient orientation   Patient education programs designed to inform patients about their disorder and its treatment and to train them in methods for coping with a disorder and its corresponding limitations.

perceived stress   The perception that an event is stressful independent of its objective characteristics.

person-environment fit   The degree to which the needs and resources of a person and the needs and resources of an environment complement each other.

pessimistic explanatory style   A chronic tendency to explain negative events as due to internal, stable, and global qualities of the self and to attribute positive events to external, unstable, and nonglobal factors; believed to contribute to the likelihood of illness.

phagocytosis   The process by which phagocytes ingest and attempt to eliminate a foreign invader.

physical dependence   A state in which the body has adjusted to the use of a substance, incorporating it into the body's normal functioning.

physical rehabilitation   A program of activities for chronically ill or disabled persons geared toward helping them use their bodies as much as possible, sense changes in the environment and in themselves so as to make appropriate physical accommodations, learn new physical and management skills if necessary, pursue a treatment regimen, and learn how to control the expenditure of energy.

physical therapists   Trained and licensed individuals who help people with muscle, nerve, joint, or bone diseases to overcome their disabilities as much as possible.

physicians' assistants   Graduates of 2-year programs who perform routine health care functions, teach patients about their treatment regimens, and record medical information.

pituitary gland   A gland located at the base of and controlled by the brain that secretes the hormones responsible for growth and organ development.

placebo   A medical treatment that produces an effect in a patient because of its therapeutic intent and not its nature.

placebo drinking   The consumption of nonalcoholic beverages in social situations in which others are drinking alcohol.

placebo effect   The medically beneficial impact of an inert treatment.

platelets   Small disks found in vertebrate blood that contribute to blood coagulation.

pons   Link between the hindbrain and the midbrain; it helps control respiration.

post-traumatic stress disorder (PTSD)   A syndrome that results after exposure to a stressor of extreme magnitude, marked by emotional numbing, the reliving of aspects of the trauma, intense responses to other stressful events, and other symptoms, such as hyperalertness, sleep disturbance, guilt, or impaired memory or concentration.

preferred provider organization (PPO)   A network of affiliated practitioners that has agreed to charge preestablished rates for particular medical services.

premature death   Death that occurs before the projected age of 75.

primary appraisal   The perception of a new or changing environment as beneficial, neutral, or negative in its consequences; believed to be a first step in stress and coping.

primary prevention   Measures designed to combat risk factors for illness before an illness has a chance to develop.

private, fee-for-service care   The condition under which patients privately contract with physicians for services and pay them for services rendered.

problem drinking   Uncontrolled drinking that leads to social, psychological, and biomedical problems resulting from alcohol; the problem drinker may show some signs associated with alcoholism, but typically problem drinking is considered to be a prealcoholic or a lesser alcoholic syndrome.

prospective research   A research strategy in which people are followed forward in time to examine the relationship between one set of variables and later occurrences. For example, prospective research can enable researchers to identify risk factors for diseases that develop at a later point in time.

psychological control   The perception that one has at one's disposal a response that will reduce, minimize, eliminate, or offset the adverse effects of an unpleasant event, such as a medical procedure.

psychoneuroimmunology   Interactions among behavioral, neuroendocrine, and immunological processes of adaptation.

psychosomatic medicine   A field within psychiatry, related to health psychology, that developed in the early 1900s to study and treat particular diseases believed to be caused by emotional conflicts, such as ulcers, hypertension, and asthma. The term is now used more broadly to mean an approach to health-related problems and diseases that examines psychological as well as somatic origins.

quality of life   The degree to which a person is able to maximize his or her physical, psychological, vocational, and social functioning; an important indicator of recovery from or adjustment to chronic illness.

randomized clinical trial   An experimental study of the effects of a variable (e.g., a drug or treatment) administered to human subjects who are randomly selected from a broad population and assigned on a random basis to either an experimental or a control group. The goal is to determine the clinical efficacy and pharmacologic effects of the drug or procedure.

reactivity   The predisposition to react physiologically to stress; believed to be genetically based in part; high reactivity is believed to be a risk factor for a range of stress-related diseases.

recurrent acute pain   Pain that involves a series of intermittent episodes of pain that are acute in character but chronic inasmuch as the condition persists for more than 6 months; migraine headaches, temporomandibular disorder (involving the jaw), and trigeminal neuralgia (involving spasms of the facial muscles) are examples.

relapse prevention   A set of techniques designed to keep people from relapsing to prior poor health habits after initial successful behavior modification; includes training in coping skills for high-risk-for-relapse situations and lifestyle rebalancing.

relaxation training   Procedures that help people relax; include progressive muscle relaxation and deep breathing; may also include guided imagery and forms of meditation or hypnosis.

renal system   Part of the metabolic system; responsible for the regulation of bodily fluids and the elimination of wastes; regulates bodily fluids by removing surplus water, surplus electrolytes, and waste products generated by the metabolism of food.

respiratory system   The system of the body responsible for taking in oxygen, excreting carbon dioxide, and regulating the relative composition of the blood.

retrospective research   A research strategy whereby people are studied for the relationship of past variables or conditions to current ones. Interviewing people with a particular disease and asking them about their childhood health behaviors or exposure to risks can identify conditions leading to an adult disease, for example.

rheumatoid arthritis (RA) A crippling form of arthritis believed to result from an autoimmune process, usually attacking the small joints of the hands, feet, wrists, knees, ankles, and neck.

role conflict Conflict that occurs when two or more social or occupational roles that an individual occupies produce conflicting standards for behavior.

secondary appraisal The assessment of one's coping abilities and resources and judgment as to whether they will be sufficient to meet the harm, threat, or challenge of a new or changing event.

secondary gains Benefits of being treated for illness, including the ability to rest, to be freed from unpleasant tasks, and to be taken care of by others.

secondhand smoke See **passive smoking.**

self-concept An integrated set of beliefs about one's personal qualities and attributes.

self-control A state in which an individual desiring to change behavior learns how to modify the antecedents and the consequences of that target behavior.

self-efficacy The perception that one is able to perform a particular action.

self-esteem A global evaluation of one's qualities and attributes.

self-help aids Materials that can be used by an individual on his or her own without the aid of a therapist to assist in the modification of a personal habit; often used to combat smoking and other health-related risk factors.

self-management Involvement of the patient in all aspects of a chronic illness and its implications, including medical management, changes in social and vocational roles and coping.

self-monitoring, self-observation Assessing the frequency, antecedents, and consequences of a target behavior to be modified.

self-reinforcement Systematically rewarding or punishing oneself to increase or decrease the occurrence of a target behavior.

self-talk Internal monologues; people tell themselves things that may undermine or help them implement appropriate health habits, such as "I can stop smoking" (positive self-talk) or "I'll never be able to do this" (negative self-talk).

separation anxiety Feelings of fear or extreme distress that result from separation from someone important, usually the mother.

set point theory of weight The concept that each individual has an ideal biological weight that cannot be greatly modified.

smoking prevention programs Programs designed to keep people from beginning to smoke, as opposed to programs that

attempt to induce people to stop once they have already become smokers.

social engineering Social or lifestyle change through legislation; for example, water purification is done through social engineering rather than by individual efforts.

social influence intervention A smoking prevention intervention that draws on the social learning principles of modeling and behavioral inoculation in inducing people not to smoke; youngsters are exposed to older peer models who deliver antismoking messages after exposure to simulated peer pressure to smoke.

socialization The process by which people learn the norms, rules, and beliefs associated with their family and society; parents and social institutions are usually the major agents of socialization.

social skills training Techniques that teach people how to relax and interact comfortably in social situations; often a part of health-behavior modification programs, on the assumption that maladaptive health behaviors, such as alcohol consumption or smoking, may develop in part to control social anxiety.

social support Information from other people that one is loved and cared for, esteemed and valued, and part of a network of communication and mutual obligation.

social workers Trained and licensed individuals who help patients and their families deal with problems by providing therapy, making referrals, and engaging in social planning; medical social workers help patients and their families ease transitions between illness and recovery states.

somaticizers People who express distress and conflict through bodily symptoms.

specific immune mechanisms Responses designed to respond to specific invaders; includes cell-mediated and humoral immunity.

stages of dying A theory, developed by Kübler-Ross, that maintains that people go through five temporal stages in adjusting to the prospect of death: denial, anger, bargaining, depression, and acceptance; believed to characterize some but not all dying people.

stimulus-control interventions Interventions designed to modify behavior that involve the removal of discriminative stimuli that evoke a behavior targeted for change and the substitution of new discriminative stimuli that will evoke a desired behavior.

stress Appraising events as harmful, threatening, or challenging and assessing one's capacity to respond to those events; events that are perceived to tax or exceed one's resources are seen as stressful.

stress carriers Individuals who create stress for others without necessarily increasing their own level of stress.

stress eating Eating in response to stress; approximately half the population increases eating in response to stress.

stress inoculation The process of identifying stressful events in one's life and learning skills for coping with them, so that when the events come up, one can put those coping skills into effect.

stress management A program for dealing with stress in which people learn how they appraise stressful events, develop skills for coping with stress, and practice putting these skills into effect.

stress moderators Internal and external resources and vulnerabilities that modify how stress is experienced and its effects.

stressful life events Events that force an individual to make changes in his or her life.

stressors Events perceived to be stressful.

stroke A condition that results from a disturbance in blood flow to the brain, often marked by resulting physical or cognitive impairments and, in the extreme, death.

sudden infant death syndrome (SIDS) A common cause of death among infants, in which an infant simply stops breathing.

support group A group of individuals who meet regularly and usually have a common problem or concern; support groups are believed to help people cope because they provide opportunities to share concerns and exchange information with similar others.

symbolic immortality The sense that one is leaving a lasting impact on the world, as through one's children or one's work, or that one is joining the afterlife and becoming one with God.

sympathetic nervous system The part of the nervous system that mobilizes the body for action.

systems theory The viewpoint that all levels of an organization in any entity are linked to each other hierarchically and that change in any level will bring about change in other levels.

tangible assistance The provision of material support by one person to another, such as services, financial assistance, or goods.

teachable moment The idea that certain times are more effective for teaching particular health practices than others; pregnancy constitutes a teachable moment for getting women to stop smoking.

terminal care Medical care of the terminally ill.

testicular self-examination (TSE) The practice of checking the testicles to detect alterations in the underlying tissue; a chief method of detecting early testicular cancer.

thalamus The portion of the forebrain responsible for the recognition of sensory stimuli and the relay of sensory impulses to the cerebral cortex.

thanatologists Those who study death and dying.

theory of planned behavior Derived from the theory of reasoned action, this theoretical viewpoint maintains that a person's behavioral intentions and behaviors can be understood by knowing the person's attitudes about the behavior, subjective norms regarding the behavior, and perceived behavioral control over that action.

time management Skills for learning how to use one's time more effectively to accomplish one's goals.

tolerance The process by which the body increasingly adapts to a substance, requiring larger and larger doses of it to obtain the same effects; a frequent characteristic of substance abuse, including alcohol and drug abuse.

transtheoretical model of behavior change An analysis of the health behavior change process that draws on the stages and processes people go through in order to bring about successful long-term behavior change. The stages include precontemplation, contemplation, preparation, action, and maintenance. Successful attitude or behavior change at each stage depends on the appropriateness of intervention. For example, attitude-change materials help move people from precontemplation to contemplation, whereas relapse prevention techniques help move people from action to maintenance.

treatment effectiveness Formal documentation of the success of an intervention.

Type A behavior pattern A behavioral and emotional style marked by an aggressive, unceasing struggle to achieve more and more in less time, often in hostile competition with other individuals or forces; a risk factor for coronary heart disease. Hostility appears to be especially implicated as the risk factor.

window of vulnerability The fact that, at certain times, people are more vulnerable to particular health problems. For example, early adolescence constitutes a window of vulnerability for beginning smoking, drug use, and alcohol abuse.

withdrawal Unpleasant physical and psychological symptoms that people experience when they stop using a substance on which they have become physically dependent; symptoms include anxiety, craving, hallucinations, nausea, headaches, and shaking.

worried well Individuals free from illness who are nonetheless concerned about their physical state and frequently and inappropriately use medical services.

yo-yo dieting The process of chronically alternating between dieting and regular eating, leading to successive weight gains and losses; over time, yo-yo dieters increase their chances of becoming obese by altering their underlying metabolism.

REFERENCES

Aaronson, N. K., Calais de Silva, F., Yoshida, O., van Dam, F. S. A. M., Fossa, S. D., Miyakawa, M., et al. (1986). Quality of life assessment in bladder cancer clinical trials: Conceptual, methodological and practical issues. *Progress in Clinical and Biological Research, 22,* 149–170.

Abbott, A. (2004, May 27). Striking back. *Nature, 429,* 338–339.

ABC News. (2004). Bitter medicine: Pills, profit, and the public health. Retrieved from: http://abcnews.go.com/onair/ABCNEWSSpecials/pharmaceuticals_020529_pjr_feature.html

Abel, G. G., Rouleau, J. L., & Coyne, B. J. (1987). Behavioral medicine strategies in medical patients. In A. Stoudemire & B. S. Fogel (Eds.), *Principles of medical psychiatry* (pp. 329–345). Orlando, FL: Grune & Stratton.

Abraham, C., Sheeran, P., Spears, R., & Abrams, D. (1992). Health beliefs and promotion of HIV-preventive intentions among teenagers: A Scottish perspective. *Health Psychology, 11,* 363–370.

Abraham, S., Collins, G., & Nordsieck, M. (1971). Relationship of childhood weight status to morbidity in adults. *Public Health Reports, 86,* 273–284.

Abrams, D. B., Orleans, C. T., Niaura, R. S., Goldstein, M. G., Prochaska, J. O., & Velicer, W. (1996). Integrating individual and public health perspectives for treatment of tobacco dependence under managed health care: A combined stepped-care and matching model. *Annals of Behavioral Medicine, 18,* 290–304.

Abrams, R. D. (1966). The patient with cancer: His changing patterns of communication. *New England Journal of Medicine, 274,* 317–322.

Academy of Sciences, Alcoholics Anonymous. (2004). A. A. at a glance. Alcoholics Anonymous. Retrieved from: http://www.alcoholics-anonymous.org.

Ackerman, K. D., Heyman, R., Rabin, B. S., Anderson, B. P., Houck, P. R., Frank, E., et al. (2002). Stressful life events precede exacerbations of multiple sclerosis. *Psychosomatic Medicine, 64,* 916–920.

Adams, J. D. (1978). Improving stress management: An action-research based OD intervention. In W. W. Burke (Ed.), *The cutting edge.* La Jolla, CA: University Associates.

Adams, S. Jr., Dammers, P., Saia, T., Brantley, P., & Gaydos, G. (1994). Stress, depression, and anxiety predict average symptom severity and daily symptom fluctuation in systemic lupus erythematosus. *Journal of Behavioral Medicine, 17,* 459–477.

Aday, L. A., & Andersen, R. (1974). A framework for the study of access to medical care. *Health Services Research, 9,* 208–220.

Adelman, R. C., & Verbrugge, L. M. (2000). Death makes news: The social impact of disease on newspaper coverage. *Journal of Health and Social Behavior, 41,* 347–367.

Ader, R. (1995). Historical perspectives on psychoneuroimmunology. In H. Friedman, T. W. Klein, & A. L. Friedman (Eds.), *Psychoneuroimmunology, stress, and infection* (pp. 1–24). Boca Raton, FL: CRC Press.

Adler, N., & Matthews, K. A. (1994). Health and psychology: Why do some people get sick and some stay well? *Annual Review of Psychology, 45,* 229–259.

Adler, N. E., Boyce, T., Chesney, M. A., Cohen, C., Folkman, S., Kahn, R. L., & Syme, L. S. (1994). Socioeconomic status and health: The challenge of the gradient. *American Psychologist, 49,* 15–24.

Adler, N. E., Boyce, W. T., Chesney, M. A., Folkman, S., et al. (1993). Socioeconomic inequalities in health: No easy solution. *Journal of the American Medical Association, 269,* 3140–3145.

Affleck, G., Tennen, H., Croog, S., & Levine, S. (1987). Causal attribution, perceived control, and recovery from a heart attack. *Journal of Social and Clinical Psychology, 5,* 339–355.

Affleck, G., Tennen, H., Pfeiffer, C., & Fifield, C. (1987). Appraisals of control and predictability in adapting to a chronic disease. *Journal of Personality and Social Psychology, 53,* 273–279.

Affleck, G., Tennen, H., Urrows, S., & Higgins, P. (1994). Person and contextual features of daily stress reactivity: Individual differences in relations of undesirable daily events with mood disturbance and chronic pain intensity. *Journal of Personality and Social Psychology, 66,* 329–340.

Affleck, G., Tennen, H., Urrows, S., Higgins, P., Abeles, M., Hall, C., et al. (1998). Fibromyalgia and women's pursuit of personal goals: A daily process analysis. *Health Psychology, 17,* 40–47.

Agras, W. S. (1992). Some structural changes that might facilitate the development of behavioral medicine. *Journal of Consulting and Clinical Psychology, 60,* 499–504.

Agras, W. S., Berkowitz, R. I., Arnow, B. A., Telch, C. F., Marnell, M., Henderson, et al. (1996). Maintenance following a very-low-calorie diet. *Journal of Consulting and Clinical Psychology, 64,* 610–613.

Agras, W. S., Kraemer, H. C., Berkowitz, R. I., Korner, A. F., & Hammer, L. D. (1987). Does a vigorous feeding style influence early development? *Journal of Pediatrics, 110,* 799–804.

Agras, W. S., Rossiter, E. M., Arnow, B., Schneider, J. A., Telch, C. F., Raeburn, S. D., et al. (1992). Pharmacologic and cognitive-behavioral treatment for bulimia nervosa: A controlled comparison. *American Journal of Psychiatry, 149,* 82–87.

Agras, W. S., Schneider, J. A., Arnow, B., Raeburn, S. D., & Telch, C. F. (1989). Cognitive-behavioral and response-prevention treatments for bulimia nervosa. *Journal of Consulting and Clinical Psychology, 57,* 215–221.

Agras, W. S., Taylor, C. B., Kraemer, H. C., Southam, M. A., & Schneider, J. A. (1987). Relaxation training for essential hypertension at the worksite: II. The poorly controlled hypertensive. *Psychosomatic Medicine, 49,* 264–273.

Aiken, L. H., & Marx, M. M. (1982). Hospices: Perspectives on the public policy debate. *American Psychologist, 37,* 1271–1279.

Ajzen, I., & Fishbein, M. (1980). *Understanding attitudes and predicting social behavior.* Englewood Cliffs, NJ: Prentice-Hall.

Ajzen, I., & Madden, T. J. (1986). Prediction of goal-directed behavior: Attitudes, intentions, and perceived behavioral control. *Journal of Experimental Social Psychology, 22,* 453–474.

Akil, H., Mayer, D. J., & Liebeskind, J. C. (1972). Comparaison chez le Rat entre l'analgesie induite par stimulation de la substance grise periaqueducale et l'analgesie morphinique. C. R. *Academy of Science, 274,* 3603–3605.

Akil, H., Mayer, D. J., & Liebeskind, J. C. (1976). Antagonism of stimulation-produced analgesia by naloxone, a narcotic antagonist. *Science, 191,* 961–962.

Akil, H., Watson, S. J., Young, E., Lewis, M. E., Khachaturian, H., & Walker, J. M. (1984). Endogenous opioids: Biology and function. *Annual Review of Neuroscience, 7,* 223–255.

Al'Absi, M., & Wittmers, L. E., Jr. (2003). Enhanced adrenocortical response to stress in hypertension-prone men and women. *Annals of Behavioral Medicine, 25,* 25–33.

Alagna, S. W., & Reddy, D. M. (1984). Predictors of proficient technique and successful lesion detection in breast self-examination. *Health Psychology, 3,* 113–127.

Albarracìn, D., McNatt, P. S., Klein, C. T. F., Ho, R. M., Mitchell, A. L., & Kumkale, G. C. (2003). Persuasive communications to change actions: An analysis of behavioral and cognitive impact in HIV prevention. *Health Psychology, 22,* 166–177.

Albom, M. (1997). *Tuesdays with Morrie.* New York: Doubleday.

Albright, C. L., Altman, D. G., Slater, M. D., & Maccoby, N. (1988). Cigarette advertisements in magazines: Evidence for a differential focus on women's and youth magazines. *Health Education Quarterly, 15,* 225–233.

Alderman, M. H., & Lamport, B. (1988). Treatment of hypertension at the workplace: An opportunity to link service and research. *Health Psychology, 7*(Suppl.), 283–295.

Alexander, F. (1950). *Psychosomatic medicine.* New York: Norton.

Alexander, J. A., Morrissey, M. A., & Shortell, S. M. (1986). Effects of competition, regulation, and corporatization on hospital-physician relationships. *Journal of Health and Social Behavior, 27,* 220–235.

Alexandrov, A., Isakova, G., Maslennikova, G., Shugaeva, E., Prokhorov, A., Olferiev, A., et al. (1988). Prevention of atherosclerosis among 11-year-old schoolchildren in two Moscow administrative districts. *Health Psychology, 7*(Suppl.), 247–252.

Alferi, S. M., Carver, C. S., Antoni, M. H., Weiss, S., & Duran, R. E. (2001). An exploratory study of social support, distress, and life disruption among low-income Hispanic women under treatment for early stage breast cancer. *Health Psychology, 20,* 41–46.

Ali, A., Toner, B. B., Stuckless, N., Gallop, R., Diamant, N. E., Gould, M. I., et al. (2000). Emotional abuse, self-blame, and self-silencing in women with irritable bowel syndrome. *Psychosomatic Medicine, 62,* 76–82.

Ali, J., & Avison, W. (1997). Employment transitions and psychological distress: The contrasting experiences of single and married mothers. *Journal of Health and Social Behavior, 38,* 345–362.

Allen, J. E. (2003a, April 7). Stroke therapy sets sights higher, farther. *Los Angeles Times,* pp. F1, F7.

Allen, J. E. (2003b, July 21). Alone in the ER. *Los Angeles Times,* p. F3.

Allen, J., Markovitz, J., Jacobs, D. R., & Knox, S. S. (2001). Social support and health behavior in hostile black and white men and women. *Psychosomatic Medicine, 63,* 609–618.

Allen, K. (2003). Are pets a healthy pleasure? The influence of pets on blood pressure. *Current Directions, 12,* 236–239.

Allen, K., Blascovich, J., & Mendes, W. B. (2002). Cardiovascular reactivity and the presence of pets, friends, and spouses: The truth about cats and dogs. *Psychosomatic Medicine, 64,* 727–739.

Allen, L. A., Escobar, J. I., Lehrer, P. M., Gara, M. A., & Woolfolk, R. L. (2002). Psychosocial treatments for multiple unexplained physical symptoms: A review of the literature. *Psychosomatic Medicine, 64,* 939–950.

Allgöwer, A., Warldle, J., & Steptoe, A. (2001). Depressive symptoms, social support, and personal health behaviors in young men and women. *Health Psychology, 20,* 223–227.

Allison, D. B., & Faith, M. S. (1996). Hypnosis as an adjunct to cognitive-behavioral psychotherapy for obesity: A meta-analytic reappraisal. *Journal of Consulting & Clinical Psychology, 64,* 513–516.

Allison, D. B., Fontaine, K. R., Manson, J. E., Stevens, J., & VanItallie, T. B. (1999). Annual deaths attributable to obesity in the United States. *Journal of the American Medical Association, 282,* 1530–1538.

Aloise-Young, P. A., Hennigan, K. M., & Graham, J. W. (1996). Role of the self-image and smoker stereotype in smoking onset during early adolescence: A longitudinal study. *Health Psychology, 15,* 494–497.

Alonso, C., & Coe, C. L. (2001). Disruptions of social relationships accentuate the association between emotional distress and menstrual pain in young women. *Health Psychology, 20,* 411–416.

Alper, J. (2000). New insights into Type II diabetes. *Science, 289,* 37–39.

Alpert, B., Field, T., Goldstein, S., & Perry, S. (1990). Aerobics enhances cardiovascular fitness and agility in preschoolers. *Health Psychology, 9,* 48–56.

Alpert, J. J. (1964). Broken appointments. *Pediatrics, 34,* 127–132.

Altman, L. K. (1991, August 6). Men, women, and heart disease: More than a question of sexism. *The New York Times,* pp. B5, B8.

Altman, L. K. (2002, July 3). U.N. forecasts big increase in AIDS death toll. *The New York Times,* pp. A1, A6.

Altman, L. K. (2002, December 18). Older way to threat hypertension found best. *The New York Times,* pp. A1, A27.

Ambler, G., Royston, P., & Head, J. (2003). Non-linear models for the relation between cardiovascular risk factors and intake of wine, beer and spirits. *Statistics in Medicine, 22,* 363–383.

Ambrosone, C. B., Flevdenheim, J. L., Graham, S., Marshall, J. R., Vena, J. E., Glasure, J. R., et al. (1996). Cigarette smoking, N-acetyltransferase 2 genetic polymorphisms, and breast cancer risk. *Journal of the American Medical Association, 276,* 1494–1501.

American Association of Health Plans. (2001). *How to choose a health plan.* Retrieved from: http://www.aahp.org

American Autoimmune Related Diseases Association. (2003). *Answers to frequently asked questions about autoimmunity.* Retrieved from: http://www.aarda.org/questions_and_answers.html

American Cancer Society. (2004b). *Can testicular cancer be found early?* Retrieved August 31, 2004, from: http://www.cancer.org/docroot/CRI/content/ CRI_2_4_3X_Can_Testicular_Cancer_Be_Found_Early_41.asp?sitearea=

American Cancer Society. (1997). *Cancer facts and figures—1996.* Atlanta, GA: Author.

American Cancer Society. (2001a). *Cancer in minorities.* Retrieved June 27, 2001, from: http://www.cancer.org/ cancerinfo/

American Cancer Society. (2001b). *Tobacco use: Smoking cessation.* Atlanta, GA: Author.

American Cancer Society. (2003). *Cancer facts & figures.* Retrieved from: http://www.cancer.org/docroot/STT/stt_0.asp

American Cancer Society. (2004a). *Secondhand smoke: What is it?* Retrieved from: http://www.cancer.org/docroot/PED/content/PED_10_2X_Environmental_Tobacco_Smoke-Clean_Indoor_Air.asp

American Cancer Society. (2004b). *Cancer Survivors' Other Medical Problems Poorly Managed.* Retrieved on August 1, 2004 from: http://www.cancer.org/docroot/MED/content/MED_2_1x_Cancer_Survivors_Other_Medical_Problems_Poorly_Managed.asp

American Diabetes Association. (2004). *All about diabetes.* Retrieved from: http://www.diabetes.org/about-diabetes.jsp

American Diabetes Association. (1999). *Diabetes facts and figures.* Alexandria, VA. Retrieved from: http://www. diabetes.org/ada/facts.asp

American Diabetes Association. (2002a). *National diabetes fact sheet.* Retrieved from: http://www.diabetes.org/diabetes-statistics/national-diabetes-fact-sheet.jsp

American Diabetes Association. (2002b). *Weight loss: How you eat may be just as important as what you eat.* Retrieved from: http://www. diabetes.org

American Heart Association. (2002). *Despite declines in heart disease deaths, racial gap remains.* Retrieved from: http://www.eurekalert.org/pub_releases/2001-11/aha-ddi110201.php

American Heart Association. (2004a). *Risk factors of cardiovascular disease.* Retrieved from: http://www.americanheart.org/presenter.jhtml?identifier=3017033

American Heart Association Meeting Report. (2001a). *Despite declines in heart disease deaths, racial gap remains.* Abstract 3700.

American Heart Association. (2000a). *Heart and stroke a–z guide.* Dallas, TX: Author.

American Heart Association. (2001b). *2001 heart and stroke statistical update.* Dallas, TX: Author.

American Heart Association. (2004b). *Heart disease and stroke statistics—2004 update.* Retrieved from: http://www.americanheart.org/presenter.jhtml? identifier=1928

American Hospital Association. (2003). *Hospital statistics.*

American Hospital Association. (2002). *Hospital Statistics.* American Hospital Association: Chicago, IL.

American Psychiatric Association. (1980). *Diagnostic and statistical manual of mental disorders* (3rd ed.). Washington, D.C.: Author.

American Psychiatric Association. (1994). *Diagnostic and statistical manual of mental disorders: DSM-IV* (4th ed.). Washington, D.C.: Author.

American Psychological Association. (1996). 1993 APA directory survey, with new member updates for 1994 and 1995. Washington, D.C.: American Psychological Association Research Office.

American Psychological Society. (1996, April). *APS observer: Special issue HCI report 4—Health living.* Washington, D.C.: Author.

American Religious Identification Survey. (2001). http://www.gc.cuny.edu/ studies/aris_index.htm

Ames, K., Wilson, L., Sawhill, R., Glick, D., & King, P. (1991, August 26). Last rights. *Newsweek,* pp. 40–41.

Amick, B. C., III, McDonough, P., Chang, H., Rodgers, W. H., Pieper, C. F., & Duncan, G. (2002). Relationship between all-cause mortality and cumulative working life course psychosocial and physical exposure in the United States labor market from 1968 to 1992. *Psychosomatic Medicine,* 64, 370–381.

Amir, M., & Haskell, E. (1997). Organ donation: Who is not willing to commit? Psychological factors influencing the individual's decision to commit to organ donation after death. *International Journal of Behavioral Medicine,* 4, 215–229.

Amkraut, A., & Solomon, G. F. (1977). From the symbolic stimulus to the pathophysiologic response: Immune mechanisms. In Z. P. Lipowski, D. R. Lipsitt, & P. C. Whybrow (Eds.), *Psychosomatic medicine: Current trends and clinical applications* (pp. 228–252). New York: Oxford University Press.

Andersen, B. L. (1992). Psychological interventions for cancer patients to enhance the quality of life. *Journal of Consulting and Clinical Psychology,* 60, 552–568.

Andersen, B. L., Anderson, B., & deProsse, C. (1989a). Controlled perspective longitudinal study of women with cancer: I. Sexual functioning outcomes. *Journal of Consulting and Clinical Psychology,* 57, 683–691.

Andersen, B. L., Anderson, B., & deProsse, C. (1989b). Controlled perspective longitudinal study of women with cancer: II. Psychological outcomes. *Journal of Consulting and Clinical Psychology,* 57, 692–697.

Andersen, B. L., Cacioppo, J. T., & Roberts, D. C. (1995). Delay in seeking a cancer diagnosis: Delay stages and psychophysiological comparison processes. *British Journal of Social Psychology,* 34, 33–52.

Andersen, B. L., Ho. J., Brackett, J., Finkelstein, D., & Laffel, L. (1997). Parental involvement in diabetes management tasks: Relationships to blood glucose monitoring adherence and metabolic control in young adolescents with insulin-dependent diabetes mellitus. *Journal of Pediatrics,* 130, 257–265.

Andersen, B. L., Kiecolt-Glaser, J., & Glaser, R. (1994). A biobehavioral model of cancer stress and disease course. *American Psychologist,* 49, 389–404.

Andersen, B. L., Woods, X. A., & Copeland, L. J. (1997). Sexual self-schema and sexual morbidity among gynecologic cancer survivors. *Journal of Consulting and Clinical Psychology,* 65, 1–9.

Andersen, R. M. (1995). Revisiting the behavioral model and access to medical care: Does it matter? *Journal of Health and Social Behavior,* 36, 1–10.

Anderson, E. S., Winett, R. A., & Wojcik, J. R. (2000). Social-cognitive determinants of nutrition behavior among supermarket food shoppers: A structural equation analysis. *Health Psychology,* 19, 479–486.

Anderson, K. O., Bradley, L. A., Young, L. D., McDaniel, L. K., & Wise, C. M. (1985). Rheumatoid arthritis: Review of psychological factors related to etiology, effects, and treatment. *Psychological Bulletin,* 98, 358–387.

Anderson, R. A., Baron, R. S., & Logan, H. (1991). Distraction, control, and dental stress. *Journal of Applied Social Psychology,* 21, 156–171.

Anderson, R. N. (2001). United States life tables, 1998. *National Vital Statistics Report,* 48, 1–39.

Andrews, J. A., & Duncan, S. C. (1997). Examining the reciprocal relation between academic motivation and substance use: Effects of family relationships, self-esteem, and general deviance. *Journal of Behavioral Medicine,* 20, 523–549.

Andrews, J. A., Tildesley, E., Hops, H., & Li, F. (2002). The influence of peers on young adult substance use. *Health Psychology,* 21, 349–357.

Andrykowski, M. A., Curran, S. L., & Lightner, R. (1998). Off-treatment fatigue in breast cancer survivors: A controlled comparison. *Journal of Behavioral Medicine,* 21, 1–18.

Aneshensel, C. S., Pearlin, L. I., & Schuler, R. H. (1993). Stress, role captivity, and the cessation of caregiving. *Journal of Health and Social Behavior,* 34, 54–70.

Angel, R. J., Frisco, M., Angel, J. L., & Chiriboga, D. A. (2003). Financial strain and health among elderly Mexican-origin individuals. *Journal of Health and Social Behavior,* 44, 536–551.

Angier, N. (2001, June 19). Researchers piecing together autoimmune disease puzzle. *The New York Times,* pp. D1, D8.

Anstey, K. J., & Luszcz, M. A. (2002). Mortality risks varies according to gender and change in depressive status in very old adults. *Psychosomatic Medicine,* 64, 880–888.

Antoni, M. H., Lehman, J. M., Kilbourne, K. M., Boyers, A. E., Culver, J. L., Alferi, S. M., et al. (2001). Cognitive-behavioral stress management intervention decreases the prevalence of depression and enhances benefit finding among women under treatment of early-stage breast cancer. *Health Psychology,* 20, 20–32.

Apanovitch, A. M., McCarthy, D., & Salovey, P. (2003). Using message framing to motivate HIV testing among low-income, ethnic minority women. *Health Psychology,* 22, 60–67.

Appels, A., Bar, F. W., Bar, J., Bruggeman, C., & DeBaets, M. (2000). Inflammation, depressive symptomatology, and coronary artery disease. *Psychosomatic Medicine,* 62, 601–605.

Armstead, C. A., Lawler, K. A., Gordon, G., Cross, J., & Gibbons, J. (1989). Relationship of racial stressors to blood pressure responses and anger expression in Black college students. *Health Psychology,* 8, 541–557.

Arnst, C. (2004, February 23). Let them eat cake-if they want to. *BusinessWeek,* pp. 110–111.

Arnst, C., & Weintraub, A. (2002, November 18). A direct hit to Parkinson's? *BusinessWeek,* pp. 58, 60.

Arthritis Foundation (2004). *Facts about arthritis.* Retrieved October 25, 2004, from: http://www.arthritis.org/resources/gettingstarted/default.asp

Ary, D. V., Biglan, A., Glasgow, R., Zoref, L., Black, C., Ochs, L., et al. (1990). The efficacy of social-influence prevention programs versus "standard care": Are new initiatives needed? *Journal of Behavioral Medicine,* 13, 281–296.

Asanuma, Y. et al. (2003). Premature coronary artery atherosclerosis in systematic lupus erythematosus. *New England Journal of Medicine,* 349, 2407–2415, http://www.nejm.org

Ashley, M. J., & Rankin, J. G. (1988). A public health approach to the prevention of alcohol-related problems. *Annual Review of Public Health, 9,* 233–271.

Aspinwall, L. G., Kemeny, M. E., Taylor, S. E., Schneider, S. G., & Dudley, J. P. (1991). Psychosocial predictors of gay men's AIDS risk-reduction behavior. *Health Psychology, 10,* 432–444.

Association for Worksite Health Promotion (1999). National Worksite Health Promotion Survey: Report of Survey Findings. William M. Mercer, Incorporated and the U.S. Department of Health and Human Services, Office of Disease Prevention and Health Promotion.

Astin, J. (1998). Why patients use alternative medicine: Results of a national study. *Journal of the American Medical Association, 279,* 1548–1553.

Astin, J. A., Beckner, W., Soeken, K., Hochberg, M. C., & Berman, B. (2002). Psychological interventions for rheumatoid arthritis: A meta-analysis of randomized controlled trials. *Arthritis and Rheumatism, 47,* 291–302.

Atkins, E., Solomon, L. J., Worden, J. K., & Foster, R. S., Jr. (1991). Relative effectiveness of methods of breast self-examination. *Journal of Behavioral Medicine, 14,* 357–368.

Audrain, J. E., Klesges, R. C., & Klesges, L. M. (1995). Relationship between obesity and the metabolic effects of smoking in women. *Health Psychology, 14,* 116–123.

Audrain, J., Schwartz, M., Herrera, J., Goldman, P., & Bush, A. (2001). Physical activity in first-degree relatives of breast cancer patients. *Journal of Behavioral Medicine, 24,* 587–603.

Auerbach, S. M., & Kilmann, P. R. (1977). Crisis intervention: A review of outcome research. *Psychological Bulletin, 84,* 1189–1217.

Auerbach, S. M., Clore, J. N., Kiesler, D. J., Orr, T., Pegg, P. O., Quick, B. G., et al. (2001). Relation of diabetic patients' health-related control appraisals and physician-patient interpersonal impacts to patients' metabolic control and satisfaction with treatment. *Journal of Behavioral Medicine, 25,* 17–32.

Avlund, K., Osler, M., Damsgaard, M. T., Christensen, U., & Schroll, M. (2000). The relations between musculoskeletal diseases and mobility among old people: Are they influenced by socio-economic, psychosocial, and behavioral factors? *International Journal of Behavioral Medicine, 7,* 322–339.

Axelrod, S., Hall, R. V., Weis, L., & Rohrer, S. (1974). Use of self-imposed contingencies to reduce the frequency of smoking behavior. In M. J. Mahoney & C. E. Thoresen (Eds.), *Self-control: Power to the person* (pp. 77–85). Monterey, CA: Brooks-Cole.

Babyak, M., Blumenthal, J. A., Herman, S., Khatri, P., Doraiswamy, M., Moore, K., et al. (2000). Exercise treatment for major depression: Maintenance of therapeutic benefit at 10 months. *Psychosomatic Medicine, 62,* 633–638.

Bach, P. B., Schrag, D., Brawley, O. W., Galaznik, A., Yakrin, S., & Begg, C. B. (2002). Survival of blacks and whites after a cancer diagnosis. *Journal of the American Association, 287,* 2106–2113.

Baer, J. S., & Marlatt, G. A. (1991). Maintenance of smoking cessation. *Clinics in Chest Medicine, 12,* 793–800.

Baer, J. S., Kivlahan, D. R., Fromme, K., & Marlatt, G. A. (1991). Secondary prevention of alcohol abuse with college students: A skills-training approach. In N. Heather, W. R. Miller, & J. Greeley (Eds.), *Self-control and the addictive behaviours* (pp. 339–356). New York: Maxwell-McMillan.

Baer, J. S., Marlatt, G. A., Kivlahan, D. R., Fromme, K., Larimer, M. E., & Williams, E. (1992). An experimental test of three methods of alcohol risk reduction with young adults. *Journal of Consulting and Clinical Psychology, 60,* 974–979.

Bages, N., Appels, A., & Falger, P. R. J. (1999). Vital exhaustion as a risk factor of myocardial infarction: A case-control study in Venezuela. *International Journal of Behavioral Medicine, 6,* 279–290.

Baig, E. (1997, February 17). The doctor is in cyberspace: Myriad sites offer feedback and support. *BusinessWeek,* p. 102E8.

Bair, M. J., Robinson, R. L., Eckert, G. J., Stang, P. E., Croghan, T. W., & Kroenke, K. (2004). Impact of pain on depression treatment response in primary care. *Psychosomatic Medicine, 66,* 17–22.

Baker, C. W., Little, T. D., & Brownell, K. D. (2003). Predicting adolescent eating and activity behaviors: The role of social norms and personal agency. *Health Psychology, 22,* 189–198.

Baker, C., Whisman, M. A., & Brownell, K. D. (2000). Studying intergenerational transmission of eating attitudes and behaviors: Methodological and conceptual questions. *Health Psychology, 19,* 376–381.

Baker, R. C., & Kirschenbaum, D. S. (1998). Weight control during the holidays: Highly consistent self-monitoring as a potentially useful coping mechanism. *Health Psychology, 17,* 367–370.

Baker, S. (1997, June 9). Apnea: The sleeper's worst nightmare. *BusinessWeek,* pp. 118–119.

Bales, D. W., Spell, N., Cullen, D. J., Burdick, E., Laird, N., Peterson, L. A., et al. for the Adverse Drug Events Prevention Study Group. (1997). The cost of adverse drug events in hospitalized patients. *Journal of the American Medical Association, 277,* 307–311.

Balfour, L., White, D. R., Schiffrin, A., Dougherty, G., & Dufresne, J. (1993). Dietary disinhibition, perceived stress, and glucose control in young, Type I diabetic women. *Health Psychology, 12,* 33–38.

Bandura, A. (1969). *Principles of behavior modification.* New York: Holt, Rinehart & Winston.

Bandura, A. (1977). Self-efficacy: Toward a unifying theory of behavioral change. *Psychological Review, 84,* 191–215.

Bandura, A. (1986). *Social foundations of thought and action: A social cognitive theory.* Englewood Cliffs, NJ: Prentice-Hall.

Bandura, A. (1989). Perceived self-efficacy in the exercise of control over AIDS infection. In S. J. Blumenthal, A. Eichler, & G. Weissman (Eds.), *Women and AIDS.* Washington, D.C.: American Psychiatric Press.

Bandura, A. (1991). Self-efficacy mechanism in physiological activation and health-promotion behavior. In J. Madden IV (Ed.), *Neurobiology of learning, emotion, and affect* (pp. 229–269). New York: Raven Press.

Banks, S. M., Salovey, P., Greener, S., Rothman, A. J., Moyer, A., Beauvais, J., et al. (1995). The effects of message framing on mammography utilization. *Health Psychology, 14,* 178–184.

Banthia, R., Malcarne, V. L., Varni, J. W., Ko, C. M., Sadler, G. R., & Greenbergs, H. L. (2003). The effects of dyadic strength and coping styles on psychological distress in couples faced with prostate cancer. *Journal of Behavioral Medicine, 26,* 31–51.

Barbarin, O. A., & Chesler, M. (1986). The medical context of parental coping with childhood cancer. *American Journal of Community Psychology, 14,* 221–235.

Barber, T. X. (1965). Physiological effects of "hypnotic suggestions": A critical review of recent research (1960–64). *Psychological Bulletin, 63,* 201–222.

Bardwell, W. A., Ancoli-Israel, S., Berry, C. C., & Dimsdale, J. E. (2001). Neuropsychological effects of one-week continuous positive airway pressure treatment in patients with obstructive sleep apnea: A placebo-controlled study. *Psychosomatic Medicine, 63,* 579–584.

Barefoot, J. C. (1992). Developments in the measurement of hostility. In H. S. Friedman (Ed.), *Hostility, coping, and health* (pp. 13–31). Washington, D.C.: American Psychological Association.

Barefoot, J. C., Maynard, K. E., Beckham, J. C., Brummett, B. H., Hooker, K., & Siegler, I. C. (1998). Trust, health, and longevity. *Journal of Behavioral Medicine, 21,* 517–526.

Barinaga, M. (1997). How much pain for cardiac gain? *Science, 276,* 1324–1327.

Barnett, R. C., & Marshall, N. L. (1993). Men, family-role quality, job-role quality, and physical health. *Health Psychology, 12,* 48–55.

Barnett, R. C., Davidson, H., & Marshall, N. L. (1991). Physical symptoms and the interplay of work and family roles. *Health Psychology, 10,* 94–101.

Barnett, R. C., Raudenbush, S. W., Brennan, R. T., Pleck, J. H., & Marshall, N. L. (1995). Change in job and marital experiences and change in psychological distress: A longitudinal study of dual-earner couples. *Journal of Personality and Social Psychology, 69,* 839–850.

Bar-On, D. (1986). Professional models vs. patient models in rehabilitation after heart attack. *Human Relations, 39,* 917–932.

Bar-On, D. (1987). Causal attributions and the rehabilitation of myocardial infarction victims. *Journal of Social and Clinical Psychology, 5,* 114–122.

Bar-On, D., & Dreman, S. (1987). When spouses disagree: A predictor of cardiac rehabilitation. *Family Systems Medicine, 5,* 228–237.

Barr, I. K. (1983). Physicians' views of patients in prepaid group practice: Reasons for visits to HMOs. *Journal of Health and Social Behavior, 24,* 244–255.

Barr, S. I. (1995). Dieting attitudes and behavior in urban high school students: Implications for calcium intake. *Journal of Adolescent Health, 16,* 458–464.

Bartholow, B. D., Sher, K. J., & Krull, J. L. (2003) Changes in heavy drinking over the third decade of life as a function of collegiate fraternity and sorority involvement: A prospective multilevel analysis. *Health Psychology, 22,* 616–626.

Barton, J., Chassin, L., Presson, C. C., & Sherman, S. J. (1982). Social image factors as motivators of smoking initiation in early and middle adolescence. *Child Development, 53,* 1499–1511.

Bartrop, R. W., Lockhurst, E., Lazarus, L., Kiloh, L. G., & Penny, R. (1977). Depressed lymphocyte function after bereavement. *Lancet, 1,* 834–836.

Bastone, E. C., & Kerns, R. D. (1995). Effects of self-efficacy and perceived social support on recovery-related behaviors after coronary artery bypass graft surgery. *Annals of Behavioral Medicine, 17,* 324–330.

Battle, E. K., & Brownell, K. D. (1996). Confronting a rising tide of eating disorders and obesity: Treatment vs. prevention and policy. *Addictive Behaviors, 21,* 755–765.

Baum, A. (1990). Stress, intrusive imagery, and chronic distress. *Health Psychology, 9,* 653–675.

Baum, A. (1994). Behavioral, biological, and environmental interactions in disease processes. In S. Blumenthal, K. Matthews, & S. Weiss (Eds.), *New research frontiers in behavioral medicine: Proceedings of the national conference* (pp. 61–70). Washington, D.C.: NIH Publications.

Baum, A., & Grunberg, N. E. (1991). Gender, stress, and health. *Health Psychology, 10,* 80–85.

Baum, A., & Valins, S. (1977). *Architecture and social behavior: Psychological studies of social density.* Hillsdale, NJ: Erlbaum.

Baum, A., Cohen, L., & Hall, M. (1993). Control and intrusive memories as possible determinants of chronic stress. *Psychosomatic Medicine, 55,* 274–286.

Baum, A., Friedman, A. L., & Zakowski, S. G. (1997). Stress and genetic testing for disease risk. *Health Psychology, 16,* 8–19.

Baum, A., Grunberg, N. E., & Singer, J. E. (1982). The use of psychological and neuroendocrinological measurements in the study of stress. *Health Psychology, 1,* 217–236.

Baum, J. G., Clark, H. B., & Sandler, J. (1991). Preventing relapse in obesity through posttreatment maintenance systems: Comparing the relative efficacy of two levels of therapist support. *Journal of Behavioral Medicine, 14,* 287–302.

Bauman, K. E., Koch, G. G., & Fisher, L. A. (1989). Family cigarette smoking and test performance by adolescents. *Health Psychology, 8,* 97–105.

Baumann, L. J., Zimmerman, R. S., & Leventhal, H. (1989). An experiment in common sense: Education at blood pressure screening. *Patient Education Counseling, 14,* 53–67.

Becker, M. H. (1993). A medical sociologist looks at health promotion. *Journal of Health and Social Behavior, 34,* 1–6.

Becker, M. H., & Janz, N. K. (1987). On the effectiveness and utility of health hazard/health risk appraisal in clinical and nonclinical settings. *Health Services Research, 22,* 537–551.

Becker, M. H., Kaback, M., Rosenstock, I., & Ruth, M. (1975). Some influences on public participation in a genetic screening program. *Journal of Community Health, 1,* 3–14.

Beckett, M. (2000). Converging health inequalities in later life—An artifact of mortality selection? *Journal of Health and Social Behavior, 41,* 106–119.

Beckman, H. B., & Frankel, R. M. (1984). The effect of physician behavior on the collection of data. *Annals of Internal Medicine, 101,* 692–696.

Beecher, H. K. (1959). *Measurement of subjective responses.* New York: Oxford University Press.

Belar, C. D. (1997). Clinical health psychology: A specialty for the 21st century. *Health Psychology, 16,* 411–416.

Belisle, M., Roskies, E., & Levesque, J. M. (1987). Improving adherence to physical activity. *Health Psychology, 6,* 159–172.

Belloc, N. D., & Breslow, L. (1972). Relationship of physical health status and family practices. *Preventive Medicine, 1,* 409–421.

Benight, C. C., Antoni, M. H., Kilbourn, K., Ironson, G., Kumar, M. A., Fletcher, M. A., et al. (1997). Coping self-efficacy buffers psychological and physiological disturbances in HIV-infected men following a natural disaster. *Health Psychology, 16,* 248–255.

Benotsch, E. G., Christensen, A. J., & McKelvey, L. (1997). Hostility, social support, and ambulatory cardiovascular activity. *Journal of Behavioral Medicine, 20,* 163–182.

Bensley, L. S., & Wu, R. (1991). The role of psychological reactance in drinking following alcohol prevention messages. *Journal of Applied Social Psychology, 21,* 1111-1124.

Benson, B. A., Gross, A. M., Messer, S. C., Kellum, G., & Passmore, L. A. (1991). Social support networks among families of children with craniofacial anomalies. *Health Psychology, 10,* 252–258.

Ben-Sira, Z. (1980). Affective and instrumental components in the physician patient relationship: An additional dimension of interaction theory. *Health and Social Behavior, 21,* 170–180.

Ben-Zur, H., Gilbar, O., & Lev, S. (2001). Coping with breast cancer: Patient, spouse, and dyad models. *Psychosomatic Medicine, 62,* 32–39.

Berkman, L. F. (1985). The relationship of social networks and social support to morbidity and mortality. In S. Cohen & S. L. Syme (Eds.), *Social support and health* (pp. 241–262). Orlando, FL: Academic Press.

Berkman, L. F., & Syme, S. L. (1979). Social networks, host resistance, and mortality: A nine-year followup study of Alameda County residents. *American Journal of Epidemiology, 109,* 186–204.

Berkowitz, R. I., Agras, W. S., Korner, A. F., Kraemer, H. C., & Zeanah, C. H. (1985). Physical activity and adiposity: A longitudinal study from birth to childhood. *Journal of Pediatrics, 106,* 734–738.

Bianco, A., & Schine, E. (1997, March 24). Doctors, Inc. *BusinessWeek,* pp. 204–206, 208–210.

Bigatti, S. M., & Cronan, T. A. (2002). An examination of the physical health, heath care use and psychological well-being of spouses of people with fibromyalgia syndrome. *Health Psychology, 21,* 157–166.

Biggs, A. M., Aziz, Q., Tomenson, B., & Creed, F. (2003). Do childhood diversity and recent social stress predict health care use in patients presenting with upper abdominal or chest pain? *Psychosomatic Medicine, 65,* 1020–1028.

Biglan, A., McConnell, S., Severson, H. H., Bavry, J., & Ary, D. (1984). A situational analysis of adolescent smoking. *Journal of Behavioral Medicine, 7,* 109–114.

Biglan, A., Metzler, C. W., Wirt, R., Ary, D., Noell, J., Ochs, L., et al. (1990). Social and behavioral factors associated with high-risk sexual behavior among adolescents. *Journal of Behavioral Medicine, 13,* 245–262.

Biglan, A., Severson, H., Ary, D., Faller, C., Gallison, C., Thompson R., et al. (1987). Do smoking prevention programs really work? Attrition and the internal and external validity of an evaluation of a refusal skills training program. *Journal of Behavioral Medicine, 10,* 159–171.

Billings, A. C., & Moos, R. H. (1982). Coping, stress, and social resources among adults with unipolar depression. *Journal of Personality and Social Psychology, 46,* 877–891.

Billings, A. C., & Moos, R. H., Miller, J. J., III, & Gottlieb, J. E. (1987). Psychosocial adaptation in juvenile rheumatoid disease: A controlled evaluation. *Health Psychology, 6,* 343–359.

Billings, A. C., & Moos, R. H. (1982). Stressful life events and symptoms: A longitudinal model. *Health Psychology, 1,* 99–117.

Bishop, G. D., & Converse, S. A. (1986). Illness representations: A prototype approach. *Health Psychology, 5,* 95–114.

Bishop S. R. (2002). What do we really know about mindfulness-based stress? *Psychosomatic Medicine, 64,* 71–84.

Bishop, S. R., & Warr, D. (2003). Coping, catastrophizing and chronic pain in breast cancer. *Journal of Behavioral Medicine, 26,* 265–281.

Bjorntorp, P. (1996). Behavior and metabolic disease. *International Journal of Behavioral Medicine, 3,* 285–302.

Black, P. H., & Garbutt, L. D. (2002). Stress, inflammation and cardiovascular disease. *Journal of Psychosomatic Research, 52,* 1–23.

Blackhall, L. J., Murphy, S. T., Frank, G., Michel, V., & Azen, S. (1995). Ethnicity and attitudes toward patient autonomy. *Journal of the American Medical Association, 274,* 820–825.

Blair, S. N., Kohl, H. W., III, Paffenbarger, R. S., Clark, D. G., Cooper, K. H., & Gibbons, L. W. (1989). Physical fitness and all-cause mortality: A prospective study of healthy men and women. *Journal of the American Medical Association, 262,* 2395–2401.

Blakeslee, S. (1998, October 13). Placebos prove so powerful even experts are surprised. *The New York Times,* Sect. F, p. 2.

Blalock, S. J., DeVellis, R. F., Giorgino, K. B., DeVellis, B. M., Gold, D. T., Dooley, M. J., et al. (1996). Osteoporosis prevention in premenopausal women: Using a stage model approach to examine the predictors of behavior. *Health Psychology, 15,* 84–93.

Blanchard, E. B., Andrasik, F., & Silver, B. V. (1980). Biofeedback and relaxation in the treatment of tension headaches: A reply to Belar. *Journal of Behavioral Medicine, 3,* 227–232.

Blanchard, E. B., McCoy, G. C., Wittrock, D., Musso, A., Gerardi, R. J., & Pangburn, L. (1988). A controlled comparison of thermal biofeedback and relaxation training in the treatment of essential hypertension: II. Effects on cardiovascular reactivity. *Health Psychology, 7,* 19–33.

Blaney, N. T., Millon, C., Morgan, R., Eisdorfer, C., & Szapocznik, J. (1990). Emotional distress, stress-related disruption and coping among healthy HIV-positive gay males. *Psychology and Health, 4,* 259–273.

Blanton, H., & Gerrard, M. (1997). Effect of sexual motivation on men's risk perception for sexually transmitted disease: There must be 50 ways to justify a lover. *Health Psychology, 16,* 374–379.

Blascovich, J., Spencer, S. J., Quinn, D., & Steele, C. (2001). African Americans and high blood pressure: The role of stereotype threat. *Psychological Science, 12,* 225–229.

Blissmer, B., & McAuley, E. (2002). Testing the requirements of stages of physical activity among adults: The comparative effectiveness of stage-matched, mismatched, standard care, and control interventions. *Annals of Behavioral Medicine, 24,* 181–189.

Blomhoff, S., Spetalen, S., Jacobsen, M. B., & Malt, U. F. (2001). Phobic anxiety changes the function of brain-gut axis in irritable bowel syndrome. *Psychosomatic Medicine, 63,* 959–965.

Bluebond-Langner, M. (1977). Meanings of death to children. In H. Feifel (Ed.), *New meanings of death* (pp. 47–66). New York: McGraw-Hill.

Blumenthal, J. A., & Emery, C. F. (1988). Rehabilitation of patients following myocardial infarction. *Journal of Consulting and Clinical Psychology, 56,* 374–381.

Blumenthal, J. A., Emery, C. F., Madden, D. J., Schniebolk, S., Walsh-Riddle, M., George, L. K., et al. (1991). Long-term effects of exercise on psychological functioning in older men and women. *Journal of Gerontology, 46,* 352–361.

Blumenthal, J. A., Emery, C. F., Walsh, M. A., Cox, D. R., Kuhn, C. M., Williams, R. B., et al. (1988). Exercise training in healthy Type A middle-aged men: Effects of behavioral and cardiovascular responses. *Psychosomatic Medicine, 50,* 418–433.

Blumenthal, J. A., Matthews, K., Fredrikson, M., Rifai, N., Schneibolk, S., German, D., et al. (1991). Effects of exercise training on cardiovascular function and plasma lipid, lipoprotein, and apolipoprotein concentrations in premenopausal and postmenopausal women. *Arteriosclerosis and Thrombosis, 11,* 912–917.

Blumenthal, J. A., Siegel, W. C., & Appelbaum, M. (1991). Failure of exercise to reduce blood pressure in patients with mild hypertension: Results of a randomized controlled trial. *Journal of the American Medical Association, 266,* 2098–2104.

Boardman, J. D., Finch, B. K., Ellison, C. G., Williams, D. R., & Jackson, J. S. (2001). Neighborhood disadvantage, stress, and drug use among adults. *Journal of Health and Social Behavior, 42,* 151–165.

Bock, B. C., Albrecht, A. E., Traficante, R. M., Clark, M. M., Pinto, B. M., Tilkemeier, P., et al. (1997). Predictors of exercise adherence following participation in a cardiac rehabilitation program. *International Journal of Behavioral Medicine, 4,* 60–75.

Bogart, L. M. (2001). Relationship of stereotypic beliefs about physicians to health-care relevant behaviors and cognitions among African American women. *Journal of Behavioral Medicine, 245,* 573–586.

Bolger, N., DeLongis, A., Kessler, R. C., & Schilling, E. A. (1989). Effects of daily stress on negative mood. *Journal of Personality and Social Psychology, 57,* 808–818.

Bolger, N., Zuckerman, A., & Kessler, R. C. (2000). Invisible support and adjustment to stress. *Journal of Personality and Social Psychology, 79,* 953–961.

Bolles, R. C., & Fanselow, M. S. (1982). Endorphins and behavior. *Annual Review of Psychology, 33,* 87–101.

Bombardier, C., Gorayeb, R., Jordan, J., Brooks, W. B., & Divine, G. (1991). The utility of the psychosomatic system checklist among hospitalized patients. *Journal of Behavioral Medicine, 14,* 369–382.

Bonanno, G. A., et al. (2002). Resilience to loss and chronic grief: A prospective study from preloss to 18-months postloss. *Journal of Personality and Social Psychology, 83,* 1150–1164.

Bonanno, G. A., Keltner, D., Holen, A., & Horowitz, M. J. (1995). When avoiding unpleasant emotions might not be such a bad thing: Verbal-autonomic response dissociation and midlife conjugal bereavement. *Journal of Personality and Social Psychology, 69,* 975–989.

Bonnet, M. H., & Arand, D. L. (1998). Heart rate variability in insomniacs and matched normal sleepers. *Psychosomatic Medicine, 60,* 610–615.

Booth, A., & Amato, P. (1991). Divorce and psychological stress. *Journal of Health and Social Behavior, 32,* 396–407.

Boscarino, J. (1997). Diseases among men 20 years after exposure to severe stress: Implications for clinical research and medical care. *Psychosomatic Medicine, 59,* 605–614.

Boscarino, J., & Chang, J. (1999). Higher abnormal leukocyte and lymphocyte counts 20 years after exposure to severe stress: Research and clinical implications. *Psychosomatic Medicine, 61,* 378–386.

Boskind-White, M., & White, W. C. (1983). *Bulimarexia: The binge/purge cycle.* New York: Norton.

Bosma, H., Marmot, M. G., Hemingway, H., Nicholson, A. C., Brunner, E., & Stanfeld, S. A. (1997). Low job control and risk of coronary heart disease in Whitehall II (prospective cohort) study. *British Medical Journal, 314,* 285.

Botvin, E. M., Botvin, G. J., Michela, J. L., Baker, E., & Filazzola, A. D. (1991). Adolescent smoking behavior and the recognition of cigarette advertisements. *Journal of Applied Social Psychology, 21,* 919–932.

Botvin, G. J., Dusenbury, L., Baker, E., James-Ortiz, S., Botvin, E. M., & Kerner, J. (1992). Smoking prevention among urban minority youth: Assessing effects on outcome and mediating variables. *Health Psychology, 11,* 290–299.

Bouchard, C. (2002). Genetic influences on body weight. In C. G. Fairburn & K. D. Brownell (Eds.), *Eating disorders and obesity: A comprehensive handbook* (pp. 16–21). New York: Guilford.

Bouchard, C., Tremblay, A., Despres, J. P., Nadeau, A., Lupien, P. J., Thierault, G., et al. (1990). The response to long-term overfeeding in identical twins. *New England Journal of Medicine, 322,* 1477–1487.

Boutelle, K. N., Kirschenbaum, D. S., Baker, R. C., & Mitchell, M. E. (1999). How can obese weight controllers minimize weight gain during the high risk holiday season? By self-monitoring very consistently. *Health Psychology, 18,* 364–368.

Bouton, M. E. (2000). A learning theory perspective on lapse, relapse, and the maintenance of behavior change. *Health Psychology, 19,* 57–63.

Bowen, D. J., Spring, B., & Fox, E. (1991). Tryptophan and high-carbohydrate diets as adjuncts to smoking cessation therapy. *Journal of Behavioral Medicine, 14,* 97–110.

Bowen, D. J., Tomoyasu, N., Anderson, M., Carney, M., & Kristal, A. (1992). Effects of expectancies and personalized feedback on fat consumption, taste, and preference. *Journal of Applied Social Psychology, 22,* 1061–1079.

Bower, J. E., Kemeny, M. E., Taylor, S. E., & Fahey, J. L. (1998). Cognitive processing, discovery of meaning, CD4 decline, and AIDS-related mortality among bereaved HIV-seropositive men. *Journal of Consulting and Clinical Psychology, 66,* 979–986.

Bower, J. E., Kemeny, M. E., Taylor, S. E., & Fahey, J. L. (2003). Finding meaning and its association with natural killer cell cytotoxicity among participants in bereavement-related disclosure intervention. *Annals of Behavioral Medicine, 25,* 146–155.

Bowlby, J. (1969). *Attachment and loss: Vol. 1. Attachment.* New York: Basic Books.

Bowlby, J. (1973). *Attachment and loss: Vol. 2. Separation.* New York: Basic Books.

Boyce, W. T., Adams, S., Tschann, J. M., Cohen, F., Wara, D., & Gunnar, M. R. (1995). Adrenocortical and behavioral predictors of immune responses to starting school. *Pediatric Research, 38,* 1009–1017.

Boyce, W. T., Alkon, A. Tschann, J. M., Chesney, M. A., & Alpert, B. S. (1995). Dimensions of psychobiologic reactivity: Cardiovascular responses to laboratory stressors in preschool children. *Annals of Behavioral Medicine, 17,* 315–323.

Boyce, W. T., Chesterman, E. A., Martin, N., Folkman, S., Cohen, F., & Wara, D. (1993). Immunologic changes occurring at kindergarten entry predict respiratory illnesses after the Loma Prieta earthquake. *Journal of Developmental and Behavioral Pediatrics, 14,* 296–303.

Bradley, L. A. (Ed.), *Coping with chronic disease: Research and applications.* New York: Academic Press, pp. 85–112.

Bradley, L. A., Young, L. D., Anderson, K. O., Turner, R. A., Agudelo, C. A., McDaniel, L. K., et al. (1987). Effects of psychological therapy on pain behavior of rheumatoid arthritis patients: Treatment outcome and six-month followup. *Arthritis and Rheumatism, 30,* 1105–1114.

Bramwell, L. (1986). Wives' experiences in the support role after husbands' first myocardial infarction. *Heart and Lung, 15,* 578–584.

Brand, A. H., Johnson, J. H., & Johnson, S. B. (1986). Life stress and diabetic control in children and adolescents with insulin-dependent diabetes. *Journal of Pediatric Psychology, 11,* 481–495.

Brandon, T. H., Copeland, A. L., & Saper, Z. L. (1995). Programmed therapeutic messages as a smoking treatment adjunct: Reducing the impact of negative affect. *Health Psychology, 14,* 41–47.

Branegan, J. (1997, March 17). I want to draw the line myself. *Time,* pp. 30–31.

Branstetter, E. (1969). The young child's response to hospitalization: Separation anxiety or lack of mothering care? *American Journal of Public Health, 59,* 92–97.

Brantley, P. J., Mosley, T. H., Jr., Bruce, B. K., McKnight, G. T., & Jones, G. N. (1990). Efficacy of behavioral management and patient education on vascular access cleansing compliance in hemodialysis patients. *Health Psychology, 9,* 103–113.

Bray, G. A., & Tartaglia, L. A. (2000). Medicinal strategies in the treatment of obesity. *Nature, 404,* 672–677.

Brenes, G. A., Rapp, S. R., Rejeski, W. J., & Miller, M. E. (2002). Do optimism and pessimism predict physical functioning? *Journal of Behavioral Medicine, 25,* 219–231.

Brennan, P. L., & Moos, R. H. (1990). Life stressors, social resources, and late-life problem drinking. *Psychology and Aging, 5,* 491–501.

Brennan, P. L., & Moos, R. H. (1995). Life context, coping responses, and adaptive outcomes: A stress and coping perspective on late-life problem drinking. In T. Beresford & E. Gomberg (Eds.), *Alcohol and aging* (pp. 230–248). New York: Oxford University Press.

Brenner, G. F., Melamed, B. G., & Panush, R. S. (1994). Optimism and coping as determinants of psychosocial adjustment to rheumatoid arthritis. *Journal of Clinical Psychology in Medical Settings, 1,* 115–134.

Breslau, N., & Davis, G. C. (1987). Posttraumatic stress disorder: The stressor criterion. *Journal of Nervous and Mental Disease, 175,* 255–264.

Breslow, L., & Enstrom, J. E. (1980). Persistence of health habits and their relationship to mortality. *Preventive Medicine, 9,* 469–483.

Brewer, N. T., Weinstein, N. D, Cuite, C. L., & Herrington, J. E. (2004). Risk perceptions and their relation to risk behavior. *Annals of Behavioral Medicine, 27,* 125–130.

Brissette, I., & Cohen, S. (2002). The contribution of individual differences in hostility to the associations between daily interpersonal conflict, affect, and sleep. *Personality and Social Psychology Bulletin, 28,* 1265–1274.

Brissette, I., Leventhal, H., & Leventhal, E. A. (2003). Observer ratings of health and sickness: Can other people tell us anything about our health that we don't already know? *Health Psychology, 22,* 471–478.

Brissette, I., Scheier, M. F., & Carver, C. S. (2002). The role of optimism and social network development, coping, and psychological adjustment during a life transition. *Journal of Personality and Social Psychology, 82,* 102–111.

Brisson, C., LaFlamme, N., Moisan, J., Milot, A., Masse, B., & Vezina, M. (1999). Effect of family responsibilities and job strain on ambulatory blood pressure among white-collar women. *Psychosomatic Medicine, 61,* 205–213.

Britton, A., & Marmot, M. (2004). Different measures of alcohol consumption and risk of coronary heart disease and all-cause mortality: 11-year follow-up of the Whitehall II Cohort Study. *Addiction, 99,* 109–116.

Broadbent, E., Petrie, K. J., Alley, P. G., & Booth, R. J. (2003). Psychological stress impairs early wound repair following surgery. *Psychosomatic Medicine, 65,* 865–869.

Broadwell, S. D., & Light, K. C. (1999). Family support and cardiovascular responses in married couples during conflict and other interactions. *International Journal of Behavioral Medicine, 6,* 40–63.

Brody, J. E. (1993, December 2). Heart attack risks shown in bursts of high activity. *The New York Times,* p. A10.

Brody, J. E. (1996a, February 28). Good habits outweigh genes as key to a healthy old age. *The New York Times,* p. B11.

Brody, J. E. (2004, January 6). Hunt for heart disease tracks a new suspect. *The New York Times*, p. D7.

Brody, J. E. (2002, January 22). Misunderstood opioids and needless pain. *The New York Times*, p. D8.

Broman, C. L. (1993). Social relationships and health-related behavior. *Journal of Behavioral Medicine, 16,* 335–350.

Bromberger, J. T., & Matthews, K. A. (1996). A longitudinal study of the effects of pessimism, trait anxiety, and life stress on depressive symptoms in middle-aged women. *Psychology and Aging, 11,* 207–213.

Brondolo, E., Rieppi, R., Erickson, S. A., Bagiella, E., Shapiro, P. A., McKinley, P., & Sloan, R. P. (2003a). Hostility, interpersonal interactions, and ambulatory blood pressure. *Psychosomatic Medicine, 65,* 1003–1011.

Brondolo, E., Rieppi, R., Kelly, K. P., & Gerin, W. (2003b). Perceived racism and blood pressure: A review of the literature and conceptual and methodological critique. *Annals of Behavioral Medicine, 25,* 55–65.

Brondolo, E., Rosen, R. C., Kostis, J. B., & Schwartz, J. E. (1999). Relationship of physical symptoms and mood to perceived and actual blood pressure in hypertensive men: A repeated-measure design. *Psychosomatic Medicine, 61,* 311–318.

Bronzaft, A. L., & McCarthy, D. P. (1975). The effects of elevated train noise on reading ability. *Environment and Behavior, 7,* 517–527.

Brosschot, J., Godaert, G., Benschop, R., Olff, M., Ballieux, R., & Heijnen, C. (1998). Experimental stress and immunological reactivity: A closer look at perceived uncontrollability. *Psychosomatic Medicine, 60,* 359–361.

Brown, G. W., & Harris, T. (1978). *Social origins of depression: A study of psychiatric disorder in women.* New York: Free Press.

Brown, J. D., & McGill, K. L. (1989). The cost of good fortune: When positive life events produce negative health consequences. *Journal of Personality and Social Psychology, 57,* 1103–1110.

Brown, J. D., & Siegel, J. M. (1988). Exercise as a buffer of life stress: A prospective study of adolescent health. *Health Psychology, 7,* 341–353.

Brown, J. H., & Raven, B. H. (1994). Power and compliance in doctor/patient relationships. *Journal of Health Psychology, 6,* 3–22.

Brown, J. L., Sheffield, D., Leary, M. R., & Robinson, M. E. (2003). Social support and experimental pain. *Psychosomatic Medicine, 65,* 276–283.

Brown, K. M., Middaugh, S. J., Haythornthwaite, J. A., & Bielory, L. (2001). The effects of stress, anxiety and outdoor temperature on the frequency and severity of Raynaud's attacks: The Raynaud treatment study. *Journal of Behavioral Medicine, 24,* 137–153.

Brown, K. W., Levy, A. R., Rosberger, Z., & Edgar, L. (2003). Psychological distress and cancer survival: A follow-up 10 years after diagnosis. *Psychosomatic Medicine, 65,* 636–643.

Brown, K. W., & Ryan, R. M. (2003). The benefits of being present: Mindfulness and its role in psychological well-being. *Journal of Personality and Social Psychology, 84,* 822–848.

Brown, P. L. (1990, November 29). For some, "retired" is an inaccurate label. *The New York Times*, pp. B1–B2.

Brown, S. L. (1997). Prevalence and effectiveness of self-regulatory techniques used to avoid drunk driving. *Journal of Behavioral Medicine, 20,* 55–66.

Brown, S. L., Nesse, R. M., Vinokur, A. D., & Smith, D. M. (2003). Providing social support may be more beneficial than receiving it: Results from a prospective study of mortality. *Psychological Science, 14,* 320–327.

Brownell, K. D. (1982). Obesity: Understanding and treating a serious, prevalent and refractory disorder. *Journal of Consulting and Clinical Psychology, 50,* 820–840.

Brownell, K. D. (2002). *Appendix A—Master List of Techniques from The LEARN Program for Weight Management.* Dallas: American Health Publishing Company.

Brownell, K. D., & Felix, M. R. J. (1987). Competitions to facilitate health promotion: Review and conceptual analysis. *American Journal of Health Promotion, 2,* 28–36.

Brownell, K. D., & Kramer, F. M. (1989). Behavioral management of obesity. *Medical Clinics of North America, 73,* 185–201.

Brownell, K. D., & Napolitano, M. A. (1995). Distorting reality for children: Body size proportions of Barbie and Ken dolls. *International Journal of Eating Disorders, 18,* 295–298.

Brownell, K. D., & Rodin, J. (1996). The dieting maelstrom: Is it possible and advisable to lose weight? *American Psychologist, 49,* 781–791.

Brownell, K. D., & Stunkard, A. J. (1981). Couples training, pharmacotherapy and behavior therapy in the treatment of obesity. *Archives of General Psychiatry, 38,* 1224–1229.

Brownell, K. D., & Wadden, T. A. (1992). Etiology and treatment of obesity: Understanding a serious, prevalent, and refractory disorder. *Journal of Consulting and Clinical Psychology, 60,* 505–517.

Brownell, K. D., Cohen, R. Y., Stunkard, A. J., Felix, M. R. J., & Cooley, B. (1984). Weight loss competitions at the work site: Impact on weight, morale, and cost-effectiveness. *American Journal of Public Health, 74,* 1283–1285.

Brownell, K. D., Greenwood, M. R. C., Stellar, E., & Shrager, E. E. (1986). The effects of repeated cycles of weight loss and regain in rats. *Physiology and Behavior, 38,* 459–464.

Brownell, K. D., Marlatt, G. A., Lichtenstein, E., & Wilson, G. T. (1986). Understanding and preventing relapse. *American Psychologist, 41,* 765–782.

Brownell, K. D., Steen, S. N., & Wilmore, J. H. (1987). Weight regulation practices in athletes: Analysis of metabolic and health effects. *Medicine and Science in Sports and Exercise, 19,* 546–556.

Brownell, K. D., Stunkard, A. J., & McKeon, P. E. (1985). Weight reduction at the work site: A promise partially fulfilled. *American Journal of Psychiatry, 142,* 47–52.

Browning, C. R., & Cagney, K. A. (2003). Moving beyond poverty: Neighboring structure, social processes, and health. *Journal of Health and Social Behavior, 44,* 552–571.

Brownley, K. A., West, S. G., Hinderliter, A. L., & Light, K. C. (1996). Acute aerobic exercise reduces ambulatory blood pressure in borderline hypertensive men and women. *American Journal of Hypertension, 9,* 200–206.

Brownson, R. C., Chang, J. C., Davis, J. R., & Smith, C. A. (1991). Physical activity on the job and cancer in Missouri. *Public Health Briefs, 81,* 639–640.

Brubaker, R. G., & Wickersham, D. (1990). Encouraging the practice of testicular self-examination: A field application of the theory of reasoned action. *Health Psychology, 9,* 154–163.

Bruhn, J. G. (1965). An epidemiological study of myocardial infarction in an Italian-American community. *Journal of Chronic Diseases, 18,* 326–338.

Brummet, B. H., Babyak, M. A., Mark, D. B., Clapp-Channing, N. E., Siegler, I. C., & Barefoot, J. C. (2004). Prospective study of perceived stress in cardiac patients. *Annals of Behavioral Medicine, 27,* 22–30.

Brummett, B. H., Babyak, M. A., Barefoot, J. C., Bosworth, H. B., Clapp-Channing, N. E., Siegler, I. C., et al. (1998). Social support and hostility as predictors of depressive symptoms in cardiac patients one month after hospitalization: A prospective study. *Psychosomatic Medicine, 60,* 707–713.

Bryan, A., Fisher, J. D., & Fisher, W. A. (2002). Tests of the mediational role of preparatory safer sexual behavior in the context of the theory or planned behavior. *Health Psychology, 21,* 71–80.

Buchwald, D., Herrell, R., Ashton, S., Belcourt, M., Schmaling, K., Sullivan, P., et al. (2001). A twin study of chronic fatigue. *Psychosomatic Medicine, 63,* 936–943.

Buckalew, L. W., & Sallis, R. E. (1986). Patient compliance and medication perception. *Journal of Clinical Psychology, 42,* 49–53.

Buckingham, R. W. (1983). Hospice care in the United States: The process begins. *Omega, 13,* 159–171.

Buckley, T. C., & Kaloupek, D. G. (2001). A meta-analytic examination of basal cardiovascular activity in posttraumatic stress disorder. *Psychosomatic Medicine, 63,* 585–594.

Budman, S. H. (2000). Behavioral health care dot-com and beyond: Computer-mediated communications in mental health and substance abuse treatment. *American Psychologist, 55,* 1290–1300.

Bukberg, J., Penman, D., & Holland, J. C. (1984). Depression in hospitalized cancer patients. *Psychosomatic Medicine, 46,* 199–212.

Bureau of Labor Statistics. (2004). *Industry-occupation employment matrix.* Retrieved from: http://data.bls.gov/oep/nioem/empiohm.jsp

Burg, M. M., Benedetto, M. C., Rosenberg, R., & Soufer, R. (2003). Presurgical depression predicts medical mortality 6 months after coronary artery bypass graft surgery. *Psychosomatic Medicine, 65,* 111–118.

Burgess, C., Morris, T., & Pettingale, K. W. (1988). Psychological response to cancer diagnosis: II. Evidence for coping styles. *Journal of Psychosomatic Research, 32,* 263–272.

Burish, T. G., & Bradley, L. A. (1983). *Coping with chronic disease: Research and applications.* New York: Academic Press.

Burish, T. G., & Jenkins, R. A. (1992). Effectiveness of biofeedback and relaxation training in reducing the side effects of cancer chemotherapy. *Health Psychology, 11,* 17–23.

Burish, T. G., & Lyles, J. N. (1979). Effectiveness of relaxation training in reducing the aversiveness of chemotherapy in the treatment of cancer. *Journal of Behavior Therapy and Experimental Psychiatry, 10,* 357–361.

Burish, T. G., & Trope, D. M. (1992). Psychological techniques for controlling the adverse side effects of cancer chemotherapy: Findings from a decade of research. *Journal of Pain and Symptom Management, 7,* 287–301.

Burish, T. G., Carey, M. P., Wallston, K. A., Stein, M. J., Jamison, R. N., & Lyles, J. N. (1984). Health locus of control and chronic disease: An external orientation may be advantageous. *Journal of Social and Clinical Psychology, 2,* 326–332.

Burish, T. G., Snyder, S. L., & Jenkins, R. A. (1991). Preparing patients for cancer chemotherapy: Effect of coping preparation and relaxation interventions. *Journal of Consulting and Clinical Psychology, 59,* 518–525.

Burnam, M. A., Timbers, D. M., & Hough, R. L. (1984). Two measures of psychological distress among Mexican Americans, Mexicans and Anglos. *Journal of Health and Social Behavior, 25,* 24–33.

Burns, J. W. (2000). Repression predicts outcome following multidisciplinary treatment of chronic pain. *Health Psychology, 19,* 75–84.

Burns, M. O., & Seligman, M. E. P. (1989). Explanatory style across the life span: Evidence for stability over 52 years. *Journal of Personality and Social Psychology, 56,* 471–477.

Burns, V. E., Drayson, M., Ring, C., & Carroll, D. (2002). Perceived stress and psychological well-being are associated with antibody status after meningitis C conjugate vaccination. *Psychosomatic Medicine, 64,* 963–970.

Burrell, G., & Granlund, B. (2002). Women's hearts need special treatment. *International Journal of Behavioral Medicine, 9,* 228–242.

Burroughs, T. E., Hong, B. A., Kappel, D. F., & Freedman, B. K. (1998). The stability of family decisions to consent or refuse organ donation: Would you do it again? *Psychosomatic Medicine, 60,* 156–162.

Burton, R. P. D. (1998). Global integrative meaning as a mediating factor in the relationship between social roles and psychological distress. *Journal of Health and Social Behavior, 39,* 201–215.

Bush, C., Ditto, B., & Feuerstein, M. (1985). A controlled evaluation of paraspinal EMG biofeedback in the treatment of chronic low back pain. *Health Psychology, 4,* 307–321.

Bush, J. P., Melamed, B. G., Sheras, P. L., & Greenbaum, P. E. (1986). Mother-child patterns of coping with anticipatory medical stress. *Health Psychology, 5,* 137–157.

Bushjahn, A., Faulhaber, H. D., Freier, K., & Luft, F. C. (1999). Genetic and environmental influences on coping styles: A twin study. *Psychosomatic Medicine, 61,* 469–475.

Buske-Kirschbaum, A., Auer, K. von, Kreiger, S., Weis, S., Rauh, W., & Hellhammer, D. (2003). Blunted cortisol responses to psychosocial stress in asthmatic children: A general feature of atopic disease? *Psychosomatic Medicine, 65,* 806–810.

Bute, B. P., Mathew, J., Blumenthal, J. A., Welsh-Bomer, K., White, W. D., Mark, D., et al. (2003). Female gender is associated with impaired quality of life 1 year after coronary artery bypass surgery. *Psychosomatic Medicine, 65,* 944–951.

Butler, D. (2004, March 18). Slim pickings. *Nature, 428,* 252–254.

Butler, L. D., Koopman, C., Classen, C., & Spiegel, D. (1999). Traumatic stress, life events, and emotional support in women with metastatic breast cancer: Cancer-related traumatic stress symptoms associated with past and current stressors. *Health Psychology, 18,* 555–560.

Butler, L. D., Koopman, C., Cordova M. J., Garlan, R. W., DiMiceli S., & Spiegel, D. (2003). Psychological distress and pain significantly increase before death in metastatic breast cancer patients. *Psychosomatic Medicine, 65,* 416–426.

Butler, R. N. (1978). The doctor and the aged patient. In W. Reichel (Ed.), *The geriatric patient* (pp. 199–206). New York: HP.

Buunk, B. (1989). Affiliation and helping within organizations: A critical analysis of the role of social support with regard to occupational stress. In W. Stroebe & M. Hewstone (Eds.), *European review of social psychology* (Vol. 1). Chichester, England: Wiley.

Buunk, B. P., Doosje, B. J., Jans, L. G. J. M., & Hopstaken, L. E. M. (1993). Perceived reciprocity, social support, and stress at work: The role of exchange and communal orientation. *Journal of Personality and Social Psychology, 65,* 801–811.

Buydens-Branchey, L., & Branchey, M. (2003). Association between low plasma levels of cholesterol and relapse in cocaine addicts. *Psychosomatic Medicine, 65,* 86–91.

Byock, I. R. (1991). Final Exit: A wake-up call to hospices. *Hospice Journal, 7,* 51–66.

Byrnes, D. M., Antoni, M. H., Goodkin, K., Efantis-Potter, J., Asthana, D., Simon, T., et al. (1998). Stressful events, pessimism, natural killer cell cytotoxicity, and cytotoxic/suppressor T cells in HIV1 Black women at risk for cervical cancer. *Psychosomatic Medicine, 60,* 714–722.

Cacioppo, J. T., Hawkley, L. C., Crawford, L. E., Ernst, J. M., Burleson, M. H., Kowalewski, R. B., et al. (2002). Loneliness and health: Potential mechanisms. *Psychosomatic Medicine, 64,* 407–417.

Calfas, K. J., et al. (1997). Mediators of change in physical activity following an intervention in primary care: PACE. *Preventive Medicine, 26,* 297–304.

Calhoun, L. G., Cann, A., Tedeschi, R. G., & McMillan, J. (2000). A correlational test of the relationship between posttraumatic growth, religion, and cognitive processing. *Journal of Traumatic Stress, 13,* 521–527.

Callahan, D. (2003). *What price better health? Hazards of the research imperative.* Berkeley, CA: University of California Press.

Calle, E. E., Rodriguez, C., Walker-Thurmond, K., & Thun, M. J. (2003). Overweight, obesity, and mortality from cancer in a prospectively studied cohort in U.S. adults. *New England Journal of Medicine, 348,* 1625–1638, http://www.nejm.org

Cameron, C. L., et al. (2001). Persistent symptoms among survivors of Hodgkin's disease: An explanatory model based on classical conditioning. *Health Psychology, 20,* 71–75.

Cameron, L., Leventhal, E. A., & Leventhal, H. (1993). Symptom representations and affect as determinants of care seeking in a community-dwelling, adult sample population. *Health Psychology, 12,* 171–179.

Cameron, L., Leventhal, E. A., & Leventhal, H. (1995). Seeking medical care in response to symptoms and life stress. *Psychosomatic Medicine, 57,* 1–11.

Cameron, N. (1963). *Personality development and psychology: A dynamic approach.* Boston: Houghton Mifflin.

Campbell, B. M., Hunter, W. W., & Stutts, J. C. (1984). The use of economic incentives and education to modify safety belt use behavior of high school students. *Health Education, 15,* 30–33.

Cannon, C. P., Braunwald, E., McCabe, C. H., Rader, D. J., Rouleau, J. L., Belder, R., et al. (2004). Intensive versus moderate lipid lowering with statins after acute coronary syndromes. *New England Journal of Medicine, 350,* 1495–1504, http://www.nejm.org

Cannon, W. B. (1932). *The wisdom of the body.* New York: Norton.

Caplan, R. D., & Jones, K. W. (1975). Effects of work load, role ambiguity, and Type A personality on anxiety, depression and heart rate. *Journal of Applied Psychology, 60,* 713–719.

Carels, R. A., Blumenthal, J. A., & Sherwood, A. (1998). Effect of satisfaction with social support on blood pressure in normotensive and borderline hypertensive men and women. *International Journal of Behavioral Medicine, 5,* 76–85.

Carey, J. (2002, November 11). Waking up a sleeping anticancer gene. *BusinessWeek,* p. 82.

Carey, M.P. (1999). Prevention of HIV infection through changes in sexual behavior. *American Journal of Health Promotion, 14,* 104–111.

Carey, M. P., & Burish, T. G. (1985). Anxiety as a predictor of behavioral therapy outcome for cancer chemotherapy patients. *Journal of Consulting and Clinical Psychology, 53,* 860–865.

Carey, M. P., & Burish, T. G. (1988). Etiology and treatment of the psychological side effects associated with cancer chemotherapy: A critical review and discussion. *Psychological Bulletin, 104,* 307–325.

Carey, M. P., Braaten, L. S., Maisto, S. A., Gleason, J. R., Forsyth, A. D., Durant, L. E., et al. (2000). Using information, motivational enhancement, and skills training to reduce the risk of HIV infection for low-income urban women: A second randomized clinical trial. *Health Psychology, 19,* 3–11.

Carey, M. P., Maisto, S. A., Kalichman, S. C., Forsyth, A. D., Wright, E. M., & Johnson, B. T. (1997). Enhancing motivation to reduce the risk of HIV infection for economically disadvantaged urban women. *Journal of Consulting and Clinical Psychology, 65,* 531–541.

Carey, R. G. (1975). Living with death: A program of service and research for the terminally ill. In E. Kübler-Ross (Ed.), *Death: The final stage of growth.* Englewood Cliffs, NJ: Prentice-Hall.

Carlier, I., Voerman, B., & Gersons, B. (2000). Intrusive traumatic recollections and comorbid posttraumatic stress disorder in depressed patients. *Psychosomatic Medicine, 62,* 26–32.

Carlson, L. E., Speca, M., Patel, K. D., & Goodey, E. (2003). Mindfulness-based stress reduction in relation to quality of life, mood, symptoms of stress, and immune parameters in breast and prostate cancer outpatients. *Psychosomatic Medicine, 65,* 571–581.

Carmin, C. N., Wiegartz, P. S., Hoff, J. A., & Kondos, G. T. (2003). Cardiac anxiety in patients self-referred for electron beam tomography. *Journal of Behavioral Medicine, 26,* 67–80.

Carmody, T. P., & Matarazzo, J. D. (1991). Health psychology. In M. Hersen, A. Kazdin, & A. Bellack (Eds.), *The clinical psychology handbook* (2nd ed., pp. 695–723). New York: Pergamon Press.

Carmody, T. P., Istvan, J., Matarazzo, J. D., Connor, S. L., & Connor, W. E. (1986). Applications of social learning theory in the promotion of heart-healthy diets: The Family Heart Study dietary intervention model. *Health Education Research, 1,* 13–27.

Carmody, T. P., Matarazzo, J. D., & Istvan, J. A. (1987). Promoting adherence to heart-healthy diets: A review of the literature. *Journal of Compliance in Health Care, 2,* 105–124.

Carney, C. P., Jones, L., Woolson, R. F., Noyes, R., & Doebbeling, B. N. (2003). Relationship between depression and pancreatic cancer in the general population. *Psychosomatic Medicine, 65,* 884–888.

Carney, R .M., Freedland, K. E., Stein, P. K., Skala, J. A., Hoffman, P., & Jaffe, A. S. (2000). Change in heart rate and heart rate variability during treatment of depression in patients with coronary heart disease. *Psychosomatic Medicine, 62,* 639–647.

Carroll, D., Smith, G. D., Shipley, M. J., Steptoe, A., Brunner, E. J., & Marmot, M. G. (2001). Blood pressure reactions to acute psychological stress and future blood pressure status: A 10-year follow-up of men in the Whitehall II study. *Psychosomatic Medicine, 63,* 737–743.

Carroll, P., Tiggemann, M., & Wade, T. (1999). The role of body dissatisfaction and bingeing in the self-esteem of women with Type II diabetes. *Journal of Behavioral Medicine, 22,* 59–74.

Cartwright, A. (1991). Balance of care for the dying between hospitals and the community: Perceptions of general practitioners, hospital consultants, community nurses, and relatives. *British Journal of General Practice, 41,* 271–274.

Cartwright, M., Wardle, J., Steggles, M., Simon, A. E., Croker, H., & Jarvis, M. J. (2003). Stress and dietary practices in adolescents. *Health Psychology, 22,* 362–369.

Carver, C. S. (1997). You want to measure coping but your protocol's too long: Consider the Brief COPE. *International Journal of Behavioral Medicine, 4,* 92–100.

Carver, C. S., & Humphries, C. (1982). Social psychology of the Type A coronary-prone behavior pattern. In G. S. Saunders & J. Suls (Eds.), *Social psychology of health and illness* (pp. 33–64). Hillsdale, NJ: Erlbaum.

Carver, C. S., Lehman, J. M., & Antoni, M. H. (2003). Dispositional pessimism predicts illness-related disruption of social and recreational activities among breast cancer patients. *Journal of Personality and Social Psychology, 84,* 813–821.

Carver, C. S., Pozo, C., Harris, S. D., Noriega, V., Scheier, M. F., Robinson, D. S., et al. (1993). How coping mediates the effect of optimism on distress: A study of women with early stage breast cancer. *Journal of Personality and Social Psychology, 65,* 375–390.

Carver, C. S., Pozo-Kaderman, C., Price, A. A., Noriega, V., Harris, S. D., Derhagopian, R. P., et al. (1998). Concern about aspects of body image and adjustment to early stage breast cancer. *Psychosomatic Medicine, 60,* 168–174.

Carver, C. S., Scheier, M. F., & Weintraub, J. K. (1989). Assessing coping strategies: A theoretically based approach. *Journal of Personality and Social Psychology, 56,* 267–283.

Case, R. B., Moss, A. J., Case, N., McDermott, M., & Eberly, S. (1992). Living alone after myocardial infarction: Impact on prognosis. *Journal of the American Medical Association, 267,* 515–519.

Cassileth, B. R., Lusk, E. J., Strouse, T. B., Miller, D. S., Brown, L. L., & Cross, P. A. (1985). A psychological analysis of cancer patients and their next-of-kin. *Cancer, 55,* 72–76.

Cassileth, B. R., Lusk, E. J., Strouse, T. B., Miller, D. S., Brown, L. L., Cross, P. A., et al. (1984). Psychosocial status in chronic illness: A comparative analysis of six diagnostic groups. *New England Journal of Medicine, 311,* 506–511.

Cassileth, B. R., Temoshok, L. Frederick, B. E., Walsh, W. P., Hurwitz, S., Guerry, D., et al. (1988). Patient and physician delay in melanoma diagnosis. *Journal of the American Academy of Dermatology, 18,* 591–598.

Castro, C. M., King, A. C., & Brassington, G. S. (2001). Telephone versus mail interventions for maintenance of physical activity in older adults. *Health Psychology, 20,* 438–444.

Castro, C. M., Wilcox, S., O'Sullivan, P., Bauman, K., & King, A. C. (2002). An exercise program for women who are caring for relatives with dementia. *Psychosomatic Medicine, 64,* 458–468.

Castro, F. G., Newcomb, M. D., McCreary, C., & Baezconde-Garbanati, L. (1989). Cigarette smokers do more than just smoke cigarettes. *Health Psychology, 8,* 107–129.

Catalano, R., Dooley, D., Wilson, C., & Hough, R. (1993). Job loss and alcohol abuse: A test using data from the epidemiologic catchment area. *Journal of Health and Social Behavior, 34,* 215–225.

Catalano, R., Hansen, H., & Hartig, T. (1999). The ecological effect of unemployment on the incidence of very low birthweight in Norway and Sweden. *Journal of Health and Social Behavior, 40,* 422–428.

Catania, J. A., Kegeles, S. M., & Coates, T. J. (1990). Towards an understanding of risk behavior: An AIDS risk reduction model (ARRM). *Health Education Quarterly, 17,* 53–72.

Catz, S. L., Kelly, J. A., Bogart, L. M., Benotsch, E. G., & McAuliffe, T. L. (2000). Patterns, correlates, and barriers to medication adherence among persons prescribed new treatments for HIV disease. *Health Psychology, 19,* 124–133.

Cella, D., Hughes, C., Peterman, A., Chang, C. H., Peshkin, B. N., Schwartz, M. D., et al. (2002). A brief assessment of concerns associated with genetic testing for cancer: The multidimensional impact of cancer risk assessment (MICRA) questionnaire. *Health Psychology, 21,* 564–572.

Center for Medicare and Medicaid Services. (2004). *Health care spending reaches $1.6 trillion in 2002.* Retrieved from: http://www.cms.hhs.gov/media/press/release.asp?Counter=935

Center for the Advancement of Health. (2004). *What we do.* Retrieved from: http://www.cfah.org/about/what_we.cfm on August 1, 2004

Center for the Advancement of Health. (December 23, 2002). "E-patients" change behavior, but don't check their sources. *Habit, 5,* 10.

Center for the Advancement of Health. (January 2004). A wake-up call on the value of sleep. *Facts of Life, 9,* 1.

Center for the Advancement of Health. (March 2004). Working out the problem of insufficient exercise. *Facts of Life, 9,* 1.

Center for the Advancement of Health. (June 2002). Point, Click, Heal: Health Information and the Internet. *Facts of Life, 7,* 6.

Center for the Advancement of Health. (November 2002). Food for thought: Prevention of eating disorders in children. *Facts of Life, 7,* 1.

Center for the Advancement of Health. (2003, April). Outside in: Environment and health. *Facts of Life, 8,* 1.

Center for the Advancement of Health. (2003, April 29). Lifestyle changes could prevent a third of world cancers. *Habit, 6.*

Center for the Advancement of Health. (2004, April). *A full partnership for the future: Essays on good behavior.*

Center for the Advancement of Health. (2002, December). Life lessons: Studying education's effect on health. *Facts of Life, 7,* 1.

Center for the Advancement of Health. (2003, December). Potential health benefits of moderate drinking. *Facts of Life, 8,* 1.

Center for the Advancement of Health. (2003, June). Shouting from the rooftops: Where we reside can affect our lives. *Facts of Life, 8,* 1.

Center for the Advancement of Health. (2003, March). Talking the talk: Improving patient-provider communication. *Facts of Life, 8,* 1.

Center for the Advancement of Health. (2003, November). Health education: Schools learn the hard way. *Facts of Life, 8,* 1.

Center for the Advancement of Health. (2002, October). An ounce of prevention: Vaccinations and immunizations. *Facts of Life, 7,* 1.

Center for the Advancement of Health. (1999). *How managed care can help older persons live well with chronic conditions.* Washington, D.C.: Author.

Center for the Advancement of Health. (2000c). *Selected evidence for behavioral approaches to chronic disease management in clinical settings: Cardiovascular disease.* Washington, D.C.: Author.

Center for the Advancement of Health. (2000d). *Selected evidence for behavioral approaches to chronic disease management in clinical settings: Chronic back pain.* Washington, D.C.: Author.

Center for the Advancement of Health. (2000e). *Selected evidence for behavioral approaches to chronic disease management in clinical settings: Depression.* Washington, D.C.: Author.

Center for the Advancement of Health. (2000f). *Selected evidence for behavioral approaches to chronic disease management in clinical settings: Diabetes.* Washington, D.C.: Author.

Center for the Advancement of Health. (2000g). *Selected evidence for behavioral approaches to chronic disease management in clinical settings: Dietary Practices.* Washington, D.C.: Author.

Center for the Advancement of Health. (2001). *Targeting the at-risk drinker with screening and advice.* Washington, D.C.: Author.

Centers for Disease Control and Prevention. (2001). *Cigarette smoking-related mortality. Tobacco information and prevention source.* Retrieved from: http://www.cdc.gov/tobacco/research_data/health_consequences/mortali.htm

Centers for Disease Control and Prevention. (2002). *HIV/AIDS surveillance report, 14.*

Centers for Disease Control and Prevention. (2004a). *Facts about prevalence of arthritis—U.S. 2004.* Retrieved from: http://www.cdc.gov/nccdphp/arthritis/

Centers for Disease Control and Prevention. (2004b). *HIV/AIDS surveillance in women.* Retrieved from http://www.cdc.gov/hiv/graphics/images/1264/1264-1.htm

Centers for Disease Control and Prevention. (2004c). *National Center for Injury Prevention and Control—Center Overview.* Retrieved from: http://www.cdc.gov/ncipc/about/about.htm

Centers for Disease Control and Prevention. (2004d). *National vital statistics report, 52.*

Centers for Disease Control and Prevention. (2004e). *National vital statistics report, 53.*

Centers for Disease Control and Prevention. (2004f). *Sudden infant death syndrome and vaccination.* Retrieved from: http://www.cdc.gov

Centers for Disease Control and Prevention. (2000a). *11 leading causes of death, United States: 1998, all races, both sexes.* Washington, D.C.: Office of Statistics and Programming, National Center for Injury Prevention and Control.

Centers for Disease Control and Prevention. (2000b). *Physical activity and good nutrition: Essential elements for good health.* Atlanta, GA. Retrieved from: http://www. cdc.gov/nccdphp/dnpa/dnpaaag.htm

Centers for Disease Control and Prevention. (2004g). *Cases by exposure category. National Center for HIV, STD and TB Prevention. Divisions of HIV/AIDS prevention. Basic statistics.* Retrieved from: http://www.cdc.gov/hiv/stats.htm#cumaids

Centers for Disease Control and Prevention. (2002b). *Prevalence of diagnosed diabetes by age, United States, 1980–2002. Diabetes health resource. Data.*

Centers for Disease Control. (1989). *Surgeon general's report on smoking: Reducing health consequences of smoking: 25 years of progress, 1964–1989.* Washington, D.C.: Central Office for Health Promotion and Education on Smoking and Health, U.S. Government Printing Office.

Centers for Disease Control. (2001). *Deaths/mortality. National Center for Health Statistics.* Retrieved from: http://www.cdc.gov/nchs/fastats/deaths.htm

Centers for Medicare & Medicaid Services. (2004). *National health expenditures and selected economic indicators, levels and average annual percent change: Selected calendar years 1990–2013.* Retrieved from: http://www.cms.hhs.gov/statistics/nhe/projections-2003/t1.asp

Centers for Medicare & Medicaid Services, Office of the Actuary. (2004). *National health expenditures and selected economic indicators, levels and average annual percent change: Selected calendar years 1980–2012—table 1.* Retrieved from: http://www.cms.hhs.gov/statistics/nhe/projections-2002/t1.asp

Cepeda-Benito, A. (1993). Meta-analytical review of the efficacy of nicotine chewing gum in smoking treatment programs. *Journal of Consulting and Clinical Psychology, 61,* 822–830.

Cesana, G., Sega, R., Ferrario, M., Chiodini, P., Corrao, G., & Mancia, G. (2003). Job strain and blood pressure in employed men and women: A pooled analysis of four northern Italian population samples. *Psychosomatic Medicine, 65,* 558–563.

Champion, V. L. (1990). Breast self-examination in women 35 and older: A prospective study. *Journal of Behavioral Medicine, 13,* 523–538.

Champion, V. L., & Springston, J. (1999). Mammography adherence and beliefs in a sample of low-income African American women. *International Journal of Behavioral Medicine, 6,* 228–240.

Champion, V. L., Skinner, C. S., Menon, U., Seshadri, R., Anzalone, D. C., & Rawl, S. M. (2002). Comparisons of tailored mammography interventions at two months postintervention. *Annals of Behavioral Medicine, 24,* 211–218.

Chang, E. C. (1998). Dispositional optimism and primary and secondary appraisal of a stressor: Controlling for confounding influences and relations to coping and psychological and physical adjustment. *Journal of Personality and Social Psychology, 74,* 1109–1120.

Chapman, C. R., & Gavrin, J. (1999). Suffering: the contributions of persisting pain. *Lancet, 353,* 2233–2237.

Chassin, L., Presson, C. C., Pitts, S. C., & Sherman, S. J. (2000). The natural history of cigarette smoking from adolescence to adulthood in a midwestern community sample: Multiple trajectories and their psychosocial correlates. *Health Psychology, 19,* 223–231.

Chassin, L., Presson, C. C., Rose, J. S., & Sherman, S. J. (1996). The natural history of cigarette smoking from adolescence to adulthood: Demographic predictors of continuity and change. *Health Psychology, 15,* 478–484.

Chassin, L., Presson, C. C., Rose, J. S., & Sherman, S. J. (2001). From adolescence to adulthood: Age-related changes in beliefs about cigarette smoking in a Midwestern community sample. *Health Psychology, 20,* 377–386.

Chassin, L., Presson, C. C., Sherman, S. J., & Kim, K. (2002). Long-term psychological sequelae of smoking cessation and relapse. *Health Psychology, 21,* 438–443.

Chassin, L., Presson, C. C., Sherman, S. J., & Kim, K. (2003). Historical changes in cigarette smoking and smoking-related beliefs after 2 decades in a Midwestern community *Health Psychology, 22,* 347–353.

Chassin, L., Presson, C., Sherman, S. J., & Kim, K. (2003). Historical changes in cigarette smoking and smoking-related beliefs over two decades in a midwestern community. *Health Psychology, 22,* 347–353.

Chaves, I. F., & Barber, T. X. (1976). Hypnotism and surgical pain. In D. Mostofsky (Ed.), *Behavioral control and modification of physiological activity.* Englewood Cliffs, NJ: Prentice-Hall.

Chen, E., Bloomberg, G. R., Fisher, E. B., Jr., & Strunk, R. C. L. (2003). Predictors of repeat hospitalizations in children with asthma: The role of psychosocial and socioenvironmental factors. *Health Psychology, 22,* 12–18.

Chen, E., Fisher, E. B., Bacharier, L. B., & Strunk, R. C. (2003). Socioeconomic status, stress, and immune markers in adolescents with asthma. *Psychosomatic Medicine, 65,* 984–992.

Chen, E., Matthews, K. A., Salomon, K., & Ewart, C. K. (2002). Cardiovascular reactivity during social and nonsocial stressors: Do children's personal goals and expressive skills matter? *Health Psychology, 21,* 16–24.

Chen, Z., Sandercock, P., Pan, P., Counsell, C., Collins, R., Liu, L., et al. (2000). Indications of early aspirin use in acute ischemic stroke: A combined analysis of 40,000 randomized patients from the Chinese acute stroke trial and the international stroke trial. *Stroke, 31,* 1240–1249.

Cheng, C. (2003). Cognitive and motivational processes underlying coping flexibility: A dual-process model. *Journal of Personality and Social Psychology, 84,* 425–438.

Cheng, C., Hui, W., & Lam, S. (1999). Coping style of individuals with functional dyspepsia. *Psychosomatic Medicine, 61,* 789–795.

Cheng, C., Hui, W., & Lam, S. (2004). Psychosocial factors and perceived severity of functional dyspeptic symptoms: A psychosocial interactionist model. *Psychosomatic Medicine, 66,* 85–91.

Cherny, N. I. (1996). The problem of inadequately relieved suffering. *Journal of Social Issues, 52,* 13–30.

Chesney, M. A., Chambers, D. B., Taylor, J. M., Johnson, L. M., & Folkman, S. (2003). Coping effectiveness training for men living with HIV: Results from a randomized clinical trial testing a group-based intervention. *Psychosomatic Medicine, 65,* 1038–1046.

Chesney, M. A., Eagleston, J. R., & Rosenman, R. H. (1981). Type A behavior: Assessment and intervention. In C. K. Prokop & L. A. Bradley (Eds.), *Medical psychology: Contributions to behavioral medicine* (pp. 485–497). New York: Academic Press.

Chilcoat, H. D., & Breslau, N. (1996). Alcohol disorders in young adulthood: Effects of transitions into adult roles. *Journal of Health and Social Behavior, 37,* 339–349.

Choi, W. S., Harris, K. J., Okuyemi, K., & Ahluwalia, J. S. (2003). Predictors of smoking initiation among college-bound high school students. *Annals of Behavioral Medicine, 26,* 69–74.

Christenfeld, N., Gerin, W., Linden, W., Sanders, M., Mathur, J., Deich, J. D., et al. (1997). Social support effects on cardiovascular reactivity: Is a stranger as effective as a friend? *Psychosomatic Medicine, 59,* 388–398.

Christenfeld, N., Glynn, L. M., Phillips, D. P., & Shrira, I. (1999). Exposure to New York City as a risk factor for heart attack mortality. *Psychosomatic Medicine, 61,* 740–743.

Christensen, A. J., Edwards, D. L., Wiebe, J. S., Benotsch, E. G., McKelvey, L., Andrews, M., et al. (1996). Effect of verbal self-disclosure on natural killer cell activity: Moderating influence of cynical hostility. *Psychosomatic Medicine, 58,* 150–155.

Christensen, A. J., Ehlers, S. L., Raichle, K. A., Bertolatus, J. A., & Lawton, W. J. (2000). Predicting change in depression following renal transplantation: Effect of patient coping preferences. *Health Psychology, 19,* 348–353.

Christensen, A. J., Ehlers, S. L., Wiebe, J. S., Moran, P. J., Raichle, K., Ferneyhough, K., et al. (2002). Patient personality and mortality: A 4-year prospective examination of chronic renal insufficiency. *Health Psychology, 21,* 315–320.

Christensen, A. J., Moran, P. J., & Wiebe, J. S. (1999). Assessment of irrational health beliefs: Relation to health practices and medical regimen adherence. *Health Psychology, 18,* 169–176.

Christensen, A. J., Moran, P. J., Wiebe, J. S., Ehlers, S. L., & Lawton, W. J. (2002). Effect of a behavioral self-regulation intervention on patient adherence in hemodialysis. *Health Psychology, 21,* 393–397.

Christensen, A. J., Wiebe, J. S., & Lawton, W. J. (1997). Cynical hostility, powerful others, control expectancies and patient adherence in hemodialysis. *Psychosomatic Medicine, 59,* 307–312.

Christensen, A. J., Wiebe, J. S., Smith, T. W., & Turner, C. W. (1994). Predictors of survival among hemodialysis patients: Effect of perceived family support. *Health Psychology, 13,* 521–525.

Christensen, K. A., Stephens, M. A. P., & Townsend, A. L. (1998). Mastery in women's multiple roles and well-being: Adult daughters providing care to impaired parents. *Health Psychology, 17,* 163–171.

Christman, N. J., McConnell, E. A., Pfeiffer, C., Webster, K. K., Schmitt, M., & Ries, J. (1988). Uncertainty, coping, and distress following myocardial infarction: Transition from hospital to home. *Research in Nursing and Health, 11,* 71–82.

Ciccone, D. S., & Natelson, B. H. (2003). Comorbid illness in women with chronic fatigue syndrome: A test of the single syndrome hypothesis. *Psychosomatic Medicine, 65,* 268–275.

Ciccone, D. S., Just, N., & Bandilla, E. (1999). A comparison of economic and social reward in patients with chronic nonmalignant back pain. *Psychosomatic Medicine, 61,* 552–563.

Clark, J. H., MacPherson, B. V., & Holmes, D. R. (1982). Cigarette smoking and the external locus of control among young adolescents. *Journal of Health and Social Behavior, 23,* 253–259.

Clark, M. (1977). The new war on pain. *Newsweek,* pp. 48–58.

Clark, M. A., Rakowski, W., & Bonacore, L. B. (2003). Repeat mammography: Prevalence estimates and considerations for assessment. *Annals of Behavioral Medicine, 26,* 201–211.

Clark, R. (2003). Parental history of hypertension and coping responses predict blood pressure changes in black college volunteers undergoing a speaking task about perceptions of racism. *Psychosomatic Medicine, 65,* 1012–1019.

Clark, R. (2003). Self-reported racism and social support predict blood pressure reactivity in Blacks. *Annals of Behavioral Medicine, 25,* 127–136.

Clark, V., Moore, C., & Adams, J. (1998). Cholesterol concentrations and cardiovascular reactivity to stress in African American college volunteers. *Journal of Behavioral Medicine, 21,* 505–515.

Clarke, V. A., Lovegrove, H., Williams, A., & Macpherson, M. (2000). Unrealistic optimism and the health belief model. *Journal of Behavioral Medicine, 23,* 367–376.

Clarke, V. A., Williams, T., & Arthey, S. (1997). Skin type and optimistic bias in relation to the sun protection and suntanning behaviors of young adults. *Journal of Behavioral Medicine, 20,* 207–222.

Classen, P. L., Pestotnik, S. L., Evans, R. S., Lloyd, J. F., & Burke, J. R. (1997). Adverse drug events in hospitalized patients: Excess length of stay, extra costs, and attributable mortality. *Journal of the American Medical Association, 277,* 301–306.

Clavel, F., Benhamou, S., & Flamant, R. (1987). Nicotine dependence and secondary effects of smoking cessation. *Journal of Behavioral Medicine, 10,* 555–558.

Clemmey, P. A., & Nicassio, P. M. (1997). Illness self-schemas in depressed and nondepressed rheumatoid arthritis patients. *Journal of Behavioral Medicine, 20,* 273–290.

Clinton, H. R. (2004, April 18). Now can we talk about health care? *The New York Times Magazine,* pp. 26–31.

Clouse, R. E., Lustman, P. J., Freedland, K. E., Griffith, L. S., McGill, J. B., & Carney, R. M. (2003). Depression and coronary heart disease in women with diabetes. *Psychosomatic Medicine, 65,* 376–383.

CNN.com (2002). *Report finds U.S. cancer death rates declining.* Retrieved October 25, 2004, from: http://archives.cnn.com/2002/HEALTH/05/14/cancer.statistics/

Cobb, S. (1976). Social support as a moderator of life stress. *Psychosomatic Medicine, 38,* 300–314.

Cochran, S. D., & Mays, V. M. (1990). Sex, lies, and HIV. *New England Journal of Medicine, 322,* 774–775.

Codori, A., Slavney, P. R., Young, C., Miglioretti, D. L., & Brandt, J. (1997). Predictors of psychological adjustment to genetic testing for Huntington's disease. *Health Psychology, 16,* 36–50.

Cody, R., & Lee, C. (1999). Development and evaluation of a pilot program to promote exercise among mothers of preschool children. *International Journal of Behavioral Medicine, 61,* 13–29.

Cogan, J. C., & Ernsberger, P. (1999). Dieting, weight, and health: Reconceptualizing research and policy. *Journal of Social Issues, 55,* 187–205.

Cohen, F., & Lazarus, R. (1979). Coping with the stresses of illness. In G. C. Stone, F. Cohen, & N. E. Adler (Eds.), *Health psychology: A handbook* (pp. 217–254). San Francisco: Jossey-Bass.

Cohen, L., Baile, W. F., Henninger, E., Agarwal, S. K., Kudelka, A. P., Lenzi, R., et al. (2003). Physiological and psychological effects of delivering medical news using a stimulated physician-patient scenario. *Journal of Behavioral Medicine, 26,* 459–471.

Cohen, L., Cohen, R., Blount, R., Schaen, E., & Zaff, J. (1999). Comparative study of distraction versus topical anesthesia for pediatric pain management during immunizations. *Health Psychology, 18,* 591–598.

Cohen, L., Marshall, G. D., Jr., Cheng, L., Agarwal, S. K., & Wei, Q. (2000). DNA repair capacity in healthy medical students during and after exam stress. *Journal of Behavioral Medicine, 23,* 531–544.

Cohen, L. L. (2002). Reducing infant immunization distress through distraction. *Health Psychology, 21,* 207–211.

Cohen, L. M., Dobscha, S. K., Hails, K. C., Pekow, P. S., & Chochinov, H. M. (2002). Depression and suicidal ideation in patients who discontinue the life-support treatment of dialysis. *Psychosomatic Medicine, 64,* 889–896.

Cohen, M. L. (2000). Changing patterns of infectious disease. *Nature, 406,* 762–767.

Cohen, R. Y., Brownell, K. D., & Felix, M. R. J. (1990). Age and sex differences in health habits and beliefs of schoolchildren. *Health Psychology, 9,* 208–224.

Cohen, R. Y., Stunkard, A., & Felix, M. R. J. (1986). Measuring community change in disease prevention and health promotion. *Preventive Medicine, 15,* 411–421.

Cohen, S. (1978). Environmental load and allocation of attention. In A. Baum, J. E. Singer, & S. Valins (Eds.), *Advances in environmental psychology* (Vol. 2, pp. 1–29). Hillsdale, NJ: Erlbaum.

Cohen, S. (1980). Aftereffects of stress on human performance and social behavior: A review of research and theory. *Psychological Bulletin, 88,* 82–108.

Cohen, S., & Herbert, T. B. (1996). Health psychology: Psychological factors and physical disease from the perspective of human psychoneuroimmunology. *Annual Review of Psychology, 47,* 113–142.

Cohen, S., & Hoberman, H. M. (1983). Positive events and social supports as buffers of life change stress. *Journal of Applied Social Psychology, 13,* 99–125.

Cohen, S., & Lichtenstein, E. (1990). Perceived stress, quitting smoking, and smoking relapse. *Health Psychology, 9,* 466–478.

Cohen, S., & McKay, G. (1984). Social support, stress, and the buffering hypothesis: A theoretical analysis. In A. Baum, S. E. Taylor, & J. Singer (Eds.), *Handbook of psychology and health* (Vol. 4, pp. 253–268). Hillsdale, NJ: Erlbaum.

Cohen, S., & Spacapan, S. (1978). The aftereffects of stress: An attentional interpretation. *Environmental Psychology and Nonverbal Behavior, 3,* 43–57.

Cohen, S., & Williamson, G. M. (1988). Perceived stress in a probability sample of the United States. In S. Spacapan & S. Oskamp (Eds.), *The social psychology of health* (pp. 31–67). Newbury Park, CA: Sage.

Cohen, S., & Williamson, G. M. (1991). Stress and infectious disease in humans. *Psychological Bulletin, 109,* 5–24.

Cohen, S., & Wills, T. A. (1985). Stress, social support, and the buffering hypothesis. *Psychological Bulletin, 98,* 310–357.

Cohen, S., Doyle, W. J., Skoner, D. P., Rabin, B. S., & Gwaltney, J. M., Jr. (1997). Social ties and susceptibility to the common cold. *Journal of the American Medical Association, 277,* 1940–1944.

Cohen, S., Doyle, W. J., Turner, R. B., Alper, C. M., & Skoner, D. P. (2003). Emotional style and susceptibility to the common cold. *Psychosomatic Medicine, 65,* 652–657.

Cohen, S., Doyle, W., & Skoner, D. (1999). Psychological stress, cytokine production, and severity of upper respiratory illness. *Psychosomatic Medicine, 61,* 175–180.

Cohen, S., Evans, G. W., Krantz, D. S., & Stokols, D. (1980). Physiological, motivational, and cognitive effects of aircraft noise on children. *American Psychologist, 35,* 231–243.

Cohen, S., Glass, D. C., & Phillip, S. (1978). Environment and health. In H. E. Freeman, S. Levine, & L. G. Reeder (Eds.), *Handbook of medical sociology* (pp. 134–149). Englewood Cliffs, NJ: Prentice-Hall.

Cohen, S., Glass, D. C., & Singer, J. E. (1973). Apartment noise, auditory discrimination, and reading ability in children. *Journal of Experimental Social Psychology, 9,* 407–422.

Cohen, S., Hamrick, N., Rodriguez, M. S., Feldman, P. J., Rabin, B. S., & Manuck, S. R. (2002). Reactivity and vulnerability to stress-associated risk for upper respiratory illness. *Psychosomatic Medicine, 64,* 302–310.

Cohen, S., Kamarck, T., & Mermelstein, R. (1983). A global measure of perceived stress. *Journal of Health and Social Behavior, 24,* 385–396.

Cohen, S., Kaplan, J. R., Cunnick, J. E., Manuck, S. B., & Rabin, B. S. (1992). Chronic social stress, affiliation, and cellular immune response in nonhuman primates. *Psychological Science, 3,* 301–304.

Cohen, S., Kessler, R. C., & Gordon, L. U. (1995). Conceptualizing stress and its relation to disease. In S. Cohen, R. C. Kessler, & L. U. Gordon (Eds.), *Measuring stress: A guide for health and social scientists* (pp. 3–26). New York: Oxford University Press.

Cohen, S., Lichtenstein, E., Prochaska, J. O., Rossi, J. S., Gritz, E. R., Carr, C. R., et al. (1989). Debunking myths about self-quitting: Evidence from ten prospective studies of persons quitting smoking by themselves. *American Psychologist, 44,* 1355–1365.

Cohen, S., Line, S., Manuck, S. B., Rabin, B. S., Heise, E. R., & Kaplan, J. R. (in press). Chronic social stress, social status, and susceptibility to upper respiratory infection in nonhuman primates. *Psychosomatic Medicine.*

Cohen, S., Sherrod, D. R., & Clark, M. S. (1986). Social skills and the stress-protective role of social support. *Journal of Personality and Social Psychology, 50,* 963–973.

Cohen, S., Tyrrell, D. A. J., & Smith, A. P. (1993). Negative life events, perceived stress, negative affect, and susceptibility to the common cold. *Journal of Personality and Social Psychology, 64,* 131–140.

Coker, A. L., Bond, S., Madeleine, M. M., Luchok, K., & Pirisi, L. (2003). Psychological stress and cervical neoplasia risk. *Psychosomatic Medicine, 65,* 644–651.

Cole, P. A., Pomerleau, C. S., & Harris, J. K. (1992). The effects of nonconcurrent and concurrent relaxation training on cardiovascular reactivity to a psychological stressor. *Journal of Behavioral Medicine, 15,* 407–427.

Cole, S. W., Kemeny, M. E., Fahey, J. L., Zack, J. A., & Naliboff, B. D. (2003). Psychological risk factors for HIV pathogenesis: Mediation by the autonomic nervous system. *Biological Psychiatry, 54,* 1444–1456.

Cole, S. W., Kemeny, M. E., Taylor, S. E., Visscher, B. R., & Fahey, J. L. (1996). Accelerated course of human immunodeficiency virus infection in gay men who conceal their homosexual identity. *Psychosomatic Medicine, 58,* 219–231.

Collijn, D. H., Appels, A., & Nijhuis, F. (1995). Psychosocial risk factors for cardiovascular disease in women: The role of social support. *International Journal of Medicine, 2,* 219–232.

Collins, B. E., & Aspinwall, L. G. (1989, May). *Impression management in negotiations for safer sex.* Paper presented at the Second Iowa Conference on Interpersonal Relationships, Iowa City, IA.

Collins, G. (1997, May 30). Trial near in new legal tack in tobacco war. *The New York Times,* p. A10.

Collins, N. L., Dunkel-Schetter, C., Lobel, M., & Scrimshaw, S. C. M. (1993). Social support in pregnancy. Psychosocial correlates of birth outcomes and postpartum depression. *Journal of Personality and Social Psychology, 6,* 1243–1258.

Collins, R. L., Kanouse, D. E., Gifford, A. L., Senterfitt, J. W., Schuster, M. A., McCaffrey, D. F., et al. (2001). Changes in health-promoting behavior following diagnosis with HIV: Prevalence and correlates in a national probability sample. *Health Psychology, 20,* 351–360.

Collins, R. L., Taylor, S. E., & Skokan, L. A. (1990). A better world or a shattered vision? Changes in perspectives following victimization. *Social Cognition, 8,* 263–285.

Compas, B. E., Barnez, G. A., Malcarne, V., & Worsham, N. (1991). Perceived control and coping with stress: A developmental perspective. *Journal of Social Issues, 47,* 23–34.

Compas, B. E., Worsham, N. L., Epping-Jordan, J. A. E., Grant, K. E., Mireault, G., Howell, D. C., et al. (1994). When mom or dad has cancer: Markers of psychological distress in cancer patients, spouses, and children. *Health Psychology, 13,* 507–515.

Compas, B. E., Worsham, N. L., Ey, S., & Howell, D. C. (1996). When mom or dad has cancer: II. Coping, cognitive appraisals, and psychological distress in children of cancer patients. *Health Psychology, 15,* 167–175.

Conger, R. D., Lorenz, F. O., Elder, G. H., Jr., Simons, R. L., & Ge, X. (1993). Husband and wife differences in response to undesirable life events. *Journal of Health and Social Behavior, 34,* 71–88.

Conis, E. (2003a, August 4). Chips for some, tofu for others. *Los Angeles Times,* p. F8.

Conis, E. (2003b, August 18). Taunts can haunt obese children. *Los Angeles Times,* p. F3.

Conn, V. S., Valentine, J. C., & Cooper, H. M. (2002). Interventions to increase physical activity among aging adults: A meta-analysis. *Annals of Behavioral Medicine, 24,* 190–200.

Contrada, R. J., Goyal, T. M., Cather, C. C., Rafalson, L., Idler, E. L., & Krause, T. J. (2004). Psychosocial factors in outcomes of heart surgery: The impact of religious involvement and depressive symptoms. *Health Psychology, 23,* 227–238.

Cook, W. W., & Medley, D. M. (1954). Proposed hostility and pharasaic-virtue scales for the MMPI. *Journal of Applied Psychology, 38,* 414–418.

Cooper, C. J., & Marshall, J. (1976). Occupational sources of stress: A review of the literature relating to coronary heart disease and mental ill health. *Journal of Occupational Psychology, 49,* 11–28.

Cooper, J. K., Love, D. W., & Raffoul, P. R. (1982). Intentional prescription nonadherence (noncompliance) by the elderly. *Journal of the American Geriatric Society, 30,* 329–333.

Cooper, M. L., Frone, M. R., Russell, M., & Mudar, P. (1995). Drinking to regulate positive and negative emotions: A motivational model of alcohol use. *Journal of Personality and Social Psychology, 69,* 990–1005.

Cooper, M. L., Wood, P. K., Orcutt, H. K., & Albino, A. (2003). Personality and the predisposition to engage in risky or problem behaviors during adolescence. *Journal of Personality and Social Psychology, 84,* 390–410.

Corbin, W. R., & Fromme, K. (2002). Alcohol use and serial monogamy as risks for sexually transmitted diseases in young adults. *Health Psychology, 21,* 229–236.

Cordova, M. J., Cunningham, L. L. C., Carlson, C. R., & Andrykoski, M. A. (2001). Posttraumatic growth following breast cancer: A controlled comparison study. *Health Psychology, 20,* 176–185.

Corle, D. K., et al. (2001). Self-rated quality of life measures: Effect of change to a low-fat, high fiber, fruit and vegetable enriched diet. *Annals of Behavioral Medicine, 23,* 198–207.

Costello, D. (2004, March 29). Insurers limit obesity surgery. Los Angeles Times, p. F1.

Courneya, K. S., & Friedenreich, C. M. (1999). Physical exercise and quality of life following cancer diagnosis: A literature review. *Annals of Behavioral Medicine, 21,* 171–179.

Courneya, K. S., & Friedenreich, C. M. (2001). Framework PEACE: An organizational model for examining physical exercise across the cancer experience. *Annals of Behavioral Medicine, 23,* 263–272.

Cousins, N. (1979). *Anatomy of an illness.* New York: Norton.

Coutu, M. F., Dupuis, G., & D'Antono, B. (2001). The impact of cholesterol lowering on patients' mood. *Journal of Behavioral Medicine, 24,* 517–536.

Coutu, M. F., Dupuis, G., D'Antono, B., & Rochon-Goyer, L. (2003). Illness representation and change in dietary habits in hypercholesterolemic patients. *Journal of Behavioral Medicine, 26,* 133–152.

Couzin, J. (2003, October 24). The twists and turns in BRCA'S path. *Science, 302,* 591–593.

Cover, H., & Irwin, W. (1994). Immunity and depression: Insomnia, retardation, and reduction in natural killer cell activity. *Journal of Behavioral Medicine, 17,* 217–223.

Cowley, G. (2002, June 24). The disappearing minds. *Newsweek,* pp. 40–50.

Cox, D. J., Tisdelle, D. A., & Culbert, J. P. (1988). Increasing adherence to behavioral homework assignments. *Journal of Behavioral Medicine, 11,* 519–522.

Coyne, J. C., & Smith, D. A. F. (1991). Couples coping with a myocardial infarction: A contextual perspective on wives' distress. *Journal of Personality and Social Psychology, 61,* 404–412.

Crandall, L. A., & Duncan, R. P. (1981). Attitudinal and situational factors in the use of physician services by low-income persons. *Journal of Health and Social Behavior, 22,* 64–77.

Criqui, M. H. (1986). Epidemiology of atherosclerosis: An updated overview. *American Journal of Cardiology, 57,* 18C–23C.

Critser, G. (2003). *Fat land: How Americans became the fattest people in the world.* Boston: Houghton Mifflin Company.

Cromwell, R. L., Butterfield, E. C., Brayfield, F. M., & Curry, J. J. (1977). *Acute myocardial infarction: Reaction and recovery.* St. Louis, MO: Mosby.

Croog, S. H. (1983). Recovery and rehabilitation of heart patients: Psychosocial aspects. In D. S. Krantz & J. S. Singer (Eds.), *Handbook of psychology and health* (Vol. 3, pp. 295–334). Hillsdale, NJ: Erlbaum.

Croog, S. H., & Fitzgerald, E. F. (1978). Subjective stress and serious illness of a spouse: Wives of heart patients. *Journal of Health and Social Behavior, 9,* 166–178.

Crosnoe, R. (2002). Academic and health-related trajectories in adolescence: The intersection of gender and athletics. *Journal of Health and Social Behavior, 43,* 317–335.

Cross, C. K., & Hirschfeld, M. A. (1986). Psychosocial factors and suicidal behavior. *Annals of the New York Academy of Sciences, 487,* 77–89.

Croyle, R. T., & Barger, S. D. (1993). Illness cognition. In S. Maes, H. Leventhal, & M. Johnston (Eds.), *International review of health psychology* (Vol. 2, pp. 29–49). New York: Wiley.

Croyle, R. T., & Ditto, P. H. (1990). Illness cognition and behavior: An experimental approach. *Journal of Behavioral Medicine, 13,* 31–52.

Croyle, R. T., & Hunt, J. R. (1991). Coping with health threat: Social influence processes in reactions to medical test results. *Journal of Personality and Social Psychology, 60,* 382–389.

Croyle, R. T., & Jemmott, J. B. III. (1991). *Psychological reactions to risk factor testing.* In J. Skelton & R. Croyle (Eds.), *The mental representation of health and illness* (pp. 85–107). New York: Springer-Verlag.

Croyle, R. T., & Lerman, C. (1993). Interest in genetic testing for colon cancer susceptibility: Cognitive and emotional correlates. *Preventive Medicine, 22,* 284–292.

Croyle, R. T., Smith, K. R., Botkin, J. R., Baty, B., & Nash, J. (1997). Psychological responses to BCRA 1 mutation testing: Preliminary findings. *Health Psychology, 16,* 63–72.

Croyle, R. T., Sun, Y. C., & Louie, D. H. (1993). Psychological minimization of cholesterol test results: Moderators of appraisal in college students and community residents. *Health Psychology, 12,* 503–507.

Cruess, D. G., Antoni, M. H., McGregor, B. A., Kilbourn, K. M., Boyers, A. E., Alferi, S. M., et al. (2000). Cognitive-behavioral stress management reduces serum cortisol by enhancing benefit finding among women being treated for early stage breast cancer. *Psychosomatic Medicine, 62,* 304–308.

Cruess, S., Antoni, M., Cruess, D., Fletcher, M., Ironson, G., Kumar, M., et al. (2000). Reduction in herpes simplex virus type 2 antibody titers after cognitive behavioral stress management and relationships with neuroendocrine function, relaxation skills, and social support in HIV-positive men. *Psychosomatic Medicine, 62,* 828–837.

Cullen, K., Bartholomew, L., Parcel, G. S., & Koehly, L. (1998). Measuring stage of change for fruit and vegetable consumption in 9- to 12-year-old girls. *Journal of Behavioral Medicine, 21,* 241–254.

Cummings, K. M., Becker, M. H., Kirscht, J. P., & Levin, N. W. (1981). Intervention strategies to improve compliance with medical regimens by ambulatory hemodialysis patients. *Journal of Behavioral Medicine, 4,* 111–128.

Curbow, B., Bowie, J., Garza, M., McDonnell, K. A., Scott, L. A., Coyne, C. A., & Chiappelli, T. (in press). Community-based cancer screening programs in older populations: making progress but can we do better? *Preventive Medicine.*

Curbow, B., Somerfield, M. R., Baker, F., Wingard, J. R., & Legro, M. W. (1993). Personal changes, dispositional optimism, and psychological adjustment to bone marrow transplantation. *Journal of Behavioral Medicine, 16,* 423–466.

Currie, S. R., Wilson, K. G., & Curran, D. (2002). Clinical significance and predictors of treatment response to cognitive-behavior therapy for insomnia secondary to chronic pain. *Journal of Behavioral Medicine, 25,* 135–153.

Curry, S. J. (1993). Self-help interventions for smoking cessation. *Journal of Consulting and Clinical Psychology, 61,* 790–803.

Curry, S. J., Ludman, E. J., Grothaus, L. C., Donovan, D., & Kim, E. (2003). A randomized trial of a brief primary-care-based intervention for reducing at-risk drinking practices. *Health Psychology, 22,* 156–165.

Cushman, L. A. (1986). Secondary neuropsychiatric complications in stroke: Implications for acute care. *Archives of Physical Medicine and Rehabilitation, 69,* 877–879.

Czaja, S. J., & Rubert, M. P. (2002). Telecommunications technology as an aid to family caregivers of persons with dementia. *Psychosomatic Medicine, 64,* 469–476.

D'Amico, E. J., & Fromme, K. (1997). Health risk behaviors of adolescent and young adult siblings. *Health Psychology, 16,* 426–432.

Dahlberg, C. C. (1977, June). Stroke. *Psychology Today,* 121–128.

Dahlquist, L. M., Pendley, J. S., Landtrip, D. S., Jones, C. L., & Steuber, C. P. (2002). Distraction intervention for preschoolers undergoing intramuscular injections and subcutaneous port access. *Health Psychology, 21,* 94–99.

Dakof, G. A., & Taylor, S. E. (1990). Victims' perceptions of social support: What is helpful from whom? *Journal of Personality and Social Psychology, 58,* 80–89.

Dallman, M. F. et al. (2003). Chronic stress and obesity: A new view of "comfort food." *Proceedings of the National Academy of Sciences, 100,* 11696–11701.

Dallman, M. F., Akana, S. F., Laugero, K. D., Gomez, F., Manalo, S., Bell, M. E., & Bhatnagar, S. (2003). A spoonful of sugar: Feedback signals of energy stores and corticosterone regulate responses to chronic stress. *Physiology & Behavior, 79,* 3–12.

Danner, M., Kasl, S. V., Abramson, J. L., & Vaccarino, V. (2003). Association between depression and elevated c-reaction protein. *Psychosomatic Medicine, 65,* 347–356.

Danoff, B., Kramer, S., Irwin, P., & Gottlieb, A. (1983). Assessment of the quality of life in long-term survivors after definitive radiotherapy. *American Journal of Clinical Oncology, 6,* 339–345.

Dar, R., Leventhal, E. A., & Leventhal, H. (1993). Schematic processes in pain perception. *Cognitive Therapy and Research, 17,* 341–357.

Dattore, P. I., Shontz, F. C., & Coyne, L. (1980). Premorbid personality differentiation of cancer and noncancer groups: A test of the hypothesis of cancer proneness. *Journal of Consulting and Clinical Psychology, 48,* 388–394.

Davidson, K., Hall, P., & MacGregor, M. Wm. (1996). Gender differences in the relations between interview-derived hostility scores and resting blood pressure. *Journal of Behavioral Medicine, 19,* 185–201.

Davidson, K., MacGregor, M. W., Stuhr, J., & Gidron, Y. (1999). Increasing constructive anger verbal behavior decreases resting blood pressure: A secondary analysis of a randomized controlled hostility intervention. *International Journal of Behavioral Medicine, 6,* 268–278.

Davidson, K. W., Reddy, S. S. K., McGrath, P., & Zitner, D. (1996). Is there an association among low untreated serum lipid levels, anger, and hazardous driving? *International Journal of Behavioral Medicine, 3,* 321–336.

Davidson, K. W., Reikmann, N., & Lesperance, F. (2004). Psychological theories of depression: Potential application for the prevention of acute coronary syndrome occurrence. *Psychosomatic Medicine, 66,* 165–173.

Davidson, R. J., Kabat-Zinn, J., Schumacher, J., Rosenkranz, M., Muller, D., Santorelli, S. F., et al. (2003). Alterations in brain and immune function produced by mindfulness meditation. *Psychosomatic Medicine, 65,* 564–570.

Davis, C., Kaptein, S., Kaplan, A., Olmstead, M., & Woodside, B. (1998). Obsessionality in anorexia nervosa: The moderating influence of exercise. *Psychosomatic Medicine, 60,* 192–197.

Davis, M., Matthews, K., & McGrath, C. (2000). Hostile attitudes predict elevated vascular resistance during interpersonal stress in men and women. *Psychosomatic Medicine, 62,* 17–25.

Davis, M., Vasterling, J., Bransfield, D., & Burish, T. G. (1987). Behavioural interventions in coping with cancer-related pain. *British Journal of Guidance and Counselling, 15,* 17–28.

Davis, M. C. (1999). Oral contraceptive use and hemodynamic, lipid, and fibrinogen responses to smoking and stress in women. *Health Psychology, 18,* 122–130.

Davis, M. C., Matthews, K. A., Meilahn, E. N., & Kiss, J. E. (1995). Are job characteristics related to fibrinogen levels in middle-aged women? *Health Psychology, 14,* 310–318.

Davis, M. C., Twamley, E. W., Hamilton, N. A., & Swan, P. D. (1999). Body fat distribution and hemodynamic stress responses in premenopausal obese women: A preliminary study. *Health Psychology, 18,* 625–633.

Davis, M. S. (1968a). Physiologic, psychological, and demographic factors in patient compliance with doctors' orders. *Medical Care, 6,* 115–122.

Davis, M. S., & Eichhorn, R. L. (1963). Compliance with medical regimen: A panel study. *Journal of Health and Social Behavior, 4,* 240–250.

Davison, G. C., Williams, M. E., Nezami, E., Bice, T. L., & DeQuattro, V. L. (1991). Relaxation, reduction in angry articulated thoughts, and improvements in borderline hypertension and heart rate. *Journal of Behavioral Medicine, 14,* 453–468.

Dawson, T. M., & Dawson, V. L. (2003, October 31). Molecular pathways of neurodegeneration in Parkinson's disease. *Science, 302,* 819–822.

de Graaf, R., & Bijl, R. V. (2002). Determinants of mental distress in adults with a severe auditory impairment: Difference between prelingual and postlingual deafness. *Psychosomatic Medicine, 64,* 61–70.

de Groot, M., Anderson, R., Freedland, K. E., Clouse, R. E., & Lustman, P. J. (2001). Association of depression and diabetes complications: A meta-analysis. *Psychosomatic Medicine, 63,* 619–630.

De Jong, P., Latour, C., & Huyse, F. J. (2003). Implementing psychiatric interventions on a medical ward: Effects on patients' quality of life and length of hospital stay. *Psychosomatic Medicine, 65,* 997–1002.

de Moor, C., Sterner, J., Hall, M., Warneke, C., Gilani, Z., Amato, R., et al. (2002). A pilot study of the side effects of expressive writing on psycholog-

ical and behavioral adjustment in patients in a phase II trial of vaccine therapy for metastatic renal cell carcinoma. *Health Psychology, 21,* 615–619.

De Vries, W. R., Bernards, N. T. M., De Rooij, M. H., & Koppeschaar, H. P. F. (2000). Dynamic exercise discloses different time-related responses in stress hormones. *Psychosomatic Medicine, 62,* 866–872.

DeAngelis, T. (2003, March). Helping young cancer patients return to normal life. *Monitor on Psychology,* 28–30.

Deaton, A. V. (1985). Adaptive noncompliance in pediatric asthma: The parent as expert. *Journal of Pediatric Psychology, 10,* 1–14.

DeBusk, R. F., Haskell, W. L., Miller, N. H., Berra, K., & Taylor, C. B. (1985). Medically directed at-home rehabilitation soon after clinically uncomplicated acute myocardial infarction: A new model for patient care. *American Journal of Cardiology, 55,* 251–257.

Delahanty, L. M., Hayden, D., Ammerman, A., & Nathan, D. M. (2002). Medical nutrition therapy for hypercholesterolemia positively affects patient satisfaction and quality of life outcomes. *Annals of Behavioral Medicine, 24,* 269–278.

DeLongis, A., Coyne, J. C., Dakof, G., Folkman, S., & Lazarus, R. S. (1982). Relationship of daily hassles, uplifts, and major life events to health status. *Health Psychology, 1,* 119–136.

DeQuattro, V., & Lee, D. D. P. (1991). Blood pressure reactivity and sympathetic hyperactivity. *American Journal of Hypertension, 4,* 624S–628S.

DeRosa, C. J., & Marks, G. (1998). Preventative counseling of HIV-positive men and self-disclosure of serostatus to sex partners: New opportunities for prevention. *Health Psychology, 17,* 224–231.

Dersh, J., Polatin, P. B., & Gatchel, R. J. (2002). Chronic pain and psychopathology: Research findings and theoretical considerations. *Psychosomatic Medicine, 64,* 773–786.

Des Jarlais, D. C. (1988). *Effectiveness of AIDS educational programs for intravenous drug users.* Unpublished manuscript, State of New York Division of Substance Abuse Services, New York.

Detweiler, J. B., Bedell, B. T., Salovey, P., Pronin, E., & Rothman, A. J. (1999). Message framing and sunscreen use: Gain-framed messages motivate beach-goers. *Health Psychology, 18,* 189–196.

DeVellis, B. M., Blalock, S. J., & Sandler, R. S. (1990). Predicting participation in cancer screening: The role of perceived behavioral control. *Journal of Applied Social Psychology, 20,* 659–660.

DeVellis, R. F., DeVellis, B. M., Sauter, S. V. H., & Cohen, J. L. (1986). Predictors of pain and functioning in arthritis. *Health Education Research, 1,* 61–67.

Devine, C. M., Connors, M. M., Sobal, J., & Bisogni, C. A. (2003). Sandwiching it in: Spillover of work onto food choices and family roles in low- and moderate-income urban households. *Social Science and Medicine, 56,* 617–630.

Devins, G. M., Mandin, H., Hons, R. B., Burgess, E. D., Klassen, J., Taub, K., et al. (1990). Illness intrusiveness and quality of life in end-stage renal disease: Comparison and stability across treatment modalities. *Health Psychology, 9,* 117–142.

Dew, M. A., Hoch, C. C., Buysse, D. J., Monk, T. H., Begley, A. E., Houck, P. R., Hall, M., Kupfer, D. J., & Reynolds, C. F. (2003). Healthy older adults' sleep predicts all-cause mortality at 4 to 19 years of follow-up. *Psychosomatic Medicine, 65,* 63–73.

DeWit, A. C. D., Duivenvoorden, H. J., Passchier, J., Niermeijer, M. F., Tibben, A., & the other members of the Rotterdam/Leiden Genetics Workgroup. (1998). Course of distress experienced by persons at risk for an autosomal dominant inheritable disorder participating in a predictive testing program: An explorative study. *Psychosomatic Medicine, 60,* 543–549.

Deykin, E. Y., Keane, T. M., Kaloupek, D., Fincke, G., Rothendler, J., Siegfried, M., et al. (2001). Posttraumatic stress disorder and the use of health services. *Psychosomatic Medicine, 63,* 835–841.

Diabetes Prevention Program Research Group. (2002). Reduction in the incidence of type 2 diabetes with lifestyle intervention or metformin. *New England Journal of Medicine, 346,* 393–403. http://www.nejm.org

Diamond, J. (2003, June 5). The double puzzle of diabetes. *Nature, 423,* 599–602.

Diamond, J., Massey, K. L., & Covey, D. (1989). Symptom awareness and blood glucose estimation in diabetic adults. *Health Psychology, 8,* 15–26.

Dias, J. A., Griffith, R. A., Ng, J. J., Reinert, S. E., Friedmann, & Moulton, A.W. (2002). Patients' use of the Internet for medical information. *Journal of General Internal Medicine, 17,* 180–185.

Dickens, C., McGowan, L., & Dale, S. (2003). Impact of depression on experimental pain perception: A systematic review of the literature with meta-analysis. *Psychosomatic Medicine, 65,* 369–375.

Dickens, C., McGowan, L., Clark-Carter, D., & Creed, F. (2002). Depression and rheumatoid arthritis: A systematic review of the literature with meta-analysis. *Psychosomatic Medicine, 64,* 52–60.

Dickerson, S. S., Kemeny, M. E., Aziz, N., Kim, K. H., & Fahey, J. L. (2004). Immunological effects of induced shame and guilt. *Psychosomatic Medicine, 66,* 124–131.

Diefenbach, M. A., Leventhal, E. A., Leventhal, H., & Patrick-Miller, L. (1996). Negative affect relates to cross-sectional but not longitudinal symptom reporting: Data from elderly adults. *Health Psychology, 15,* 282–288.

Dienstbier, R. A. (1989). Arousal and physiological toughness: Implications for mental and physical health. *Psychological Review, 96,* 84–100.

Dietz, W. H. (2004). Overweight in childhood and adolescence. *New England Journal of Medicine, 350,* 855–857.

Dietz, W. H., & Gortmaker, S. L. (2001). Preventing obesity in children and adolescents. *Annual Review of Public Health, 22,* 337–353.

Dijkstra, A., & Borland, R. (2003). Residual outcome expectations and relapse in ex-smokers. *Health Psychology, 22,* 340–346.

Diller, L. (1976). A model of cognitive retraining in rehabilitation. *Journal of Clinical Psychology, 29,* 74–79.

DiMatteo, M. R. (2004). Social support and patient adherence to medical treatment: A meta-analysis. *Health Psychology, 23,* 207–218.

DiMatteo, M. R., & DiNicola, D. D. (1982). *Achieving patient compliance: The psychology of the medical practitioner's role.* New York: Pergamon Press.

DiMatteo, M. R., Friedman, H. S., & Taranta, A. (1979). Sensitivity to bodily nonverbal communication as a factor in physician-patient rapport. *Journal of Nonverbal Behavior, 4,* 18–26.

DiMatteo, M. R., Giordani, P. J., Lepper, H. S., & Croghan, T. W. (2002). Patient adherence and medical treatment outcomes: A meta-analysis. *Medical Care, 40,* 794–811.

DiMatteo, M. R., Hays, R. D., & Prince, L. M. (1986). Relationship of physicians' nonverbal communication skill to patient satisfaction, appointment noncompliance, and physical workload. *Health Psychology, 5,* 581–594.

DiMatteo, M. R., Lepper, H. S., & Croghan, T. W. (2000). Depression is a risk factor for noncompliance with medical treatment. *Archives of Internal Medicine, 160,* 2101–2107.

DiMatteo, M. R., Sherbourne, C. D., Hays, R. D., Ordway, L., Kravitz, R. L., McGlynn, E. A., et al. (1993). Physicians' characteristics influence patients' adherence to medical treatment: Results from the medical outcomes study. *Health Psychology, 12,* 93–102.

Dimond, M. (1979). Social support and adaptation to chronic illness: The case of maintenance hemodialysis. *Research in Nursing and Health, 2,* 101–108.

Dimsdale, J. E. (2000). Stalked by the past: The influence of ethnicity on health. *Psychosomatic Medicine, 62,* 161–170.

Dimsdale, J. E., & Herd, J. A. (1982). Variability of plasma lipids in response to emotional arousal. *Psychosomatic Medicine, 44,* 413–430.

Dimsdale, J. E., Pierce, C., Schoenfeld, D., Brown, A., Zusman, R., & Graham, R. (1986). Suppressed anger and blood pressure: The effects of race, sex, social class, obesity, and age. *Psychosomatic Medicine, 48,* 430–436.

Dimsdale, J. E., Young, D., Moore, R., & Strauss, H. W. (1987). Do plasma norepinephrine levels reflect behavioral stress? *Psychosomatic Medicine, 49,* 375–382.

Dinh, K. T., Sarason, I. G., Peterson, A. V., & Onstad, L. E. (1995). Children's perceptions of smokers and nonsmokers: A longitudinal study. *Health Psychology, 14,* 32–40.

Dishman, R. K. (1982). Compliance/adherence in health-related exercise. *Health Psychology, 1,* 237–267.

Ditto, P. H., Druley, J. A., Moore, K. A., Danks, H. J., & Smucker, W. D. (1996). Fates worse than death: The role of valued life activities in health-state evaluations. *Health Psychology, 15,* 332–343.

Ditto, P. H., Munro, G. D., Apanovich, A. M., Scepansky, J. A., & Lockhart, L. K. (2003). Spontaneous skepticism: The interplay of motivation and expectation in response to favorable and unfavorable medical diagnoses. *Personality and Social Psychology Bulletin, 29,* 1120–1132.

Dobbins, T. A., Simpson, J. M., Oldenburg, B., Owen, N., & Harris, D. (1998). Who comes to a workplace health risk assessment? *International Journal of Behavioral Medicine, 5,* 323–334.

Dobkin, P. L., et al. (2002). Counterbalancing patient demands with evidence: Results from a Pan-Canadian randomized clinical trial of brief supportive-expressive group psychotherapy for women with systemic lupus erythematosus. *Annals of Behavioral Medicine, 24,* 88–99.

Doering, S., Katzleberger, F., Rumpold, G., Roessler, S., Hofstoetter, B., Schatz, D. S., et al. (2000). Videotape preparation of patients before hip replacement surgery reduces stress. *Psychosomatic Medicine, 62,* 365–373.

Doll, J., & Orth, B. (1993). The Fishbein and Ajzen theory of reasoned action applied to contraceptive behavior: Model variants and meaningfulness. *Journal of Applied Social Psychology, 23,* 341–395.

Doll, L. S., O'Malley, P. M., Pershing, A. L., Darrow, W. W., Hessol, N. A., & Lifson, A. R. (1990). High-risk sexual behavior and knowledge of HIV antibody status in the San Francisco City Clinic Cohort. *Health Psychology, 9,* 253–265.

Donaldson, S. I., Graham, J. W., & Hansen, W. B. (1994). Testing the generalizability of intervening mechanism theories: Understanding the effects of adolescent drug use prevention interventions. *Journal of Behavioral Medicine, 17,* 195–216.

Donaldson, S. I., Graham, J. W., Piccinin, A. M., & Hansen, W. B. (1995). Resistance-skills training and onset of alcohol use: Evidence for beneficial and potentially harmful effects in public schools and in private Catholic schools. *Health Psychology, 14,* 291–300.

Donovan, J. E., & Jessor, R. (1985). Structure of problem behavior in adolescence and young adulthood. *Journal of Consulting and Clinical Psychology, 53,* 890–904.

Donovan, J. E., Jessor, R., & Costa, F. M. (1991). Adolescent health behavior and conventionality-unconventionality: An extension of problem-behavior theory. *Health Psychology, 10,* 52–61.

Dorgan, C., & Editue, A. (1995). *Statistical record of health and medicine: 1995.* Detroit, MI: Oracle Research.

Doshi, A., Patrick, K., Sallis, J. F., & Calfas, K. (2003). Evaluation of physical activity web sites for use of behavior change theories. *Annals of Behavioral Medicine, 25,* 105–111.

Downey, G., Silver, R. C., & Wortman, C. B. (1990). Reconsidering the attribution-adjustment relation following a major negative event: Coping with the loss of a child. *Journal of Personality and Social Psychology, 59,* 925–940.

Dracup, K. (1985). A controlled trial of couples' group counseling in cardiac rehabilitation. *Journal of Cardiopulmonary Rehabilitation, 5,* 436–442.

Dracup, K., & Moser, D. (1991). Treatment-seeking behavior among those with signs and symptoms of acute myocardial infarction. *Heart and Lung, 20,* 570–575.

Dracup, K., Guzy, P. M., Taylor, S. E., & Barry, J. (1986). Cardiopulmonary resuscitation (CPR) training: Consequences for family members of high-risk cardiac patients. *Archives of Internal Medicine, 146,* 1757–1761.

Dracup, K., Meleis, A., Clark, S., Clyburn, A., Shields, L., & Staley, M. (1984). Group counseling in cardiac rehabilitation: Effect on patient compliance. *Patient Education and Counseling, 6,* 169–177.

Droge, D., Arntson, P., & Norton, R. (1986). The social support function in epilepsy self-help groups. *Small Group Behavior, 17,* 139–163.

Droomers, M., Schrijvers, C. T. M., & Mackenbach, J. P. (2002). Why do lower educated people continue smoking? Explanations from the longitudinal GLOBE study. *Health Psychology, 21,* 263–272.

Drossman, D. A., Leserman, J., Li, Z., Keefe, F., Hu, Y. J. B., & Toomey, T. C. (2000). Effects of coping on health outcome among women with gastrointestinal disorders. *Psychosomatic Medicine, 62,* 309–317.

Duenwald, M. (2002, September 17). Students find another staple of campus life: Stress. *The New York Times,* p. F 5.

Duff, R. S., & Hollingshead, A. B. (1968). *Sickness and society.* New York: Harper & Row.

DuHamel, K. N., Manne, S., Nereo, N., Ostroff, J., Martini, R., Parsons, S., et al. (2004). Cognitive processing among mothers of children undergoing bone marrow/stem cell transplantation. *Psychosomatic Medicine, 66,* 92–103.

Duits, A. A., Boeke, S., Taams, M. A., Passchier, J., & Erdman, R. A. M. (1997). Prediction of quality of life after coronary artery bypass graft surgery: A review and evaluation of multiple, recent studies. *Psychosomatic Medicine, 59,* 257–268.

Dujovne, V. F., & Houston, B. K. (1991). Hostility-related variables and plasma lipid levels. *Journal of Behavioral Medicine, 14,* 555–565.

Dunbar, F. (1943). *Psychosomatic diagnosis.* New York: Hoeber.

Dunbar, J. M., & Agras, W. S. (1980). Compliance with medical instructions. In J. M. Ferguson & C. B. Taylor (Eds.), *Comprehensive handbook of behavioral medicine* (Vol. 3). New York: Spectrum.

Dunbar-Jacob, J., Dwyer, K., & Dunning, E. J. (1991). Compliance with antihypertensive regimen: A review of the research in the 1980s. *Annals of Behavioral Medicine, 13,* 31–39.

Duncan, S. C., Duncan, T. E., Strycker, L. A., & Chaumeton, N. R. (2002). Relations between youth antisocial and prosocial activities. *Journal of Behavioral Medicine, 25,* 425–438.

Duncan, T. E., Duncan, S. C., Beauchamp, N., Wells, J., & Ary, D. V. (2000). Development and evaluation of an interactive CD-ROM refusal skills program to prevent youth substance use: "Refuse to use." *Journal of Behavioral Medicine, 23,* 59–72.

Dunkel-Schetter, C., Feinstein, L. G., Taylor, S. E., & Falke, R. L. (1992). Patterns of coping with cancer. *Health Psychology, 11,* 79–87.

Dunkel-Schetter, C., Folkman, S., & Lazarus, R. S. (1987). Correlates of social support receipt. *Journal of Personality and Social Psychology, 53,* 71–80.

Dunlop, D. (1970). Abuse of drugs by the public and by doctors. *British Medical Bulletin, 6,* 236–239.

Dunnell, K., & Cartwright, A. (1972). *Medicine takers, prescribers, and hoarders.* Boston: Routledge & Kegan Paul.

DuPont, R. L. (1988). The counselor's dilemma: Treating chemical dependence at college. In T. M. Rivinus (Ed.), *Alcoholism/chemical dependency and the college student* (pp. 41–61). New York: Haworth Press.

DuPont, R. L., & Gold, M. S. (1995). Withdrawal and reward: Implications for detoxification and relapse prevention. *Psychiatric Annals, 25,* 663–668.

Dusseldorp, E., van Elderen, T., Maes, S., Meulman, J., & Kraaij, V. (1999). A meta-analysis of psychoeducational programs for coronary heart disease patients. *Health Psychology, 18,* 506–519.

Duxbury, M. L., Armstrong, G. D., Dren, D. J., & Henley, S. J. (1984). Head nurse leadership style with staff nurse burnout and job satisfaction in neonatal intensive care units. *Nursing Research, 33,* 97–101.

Dwyer, J. W., Clarke, L. L., & Miller, M. K. (1990). The effect of religious concentration and affiliation on county cancer mortality rates. *Journal of Health and Social Behavior, 31,* 185–202.

Eaton, W. W., Muntaner, C., Bovasso, G., & Smith, C. (2001). Socioeconomic status and depressive syndrome: The role of inter- and intra-generational mobility, government assistance, and work environment. *Journal of Health and Social Behavior, 42,* 277–294.

Ebbesen, B. L., Prkhachin, K. M., Mills, D. E., & Green, H. J. (1992). Effects of acute exercise on cardiovascular reactivity. *Journal of Behavioral Medicine, 15,* 489–508.

Echteld, M. A., van Elderen, T., & van der Kamp, L. J. Th. (2003). Modeling predictors of quality of life after coronary angioplasty. *Annals of Behavioral Medicine, 26,* 49–60.

Eckenrode, J., & Gore, S. (Eds.). (1990). *Stress between work and family.* New York: Plenum Press.

Edwards, R., Telfair, J., Cecil, H., & Lenoci, J. (2001). Self-efficacy as a predictor of adult adjustment to sickle cell disease: One-year outcomes. *Psychosomatic Medicine, 63,* 850–851.

Edwards, R., & Fillingim, R. (1999). Ethnic differences in thermal pain responses. *Psychosomatic Medicine, 61,* 346–354.

Edwards, S., Hucklebridge, F., Clow, A., & Evans, P. (2003). Components of the diurnal cortisol cycle in relation to upper respiratory symptoms and perceived stress. *Psychosomatic Medicine, 65,* 320–327.

Egbert, L. D., Battit, C. E., Welch, C. E., & Bartlett, M. K. (1964). Reduction of postoperative pain by encouragement and instruction of patients. A study of doctor-patient rapport. *New England Journal of Medicine, 270,* 825–827.

Eichner, E. R. (1983). Exercise and heart disease. *American Journal of Medicine, 75,* 1008–1023.

Eifert, G. H., Hodson, S. E., Tracey, D. R., Seville, J. L., & Gunawardane, K. (1996). Heart-focused anxiety, illness beliefs, and behavioral impairment: Comparing healthy heart-anxious patients with cardiac and surgical inpatients. *Journal of Behavioral Medicine, 19,* 385–400.

Eisenberg, D., & Sieger, M. (2003, June 9). The doctor won't see you now. *Time,* 46–60.

Eisenberg, D. M., Kessler, R. C., Foster, C., Norlock, F. E., Calkins, D. R., & Delbanco, T. L. (1993). Unconventional medicine in the United States: Prevalence, costs, and patterns of use. *New England Journal of Medicine, 328,* 246–252.

Eiser, J. R., van der Plight, J., Raw, M., & Sutton, S. R. (1985). Trying to stop smoking: Effects of perceived addiction, attributions for failure, and expectancy of success. *Journal of Behavioral Medicine, 8,* 321–342.

Eiser, R., & Gentle, P. (1988). Health behavior as goal-directed action. *Journal of Behavioral Medicine, 11,* 523–536.

Ekkekakis, P., Hall, E. E., VanLanduyt, L. M., & Petruzzello, S. J. (2000). Walking in (affective) circles: Can short walks enhance affect? *Journal of Behavioral Medicine, 23,* 245–275.

Elchisak, M. A. (2001). *Acamprosate (Campral): Medication for alcohol abuse and alcoholism treatment.* Retrieved from: www.doctordeluca.com/Documents/AcamprosateSummary.htm

Elder, J. P., Sallis, J. F., Woodruff, S. I., & Wildey, M. B. (1993). Tobacco-refusal skills and tobacco use among high-risk adolescents. *Journal of Behavioral Medicine, 16,* 629–642.

Elizur, Y., & Hirsh, E. (1999). Psychosocial adjustment and mental health two months after coronary artery bypass surgery: A multisystemic analysis of patients' resources. *Journal of Behavioral Medicine, 22,* 157–177.

Ellickson, P. L., Bird, C. E., Orlando, M., Klein, D. J., & McCaffrey, D. F. (2003). Social context and adolescent health behavior: Does school-level smoking prevalence affect students' subsequent smoking behavior? *Journal of Health and Social Behavior, 44,* 525–535.

Ellickson, P. L., Tucker, J. S., & Klein, D. J. (2001). Sex differences in predictors of adolescent smoking cessation. *Health Psychology, 20,* 186–195.

Ellington, L., & Wiebe, D. (1999). Neuroticism, symptom presentation, and medical decision making. *Health Psychology, 18,* 634–643.

Ellis, A. (1962). *Reason and emotion in psychotherapy.* New York: Lyle Stuart.

Emanuel, E. J., Fariclough, D., Clarridge, B. C., Blum, D., Bruera, E., Penlye, W. C., et al. (2000). Attitudes and practices of U.S. oncologists regarding euthanasia and physician-assisted suicide. *Annals of Internal Medicine, 133,* 527–532.

Emedicine.com. (2004). *Asthma resource center.* Retrieved from: http://www.emedicine.com/med/topic177.htm

Emery, C. F., Frid, D. J., Engebretson, T. O., Alonzo, A. A., Fish, A., Ferketich, A. K., et al. (2004). Gender differences in quality of life among cardiac patients. *Psychosomatic Medicine, 66,* 190–197.

Emery, C. F., Schein, R. L., Hauck, E. R., & MacIntyre, N. R. (1998). Psychological and cognitive outcomes of a randomized trial of exercise among patients with chronic obstructive pulmonary disease. *Health Psychology, 17,* 232–240.

Emery, C. F., Shermer, R. L., Hauck, E. R., Hsaio, E. T., & MacIntyre, N. R. (2003). Cognitive and psychological outcomes of exercise in a 1-year follow-up study of patients with chronic obstructive pulmonary disease. *Health Psychology, 22,* 598–604.

Emmons, C., Biernat, M., Teidje, L. B., Lang, E. L., & Wortman, C. B. (1990). Stress, support, and coping among women professionals with preschool children. In J. Eckenrode & S. Gore (Eds.), *Stress between work and family* (pp. 61–93). New York: Plenum Press.

Emmons, K. M., Hammond, S. K., Fava, J. L., Velicer, W. F., Evans, J. L., & Monroe, A. D. (2001). A randomized trial to reduce passive smoke exposure in low-income households with young children. *Pediatrics, 108,* 18–24.

Eng, P. M., Fitzmaurice, G., Kubansky, L. D., Rimm, E. B., & Kawachi, I. (2003). Anger in expression and risk of stroke and coronary heart disease among male health professionals. *Psychosomatic Medicine, 65,* 100–110.

Engel, B. T. (1986). Psychosomatic medicine, behavioral medicine, just plain medicine. *Psychosomatic Medicine, 48,* 466–479.

Engel, G. L. (1977). The need for a new medical model: A challenge for biomedicine. *Science, 196,* 129–136.

Engel, G. L. (1980). The clinical application of the biopsychosocial model. *American Journal of Psychiatry, 137,* 535–544.

Engebretson, T. O., & Matthews, K. A. (1992). Dimensions of hostility in men, women, and boys: Relationships to personality and cardiovascular responses to stress. *Psychosomatic Medicine, 54,* 311–323.

English, E. H., & Baker, T. B. (1983). Relaxation training and cardiovascular response to experimental stressors. *Health Psychology, 2,* 239–259.

Ennett, S. T., & Bauman, K. E. (1991). Mediators in the relationship between parental and peer characteristics and beer drinking by early adolescents. *Journal of Applied Social Psychology, 21,* 1699–1711.

Ennett, S. T., & Bauman, K. E. (1993). Peer group structure and adolescent cigarette smoking: A social network analysis. *Journal of Health and Social Behavior, 34,* 226–236.

Enright, M. F., Resnick, R., DeLeon, P. H., Sciara, A. D., & Tanney, F. (1990). The practice of psychology in hospital settings. *American Psychologist, 45,* 1059–1065.

ENRICHD Investigators. (2001). Enhancing recovery in coronary heart disease (ENRICHD) study intervention: rational and design. *Psychosomatic Medicine, 63,* 747–755.

Environmental Health Perspective. (2004). *Study finds that combined exposure to second-hand smoke and urban air pollutants during pregnancy adversely affects birth outcomes.* Retrieved from: http://ehp.niehs.nih.gov/press/012304.html

Epel, E. S., McEwen, B., Seeman, T., Matthews, K., Catellazzo, G., Brownell, K., et al. (2000). Stress and body shape: Stress-induced cortisol secretion is consistently greater among women with central fat. *Psychosomatic Medicine, 62,* 623–632.

Epilepsy Foundation. (2003). *Epilepsy and seizure statistics.* Retrieved from: http://www.epilepsyfoundation.org/answerplace/statistics.cfm

Epker, J., & Gatchel, R. J. (2000). Coping profile differences in the biopsychosocial functioning of patients with temporomandibular disorder. *Psychosomatic Medicine, 62,* 69–75.

Epping-Jordan, J. A., Compas, B. E., & Howell, D. C. (1994). Predictors of cancer progression in young adult men and women: Avoidance, intrusive thoughts, and psychological symptoms. *Health Psychology, 13,* 539–547.

Epping-Jordan, J., Williams, R., Pruitt, S., Patterson, T., Grant, I., Wahlgren, D., et al. (1998). Transition to chronic pain in men with low back pain: Predictive relationships among pain intensity, disability, and depressive symptoms. *Health Psychology, 17,* 421–427.

Epping-Jordan, J. E., Compas, B. E., Osowiecki, D. M., Oppedisano, G., Gerhardt, C., Primo, K., et al. (1999). Psychological adjustment in breast cancer: Processes of emotional distress. *Health Psychology, 18,* 315–326.

Epstein, L. H., Kilanowski, C. K., Consalvi, A. R., & Paluch, R. A. (1999). Reinforcing value of physical activity as a determinant of child activity level. *Health Psychology, 18,* 599–603.

Epstein, L. H., Saelens, B. E., Myers, M. D., & Vito, D. (1997). Effects of decreasing sedentary behaviors on activity choice in obese children. *Health Psychology, 16,* 107–113.

Epstein, L. H., Valoski, A. M., Vara, L. S., McCurley, J., Wisniewski, L., Kalarchian, M. A., Klein, et al. (1995). Effects of decreasing sedentary behavior and increasing activity on weight change in obese children. *Health Psychology, 14,* 109–115.

Epstein, L. H., Valoski, A., Wing, R. R., & McCurley, J. (1994). Ten-year outcomes of behavioral family-based treatment for childhood obesity. *Health Psychology, 13,* 373–383.

Epstein, S., & Katz, L. (1992). Coping ability, stress, productive load, and symptoms. *Journal of Personality and Social Psychology, 62,* 813–825.

Ernsberger, P., & Koletsky, R. J. (1999). Biomedical rationale for a wellness approach to obesity: An alternate to a focus on weight loss. *Journal of Social Issues, 55,* 221–260.

Esposito-Del Puente, A., Lillioja, S., Bogardus, C., McCubbin, J. A., Feinglos, M. N., Kuhn, C. M., et al. (1994). Glycemic response to stress is altered in euglycemic Pima Indians. *International Journal of Obesity, 18,* 766–770.

Estabrooks, P. A., & Carron, A. V. (1999). Group cohesion in older adult exercisers: Prediction and intervention effects. *Journal of Behavioral Medicine, 22,* 575–588.

Estabrooks, P. A., Lee, R. E., & Gyurcsik, N. C. (2003). Resources for physical activity participation: Does availability and accessibility differ by neighborhood socioeconomic status? *Annals of Behavioral Medicine, 25,* 100–104.

Esterling, B. A., Kiecolt-Glaser, J. K., & Glaser, R. (1996). Psychosocial modulation of cytokine-induced natural killer cell activity in older adults. *Psychosomatic Medicine, 58,* 264–272.

Esterling, B. A., Kiecolt-Glaser, J. K., Bodnar, J. C., & Glaser, R. (1994). Chronic stress, social support, and persistent alterations in the natural killer cell response to cytokines in older adults. *Health Psychology, 13,* 291–298.

Evans, G. W., & Kantrowitz, E. (2001). *Socioeconomic status and health: The potential role of suboptimal physical environments.* John D. and Catherine T. MacArthur Research Network on Socioeconomic Status and Health. Retrieved from: http://www.macses.ucsf.edu/

Evans, R. I., Dratt, L. M., Raines, B. E., & Rosenberg, S. S. (1988). Social influences on smoking initiation: Importance of distinguishing descriptive versus mediating process variables. *Journal of Applied Social Psychology, 18,* 925–943.

Everson, S. A., Goldberg, D. E., Kaplan, G. A., Cohen, R. D., Pukkala, E., Tuomilehto, J., et al. (1996). Hopelessness and risk of mortality and incidence of myocardial infarction and cancer. *Psychosomatic Medicine, 58,* 113–121.

Everson, S. A., Goldberg, D. E., Kaplan, G. A., Julkunen, J., & Salonen, J. T. (1998). Anger expression and incident hypertension. *Psychosomatic Medicine, 60,* 730–735.

Everson, S. A., Lovallo, W. R., Sausen, K. P., & Wilson, M. F. (1992). Hemodynamic characteristics of young men at risk for hypertension at rest and during laboratory stressors. *Health Psychology, 11,* 24–31.

Ewart, C. K. (1991). Familial transmission of essential hypertension: Genes, environments, and chronic anger. *Annals of Behavioral Medicine, 13,* 40–47.

Ewart, C. K., & Jorgensen, R. S. (2004). Agonistic interpersonal striving: Social-cognitive mechanism of cardiovascular risk in youth? *Health Psychology, 23,* 75–85.

Ewart, C. K., & Suchday, S. (2002). Discovering how urban poverty and violence affect health: Development and validation of a neighborhood stress index. *Health Psychology, 21,* 254–262.

Ezekiel, J. E., Fairclough, D., Clarridge, B. C., Blum, D., Bruera, E., Charles Penley, W., Schnipper, L. E., & Mayer, R. J. (2000). Attitudes and practices of U.S. oncologists regarding euthanasia and physician-assisted suicide. *Annals of Internal Medicine, 133,* 527–532.

Ezzel, C. (1993). Drug companies told to assess effects of drugs in women. *Journal of NIH Research, 5,* 37–38.

Facts of life: Issue briefing for health reporters. (2002). Center for the Advancement of Health, 7, Washington, D.C.

Faden, R. R., & Kass, N. E. (1993). Genetic screening technology: Ethical issues in access to tests by employers and health insurance companies. *Journal of Social Issues, 49,* 75–88.

Fagan, J., Galea, S., Ahern, J., Bonner, S., & Vlahov, D. (2003). Relationship of self-reported asthma severity and urgent health care utilization to psychological seguelae of the September 11, 2001, terrorist attacks on the world trade center among New York City area residents. *Psychosomatic Medicine, 65,* 993–996.

Fagerlin, A., Ditto, P. H., Danks, J. H., Houts, R. M., & Smucker, W. D. (2001). Projection in surrogate decisions about life-sustaining medical treatments. *Health Psychology, 20,* 166–175.

Fahrenwald, N. L., Atwood, J. R., Walker, S. N., Johnson, D. R., & Berg, K. (2004). A randomized pilot test of "moms on the move": A physical activity intervention on WIC mothers. *Annals of Behavioral Medicine, 27,* 82–90.

Falk, A., Hanson, B. S., Isacsson, C., & Ostergren, P. (1992). Job strain and mortality in elderly men: Social network support and influence as buffers. *American Journal of Public Health, 82,* 1136–1139.

Fang, C. Y., & Myers, H. F. (2001). The effects of racial stressors and hostility on cardiovascular reactivity in African American and Caucasian men. *Health Psychology, 20,* 64–70.

Fang, C. Y., Manne, S. L., & Pape, S. J. (2001). Functional impairment, marital quality, and patient psychological distress as predictors of psychological distress among cancer patients' spouses. *Health Psychology, 20,* 452–457.

Farkas, A. J., Pierce, J. P., Gilpin, E. A., Zhu, S. H., Rosbrook, B., Berry, C., et al. (1996). Is stage-of-change a useful measure of the likelihood of smoking cessation? *Annals of Behavioral Medicine, 18,* 79–86.

Fauerbach, J. A., Heinberg, L. J., Lawrence, J. W., Bryant, A. G., Richter, L., & Spence, R. J. (2002). Coping with body image changes following a disfiguring burn injury. *Health Psychology, 21,* 115–121.

Fawzy, F. I., Cousins, N., Fawzy, N. W., Kemeny, M. E., Elashoff, R., & Morton, D. (1990). A structured psychiatric intervention for cancer patients, I: Changes over time in methods of coping and affective disturbance. *Archives of General Psychiatry, 47,* 720–725.

Fawzy, F. I., et al. (1993). Malignant melanoma: Effects of an early structured psychiatric intervention, coping, and affective state on recurrence and survival six years later. *Archives of General Psychiatry, 9,* 681–689.

Fawzy, F. I., Kemeny, M. E., Fawzy, M. W., Elashoff, R., Morton, D., Cousins, N., et al. (1990). A structured psychiatric intervention for cancer patients, II: Changes over time in immunological measures. *Archives of General Psychiatry, 47,* 729–735.

Feder, B. J. (1997, April 20). Surge in teen-age smoking left an industry vulnerable. *The New York Times,* pp. 1, 14.

Federspiel, J. F. (1983). *The ballad of Typhoid Mary.* New York: Dutton.

Feifel, H. (Ed.). (1977). *New meanings of death.* New York: McGraw-Hill.

Feinglos, M. N., & Surwit, R. S. (1988). *Behavior and diabetes mellitus.* Kalamazoo, MI: Upjohn.

Feldman, J., Makuc, D., Kleinman, J., & Cornoni-Huntley, J. (1998). National trends in educational differentials in mortality. *American Journal of Epidemiology, 129,* 919–933.

Feldman, P. E. (1956). The personal element in psychiatric research. *American Journal of Psychiatry, 113,* 52–54.

Feldman, P., Cohen, S., Doyle, W., Skoner, D., & Gwaltney, J. (1999). The impact of personality on the reporting of unfounded symptoms and illness. *Journal of Personality and Social Psychology, 77,* 370–378.

Feldman, P. J., & Steptoe, A. (2004). How neighborhoods and physical functioning are related: The roles of neighborhood socioeconomic status, perceived neighborhood strain, and individual health risk factors. *Annals of Behavioral Medicine, 27,* 91–99.

Felitti, V. J., Anda, R. F., Nordenberg, D., Williamson, D. F., Apitz, A. M., Edwards, V., et al. (1998). Relationship of childhood abuse and household dysfunction to many of the leading causes of death in adults. *American Journal of Preventive Medicine, 14,* 245–258.

Felton, B. J., & Revenson, T. A. (1984). Coping with chronic illness: A study of illness controllability and the influence of coping strategies on psychological adjustment. *Journal of Consulting and Clinical Psychology, 52,* 343–353.

Fernandez, E., & Turk, D. C. (1992). Sensory and affective components of pain: Separation and synthesis. *Psychological Bulletin, 112,* 205–217.

Ferrando, S., Evans, S., Goggin, K., Sewell, M., Fishman, B., & Rabkin, J. (1998). Fatigue in HIV illness: Relationship to depression, physical limitations, and disability. *Psychosomatic Medicine, 60,* 759–764.

Fiatarone, M. A., Morley, J. E., Bloom, E. T., Benton, D., Makinodan, T., & Solomon, G. F. (1988). Endogenous opioids and the exercise-induced augmentation of natural killer cell activity. *Journal of Laboratory and Clinical Medicine, 112,* 544–552.

Fichten, C. S., Libman, E., Creti, L., Balles, S., & Sabourin, S. (2004). Long sleepers sleep more and short sleepers sleep less: A comparison of older adults who sleep well. *Behavioral Sleep Medicine, 2,* 2–23.

Fielding, J. E. (1978). Successes of prevention. *Milbank Memorial Fund Quarterly, 56,* 274–302.

Fielding, J. E. (1991). The challenge of workplace health promotion. In S. M. Weiss, J. E. Fielding, & A. Baum (Eds.), *Perspectives in behavioral medicine* (pp. 13–28). Hillsdale, NJ: Erlbaum.

Fifield, J., McQuinlan, J., Tennen, H., Sheehan, T. J., Reisine, S., Hesselbrock, V., et al. (2001). History of affective disorder and the temporal trajectory of fatigue in rheumatoid arthritis. *Annals of Behavioral Medicine, 23,* 34–41.

Fife, B. L., & Wright, E. R. (2000). The dimensionality of stigma: A comparison of its impact on the self of persons with HIV/AIDS and cancer. *Journal of Health and Social Behavior, 41,* 50–67.

Fillingham, R. B., & Maixner, W. (1996). The influence of resting blood pressure and gender on pain responses. *Psychosomatic Medicine, 58,* 326–332.

Findley, J. C., Kerns, R., Weinberg, L. D., & Rosenberg, R. (1998). Self-efficacy as a psychological moderator of chronic fatigue syndrome. *Journal of Behavioral Medicine, 21,* 351–362.

Findley, T. (1953). The placebo and the physician. *Medical Clinics of North America, 37,* 1821–1826.

Finkelstein, E. A., Fiebelkorn, I. C., & Wang, G. (2003). National medical spending attributable to overweight and obesity. *Health Affairs,* Suppl:W3-219–26.

Finney, J. W., & Moos, R. H. (1992). The long-term course of treated alcoholism, II: Predictors and correlates of 10-year functioning and mortality. *Journal of Studies on Alcoholism, 53,* 142–153.

Finney, J. W., & Moos, R. H. (1995). Entering treatment for alcohol abuse: A stress and coping method. *Addiction, 90,* 1223–1240.

Finney, J. W., Lemanek, K. L., Brophy, C. J., & Cataldo, M. F. (1990). Pediatric appointment keeping: Improving adherence in a primary care allergy clinic. *Journal of Pediatric Psychology, 15,* 571–579.

Firestein, G. S. (2003, May 15). Evolving concepts of rheumatoid arthritis. *Nature, 423,* 356–361.

Fishbain, D., Cutler, R., Rosomoff, H., & Rosomoff, R. (1998). Do antidepressants have an analgesic effect in psychogenic pain and somatoform pain disorder? A meta-analysis. *Psychosomatic Medicine, 60,* 503–509.

Fishbein, M., & Ajzen, I. (1975). *Belief, attitude, intention, and behavior: An introduction to theory and research.* Reading, MA: Addison-Wesley.

Fisher , J. D., Fisher, W. A., Bryan, A. D., & Misovich, S. J. (2002). Information-motivation-behavioral skills model-based HIV risk behavior change intervention for inner-city high school youth. *Health Psychology, 21,* 177–186.

Fisher, L., Soubhi, H., Mansi, O., Paradis, G., Gauvin, L., & Potvin, L. (1998). Family process in health research: Extending a family typology to a new cultural context. *Health Psychology, 17,* 358–366.

Fisher, W. A., Fisher, J. D., & Rye, B. J. (1995). Understanding and promoting AIDS-preventive behavior: Insights from the theory of reasoned action. *Health Psychology, 14,* 255–264.

Fitzgerald, S. T., Haythornthwaite, J. A., Suchday, S., & Ewart, C. K. (2003). Anger in young black and white workers: Effects of job control, dissatisfaction, and support. *Journal of Behavioral Medicine, 26,* 283–296.

Fitzgerald, T. E., Tennen, H., Affleck, G., & Pransky, G. S. (1993). The relative importance of dispositional optimism and control appraisals in quality of life after coronary artery bypass surgery. *Journal of Behavioral Medicine, 16,* 25–43.

Fitzgibbon, M. L., Stolley, M. R., & Kirschenbaum, D. S. (1993). Obese people who seek treatment have different characteristics than those who do not seek treatment. *Health Psychology, 12,* 342–345.

Fitzgibbon, M. L., Stolley, M. R., Avellone, M. E., Sugerman, S., & Chavez, N. (1996). Involving parents in cancer risk reduction: A program for Hispanic American families. *Health Psychology, 15,* 413–422.

Flay, B. R. (1985). Psychosocial approaches to smoking prevention: A review of findings. *Health Psychology, 4,* 448–488.

Flay, B. R., Koepke, D., Thomson, S. J., Santi, S., Best, J. A., & Brown, K. S. (1992). Six year follow-up of the first Waterloo school smoking prevention trial. *American Journal of Public Health, 68,* 458–478.

Flay, B. R., McFall, S., Burton, D., Cook, T. D., & Warnecke, R. B. (1993). Health behavior changes through television: The roles of de facto and motivated selection processes. *Journal of Health and Social Behavior, 34,* 322–335.

Fleming, R., Baum, A., Davidson, L. M., Rectanus, E., & McArdle, S. (1987). Chronic stress as a factor in physiologic reactivity to challenge. *Health Psychology, 6,* 221–237.

Fleming, R., Baum, A., Gisriel, M. M., & Gatchel, R. J. (1982, September). Mediating influences of social support on stress at Three Mile Island. *Journal of Human Stress, 8,* 14–23.

Fleming, R., Leventhal, H., Glynn, K., & Ershler, J. (1989). The role of cigarettes in the initiation and progression of early substance use. *Addictive Behaviors, 14,* 261–272.

Flor, H., Birbaumer, N., & Turk, D. C. (1990). The psychology of chronic pain. *Advances in Behavior Research and Therapy, 12,* 47–84.

Focht, B. C., Ewing, V., Gauvin, L., & Rejeski, W. J. (2002). The unique and transient impact of exercise on pain perception in older, overweight, or obese adults with knee osteoarthritis. *Annals of Behavioral Medicine, 24,* 201–210.

Fogel, J., Albert, S. M., Schnabel, F., Ditkoff, B. A., & Neuget, A. I. (2002). Internet use and support in women with breast cancer. *Health Psychology, 21,* 398–404.

Folkman, S., & Lazarus, R. S. (1980). An analysis of coping in a middle-aged community sample. *Journal of Health and Social Behavior, 21,* 219–239.

Folkman, S., Schaefer, C., & Lazarus, R. S. (1979). Cognitive processes as mediators of stress and coping. In V. Hamilton & D. M. Warburton (Eds.), *Human stress and cognition: An information processing approach* (pp. 265–298). London, England: Wiley.

Fontana, A., Diegnan, T., Villeneuve, A., & Lepore, S. (1999). Nonevaluative social support reduces cardiovascular reactivity in young women during acutely stressful performance situations. *Journal of Behavioral Medicine, 22,* 75–91.

Ford, J. D., Campbell, K. A., Storzbach, D., Binder, L. M., Anger, W. K., & Rohlman, D. S. (2001). Posttraumatic stress symptomatology is associated with unexplained illness attributed to Persian Gulf War military service. *Psychosomatic Medicine, 63,* 842–849.

Foreyt, J. P., Scott, L. W., Mitchell, R. E., & Gotto, A. M. (1979). Plasma lipid changes in the normal population following behavioral treatment. *Journal of Consulting and Clinical Psychology, 47,* 440–452.

Forman, T. A. (2003). The social psychological costs of racial segmentation in the workplace: A study of African Americans' well being. *Journal of Health and Social Behavior, 44,* 332–352.

Forsyth, A. D., & Carey, M. P. (1998). Measuring self-efficacy in the context of HIV risk reduction: Research challenges and recommendations. *Health Psychology, 6,* 559–568.

Foshee, V., & Bauman, K. E. (1992). Parental and peer characteristics as modifiers of the bond-behavior relationship: An elaboration of control theory. *Journal of Health and Social Behavior, 33,* 66–76.

Foster, G. D., Wadden, T. A., & Vogt, R. A. (1997). Body image in obese women before, during, and after weight loss treatment. *Health Psychology, 16,* 226–229.

Foster, G. D., Wadden, T. A., & Vogt, R. A., & Brewer, G. (1997). What is a reasonable weight loss? Patients' expectations and evaluations of obesity treatment outcomes. *Journal of Consulting and Clinical Psychology, 65,* 79–85.

Fox, B. H. (1978). Premorbid psychological factors as related to cancer incidence. *Journal of Behavioral Medicine, 1,* 45–134.

Frances, R. J., Franklin, J., & Flavin, D. (1986). Suicide and alcoholism. *Annals of the New York Academy of Sciences, 487,* 316–326.

Francis, A., Fyer, M., & Clarkin, J. (1986). Personality and suicide. *Annals of the New York Academy of Sciences, 487,* 281–293.

Frankenhaeuser, M. (1975). Sympathetic-adrenomedullary activity behavior and the psychosocial environment. In P. H. Venables & M. J. Christie (Eds.), *Research in psychophysiology* (pp. 71–94). New York: Wiley.

Frankenhaeuser, M. (1991). The psychophysiology of workload, stress, and health: Comparison between the sexes. *Annals of Behavioral Medicine, 13,* 197–204.

Frankenhaeuser, M., Lundberg, U., Fredrikson, M., Melin, B., Tuomisto, M., Myrsten, A., et al. (1989). Stress on and off the job as related to sex and oc-

References **467**

cupational status in white-collar workers. *Journal of Organizational Behavior, 10,* 321–346.

Frankish, C. J., & Linden, W. (1996). Spouse-pair risk factors and cardiovascular reactivity. *Journal of Psychosomatic Research, 40,* 37–51.

Fredrickson, B. L., Maynard, K. E., Helms, M. J., Haney, T. L., Siegler, I. C., & Barefoot, J. C. (2000). Hostility predicts magnitude and duration of blood pressure response to anger. *Journal of Behavioral Medicine, 23,* 229–243.

Fredrickson, B. L., Tugade, M. M., Waugh, C. E. & Larkin, G. R. (2003). What good are positive emotions in crises? A prospective study of resilience and emotions following the terrorist attacks on the United States on September 11th, 2001. *Journal of Personality and Social Psychology, 84,* 365–376.

Fredrickson, M., & Matthews, K. A. (1990). Cardiovascular responses to behavioral stress and hypertension: A meta-analytic review. *Annals of Behavioral Medicine, 12,* 30–39.

Fredrikson, M., Robson, A., & Ljungdell, T. (1991). Ambulatory and laboratory blood pressure in individuals with negative and positive family history of hypertension. *Health Psychology, 10,* 371–377.

Freedland, K. E., Rich, M. W., Skala, J. A., Carney, R. M., Davila-Roman, V. G., & Jaffe, A. S. (2003). Prevalence of depression in hospitalized patients with congestive heart failure. *Psychosomatic Medicine, 65,* 119–128.

Freedman, V. A. (1993). Kin and nursing home lengths of stay: A backward recurrence time approach. *Journal of Health and Social Behavior, 34,* 138–152.

Freeman, A., Simon, K., Beutler, L., & Arkowitz, H. (1989). *Comprehensive handbook of cognitive theory.* New York: Plenum Press.

Freidson, E. (1960). Client control and medical practice. *American Journal of Sociology, 65,* 374–382.

French, A. P., & Tupin, J. P. (1974). Therapeutic application of a simple relaxation method. *American Journal of Psychotherapy, 28,* 282–287.

French, J. R. P., Jr., & Caplan, R. D. (1973). Organizational stress and the individual strain. In A. J. Marrow (Ed.), *The failure of success.* New York: Amacon.

French, S. A., Hennrikus, D. J., & Jeffery, R. W. (1996). Smoking status, dietary intake, and physical activity in a sample of working adults. *Health Psychology, 15,* 448–454.

Frenzel, M. P., McCaul, K. D., Glasgow, R. E., & Schafer, L. C. (1988). The relationship of stress and coping to regimen adherence and glycemic control of diabetes. *Journal of Social and Clinical Psychology, 6,* 77–87.

Freudenheim, M. (1993, August 18). Many patients unhappy with H.M.O.'s. *The New York Times,* pp. 5, 16.

Friedman, E. M., & Irwin, M. R. (1995). A role for CRH and the sympathetic nervous system in stress-induced immunosuppression. *Annals of the New York Academy of Science, 771,* 396–418.

Friedman, H. S., & Booth-Kewley, S. (1987). The "disease-prone" personality: A meta-analytic view of the construct. *American Psychologist, 42,* 539–555.

Friedman, H. S., Tucker, J. S., Schwartz, J. E., Martin, L. R., Tomlinson-Keasey, C., Wingard, D. L., et al. (1995). Childhood conscientiousness and longevity: Health behaviors and cause of death. *Journal of Personality and Social Psychology, 68,* 696–703.

Friedman, H. S., Tucker, J. S., Schwartz, J. E., Tomlinson-Keasey, C., Martin, L. R., Wingard, D. L., et al. (1995). Psychosocial and behavioral predictors of longevity: The aging and death of the "Termites." *American Psychologist, 50,* 69–78.

Friedman, H. S., Tucker, J. S., Tomlinson-Keasey, C., Schwartz, J. E., Wingard, D. L., & Criqui, M. H. (1993). Does childhood personality predict longevity? *Journal of Personality and Social Psychology, 65,* 176–185.

Friedman, J. M. (2000). Obesity in the new millennium. *Nature, 404,* 632–634.

Friedman, M., & Rosenman, R. H. (1974). *Type A behavior and your heart.* New York: Knopf.

Friedman, M., Thoresen, C. E., Gill, J. J., Powell, L. H., Ulmer, D., Thompson, L., et al. (1986). Alteration of Type A behavior and its effect on cardiac recurrences in post myocardial infarction patients: Summary results of the recurrent coronary prevention project. *American Heart Journal, 112,* 653–665.

Friman, P. C., & Christophersen, E. R. (1986). Biobehavioral prevention in primary care. In N. A. Krasnegor, J. Arasteh, & M. F. Cataldo (Eds.), *Child health behavior: A behavioral pediatrics perspective* (pp. 254–280). New York: Wiley.

Friman, P. C., Finney, J. W., Glasscock, S. G., Weigel, J. W., & Christophersen, E. R. (1986). Testicular self-examination: Validation of a training strategy for early cancer detection. *Journal of Applied Behavior Analysis, 19,* 87–92.

Fritz, H. L. (2000). Gender-linked personality traits predict mental health and functional status following a first coronary event. *Health Psychology, 19,* 420–428.

Fromm, K., Andrykowski, M. A., & Hunt, J. (1996). Positive and negative psychosocial sequelae of bone marrow transplantation: Implications for quality of life assessment. *Journal of Behavioral Medicine, 19,* 221–240.

Fukudo, S., Lane, J. D., Anderson, N. B., Kuhn, C. M., Schanberg, S. M., McCown, N., et al. (1992). Accentuated vagal antagonism of beta-adrenergic effects on ventricular repolarization: Evidence of weaker antagonism in hostile Type A men. *Circulation, 85,* 2045–2053.

Fuller, R. K., & Hiller-Strumhofel, S. (1999). Alcoholism treatment in the United States. An overview. Alcohol research and health. *Journal of the National Institute on Alcohol Abuse and Alcoholism 23,* 69–77.

Fuller, T. D., Edwards, J. N., Sermsri, S., & Vorakitphokatorn, S. (1993). Gender and health: Some Asian evidence. *Journal of Health and Social Behavior, 34,* 252–271.

Fullerton, J. T., Kritz-Silverstein, D., Sadler, G. R., & Barrett-Connor, E. (1996). Mammography usage in a community-based sample of older women. *Annals of Behavioral Medicine, 18,* 67–72.

Fung, T. T., Willett, W. C., Stampfer, M. J., Manson, J. E., & Hu, F. B. (2001). Dietary patterns and the risk of coronary heart disease in women. *Archives of Internal Medicine, 161,* 1857–1862.

Fyrand, L., Moum, T., Finset, A., & Glennas, A. (2002). The impact of disability and disease duration on social support of women with rheumatoid arthritis. *Journal of Behavioral Medicine, 25,* 251–268.

Gaab, J., Hüster, D., Peisen, R., Engert, V., Schad, T., Schürmeyer, T. H., et al. (2002). Low-dose dexamethasone suppression test in chronic fatigue syndrome and health. *Psychosomatic Medicine, 64,* 311–318.

Gallacher, J. E. J., Sweetnam, P. M., Yarnell, J. W. G., Elwood, P. C., & Stansfeld, S. A. (2003). Is type A behavior really a trigger for coronary heart disease events. *Psychosomatic Medicine, 65,* 338–349.

Gallacher, J. E. J., Yarnell, J. W. G., Sweetnam, P. M., Elwood, P. C., & Stansfeld, S. A. (1999). Anger and incident heart disease in the Caerphilly study. *Psychosomatic Medicine, 61,* 446–453.

Gallo, L. C., Matthews, K. A., Kuller, L. H., Sutton-Tyrell, K., & Edmundowicz, D. (2001). Educational attainment and coronary and aortic calcification in postmenopausal women. *Psychosomatic Medicine, 63,* 925–935.

Gallo, L. C., Troxel W. M., Kuller, L. H., Sutton-Tyrell, K., Edmundowicz, D., & Matthews, K. A. (2003). Marital status, marital quality and atherosclerotic burden in postmenopausal women. *Psychosomatic Medicine, 65,* 952–962.

Gallo, L. C., Troxel, W. M., Matthews, K. A., Jansen-McWilliams, L., Kuller, L. H., & Sutton-Tyrell, K. (2003). Occupation and subclinical carotid artery disease in women: Are clerical workers at greater risk? *Health Psychology, 22,* 19–29.

Gallup Organization. (2003, December 3). *Religion and gender: A congregation divided.* Retrieved August 2 from: http://www.gallup.com

Galuska, D. A., Will, J. C., Serdula, M. K., & Ford, E. S. (1999). Are health care professionals advising obese patients to lose weight? *Journal of the American Medical Association, 282,* 1576–1578.

Gan, S. C., Beaver, S. K., Houck, P. M., MacLehose, R. F., Lawson, H. W., & Chan, L. (2000). Treatment of acute myocardial infarction and 30-day mortality among women and men. *New England Journal of Medicine, 343,* 8–15.

Ganster, D. C., Mayes, B. T., Sime, W. E., & Tharp, G. D. (1982). Managing organizational stress: A field experiment. *Journal of Applied Psychology, 67,* 533–542.

Garfinkel, P. E., & Garner, D. M. (1982). *Anorexia nervosa: A multidimensional perspective.* New York: Brunner/Mazel.

Garfinkel, P. E., & Garner, D. M. (1983). The multidetermined nature of anorexia nervosa. In P. L. Darby, P. E. Garfinkel, D. M. Garner, & D. V. Coscina (Eds.), *Anorexia nervosa: Recent developments in research.* New York: Liss.

Garner, D. M., & Wooley, S. C. (1991). Confronting the failure of behavioral and dietary treatments for obesity. *Clinical Psychology Review, 11,* 729–780.

Garrett, V. D., Brantley, P. J., Jones, G. N., & McKnight, G. T. (1991). The relation between daily stress and Crohn's disease. *Journal of Behavioral Medicine, 14,* 87–96.

Gartner, A., & Reissman, F. (1976). Health care in a technological age. In *Self-help and health: A report.* New York: New Human Services Institute.

Gatchel, R. J., Gaffney, F. A., & Smith, J. E. (1986). Comparative efficacy of behavioral stress management versus propranolol in reducing psychophysiological reactivity in postmyocardial infarction patients. *Journal of Behavioral Medicine, 9,* 503–513.

Geersten, R., Klauber, M. R., Rindflesh, M., Kane, R. L., & Gray, R. (1975). A re-examination of Suchman's reviews of social factors in health care utilization. *Journal of Health and Social Behavior, 16,* 426–437.

Gemming, M. G., Runyan, C. W., Hunter, W. W., & Campbell, B. J. (1984). A community health education approach to occupant protection. *Health Education Quarterly, 11,* 147–158.

George, L. K., & Lynch, S. M. (2003). Race differences in depressive symptoms: A dynamic perspective on stress exposure and vulnerability. *Journal of Health and Social Behavior, 44,* 353–369.

George, L. K., Ellison, C. G., & Larson, D. B. (2002). Explaining the relationships between religious involvement and health. *Psychology Inquiry, 13,* 190–200.

Gerardo-Gettens, T., Miller, G. D., Horwitz, B. A., McDonald, R. B., Brownell, K. D., Greenwood, M. R. C., et al. (1991). Exercise decreases fat selection in female rats during weight cycling. *American Journal of Physiology, 260,* R518–R524.

Gerbert, B., Stone, G., Stulbarg, M., Gullion, D. S., & Greenfield, S. (1988). Agreement among physician assessment methods: Searching for the truth among fallible methods. *Medical Care, 26,* 519–535.

Gerin, W., & Pickering, T. G. (1995). Association between delayed recovery of blood pressure after acute mental stress and parental history of hypertension. *Journal of Hypertension, 13,* 603–610.

Gerrard, M., Gibbons, F. X., Benthin, A. C., & Hessling, R. M. (1996). A longitudinal study of the reciprocal nature of risk behaviors and cognitions in adolescents: What you do shapes what you think, and vice versa. *Health Psychology, 15,* 344–354.

Gerritson, W., Heijnen, C. J., Wiegant, V. M., Bermond, B., & Frijda, N. H. (1996). Experimental social fear: Immunological, hormonal, and autonomic concomitants. *Psychosomatic Medicine, 58,* 273–286.

Gibbons, F. X., & Eggleston, T. J. (1996). Smoker networks and the "typical smoker": A prospective analysis of smoking cessation. *Health Psychology, 15,* 469–477.

Gibbons, F. X., & Gerrard, M. (1995). Predicting young adults' health risk behavior. *Journal of Personality and Social Psychology, 69,* 505–517.

Gibson, B. (1997). Suggestions for the creation and implementation of tobacco policy. *Journal of Social Issues, 53,* 187–192.

Gidron, Y., & Davidson, K. (1996). Development and preliminary testing of a brief intervention for modifying CHD-predictive hostility components. *Journal of Behavioral Medicine, 19,* 203–220.

Gidron, Y., Davidson, K., & Bata, I. (1999). The short-term effects of a hostility-reduction intervention on male coronary heart disease patients. *Health Psychology, 18,* 416–420.

Gil, K. M., Carson, J. W., Porter, L. S., Scipio, C., Bediako, S. M., & Orringer, E. (2004). Daily mood and stress predict pain, health care use, and work activity in African American adults with sickle-cell disease. *Health Psychology, 23,* 267–274.

Gil, K. M., Wilson, J. J., Edens, J. L., Webster, D. A., Abrams, M. A., Orringer, E., et al. (1996). Effects of cognitive coping skills training on coping strategies and experimental pain sensitivity in African American adults with sickle cell disease. *Health Psychology, 15,* 3–10.

Gill, T. M., Baker, D. I., Gottschalk, M., Peduzzi, P. N., Allore, H., & Byers, A. (2002). A randomized trial of a prehabilitation program to prevent functional decline among frail community-living older persons. *New England Journal of Medicine, 347,* 1068–1074.

Gillespie, M. (1999, March 19). *Latest round in public debate over assisted suicide.* Retrieved June 19, 2001, from: www.gallup.com/poll/releases/

Girdler, S. S., Hinderliter, A. L., Brownley, K. A., Turner, J. R., Sherwood, A., & Light, K. C. (1996). The ability of active versus passive coping tasks to predict future blood pressure levels in normotensive men and women. *International Journal of Behavioral Medicine, 3,* 233–250.

Girdler, S. S., Jamner, L. D., Jarvik, M., Soles, J. R., & Shapiro, D. (1997). Smoking status and nicotine administration differentially modify hemodynamic stress reactivity in men and women. *Psychosomatic Medicine, 59,* 294–306.

Given, C. W., Stommel, M., Given, B., Osuch, J., Kurtz, M. E., & Kurtz, J. C. (1993). The influence of cancer patients' symptoms and functional states on patients' depression and family caregivers' reaction and depression. *Health Psychology, 12,* 277–285.

Glantz, S. A. (2004). Effect of public smoking ban in Helena, Montana: Author's reply. *British Medical Journal, 328,* 1380.

Glanz, K., Croyle, R. T., Chollete, V. Y., & Pinn, V. W. (2003). Cancer-related health disparities in women. *American Journal of Public Health, 93,* 292–298.

Glaros, A. G., & Burton, E. (2004). Parafunctional clenching, pain, and effort in temporomandibular disorders. *Journal of Behavioral Medicine, 27,* 91–100.

Glaser, R., Kiecolt-Glaser, J. K., Bonneau, R. H., Malarkey, W., Kennedy, S., & Hughes, J. (1992). Stress-induced modulation of the immune response to recombinant hepatitis B vaccine. *Psychosomatic Medicine, 54,* 22–29.

Glaser, R., Kiecolt-Glaser, J. K., Marucha, P. T., MacCallum, R. C., Laskowski, B. F., & Malarkey, W. B. (1999). Stress-related changes in proinflammatory cytokine production in wounds. *Archives of General Psychiatry, 56,* 450–456.

Glaser, R., Kiecolt-Glaser, J. K., Speicher, C. E., & Holliday, J. E. (1985). Stress, loneliness, and changes in herpesvirus latency. *Journal of Behavioral Medicine, 8,* 249–260.

Glaser, R., Kiecolt-Glaser, J. K., Stout, J. C., Tarr, K. L., Speicher, C. E., & Holliday, J. E. (1985). Stress-related impairments in cellular immunity. *Psychiatry Research, 16,* 233–239.

Glaser, R., Rice, J., Speicher, C. E., Stout, J. C., & Kiecolt-Glaser, J. K. (1986). Stress depresses interferon production by leukocytes concomitant with a decrease in natural killer cell activity. *Behavioral Neuroscience, 100,* 675–678.

Glaser, R., Sheridan, J., Malarkey, W. B., MacCallum, R. C., & Kiecolt-Glaser, J. K. (2000). Chronic stress modulates the immune response to a pneumococcal pneumonia vaccine. *Psychosomatic Medicine, 62,* 804–807.

Glasgow, M. S., & Engel, B. T. (1987). Clinical issues in biofeedback and relaxation therapy for hypertension. In J. P. Hatch, J. G. Fisher, & J. D. Rugh (Eds.), *Biofeedback* (pp. 81–121). New York: Plenum Press.

Glasgow, M. S., Engel, B. T., & D'Lugoff, B. C. (1989). A controlled study of a standardized behavioral stepped treatment for hypertension. *Psychosomatic Medicine, 51,* 10–26.

Glasgow, R. E., & Anderson, B. J. (1995). Future directions for research on pediatric chronic disease management: Lessons from diabetes. *Journal of Pediatric Psychology, 20,* 389–402.

Glasgow, R. E., Funnell, M. M., Bonomi, A. E., Davis, C., Beckham, V., & Wagner, E. H. (2002). Self-management aspects of the improving chronic illness care breakthrough series: Implementation with diabetes and heart failure teams. *Annals of Behavioral Medicine, 24,* 80–87.

Glasgow, R. E., Klesges, L. M., Dzewaltowski, D. A., Bull, S. S., & Estabrooks, P. (2004). The future of health behavior change research: What is needed to improve translation of research into health promotion practice? *Annals of Behavioral Medicine, 27,* 3–12.

Glasgow, R. E., Stevens, V. J., Vogt, T. M., Mullooly, J. P., & Lichtenstein, E. (1991). Changes in smoking associated with hospitalization: Quit rates, predictive variables, and intervention implications. *American Journal of Health Promotion, 6,* 24–29.

Glasgow, R. E., Terborg, J. R., Strycker, L. A., Boles, S. M., & Hollis, J. F. (1997). Take heart II: Replication of a worksite health promotion trial. *Journal of Behavioral Medicine, 20,* 143–161.

Glasgow, R. E., Toobert, D. J., Hampson, S. E., & Wilson, W. (1995). Behavioral research on diabetes at the Oregon Research Institute. *Annals of Behavioral Medicine, 17,* 32–40.

Glasgow, R. E., Toobert, D. J., Mitchell, D. L., Donnelly, J. E., & Calder, D. (1989). Nutrition education and social learning interventions for type II diabetes. *Diabetes Care, 12,* 150–152.

Glass, D. C., & Singer, J. E. (1972). *Urban stress.* New York: Academic Press.

Glass, J., & Fujimoto, T. (1994). Housework, paid work, and depression among husbands and wives. *Journal of Health and Social Behavior, 35,* 179–191.

Glass, T. A., DeLeon, C. M., Marottoli, R. A., & Berkman, L. F. (1999). Population based study of social and productive activities as predictors of survival among elderly Americans. *British Medical Journal, 319,* 478–483.

Glenn, B., & Burns, J. W. (2003). Pain self-management in the process and outcome of multidisciplinary treatment of chronic pain: Evaluation of a stage of change model. *Journal of Behavioral Medicine, 26,* 417–433.

Glick, I. O., Weiss, R. S., & Parkes, C. M. (1974). *The first year of bereavement.* New York: Wiley.

Glinder, J. G., & Compas, B. E. (1999). Self-blame attributions in women with newly diagnosed breast cancer: A prospective study of psychological adjustment. *Health Psychology, 18,* 475–481.

Global Information Incorporated. (2003). *Pain management: World prescription drug markets.* Retrieved from: http://www.the-infoshop.com/study/tv12667_pain_management.html

Glynn, L. M., Christenfeld, N., & Gerin, W. (1999). Gender, social support, and cardiovascular responses to stress. *Psychosomatic Medicine, 61,* 234–242.

Glynn, L. M., Christenfeld, N., & Gerin, W. (2002). The role of rumination in recovery from reactivity: Cardiovascular consequences of emotional states. *Psychosomatic Medicine, 64,* 714–726.

Goede, P., Vedel, P., Larsen, N., Jensen, G. V. H., Parving, H., & Pedersen, O. (2003). Multifactorial intervention and cardiovascular disease in patients with type 2 diabetes. *New England Journal of Medicine, 348,* 383–393, http://www.nejm.org

Goffman, E. (1961). *Asylums.* Garden City, NY: Doubleday.

Goffman, E. (1963). *Stigma: Notes on the management of spoiled identity.* Englewood Cliffs, NJ: Prentice-Hall.

Goldberg, J. H., Halpern-Felsher, B. L., & Millstein, S. G. (2002). Beyond invulnerability: The importance of benefits in adolescents' decision to drink alcohol. *Health Psychology, 21,* 477–484.

Goldberg, R. J. (1981). Management of depression in the patient with advanced cancer. *Journal of the American Medical Association, 246,* 373–376.

Golden, J. S., & Johnston, G. D. (1970). Problems of distortion in doctor-patient communications. *Psychiatry in Medicine, 1,* 127–149.

Goldman, M. S. (1983). Cognitive impairment in chronic alcoholics: Some cause for optimism. *American Psychologist, 38,* 1045–1054.

Goldman, S. L., Whitney-Saltiel, D., Granger, J., & Rodin, J. (1991). Children's representations of "everyday" aspects of health and illness. *Journal of Pediatric Psychology, 16,* 747–766.

Goldring, A. B., Taylor, S. E., Kemeny, M. E., & Anton, P. A. (2002). Impact of health beliefs, quality of life and the physician-patient relationship on the treatment intentions of inflammatory bowel disease patients? *Health Psychology, 21,* 219–228.

Goldstein, M. S., Jaffe, D. T., Garell, D., & Berk, R. E. (1986). Holistic doctors: Becoming a non-traditional medical practitioner. *Urban Life, 14,* 317–344.

Goldstein, M. S., Jaffe, D. T., Sutherland, C., & Wilson, J. (1987). Holistic physicians: Implications for the study of the medical profession. *Journal of Health and Social Behavior, 28,* 103–119.

Gonder-Frederick, L. A., Carter, W. R., Cox, D. J., & Clarke, W. L. (1990). Environmental stress and blood glucose change in insuring insulin-dependent diabetes mellitus. *Health Psychology, 9,* 503–515.

Gonder-Frederick, L. A., Cox, D. J., Bobbitt, S. A., & Pennebaker, J. W. (1986). Blood glucose symptom beliefs of diabetic patients: Accuracy and implications. *Health Psychology, 5,* 327–341.

Goodall, T. A., & Halford, W. K. (1991). Self-management of diabetes mellitus: A critical review. *Health Psychology, 10,* 1–8.

Goode, K. T., Haley, W. E., Roth, D. L., & Ford, G. R. (1998). Predicting longitudinal changes in caregiver physical and mental health: A stress process model. *Health Psychology, 17,* 190–198.

Goodenow, C., Reisine, S. T., & Grady, K. E. (1990). Quality of social support and associated social and psychological functioning in women with rheumatoid arthritis. *Health Psychology, 9,* 266–284.

Goodman, E., & Capitman, J. (2000). Depressive symptoms and cigarette smoking among teens. *Pediatrics, 106,* 748–755.

Goodstein, R. (1983). Overview: Cerebrovascular accident and the hospitalized elderly—A multi-dimensional clinical problem. *American Journal of Psychiatry, 140,* 141–147.

Goodwin, R. D., & Stein, M. B. (2002). Generalized anxiety disorder and peptic ulcer disease among adults in the United States. *Psychosomatic Medicine, 64,* 862–866.

Goodwin, R. D., Kroenke, K., Hoven, C. W., & Spitzer, R. L. (2003). Major depression, physical illness and suicidal ideation in primary care. *Psychosomatic Medicine, 65,* 501–505.

Gorbatenko-Roth, K. G., Levin, I. P., Altmaier, E. M., & Doebbling, B. N. (2001). Accuracy of health-related quality of life assessment: What is the benefit of incorporating patients' preferences for domain functioning? *Health Psychology, 20,* 136–140.

Gordon, C. M., Carey, M. P., & Carey, K. B. (1997). Effects of a drinking event on behavioral skills and condom attitudes in men: Implications for HIV risk from a controlled experiment. *Health Psychology, 16,* 490–495.

Gordon, J. R., & Marlatt, G. A. (1981). Addictive behaviors. In J. L. Shelton & R. L. Levy (Eds.), *Behavioral assignments and treatment compliance* (pp. 167–186). Champaign, IL: Research Press.

Gordon, W. A., & Diller, L. (1983). Stroke: Coping with a cognitive deficit. In T. G. Burish & L. A. Bradley (Eds.), *Coping with chronic disease: Research and applications* (pp. 113–135). New York: Academic Press.

Gordon, W. A., & Hibbard, M. R. (1992). Critical issues in cognitive remediation. *Neuropsychology, 6,* 361–370.

Gore, S. A., Brown, D. M., & West, D. S. (2003). The role of postpartum weight retention in obesity among women: A review of the evidence. *Annals of Behavioral Medicine, 26,* 149–159.

Gorman, C. (1999, March 29). Get some sleep. *Time,* 225.

Gorman, C. (2003, April 28). The no. 1 killer of women. *Time,* 61–66.

Gorman, Christine. (September 18, 1996). Damage Control. *Time Magazine.*

Gornick, M. E. (2000). *Vulnerable populations and Medicare services: Why do disparities exist?* New York, NY: The Century Foundation Press.

Gottlieb, B. H. (1983). *Social support strategies: Guidelines for mental health practice.* Beverly Hills, CA: Sage.

Gottlieb, B. H. (Ed.). (1988). *Marshalling social support: Formats, processes, and effects.* Newbury Park, CA: Sage.

Gottlieb, J., & Yi, D. (2003, April 28). Hepatitis B a deadly threat to U.S. Asians. *Los Angeles Times,* p. B6.

Gottlieb, N. H., & Green, L. W. (1984). Life events, social network, life-style, and health: An analysis of the 1979 national survey on personal health practices and consequences. *Health Education Quarterly, 11,* 91–105.

Gould, R. (1972). The phases of adult life: A study in developmental psychology. *American Journal of Psychiatry, 129,* 521–531.

Gove, W. R., & Zeiss, C. (1987). Multiple roles and happiness. In F. Crosby (Ed.), *Spouse, parent, worker* (pp. 125–137). New Haven, CT: Yale University Press.

Grady, D. (2000b, February 3). Study says children with cancer suffer more than necessary. *The New York Times,* p. A16.

Grady, D. (2002, May 23). Hormones may explain difficulty dieters have keeping weight off. *The New York Times,* pp. A1, A24.

Grady, D. (2003, October 24). Women with genetic mutation at high risk for breast cancer, study confirms. *The New York Times,* p. A15.

Grady, D. (2004, April 14). Lung cancer affects sexes differently. *The New York Times,* p. A18.

Graham, M. A., Thompson, S. C., Estrada, M., & Yonekura, M. L. (1987). Factors affecting psychological adjustment to a fetal death. *American Journal of Obstetrics and Gynecology, 157,* 254–257.

Gramling, S. E., Clawson, E. P., & McDonald, M. K. (1996). Perceptual and cognitive abnormality model of hypochondriasis: Amplification and physiological reactivity in women. *Psychosomatic Medicine, 58,* 423–431.

Grandner, M. A., & Kripke, D. F. (2004). Self-reported sleep complaints with long and short sleep: A nationally representative sample. *Psychosomatic Medicine, 66,* 239–241.

Grant, I., Adler, K. A., Patterson, T. L., Dimsdale, J. E., Zeigler, M. G., & Irwin, M. R. (2002). Health consequences of Alzheimer's caregiving transitions: Effects of placement and bereavement. *Psychosomatic Medicine, 64,* 477–486.

Grassi, L., & Molinari, S. (1986). Intrafamilial dynamics and neoplasia: Prospects for a multidisciplinary analysis. *Rivista di Psichiatria, 21,* 329–341.

Graugaard, P., & Finset, A. (2000). Trait anxiety and reactions to patient-centered and doctor-centered styles of communication: An experimental study. *Psychosomatic Medicine, 62,* 33–39.

Graves, K. D. (2003). Social cognitive theory and cancer patients' quality of life: A meta-analysis of psychosocial intervention components. *Health Psychology, 22,* 210–219.

Green, C. A., Freeborn, D. K., & Polen, M. R. (2001). Gender and alcohol use: The roles of social support, chronic illness, and psychological well-being. *Journal of Behavioral Medicine, 24,* 383–399.

Green, J. H. (1978). *Basic clinical psychology* (3rd ed.). New York: Oxford University Press.

Greenberg, E. S., & Grunberg, L. (1995). Work alienation and problem alcohol behavior. *Journal of Health and Social Behavior, 36,* 83–102.

Greenberg, R. A., Strecher, V. J., Bauman, K. E., Boat, B. W., Fowler, M. G., Keyes, L. L., et al. (1994). Evaluation of a home-based intervention program to reduce infant passive smoking and lower respiratory illness. *Journal of Behavioral Medicine, 17,* 273–290.

Greene, R. E., Houston, B. K., & Holleran, S. A. (1995). Aggressiveness, dominance, developmental factors, and serum cholesterol level in college males. *Journal of Behavioral Medicine, 18,* 569–580.

Greenfield, S., Kaplan, S. H., Ware, J. E., Jr., Yano, E. M., & Frank, H. J. L. (1988). Patients' participation in medical care: Effects on blood sugar control and quality of life in diabetes. *Journal of General Internal Medicine, 3,* 448–457.

Gregerson, M.B. (2000). The curious 2000-year case of asthma. *Psychosomatic Medicine, 62,* 816–827.

Grembowski, D., Patrick, D., Diehr, P., Durham, M., Beresford, S., Kay, E., et al. (1993). Self-efficacy and health behavior among older adults. *Journal of Health and Social Behavior, 34,* 89–104.

Grodner, S., Prewitt, L. M., Jaworski, B. A., Myers, R., Kaplan, R. M., & Ries, A. L. (1996). The impact of social support in pulmonary rehabilitation of patients with chronic obstructive pulmonary disease. *Annals of Behavioral Medicine, 18,* 139–145.

Gross, A. M., Eudy, C., & Drabman, R. S. (1982). Training parents to be physical therapists with their physically handicapped child. *Journal of Behavioral Medicine, 5,* 321–328.

Grossman, H. Y., Brink, S., & Hauser, S. T. (1987). Self-efficacy in adolescent girls and boys with insulin-dependent diabetes mellitus. *Diabetes Care, 10,* 324–329.

Groth-Marnat, G., & Fletcher, A. (2000). Influence of neuroticism, catastrophizing, pain, duration, and receipt of compensation on short-term response to nerve block treatment for chronic back pain. *Journal of Behavioral Medicine, 23,* 339–350.

Gruman, J. (2003, January). *Ship happens. Good behavior.* Center for the Advancement of Health.

Grunberg, N. E. (1985). Specific taste preferences: An alternative explanation for eating changes in cancer patients. In T. G. Burish, S. M. Levy, & B. E. Meyerowitz (Eds.), *Cancer, nutrition, and eating behavior: A biobehavioral perspective* (pp. 43–61). Hillsdale, NJ: Erlbaum.

Grunberg, N. E. (1986). Nicotine as a psychoactive drug: Appetite regulation. *Psychopharmacology Bulletin, 22,* 875–881.

Grunberg, N. E., & Acri, J. B. (1991). Conceptual and methodological considerations for tobacco addiction research. *British Journal of Addiction, 86,* 637–641.

Grunberg, N. E., & Straub, R. O. (1992). The role of gender and taste class in the effects of stress on eating. *Health Psychology, 11,* 97–100.

Grzywacz, J. G., Almeida, D. M., Neupert, S. D., & Ettner, S. L. (2004). Socioeconomic status and health: A micro-level analysis of exposure and vulnerability to daily stressors. *Journal of Health and Social Behavior, 45,* 1–16.

Gump, B. B., & Matthews, K. A. (1998). Vigilance and cardiovascular reactivity to subsequent stressors in men: A preliminary study. *Health Psychology, 17,* 93–96.

Gump, B. B., & Matthews, K. A. (2000). Are vacations good for your health? The 9-year mortality experience after the multiple risk factor intervention trial. *Psychosomatic Medicine, 62,* 608–612.

Gunthert, K. C., Cohen, L. H., & Armeli, S. (1999). The role of neuroticism in daily stress and coping. *Journal of Personality and Social Psychology, 77,* 1087–1100.

Gupta, S. (2002, August 26). Don't ignore heart-attack blues. *Time,* 71.

Gurevich, M., Devins, G. M., Wilson, C., McCready, D., Marmar, C. R., & Rodin, G. M. (2004). Stress responses syndromes in women undergoing mammography: A comparison of women with and without a history of breast cancer. *Psychosomatic Medicine, 66,* 104–112.

Guyll, M., & Contrada, R. J. (1998). Trait hostility and ambulatory cardiovascular activity: Responses to social interaction. *Health Psychology, 17,* 30–39.

Guyll, M., Matthews, K. A., & Bromberger, J. T. (2001). Discrimination and unfair treatment: Relationship to cardiovascular reactivity among African American and European American women. *Health Psychology, 20,* 315–325.

Guzman, S. J., & Nicassio, P. M. (2003). The contribution of negative and positive illness to depression in patients with end-stage renal disease. *Journal of Behavioral Medicine, 26,* 517–534.

Gynecological Cancer Foundation. (2003, June 19). *Over 80,000 women newly diagnosed every year. Women's cancer network.* Retrieved from: http://www.wcn.org/interior.cfm?featureid=2&contentfile=fa.cfm& contentid=10514&contenttypeid=8&featureid=2&diseaseid=13

Hackett, T. P., & Cassem, N. H. (1973). Psychological adaptation to convalescence in myocardial infarction patients. In J. P. Naughton, H. K. Hellerstein, & I. C. Mohler (Eds.), *Exercise testing and exercise training in coronary heart disease.* New York: Academic Press.

Hagedoorn, M., Kuijer, R. G., Buunk, B. P., DeJong, G., Wobbes, T., & Sanderman, R. (2000). Marital satisfaction in patients with cancer: Does support from intimate partners benefit those who need it the most? *Health Psychology, 19,* 274–282.

Haines, V. A., Hurlbert, J. S., & Beggs, J. J. (1996). Exploring the determinants of support provision: Provider characteristics, personal networks, community contexts, and support following life events. *Journal of Health and Social Behavior, 37,* 252–264.

Halberstam, M. J. (1971, February 14). The doctor's new dilemma: Will I be sued? *New York Times Magazine,* pp. 8–9, 33–39.

Halford, W. K., Cuddihy, S., & Mortimer, R. H. (1990). Psychological stress and blood glucose regulation in Type I diabetic patients. *Health Psychology, 9,* 516–528.

Hall, A., & Crisp, A. H. (1983). Brief psychotherapy in the treatment of anorexia nervosa: Preliminary findings. In P. L. Darby, P. E. Garfinkel, D. M. Garner, & D. V. Coscina (Eds.), *Anorexia nervosa: Recent developments in research* (pp. 41–56). New York: Liss.

Hall, C. (1999, April 5). Living in pain affliction: For chronic pain sufferers, even hope can hurt (first of two parts). *San Francisco Chronicle.* Retrieved March 27, 2001, from: http://www.sfgate.com/

Hall, J. A., Epstein, A. M., DeCiantis, M. L., & McNeil, B. J. (1993). Physicians' liking for their patients: More evidence for the role of affect in medical care. *Health Psychology, 12,* 140–146.

Hall, J. A., Irish, J. T., Roter, D. L., Ehrlich, C. M., & Miller, L. H. (1994). Gender in medical encounters: An analysis of physician and patient communication in a primary care setting. *Health Psychology, 13,* 384–392.

Hall, J. A., Rotter, D. L., & Katz, N. R. (1988). Meta-analysis of correlates of provider behavior in medical encounters. *Medical Care, 26,* 657–675.

Hall, M., Buysse, D. J., Nowell, P. D., Nofzinger, E. A., Houck, P., Reynolds, C. F., et al. (2000). Symptoms of stress and depression as correlates of sleep in primary insomnia. *Psychosomatic Medicine, 62,* 227–230.

Hall, S. C., Adams, C. K., Stein, C. H., Stephenson, H. S., Goldstein, M. K., & Pennypacker, H. S. (1980). Improved detection of human breast lesions following experimental training. *Cancer, 46,* 408–414.

Hall, S. M., Ginsberg, D., & Jones, R. T. (1986). Smoking cessation and weight gain. *Journal of Consulting and Clinical Psychology, 54,* 342–346.

Halpern-Felsher, B. L., Millstein, S. G., Ellen, J. M., Adler, N. E., Tschann, J. M., & Biehl, M. (2001). The role of behavioral experience in judging risks. *Health Psychology, 20,* 120–126.

Ham, B. (Ed.). (2003). Health behavior information transfer. *Habit, 6.* Retrieved from: http://www.cfah.org/habit/

Hamburg, D. A., & Adams, J. E. (1967). A perspective on coping behavior: Seeking and utilizing information in major transitions. *Archives of General Psychiatry, 19,* 277–284.

Hamilton, M. K., Gelwick, B. P., & Meade, C. J. (1984). The definition and prevalence of bulimia. In R. C. Hawkins, W. J. Fremouw, & P. F. Clement (Eds.), *The binge-purge syndrome* (pp. 3–26). New York: Springer.

Hamilton, V. L., Broman, C. L., Hoffman, W. S., & Renner, D. S. (1990). Hard times and vulnerable people: Initial effects of plant closing on autoworkers' mental health. *Journal of Health and Social Behavior, 31,* 123–140.

Hammen, C., Marks, T., Mayol, A., & DeMayo, R. (1985). Depressive self-schemas, life stress, and vulnerability to depression. *Journal of Abnormal Psychology, 94,* 308–319.

Hampson, S. E., Andrews, J. A., Barckley, M., Lichtenstein, E., & Lee, M. E. (2000). Conscientiousness, perceived risk, and risk-reduction behaviors: A preliminary study. *Health Psychology, 19,* 496–500.

Hampson, S. E., Glasgow, R. E., & Toobert, D. J. (1990). Personal models of diabetes and their relations to self-care activities. *Health Psychology, 9,* 632–646.

Hampson, S. E., Glasgow, R. E., & Zeiss, A. M. (1994). Personal models of osteoarthritis and their relation to self-management activities and quality of life. *Journal of Behavioral Medicine, 17,* 143–158.

Hamrick, N., Cohen, S., & Rodriguez, M. S. (2002). Being popular can be healthy or unhealthy: Stress, social network diversity, and incidence of upper respiratory infection. *Health Psychology, 21,* 294–298.

Han, S., & Shavitt, S. (1994). Persuasion and culture: Advertising appeals in individualistic and collectivistic societies. *Journal of Experimental Social Psychology, 30,* 326–350.

Hansen, C. J., Stevens, L. C., & Coast, J. R. (2001). Exercise duration and mood state: How much is enough to feel better? *Health Psychology, 20,* 267–275.

Hanson, C. L., & Pichert, J. W. (1986). Perceived stress and diabetes control in adolescents. *Health Psychology, 5,* 439–452.

Hanson, C. L., Henggeler, S. W., & Burghen, G. A. (1987). Models of associations between psychosocial variables and health-outcome measures of adolescents with IDDM. *Diabetes Care, 10,* 752–758.

Hanson, C. L., Henggeler, S. W., Harris, M. A., Burghen, G. A., & Moore, M. (1989). Family system variables and the health status of adolescents with insulin-dependent diabetes mellitus. *Health Psychology, 8,* 239–253.

Harburg, E., Erfurt, J. C., Havenstein, L. S., Chape, C., Schull, W. J., & Schork, M. A. (1973). Socio-ecological stress, suppressed hostility, skin color, and Black-White male blood pressure: Detroit. *Psychosomatic Medicine, 35,* 276–296.

Harburg, E., Julius, M., Kaciroti, N., Gleiberman, L., & Schork, M. A. (2003). Expressive/suppressive anger-coping responses, gender, and types of mortality: a 17-year follow-up (Tecumseh, Michigan, 1971–1988). *Psychosomatic Medicine, 65,* 588–597.

Harmon, A. (2004, July 21). As gene test menu grows, who gets to choose? *The New York Times,* pp. A1, A15.

Harnish, J. D., Aseltine, R. H., & Gore, S. (2000). Resolution of stressful experiences as an indicator of coping effectiveness in young adults: An event history analysis. *Journal of Health and Social Behavior, 41,* 121–136.

Harrell, J. P. (1980). Psychological factors and hypertension: A status report. *Psychological Bulletin, 87,* 482–501.

Harrington, L., Affleck, G., Urrows, S., Tennen, H., Higgins, P., Zautra, A., et al. (1993). Temporal covariation of soluable interleukin-2 receptor levels, daily stress, and disease activity in rheumatoid arthritis. *Arthritis and Rheumatism, 36,* 199–207.

Harris, K. F., & Matthews, K. A. (2004). Interactions between autonomic nervous system activity and the endothelial function: A model for the development of cardiovascular disease. *Psychosomatic Medicine, 66,* 153–164.

Harris, M. B., Walters, L. C., & Waschull, S. (1991). Gender and ethnic differences in obesity-related behaviors and attitudes in a college sample. *Journal of Applied Social Psychology, 21,* 1545–1566.

Hartley, H. (1999). The influence of managed care on supply of certified nurse-midwives: An evaluation of the physician dominance thesis. *Journal of Health and Social Behavior, 40,* 87–101.

Harwood, H. *Updating Estimates of the Economic Costs of Alcohol Abuse in the United States: Estimates, Update Methods, and Data.* Report prepared by The Lewin Group for the National Institute on Alcohol Abuse and Alcoholism, 2000. Based on estimates, analyses, and data reported in Harwood, H.; Fountain, D.; and Livermore, G. *The Economic Costs of Alcohol and Drug Abuse in the United States 1992.* Report prepared for the National Institute on Drug Abuse and Alcoholism, National Institutes of Health, Department of Health and Human Services. NIH Publication No. 98-4327. Rockville, MD: National Institutes of Health, 1998.

Hassinger, H., Semenchuk, E., & O'Brien, W. (1999). Appraisal and coping responses to pain and stress in migraine headache sufferers. *Journal of Behavioral Medicine, 22,* 327–340.

Hastrup, J. L. (1985). Inaccuracy of family health information: Implications for prevention. *Health Psychology, 4,* 389–397.

Hatfield, M. O. (1990). Stress and the American worker. *American Psychologist, 45,* 1162–1164.

Hatsukami, D., LaBounty, L., Hughes, J., & Laine, D. (1993). Effects of tobacco abstinence on food intake among cigarette smokers. *Health Psychology, 12,* 499–502.

Hauenstein, M. S., Schiller, M. R., & Hurley, R. S. (1987). Motivational techniques of dieticians counseling individuals with Type II diabetes. *Journal of the American Diabetic Association, 87,* 37–42.

Haug, M. R. (1994). Elderly patients, caregivers, and physicians: Theory and research on health care trends. *Journal of Health and Social Behavior, 35,* 1–12.

Haug, M. R., & Folmar, S. J. (1986). Longevity, gender, and life quality. *Journal of Health and Social Behavior, 27,* 332–345.

Haug, M. R., & Ory, M. G. (1987). Issues in elderly patient-provider interactions. *Research on Aging, 9,* 3–44.

Hawk, L., Dougall, L., Ursano, R., & Baum, A. (2000). Urinary catecholamines and cortisol in recent-onset posttraumatic stress disorder after motor vehicle accidents. *Psychosomatic Medicine, 62,* 423–434.

Hawkley, L. C., Burleson, M. H., Berntson, G. G., & Cacioppo, J. T. (2003). Loneliness in everyday life: Cardiovascular activity, psychosocial context, and health behaviors. *Journal of Personality and Social Psychology, 85,* 105–120.

Hayes, D., & Ross, C. E. (1987). Concern with appearance, health beliefs, and eating habits. *Journal of Health and Social Behavior, 28,* 120–130.

Hayes-Bautista, D. E. (1976). Modifying the treatment: Patient compliance, patient control, and medical care. *Social Science and Medicine, 10,* 233–238.

Haynes, R. B. (1979a). Determinants of compliance: The disease and the mechanics of treatment. In R. B. Haynes, D. W. Taylor, & D. L. Sackett (Eds.), *Compliance in health care* (pp. 49–62). Baltimore, MD: Johns Hopkins University Press.

Haynes, R. B. (1979b). Strategies to improve compliance with referrals, appointments, and prescribed medical regimens. In R. B. Haynes, D. W. Taylor, & D. L. Sackett (Eds.), *Compliance in health care* (pp. 121–143). Baltimore, MD: Johns Hopkins University Press.

Haynes, R. B., McKibbon, K. A., & Kanani, R. (1996). Systematic review of randomized controlled trials of the effects on patient adherence and outcomes of interventions to assist patients to follow prescriptions for medications. *The Cochrane Library, 2,* 1–26.

Haynes, R. B., Wang, B., & da-Mota-Gomes, M. (1987). A critical review of intentions to improve compliance with prescribed medications. *Patient Education and Counseling, 10,* 155–166.

Haynes, S. G., Odenkirchen, J., & Heimendinger, J. (1990). Worksite health promotion for cancer control. *Seminars in Oncology, 17,* 463–484.

Haynes, S. N., Gannon, L. R., Bank, J., Shelton, D., & Goodwin, J. (1990). Cephalic blood flow correlates of induced headaches. *Journal of Behavioral Medicine, 13,* 467–480.

Hays, J., et al. (2003). Effects of estrogen plus progestin on health-related quality of life. *New England Journal of Medicine, 348,* 1839–1854. Retrieved from: http://www.nejm.org

Hays, R. B., Turner, H., & Coates, T. J. (1992). Social support, AIDS-related symptoms, and depression among gay men. *Journal of Consulting and Clinical Psychology, 60,* 463–469.

Haythornthwaite, J. A., Lawrence, J. W., & Fauerbach, J. A. (2001). Brief cognitive interventions for burn pain. *Annals of Behavioral Medicine, 23,* 42–49.

Hazuda, H. P., Gerety, M. B., Lee, S., Mulrow, C. D., & Lichtenstein, M. J. (2002). Measuring subclinical disability in older Mexican Americans. *Psychosomatic Medicine, 64,* 520–530.

Heaney, C. A., Israel, B. A., & House, J. A. (1994). Chronic job insecurity among automobile workers: Effects on job satisfaction and health. *Social Science and Medicine, 38,* 1431–1437.

Heath, A. C., & Madden, P. A. F. (1995). Genetic influences on smoking behavior. In J. R. Turner et al. (Eds.), *Behavior genetic approaches in behavioral medicine.* New York: Plenum Press.

Heatherton, T. F., Herman, C. P., & Polivy, J. (1992). Effects of distress on eating: The importance of ego-involvement. *Journal of Personality and Social Psychology, 62,* 801–803.

Hebert, L. E., Scherr, P. A., Bienias, J. L., Bennett, D. A., & Evans, D. A. (2003). Alzheimer's disease in the U.S. population: prevalence estimates using the 2000 census. *Archives of Neurology, 60,* 1119–1122.

Heckman, T. G. (2003). The chronic illness quality of life (CIQOL) model: Explaining life satisfaction in people living with HIV disease. *Health Psychology, 22,* 140–147.

Heckman, T. G., Anderson, E. S., Sikkema, K. J., Kochman, A., Kalichman, S. C., & Anderson, T. (2004). Emotional distress in nonmetropolitan persons living with HIV disease enrolled in a telephone-delivered, coping improvement group intervention. *Health Psychology, 23,* 94–100.

Heckman, T. G., Miller, J., Kochman, A., Kalichman, S. C., Carlson, B., & Silverthorn, M. (2002). Thoughts of suicide among HIV-infected rural persons enrolled in telephone-delivered mental health intervention. *Annals of Behavioral Medicine, 2002,* 141–148.

Heesch, K. C., Mâsse, L. C., Dunn, A. L., Frankowski, R. F., & Mullen, P. D. (2003). Does adherence to a lifestyle physical activity intervention predict changes in physical activity? *Journal of Behavioral Medicine, 26,* 333–348.

Heim, E., Valach, L., & Schaffner, L. (1997). Coping and psychosocial adaptation: Longitudinal effects over time and stages in breast cancer. *Psychosomatic Medicine, 59,* 408–418.

Heishman, S. J., Kozlowski, L. T., & Henningfield, J. E. (1997). Nicotine addiction: Implications for public health policy. *Journal of Social Issues, 53,* 13–33.

Helgeson, V. S. (1992). Moderators of the relation between perceived control and adjustment to chronic illness. *Journal of Personality and Social Psychology, 63,* 656–666.

Helgeson, V. S. (1993). Implications of agency and communion for patient and spouse adjustment to a first coronary event. *Journal of Personality and Social Psychology, 64,* 807–816.

Helgeson, V. S. (1999). Applicability of cognitive adaptation theory to predicting adjustment to heart disease after coronary angioplasty. *Health Psychology, 18,* 561–569.

Helgeson, V. S. (2003). Cognitive adaptation, psychological adjustment and disease progression among angioplasty patients: 4 years later. *Health Psychology, 22,* 30–38.

Helgeson, V. S., & Cohen, S. (1996). Social support and adjustment to cancer: Reconciling descriptive, correlational, and intervention research. *Health Psychology, 15,* 135–148.

Helgeson, V. S., & Fritz, H. L. (1998). A theory of unmitigated communion. *Personality & Social Psychology Review, 2,* 173–183.

Helgeson, V. S., & Fritz, H. L. (1999). Cognitive adaptation as a predictor of new coronary events after percutaneous transluminal coronary angioplasty. *Psychosomatic Medicine, 61,* 488–495.

Helgeson, V. S., & Lepore, S. J. (1997). Men's adjustment to prostate cancer: The role of agency and unmitigated agency. *Sex Roles, 37,* 251–267.

Helgeson, V. S., Cohen, S., Schulz, R., & Yasko, J. (2000). Group support interventions for women with breast cancer: Who benefits from what? *Health Psychology, 19,* 107–117.

Helgeson, V. S., Cohen, S., Schulz, R., & Yasko, J. (2001). Long-term effects of educational and peer discussion group interventions on adjustment to breast cancer. *Health Psychology, 20,* 387–392.

Helgeson, V. S., Snyder, P., & Seltman, H. (2004). Psychological and physical adjustment to breast cancer over 4 years: Identifying distinct trajectories of change. *Health Psychology, 23,* 3–15.

Helmers, K. F., & Krantz, D. S. (1996). Defensive hostility, gender and cardiovascular levels and responses to stress. *Annals of Behavioral Medicine, 18,* 246–254.

Hemenover, S. H. (2001). Self-reported processing bias and naturally occurring mood: Mediators between personality and stress appraisals. *Personality and Social Psychology Bulletin, 27,* 387–394.

Hemenover, S. H. (2003). The good, the bad, and the healthy: Impacts of emotional disclosure of trauma on resilient self-concept and psychological distress. *Personality and Social Psychology Bulletin, 29,* 1236–1244.

Henifin, M. S. (1993). New reproductive technologies: Equity and access to reproductive health care. *Journal of Social Issues, 49,* 62–74.

Henry, J. P., & Cassel, J. C. (1969). Psychosocial factors in essential hypertension: Recent epidemiologic and animal experimental evidence. *American Journal of Epidemiology, 90,* 171–200.

Herbert, L. E., Scherr, P. A., Bienias, J. L., Bennett, B. D., & Evans, D. A. (2003). Alzheimer's disease in the U. S. population. *Archives of Neurology, 60,* 1119–1122.

Herbert, T. B., & Cohen, S. (1993). Stress and immunity in humans: A meta-analytic review. *Psychosomatic Medicine, 5,* 364–379.

Herek, G. M., Capitanio, J. P., & Widaman, K. F. (2003). Stigma, social risk, and health policy: Public attitudes toward HIV surveillance policies and the social construction of illness. *Health Psychology, 22,* 533–540.

Herman, C. P. (1987). Social and psychological factors in obesity: What we don't know. In H. Weiner & A. Baum (Eds.), *Perspectives in behavioral medicine: Eating regulation and discontrol* (pp. 175–187). Hillsdale, NJ: Erlbaum.

Herman, M. (1972). The poor: Their medical needs and the health services available to them. *Annals of the American Academy of Political and Social Science, 399,* 12–21.

Herman, S., Blumenthal, J. A., Babyak, M., Khatri, P., Craighead, W. E., Krishnan, K. R., et al. (2002). Exercise therapy for depression in middle-aged and older adults: Predictors of early dropout and treatment failure. *Health Psychology, 21,* 553–563.

Hermand, D., Mullet, E., & Lavieville, S. (1997). Perception of the combined effects of smoking and alcohol on health. *Journal of Health Psychology, 2,* 481–491.

Herrmann, C., Brand-Driehorst, S., Kaminsky, B., Leibing, E., Staats, H., & Ruger, U. (1998). Diagnostic groups and depressed mood as predictors of 22-month mortality in medical inpatients. *Psychosomatic Medicine, 60,* 570–577.

Herschbach, P., Duran, G., Waadt, S., Zettler, A., Amm, C., Marten-Mittag, B., et al. (1997). Psychometric properties of the questionnaire on stress in patients with diabetes-revised (QSD-F). *Health Psychology, 16,* 171–174.

Herzog, A. R., House, J. D., & Morgan, J. N. (1991). Relation of work and retirement to health and well-being in older age. *Psychology and Aging, 6,* 202–211.

Hibbard, M. R., Gordon, W. A., Stein, P. N., Grober, S., & Sliwinski, M. (1992). Awareness of disability in patients following stroke. *Rehabilitation Psychology, 37,* 103–120.

Hibbard, M. R., Grober, S. E., Stein, P. N., & Gordon, W. A. (1992). Post-stroke depression. In A. Freeman & F. M. Dattilio (Eds.), *Comprehensive casebook of cognitive therapy* (pp. 303–310). New York: Plenum Press.

Higgins-Biddle, J. C., Babor, T. F., Mullahyl, J., Daniels, J., & McRee, B. (1997). Alcohol screening and brief intervention: Where research meets practice. *Connecticut Medicine, 61,* 565–575.

Hilgard, E. R. (1965). *Hypnotic susceptibility.* New York: Harcourt, Brace & World.

Hilgard, E. R. (1971). Hypnotic phenomena: The struggle for scientific acceptance. *American Scientist, 59,* 567–577.

Hilgard, E. R. (1978). Hypnosis and pain. In R. A. Sternbach (Ed.), *The psychology of pain.* New York: Raven Press.

Hill-Briggs, F. (2003). Problem solving in diabetes self-management: A model of chronic illness self-management behavior. *Annals of Behavior Medicine, 25,* 182–193.

Hillhouse, J. J., & Turrisi, R. (2002). Examination of efficacy of an appearance-focused intervention to reduce UV exposure. *Journal of Behavioral Medicine, 25,* 395–409.

Hillhouse, J. J., Stair, A. W., III, & Adler, C. M. (1996). Predictors of sun-bathing and sunscreen use in college undergraduates. *Journal of Behavioral Medicine, 19,* 543–562.

Hinton, J. M. (1967). *Dying.* Baltimore, MD: Penguin.

Hirayama, T. (1981). Non-smoking wives of heavy smokers have a higher risk of lung cancer: A study from Japan. *British Medical Journal, 282,* 183–185.

Hobfoll, S. E. (1989). Conservation of resources: A new attempt at conceptualizing stress. *American Psychologist, 44,* 513–524.

Hobfoll, S. E., Jackson, A. P., Lavin, J., Britton, P. J., & Shepherd, J. B. (1993). Safer sex knowledge, behavior, and attitudes of inner-city women. *Health Psychology, 12,* 481–488.

Hochbaum, G. (1958). Public participation in medical screening programs (DHEW Publication No. 572, Public Health Service). Washington, D.C.: U.S. Government Printing Office.

Hochschild, A. (1989). *The second shift: Working parents and the revolution at home.* New York: Viking Penguin.

Hodis, H. N., et al. (2003). Hormone therapy and the progression of coronary-artery atherosclerosis in postmenopausal women. *New England Journal of Medicine, 349,* 535–545. http://www.nejm.org

Hoelscher, T. J., Lichstein, K. L., & Rosenthal, T. L. (1986). Home relaxation practice in hypertension treatment: Objective assessment and compliance induction. *Journal of Consulting and Clinical Psychology, 54,* 217–221.

Hoffman, C., Rice, D., & Sung, H. Y. (1996). Persons with chronic conditions: Their prevalence and costs. *Journal of the American Medical Association, 276,* 1473–1479.

Hogan, B. E., & Linden, W. (2004). Anger response style and blood pressure: At least don't ruminate about it! *Annals of Behavioral Medicine, 27,* 38–49.

Holaday, J. W. (1983). Cardiovascular effects of endogenous opiate systems. *Annual Review of Pharmacology and Toxicology, 23,* 541–594.

Holahan, C. J., & Moos, R. H. (1986). Personality, coping, and family resources in stress resistance: A longitudinal analysis. *Journal of Personality and Social Psychology, 51,* 389–395.

Holahan, C. J., & Moos, R. H. (1987). Personal and contextual determinants of coping strategies. *Journal of Personality and Social Psychology, 52,* 946–955.

Holahan, C. J., & Moos, R. H. (1990). Life stressors, resistance factors, and improved psychological functioning: An extension of the stress resistance paradigm. *Journal of Personality and Social Psychology, 58,* 909–917.

Holahan, C. J., & Moos, R. H. (1991). Life stressors, personal and social resources, and depression: A four-year structural model. *Journal of Abnormal Psychology, 100,* 31–38.

Holahan, C. J., Moos, R. H., Holahan, C. K., & Brennan, P. L. (1997). Social context, coping strategies, and depressive symptoms: An expanded model with cardiac patients. *Journal of Personality and Social Psychology, 72,* 918–928.

Holden, C. (1980). Love Canal residents under stress. *Science, 208,* 1242–1244.

Holden, C. (1987). Is alcoholism treatment effective? *Science, 236,* 20–22.

Holland, J. C. (2002). History of psycho-oncology: Overcoming attitudinal and conceptual barriers. *Psychosomatic Medicine, 64,* 206–221.

Holland, J. C., & Rowland, J. H. (1981). Psychiatric, psychosocial, and behavioral interventions in the treatment of cancer: A historical overview. In S. M. Weiss, J. A. Herd, & B. H. Fox (Eds.), *Perspectives on behavioral medicine.* New York: Academic Press.

Hollis, J. F., Carmody, T. P., Connor, S. L., Fey, S. G., & Matarazzo, J. D. (1986). The nutrition attitude survey: Associations with dietary habits, psychological and physical well-being, and coronary risk factors. *Health Psychology, 5,* 359–374.

Hollon, S. D., & Beck, A. T. (1986). Cognitive and cognitive-behavioral therapies. In S. L. Garfield & A. E. Bergin (Eds.), *Handbook of psychotherapy and behavior change* (3rd ed., pp. 443–482). New York: Wiley.

Holmes, D. S. (1981). The use of biofeedback for treating patients with migraine headaches, Raynaud's disease, and hypertension: A critical evaluation. In C. K. Prokop & L. A. Bradley (Eds.), *Medical psychology: Contributions to behavioral medicine* (pp. 423–441). New York: Academic Press.

Holmes, J. A., & Stevenson, C. A. Z. (1990). Differential effects of avoidant and attentional coping strategies on adaptation to chronic and recent-onset pain. *Health Psychology, 9,* 577–584.

Holmes, T. H., & Rahe, R. H. (1967). The social readjustment rating scale. *Journal of Psychosomatic Research, 11,* 213–218.

Holroyd, K. A., Andrasik, F., & Westbrook, T. (1977). Cognitive control of tension headache. *Cognitive Therapy and Research, 1,* 121–133.

Holt, C. L., Clark, E. M., Kreuter, M. W., & Rubio, D. M. (2003). Spiritual health locus of control and breast cancer beliefs among urban African American women. *Health Psychology, 22,* 294–299.

Homme, L. E. (1965). Perspectives in psychology, XXIV: Control of coverants, the operants of the mind. *Psychological Record, 15,* 501–511.

Hongladrom, T., & Hongladrom, G. C. (1982). The problem of testicular cancer: How health professionals in the armed services can help. *Military Medicine, 147,* 211–213.

Hops, H., Duncan, T. E., Duncan, S. C., & Stoolmiller, M. (1996). Parent substance use as a predictor of adolescent use: A six-year lagged analysis. *Annals of Behavioral Medicine, 18,* 157–164.

Horan, M. J., & Roccella, E. J. (1988). Non-pharmacologic treatment of hypertension in the United States. *Health Psychology, 7*(Suppl.), 267–282.

Horgen, K. B., & Brownell, K. D. (2002). Comparison of price change and health message interventions in promoting healthy food choices. *Health Psychology, 21,* 505–512.

Horowitz, M. J. (1975). Sliding meanings: A defense against threat in narcissistic personalities. *International Journal of Psychoanalysis and Psychotherapy, 4,* 167–180.

Horwitz, A. V., Reinhard, S. C., & Howell-White, S. (1996). Caregiving as reciprocal exchange in families with seriously mentally ill members. *Journal of Health and Social Behavior, 37,* 149–162.

House, J. A. (1981). *Work stress and social support.* Reading, MA: Addison-Wesley.

House, J. S. (1987). Chronic stress and chronic disease in life and work: Conceptual and methodological issues. *Work and Stress, 1,* 129–134.

House, J. S. (2001). Understanding social factors and inequalities in health: 20th century progress and 21st century prospects. *Journal of Health and Social Behavior, 43,* 125–142.

House, J. S., & Smith, D. A. (1985). Evaluating the health effects of demanding work on and off the job. In T. F. Drury (Ed.), *Assessing physical fitness and physical activity in population-base surveys* (pp. 481–508). Hyattsville, MD: National Center for Health Statistics.

House, J. S., Kessler, R. C., Herzog, A. R., Mero, R. P., Kinney, A. M., & Breslow, M. J. (1990). Age, socioeconomic status, and health. *The Milbank Quarterly, 68,* 383–411.

House, J. S., Landis, K. R., & Umberson, D. (1988). Social relationships and health. *Science, 241,* 540–545.

House, J. S., Strecher, V., Meltzner, H. L., & Robbins, C. A. (1986). Occupational stress and health among men and women in the Tecumseh Community Health Study. *Journal of Health and Social Behavior, 27,* 62–77.

House, W. C., Pendelton, L., & Parker, L. (1986). Patients' versus physicians' attributions of reasons for diabetic patients' noncompliance with diet. *Diabetes Care, 9,* 434.

Houston, B. K., & Vavak, C. R., (1991). Cynical hostility: Developmental factors, psychosocial correlates, and health behaviors. *Health Psychology, 10,* 9–17.

Houston, B. K., Babyak, M. A., Chesney, M. A., Black, G., & Ragland, D. R. (1997). Social dominance and 22-year all-cause mortality in men. *Psychosomatic Medicine, 59,* 5–12.

Hu, F. B., Stampfer, M. J., Manson, J. E., Grodstein, F., Colditz, G. A., Speizer, F. E., & Willett, W. C. (2000). Trends in the incidence of coronary heart disease and changes in diet and lifestyle in women. *New England Journal of Medicine, 343,* 530–537.

Huebner, D. M., & Gerend, M. A. (2001). The relation between beliefs about drug treatments for HIV and sexual risk behavior in gay and bisexual men. *Annals of Behavioral Medicine, 23,* 304–312.

Hughes, J. R. (1993). Pharmacotherapy for smoking cessation: Unvalidated assumptions, anomalies, and suggestions for future research. *Journal of Consulting and Clinical Psychology, 61,* 751–760.

Hughes, J. R., Gulliver, S. B., Fenwick, J. W., Valliere, W. A., Cruser, K., Pepper, S., et al. (1992). Smoking cessation among self-quitters. *Health Psychology, 11,* 331–334.

Hughes, M. E., & Waite, L. J. (2002). Health in household context: Living arrangements and health in late middle age. *Journal of Health and Social Behavior, 43,* 1–21.

Huizink, A. C., Robles de Medina, P. G., Mulder, E. J. H., Visser, G. H. A., & Buitelaar, J. K. (2002). Coping in normal pregnancy. *Annals of Behavioral Medicine, 24,* 132–140.

Hultquist, C. M., Meyers, A. W., Whelan, J. P., Klesges, R. C., Peacher-Ryan, H., & DeBon, M. W. (1995). The effect of smoking and light activity on metabolism in men. *Health Psychology, 14,* 124–131.

Humpel, N., Marshall, A. L., Leslie, E., Bauman, A., & Owen, N. (2004). Changes in neighborhood walking are related to changes in perceptions of environmental attributes. *Annals of Behavioral Medicine, 27,* 60–67.

Hunt, W. A., & Matarazzo, J. D. (1973). Three years later: Recent developments in the experimental modification of smoking behavior. *Journal of Abnormal Psychology, 81,* 107–114.

Hunter, C. E., & Ross, M. W. (1991). Determinants of health-care workers' attitudes toward people with AIDS. *Journal of Applied Social Psychology, 21,* 947–956.

Huntington, R., & Metcalf, P. (1979). *Celebrations of death: The anthropology of mortuary ritual.* New York: Cambridge University Press.

Huntington's Outreach Project for Education. (2004). *The basics of Huntington's disease: Part 1.* Stanford University, CA, http://www.stanford.edu/group/hopes/basics/basichd/a1.html

Hutchison, K. E., McGeary, J., Smolen, A., Bryan, A., & Swift, R. M. (2002). The DRD4 VNTR polymorphism moderates craving after alcohol consumption. *Health Psychology, 21,* 139–146.

Hymowitz, N., Campbell, K., & Feuerman, M. (1991). Long-term smoking intervention at the worksite: Effects of quit-smoking groups and an "enriched milieu" on smoking cessation in adult white-collar employees. *Health Psychology, 10,* 366–369.

Ickovics, J. R., Hamburger, M. E., Vlahov, D., Schoenbaum, E. E., Schuman, P., Boland, R. J., et al. (2001). Mortality, CD4 cell count decline, and depressive symptoms among HIV-seropositive women. *Journal of the American Medical Association, 285,* 1466–1474.

Ickovics, J. R., Viscoli, C. M., & Horwitz, R. I. (1997). Functional recovery after myocardial infarction in men: the independent effects of social class. *Annals of Internal Medicine, 127,* 518–525.

Iezzi, T., Archibald, Y., Barnett, P., Klinck, A., & Duckworth, M. (1999). Neurocognitive performance and emotional status in chronic pain patients. *Journal of Behavioral Medicine, 22,* 205–216.

Ingelfinger, J. R. (2004). Pediatric antecedents of adult cardiovascular disease-awareness and intervention. *The New England Journal of Medicine, 350,* 2123–2126, http://www.nejm.org

Ingram, R. E., Atkinson, J. H., Slater, M. A., Saccuzzo, D. P., & Garfin, S. R. (1990). Negative and positive cognition in depressed and nondepressed chronic-pain patients. *Health Psychology, 9,* 300–314.

Institute of Medicine. (1999). *To err is human: Building a safer health system.* Retrieved from: http://www.iom.edu/report.asp?id=5575

Institute of Medicine. (2002). *Unequal treatment: Confronting racial and ethnic disparities in health care.* Washington, D.C.: National Academic Press.

Interian, A., Gara, M., Díaz-Martínez, A. M., Warman, M. J., Escobar, J. I., Allen, L. A., & Manetti-Cusa, J. (2004) The value of pseudoneurological symptoms for assessing psychopathology in primary care. *Psychosomatic Medicine, 66,* 141–146.

Ironson, G., Solomon, G. F., Balbin, E. G., O'Cleirigh, C., George, A., Kumar, M., Larson, D., & Woods, T. E. (2002). The Ironson-Woods Spirituality/Religiousness Index is associated with long survival, health behaviors, less distress, and low cortisol in people with HIV/AIDS. *Annals of Behavioral Medicine, 24,* 34–48.

Ironson, G., Wynings, C., Schneiderman, N., Baum, A., Rodriguez, M., Greenwood, D., et al. (1997). Posttraumatic stress symptoms, intrusive thoughts, loss, and immune function after Hurricane Andrew. *Psychosomatic Medicine, 59,* 128–141.

Irvine, J., Baker, B., Smith, J., Janice, S., Paquette, M., Cairns, J., et al. (1999). Poor adherence to placebo or amiodarone therapy predicts mortality: Results from the CAMIAT study. *Psychosomatic Medicine, 61,* 566–575.

Irwin, M. (1999). Immune correlates of depression. Advances in Experimental Medicine and Biology, *461,* 1–24.

Irwin, M. R., Pike, J. L., Cole, J. C., & Oxman, M. N. (2003). Effects of a behavioral intervention, tai chi chih, on varicella-zoster virus specific immunity and health functioning in older adults. *Psychosomatic Medicine, 65,* 824–830.

Irwin, M., Mascovich, A., Gillin, J. C., Willoughby, R., Pike, J., & Smith, T. L. (1994). Partial sleep deprivation reduces natural killer cell activity in humans. *Psychosomatic Medicine, 56,* 493–498.

Ishigami, T. (1919). The influence of psychic acts on the progress of pulmonary tuberculosis. *American Review of Tuberculosis, 2,* 470–484.

Itkowitz, N. I., Kerns, R. D., & Otis, J. D. (2003). Support and coronary heart disease: The importance of significant other responses. *Journal of Behavioral Medicine, 26,* 19–30.

Ituarte, P. H., Kamarck, T. W., Thompson, H. S., & Bacanu, S. (1999). Psychosocial mediators of racial differences in nighttime blood pressure dipping among normotensive adults. *Health Psychology, 18,* 393–402.

Iwanaga, M., Yokoyama, H., & Seiwa, H. (2000). Effects of personal responsibility and latitude of Type A and B individuals on psychological and physiological stress responses. *International Journal of Behavioral Medicine, 7,* 204–215.

Jachuck, S. J., Brierley, H., Jachuck, S., & Willcox, P. M. (1982). The effect of hypotensive drugs on the quality of life. *Journal of the Royal College of General Practitioners, 32,* 103–105.

Jackson, K. M., & Aiken, L. S. (2000). A psychosocial model of sun protection and sunbathing in young women: The impact of health beliefs, attitudes, norms, and self-efficacy for sun protection. *Health Psychology, 19,* 469–478.

Jacob, R. G., Chesney, M. A., Williams, D. M., Ding, Y., & Shapiro, A. P. (1991). Relaxation therapy for hypertension: Design effects and treatment effects. *Annals of Behavioral Medicine, 13,* 5–17.

Jacobsen, P. B., Bovbjerg, D. H., & Redd, W. H. (1993b). Anticipatory anxiety in women receiving chemotherapy for breast cancer. *Health Psychology, 12,* 469–475.

Jacobsen, P. B., Bovbjerg, D. H., Schwartz, M. D., Andrykowski, M. A., Futterman, A. D., Gilewski, T., et al. (1993a). Formation of food aversions in cancer patients receiving repeated infusions of chemotherapy. *Behaviour Research and Therapy, 8,* 739–748.

Jacobsen, P. B., Bovbjerg, D. H., Schwartz, M. D., Hudis, C. A., Gilewski, T. A., & Norton, L. (1995). Conditioned emotional distress in women receiving chemotherapy for breast cancer. *Journal of Consulting and Clinical Psychology, 63,* 108–114.

Jacobsen, P. B., Manne, S. L., Gorfinkle, K., Schorr, O., Rapkin, B., & Redd, W. H. (1990). Analysis of child and parent behavior during painful medical procedures. *Health Psychology, 9,* 559–576.

Jacobsen, P. B., Valdimarsdottir, H. B., Brown, K. L., & Offit, K. (1997). Decision-making about genetic testing among women at familial risk for breast cancer. *Psychosomatic Medicine, 59,* 459–466.

Jacobson, E. (1938). *Progressive relaxation* (2nd ed.). Chicago: University of Chicago Press.

Jacobson, M. F., & Brownell, K. D. (2000). Small taxes on soft drinks and snack foods to promote health. *American Journal of Public Health, 90,* 854–857.

Jacobson, P. B., Wasserman, J., & Anderson, J. R. (1997). Historical overview of tobacco legislation and regulation. *Journal of Social Issues, 53,* 75–95.

Jacoby, D. B. (1986). Letter to the editor. *New England Journal of Medicine, 315,* 399.

James, J. E. (2004). Critical review of dietary caffeine and blood pressure: A relationship that should be taken more seriously. *Psychosomatic Medicine, 66,* 63–71.

James, S. A., Hartnett, S. A., & Kalsbeek, W. D. (1983). John Henryism and blood pressure differences among Black men. *Journal of Behavioral Medicine, 6,* 259–278.

James, S. A., Keenan, N. L., Strogatz, D. S., Browning, S. R., & Garrett, J. M. (1992). Socioeconomic status, John Henryism, and blood pressure in

Black adults: The Pitt County study. *American Journal of Epidemiology, 135,* 59–67.

Jameson, M. (2004, January 19). No standing pat. *Los Angeles Times,* p. F7.

Janis, I. L. (1958). *Psychological stress.* New York: Wiley.

Janis, I. L. (1983). Improving adherence to medical recommendations: Prescriptive hypotheses derived from recent research in social psychology. In A. Baum, S. E. Taylor, & J. Singer (Eds.), *Handbook of psychology and health* (Vol. 4, pp. 113–148). Hillsdale, NJ: Erlbaum.

Janson, M. A. H. (1986). A comprehensive bereavement program. *Quality Review Bulletin, 12,* 130–135.

Jarvinen, K. A. J. (1955). Can ward rounds be dangerous to patients with myocardial infarction? *British Medical Journal, 1,* 318–320.

Jason, H., Kagan, N., Werner, A., Elstein, A. S., & Thomas, J. B. (1971). New approaches to teaching basic interview skills to medical students. *American Journal of Psychiatry, 127,* 140–143.

Jay, S. M., Elliott, C. H., Woody, P. D., & Siegel, S. (1991). An investigation of cognitive-behavior therapy combined with oral valium for children undergoing painful medical procedures. *Health Psychology, 10,* 317–322.

Jeffery, R. W. (1991). Weight management and hypertension. *Annals of Behavioral Medicine, 13,* 18–22.

Jeffery, R. W. (1992). Is obesity a risk factor for cardiovascular disease? *Annals of Behavioral Medicine, 14,* 109–112.

Jeffery, R. W., & Wing, R. R. (1995). Long-term effects of interventions for weight loss using food provision and money incentives. *Journal of Consulting and Clinical Psychology, 63,* 793–796.

Jeffery, R. W., Boles, S. M., Strycker, L. A., & Glasgow, R. E. (1997). Smoking-specific weight gain concerns and smoking cessation in a working population. *Health Psychology, 16,* 487–489.

Jeffery, R. W., French, S. A., & Rothman, A. J. (1999). Stage of change as a predictor of success in weight control in adult women. *Health Psychology, 18,* 543–546.

Jeffery, R. W., Hennrikus, D. J., Lando, H. A., Murray, D. M., & Liu, J. W. (2000). Reconciling conflicting findings regarding postcessation weight concerns and success in smoking cessation. *Health Psychology, 19,* 242–246.

Jeffery, R. W., Pirie, P. L., Rosenthal, B. S., Gerber, W. M., & Murray, D. M. (1982). Nutritional education in supermarkets: An unsuccessful attempt to influence knowledge and produce sales. *Journal of Behavioral Medicine, 5,* 189–200.

Jeffrey, R. W., Kelly, K. M., Rothman, A. J., Sherwood, N. E., & Boutelle, K. N. (2004). The weight loss experience: A descriptive analysis. *Annals of Behavioral Medicine, 27,* 100–106.

Jellinek, E. M. (1960). *The disease concept of alcoholism.* Highland Park, NJ: Hillhouse Press.

Jemmott, J. B., III, Jemmott, L. S., Spears, H., Hewitt, N., & Cruz-Collins, M. (1992). Self-efficacy, hedonistic expectancies, and condom-use intentions among inner-city Black adolescent women: A social cognitive approach to AIDS risk behavior. *Journal of Adolescent Health, 13,* 512–519.

Jemmott, J. B., III, & Jones, J. M. (1993). Social psychology and AIDS among ethnic minorities: Risk behaviors and strategies for changing them. In J. Pryor & G. Reeder (Eds.), *The social psychology of HIV infection* (pp. 183–244). Hillsdale, NJ: Erlbaum.

Jemmott, J. B., III, Croyle, R. T., & Ditto, P. H. (1988). Commonsense epidemiology: Self-based judgments from laypersons and physicians. *Health Psychology, 7,* 55–73.

Jemmott, J. B., III, Jemmott, L. S., & Fong, G. (1992). Reductions in HIV risk–associated sexual behaviors among Black male adolescents: Effects of an AIDS prevention intervention. *American Journal of Public Health, 82,* 372–377.

Jemmott, J. B., III, Jemmott, L. S., & Hacker, C. I. (1992). Predicting intentions to use condoms among African American adolescents: The theory of planned behavior as a model of HIV risk–associated behavior. *Ethnicity Discussions, 2,* 371–380.

Jemmott, J. B., III, Jemmott, L. S., Spears, H., Hewitt, N., & Cruz-Collins. (1992). Self-efficacy, hedonistic expectancies, and condom-use intentions among inner-city Black adolescent women: A social cognitive approach to AIDS risk behavior. *Journal of Adolescent Health, 13,* 512–519.

Jenkins, C. D. (1990a). Health for all by the year 2000: A challenge to behavioural sciences and health education. *International Journal of Health Education, 9,* 8–12.

Jenkins, C. D. (1990b). *Model for an integrated patient motivation, management and evaluation programme for persons with diabetes mellitus.* Review, World Health Organization, Geneva, Switzerland.

Jiang, W., Babyak, M., Krantz, D. S., Waugh, R. A., Coleman, R. E., Hanson, M. M., et al. (1996). Mental stress-induced myocardial ischemia and cardiac events. *Journal of the American Medical Association, 275,* 1651–1656.

Joffres, M., Reed, D. M., & Nomura, A. M. Y. (1985). Psychosocial processes and cancer incidence among Japanese men in Hawaii. *American Journal of Epidemiology, 121,* 488–500.

Johansson, E., & Lindberg, P. (2000). Low back pain patients in primary care: Subgroups based on the multidimensional pain inventory. *International Journal of Behavioral Medicine, 7,* 340–352.

Johnsen, L., Spring, B., Pingitore, R., Sommerfeld, B. K., & MacKirnan, D. (2002). Smoking as subculture? Influence on Hispanic and Non-Hispanic White women's attitudes toward smoking and obesity. *Health Psychology, 21,* 279–287.

Johnson, C. G., Levenkron, J. C., Suchman, A. L., & Manchester, R. (1988). Does physician uncertainty affect patient satisfaction? *Journal of General Internal Medicine, 3,* 144–149.

Johnson, E. H., Schork, N. J., & Spielberger, C. D. (1987). Emotional and familial determinants of elevated blood pressure in Black and White adolescent females. *Journal of Psychosomatic Research, 31,* 731–741.

Johnson, J. (1982). The effects of a patient education course on persons with a chronic illness. *Cancer Nursing, 5,* 117–123.

Johnson, J. E. (1984). Psychological interventions and coping with surgery. In A. Baum, S. E. Taylor, & J. E. Singer (Eds.), *Handbook of psychology and health* (Vol. 4, pp. 167–188). Hillsdale, NJ: Erlbaum.

Johnson, J. E., & Leventhal, H. (1974). Effects of accurate expectations and behavioral instructions on reactions during a noxious medical examination. *Journal of Personality and Social Psychology, 29,* 710–718.

Johnson, J. E., Christman, N., & Stitt, C. (1985). Personal control interventions: Short- and long-term effects on surgical patients. *Research in Nursing and Health, 8,* 131–145.

Johnson, J. E., Lauver, D. R., & Nail, L. M. (1989). Process of coping with radiation therapy. *Journal of Consulting and Clinical Psychology, 57,* 358–364.

Johnson, J. G., Cohen, P., Pine, D. S., Klein, D. F., Kasen, S., & Brook, J. S. (2000). Association between cigarette smoking and anxiety disorders during adolescence and early adulthood. *Journal of the American Medical Association, 284,* 2348–2351.

Johnson, R. J., & Wolinsky, F. D. (1993). The structure of health status among older adults: Disease, disability, functional limitation, and perceived health. *Journal of Health and Social Behavior, 34,* 105–121.

Johnson, R. J., McCaul, K. D., & Klein, W. M. P. (2002). Risk involvement and risk perception among adolescents and young adults. *Journal of Behavioral Medicine, 25,* 67–82.

Johnson, S. (2003). *Arthritis has plagued mankind throughout the ages.* DeWitt Publishing.

Johnson, S. B., Freund, A., Silverstein, J., Hansen, C. A., & Malone, J. (1990). Adherence-health status relationships in childhood diabetes. *Health Psychology, 9,* 606–631.

Johnson, S. B., Tomer, A., Cunningham, W. R., & Henretta, J. C. (1990). Adherence in childhood diabetes: Results of a confirmatory factor analysis. *Health Psychology, 9,* 493–501.

Jonas, B. S., & Lando, J. F. (2000). Negative affect as a prospective risk factor for hypertension. *Psychosomatic Medicine, 62,* 188–196.

Jonas, B. S., & Mussolino, M. E. (2000). Symptoms of depression as a prospective risk factor of stroke. *Psychosomatic Medicine, 62,* 463–471.

Jones, D. J., Beach, S. R. H., Forehand, R., & Foster, S. E. (2003). Self reported health in HIV-positive African American women: The role of family stress and depressive symptoms. *Journal of Behavioral Medicine, 26,* 577–599.

Jones, J. L., & Leary, M. R. (1994). Effects of appearance-based admonitions against sun exposure on tanning intentions in young adults. *Health Psychology, 13,* 86–90.

Jorgensen, R. S., & Houston, B. K. (1981). Family history of hypertension, gender and cardiovascular reactivity and stereotypy during stress. *Journal of Behavioral Medicine, 4,* 175–190.

Jorgensen, R. S., Frankowski, J. J., & Carey, M. P. (1999). Sense of coherence, negative life events and appraisal of physical health among university students. *Personality and Individual Differences, 27,* 1079–1089.

Jung, W., & Irwin, M. (1999). Reduction of natural killer cytotoxic activity in major depression: Interaction between depression and cigarette smoking. *Psychosomatic Medicine, 61,* 263–270.

Kabat-Zinn, J., & Chapman-Waldrop, A. (1988). Compliance with an outpatient stress reduction program: Rates and predictors of program completion. *Journal of Behavioral Medicine, 11,* 333–352.

Kagan, N. I. (1974). Teaching interpersonal relations for the practice of medicine. *Lakartidningen, 71,* 4758–4760.

Kahana, E., Lawrence, R. H., Kahana, B., Kercher, K., Wisniewski, A., Stoller, E., et al. (2002). Long-term impact of preventive proactivity on quality of life of the old-old. *Psychosomatic Medicine, 64,* 382–394.

Kahn, R. L. (1981). *Work and health.* New York: Wiley.

Kahn, R. L., & Juster, F. T. (2002). Well-being: Concepts and measures. *Journal of Social Issues, 58,* 627–644.

Kalichman, S. C., & Coley, B. (1996). Context framing to enhance HIV-antibody-testing messages targeted to African American women. *Health Psychology, 14,* 247–254.

Kalichman, S. C., & Nachimson, D. (1999). Self-efficacy and disclosure of HIV-positive serostatus to sex partners. *Health Psychology, 18,* 281–287.

Kalichman, S. C., Carey, M. P., & Johnson, B. T. (1996). Prevention of sexually transmitted HIV infection: A meta-analytic review of the behavioral outcome literature. *Annals of Behavioral Medicine, 18,* 6–15.

Kalichman, S. C., DiMarco, M., Austin, J., Luke, W., & DiFonzo, K. (2003). Stress, social support, and HIV-status disclosure to family and friends among HIV-positive men and women. *Journal of Behavioral Medicine, 26,* 315–332.

Kalichman, S. C., Kelly, J. A., & Rompa, D. (1997). Continued high-risk sex among HIV seropositive gay and bisexual men seeking HIV prevention services. *Health Psychology, 16,* 369–373.

Kalichman, S. C., Nachimson, D., Cherry, C., & Williams, E. (1998). AIDS treatment advances and behavioral prevention setbacks: Preliminary assessment of reduced perceived threat of HIV-AIDS. *Health Psychology, 17,* 546–550.

Kalichman, S. C., Weinhardt, L., DiFonzo, K., Austin, J., & Luke, W. (2002). Sensation seeking and alcohol use as markers of sexual transmission risk behavior in HIV-positive men. *Annals of Behavioral Medicine, 24,* 229–235.

Kalish, R. A. (1977). Dying and preparing for death: A view of families. In H. Feifel (Ed.), *New meanings of death.* New York: McGraw-Hill.

Kamarck, T. W., & Lichtenstein, E. (1998). Program adherence and coping strategies as predictors of success in a smoking treatment program. *Health Psychology, 7,* 557–574.

Kamarck, T. W., Muldoon, M. F., Shiffman, S., Sutton-Tyrell, K., Gwaltney, C., & Janieki, D. L. (2004). Experiences of demand and control in daily life as correlates of subclinical carotid atherosclerosis in a healthy older sample. *Health Psychology, 23,* 24–32.

Kamen-Siegel, L., Rodin, J., Seligman, M. E. P., & Dwyer, J. (1991). Explanatory style and cell-mediated immunity in elderly men and women. *Health Psychology, 10,* 229–235.

Kanner, A. D., Coyne, J. C., Schaeffer, C., & Lazarus, R. S. (1981). Comparison of two modes of stress measurement: Daily hassles and uplifts versus major life events. *Journal of Behavioral Medicine, 4,* 1–39.

Kapel, L., Glaros, A. G., & McGlynn, F. D. (1989). Psychophysiological responses to stress in patients with myofascial pain-dysfunction syndrome. *Journal of Behavioral Medicine, 12,* 397–406.

Kaplan, G. A., & Reynolds, P. (1988). Depression and cancer mortality and morbidity: Prospective evidence from the Alameda County Study. *Journal of Behavioral Medicine, 11,* 1–13.

Kaplan, H. I. (1975). Current psychodynamic concepts in psychosomatic medicine. In R. O. Pasnau (Ed.), *Consultation-liaison psychiatry.* New York: Grune & Stratton.

Kaplan, J. R., Manuck, S. B., & Shively, C. (1991). The effects of fat and cholesterol on social behavior in monkeys. *Psychosomatic Medicine, 53,* 634–642.

Kaplan, R. M. (1985). Quality of life measurement. In P. Karoly (Ed.), *Measurement strategies in health psychology* (pp. 115–146). New York: Wiley.

Kaplan, R. M. (1989). Health outcome models for policy analysis. *Health Psychology, 8,* 723–735.

Kaplan, R. M. (1990). Behavior as the central outcome in health care. *American Psychologist, 45,* 1211–1220.

Kaplan, R. M. (1991a). Assessment of quality of life for setting priorities in health policy. In H. E. Schroeder (Ed.), *New directions in health psychology assessment* (pp. 1–26). Washington, D.C.: Hemisphere.

Kaplan, R. M. (1991b). Health-related quality of life in patient decision making. *Journal of Social Issues, 47,* 69–90.

Kaplan, R. M. (2000). Two pathways to prevention. *American Psychologist, 55,* 382–396.

Kaplan, R. M., & Bush, J. W. (1982). Health-related quality of life measurement for evaluation research and policy analysis. *Health Psychology, 1,* 61–80.

Kaplan, R. M., & Hartwell, S. L. (1987). Differential effects of social support and social network on physiological and social outcomes in men and women with Type II diabetes mellitus. *Health Psychology, 6,* 387–398.

Kaplan, R. M., & Simon, H. J. (1990). Compliance in medical care: Reconsideration of self-predictions. *Annals of Behavioral Medicine, 12,* 66–71.

Kaplan, R. M., & Toshima, M. T. (1990). The functional effects of social relationships on chronic illnesses and disability. In B. R. Sarason, I. G. Sarason, & G. R. Pierce (Eds.), *Social support: An interactional view* (pp. 427–453). New York: Wiley-Interscience.

Kaplan, R. M., Atkins, C. I., & Lenhard, L. (1982). Coping with a stressful sigmoidoscopy: Evaluation of cognitive and relaxation preparations. *Journal of Behavioral Medicine, 5,* 67–82.

Kaplan, R. M., Orleans, C. T., Perkins, K. A., & Pierce, J. P. (1995). Marshaling the evidence for greater regulation and control of tobacco products: A call for action. *Annals of Behavioral Medicine, 17,* 3–14.

Kaplan, R. M., Ries, A. L., Prewitt, L. M., & Eakin, E. (1994). Self-efficacy expectations predict survival for patients with chronic obstructive pulmonary disease. *Health Psychology, 13,* 366–368.

Kapp, M. B. (1993). Life-sustaining technologies: Value issues. *Journal of Social Issues, 49,* 151–167.

Karasek, R., Baker, D., Marxer, F., Ahlbom, A., & Theorell, T. (1981). Job decision latitude, job demands, and cardiovascular disease: A prospective study of Swedish men. *American Journal of Public Health, 71,* 694–705.

Karlin, W. A., Brondolo, E., & Schwartz, J. (2003). Workplace social support and ambulatory cardiovascular activity in New York city traffic agents. *Psychosomatic Medicine, 65,* 167–176.

Karoly, P., & Ruehlman, L. S. (1996). Motivational implications of pain: Chronicity, psychological distress, and work global construal in a national sample of adults. *Health Psychology, 15,* 383–390.

Kasl, S. V., & Berkman, L. (1983). Health consequences of the experience of migration. *Annual Review of Public Health, 4,* 69–90.

Kassem, N. O. & Lee, J. W. (2004). Understanding soft drink consumption among male adolescents using the theory of planned behavior. *Journal of Behavioral Medicine, 27,* 273–296.

Kastenbaum, R. J. (1977). *Death, society, & human experience.* St. Louis: Mosby.

Katon, W. J., Richardson, L., Lozano, P., & McCauley, E. (2004). The relationship of asthma and anxiety disorder. *Psychosomatic Medicine, 66,* 349–355.

Katz, R. C., & Jernigan, S. (1991). An empirically derived educational program for detecting and preventing skin cancer. *Journal of Behavioral Medicine, 14,* 421–428.

Katz, R. C., Flasher, L., Cacciapaglia, H., & Nelson, S. (2001). The psychological impact of cancer and lupus: A cross validation study that extends the generality of "benefit finding" in patients with chronic disease. *Journal of Behavioral Medicine, 24,* 561–571.

Katz, S. T., Ford, A. B., Moskowitz, R. W., Jackson, B. A., & Jaffee, M. W. (1983). Studies of illness in the aged: The index of ADL. *Journal of the American Medical Association, 185,* 914–919.

Kaufman, M. R. (1970). Practicing good manners and compassion. *Medical Insight, 2,* 56–61.

Kavanaugh, D. J., Gooley, S., & Wilson, P. H. (1993). Prediction of adherence and control in diabetes. *Journal of Behavioral Medicine, 16,* 509–522.

Kazdin, A. E. (1974). Self-monitoring behavior change. In M. J. Mahoney & C. E. Thoresen (Eds.), *Self-control: Power to the person* (pp. 218–246). Monterey, CA: Brooks-Cole.

Keane, T. M., & Wolfe, J. (1990). Comorbidity in post-traumatic stress disorder: An analysis of community and clinical studies. *Journal of Applied Social Psychology, 20,* 1776–1788.

Kearney, M. H., Rosal, M. C., Ockene, J. K., & Churchill, L. C. (2002). Influences on older women's adherence to a low-fat diet in the women's health initiative. *Psychosomatic Medicine, 64,* 450–457.

Keefe, F. J., & Van Horn, Y. (1993). Cognitive-behavioral treatment of rheumatoid arthritis pain. *Arthritis Care and Research, 6,* 213–222.

Keefe, F. J., Caldwell, D. S., Queen, K. T., Gil, K. M., Martinez, S., Crisson, J. E., et al. (1987). Pain coping strategies in osteoarthritis patients. *Journal of Consulting and Clinical Psychology, 55,* 208–212.

Keefe, F. J., Dunsmore, J., & Burnett, R. (1992). Behavioral and cognitive-behavioral approaches to chronic pain: Recent advances and future directions. *Journal of Consulting and Clinical Psychology, 60,* 528–536.

Keefe, F. J., Lumley, M. A., Buffington, A. L. H., Carson, J. W., Studts, J. L., Edwards, C. L., et al. (2002). Changing face of pain: Evolution of pain research in psychosomatic medicine. *Psychosomatic Medicine, 64,* 921–938.

Keene, R. J. (1980). Follow-up studies of World War II and Korean conflict prisoners. *American Journal of Epidemiology, 111,* 194–200.

Kegeles, S. S. (1985). Education for breast self-examination: Why, who, what, and how? *Preventive Medicine, 14,* 702–720.

Keita, G. P., & Jones, J. M. (1990). Reducing adverse reaction to stress in the workplace: Psychology's expanding role. *American Psychologist, 45,* 1137–1141.

Kelder, G. E., Jr., & Daynard, R. A. (1997). Judicial approaches to tobacco control: The third wave of tobacco litigation as a tobacco control mechanism. *Journal of Social Issues, 53,* 169–186.

Kellerman, J., Rigler, D., & Siegel, S. E. (1979). Psychological responses of children to isolation in a protected environment. *Journal of Behavioral Medicine, 2,* 263–274.

Kelly, J. A., Lawrence, J. S., Hood, H. V., & Brasfield, T. L. (1989). Behavioral intention to reduce AIDS risk activities. *Journal of Consulting and Clinical Psychology, 57,* 60–67.

Kelly, J. A., Murphy, D. A., Bahr, G. R., Koob, J. J., Morgan, M. G., Kalichman, S. C., et al. (1993). Factors associated with severity of depression and high-risk sexual behavior among persons diagnosed with human immunodeficiency virus (HIV) infection. *Health Psychology, 12,* 215–219.

Kelly-Hayes, M., Wolf, P. A., Kannel, W. B., Sytkowski, D., D'Agostino, R. B., & Gresham, G. E. (1988). Factors influencing survival and need for institutionalization following stroke: The Framingham Study. *Archives of Physical and Medical Rehabilitation, 69,* 415–418.

Kemeny, M. E. (2003). The psychobiology of stress. *Current Directions, 12,* 124–129.

Kemeny, M. E., Cohen, R., Zegans, L. S., & Conant, M. A. (1989). Psychological and immunological predictors of genital herpes recurrence. *Psychosomatic Medicine, 51,* 195–208.

Kemeny, M. E., Weiner, H., Duran, R., Taylor, S. E., et al. (1995). Immune system changes after the death of a partner in HIV-positive gay men. *Psychosomatic Medicine, 57,* 547–554.

Kemeny, M. E., Weiner, H., Taylor, S. E., Schneider, S., Visscher, B., & Fahey, J. L. (1994). Repeated bereavement, depressed mood, and immune parameters in HIV seropositive and seronegative homosexual men. *Health Psychology, 13,* 14–24.

Kempen, G. I. J. M., Jelicic, M., & Ormel, J. (1997). Personality, chronic medical morbidity, and health-related quality of life among older persons. *Health Psychology, 16,* 539–546.

Kenchaiah, S., Evans, J. C., Levy, D., Wilson, P. W. F., Benjamin, E. J., Larson, M. G., et al. (2002). Self-appraised problem solving and pain-relevant social support as predictors of the experience of chronic pain. *Annals of Behavioral Medicine, 24,* 100–105.

Kendall, P. C., Williams, L., Pechacek, T. F., Graham, L. E., Shisslak, C., & Herzoff, N. (1979). Cognitive-behavioral and patient education interventions in cardiac catheterization procedures: The Palo Alto medical psychology project. *Journal of Consulting and Clinical Psychology, 47,* 49–58.

Kendler, K. S., Kessler, R. C., Heath, A. C., Neale, M. C., & Eaves, L. J. (1991). Coping: A genetic epidemiological investigation. *Psychological Medicine, 21,* 337–346.

Kendler, K. S., Silberg, J. L., Neale, M. C., Kessler, R. C., Heath, A. C., & Eaves, L. J. (1992). Genetic and environmental factors in the aetiology of menstrual, premenstrual, and neurotic symptoms: A population-based twin study. *Psychological Medicine, 22,* 85–100.

Kerckhoff, A. C., & Back, K. W. (1968). *The June bug: A study of hysterical contagion.* New York: Appleton-Century-Crofts.

Kerns, R. D., Rosenberg, R., & Otis, J. D. (2002). Self-appraised problem solving and pain-relevant social support as predictors of the experience of chronic pain. *Annals of Behavioral Medicine, 24,* 100–105.

Kerr, L. R., Hundal, R., Silva, W. A., Emerman, J. T., & Weinberg, J. (2001). Effects of social housing condition on chemotherapeutic efficacy in a shionogi carcinoma (sc115) mouse tumor model: Influences if temporal factors, tumor size, and tumor growth rate. *Psychosomatic Medicine, 63,* 973–984.

Kerry, B., & Hofshire, P. J. (1993). Hidden problems in current health-care financing and potential changes. *American Psychologist, 48,* 261–264.

Kershaw, T. S., Ethier, K. A., Niccolai, L. M., Lewis J. B., & Ickovics, J. R. (2003). Misperceived risk among female adolescents: Social and psychological factors associated with sexual risk accuracy. *Health Psychology, 22,* 523–532.

Kessler, R. C., & McRae, J. A., Jr. (1982). The effects of wives' employment on the mental health of married men and women. *American Sociological Review, 47,* 216–227.

Kessler, R. C., & Wethington, E. (1991). The reliability of life event reports in a community survey. *Psychological Medicine, 21,* 723–738.

Kessler, R. C., Kendler, K. S., Heath, A. C., Neale, M. C., & Eaves, L. J. (1992). Social support, depressed mood, and adjustment to stress: A genetic epidemiological investigation. *Journal of Personality and Social Psychology, 62,* 257–272.

Kessler, R. C., Turner, J. B., & House, J. S. (1987). Intervening processes in the relationship between unemployment and health. *Psychological Medicine, 17,* 949–961.

Kessler, R. C., Turner, J. B., & House, J. S. (1988). Effects of unemployment on health in a community survey: Main, modifying, and mediating effects. *Journal of Social Issues, 44,* 69–85.

Ketterer, M. W., Fitzgerald, F., Keteyian, S., Thayer, B., Jordon, M., McGowan, C., et al. (2000). Chest pain and the treatment of psychosocial/emotional distress in CAD patients. *Journal of Behavioral Medicine, 23,* 437–450.

Kiberstis, P., & Marx, J. (2002, July 26). The unstable path to cancer. *Science, 297,* 543–569.

Kiecolt-Glaser, J. K., & Glaser, R. (1987). Psychosocial influences on herpesvirus latency. In E. Kurstak, Z. J. Lipowski, & P. V. Morozov (Eds.), *Viruses, immunity, and mental disorders* (pp. 403–412). New York: Plenum Press.

Kiecolt-Glaser, J. K., & Newton, T. L. (2001). Marriage and health: His and hers. *Psychological Bulletin, 127,* 472–503.

Kiecolt-Glaser, J. K., Dura, J. R., Speicher, C. E., Trask, O. J., & Glaser, R. (1991). Spousal caregivers of dementia victims: Longitudinal changes in immunity and health. *Psychosomatic Medicine, 53,* 345–362.

Kiecolt-Glaser, J. K., Fisher, L., Ogrocki, P., Stout, J. C., Speicher, C. E., & Glaser, R. (1987). Marital quality, marital disruption, and immune function. *Psychosomatic Medicine, 49,* 13–34.

Kiecolt-Glaser, J. K., Glaser, R., Cacioppo, J. T., MacCallum, R. C., Snydersmith, M., Kim, C., et al. (1997). Marital conflict in older adults: Endocrinological and immunological correlates. *Psychosomatic Medicine, 59,* 339–349.

Kiecolt-Glaser, J. K., Glaser, R., Gravenstein, S., Malarkey, W. B., & Sheridan, J. (1996). Chronic stress alters the immune response to influenza virus vaccine in older adults. *Proceedings of the National Academy of Science USA, 93,* 3043–3047.

Kiecolt-Glaser, J. K., Glaser, R., Williger, D., Stout, J., Messick, G., Sheppard, S., et al. (1985). Psychosocial enhancement of immunocompetence in a geriatric population. *Health Psychology, 4,* 25–41.

Kiecolt-Glaser, J. K., Malarkey, W. B., Chee, M. A., Newton, T., Cacioppo, J. T., Mao, H. Y., et al. (1993). Negative behavior during marital conflict is associated with immunological down-regulation. *Psychosomatic Medicine, 55,* 395–409.

Kiecolt-Glaser, J. K., Marucha, P. T., Malarkey, W. B., Mercado, A. M., & Glaser, R. (1995). Slowing of wound healing by psychological stress. *Lancet, 346,* 1194–1196.

Kielcolt-Glaser, J. K., McGuire, L., Robles, T. F., & Glaser, R. (2002). Psychoneuroimmunology and psychosomatic medicine: Back to the future. *Psychosomatic Medicine, 64,* 15–28.

Kiecolt-Glaser, J. K., Newton, T., Cacioppo, J. T., MacCallum, R. C., Glaser, R., & Malarkey, W. B. (1996). Marital conflict and endocrine function: Are men really more psychologically affected than women? *Journal of Consulting and Clinical Psychology, 64,* 324–332.

Kim, Y., Valdimarsdottir, H. B., & Bovbjerg, D. H. (2003). Family histories of breast cancer, coping styles, and psychological adjustment. *Journal of Behavioral Medicine, 26,* 225–243.

Kimm, S. Y. S., Glynn, N. W., Kriska, A. M., Barton, B. A., Kronsberg, S. S., Daniels, S. R., et al. (2002). Decline in physical activity in Black girls and White girls during adolescence. *New England Journal of Medicine, 347,* 709–715, http://www.nejm.org

Kinder, L. S., Carnethon, M. R., Palaniappan, L. P., King, A. C., & Fortmann, S. P. (2004). Depression and the metabolic syndrome in young adults: Findings from the Third National Health and Nutrition Examination Survey. *Psychosomatic Medicine, 66,* 316–322.

Kinder, L. S., Kamarck, T. W., Baum, A., & Orchard, T. J. (2002). Depressive symptomology and coronary heart disease in type I diabetes mellitus: A study of possible mechanisms. *Health Psychology, 21,* 542–552.

King, A. C., Castro, C., Wilcox, S., Eyler, A. A., Sallis, J. F., & Brownson, R. C. (2000). Personal and environmental factors associated with physical inactivity among different racial-ethnic groups of U.S. middle-aged and older-aged women. *Health Psychology, 19,* 354–364.

King, D. W., King, L. A., Gudanowski, D. M., & Vreven, D. L. (1995). Alternative representations of war zone stressors: Relationships to posttraumatic stress disorder in male and female Vietnam veterans. *Journal of Abnormal Psychology, 104,* 184–196.

King, K. B., Reis, H. T., Porter, L. A., & Norsen, L. H. (1993). Social support and long-term recovery from coronary artery surgery: Effects on patients and spouses. *Health Psychology, 12,* 56–63.

Kirby, J. B. (2002). The influence of parental separation on smoking initiation in adolescents. *Journal of Health and Social Behavior, 43,* 56–71.

Kirchheimer, S. (2003). *Racism should be a public health issue. Medscape.* Retrieved January 9, 2003, from: http://www.medscape.com/viewarticle/447757

Kirkley, B. G., & Fisher, E. B., Jr. (1988). Relapse as a model of nonadherence to dietary treatment of diabetes. *Health Psychology, 7,* 221–230.

Kirkley, B. G., Agras, W. S., & Weiss, J. J. (1985). Nutritional inadequacy in the diets of treated bulimics. *Behavior Therapy, 16,* 287–291.

Kirkley, B. G., Schneider, J. A., Agras, W. J., & Bachman, J. A. (1985). Comparison of two group treatments for bulimia. *Journal of Consulting and Clinical Psychology, 53,* 43–48.

Kirmayer, L. J., & Young, A. (1998). Culture and somatization: Clinical, epidemiological, and ethnographic perspectives. *Psychosomatic Medicine, 60,* 420–430.

Kirschbaum, C., Klauer, T., Filipp, S., & Hellhammer, D. H. (1995). Sex-specific effects of social support on cortisol and subjective responses to acute psychological stress. *Psychosomatic Medicine, 57,* 23–31.

Kirschenbaum, D. S., Sherman, J., & Penrod, J. D. (1987). Promoting self-directed hemodialysis: Measurement and cognitive-behavioral intervention. *Health Psychology, 6,* 373–385.

Kirscht, J. P. (1983). Preventive health behavior: A review of research and issues. *Health Psychology, 2,* 277–301.

Kirscht, J. P., & Rosenstock, I. M. (1979). Patients' problems in following recommendations of health experts. In G. C. Stone, F. Cohen, & N. E. Adler (Eds.), *Health psychology—A handbook* (pp. 189–216). San Francisco: Jossey-Bass.

Kivimaki, M., Vahtera, J., Elovainio, M., Lillrank, B., & Kevin, M. V. (2002). Death or illness of a family member, violence, interpersonal conflict, and financial difficulties as predictors of sickness absence: Longitudinal cohort study on psychological and behavioral links. *Psychosomatic Medicine, 64,* 817–825.

Kivlahan, D. R., Marlatt, G. A., Fromme, K., Coppel, D. B., & Williams, E. (1990). Secondary prevention with college drinkers: Evaluation of an alcohol skills training program. *Journal of Consulting and Clinical Psychology, 58,* 805–810.

Klebanov, P. K., & Jemmott, J. J., III. (1992). Effects of expectations and bodily sensations on self-reports of premenstrual symptoms. *Psychology of Women Quarterly, 16,* 210–289.

Klem, M., Wing, R R., McGuire, M. T., Seagle, H. M., & Hill, J. O. (1998). Psychological symptoms in individuals successful at long-term maintenance of weight loss. *Health Psychology, 17,* 336–345.

Klepp, K. I., Kelder, S. H., & Perry, C. L. (1995). Alcohol and marijuana use among adolescents: Long-term outcomes of the class of 1989 study. *Annals of Behavioral Medicine, 17,* 19–24.

Klesges, R. C., Eck, L. H., Hanson, C. L., Haddock, C. K., & Klesges, L. M. (1990). Effects of obesity, social interactions, and physical environment on physical activity in preschoolers. *Health Psychology, 9,* 435–449.

Klesges, R. C., Meyers, A. W., Klesges, L. M., & LaVasque, M. E. (1989). Smoking, body weight, and their effects on smoking behavior: A comprehensive review of the literature. *Psychological Bulletin, 106,* 204–230.

Klohn, L. S., & Rogers, R. W. (1991). Dimensions of the severity of a health threat: The persuasive effects of visibility, time of onset, and rate of onset on young women's intentions to prevent osteoporosis. *Health Psychology, 10,* 323–329.

Klonoff, E. A., & Landrine, H. (1992). Sex roles, occupational roles, and symptom-reporting: A test of competing hypotheses on sex differences. *Journal of Behavioral Medicine, 15,* 355–364.

Klonoff, E. A., & Landrine, H. (1999). Acculturation and cigarette smoking among African Americans: Replication and implications for prevention and cessation programs. *Journal of Behavioral Medicine, 22,* 195–204.

Klonoff, E. A., & Landrine, H. (2000). Is skin color a marker for racial discrimination? Explaining the skin color–hypertension relationship. *Journal of Behavioral Medicine, 23,* 329–338.

Klopfer, B. (1959). Psychological variables in human cancer. *Journal of Projective Techniques, 21,* 331–340.

Koenig, H. G., George, L. K., & Siegler, I. C. (1988). The use of religion and other emotion-regulating coping strategies among older adults. *The Gerontologist, 28,* 303–323.

Koetting O'Byrne, K., Peterson, L., & Saldana, L. (1997). Survey of pediatric hospitals' preparation programs: Evidence of the impact of health psychology research. *Health Psychology, 16,* 147–154.

Kogan, M. M., et al. (1997). Effect of medical and psychotherapeutic treatment on the survival of women with metastatic breast carcinoma. *Cancer, 80,* 225–230.

Kohler, C. L., Fish, L., & Greene, P. G. (2002). The relationship of perceived self-efficacy to quality of life in chronic obstructive pulmonary disease. *Health Psychology, 21,* 610–614.

Kohn, P. M., Lafreniere, K., & Gurevich, M. (1990). The inventory of college students' recent life experiences: A decontaminated hassles scale for a special population. *Journal of Behavioral Medicine, 13,* 619–630.

Kohn, P. M., Lafreniere, K., & Gurevich, M. (1991). Hassles, health, and personality. *Journal of Personality and Social Psychology, 61,* 478–482.

Kolata, G. (1994, January 6). Fetal ovary transplant is envisioned. *The New York Times,* p. 8.

Koltun, A., & Stone, G. A. (1986). Past and current trends in patient noncompliance research: Focus on diseases, regimens-programs, and provider-disciplines. *Journal of Compliance in Health Care, 1,* 21–32.

Koo-Loeb, J. H., Costello, N., Light, K., & Girdler, S. S. (2000). Women with eating disorder tendencies display altered cardiovascular, neuroendocrine, and psychosocial profiles. *Psychosomatic Medicine, 62,* 539–548.

Koop, C. E. (1996, Fall). Manage with care. *Time,* p. 69.

Kop, W. J., Appels, A. P. W. M., Mendes de Leon, C. F., de Swart, H. B., & Bar, F. W. (1994). Vital exhaustion predicts new cardiac events after successful coronary angioplasty. *Psychosomatic Medicine, 56,* 281–287.

Kopelman, P. G. (2000, April 6). Obesity as a medical problem. *Nature, 404,* 635–643.

Koretz, G. (2000, August 7). A health-cost time bomb? Aging boomers will test the system. *BusinessWeek,* 26.

Koretz, G. (2001, January 15). Extra pounds, slimmer wages. *BusinessWeek,* 28.

Koretz, G. (2003a, May 19). Stub out that cigarette, lady: Smoking narrows the mortality gap. BusinessWeek, 25.

Koretz, G. (2003b, November 10). Those heavy Americans. BusinessWeek, 34.

Kouyanou, K., Pither, C., & Wessely, S. (1997). Iatrogenic factors and chronic pain. *Psychosomatic Medicine, 59,* 597–604.

Krantz, D. S. (1980). Cognitive processes and recovery from heart attack: A review and theoretical analysis. *Journal of Human Stress, 6,* 27–38.

Krantz, D. S., & Deckel, A. W. (1983). Coping with coronary heart disease and stroke. In T. G. Burish & L. A. Bradley (Eds.), *Coping with chronic disease: Research and applications.* New York: Academic Press, pp. 85–112.

Krantz, D. S., & McCeney, M. K. (2002). Effects of psychological and social factors on organic disease: A critical assessment of research on coronary heart disease. *Annual Review Psychology, 53,* 341–369.

Krause, N., Ingersoll-Dayton, B., Liang, L., & Sugisawa (1999). Religion, social support, and health among the Japanese elderly. *Journal of Health and Social Behavior, 40,* 405–421.

Krause, N., & Markides, K. S. (1985). Employment and psychological well-being in Mexican American women. *Journal of Health and Social Behavior, 26,* 15–26.

Krause, Ingersoll-Dayton, Liang & Sugisawa (1999). Religion, social support, and health among Japanese elderly. *Journal of Health and Social Behavior, 40,* 405–421.

Kreuter, M. W., & Strecher, V. J. (1995). Changing inaccurate perceptions of health risk: Results from a randomized trial. *Health Psychology, 14,* 56–63.

Kreuter, M. W., Bull, F. C., Clark, E. M., & Oswald, D. L. (1999). Understanding how people process health information: A comparison of tailored and nontailored weight-loss materials. *Health Psychology, 18,* 487–494.

Kristal-Boneh, E., Melamed, S., Bernheim, J., Peled, I., & Green, M. S. (1995). Reduced ambulatory heart rate response to physical work and complaints of fatigue among hypertensive males treated with beta-blockers. *Journal of Behavioral Medicine, 18,* 113–126.

Kristof, K. M. (2002, April 3). Weight-loss programs tax-deductible. *Los Angeles Times,* pp. C1, C11.

Krittayaphong, R., Cascio, W. E., Light, K. C., Sheffield, D., Golden, R. N., Finkel, J. B., et al. (1997). Heart rate variability in patients with coronary artery disease: Differences in patients with higher and lower depression scores. *Psychosomatic Medicine, 59,* 231–235.

Kroeber, A. L. (1948). *Anthropology.* New York: Harcourt.

Kroner-Herwig, B., Jakle, C., Frettloh, J., Peters, K., Seemann, H., Franz, C., et al. (1996). Predicting subjective disability in chronic pain patients. *International Journal of Behavioral Medicine, 3,* 30–41.

Kübler-Ross, E. (1969). *On death and dying.* New York: Macmillan.

Kübler-Ross, E. (1975). *Death: The final stage of growth.* Englewood Cliffs, NJ: Prentice-Hall.

Kubzansky, L. D., Berkman, L. F., Glass, T. A., & Seeman, T. E. (1998). Is educational attainment associated with shared determinants of health in the elderly? Findings from the MacArthur studies of successful aging. *Psychosomatic Medicine, 60,* 578–585.

Kubzansky, L. D., Sparrow, D., Vokonas, P., & Kawachi, I. (2001). Is the glass half empty or half full? A prospective study of optimism and coronary heart disease in the normative aging study. *Psychosomatic Medicine, 63,* 910–916.

Kubzansky, L. D., Wright, R. J., Cohen, S., Weiss, S., Rosner, B., & Sparrow, D. (2002). Breathing easy: A prospective study of optimism and pulmonary function in the normative aging study. *Annals of Behavioral Medicine, 24,* 345–353.

Kugler, J., Dimsdale, J. E., Hartley, L. H., & Sherwood, J. (1990). Hospital supervised versus home exercise in cardiac rehabilitation: Effects on aerobic fitness, anxiety, and depression. *Archives of Physical Medicine and Rehabilitation, 71,* 322–325.

Kulik, J. A., & Carlino, P. (1987). The effect of verbal communication and treatment choice on medication compliance in a pediatric setting. *Journal of Behavioral Medicine, 10,* 367–376.

Kulik, J. A., & Mahler, H. I. M. (1987). Effects of preoperative roommate assignment on preoperative anxiety and recovery from coronary-bypass surgery. *Health Psychology, 6,* 525–543.

Kulik, J. A., & Mahler, H. I. M. (1989). Social support and recovery from surgery. *Health Psychology, 8,* 221–238.

Kulik, J. A., & Mahler, H. I. M. (1993). Emotional support as a moderator of adjustment and compliance after coronary artery bypass surgery: A longitudinal study. *Journal of Behavioral Medicine, 16,* 45–64.

Kulik, J. A., Moore, P. J., & Mahler, H. I. M. (1993). Stress and affiliation: Hospital roommate effects on preoperative anxiety and social interaction. *Health Psychology, 12,* 118–124.

Kumanyika, S. K., Van Horn, L., Bowen, D., Perri, M. G., Rolls, B. J., Czajkowski, S. M., et al. (2000). Maintenance of dietary behavior change. *Health Psychology, 19,* 42–56.

Kunkel, L. E., & Temple, L. L. (1992). Attitudes towards AIDS and homosexuals: Gender, marital status, and religion. *Journal of Applied Social Psychology, 22,* 1030–1040.

Kunz, J. R. M. (Ed.). (1982). *The American Medical Association family medical guide.* New York: Random House.

Kutner, N. G. (1987). Issues in the application of high cost medical technology: The case of organ transplantation. *Journal of Health and Social Behavior, 28,* 23–36.

Lacroix, J. M., Martin, B., Avendano, M., & Goldstein, R. (1991). Symptom schemata in chronic respiratory patients. *Health Psychology, 10,* 268–273.

Laforge, R. G., Greene, G. W., & Prochaska, J. O. (1994). Psychosocial factors influencing low fruit and vegetable consumption. *Journal of Behavioral Medicine, 17,* 361–374.

Lai, H., Lai, S., Krongrad, A., Trapido, E., Page, J. B., & McCoy, C. B. (1999). The effect of marital status on survival in late-stage cancer patients: An analysis based on surveillance, epidemiology, and end results (SEER) data, in the United States. *International Journal of Behavioral Medicine, 6,* 150–176.

Lam, T. H., Stewart, M., & Ho, L. M. (2001). Smoking and high-risk sexual behavior among young adults in Hong Kong. *Journal of Behavioral Medicine, 24,* 503–518.

LaManca, J. J., Peckerman, A., Sisto, S., DeLuca, J., Cook, S., & Natelson, B. H. (2001). Cardiovascular responses of women with chronic fatigue syndrome to stressful cognitive testing before and after strenuous exercise. *Psychosomatic Medicine, 63,* 756–764.

Lamb, R., & Joshi, M.S. (1996). The stage model and processes of change in dietary fat reduction. *Journal of Human Nutrition and Dietetics, 9,* 43–53.

Lamprecht, F., & Sack, M. (2002). Posttraumatic stress disorder revisited. *Psychosomatic Medicine, 64,* 222–237.

Landsbergis, P. A., Schnall, P. L., Deitz, D., Friedman, R., & Pickering, T. (1992). The patterning of psychological attributes and distress by "job strain" and social support in a sample of working men. *Journal of Behavioral Medicine, 15,* 379–414.

Lang, A. R., & Marlatt, G. A. (1982). Problem drinking: A social learning perspective. In R. J. Gatchel, A. Baum, & J. E. Singer (Eds.), *Handbook of psychology and health: Vol. 1. Clinical psychology and behavioral medicine: Overlapping disciplines* (pp. 121–169). Hillsdale, NJ: Erlbaum.

Lange, T., Perras, B., Fehm, H. L., & Born, J. (2003). Sleep enhances the human antibody response to Hepatitis A vaccination. *Psychosomatic Medicine, 65,* 831–835.

Langewitz, W., Eich, P., Kiss, A., & Wossmer, B. (1998). Improving communication skills—A randomized controlled behaviorally oriented intervention study for residents in internal medicine. *Psychosomatic Medicine, 60,* 268–276.

Langner, T., & Michael, S. (1960). *Life stress and mental health.* New York: Free Press.

Langston, C. A. (1994). Capitalizing on and coping with daily-life events: Expressive responses to positive events. *Journal of Personality and Social Psychology, 67,* 1112–1125.

Lankford, T. R. (1979). Integrated science for health students (2nd ed.). Reston, VA: Reston.

Lantz, P. M., Weigers, M. E., & House, J. S. (1997). Education and income differentials in breast and cervical cancer screening: Policy implications for rural women. *Medical Care, 35,* 219–236.

Larkin, K. T., & Zayfert, C. (1996). Anger management training with mild essential hypertensive patients. *Journal of Behavioral Medicine, 19,* 415–434.

Larsen, D. (1990, March 18). Future of fear. *Los Angeles Times,* pp. E1, E8.

Latkin, C. A., Sherman, S., & Knowlton, A. (2003). HIV prevention among drug users: Outcome of network-oriented peer outreach intervention. *Health Psychology, 22,* 332–339.

Lau, R. R., Kane, R., Berry, S., Ware, J. E., Jr., & Roy, D. (1980). Channeling health: A review of televised health campaigns. *Health Education Quarterly, 7,* 56–89.

Lau, R. R., Quadrel, M. J., & Hartman, K. A. (1990). Development and change of young adults' preventive health beliefs and behavior: Influence from parents and peers. *Journal of Health and Social Behavior, 31,* 240–259.

Laubmeier, K. K., Zakowski, S. G., & Bair, J. P. (2004). The role of spirituality in the psychological adjustment to cancer: A test of the transactional model of stress and coping. *International Journal of Behavioral Medicine, 11,* 48–55.

Lautenbacher, S., Spernal, J., Schreiber, W., & Krieg, J. (1999). Relationship between clinical pain complaints and pain sensitivity in patients with depression and panic disorder. *Psychosomatic Medicine, 61,* 822–827.

Lauver, D. R., Henriques, J. B., Settersten, L., & Bumann, M. C. (2003). Psychosocial variables, external barriers, and stage of mammography adoption. *Health Psychology, 22,* 649–653.

Laveist, T. A., & Nuru-Jeter, A. (2002). Is doctor-patient race concordance associated with greater satisfaction with care? *Journal of Health and Social Behavior, 43,* 296–306.

Lavigne, J. V., Gidding, S., Stevens, V. J., Ewart, C., Brown, K. M., Evans, M., et al. (1999). A cholesterol-lowering diet does not produce adverse psychological effects in children: Three-year results from the dietary intervention study in children. *Health Psychology, 18,* 604–613.

Lavin, B., Haug, M., Belgrave, L. L., & Breslau, N. (1987). Change in student physicians' views on authority relationships with patients. *Journal of Health and Social Behavior, 28,* 258– 272.

Lazarus, A. A. (1971). *Behavior therapy and beyond.* New York: McGraw-Hill.

Lazarus, R. S. (1968). Emotions and adaptation: Conceptual and empirical relations. In W. Arnold (Ed.), *Nebraska symposium on motivation* (pp. 175–266). Lincoln: University of Nebraska Press.

Lazarus, R. S. (1983). The costs and benefits of denial. In S. Bresnitz (Ed.), *Denial of stress* (pp. 1–30). New York: International Universities Press.

Lazarus, R. S., & Folkman, S. (1984a). Coping and adaptation. In W. D. Gentry (Ed.), *The handbook of behavioral medicine* (pp. 282–325). New York: Guilford Press.

Lazarus, R. S., & Folkman, S. (1984b). *Stress, appraisal, and coping*. New York: Springer.

Lazarus, R. S., & Launier, R. (1978). Stress-related transactions between person and environment. In L. A. Pervin & M. Lewis (Eds.), *Internal and external determinants of behavior* (pp. 287–327). New York: Plenum Press.

Lazarus, R. S., DeLongis, A., Folkman, S., & Gruen, R. (1985). Stress and adaptational outcomes: The problem of confounded measures. *American Psychologist, 40,* 770–779.

Leary, M. R., & Jones, J. L. (1993). The social psychology of tanning and sunscreen use: Self-presentational motives as a predictor of health risk. *Journal of Applied Social Psychology, 23,* 1390–1406.

LeBlanc, A. J. (1993). Examining HIV-related knowledge about adults in the U.S. *Journal of Health and Social Behavior, 34,* 23–26.

Lecci, L., & Cohen, D. J. (2002). Perceptual consequences of an illness-concern induction and its relation to hypochondriacal tendencies. *Health Psychology, 21,* 147–156.

Leclere, F. B., Rogers, R. G., & Peters, K. (1998). Neighborhood social context and racial differences in women's heart disease mortality. *Journal of Health and Social Behavior, 39,* 91–107.

Lee, C. (1993). Factors related to the adoption of exercise among older women. *Journal of Behavioral Medicine, 16,* 323–334.

Lee, J. (2000, November). Easing the pain. *Money,* 179–180.

Lee, R. E., & King, A. C. (2003). Discretionary time among older adults: How do physical activity promotion interventions affect sedentary and active behaviors? *Annals of Behavioral Medicine, 25,* 112–119.

Lee, S. S., & Ruvkun, G. (2002, July 18). Don't hold your breath. *Nature, 418,* 287–288.

Leffall, L. D., Jr., White, J. E., & Ewing, J. (1963). Cancer of the breast in Negroes. *Surgery, Gynecology, Obstetrics, 117,* 97–104.

Leger, D., Scheuermaier, K., Phillip, P., Paillard, M., & Guilleminault, C. (2001). SF-36: Evaluation of quality of life in severe and mild insomniacs compared with good sleepers. *Psychosomatic Medicine, 63,* 49–55.

Lehman, C. D., Rodin, J., McEwen, B., & Brinton, R. (1991). Impact of environmental stress on the expression of insulin-dependent diabetes mellitus. *Behavioral Neuroscience, 105,* 241–245.

Lehrer, P., Feldman, J., Giardino, N., Song, H. S., & Schmaling, K. (2002). Psychological aspects of asthma. *Journal of Consulting and Clinical Psychology, 70,* 691–711.

Leigh, H., & Reiser, M. F. (1986). Comparison of theoretically oriented and patient-oriented behavioral science courses. *Journal of Medical Education, 61,* 169–174.

Lekander, M., Furst, C., Rotstein, S., Blomgren, H., & Fredrikson, M. (1995). Anticipatory immune changes in women treated with chemotherapy for ovarian cancer. *International Journal of Behavioral Medicine, 2,* 1–12.

Lemonick, M. D. (2004, April 19). The other lung disease. *Time,* 62–63.

Lenert, L., & Skoczen, S. (2002). The Internet as a research tool: Worth the price of admission? *Annals of Behavioral Medicine, 24,* 251–256.

Lennon, M. C., & Rosenfield, S. (1992). Women and mental health: The interaction of job and family conditions. *Journal of Health and Social Behavior, 33,* 316–327.

Lepore, S. J. (1995). Cynicism, social support, and cardiovascular reactivity. *Health Psychology, 14,* 210–216.

Lepore, S. J., Evans, G. W., & Palsane, M. N. (1991). Social hassles and psychological health in the context of chronic crowding. *Journal of Health and Social Behavior, 32,* 357–367.

Lepore, S. J., Helgeson, V. S., Eton, D. T., & Schulz, R. (2003). Improving quality of life in men with prostate cancer: A randomized controlled trial of group education interventions. *Health Psychology, 22,* 443–452.

Lepore, S. J., Miles, H. J., & Levy, J. S. (1997). Relation of chronic and episodic stressors to psychological distress, reactivity, and health problems. *International Journal of Behavioral Medicine, 4,* 39–59.

Lepore, S. J., Ragan, J. D., & Jones, S. (2000). Talking facilitates cognitive-emotional processes of adaptation to an acute stressor. *Journal of Personality and Social Psychology, 78,* 499–508.

Lepore, S. J., & Smyth, J. M. (Eds.). (2002). *The writing cure: How expressive writing promotes health and emotional well-being.* (pp. 3–14). Washington, D.C., US: American Psychological Association.

Lerman, C., Caporaso, N. E., Audrain, J., Main, D., Bowman, E. D., Lockshin, B., et al. (1999). Evidence suggesting the role of specific genetic factors in cigarette smoking. *Health Psychology, 18,* 14–20.

Lerman, C., Gold, K., Audrain, J., Lin, T. H., Boyd, N. R., Orleans, C. T., et al. (1997). Incorporating biomarkers of exposure and genetic susceptibility into smoking cessation treatment: Effects on smoking-related cognitions, emotions, and behavior change. *Health Psychology, 16,* 87–99.

Lerman, C., Shields, P. G., Wileyto, E. P., Audrain, J., Hawk, L. H., Jr., Pinto, A., et al. (2003). Effects of dopamine transporter and receptor polymorphisms of smoking cessation in a bupropion clinical trial. *Health Psychology, 22,* 541–548.

Lerman, C., Schwartz, M. D., Miller, S. M., Daly, M., Sands, C., & Rimer, B. K. (1996). A randomized trial of breast cancer risk counseling: Interacting effects of counseling, educational level, and coping style. *Health Psychology, 5,* 75–83.

Lesar, T. S., Briceland, L., & Stein, D. S. (1997). Factors related to errors in medication prescribing. *Journal of the American Medical Association, 277,* 312–317.

Leserman, J., Jackson, E. D., Petitto, J. M., Golden, R. N., Silva, S. G., Perkins, D. O., et al. (1999). Progression to AIDS: The effects of stress, depressive symptoms, and social support. *Psychosomatic Medicine, 61,* 397–406.

Leserman, J., Li, Z., Hu, Y., & Drossman, D. (1998). How multiple types of stressors impact on health. *Psychosomatic Medicine, 60,* 175–181.

LeShan, L. L., & Worthington, R. E. (1956). Personality as a factor in the pathogenesis of cancer: Review of literature. *British Journal of Medical Psychology, 29,* 49.

Lett, H. S., Blumenthal, J. A., Babyak, M. A., Sherwood, A., Strauman, T., Robins, C., et al. (2004). Depression as a risk factor for coronary artery disease: Evidence, mechanisms, and treatment. *Psychosomatic Medicine, 66,* 305–315.

Leveille, S. G., et al. (1998). Preventing disability and managing chronic illness in frail older adults: A randomized trial of community-based partnership with primary care. *Journal of the American Geriatrics Society, 46,* 191–198.

Levenkron, J. C., Greenland, P., & Bowlby, N. (1987). Using patient instructors to teach behavioral counseling skills. *Journal of Medical Education, 62,* 665–672.

Leventhal, E. A., Easterling, D., Leventhal, H., & Cameron, L. (1995). Conservation of energy, uncertainty reduction, and swift utilization of medical care among the elderly: Study II. *Medical Care, 33,* 988–1000.

Leventhal, E. A., Hansell, S., Diefenbach, M., Leventhal, H., & Glass, D. C. (1996). Negative affect and self-report of physical symptoms: Two longitudinal studies of older adults. *Health Psychology, 15,* 193–199.

Leventhal, E. A., Leventhal, H., Schacham, S., & Easterling, D. V. (1989). Active coping reduces reports of pain from childbirth. *Journal of Consulting and Clinical Psychology, 57,* 365–371.

Leventhal, H. (1970). Findings and theory in the study of fear communications. In L. Berkowitz (Ed.), *Advances in experimental social psychology* (Vol. 5, pp. 120–186). New York: Academic Press.

Leventhal, H., & Baker, T. B. (1986). Strategies for smoking withdrawal. *Wisconsin Medical Journal, 85,* 11–13.

Leventhal, H., & Benyamini, Y. (1997). Lay beliefs about health and illness. In A. Baum, C. McManus, S. Newman, J. Weinman, & R. West (Eds.), *Cambridge handbook of psychology, health, and medicine.* Cambridge, England: Cambridge University Press.

Leventhal, H., & Cleary, P. D. (1980). The smoking problem: A review of the research and theory in behavioral risk modification. *Psychological Bulletin, 88,* 370–405.

Leventhal, H., & Nerenz, D. R. (1982). A model for stress research and some implications for the control of stress disorders. In D. Meichenbaum & M. Jaremko (Eds.), *Stress prevention and management: A cognitive behavioral approach.* New York: Plenum Press.

Leventhal, H., Diefenbach, M., & Leventhal, E. A. (1992). Illness cognition: Using common sense to understand treatment adherence and affect cognition interactions. *Cognitive Therapy and Research, 16,* 143–163.

Leventhal, H., Glynn, K., & Fleming, R. (1987). Is the smoking decision an "informed choice"? Effect of smoking risk factors on smoking beliefs. *Journal of the American Medical Association, 257,* 3373–3376.

Leventhal, H., Nerenz, D. R., & Steele, D. J. (1984). Illness representations and coping with health threats. In A. Baum & J. Singer (Eds.), *A handbook of psychology and health* (Vol. 4, pp. 219–252). Hillsdale, NJ: Erlbaum.

Leventhal, H., Nerenz, D., & Strauss, A. (1982). Self-regulation and the mechanisms for symptom appraisal. In D. Mechanic (Ed.), *Monograph series in psychosocial epidemiology, 3: Symptoms, illness behavior, and help-seeking* (pp. 55–86). New York: Neale Watson.

Leventhal, H., Prohaska, T. R., & Hirschman, R. S. (1985). Preventive health behavior across the life span. In J. C. Rosen & L. J. Solomon (Eds.), *Prevention in health psychology* (Vol. 8, pp. 190–235). Hanover, NH: University Press of New England.

Leventhal, H., Safer, M. A., Cleary, P. D., & Gutmann, M. (1980). Cardiovascular risk modification by community-based programs for lifestyle change: Comments on the Stanford study. *Journal of Consulting and Clinical Psychology, 48,* 150–158.

Levin, M. (2003, November 9). States' tobacco settlement has failed to clear the air. *Los Angeles Times,* pp. C1, C4.

Levine, J. D., Gordon, N. C., & Fields, H. L. (1978). The mechanism of placebo analgesia. *Lancet, 2,* 654–657.

Levine, M. N., Guyatt, G. H., Gent, M., De Pauw, S., Goodyear, M. D., Hryniuk, W. M., et al. (1988). Quality of life in stage II breast cancer: An instrument for clinical trials. *Journal of Clinical Oncology, 6,* 1798–1810.

Levinson, R. M., McCollum, K. T., & Kutner, N. G. (1984). Gender homophily in preferences for physicians. *Sex Roles, 10,* 315–325.

Levitsky, L. L., (2004). Childhood immunizations and chronic illness. *New England Journal of Medicine, 350,* 1380–1382, http://www.nejm.org

Levy, R., Cain, K., Jarrett, M., & Heikemper, M. (1997). The relationship between daily life stress and gastrointestinal symptoms in women with irritable bowel syndrome. *Journal of Behavioral Medicine, 20,* 177–193.

Levy, S. M. (1983). Host differences in neoplastic risk: Behavioral and social contributors to disease. *Health Psychology, 2,* 21–44.

Levy, S. M., Fernstrom, J., Herberman, R. B., Whiteside, T., Lee, J., Ward, M., et al. (1991). Persistently low natural killer cell activity and circulating levels of plasma beta endorphin: Risk factors for infectious disease. *Life Sciences, 48,* 107–116.

Levy, S. M., Herberman, R. B., Lee, J. K., Lippman, M. E., & d'Angelo, T. (1989). Breast conservation versus mastectomy: distress sequelae as a function of choice. *Journal of Clinical Oncology, 7,* 367–375.

Levy, S. M., Herberman, R. B., Lippman, M., & D'Angelo, T. (1989). Breast conservation versus mastectomy: Distress sequelae as a function of choice. *Journal of Clinical Oncology, 7,* 367–375.

Levy, S. M., Herberman, R. B., Lippman, M., D'Angelo, T., & Lee, J. (1991, Summer). Immunological and psychosocial predictors of disease recurrence in patients with early-stage breast cancer. *Behavioral Medicine 17,* 67–75.

Levy, S. M., Herberman, R. B., Simons, A., Whiteside, T., Lee, J., McDonald, R., et al. (1989). Persistently low natural killer cell activity in normal adults: Immunological, hormonal and mood correlates. *Natural Immune Cell Growth Regulation, 8,* 173–186.

Levy, S. M., Herberman, R. B., Whiteside, T., Sanzo, K., Lee, J., & Kirkwood, J. (1990). Perceived social support and tumor estrogen/progesterone receptor status as predictors of natural killer cell activity in breast cancer patients. *Psychosomatic Medicine, 52,* 73–85.

Levy, S. M., Lee, J. K., Bagley, C., & Lippman, M. (1988). Survival hazards analysis in first recurrent breast cancer patients: Seven-year follow-up. *Psychosomatic Medicine, 50,* 520–528.

Lewis, J. A., Manne, S. L., DuHamel, K. N., Vicksburg, S. M. J., Bovbjerg, D. H., Currie, V. et al. (2001). Social support, intrusive thoughts, and quality of life in breast cancer survivors. *Journal of Behavioral Medicine, 24,* 231–245.

Lewis, J. W., Terman, S. W., Shavit, Y., Nelson, L. R., & Liebeskind, J. C. (1984). Neural, neurochemical, and hormonal bases of stress-induced analgesia. In L. Kruger & J. C. Liebeskind (Eds.), *Advances in pain research and therapy* (Vol. 6, pp. 277–288). New York: Raven Press.

Lewis, M. A., & Rook, K. S. (1999). Social control in personal relationships: Impact on health behaviors and psychological distress. *Health Psychology, 18,* 63–71.

Ley, P. (1977). Psychological studies of doctor-patient communication. In S. Richman (Ed.), *Contributions to medical psychology* (Vol. 1). Oxford, England: Pergamon Press.

Li, F., Barrera, M., Jr., Hops, H., & Fisher, K. J. (2002). The longitudinal influence of peers on the development of alcohol use in late adolescence: A growth mixture analysis. *Journal of Behavioral Medicine, 25,* 293–315.

Liberman, A., & Chaiken, S. (1992). Defensive processing of personally relevant health messages. *Personality and Social Psychology Bulletin, 18,* 669–679.

Liberman, R. (1962). An analysis of the placebo phenomenon. *Journal of Chronic Diseases, 15,* 761–783.

Lichtenstein, E. (1982). The smoking problem: A behavioral perspective. *Journal of Consulting and Clinical Psychology, 50,* 804–819.

Lichtenstein, E., & Cohen, S. (1990). Prospective analysis of two modes of unaided smoking cessation. *Health Education Research, 5,* 63–72.

Lichtenstein, E., & Glasgow, R. E. (1992). Smoking cessation: What have we learned over the past decade? *Journal of Consulting and Clinical Psychology, 4,* 518–527.

Lichtenstein, E., Glasgow, R. E., Lando, H. A., Ossip-Klein, D. J., & Boles, S. M. (1996). Telephone counseling for smoking cessation: Rationales and meta-analytic review of evidence. *Health Education Research: Theory and Practice, 11,* 243–257.

Lichtenstein, P., Holm, N. V., Verkasalo, P. K., Iliadou, A., Kaprio, J., Koskenvuo, M., et al. (2000). Environmental and heritable factors in the causation of cancer: Analyses of cohorts of twins from Sweden, Denmark, and Finland. *New England Journal of Medicine, 343,* 78–85.

Lichtman, R. R., Taylor, S. E., Wood, J. V., Bluming, A. Z., Dosik, G. M., & Leibowitz, R. L. (1984). Relations with children after breast cancer: The mother-daughter relationship at risk. *Journal of Psychosocial Oncology, 2,* 1–19.

Lieberman, M. D., Jarcho, J. M., Berman, S., Naliboff, B. D., Suyenobu, B. Y., Mandelkern, M., et al. (2004). The neural correlates of placebo effects: A disruption account. *NeuroImage, May,* 447–495.

Liegner, L. M. (1986–1987). Suffering. *Loss, Grief and Care, 1,* 93–96.

Lifton, R. J. (1977). The sense of immortality: On death and the continuity of life. In H. Feifel (Ed.), *New meanings of death.* New York: McGraw-Hill.

Lin, N., Ye, X., & Ensel, W. (1999). Social support and depressed mood: A structural analysis. *Journal of Health and Social Behavior, 40,* 344–359.

Linden, W. (1994). Autogenic training: A narrative and quantitative review of clinical outcome. *Biofeedback and Self-regulation, 19,* 227–264.

Linden, W., & Chambers, L. (1994). Clinical effectiveness of non-drug treatment for hypertension: A meta-analysis. *Annals of Behavioral Medicine, 16,* 35–45.

Linden, W., Chambers, L., Maurice, J., & Lenz, J. W. (1993). Sex differences in social support, self-deception, hostility, and ambulatory cardiovascular activity. *Health Psychology, 12,* 376–380.

Linden, W., Stossel, C., & Maurice, J. (1996). Psychosocial interventions for patients with coronary artery disease. *Archives of Internal Medicine, 156,* 745–752.

Lindsay, M., & McCarthy, D. (1974). Caring for the brothers and sisters of a dying child. In T. Burton (Ed.), *Care of the child, facing death* (pp. 189–206). Boston: Routledge & Kegan Paul.

Lingsweiler, V. M., Crowther, J. H., & Stephens, M. A. P. (1987). Emotional reactivity and eating in binge eating and obesity. *Journal of Behavioral Medicine, 10,* 287–300.

Linkins, R. W. & Comstock, G. W. (1990). Depressed mood and development of cancer. *American Journal of Epidemiology, 132,* 962–972.

Linkins, R. W., & Comstock, G. W. (1988). Depressed mood and development of cancer. *American Journal of Epidemiology, 128* (Abstract), 894.

Linnan, L. A., Emmons, K. M., Klar, N., Fava, J. L., LaForge, R. G., & Abrams, D. B. (2002). Challenges to improving the impact of worksite cancer prevention programs: Comparing reach, enrollment, and attrition using active versus passive recruitment strategies. *Annals of Behavioral Medicine, 24,* 157–166.

Linton, S. J., & Buer, N. (1995). Working despite pain: Factors associated with work attendance versus dysfunction. *International Journal of Behavioral Medicine, 2,* 252–262.

Lipkus, I. M., Barefoot, J. C., Williams, R. B., & Siegler, I. C. (1994). Personality measures as predictors of smoking initiation and cessation in the UNC Alumni Heart Study. *Health Psychology, 13,* 149–155.

Lipkus, I. M., McBride, C. M., Pollack, K. I., Lyna, P., & Bepler, G. (2004). Interpretation of genetic risk feedback among African American smokers with low socioeconomic status. *Health Psychology, 23,* 178–188.

Lipsitt, L. P. (2003). Crib death: A biobehavioral phenomenon? *Current Directions in Psychological Science, 12,* 164–170.

Liss-Levinson, W. S. (1982). Reality perspectives for psychological services in a hospice program. *American Psychologist, 37,* 1266–1270.

Litt, M. D., Kleppinger, A., & Judge, J. O. (2002). Initiation and maintenance of exercise behavior in older women: Predictors from the social learning model. *Journal of Behavioral Medicine, 25,* 83–97.

Little, S. J., Holte, S., Routy, J., Daar, E. S., Markowitz, M., Collier, A. C., et al. (2002). Antiretroviral-drug resistance among patients recently infected with HIV. *New England Journal of Medicine, 347,* 385–394. http://www. nejm.org

Littlebrant, C. K. (January 12, 1976). Death is a personal matter. *Newsweek.* Originally published under the name of Carol K. Gross.

Littlefield, C. H., Rodin, G. M., Murray, M. A., & Craven, J. L. (1990). Influence of functional impairment and social support on depressive symptoms in persons with diabetes. *Health Psychology, 9,* 737–749.

Liu, Y., Tanaka, H., & The Fukuda Heart Study Group. (2002). Overtime work, insufficient sleep , and risk of non-fatal acute myocardial infarction in Japanese men. *Occupational and Environmental Medicine, 59,* 447–451.

Lobel, M., Dunkel-Schetter, C., & Scrimshaw, S. C. M. (1992). Prenatal maternal stress and prematurity: A prospective study of socioeconomically disadvantaged women. *Health Psychology, 11,* 32–40.

Locke, S. E., Kraus, L., & Leserman, J. (1984). Life change, stress, psychiatric symptoms, and natural killer cell activity. *Psychosomatic Medicine, 46,* 441–453.

Logsdon, R. G., Gibbons, L. E., McCurry, S. M., & Teri, L. (2002). Assessing quality of life in older adults with cognitive impairment. *Psychosomatic Medicine, 64,* 510–519.

Lombard, D. N., Lombard, T. N., & Winett, R. A. (1995). Walking to meet health guidelines: The effect of prompting frequency and prompt structure. *Health Psychology, 14,* 164–170.

Lombardo, T., & Carreno, L. (1987). Relationship of Type A behavior pattern in smokers to carbon monoxide exposure and smoking topography. *Health Psychology, 6,* 445–452.

Longmore, M. A., Manning, W. D., Giordano, P. C., & Rudolph, J. L. (2003). Contraceptive self-efficacy: Does it influence adolescents' contraceptive use? *Journal of Health & Social Behavior, 44,* 45–60.

Lorig, K. R., & Holman, H. R. (2003). Self-management education: History, definition, outcomes, and mechanisms. *Annals of Behavioral Medicine, 26,* 1–7.

Lorig, K., Chastain, R. L., Ung, E., Shoor, S., & Holman, H. (1989). Development and evaluation of a scale to measure perceived self-efficacy in people with arthritis. *Arthritis and Rheumatism, 32,* 37–44.

Los Angeles Times. (1993, March 30). Three-hundred-sixty days in row not overwork.

Los Angeles Times. (1993a, June 28). Health reform may expand nurses' role.

Los Angeles Times. (1997, May 30). Jenny Craig agrees to settle ad complaint, pp. D1, D5.

Loscocco, K. A., & Spitze, G. (1990). Working conditions, social support, and the well-being of female and male factory workers. *Journal of Health and Social Behavior, 31,* 313–327.

Lovallo, W. R., & Gerin, W. (2003). Psychophysical reactivity: Mechanisms and pathways to cardiovascular disease. *Psychosomatic Medicine, 65,* 36–45.

Lovallo, W. R., al'Absi, M., Pincomb, G. A., Passey, R. B., Sung, B., & Wilson, M. F. (2000). Caffeine, extended stress, and blood pressure in borderline hypertensive men. *International Journal of Behavioral Medicine, 7,* 183–188.

Love, R. R., Cameron, L., Connell, B. L., & Leventhal, H. (1991). Symptoms associated with tamoxifen treatment in postmenopausal women. *Archives of Internal Medicine, 151,* 1842–1847.

Love, R. R., Leventhal, H., Easterling, D. V., & Nerenz, D. R. (1989). Side effects and emotional distress during cancer chemotherapy. *Cancer, 63,* 604–612.

Löwe, B., Grafe, K., Kroenke, K., Zipfel, S., Quentier, A., Wild, B., et al. (2003). Predictors of psychiatric comorbidity in medical outpatients. *Psychosomatic Medicine, 65,* 764–770.

Lowery, D., Fillingim, R. B., & Wright, R. A. (2003). Sex differences and incentive effects on perceptual and cardiovascular responses to cold pressor pain. *Psychosomatic Medicine, 65,* 284–291.

Lubeck, D. P., & Yelin, E. H. (1988). A question of value: Measuring the impact of chronic disease. *The Millbank Quarterly, 66,* 444–464.

Lucini, D., Covacci, G., Milani, R., Mela, G. S., Malliani, A., & Pagani, M. (1997). A controlled study of the effects of mental relaxation on autonomic excitatory responses in healthy subjects. *Psychosomatic Medicine, 59,* 541–552.

Luckow, A., Reifman, A., & McIntosh, D. N. (1998, August). *Gender differences in coping: A meta-analysis.* Poster session presented at the 106th annual convention of the American Psychological Association, San Francisco, CA.

Ludwick-Rosenthal, R., & Neufeld, R. W. J. (1988). Stress management during noxious medical procedures: An evaluative review of outcome studies. *Psychological Bulletin, 104,* 326–342.

Ludwig, D. S., Pereira, M. A., Kroenke, C. H., Hilner, J. E., Van Horn, L., Slattery, M., & Jacobs, D.R., Jr. (1999). Dietary fiber, weight gain, and cardiovascular disease risk factors in young adults. *Journal of the American Medical Association, 282,* 1539–1546.

Luecken, L. J., & Compas, B. E. (2002). Stress, coping, and immune function in breast cancer. *Annals of Behavioral Medicine, 24,* 336–344.

Lumley, M. A., Abeles, L. A., Melamed, B. G., Pistone, L. M., & Johnson, J. H. (1990). Coping outcomes in children undergoing stressful medical procedures: The role of child-environment variables. *Behavioral Assessment, 12,* 223–238.

Lundberg, U., & Frankenhaeuser, M. (1976). *Adjustment to noise stress.* Stockholm, Sweden: Department of Psychology, University of Stockholm.

Lustman, P. J. (1988). Anxiety disorders in adults with diabetes mellitus. *Psychiatric Clinics of North America, 11,* 419–432.

Lustman, P. J., & Harper, G. W. (1987). Nonpsychiatric physicians' identification and treatment of depression in patients with diabetes. *Comprehensive Psychiatry, 28,* 22–27.

Lustman, P. J., Griffith, L. S., & Clouse, R. E. (1988). Depression in adults with diabetes: Results of a 5-year follow-up study. *Diabetes Care, 11,* 605–612.

Lustman, P. J., Griffith, L. S., Clouse, R. E., Freedland, K. E., Eisen, S. A., Rubin, E. H., et al. (1997). Effects of nortriptyline on depression and glycemic control in diabetes: Results of a double-blind, placebo-controlled trial. *Psychosomatic Medicine, 59,* 241–250.

Lutgendorf, S. K., Anderson, B., Sorosky, J. I., Buller, R. E., & Lubaroff, D. M. (2000). Interleukin-6 and use of social support in gynecologic cancer patients. *International Journal of Behavioral Medicine, 7,* 127–142.

Lutgendorf, S. K., Antoni, M. H., Ironson, G., Starr, K., Costello, N., Zuckerman, M., et al. (1998). Changes in cognitive coping skills and social support during cognitive behavioral stress management intervention and distress outcomes in symptomatic human immunodeficiency virus (HIV)–seropositive gay men. *Psychosomatic Medicine, 60,* 204–214.

Lynch, D. J., Birk, T. J., Weaver, M. T., Gohara, A. F., Leighton, R. F., Repka, F. J., et al. (1992). Adherence to exercise interventions in the treatment of hypercholesterolemia. *Journal of Behavioral Medicine, 15,* 365–378.

Macrodimitris, S. D., & Endler, N. S. (2001). Coping, control and adjustment in type 2 diabetes. *Health Psychology, 20,* 208–216.

Madden, T. J., Ellen, P. S., & Ajzen, I. (1992). A comparison of the theory of planned behavior and the theory of reasoned action. *Personality and Social Psychology Bulletin, 18,* 3–9.

Maddox, G. L., & Clark, D. O. (1992). Trajectories of functional impairment in later life. *Journal of Health and Social Behavior, 33,* 114–125.

Maddux, J. E., Roberts, M. C., Sledden, E. A., & Wright, L. (1986). Developmental issues in child health psychology. *American Psychologist, 41,* 25–34.

Maeland, J. G., & Havik, O. E. (1987). Psychological predictors for return to work after a myocardial infarction. *Journal of Psychosomatic Research, 31,* 471–481.

Maes, S., Leventhal, H., & DeRidder, D. T. D. (1996). Coping with chronic diseases. In M. Zeidner & N. S. Endler (Eds.), *Handbook of coping: Theory, research, and applications* (pp. 221–251). New York: Wiley.

Magni, G., Silvestro, A., Tamiello, M., Zanesco, L., & Carl, M. (1988). An integrated approach to the assessment of family adjustment to acute lymphocytic leukemia in children. *Acta Psychiatrica Scandinavia, 78,* 639–642.

Magnus, K., Diener, E., Fujita, F., & Pavot, W. (1993). Extraversion and neuroticism as predictors of objective life events: A longitudinal analysis. *Journal of Personality and Social Psychology, 65,* 1046–1053.

Maguire, P. (1975). The psychological and social consequences of breast cancer. *Nursing Minor, 140,* 54–57.

Mahler, H. I. M., & Kulik, J. A. (1998). Effects of preparatory videotapes on self-efficacy beliefs and recovery from coronary bypass surgery. *Annals of Behavioral Medicine, 20,* 39–46.

Mahler, H. I. M., & Kulik, J. A. (2002). Effects of videotape information intervention for spouses on spouse distress and patient recovery from surgery. *Health Psychology, 21,* 427–437.

Mahler, H. I. M., Kulick, J. A., Gibbons, F. X., Gerrard, M., & Harrell, J. (2003). Effects of appearance-based interventions on sun protection intentions and self-reported behaviors. *Health Psychology, 22,* 199–209.

Mahoney, M. J. (1974). Self-reward and self-monitoring techniques for weight control. *Behavioral Therapy, 5,* 48–57.

Maier, K. J., Waldstein, S. R., & Synowski, S. J. (2003). Relation of cognitive appraisal to cardiovascular reactivity, affect, and task engagement. *Annals of Behavioral Medicine, 26,* 32–41.

Maixner, W., Fillingim, R., Kincaid, S., Sigurdsson, A., Odont, C., & Harris, B. (1997). Relationship between pain sensitivity and resting arterial blood pressure in patients with painful temporomandibular disorders. *Psychosomatic Medicine, 59,* 503–511.

Malarkey, W. B., Kiecolt-Glaser, J. K., Pearl, D., & Glaser, R. (1994). Hostile behavior during marital conflict alters pituitary and adrenal hormones. *Psychosomatic Medicine, 56,* 41–51.

Mallett, K., Price, J. H., Jurs, S. G., & Slenker, S. (1991). Relationships among burnout, death anxiety, and social support in hospice and critical care nurses. *Psychological Reports, 68,* 1347–1359.

Manber, R., Kuo, T. F., Cataldo, N., & Colrain, I. M. (2003). The effects of hormone replacement therapy on sleep-disordered breathing in postmenopausal women: A pilot study. *Journal of Sleep & Sleep Disorders Research, 26,* 163–168.

Mann, T. (2001). Effects of future writing and optimism on health behaviors in HIV-infected women. *Annals of Behavioral Medicine, 23,* 26–33.

Mann, T., Nolen-Hoeksema, S., Huang, K., Burgard, D., Wright, A., & Hanson, K. (1997). Are two interventions worse than none? Joint primary and secondary prevention of eating disorders in college females. *Health Psychology, 16,* 215–225.

Manne, S. L., & Zautra, A. J. (1990). Couples coping with chronic illness: Women with rheumatoid arthritis and their healthy husbands. *Journal of Behavioral Medicine, 13,* 327–342.

Manne, S. L., Bakeman, R., Jacobsen, P. B., Gorfinkle, K., & Redd, W. H. (1994). An analysis of a behavioral intervention for children undergoing venipuncture. *Health Psychology, 13,* 556–566.

Manne, S. L., Bakeman, R., Jacobsen, P. B., Gorfinkle, K., Bernstein, D., & Redd, W. H. (1992). Adult-child interaction during invasive medical procedures. *Health Psychology, 11,* 241–249.

Manne, S. L., Jacobsen, P. B., Gorfinkle, K., Gerstein, F., & Redd, W. H. (1993). Treatment adherence difficulties among children with cancer: The role of parenting style. *Journal of Pediatric Psychology, 18,* 47–62.

Manne, S. L., Redd, W. H., Jacobsen, P. B., Gorfinkle, K., Schorr, O., & Rapkin, B. (1990). Behavioral intervention to reduce child and parent distress during venipuncture. *Journal of Consulting and Clinical Psychology, 58,* 565–572.

Manne, S., Glassman, M., & Du Hamel, K. (2000). Intrusion, avoidance, and psychological distress among individuals with cancer. *Psychosomatic Medicine, 63,* 658–667.

Manne, S. L., Taylor, K. L., Dougherty, J., & Kemeny, N. (1997). Supportive and negative responses in the partner relationship: Their association with psychological adjustment among individuals with cancer. *Journal of Behavioral Medicine, 20,* 101–126.

Manne, S. L., & Glassman, M. (2000). Perceived control, coping efficacy, and avoidance coping as mediators between spouses' unsupportive behaviors and cancer patients' psychological distress. *Health Psychology, 19,* 155–164.

Manson, J. E., Colditz, G. A., Stampfer, M. J., Willett, W. C., Rosner, B., Monson, R. R., et al. (1990). A prospective study of obesity and risk of coronary heart disease in women. *New England Journal of Medicine, 322,* 882–888.

Manson, J. E., Hsia, J., Johnson, K. C., Rossouw, J. E., Assaf, A. R., Lasser, N. L., et al. (2003). Estrogen plus progestin and the risk of coronary heart disease. *New England Journal of Medicine, 349,* 523–534, http://www.nejm.org

Manson, J. E., Willett, W. C., Stampfer, M. J., Loiditz, G. A., Hunter, D. J., Hankinson, S. E., et al. (1995). Body weight and mortality among women. *New England Journal of Medicine, 333,* 677–685.

Mapou, R. L., Kay, G. G., Rundell, J. R., & Temoshok, L. R. (1993). Measuring performance decrements in aviation personnel infected with the human immunodeficiency virus. *Aviation, Space, and Environmental Medicine, 64,* 158–164.

Marbach, J. J., Lennon, M. C., Link, B. G., & Dohrenwend, B. P. (1990). Losing face: Sources of stigma as perceived by chronic facial pain patients. *Journal of Behavioral Medicine, 13,* 583–604.

Marcus, A. C., & Siegel, J. M. (1982). Sex differences in the use of physician services: A preliminary test of the fixed role hypothesis. *Journal of Health and Social Behavior, 23,* 186–197.

Marcus, B. H., & Owen, N. (1992). Motivational readiness, self-efficacy and decision-making for exercise. *Journal of Applied Social Psychology, 22,* 3–16.

Marcus, B. H., Dubbert, P. M., Forsyth, L. H., McKenzie, T. L., Stone, E. J., Dunn, A. L., et al. (2000). Physical activity behavior change: Issues in adoption and maintenance. *Health Psychology, 19,* 32–41.

Margolin, A., Avants, S. K., Warburton, L. A., Hawkins, K. A., & Shi, J. (2003). A randomized clinical trial of a manual-guided risk reduction intervention for HIV-positive injection drug users. *Health Psychology, 22,* 223–228.

Margolis, S., & Moses, H., III. (Eds.). (1992). *The Johns Hopkins medical handbook: The 100 major medical disorders of people over the age of 50.* New York: Rebus.

Marin, B. V., & Marin, G. (1990). Effects of acculturation on knowledge of AIDS and HIV among Hispanics. *Hispanic Journal of Behavioral Sciences* [Special issue on Hispanics and AIDS], *12,* 153–164.

Markovitz, J. H. (1998). Hostility is associated with increased platelet activation in coronary heart disease. *Psychosomatic Medicine, 60,* 586–591.

Markovitz, J. H., Matthews, K. A., Wing, R. R., Kuller, L. H., & Meilahn, E. N. (1991). Psychological, biological and health behavior predictors of blood pressure changes in middle-aged women. *Journal of Hypertension, 9,* 399–406.

Marks, M., Sliwinski, M., & Gordon, W. A. (1993). An examination of the needs of families with a brain injured child. *Journal of Neurorehabilitation, 3,* 1–12.

Marlatt, G. A. (1990). Cue exposure and relapse prevention in the treatment of addictive behaviors. *Addictive Behaviors, 15,* 395–399.

Marlatt, G. A., & George, W. H. (1988). Relapse prevention and the maintenance of optimal health. In S. Shumaker, E. Schron, & J. K. Ockene (Eds.), *The adoption and maintenance of behaviors for optimal health.* New York: Springer.

Marlatt, G. A., & Gordon, J. R. (1980). Determinants of relapse: Implications for the maintenance of behavior change. In P. O. Davidson & S. M. Davidson (Eds.), *Behavioral medicine: Changing health life-styles.* New York: Brunner/Mazel.

Marlatt, G. A., & Gordon, J. R. (1985). *Relapse prevention: Maintenance strategies in the treatment of addictive behaviors.* New York: Guilford Press.

Marlatt, G. A., Baer, J. S., & Larimer, M. (1995). Preventing alcohol abuse in college students: A harm-reduction approach. In G. M. Boyd, Jr., J. Howard, & R. A. Zucker (Eds.), *Alcohol problems among adolescents* (pp. 147–172). Northvale, NJ: Erlbaum.

Marlatt, G. A., Baer, J. S., Kivlahan, D. R., Dimeff, L. A., Larimer, M. E., Quigley, L. A., et al. (1998). Screening and brief intervention for high-risk college student drinkers: Results from a 2-year follow-up assessment. *Journal of Consulting and Clinical Psychology, 66,* 604–615.

Marlatt, G. A., Larimer, M. E., Baer, J. S., & Quigley, L. A. (1993). Harm reduction for alcohol problems: Moving beyond the controlled drinking controversy. *Behavior Therapy, 24,* 461–504.

Marmot, M. G. (1998). Improvement of social environment to improve health. *Lancet, 331,* 57–60.

Marsh, B. (2002, September 10). A primer on fat, some of it good for you. *The New York Times,* p. D7.

Marshall, A. L., Bauman, A. E., Owen, N., Booth, M. L., Crawford, D., & Marcus, B. H. (2003). Population-based randomized controlled trial of a stage-targeted physical activity intervention. *Annals of Behavioral Medicine, 25,* 194–202.

Marshall, E. (1986). Involuntary smokers face health risks. *Science, 234,* 1066–1067.

Marshall, J., Burnett, W., & Brasure, J. (1983). On precipitating factors: Cancer as a cause of suicide. *Suicide and Life-Threatening Behavior, 13,* 15–27.

Marshall, S. J., & Biddle, S. J. H. (2001). The transtheoretical model of behavior change: A meta-analysis of applications to physical activity and exercise. *Annals of Behavioral Medicine, 23,* 229–246.

Marsland, A. L., Cohen, S., Rabin, B. S., & Manuck, S. B. (2001). Associations between stress, trait negative affect, acute immune reactivity, and antibody response to hepatitis B injection in healthy young adults. *Health Psychology, 20,* 4–11.

Marteau, T. M., Bloch, S., & Baum, J. D. (1987). Family life and diabetic control. *Journal of Child Psychology and Psychiatry, 28,* 823–833.

Marteau, T. M., Dundas, R., & Axworthy, D. (1997). Long-term cognitive and emotional impact of genetic testing for carriers of cystic fibrosis: The effects of test result and gender. *Health Psychology, 16,* 51–62.

Marteau, T. M., Johnston, M., Baum, J. D., & Bloch, S. (1987). Goals of treatment in diabetes: A comparison of doctors and parents of children with diabetes. *Journal of Behavioral Medicine, 10,* 33–48.

Martin, J. E., & Dubbert, P. M. (1982). Exercise applications and promotion in behavioral medicine: Current status and future directions. *Journal of Consulting and Clinical Psychology, 50,* 1004–1017.

Martin, J. K., Tuch, S. A., & Roman, P. M. (2003). Problem drinking patterns among African Americans: The impacts of reports of discrimination, perceptions of prejudice, and "risky" coping strategies. *Journal of Health and Social Behavior, 44,* 408–425.

Martin, L. R., Friedman, H. S., Tucker, J. S., Tomlinson-Keasey, C., Criqui, M. H., & Schwartz, J. E. (2002). Life course perspective on childhood cheerfulness and its relations to mortality risk. *Personality and Social Psychology Bulletin, 28,* 1155–1165.

Martin, R., & Lemos, K. (2002). From heart attacks to melanoma: Do common sense models of somatization influence symptom interpretation for female victims? *Health Psychology, 21,* 25–32.

Martin, R., Davis, G. M., Baron, R. S., Suls, J., & Blanchard, E. B. (1994). Specificity in social support: Perceptions of helpful and unhelpful provider behaviors among irritable bowel syndrome, headache, and cancer patients. *Health Psychology, 13,* 432–439.

Martire, L. M., Stephens, M. A. P., Druley, J. A., & Wojno, W. C. (2002). Negative reactions to received spousal care: Predictors and consequences of miscarried support. *Health Psychology, 21,* 167–176.

Maruta, T., Colligan, R. C., Malinchoc, M., & Offord, K. P. (2002). Optimism-pessimism assessed in the 1960s and self-reported health status 30 years later. *Mayo Clinic Proceedings, 77,* 748–753.

Maslach, C. (1979). The burn-out syndrome and patient care. In C. Garfield (Ed.), *The emotional realities of life-threatening illness* (pp. 111–120). St. Louis, MO: Mosby.

Maslach, C. (2003). Job burnout: New directions in research and intervention. *Current Directions, 12,* 189–192.

Mason, E. (1970). Obesity in pet dogs. *Veterinary Record, 86,* 612–616.

Mason, H. R. C., Marks, G., Simoni, J. M., Ruiz, M. S., & Richardson, J. L. (1995). Culturally sanctioned secrets? Latino men's nondisclosure of HIV infection to family, friends, and lovers. *Health Psychology, 14,* 6–12.

Mason, J. W., Brady, J. V., & Tolliver, G. A. (1968). Plasma and urinary 17-hydroxycorticosteroid responses to 72-hour avoidance sessions in the monkey. *Psychosomatic Medicine, 30,* 608–630.

Mason, J. W., Kosten, T. R., Southwick, S. M., & Giller, E. L., Jr. (1990). The use of psychoendocrine strategies in post-traumatic stress disorder. *Journal of Applied Social Psychology, 20,* 1822–1846.

Mason, J. W., Wang, S., Yehuda, R., Lubin, H., Johnson, D., Bremner, J. D., et al. (2002). Marked lability in urinary cortisol levels in subgroups of combat veterans with posttraumatic stress disorder during an intensive exposure treatment program. *Psychosomatic Medicine, 64,* 238–246.

Massie, M. J., & Holland, J. C. (1987). Consultation and liaison issues in cancer care. *Psychiatric Medicine, 5,* 343–359.

Masters, J. C., Cerreto, M. C., & Mendlowitz, D. R. (1983). The role of the family in coping with childhood chronic illness. In T. G. Burish & L. A. Bradley (Eds.), *Coping with chronic disease: Research and applications* (pp. 381–408). New York: Academic Press.

Masuda, A., Munemoto, T., Yamanaka, T., Takei, M., & Tei, C. (2002). Psychological characteristics and immunological functions in patients with postinfectious chronic fatigue syndrome and noninfectious chronic fatigue syndrome. *Journal of Behavioral Medicine, 25,* 477–485.

Matarazzo, J. (1994). Health and behavior: The coming together of science and practice in psychology and medicine after a century of benign neglect. *Journal of Clinical Psychology in Medical Settings, 1,* 7–37.

Matarazzo, J. D. (1980). Behavioral health and behavioral medicine: Frontiers for a new health psychology. *American Psychologist, 35,* 807–817.

Matarazzo, J. D. (1982). Behavioral health's challenge to academic, scientific, and professional psychology. *American Psychologist, 37,* 1–14.

Matt, G. E., & Dean, A. (1993). Social support from friends and psychological distress among elderly persons: Moderator effects of age. *Journal of Health and Social Behavior, 34,* 187–200.

Matt, G. E., Quintana, P. J. E., Hovell, M. F., Bernert, J. T., Song, S., Novianti, N., et al. (2004). Households contaminated by environmental tobacco smoke: Sources of infant exposures. *Tobacco Control, 13,* 29–37.

Mattar, M. E., Markello, J., & Yaffe, S. J. (1975). Inadequacies in the pharmacologic management of ambulatory children. *Journal of Pediatrics, 87,* 137–141.

Matthews, J. R., Friman, P. C., Barone, V. J., Ross, L. V., & Christophersen, E. R. (1987). Decreasing dangerous infant behaviors through parent instruction. *Journal of Applied Behavior Analysis, 20,* 165–169.

Matthews, K. A. (1982). Psychological perspectives on the Type A behavior pattern. *Psychological Bulletin, 91,* 293–323.

Matthews, K. A., & Rodin, J. (1992). Pregnancy alters blood pressure responses to psychological and physical challenge. *Psychophysiology, 29,* 232–240.

Matthews, K. A., Gump, B. B., & Owens, J. F. (2001). Chronic stress influences cardiovascular and neuroendocrine responses during acute stress and recovery, especially in men. *Health Psychology, 20,* 403–410.

Matthews, K. A., Gump, B. B., Block, D. R., & Allen, M. T. (1997). Does background stress heighten or dampen children's cardiovascular responses to acute stress? *Psychosomatic Medicine, 59,* 488–496.

Matthews, K. A., Owens, J. F., Allen, M. T., & Stoney, C. M. (1992). Do cardiovascular responses to laboratory stress relate to ambulatory blood pressure levels? Yes, in some of the people, some of the time. *Psychosomatic Medicine, 54,* 686–697.

Matthews, K. A., Owens, J. F., Kuller, L. H., Sutton-Tyrrell, K., & Jansen-McWilliams, L. (1998). Are hostility and anxiety associated with carotid atherosclerosis in healthy postmenopausal women? *Psychosomatic Medicine, 60,* 633–638.

Matthews, K. A., Räikkönen, K., Everson, S. A., Flory, J. D., Marco, C. A., Owens, J. F., et al. (2000). Do the daily experiences of healthy men and women vary according to occupational prestige and work strain? *Psychosomatic Medicine, 62,* 346–353.

Matthews, K. A., Salomon, K., Brady, S. S., & Allen, M. T. (2003). Cardiovascular reactivity to stress predicts future blood pressure in adolescence. *Psychosomatic Medicine, 65,* 410–415.

Matthews, K. A., Shumaker, S. A., Bowen, D. J., Langer, R. D., Hunt, J. R., Kaplan, R. M., et al. (1997). Women's health initiative: Why now? What is it? What's new? *American Psychologist, 52,* 101–116.

Matthews, K. A., Woodall, K. L., & Allen, M. T. (1993). Cardiovascular reactivity to stress predicts future blood pressure status. *Hypertension, 22,* 479–485.

Matthews, K. A., Woodall, K. L., Kenyon, K., & Jacob, T. (1996). Negative family environment as a predictor of boys' future status on measures of hostile attitudes, interview behavior, and anger expression. *Health Psychology, 15,* 30–37.

Mauksch, H. O. (1973). Ideology, interaction, and patient care in hospitals. *Social Science and Medicine, 7,* 817–830.

Maunder, R. G., & Hunter, J. J. (2001). Attachment and psychosomatic medicine: Developmental contributions to stress and disease. *Psychosomatic Medicine, 63,* 556–567.

Maxwell, T. D., Gatchel, R. J., & Mayer, T. G. (1998). Cognitive predictors of depression in chronic low back pain: Toward an inclusive model. *Journal of Behavioral Medicine, 21,* 131–143.

May, M., McCarron, P., Stansfeld, S., Ben-Schlomo, Y., Gallacher, J., Yarnell, J., et al. (2002). Does psychological distress predict the risk of ischemic stroke and transient ischemic attack? *Stroke, 33,* 7–12.

Mayer, D. J., Price, D. D., Barber, J., & Rafii, A. (1976). Acupuncture analgesia: Evidence for activation of a pain inhibitor system as a mechanism of action. In J. J. Bonica & D. Albe-Fessard (Eds.), *Advances in pain research and therapy* (Vol. 1, pp. 751–754). New York: Raven Press.

Mayer, J. A., & Kellogg, M. C. (1989). Promoting mammography appointment making. *Journal of Behavioral Medicine, 12,* 605–611.

Mayne, T. J., Acree, M., Chesney, M. A., & Folkman, S. (1998). HIV sexual risk behavior following bereavement in gay men. *Health Psychology, 17,* 403–411.

Mayo Clinic (2001). Retrieved August 1, 2004 from http://www.mayoclinic.org/news2001-rst/790.html

Mazor, K. M., Simon, S. R., Yood, R. A., Martinson, B. C., Gunter, M. J., Reed, G. W., & Gurwitz, J. H. (2004). Health plan members' views about disclosure of medical errors. *Annals of Internal Medicine, 140,* 409–418.

McAuley, E. (1992). The role of efficacy cognitions in the prediction of exercise behavior in middle-aged adults. *Journal of Behavioral Medicine, 15,* 65–88.

McAuley, E. (1993). Self-efficacy and the maintenance of exercise participation in older adults. *Journal of Behavioral Medicine, 16,* 103–113.

McAuley, E., & Courneya, K. S. (1992). Self-efficacy relationships with affective and exertion responses to exercise. *Journal of Applied Social Psychology, 22,* 312–326.

McAuley, E., Jerome, G. J., Marquez, D. X., Elavsky, S., & Blissmer, B. (2003). Exercise self-efficacy in older adults: Social, affective, and behavioral influences. *Annals of Behavioral Medicine, 25,* 1–7.

McAuley, E., Mihalko, S. L., & Bane, S. M. (1997). Exercise and self-esteem in middle-aged adults: Multidimensional relationships and physical fitness and self-efficacy influences. *Journal of Behavioral Medicine, 20,* 67–84.

McAuley, E., Talbot, H., & Martinez, S. (1999). Manipulating self-efficacy in the exercise environment in women: Influences on affective responses. *Health Psychology, 18,* 288–294.

McBride, C. M., Pollack, K. I., Lyna, P., Lipkus, I. M., Samsa, G. P., & Bepler, G. (2001). Reasons for quitting smoking among low-income African American smokers. *Health Psychology, 20,* 334–340.

McCaffery, J. M., Niaura, R., Todaro, J. F., Swan, G. E., & Carmelli, D. (2003). Depressive symptoms and metabolic risk in adult male twins enrolled in the national heart, lung and blood study. *Psychosomatic Medicine, 65,* 490–497.

McCaffery, J. M., Pogue-Geile, M. F., Muldoon, M. F., Debski, T. T., Wing, R. R., & Manuck, S. B. (2001). The nature of the association between diet and serum lipids in the community: A twin study. *Health Psychology, 20,* 341–350.

McCann, B., Benjamin, A., Wilkinson, C., Retzlaff, B., Russo, J., & Knopp, R. (1999). Plasma lipid concentrations during episodic occupational stress. *Annals of Behavioral Medicine, 21,* 103–110.

McCann, B. S., Bovbjerg, V. E., Curry, S. J., Retzlaff, B. M., Walden, C. E., & Knopp, R. H. (1996). Predicting participation in a dietary intervention to lower cholesterol among individuals with hyperlipidemia. *Health Psychology, 15,* 61–64.

McCarroll, J. E., Ursano, R. J., Fullerton, C. S., Liu, X., & Lundy, A. (2002). Somatic symptoms in Gulf War mortuary workers. *Psychosomatic Medicine, 64,* 29–33.

McCarthy, C. J. (1995). The relationship of cognitive appraisals and stress coping resources to emotion-eliciting events. *Dissertation Abstracts International: Section B: The Sciences & Engineering, 56,* 1746.

McCaul, K. D., Branstetter, A. D., O'Donnell, S. M., Jacobson, K., & Quinlan, K. B. (1998). A descriptive study of breast cancer worry. *Journal of Behavioral Medicine, 21,* 565–579.

McCaul, K. D., Branstetter, A. D., Schroeder, D. M., & Glasgow, R. E. (1996). What is the relationship between breast cancer risk and mammography screening? A meta-analytic review. *Health Psychology, 15,* 423–429.

McCaul, K. D., Glasgow, R. E., & O'Neill, H. K. (1992). The problem of creating habits: Establishing health-protective dental behaviors. *Health Psychology, 11,* 101–110.

McCaul, K. D., Johnson, R. J., & Rothman, A. J. (2002). The effects of framing and action instructions on whether older adults obtain flu shots. *Health Psychology, 21,* 624–628.

McCaul, K. D., Monson, N., & Maki, R. H. (1992). Does distraction reduce pain-produced distress among college students? *Health Psychology, 11,* 210–217.

McClearn, G., Johansson, B., Berg, S., Pedersen, N., Ahern, F., Petrill, S. A., et al. (1997). Substantial genetic influence on cognitive abilities in twins 80 or more years old. *Science, 276,* 1560–1563.

McConnell, S., Biglan, A., & Severson, H. H. (1984). Adolescents' compliance with self-monitoring and physiological assessment of smoking in natural environments. *Journal of Behavioral Medicine, 7,* 115–122.

McCoy, S. B., Gibbons, F. X., Reis, T. J., Gerrard, M., Luus, C. A. E., & Sufla, A. V. W. (1992). Perceptions of smoking risk as a function of smoking status. *Journal of Behavioral Medicine, 15,* 469–488.

McCracken, L. M. (1991). Cognitive-behavioral treatment of rheumatoid arthritis: A preliminary review of efficacy and methodology. *Annals of Behavioral Medicine, 13,* 57–65.

McCullough, M. E., Hoyt, W. T., Larson, D. B., Koenig, H. G., & Thoresen, C. (2000). Religious involvement and mortality: A meta-analytic review. *Health Psychology, 19,* 211–222.

McDonough, P., Williams, D. R., House, J. S., & Duncan, G. J. (1999). Gender and the socioeconomic gradient in mortality. *Journal of Health and Social Behavior, 40,* 17–31.

McEwen, B. S. (1998). Protective and damaging effects of stress mediators. *New England Journal of Medicine, 338,* 171–179.

McEwen, B. S., & Stellar, E. (1993). Stress and the individual: Mechanisms leading to disease. *Archives of Internal Medicine, 153,* 2093–2101.

McFarland, C., & Alvaro, C. (2000). The impact of motivation on temporal comparisons: Coping with traumatic events by perceiving personal growth. *Journal of Personality and Social Psychology, 79,* 327–343.

McFarland, C., Ross, M., & DeCourville, N. (1989). Women's theories of menstruation and biases in recall of menstrual symptoms. *Journal of Personality and Social Psychology, 57,* 522–531.

McFarlane, T., Polivy, J., & McCabe, R. E. (1999). Help, not harm: Psychological foundation for a nondieting approach toward health. *Journal of Social Issues, 55,* 261–276.

McGinnis, M. (1994). The role of behavioral research in national health policy. In S. Blumenthal, K. Matthews, & S. Weiss (Eds.), *New research frontiers in behavioral medicine: Proceedings of the national conference* (pp. 217–222). Washington, D.C.: NIH Publications.

McGinnis, M., Richmond, J. B., Brandt, E. N., Windom, R. E., & Mason, J. O. (1992). Health progress in the United States: Results of the 1990 objectives for the nation. *Journal of the American Medical Association, 268,* 2545–2552.

McGonagle, K. A., & Kessler, R. C. (1990). Chronic stress, acute stress, and depressive symptoms. *American Journal of Community Psychology, 18,* 681–706.

McGrady, A., Conran, P., Dickey, D., Garman, D., Farris, E., & Schumann-Brzezinski, C. (1992). The effects of biofeedback-assisted relaxation on cell-mediated immunity, cortisol, and white blood cell count in healthy adult subjects. *Journal of Behavioral Medicine, 15,* 343–354.

McGregor, D. (1967). *The professional manager.* New York: McGraw-Hill.

McGuire, F. L. (1982). Treatment of the drinking driver. *Health Psychology, 1,* 137–152.

McGuire, W. J. (1964). Inducing resistance to persuasion: Some contemporary approaches. In L. Berkowitz (Ed.), *Advances in experimental social psychology* (Vol. 1, pp. 192–231). New York: Academic Press.

McGuire, W. J. (1973). Persuasion, resistance and attitude change. In I. de Sola Pool, F. W. Frey, W. Schramm, N. Maccoby, & E. B. Parker (Eds.), *Handbook of communication* (pp. 216–252). Chicago: Rand-McNally.

McGuire, W. J. (1984). Public communication as a strategy for inducing health-promoting behavioral change. *Preventive Medicine, 13,* 299–319.

McIntosh, D. N., Silver, R. C., & Wortman, C. B. (1993). Religion's role in adjustment to a negative life event: Coping with the loss of a child. *Journal of Personality and Social Psychology, 65,* 812–821.

McKenna, M. C., Zevon, M. A., Corn, B., & Rounds, J. (1999). Psychological factors and the development of breast cancer: A meta-analysis. *Health Psychology, 18,* 520–531.

McKinlay, J. B. (1975). Who is really ignorant—physician or patient? *Journal of Health and Social Behavior, 16,* 3–11.

McKinnon, W., Weisse, C. S., Reynolds, C. P., Bowles, C. A., & Baum, A. (1989). Chronic stress, leukocyte subpopulations, and humoral response to latent viruses. *Health Psychology, 8,* 389–402.

McKusick, L., Coates, T. J., Morin, S. F., Pollack, L., & Hoff, C. (1990). Longitudinal predictors of reductions in unprotected anal intercourse among gay men in San Francisco: The AIDS Behavioral Research Project. *American Journal of Public Health, 80,* 978–983.

McKusick, L., Horstman, W., & Coates, T. (1985). AIDS and sexual behavior reported by gay men in San Francisco. *American Journal of Public Health, 75,* 493–496.

McKusick, V. A. (1993). Medical genetics: A 40-year perspective on the evolution of a medical speciality from a basic science. *Journal of the American Medical Association, 270,* 2351–2357.

McLeod, J. D., Kessler, R. C., & Landis, K. R. (1992). Speed of recovery from major depressive episodes in a community sample of married men and women. *Journal of Abnormal Psychology, 101,* 277–286.

McNeil, D. G., Jr. (2002, May 17). With folk medicine on rise, health group is monitoring. *The New York Times,* p. A9.

McQuade, D. V. (2002). Negative social perception of hypothetical workers with rheumatoid arthritis. *Journal of Behavioral Medicine, 25,* 205–217.

McQuillen, A. D., Licht, M. H., & Licht, B. G. (2003). Contributions of disease severity and perceptions of primary and secondary control to the prediction of psychological adjustment to Parkinson's disease. *Health Psychology, 22,* 504–512.

Meagher, M., Arnau, R., & Rhudy, J. (2001). Pain and emotion: Effects of affective picture modulation. *Psychosomatic Medicine, 63,* 79–90.

Mechanic, D. (1972). Social psychologic factors affecting the presentation of bodily complaints. *New England Journal of Medicine, 286,* 1132–1139.

Mechanic, D. (1975). The organization of medical practice and practice orientation among physicians in prepaid and nonprepaid primary care settings. *Medical Care, 13,* 189–204.

Medicinenet.com. (2002). *Alcohol abuse.* Retrieved from: http://www.medicinenet.com/script/main/art.asp?articlekey=38054&page=2

Medzhitov, R., & Janeway, C. A., Jr. (2002). Decoding the Patterns of Self and Nonself by the Innate Immune System, *Science, 296,* 298–300.

Medzhitov, R., & Janeway Jr., C. A. (2002, April 12). Decoding the patterns of self and nonself by the innate immune system. *Science, 296,* 298–316.

Meechan, G., Collins, J., & Petrie, K. J. (2003). The relationship of symptoms and psychological factors to delay in seeking medical care for breast symptoms. *Preventive Medicine, 36,* 374–378.

Meichenbaum, D. H. (1971, September). *Cognitive factors in behavior modification: Modifying what clients say to themselves.* Paper presented at the annual meeting of the Association for Advancement of Behavior Therapy, Washington, D.C.

Meichenbaum, D. H. (1975). A self-instructional approach to stress management: A proposal for stress inoculation training, In C. D. Spielberger & I. Sarason (Eds.), *Stress and anxiety* (Vol. 2, pp. 237–264). New York: Wiley.

Meichenbaum, D. H., & Cameron, R. (1974). The clinical potential and pitfalls of modifying what clients say to themselves. In M. J. Mahoney & C. E. Thoresen (Eds.), *Self-control: Power to the person* (pp. 263–290). Monterey, CA: Brooks-Cole.

Meichenbaum, D. H., & Jaremko, M. E. (Eds.). (1983). *Stress reduction and prevention.* New York: Plenum Press.

Meichenbaum, D. H., & Turk, D. (1982). Stress, coping, and disease: A cognitive-behavioral perspective. In R. W. J. Neufield (Ed.), *Psychological stress and psychopathology* (pp. 289–306). New York: McGraw-Hill.

Meichenbaum, D. H., & Turk, D. C. (1987). *Facilitating treatment adherence: A practitioner's guidebook.* New York: Plenum Press.

Mei-Tal, V., Meyerowitz, S., & Engel, G. I. (1970). The role of psychological process in a somatic disorder: M.S. 1. The emotional setting of illness onset and exacerbation. *Psychosomatic Medicine, 32,* 67–85.

Melamed, B. (1995). The interface between physical and mental disorders: The need to dismantle the biopsychosocialneuroimmunological model of disease. *Journal of Clinical Psychology in Medical Setting, 2,* 225–231.

Melamed, B. G., & Brenner, G. F. (1990). Social support and chronic medical stress: An interaction-based approach. *Journal of Social and Clinical Psychology, 9,* 104–117.

Melamed, B. G., & Siegel, L. (1975). Reduction of anxiety in children facing hospitalization and surgery by use of filmed modeling. *Journal of Consulting and Clinical Psychology, 43,* 511–521.

Melamed, S., Shirom, A., Toker, S., Berliner, S., & Shapira, I. (2004). Association of fear of terror with low-grade inflammation among apparently healthy adults. *Psychosomatic Medicine, 66,* 484–491.

Melzack, R., & Wall, P. D. (1982). *The challenge of pain.* New York: Basic Books.

Menaghan, E., Kowaleski-Jones, L., & Mott, F. (1997). The intergenerational costs of parental social stressors: Academic and social difficulties in early adolescence for children of young mothers. *Journal of Health and Social Behavior, 38,* 72–86.

Mendes de Leon, C. F. (1992). Anger and impatience/irritability in patients of low socioeconomic status with acute coronary heart disease. *Journal of Behavioral Medicine, 15,* 273–284.

Mendes de Leon, C. F., Dilillo, V., Czajkowski, S., Norten, J., Schaefer, J., Catellier, D., & Blumenthal, J. A., Enhancing Recovery in Coronary Heart Disease (ENRICHD) Pilot Study. (2001). Psychosocial characteristics after acute myocardial infarction: the ENRICHD pilot study. Enhancing Recovery in Coronary Heart Disease. *Journal of Cardiopulmonary Rehabilitation, 21,* 353–362.

Mendes de Leon, C. F., Kop, W. J., de Swart, H. B., Bar, F. W., & Appels, A. P. W. M. (1996). Psychosocial characteristics and recurrent events after percutaneous transluminal coronary angioplasty. *American Journal of Cardiology, 77,* 252–255.

Mensch, B. S., & Kandel, D. B. (1988). Do job conditions influence the use of drugs? *Journal of Health and Social Behavior, 29,* 169–184.

Mercado, A. C., Carroll, L. J., Cassidy, J. D., & Cote, P. (2000). Coping with neck and low back pain in the general population. *Health Psychology, 19,* 333–338.

Mermelstein, R., Cohen, S., Lichtenstein, E., Baer, J. S., & Kamarck, T. (1986). Social support and smoking cessation and maintenance. *Journal of Consulting and Clinical Psychology, 54,* 447–453.

Merritt, M. M., Bennett, G. G., Williams, R. B., Sollers, J. J., III, & Thayer, J. F. (2004). Low educational attainment, John Henryism and cardiovascular reactivity to and recovery from personally relevant stress. *Psychosomatic Medicine, 66,* 49–55.

Messeri, P., Silverstein, M., & Litwak, E. (1993). Choosing optimal support groups: A review and reformulation. *Journal of Health and Social Behavior, 34,* 122–137.

Messina, C. R., Lane, D. S., & Grimson, R. (2002). Effectiveness of women's telephone counseling and physician education to improve mammography screening among women who underuse mammography. *Annals of Behavioral Medicine, 24,* 279–289.

Meyer, A. J., Maccoby, N., & Farquhar, J. W. (1980). Reply to Kasl and Leventhal et al. *Journal of Consulting and Clinical Psychology, 48,* 159–163.

Meyer, D., Leventhal, H., & Gutmann, M. (1985). Common-sense models of illness: The example of hypertension. *Health Psychology, 4,* 115–135.

Meyer, J. M., & Stunkard, A. J. (1994). Twin studies of human obesity. In C. Bouchard (Ed.), *The genetics of obesity* (pp. 63–78). Boca Raton, FL: CRC Press.

Meyer, M. H., & Pavalko, E. K. (1996). Family, work, and access to health insurance among mature women. *Journal of Health and Social Behavior, 37,* 311–325.

Meyerowitz, B. E. (1980). Psychosocial correlates of breast cancer and its treatments. *Psychological Bulletin, 87,* 108–131.

Meyerowitz, B. E. (1983). Postmastectomy coping strategies and quality of life. *Health Psychology, 2,* 117–132.

Meyerowitz, B. E., & Hart, S. (1993, April*). Women and cancer: Have assumptions about women limited our research agenda?* Paper presented at the Women's Psychological and Physical Health Conference, Lawrence, KS.

Mezzacappa, E. S., Kelsey, R. M., Katkin, E. S., & Sloan, R. P. (2001). Vagal rebound and recovery from psychological stress. *Psychosomatic Medicine, 63,* 650–657.

Michael, B. E., & Copeland, D. R. (1987). Psychosocial issues in childhood cancer: An ecological framework for research. *American Journal of Pediatric Hematology and Oncology, 9,* 73–83.

Michaud, D. S., Liu, S., Giovannucci, E., Willett, W. C., Colditz, G. A., & Fuchs, C. S. (2002). Dietary sugar, glycemic load, and pancreatic cancer risk in a prospective study. *Journal of the National Cancer Institute, 94,* 1293–1300.

Michela, J. L. (1987). Interpersonal and individual impacts of a husband's heart attack. In A. Baum & J. E. Singer (Eds.), *Handbook of psychology and health* (Vol. 5, pp. 255–301). Hillsdale, NJ: Erlbaum.

Millar, M. G., & Millar, K. (1995). Negative affective consequences of thinking about disease detection behaviors. *Health Psychology, 14,* 141–146.

Millar, M. G., & Millar, K. (1996). The effects of anxiety on response times to disease detection and health promotion behaviors. *Journal of Behavioral Medicine, 19,* 401–414.

Miller, G. E. & Cohen, S. (2001). Psychological interventions and the immune system: A meta-analytic review and critique. *Health Psychology, 20,* 47–63.

Miller, G. E., Cohen, S., & Herbert, T. B. (1999). Pathways linking major depression and immunity in ambulatory female patients. *Psychosomatic Medicine, 61,* 850–860.

Miller, G. E., Cohen, S., & Ritchey, A. K. (2002). Chronic psychological stress and the regulation of pro-inflammatory cytokines: A glucocorticoid-resistance model. *Health Psychology, 21,* 531–541.

Miller, G. E., Cohen, S., Pressman, S., Barkin, A., Rabin, B. S., & Treanor, J. J. (2004). Psychological stress and antibody response to influenza vaccination: When is the critical period for stress, and how does it get inside the body? *Psychosomatic Medicine, 66,* 215–223.

Miller, G. E., Freedland, K. E., Carney, R. M., Stetler, C. A., & Banks, W. A. (2003). Cynical hostility, depressives symptoms and the expression of inflammatory risk markers for coronary heart disease. *Journal of Behavioral Medicine, 26,* 501–516.

Miller, G. J., Cruickshank, J. K., Ellis, L. J., Thompson, R. L., Wilkes, H. C., Stirling, Y., et al. (1989). Fat consumption and factor VII coagulant activity in middle-aged men. *Atherosclerosis, 78,* 19–24.

Miller, L. C., Bettencourt, B. A., DeBro, S., & Hoffman, V. (1993). Negotiating safer sex: Interpersonal dynamics. In J. Pryor & G. Reeder (Eds.), *The social psychology of HIV infection* (pp. 85–123). Hillsdale, NJ: Erlbaum.

Miller, N. E. (1989). Placebo factors in types of treatment: Views of a psychologist. In M. Shepherd & N. Sartorius (Eds.), *Non-specific aspects of treatment* (pp. 39–56). Lewiston, NY: Hans Huber.

Miller, N. E. (1992). Some trends from the history to the future of behavioral medicine. *Annals of Behavioral Medicine, 14,* 307–309.

Miller, S. M., & Mangan, C. E. (1983). Interacting effects of information and coping style in adapting to gynecologic stress: Should the doctor tell all? *Journal of Personality and Social Psychology, 45,* 223–236.

Miller, W. R. & Rollnick, S. (1991). *Motivational interviewing: Preparing people to change addictive behavior.* New York, NY, Guilford Press.

Miller, W. R., & Thoresen, C. E. (2003). Spirituality, religion, and health: An emerging research field. *American Psychologist, 58,* 24–35.

Millman, M. (1980). *Such a pretty face: Being fat in America.* New York: Norton.

Mills, P., Yu, H., Ziegler, M. G., Patterson, T., & Grant, I. (1999). Vulnerable caregivers of patients with Alzheimer's disease have a deficit in circulating CD62L T lymphocytes. *Psychosomatic Medicine, 61,* 168–174.

Mills, P. J., Meck, J. V., Waters, W. W., D'Aunno, D., & Ziegler, M. G. (2001). Peripheral leukocyte subpopulations and catecholamine levels in astronauts as a function of mission duration. *Psychosomatic Medicine, 63,* 886–890.

Mills, R. T., & Krantz, D. S. (1979). Information, choice, and reactions to stress: A field experiment in a blood bank with laboratory analogue. *Journal of Personality and Social Psychology, 4,* 608–620.

Mintzer, J. E., Rubert, M. P., Loewenstein, D., Gamez, E., Millor, A., Quinteros, R., et al. (1992). Daughters caregiving for Hispanic and non-Hispanic Alzheimer patients: Does ethnicity make a difference? *Community Mental Health Journal, 28,* 293–303.

Minuchen, S., Rosman, B. L., & Baker, L. (1978). *Psychosomatic families.* Cambridge, MA: Harvard University Press.

Miranda, J., Perez-Stable, E. J., Munoz, R. F., Hargreaves, W., & Henke, C. J. (1991). Somatization, psychiatric disorder, and stress in utilization of ambulatory medical services. *Health Psychology, 10,* 46–51.

Mishra, K. D., Gatchel, R. J., & Gardea, M. A. (2000). The relative efficacy of three cognitive-behavioral treatment approaches to temporomandibular disorders. *Journal of Behavioral Medicine, 23,* 293–309.

Mitchell, J. E., Laine, D. E., Morley, J. E., & Levine, A. S. (1986). Naloxone but not CCK-8 may attenuate binge-eating behavior in patients with the bulimia syndrome. *Biological Psychiatry, 21,* 1399–1406.

Mittag, W., & Schwarzer, R. (1993). Interaction of employment status and self-efficacy on alcohol consumption: A two-wave study on stressful life transitions. *Psychology and Health, 8,* 77–87.

Mittermaier, C., Dejaco, C., Waldhoer, T., Oefferlbauer-Ernst, A., Miehsler, W., Beier, M., et al. (2004). Impact of depressive mood on relapse in patients with inflammatory bowel disease: A prospective 18-month follow up study. *Psychosomatic Medicine, 66,* 79–84.

Mohr, D., Bedantham, K., Neylan, T., Metzler, T. J., Best, S., & Marmar, C. R. (2003). The mediating effects of sleep in the relationship between traumatic stress and health symptoms in urban police officers. *Psychosomatic Medicine, 65,* 485–489.

Mohr, D. C., Dick, L. P., Russo, D., Pinn, J., Boudewyn, A. C., Likosky, W., et al. (1999). The psychological impact of multiple sclerosis: Exploring the patient's perspective. *Health Psychology, 18,* 376–382.

Mohr, D. C., Goodkin, D. E., Nelson, S., Cox, D., & Weiner, M. (2002). Moderating effects of coping on the relationship between stress and the development of new brain lesions in multiple sclerosis. *Psychosomatic Medicine, 64,* 803–809.

Mohr, D., Hart, S. L., & Goldberg, A. (2003). Effects of treatment for depression on fatigue in multiple sclerosis. *Psychosomatic Medicine, 65,* 542–547.

Mokdad, A. H., Marks, J. S., Stroup, D. F., & Gerberding, J. L. (2004). Actual cause of death in the United States, 2000. *Journal of the American Medical Society, 291,* 1238–1245.

Mokdad, A. H., Serdula, M. K., Dietz, W. H., Bowman, B. A., Marks, J. S., & Koplan, J. P. (1999). The spread of the obesity epidemic in the United States, 1991–1998. *Journal of the American Medical Association, 282,* 1519–1522.

Moller, J., Hallqvist, J., Diderichsen, F., Theorell, T., Reuterwall, C., & Ahlbom, A. (1999). Do episodes of anger trigger myocardial infarction? A case-crossover analysis in the Stockholm Heart Epidemiology Program (SHEEP). *Psychosomatic Medicine, 61,* 842–849.

Monroe, S. (1983). Major and minor life events as predictors of psychological distress: Further issues and findings. *Journal of Behavioral Medicine, 6,* 189–205.

Montano, D. E., & Taplin, S. H. (1991). A test of an expanded theory of reasoned action to predict mammography participation. *Social Science and Medicine, 32,* 733–741.

Monteleone, P., Luisi, M., Colurcio, B., Casarosa, E., Ioime, R., Genazzani, A. R., et al. (2001). Plasma levels of neuroactive steroids are increased in untreated women with anorexia nervosa or bulimia nervosa. *Psychosomatic Medicine, 63,* 62–68.

Monteleone, P., Martiadis, V., Colurcio, B., & Maj, M. (2002). Leptin secretion is related to chronicity and severity of the illness in bulimia nervosa. *Psychosomatic Medicine, 64,* 874–879.

Montgomery, G. H., & Bovjerg, D. H. (2003). Expectations of chemotherapy-related nausea: Emotional and experiential predictors. *Annals of Behavioral Medicine, 25,* 48–54.

Moody, L., McCormick, K., & Williams, A. (1990). Disease and symptom severity, functional status, and quality of life in chronic bronchitis and emphysema (CBE). *Journal of Behavioral Medicine, 13,* 297–306.

Moody, R. A. (1978). *Laugh after laugh: The healing power of humor.* Jacksonville, FL: Headwaters Press.

Mooradian, A. D., Perryman, K., Fitten, J., Kavonian, G. D., & Morley, J. E. (1988). Cortical function in elderly non-insulin dependent diabetic patients. *Archives of Internal Medicine, 148,* 2369–2372.

Moore, P. J., Adler, N. E., Williams, D. R., & Jackson, J. S. (2002). Socioeconomic status and health: The role of sleep. *Psychosomatic Medicine, 64,* 337–344.

Moos, R. H. (1988). Life stressors and coping resources influence health and well-being. *Psychological Assessment, 4,* 133–158.

Moos, R. H., & Finney, J. W. (1983). The expanding scope of alcoholism treatment evaluation. *American Psychologist, 38,* 1036–1044.

Moos, R. H., & Schaefer, J. A. (1987). Evaluating health care work settings: A holistic conceptual framework. *Psychology and Health, 1,* 97–122.

Moos, R. H., Brennan, P. L., & Moos, B. S. (1991). Short-term processes of remission and nonremission among later-life problem drinkers. *Alcoholism: Clinical and Experimental Review, 15,* 948–955.

Mor, V., & Hiris, J. (1983). Determinants of site of death among hospice cancer patients. *Journal of Health and Social Behavior, 24,* 375–385.

Morell, V. (1993). Huntington's gene finally found. *Science, 260,* 28–30.

Morens, D. M., Folkers, G. K., & Fauci, A. S. (2004, July 8). The challenge of emerging and re-emerging infectious diseases. *Nature, 430,* 242–249.

Morgan, D. L. (1985). Nurses' perceptions of mental confusion in the elderly: Influence of resident and setting characteristics. *Journal of Health and Social Behavior, 26,* 102–112.

Morimoto, Y., Dishi, T., Hanasaki, N., Miyatake, A., Sato, B., Noma, K., et al. (1980). Interrelations among amenorrhea, serum gonadotropins and body weight in anorexia nervosa. *Endocrinology in Japan, 27,* 191–200.

Morin, C. M., Rodrigue, S., & Ivers, H. (2003). Role of stress, arousal, and coping skills in primary insomnia. *Psychosomatic Medicine, 65,* 259–267.

Morley, J. E., Kay, N. E., & Solomon, G. P. (1988). Opioid peptides, stress, and immune function. In Y. Tache, J. E. Morley, & M. R. Brown (Eds.), *Neuropeptides and stress* (pp. 222–234). New York: Springer.

Morris, P. L. P., & Raphael, B. (1987). Depressive disorder associated with physical illness: The impact of stroke. *General Hospital Psychiatry, 9,* 324–330.

Moser, D. K., Dracup, K., McKinley, S., Yamaski, K., Kim, C., Reigel, B., et al. (2003). An international perspective on gender differences in anxiety early after acute myocardial infarction. *Psychosomatic Medicine, 65,* 511–516.

Moses, H. (Producer). (1984, February 18). *Helen.* In *60 Minutes.* New York: CBS Television Network.

Moskowitz, J. T. (2003). Positive affect predicts lower risk of AIDS mortality. *Psychosomatic Medicine, 65,* 620–626.

Moss-Morris, R., & Petrie, K. J. (2001). Discriminating between chronic fatigue syndrome and depression: A cognitive analysis. *Psychological Medicine, 31,* 469–479.

Moss-Morris, R., Petrie, K. J., & Weinman, J. (1996). Functioning in chronic fatigue syndrome: Do illness perceptions play a regulatory role? *British Journal of Health Psychology, 1,* 15–25.

Mostofsky, D. I. (1998). Behavior modification and therapy in the management of epileptic disorders. In D. I. Mostofsky & Y. Loyning (Eds.), *The neurobehavioral treatment of epilepsy.* Hillsdale, NJ: Erlbaum.

Motivala, S. J., Hurwitz, B. E., Llabre, M. M., Klimas, N. G., Fletcher, M. A., Antoni, M. H., et al. (2003). Psychological distress is associated with decreased memory and helper T-cell and B-cell counts in pre-AIDS HIV

seropositive men and women but only in those with low viral load. *Psychosomatic Medicine, 65,* 627–635.

Motl, R. W., Dishman, R. K., Saunders, R. P., Dowda, M., Felton, G., Ward, D. S., et al. (2002). Examining social-cognitive determinants of intention and physical activity among Black and White adolescent girls under structural equation modeling. *Health Psychology, 21,* 459–467.

Moyer, A. (1997). Psychosocial outcomes of breast-conserving surgery versus mastectomy: A meta-analytic review. *Health Psychology, 16,* 284–298.

Moyer, A., & Salovey, P. (1996). Psychosocial sequelae of breast cancer and its treatment. *Annals of Behavioral Medicine, 18,* 110–125.

Moynihan, J. A., & Ader, R. (1996). Psychoneuroimmunology: Animal models of disease. *Psychosomatic Medicine, 58,* 546–558.

Mroczek, D. K., Spiro, A., III, Aldwin, C. M., Ozer, D. J., & Bosse, R. (1993). Construct validation of optimism and pessimism in older men: Findings from the normative aging study. *Health Psychology, 12,* 406–409.

Muhonen, T., & Torkelson, E. (2003). The demand-control-support model and health among women and men in similar occupations. *Journal of Behavioral Medicine, 26,* 601–613.

Mulder, C. L., de Vroome, E. M. M., van Griensven, G. J. P., Antoni, M. H., & Sandfort, T. G. M. (1999). Avoidance as a predictor of the biological course of HIV infection over a 7-year period in gay men. *Health Psychology, 18,* 107–113.

Muldoon, M. F., Kaplan, R., Manuck, S. B., & Mann, J. J. (1992). Effects of a low-fat diet on brain serotonergic responsivity in cynomolgus monkeys. *Biological Psychiatry, 31,* 739–742.

Muldoon, M. F., Ryan, C. M., Matthews, K. A., & Manuck, S. B. (1997). Serum cholesterol and intellectual performance. *Psychosomatic Medicine, 59,* 382–387.

Mullen, B., & Smyth, J. M. (2004). Immigrant suicide rates as a function of ethnophaulisms: Hate speech predicts death. *Psychosomatic Medicine, 66,* 343–348.

Mullen, B., & Suls, J. (1982). The effectiveness of attention and rejection as coping styles: A meta-analysis of temporal differences. *Journal of Psychosomatic Research, 26,* 43–49.

Mullen, P. D., & Green, L. W. (1985, November–December). Meta-analysis points way toward more effective medication teaching. *Promoting Health,* 6–8.

Murphy, D. A., Mann, T., O'Keefe, Z., & Rotheram-Borus, M. (1998). Number of pregnancies, outcome expectancies, and social norms among HIV-infected young women. *Health Psychology, 17,* 470–475.

Murphy, D. A., Stein, J. A., Schlenger, W., Maibach, E., & National Institute of Mental Health Multisite HIV Prevention Trial Group. (2001). Conceptualizing the multidimensional nature of self-efficacy: Assessment of situational context and level of behavioral challenge to maintain safer sex. *Health Psychology, 20,* 281–290.

Murphy, K. (2000, May 8). An "epidemic" of sleeplessness. *Business Week,* 161–162.

Murphy, S. L. (2000, July 24). *Deaths: Final data for 1998.* National Vital Statistics Reports (NCHS), pp. 26, 73.

Murphy, T. J., Pagano, R. R., & Marlatt, G. A. (1986). Lifestyle modification with heavy alcohol drinkers: Effects of aerobic exercise and meditation. *Addictive Behaviors, 11,* 175–186.

Murray, D. M., Davis-Hearn, M., Goldman, A. I., Pirie, P., & Luepker, R. V. (1988). Four- and five-year follow-up results from four seventh-grade smoking prevention strategies. *Journal of Behavioral Medicine, 11,* 395–406.

Murray, D. M., Richards, P. S., Luepker, R. V., & Johnson, C. A. (1987). The prevention of cigarette smoking in children: Two- and three-year follow-up comparisons of four prevention strategies. *Journal of Behavioral Medicine, 10,* 595–612.

Musselman, D. L., & Nemeroff, C. B. (2000). Depression really does hurt your heart: Stress, depression, and cardiovascular disease. *Progress in Brain Research, 122,* 43–59.

Mutterperl, J. A., & Sanderson, C. A. (2002). Mind over matter: Internalization of the thinness norm as a moderator of responsiveness to norm misperception education in college women. *Health Psychology, 21,* 519–523.

Myers, C. D., Robinson, M. E., Riley, J. L., & Sheffield, D. (2001). Sex, gender, and blood pressure: Contributions to experimental pain report. *Psychosomatic Medicine, 63,* 545–550.

Myers, M. M. (1996). Enduring effects of infant feeding experiences on adult blood pressure. *Psychosomatic Medicine, 58,* 612–621.

Myers, R. S., & Roth, D. L. (1997). Perceived benefits of and barriers to exercise and stage of exercise adoption in young adults. *Health Psychology, 16,* 277–283.

Nagourney, E. (2001, September 9). Quitters never win? Not true. *The New York Times,* p. D6.

Nail, L. M., King, K. B., & Johnson, J. E. (1986). Coping with radiation treatment for gynecologic cancer: Mood and disruption in usual function. *Journal of Psychosomatic Obstetrics and Gynaecology, 5,* 271–281.

Nakao, M., Nomura, S., Shimosawa, T., Yoshiuchi, K., Kumano, H., Kuboki, T., et al. (1997). Clinical effects of blood pressure biofeedback treatment on hypertension by auto-shaping. *Psychosomatic Medicine, 59,* 331–338.

Naliboff, B. D., Mayer, M., Fass, R., Fitzgerald, L. Z., Chang, L., Bolus, R., et al. (2004). The effect of life stress on symptoms of heartburn. *Psychosomatic Medicine, 66,* 426–434.

Napolitano, M. A., Fotheringham, M., Tate, D., Sciamanna, C., Leslie, E., Owen, N., et al. (2003). Evaluation of an Internet-based physical activity intervention: A preliminary investigation. *Annals of Behavioral Medicine, 25,* 92–99.

Nash, J. M. (2003, August 25). Obesity goes global. *Time,* 53–54.

Nashold, B. S., & Friedman, H. (1972). Dorsal column stimulation for pain: A preliminary report on thirty patients. *Journal of Neurosurgery, 36,* 590–597.

National Cancer Institute Breast Cancer Screening Consortium. (1990). Screening mammography: A missing clinical opportunity? Results of the NCI Breast Cancer Screening Consortium and National Health Interview survey studies. *Journal of the American Medical Association, 264,* 54–58.

National Cancer Institute. (1987). *1986 annual cancer statistics review* (NIH Publication No. 87-2789). Bethesda, MD: National Institutes of Health.

National Center for Health Statistics. (1996). *Health, United States, 1995.* Hyattsville, MD: U.S. Public Health Service.

National Center for Health Statistics. (1999). *Healthy people 2000 review, 1998–99.* Hyattsville, MD: U.S. Public Health Service.

National Center for Health Statistics. (2001). *Current smoking trends among adults, by sex, race, and education, 1974–2001. Smoking.* Retrieved from: http://www.cdc.gov/nchs/fastats/smoking.htm

National Center for Health Statistics. (2001). *Health expenditures.* Retrieved July 5, 2001, from: http://www. cdc.gov/nchs/fastats/hexpense.htm

National Center for Health Statistics. (2002). *Health, United States—Table 70.*

National Center for Health Statistics. (2004a). *Prevalence of overweight among children and adolescents: United States, 1999–2000.* Retrieved from: http://www.cdc.gov/nchs/products/pubs/pubd/hestats/overwght99.htm

National Center for Health Statistics. (2004b). *U.S. life expectancy at all-time high, but infant mortality increases.* Retrieved October 25, 2004, from: http://www.cdc.gov/nchs/pressroom/04news/infantmort.htm

National Center for Health Statistics. (2004c). *LCWK1—Deaths, percent of total deaths, and death rates for the 15 leading causes of death in 5-year age groups, by race and sex: United States, 1999–2001.* Retrieved from: http://www.cdc.gov/nchs/datawh/statab/unpubd/mortabs/lcwk1_10.htm

National Center for Health Statistics. *Health, United States, 2002: Table 70.* Retrieved from http://www.cdc.gov/nchs/data/hus/tables/2002/02hus070. pdf

National Center for Injury Prevention and Control. (2001). *Unintentional injury deaths.* http://www.cdc.gov/ncipc/pub-res/unintentional_activity/02_effects.htm

National Committee for Quality Assurance. (2001). *Health plan report card.* Retrieved from: http://www.ncqa.org/ index.asp

National Health Education Committee. (1976). *The killers and cripplers: Facts on major diseases in the United States today.* New York: David McKay.

National Heart, Lung, and Blood Institute. (1999). *Data Fact Sheet – Asthma Statistics.* Retrieved August 1, 2004 from http://www.nhlbi.nih.gov/health/prof/lung/asthma/asthstat.pdf

National Heart, Lung, and Blood Institute. (2004). *Body mass index table.* Retrieved from: http://www.nhlbi.nih.gov/guidelines/obesity/bmi_tbl.htm

National Highway Traffic Safety Administration. (2003a). U.S. Department of Transportation. *Traffic safety facts 2002: Alcohol.* Washington, D.C.: NHTSA; [cited 2003, November 25]. Available from: http://www-nrd. nhtsa.dot.gov/pdf/nrd-30/NCSA/TSF2002/2002alcfacts.pdf

National Institute on Alcohol Abuse and Alcoholism. (2004). *A snapshot of annual high-risk college drinking consequences.* Retrieved from http://www.collegedrinkingprevention.gov/facts/snapshot.aspx on October 1, 2004

National Institute for Health Care Management. (2000, October 12). Prescription spending. *The New York Times,* p. C2.

National Institute of Arthritis and Musculoskeletal and Skin Diseases. (2002). *Questions and answers about arthritis and rheumatic diseases.* Retrieved from: http://www.niams.nih.gov/hi/topics/arthritis/artrheu.htm

National Institute of Diabetes and Digestive and Kidney Diseases. (2001). *Statistics related to overweight and obesity.* Retrieved from: http://www.niddk.nih.gov/health/nutrit/pubs/statobes.htm

National Institute of Mental Health. (2002) *Facts about post-traumatic stress disorder.* Retrieved from: http://www.nimh.nih.gov/publicat/ptsdfacts.cfm

National Institute of Mental Health Multisite HIV Prevention Trial Group. (2001). Social-cognitive theory mediators of behavior change in the national institute of mental health multisite HIV prevention trial. *Health Psychology, 20,* 369–376.

National Institute on Alcohol Abuse and Alcoholism. (2000b). *10th special report to the U.S. Congress on alcohol and health.* Bethesda, MD: Author. Retrieved from: http://silk.nih.gov/silk/niaaa1/publication/10report/10-order.htm

National Institute on Alcohol Abuse and Alcoholism. (2000a, October). *Alcohol alert: New advances in alcoholism treatment.* Bethesda, MD: Author. Retrieved from: www.niaaa. nih.gov

National Institute on Diabetes and Digestive and Kidney Disorders. (1999). *Diabetes control and complications trial (DCCT).* National Institutes of Health Publication No. 97-3874. Retrieved from: http://www. niddk.nih.gov/health/diabetes/pubs/dcct1/dcct.htm

National Multiple Sclerosis Society. (2003). *About MS: Who gets MS?* Retrieved from: http://www.nationalmssociety.org/Who%20gets%20MS.asp

National Safety Council. (2002). *Injury Facts®, 2002 edition.* pp. 36–37.

National Vital Statistics Report. (2001). *Deaths: Preliminary data for 2002.* Volume 52. Retrieved from: http://www.cdc.gov/nchs/fastats/deaths.htm

Navarro, A. M. (1996). Cigarette smoking among adult Latinos: The California tobacco baseline survey. *Annals of Behavioral Medicine, 18,* 238–245.

Nemeroff, C. J. (1995). Magical thinking about illness virulence: Conceptions of germs from "safe" versus "dangerous" others. *Health Psychology, 14,* 147–151.

Nerenz, D. R. (1979). *Control of emotional distress in cancer chemotherapy.* Unpublished doctoral dissertation, University of Wisconsin, Madison.

Nerenz, D. R., & Leventhal, H. (1983). Self-regulation theory in chronic illness. In T. G. Burish & L. A. Bradley (Eds.), *Coping with chronic disease: Research and applications* (pp. 13–38). New York: Academic Press.

Nestle, M. (2003, February 7). The ironic politics of obesity. *Science, 299,* 781.

Neu, P., Sclattmann, P., Schilling, A., & Hartman, A. (2004). Cerebrovascular reactivity in major depression: A pilot study. *Psychosomatic Medicine, 66,* 6–8.

Neu, S., & Kjellstrand, C. M. (1986). Stopping long-term dialysis: An empirical study of withdrawal of life-supporting treatment. *New England Journal of Medicine, 314,* 14–19.

Neugebauer, A., Katz, P. P., & Pasch, L. A. (2003). Effect of valued activity disability, social comparisons, and satisfaction with ability on depressive symptoms in rheumatoid arthritis. *Health Psychology, 22,* 253–262.

Neuling, S. J., & Winefield, H. R. (1988). Social support and recovery after surgery for breast cancer: Frequency and correlates of supportive behaviors by family, friends, and surgeon. *Social Science and Medicine, 27,* 385–392.

Neumark-Sztainer, D., Wall, M. M., Story, M., & Perry C. L. (2003). Correlates of unhealthy weight-control behaviors among adolescents: Implications for prevention programs. *Health Psychology, 22,* 88–98.

New York Times. (1995, June 26). "Back to sleep" effort is said to save 1500, p. 5.

New York Times. (2000a, September 12). Men, women, and battles of the bulges, p. D8.

New York Times. (2000b, October 3). Passing along the diet-and-binge habit, p. D8.

New York Times. (2001, May 22). Diabetics reminded of heart risk, p. D8.

New York Times. (2002a, March 25). Drinking still on rise at women's colleges. p. A16.

Newcomb, M. D., Rabow, J., Monte, M., & Hernandez, A. C. R. (1991). Informal drunk driving intervention: Psychosocial correlates among young adult women and men. *Journal of Applied Social Psychology, 21,* 1988–2006.

Newman, S. (1984). The psychological consequences of cerebrovascular accident and head injury. In R. Fitzpatrick et al. (Eds.), *The experience of illness.* London, England: Tavistock.

Newsom, J. T., & Schulz, R. (1998). Caregiving from the recipient's perspective: Negative reactions to being helped. *Health Psychology, 17,* 172–181.

Newsom, J. T., Knapp, J. E., & Schulz, R. (1996). Longitudinal analysis of specific domains of internal control and depressive symptoms in patients with recurrent cancer. *Health Psychology, 15,* 323–331.

Newton, T. L., & Sanford, J. M. (2003). Conflict structure moderates associations between cardiovascular reactivity and negative marital interaction. *Health Psychology, 22,* 270–278.

Neylan, T. C., et al. (2002). Critical incident exposure and sleep quality in police officers. *Psychosomatic Medicine, 64,* 345–352.

Neylan, T. C., Metzler, T. J., Best, S. R., Weiss, D. S., Fagan, J. A., Liberman, A., et al. (2002). Critical incident exposure and sleep quality in police officers. *Psychosomatic Medicine, 64,* 345–352.

Ng, D. M., & Jeffery, R. W. (2003). Relationships between perceived stress and health behaviors in a sample of working adults. *Health Psychology, 22,* 638–642.

Ni, H., & Cohen, R. (2002). *Trends in health insurance coverage by race/ethnicity among persons under 65 years of age: United States, 1997–2001.* National Center for Health Statistics. Retrieved from: www.cdc.gov/nchs/products/pubs/pubd/hestats/healthinsur.htm

Niaura, R., Banks, S. M., Ward, K. D., Stoney, C. M., Spiro, A., Aldwin, C. M., et al. (2000). Hostility and the metabolic syndrome in older males: The normative aging study. *Psychosomatic Medicine, 62,* 7–16.

Niaura, R., Todaro, J. F., Stroud, L., Spiro, A., III, Ward, K. D., & Weiss, S. (2002). Hostility, the metabolic syndrome and incident coronary heart disease. *Health Psychology, 21,* 588–593.

Nicassio, P. M., Radojevic, V., Schoenfeld-Smith, K., & Dwyer, K. (1995). The contribution of family cohesion and the pain-coping process to depressive symptoms in fibromyalgia. *Annals of Behavioral Medicine, 17,* 349–356.

Nichol, K. L., Nordin, J., Mullooly, J., Lask, R., Fillbrandt, K., & Iwane, M. (2003). Influenza vaccination and reduction in hospitalizations for cardiac disease and stroke among the elderly. *New England Journal of Medicine, 348,* 1322–1332, http:// www.nejm.org

Nides, M. A., Rakos, R. F., Gonzales, D., Murray, R. P., Tashkin, D. P., Bjornson-Benson, W. M., et al. (1995). Predictors of initial smoking cessation and relapse through the first two years of the Lung Health Study. *Journal of Consulting and Clinical Psychology, 63,* 60–69.

Nides, M. A., Rand, C., Dolce, J., Murray, R., O'Hara, P., Voelker, H., et al. (1994). Weight gain as a function of smoking cessation and 2-mg. nicotine gum use among middle-aged smokers with mild lung impairment in the first two years of the Lung Health Study. *Health Psychology, 13,* 354–361.

Nielsen, S. J., & Popkin, B. M. (2003). Patterns and trends in food portion sizes, 1977–1998. *Journal of the American Medical Association, 289,* 450–453.

Niemcryk, S. J., Jenkins, S. D., Rose, R. M., & Hurst, M. W. (1987). The prospective impact of psychosocial variables on rates of illness and injury in professional employees. *Journal of Occupational Medicine, 29,* 645–652.

Niemi, M. L., Laaksonen, R., Kotila, M., & Waltimo, O. (1988). Quality of life 4 years after stroke. *Stroke, 19,* 1101–1107.

Nigg, C. R. (2001). Explaining adolescent exercise behavior change: A longitudinal application of the transtheoretical model. *Annals of Behavioral Medicine, 23,* 11–20.

Nivison, M. E., & Endresen, I. M. (1993). An analysis of relationships among environmental noise, annoyance and sensitivity to noise, and the consequences for health and sleep. *Journal of Behavioral Medicine, 16,* 257–271.

Nolan, R. P., Wilson, E., Shuster, M., Rowe, B. H., Stewart, D., & Zambon, S. (1999). Readiness to perform cardiopulmonary resuscitation: An emerging strategy against sudden cardiac death. *Psychosomatic Medicine, 61,* 546–551.

Nolen-Hoeksema, S., McBride, A., & Larson, J. (1997). Rumination and psychological distress among bereaved partners. *Journal of Personality and Social Psychology, 72,* 855–862.

Norman, P., Conner, M., & Bell, R. (1999). The theory of planned behavior and smoking cessation. *Health Psychology, 18,* 89–94.

Northouse, L., Templin, T., & Mood, D. (2001). Couples' adjustment to breast disease during the first year following diagnosis. *Journal of Behavioral Medicine, 24,* 115–136.

Novak, S. P., & Clayton, R. R. (2001). The influence of school environment and self-regulation on transitions between stages of cigarette smoking: A multilevel analysis. *Health Psychology, 20,* 196–207.

Novotny, T. E., Romano, R. A., Davis, R. M., & Mills, S. L. (1992). The public health practice of tobacco control: Lessons learned and directions for the states in the 1990s. *Annual Review of Public Health, 13,* 287–318.

Nowack, R. (1992). Final ethics: Dutch discover euthanasia abuse. *Journal of NIH Research, 4,* 31–32.

Noyes, R., et al. (2000). Illness fears in the general population. *Psychosomatic Medicine, 62,* 318–325.

Noyes, R., Jr., Stuart, S. P., Langbehn, D. R., Happel, R. L., Longley, S. L., Muller, B. A., et al. (2003). Test of an interpersonal model of hypochondriasis. *Psychosomatic Medicine, 65,* 292–300.

Nurses' Health Study (2004). History. Retrieved August 1, 2004 from http://www.channing.harvard.edu/nhs/history/index.shtml

Nyamathi, A., Stein, J. A., & Brecht, M. L. (1995). Psychosocial predictors of AIDS risk behavior and drug use behavior in homeless and drug addicted women of color. *Health Psychology, 14,* 265–273.

Nyklicek, I., Vingerhoets, A. J. J. M., Van Heck, G. L., & Van Limpt, M. C. A. M. (1998). Defensive coping in relation to casual blood pressure and self-reported daily hassles and life events. *Journal of Behavioral Medicine, 21,* 145–161.

O'Brien, A., Fries, E., & Bowen, D. (2000). The effect of accuracy of perceptions of dietary-fat intake on perceived risk and intentions to change. *Journal of Behavioral Medicine, 23,* 465–473.

O'Byrne, K. K., Peterson, L., & Saldana, L. (1997). Survey of pediatric hospitals' preparation programs: Evidence of the impact of health psychology research. *Health Psychology, 16,* 147–154.

O'Carroll, R. E., Ayling, R., O'Reilly, S. M., & North, N. T. (2003). Alexithymia and sense of coherence in patients with total spinal cord transection. *Psychosomatic Medicine, 65,* 151–155.

O'Leary, A., Goodhardt, F., Jemmott, L. S., & Boccher-Lattimore, D. (1992). Predictors of safer sex on the college campus: A social cognitive theory analysis. *Journal of American College Health, 40,* 254–263.

O'Leary, A., Shoor, S., Lorig, K., & Holman, H. R. (1988). A cognitive-behavioral treatment for rheumatoid arthritis. *Health Psychology, 7,* 527–544.

O'Neil, J. (2003, January 21). When aspirin can't help a heart. *The New York Times,* p. D6.

O'Neil, J. (2004, April 20). Statins and diabetes: New advice. *The New York Times,* p. D6.

Obesity: Definitions, facts, statistics. (2000). Retrieved June 6, 2001, from: http://www.coloradohealthnet.org/obesity/obs_stats.html

Ockene, J. K. (1992). Are we pushing the limits of public health interventions for smoking cessation? *Health Psychology, 11,* 277–279.

Ockene, J. K., Emmons, K. M., Mermelstein, R. J., Perkins, K. A., Bonollo, D. S., Voorhees, C. C., et al. (2000). Relapse and maintenance issues for smoking cessation. *Health Psychology, 19,* 17–31.

Odendaal, J. S. J., & Meintjes, R. A. (2002). Neurophysiological correlates of affiliative behaviour between humans and dogs. *Veterinary Journal, 165,* 296–301.

Offerman, L. R., & Gowing, M. K. (1990). Organizations of the future: Changes and challenges. *American Psychologist, 45,* 95–109.

Ogden, J. (2003). Some problems with social cognition models: A pragmatic and conceptual analysis. *Health Psychology, 22,* 424–428.

Oken, D. (2002). Multiaxial diagnosis and the psychosomatic model of disease. *Psychosomatic Medicine, 62,* 171–175.

Oleck, J. (2001, April 23). Dieting: More fun with a buddy? *BusinessWeek,* 16.

Oliver, G., Wardle, J., & Gibson, E. L. (2000). Stress and food choice: A laboratory study. *Psychosomatic Medicine, 62,* 853–865.

Organisation for Economic Co-operation and Development. (2004). *OECD health data, 2004.* Retrieved from: http://www.oecd.org/dataoecd/3/62/31938359.pdf

Orleans, C. T. (2000). Promoting the maintenance of health behavior change: Recommendations for the next generation of research and practice. *Health Psychology, 19,* 76–83.

Orleans, C. T., & Barnett, L. R. (1984). Bulimarexia: Guidelines for behavioral assessment and treatment. In R. C. Hawkins, W. J. Fremouw, & P. F. Clement (Eds.), *The binge-purge syndrome* (pp. 144–182). New York: Springer.

Oslin, D. W., Sayers, S., Ross, J., Kane, V., Have, T. T., Conigliaro, J., et al. (2003). Disease management for depression and at-risk drinking via telephone in an older population of veterans. *Psychosomatic Medicine, 65,* 931–937.

Osman, A., Breitenstein, J. L., Barrios, F. X., Gutierrez, P. M., & Kopper, B. A. (2002). The Fear of Pain questionnaire-III: Further reliability and validity with nonclinical samples. *Journal of Behavioral Medicine, 25,* 155–173.

Osterhaus, S., Lange, A., Linssen, W., & Passchier, J. (1997). A behavioral treatment of young migrainous and nonmigrainous headache patients: Prediction of treatment success. *International Journal of Behavioral Medicine, 4,* 378–396.

Osterweis, M. (1985). Bereavement care: Special opportunities for hospice. In K. Gardner (Ed.), *Quality of care for the terminally ill: An examination of the issues* (pp. 131–135). Chicago: Joint Commission on Accreditation of Hospitals.

Owens, I. P. F. (2002, September 20). Sex differences in mortality rate. *Science's Compass,* 2008–2009.

Owens, J. F., Matthews, K. A., Wing, R. R., & Kuller, L. H. (1990). Physical activity and cardiovascular risk: A cross-sectional study of middle-aged premenopausal women. *Preventive Medicine, 19,* 147–157.

Pacchetti, C., Mancini, F., Aglieri, R., Fundaro, C., Martignoni, E., & Nappi, G. (2000). Active music therapy in Parkinson's disease: An integrative method for motor and emotional rehabilitation. *Psychosomatic Medicine, 62,* 386–393.

Paffenbarger, R. S., Jr., Hyde, R. T., Wing, A. L., & Hsieh, C. C. (1986). Physical activity, all-cause mortality, and longevity of college alumni. *New England Journal of Medicine, 314,* 605–613.

Paffenbarger, R. S., Jr., Hyde, R. T., Wing, A. L., & Steinmetz, C. H. (1984). A natural history of athleticism and cardiovascular health. *Journal of the American Medical Association, 222,* 491–495.

Pagoto, S., McChargue, D., & Fuqua, R. W. (2003). Effects of a multicomponent intervention on motivation and sun protection behaviors among Midwestern beachgoers. *Health Psychology, 22,* 429–433.

Pakenham, K. I. (1999). Adjustment to multiple sclerosis: Application of a stress and coping model. *Health Psychology, 18,* 383–392.

Palmer, C. E., & Noble, D. N. (1986). Premature death: Dilemmas of infant mortality. *Social Casework: Journal of Contemporary Social Work, 67,* 332–339.

Palmer, S. C., Kagee, A., Coyne, J. C., & DeMichele, A. (2004). Experience of trauma, distress, and posttraumatic stress disorder among breast cancer patients. *Psychosomatic Medicine, 66,* 258–264.

Pampel, F. C. (2001). Cigarette diffusion and sex differences in smoking. *Journal of Health and Social Behavior, 42,* 388–404.

Pardine, P., & Napoli, A. (1983). Physiological reactivity and recent life-stress experience. *Journal of Consulting and Clinical Psychology, 51,* 467–469.

Park, C. L., & Adler, N. E. (2003). Coping style as a predictor of health and well-being across the first year of medical school. *Health Psychology, 22,* 627–631.

Park, E., Eaton, C. A., Goldstein, M. G., DePue, J., Niaura, R., Guadagnoli, E., MacDonald Gross, N., & Dube, C. (2001). The development of a decisional balance measure of physician smoking cessation interventions. *Preventive Medicine, 33,* pp. 261–267.

Park, E. R., DePue, J. D., Goldstein, M. G., Niaura, R., Harlow, L. L., Willey, C., Rakowski, W., Prokhorov, A. V., (2003). Assessing the transtheoretical model of change constructs for physicians counseling smokers. *Annals of Behavioral Medicine, 25,* 120–126.

Parker, J. C., Frank, R. G., Beck, N. C., Smarr, K. L., Buescher, K. L., Phillips, L. R., et al. (1988). Pain management in rheumatoid arthritis patients: A cognitive-behavioral approach. *Arthritis and Rheumatism, 31,* 593–601.

Parker, P. A., & Kulik, J. A. (1995). Burnout, self- and supervisor-rated job performance, and absenteeism among nurses. *Journal of Behavioral Medicine, 18,* 581–600.

Parker, S. L., Tong, T., Bolden, S., & Wingo, P. A. (1996). Cancer statistics. *CA: A Cancer Journal for Clinicians, 46,* 5–28.

Parkinson's Disease Foundation. (2002). *Parkinson's disease: An overview. What is Parkinson's disease?* Retrieved from: http://www.pdf.org/AboutPD/

Parsons, T. (1954). The professions and the social structure. In T. Parsons, (Ed.), *Essays in sociological theory* (pp. 34–49). New York: Free Press.

Pasch, L. A., & Dunkel-Schetter, C. (1997). Fertility problems: Complex issues faced by women and couples. In S. J. Gallant, G. P. Keita, & R. Royak-Schaler (Eds.), *Health care for women: Psychological, social, and behavioral influences* (pp. 187–202). Washington, D.C.: American Psychological Association.

Pasic, J., Levy, W. C., & Sullivan, M.D. (2003). Cytokines in depression and heart failure. *Psychosomatic Medicine, 65,* 181–193.

Patenaude, A. F., Guttmacher, A. E., & Collins, F. S. (2002). Genetic testing and psychology: New roles, new responsibilities. *American Psychologist, 57,* 271–282.

Patterson, S. M., Marsland, A. L., Manuck, S. B., Kameneva, M., & Muldoon, M. F. (1998). Acute hemoconcentration during psychological stress: Assessment of hemorheologic factors. *International Journal of Behavioral Medicine, 5,* 204–212.

Patterson, T. L., Sallis, J. F., Nader, P. R., Rupp, J. W., McKenzie, T. L., Roppe, B., et al. (1988). Direct observation of physical activity and dietary behaviors in a structured environment: Effects of a family-based health promotion program. *Journal of Behavioral Medicine, 11,* 447–458.

Patterson, T. L., Shaw, W. S., & Semple, S. J. (2003). Reducing the sexual risk behaviors of HIV + individuals: Outcome of a randomized controlled trial. *Annals of Behavioral Medicine, 25,* 137–145.

Pavalko, E. K., & Woodbury, S. (2000). Social roles as process: Caregiving careers and women's health. *Journal of Health and Social Behavior, 41,* 91–105.

Pavalko, E. K., Elder, G. H., Jr., & Clipp, E. C. (1993). Worklives and longevity: Insights from a life course perspective. *Journal of Health and Social Behavior, 34,* 363–380.

Pavalko, E. K., Mossakowski, K. N., & Hamilton, V. J. (2003). Does perceived discrimination affect health? Longitudinal relationships between work discrimination and women's physical and emotional health. *Journal of Health and Social Behavior, 43,* 18–33.

Pearlin, L. I., & Schooler, C. (1978). The structure of coping. *Journal of Health and Social Behavior, 19,* 2–21.

Pearson, H. (2004, April 8). Public health: The demon drink. *Nature, 428,* 598–600.

Peck, C. L., & King, N. J. (1982). Increasing patient compliance with prescriptions. *Journal of the American Medical Association, 248,* 2874–2877.

Peckerman, A., LaManca, J. J., Qureishi, B., Dahl, K. A., Golfetti, R., Yamamoto, Y., et al. (2003). Baroreceptor reflex and integrative stress responses in chronic fatigue syndrome. *Psychosomatic Medicine, 65,* 889–895.

Peeters, A., Barendregt, J. J., Willekens, F., Mackenbach, J. P., Mamun, A. A., & Bonneux, L. (2003). Obesity in adulthood and its consequences for life expectancy: A life-table analysis. *Annals of Internal Medicine, 138,* 24–32.

Peirce, R. S., Frone, M. R., Russell, M., & Cooper, M. L. (1994). Relationship of financial strain and psychosocial resources to alcohol use and abuse: The mediating role of negative affect and drinking motives. *Journal of Health and Social Behavior, 35,* 291–308.

Penedo, F. J., Gonzalez, J. S., Davis, C., Dahn, J., Antoni, M. H., Ironson, G., et al. (2003). Coping and psychological distress among symptomatic HIV+ men who have sex with men. *Annals of Behavioral Medicine, 25,* 203–213.

Penick, S. B., Filion, R., Fox, S., & Stunkard, A. J. (1971). Behavior modification in the treatment of obesity. *Psychosomatic Medicine, 33,* 49–55.

Penley, J. A., Tomaka, J., & Wiebe, J. S. (2002). The association of coping to physical and psychological health outcomes: A meta-analytic review. *Journal of Behavioral Medicine, 25,* 551–603.

Pennebaker, J. W. (1980). Perceptual and environmental determinants of coughing. *Basic and Applied Social Psychology, 1,* 83–91.

Pennebaker, J. W. (1983). Accuracy of symptom perception. In A. Baum, S. E. Taylor, & J. Singer (Eds.), *Handbook of psychology and health* (Vol. 4, pp. 189–218). Hillsdale, NJ: Erlbaum.

Pennebaker, J. W. (1997). Writing about emotional experiences as a therapeutic process. *Psychological Science, 8,* 162–166.

Pennebaker, J. W., & Beall, S. (1986). Confronting a traumatic event: Toward an understanding of inhibition and disease. *Journal of Abnormal Psychology, 95,* 274–281.

Pennebaker, J. W., & O'Heeron, R. C. (1984). Confiding in others and illness rates among spouses of suicide and accidental death victims. *Journal of Abnormal Psychology, 93,* 473–476.

Pennebaker, J. W., Colder, M., & Sharp, L. K. (1990). Accelerating the coping process. *Journal of Personality and Social Psychology, 58,* 528–537.

Pennebaker, J. W., Hughes, C., & O'Heeron, R. C. (1987). The psychophysiology of confession: Linking inhibitory and psychosomatic processes. *Journal of Personality and Social Psychology, 52,* 781–793.

Pennebaker, J. W., Kiecolt-Glaser, J., & Glaser, R. (1988). Disclosure of traumas and immune function: Health implications for psychotherapy. *Journal of Consulting and Clinical Psychology, 56,* 239–245.

Penninx, B. W. J. H., van Tilburg, T., Boeke, A. J. P., Deeg, D. J. H., Kriegsman, D. M. W., & van Eijk, J. T. M. (1998). Effects of social support and personal coping resources on depressive symptoms: Different for various chronic diseases? *Health Psychology, 17,* 551–558.

Pereira, D. B., Antoni, M. H., Danielson, A., Simon, T., Efantis-Potter, J., Carver, C. S., Duran, R. E. F., Ironson, G., Klimas, N., & O'Sullivan, M. (2003). Life stress and cervical squamous intraepithelial lesions in women with human papillomavirus and human immunodeficiency virus. *Psychosomatic Medicine, 65,* 427–434.

Perez, M. A., Skinner, E. C., & Meyerowitz, B. E. (2002). Sexuality and intimacy following radical prostatectomy: Patient and partner. *Health Psychology, 21,* 288–293.

Pérez-Peña, R., & Glickson, G. (2003, November 29). As obesity rises, so do indignities in health care. *The New York Times,* pp. A1, A13.

Perkins, K. A. (1985). The synergistic effect of smoking and serum cholesterol on coronary heart disease. *Health Psychology, 4,* 337–360.

Perkins, K. A., Broge, M., Gerlach, D., Sanders, M., Grobe, J. E., Cherry, C., et al. (2002). Acute nicotine reinforcement, but not chronic tolerance, predicts withdrawal and relapse after quitting smoking. *Health Psychology, 21,* 332–339.

Perkins, K. A., Dubbert, P. M., Martin, J. E., Faulstich, M. E., & Harris, J. K. (1986). Cardiovascular reactivity to psychological stress in aerobically trained versus untrained mild hypertensives and normotensives. *Health Psychology, 5,* 407–421.

Perkins, K. A., Levine, M., Marcus, M. D., & Shiffman, S. (1997). Addressing women's concerns about weight gain due to smoking cessation. *Journal of Substance Abuse Treatment, 14,* 1–10.

Perkins, K. A., Rohay, J., Meilahn, E. N., Wing, R. R., Matthews, K. A., & Kuller, L. H. (1993). Diet, alcohol, and physical activity as a function of smoking status in middle-aged women. *Health Psychology, 12,* 410–415.

Perlis, M., Aloia, M., Millikan, A., Boehmler, J., Smith, M., Greenblatt, D., et al. (2000). Behavioral treatment of insomnia: A clinical case series study. *Journal of Behavioral Medicine, 23,* 149–161.

Perlis, M. L., Sharpe, M., Smith, M. T., Greenblatt, D., & Giles, D. (2001). Behavioral treatment of insomnia: Treatment outcome and the relevance of medical and psychiatric morbidity. *Journal of Behavioral Medicine, 24,* 281–296.

Perna, F. M., & McDowell, S. L. (1995). Role of psychological stress in cortisol recovery from exhaustive exercise among elite athletes. *International Journal of Behavioral Medicine, 2,* 13–26.

Perri, M. G., Anton, S. D., Durning, P. E., Ketterson, T. U., Sydeman, S. J., Berlant, N. E., et al. (2002). Adherence to exercise prescriptions: Effects of prescribing moderate versus higher levels of intensity and frequency. *Health Psychology, 21,* 452–458.

Persky, V. W., Kempthorne-Rawson, J., & Shekelle, R. B. (1987). Personality and risk of cancer: 20-year follow-up of the Western Electric study. *Psychosomatic Medicine, 49,* 435–449.

Pervin, L. A. (1968). Performance and satisfaction as a function of individual-environment fit. *Psychological Bulletin, 69,* 56–68.

Perz, C. A., DiClemente, C. C., & Carbonari, J. P. (1996). Doing the right thing at the right time? The interaction of stages and processes of change in successful smoking cessation. *Health Psychology, 15,* 462–468.

Pescosolido, B. A., Tuch, S. A., & Martin, J. K. (2001). The profession of medicine and the public: Examining Americans' changing confidence in physician authority from the beginning of the 'health care crisis' to the era of health care reform. *Journal of Health and Social Behavior, 42,* 1–16.

Peters, M., Godaert, G., Ballieux, R., Brosschot, J., Sweep, F., Swinkels, L., et al. (1999). Immune responses to experimental stress: Effects of mental effort and uncontrollability. *Psychosomatic Medicine, 61,* 513–524.

Peterson, C., Seligman, M. E. P., & Vaillant, G. E. (1988). Pessimistic explanatory style is a risk factor for physical illness: A thirty-five-year longitudinal study. *Journal of Personality and Social Psychology, 55,* 23–27.

Peterson, L. & Soldana, L. (1996). Accelerating children's risk for injury: Mother's decisions regarding common safety rules. *Journal of Behavioral Medicine, 19,* 317–332.

Peterson, L., & Toler, S. M. (1986). An information seeking disposition in child surgery patients. *Health Psychology, 5,* 343–358.

Peterson, L., Farmer, J., & Kashani, J. H. (1990). Parental injury prevention endeavors: A function of health beliefs? *Health Psychology, 9,* 177–191.

Petrie, K. J., & Weinman, J. A. (Eds.). (1997). *Perceptions of health and illness: Current research and applications.* Reading, England: Harwood Academic.

Petrie, K. J., & Wessely, S. (2002). Modern worries, new technology, and medicine. *British Journal of Medicine, 324,* 690–691.

Petrie, K. J., Booth, R. J., Pennebaker, J. W., Davison, K. P., & Thomas, M. G. (1995). Disclosure of trauma and immune response to a hepatitis B vaccination program. *Journal of Consulting and Clinical Psychology, 63,* 787–792.

Petrie, K. J., Buick, D., Weinman, J., & Booth, R. J. (1999). Positive effects of illness reported by myocardial infarction and breast cancer patients. *Journal of Psychosomatic Research, 47,* 537–543.

Petrie, K. J., Fontanilla, I., Thomas, M. G., Booth, R. J., & Pennebaker, J. W. (2004). Effect of written emotional expression on immune function in patients with human immunodeficiency virus: A randomized trial. *Psychosomatic Medicine, 66,* 272–275.

Petrovic, P., Kalso, E., Peterson, K. M., & Ingvar, M. (2002, March 1). Placebo and opioid analgesia – Imaging a shared neuronal network. *Science, 295,* 1737–1740.

Peyrot, M., McMurry, J. F., Jr., & Kruger, D. F. (1999). A biopsychosocial model of glycemic control in diabetes: Stress, coping and regimen adherence. *Journal of Health and Social Behavior, 40,* 141–158.

Pfeifer, J. E., & Brigham, J. C. (Eds.). (1996). Psychological perspectives on euthanasia. *Journal of Social Issues, 52* (entire issue).

Philips, H. C. (1983). Assessment of chronic headache behavior. In R. Meizack (Ed.), *Pain measurement and assessment* (pp. 97–104). New York: Raven Press.

Phillips, K. A., Kerlikowske, K., Baker, L. C., Chang, S. W., & Brown, M. L. (1998). Factors associated with women's adherence to mammography screening guidelines. *Health Services Research, 33,* 29–53.

Phipps, S., & Steele, R. (2002). Repressive adaptive style in children with chronic illness. *Psychosomatic Medicine, 64,* 34–42.

Phipps, S., Steele, R. G., Hall, K., & Leigh, L. (2001). Repressive adaptation in children with cancer: A replication and extension. *Health Psychology, 20,* 445–451.

Pickering, T. G., Devereux, R. B., James, G. D., Gerin, W., Landsbergis, P., Schnall, P. L., et al. (1996). Environmental influences on blood pressure and the role of job strain. *Journal of Hypertension, 14*(Suppl.), S179–S185.

Pickering, T. G., Schwartz, J. E., & James, G. D. (1995). Ambulatory blood pressure monitoring for evaluating the relationships between lifestyle, hypertension, and cardiovascular risk. *Clinical and Experimental Pharmacology and Physiology, 22,* 226–231.

Pickett, M. (1993). Cultural awareness in the context of terminal illness. *Cancer Nursing, 16,* 102–106.

Pierce, J. P., Choi, W. S., Gilpin, E. A., Farkas, A. J., & Merritt, R. K. (1996). Validation of susceptibility as a predictor of which adolescents take up smoking in the United States. *Health Psychology, 15,* 355–361.

Pignone, M. P., Gaynes, B. N., Rushton, J. L., Burchell, C. M., Orleans, C. T., Mulrow, C. D., et al. (2002). Screening for depression in adults: A summary of the evidence for the U.S. preventive services task force. *Annals of Internal Medicine, 136,* 765–776.

Pike, J., Smith, T., Hauger, R., Nicassio, P., Patterson, T., McClintock, J., et al. (1997). Chronic life stress alters sympathetic, neuroendocrine, and immune responsivity to an acute psychological stressor in humans. *Psychosomatic Medicine, 59,* 447–457.

Pike, K. M., & Rodin, J. (1991). Mothers, daughters, and disordered eating. *Journal of Abnormal Psychology, 100,* 1–7.

Pillow, D. R., Zautra, A. J., & Sandler, I. (1996). Major life events and minor stressors: Identifying mediational links in the stress process. *Journal of Personality and Social Psychology, 70,* 381–394.

Pinkerton, S. D., & Abramson, P. R. (1993). Evaluating the risks: A Bernoulli process model of HIV infection and risk reduction. *Evaluation Review, 17,* 504–528.

Pitman, D. L., Ottenweller, J. E., & Natelson, B. H. (1988). Plasma corticosterone levels during repeated presentation of two intensities of restraint stress: Chronic stress and habituation. *Physiology and Behavior, 43,* 47–55.

Plante, T. G., & Rodin, J. (1990). Physical fitness and enhanced psychological health. *Current Psychology: Research and Reviews, 9,* 3–24.

Plehn, K., Peterson, R. A., & Williams, D. A. (1998). Special anxiety, pain, and disability. *Journal of Occupational Rehabilitation, 8,* 213–222.

Plomin, R. (1998). Using DNA in health psychology. *Health Psychology, 17,* 53–55.

Plomin, R., Scheier, M. F., Bergeman, S. C., Pedersen, N. L., Nesselroade, J. R., & McClearn, G. E. (1992). Optimism, pessimism, and mental health: A twin/adoption study. *Personality and Individual Differences, 13,* 921–930.

Plumb, J. D., & Ogle, K. S. (1992). Hospice care. *Primary Care: Clinics in Office Practice, 19,* 807–820.

Polivy, J., & Herman, C. P. (1985). Dieting and binging: A causal analysis. *American Psychologist, 40,* 193–201.

Pollack, K. I., McBride, C. M., Baucom, D. H., Curry, S. J., Lando, H., Pirie, P. L., et al. (2001). Women's perceived and partners' reported support for smoking cessation during pregnancy. *Annals of Behavioral Medicine, 23,* 208–214.

Pollard, T. M., & Schwartz, J. E. (2003). Are changes in blood pressure and total cholesterol related to changes in mood? An 18-month study of men and women. *Health Psychology, 22,* 47–53.

Porter, L., Gil, K., Sedway, J., Ready, J., Workman, E., & Thompson, R., Jr. (1998). Pain and stress in sickle cell disease: An analysis of daily pain records. *International Journal of Behavioral Medicine, 5,* 185–203.

Porter, L. S., Mishel, M., Neelon, V., Belyea, M., Pisano, E., & Soo, M. S. (2003). Cortisol levels and responses to mammography screening in breast cancer survivors: A pilot study. *Psychosomatic Medicine, 65,* 842–848.

Powell, L. H., Hoffman, A., & Shahabi, L. (2001). Socioeconomic differential in health and disease: Let's take the next step. *Psychosomatic Medicine, 63,* 722–723.

Powell, L. H., Shahabi, L., & Thoresen, C. E. (2003). Religion and spirituality: Linkages to physical health. *American Psychologist, 58,* 36–52.

Powell, L. H., William, R. L., Matthews, K. A., Meyer, P., Midgley, A. R., Baum, A., et al. (2002). Physiologic markers of chronic stress in premenopausal, middle-aged women. *Psychosomatic Medicine, 64,* 502–509.

Power, M., Bullinger, M., Harper, A., & The World Health Organization Quality of Life Group. (1999). The World Health Organization WHOQOL-100: Tests of the universality of quality of life in 15 different cultural groups worldwide. *Health Psychology, 18,* 495–505.

Pradhan, A. D., Rifai, N., & Ridker, P. (2002). Soluble intercellular adhesion molecule-1, soluble vascular adhesion molecule-1, and the development of symptomatic peripheral arterial disease in men. *Circulation, 106,* 820–825.

Pratt, L. A., Ford, D. E., Crum, R. M., Armenian, H. K., Gallo, J. J., & Eaton, W. W. (1996). Depression, psychotropic medication, and risk of myocardial infarction. Prospective data from the Baltimore ECA follow-up. *Circulation, 94,* 3123–3129.

Pressman, E., & Orr, W. C. (Eds.). (1997). *Understanding sleep: The evolution and treatment of sleep disorders.* Washington, D.C.: American Psychological Association.

Presti, D. E., Ary, D. V., & Lichtenstein, E. (1992). The context of smoking initiation and maintenance: Findings from interviews with youths. *Journal of Substance Abuse, 4,* 35–45.

Preston, J., et al. (1998, December). The impact of a physician intervention program on older women's mammography use. *Evaluation and the Health Professions, 21,* 502–513.

Price, D. (2000, June 9). Psychological and neural mechanisms of the affective dimension of pain. *Science, 288,* 1769–1771.

Primeau, F. (1988). Post-stroke depression: A critical review of the literature. *Canadian Journal of Psychiatry, 33,* 757–765.

Pringle, B., Dahlquist, L. M., & Eskenazi, A. (2003). Memory in pediatric patients undergoing conscious sedation for aversive medical procedures. *Health Psychology, 22,* 263–269.

Prohaska, J. O. (1994). Strong and weak principles for progressing from precontemplation to action on the basis of 12 problem behaviors. *Health Psychology, 13,* 47–51.

Prohaska, J. O., & DiClemente, C. C. (1984a). Self change processes, self-efficacy, and decisional balance across five stages of smoking cessation. In A. R. Liss (Ed.), *Advances in cancer control: Epidemiology and research.* New York: Liss.

Prohaska, J. O., & DiClemente, C. C. (1984b). *The transtheoretical approach: Crossing traditional boundaries of therapy.* Chicago: Dow Jones/Irwin.

Prohaska, J. O., DiClemente, C. C., & Norcross, J. C. (1992). In search of how people change: Applications to addictive behaviors. *American Psychologist, 47,* 1102–1114.

Prohaska, J. O., Velicer, W. F., Rossi, J. S., Goldstein, M. G., Marcus, B. H., Rakowski, W., et al. (1994). Stages of change and decisional balance for 12 problem behaviors. *Health Psychology, 13,* 39–46.

Pruessner, J. C., Hellhammer, D. H., & Kirschbaum, C. (1999). Burnout, perceived stress, and cortisol responses to awakening. *Psychosomatic Medicine, 61,* 197–204.

Pruessner, M., Hellhammer, D. H., Pruessner, J. C., & Lupien, S. J. (2003). Self-reported depressive symptoms and stress levels in healthy young men: Associations with the cortisol response to awakening. *Psychosomatic Medicine, 65,* 92–99.

Pryor, D. B., Harrell, F. E., Lee, K. L., Califf, R. M., & Rosati, R. A. (1983). Estimating the likelihood of significant coronary artery disease. *American Journal of Medicine, 75,* 771–780.

Putt, A. M. (1970). One experiment in nursing adults with peptic ulcer. *Nursing Research, 19,* 484–494.

Quick, J. C. (1999). Occupational health psychology: Historical roots and future directions. *Health Psychology, 18,* 82–88.

Quinlan, K. B., & McCaul, K. D. (2000). Matched and mismatched interventions with young adult smokers: Testing a stage theory. *Health Psychology, 19,* 165–171.

Quittner, A. L., Espelage, D. L., Opipari, L. C., Carter, B., Eid, N., & Eigen, H. (1998). Role strain in couples with and without a child with a chronic illness: Associations with marital satisfaction, intimacy, and daily mood. *Health Psychology, 17,* 112–124.

Rabin, C., Ward, S., Leventhal, H., & Schmitz, M. (2001). Explaining retrospective reports of symptoms in patients undergoing chemotherapy: Anxiety, initial symptom experience and posttreatment symptoms. *Health Psychology, 20,* 91–98.

Rabkin, J. G., Ferrando, S. J., Lin, S., Sewell, M., & McElhiney, M. (2000). Psychological effects of HAART: A 2-year study. *Psychosomatic Medicine, 62,* 413–422.

Rabkin, J. G., McElhiney, M., Ferrando, S. J., Van Gorp, W., & Lin, S. H. (2004). Predictors of employment of men with HIV /AIDS: A longitudinal study. *Psychosomatic Medicine, 66,* 72–78.

Rachman, S. J., & Phillips, C. (1978). *Psychology and medicine.* Baltimore, MD: Penguin.

Radcliffe-Brown, A. R. (1964). *The Andaman Islanders.* New York: Free Press.

Radecki, C. M., & Jaccard, J. (1997). Psychological aspects of organ donation: A critical review and synthesis of individual and next-of-kin donation decisions. *Health Psychology, 16,* 183–195.

Raeburn, P., Forster, D., Foust, D., & Brady, D. (2002, October 21). Why we're so fat. *BusinessWeek,* pp. 112–114.

Raether, H. C., & Slater, R. C. (1977). Immediate postdeath activities in the United States. In H. Feifel (Ed.), *New meanings of death* (pp. 233–250). New York: McGraw-Hill.

Rahe, R. H., Mahan, J. L., & Arthur, R. J. (1970). Prediction of near-future health change from subjects' preceding life changes. *Journal of Psychosomatic Research, 14,* 401–406.

Rahe, R. H., Taylor, C. B., Tolles, R. L., Newhall, L. M., Veach, T. L., & Bryson, S. (2002). A novel stress and coping workplace program reduces illness and healthcare utilization. *Psychosomatic Medicine, 64,* 278–286.

Räikkönen, K., Matthews, K. A., & Salomon, K. (2003). Hostility predicts metabolic syndrome risk factors in children and adolescents. *Health Psychology, 22,* 297–286.

Räikkönen, K., Matthews, K. A., Flory, J. D., & Owens, J. F. (1999). Effects of hostility on ambulatory blood pressure and mood during daily living in healthy adults. *Health Psychology, 18,* 44–53.

Räikkönen, K., Matthews, K. A., Flory, J. D., Owens, J. F., & Gump, B. B. (1999). Effects of optimism, pessimism, and trait anxiety on ambulatory blood pressure and mood during everyday life. *Journal of Personality and Social Psychology, 76,* 104–113.

Räikkönen, K., Matthews, K. A., Kondwani, K. A., Bunker, C. H., Melhem, N. M., Ukoli, F. A. M., et al. (2004). Does nondipping of blood pressure at night reflect a trait of blunted cardiovascular responses to daily activities? *Annals of Behavioral Medicine, 27,* 131–137.

Rains, J. C., Penzien, D. B., & Jamison, R. N. (1992). A structured approach to the management of chronic pain. In L. VandeCreek, S. Knapp, & T. L. Jackson (Eds.), *Innovations in clinical practice: A source book* (Vol. 11, pp. 521–539). Sarasota, FL: Professional Resource Press.

Rakoff, V. (1983). Multiple determinants of family dynamics in anorexia nervosa. In P. L. Darby, P. E. Garfinkel, D. M. Garner, & D. V. Coscina (Eds.), *Anorexia nervosa: Recent developments in research* (pp. 29–40). New York: Liss.

Rakowski, W., Fulton, J. P., & Feldman, J. P. (1993). Women's decision making about mammography: A replication of the relationship between stages of adoption and decisional balance. *Health Psychology, 12,* 209–214.

Ramos, J. C. (1996, Fall). Doc in a box. *Time,* 55–57.

Raphael, K. G., Cloitre, M., & Dohrenwend, B. P. (1991). Problems of recall and misclassification with checklist methods of measuring stressful life events. *Health Psychology, 10,* 62–74.

Rapoff, M. A., & Christophersen, E. R. (1982). Improving compliance in pediatric practice. *Pediatric Clinics of North America, 29,* 339–357.

Raven, B. H., Freeman, H. E., & Haley, R. W. (1982). Social science perspectives in hospital infection control. In A. W. Johnson, O. Grusky, & B. Raven (Eds.), *Contemporary health services: Social science perspectives* (pp. 139–176). Boston, MA: Auburn House.

Raynor, D. A., Pogue-Geile, M. F., Kamarck, T. W., McCaffery, J. M., & Manuck, S. B. (2002). Covariation of psychosocial characteristics associated with cardiovascular disease: Genetic and environmental influences. *Psychosomatic Medicine, 64,* 191–203.

Reaby, L. L., & Hort, L. K. (1995). Postmastectomy attitudes in women who wear external breast prostheses compared to those who have undergone breast reconstruction. *Journal of Behavioral Medicine, 18,* 55–68.

Reaney, P. (1998, November 19). *Chinese tobacco deaths to soar to 3 million.* Reuters News Service, www.reuters.com

Rebuffe-Scrive, M., Walsh, U. A., McEwen, B., & Rodin, J. (1992). Effect of chronic stress and exogenous glucocorticoids on regional fat distribution and metabolism. *Physiology and Behavior, 52,* 583–590.

Redd, W. H., Jacobsen, P. B., Die-Trill, M., Dematis, H., McEvoy, M., & Holland, J. C. (1987). Cognitive/attentional distraction in the control of conditioned nausea in pediatric cancer patients receiving chemotherapy. *Journal of Consulting and Clinical Psychology, 3,* 391–395.

Redman, S., Webb, G. R., Hennrikus, D. J., Gordon, J. J., & Sanson-Fisher, R. W. (1991). The effects of gender on diagnosis of psychological disturbance. *Journal of Behavioral Medicine, 14,* 527–540.

Redwine, L., Dang, J., Hall, M., & Irwin, M. (2003). Disordered sleep, nocturnal cytokines, and immunity in alcoholics. *Psychosomatic Medicine, 65,* 75–85.

Redwine, L., Snow, S., Mills, P., & Irwin, M. (2003). Acute psychological stress: Effects in chemotaxosis and cellular adhesion molecule expression. *Psychosomatic Medicine, 65,* 598–603.

Reed, G. M. (1989). *Stress, coping, and psychological adaptation in a sample of gay and bisexual men with AIDS.* Unpublished doctoral dissertation, University of California, Los Angeles.

Reed, G. M., Kemeny, M. E., Taylor, S. E., Wang, H. Y. J., & Visscher, B. R. (1994). Realistic acceptance as a predictor of decreased survival time in gay men with AIDS. *Health Psychology, 13,* 299–307.

Reed, G. M., Kemeny, M. E., Taylor, S. E., & Visscher, B. R. (1999). Negative HIV-specific expectancies and AIDS-related bereavement as predictors of symptom onset in asymptomatic HIV-positive gay men. *Health Psychology, 18,* 354–363.

Reid, G., Chambers, C., McGrath, P., & Finley, G. A. (1997). Coping with pain and surgery: Children's and parents' perspectives. *International Journal of Behavioral Medicine, 4,* 339–363.

Reif, J. S., Dunn, K., Ogilvie, G. K., & Harris, C. K. (1992). Passive smoking and canine lung cancer risk. *American Journal of Epidemiology, 135,* 234–239.

Reinhardt, U. E. (2004, March 12). Health care in the service of science? *Science, 303,* 1613–1614.

Reitman, V. (2003a, March 24). Healing sound of a word: 'Sorry.' *Los Angeles Times,* pp. F1, F8.

Reitman, V. (2003b, July 7). Heart attacks in young women. *Los Angeles Times,* pp. F1, F4.

Rejeski, W. J., Brawley, L. R., Ambrosius, W. T., Brubaker, P. H., Focht, B. C., Foy, C. G., & Fox, L. D. (2003). Older adults with chronic disease: Benefits of group-mediated counseling in the promotion of physically active lifestyles. *Health Psychology, 22,* 414–423.

Religioustolerance.org (2004). *Religious beliefs of Americans: Reliability of polling data.* Retrieved August 1, 2004 from http://www.religioustolerance.org/chr_poll2.htm

Remennick, L., & Shtarkshall, R. (1997). Technology versus responsibility: Immigrant physicians from the former Soviet Union on Israeli health care. *Journal of Health and Social Behavior, 38,* 191–202.

Renneker, R., & Cutler, M. (1952). Psychological problems of adjustment to cancer of the breast. *Journal of the American Medical Association, 148,* 833–838.

Repetti, R. L. (1989). Effects of daily workload on subsequent behavior during marital interactions: The role of social withdrawal and spouse support. *Journal of Personality and Social Psychology, 57,* 651–659.

Repetti, R. L. (1993a). The effects of workload and the social environment at work on health. In L. Goldberger & S. Bresnitz (Eds.), *Handbook of stress* (pp. 368–385). New York: Free Press.

Repetti, R. L. (1993b). Short-term effects of occupational stressors on daily mood and health complaints. *Health Psychology, 12,* 125–131.

Repetti, R. L., & Pollina, S. L. (1994). *The effects of daily social and academic failure experiences on school-age children's subsequent interactions with parents.* Unpublished manuscript, University of California, Los Angeles.

Repetti, R. L., Matthews, K. A., & Waldron, I. (1989). Employment and women's health. *American Psychologist, 44,* 1394–1401.

Repetti, R. L., Taylor, S. E., & Seeman, T. E. (2002). Risky families: Family social environments and the mental and physical health of offspring. *Psychological Bulletin, 128,* 330–366.

Resnicow, K., DiIorio, C., Soet, J. E., Borrelli, B., Hecht, J., & Ernst, D. (2002). Motivational interviewing in health promotion: It sounds like something is changing. *Health Psychology, 21,* 444–451.

Revicki, D. A., & May, H. J. (1985). Occupational stress, social support, and depression. *Health Psychology, 4,* 61–77.

Reynolds, D. V. (1969). Surgery in the rat during electrical analgesia induced by focal brain stimulation. *Science, 164,* 444–445.

Reynolds, J. R. (1997). The effects of industrial employment conditions on job-related distress. *Journal of Health & Social Behavior, 38,* 105–116.

Reynolds, P., & Kaplan, G. (1986, March). *Social connections and cancer: A prospective study of Alameda County residents.* Paper presented at the annual meeting of the Society of Behavioral Medicine, San Francisco, CA.

Richards, J. C., Hof, A., & Alvarenga, M. (2000). Serum lipids and their relationships with hostility and angry affect and behaviors in men. *Health Psychology, 19,* 393–398.

Richardson, J. L., Marks, G., Johnson, C. A., Graham, J. W., Chan, K. K., Selser, J. N., et al. (1987). Path model of multidimensional compliance with cancer therapy. *Health Psychology, 6,* 183–207.

Richardson, L. (2004, January 9). Obesity blamed as disability rates soar for those under 60. *Los Angeles Times,* p. A22.

Richardson, S. A., Goodman, N., Hastorf, A. H., & Dornbusch, S. M. (1961). Cultural uniformity in reaction to physical disabilities. *American Sociological Review, 26,* 241–247.

Ridker, P. M., Rifai, N., Rose, L., Buring, J. E., & Cook, N. R. (2002). Comparison of c-reactive proteins and low-density lipoprotein cholesterol levels in the prediction of first cardiovascular events. *New England Journal of Medicine, 347,* 1557–1565. http://www.nejm.org

Rief, W., Hessel, A., & Braehler, E. (2001). Somatization symptoms and hypochondriachal features in the general population. *Psychosomatic Medicine, 63,* 595–602.

Riese, H., Houtman, I. L. D., Van Doornen, L. J. P., & De Geus, E. J. C. (2000). Job strain and risk indicators for cardiovascular disease in young female nurses. *Health Psychology, 19,* 429–440.

Rietschlin, J. (1998). Voluntary association membership and psychological distress. *Journal of Health and Social Behavior, 39,* 348–355.

Rigotti, N. A., Thomas, G. S., & Leaf, A. (1983). Exercise and coronary heart disease. *Annual Review of Medicine, 34,* 391–412.

Riley, M. W., Matarazzo, J. D., & Baum, A. (Eds.). (1987). *Perspectives in behavioral medicine: The aging dimension.* Hillsdale, NJ: Erlbaum.

Ringler, K. E. (1981). *Processes of coping with cancer chemotherapy.* Unpublished doctoral dissertation, University of Wisconsin, Madison.

Rini, C., Dunkel-Schetter, C., Wadhwa, P., & Sandman, C. (1999). Psychological adaptation and birth outcomes: The role of personal resources, stress, and sociocultural context in pregnancy. *Health Psychology, 18,* 333–345.

Ritz, T., & Steptoe, A. (2000). Emotion and pulmonary function in asthma: Reactivity in the field and relationship with laboratory induction of emotion. *Psychosomatic Medicine, 62,* 808–815.

Roan, S. (1993, April 6). Medicine turning its attention to women and heart disease. *Los Angeles Times.*

Roan, S. (2003, March 10). Diabetes study has wide reach. *Los Angeles Times,* p. F3.

Robbins, C. A., & Martin, S. S. (1993). Gender, styles of deviance, and drinking problems. *Journal of Health and Social Behavior, 34,* 302–321.

Robbins, M. A., Elias, M. F., Croog, S. H., & Colton, T. (1994). Unmedicated blood pressure levels and quality of life in elderly hypertensive women. *Psychosomatic Medicine, 56,* 251–259.

Roberts, A. H., Kewman, D. G., Mercier, L., & Hovell, M. (1993). The power of nonspecific effects in healing: Implications for psychosocial and biological treatments. *Clinical Psychology Review, 13,* 375–391.

Roberts, M. C., & Turner, D. S. (1984). Preventing death and injury in childhood: A synthesis of child safety seat efforts. *Health Education Quarterly, 11,* 181–193.

Roberts, R. E., Strawbridge, W. J., Deleger, S., & Kaplan, G. A. (2002). Are the fat more jolly? *Annals of Behavioral Medicine, 24,* 169–180.

Robertson, E. K., & Suinn, R. M. (1968). The determination of rate of progress of stroke patients through empathy measures of patient and family. *Journal of Psychosomatic Research, 12,* 189–191.

Robinson, D. (1979). *Talking out of alcoholism: The self-help process of Alcoholics Anonymous.* London, England: Croom, Helm.

Robinson, R. G. (1986). Post-stroke mood disorder. *Hospital Practice, 21,* 83–89.

Robinson, R. G., & Price, T. R. (1982). Poststroke depressive disorders: A follow-up study of 103 patients. *Stroke, 13,* 635–640.

Robinson, R. R. (Ed.). (1974). *Proceedings of the Frances E. Camp International Symposium on Sudden and Unexpected Deaths in Infancy.* Toronto: Canadian Foundation for the Study of Infant Deaths.

Robinson, T. N. (1999). Reducing children's television viewing to prevent obesity. *Journal of the American Medical Association, 282,* 1561–1567.

Rodin, G., & Voshart, K. (1986). Depression in the medically ill: An overview. *American Journal of Psychiatry, 143,* 696–705.

Rodin, J. (1990). Comparative effects of fructose, aspartame, glucose, and water preloads on calorie and macronutrient intake. *American Journal of Clinical Nutrition, 51,* 428–435.

Rodin, J. (1991). Effects of pure sugar versus mixed starch fructose loads on food intake. *Appetite, 17,* 213–219.

Rodin, J., & Ickovics, J. R. (1990). Women's health: Review and research agenda as we approach the 21st century. *American Psychologist, 45,* 1018–1034.

Rodin, J., & McAvay, G. (1992). Determinants of change in perceived health in a longitudinal study of older adults. *Journal of Gerontology, 47,* P373–P384.

Rodin, J., & Plante, T. (1989). The psychological effects of exercise. In R. S. Williams & A. Wellece (Eds.), *Biological effects of physical activity* (pp. 127–137). Champaign, IL: Human Kinetics.

Rodin, J., Elias, M., Silberstein, L. R., & Wagner, A. (1988). Combined behavioral and pharmacologic treatment for obesity: Predictors of successful weight maintenance. *Journal of Consulting and Clinical Psychology, 56,* 399–404.

Roitt, I., Brostoff, J., & Male, D. (1998). *Immunology* (5th ed.). London, England: Mosby International Limited.

Rokke, P. D., & Al Absi, M. (1992). Matching pain coping strategies to the individual: A prospective validation of the cognitive coping strategy inventory. *Journal of Behavioral Medicine, 15,* 611–626.

Rollman, B. L., & Shear, M. K. (2003). Depression and medical comorbidity: Red flags for current suicidal ideation in primary care. *Psychosomatic Medicine, 65,* 506–507.

Roman, M. J., Shanker, B. A., Davis, A., Lockshin, M. D., Sammaritano, L., Simantov, R., et al. (2003). Prevalence and correlates of accelerated atherosclerosis in systematic lupus erythematosus. *New England Journal of Medicine, 349,* 2399–2406, http://www.nejm.org

Ronis, D. L. (1992). Conditional health threats: Health beliefs, decisions, and behaviors among adults. *Health Psychology, 11,* 127–134.

Rook, K. S. (1984). The negative side of social interaction: Impact on psychological well-being. *Journal of Personality and Social Psychology, 46,* 1097–1108.

Rosal, M. C., Ockene, J. K., Yunsheng, M., Hebert, J. R., Ockene, I. S., Merriam, P., & Hurley, T. G. (1998). Coronary artery smoking intervention study (CASIS): 5-year follow-up. *Health Psychology, 17,* 476–478.

Rose, J. S., Chassin, L., Presson, C. C., & Sherman, S. J. (1996). Prospective predictors of quit attempts and smoking cessation in young adults. *Health Psychology, 15,* 261–268.

Rose, L. A., DeVellis, B. M., Howard, G., & Mutran, E. (1996). Prescribing of schedule II pain medications in ambulatory medical care settings. *Annals of Behavioral Medicine, 18,* 165–171.

Rosen, J. C., & Gross, J. (1987). Prevalence of weight reducing and weight gaining in adolescent girls and boys. *Health Psychology, 6,* 131–147.

Rosenblatt, R. A. (2001, May 5). Gains found in numbers, health of the elderly. *Los Angeles Times,* pp. A1, A6.

Rosenfield, S. (1992). The costs of sharing: Wives' employment and husbands' mental health. *Journal of Health and Social Behavior, 33,* 213–225.

Rosenman, R. H. (1978). The interview method of assessment of the coronary-prone behavior pattern. In T. Dembroski, S. Weiss, J. Shields, S. Haynes, & M. Feinleib (Eds.), *Coronary-prone behavior.* New York: Springer.

Rosenstock, I. M. (1966). Why people use health services. *Milbank Memorial Fund Quarterly, 44,* 94ff.

Rosenstock, I. M. (1974). Historical origins of the health belief model. *Health Education Monographs, 2,* 328–335.

Roskies, E. (1980). Considerations in developing a treatment program for the coronary-prone (Type A) behavior pattern. In P. O. Davidson & S. M. Davidson (Eds.), *Behavioral medicine: Changing health lifestyles* (pp. 38–69). New York: Brunner/Mazel.

Roskies, E., Spevack, M., Surkis, A., Cohen, C., & Gilman, S. (1978). Changing the coronary-prone (Type A) behavior pattern in a nonclinical population. *Journal of Behavioral Medicine, 1,* 201–216.

Ross, C. E. (1994). Overweight and depression. *Journal of Health and Social Behavior, 35,* 63–78.

Ross, C. E., & Bird, C. E. (1994). Sex stratification and health lifestyle: Consequences for men's and women's perceived health. *Journal of Health and Social Behavior, 35,* 161–178.

Ross, C. E., & Duff, R. S. (1982). Returning to the doctor: The effect of client characteristics, type of practice, and experiences with care. *Journal of Health and Social Behavior, 23,* 119–131.

Ross, C. E., & Mirowsky, J. (1988). Child care and emotional adjustment to wives' employment. *Journal of Health and Social Behavior, 29,* 127–138.

Ross, C. E., & Mirowsky, J. (2001). Neighborhood disadvantages, disorder, and health. *Journal of Health and Social Behavior, 42,* 258–276.

Ross, C. E., Mirowsky, J., & Duff, R. S. (1982). Physician status characteristics and client satisfaction in two types of medical practice. *Journal of Health and Social Behavior, 23,* 317–329.

Ross, J. W. (1985). Hospice care for children: Psychosocial considerations. In K. Gardner (Ed.), *Quality of care for the terminally ill: An examination of the issues* (pp. 124–130). Chicago: Joint Commission on Accreditation of Hospitals.

Rossy, L. A., Buckelew, S. P., Dorr, N., Hagglund, K. J., Thayer, J. F., McIntosh, M. J., et al. (1999). A meta-analysis of fibromyalgia treatment interventions. *Annals of Behavioral Medicine, 21,* 180–191.

Roter, D. L., Hall, J. A., Merisca, R., Nordstrom, B., Cretin, D., & Svarstad, B. (1998). Effectiveness of interventions to improve patient compliance. *Medical Care, 36,* 1138–1161.

Roth, B., & Robbins, D. (2004). Mindfulness-based stress reduction and health related quality of life: Findings from a bilingual inner-city patient population. *Psychosomatic Medicine, 66,* 113–123.

Roth, G. S., Lane, M. A., Ingram, D. K., Mattison, J. A., Elahi, D., Tobin, J. D., et al. (2002, August 2). Biomarkers of caloric restriction may predict longevity in humans. *Science, 297,* 811.

Roth, H. P. (1987). Measurement of compliance. *Patient Education and Counseling, 10,* 107–116.

Roth, J. (1977). Some contingencies of the moral evaluation and control of clientele: The case of the hospital emergency service. *American Journal of Sociology, 1972,* 836–839.

Rotheram-Borus, M. J., Murphy, D. A., Reid, H. M., & Coleman, C. L. (1996). Correlates of emotional distress among HIV1 youths: Health status, stress, and personal resources. *Annals of Behavioral Medicine, 18,* 16–23.

Rothman, A. J. (2000). Toward a theory-based analysis of behavioral maintenance. *Health Psychology, 19,* 64–69.

Rothman, A. J., & Salovey, P. (1997). Shaping perceptions to motivate healthy behavior: The role of message framing. *Psychological Bulletin, 121,* 3–19.

Rovniak, L. S., Anderson, E. S., Winett, R. A., & Stephens, R. S. (2002). Social cognitive determinants of physical activity in young adults: A prospective structural equation analysis. *Annals of Behavioral Medicine, 24,* 149–156.

Rowe, M. M. (1999). Teaching health-care providers coping: Results of a two-year study. *Journal of Behavioral Medicine, 22,* 511–527.

Rubenstein, E., & Federman, D. D. (Eds.). (1983). *Medicine.* New York: Scientific American.

Ruble, D. N. (1972). Premenstrual symptoms: A reinterpretation. *Science, 197,* 291–292.

Ruchlin, H. (1997, July). Prevalence and correlates of breast and cervical cancer screening among older women. *Obstetrics and Gynecology, 90,* 16–21.

Rummans, T. A., Bostwick, J. M., & Clark, M. M. (2000). Maintaining the quality of life at the end of life. *Mayo Clinic Proceedings, 75,* 1305–1310.

Rundall, T. G., & Wheeler, J. R. C. (1979). The effect of income on use of preventive care: An evaluation of alternative explanations. *Journal of Health and Social Behavior, 20,* 397–406.

Rushing, B., Ritter, C., & Burton, R. P. D. (1992). Race differences in the effects of multiple roles on health: Longitudinal evidence from a national sample of older men. *Journal of Health and Social Behavior, 33,* 126–139.

Russek, L. G., & Schwartz, G. E. (1997). Feelings of parental caring can predict health status in midlife: A 35-year follow-up of the Harvard Mastery of Stress study. *Journal of Behavioral Medicine, 20,* 1–13.

Russek, L. G., Schwartz, G. E., Bell, I. R., & Baldwin, C. M. (1998). Positive perceptions of parental caring are associated with reduced psychiatric and somatic symptoms. *Psychosomatic Medicine, 60,* 654–657.

Rutledge, T., & Hogan, B. E. (2002). A quantitative review of prospective evidence linking psychological factors with hypertension development. *Psychosomatic Medicine, 64,* 758–766.

Rutledge, T., Linden, W., & Paul, D. (2000). Cardiovascular recovery from acute laboratory stress: Reliability and concurrent validity. *Psychosomatic Medicine, 62,* 648–654.

Rutledge, T., Linden, W., & Davies, R. F. (1999). Psychological risk factors may moderate pharmacological treatment effects among ischemic heart disease patients. *Psychosomatic Medicine, 61,* 834–841.

Rutledge, T., Matthews, K. A., Lui, L. Y., Stone, K. L., & Cauley, J. A. (2003). Social networks and marital status predict mortality in older women: Prospective evidence from the Study of Osteoporotic Fractures (SOF). *Psychosomatic Medicine, 65,* 688–694.

Rutman, D., & Parke, B. (1992). Palliative care needs of residents, families, and staff in long-term care facilities. *Journal of Palliative Care, 8,* 23–29.

Ryan, J., Zwerling, C., & Orav, E. J. (1992). Occupational risks associated with cigarette smoking: A prospective study. *American Journal of Public Health, 82,* 29–32.

Rydén, A., Karlsson, J., Sullivan, M., Torgerson, J. S., & Taft, C. (2003). Coping and distress: What happens after intervention? A 2-year follow-up from the Swedish Obese Subjects (SOS) Study. *Psychosomatic Medicine, 65,* 435–442.

Ryff, C. D., & Singer, B. (1996). Psychological well-being: Meaning, measurement, and implications for psychotherapy research. *Psychotherapy and Psychosomatics, 65,* 14–23.

Ryff, C. D., & Singer, B. (1998). The contours of positive human health. *Psychological Inquiry, 9,* 1–28.

Ryff, C. D., & Singer, B. (2000). Interpersonal flourishing: A positive health agenda for the new millennium. *Personality and Social Psychology Review, 4,* 30–44.

Ryff, C. D., Keyes, C. L. M., & Hughes, D. L. (2003). Status inequalities, perceived discrimination, and eudaimonic well-being: Do the challenges of minority life hone purpose and growth? *Journal of Health and Social Behavior, 44,* 275–291.

Saab, P. G., Llabre, M. M., Schneiderman, N., Hurwitz, B. E., McDonald, P. G., Evans, J., et al. (1997). Influence of ethnicity and gender on cardiovascular responses to active coping and inhibitory-passive coping challenges. *Psychosomatic Medicine, 59,* 434–446.

Sabol, S. Z., Nelson, M. L, Fisher, C., Gunzerath, L., Brody, C. L., Hu, S., et al. (1999). A genetic association for cigarette smoking behavior. *Health Psychology, 18,* 7–13.

Sadava, S. W., & Pak, A. W. (1994). Problem drinking and close relationships during the third decade of life. *Psychology of Addictive Behaviors, 8,* 251–258.

Safer, M. A., Tharps, Q. J., Jackson, T. C., & Leventhal, H. (1979). Determinants of three stages of delay in seeking care at a medical care clinic. *Medical Care, 17,* 11–29.

Sallis, J. F., Nader, P. R., Broyles, S. L., Berry, C. C., Elder, J. P., McKenzie, R. L., et al. (1993). Correlates of physical activity at home in Mexican-American and Anglo-American preschool children. *Health Psychology, 12,* 390–398.

Sallis, J. F., Patterson, T. L., Buono, M. J., Atkins, C. J., & Nader, P. R. (1988). Aggregation of physical activity habits in Mexican-American and Anglo families. *Journal of Behavioral Medicine, 11,* 31–42.

Sallis, J. F., Prochaska, J. J., Taylor, W. C., Hill, J. O., & Geraci, J. C. (1999). Correlates of physical activity in a national sample of girls and boys in grades 4 through 12. *Health Psychology, 18,* 410–415.

Salmon, J., Owen, N., Crawford, D., Bauman, A., & Sallis, J. F. (2003). Physical activity and sedentary behavior: A population-based study of barriers, enjoyment, and preference. *Health Psychology, 22,* 178–188.

Salovey, P., O'Leary, A., Stretton, M. S., Fishkin, S. A., & Drake, C. A. (1991). Influence of mood on judgments about health and illness. In J. P. Firgas (Ed.), *Emotion and social judgments* (pp. 241–262). New York: Pergamon Press.

Sanchez, L. M., & Turner, S. M. (2003). Practicing psychology in the era of managed care: Implications for practice and training. *American Psychologist, 58,* 116–129.

Sanderson, C. A. (1999). Role of relationship context in influencing college students' responsiveness to HIV prevention videos. *Health Psychology, 18,* 295–300.

Sanderson, C. A., Darley, J. M., & Messinger, C. S. (2002). "I'm not as thin as you think I am": The development and consequences of feeling discrepant from the thinness norm. *Personality and Social Psychology Bulletin, 28,* 172–183.

Sandgren, A. K., & McCaul, K. D. (2003). Short-term effects of telephone therapy for breast cancer patients. *Health Psychology, 22,* 310–315.

Sarason, I. G., Sarason, B. R., Pierce, G. R., Shearin, E. N., & Sayers, M. H. (1991). A social learning approach to increasing blood donations. *Journal of Applied Social Psychology, 21,* 896–918.

Sarason, I. G., Johnson, J. H., & Siegel, J. M. (1978). Assessing the impact of life changes: Development of the Life Experiences Survey. *Journal of Consulting and Clinical Psychology, 46,* 932–946.

Sarlio-Lahteenkorva, S., Stunkard, A., & Rissanen, A. (1995). Psychosocial factors and quality of life in obesity. *International Journal of Obesity, 19,* S1–S5.

Sausen, K. P., Lovallo, W. R., Pincomb, G. A., & Wilson, M. F. (1992). Cardiovascular responses to occupational stress in male medical students: A paradigm for ambulatory monitoring studies. *Health Psychology, 11,* 55–60.

Sauter, S. L., Murphy, L. R., & Hurrell, J. J., Jr. (1990). Prevention of work-related psychological disorders: A national strategy proposed by the National Institute for Occupational Safety and Health (NIOSH). *American Psychologist, 45,* 1146–1158.

Savard, J., Laroche, L., Simard, S., Ivers, H., & Morin, C. M. (2003). Chronic insomnia and immune functioning. *Psychosomatic Medicine, 65,* 211–221.

Saxby, B. K., Harrington, F., McKeith, I. G., Wesnes, K., & Ford, G. A. (2003). Effects of hypertension in attention, memory and executive function in older adults. *Health Psychology, 22,* 587–591.

Scanlan, J. M., Vitaliano, P. P., Zhang, J., Savage, M., & Ochs, H. D. (2001). Lymphocyte proliferation is associated with gender, caregiving, and psychosocial variables in older adults. *Journal of Behavioral Medicine, 24,* 537–559.

Scarr, S., Phillips, D., & McCartney, K. (1989). Working mothers and their families. *American Psychologist, 44,* 1402–1409.

Schachter, S. (1982). Recidivism and self-cure of smoking and obesity. *American Psychologist, 37,* 436–444.

Schaefer, J. A., & Moos, R. H. (1992). Life crises and personal growth. In B. N. Carpenter (Ed.), *Personal coping, theory, research, and application* (pp. 149–170). Westport, CT: Praeger.

Schaeffer, J. J. W., Gil, K. M., Burchinal, M., Kramer, K. D., Nash, K. B., Orringer, E., et al. (1999). Depression, disease severity, and sickle cell disease. *Journal of Behavioral Medicine, 22,* 115–126.

Schaeffer, M. A., McKinnon, W., Baum, A., Reynolds, C. P., Rikli, P., Davidson, L. M., et al. (1985). Immune status as a function of chronic stress at Three Mile Island. *Psychosomatic Medicine, 47 (*abstract), 85.

Schag, C. A. C., & Heinrich, R. L. (1986). The impact of cancer on daily living: A comparison with cardiac patients and healthy controls. *Rehabilitation Psychology, 31,* 157–167.

Schaie, K. W., Blazer, D., & House, J. S. (Eds.). (1992). *Aging, health behaviors, and health outcomes.* Hillsdale, NJ: Erlbaum.

Schechtman, K. B., Ory, M. G., & The FICSIT Group (2001). The effects of exercise on the quality of life of frail older adults: A preplanned meta-analysis of the FICSIT trials. *Annals of Behavioral Medicine, 23,* 186–197.

Scheier, M. F., & Bridges, M. W. (1995). Person variables and health: Personality predispositions and acute psychological states as shared determinants for disease. *Psychosomatic Medicine, 57,* 255–268.

Scheier, M. F., & Carver, C. S. (1985). Optimism, coping, and health: Assessment and implications of generalized outcome expectancies. *Health Psychology, 4,* 219–247.

Scheier, M. F., Matthews, K. A., Owens, J., Magovern, G. J., Sr., Lefebvre, R. C., Abbott, R. A., et al. (1989). Dispositional optimism and recovery from coronary artery bypass surgery: The beneficial effects on physical and psychological well-being. *Journal of Personality and Social Psychology, 57,* 1024–1040.

Scheier, M. F., Weintraub, J. K., & Carver, C. S. (1986). Coping with stress: Divergent strategies of optimists and pessimists. *Journal of Personality and Social Psychology, 51,* 1257–1264.

Scherrer, J. F., Xian, H., Bucholz, K. K., Eisen, S. E., Lyons, M. J., Goldberg, J., et al. (2003). A twin study of depression symptoms, hypertension, and heart disease in middle-aged men. *Psychosomatic Medicine, 65,* 548–557.

Scheufele, P. M. (2000). Effects of progressive relaxation and classical music on measurements of attention, relaxation, and stress responses. *Journal of Behavioral Medicine, 23,* 207–228.

Schiaffino, K. M., & Revenson, T. A. (1992). The role of perceived self-efficacy, perceived control, and causal attributions in adaptation to rheumatoid arthritis: Distinguishing mediator from moderator effects. *Personality and Social Psychology Bulletin, 18,* 709–718.

Schieken, R. M. (1988). Preventive Cardiology: An overview. *Journal of the American College of Cardiology, 12,* 1090–1091.

Schins, A., Honig, A., Crijns, H., Baur, L., & Hamulyak, K. (2003). Increased coronary events in depressed cardiovascular patients: 5HT2A receptor as missing link? *Psychosomatic Medicine, 65,* 729–737.

Schleifer, S. J., Scott, B., Stein, M., & Keller, S. E. (1986). Behavioral and developmental aspects of immunity. *Journal of the American Academy of Child Psychiatry, 26,* 751–763.

Schlotz, W., Hellhammer, J., Schulz, P., & Stone, A. A. (2004). Perceived work overload and chronic worrying predict weekend-weekday differences in the cortisol awakening response. *Psychosomatic Medicine, 66,* 207–214.

Schmaling, K. B., Fiedelak, J. I., Katon, W. J., Bader, J. O., & Buchwald, D. S. (2003). Prospective study of the prognosis of unexplained chronic fatigue in a clinic-based cohort. *Psychosomatic Medicine, 65,* 1047–1054.

Schmaling, K. B., Smith, W. R., & Buchwald, D. S. (2000). Significant other responses are associated with fatigue and functional status among patients with chronic fatigue syndrome. *Psychosomatic Medicine, 62,* 444–450.

Schmelkin, L. P., Wachtel, A. B., Schneiderman, B. E., & Hecht, D. (1988). The dimensional structure of medical students' perceptions of diseases. *Journal of Behavioral Medicine, 11,* 171–184.

Schneider, J. A., O'Leary, A., & Agras, W. S. (1987). The role of perceived self-efficacy in recovery from bulimia: A preliminary examination. *Behavioral Research and Therapy, 25,* 429–432.

Schneider, M. S., Friend, R., Whitaker, P., & Wadhwa, N. K. (1991). Fluid noncompliance and symptomatology in end-stage renal disease: Cognitive and emotional variables. *Health Psychology, 10,* 209–215.

Schneiderman, L. J., Kronick, R., Kaplan, R. M., Anderson, J. P., & Langer, R. D. (1992). Effects of offering advance directives on medical treatments and costs. *Annals of Internal Medicine, 117,* 599–606.

Schneiderman, N. (1999). Behavioral medicine and the management of HIV/AIDS. *International Journal of Behavioral Medicine, 6,* 3–12.

Schommer, N. C., Hellhammer, D. H., & Kirschbaum, C. (2003). Dissociation between reactivity of the hypothalamus-pituitary-adrenal axis and the sympathetic-adrenal-medullary system to repeated psychosocial stress. *Psychosomatic Medicine, 65,* 450–460.

Schrimshaw, E. W. (2003). Relationship-specific unsupportive social interactions and depressive symptoms among women living with HIV/AIDS: Direct and moderating effects. *Journal of Behavioral Medicine, 26,* 297–313.

Schroeder, D. H., & Costa, P. T., Jr. (1984). Influence of life event stress on physical illness: Substantive effects or methodological flaws? *Journal of Personality and Social Psychology, 46,* 853–863.

Schulz, R. (1978). *The psychology of death, dying, and bereavement.* Reading, MA: Addison-Wesley.

Schulz, R., & Beach, S.R. (1999). Caregiving as a risk factor for mortality: The caregiver health effects study. *Journal of the American Medical Association, 282,* 2215–2219.

Schulz, R., & Decker, S. (1985). Long-term adjustment to physical disability: The role of social support, perceived control, and self-blame. *Journal of Personality and Social Psychology, 48,* 1162–1172.

Schulz, R., Bookwala, J., Knapp, J. E., Scheier, M., & Williamson, G. (1996). Pessimism, age, and cancer mortality. *Psychology and Aging, 11,* 304–309.

Schulz, R., O'Brien, A.T., Bookwala, J., & Fleissner, K. (1995). Psychiatric and physical morbidity effects of dementia caregiving: Prevalence, correlates, and causes. *The Gerontologist, 35,* 771–791.

Schum, J. L., Jorgensen, R. S., Verhaeghen, P., Sauro, M., & Thibodeau. (2003). Trait anger, anger expression and ambulatory blood pressure: A meta-analytic review. *Journal of Behavioral Medicine, 26,* 395–416.

Schumaker, S. A., & Grunberg, N. E. (Eds.). (1986). Proceedings of the National Working Conference on Smoking Relapse. *Health Psychology, 5*(Suppl.), 1–99.

Schuster, T. L., Kessler, R. C., & Aseltine, R. H., Jr. (1990). Supportive interactions, negative interactions, and depressed mood. *American Journal of Community Psychology, 18,* 423–438.

Schwab, J. J., & Hameling, J. (1968). Body image and medical illness. *Psychosomatic Medicine, 30,* 51–71.

Schwartz, C., Meisenhelder, J. B., Ma, Y., & Reed, G. (2003). Altruistic social interest behaviors are associated with better mental health. *Psychosomatic Medicine, 65,* 778–785.

Schwartz, G. E. (1982). Testing the biopsychosocial model: The ultimate challenge facing behavioral medicine? *Journal of Consulting and Clinical Psychology, 50,* 1040–1053.

Schwartz, J. E., Neale, J., Marco, C., Shiffman, S. S., & Stone, A. A. (1999). Does trait coping exist? A momentary assessment approach to the evaluation of traits. *Journal of Personality and Social Psychology, 77,* 360–369.

Schwartz, L. S., Springer, J., Flaherty, J. A., & Kiani, R. (1986). The role of recent life events and social support in the control of diabetes mellitus. *General Hospital Psychiatry, 8,* 212–216.

Schwartz, M. B., & Brownell, K. D. (1995). Matching individuals to weight loss treatments: A survey of obesity experts. *Journal of Consulting and Clinical Psychology, 63,* 149–153.

Schwartz, M. D., Lerman, C., Miller, S. M., Daly, M., & Masny, A. (1995). Coping disposition, perceived risk, and psychological distress among women at increased risk for ovarian cancer. *Health Psychology, 14,* 232–235.

Schwartz, M. D., Taylor, K. L., Willard, K. S., Siegel, J. E., Lamdan, R. M., & Moran, K. (1999). Distress, personality, and mammography utilization among women with a family history of breast cancer. *Health Psychology, 18,* 327–332.

Schwarzer, R., & Renner, B. (2000). Social-cognitive predictors of health behavior: Action self-efficacy and coping self-efficacy. *Health Psychology, 19,* 487–495.

Scrimshaw, S. M., Engle, P. L., & Zambrana, R. E. (1983, August). *Prenatal anxiety and birth outcome in U.S. Latinas: Implications for psychosocial interventions.* Paper presented at the annual meeting of the American Psychological Association, Anaheim, CA.

Sears, S. R., & Stanton, A. L. (2001). Physician-assisted dying: Review of issues and roles for health psychologists. *Health Psychology, 20,* 302–310.

Sears, S. R., Stanton, A. L., & Danoff-Burg, S. (2003). The yellow brick road and the emerald city: Benefit finding, positive reappraisal coping and post-traumatic growth in women with early-stage breast cancer. *Health Psychology, 22,* 487–497.

Seelman, K. D. (1993). Assistive technology policy: A road to independence for individuals with disabilities. *Journal of Social Issues, 49,* 115–136.

Seeman, M., Seeman, A. Z., & Budros, A. (1988). Powerlessness, work, and community: A longitudinal study of alienation and alcohol use. *Journal of Health and Social Behavior, 29,* 185–198.

Seeman, T. E., & McEwen, B. (1996). Impact of social environment characteristics on neuroendocrine regulation. *Psychosomatic Medicine, 58,* 459–471.

Seeman, T. E., Berkman, L. F., Blazer, D., & Rowe, J. W. (1994). Social ties and support and neuroendocrine function: MacArthur studies of successful aging. *Annals of Behavioral Medicine, 16,* 95–106.

Seeman, T. E., Berkman, L. F., Gulanski, B. I., Robbins, R. J., Greenspan, S. L., Charpentier, P. A., et al. (1995). Self-esteem and neuroendocrine response to challenge: MacArthur studies of successful aging. *Journal of Psychosomatic Research, 39,* 69–84.

Seeman, T. E., Dubin, L. F., & Seeman, M. (2003). Religiosity/spirituality and health: A critical review of the evidence for biological pathways. *American Psychologist, 58,* 53–63.

Seeman, T. E., Lusignolo, T. M., Albert, M., & Berkman, L. (2001). Social relationships, social support, and patterns of cognitive aging in healthy, high-functioning older adults: MacArthur studies of successful aging. *Health Psychology, 20,* 243–255.

Seeman, T. E., Singer, B., Horwitz, R., & McEwen, B. S. (1997). The price of adaptation—Allostatic load and its health consequences: MacArthur studies of successful aging. *Archives of Internal Medicine, 157,* 2259–2268.

Seeman, T. E., Singer, B. H., Ryff, C. D., Love, G. D., & Levy-Storms, L. (2002). Social relationships, gender, and allostatic load across two age cohorts. *Psychosomatic Medicine, 64,* 395–406.

Segan, C. J., Borland, R., & Greenwood, K. M. (2004). What is the right thing at the right time? Interactions between stages and processes of change among smokers who make a quit attempt. *Health Psychology, 23,* 86–93.

Segerstrom, S. C. (2001). Optimism, goal conflict, and stressor-related immune change. *Journal of Behavioral Medicine, 24,* 441–467.

Segerstrom, S. C., & Miller, G. E. (2004). Psychological stress and the human immune system: A meta-analytic study of 30 years of inquiry. *Psychological Bulletin, 130,* 601–630.

Segerstrom, S. C., Castañeda, J. O., & Spencer, T. E. (2003). Optimism effects on cellular immunity: Testing the affective and persistence models. *Personality and Individual Differences, 35,* 1615–1624.

Segerstrom, S. C., Taylor, S. E., Kemeny, M. E., & Fahey, J. L. (1998). Optimism is associated with mood, coping, and immune change in response to stress. *Journal of Personality and Social Psychology, 74,* 1646–1655.

Segerstrom, S. C., Taylor, S. E., Kemeny, M. E., Reed, G. M., & Visscher, B. R. (1996). Causal attributions predict rate of immune decline in HIV-seropositive gay men. *Health Psychology, 15,* 485–493.

Segerstrom, S.C., & Miller, G.E. (2004). Psychological stress and the human immune system: A meta-analytic study of 20 years of inquiry. *Psychological Bulletin, 130,* 601–630.

Self, C. A., & Rogers, R. W. (1990). Coping with threats to health: Effects of persuasive appeals on depressed, normal, and antisocial personalities. *Journal of Behavioral Medicine, 13,* 343–358.

Selye, H. (1956). *The stress of life.* New York: McGraw-Hill.

Selye, H. (1974). *Stress without distress.* Philadelphia: Lippincott.

Selye, H. (1976). *Stress in health and disease.* Woburn, MA: Butterworth.

Senecal, C., Nouwen, A., & White, D. (2000). Motivation and dietary self-care in adults with diabetes: Are self-efficacy and autonomous self-regulation complementary or competing constructs? *Health Psychology, 19,* 452–457.

Seneff, M. G., Wagner, D. P., Wagner, R. P., Zimmerman, J. E., & Knaus, W. A. (1995). Hospital and 1-year survival of patients admitted to intensive care units with acute exacerbation of chronic obstructive pulmonary disease. *Journal of the American Medical Association, 274,* 1852–1857.

Serido, J., Almeida, D. M., & Wethington, E. (2004). Chronic stress and daily hassles: Unique and interactive relationships with psychological distress. *Journal of Health and Social Behavior, 45,* 17–33.

Severeijns, R., Vlaeyen, J. W. S., van den Hout, M. A., & Picavet, H. S. J. (2004). Pain catastrophizing is associated with health indices in musculoskeletal pain: A cross-sectional study in the Dutch community. *Health Psychology, 23,* 49–57.

Sexton, M., Bross, D., Hebel, J. H., Schumann, B. C., Gerace, T. A., Lasser, N., et al. (1987). Risk-factor changes in wives with husbands at high risk of coronary heart disease (CHD): The spin-off effect. *Journal of Behavioral Medicine, 10,* 251–262.

Sexton, M. M. (1979). Behavioral epidemiology. In O. F. Pomerleau & J. P. Brady (Eds.), *Behavioral medicine: Theory and practice* (pp. 3–22). Baltimore, MD: Williams & Wilkins.

Shadel, W. G., & Mermelstein, R. J. (1993). Cigarette smoking under stress: The role of coping expectancies among smokers in a clinic-based smoking cessation program. *Health Psychology, 12,* 443–450.

Shadel, W. G., & Mermelstein, R. J. (1996). Individual differences in self-concept among smokers attempting to quit: Validation and predictive utility of measures of the smoker self-concept and abstainer self-concept. *Annals of Behavioral Medicine, 18,* 151–156.

Shaffer, W. J., Duszynski, K. R., & Thomas, C. B. (1982). Family attitudes in youth as a possible precursor of cancer among physicians: A search for explanatory mechanisms. *Journal of Behavioral Medicine, 15,* 143–164.

Shaham, Y., Singer, J. E., & Schaeffer, M. H. (1992). Stability/instability of cognitive strategies across tasks determine whether stress will affect judgmental processes. *Journal of Applied Social Psychology, 22,* 691–713.

Shalev, A. Y., Bonne, M., & Eth, S. (1996). Treatment of posttraumatic stress disorder: A review. *Psychosomatic Medicine, 58,* 165–182.

Shapiro, A. K. (1960). A contribution to a history of the placebo effect. *Behavioral Science, 5,* 109–135.

Shapiro, A. K. (1964). Factors contributing to the placebo effect: Their implications for psychotherapy. *American Journal of Psychotherapy, 18,* 73–88.

Shapiro, A. P., Schwartz, G. E., Ferguson, D. C. E., Redmond, D. P., & Weiss, S. M. (1977). Behavioral methods in the treatment of hypertension: A review of their clinical status. *Annals of Internal Medicine, 86,* 626–636.

Shapiro, D., Hui, K. K., Oakley, M. E., Pasic, J., & Jamner, L. D. (1997). Reduction in drug requirements for hypertension by means of a cognitive-behavioral intervention. *American Journal of Hypertension, 10,* 9–17.

Shapiro, D. E., Boggs, S. R., Melamed, B. G., & Graham-Pole, J. (1992). The effect of varied physician affect on recall, anxiety, and perceptions in women at risk for breast cancer: An analogue study. *Health Psychology, 11,* 61–66.

Shapiro, S., Venet, W., Strax, P., Venet, L., & Roeser, R. (1985). Selection, follow-up, and analysis in the Health Insurance Plan Study: A randomized trial with breast cancer screening. *National Cancer Institute Monographs, 67,* 65–74.

Sharpe, M., et al. (1994). Why do doctors find some patients difficult to help? *Quarterly Journal of Medicine, 87,* 187–193.

Sharpe, T. R., Smith, M. C., & Barbre, A. R. (1985). Medicine use among the rural elderly. *Journal of Health and Social Behavior, 26,* 113–127.

Shattuck, F. C. (1907). The science and art of medicine in some of their aspects. *Boston Medical and Surgical Journal, 157,* 63–67.

Shaver, J. L. F., Johnston, S. K., Lentz, M. J., & Landis, C. A. (2002). Stress exposure, psychological distress, and physiological stress activation in midlife women with insomnia. *Psychosomatic Medicine, 64,* 793–802.

Sheahan, S. L., Coons, S. J., Robbins, C. A., Martin, S. S., Hendricks, J., & Latimer, M. (1995). Psychoactive medication, alcohol use, and falls among older adults. *Journal of Behavioral Medicine, 18,* 127–140.

Sheehy, G. (1974). *Passages.* New York: Dutton.

Sheeran, P., Conner, M., & Norman, P. (2001). Can the theory of planned behavior explain patterns of health behavior change? *Health Psychology, 20,* 12–19.

Sheffield, D., Biles, P., Orom, H., Maixner, W., & Sheps, D. (2000). Race and sex differences in cutaneous pain perception. *Psychosomatic Medicine, 62,* 517–523.

Shelton, J. L., & Levy, R. L. (1981). *Behavioral assignments and treatment compliance: A handbook of clinical strategies.* Champaign, IL: Research Press.

Shen, B., McCreary, C. P., & Myers, H. F. (2004). Independent and mediated contributions of personality, coping, social support, and depressive symptoms to physical functioning outcome among patients in cardiac rehabilitation. *Journal of Behavioral Medicine, 27,* 39–62.

Shepperd, S. L., Solomon, L. H., Atkins, E., Foster, R. S., Jr., & Frankowski, B. (1990). Determinants of breast self-examination among women of lower income and lower education. *Journal of Behavioral Medicine, 13,* 359–372.

Sherbourne, C. D., Hays, R. D., Ordway, L., DiMatteo, M. R., & Kravitz, R. L. (1992). Antecedents of adherence to medical recommendations: Results from the medical outcomes study. *Journal of Behavioral Medicine, 15,* 447–468.

Sheridan, E. P., Perry, N. W., Johnson, S. B., Clayman, D., Ulmer, R., Prohaska, T., et al. (1989). Research and practice in health psychology. *Health Psychology, 8,* 777–779.

Sherman, B. F., Bonanno, G. A., Wiener, L. S., & Battles, H. B. (2000). When children tell their friends they have AIDS: Possible consequences for psychological well-being and disease progression. *Psychosomatic Medicine, 62,* 238–247.

Sherwood, A., Hinderliter, A. L., & Light, K. C. (1995). Physiological determinants of hyperreactivity to stress in borderline hypertension. *Hypertension, 25,* 384–390.

Shewchuk, R. M., Richards, J. S., & Elliott, T. R. (1998). Dynamic processes in health outcomes among caregivers of patients with spinal cord injuries. *Health Psychology, 17,* 125–129.

Shiffman, S., Balabanis, M. H., Paty, J. A., Engberg, J., Gwaltney, C. J., Liu, K. S., et al. (2000). Dynamic effects of self-efficacy on smoking lapse and relapse. *Health Psychology, 19,* 315–323.

Shiffman, S., Fischer, L. A., Paty, J. A., Gnys, M., Hickcox, M., & Kassel, J. D. (1994). Drinking and smoking: A field study of their association. *Annals of Behavioral Medicine, 16,* 203–209.

Shiffman, S., Hickcox, M., Paty, J. A., Gnys, M., Kassel, J. D., & Richards, T. J. (1996). Progression from a smoking lapse to relapse: Prediction from abstinence violation effects, nicotine dependence, and lapse characteristics. *Journal of Consulting and Clinical Psychology, 64,* 993–1002.

Shiffman, S., Kassel, J. D., Paty, J., Gnys, M., & Zettler-Segal, M. (1994). Smoking typology profiles of clippers and regular smokers. *Journal of Substance Abuse, 6,* 21–35.

Shifren, K., Park, D. C., Bennett, J. M., & Morrell, R. W. (1999). Do cognitive processes predict mental health in individuals with rheumatoid arthritis? *Journal of Behavioral Medicine, 22,* 529–547.

Shih, F., Lai, M., Lin, M., Lin, H., Tsao, C., Chou, L., et al. (2001). Impact of cadaveric organ donation on Taiwanese donor families during the first 6 months after donation. *Psychosomatic Medicine, 63,* 69–78.

Shiloh, S., Rashuk-Rosenthal, D., & Benyamini, Y. (2002). Illness causal attributions: An exploratory study of their structure and associations with other illness cognitions and perceptions of control. *Journal of Behavioral Medicine, 25,* 373–394.

Shilts, R. (1987). *And the band played on: Politics, people, and the AIDS epidemic.* New York: St. Martin's Press.

Shimizu, M., & Pelham, B. W. (2004). The unconsciousness cost of good fortune: Implicit and explicit self-esteem, positive life events, and health. *Health Psychology, 23,* 101–105.

Shinn, M., Rosario, M., Morch, H., & Chestnut, D. E. (1984). Coping with job stress and burnout in the human services. *Journal of Personality and Social Psychology, 46,* 864–876.

Shnayerson, M. (2002, September 30). The killer bug. *Fortune, 149.*

Shnek, Z. M., Irvine, J., Stewart, D., & Abbey, S. (2001). Psychological factors and depressive symptoms in ischemic heart disease. *Health Psychology, 20,* 141–145.

Shumaker, S. A., & Hill, D. R. (1991). Gender differences in social support and physical health. *Health Psychology, 10,* 102–111.

Sicotte, C., Pineault, R., Tilquin, C., & Contandriopoulos, A. P. (1996). The diluting effect of medical work groups on feedback efficiency in changing physician's practice. *Journal of Behavioral Medicine, 19,* 367–384.

Sidney, S., Friedman, G. D., & Siegelaub, A. B. (1987). Thinness and mortality. *American Journal of Public Health, 77,* 317–322.

Sieber, W. J., Rodin, J., Larson, L., Ortega, S., Cummings, N., Levy, S., et al. (1992). Modulation of human natural killer cell activity by exposure to uncontrollable stress. *Brain, Behavior, and Immunity, 6,* 1–16.

Siegel, K., Karus, D., & Raveis, V. H. (1997). Correlates of change in depressive symptomatology among gay men with AIDS. *Health Psychology, 16,* 230–238.

Siegel, K., Mesagno, E. P., Chen, J.-Y., & Christ, G. (1989). Factors distinguishing homosexual males practicing risky and safer sex. *Social Science and Medicine, 28,* 561–569.

Siegler, I. C., Costa, P. T., Brummett, B. H., Helms, M. J., Barefoot, J. C., Williams, R. B., et al. (2003). Patterns of change in hostility from college to midlife in the UNC alumni heart study predict high-risk status. *Psychosomatic Medicine, 65,* 738–745.

Siegler, I. C., Peterson, B. L., Barefoot, J. C., & Williams, R. B. (1992). Hostility during late adolescence predicts coronary risk factors at mid-life. *American Journal of Epidemiology, 136,* 146–154.

Siegman, A. W., & Snow, S. C. (1997). The outward expression of anger, the inward experience of anger, and CVR: The role of vocal expression. *Journal of Behavioral Medicine, 20,* 29–46.

Siegman, A. W., Dembroski, T. M., & Crump, D. (1992). Speech rate, loudness, and cardiovascular reactivity. *Journal of Behavioral Medicine, 15,* 519–532.

Siegman, A. W., Townsend, S. T., Civelek, A. C., & Blumenthal, R. S. (2000). Antagonistic behavior, dominance, hostility, and coronary heart disease. *Psychosomatic Medicine, 62,* 248–257.

Siegrist, J., Peter, R., Runge, A., Cremer, P., & Seidel, D. (1990). Low status control, high effort at work, and ischemic heart disease: Prospective evidence from blue-collar men. *Social Science and Medicine, 31,* 1127–1134.

Sikkema, K. J., Kochman, A., DiFrancesico, W., Kelly, J. A., & Hoffman, R. G. (2003). AIDS-related grief and coping with loss among HIV-positive men and women. *Journal of Behavioral Medicine, 26,* 165–181.

Silberstein, L. R., Striegel-Moore, R. H., & Rodin, J. (1987). Feeling fat: A woman's shame. In H. B. Lewis (Ed.), *The role of shame in symptom formation.* Hillsdale, NJ: Erlbaum.

Silver, E. J., Bauman, L. J., & Ireys, H. T. (1995). Relationships of self-esteem and efficacy to psychological distress in mothers of children with chronic physical illnesses. *Health Psychology, 14,* 333–340.

Silver, R. L., & Wortman, C. B. (1980). Coping with undesirable life events. In J. Garber & M. E. P. Seligman (Eds.), *Human helplessness: Theory and applications.* New York: Academic Press.

Silver, R. L., Boon, C., & Stones, M. (1983). Searching for meaning in misfortune: Making sense of incest. *Journal of Social Issues, 39,* 81–102.

Silverstein, M., & Bengtson, V. L. (1991). Do close parent-child relations reduce the mortality risk of older parents? *Journal of Health and Social Behavior, 32,* 382–395.

Simkin-Silverman, L. R., Wing, R. R., Boraz, M. A., & Kuller, L. H. (2003). Lifestyle intervention can prevent weight gain during menopause: Results from a 5-year randomized clinical trial. *Annals of Behavioral Medicine, 26,* 212–220.

Simkin-Silverman, L., Wing, R. R., Hansen, D. H., Klem, M. L., Pasagian-Macaulay, A., et al. (1995). Prevention of cardiovascular risk factor elevations in healthy premenopausal women. *Preventive Medicine, 24,* 509–571.

Simon, N. (2003, September). Can you hear me now? *Time.* Retrieved from: http://www.time.com/time/archive/preview/0,10987,1005468,00.htm

Simon, R. W. (1992). Parental role strains, salience of parental identity and gender differences in psychological distress. *Journal of Health and Social Behavior, 33,* 25–35.

Simon, R. W. (1998). Assessing sex differences in vulnerability among employed parents: The importance of marital status. *Journal of Health and Social Behavior, 39,* 38–54.

Simoni, J. M., & Ng, M. T. (2002). Abuse, health locus of control, and perceived health among HIV-positive women. *Health Psychology, 21,* 89–93.

Simrén, M., Ringström, G., Björnsson, E. S., & Abrahamsson, H. (2004). Treatment with hypnotherapy reduces the sensory and motor component of the gastrocolonic response in irritable bowel syndrome. *Psychosomatic Medicine, 66,* 233–238.

Singer, B. H. (Ed.). (2000). *Future directions for behavioral and social sciences research at the National Institutes of Health.* Washington, D.C.: National Academy of Sciences Press.

Singer, J. E., Lundberg, U., & Frankenhaeuser, M. (1978). Stress on the train: A study of urban commuting. In A. Baum, J. E. Singer, & S. Valins (Eds.), *Advances in environmental psychology* (Vol. 1). Hillsdale, NJ: Erlbaum.

Singh, M., Katz, R. C., Beauchamp, K., & Hannon, R. (2002). Effects of anonymous information about potential organ transplant recipients on attitudes toward organ transplantation and the willingness to donate organs. *Journal of Behavioral Medicine, 25,* 469–476.

Sinha, R., Fisch, G., Teague, B., Tamborlane, W. V., Banyas, B., Allen, K., et al. (2002). Prevalence of impaired glucose tolerance among children and adolescents with marked obesity. *New England Journal of Medicine, 346,* 802–810, http://www.nejm.org

Sinyor, D., Amato, P., Kaloupek, D. G., Becker, R., Goldenberg, M., & Coopersmith, H. (1986). Post-stroke depression: Relationships to functional impairment, coping strategies, and rehabilitation outcomes. *Stroke, 17,* 1102–1107.

Skapinakis, P., Lewis, G., & Mavreas, V. (2004). Temporal relations between unexplained fatigue and depression: Longitudinal data from an international study in primary care. *Psychosomatic Medicine, 66,* 330–335.

Skelton, M., & Dominian, J. (1973). Psychological stress in wives of patients with myocardial infarction. *British Medical Journal, 2,* 101.

Skinner, N., & Brewer, N. (2002). The dynamics of threat and challenge appraisals prior to stressful achievement events. *Journal of Personality and Social Psychology, 83,* 678–692.

Skinner, T. C., Hampson, S. E., & Fife-Schaw, C. (2002). Personality, personal model beliefs, and self-care in adolescents and young adults with type 1 diabetes. *Health Psychology, 21,* 61–70.

Sklar, L. S., & Anisman, H. (1981). Stress and cancer. *Psychological Bulletin, 89,* 369–406.

Slaven, L., & Lee, C. (1997). Mood and symptom reporting among middle-aged women: The relationship between menopausal status, hormone replacement therapy, and exercise participation. *Health Psychology, 16,* 203–208.

Sloan, R. P., Shapiro, P. A., Bagiella, E., Myers, M. M., & Gorman, J. M. (1999). Cardiac autonomic control buffers blood pressure variability responses to challenge: A psychophysiologic model of coronary artery disease. *Psychosomatic Medicine, 61,* 58–68.

Smalec, J. L., & Klingle, R. S. (2000). Bulimia interventions via interpersonal influence: The role of threat and efficacy in persuading bulimics to seek help. *Journal of Behavioral Medicine, 23,* 37–57.

Smith, B. W., & Zautra, A. J. (2002). The role of personality in exposure and reactivity to interpersonal stress in relation to arthritis disease activity and negative effects in women. *Health Psychology, 21,* 81–88.

Smith, C. A., & Wallston, K. A. (1992). Adaptation in patients with chronic rheumatoid arthritis: Application of a general model. *Health Psychology, 11,* 151–162.

Smith, C. A., Wallston, K. A., & Dwyer, K. A. (1995). On babies and bathwater: Disease impact and negative affectivity in the self-reports of persons with rheumatoid arthritis. *Health Psychology, 14,* 64–73.

Smith, G. E., Gerrard, M., & Gibbons, F. X. (1997). Self-esteem and the relation between risk behavior and perceptions of vulnerability to unplanned pregnancy in college women. *Health Psychology, 16,* 137–146.

Smith, J. A., Lumley, M. A., & Longo, D. J. (2002). Contrasting emotional approach coping with passive coping for chronic myofascial pain. *Annals of Behavioral Medicine, 24,* 326–335.

Smith, L., Adler, N., & Tschann, J. (1999). Underreporting sensitive behaviors: The case of young women's willingness to report abortion. *Health Psychology, 18,* 37–43.

Smith, T. W., & Gallo, L. C. (1999). Hostility and cardiovascular reactivity during marital interaction. *Psychosomatic Medicine, 61,* 436–445.

Smith, T. W., & Ruiz, J. M. (2002). Psychosocial influences on the development and course of coronary heart disease: Current status and implications for research and practice. *Journal of Consulting and Clinical Psychology, 70,* 548–568.

Smith, T. W., Christensen, A. J., Peck, J. R., & Ward, J. R. (1994). Cognitive distortion, helplessness, and depressed mood in rheumatoid arthritis: A four-year longitudinal analysis. *Health Psychology, 13,* 313–317.

Smith, T. W., Peck, J. R., Milano, R. A., & Ward, J. R. (1988). Cognitive distortion in rheumatoid arthritis: Relation to depression and disability. *Journal of Consulting and Clinical Psychology, 56,* 412–416.

Smith, T. W., Ruiz, J. M., & Uchino, B. N. (2000). Vigilance, active coping, and cardiovascular reactivity during social interaction in young men. *Health Psychology, 19,* 382–392.

Smith, T. W., Turner, C. W., Ford, M. H., Hunt, S. C., Barlow, G. K., Stults, B. M., et al. (1987). Blood pressure reactivity in adult male twins. *Health Psychology, 6,* 209–220.

Smyth, J. M., Soefer, M. H., Hurewitz, A., & Stone, A. A. (1999). The effect of tape-recorded relaxation training on well-being, symptoms and peak expiratory flow rate in adult asthmatics: A pilot study. *Psychology and Health, 14,* 487–501.

Smyth, J. M., Stone, A. A., Hurewitz, A., & Kaell, A. (1999). Effects of writing about stressful experiences on symptom reduction in patients with asthma or rheumatoid arthritis. *Journal of the American Medical Association, 281,* 1304–1309.

Sobel, H. (1981). Toward a behavioral thanatology in clinical care. In H. Sobel (Ed.), *Behavioral therapy in terminal care: A humanistic approach* (pp. 3–38). Cambridge, MA: Ballinger.

Solano, L., Donati, V., Pecci, F., Persichetti, S., & Colaci, A. (2003). Postoperative course after papilloma resection: Effects of written disclosure of the experience in subjects with different alexithymia levels. *Psychosomatic Medicine, 65,* 477–484.

Solomon, G. F., Amkraut, A. A., & Kasper, P. (1974). Immunity, emotions, and stress (with special reference to the mechanism of stress effects on the immunity system). *Annals of Clinical Research, 6,* 313–322.

Solomon, L. J., Secker-Walker, R. H., Skelly, J. M., & Flynn, B. S. (1996). Stages of change in smoking during pregnancy in low-income women. *Journal of Behavioral Medicine, 19,* 333–344.

Solomon, M. Z., & De Jong, W. (1989). Preventing AIDS and other STDs through condom promotion: A patient education intervention. *American Journal of Public Health, 79,* 453–458.

Solomon, Z., Mikulincer, M., & Avitzur, E. (1988). Coping, locus of control, social support, and combat-related posttraumatic stress disorder: A prospective study. *Journal of Personality and Social Psychology, 55,* 279–285.

Somerfield, M. R., Curbow, B., Wingard, J. R., Baker, F., & Fogarty, L. A. (1996). Coping with the physical and psychosocial sequelae of bone marrow transplantation among long-term survivors. *Journal of Behavioral Medicine, 19,* 163–184.

Sommers-Flanagan, J., & Greenberg, R. P. (1989). Psychosocial variables and hypertension: A new look at an old controversy. *Journal of Nervous and Mental Disease, 177,* 15–24.

Sorensen, G., Pirie, P., Folson, A., Luepker, R., Jacobs, D., & Gillum, R. (1985). Sex differences in the relationship between work and health: The Minnesota heart survey. *Journal of Health and Social Behavior, 26,* 379–394.

Sorensen, G., Thompson, B., Basen-Engquist, K., Abrams, D., Kuniyuki, A., DiClemente, C., et al. (1998). Durability, dissemination, and institutionalization of worksite tobacco control programs: Results from the working well trial. *International Journal of Behavioral Medicine, 5,* 335–351.

Sorkin, D. H., Rook, K. S., & Lu, J. (2002). Loneliness, lack of emotional support, lack of companionship and the likelihood of having a heart condition in an elderly sample. *Annals of Behavioral Medicine, 24,* 290–298.

Sorrentino, E. A. (1992). Hospice care: A unique clinical experience for MSN students. *American Journal of Hospice and Palliative Care, 9,* 29–33.

Spalletta, G., Pasini, A., Costa, A., De Angelis, D., Ramundo, N., Paolucci, S., & Cartagirone, C. (2001). Alexithymic features in stroke: Effects of laterality and gender. *Psychosomatic Medicine, 63,* 944–950.

Speca, M., Carlson, L. E., Goodey, E., & Angen, M. (2000). A randomized, wait-list controlled clinical trial: The effect of a mindfulness meditation–based stress reduction program on mood and symptoms of stress in cancer outpatients. *Psychosomatic Medicine, 62,* 613–622.

Spector, I. P., Leiblum, S. R., Carey, M. P., & Rosen, R. C. (1993). Diabetes and female sexual function: A critical review. *Annals of Behavioral Medicine, 15,* 257–264.

Speisman, J., Lazarus, R. S., Mordkoff, A., & Davidson, L. (1964). Experimental reduction of stress based on ego defense theory. *Journal of Abnormal and Social Psychology, 68,* 367–380.

Spencer, S. M., Lehman, J. M., Wynings, C., Arena, P., Carver, C. S., Antoni, M. H., et al. (1999). Concerns about breast cancer and relations to psychosocial well-being in a multiethnic sample of early-stage patients. *Health Psychology, 18,* 159–168.

Spiegel, D., & Bloom, J. R. (1983). Group therapy and hypnosis reduce metastatic breast carcinoma pain. *Psychosomatic Medicine, 45,* 333–339.

Spiegel, D., Bloom, J. R., Kraemer, H. C., & Gottheil, E. (1989). Effect of psychosocial treatment on survival of patients with metastatic breast cancer. *Lancet, 14,* 888–891.

Spinetta, J. J. (1974). The dying child's awareness of death: A review. *Psychological Bulletin, 81,* 256–260.

Spinetta, J. J. (1982). Behavioral and psychological research in childhood cancer: An overview. *Cancer, 50*(Suppl.), 1939–1943.

Spinetta, J. J., Spinetta, P. D., Kung, F., & Schwartz, D. B. (1976). *Emotional aspects of childhood cancer and leukemia: A handbook for parents.* San Diego, CA: Leukemia Society of America.

Spitzer, R. L., Yanovski, S., Wadden, T., Wing, R., Marcus, M. D., Stunkard, A., Devlin, M., et al. (1993). Binge eating disorder: Its further validation in a multisite study. *International Journal of Eating Disorders, 13,* 137–153.

Spragins, E. (1996, June 24). Does your HMO stack up? *Newsweek,* 56–61, 63.

Spring, B., Wurtman, J., Gleason, R., Wurtman, R., & Kessler, K. (1991). Weight gain and withdrawal symptoms after smoking cessation: A preventive intervention using d-Fenfluramine. *Health Psychology, 10,* 216–223.

Stacy, A. W., Sussman, S., Dent, C. W., Burton, D., & Flay, B. R. (1992). Moderators of peer social influence in adolescent smoking. *Personality and Social Psychology Bulletin, 18,* 163–172.

Stall, R., & Biernacki, P. (1986). Spontaneous remission from the problematic use of substances: An inductive model derived from a comparative analysis of the alcohol, opiate, tobacco, and food/obesity literatures. *International Journal of the Addictions, 21,* 1–23.

Stampfer, M. J., Hu, F. B., Manson, J. E., Rimm, E. B., & Willett, W. C. (2000). Primary prevention of coronary heart disease in women through diet and lifestyle. *New England Journal of Medicine, 343,* 16–22.

Stansfield, S. A., Bosma, H., Hemingway, H., & Marmot, M. G. (1998). Psychosocial work characteristics and social support as predictors of SF-36 health functioning: The Whitehall II study. *Psychosomatic Medicine, 60,* 247–255.

Stansfeld, S. A., Fuhrer, R., Shipley, M. J., & Marmot, M. G. (2002). Psychological distress as a risk factor for coronary heart disease in the Whitehall II Study. *International Journal of Epidemiology, 31,* 248–255.

Stanton, A. L. (1987). Determinants of adherence to medical regimens by hypertensive patients. *Journal of Behavioral Medicine, 10,* 377–394.

Stanton, A. L., Danoff-Burg, S., Cameron, C. L., & Ellis, A. P. (1994). Coping through emotional approach: Problems of conceptualizaton and confounding. *Journal of Personality & Social Psychology, 66,* 350–362.

Stanton, A. L., Danoff-Burg, S., Cameron, C. L., Snider, P. R., & Kirk, S. B. (1999). Social comparison and adjustment to breast cancer: An experimental examination of upward affiliation and downward evaluation. *Health Psychology, 18,* 151–158.

Stanton, A. L., Kirk, S. B., Cameron, C. L., & Danoff-Burg, S. (2000). Coping through emotional approach: Scale construction and validation. *Journal of Personality and Social Psychology, 78,* 1150–1169.

Starkman, M. N., Giordani, B., Berent, S., Schork, M. A., & Schteingart, D. E. (2001). Elevated cortisol levels in Cushing's Disease are associated with cognitive decrements. *Psychosomatic Medicine, 63,* 985–993.

Starr, K. R., Antoni, M. H., Hurwitz, B. E., Rodriguez, M. S., Ironson, G., Fletcher, M. A., et al. (1996). Patterns of immune, neuroendocrine, and cardiovascular stress responses in asymptomatic HIV seropositive and seronegative men. *International Journal of Behavioral Medicine, 3,* 135–162.

Stauder, A., & Kovacs, M. (2003). Anxiety symptoms in allergic patients: Identification and risk factors. *Psychosomatic Medicine, 65,* 816–823.

Steegmans, P. H. A., Hoes, A. W., Bak, A. A. A., van der Does, E., & Grobbee, D. E. (2000). Higher prevalence of depressive symptoms in middle-aged men with low serum cholesterol levels. *Psychosomatic Medicine, 62,* 205–211.

Steele, C., & Josephs, R. A. (1990). Alcohol myopia: Its prized and dangerous effects. *American Psychologist, 45,* 921–933.

Steen, S. N., Oppliger, R. A., & Brownell, K. D. (1988). Metabolic effects of repeated weight loss and regain in adolescent wrestlers. *Journal of the American Medical Association, 260,* 47–50.

Steffen, P. R., Hinderliter, A. L., Blumenthal, J. A., & Sherwood, A. (2001). Religious coping, ethnicity, and ambulatory blood pressure. *Psychosomatic Medicine, 63,* 523–530.

Steffen, P. R., McNeilly, M., Anderson, N., & Sherwood, A. (2003). Effects of perceived racism and anger inhibition on ambulatory blood pressure in African Americans. *Psychosomatic Medicine, 65,* 746–750.

Stein, J. (2003, August 18). It hasn't gone away; Rising HIV infection rates are causing worries about a resurgence of AIDS amid public complacency. *Los Angeles Times,* pp. F1, F5.

Stein, N., Folkman, S., Trabasso, T., & Richards, T. A. (1997). Appraisal and goal processes as predictors of psychological well-being in bereaved caregivers. *Journal of Personality and Social Psychology, 72,* 872–884.

Stein, P. N., Gordon, W. A., Hibbard, M. R., & Sliwinski, M. J. (1992). An examination of depression in the spouses of stroke patients. *Rehabilitation Psychology, 37,* 121–130.

Stein, R. (July 29, 2003). AIDS cases in U.S. increase. *The Washington Post,* p. A1.

Steinbrook, R. (2004a). Disparities in health care-from politics to policy. *New England Journal of Medicine, 350,* 1486–1488, http://www.nejm.org

Steinbrook, R. (2004b). Surgery for severe obesity. *New England Journal of Medicine, 350,* 1075–1079, http://www.nejm.org

Steinman, L. (1993). Autoimmune disease. *Scientific American, 269,* 107–114.

Steinmetz, K. A., Kushi, L., Bostick, R., Folsom, A., & Potter, J. (1994). Vegetables, fruit, and colon cancer in the Iowa Women's Health Study. *American Journal of Epidemiology, 139,* 1–15.

Stephens, M. A. P., Druley, J. A., & Zautra, A. J. (2002). Older adults' recovery from surgery for osteoarthritis of the knee: Psychological resources and constraints as predictors of outcomes. *Health Psychology, 21,* 377–383.

Stephenson, H. S., Adams, C. K., Hall, D. C., & Pennypacker, H. S. (1979). Effects of certain training parameters on detection of simulated breast cancer. *Journal of Behavioral Medicine, 2,* 239–250.

Steptoe, A., & Marmot, M. (2003). Burden of psychosocial adversity and vulnerability in middle age: Associations with biobehavioral risk factors and quality of life. *Psychosomatic Medicine, 65,* 1029–1037.

Steptoe, A., Doherty, S., Kerry, S., Rink, E., & Hilton, S. (2000). Sociodemographic and psychological predictors of changes in dietary fat consumption in adults with high blood cholesterol following counseling in primary care. *Health Psychology, 19,* 411–419.

Steptoe, A., Kerry, S., Rink, E., & Hilton, S. (2001). The impact of behavioral counseling on stage of change in fat intake, physical activity, and cigarette smoking in adults at increased risk coronary heart disease. *American Journal of Public Health, 91,* 265–269.

Steptoe, A., Kunz-Ebrecht, S., Owen, N., Feldman, P. J., Rumley, A., Lowe, G. D. O., et al. (2003). Influence of socioeconomic status and job control on plasma fibrinogen responses to acute mental stress. *Psychosomatic Medicine, 65,* 137–144.

Steptoe, A., Kunz-Ebrecht, S., Owen, N., Feldman, P. J., Willemsen, G., Kirschbaum, C., & Marmot, M. (2003). Socioeconomic status and stress-related biological responses over the working day. *Psychosomatic Medicine, 65,* 461–470.

Steptoe, A., Roy, M. P., & Evans, O. (1996). Psychosocial influences on ambulatory blood pressure over working and non-working days. *Journal of Psychophysiology, 10,* 218–227.

Steptoe, A., Siegrist, J., Kirschbaum, C., et al. (2004). Effort-reward imbalance, overcommitment, and measures of cortisol and blood pressure over the working day. *Psychosomatic Medicine, 66,* 323–329.

Stern, M. J., Pascale, L., & Ackerman, A. (1977). Life adjustment postmyocardial infarction: Determining predictive variables. *Archives of Internal Medicine, 137,* 1680–1685.

Stetson, B. A., Rahn, J. M., Dubbert, P. M., Wilner, B. I., & Mercury, M. G. (1997). Prospective evaluation of the effects of stress on exercise adherence in community-residing women. *Health Psychology, 16,* 515–520.

Stevens, V. M., Hatcher, J. W., & Bruce, B. K. (1994). How compliant is compliant? Evaluating adherence with breast self-exam positions. *Journal of Behavioral Medicine, 17,* 523–535.

Stevens, V., Peterson, R., & Maruta, T. (1988). Changes in perception of illness and psychosocial adjustment. *The Clinical Journal of Pain, 4,* 249–256.

Stewart, A. L., King, A. C., Killen, J. D., & Ritter, P. L. (1995). Does smoking cessation improve health-related quality-of-life? *Annals of Behavioral Medicine, 17,* 331–338.

Stewart, D. E., Abbey, S. E., Shnek, Z. M., Irvine, J., & Grace, S. L. (2004). Gender differences in health information needs and decisional preferences in patients recovering from an acute ischemic coronary event. *Psychosomatic Medicine, 66,* 42–48.

Stewart-Williams, S. (2004). The placebo puzzle: Putting together the pieces. *Health Psychology, 23,* 198–206.

Stice, E., Presnell, K., & Spangler, D. (2002). Risk factors for binge eating onset in adolescent girls: A 2-year prospective investigation. *Health Psychology, 21,* 131–138.

Stilley, C. S., Sereika, S., Muldoon, M. F., Ryan, C. M., & Dunbar-Jacob, J. (2004). Psychological and cognitive function: Predictors of adherence with cholesterol lowering treatment. *Annals of Behavioral Medicine, 27,* 117–124.

Stokols, D., Novaco, R. W., Stokols, J., & Campbell, J. (1978). Traffic congestion, Type A behavior, and stress. *Journal of Applied Psychology, 63,* 467–480.

Stolberg, S. G. (1999a, April 25). Sham surgery returns as a research tool. *The New York Times,* p. 3.

Stolberg, S. G. (1999b, September 23). Study finds shortcomings in care for chronically ill. *The New York Times,* p. A21.

Stolberg, S. G. (2002, May 2). Racial disparity is found in AIDS clinical studies. *The New York Times,* p. A24.

Stone, A. A., Kennedy-Moore, E., & Neale, J. M. (1995). Association between daily coping and end-of-day mood. *Health Psychology, 14,* 341–349.

Stone, A. A., Mezzacappa, E. S., Donatone, B. A., & Gonder, M. (1999). Psychosocial stress and social support are associated with prostate-specific antigen levels in men: Results from a community screening program. *Health Psychology, 18,* 482–486.

Stoney, C., Niaura, R., Bausserman, L., & Matacin, M. (1999). Lipid reactivity to stress: I. Comparison of chronic and acute stress responses in middle-aged airline pilots. *Health Psychology, 18,* 241–250.

Stoney, C. M., & Finney, M. L. (2000). Social support and stress: Influences on lipid reactivity. *International Journal of Behavioral Medicine, 7,* 111–126.

Stoney, C. M., Owens, J. F., Guzick, D. S., & Matthews, K. A. (1997). A natural experiment on the effects of ovarian hormones on cardiovascular risk factors and stress reactivity: Bilateral salpingo oophorectomy versus hysterectomy only. *Health Psychology, 16,* 349–358.

Storer, J. H., Frate, D. M., Johnson, S. A., & Greenberg, A. M. (1987). When the cure seems worse than the disease: Helping families adapt to hypertension treatment. *Family Relations, 36,* 311–315.

Stotts, A. L., DiClemente, C. C., Carbonari, J. P., & Mullen, P. D. (2000). Postpartum return to smoking: Staging a "suspended" behavior. *Health Psychology, 19,* 324–332.

Stowe, R. P., Pierson, D. L., & Barrett, A. D. T. (2001). Elevated stress hormone levels relate to Epstein-Barr virus reactivation in astronauts. *Psychosomatic Medicine, 63,* 891–895.

Stowell, J. R., Kiecolt-Glaser, J. K., & Glaser, R. (2001). Perceived stress and cellular immunity: When coping counts. *Journal of Behavioral Medicine, 24,* 323–339.

Straus, R. (1988). Interdisciplinary biobehavioral research on alcohol problems: A concept whose time has come. *Drugs and Society, 2,* 33–48.

Strauss, A., Schatzman, L., Bucher, R., Erlich, D., & Sarshim, M. (1963). The hospital and its negotiated social order. In E. Freidson (Ed.), *The hospital in modern society* (pp. 147–169). New York: Free Press.

Straw, M. K. (1983). Coping with obesity. In T. G. Burish & L. A. Bradley (Eds.), *Coping with chronic disease: Research and applications* (pp. 219–258). New York: Academic Press.

Strax, P. (1984). Mass screening for control of breast cancer. *Cancer, 53,* 665–670.

Strecher, V. J., DeVellis, B. M., Becker, M. H., & Rosenstock, I. M. (1986). The role of self-efficacy in achieving health behavior change. *Health Education Quarterly, 13,* 73–92.

Striegel-Moore, R. H., Silberstein, L. R., Frensch, P., & Rodin, J. (1989). A prospective study of disordered eating among college students. *International Journal of Eating Disorders, 8,* 499–511.

Strober, M., et al. (2000). Controlled family study of anorexia nervosa and bulimia nervosa: Evidence of shared liability and transmission of partial syndromes. *American Journal of Psychiatry, 157,* 393–401.

Stroebe, M., Gergen, M. M., Gergen, K. J., & Stroebe, W. (1992). Broken hearts or broken bonds: Love and death in historical perspective. *American Psychologist, 47,* 1205–1212.

Stroebe, W., & Stroebe, M. S. (1987). *Bereavement and health: The psychological and physical consequences of partner loss.* New York: Cambridge University Press.

Strube, M. J., Smith, J. A., Rothbaum, R., & Sotelo, A. (1991). Measurement of health care attitudes in cystic fibrosis patients and their parents. *Journal of Applied Social Psychology, 21,* 397–408.

Stuber, M. L., Christakis, D. A., Houskamp, B., & Kazak, A. E. (1996). Post trauma symptoms in childhood leukemia survivors and their parents. *Journal of Consulting and Clinical Psychology, 37,* 254–261.

Stunkard, A. J. (1979). Behavioral medicine and beyond: The example of obesity. In O. F. Pomerleau & J. P. Brady (Eds.), *Behavioral medicine: Theory and practice* (pp. 279–298). Baltimore: Williams & Wilkins.

Stunkard, A. J. (1988). Some perspectives on human obesity: Its causes. *Bulletin of the New York Academy of Medicine, 64,* 902–923.

Stunkard, A. J., Cohen, R. Y., & Felix, M. R. J. (1989). Weight loss competitions at the work site: How they work and how well. *Journal of Preventive Medicine, 18,* 460–474.

Stunkard, A. J., Sorensen, T. I. A., Hanis, C., Teasdale, T. W., Chakraborty, R., Schull, W. J., et al. (1986). An adoption study of human obesity. *New England Journal of Medicine, 314,* 193–198.

Sturges, J. W., & Rogers, R. W. (1996). Preventive health psychology from a developmental perspective: An extension of protection motivation theory. *Health Psychology, 15,* 158–166.

Suarez, E. C. (2003). Joint effect of hostility and severity of depressive symptoms on plasma interleukin-6 concentration. *Psychosomatic Medicine, 65,* 523–527.

Suarez, E. C., Krishnan, R. R., & Lewis, J. G. (2003). The relation of severity of depressive symptoms in monocyte-associated proinflammatory cytokines and chemokines in apparently healthy men. *Psychosomatic Medicine, 65,* 362–368.

Suarez, E. C., Kuhn, C. M., Schanberg, S. M., Williams, R. B., & Zimmermann, E. (1998). Neuroendocrine, cardiovascular, and emotional responses of hostile men: The role of interpersonal challenge. *Psychosomatic Medicine, 60,* 78–88.

Suarez, E. C., Shiller, A. D., Kuhn, C. M., Schanberg, S., Williams, R. B., Jr., & Zimmermann, E. A. (1997). The relationship between hostility and B-adrenergic receptor physiology in healthy young males. *Psychosomatic Medicine, 59,* 481–487.

Suhr, J. A., Stewart, J. C., & France, C. R. (2004). The relationship between blood pressure and cognitive performance in the Third National Health and Nutrition Examination Survey (NHANES III). *Psychosomatic Medicine, 66,* 291–297.

Sullivan, M. D., LaCroix, A. Z., Russo, J., & Katon, W. J. (1998). Self-efficacy and self-reported functional status in coronary heart disease: A six-month prospective study. *Psychosomatic Medicine, 60,* 473–478.

Sullivan, M. D., LaCroix, A. Z., Spertus, J. A., Hecht, J., & Russo, J. (2003). Depression predicts revascularization procedures for 5 years after coronary heart angiography. *Psychosomatic Medicine, 65,* 229–236.

Suls, J., & Fletcher, B. (1985). The relative efficacy of avoidant and nonavoidant coping strategies: A meta-analysis. *Health Psychology, 4,* 249–288.

Suls, J., & Green, P. (2003). Pluralistic ignorance and college student perceptions of gender-specific alcohol norms. *Health Psychology, 22,* 479–486.

Suls, J., & Wan, C. K. (1993). The relationship between trait hostility and cardiovascular reactivity: A quantitative review and analysis. *Psychophysiology, 30,* 1–12.

Suls, J., Wan, C. K., & Sanders, G. S. (1988). False consensus and false uniqueness in estimating the prevalence of health-protective behaviors. *Journal of Applied Social Psychology, 18,* 66–79.

Surwit, R. S., & Schneider, M. S. (1993). Role of stress in the etiology and treatment of diabetes mellitus. *Psychosomatic Medicine, 55,* 380–393.

Surwit, R. S., & Williams, P. G. (1996). Animal models provide insight into psychosomatic factors in diabetes. *Psychosomatic Medicine, 58,* 582–589.

Surwit, R. S., Feinglos, M. N., McCaskill, C. C., Clay, S. L., Babyak, M. A., Brownlow, B. S., et al. (1997). Metabolic and behavioral effects of a high-sucrose diet during weight loss. *American Journal of Clinical Nutrition, 65,* 908–915.

Surwit, R. S., Schneider, M. S., & Feinglos, M. N. (1992). Stress and diabetes mellitus. *Diabetes Care, 15,* 1413–1422.

Sutton, S. R., & Eiser, J. R. (1984). The effect of fear-arousing communications on cigarette smoking: An expectancy-value approach. *Journal of Behavioral Medicine, 7,* 13–34.

Sutton, S. R., & Kahn, R. L. (1986). Prediction, understanding, and control as antidotes to organizational stress. In J. Lorsch (Ed.), *Handbook of organizational behavior* (pp. 272–285). Boston: Harvard University Press.

Sutton, S., McVey, D., & Glanz, A. (1999). A comparative test of the theory of reasoned action and the theory of planned behavior in the prediction of condom use intentions in a national sample of English young people. *Health Psychology, 18,* 72–81.

Swaim, R. C., Oetting, E. R., & Casas, J. M. (1996). Cigarette use among migrant and nonmigrant Mexican American youth: A socialization latent-variable model. *Health Psychology, 15,* 269–281.

Swaveley, S. M., Silverman, W. H., & Falek, A. (1987). Psychological impact of the development of a presymptomatic test for Huntington's disease. *Health Psychology, 6,* 149–157.

Swindle, R. E., Jr., & Moos, R. H. (1992). Life domains in stressors, coping, and adjustment. In W. B. Walsh, R. Price, & K. B. Crak (Eds.), *Person environment psychology: Models and perspectives* (pp. 1–33). New York: Erlbaum.

Szapocznik, J. (1995). Research on disclosure of HIV status: Cultural evolution finds an ally in science. *Health Psychology, 14,* 4–5.

Talbot, F., Nouwen, A., Gingras, J., Belanger, A., & Audet, J. (1999). Relations of diabetes intrusiveness and personal control to symptoms of depression among adults with diabetes. *Health Psychology, 18,* 537–542.

Talbot, F., Nouwen, A., Gingras, J., Gosselin, M., & Audet, J. (1997). The assessment of diabetes-related cognitive and social factors: The multidimensional diabetes questionnaire. *Journal of Behavioral Medicine, 20,* 291–312.

Tamres, L., Janicki, D., & Helgeson, V. S. (2002). Sex differences in coping behavior: A meta-analytic review. *Personality and Social Psychology Review, 6,* 2–30.

Tapp, W. N., & Natelson, B. H. (1988). Consequences of stress: A multiplicative function of health status. *The FASEB Journal, 2,* 2268–2271.

Taubes, G. (1993). Claim of higher risk for women smokers attacked. *Science, 262,* 1375.

Taubes, G. (2001). The soft science of dietary fat. *Science, 291,* 2536–2545.

Taylor, C. B., & Curry, S. J. (2004). Implementation of evidence-based tobacco use cessation guidelines in managed care organizations. *Annals of Behavioral Medicine, 27,* 13–21.

Taylor, C. B., Bandura, A., Ewart, C. K., Miller, N. H., & DeBusk, R. F. (1985). Exercise testing to enhance wives' confidence in their husbands' cardiac capability soon after clinically uncomplicated acute myocardial infarction. *American Journal of Cardiology, 55,* 635–638.

Taylor, J., & Turner, R. J. (2001). A longitudinal study of the role and significance of mattering to others for depressive symptoms. *Journal of Health and Social Behavior, 42,* 310–325.

Taylor, K. L., Lamdan, R. M., Siegel, J. E., Shelby, R., Moran-Klimi, K., & Hrywna, M. (2003). Psychological adjustment among African American patients: One-year follow-up results of a randomized psychoeducational group intervention. *Health Psychology, 22,* 316–323.

Taylor, L. A., & Rachman, S. J. (1988). The effects of blood sugar level changes on cognitive function, affective state, and somatic symptoms. *Journal of Behavioral Medicine, 11,* 279–292.

Taylor, R. (2004). Causation of type 2 diabetes—The Gordian Knot unravels. *New England Journal of Medicine, 350,* 639–641, http://www.nejm.org

Taylor, R. R., Jason, L. A., & Jahn, S. C. (2003). Chronic fatigue and socio-demographic characteristics as predictors of psychiatric disorders in a community-based sample. *Psychosomatic Medicine, 65,* 896–901.

Taylor, S. E. (1983). Adjustment to threatening events: A theory of cognitive adaptation. *American Psychologist, 41,* 1161–1173.

Taylor, S. E. (1989). *Positive illusions: Creative self-deception and the healthy mind.* New York: Basic Books.

Taylor, S. E. (2002). *The tending instinct: How nurturing is essential to who we are and how we live.* New York: Holt.

Taylor, S. E., & Aspinwall, L. G. (1990). Psychological aspects of chronic illness. In G. R. VandenBos & P. T. Costa, Jr. (Eds.), *Psychological aspects of serious illness.* Washington, D.C.: American Psychological Association.

Taylor, S. E., & Brown, J. D. (1988). Illusion and well-being: A social psychological perspective on mental health. *Psychological Bulletin, 103,* 193–210.

Taylor, S. E., & Clark, L. F. (1986). Does information improve adjustment to noxious events? In M. J. Saks & L. Saxe (Eds.), *Advances in applied social psychology* (Vol. 3, pp. 1–28). Hillsdale, NJ: Erlbaum.

Taylor, S. E., & Thompson, S. C. (1982). Stalking the elusive "vividness" effect. *Psychological Review, 89,* 155–181.

Taylor, S. E., Falke, R. L., Shoptaw, S. J., & Lichtman, R. R. (1986). Social support, support groups, and the cancer patient. *Journal of Consulting and Clinical Psychology, 54,* 608–615.

Taylor, S. E., Helgeson, V. S., Reed, G. M., & Skokan, L. A. (1991). Self-generated feelings of control and adjustment to physical illness. *Journal of Social Issues, 47,* 91–109.

Taylor, S. E., Kemeny, M. E., Reed, G. M., Bower, J. E., & Gruenewald, T. L. (2000). Psychological resources, positive illusions, and health. *American Psychologist, 55,* 99–109.

Taylor, S. E., Klein, L. C., Lewis, B. P., Gruenewald, T. L., Gurung, R. A. R., & Updegraff, J. A. (2000). Biobehavioral responses to stress in females: Tend-and-befriend, not fight-or-flight. *Psychological Review, 107,* 411–429.

Taylor, S. E., Lichtman, R. R., & Wood, J. V. (1984a). Attributions, beliefs about control, and adjustment to breast cancer. *Journal of Personality and Social Psychology, 46,* 489–502.

Taylor, S. E., Lichtman, R. R., & Wood, J. V. (1984b). Compliance with chemotherapy among breast cancer patients. *Health Psychology, 3,* 553–562.

Taylor, S. E., Repetti, R. L., & Seeman, T. (1997). Health psychology: What is an unhealthy environment and how does it get under the skin? *Annual Review of Psychology, 48,* 411–447.

Taylor, S. E., Wood, J. V., & Lichtman, R. R. (1983). *Life change following cancer.* Unpublished manuscript, University of California, Los Angeles.

Teachman, B. A., Gapinski, K. D., Brownell, K. D., & Jeyaram, S. (2003). Demonstrations of implicit anti-fat bias: The impact of providing casual information and evoking empathy. *Health Psychology, 22,* 68–78.

Teixeira, P. J., Going, S. B., Houtkooper, L. B., Cussler, E. C., Martin, C. J., Metcalfe, L. L., et al. (2002). Weight loss readiness in middle-aged women: Psychosocial predictors of success for behavioral weight reduction. *Journal of Behavioral Medicine, 25,* 499–523.

Telch, C. F., & Agras, W. S. (1996). Do emotional states influence binge eating in the obese? *International Journal of Eating Disorders, 20,* 271–279.

Telch, C. F., & Telch, M. J. (1986). Group coping skills instruction and supportive group therapy for cancer patients: A comparison of strategies. *Journal of Consulting and Clinical Psychology, 54,* 802–808.

Tempelaar, R., de Haes, J. C. J. M., de Ruiter, J. H., Bakker, D., van den Heuvel, W. J. A., & van Nieuwenhuijzen, M. G. (1989). The social experiences of cancer patients under treatment: A comparative study. *Social Science and Medicine, 29,* 635–642.

Tennen, H., Affleck, G., Urrows, S., Higgins, P., & Mendola, R. (1992). Perceiving control, construing benefits, and daily processes in rheumatoid arthritis. *Canadian Journal of Behavioral Science, 24,* 186–203.

Teno, J. M., Fisher, E. S., Hamel, M. B., Coppola, K., & Dawson, N. V. (2002). Medical care inconsistent with patients' treatment goals: Association with 1-year medicare resource use and survival. *Journal of the American Geriatrics Society, 50,* 496–500.

Tercyak, K. P., Lerman, C., Peshkin, B. N., Hughes, C., Main, D., Isaacs, C., et al. (2001). Effects of coping style and BRCA1 and BRCA2 test results on anxiety among women participating in genetic counseling and testing for breast and ovarian cancer risk. *Health Psychology, 20,* 217–222.

Thayer, R. E., Newman, R., & McClain, T. M. (1994). Self-regulation of mood: Strategies for changing a bad mood, raising energy, and reducing tension. *Journal of Personality and Social Psychology, 67,* 910–923.

The Columbia Encyclopedia, 6th ed. (2004). *Alcoholics Anonymous.* Columbia University Press.

The National Institute of Mental Health (NIMH) Multisite HIV Prevention Trial Group. (1998). The NIMH Multisite HIV Prevention Trial: Reducing HIV Sexual Risk Behavior. *Science, 280,* 1889–1894.

Theorell, T., Blomkvist, V., Lindh, G., & Evengard, B. (1999). Critical life events, infections, and symptoms during the year preceding chronic fatigue syndrome (CFS): An examination of CFS patients and subjects with a nonspecific life crisis. *Psychosomatic Medicine, 61,* 304–310.

Theorell, T., Emdad, R., Arnetz, B., & Weingarten, A. M. (2001). Employee effects of an educational program for managers at an insurance company. *Psychosomatic Medicine, 63,* 724–733.

Thernstrom, M. (2001, December 16). Pain, the disease: When chronic suffering is more than a symptom. *The New York Times Magazine,* pp. 66–71.

Thoits, P. A. (1986). Social support as coping assistance. *Journal of Consulting and Clinical Psychology, 54,* 416–423.

Thoits, P. A., & Hewitt, L. N. (2001). Volunteer work and well-being. *Journal of Health and Social Behavior, 42,* 115–131.

Thoits, P. A., Harvey, M. R., Hohmann, A. A., & Fletcher, B. (2000). Similar-other support for men undergoing coronary artery bypass surgery. *Health Psychology, 19,* 264–273.

Thomas, C. (1995, April 10). H. M. overdose. *The New Republic,* pp. 11–12.

Thomas, C. B., & Duszynski, K. R. (1974). Closeness to parents and the family constellation in a prospective study of five disease states: Suicide, mental illness, malignant tumor, hypertension, and coronary heart disease. *Johns Hopkins Medical Journal, 134,* 251–270.

Thomas, K. S., Nelesen, R. A., & Dimsdale, J. E. (2004). Relationships between hostility, anger expression, and blood pressure dipping in an ethnically diverse sample. *Psychosomatic Medicine, 66,* 298–304.

Thompson, D. R., & Cordle, C. J. (1988). Support of wives of myocardial infarction patients. *Journal of Advanced Nursing, 13,* 223–228.

Thompson, J. K., & Heinberg, L. J. (1999). The media's influence on body image disturbance and eating disorders: We've reviled them, now can we rehabilitate them? *Journal of Social Issues, 55,* 339–353.

Thompson, R. F., & Glanzman, D. L. (1976). Neural and behavioral mechanism of habituation and sensitization. In T. J. Tighe & R. N. Leatron (Eds.), *Habituation* (pp. 49–94). Hillsdale, NJ: Erlbaum.

Thompson, S. C. (1981). Will it hurt less if I can control it? A complex answer to a simple question. *Psychological Bulletin, 90,* 89–101.

Thompson, S. C., & Spacapan, S. (1991). Perceptions of control in vulnerable populations. *Journal of Social Issues, 47,* 1–22.

Thompson, S. C., Cheek, P. R., & Graham, M. A. (1988). The other side of perceived control: Disadvantages and negative effects. In S. Spacapan & S. Oskamp (Eds.), *The social psychology of health: The Claremont Applied Social Psychology Conference* (Vol. 2, pp. 69–94). Beverly Hills, CA: Sage.

Thompson, S. C., Nanni, C., & Levine, A. (1994). Primary versus secondary and central versus consequence-related control in HIV-positive men. *Journal of Personality and Social Psychology, 67,* 540–547.

Thompson, S. C., Nanni, C., & Schwankovsky, L. (1990). Patient-oriented interventions to improve communication in a medical office visit. *Health Psychology, 9,* 390–404.

Thompson, S. C., Sobolew-Shubin, A., Galbraith, M. E., Schwankovsky, L., & Cruzen, D. (1993). Maintaining perceptions of control: Finding perceived control in low-control circumstances. *Journal of Personality and Social Psychology, 64,* 293–304.

Thompson, S. C., Sobolew-Shubin, A., Graham, M. A., & Janigian, A. S. (1989). Psychosocial adjustment following a stroke. *Social Science and Medicine, 28,* 239–247.

Thomsen, D. K., Mehlsen, M. Y., Hokland, M., Viidik, A., Olesen, F., Avlund, K., et al. (2004). Negative thoughts and health: Associations among rumination, immunity, and health care utilization in an young and elderly sample. *Psychosomatic Medicine, 66,* 363–371.

Thoresen, C. E., & Mahoney, M. J. (1974). *Behavioral self-control.* New York: Holt.

Thornton, B., Gibbons, F. X., & Gerrard, M. (2002). Risk perception and prototype perception: Independent processes predicting risk behaviors. *Personality and Social Psychology Bulletin, 28,* 986–999.

Thorsteinsson, E. B., James, J. E., & Gregg, M. E. (1998). Effects of video-relayed social support on hemodynamic reactivity and salivary cortisol during laboratory-based behavioral challenge. *Health Psychology, 17,* 436–444.

Tibben, A., Timman, R., Bannink, E. C., & Duivenvoorden, H. J. (1997). Three-year follow-up after presymptomatic testing for Huntington's disease in tested individuals and partners. *Health Psychology, 16,* 20–35.

Time. (1970, November 2). The malpractice mess, pp. 36, 39.

Time. (1996, October 7). Notebook: The bad news, p. 30.

Time. (2001, June 25). Notebook: Verbatim, p. 19.

Timko, C., Baumgartner, M., Moos, R. H., & Miller, J. J., III. (1993). Parental risk and resistance factors among children with juvenile rheumatic disease: A four-year predictive study. *Journal of Behavioral Medicine, 16,* 571–589.

Timko, C., Finney, J. W., Moos, R. H., & Moos, B. S. (1995). Short-term treatment careers and outcomes of previously untreated alcoholics. *Journal of Studies on Alcohol, 56,* 597–610.

Timko, C., Stovel, K. W., Moos, R. H., & Miller, J. J., III. (1992). A longitudinal study of risk and resistance factors among children with juvenile rheumatic disease. *Journal of Clinical Child Psychology, 21,* 132–142.

Timman, R., Roos, R., Maat-Kievit, A., & Tibben, A. (2004). Adverse effects of predictive testing for Huntington Disease underestimated: Long-term effects 7–10 years after the test. *Health Psychology, 23,* 189–197.

Timmermans, S., & Angell, A. (2001). Evidence-based medicine, clinical uncertainty, and learning to doctor. *Journal of Health and Social Behavior, 42,* 342–359.

Tomei, L. D., Kiecolt-Glaser, J. K., Kennedy, S., & Glaser, R. (1990). Psychological stress and phorbol ester inhibition of radiation-induced apoptosis in human peripheral blood leukocytes. *Psychiatry Research, 33,* 59–71.

Tomich, P. L., & Helgeson, V. S. (2004). Is finding something good in the bad always good? Benefit finding among women with breast cancer. *Health Psychology, 23,* 16–23.

Tomporowski, P. D., & Ellis, N. R. (1986) The effects of exercise on cognitive processes: A review. *Psychological Bulletin, 99,* 338–346.

Toobert, D. J., & Glasgow, R. E. (1991). Problem solving and diabetes self-care. *Journal of Behavioral Medicine, 14,* 71–86.

Topol, E. J. (2004). Intensive strain therapy—A sea change in cardiovascular prevention. *New England Journal of Medicine, 350,* 1562–1564, http://www.nejm.org

Toshima, M. T., Kaplan, R. M., & Ries, A. L. (1992). Self-efficacy expectancies in chronic obstructive pulmonary disease rehabilitation. In R. Schwarzer (Ed.), *Self-efficacy: Thought control of action* (pp. 325–354). London, England: Hemisphere.

Toynbee, P. (1977). *Patients.* New York: Harcourt Brace.

Traue, H., & Kosarz, P. (1999). Everyday stress and Crohn's disease activity: A time series analysis of 20 single cases. *International Journal of Behavioral Medicine, 6,* 101–119.

Treiber, F. A., Kamarck, T., Schneiderman, N., Sheffield, D., Kapuku, G., & Taylor, T. (2003). Cardiovascular reactivity and development of preclinical and clinical disease states. *Psychosomatic Medicine, 65,* 46–62.

Treue, W. (1958). *Doctor at court* (translated from the German by Frances Fawcett). London: Weidenfeld and Nicolson.

Trikas, P., Vlachonikolis, I., Fragkiadakis, N., Vasilakis, S., Manousos, O., & Paritsis, N. (1999). Core mental state in irritable bowel syndrome. *Psychosomatic Medicine, 61,* 781–788.

Troxel, W. M., Matthews, K. A., Bromberger, J. T., & Sutton-Tyrrell, K. (2003). Chronic stress burden, discrimination, and subclinical carotid artery disease in African American and Caucasian women. *Health Psychology, 22,* 300–309.

Tsutsumi, A., Tsutsumi, K., Kayaba, K., Theorell, T., Nago, N., Kario, K., et al. (1998). Job strain and biological coronary risk factors: A cross-sectional study of male and female workers in a Japanese rural district. *International Journal of Behavioral Medicine, 5,* 295–311.

Tugade, M. M., & Fredrickson, B. L. (2004). Resilient individuals use positive emotions to bounce back from negative emotional experiences. *Journal of Personality and Social Psychology, 86,* 320–333.

Tuomilehto, J., Geboers, J., Salonen, J. T., Nissinen, A., Kuulasmaa, K., & Puska, P. (1986). Decline in cardiovascular mortality in North Karelia and other parts of Finland. *British Medical Journal, 293,* 1068–1071.

Tuomilehto, J., Lindstrom, J., Eriksson, J. G., Valle, T. T., Hamalainen, H., Ilanne-Parikka, P., et al. (2001). Prevention of Type 2 diabetes mellitus by changes in lifestyle among subjects with impaired glucose tolerance. *New England Journal of Medicine, 344,* 1343–1350.

Tuomisto, M. T. (1997). Intra-arterial blood pressure and heart rate reactivity to behavioral stress in normotensive, borderline, and mild hypertensive men. *Health Psychology, 16,* 554–565.

Turk, D. C. (1994). Perspectives on chronic pain: The role of psychological factors. *Current Directions in Psychological Science, 3,* 45–48.

Turk, D. C., & Feldman, C. S. (1992a). Facilitating the use of noninvasive pain management strategies with the terminally ill. In D. C. Turk & C. S. Feldman (Eds.), *Non-invasive approaches to pain management in the terminally ill* (pp. 1–25). New York: Haworth Press.

Turk, D. C., & Feldman, C. S. (1992b). Noninvasive approaches to pain control in terminal illness: The contribution of psychological variables. In D. C. Turk & C. S. Feldman (Eds.), *Non-invasive approaches to pain management in the terminally ill* (pp. 193–214). New York: Haworth Press.

Turk, D. C., & Fernandez, E. (1990). On the putative uniqueness of cancer pain: Do psychological principles apply? *Behavioural Research and Therapy, 28,* 1–13.

Turk, D. C., & Meichenbaum, D. (1991). Adherence to self-care regimens: The patient's perspective. In R. H. Rozensky, J. J. Sweet, & S. M. Tovian (Eds.), *Handbook of clinical psychology in medical settings* (pp. 249–266). New York: Plenum Press.

Turk, D. C., & Rudy, T. E. (1991a). Neglected topics in the treatment of chronic pain patients—Relapse, noncompliance, and adherence enhancement. *Pain, 44,* 5–28.

Turk, D. C., Kerns, R. D., & Rosenberg, R. (1992). Effects of marital interaction on chronic pain and disability: Examining the downside of social support. *Rehabilitation Psychology, 37,* 259–274.

Turk, D. C., Meichenbaum, D. H., & Berman, W. H. (1979). Application of biofeedback for the regulation of pain: A critical review. *Psychological Bulletin, 86,* 1322–1338.

Turk, D. C., Wack, J. T., & Kerns, R. D. (1995). An empirical examination of the "pain-behavior" construct. *Journal of Behavioral Medicine, 8,* 119–130.

Turner, H. A., Hays, R. B., & Coates, T. J. (1993). Determinants of social support among gay men: The context of AIDS. *Journal of Health and Social Behavior, 34,* 37–53.

Turner, J. B., Kessler, R. C., & House, J. S. (1991). Factors facilitating adjustment to unemployment: Implications for intervention. *American Journal of Community Psychology, 19,* 521–542.

Turner, R. J., & Avison, W. R. (1992). Innovations in the measurement of life stress: Crisis theory and the significance of event resolution. *Journal of Health and Social Behavior, 33,* 36–50.

Turner, R. J., & Avison, W. R. (2003). Status variations in stress exposure: Implications for the interpretation of research on race, socioeconomic status, and gender. *Journal of Health and Social Behavior, 44,* 488–505.

Turner, R. J., & Lloyd, D. A. (1999). The stress process and the social distribution of depression. *Journal of Health and Social Behavior, 40,* 374–404.

Turner, R. J., & Noh, S. (1988). Physical disability and depression: A longitudinal analysis. *Journal of Health and Social Behavior, 29,* 23–37.

Turner-Cobb, J. M., Gore-Felton, C., Marouf, F., Koopman, C., Kim, P., Israelski, D., & Spiegel, D. (2002). Coping, social support, and attachment style as psychosocial correlates of adjustment in men and women with HIV/AIDS. *Journal of Behavioral Medicine, 25,* 337–353.

Turner-Cobb, J. M., Sephton, S. E., Koopman, C., Blake-Mortimer, J., & Spiegel, D. (2000). Social support and salivary cortisol in women with metastatic breast cancer. *Psychosomatic Medicine, 62,* 337–345.

Turrisi, R., Hillhouse, J., Gebert, C., & Grimes, J. (1999). Examination of cognitive variables relevant to sunscreen use. *Journal of Behavioral Medicine, 22,* 493–509.

U.S. Census Bureau. (2003). Health Insurance coverage in the United States: 2002.

U.S. Department of Economic Research Service. (2002). Health concerns or price: Which takes credit for declining cigarette consumption in the U.S.? *Choices,* 1st Quarter.

U.S. Department of Health and Human Services. (2001). *Diet and exercise dramatically delay type 2 diabetes: Diabetes medication metformin also effective.* Retrieved from: http://www.nih.gov/news/pr/aug2001/niddk-08.htm

U.S. Department of Health and Human Services. (1986). *Utilization of short-stay hospitals* (USDHHS Publication No. 86-1745). Washington, D.C.: U.S. Government Printing Office.

U.S. Department of Health and Human Services. (1981). *Alcohol and health.* Rockville, MD: National Institute on Alcohol Abuse and Alcoholism.

U.S. Department of Health, Education, and Welfare and U.S. Public Health Service, Centers for Disease Control and Prevention. (1964). *Smoking and health: Report of the advisory committee to the surgeon general of the Public Health Service* (Publication No. PHS-1103). Washington, D.C.: U.S. Government Printing Office.

U.S. Department of Labor. (1998). *Bureau of Labor Statistics.* Retrieved from: http://stats.bls.gov

U.S. Department of Labor – Bureau of Labor Statistics, May 2003, http://www.bls.gov/news.release/pdf/ocwage.pdf

U.S. Public Health Service. (1982). *The health consequences of smoking: Cancer. A report to the surgeon general: 1982* (Publication of Superintendent of Documents). Washington, D.C.: U.S. Government Printing Office.

Uchino, B. N., & Garvey, T. S. (1997). The availability of social support reduces cardiovascular reactivity to acute psychological stress. *Journal of Behavioral Medicine, 20,* 15–27.

Uchino, B. N., Cacioppo, J. T., & Kiecolt-Glaser, J. K. (1996). The relationship between social support and physiological processes: A review with emphasis on underlying mechanisms and implications for health. *Psychological Bulletin, 119,* 488–531.

Uchino, B. N., Cacioppo, J. T., Malarkey, W., & Glaser, R. (1995). Individual differences in cardiac sympathetic control predict endocrine and immune responses to acute psychological stress. *Journal of Personality and Social Psychology, 69,* 736–743.

Uchino, B. N., Kiecolt-Glaser, J. K., & Cacioppo, J. T. (1992). Age-related changes in cardiovascular response as a function of a chronic stressor and social support. *Journal of Personality and Social Psychology, 63,* 839–846.

Ueda, H., et al. (2003, May 29). Association of the T-cell regulatory gene CTLA-4 with susceptibility to autoimmune disease. *Nature, 423,* 506–511.

Ukestad, L. K., & Wittrock, D. A. (1996). Pain perception and coping in female tension headache sufferers and headache-free controls. *Health Psychology, 15,* 65–68.

Ullrich, P. M., & Lutgendorf, S. K. (2002). Journaling about stressful events: Effects of cognitive processing and emotional expression. *Annals of Behavioral Medicine, 24,* 244–250.

Umberson, D. (1987). Family status and health behaviors: Social control as a dimension of social integration. *Journal of Health and Social Behavior, 28,* 306–319.

Umberson, D., Wortman, C. B., & Kessler, R. C. (1992). Widowhood and depression: Explaining long-term gender differences in vulnerability. *Journal of Health and Social Behavior, 33,* 10–24.

UNAIDS (2003). *AIDS epidemic update: December 2003.*

UNAIDS (2004). *Report on the global AIDS epidemic.*

Unger, J. B., Hamilton, J. E., & Sussman, S. (2004). A family member's job loss as a risk factor for smoking among adolescents. *Health Psychology, 23,* 308–313.

United Cerebral Palsy Research and Educational Foundation. (2002). *Research foundation and fact sheets. The diagnosis of cerebral palsy.* Retrieved from: http://www.ucp.org/ucp_generaldoc.cfm/1/4/11654/11654-11654/3968

United Network for Organs Sharing (UNOS). (1996). *UNOS bulletin.* Retrieved from: www.unos.org

University of Alabama, Birmingham Health System. (2004). *Chronic pain.* Retrieved from: http://www.health.uab.edu/show.asp?durki=17936

Uno, D., Uchino, B. N., & Smith, T. W. (2002). Relationship quality moderates the effect of social support given by close friends on cardiovascular re-

activity in women. *International Journal of Behavioral Medicine, 9,* 243–262.

Updegraff, J. A., Taylor, S. E., Kemeny, M. E., & Wyatt, G. E. (2002). Positive and negative effects of HIV infection in women with low socioeconomic resources. *Personality and Social Psychology Bulletin, 28,* 382–394.

Uzark, K. C., Becker, M. H., Dielman, T. E., & Rocchini, A. P. (1987). Psychosocial predictors of compliance with a weight control intervention for obese children and adolescents. *Journal of Compliance in Health Care, 2,* 167–178.

Valdimarsdottir, H. B., Zakowski, S. G., Gerin, W., Mamakos, J., Pickering, T., & Bovbjerg, D. H. (2002). Heightened psychobiological reactivity to laboratory stressors in healthy women at familial risk for breast cancer. *Journal of Behavioral Medicine, 25,* 51–65.

Valentiner, D. P., Holahan, C. J., & Moos, R. H. (1994). Social support, appraisals of event controllability, and coping: An integrative model. *Journal of Personality and Social Psychology, 66,* 1094–1102.

Valois, P., Desharnais, R., & Godin, G. (1988). A comparison of the Fishbein and Ajzen and the Triandis attitudinal models for the prediction of exercise intention and behavior. *Journal of Behavioral Medicine, 11,* 459–472.

Valois, R. F., Adams, K. G., & Kammermann, S. K. (1996). One-year evaluation results from CableQuit: A community cable television smoking cessation pilot program. *Journal of Behavioral Medicine, 19,* 479–500.

van der Velde, F. W., & Van der Pligt, J. (1991). AIDS-related health behavior: Coping, protection, motivation, and previous behavior. *Journal of Behavioral Medicine, 14,* 429–452.

van Dulmen, A. M., Fennis, J. F. M., & Bleijenberg, G. (1996). Cognitive-behavioral group therapy for irritable bowel syndrome: Effects and long-term follow-up. *Psychosomatic Medicine, 58,* 508–514.

van Eck, M., Berkhof, H., Nicolson, N., & Sulon, J. (1996). The effects of perceived stress, traits, mood states, and stressful daily events on salivary cortisol. *Psychosomatic Medicine, 58,* 447–458.

van Lankveld, W., Naring, G., van der Staak, C., van't Pad Bosch, P., & van de Putte, L. (1993). Stress caused by rheumatoid arthritis: Relation among subjective stressors of the disease, disease status, and well-being. *Journal of Behavioral Medicine, 16,* 309–322.

Van Rood, Y. R., Bogaards, M., Goulmy, E., & van Houwelingen, H. C. (1993). The effects of stress and relaxation on the in vitro immune response in man: A meta-analytic study. *Journal of Behavioral Medicine, 16,* 163–182.

van Ryn, M., & Fu, S. S. (2003). Paved with good intensions: Do public health and human service providers contribute to racial/ethnic disparities in health? *American Journal of Public Health, 93,* 248–255.

Van Tilberg, M. A. L., McCaskill C. C., Lane, J. D., Edwards, C. L., Bethel, A. Feinglos, M. N., et al. (2001). Depressed mood is a factor in glycemic control in type 1 diabetes. *Psychosomatic Medicine, 65,* 551–555.

Van YPeren, N. W., Buunk, B. P., & Schaufelli, W. B. (1992). Communal orientation and the burnout syndrome among nurses. *Journal of Applied Social Psychology, 22,* 173–189.

van't Spijker, A., Trijsburg, R. W., & Duivenvoorden, H. J. (1997). Psychological sequelae of cancer diagnosis: A meta-analytic review of 58 studies after 1980. *Psychosomatic Medicine, 59,* 280–293.

Vanable, P. A., Ostrow, D. G., McKirnan, D. J., Taywaditep, K. J., & Hope, B. A. (2000). Impact of combination therapies on HIV risk perceptions and sexual risk among HIV-positive and HIV-negative gay and bisexual men. *Health Psychology, 19,* 134–145.

VanderPlate, C., Aral, S. O., & Magder, L. (1988). The relationship among genital herpes simplex virus, stress, and social support. *Health Psychology, 7,* 159–168.

Vasterling, J., Jenkins, R. A., Tope, D. M., & Burish, T. G. (1993). Cognitive distraction and relaxation training for the control of side effects due to cancer chemotherapy. *Journal of Behavioral Medicine, 16,* 65–80.

Vedhara, K., & Nott, K. (1996). The assessment of the emotional and immunological consequences of examination stress. *Journal of Behavioral Medicine, 19,* 467–478.

Velicer, W. F., Prochaska, J. O., Fava, J. L., Laforge, R. G., & Rossi, J. S. (1999). Interactive versus noninteractive interventions and dose-response relationships for stage-matched smoking cessation programs in a managed care setting. *Health Psychology, 18,* 21–28.

Vendrig, A. (1999). Prognostic factors and treatment-related changes associated with return to working: The multimodal treatment of chronic back pain. *Journal of Behavioral Medicine, 22,* 217–232.

Verbrugge, L. M. (1983). Multiple roles and physical health of women and men. *Journal of Health and Social Behavior, 24,* 16–30.

Verbrugge, L. M. (1985). Gender and health: An update on hypotheses and evidence. *Journal of Health and Social Behavior, 26,* 156–182.

Verbrugge, L. M. (1990). Pathways of health and death. In R. D. Apple (Ed.), *Women, health, and medicine in America: A historical handbook* (pp. 41–79). New York: Garland.

Verbrugge, L. M. (1995). Women, men, and osteoarthritis. *Arthritis Care and Research, 8,* 212–220.

Vernon, D. T. A. (1974). Modeling and birth order in response to painful stimuli. *Journal of Personality and Social Psychology, 29,* 794–799.

Vickberg, S. M. J. (2003). The concerns about recurrence scale (CARS): A systematic measure of women's fears about the possibility of breast cancer recurrence. *Annals of Behavioral Medicine, 25,* 16–24.

Vickers, K. S., Patten, C. A., Lane, K., Clark, M. M., Croghan, I. T., Schroeder, D. R., & Hurt, R. D. (2003). Depressed versus nondepressed young adult tobacco users: Differences in coping style, weight concerns, and exercise level. *Health Psychology, 22,* 498–503.

Vila, G., Porche, L., & Mouren-Simeoni, M. (1999). An 18-month longitudinal study of posttraumatic disorders in children who were taken hostage in their school. *Psychosomatic Medicine, 61,* 746–754.

Villarosa, L. (2002, September 23). As black men move into middle age, dangers rise. *The New York Times,* pp. E1, E8.

Visintainer, M. A., Volpicelli, T. R., & Seligman, M. E. P. (1982). Tumor rejection in rats after inescapable or escapable electric shock. *Science, 216,* 437–439.

Visotsky, H. M., Hamburg, D. A., Goss, M. E., & Lebovitz, B. Z. (1961). Coping behavior under extreme stress. *Archives of General Psychiatry, 5,* 423–428.

Vitaliano, P. P., Maiuro, R. D., Russo, J., Katon, W., DeWolfe, D., & Hall, G. (1990). Coping profiles associated with psychiatric, physical health, work, and family problems. *Health Psychology, 9,* 348–376.

Vitaliano, P. P., Scanlan, J. M., Krenz, C., & Fujimoto, W. (1996). Insulin and glucose: Relationships with hassles, anger, and hostility in nondiabetic older adults. *Psychosomatic Medicine, 58,* 489–499.

Vitaliano, P. P., Scanlan, J. M., Zhang, J., Savage, M. V., Hirsch, I. B., & Siegler, I. C. (2002). A path model of chronic stress, the metabolic syndrome, and coronary heart disease. *Psychosomatic Medicine, 64,* 418–435.

Vittinghoff, E., Shlipak, M. G., Varosy, P. D., Furberg, C. D., Ireland, C. C., Khan, S. S., et al. (2003). Risk factors and secondary prevention in women with heart disease: The heart and estrogen/progestin replacement study. *Annals of Internal Medicine, 138,* 81–89.

Vogele, C., Jarvis, A., & Cheeseman, K. (1997). Anger suppression, reactivity, and hypertension risk: Gender makes a difference. *Annals of Behavioral Medicine, 19,* 61–69.

Volgyesi, F. A. (1954). "School for Patients" hypnosis-therapy and psychoprophylaxis. *British Journal of Medical Hypnotism, 5,* 8–17.

von Kaenel, R., Dimsdale, J. E., Patterson, T. L., & Grant, I. (2003). Acute procoagulant stress response as a dynamic measure of allostatic load in Alzheimer caregivers. *Annals of Behavioral Medicine, 26,* 42–48.

von Kaenel, R., Mills, P. J., Fainman, C., & Dimsdale, J. E. (2001). Effects of psychobiological stress and psychiatric disorders on blood coagulation and fibrinolysis: A biobehavioral pathway to coronary artery disease? *Psychosomatic Medicine, 63,* 531–544.

Vowles, K. E., Zvolensky, M. J., Gross, R. T., & Sperry, J. A. (2004). Pain-related anxiety in the prediction of chronic low-back pain distress. *Journal of Behavioral Medicine, 27,* 77–89.

Vrijkotte, T., van Doornen, L., & de Geus, E. (1999). Work stress and metabolic and hemostatic risk factors. *Psychosomatic Medicine, 61,* 796–805.

Wadden, T. A., Stunkard, A. J., & Brownell, K. D. (1983). Very low calorie diets: Their efficacy, safety and future. *Annals of Internal Medicine, 99,* 675–684.

Wadden, T. A., Vogt, R. A., Andersen, R. E., Bartlett, S. J., Foster, G. D., Kuehnel, R. H., et al. (1997). Exercise in the treatment of obesity: Effects of four interventions on body composition, resting energy expenditure, appetite, and mood. *Journal of Consulting and Clinical Psychology, 65,* 269–277.

Wade, T. D., Bulik, C. M., Sullivan, P. F., Neale, M. C., & Kendler, K. S. (2000). The relation between risk factors for binge eating and bulimia nervosa: A population-based female twin study. *Health Psychology, 19,* 115–123.

Wager, T. D., Rilling, J. K., Smith, E. E., Sokolik, A., Casey, K. L., Davidson, R. J., et al. (2004, February 20). Placebo-induced changes in fMRI in the anticipation and experience of pain. *Science, 303,* 1162–1167.

Waggoner, C. D., & LeLieuvre, R. B. (1981). A method to increase compliance to exercise regimens in rheumatoid arthritis patients. *Journal of Behavioral Medicine, 4,* 191–202.

Wagner, P. J., & Curran, P. (1984). Health beliefs and physician identified "worried well." *Health Psychology, 3,* 459–474.

Waitzkin, H. (1985). Information giving in medical care. *Journal of Health and Social Behavior, 26,* 81–101.

Waldron, I., Weiss, C. C., & Hughes, M. E. (1998). Interacting effects of multiple roles on women's health. *Journal of Health and Social Behavior, 39,* 216–236.

Waldstein, S. R., & Burns, H. O. (2003). Interactive relation of insulin and gender to cardiovascular reactivity in healthy young adults. *Annals of Behavioral Medicine, 25,* 163–171.

Waldstein, S. R., Burns, H. O., Toth, M. J., & Poehlman, E. T. (1999). Cardiovascular reactivity and central adiposity in older African Americans. *Health Psychology, 18,* 221–228.

Waldstein, S. R., Jennings, J. R., Ryan, C. M., Muldoon, M. F., Shapiro, A. P., Polefrone, J. M., et al. (1996). Hypertension and neuropsychological performance in men: Interactive effects of age. *Health Psychology, 15,* 102–109.

Waller, J., McCaffery, K. J., Forrest, S., & Wardle, J. (2004). Human papillomavirus and cervical cancer: Issues for biobehavioral and psychosocial research. *Annals of Behavioral Medicine, 27,* 68–79.

Wallston, B. S., Alagna, S. W., DeVellis, B. M., & DeVellis, R. F. (1983). Social support and physical health. *Health Psychology, 2,* 367–391.

Wallston, K. A., Wallston, B. S., & DeVellis, R. (1978). Development of the Multidimensional Health Locus of Control (MHLC) Scale. *Health Education Monographs, 6,* 161–170.

Walsh, D. C., & Gordon, N. P. (1986). Legal approaches to smoking deterrence. *Annual Review of Public Health, 7,* 127–149.

Wanburg, K. W., & Horn, J. L. (1983). Assessment of alcohol use with multidimensional concepts and measures. *American Psychologist, 38,* 1055–1069.

Wang, S., & Mason, J. (1999). Elevations of serum T3 levels and their association with symptoms in World War II veterans with combat-related posttraumatic stress disorder: Replication findings in Vietnam combat veterans. *Psychosomatic Medicine, 61,* 131–138.

Ward, A., & Mann, T. (2000). Don't mind if I do: Disinhibited eating under cognitive load. *Journal of Personality and Social Psychology, 78,* 753–763.

Ward, K. D., Klesges, R. C., & Halpern, M. T. (1997). Predictors of smoking cessation and state-of-the-art smoking interventions. *Journal of Social Issues, 53,* 129–145.

Ward, S., & Leventhal, H. (1993). *Explaining retrospective reports of side effects: Anxiety, initial side effect experience, and post-treatment side effects.* Series paper from the School of Nursing, University of Wisconsin, Madison.

Ward, S. E., Leventhal, H., & Love, R. (1988). Repression revisited: Tactics used in coping with a severe health threat. *Personality and Social Psychology Bulletin, 14,* 735–746.

Wardle, J., Waller, J., & Jarvis, M. J. (2002). Sex differences in the association of socioeconomic status with obesity. *American Journal of Public Health, 92,* 1299–1304.

Wardle, J., Williamson, S., McCaffery, K., Sutton, S., Taylor, T., Edwards, R., et al. (2003). Increasing attendance at colorectal cancer screening: Testing the efficacy of a mailed, psychoeducational intervention in a community sample of older adults. *Health Psychology, 22,* 99–105.

Wardle, J., Williamson, S., Sutton, S., Biran, A., McCaffery, K., Cuzik, J., et al. (2003). Psychological impact of colorectal cancer screening. *Health Psychology, 22,* 54–59.

Ware, J. E., Jr. (1994). Norm-based interpretation. *Medical Outcomes Trust Bulletin, 2,* 3.

Ware, J. E., Jr., Bayliss, M. S., Rogers, W. H., & Kosinski, M. (1996). Differences in four-year health outcomes for elderly and poor, chronically ill patients in HMO and fee-for-service systems: Results from the Medical Outcomes Study. *Journal of the American Medical Association, 276,* 1039–1047.

Ware, J. E., Jr., Davies-Avery, A., & Stewart, A. L. (1978). The measurement and meaning of patient satisfaction: A review of the literature. *Health and Medical Care Services Review, 1,* 1–15.

Warnecke, R. B., Morera, O., Turner, L., Mermelstein, R., Johnson, T. P., Parsons, J., et al. (2001). Changes in self-efficacy and readiness for smoking cessation among women with high school or less education. *Journal of Health and Social Behavior, 42,* 97–110.

Warner, K. E., & Murt, H. A. (1982). Impact of the antismoking campaign on smoking prevalence: A cohort analysis. *Journal of Public Health Policy, 3,* 374–390.

Warren, M., Weitz, R., & Kulis, S. (1998). Physician satisfaction in a changing health care environment: The impact of challenges to professional autonomy, authority, and dominance. *Journal of Health and Social Behavior, 39,* 356–367.

Watkins, J. D., Roberts, D. E., Williams, T. F., Martin, D. A., & Coyle, I. V. (1967). Observations of medication errors made by diabetic patients in the home. *Diabetes, 16,* 882–885.

Watkins, L. L., Grossman, P., Krishnan, R., & Sherwood, A. (1998). Anxiety and vagal control of heart rate. *Psychosomatic Medicine, 60,* 498–502.

Watson, D., & Clark, L. A. (1984). Negative affectivity: The disposition to experience aversive emotional states. *Psychological Bulletin, 96,* 465–490.

Watson, D., & Pennebaker, J. W. (1989). Health complaints, stress, and distress: Exploring the central role of negative affectivity. *Psychological Review, 96,* 234–264.

Weber-Hamann, B., Hentschel, F., Kniest, A., Deuschle, M., Colla, M., Lederbogen, F., et al. (2002). Hypercortisolemic depression is associated with increased intra-abdominal fat. *Psychosomatic Medicine, 64,* 274–277.

Wechsler, H., Lee, J. E., Kuo, M., Seibring, M., Nelson, T. F., & Lee, H. (2002). Trends in college binge drinking during a period of increased prevention efforts. *Journal of American College Health, 50,* 203–217.

Wechsler, H., Levine, S., Idelson, R. K., Rothman, M., & Taylor, J. O. (1983). The physician's role in health promotion: A survey of primary care physicians. *New England Journal of Medicine, 308,* 97–100.

Wechsler, H., Seibring, M., Liu, I. C., & Ahl, M. (2004). Colleges respond to student binge drinking: Reducing student demand or limiting access. *Journal of American College Health, 52,* 159–168.

Weidner, G., Archer, S., Healy, B., & Matarazzo, J. D. (1985). Family consumption of low fat foods: Stated preference versus actual consumption. *Journal of Applied Social Psychology, 15,* 773–779.

Weidner, G., Boughal, T., Connor, S. L., Pieper, C., & Mendell, N. R. (1997). Relationship of job strain to standard coronary risk factors and psychological characteristics in women and men of the family heart study. *Health Psychology, 16,* 239–247.

Weidner, G., Rice, T., Knox, S. S., Ellison, C., Province, M. A., Rao, D. C., et al. (2000). Familial resemblance for hostility: The National Heart, Lung, and Blood Institute Family Heart Study. *Psychosomatic Medicine, 62,* 197–204.

Weinberg, J., Diller, L., Gordon, W. A., Gerstman, L. J., Lieberman, A., Lakin, P., et al. (1977). Visual scanning training effect in reading-related tasks in acquired right brain damage. *Archives of Physical Medicine and Rehabilitation, 58,* 479–486.

Weinhardt, L. S., & Carey, M. P. (1996). Prevalence of erectile disorder among men with diabetes mellitus: Comprehensive review, methodological critique, and suggestions for future research. *Journal of Sex Research, 33,* 205–214.

Weinhardt, L. S., Carey, M. P., Carey, K. B., Maisto, S. A., & Gordon, C. M. (2001). The relation of alcohol use to sexual HIV risk behavior among adults with severe and persistent mental illness. *Journal of Consulting and Clinical Psychology, 69,* 77–84.

Weinhardt, L. S., Carey, M. P., Johnson, B. T., & Bickman, N. L. (1999). Effects of HIV counseling and testing on sexual risk behavior: A meta-analytic review of published research, 1985–1997. *American Journal of Public Health, 89,* 1397–1405.

Weinman, J., Petrie, K. J., Moss-Morris, R., & Horne, R. (1996). The illness perception questionnaire: A new method for assessing the cognitive representation of illness. *Psychology and Health, 11,* 431–445.

Weinstein, N. D. (1988). The precaution adoption process. *Health Psychology, 7,* 355–386.

Weinstein, N. D. (1993). Testing four competing theories of health-protective behavior. *Health Psychology, 12,* 324–333.

Weinstein, N. D., & Klein, W. M. (1995). Resistance of personal risk perceptions to debiasing interventions. *Health Psychology, 14,* 132–140.

Weinstein, N. D., Rothman, A. J., & Sutton, S. R. (1998). Stage theories of health behavior: Conceptual and methodological issues. *Health Psychology, 17,* 290–299.

Weintraub, A. (2004, January 26). "I can't sleep." *BusinessWeek,* 67–70, 72, 74.

Weisman, A. D. (1972). *On death and dying.* New York: Behavioral Publications.

Weisman, A. D. (1977). The psychiatrist and the inexorable. In H. Feifel (Ed.), *New meanings of death* (pp. 107–122). New York: McGraw-Hill.

Weisman, C. S., & Teitelbaum, M. A. (1985). Physician gender and the physician-patient relationship: Recent evidence and relevant questions. *Social Sciences and Medicine, 20,* 1119–1127.

Weiss, R. S., & Richards, T. A. (1997). A scale for predicting quality of recovery following the death of a partner. *Journal of Personality and Social Psychology, 72,* 885–891.

Welch-McCaffrey, S. (1985). Cancer, anxiety, and quality of life. *Cancer Nursing, 8,* 151–158.

Wellisch, D. K. (1979). Adolescent acting out when a parent has cancer. *International Journal of Family Therapy, 1,* 230–241.

Wellisch, D. K. (1981). Intervention with the cancer patient. In C. K. Prokop & L. A. Bradley (Eds.), *Medical psychology: Contributions to behavioral medicine* (pp. 224–241). New York: Academic Press.

Wellisch, D. K., Gritz, E. R., Schain, W., Wang, H. J., & Siau, J. (1991). Psychological functioning of daughters of breast cancer patients: I. Daughters and comparison subjects. *Psychosomatics, 32,* 324–336.

Wells, S., Mullin, B., Norton, R., Langley, J., Connor, J., Lay-Yee, R., et al. (2004). Motorcycle rider conspicuity and crash related injury: Case control study. *British Medical Journal, 328,* 857–860.

Wenninger, K., Weiss, C., Wahn, U., & Staab, D. (2003). Body image in cystic fibrosis—Development of a brief diagnostic scale. *Journal of Behavioral Medicine, 26,* 81–94.

Westmaas, J. L., Wild, T. C., Ferrence, R. (2002). Effects of gender in social control of smoking cessation. *Health Psychology, 21,* 368–376.

Wetter, D. W., Kenford, S. L., Welsch, S. K., Smith, S. S., Fouladi, R. T., Fiore, M. C., et al.. (2004). Prevalence and predictors of transitions in smoking behavior among college students. *Health Psychology, 23,* 168–177.

Whalen, C. K., Jamner, L. D., Henker, B., & Delfino, R. J. (2001). Smoking and moods in adolescents with depressive and aggressive dispositions: Evidence from surveys and electronic diaries. *Health Psychology, 20,* 99–111.

Whisman, M. A., & Kwon, P. (1993). Life stress and dysphoria: The role of self-esteem and hopelessness. *Journal of Personality and Social Psychology, 65,* 1054–1060.

Whitbeck, L. B., Hoyt, D. R., McMorris, B. J., Chen, X., & Stubben, J. D. (2001). Perceived discrimination and early substance abuse among American Indian children. *Journal of Health and Social Behavior, 42,* 05–424.

Whitbeck, L. B., McMorris, B. J., Hoyt, D. R., Stubben, J. D., & LaFromboise, T. (2002). Perceived discrimination, traditional practices, and depressive symptoms among American Indians in the upper Midwest. *Journal of Health and Social Behavior, 43,* 400–418.

White, L. P., & Tursky, B. (1982). Where are we where are we going? In L. White & B. Tursky (Eds.), *Clinical biofeedback: Efficacy and mechanisms* (pp. 438–448). New York: Guilford Press.

Whittam, E. H. (1993). Terminal care of the dying child: Psychosocial implications of care. *Cancer, 71,* 3450–3462.

Wholey, D. R., & Burns, L. R. (1991). Convenience and independence: Do physicians strike a balance in admitting decisions? *Journal of Health and Social Behavior, 32,* 254–272.

Wichstrom, L. (1994). Predictors of Norwegian adolescents' sunbathing and use of sunscreen. *Health Psychology, 13,* 412–420.

Wickrama, K. A. S., Conger, R. D., & Lorenz, F. O. (1995). Work, marriage, lifestyle, and changes in men's physical health. *Journal of Behavioral Medicine, 18,* 97–112.

Wickrama, K. A. S., Conger, R. D., Wallace, L. E., & Elder, G. H., Jr. (2003). Linking early social risks to impaired physical health during the transition to adulthood. *Journal of Health and Social Behavior, 44,* 61–74.

Widows, M. R., Jacobsen, P. B., & Fields, K. K. (2000). Relation of psychological vulnerability factors to posttraumatic stress disorder symptomatology in bone marrow transplant recipients. *Psychosomatic Medicine, 62,* 873–882.

Wilcox, S., & Stefanick, M. L. (1999). Knowledge and perceived risk of major diseases in middle-aged and older women. *Health Psychology, 18,* 346–353.

Wilcox, S., & Storandt, M. (1996). Relations among age, exercise, and psychological variables in a community sample of women. *Health Psychology, 15,* 110–113.

Wilcox, S., Evenson, K. R., Aragaki, A., Wassertheil-Smoller, S., Mouton, C. P., & Loevinger, B. L. (2003). The effects of widowhood on physical and mental health, health behaviors, and health outcomes: The women's health initiative. *Health Psychology, 22,* 513–522.

Wilcox, V. L., Kasl, S. V., & Berkman, L. F. (1994). Social support and physical disability in older people after hospitalization: A prospective study. *Health Psychology, 13,* 170–179.

Willenbring, M. L., Levine, A. S., & Morley, J. E. (1986). Stress induced eating and food preference in humans: A pilot study. *International Journal of Eating Disorders, 5,* 855–864.

Williams, C. J. (2001, April 24). Entertained into social change. *Los Angeles Times,* pp. A1, A6–A7.

Williams, D. R. (2002). Racial/ethnic variations in women's health: The social embeddedness of health. *American Journal of Public Health, 92*(4), 588–597.

Williams, D. R. (2003). The health of men: Structured inequalities and opportunities. *American Journal of Public Health, 93,* 724–731.

Williams, D. R., & Collins, C. (2001). Racial residential segregation: a fundamental cause of racial disparities in health. *Public Health Reports, 116,* 404–416.

Williams, G. C., Gagne, M., Ryan, R. M., & Deci, E. L. (2002). Supporting autonomy to motivate smoking cessation: A test of self-determination theory. *Health Psychology, 21,* 40–50.

Williams, G. C., McGregor, H. A., Zeldman, A., Freedman, Z. R., & Deci, E. L. (2004). Testing a self-determination theory process model for promoting glycemic control through diabetes self-management. *Health Psychology, 23,* 58–66.

Williams, K. J., Suls, J., Alliger, G. M., Learner, S. M., & Wan, C. K. (1991). Multiple role juggling and daily mood states in working mothers: An experience sampling study. *Journal of Applied Psychology, 76,* 664–674.

Williams, P. D., Williams, A. R., Graff, J. C., Hanson, S., Stanton, Hafeman, C., et al. (2002). Interrelationships among variables affecting wall siblings and mothers in families of children with chronic illness or disability. *Journal of Behavioral Medicine, 25,* 411–424.

Williams, P. G., Colder, C. R., Lane, J. D., McCaskill, C. C., Feinglos, M. N., & Surwit, R. S. (2002). Examination of the neuroticism-symptom reporting relationship in individuals with type-2 diabetes. *Personality and Social Psychology Bulletin, 28,* 1015–1025.

Williams, R. B. (1984). An untrusting heart. *The Sciences, 24,* 31–36.

Williams, R. B., Barefoot, J. C., & Shekelle, R. B. (1985). The health consequences of hostility. In M. A. Chesney & R. H. Rosenman (Eds.), *Anger and hostility in cardiovascular and behavioral disorders* (pp. 173–185). New York: Hemisphere/McGraw-Hill.

Williams, R. B., Barefoot, J. C., Califf, R. M., Haney, T. L., Saunders, W. B., Pryor, D. B., et al. (1992). Prognostic importance of social and economic resources among medically treated patients with angiographically documented coronary artery disease. *Journal of the American Medical Association, 267,* 520–524.

Williams, R. B., Sasaki, M., Lewis, J. G., Kuhn, C. M., Schanberg, S. M., Suarez, E. C., et al. (1997). Differential responsivity of monocyte cytokine and adhesion proteins in high- and low-hostile humans. *International Journal of Behavioral Medicine, 4,* 262–272.

Williams, S., & Kohout, J. L. (1999). Psychologists in medical schools in 1997. *American Psychologist, 54,* 272–276.

Williams, S. A., Kasil, S. V., Heiat, A., Abramson, J. L., Krumholtz, H. M., & Vaccarino, V. (2002). Depression and risk of heart failure among the elderly: A prospective community-based study. *Psychosomatic Medicine, 64,* 6–12.

Williamson, G. M. (2000). Extending the activity restriction model of depressed affect: Evidence from a sample of breast cancer patients. *Health Psychology, 19,* 339–347.

Williamson, G. M., Shaffer, D. R., & Schulz, R. (1998). Activity restriction and prior relationship history as contributors to mental health outcomes among middle-aged and older spousal caregivers. *Health Psychology, 17,* 152–162.

Williamson, G. M., Walters, A. S., & Shaffer, D. R. (2002). Caregiver models of self and others, coping, and depression: Predictors of depression in children with chronic pain. *Health Psychology, 21,* 405–410.

Wills, T. A. (1984). Supportive functions of interpersonal relationships. In S. Cohen & L. Syme (Eds.), *Social support and health* (pp. 61–82). New York: Academic Press.

Wills, T. A., & Cleary, S. D. (1999). Peer and adolescent substance use among 6th–9th graders: Latent growth analyses of influence versus selection mechanisms. *Health Psychology, 18,* 453–463.

Wills, T. A., & Vaughan, R. (1989). Social support and substance use in early adolescence. *Journal of Behavioral Medicine, 12,* 321–340.

Wills, T. A., Gibbons, F. X., Gerrard, M., & Brody, G. H. (2000). Protection and vulnerability processes relevant for early onset of substance use: A test among African American children. *Health Psychology, 19,* 253–263.

Wills, T. A., Pierce, J. P., & Evans, R. I. (1996). Large-scale environmental risk factors for substance use. *American Behavioral Scientist, 39,* 808–822.

Wills, T. A., Sandy, J. M., & Yaeger, A. M. (2002). Stress and smoking in adolescence: A test of directional hypotheses. *Health Psychology, 21,* 122–130.

Wilson, D. K., & Ampey-Thornhill, G. (2001). The role of gender and family support on dietary compliance in an African American adolescent hypertension prevention study. *Annals of Behavioral Medicine, 23,* 59–67.

Wilson, D. K., Friend, R., Teasley, N., Green, S., Reaves, I. L., & Sica, D. A. (2002). Motivational versus social cognitive interventions for promoting fruit and vegetable intake and physical activity in African American adolescents. *Annals of Behavioral Medicine, 24,* 310–319.

Wilson, D. K., Kliewer, W., Teasley, N., Plybon, L., & Sica, D. A. (2002). Violence exposure, catecholamine excretion, and blood pressure nondipping status in African American male versus female adolescents. *Psychosomatic Medicine, 64,* 906–915.

Wilson, G. T. (1984). Toward the understanding and treatment of binge eating. In R. C. Hawkins, W. J. Fremouw, & P. F. Clement (Eds.), *The binge-purge syndrome* (pp. 77–103). New York: Springer.

Wilson, G. T. (1985). Psychological prognostic factors in the treatment of obesity. In J. Hirsch & T. B. Van Italie (Eds.), *Recent advances in obesity research* (Vol. 4, pp. 301–311). London, England: Libbey.

Wilson, G. T. (1994). Behavioral treatment of childhood obesity: Theoretical and practical implications. *Health Psychology, 13,* 371–372.

Wilson, R. (1963). The social structure of a general hospital. *Annals of the American Academy of Political and Social Science, 346,* 67–76.

Winett, R. A. (1995). A framework for health promotion and disease prevention programs. *American Psychologist, 50,* 341–350.

Winett, R. A. (2003). Comments on "challenges to improving the impact of worksite cancer prevention programs": Paradigm lost? *Annals of Behavioral Medicine, 26,* 221.

Winett, R. A., Wagner, J. L., Moore, J. F., Walker, W. B., Hite, L. A., Leahy, M., et al. (1991). An experimental evaluation of a prototype public access nutrition information system for supermarkets. *Health Psychology, 10,* 75–78.

Wing, R. R. (2000). Cross-cutting themes in maintenance of behavior change. *Health Psychology, 19,* 84–88.

Wing, R. R., & Jeffery, R. W. (1999). Benefits of recruiting participants with friends and increasing social support for weight loss and maintenance. *Journal of Consulting and Clinical Psychology, 67,* 132–138.

Wing, R. R., Blair, E., Marcus, M., Epstein, L. H., & Harvey, J. (1994). Year-long weight loss treatment for obese patients with Type II diabetes: Does including an intermittent very-low-calorie diet improve outcome? *American Journal of Medicine, 97,* 354–362.

Wing, R. R., Epstein, L. H., Nowalk, M. P., & Lamparski, D. M. (1986). Behavioral self-regulation in the treatment of patients with diabetes mellitus. *Psychological Bulletin, 99,* 78–89.

Wing, R. R., Epstein, L. H., Nowalk, M. P., Scott, N., Koeske, R., & Hagg, S. (1986). Does self-monitoring of blood glucose levels improve dietary competence for obese patients with Type II diabetes? *American Journal of Medicine, 81,* 830–836.

Wing, R. R., Jeffery, R. W., Burton, L. R., Thorson, C., Nissinoff, K. S., & Baxter, J. E. (1996). Food provision versus structured meal plans in the behavioral treatment of obesity. *International Journal of Obesity, 20,* 56–62.

Wing, R. R., Matthews, K. A., Kuller, L. H., Meilahn, E. N., & Plantinga, P. L. (1991). Weight gain at the time of menopause. *Archives of Internal Medicine, 151,* 97–102.

Wing, R. R., Nowalk, L. H., Marcus, M. D., Koeske, R., & Finegold, D. (1986). Subclinical eating disorders and glycemic control in adolescents with Type I diabetes. *Diabetes Care, 9,* 162–167.

Winkleby, M. A., Kraemer, H. C., Ahn, D. K., & Varady, A. N. (1998). Ethnic and socioeconomic differences in cardiovascular disease risk factors. *Journal of the American Medical Association, 280,* 356–362.

Winslow, R. W., Franzini, L. R., & Hwang, J. (1992). Perceived peer norms, casual sex, and AIDS risk prevention. *Journal of Applied Social Psychology, 22,* 1809–1827.

Wirtz, P. H., Von Kanel, R., Schnorpfeil, P., Ehlert, U., Frey, K., & Fischer, J. E. (2003). Reduced glucocorticoid sensitivity of monocyte interleukin-6 production in male industrial employees who are vitally exhausted. *Psychosomatic Medicine, 65,* 672–678.

Wisniewski, L., Epstein, L., Marcus, M. D., & Kaye, W. (1997). Differences in salivary habituation to palatable foods in bulimia nervosa patients and controls. *Psychosomatic Medicine, 59,* 427–433.

Witkiewitz, K., & Marlatt, G. A. (2004). Relapse prevention for alcohol and drug problems. *American Psychologist, 59,* 224–235.

Wolpe, J. (1958). *Psychotherapy by reciprocal inhibition.* Stanford, CA: Stanford University Press.

Wong, M., & Kaloupek, D. G. (1986). Coping with dental treatment: The potential impact of situational demands. *Journal of Behavioral Medicine, 9,* 579–598.

Wong, M. D., Shapiro, M. F., Boscardin, W. J., & Ettner, S. L. (2002). Contribution of major diseases to disparities in mortality. *New England Journal of Medicine, 347,* 1585–1592, http://www.nejm.org

Woodall, K. L., & Matthews, K. A. (1993). Changes in and stability of hostile characteristics: Results from a 4-year longitudinal study of children. *Journal of Personality and Social Psychology, 64,* 491–499.

Worden, J. W., & Weisman, A. D. (1975). Psychosocial components of lag-time in cancer diagnosis. *Journal of Psychosomatic Research, 19,* 69–79.

World Health Organization. (1948). *Constitution of the World Health Organization.* Geneva, Switzerland: World Health Organization Basic Documents.

World Health Organization. (1995–1996). *Cancer around the world: World health statistics annual.* Geneva, Switzerland: Author.

World Health Organization. (1996). *The global burden of disease: A comprehensive assessment of mortality and disability from diseases, injuries, and risk factors in 1990 and projected to 2020.* (C. J. L. Murray & A. D. Lopez, Eds.). Cambridge, MA: Harvard University Press.

World Health Organization. (2003). *Adult health at risk: Slowing gains and widening gaps. Chapter 1: Today's health: Global challenges.* Retrieved from: http://www.who.int/whr/2003/chapter1/en/index3.html

World Health Organization. (2004). World Report on road traffic injury prevention.

Wortman, C. B., & Dunkel-Schetter, C. (1979). Interpersonal relationships and cancer: A theoretical analysis. *Journal of Social Issues, 35,* 120–155.

Wright, L. (1988). The Type A behavior pattern and coronary artery disease: Quest for the active ingredients and the elusive mechanism. *American Psychologist, 43,* 2–14.

Wroe, A. L. (2001). Intentional and unintentional nonadherence: A study of decision making. *Journal of Behavioral Medicine, 25,* 355–372.

Wrosch, C., Schulz, R., & Heckhausen, J. (2002). Health stresses and depressive symptomatology in the elderly: The importance of health engagement control strategies. *Health Psychology, 21,* 340–348.

Wulfert, E., & Wan, C. K. (1993). Condom use: A self-efficacy model. *Health Psychology, 12,* 346–353.

Wulfert, E., Wan, C. K., & Backus, C. A. (1996). Gay men's safer sex behavior: An integration of three models. *Journal of Behavioral Medicine, 19,* 345–366.

Wulsin, L. R., & Singal, B. M. (2003). Do depressive symptoms increase the risk for the onset of coronary disease? Systemic quantitative review. *Psychosomatic Medicine, 65,* 201–210.

Wulsin, L. R., Vaillant, G. E., & Wells, V. E. (1999). A systematic review of the mortality of depression. *Psychosomatic Medicine, 61,* 6–17.

Wynder, E. L., Kajitani, T., Kuno, I. J., Lucas, J. C., Jr., DePalo, A., & Farrow, J. (1963). A comparison of survival rates between American and Japanese patients with breast cancer. *Surgery, Gynecology, Obstetrics, 117,* 196–200.

Wysocki, T., Green, L., & Huxtable, K. (1989). Blood glucose monitoring by diabetic adolescents: Compliance and metabolic control. *Health Psychology, 8,* 267–284.

Yamada, Y., Izawa, H., Ichihara, S., Takatsu, F., Ishihara, H., Hirayama, H., et al. (2002). Prediction of the risk of myocardial infarction from polymorphisms in candidate genes. *New England Journal of Medicine, 347,* 1916–1923, http://www.nejm.org

Yarnold, P., Michelson, E., Thompson, D., & Adams, S. (1998). Predicting patient satisfaction: A study of two emergency departments. *Journal of Behavioral Medicine, 21,* 545–563.

Yazdanbakhsh, M., Kremsner, P. G., & van Ree, R. (2002, April 19). Allergy, parasites, and the hygiene hypothesis. *Science, 296,* 490–494.

Ybema, J. F., Kuijer, R. G., Buunk, B. P., DeJong, G. M., & Sanderman, R. (2001). Depression and perceptions of inequity among couples facing cancer. *Personality and Social Psychology Bulletin, 27,* 3–13.

Yoshimasu, K., & The Fukuoka Heart Study Group. (2001). Relation of type A behavior pattern and job-related psychosocial factors to nonfatal myocardial infarction: A case-control study of Japanese male workers and women. *Psychosomatic Medicine, 63,* 797–804.

Yoshiuchi, Z., Kumano, H., Nomura, S., Yoshimura, H., Ito, K., Kanaji, Y., et al. (1998). Stressful life events and smoking were associated with Graves' disease in women, but not in men. *Psychosomatic Medicine, 60,* 182–185.

Young-Brockopp, D. (1982). Cancer patients' perceptions of five psychosocial needs. *Oncology Nursing Forum, 9,* 31–35.

Zabinski, M. F., Calfas, K. J., Gehrman, C. A., Wilfley, D. E., & Sallis, J. F. (2001). Effects of a physical activity intervention on body image in university seniors: Project GRAD. *Annals of Behavioral Medicine, 23,* 247–252.

Zakowski, S. G., Hall, M. H., Klein, L. C., & Baum, A. (2001). Appraised control, coping, and stress in a community sample: A test of the goodness-of-fit hypothesis. *Annals of Behavioral Medicine, 23,* 158–165.

Zastowny, T. R., Kirschenbaum, D. S., & Meng, A. L. (1986). Coping skills training for children: Effects on distress before, during, and after hospitalization for surgery. *Health Psychology, 5,* 231–247.

Zatzick, D. F., & Dimsdale, J. E. (1990). Cultural variations in response to painful stimuli. *Psychosomatic Medicine, 52,* 544–557.

Zautra, A. J., & Manne, S. L. (1992). Coping with rheumatoid arthritis: A review of a decade of research. *Annals of Behavioral Medicine, 14,* 31–39.

Zautra, A. J., & Smith, B. W. (2001). Depression and reactivity to stress in older women with rheumatoid arthritis and osteoarthritis. *Psychosomatic Medicine, 63,* 687–696.

Zautra, A. J., Burleson, M. H., Matt, K. S., Roth, S., & Burrows, L. (1994). Interpersonal stress, depression, and disease activity in rheumatoid arthritis and osteoarthritis patients. *Health Psychology, 13,* 139–148.

Zautra, A. J., Maxwell, B. M., & Reich, J. W. (1989). Relation among physical impairment, distress, and well-being in older adults. *Journal of Behavioral Medicine, 12,* 543–557.

Zautra, A. J., Okun, M. A., Roth, S. H., & Emmanual, J. (1989). Life stress and lymphocyte alterations among patients with rheumatoid arthritis. *Health Psychology, 8,* 1–14.

Zelinski, E. M., Crimmins, E., Reynolds, S., & Seeman, T. (1998). Do medical conditions affect cognition in older adults? *Health Psychology, 17,* 504–512.

Zheng, Z. J., Croft, J. B., Labarthe, D., Williams, J. E., & Mensah, G. A. Racial disparity in coronary heart disease mortality in the United States: Has the gap narrowed? *Circulation 2001; 104*: 787 (abstract).

Zhu, S. H., Sun, J., Hawkins, S., Pierce, J., & Cummins, S. (2003). A population study of low-rate smokers: Quitting history and instability over time. *Health Psychology, 22,* 245–252.

Zillman, D., de Wied, M., King-Jablonski, C., & Jenzowsky, S. (1996). Drama-induced affect and pain sensitivity. *Psychosomatic Medicine, 58,* 333–341.

Zimbardo, P. G. (1969). The human choice: Individuation, reason, and order versus deindividuation, impulse, and chaos. In W. J. Arnold & D. Levine (Eds.), *Nebraska symposium on motivation.* Lincoln: University of Nebraska Press.

Zimet, G. D., Lazebnik, R., DiClemente, R. J., Anglin, T. M., Williams, P., & Ellick, E. M. (1993). The relationship of Magic Johnson's announcement of HIV infection to the AIDS attitudes of junior high school students. *Journal of Sex Research, 30,* 129–134.

Zimmer, C. (2001, September 14). Do chronic diseases have an infectious root? *Science, 293,* 1974–1977.

Zimmerman, R. S., Safer, M. A., Leventhal, H., & Baumann, L. J. (1986). The effects of health information in a worksite hypertension screening program. *Health Education Quarterly, 13,* 261–280.

Zipfel, S., Löwe, B., Schneider, A., Herzog, W., & Bergmann, G. (1999). Quality of life, depression, and coping in patients awaiting heart transplantation. *Psychotherapie Psychosomatik Medizinische Psychologie, 49,* 187–194.

Zisook, S., Shuchter, S. R., Irwin, M., Darko, D. F., Sledge, P., & Resovsky, K. (1994). Bereavement, depression, and immune function. *Psychiatry Research, 52,* 1–10.

Zola, I. K. (1966). Culture and symptoms—An analysis of patients' presenting complaints. *American Sociological Review, 31,* 615–630.

Zola, I. K. (1973). Pathways to the doctor—From person to patient. *Social Science and Medicine, 7,* 677–689.

Zucker, R. A., & Gomberg, E. S. L. (1986). Etiology of alcoholism reconsidered: The case for a biopsychosocial process. *American Psychologist, 41,* 783–793.

Zuger, A. (1999, May 4). A simpler, cheaper plan for fighting high blood pressure. *The New York Times,* p. D12.

CREDITS

Text and Line Art Credits

Chapter 3   **Box 3.1** J. R. Gordon and G. A. Marlatt, 1981, "Addictive Behavior" in J. L. Shelton and R. L. Levy (eds.), *Behavioral Assignments and Treatment Compliance*, pp. 167–186, Research Press. Used with permission from Dr. J. L. Shelton. **Fig. 3.5:** G.A. Marlatt and J. R. Gordon. "A Cognitive Behavioral Model of the Relapse Process" from *Relapse Prevention: Maintenance in the Treatment of Addictive Behaviors*, 1985. Used by permission of Guilford Publications, Inc. **Fig. 3.7** Association for Worksite Promotion et al., *National Worksite Health Promotion Survey*, 2000.

Chapter 4   **Box 4.2:** Marcia Millman. From *Such a Pretty Face: Being Fat in America* by Marcia Millman. Copyright © 1980 Marcia Millman. Used by permission of W. W. Norton & Company, Inc.

Chapter 5   **Fig. 5.3:** B.J. Feder. *The New York Times,* April 20, 1997. Copyright © 1997 The New York Times Company. Reprinted with permission. **Table 5.6:** © 2003 American Cancer Society, Inc. www.cancer.org. Reprinted with permission.

Chapter 6   **Fig. 6.1** From *Stress Without Distress* by Hans Selye, M.D., p. 39. Copyright © 1974 by Hans Selye, M.D. Reprinted by permission of HarperCollins Publishers, Inc. **Table 6.1:** The Social Readjustment Rating Scale. Reprinted from *Journal of Psychosomatic Research,* 11, pp. 213–218. Copyright © 1967, with permission from Elsevier.

Chapter 7   **Box 7.1:** M. F. Scheier and C. S. Carver, 1985. "Optimism, Coping & Health: Assessment and Implications of Generalized Outcome Expectancies." *Health Psychology* 4, pp. 219–247. Used with permission by Lawrence Erlbaum Associates, Inc. and M. F. Scheier. **Box 7.3:** C. S. Carver. "You Want to Measure Coping but Your Protocol's too Long: Consider the Brief COPE." *International Journal of Behavioral Medicine* 4, pp. 92–100. Reprinted by permission of the author.

Chapter 8   **Fig. 8.1:** B. L. Anderson, J. T. Cacioppo, and D. C. Roberts. "Delay in Seeking a Cancer Diagnosis: Delay Stages with Psychophysiological Comparison Processes." *British Journal of Social Psychology* 34, 1995, Fig. 1, p. 35. Used with permission by The British Psychological Society.

Chapter 9   **Box 9.1:** C. Thomas. "H.M. Overdose." *The New Republic,* April 10, 1995. Used with permission.

Chapter 12   **Box 12.2** From *Passages* by Gail Sheehy. Copyright © 1974, 1976 by Gail Sheehy. Used by permission of Dutton, a division of Penguin Group, USA, Inc. and International Creative Management, Inc. **Table 12.3:** R. Schultz. From *Psychology of Death, Dying, and Bereavement.* Copyright © 1978 The McGraw-Hill Companies. Used by permission of The McGraw-Hill Companies. **Box 12.4:** "A Letter to My Physician." From Compassion & Choices (formerly the Hemlock Society). For more information, visit www.compassionandchoices.org. Used with permission. **Box 12.5:** J. Branegan. "I Want To Draw the Line Myself." *Time,* March 17, 1977, pp. 30–31. © 1977 Time Inc. Reprinted by permission. **Box 12.6:** Carol K. Littlebrant. Selected excerpts from "Death is a Personal Matter," an essay originally published in *Newsweek,* January 12, 1976, under the name of Carol K. Gross. Used with permission of the author.

Chapter 14   **Fig. 14.1:** Reprinted from Roitt, Brostoff & Male, *Immunology* 5th Edition, 1998, Mosby International Ltd. With permission from Elsevier. **Fig. 14.2:** Reprinted from Roitt, Brostoff & Male, *Immunology* 5th Edition, 1998, Mosby International Ltd. With permission from Elsevier. **Fig. 14.4:** American Cancer Society. Reprinted with permission. **Box 14.3:** Randy Shilts. "A Profile of Patient Zero." From *And the Band Played On: People, Politics, and the AIDs Epidemic."* Copyright © 2000 by the author and reprinted by permission of St. Martin's Press, LLC, and Frederick Hill Agency.

Chapter 15   **Fig. 15.2:** From Population Division of the Department of Economic and Social Affairs of the United Nations Secretariat, *World Population Prospects: The 2002 Revision and World Urbanization Prospects: The 2001 Revision*, http://esa.un.org/unpp, 20 October 2004. Used with permission.

Photo Credits

Chapter 1   **page 1, 2**: © David Young-Wolff/PhotoEdit; **3**: © Richard Hutchings/PhotoEdit; **5**: Courtesy The National Library of Medicine; **12**: © Will and Deni McIntyre/Photo Researchers

Chapter 2   **16**: © David Young-Wolff/PhotoEdit

Chapter 3   **43**: © Randy M. Ury/Corbis Images; **44**: © Arnold Gold/New Haven Register/Image Works; **50**: © Myrleen Ferguson Cate/PhotoEdit; **51**: © Larry Bray/Getty Images; **53**: © Bob Daemmrich/Stock Boston; **55**: © A. Ramey\PhotoEdit; **70**: © Jeff Greenberg/PhotoEdit; **73**: © Tony Freeman/PhotoEdit; **76**: © Michael A. Dwyer/Stock Boston; **77**: © Lincoln Russell/Stock Boston

Chapter 4   **81**: © Randy M. Ury/Corbis Images; **84**: © Kathy Ferguson-Johnson/PhotoEdit; **88**: © PhotoDisc/Vol.#73; **90**: © PhotoDisc/Vol. 40; **93**: © Royalty-Free/Corbis; **101**: © Chet Gordon/Image Works; **102**: © AP/Wide World Photos; **106**: © Weisbrot/Image Works; **108**: © AP/Wide World Photos; **112**: © AP/Wide World Photos; **116**: © Mary Kate Denny/PhotoEdit

Chapter 5   **120**: © Dennis MacDonald/PhotoEdit; **123**: © Alex Adams/Stock Connection/PictureQuest; **125**: © Richard Hutchings/PhotoEdit; **129**: © Drew Crawford/Image Works; **134**: © Dennis MacDonald/PhotoEdit; **135**: Courtesy, State of Health Products, Minneapolis, MN, www.buttout.com; **148**: © PhotoDisc/Vol. 18

Chapter 6   **151**: © Bill Aron/PhotoEdit; **152**: © David Bases/Index Stock Imagery; **159, 162, 165**: © AP/Wide World Photos; **168**: © Billy E. Barnes/PhotoEdit; **176, 180**: © Bill Bachmann/Photo Researchers

Chapter 7   **183**: © Bill Aron/PhotoEdit; **191**: © Alan Oddie/PhotoEdit; **198**: © David Young-Wolff/PhotoEdit/PictureQuest; **199**: © Cleo

Note: page numbers with *f* indicate additional figures